KV-418-983

STATUTORY INSTRUMENTS

1977

PART II
(in two Sections)

SECTION 2

Published by Authority

LONDON
HER MAJESTY'S STATIONERY OFFICE
1978

STOKE-ON-TRENT
CITY
LIBRARIES

©*Crown copyright* 1978

PRINTED AND PUBLISHED BY HER MAJESTY'S STATIONERY OFFICE

To be purchased from
49 High Holborn, LONDON, EC1V 6HB
13a Castle Street, EDINBURGH, EH2 3AR   41 The Hayes, CARDIFF, CF1 1JW
Brazennose Street, MANCHESTER, M60 8AS   Southey House, Wine Street, BRISTOL, BS1 2BQ
258 Broad Street, BIRMINGHAM, B1 2HE   80 Chichester Street, BELFAST, BT1 4JY

or through booksellers

1978

Price for the two Sections: £36.75 net

PRINTED IN ENGLAND

STAFFORDSHIRE
COUNTY
LIBRARY

A   1/2/78
C

0 11 840161 0*

HORACE BARKS
REFERENCE LIBRARY

STOKE-ON-TRENT

Contents of the Edition

PART I,
Section 1

Section 2

PART II,
Section 1

Section 2

PART III

STATUTORY INSTRUMENTS

1977 No. 1174 (L. 21)

MAGISTRATES' COURTS
PROCEDURE

The Magistrates' Courts (Amendment) Rules 1977

Made - - - -	13*th July* 1977
Laid before Parliament	22*nd July* 1977
Coming into Operation	5*th September* 1977

The Lord Chancellor in exercise of the power conferred on him by section 15 of the Justices of the Peace Act 1949(**a**), as extended by section 122 of the Magistrates' Courts Act 1952(**b**), after consultation with the Rule Committee appointed under the said section 15, hereby makes the following Rules:—

1. These Rules may be cited as the Magistrates' Courts (Amendment) Rules 1977 and shall come into operation on 5th September 1977.

2. After rule 38 of the Magistrates' Courts Rules 1968(**c**), as amended(**d**), there shall be inserted the following rule:—

"Registration and notification of financial penalty enforcement order

38A.—(1) The clerk of a magistrates' court receiving a financial penalty enforcement order made by the Defence Council or an officer authorised by them shall cause the said order to be registered in his courts by means of a memorandum entered in the register kept pursuant to rule 54 of these Rules and signed by him and shall send notice in writing to the Defence Council or the authorised officer, as appropriate, stating that the order has been so registered.

(2) Where a financial penalty enforcement order has been registered in accordance with the provisions of paragraph (1) above, the clerk shall forthwith serve on the person against whom the order was made a notice of registration in the prescribed form.

(3) A notice required by paragraph (2) of this rule shall be served on the person by delivering it to him or by sending it by post addressed to him at the address shown on the financial penalty enforcement order.

(4) In this rule "financial penalty enforcement order" means an order made under section 133A(1) of the Army Act 1955(**e**), section 133A(1) of the Air Force Act 1955(**f**) or section 128F(1) of the Naval Discipline Act 1957(**g**).".

Dated 13th July 1977. *Elwyn-Jones,* C.

(**a**) 1949 c. 101. (**b**) 1952 c. 55.
(**c**) S.I. 1968/1920 (1968 III, p. 5175). (**d**) There are no relevant amendments.
(**e**) 1955 c.18. (**f**) 1955 c.19
(**g**) 1957 c. 53.

EXPLANATORY NOTE

(This Note is not part of the Rules.)

These Rules provide for the registration in magistrates' courts of financial penalty enforcement orders made under the Army Act 1955, the Air Force Act 1955 and the Naval Discipline Act 1957 (as amended by section 16 of, and Schedule 8 to, the Armed Forces Act 1976 (c. 52)) and for the service of notification of the registration on the person against whom the order was made.

STATUTORY INSTRUMENTS

1977 No. 1175 (L.22)

MAGISTRATES' COURTS

PROCEDURE

The Magistrates' Courts (Forms) (Amendment) Rules 1977

Made - - - -	*13th July* 1977
Laid before Parliament	*22nd July* 1977
Coming into Operation	*5th September* 1977

The Lord Chancellor in exercise of the power conferred on him by section 15 of the Justices of the Peace Act 1949(a), as extended by section 122 of the Magistrates' Courts Act 1952(b), after consultation with the Rule Committee under the said section 15, hereby makes the following Rules:—

1. These Rules may be cited as the Magistrates' Courts (Forms) (Amendment) Rules 1977 and shall come into operation on 5th September 1977.

2. In the Schedule to the Magistrates' Courts (Forms) Rules 1968(c), as amended(d), after Form 49 there shall be inserted the form contained in the Schedule to these Rules.

Dated 13th July 1977.

Elwyn-Jones, C.

(a) 1949 c. 101.   (b) 1952 c. 55.   (c) S.I. 1968/1919 (1968 III, p. 5075)
(d) There are no relevant amendments.

Rule 2.

SCHEDULE

49A.

Notice of registration of financial penalty enforcement order
(*Army Act* 1955, *s.* 133A; *Air Force Act* 1955, *s.* 133A; *Naval Discipline Act* 1957,
s. 128F; *M.C. Rules*, 1968, *r.* 38A)

	.....................Magistrates' Court
(as parent/guardian	
of.....................)	Date ....
	Convicted on..........(date)...........
	by the...............................

Offence(s)	Sum certified as outstanding			
	Fine £	Stoppages £	Compensation £	Total £

You are hereby given notice that a financial penalty enforcement order made against you on.............................by...............................has been registered in this Court.

Payment of the outstanding amount shown above should be made either in person at the address shown below on (   ) between....................or sent by post to the address shown below. Cheques and postal orders should be crossed and made payable to The Justices' Clerk. Cash should not be sent in unregistered envelopes. Any communication sent by post must be properly stamped.

The address of the Court is:

The .... Magistrates' Court

....

....

Correspondence should be addressed to the Justices' Clerk.

In the event of your failure to pay the sum due a distress warrant may be issued against you or you may be required to appear or be arrested and brought before the Court for an inquiry into your means. Application for further time for payment may be made in writing to the Justices' Clerk at the above address stating the grounds of the application.

[NOTE: This notice should be sent with any payment or on application.]

A.B.
Justices' Clerk.

EXPLANATORY NOTE
(This Note is not part of the Rules.)

These Rules prescribe the form of notice of registration to be given to a person against whom a financial penalty enforcement order has been made under the Army Act 1955 (c.18), the Air Force Act 1955 (c.19) or the Naval Discipline Act 1957 (c.53) when the order has been registered in a magistrates' court in accordance with provisions of those Acts as amended by section 16, of and Schedule 8 to, the Armed Forces Act 1976. (c.52).

STATUTORY INSTRUMENTS

1977 No. 1176

BETTING, GAMING AND LOTTERIES
The Amusements with Prizes (Variation of Fees) Order 1977

Made	-	- -	*14th July* 1977
Laid before Parliament			26th July 1977
Coming into Operation			22nd August 1977

In pursuance of section 18(1) of the Lotteries and Amusements Act 1976(**a**), I hereby make the following Order:—

1.—(1) This Order may be cited as the Amusements with Prizes (Variation of Fees) Order 1977 and shall come into operation on 22nd August 1977.

(2) This Order shall not extend to Scotland.

2. The Interpretation Act 1889(**b**) shall apply for the interpretation of this Order as it applies for the interpretation of an Act of Parliament.

3. The fee payable under paragraph 18 of Schedule 3 to the Lotteries and Amusements Act 1976 (which relates to permits for the commercial provision of amusements with prizes) shall, instead of £2·50, be £3·75.

Merlyn Rees,
One of Her Majesty's Principal
Secretaries of State.

Home Office.
14th July 1977.

EXPLANATORY NOTE.
(*This Note is not part of the Order.*)

This Order increases the fee payable to a local authority or other appropriate authority on the grant or renewal of a permit for amusements with prizes provided under section 16 of the Lotteries and Amusements Act 1976.

(**a**) 1976 c.32. (**b**) 1889 c.63.

STATUTORY INSTRUMENTS

1977 No. 1179 (S.91)

BETTING, GAMING AND LOTTERIES

The Amusements with Prizes (Variation of Fees) (Scotland) Order 1977

Made - - - -	*12th July* 1977
Laid before Parliament	*26th July* 1977
Coming into Operation	*22nd August* 1977

In exercise of the powers conferred on me by section 18(1) of the Lotteries and Amusements Act 1976(a), and of all other powers enabling me in that behalf, I hereby make the following order:—

1.—(1) This order may be cited as the Amusements with Prizes (Variation of Fees) (Scotland) Order 1977 and shall come into operation on 22nd August 1977.

(2) This order shall extend to Scotland only.

2. The Interpretation Act 1889(b) shall apply for the interpretation of this order as it applies for the interpretation of an Act of Parliament.

3. The fee payable under paragraph 18 of Schedule 3 to the Lotteries and Amusements Act 1976 (which relates to permits for the commercial provision of amusements with prizes) shall, instead of £2.50, be £3.75.

> *Bruce Millan,*
> One of Her Majesty's Principal
> Secretaries of State.

New St. Andrew's House,
Edinburgh.
12th July 1977.

EXPLANATORY NOTE

(This Note is not part of the Order.)

This Order increases the fee payable to a local authority or other appropriate authority on the grant or renewal of a permit for amusements with prizes provided under Section 16 of the Lotteries and Amusements Act 1976.

(a) 1976 c. 32.   **(b)** 1889 c. 63.

STATUTORY INSTRUMENTS

1977 No. 1180 (S.92)

SHERIFF COURT, SCOTLAND

Act of Sederunt (Sheriff Court Procedure, Consumer Credit) 1977

Made - - - -	*14th July* 1977
Coming into Operation	*8th August* 1977

The Lords of Council and Session, considering that it is necessary to regulate proceedings in the Sheriff Court under section 75 of the Consumer Credit Act 1974(a) under and by virtue of the powers conferred on them by section 32 of the Sheriff Courts (Scotland) Act 1971(b) and of all other powers competent to them in that behalf, do hereby enact and declare:—

Citation, commencement and interpretation

1.—(1) This Act of Sederunt may be cited as the Act of Sederunt (Sheriff Court Procedure, Consumer Credit) 1977 and shall come into operation on 8th August 1977.

(2) The Interpretation Act 1889(c) shall apply for the interpretation of this Act of Sederunt as it applies for the interpretation of an Act of Parliament.

Procedure in Ordinary Causes

2. In addition to the rules for regulating the procedure in an ordinary cause contained in the Sheriff Courts (Scotland) Act 1907(d) as amended, the rules contained in Schedule 1 to this Act of Sederunt shall apply in relation to proceedings under section 75 of the Consumer Credit Act 1974.

Procedure in Summary Causes

3. In addition to the rules for regulating the procedure in a summary cause contained in the Act of Sederunt (Summary Cause Rules, Sheriff Court) 1976(e) the rules contained in Schedule 2 to this Act of Sederunt shall apply in relation to proceedings under section 75 of the Consumer Credit Act 1974.

And the Lords appoint this Act of Sederunt to be entered in the Books of Sederunt.

G. C. Emslie,
I.P.D.

Edinburgh.
14th July 1977.

(a) 1974 c. 39.   (b) 1971 c. 58.   (c) 1889 c. 63.   (d) 1907 c. 51.
(e) S.I. 1976/476 (1976 I, p. 1390).

SCHEDULE 1

Third party procedure in an ordinary cause.

Where, in an action under Section 75 of the Consumer Credit Act 1974 a defender has a claim against a third party who is not already a party to the action or whom the pursuer is not bound to call as a defender in respect that that party is jointly and severally liable with the defender to the pursuer in respect of the subject matter of the action, the defender may set out in his defences or in a separate statement of facts the grounds on which he maintains that the third party should be made a party to the action. The defences or statement of facts shall also contain appropriate pleas-in-law directed against such third party. Thereafter the defender may enrol a motion for the purpose of obtaining an order of court for the service of a third party notice upon such third party. If the motion be granted, the third party shall be constituted a party to the action and it shall be competent to such third party to lodge answers on or before a date appointed by the court for the regulation of further procedure. Averments directed against a third party should ordinarily be made prior to the closing of the record, but may, in the discretion of the court and subject to such conditions as the court may attach, be made at a later stage, provided that no such averments shall be made later than the commencement of the hearing of the cause on its merits. A third party notice shall be as nearly as may be in the form shown in the form in the Appendix to this Schedule; and the answers by a third party shall be headed 'Answers for E. F. Third Party in the action at the instance of A. B. Pursuer against C. D. Defender;' and the following provisions shall apply to the procedure under such third party notice:

(a) The third party notice shall be served on the third party in any manner in which an initial writ may competently be served on a defender and shall be accompanied by a copy of the initial writ and defences, or the record, if any. A copy of the third party notice shall be lodged in process with a certificate of execution thereon.

(b) The order granting leave to serve a third party notice may contain a warrant for arrestment to found jurisdiction, or for arrestment on the dependence.

(c) On the date appointed by the court for the regulation of further procedure or at any time thereafter the court may grant such decree, interlocutor or order as it thinks fit.

(d) Any decree, interlocutor or order against the third party shall take effect and be extractable in the same way as a decree, interlocutor or order against the defender.

APPENDIX TO SCHEDULE 1

Third Party Notice in the Cause between

> A. B. Pursuer
> and
> C. D. Defender
> and
> E. F. Third Party

to E. F.

This Notice is served upon you by the above named C. D. by virtue of an order granted by Sheriff   in the action in which the above-named A. B. is the pursuer and C. D. the defender. In the action the pursuer claims against the defender £   in respect of
as more fully appears in the copy initial writ and condescendence (or copy record in the action) enclosed herewith.

> The defender admits (or denies) liability to the pursuer but claims that (if he is liable to the pursuer) you are liable to relieve him wholly (or partially) of his liability in respect of (set forth contract or other right of contribution, relief, or indemnity) as more fully appears from his defences lodged in the above action and enclosed herewith,

or

> (otherwise as the case may be).
> And take notice that if you wish to resist either the claim of the pursuer against the defender, or the claim of the defender against you, you must lodge answers in the action not later than   being the date appointed by the court for the regulation of further procedure and must appear or be represented in court on that date, otherwise the Court may pronounce such decree against you as it thinks fit.

Dated this   day of   19

(Signed)   (Solicitor for the Defender).

SCHEDULE 2

Third party procedure in a summary cause.

Where in an action under Section 75 of the Consumer Credit Act 1974 a defender has a claim against a third party who is not already a party to the action or whom the pursuer is not bound to call as a defender in respect that that party is jointly and severally liable with the defender to the pursuer in respect of the subject matter of the action, the defender may apply under Rule 93 of the Act of Sederunt (Summary Cause Rules, Sheriff Court) 1976 to the court for an order constituting that third party as a party to the action.

If the application be granted the following provisions shall apply:—

(a) The court shall fix a date on which it shall regulate further procedure and shall grant warrant to serve on the third party on such notice as the court may specify:

a copy of the order,

a copy of the summons,

a note of the defences and the grounds on which it is alleged the third party is liable,

a notice in a form as near as may be to the form of the notice shown in the Appendix to this Schedule.

(b) On the date fixed by the court to regulate further procedure or at any time thereafter, the court may grant such decree, interlocutor or order as it thinks fit.

(c) Such decree, interlocutor or order against the third party shall take effect and be extractable in the same way as a decree, interlocutor or order against the defender.

APPENDIX TO SCHEDULE 2

Third Party Notice in the case of

> A. B. Pursuer
> against
> C. D. Defender
> and
> E. F. Third Party

To E. F.

This Notice is served upon you by C. D. by virtue of an order granted by Sheriff
in the case in which A. B. is the pursuer and C. D. the defender. In
the case the pursuer claims against the defender for   in
respect of   as more fully appears in the copy summons.

The defender admits (or denies) liability to the pursuer but (and) claims that (if he
is liable to the pursuer) you are liable to relieve him wholly (or partially) of his
liability for the reasons set out in the statement enclosed herewith.

Take notice that if you wish to resist either the claim of the pursuer against the
defender or the claim of the defender against you or to pay any sum of instalments,
you are required to appear at the Sheriff Court at (address)
                          on (day and date)   at (time)

If you do not appear decree may be granted against you in your absence.

Dated this   day of   19

                         (Signed)   (Solicitor for Defender)

NOTES:

  (1) You may attend court in person or be represented by an advocate or solicitor.

  (2) If you are ordered to pay a sum of money by instalments any failure to pay such
instalments at the proper time may result in your forfeiting the right to pay by instalments
and the whole amount outstanding will then become due.

  (3) If decree is granted against you this amongst other things may lead to the arrestment
of your wages and/or the seizure of your possessions.

EXPLANATORY NOTE

(This Note is not part of the Act of Sederunt.)

   This Act of Sederunt makes rules to enable third party procedure to operate
in actions brought against a creditor under Section 75 of the Consumer Credit
Act 1974 in the Sheriff Court.

STATUTORY INSTRUMENTS

1977 No. 1181

MERCHANT SHIPPING

MASTERS AND SEAMEN

The Merchant Shipping (Seamen's Documents) (Amendment) Regulations 1977

Made - - - -	*15th July* 1977
Laid before Parliament	*25th July* 1977
Coming into Operation	*15th August* 1977

The Secretary of State, after consulting with the organisations referred to in section 99(2) of the Merchant Shipping Act 1970(a), in exercise of powers conferred by section 71 of that Act and now vested in him(b), and of all other powers enabling him in that behalf, hereby makes the following Regulations:—

1. These Regulations may be cited as the Merchant Shipping (Seamen's Documents) (Amendment) Regulations 1977 and shall come into operation on 15th August 1977.

2. The Merchant Shipping (Seamen's Documents) Regulations 1972(c), as amended(d), shall be further amended as follows:—

(1) In Regulation 20 for paragraph (*d*) there shall be substituted:
"(*d*) (i) dates of any Merchant Navy Training Board training courses he attends for instruction in survival at sea and the certificates or other qualifications (if any) obtained;
(ii) dates and nature of any other training courses (including pre-sea training courses) he attends and the certificates or other qualifications (if any) obtained;".

(2) In Regulation 21(1)(*a*) for "(*d*)" there shall be substituted "(*d*)(i) and (*d*)(ii)".

(3) After paragraph (*f*) of Regulation 21(1) there shall be added:
"(*g*) referred to in Regulation 20(*d*)(i) may be made by an official of the Merchant Navy Establishment Administration, the Principal of the training establishment attended or the Instructor in charge of the holder's training;".

Stanley Clinton Davis,
Parliamentary Under-Secretary of State,
Department of Trade.

15th July 1977.

(a) 1970 c. 36.   (b) *See* S.I. 1970/1537 (1970 III, p. 5293).
(c) S.I. 1972/1295 (1972 II, p. 3874).
(d) The amendment is not relevant to the subject matter of these Regulations.

EXPLANATORY NOTE

(This Note is not part of the Regulations.)

These Regulations further amend the Merchant Shipping (Seamen's Documents) Regulations 1972 by providing that details of Merchant Navy Training Board training courses in survival at sea may be recorded in Discharge Books by an official of the Merchant Navy Establishment Administration, the Principal of the training establishment attended or the Instructor in charge of the training.

STATUTORY INSTRUMENTS

1977 No. 1185

PUBLIC HEALTH, ENGLAND AND WALES

The Control of Pollution (Licensing of Waste Disposal) (Amendment) Regulations 1977

Made - - -	*14th July* 1977
Laid before Parliament	*26th July* 1977
Coming into Operation	*16th August* 1977

The Secretary of State for the Environment, as respects England, and the Secretary of State for Wales, as respects Wales, in exercise of the powers conferred on them by sections 3(1), 10(1), 30(4) and 104(1) of the Control of Pollution Act 1974(a) and of all other powers enabling them in that behalf, hereby make the following regulations:—

Citation, commencement and interpretation

1.—(1) These regulations may be cited as the Control of Pollution (Licensing of Waste Disposal) (Amendment) Regulations 1977 and shall come into operation on 16th August 1977.

(2) The Interpretation Act 1889(b) shall apply for the interpretation of these regulations as it applies for the interpretation of an Act of Parliament.

(3) In these regulations "the principal regulations" means the Control of Pollution (Licensing of Waste Disposal) Regulations 1976(c).

Amendment of principal regulations

2. The principal regulations are hereby amended as follows:—

(a) at the end of paragraph (c) of regulation 3 (which regulation provides that waste of certain descriptions shall be treated as being industrial waste, subject to certain exceptions specified in paragraph (c) thereof) there shall be inserted the following sub-paragraphs:—

"(iii) sewage deposited on land from a sanitary convenience forming part of a moving or stationary vehicle which is being used for the conveyance of passengers; and

(iv) sewage buried on land, being matter taken from a moveable receptacle contained in a sanitary convenience serving a camp site, caravan site, building site, signal box, or other land or premises not being a dwelling-house.";

(a) 1974 c. 40. (b) 1889 c. 63. (c) S.I. 1976/732 (1976 II, p. 1945).

(*b*) at the end of paragraph (1) of regulation 4 (which regulation exempts the disposal of certain categories of controlled waste from the requirement to be licensed) there shall be inserted the following sub-paragraph:—

"(*l*) waste is deposited by means of a line of pipes—

(i) on the foreshore, or

(ii) on any land above high-water mark which is covered by the sea from time to time.";

(*c*) at the end of regulation 4 there shall be inserted the following paragraph:—

"(4) In this regulation 'high-water mark' means the high-water mark of ordinary spring tides, and 'low-water mark' shall be construed accordingly; and 'the foreshore' means the land between high-water mark and low-water mark.";

(*d*) the following regulation shall be substituted for regulation 7 (appeals under section 10(1)):—

"**7.**—(1) Notice of appeal under section 10(1) (appeals to Secretary of State from decisions with respect to licences) shall be given in writing within six months of the date of the decision in question (or, as the case may be, of the deemed rejection under section 6(5)) or such longer period as the Secretary of State may at any time allow.

(2) The Secretary of State may, if he thinks fit, require a person who has appealed under section 10(1) to furnish him within a specified period with two copies of a statement of the reasons for his appeal and two copies of any or all of the following documents:—

(*a*) the application, if any, to the disposal authority for a disposal licence or for a modification of such a licence;

(*b*) any relevant plans, drawings, particulars and documents submitted to the disposal authority in support of the application;

(*c*) any relevant record, consent, determination, notice or other notification made or issued by the disposal authority;

(*d*) any relevant planning permission in force under the Town and Country Planning Act 1971(**a**);

(*e*) all other relevant correspondence with other authorities.

(3) The Secretary of State shall send to the disposal authority a copy of the notice of appeal and of every other document submitted by the appellant with that notice or furnished by him under paragraph (2) above.

(4) The Secretary of State may, if he thinks fit, require the appellant or the disposal authority to submit within a specified period a further statement in writing in respect of any of the matters to which the appeal relates and if, after considering the

_____

(**a**) 1971 c. 78.

grounds of the appeal and any such further statement, the Secretary of State is satisfied that he is sufficiently informed for the purpose of reaching a decision as to the matters to which the appeal relates, he may decide that appeal without further investigation; but if he does not so decide it, the Secretary of State shall (except in a case where he causes a local inquiry to be held under section 96), if either party so desire, afford to each of them an opportunity of appearing before, and being heard by, a person appointed by the Secretary of State for that purpose."

Peter Shore,

12th July 1977.   Secretary of State for the Environment.

John Morris,

14th July 1977.   Secretary of State for Wales.

EXPLANATORY NOTE.
(This Note is not part of the Regulations.)

The Control of Pollution (Licensing of Waste Disposal) Regulations 1976 provide, among other things, that waste of certain descriptions is to be treated as industrial waste for the purposes of the Control of Pollution Act 1974, and that the deposit of certain categories of controlled waste is to be exempted from the need to be licensed under that Act; they also make certain provision for the making of appeals to the Secretary of State under section 10(1) of the Act.

These Regulations amend the 1976 Regulations as follows:—

(*a*) the provisions of the Act controlling industrial waste are not to apply to sewage deposited on land from sanitary conveniences on railway trains, nor to sewage buried on land from conveniences used at camp sites, caravan sites, and other similar premises;

(*b*) the requirement of the Act that the deposit of certain categories of waste is to be made only on sites licensed under Part I of the Act is not to apply to waste deposited on the foreshore through a pipe;

(*c*) regulation 7 of the 1976 Regulations, which relates to the method of making an appeal to the Secretary of State under section 10(1) of the Act, is extended so as to prescribe the procedure to be followed by the Secretary of State before he determines an appeal.

STATUTORY INSTRUMENTS

1977 No. 1186 (S. 93)

COURT OF SESSION, SCOTLAND

Act of Sederunt (Extension of Sessions of Court) 1977

Made - - - - 14th July 1977

Coming into Operation 3rd August 1977

The Lords of Council and Session, by virtue of the powers conferred by section 4(2) of the Administration of Justice (Scotland) Act 1933(a) DO HEREBY ENACT AND DECLARE that Thursday, 4th August 1977, Thursday, 25th August 1977 and Thursday, 15th September 1977 shall be Sederunt Days for the purposes of passing any required Acts of Sederunt.

This Act of Sederunt may be cited as the Act of Sederunt (Extension of Sessions of Court) 1977 and shall come into operation on 3rd August 1977.

And the Lords appoint this Act of Sederunt to be inserted in the Books of Sederunt.

G. C. Emslie,
I.P.D.

Edinburgh.
14th July 1977.

(a) 1933 c. 41.

STATUTORY INSTRUMENTS

1977 No. 1187

PENSIONS

The Occupational Pension Schemes (Preservation of Benefit) Amendment Regulations 1977

Made - - - -	*18th July* 1977
Laid before Parliament	*26th July* 1977
Coming into Operation	*16th August* 1977

The Secretary of State for Social Services, in exercise of the powers conferred upon him by paragraphs 12 and 22 of Schedule 16 to the Social Security Act 1973(a), and of all other powers enabling him in that behalf, after considering the report of the Occupational Pensions Board on the preliminary draft submitted to them, hereby makes the following regulations:—

Citation, interpretation and commencement

1. These regulations, which may be cited as the Occupational Pension Schemes (Preservation of Benefit) Amendment Regulations 1977, shall be read as one with the Occupational Pension Schemes (Preservation of Benefit) Regulations 1973(b) (hereinafter called "the principal regulations") as amended (c), and shall come into operation on 16th August 1977.

Amendments of principal regulations

2.—(1) Regulation 6 of the principal regulations (alternatives to short service benefit) shall be amended by substituting for the references in paragraphs (2) and (3) to paragraph (1)(*d*)(ii) references to paragraph (1)(*d*)(iii).

(2) Regulation 10 (termination of service) of the principal regulations shall be amended as mentioned in paragraphs (3) and (4) below.

(3) At the end of paragraph (3)(*b*) there shall be added the following, namely—
"or
  (iv) an interval of any length if it is between 2 employments the second of which results from the exercise of a right to return to work under section 48(1) of the Employment Protection Act 1975(d) (right to return to work following pregnancy or confinement)."

(a) 1973 c. 38.   (b) S.I. 1973/1469 (1973 II, p. 4471).
  (c) The relevant amending instrument is the Occupational Pension Schemes (Preservation of Benefit) Amendment Regulations 1976 (S.I. 1976/140 (1976 I, p. 396)).
  (d) 1975 c. 71.

(4) For paragraph (5)(c) there shall be substituted the following, namely—

"(c) the contract is not renewed (or, as the case may be, the service resumed) with the same employer or his successor—

(i) immediately, or

(ii) after an interval not exceeding one month, or

(iii) pursuant to the exercise of a right to return to work under section 48(1) of the Employment Protection Act 1975,".

Deductions from short service benefit

3.—(1) Where a scheme provides that in computing the amount of long service benefit payable to a member a deduction shall be made, either on account of benefit payable to that member under the Social Security Act 1975(a) or otherwise, any corresponding provision in relation to short service benefit shall be permissible only if the basis on which the amount of the deduction is computed is such as the Board may consider reasonable having regard to all the circumstances of the case.

(2) This regulation does not apply to any deduction made in computing short service benefit pursuant to a right of charge or lien on, or set-off against, such benefit which is permitted by paragraph 18 of Schedule 16 to the Act.

David Ennals,
Secretary of State for Social Services.
18th July 1977.

EXPLANATORY NOTE
(*This Note is not part of the Regulations.*)

These Regulations amend the Occupational Pension Schemes (Preservation of Benefit) Regulations 1973. Regulation 2 amends regulations 6 and 10 of those regulations to take account of the amendment made to regulation 6 by the Occupational Pensions Schemes (Preservation of Benefit) Amendment Regulations 1976 and to provide that, for the purposes of the preservation requirements set out in Part I of Schedule 16 to the Social Security Act 1973, a woman's service in an employment is not treated as terminated if it is followed by another employment which results from the exercise of a right to return to work under section 48(1) of the Employment Protection Act 1975. Regulation 3 provides that where a scheme provides that in computing long service benefit a deduction is to be made for any reason, any corresponding provision in relation to short service benefit shall be permissible only if the Occupational Pensions Board consider the basis for computing the amount of the deduction to be reasonable.

The report of the Occupational Pensions Board on the preliminary draft of these regulations, dated 7th July 1977, is contained in House of Commons Paper No. 454 (Session 1976-77) published by Her Majesty's Stationery Office.

(a) 1975 c. 14.

STATUTORY INSTRUMENTS

1977 No. 1188

PENSIONS

The Contracted-out Employment (Miscellaneous Provisions) Regulations 1977

Made - - - -	18*th July* 1977
Laid before Parliament	26*th July* 1977
Coming into Operation	6*th April* 1978

The Secretary of State for Social Services, in exercise of the powers conferred upon him by section 40(2) and (3) of the Social Security Pensions Act 1975(a) and sections 21(1) and (2) and 22(9) and (13) of the Social Security (Miscellaneous Provisions) Act 1977(b) and of all other powers enabling him in that behalf, after considering the report of the Occupational Pensions Board on the preliminary draft submitted to them, hereby makes the following regulations:—

Citation, interpretation and commencement

1.—(1) These regulations may be cited as the Contracted-out Employment (Miscellaneous Provisions) Regulations 1977 and shall come into operation on 6th April 1978.

(2) In these regulations, unless the context otherwise requires—

"the 1977 Act" means the Social Security (Miscellaneous Provisions) Act 1977;

"the Pensions Act" means the Social Security Pensions Act 1975;

"relevant year", in relation to an earner, means any tax year in his working life (not being earlier than the first tax year for which lower and upper earnings limits are specified under section 1 of the Pensions Act);

"trustees", in relation to a scheme which is not set up or established under a trust, means the administrator of the scheme;

and other expressions have the same meaning as in the Pensions Act.

(3) Any reference in these regulations to any provision made by or contained in any enactment or instrument shall, except in so far as the context otherwise requires, be construed as a reference to that provision as amended or extended by any enactment or instrument and as including a reference to any provision which it re-enacts or replaces, or which may re-enact or replace it, with or without modification.

(4) The rules for the construction of Acts of Parliament contained in the Interpretation Act 1889(c) shall apply in relation to this instrument and in relation to the revocations effected by it as if this instrument and the regulations revoked by it were Acts of Parliament and as if the revocations were repeals.

(a) 1975 c. 60.   (b) 1977 c. 5.
(c) 1889 c. 63.

Policies of insurance and annuity contracts

2. For the purposes of section 22(9) of the 1977 Act, which makes provisions dependent upon the existence in force of a certificate issued by the Secretary of State stating that in his opinion the payment of a guaranteed minimum pension to which a person is entitled or has accrued rights is secured by means of a policy of insurance or annuity contract which satisfies prescribed conditions, the prescribed conditions are—

(a) that the policy is taken out, or the contract entered into, with an insurance company to which Part II of the Insurance Companies Act 1974(**a**) or the Insurance Companies (Northern Ireland) Order 1976(**b**) applies and which is authorised by or under section 3 of that Act or Article 7 of that Order to carry on ordinary long-term insurance business as defined in that Act or that Order; and

(b) that the policy or contract contains, or is endorsed with, terms so as to provide—

(i) that the annuity to be paid thereunder to or for the benefit of that person will be at least equal to the guaranteed minimum pension due to him, or, as the case may be, prospectively due to him at pensionable age, subject to any revaluation or increase under section 35(7) of the Pensions Act as amended by section 22(7) of the 1977 Act,

(ii) if that person is a man, that if he dies leaving a widow the annuity to be paid thereunder to her or for her benefit will be at least equal to the guaranteed minimum pension prospectively due to her in the event of her being left as that person's widow,

(iii) that the annuity or annuities (or such part of it or them as relates to the guaranteed minimum pensions of that person and, if he is a man, his widow) is or are (subject to the provisions of section 39(1) of the Pensions Act and regulations from time to time made thereunder(**c**)) non-commutable and non-assignable, and

(iv) that the insurance company assumes an enforceable obligation to pay the guaranteed minimum pensions either to that person and, if appropriate, his widow, or, as the case may be, to trustees of a trust for the benefit of that person and, if appropriate, his widow, under the terms of which the sums paid by the insurance company in respect of those guaranteed minimum pensions can be used for no other purpose.

Modification of section 44(6) of the Pensions Act

3. In relation to a scheme which has ceased to be contracted-out and, immediately before it so ceased, contained provisions authorised by section 35(7) of the Pensions Act as amended by section 22(7) of the 1977 Act, section 44(6) of the Pensions Act as amended by section 22(12) of the 1977 Act shall have effect with the modification that, where under the provisions authorised by section 35(7) an earner's earnings factors are determined for the purposes of section 35(2) of the Pensions Act without reference to any order made under section 21 of the Pensions Act, that order shall also be disregarded for the purpose of calculating the costs, referred to in section 44(5)(a) and (b) of the Pensions Act, of providing guaranteed minimum pensions for or in respect of that earner, so however that those costs shall be calculated on the basis that the

---

(a) 1974 c. 49.   (b) S.I. 1976/59 (N.I.3).
(c) *See* regulation 8 of S.I. 1975/2101 (1975 III, p. 7879).

weekly equivalent mentioned in section 35(2) has been increased, in the manner for which the scheme is required to provide by section 35(7), for each relevant year after the year in which the earner's service is terminated except those years (if any) for which his earnings factors are increased by 12 per cent. in accordance with section 44(6).

Modification of section 21(1) of the 1977 Act

4. In relation to a scheme which has ceased to be contracted-out and, immediately before it so ceased, contained provisions authorised by section 35(7) of the Pensions Act as amended by section 22(7) of the 1977 Act, section 21(1) of the 1977 Act shall be so modified as to provide that, in the case of an earner whose service in contracted-out employment by reference to the scheme is terminated before he attains pensionable age—

(a) if it is so terminated before the period of 5 years ending with the tax year in which the scheme ceases to be contracted-out, the provision for taking his earnings factor for any relevant year to be that factor as increased by 12 per cent. for some or all of those tax years shall not apply; and

(b) if it is so terminated within that period of 5 years and unless an election is made as provided in section 21(1), the provision for taking his earnings factor for any relevant year to be that factor as increased by 12 per cent. for some or all of those tax years shall apply, so however that his weekly equivalent shall not be increased, pursuant to any provision required by section 35(7), for the years for which that factor is taken to be that factor as increased by 12 per cent.

Miscellaneous provisions affecting section 21 of the 1977 Act

5.—(1) For the purposes of section 21 of the 1977 Act the prescribed person is the trustees of the scheme.

(2) An election under section 21 of the 1977 Act shall be notified to the Secretary of State in writing in such form as the Secretary of State may reasonably require for the purpose of identifying the earner to whom the election relates.

(3) Section 21 of the 1977 Act shall not apply where the arrangements approved by the Occupational Pensions Board in respect of an earner's accrued rights to guaranteed minimum pensions under the scheme which is ceasing to be contracted-out consist of or include the transfer of those rights to another contracted-out scheme.

Priorities on the winding-up of a scheme

6. An occupational pension scheme (not being a public service scheme) which contains provision for the payment of pensions or other benefits (not being pensions or other benefits payable by reason of a death) to persons who have not attained normal pension age shall be exempt from the requirements of section 40(3) of the Pensions Act (as amended by section 22(8) of the 1977 Act) to the following extent only, namely that it shall not be required to accord priority on a winding-up to the liabilities specified in paragraphs (a) to (d) of the said section 40(3) over liabilities of the scheme in respect of pensions and other benefits to which the widow or widower or any dependant of a person who is already entitled to payment of a pension or benefit under the scheme but has not attained normal pension age will be entitled on that person's death.

Revocations

7. Regulation 4(3) of the Occupational Pension Schemes (Contracting-out) Regulations 1975**(a)**, sub-paragraph (c) in the definition of "responsible paying authority" in regulation 1(2) of those regulations, and sub-paragraph (c) in the definition of "responsible paying authority" in regulation 1(2) of the Contracted-out Employment (Notifications, Premium Payment and Miscellaneous Provisions) Regulations 1976**(b)**, are hereby revoked.

David Ennals,
Secretary of State for Social Services.

18th July 1977.

EXPLANATORY NOTE

(This Note is not part of the Regulations.)

These Regulations make miscellaneous provisions regarding the contracting-out of occupational pension schemes pursuant to Part III of the Social Security Pensions Act 1975 ("the Pensions Act") as amended by the Social Security (Miscellaneous Provisions) Act 1977.

Regulation 2 sets out the conditions which a policy of insurance or annuity contract must satisfy in order that a Secretary of State's certificate may be issued under section 22(9) of the 1977 Act, thereby bringing about a relaxation of some of the requirements of sections 41 and 44 of the Pensions Act. This regulation supersedes regulation 4(3) of the Occupational Pension Schemes (Contracting-out) Regulations 1975, which is revoked by regulation 7.

Regulation 3 modifies the provisions of section 44(6) of the Pensions Act as amended by section 22(12) of the 1977 Act (which provides for state scheme premiums to be calculated as if earnings factors were increased for certain years by 12 per cent. instead of in accordance with orders made under section 21 of the Pensions Act) as they apply to schemes which contain special provisions, authorised under section 35(7) of the Pensions Act as amended by section 22(7) of the 1977 Act, for the calculation of guaranteed minimum pensions of earners whose service in contracted-out employment by reference to the scheme is terminated before they reach pensionable age.

Regulation 4 modifies the provisions of section 21(1) of the 1977 Act (which provides for guaranteed minimum pensions, in the case of schemes which cease to be contracted-out, to be calculated as if earnings factors were increased for certain years by 12 per cent.) as they apply to schemes containing provisions authorised by section 35(7) of the Pensions Act.

Regulation 5 makes ancillary provisions for the purposes of section 21 of the 1977 Act, and provides that it shall not apply in cases where accrued rights to guaranteed minimum pensions are transferred from one contracted-out scheme to another.

(a) S.I. 1975/2101 (1975 III, p. 7879).   (b) S.I. 1976/143 (1976 I, p. 411).

Regulation 6 provides a limited exemption for certain schemes from the requirements of section 40(3) of the Pensions Act (which relate to priorities among liabilities on the winding-up of a scheme).

The report of the Occupational Pensions Board on the preliminary draft of these regulations, dated 20th June 1977, is contained in House of Commons Paper No. 513 (Session 1976/77) published by Her Majesty's Stationery Office.

STATUTORY INSTRUMENTS

1977 No. 1189 (L. 23)

COUNTY COURTS

The County Court Districts (Camborne and Redruth) Order 1977

Made - - -		*14th July* 1977
Coming into Operation		*29th August* 1977

The Lord Chancellor, in exercise of the powers conferred on him by section 2 of the County Courts Act 1959 **(a)**, hereby makes the following Order:—

1. This Order may be cited as the County Court Districts (Camborne and Redruth) Order 1977 and shall come into operation on 29th August 1977.

2. The Redruth County Court shall cease to be held at Redruth and shall hereafter be held at Camborne under the name of the Camborne and Redruth County Court; and accordingly Schedule 1 to the County Court Districts Order 1970 **(b)**, as amended **(c)**, (in this Order referred to as "the principal Order"), shall be further amended:—

(*a*) by substituting "CAMBORNE AND REDRUTH" for "RED-RUTH" in column 1; and

(*b*) by transferring the whole of the entry relating to "CAMBORNE AND REDRUTH" to its proper alphabetical position therein.

3. In Schedule 2 to the principal Order there shall be inserted, after the entry relating to the Bury St. Edmunds County Court the following entry:—

Column 1	Column 2
"Camborne and Redruth	Camborne"

4. No process shall be invalid only because the court is described therein by the name by which it was known prior to the coming into operation of this Order.

Dated 14th July 1977

Elwyn-Jones, C.

(a) 1959 c. 22. **(b)** S.I. 1970/16 (170 I, p. 17).
(c) The relevant amending instruments are S.I. 1970/904, 1973/2045, 1976/29, 850, 890 1977/348 (1970 II, p. 2833; 1973 III, p. 7065; 1976 I, p. 43; II, pp. 2193, 2244; 1977 I, p. 1185).

EXPLANATORY NOTE

(This Note is not part of the Order.)

This Order transfers the Redruth County Court to Camborne and changes the name of the court to Camborne and Redruth County Court.

STATUTORY INSTRUMENTS

1977 No. 1190

CUSTOMS AND EXCISE

The Export of Goods (Control) (Amendment No. 2) Order 1977

Made - - - - 18*th July* 1977

Coming into Operation 8*th August* 1977

The Secretary of State, in exercise of the powers conferred by section 1 of the Import, Export and Customs Powers (Defence) Act 1939(**a**) and now vested in him(**b**), hereby orders as follows:

1.—(1) This Order may be cited as the Export of Goods (Control) (Amendment No. 2) Order 1977 and shall come into operation on 8th August 1977.

(2) The Interpretation Act 1889(**c**) shall apply for the interpretation of this Order as it applies for the interpretation of an Act of Parliament and as if this Order and the Order hereby revoked were Acts of Parliament.

2. The Export of Goods (Control) Order 1970(**d**), as amended(**e**), shall have effect as if in Schedule 1, Group 8, the following was deleted namely:

"Potatoes ... ... A"

3. The Export of Goods (Control) (Amendment No. 2) Order 1975(**e**) is hereby revoked.

B. M. Eyles,
An Assistant Secretary,
18th July 1977. Department of Trade.

EXPLANATORY NOTE

(*This Note is not part of the Order.*)

This Order further amends the Export of Goods (Control) Order 1970 by removing potatoes from export control.

(**a**) 1939 c. 69.   (**b**) *See* S.I. 1970/1537 (1970 III, p. 5293).
(**c**) 1889 c. 63.   (**d**) S.I. 1970/1288 (1970 III, p. 4270).
(**e**) The relevant amending Order is S.I. 1975/1582 (1975 III, p. 5472).

STATUTORY INSTRUMENTS

1977 No. 1191

INDUSTRIAL TRAINING

The Industrial Training Levy (Road Transport) Order 1977

Made - - -	*18th July* 1977
Laid before Parliament	*28th July* 1977
Coming into Operation	*31st August* 1977

Whereas proposals made by the Road Transport Industry Training Board for the raising and collection of a levy have been submitted to, and approved by, the Manpower Services Commission under section 7 of the Industrial Training Act 1964 (a) ("the 1964 Act"), as amended by section 6 of and Schedule 2 to the Employment and Training Act 1973(b) ("the 1973 Act") and have thereafter been submitted by the said Commission to the Secretary of State under section 7(1C) of the 1964 Act as inserted by the 1973 Act;

And whereas in pursuance of section 7(1A)(*a*) of the 1964 Act as inserted by the 1973 Act the said proposals include provision for the exemption from the levy of employers who, in view of the small number of their employees, ought in the opinion of the Secretary of State to be exempted from it;

And whereas the Secretary of State estimates that the amount which, disregarding any exemptions, will be payable by virtue of this Order by any employer in the road transport industry, does not exceed an amount which the Secretary of State estimates is equal to one per cent. of the aggregate of the emoluments and payments intended to be disbursed as emoluments which have been paid or are payable by any such employer to or in respect of persons employed in the industry, in respect of the period specified in the said proposals as relevant, that is to say the period hereafter referred to in this Order as "the eleventh base period";

And whereas the Secretary of State is satisfied that proposals published by the said Board in pursuance of section 4A of the 1964 Act, as inserted by the 1973 Act, provide for exemption certificates relating to the levy in such cases as he considers necessary;

Now, therefore, the Secretary of State in exercise of the powers conferred on him by section 4 of the 1964 Act, as amended by section 6 of and Schedule 2 to the 1973 Act, and of all other powers enabling him in that behalf hereby makes the following Order:—

Citation and commencement

1. This Order may be cited as the Industrial Training Levy (Road Transport) Order 1977 and shall come into operation on 31st August 1977.

(a) 1964 c. 16. (b) 1973 c. 50.

2b

Interpretation

2.—(1) In this Order unless the context otherwise requires:—

(a) "an appeal tribunal" means an industrial tribunal established under section 12 of the Industrial Training Act 1964;

(b) "assessment" means an assessment of an employer to the levy;

(c) "the Board" means the Road Transport Industry Training Board;

(d) "business" means any activities of industry or commerce;

(e) "the eleventh base period" means the period of twelve months that commenced on 6th April 1976;

(f) "the eleventh levy period" means the period commencing with the day upon which this Order comes into operation and ending on 31st July 1978;

(g) "employer" means a person who is an employer in the road transport industry at any time in the eleventh levy period;

(h) "the industrial training order" means the Industrial Training (Road Transport Board) Order 1966(a) as amended by the Industrial Training (Road Transport Board) Order 1972(b) and the Industrial Training (Road Transport Board) Order 1966 (Amendment) Order 1973(c);

(i) "the levy" means the levy imposed by the Board in respect of the eleventh levy period;

(j) "notice" means a notice in writing;

(k) "road transport establishment" means an establishment in Great Britain engaged in the eleventh base period wholly or mainly in the road transport industry for a total of twenty-seven or more weeks or, being an establishment that commenced to carry on business in the eleventh base period, for a total number of weeks exceeding one-half of the number of weeks in the part of the said period commencing with the day on which business was commenced and ending on the last day thereof;

(l) "the road transport industry" does not include any activities which have been transferred from the industry of the Board to the industry of another industrial training board by one of the transfer orders but save as aforesaid means any one or more of the activities which, subject to the provisions of paragraph 2 of Schedule 1 to the industrial training order, are specified in paragraph 1 of that Schedule as the activities of the road transport industry or, in relation to an establishment whose activities have been transferred to the industry of the Board by one of the transfer orders, any activities so transferred;

(m) "the transfer orders" means:—

(i) the Industrial Training (Transfer of the Activities of Establishments) (No. 2) Order 1974(d),

(ii) the Industrial Training (Transfer of the Activities of Establishments) (No. 2) Order 1975(e),

(iii) the Industrial Training (Transfer of the Activities of Establishments) Order 1976(f), and

---

(a) S.I. 1966/1112 (1966 III, p. 2712).   (b) S.I. 1972/772 (1972 II, p. 2471).
(c) S.I. 1973/860 (1973 II, p. 2663).   (d) S.I. 1974/1495 (1974 III, p. 5739).
(e) S.I. 1975/1157 (1975 II, p. 4109).   (f) S.I. 1976/396 (1976 I, p. 1055).

(iv) the Industrial Training (Transfer of the Activities of Establishments) (No. 3) Order 1976(a).

(2) Any reference in this Order to persons employed at or from a road transport establishment shall in any case where the employer is a company be construed as including a reference to any director of the company (or any person occupying the position of director by whatever name he is called) who devotes substantially the whole of his time to the service of the company.

(3) Any reference in this Order to an establishment that commences to carry on business or that ceases to carry on business shall not be taken to apply where the location of the establishment is changed but its business is continued wholly or mainly at or from the new location, or where the suspension of activities is of a temporary or seasonal nature.

(4) The Interpretation Act 1889(b) shall apply to the interpretation of this Order as it applies to the interpretation of an Act of Parliament.

Imposition of the levy

3. The levy to be imposed by the Board on employers in respect of the eleventh levy period shall be assessed in accordance with the provisions of the Schedule to this Order.

Assessment notices

4.—(1) The Board shall serve an assessment notice on every employer assessed to the levy.

(2) The amount payable under an assessment notice shall be rounded down to the nearest £1.

(3) An assessment notice shall state the Board's address for the service of a notice of appeal or of an application for an extension of time for appealing.

(4) An assessment notice may be served on the person assessed to the levy either by delivering it to him personally or by leaving it, or sending it to him by post, at his last known address or place of business in the United Kingdom or, if that person is a corporation, by leaving it, or sending it by post to the corporation at such address or place of business or at its registered or principal office.

Payment of levy

5.—(1) Subject to the provisions of this Article and of Articles 6 and 7, the amount of the levy payable under an assessment notice served by the Board shall be due and payable to the Board on 1st December 1977, or one month after the date of the assessment notice, whichever is the later.

(2) The amount of an assessment shall not be recoverable by the Board until there has expired the time allowed for appealing against the assessment by Article 7(1) of this Order and any further period or periods of time that the Board or an appeal tribunal may have allowed for appealing under paragraph (2) or (3) of that Article or, where an appeal is brought, until the appeal is decided or withdrawn.

(a) S.I. 1976/2110 (1976 III, p. 5851).   (b) 1889 c. 63.

Withdrawal of assessment

6.—(1) The Board may, by a notice served on the person assessed to the levy in the same manner as an assessment notice, withdraw an assessment if that person has appealed against that assessment under the provisions of Article 7 of this Order and the appeal has not been entered in the Register of Appeals kept under the appropriate Regulations specified in paragraph (5) of that Article.

(2) The withdrawal of an assessment shall be without prejudice to the power of the Board to serve a further assessment notice on the employer.

Appeals

7.—(1) A person assessed to the levy may appeal to an appeal tribunal against the assessment within one month from the date of the service of the assessment notice or within any further period or periods of time that may be allowed by the Board or an appeal tribunal under the following provisions of this Article.

(2) The Board by notice may for good cause allow a person assessed to the levy to appeal to an appeal tribunal against the assessment at any time within the period of four months from the date of the service of the assessment notice or within such further period or periods as the Board may allow before such time as may then be limited for appealing has expired.

(3) If the Board shall not allow an application for extension of time for appealing, an appeal tribunal shall upon application made to the tribunal by the person assessed to the levy have the like powers as the Board under the last foregoing paragraph.

(4) In the case of an assessment that has reference to an establishment that ceases to carry on business in the eleventh levy period on any day after the date of the service of the assessment notice, the foregoing provisions of this Article shall have effect as if for the period of four months from the date of the service of the assessment notice mentioned in paragraph (2) of this Article there were substituted the period of six months from the date of the cessation of business.

(5) An appeal or an application to an appeal tribunal under this Article shall be made in accordance with the Industrial Tribunals (England and Wales) Regulations 1965(**a**) as amended by the Industrial Tribunals (England and Wales) (Amendment) Regulations 1967(**b**) except where the assessment relates to persons employed at or from one or more establishments which are wholly in Scotland and to no other persons in which case the appeal or application shall be made in accordance with the Industrial Tribunals (Scotland) Regulations 1965(**c**) as amended by the Industrial Tribunals (Scotland) (Amendment) Regulations 1967(**d**).

(6) The powers of an appeal tribunal under paragraph (3) of this Article may be exercised by the President of the Industrial Tribunals (England and Wales) or by the President of the Industrial Tribunals (Scotland) as the case may be.

Evidence

8.—(1) Upon the discharge by a person assessed to the levy of his liability under an assessment the Board shall if so requested issue to him a certificate to that effect.

(**a**) S.I. 1965/1101 (1965 II, p. 2805).   (**b**) S.I. 1967/301 (1967 I, p. 1040).
(**c**) S.I. 1965/1157 (1965 II, p. 3266).   (**d**) S.I. 1967/302 (1967 I, p. 1050).

(2) The production in any proceedings of a document purporting to be certified by the Secretary of the Board to be a true copy of an assessment or other notice issued by the Board or purporting to be a certificate such as is mentioned in the foregoing paragraph of this Article shall, unless the contrary is proved, be sufficient evidence of the document and of the facts stated therein.

Signed by order of the Secretary of State.
18th July 1977.

John Golding,

Joint Parliamentary Under Secretary of State,
Department of Employment.

Article 3   SCHEDULE

1.—(1) In this Schedule unless the context otherwise requires—

(a) "emoluments" means all emoluments assessable to income tax under Schedule E (other than pensions), being emoluments from which tax under that Schedule is deductible, whether or not tax in fact falls to be deducted from any particular payment thereof;

(b) "exemption certificate" means a certificate issued by the Board under section 4B of the 1964 Act as inserted by the 1973 Act;

(c) "the relevant date" means the 5th April 1977;

(d) "the relevant establishment" means the road transport establishment of an employer other than an establishment in respect of which an exemption certificate has been issued to the employer, or one which is an establishment of an employer who is exempted by virtue of paragraph 3 of this Schedule;

(e) other expressions have the meanings assigned to them respectively by paragraph 3 or 4 of the Schedule to the industrial training order or by Article 2 of this Order.

(2) For the purposes of this Schedule no regard shall be had to the emoluments of any person employed as follows:—

(a) by the London Transport Executive wholly in any activities to which paragraph 1(p) of Schedule 1 to the industrial training order applies, not being activities that are specified in head (ii), (v) or (vi) of the definition of related activities in paragraph 3 of that Schedule and are incidental or ancillary to principal activities of the road transport industry;

(b) by a local authority or a joint board or joint committee of such authorities in any activities, not being activities carried out for the purposes of a passenger road transport service provided by the authority, board or committee;

(c) wholly in agriculture;

(d) wholly as a registered dock worker on dock work; or

(e) wholly in the supply of food or drink for immediate consumption.

2. Subject to the provisions of this Schedule, the levy shall be assessed by the Board in respect of each employer and the amount thereof shall be equal to 1·0 per cent. of the sum of the emoluments of all the persons employed by the employer in the eleventh base period at or from the relevant establishment or establishments.

3. There shall be exempt from the levy an employer—

(a) in whose case the sum of the emoluments of all the persons employed by him in the eleventh base period at or from his road transport establishment or establishments (whether or not any such establishment is a relevant establishment) is £16,000 or less (£19,000 or less in the case of an employer wholly or mainly engaged on the relevant date in any of the activities comprised in Group 1 of the Appendix to this Schedule, or £36,000 or less in the case of an employer wholly or mainly engaged on the relevant date in any of the activities comprised in Groups 2 and 3 of the said Appendix);

(b) who was wholly or mainly engaged on the relevant date in giving instruction by way of business in the driving of motor vehicles or goods vehicles.

4. Where any persons whose emoluments are taken into account for the purpose of the preceding paragraphs of this Schedule were employed at or from an establishment that ceases to carry on business in the eleventh levy period, the sum of the emoluments of those persons shall, for the purposes of the assessment, be reduced in the same proportion as the number of days between the commencement of the said levy period and the date of cessation of business (both dates inclusive) bears to the number of days in the said levy period.

APPENDIX

Column 1 Group No.	Column 2 Description of Activities
1.	Dealing in, letting out on hire or the repair by way of business of, agricultural machinery and equipment.
2.	The carriage of passengers by motor vehicles on roads for hire or reward.
3.	The letting out on hire (with or without the services of the drivers) of motor vehicles for the conveyance of persons.

EXPLANATORY NOTE

(This Note is not part of the Order.)

This Order gives effect to proposals of the Road Transport Industry Training Board which were submitted to and approved by the Manpower Services Commission, and thereafter submitted by the Manpower Services Commission to the Secretary of State. The proposals are for the imposition of a levy on employers in the road transport industry for the purpose of encouraging adequate training in the industry.

The levy is to be imposed in respect of the eleventh levy period commencing with the day upon which this Order comes into operation and ending on 31st July 1978. The levy will be assessed by the Board and there will be a right of appeal against an assessment to an industrial tribunal.

STATUTORY INSTRUMENTS

1977 No. 1192

INDUSTRIAL TRAINING

The Industrial Training Levy (Furniture and Timber) Order 1977

Made - - - -		*18th July* 1977
Laid before Parliament		*28th July* 1977
Coming into Operation		*31st August* 1977

Whereas proposals made by the Furniture and Timber Industry Training Board for the raising and collection of a levy have been submitted to, and approved by, the Manpower Services Commission under section 7 of the Industrial Training Act 1964(a) ("the 1964 Act"), as amended by section 6 of and Schedule 2 to the Employment and Training Act 1973(b) ("the 1973 Act") and have thereafter been submitted by the said Commission to the Secretary of State under section 7(1C) of the 1964 Act as inserted by the 1973 Act;

And whereas in pursuance of section 7(1A)(*a*) of the 1964 Act as inserted by the 1973 Act the said proposals include provision for the exemption from the levy of employers who, in view of the small number of their employees, ought in the opinion of the Secretary of State to be exempted from it;

And whereas the Secretary of State estimates that the amount which, disregarding any exemptions, will be payable by virtue of this Order by any employer in the furniture and timber industry, does not exceed an amount which the Secretary of State estimates is equal to one per cent. of the aggregate of the emoluments and payments intended to be disbursed as emoluments which have been paid or are payable by any such employer to or in respect of persons employed in the industry, in respect of the period specified in the said proposals as relevant, that is to say the period hereafter referred to in this Order as "the eleventh base period";

And whereas the Secretary of State is satisfied that proposals published by the said Board in pursuance of section 4A of the 1964 Act, as inserted by the 1973 Act, provide for exemption certificates relating to the levy in such cases as he considers necessary;

Now, therefore, the Secretary of State in exercise of the powers conferred on him by section 4 of the 1964 Act, as amended by section 6 of and Schedule 2 to the 1973 Act, and of all other powers enabling him in that behalf hereby makes the following Order:—

Citation and commencement

1. This Order may be cited as the Industrial Training Levy (Furniture and Timber) Order 1977 and shall come into operation on 31st August 1977.

(a) 1964 c. 16.   (b) 1973 c. 50.

Interpretation

2.—(1) In this Order unless the context otherwise requires:—

(*a*) "agriculture" has the same meaning as in section 109(3) of the Agriculture Act 1947(**a**) or, in relation to Scotland, as in section 86(3) of the Agriculture (Scotland) Act 1948(**b**);

(*b*) "an appeal tribunal" means an industrial tribunal established under section 12 of the Industrial Training Act 1964;

(*c*) "assessment" means an assessment of an employer to the levy;

(*d*) "the Board" means the Furniture and Timber Industry Training Board;

(*e*) "business" means any activities of industry or commerce;

(*f*) "charity" has the same meaning as in section 360 of the Income and Corporation Taxes Act 1970(**c**);

(*g*) "dock work" and "registered dock worker" have the same meanings as in the Docks and Harbours Act 1966(**d**);

(*h*) "the eleventh base period" means the period of twelve months that commenced on 6th April 1976;

(*i*) "the eleventh levy period" means the period commencing with the day upon which this Order comes into operation and ending on 5th April 1978;

(*j*) "emoluments" means all emoluments assessable to income tax under Schedule E (other than pensions), being emoluments from which tax under that Schedule is deductible, whether or not tax in fact falls to be deducted from any particular payment thereof;

(*k*) "employer" means a person who is an employer in the furniture and timber industry at any time in the eleventh levy period;

(*l*) "furniture and timber establishment" means an establishment in Great Britain engaged in the eleventh base period wholly or mainly in the furniture and timber industry for a total of twenty-seven or more weeks or, being an establishment that commenced to carry on business in the eleventh base period, for a total number of weeks exceeding one half of the number of weeks in the part of the said period commencing with the day on which business was commenced and ending on the last day thereof;

(*m*) "the furniture and timber industry" does not include any activities of an establishment which have been transferred from the industry of the Board to the industry of another industrial training board by one of the transfer orders, but save as aforesaid means any one or more of the activities which, subject to the provisions of paragraph 2 of Schedule 1 to the industrial training order, are specified in paragraph 1 of that Schedule as the activities of the furniture and timber industry, or in relation to an establishment whose activities have been transferred to the industry of the Board by one of the transfer orders, any activities so transferred;

(*n*) "the industrial training order" means the Industrial Training (Furniture and Timber Industry Board) Order 1965(**e**) as amended by the Industrial Training (Furniture and Timber Industry Board) Order 1969(**f**), the Industrial Training (Furniture and Timber Industry Board) Order

---

(**a**) 1947 c. 48.   (**b**) 1948 c. 45.   (**c**) 1970 c. 10.
(**d**) 1966 c. 28.   (**e**) S.I. 1965/2028 (1965 III, p. 5998).
(**f**) S.I. 1969/1290 (1969 III, p. 3820).

1969 (Amendment) Order 1970(a) and the Industrial Training (Furniture and Timber Industry Board) Order 1965 (Amendment) Order 1973(b);

(*o*) "the levy" means the levy imposed by the Board in respect of the eleventh levy period;

(*p*) "notice" means a notice in writing;

(*q*) "the transfer orders" means—

(i) the Industrial Training (Transfer of the Activities of Establishments) Order 1975(c);

(ii) the Industrial Training (Transfer of the Activities of Establishments) (No. 2) Order 1975(d);

(iii) the Industrial Training (Transfer of the Activities of Establishments) Order 1976(e); and

(iv) the Industrial Training (Transfer of the Activities of Establishments) (No. 2) Order 1976(f).

(2) Any reference in this Order to persons employed at or from a furniture and timber establishment shall in any case where the employer is a company be construed as including a reference to any director of the company (or any person occupying the position of director by whatever name he was called) who was, at the material time, in receipt of a salary from the company.

(3) Any reference in this Order to an establishment that commences to carry on business or that ceases to carry on business shall not be taken to apply where the location of the establishment is changed but its business is continued wholly or mainly at or from the new location, or where the suspension of activities is of a temporary or seasonal nature.

(4) The Interpretation Act 1889(g) shall apply to the interpretation of this Order as it applies to the interpretation of an Act of Parliament.

Imposition of the levy

3.—(1) The levy to be imposed by the Board on employers in respect of the eleventh levy period shall be assessed in accordance with the provisions of this Article.

(2) The levy shall be assessed by the Board separately in respect of each furniture and timber establishment of an employer (not being an employer who is exempt from the levy by virtue of paragraph (5) of this Article) but in agreement with the employer one assessment may be made in respect of any number of such establishments, in which case those establishments shall be deemed for the purposes of that assessment to constitute one establishment.

(3) Subject to the provisions of this Article, the levy assessed in respect of a furniture and timber establishment of an employer shall be an amount equal to 0·7 per cent. of the sum of the emoluments of all the persons employed by the employer in the eleventh base period at or from the relevant establishment (that is to say the furniture and timber establishment or establishments of the employer other than any establishment in respect of which an exemption certificate has been issued to the employer, or one which is an establishment of an employer who is exempted by virtue of paragraph (5) of this Article).

(a) S.I. 1970/1634 (1970 III, p. 5372).
(b) S.I. 1973/1224 (1973 II, p. 3662).
(c) S.I. 1975/434 (1975 I, p. 1371).
(d) S.I. 1975/1157 (1975 I, p. 4019).
(e) S.I. 1976/396 (1976 I, p. 1055).
(f) S.I. 1976/1635 (1976 III, p. 4163).
(g) 1889 c. 63.

(4) The amount of the levy imposed in respect of an establishment that ceases to carry on business in the eleventh levy period shall be in the same proportion to the amount that would otherwise be due under paragraph (3) of this Article as the number of days between the commencement of the said levy period and the date of cessation of business (both dates inclusive) bears to the number of days in the said levy period.

(5) There shall be exempt from the levy—

    (*a*) an employer in whose case the number of all the persons employed by him under contracts of service on 2nd April 1976 or on 1st April 1977 at or from the furniture and timber establishment or establishments of the employer did not exceed fifteen;

    (*b*) a charity.

(6) In determining for the purposes of this Article the number of persons employed by an employer account shall be taken of one half only of the number of any such persons normally employed by the employer for less than twenty-two hours a week, and, in the case of any such persons who are directors of the employing company, for more than eight hours a week. No account shall be taken of directors who work for eight hours or less a week.

(7) For the purposes of this Article no regard shall be had to the emoluments of any person wholly employed—

    (*a*) in agriculture;

    (*b*) as a registered dock worker on dock work; or

    (*c*) in the supply of food or drink for immediate consumption.

Assessment Notices

4.—(1) The Board shall serve an assessment notice on every employer assessed to the levy, but one notice may comprise two or more assessments.

(2) An assessment notice shall state the amount (rounded down, where necessary to the nearest £1) of the levy payable thereunder, and where the notice comprises two or more assessments the said amount shall, before any such rounding down, be equal to the total amount of the levy assessed by the Board under Article 3 of this Order in respect of each establishment included in the notice.

(3) An assessment notice shall state the Board's address for the service of a notice of appeal or of an application for an extension of time for appealing.

(4) An assessment notice may be served on the person assessed to the levy either by delivering it to him personally or by leaving it, or sending it to him by post, at his last known address or place of business in the United Kingdom or, if that person is a corporation, by leaving it, or sending it by post to the corporation, at such address or place of business or at its registered or principal office.

Payment of levy

5.—(1) Subject to the provisions of this Article and of Articles 6 and 7, the amount of the levy payable under an assessment notice served by the Board shall be due and payable to the Board one month after the date of the notice.

(2) The amount of an assessment shall not be recoverable by the Board until there has expired the time allowed for appealing against the assessment by Article 7(1) of this Order and any further period or periods of time that the

Board or an appeal tribunal may have allowed for appealing under paragraph (2) or (3) of that Article or, where an appeal is brought, until the appeal is decided or withdrawn.

Withdrawal of assessment

6.—(1) The Board may, by a notice served on the person assessed to the levy in the same manner as an assessment notice, withdraw an assessment if that person has appealed against that assessment under the provisions of Article 7 of this Order and the appeal has not been entered in the Register of Appeals kept under the appropriate Regulations specified in paragraph (5) of that Article.

(2) The withdrawal of an assessment shall be without prejudice—

> (*a*) to the power of the Board to serve a further assessment notice in respect of any establishment to which that assessment related;

> (*b*) to any other assessment included in the original assessment notice, and such notice shall thereupon have effect as if any assessment withdrawn by the Board had not been included therein.

Appeals

7.—(1) A person assessed to the levy may appeal to an appeal tribunal against the assessment within one month from the date of the service of the assessment notice or within any further period or periods of time that may be allowed by the Board or an appeal tribunal under the following provisions of this Article.

(2) The Board by notice may for good cause allow a person assessed to the levy to appeal to an appeal tribunal against the assessment at any time within the period of four months from the date of the service of the assessment notice or within such further period or periods as the Board may allow before such time as may then be limited for appealing has expired.

(3) If the Board shall not allow an application for extension of time for appealing, an appeal tribunal shall upon application made to the tribunal by the person assessed to the levy have the like powers as the Board under the last foregoing paragraph.

(4) In the case of an establishment that ceases to carry on business in the eleventh levy period on any day after the date of the service of the relevant assessment notice, the foregoing provisions of this Article shall have effect as if for the period of four months from the date of the service of the assessment notice mentioned in paragraph (2) of this Article there were substituted the period of six months from the date of the cessation of business.

(5) An appeal or an application to an appeal tribunal under this Article shall be made in accordance with the Industrial Tribunals (England and Wales) Regulations 1965(**a**) as amended by the Industrial Tribunals (England and Wales) (Amendment) Regulations 1967(**b**) except where the establishment to which the relevant assessment relates is wholly in Scotland in which case the appeal or application shall be made in accordance with the Industrial Tribunals (Scotland) Regulations 1965(**c**) as amended by the Industrial Tribunals (Scotland) (Amendment) Regulations 1967(**d**).

(a) S.I. 1965/1101 (1965 II, p. 2805).   (b) S.I. 1967/301 (1967 I, p. 1040).
(c) S.I. 1965/1157 (1965 II, p. 3266).   (d) S.I. 1967/302 (1967 I, p. 1050).

(6) The powers of an appeal tribunal under paragraph (3) of this Article may be exercised by the President of the Industrial Tribunals (England and Wales) or by the President of the Industrial Tribunals (Scotland) as the case may be.

Evidence

8.—(1) Upon the discharge by a person assessed to the levy of his liability under an assessment the Board shall if so requested issue to him a certificate to that effect.

(2) The production in any proceedings of a document purporting to be certified by the Secretary of the Board to be a true copy of an assessment or other notice issued by the Board or purporting to be a certificate such as is mentioned in the foregoing paragraph of this Article shall, unless the contrary is proved, be sufficient evidence of the document and of the facts stated therein.

Signed by order of the Secretary of State.

18th July 1977.

John Golding,
Joint Parliamentary Under Secretary of State,
Department of Employment.

EXPLANATORY NOTE

(This Note is not part of the Order.)

This Order gives effect to proposals of the Furniture and Timber Industry Training Board which were submitted to and approved by the Manpower Services Commission, and thereafter submitted by the Manpower Services Commission to the Secretary of State. The proposals are for the imposition of a levy upon employers in the furniture and timber industry for the purpose of encouraging adequate training in the industry.

The levy is to be imposed in respect of the eleventh levy period commencing with the day upon which this Order comes into operation and ending on 5th April 1978. The levy will be assessed by the Board and there will be a right of appeal against an assessment to an industrial tribunal.

STATUTORY INSTRUMENTS

1977 No. 1193

EDUCATION, ENGLAND AND WALES

The Provision of Milk and Meals (Amendment) (No. 2) Regulations 1977

Made - - - -	18th July 1977
Laid before Parliament	26th July 1977
Coming into Operation	16th August 1977

The Secretary of State for Education and Science and the Secretary of State for Wales, in joint exercise of the powers conferred by section 49 of the Education Act 1944(a) (read with section 1 of the Education (Milk) Act 1971(b) as amended by section 9 of the Education Act 1976(c), and vested in them(d), hereby make the following regulations:—

1. These regulations may be cited as the Provision of Milk and Meals (Amendment) (No. 2) Regulations 1977 and shall come into operation on 16th August 1977.

2. In these regulations a reference to the principal regulations is a reference to the Provision of Milk and Meals Regulations 1969(e), as amended(f).

3. In regulation 10(3)(a) of the principal regulations (charge for school dinner in nursery schools and in county and voluntary schools) for the sum "15p" there shall be substituted the sum "25p".

4.—(1) In paragraph 1 of schedule 1 to the principal regulations (determination of financial hardship) for the table and the first note following thereon there shall be substituted the following table and note:—

"Part A	Part B					
Size of Family	1	2	3	4	5	6
	£	£	£	£	£	£
1	34·35					
2	41·00	39·75				
3	47·65	46·40	45·15			
4	54·30	53·05	51·80	50·55		
5	60·95	59·70	58·45	57·20	55·95	
6	67·60	66·35	65·10	63·85	62·60	61·35

For larger families, in respect of each child—
(a) £6·65 is to be added at each incremental point in every additional line, and
(b) £1·25 is to be deducted at each incremental point in every additional column.".

(a) 1944 c. 31. (b) 1971 c. 74. (c) 1976 c. 81.
(d) S.I. 1964/490, 1970/1536 (1964 I, p. 800; 1970 III, p. 5289).
(e) S.I. 1969/483 (1969 I, p. 1382).
(f) The relevant amending instruments are S.I. 1971/1368, 1975/311, 1619, 1976/1705, 1977/385 (1971 II, p. 3844; 1975 I, p. 831; III, p. 5617; 1976 III, p. 4552; 1977 I, p. 1257).

(2) Paragraph 3(4A) of the said schedule 1 shall be omitted.

Given under the Official Seal of the Secretary of State for Education and Science on 15th July 1977.

Shirley Williams,
Secretary of State for Education
and Science.

(L.S.)

Given under my hand on 18th July 1977.

John Morris,
Secretary of State for Wales.

EXPLANATORY NOTE
(This Note is not part of the Regulations.)

These Regulations amend the Provision of Milk and Meals Regulations 1969.

Regulation 3 increases the charge for school dinners in nursery schools and in county and voluntary schools from 15p to 25p.

Regulation 4 relates to the remission of charges for school meals. The levels of net weekly income below which a parent qualifies for remission are raised (paragraph (1)). The provision relating to the disregard of child benefit for the purpose of determining whether a parent is entitled to remission is revoked (paragraph (2)).

STATUTORY INSTRUMENTS

1977 No. 1203 (S. 94)

EDUCATION, SCOTLAND

Milk and Meals (Education) (Scotland) Amendment (No. 2) Regulations 1977

Made - - - -	15th July 1977
Laid before Parliament	26th July 1977
Coming into Operation	16th August 1977

In exercise of the powers conferred on me by sections 53(3) and 144(5) of the Education (Scotland) Act 1962(a) and of all other powers enabling me in that behalf, I hereby make the following regulations:—

Citation, commencement and interpretation

1.—(1) These regulations may be cited as the Milk and Meals (Education) (Scotland) Amendment (No. 2) Regulations 1977 and these regulations and the Milk and Meals (Education) (Scotland) Regulations 1971 to 1977 shall be cited as the Milk and Meals (Education) (Scotland) Regulations 1971 to 1977.

(2) These regulations shall come into operation on 16th August 1977.

(3) The Interpretation Act 1889(b) shall apply for the interpretation of these regulations as it applies for the interpretation of an Act of Parliament.

Amendment of Regulations

2. The Milk and Meals (Education) (Scotland) Regulations 1971(c) as amended(d) shall be amended as follows—

(a) in Regulation 7(2)(a) (which prescribes the charge for midday meals) there shall be substituted for the reference to "15p", a reference to "25p".

(b) in Regulation 7(2)(b) (which prescribes the maximum charge for midday meals provided for pupils receiving special education) there shall be substituted for the reference to "7½p", a reference to "12½p".

(a) 1962 c. 47.   (b) 1889 c. 63.   (c) S.I. 1971/1537 (1971 III, p. 4340).

(d) The relevant amending instruments are S.I. 1972/1220, 1973/1258, 1974/1134, 1975/296, 1629, 1976/1702, 1977/362 (1972 II, p. 3612; 1973 II, p. 3729; 1974 II, p. 4313; 1975 I, p. 759, III, p. 5625; 1976 III, p. 4550; 1977 I, p. 1235).

(c) for the Schedule to the regulations there shall be substituted the following Schedule—

"Regulation 7(4)

SCHEDULE

DETERMINATION OF FINANCIAL HARDSHIP

Where the net weekly income of the parent of a family of any size specified in Part A of the following table is less than the amount of the corresponding entry in column 1 of Part B, the number of children in respect of whom the charge for the meal shall be remitted is the number at the head of the column in Part B in which there appears the lowest amount in that entry which exceeds his income.

Part A	Part B					
Size of Family	Net weekly income in £p					
	1	2	3	4	5	6
1	34.35					
2	41.00	39.75				
3	47.65	46.40	45.15			
4	54.30	53.05	51.80	50.55		
5	60.95	59.70	58.45	57.20	55.95	
6	67.60	66.35	65.10	63.85	62.60	61.35

For larger families, in respect of each child—

(a) £6.65 is to be added at each incremental point in every additional line; and

(b) £1.25 is to be subtracted at each incremental point in every additional column.

For the purpose of this Schedule—

'net weekly income' means the weekly resources of the parent calculated in accordance with the provisions of Part III of Schedule 1 to the Supplementary Benefits Act 1976 reduced by payments made for rent and rates and disregarding any attendance allowance under section 35 of the Social Security Act 1975(a);

'Size of Family' means the number of dependent children in the family who have not attained the age of 19."

Bruce Millan,
One of Her Majesty's Principal Secretaries of State.

New St Andrew's House,
Edinburgh.
15th July 1977.

(a) 1975 c. 14.

EXPLANATORY NOTE

(This Note is not part of the Regulations.)

These Regulations amend the Milk & Meals (Education) (Scotland) Regulations 1971 to provide for an increase in the charge for the school mid-day meal from 15p to 25p and in the case of pupils receiving special education for an increase in the maximum charge for the mid-day meal from 7½p to 12½p. They also amend the provisions of these Regulations for the calculation of a parent's income for the purpose of determining his entitlement to remission of the charge for school meals.

1977 No. 1204

NATIONAL HEALTH SERVICE, ENGLAND AND WALES

The National Health Service (Association of Community Health Councils—Establishment) Order 1977

Made - - - -	*19th July* 1977
Laid before Parliament	*22nd July* 1977
Coming into Operation	*15th August* 1977

The Secretary of State for Social Services in exercise of the powers conferred upon him by section 54(2) of the National Health Service Reorganisation Act 1973(a) and of all other powers enabling him in that behalf hereby makes the following order:—

Citation, commencement and interpretation

1.—(1) This order may be cited as the National Health Service (Association of Community Health Councils—Establishment) Order 1977 and shall come into operation on 15th August 1977.

(2) The rules for the construction of Acts of Parliament in the Interpretation Act 1889(b) shall apply for the purposes of the interpretation of this order as they apply for the purposes of the interpretation of an Act of Parliament.

Establishment of Association

2. At the request of a meeting of representatives of Community Health Councils on 15th June 1977 a body called the Association of Community Health Councils for England and Wales is established, which shall have the functions set out in regulation 3 of the National Health Service (Association of Community Health Councils) Regulations 1977(c).

David Ennals,
Secretary of State for Social Services.

19th July 1977.

EXPLANATORY NOTE

(This Note is not part of the Order.)

This order establishes an Association of Community Health Councils for England and Wales.

(a) 1973 c. 32.　　　(b) 1889 c. 63.　　　(c) S.I. 1977/874 (1977 II, p. 2382).

STATUTORY INSTRUMENTS

1977 No. 1205

HEALTH AND SAFETY
MINES AND QUARRIES

The Coal and Other Mines (Electricity) (Third Amendment) Regulations 1977

Made - - - -	20th July 1977
Laid before Parliament	28th July 1977
Coming into Operation	17th August 1977

The Secretary of State, in exercise of the powers conferred on him by sections 15(1), (3)(a) and (4)(a) of the Health and Safety at Work etc. Act 1974(a) ("the 1974 Act"), as amended by section 116 of, and paragraph 6 of Schedule 15 to, the Employment Protection Act 1975(b), and of all other powers enabling him in that behalf, and for the purpose of giving effect without modifications to proposals submitted to him by the Health and Safety Commission under section 11(2)(d) of the 1974 Act after the carrying out by the said Commission of consultations in accordance with section 50(3) of that Act, hereby makes the following Regulations:—

Citation, commencement and interpretation

1.—(1) These Regulations may be cited as the Coal and Other Mines (Electricity) (Third Amendment) Regulations 1977 and shall come into operation on 17th August 1977.

(2) The Interpretation Act 1889(c) shall apply for the interpretation of these Regulations as it applies for the interpretation of an Act of Parliament.

Amendment of the Coal and Other Mines (Electricity) Regulations 1956

2. Regulation 20 of the Coal and Other Mines (Electricity) Regulations 1956(d), as amended(e), shall be further amended by adding the following sub-paragraph at the end of paragraph (3)—

"(c) that such a circuit may be connected to earth if it includes apparatus of a type approved by the Health and Safety Executive for the purpose of this paragraph and is so connected by a method which is also approved by the Executive for that type of apparatus."

Alexander Eadie,
Parliamentary Under Secretary of State,
Department of Energy.

John Grant,
Parliamentary Under Secretary of State,
Department of Employment.

20th July 1977.

(a) 1974 c. 37.   (b) 1975 c. 71.   (c) 1889 c. 63.   (d) S.I. 1956/1766 (1956 I, p. 1314).
(e) The relevant amending instrument is S.I. 1974/2013 (1974 III, p. 7047).

EXPLANATORY NOTE

(This Note is not part of the Regulations.)

These Regulations amend the Coal and Other Mines (Electricity) Regulations 1956 by enabling certain electrical circuits to be connected to earth if they include apparatus of a type approved by the Health and Safety Executive and if the connection to earth is by a method which is also approved by the Executive.

STATUTORY INSTRUMENTS

1977 No. 1206 (L. 24)

COUNTY COURTS

PROCEDURE

The County Court (Amendment No. 3) Rules 1977.

Made - - - *20th July* 1977
Coming into Operation 22nd August 1977

1.—(1) These Rules may be cited as the County Court (Amendment No. 3) Rules 1977.

(2) In these Rules, unless the context otherwise requires, an Order and Rule referred to by number means the Order and Rule so numbered in the County Court Rules 1936(**a**), as amended(**b**); Appendices A and D mean Appendices A and D to those Rules, and a form referred to by number means the form so numbered in Appendix A.

(3) The Interpretation Act 1889(**c**) shall apply for the interpretation of these Rules as it applies for the interpretation of an Act of Parliament.

2. Part I of Order 26 shall be amended as follows:—

(1) For paragraph (3) of Rule 1 there shall be substituted the following paragraph:—

"(3) Where the applicant does not know the name of every person occupying the land for the purpose of making him a respondent, the conclusion of Form 26 shall be in Form 399 instead of Form 3."

Form 399

(2) For paragraph (*c*) of Rule 2 there shall be substituted the following paragraph:—

"(*c*) in a case to which Rule 1(3) relates, that he does not know the name of any person occupying the land who is not named in the originating application."

(3) In Rule 3(1) for the words from the beginning to "originating application" there shall be substituted the words "Where any person in occupation of the land is named in the originating application, the application".

(**a**) S.R. & O. 1936/626 (1936 I, p. 282).

(**b**) The relevant amending instruments are S.I. 1950/1993, 1970/673, 1201, 1871, 1971/2152 (1950 I p. 440; 1970 II, pp. 2180, 3984; III, p. 6154; 1971 III, p. 6305).

(**c**) 1889 c. 63.

(4) For paragraph (2) of Rule 3 there shall be substituted the following paragraph:—

"(2) In a case to which Rule 1(3) relates, the originating application shall, in addition to being served on the named respondents (if any) in accordance with paragraph (1), be served, unless the court otherwise directs, by—

(a) affixing a copy of the originating application to the main door or other conspicuous part of the premises, and

(b) if practicable, inserting through the letterbox at the premises a copy of the originating application enclosed in a sealed envelope addressed to "the occupiers.""

(5) In Rule 5(1) for the words "7 clear days" there shall be substituted the words "5 clear days".

(6) In Rule 6 at the beginning of paragraph (1) there shall be inserted the words "Subject to paragraph (3)" and at the end of the Rule there shall be added the following paragraph:—

"(3) No warrant of possession shall be issued after the expiry of 3 months from the date of the order without the leave of the court, and an application for such leave may be made *ex parte* unless the court otherwise directs."

3. Form 398 shall be amended as follows:—

(1) In the title after the word "*Respondent*" there shall be inserted the words "*if any*".

(2) For the words "*whom the applicant has identified*" there shall be substituted the words "*whose name the applicant knows*".

(3) For the words "whom I have been unable to identify" there shall be substituted the words "whose names I do not know".

4. In Form 399 for the words "To all persons concerned" there shall be substituted the words "To [*named respondent* and] every [other] person in occupation of   ".

5. Part III of Appendix D shall be amended as follows:—

(1) For the words "Rule 66(2)(*b*)" there shall be substituted the words "Rule 24(2) or 66(2)(*b*)".

(2) After item 3 there shall be added the following item:—

"4. For attending at the court office to issue a warrant of execution for a sum exceeding £20 . . . . £0.50".

We, the undersigned members of the Rule Committee appointed by the Lord Chancellor under section 102 of the County Courts Acts 1959(a), having by virtue of the powers vested in us in this behalf made the foregoing rules, do hereby certify the same under our hands and submit them to the Lord Chancellor accordingly.

Conolly H. Gage.
H. S. Ruttle.
David Pennant.
W. Granville Wingate.
T. Richard Nevin.
E. A. Everett.
A. A. Hibbert.
Arnold Russell Vick.
E. Somerset Jones.
D. A. Marshall.
Emyr O. Parry.

I allow these Rules, which shall come into operation on 22nd August 1977.

Dated 20th July 1977.

Elwyn-Jones, C.

EXPLANATORY NOTE

(This Note is not part of the Rules.)

These Rules simplify and expedite the summary procedure in the county court for the recovery of land against trespassers. The amendments follow those recently made by the Rules of the Supreme Court (Amendment No. 2) 1977 (S.I. 1977/960) to the corresponding procedure in the High Court. Their principal effect is to substitute for the requirement to take reasonable steps to identify the occupiers an obligation to name those who are known to the applicant.

The Rules also insert in the lower scale of costs a charge for a solicitor's attendance at the court office to issue a warrant of execution for a sum exceeding £20.

(a) 1959 c. 22.

STATUTORY INSTRUMENTS

1977 No. 1207

BUILDING SOCIETIES

The Building Societies (Designation for Trustee Investment) (Amendment) Regulations 1977

Made - - - -	*18th July* 1977
Laid before Parliament	*29th July* 1977
Coming into Operation	*19th August* 1977

The Treasury, in exercise of the powers conferred upon them by section 1(1) of the House Purchase and Housing Act 1959(a), and of all other powers enabling them in that behalf, hereby make the following Regulations:—

1.—(1) These Regulations may be cited as the Building Societies (Designation for Trustee Investment) (Amendment) Regulations 1977, and shall come into operation on 19th August 1977.

(2) The Interpretation Act 1889(b) shall apply to the interpretation of these Regulations as it applies to the interpretation of an Act of Parliament.

2. The Building Societies (Designation for Trustee Investment) Regulations 1972(c) (hereinafter called "the principal Regulations") shall be amended in paragraph 1 of the Schedule thereto by substituting for the words "one million" the words "two million five hundred thousand".

3. Where—

(*a*) the annual return of a building society for its last financial year shows that at the end of that year the amount of its assets was not less than one million pounds; and

(*b*) the society has before 18th July 1977 applied to the Chief Registrar of Friendly Societies for designation under section 1 of the House Purchase and Housing Act 1959,

such building society shall not be required to fulfil the requirements of paragraph 1 of the Schedule to the principal Regulations, as amended by these Regulations, if the Chief Registrar of Friendly Societies before 1st January 1978 so designates the society.

T. E. Graham,
David Stoddart,

Two of the Lords Commissioners
of Her Majesty's Treasury.

18th July 1977.

(**a**) 1959 c. 33.   (**b**) 1889 c. 63.   (**c**) S.I. 1972/1577 (1972 III, p. 4572).

EXPLANATORY NOTE

(*This Note is not part of the Regulations.*)

These Regulations amend the Building Societies (Designation for Trustee Investment) Regulations 1972, which set out the requirements to be fulfilled by building societies in order to qualify them for designation under section 1 of the House Purchase and Housing Act 1959. Subject to certain transitional provisions, the amendment raises to £2,500,000 the minimum assets to be held by a society in order to qualify for such designation.

STATUTORY INSTRUMENTS

1977 No. 1210

SAVINGS BANKS

The National Savings Bank (Investment Deposits) (Limits) Order 1977

Laid before Parliament in draft

Made - - - -	*21st July* 1977
Coming into Operation	*22nd July* 1977

The Treasury, in exercise of the powers conferred on them by section 4 of the National Savings Bank Act 1971(a), and of all other powers enabling them in that behalf, hereby make the following Order:—

1. This Order may be cited as the National Savings Bank (Investment Deposits) (Limits) Order 1977, and shall come into operation on 22nd July 1977.

2. The Interpretation Act 1889(b) shall apply for the interpretation of this Order as it applies for the interpretation of an Act of Parliament.

3. Subject to the provisions of this Order, it shall not be lawful for the Director of Savings to receive a deposit from, or make a credit to an account of, any person by way of investment deposit in any case where the amount standing to the credit of that person by way of investment deposit in the National Savings Bank, whether solely or jointly with any other person, and whether in one or more accounts, exceeds, or would as a result of the receipt of the said deposit or the making of the said credit, exceed £50,000.

4.—(1) Nothing in Article 3 of this Order shall operate to prevent the receipt or crediting of—

(*a*) any amount allowed by the National Savings Bank to a depositor by way of interest in respect of his investment deposit account, or

(*b*) any amount transferred from the investment deposit account of another depositor in the National Savings Bank who has died.

(2) For the purposes of this Order, a person who is a trustee shall be treated separately in his personal capacity and in his capacity as trustee and in the latter capacity separately in respect of each separate trust fund; and so much of the property in the hands of a trustee shall be treated as a separate trust fund as is held on trusts which (as respects the beneficiaries or their respective interests or the purposes of the trust or as respects the powers of the trustee) are not identical with those on which other property in his hands is held.

(3) In computing for the purposes of this Order the amount standing to the credit of any person, there shall not be taken into account any amounts

---

(**a**) 1971 c. 29.   (**b**) 1889 c. 63.

received from a trustee on behalf of that person for an account in the joint names of the trustee and that person.

> *T. E. Graham,*
> *D. Stoddart,*
> Two of the Lords Commissioners
> of Her Majesty's Treasury.

21st July 1977.

EXPLANATORY NOTE
(*This Note is not part of the Order.*)

This Order introduces a limit of £50,000 on the aggregate amount which can be accepted by the Director of Savings from any person by way of investment deposit in the National Savings Bank.

STATUTORY INSTRUMENTS

1977 No. 1211

HOUSING, ENGLAND AND WALES

The Improvement Grant (Eligible Expense Limits) Order 1977

Made - - - - - -	*21st July* 1977
Laid before the House of Commons	*25th July* 1977
Coming into operation - - -	*15th August* 1977

The Secretary of State for the Environment as respects England and the Secretary of State for Wales as respects Wales, in exercise of the powers conferred on them by sections 64(3) and 128(2) of the Housing Act 1974(a), and of all other powers enabling them in that behalf, hereby make the following order:—

Citation, commencement and interpretation

1.—(1) This order may be cited as the Improvement Grant (Eligible Expense Limits) Order 1977 and shall come into operation on 15th August 1977.

(2) The Interpretation Act 1889(b) shall apply for the interpretation of this order as it applies for the interpretation of an Act of Parliament.

Eligible expense limits

2. The amount of £5,000 is hereby specified for the purposes of paragraph (*a*) of section 64(3) of the Housing Act 1974, and the amount of £5,800 is hereby specified for the purposes of paragraph (*b*) of the said section 64(3).

Revocation

3. The Improvement Grant (Eligible Expense Limits) Order 1974(c) is hereby revoked.

	Peter Shore,
21st July 1977.	Secretary of State for the Environment.

	John Morris,
21st July 1977.	Secretary of State for Wales.

(a) 1974 c. 44.　　(b) 1889 c. 63.　　(c) S.I. 1974/2004 (1974 III, p. 7009).

EXPLANATORY NOTE

(This Note is not part of the Order.)

This Order, which applies to England and Wales, specifies new limits of eligible expense for the purposes of improvement grants, in place of the limits specified in the revoked Improvement Grant (Eligible Expense Limits) Order 1974 (which themselves replaced the limits set out in paragraphs (*a*) and (*b*) of section 64(3) of the Housing Act 1974). The Order specifies the amount of £5,000 (in place of the amount of £3,200) as the limit for a dwelling improved, or provided otherwise than by the conversion of a house or other building consisting of three or more storeys, and the amount of £5,800 (in place of the amount of £3,700) for a dwelling provided by the conversion of a house or other building consisting of three or more storeys.

STATUTORY INSTRUMENTS

1977 No. 1212

HOUSING, ENGLAND AND WALES

The Grants by Local Authorities Order 1977

Made - - - -	21st July 1977
Laid before Parliament	25th July 1977
Coming into Operation	15th August 1977

The Secretary of State for the Environment as respects England and the Secretary of State for Wales as respects Wales, in exercise of the powers conferred on them by sections 58(2), 68(3) and 72(3) of the Housing Act 1974(a), and of all other powers enabling them in that behalf, hereby make the following order:—

Citation, commencement and interpretation

1.—(1) This order may be cited as the Grants by Local Authorities Order 1977 and shall come into operation on 15th August 1977.

(2) The Interpretation Act 1889(b) shall apply for the interpretation of this order as it applies for the interpretation of an Act of Parliament.

Standard amenities

2. Schedule 6 to the Housing Act 1974 is hereby varied by substituting for Part I thereof the following:—

"PART I

LIST OF AMENITIES AND MAXIMUM ELIGIBLE AMOUNTS

Description of Amenity	Maximum eligible amount £
A fixed bath or shower	180
A hot and cold water supply at a fixed bath or shower	230
A wash-hand basin	70
A hot and cold water supply at a wash-hand basin	120
A sink	180
A hot and cold water supply at a sink	150
A water closet	270".

(a) 1974 c. 44.   (b) 1889 c. 63.

Eligible expense

3. The amount of £1,500 is hereby prescribed for the purposes of—

(*a*) section 68(3)(*a*), and

(*b*) section 72(3)

of the Housing Act 1974.

Peter Shore,
Secretary of State for the Environment.

21st July 1977.

John Morris,
Secretary of State for Wales.

21st July 1977.

EXPLANATORY NOTE

(This Note is not part of the Order.)

This Order, which applies to England and Wales, increases the maximum eligible amounts specified in Part I of Schedule 6 to the Housing Act 1974 in relation to the standard amenities there described (the descriptions remaining unchanged). This has the effect of increasing for the purposes of section 68(3)(*b*) of that Act (intermediate grant) the maximum eligible expense for works relating to the provision of standard amenities, and of increasing the maximum eligible expense for the purposes of section 70(4) (special grant). The Order also increases (from £800 to £1,500) the maximum eligible expense for works of repair or replacement for the purposes of section 68(3)(*a*) (intermediate grant) and the maximum eligible expense for the purposes of section 72(3) (repairs grant).

STATUTORY INSTRUMENTS

1977 No. 1213

HOUSING, ENGLAND AND WALES

The Improvement Grant (Rateable Value Limits) Order 1977

Made - - - -	21st *July* 1977
Laid before Parliament	25th *July* 1977
Coming into Operation	15th *August* 1977

The Secretary of State for the Environment as respects England and the Secretary of State for Wales as respects Wales, with the consent of the Treasury, in exercise of the powers conferred on them by sections 62(3) and 128(2) of the Housing Act 1974(**a**), and of all other powers enabling them in that behalf, hereby make the following order:—

Citation, commencement and interpretation

1.—(1) This order may be cited as the Improvement Grant (Rateable Value Limits) Order 1977 and shall come into operation on 15th August 1977.

(2) The Interpretation Act 1889(**b**) shall apply for the interpretation of this order as it applies for the interpretation of an Act of Parliament.

Limits of rateable value

2. For the purposes of section 62 of the Housing Act 1974 (rateable value limit on improvement grants for dwellings for owner-occupation) the following limits of rateable value are hereby specified—

(*a*) in relation to dwellings falling within subsection (1) of the said section 62 which are—

(i) in Greater London, £400;

(ii) elsewhere in England and Wales, £225;

(*b*) in relation to houses converted as mentioned in subsection (2) of the said section 62 which are—

(i) in Greater London, £600;

(ii) elsewhere in England and Wales, £350.

(**a**) 1974 c. 44.   (**b**) 1889 c. 63.

2c

Revocation

3. The Improvement Grant (Rateable Value Limits) Order 1976(a) is hereby revoked.

21st July 1977.

Peter Shore,
Secretary of State for the Environment.

21st July 1977.

John Morris,
Secretary of State for Wales.

We consent

21st July 1977.

J. Dormand,
T. E. Graham,
Two of the Lords Commissioners of
Her Majesty's Treasury.

EXPLANATORY NOTE

(This Note is not part of the Order.)

This Order, which applies to England and Wales, specifies limits of rateable value for the purposes of section 62 of the Housing Act 1974 (which sets a rateable value limit on improvement grants for dwellings for owner-occupation). The limits specified by the Improvement Grant (Rateable Value Limits) Order 1976, which is revoked by this Order, are unchanged in relation to houses converted as mentioned in subsection (2) of that section (provision of a dwelling or dwellings by the conversion of any premises which consist of or include a house or two or more houses), but higher limits are specified in relation to dwellings falling within subsection (1) (improvement of a dwelling or dwellings). As before, different limits are specified for property in Greater London and property elsewhere in England and Wales.

(a) S.I. 1976/526 (1976 I, p. 1556).

STATUTORY INSTRUMENTS

1977 No. 1215

AGRICULTURE

The Agriculture (Miscellaneous Provisions) Act 1976 (Application of Provisions) Regulations 1977

Made - -- - -	*21st July* 1977
Laid before Parliament	*1st August* 1977
Coming into Operation	*23rd August* 1977

The Lord Chancellor, in exercise of the powers conferred on him by section 23(8) of the Agriculture (Miscellaneous Provisions) Act 1976**(a)**, hereby makes the following Regulations:—

Citation, commencement and interpretation

1.—(1) These Regulations may be cited as the Agriculture (Miscellaneous Provisions) Act 1976 (Application of Provisions) Regulations 1977 and shall come into operation on 23rd August 1977.

(2) In these Regulations "the Act" means the Agriculture (Miscellaneous Provisions) Act 1976.

(3) The Interpretation Act 1889**(b)** shall apply to the interpretation of these Regulations as it applies to the interpretation of an Act of Parliament.

Application of the Act in cases of death before succession

2.—(1) Where a person entitled to a joint tenancy of an agricultural holding by virtue of a direction under section 20(9) of the Act dies before the relevant time (as defined in section 23(2) of the Act) without having become the tenant or a joint tenant of that holding, that direction shall from the date of his death cease to have effect in relation to that person if he is survived by any other person jointly entitled under the direction; but the direction shall continue to have effect (subject to the provisions of the Act) in relation to the other person or persons as if the dead person had not been named therein; and the provisions of Part II of the Act, so far as relevant, shall apply accordingly.

(2) Where—

(*a*) a person entitled to a tenancy of an agricultural holding by virtue of a direction under section 20(5) or (6) of the Act; or

(*b*) the sole survivor of two or more persons entitled to a joint tenancy of an agricultural holding by virtue of a direction under section 20(9) of the Act

---

(a) 1976 c. 55.   **(b)** 1889 c. 63.

dies before the relevant time (as defined in section 23(2) of the Act) without having become the tenant or joint tenant of that holding, the provisions of Part II of the Act, except section 23(8), shall apply in accordance with the provisions of the Schedule to these Regulations subject to the exceptions, additions and modifications set out therein.

(3) Where two or more persons who are jointly entitled to a tenancy of the holding by virtue of a direction under section 20(9) of the Act have died in circumstances rendering it uncertain which of them survived the other, such deaths shall for the purposes of these Regulations be presumed to have occurred in order of seniority, and accordingly the younger shall be deemed to have survived the elder.

Dated 21st July 1977.

Elwyn-Jones, C.

SCHEDULE

APPLICATION OF PART II OF THE ACT

1. Sections 16 and 17 shall not apply.

2. Section 18 shall apply—

(a) with the addition of the following subsection after subsection (1):—

"(1A) In subsection (1) and in the definition of "the deceased" in subsection (2), the expression "tenant" includes a person who is—

(i) entitled to a tenancy of an agricultural holding by virtue of a direction by the Tribunal under section 20(5) or (6) of this Act; or

(ii) the sole survivor of two or more persons entitled to a joint tenancy of an agricultural holding by virtue of such a direction under section 20(9) of this Act,

and who dies before the time at which, had he survived, he would have been deemed to have been granted and to have accepted that tenancy or joint tenancy";

(b) with the addition in subsection (4) of the words "(except section 19A)" after the words "this Part of this Act";

(c) as if the reference in subsection (4)(e) to subsection (1) included a reference to subsection (1A);

(d) with the exception of subsection (5).

3. Section 19 shall not apply, but instead the following section shall be added:—

"19A—(1) Where at the date of death of the deceased the holding is the subject of a relevant notice to quit, the operation of that notice shall, subject to subsection (2) below and notwithstanding any provision of this Act having effect prior to the death of the deceased, take effect at the date specified in the notice for the termination of the tenancy to which it relates:

Provided that where, in the case of a relevant notice to quit, there remains at the date of death of the deceased a period of less than twelve months before the date specified in the notice for the termination of the tenancy of the holding, the operation of the notice shall be postponed for a period of twelve months.

(2) A relevant notice to quit shall not have effect unless either—

(a) no application to become the tenant of the holding is made under section 20 of this Act within the relevant period; or

(b) one or more such applications having been made within that period, either—

(i) none of the applicants is determined by the Tribunal to be in their opinion a suitable person to become the tenant of the holding; or

(ii) the Tribunal consent under section 22 of this Act to the operation of the notice to quit.

(3) In this section "relevant notice to quit" means a notice to quit the holding falling within section 24(2)(g) of the 1948 Act.".

4. Sections 20 and 21 shall apply.

5. Section 22 shall apply as if the references to section 19 of the Act were references to section 19A.

6. Section 23 shall apply:—

(a) as if, in subsection (1), for the words "the date of death", there were substituted the words "the date when the original tenant died";

(b) as if for subsection (2) there were substituted the following subsection:—

"(2A) In this and the following section "the relevant time" means the end of the twelve months immediately following the end of the year of tenancy in which the deceased died.";

(c) as if, in subsection (3), for the words "on the date of death the holding was held by the deceased" there were substituted the words "immediately before the death of the original tenant he held the holding";

(d) as if the following subsection were added:—

"(9) In this and the next following section "the original tenant" means the tenant of the holding to whose tenancy the deceased would have succeeded, had he survived, by virtue of the provisions of this Part of this Act.".

7. Section 24 shall apply as if in subsection (5)(a) for the word "deceased's" there were substituted the words "the original tenant's".

EXPLANATORY NOTE

(This Note is not part of the Regulations.)

These Regulations apply, with certain exceptions, additions and modifications, the provisions of Part II of the Agriculture (Miscellaneous Provisions) Act 1976 (which make provision for succession on the death of a tenant of an agricultural holding) in cases where the person or any of the persons whom a direction by an Agricultural Land Tribunal entitles to a tenancy or joint tenancy of the holding dies before he becomes the tenant thereof.

STATUTORY INSTRUMENTS

1977 No. 1216 (L. 25)

SUPREME COURT OF JUDICATURE, ENGLAND

OFFICERS AND OFFICES

The District Registries (Amendment No. 3) Order 1977

Made - - -	*20th July* 1977
Coming into Operation	*1st September* 1977

The Lord Chancellor, in exercise of the powers conferred on him by section 84(1) of the Supreme Court of Judicature (Consolidation) Act 1925(**a**), as amended by paragraph 18(3) of Schedule 8 to the Courts Act 1971(**b**), hereby makes the following Order:—

1. This Order may be cited as the District Registries (Amendment No. 3) Order 1977 and shall come into operation on 1st September 1977.

2. The District Registries Order 1971(**c**), as amended(**d**), shall have effect subject to the following further amendments to the Schedule thereto:—

(*a*) after the entry relating to Manchester, there shall be inserted the following new entry:

First Column	*Second Column*
"Mansfield	Mansfield";

(*b*) the entry relating to Mansfield shall be deleted from the second column where it appears in the entry relating to Chesterfield.

Dated 20th July 1977.

Elwyn-Jones, C.

EXPLANATORY NOTE

(*This Note is not part of the Order.*)

This Order establishes a district registry at Mansfield.

(a) 1925 c. 49. (b) 1971 c. 23. (c) S.I. 1971/392 (1971 I, p. 1189).
(d) S.I. 1975/1781, 1976/434, 891, 1977/152, 351, (1975 III, p. 6755; 1976 I, p. 1300; II, p. 2245; 1977 I, pp. 478, 1201).

STATUTORY INSTRUMENTS

1977 No. 1220

COUNTER-INFLATION

The Prices and Charges (Adaptation of the Counter-Inflation Act 1973) Regulations 1977

Made -	-	-	-	*26th July* 1977
Laid before Parliament				*29th July* 1977
Coming into Operation				*1st August* 1977

The Secretary of State, in exercise of the powers conferred on him by Sections 15(4) and 22(3) of, and paragraph 8 of Schedule 2 to, the Price Commission Act 1977(**a**) and of all other powers enabling him in that behalf, hereby makes the following Regulations:—

Citation, commencement and interpretation

1.—(1) These Regulations may be cited as the Prices and Charges (Adaptation of the Counter-Inflation Act 1973) Regulations 1977 and shall come into operation on 1st August 1977.

(2) The Interpretation Act 1889(**b**) shall apply for the interpretation of these Regulations as it applies for the interpretation of an Act of Parliament.

Adaptation of the Counter-Inflation Act 1973

2. The Counter-Inflation Act 1973(**c**) as amended(**d**) is hereby varied—

(*a*) in Schedule 3—

(i) in paragraph 2(1) by the insertion after "Act" of "and sections 4 to 9 of the Price Commission Act 1977 (in this Part of this Schedule and in Schedule 4 referred to as "the 1977 Act")" and by the insertion at the end of "Provided that nothing in this sub-paragraph shall be construed as requiring the Commission to give a copy of a notification under subsection (2) of section 4 or of section 5 of the 1977 Act—

(i) in relation to an investigation pursuant to a notification by the Commission under subsection (1) of the said section 4, to any person other than the person who gave notice of the proposed increase under section 5 of this Act to which the investigation relates, and

(ii) in relation to an investigation pursuant to a notification by the Commission under subsection (1) of the said section 5, to more than one person,

or to require the Commission to give any notice or a copy of any report, or the Secretary of State to give any notice, to any other person.",

---

(**a**) 1977 c. 33.   (**b**) 1889 c. 63.   (**c**) 1973 c. 9.
(**d**) *See* S.I. 1974/1218 (1974 II, p. 4631) and 1977 c. 33.

(ii) in paragraph 2(2), by the insertion after "Act" of "and sections 7, 12 and 13 of the 1977 Act, a variation notice given under subsection (5) of section 4 of that Act or under that subsection as applied by section 5(4) of that Act, any recommendation included in a report by the Commission in pursuance of section 6(5)(b) of that Act and regulations under section 9 of that Act" and by the substitution for "or notice" where it last occurs of "notice, recommendation or regulations",

(iii) by the insertion after sub-paragraph (2) of paragraph 2 of the following sub-paragraph—

"(3) For the purposes of section 15(3) of the 1977 Act, "employer" includes any person with whom under sub-paragraph (1) above the employer is to be treated as one.",

(iv) in paragraph 3(1), by the insertion after "Part II" of "of this Act (including a notice under section 5 of this Act as applied by section 4(2)(b) of the 1977 Act), subsection (5)(a) of section 7 of that Act or section 13 of that Act or by virtue of section 5(3)(a) of that Act or subsection (1) of the said section 7",

(v) in paragraph 3(2), by the insertion after "charge" where it first occurs of "or of any restriction imposed by virtue of section 5(3)(a) of the 1977 Act or of subsection (1) of the said section 7",

(vi) in paragraph 5(1), by the insertion after "Act" of "or the 1977 Act or in which any notification or report or copy of a notification or report is to be given under that Act",

(vii) in paragraph 5(2)(a), by the insertion after "Act" of "or notification, notice, undertaking or direction under the 1977 Act",

(viii) in paragraph 5(2)(b), by the insertion after "Act" of "or notice under section 13 of the 1977 Act",

(ix) in paragraph 5(3), by the insertion after "Act" of "or notice under section 13 of the 1977 Act",

(x) in paragraph 7, by the insertion after "Act" in the first place where it occurs of "or of the 1977 Act" and after "Act" in the second place where it occurs of "or the 1977 Act, as the case may be,";

(b) in Schedule 4—

(i) in paragraph 1, by the insertion after sub-paragraph (4) of the following sub-paragraph—

"(5) An authority specified in an order under section 12 of the 1977 Act in pursuance of subsection (6)(c) of that section may in relation to a notice under section 13 of that Act make, or may authorise any of its officers to make on its behalf, any purchase of goods, and may authorise any of its officers to obtain any services.",

(ii) in paragraph 2(1), by the insertion after "Act" of "or the 1977 Act",

(iii) in paragraph 3, by the insertion after sub-paragraph (5) of the following sub-paragraph—

"(6) This paragraph shall have effect in relation to a notice under section 13 of the 1977 Act as it has effect in relation to a notice under section 6 of this Act and, in relation to a notice under the said section 13, as if references to a duly authorised officer of a local weights and measures authority were references to a duly authorised officer of an authority specified in an order under section 12 of the 1977 Act in pursuance of subsection (6)(c) of that section.",

(iv) in paragraph 5(1), by the insertion after "Act" of "or of the 1977 Act".

26th July 1977.   *Roy Hattersley,*

                                        Secretary of State for
                                  Prices and Consumer Protection.

EXPLANATORY NOTE

(This Note is not part of the Regulations.)

These Regulations modify certain provisions of the Counter-Inflation Act 1973 to apply them for the purposes of the Price Commission Act 1977. The provisions concerned treat as one person certain different persons who are closely connected with one another, the validity of transactions affected by the operation of the 1977 Act, procedural matters relating to notices and orders, consultation in relation to statutory instruments where consultation has been conducted before the 1977 Act came into operation and enforcement of provisions of the 1977 Act.

STATUTORY INSTRUMENTS

1977 No. 1221

PRICES

The Prices and Charges (Definitions) Regulations 1977

Made - - - -	26th July 1977
Laid before Parliament	29th July 1977
Coming into Operation	1st August 1977

The Secretary of State, in exercise of his powers under sections 5(6) and 22(3) of the Price Commission Act 1977(a) and of all other powers enabling him in that behalf, hereby makes the following Regulations:—

Citation, commencement and interpretation

1.—(1) These Regulations may be cited as the Prices and Charges (Definitions) Regulations 1977 and shall come into operation on 1st August 1977.

(2) In these Regulations—

"the Act" means the Price Commission Act 1977;

"distributor" means a distributor of goods within the meaning of regulation 4; and

"price", except in regulation 5, includes charge,

and all other expressions have the same meanings as they have for the purposes of the Act.

(3) The Interpretation Act 1889(b) shall apply for the interpretation of these Regulations as it applies for the interpretation of an Act of Parliament.

Meaning of increase in a price (other than of a distributor) for the purposes of section 5(1) of the Act

2.—(1) For the purposes of subsection (1) of section 5 of the Act, an increase in a price which is not a price of a distributor made after 31st May 1977 shall be ascertained in accordance with the following provisions of this regulation and the provisions of regulation 3.

(2) If, at 31st May 1977 or at the time when the said subsection (1) falls to be applied, the relevant person has quoted a higher amount than its amount at that date or time as the amount of a price, the amount of the price at 31st May 1977 or at that date, as the case may be, shall be taken to be that higher amount; and a person shall be taken to have quoted a price if he has given notice, by display, advertisement, circular or other public notice, of his intention to do business at a price of that amount before the expiration of the period of 28 days beginning with 31st May 1977 or that date, as the case may require.

(a) 1977 c. 33.   (b) 1889 c. 63.

(3) In this regulation and in regulation 3, "relevant person" means the person who would be the relevant person for the purposes of the Act in relation to the price in question if, at the time when the said subsection (1) falls to be applied, the Price Commission were to give a notification to the Secretary of State in pursuance of the said subsection.

Determination of increase for the purposes of regulation 2

3.—(1) The amount of the price at the time when subsection (1) of the said section 5 falls to be applied shall be compared with that charged by the relevant person in the course of business for comparable transactions as regards goods of the same description on 31st May 1977 or last so charged before that date.

(2) If there is no price which can be taken for comparison under paragraph (1) above, the comparison may be with prices charged by the relevant person in the course of business for transactions which are not in all respects comparable and as regards goods which are not of precisely the same description with a fair adjustment to take account of the differences; and as between different transactions or different descriptions of goods, those taken for comparison under this paragraph shall be those which are most closely comparable.

(3) Where a relevant person charges prices of different amounts for the same goods in relation to different persons or to persons of different descriptions or to the same persons or descriptions of persons in different circumstances, a price shall be treated as an increased price in relation to any person only if it exceeds the price charged in relation to the same person, persons of the same description or persons of the same description in the same circumstances, as the case may be.

(4) A price shall not be treated for the purposes of regulation 2 as being of an increased amount only because it exceeds the amount of an earlier price if the increase does not exceed the cash amount of any increase (including a change from a nil amount) in—

(*a*) excise duties, customs duties or car tax on, or on anything comprised in, the goods in question which, whether by virtue of a contract or otherwise, is, or is to be, borne in the particular case by the relevant person; or

(*b*) value added tax chargeable by the relevant person on the supply of the goods in question; or

(*c*) any fee prescribed(a) under subsection (3) of section 11 of the Weights and Measures Act 1963(b) or subsection (3) of section 5 of the Weights and Measures Act (Northern Ireland) 1967(c) (both of which provisions relate to the passing and stamping as fit for use for trade of weighing or measuring equipment) which is payable in respect of, or of anything comprised in, the goods in question by the person intending to implement the increase.

(5) In this Regulation "goods" includes services.

Meaning of "distributor of goods"

4. For the purposes of the Act, a distributor of goods—

(*a*) means a person who carries on in the course of business activities falling within Order XXIII (other than the wholesale slaughtering of animals for human consumption, leasing industrial or office machinery,

---

(a) See S.I. 1975/1381 (1975 II, p. 4737).   (b) 1963 c. 31.   (c) 1967 c. 6 (N.I.).

the hiring of furniture, radio and television sets and other domestic appliances or the activities of bakers or processors of scrap metals) or falling within minimum list heading 894 of Order XXVI (other than the repairing of motor vehicles) of the Standard Industrial Classification; and

(b) in the case of a person carrying on activities within sub-paragraph (a) above and other activities, means only the former activities if—

(i) separate accounts for the former activities and those other activities can be provided for all relevant periods;

(ii) such accounts are not materially distorted by transactions otherwise than at arm's length; and

(iii) such accounts would, if combined with one another, show results consistent with those shown by the accounts of his enterprise taken as a whole,

and, in any other case, he shall be treated as a distributor of goods if activities within sub-paragraph (a) above are his main activity,

and in this Regulation "the Standard Industrial Classification" means the edition thereof published by Her Majesty's Stationery Office in 1968, as amended by Amendment List No. 1 so published in 1977, together with the alphabetical list of industries so published in 1968 as amended by Amendment List Nos. 1 and 2 so published in 1970 and 1977 respectively.

Meaning of "margin" and "price" of a distributor of goods

5. For the purposes of subsection (1) of section 5 of the Act—

(a) the margin of a distributor of goods is his gross percentage margin, that is to say, the difference, expressed as a percentage of the value of sales, between the value of sales of all goods (other than liquid milk and goods supplied, whether by the person in question or another, to a person outside the United Kingdom) sold by the person in question in the course of business as a distributor of goods in a period and the cost to him of those goods; and

(b) the prices of a distributor of goods are the prices charged by him for sales of goods (other than goods supplied, whether by him or another, to persons outside the United Kingdom) in the course of his business as such a distributor.

Roy Hattersley,
26th July 1977.   Secretary of State for Prices and
Consumer Protection.

EXPLANATORY NOTE

(This Note is not part of the Regulations.)

These Regulations prescribe how an increase in a price (other than a price charged by a distributor of goods), the margin of a distributor of goods and the prices of a distributor of goods are to be determined for the purposes of section 5(1) of the Price Commission Act 1977. Under that subsection, the Price Commission may notify the Secretary of State that they consider that a price, not being a price of a distributor, for an increase of which no prior notice is required to be given to the Commission and which has been increased after 31st May 1977, or the margin of a distributor of goods, should be the subject of an investigation by them.

STATUTORY INSTRUMENTS

1977 No. 1222

COUNTER-INFLATION

The Prices and Charges (Notices and Orders) Regulations 1977

Made - - - -	26th July 1977
Laid before Parliament	29th July 1977
Coming into Operation	1st August 1977

The Secretary of State, in exercise of the powers conferred on him by section 23(2) of, and paragraph 5(1) and (2) of Schedule 3 to, the Counter-Inflation Act 1973(a) as amended(b) and having effect with the additions and amendments contained in the Prices and Charges (Adaptation of the Counter-Inflation Act 1973) Regulations 1977(c) and of all other powers enabling him in that behalf, hereby makes the following Regulations:—

Citation, commencement, interpretation and revocation

1.—(1) These Regulations may be cited as the Prices and Charges (Notices and Orders) Regulations 1977 and shall come into operation on 1st August 1977.

(2) In these Regulations—

"the 1973 Act" means the Counter-Inflation Act 1973;

"the 1977 Act" means the Price Commission Act 1977(d);

"the Commission" means the Price Commission;

"Gazette" has the same meaning as in section 21(6) of the 1973 Act.

(3) The Interpretation Act 1889(e) shall apply for the interpretation of these Regulations as it applies for the interpretation of an Act of Parliament and as if these Regulations and the Regulations hereby revoked were Acts of Parliament.

(4) The Counter-Inflation (Notices and Orders) Regulations 1973(f) are hereby revoked.

Manner of giving notices etc.

2. A notice, notification, copy of a notification, report or copy of a report to be given to or served on any person under the 1973 Act or the 1977 Act may be given either—

(a) in the case of an incorporated company or body, by delivering it, or sending it by registered post or the recorded delivery service, to a director or the secretary, clerk or other similar officer of the company or body at its registered office or other principal place of business in the United Kingdom; or

---

(a) 1973 c. 9. (b) *See* S.I. 1974/1218 (1974 II, p. 4631) and 1977 c. 33.
(c) S.I. 1977/1220 (1977 II, p. 3385). (d) 1977 c. 33.
(e) 1889 c. 63. (f) S.I. 1973/621 (1973 I, p. 1956).

(*b*) in the case of an unincorporated body, by delivering it, or sending it by registered post or the recorded delivery service, to the secretary, manager or other similar officer of the body at its principal office in the United Kingdom or, in the case of a partnership, to a partner; or

(*c*) in the case of a partner and of any other person not mentioned in sub-paragraph (*b*) above, by delivering it or sending it by registered post or the recorded delivery service to that person at his usual or last known place of business in the United Kingdom or last known place of abode;

Provided that a notice to be given to the Commission or a notice, notification or report to be given to the Secretary of State shall not be deemed to have been given until it is received at the offices of the Commission or of the Secretary of State, as the case may be.

Evidence as to orders and notices

3.—(1) Every document purporting to be an order made by the Commission, a notification given by the Commission or notice given or served by the Commission or the Secretary of State, under the 1973 Act or the 1977 Act and to be signed on behalf of the Commission, or by or on behalf of the Secretary of State, shall be received in evidence and shall, until the contrary is proved, be deemed to be an order made by the Commission or, as the case may be, a notice or notification given or served by the Commission or the Secretary of State, as the case may be.

(2) Prima facie evidence of an order made by the Commission, or a notice, notification or copy of a notification given or served by the Commission or the Secretary of State, under the 1973 Act or the 1977 Act, of a notice served or published in accordance with section 13(1) (*c*) of the 1977 Act by an authority specified in an order under section 12 of that Act in pursuance of subsection (6)(*c*) of that section or of a report or copy of a report made by the Commission under the 1977 Act may in any legal proceedings be given—

(*a*) by the production of a document purporting to be certified to be a true copy of the order, notice, notification, copy of a notification, report or copy of a report in question, or

(*b*) in the case of an order made by the Commission under the 1973 Act or the 1977 Act, or a notice given by the Commission under section 6(5), or by the Secretary of State under section 9(5), of the 1973 Act, by the production of a copy of the Gazette purporting to contain such an order or notice.

Publication of orders, notices and consents

4.—(1) Any order made by the Commission under section 6 of the 1973 Act or under the 1977 Act and any notice given by the Commission under section 6(5) of the 1973 Act or by the Secretary of State under section 9(5) of that Act shall be published in one or more newspapers of general circulation in the area affected by the order or notice.

(2) Particulars of—

(a) any notice given by the Commission or the Secretary of State under section 6(3) or 9(2) of the 1973 Act;

(b) any direction given by the Secretary of State under section 10(1) of the 1977 Act; and

(c) any consent granted by the Commission or the Secretary of State under the 1973 Act,

shall be published in one or more newspapers of general circulation in the area affected by the notice, direction or consent.

26th July 1977.

Roy Hattersley,
Secretary of State
for Prices and Consumer Protection.

EXPLANATORY NOTE

(This Note is not part of the Regulations.)

These Regulations prescribe the manner in which notices and notifications and copies of notifications are to be given under the Counter-Inflation Act 1973 and the Price Commission Act 1977 and the method of proving in legal proceedings orders and other documents made or given by the Commission and notices given under those Acts.

The Regulations also prescribe the manner in which certain orders, notices, directions and consents under those Acts are to be published.

STATUTORY INSTRUMENTS

1977 No. 1223

COUNTER-INFLATION

The Prices and Charges (Designated Officers) Order 1977

Made -	-	-	-	*26th July* 1977
Coming into Operation				*22nd August* 1977

The Secretary of State, in exercise of the powers conferred on him by section 23(2) of, and paragraph 2(1) and (4) of Schedule 4 to, the Counter-Inflation Act 1973(a) as amended (b) and having effect with the additions and amendments made by the Prices and Charges (Adaptation of the Counter-Inflation Act 1973) Regulations 1977(c), and of all other powers enabling him in that behalf, hereby makes the following Order:—

1.—(1) This Order may be cited as the Prices and Charges (Designated Officers) Order 1977 and shall come into operation on 22nd August 1977.

(2) The Interpretation Act 1889(d) shall apply for the interpretation of this Order as it applies for the interpretation of an Act of Parliament and as if this Order and the Order hereby revoked were Acts of Parliament.

2.—(1) The persons specified in paragraph (2) below are hereby designated as persons to execute the Counter-Inflation Act 1973 and the Price Commission Act 1977 in the United Kingdom in accordance with paragraph 2 of Schedule 4 to the first-mentioned Act having effect as amended(c) by doing what may be done by officers of the Secretary of State.

(2) The persons referred to in paragraph (1) above are all officers of the Price Commission of or above the rank of higher executive officer or equivalent rank.

3. The Counter-Inflation (Designated Officers) (No. 2) Order 1973(e) is hereby revoked.

Roy Hattersley,
26th July 1977.   Secretary of State
for Prices and Consumer Protection.

(a) 1973 c. 9.
(c) S.I. 1977/1220 (1977 II, p. 3385).
(d) 1889 c. 63.

(b) *See* S.I. 1974/1218 (1974 II, p. 4631) and 1977 c. 33.
(e) S.I. 1973/1065 (1973 II, p. 3202).

EXPLANATORY NOTE

(This Note is not part of the Order.)

By this Order, officers of the Price Commission of or above the rank of higher executive officer or equivalent are designated officers for the purpose of enforcement in accordance with Schedule 4 to the Counter-Inflation Act 1973 of provisions of that Act and of the Price Commission Act 1977.

This Order supersedes the Counter-Inflation (Designated Officers) (No. 2) Order 1973 which it revokes.

STATUTORY INSTRUMENTS

1977 No. 1224

CONSUMER PROTECTION

PRICES

The Prices and Charges (Recommended Resale Prices) (Enforcement) Regulations 1977

Made - - - -	*26th July* 1977
Laid before Parliament	*29th July* 1977
Coming into Operation	*22nd August* 1977

The Secretary of State, in pursuance of the powers conferred on him by sections 13(5) and 22(3) of the Price Commission Act 1977(a) and of all other powers enabling him in that behalf, hereby makes the following Regulations:—

Citation, commencement and interpretation

1.—(1) These Regulations may be cited as the Prices and Charges (Recommended Resale Prices) (Enforcement) Regulations 1977 and shall come into operation on 22nd August 1977.

(2) The Interpretation Act 1889(b) shall apply for the interpretation of these Regulations as it applies for the interpretation of an Act of Parliament.

(3) In these Regulations "resale prices order" means an order in pursuance of sub-section (3)(b) of section 12 of the Price Commission Act 1977 so far as it contains such provisions as are mentioned in sub-section (4) of that section (which enables the Secretary of State in consequence of a report by the Price Commission under section 11 of that Act to prohibit certain practices relating to recommended resale prices and charges).

Adaptation of Schedule to Prices Act 1974

2. For the purposes of enforcement of a resale prices order, the Schedule to the Prices Act 1974(c) shall have effect with the following variations—

    (*a*) in paragraph 5(2), the insertion after "Act" of "or a resale prices order" and the omission of all the words after the semi-colon;

    (*b*) in paragraph 5(3), the insertion after "this Act" of "or a resale prices order"; and

    (*c*) the insertion after paragraph 14 of the following paragraph—

"Interpretation

    15. In this Schedule "resale prices order" means an order in pursuance of sub-section (3)(b) of section 12 of the Price Commission Act 1977 so far as it contains such provisions as are mentioned in sub-section (4)

(a) 1977 c. 33.   **(b)** 1889 c. 63.   **(c)** 1974 c. 24.

of that section (which enables the Secretary of State in consequence of a report by the Price Commission under section 11 of that Act to prohibit certain practices relating to recommended resale prices and charges); and in relation to a resale prices order references to a local weights and measures authority and to their officers shall be construed as references to the authority specified in the order in pursuance of sub-section (6)(*c*) of the said section 12 and to its officers."

Roy Hattersley,
Secretary of State
26th July 1977.   for Prices and Consumer Protection.

EXPLANATORY NOTE

(*This Note is not part of the Regulations.*)

These Regulations adapt the provisions of the Schedule to the Prices Act 1974 for the purpose of enforcement of orders relating to recommended resale prices and charges made by the Secretary of State in consequence of a report to him by the Price Commission under the Price Commission Act 1977.

STATUTORY INSTRUMENTS

1977 No. 1225

COUNTER-INFLATION

The Counter-Inflation (Validity of Transactions) Order 1977

Made - - - -	*26th July* 1977
Coming into Operation	*1st August* 1977

The Secretary of State in exercise of the powers conferred on him by section 23(2) of, and by paragraph 3 of Schedule 3 to, the Counter-Inflation Act 1973(**a**) as amended(**b**) and having effect with the additions and amendments made by the Prices and Charges (Adaptation of the Counter-Inflation Act 1973) Regulations 1977(**c**) and of all other powers enabling him in that behalf, hereby makes the following Order:—

Citation, commencement, interpretation and revocation

1.—(1) This Order may be cited as the Counter-Inflation (Validity of Transactions) Order 1977 and shall come into operation on 1st August 1977.

(2) In this Order—

"the 1973 Act" means the Counter-Inflation Act 1973;

"the 1977 Act" means the Price Commission Act 1977(**d**).

(3) The Interpretation Act 1889(**e**) shall apply for the interpretation of this Order as it applies for the interpretation of an Act of Parliament and as if this Order and the Order hereby revoked were Acts of Parliament.

(4) The Counter-Inflation (Validity of Transactions) Order 1973(**f**) is hereby revoked.

Validity of transactions relating to goods, services and insurance premiums

2.—(1) A transaction shall not be invalid because it involves—

(*a*) a price or charge which has been increased in contravention of an order made under section 5 of, or paragraph 1 of Schedule 2 to, the 1973 Act and having the effect of restricting that price or charge; or

(*b*) a price or charge in excess of a price or charge restricted by an order or notice under section 6 of that Act; or

(*c*) an insurance premium in excess of a premium restricted by an order or notice under section 9 of that Act; or

---

(**a**) 1973 c. 9.   (**b**) See S.I. 1974/1218 (1974 II, p. 4631) and 1977 c. 33.
(**c**) S.I. 1977/1220 (1977 II, p. 3385). (**d**) 1977 c. 33.
(**e**) 1889 c. 63.   (**f**) S.I. 1973/660 (1973 I, p. 2139).

(*d*) a price or charge which has been increased—

   (i) in contravention of section 4(2)(*b*) or section 5(3)(*a*) of the 1977 Act, or

   (ii) in contravention of subsection (1) of section 7 of that Act, an order under subsection (5)(*a*) of the said section 7 or of a notice under subsection (1) of section 13 of that Act if contravention of that notice is an offence under subsection (4) of that section.

(2) The person paying a price, charge or premium referred to in paragraph (1) above shall be entitled to recover the excess over the restriction—

(*a*) unless he is himself liable to punishment by reason of his having aided, abetted, counselled or procured the contravention of the order or notice by the other party to the transaction; or

(*b*) in the case of—

   (i) a price or charge falling within head (*d*)(i) of that paragraph, unless the excess is permitted by a variation notice under section 4(5) of the 1977 Act or under that section as applied by section 5(4) of that Act, and

   (ii) a price or charge falling within head (*d*)(ii) of that paragraph, unless the excess is permitted under section 9 of the 1977 Act.

Validity of declaration of dividends

3. The declaration of a dividend contrary to an order or notice under section 10 of the 1973 Act shall not be invalidated except to the extent to which it contravenes the order or notice.

Roy Hattersley,
Secretary of State for
Prices and Consumer Protection.

26th July 1977.

EXPLANATORY NOTE

(This Note is not part of the Order.)

This Order prescribes the degree to which transactions made illegal or otherwise affected by certain orders or notices made or given under the Counter-Inflation Act 1973 and the Price Commission Act 1977 are to be valid or invalid. The orders or notices are those relating to prices for the sale of goods and charges for the performance of services, insurance premiums and dividends.

STATUTORY INSTRUMENTS

1977 No. 1226

SOCIAL SECURITY

The Supplementary Benefits (General) Amendment Regulations 1977

Made - - -	*25th July* 1977
Laid before Parliament	*26th July* 1977
Coming into Operation	*29th July* 1977

The Secretary of State for Social Services, in exercise of the powers conferred upon him by section 2(2) of the Supplementary Benefits Act 1976(a), as amended by section 14(4) of the Social Security (Miscellaneous Provisions) Act 1977(b), and of all other powers enabling him in that behalf, and with the consent of the Treasury, hereby makes the following regulations:—

Citation, interpretation and commencement

1. These regulations, which may be cited as the Supplementary Benefits (General) Amendment Regulations 1977, shall be read as one with the Supplementary Benefits (General) Regulations 1977(c) (hereinafter referred to as "the principal regulations") and shall come into operation on 29th July 1977.

Amendment of regulation 11 of the principal regulations

2. In regulation 11 of the principal regulations (date of commencement, change and termination of entitlement to pensions and allowances), in paragraph (2)(*d*) for "within head (iv)" there shall be substituted "within head (iii)" and for "within head (v)" there shall be substituted "within head (iv)".

Signed by authority of the Secretary of State for Social Services.

Stanley Orme,

Minister for Social Security,
Department of Health and
Social Security.

25th July 1977.

We consent.

David Stoddart,

T. M. Cox,

Two of the Lords Commissioners of
Her Majesty's Treasury.

25th July 1977.

(a) 1976 c. 71.   (b) 1977 c. 5.   (c) S.I. 1977/1141 (1977 II, p. 3190).

EXPLANATORY NOTE

(This Note is not part of the Regulations.)

These Regulations amend the Supplementary Benefits (General) Regulations 1977 ("the Principal Regulations"). Regulation 1 is formal; and regulation 2 corrects an error of reference contained in regulation 11 of the Principal Regulations.

STATUTORY INSTRUMENTS

1977 No. 1227

INDUSTRIAL TRAINING
The Industrial Training Levy (Ceramics, Glass and Mineral Products) Order 1977

Made - - - -	*25th July* 1977
Laid before Parliament	*5th August* 1977
Coming into Operation	*6th September* 1977

Whereas proposals made by the Ceramics, Glass and Mineral Products Industry Training Board for the raising and collection of a levy have been submitted to, and approved by, the Manpower Services Commission under section 7 of the Industrial Training Act 1964(a) (" the 1964 Act"), as amended by section 6 of and Schedule 2 to the Employment and Training Act 1973(b) ("the 1973 Act") and have thereafter been submitted by the said Commission to the Secretary of State under section 7(1C) of the 1964 Act as inserted by the 1973 Act;

And whereas in pursuance of section 7(1A)(*a*) of the 1964 Act as inserted by the 1973 Act the said proposals include provision for the exemption from the levy of employers who, in view of the small number of their employees, ought in the opinion of the Secretary of State to be exempted from it;

And whereas the Secretary of State estimates that the amount which, disregarding any exemptions, will be payable by virtue of this Order by any employer in the ceramics, glass and mineral products industry, does not exceed an amount which the Secretary of State estimates is equal to one per cent. of the aggregate of the emoluments and payments intended to be disbursed as emoluments which have been paid or are payable by any such employer to or in respect of persons employed in the industry, in respect of the period specified in the said proposals as relevant, that is to say the period hereafter referred to in this order as "the eleventh base period";

And whereas the Secretary of State is satisfied that proposals published by the said Board in pursuance of section 4A of the 1964 Act, as inserted by the 1973 Act, provide for exemption certificates relating to the levy in such cases as he considers appropriate;

Now, therefore, the Secretary of State in exercise of the powers conferred by section 4 of the 1964 Act, as amended by section 6 of and Schedule 2 to the 1973 Act, and of all other powers enabling him in that behalf hereby makes the following Order:—

Citation and commencement

1. This Order may be cited as the Industrial Training Levy (Ceramics, Glass and Mineral Products) Order 1977 and shall come into operation on 6th September 1977.

(a) 1964 c. 16.　　　　　　　(b) 1973 c. 50.

Interpretation

2.—(1) In this Order unless the context otherwise requires:—

(*a*) "an appeal tribunal" means an industrial tribunal established under section 12 of the Industrial Training Act 1964;

(*b*) "assessment" means an assessment of an employer to the levy;

(*c*) "the Board" means the Ceramics, Glass and Mineral Products Industry Training Board;

(*d*) "business" means any activities of industry or commerce;

(*e*) "ceramics, glass and mineral products establishment" means an establishment in Great Britain engaged in the eleventh base period wholly or mainly in the ceramics, glass and mineral products industry for a total of twenty-seven or more weeks or, being an establishment that commenced to carry on business in the eleventh base period, for a total number of weeks exceeding one-half of the number of weeks in the part of the said period commencing with the day on which business was commenced and ending on the last day thereof;

(*f*) "the ceramics, glass and mineral products industry" does not include any activities which have been transferred from the industry of the Board to the industry of another industrial training board by one of the transfer orders but save as aforesaid means any one or more of the activities which, subject to the provisions of paragraph 2 of the Schedule to the industrial training order, are specified in paragraph 1 of that Schedule as the activities of the ceramics, glass and mineral products industry or, in relation to activities which have been transferred to the industry of the Board by one of the transfer orders, any activities so transferred;

(*g*) "the eleventh base period" means the period of twelve months that commenced on 6th April 1976;

(*h*) "the eleventh levy period" means the period commencing with the day upon which this Order comes into operation and ending on 31st March 1978;

(*i*) "employer" means a person who is an employer in the ceramics, glass and mineral products industry at any time in the eleventh levy period;

(*j*) "exemption certificate" means a certificate issued by the Board under section 4B of the 1964 Act as inserted by the 1973 Act;

(*k*) "the industrial training order" means the Industrial Training (Ceramics, Glass and Mineral Products Board) Order 1965**(a)** as amended by the Industrial Training (Ceramics, Glass and Mineral Products Board) Order 1969**(b)**;

(*l*) "the levy" means the levy imposed by the Board in respect of the eleventh levy period;

(*m*) "notice" means a notice in writing;

(*n*) "the tenth base period" means the period of twelve months that commenced on 6th April 1975;

(*o*) "the transfer orders" means—

    (i) the Industrial Training (Transfer of the Activities of Establishments) (No. 2) Order 1974**(c)**,

    (ii) the Industrial Training (Transfer of the Activities of Establishments) Order 1975**(d)**;

(a) S.I. 1965/1391 (1965 II, p. 4062).   (b) S.I. 1969/689 (1969 II, p. 1860).
(c) S.I. 1974/1495 (1974 III, p. 5739).   (d) S.I. 1975/434 (1975 I, p. 1371).

    (iii) the Industrial Training (Transfer of the Activities of Establishments) Order 1976**(a)**;

    (iv) the Industrial Training (Transfer of the Activities of Establishments) (No. 2) Order 1976**(b)**; and

    (v) the Industrial Training (Transfer of the Activities of Establishments) (No. 3) Order 1976**(c)**.

(2) Any reference in this Order to an establishment that commences to carry on business or that ceases to carry on business shall not be taken to apply where the location of the establishment is changed but its business is continued wholly or mainly at or from the new location, or where the suspension of activities is of a temporary or seasonal nature.

(3) The Interpretation Act 1889**(d)** shall apply to the interpretation of this Order as it applies to the interpretation of an Act of Parliament.

Imposition of the levy

3.—(1) The levy to be imposed by the Board on employers in respect of the eleventh levy period shall be assessed in accordance with the provisions of this Article and of the Schedule to this Order.

(2) The levy shall be assessed by the Board separately in respect of each relevant establishment (that is to say, each ceramics, glass and mineral products establishment other than one which is exempted by an exemption certificate or one which is an establishment of an employer who is exempted by virtue of paragraph 3 of the Schedule to this Order), but in agreement with the employer one assessment may be made in respect of any number of relevant establishments, in which case those establishments shall be deemed for the purpose of that assessment to constitute one establishment.

Assessment notices

4.—(1) The Board shall serve an assessment notice on every employer assessed to the levy, but one notice may comprise two or more assessments.

(2) An assessment notice shall state the amount of the levy payable by the person assessed to the levy, and that amount shall be equal to the total amount (rounded down where necessary to the nearest £1) of the levy assessed by the Board under this Order in respect of each establishment included in the notice.

(3) An assessment notice shall state the Board's address for the service of a notice of appeal or of an application for an extension of time for appealing.

(4) An assessment notice may be served on the person assessed to the levy either by delivering it to him personally or by leaving it, or sending it to him by post, at his last known address or place of business in the United Kingdom or, if that person is a corporation, by leaving it, or sending it by post to the corporation, at such address or place of business or at its registered or principal office.

Payment of the levy

5.—(1) Subject to the provisions of this Article and of Articles 6 and 7, the amount of the levy payable under an assessment notice served by the Board shall be due and payable to the Board one month after the date of the notice.

(2) The amount of an assessment shall not be recoverable by the Board until there has expired the time allowed for appealing against the assessment by

(a) S.I. 1976/396 (1976 I, p. 1055).   (b) S.I. 1976/1635 (1976 III, p. 4103).
(c) S.I. 1976/2110 (1976 III, p. 5851).   (d) 1889 c. 63.

Article 7(1) of this Order and any further period or periods of time that the Board or an appeal tribunal may have allowed for appealing under paragraph (2) or (3) of that Article, or, where an appeal is brought, until the appeal is decided or withdrawn.

Withdrawal of assessment

6.—(1) The Board may, by a notice served on the person assessed to the levy in the same manner as an assessment notice, withdraw an assessment if that person has appealed against that assessment under the provisions of Article 7 of this Order and the appeal has not been entered in the Register of Appeals kept under the appropriate Regulations specified in paragraph (5) of that Article.

(2) The withdrawal of an assessment shall be without prejudice—

(a) to the power of the Board to serve a further assessment notice in respect of any establishment to which that assessment related; or

(b) to any other assessment included in the original assessment notice, and such notice shall thereupon have effect as if any assessment withdrawn by the Board had not been included therein.

Appeals

7.—(1) A person assessed to the levy may appeal to an appeal tribunal against the assessment within one month from the date of the service of the assessment notice or within any further period or periods of time that may be allowed by the Board or an appeal tribunal under the following provisions of this Article.

(2) The Board by notice may for good cause allow a person assessed to the levy to appeal to an appeal tribunal against the assessment at any time within the period of four months from the date of the service of the assessment notice or within such further period or periods as the Board may allow before such time as may then be limited for appealing has expired.

(3) If the Board shall not allow an application for extension of time for appealing, an appeal tribunal shall upon application made to the tribunal by the person assessed to the levy have the like powers as the Board under the last foregoing paragraph.

(4) In the case of an establishment that ceases to carry on business in the eleventh levy period on any day after the date of the service of the relevant assessment notice, the foregoing provisions of this Article shall have effect as if for the period of four months from the date of the service of the assessment notice mentioned in paragraph (2) of this Article there were substituted the period of six months from the date of the cessation of business.

(5) An appeal or an application to an appeal tribunal under this Article shall be made in accordance with the Industrial Tribunals (England and Wales) Regulations 1965(a) as amended by the Industrial Tribunals (England and Wales) (Amendment) Regulations 1967(b) except where the establishment to which the relevant assessment relates is wholly in Scotland, in which case the appeal or application shall be made in accordance with the Industrial Tribunals (Scotland) Regulations 1965(c) as amended by the Industrial Tribunals (Scotland) (Amendment) Regulations 1967(d).

(a) S.I. 1965/1101 (1965 II, p. 2805).   (b) S.I. 1967/301 (1967 I, p. 1040).
(c) S.I. 1965/1157 (1965 II, p. 3266).   (d) S.I. 1967/302 (1967 I, p. 1050).

(6) The powers of an appeal tribunal under paragraph (3) of this Article may be exercised by the President of the Industrial Tribunals (England and Wales) or by the President of the Industrial Tribunals (Scotland) as the case may be.

Evidence

8.—(1) Upon the discharge by a person assessed to the levy of his liability under an assessment the Board shall if so requested issue to him a certificate to that effect.

(2) The production in any proceedings of a document purporting to be certified by the Secretary of the Board to be a true copy of an assessment or other notice issued by the Board or purporting to be a certificate such as is mentioned in the foregoing paragraph of this Article shall, unless the contrary is proved, be sufficient evidence of the document and of the facts stated therein.

Signed by order of the Secretary of State.

25th July 1977.

John Golding,
Joint Parliamentary Under Secretary of State,
Department of Employment.

Article 3

SCHEDULE

1.—(1) In this Schedule unless the context otherwise requires—

(a) "agriculture" has the same meaning as in section 109(3) of the Agriculture Act 1947(a) or, in relation to Scotland, as in section 86(3) of the Agriculture (Scotland) Act 1948(b);

(b) "the appropriate percentage", in relation to the emoluments of persons employed at or from a ceramics, glass and mineral products establishment, means—

(i) where the establishment was engaged wholly or mainly in any one or more of the activities comprised in one of the two Categories specified in column 1 and column 2 of Appendix 1 to this Schedule, the percentage specified in relation to that Category in column 3 of that Appendix;

(ii) in any other case, the lowest percentage specified in relation to any Category in column 3 of that Appendix which comprises an activity in which the establishment was engaged;

(c) "charity" has the same meaning as in section 360 of the Income and Corporation Taxes Act 1970(c);

(d) "emoluments" means all emoluments assessable to income tax under Schedule E (other than pensions), being emoluments from which tax under that Schedule is deductible, whether or not tax in fact falls to be deducted from any particular payment thereof;

(e) "pottery" includes bone china, vitreous china, porcelain, earthernware, wall tiles, sanitary fire clay ware, sanitary earthenware and similar wares;

(f) "related or administive activities" means activities of a kind to which paragraph 1(o) of the Schedule to the industrial training order applies;

(g) other expressions have the meanings assigned to them respectively by paragraph 3 or 4 of the Schedule to the industrial training order or by Article 2 of this Order.

(2) The activities in a Category specified in column 1 and column 2 of Appendices 1 and 2 to this Schedule include any related or administrative activities undertaken in relation to any activities comprised in such Category.

(3) In reckoning any sum of emoluments for the purposes of this Schedule no regard shall be had to the emoluments of any person employed as follows:—

(a) wholly as a registered dock worker in dock work;

(b) wholly in agriculture; or

(c) wholly in the supply of food or drink for immediate consumption.

2. Subject to the provisions of this Schedule, the amount of the levy imposed on an employer in respect of a ceramics, glass and mineral products establishment shall be equal to the appropriate percentage of the sum of the emoluments of all the persons employed by the employer in the eleventh base period at or from the establishment.

3.—(1) There shall be exempt from the levy an employer in whose case the sum of the emoluments of all the persons employed by him in either the tenth or eleventh base period at or from the ceramics, glass and mineral products establishment or establishments of the employer (including any persons employed at or from a ceramics, glass and mineral products establishment by an associated company of the employer) was less than the appropriate minimum amount specified in column 3 of Appendix 2 to this Schedule for the appropriate Category:

Provided that in the case of an employer who was exempt from the levy imposed under the Industrial Training Levy (Ceramics, Glass and Mineral Products) Order 1976(d) by reason of paragraph 3(1) of the Schedule to that Order the appropriate

---

(a) 1947 c. 48.   (b) 1948 c. 45.   (c) 1970 c. 10.
(d) S.I. 1976/1633 (1976 III, p. 4088).

minimum amount referred to above shall, in relation to the sum of the emoluments in the tenth base period, be that specified in column 4 of Appendix 2 to this Schedule.

(2) A charity shall be exempted from the levy.

(3) In order to determine, in relation to either the tenth or eleventh base period, the appropriate Category for the purposes of sub-paragraph (1) of this paragraph, an establishment shall be taken to fall within that Category specified in column 1 and column 2 of Appendix 2 to this Schedule in which are comprised the ceramics, glass and mineral products activities in which the establishment was wholly or mainly engaged. The appropriate Category is that Category if in the base period the employer had only one establishment and there were no persons employed at or from a ceramics, glass and mineral products establishment by an associated company of the employer. In any other case, the appropriate Category, in relation to either the tenth or eleventh base period, is the one in which the total emoluments of all the persons employed by the employer and any associated company of the employer at establishments falling within that Category was the highest.

4. The amount of the levy imposed in respect of a ceramics, glass and mineral products establishment that ceases to carry on business in the eleventh levy period shall be in the same proportion to the amount that would otherwise be due in accordance with the foregoing provisions of this Schedule as the number of days between the commencement of the said levy period and the date of cessation of business (both dates inclusive) bears to the number of days in the said levy period.

APPENDIX 1

Column 1 Category No.	Column 2 Description of activities	Column 3 Appropriate percentage
1.	The following activities or any of them—	0·65
	(a) the manufacture of glass;	
	(b) the manufacture of articles or other products wholly or mainly from glass;	
	(c) the calibrating, graduating or toughening of glass or glass articles;	
	(d) the milling, grinding or mixing of any material for the purpose of the manufacture of pottery;	
	(e) the manufacture of pottery;	
	(f) the manufacture, wholly or mainly from plaster, of effigies, models or toys.	
2.	Any activities of the ceramics, glass and mineral products industry, not being activities comprised in Category 1.	0·50

APPENDIX 2

Column 1 Category No.	Column 2 Description of activities	Column 3 Appropriate minimum amount	Column 4 Appropriate minimum amount
	The following activities or any of them—	£	£
1.	(a) the lifting or extracting of mineral deposits or products of minerals from the earth or of mineral deposits from the bed of a lake or river or of the sea;	62,000	67,000

APPENDIX 2 (*Continued*)

Column 1	Column 2	Column 3	Column 4
Category No.	*Description of activities*	*Appropriate minimum amount £*	*Appropriate minimum amount £*

(*b*) the crushing, grinding, washing, drying, grading or screening of sand, gravel or fluorspar;

(*c*) the crushing, grinding, washing, drying, foaming, grading, screening, cutting, splitting, dressing, polishing, or mixing of mineral deposits (not being sand, gravel or fluorspar) or products of minerals or any similar operation, being activities carried out—

    (i) by an employer (or an associated company of the employer, being a company) engaged in any activities specified in sub-paragraph (*a*) of this paragraph; and

    (ii) on land in or adjacent to a mine or quarry and in conjunction with the operation thereof;

(*d*) the burning of limestone or the hydration of lime;

(*e*) the production of cement plaster or whiting;

(*f*) the production of ready-mixed concrete or ready-mixed mortar or the batching or mixing of ingredients in connection with such production;

(*g*) the production of coated material for the purpose of the construction or repair of roads or footways;

(*h*) the processing of slag, clinker or breeze;

(*i*) the manufacture of articles or other products wholly or mainly from—

    (i) asbestos cement;

    (ii) concrete, cast stone, or cement, or from any mixture of aggregate together with a cementing or bonding agent;

    (iii) plaster, other than the manufacture of effigies, models or toys;

(*j*) the manufacture, wholly or mainly from concrete and tiles or from stone set in concrete, of fireplaces;

2.	(*a*) the exfoliation of vermiculite or any similar material;	124,000	134,000

(*b*) the manufacture of—

    (i) articles consisting mainly of bonded abrasive material or coated with abrasive material;

    (ii) calcium silicate bricks;

(*c*) the manufacture of articles or other products wholly or mainly from—

    (i) clay or any mixture of clay and calcined or burnt animal bones;

    (ii) one or more refractory materials;

(*d*) the manufacture, wholly or mainly from plaster, of effigies, models or toys;

(*e*) the milling, grinding or mixing of any material for the purpose of the manufacture of pottery;

3.	(*a*) the manufacture of glass and of articles or other products wholly or mainly from glass;	162,000	177,000

(*b*) the calibrating, graduating or toughening of glass or glass aticles.

EXPLANATORY NOTE

(This Note is not part of the Order.)

This Order gives effect to proposals of the Ceramics, Glass and Mineral Products Industry Training Board which were submitted to and approved by the Manpower Services Commission, and thereafter submitted by the Manpower Services Commission to the Secretary of State. The proposals are for the imposition of a levy on employers in the ceramics, glass and mineral products industry for the purpose of encouraging adequate training in the industry.

The levy is to be imposed in respect of the eleventh levy period commencing with the date upon which this Order comes into operation and ending on 31st March 1978. The levy will be assessed by the Board and there will be a right of appeal against an assessment to an industrial tribunal.

STATUTORY INSTRUMENTS

1977 No. 1228

INDUSTRIAL TRAINING

The Industrial Training Levy (Cotton and Allied Textiles) Order 1977

Made - - - -	*25th July* 1977
Laid before Parliament	*5th August* 1977
Coming into Operation	*6th September* 1977

Whereas proposals made by the Cotton and Allied Textiles Industry Training Board for the raising and collection of a levy have been submitted to, and approved by, the Manpower Services Commission under section 7 of the Industrial Training Act 1964(a) ("the 1964 Act"), as amended by section 6 of and Schedule 2 to the Employment and Training Act 1973(b) ("the 1973 Act") and have thereafter been submitted by the said Commission to the Secretary of State under section 7(1C) of the 1964 Act as inserted by the 1973 Act:

And whereas in pursuance of section 7(1A)(*a*) of the 1964 Act as inserted by the 1973 Act the said proposals include provision for the exemption from the levy of employers who, in view of the small number of their employees, ought in the opinion of the Secretary of State to be exempted from it;

And whereas the Secretary of State estimates that the amount which, disregarding any exemptions, will be payable by virtue of this Order by any employer in the cotton and allied textiles industry, does not exceed an amount which the Secretary of State estimates is equal to one per cent. of the aggregate of the emoluments and payments intended to be disbursed as emoluments which have been paid or are payable by any such employer to or in respect of persons employed in the industry, in respect of the period specified in the said proposals as relevant, that is to say the period hereafter referred to in this order as "the eleventh base period";

And whereas the Secretary of State is satisfied that proposals published by the said Board in pursuance of section 4A of the 1964 Act, as inserted by the 1973 Act, provide for exemption certificates relating to the levy in such cases as he considers appropriate;

Now, therefore, the Secretary of State in exercise of the powers conferred by section 4 of the 1964 Act, as amended by section 6 of and Schedule 2 to the 1973 Act, and of all other powers enabling him in that behalf hereby makes the following Order:—

Citation and commencement

1. This Order may be cited as the Industrial Training Levy (Cotton and Allied Textiles) Order 1977 and shall come into operation on 6th September 1977.

(a) 1964 c. 16.　　　　　　　　　　　　　　　　(b) 1973 c. 50.

Interpretation

2.—(1) In this Order unless the context otherwise requires:—

(*a*) "agriculture" has the same meaning as in section 109(3) of the Agriculture Act 1947(a) or, in relation to Scotland, as in section 86(3) of the Agriculture (Scotland) Act 1948(b);

(*b*) "an appeal tribunal" means an industrial tribunal established under section 12 of the Industrial Training Act 1964;

(*c*) "assessment" means an assessment of an employer to the levy;

(*d*) "the Board" means the Cotton and Allied Textiles Industry Training Board;

(*e*) "business" means any activities of industry or commerce;

(*f*) "charity" has the same meaning as in section 360 of the Income and Corporation Taxes Act 1970(c);

(*g*) "cotton and allied textiles establishment" means an establishment in Great Britain engaged in the eleventh base period wholly or mainly in the cotton and allied textiles industry for a total of twenty-seven or more weeks or, being an establishment that commenced to carry on business in the eleventh base period, for a total number of weeks exceeding one half of the number of weeks in the part of the said period commencing with the day on which business was commenced and ending on the last day thereof;

(*h*) "the cotton and allied textiles industry" does not include any activities of an establishment which have been transferred from the industry of the Board to the industry of another industrial training board by one of the transfer orders but save as aforesaid means any one or more of the activities which, subject to the provisions of paragraph 2 of Schedule 1 to the industrial training order, are specified in paragraph 1 of that Schedule as the activities of the cotton and allied textiles industry or, in relation to an establishment whose activities have been transferred to the industry of the Board by one of the transfer orders, any activities so transferred;

(*i*) "the eleventh levy period" means the period commencing with the day upon which this Order comes into operation and ending on 31st March 1978;

(*j*) "emoluments" means all emoluments assessable to income tax under Schedule E (other than pensions), being emoluments from which tax under that Schedule is deductible, whether or not tax in fact falls to be deducted from any particular payment thereof;

(*k*) "employer" means a person who is an employer in the cotton and allied textiles industry at any time in the eleventh levy period;

(*l*) "exemption certificate" means a certificate issued by the Board under section 4B of the 1964 Act, as inserted by the 1973 Act;

(*m*) "the industrial training order" means the Industrial Training (Cotton and Allied Textiles Board) Order 1966(d);

(*n*) "the levy" means the levy imposed by the Board in respect of the eleventh levy period;

(a) 1947 c. 48.　　　　　　　　　　(b) 1948 c. 45.
(c) 1970 c. 10.　　　　　　　　　　(d) S.I. 1966/823 (1966 II, p. 1907).

(*o*) "notice" means a notice in writing;

(*p*) "the tenth base period" and "the eleventh base period" respectively mean the period of twelve months that commenced on the 6th April 1975 and the period of twelve months that commenced on 6th April 1976;

(*q*) "the transfer orders" means—

(i) the Industrial Training (Transfer of the Activities of Establishments) Order 1974**(a)**, and

(ii) the Industrial Training (Transfer of the Activities of Establishments) Order 1975**(b)**, and

(iii) the Industrial Training (Transfer of the Activities of Establishments) (No. 2) Order 1976**(c)**.

(2) Any reference in this Order to an establishment that commences to carry on business or that ceases to carry on business shall not be taken to apply where the location of the establishment is changed but its business is continued wholly or mainly at or from the new location, or where the suspension of activities is of a temporary or seasonal nature.

(3) Any reference in this Order to a person employed at or from a cotton and allied textiles establishment shall in any case where the employer is a company be construed as including a reference to any director of the company (or any person occupying the position of director by whatever name he is called) who is required to devote substantially the whole of his time to the service of the company.

(4) The Interpretation Act 1889**(d)** shall apply to the interpretation of this Order as it applies to the interpretation of an Act of Parliament.

Imposition of the levy

3.—(1) The levy to be imposed by the Board on employers in respect of the eleventh levy period shall be assessed in accordance with the provisions of this Article.

(2) The levy shall be assessed separately in respect of each relevant establishment of an employer (that is to say each cotton and allied textiles establishment other than one in respect of which an exemption certificate has been issued to the employer, or one which is an establishment of an employer who is exempt from the levy by virtue of paragraph (7) of this Article) but in agreement with the employer one assessment may be made in respect of any number of such establishments, in which case those establishments shall be deemed for the purposes of that assessment to constitute one establishment.

(3) Subject to the provisions of this Article, the levy assessed in respect of a cotton and allied textiles establishment of an employer shall be an amount equal to 0·75 per cent. of the appropriate sum (calculated in accordance with the Schedule to this Order).

(**a**) S.I. 1974/1154 (1974 II, p. 4402).   (**b**) S.I. 1975/434 (1975 I, p. 1371).
(**c**) S.I. 1976/1635 (1976 III, p. 4103).   (**d**) 1889 c. 63.

(4) In the case of one establishment only of an employer, the appropriate sum shall be treated for the purposes of the assessment of the levy in respect of that establishment as if that sum were reduced by £45,000.

(5) For the purposes of the application of the provisions of the last foregoing paragraph the Board shall, if necessary—

(a) select the establishment in relation to which the provisions of the said paragraph are to apply; or

(b) aggregate the appropriate sums in respect of any two or more cotton and allied textiles establishments of the employer, in which case the said establishments shall be deemed for the purposes of the assessment to constitute one establishment.

(6) The amount of the levy imposed in respect of a cotton and allied textiles establishment that ceases to carry on business in the eleventh levy period shall be in the same proportion to the amount that would otherwise be due under the foregoing provisions of this Article as the number of days between the commencement of the said levy period and the date of cessation of business (both dates inclusive) bears to five times the number of days in the said levy period.

(7) There shall be exempt from the levy—

(a) an employer in whose case the appropriate sum, or where there is more than one cotton and allied textiles establishment of the employer, the aggregate of the appropriate sums, is less than £46,334;

(b) a charity.

Assessment notices

4.—(1) The Board shall serve an assessment notice on every employer assessed to the levy, but one notice may comprise two or more assessments.

(2) An assessment notice shall state the amount of the levy payable by the person assessed to the levy, and that amount shall be equal to the total amount (rounded down where necessary to the nearest £1) of the levy assessed by the Board under Article 3 of this Order in respect of each establishment included in the notice.

(3) An assessment notice shall state the Board's address for the service of a notice of appeal or of an application for an extension of time for appealing.

(4) An assessment notice may be served on the person assessed to the levy either by delivering it to him personally or by leaving it, or sending it to him by post, at his last known address or place of business in the United Kingdom, or, if that person is a corporation, by leaving it, or sending it by post to the corporation, at such address or place of business or at its registered or principal office.

Payment of the levy

5.—(1) Subject to the provisions of this Article and of Articles 6 and 7, the amount of the levy payable under an assessment notice served by the Board shall be due and payable to the Board one month after the date of the notice.

(2) The amount of an assessment shall not be recoverable by the Board until there has expired the time allowed for appealing against the assessment by Article 7(1) of this Order and any further period or periods of time that the Board or an appeal tribunal may have allowed for appealing under paragraph (2) or (3) of that Article or, where an appeal is brought, until the appeal is decided or withdrawn.

Withdrawal of assessment

6.—(1) The Board may, by a notice served on the person assessed to the levy in the same manner as an assessment notice, withdraw an assessment if that person has appealed against that assessment under the provisions of Article 7 of this Order and the appeal has not been entered in the Register of Appeals kept under the appropriate Regulations specified in paragraph (5) of that Article, and such withdrawal may be extended by the Board to any other assessment appearing in the assessment notice.

(2) The withdrawal of an assessment shall be without prejudice—

(*a*) to the power of the Board to serve a further assessment notice in respect of any establishment to which that assessment related;

(*b*) to any other assessment included in the original assessment notice and not withdrawn by the Board, and such notice shall thereupon have effect as if any assessment withdrawn by the Board had not been included therein.

Appeals

7.—(1) A person assessed to the levy may appeal to an appeal tribunal against the assessment within one month from the date of the service of the assessment notice or within any further period or periods of time that may be allowed by the Board or an appeal tribunal under the following provisions of this Article.

(2) The Board by notice may for good cause allow a person assessed to the levy to appeal to an appeal tribunal against the assessment at any time within the period of four months from the date of the service of the assessment notice or within such further period or periods as the Board may allow before such time as may then be limited for appealing has expired.

(3) If the Board shall not allow an application for extension of time for appealing, an appeal tribunal shall upon application made to the tribunal by the person assessed to the levy have the like powers as the Board under the last foregoing paragraph.

(4) In the case of an establishment that ceases to carry on business in the eleventh levy period on any day after the date of the service of the relevant assessment notice, the foregoing provisions of this Article shall have effect as if for the period of four months from the date of the service of the assessment notice mentioned in paragraph (2) of this Article there were substituted the period of six months from the date of the cessation of business.

(5) An appeal or an application to an appeal tribunal under this Article shall be made in accordance with the Industrial Tribunals (England and Wales) Regulations 1965(a) as amended by the Industrial Tribunals (England and Wales) (Amendment) Regulations 1967(b) except where the establishment to which the relevant assessment relates is wholly in Scotland in which case the appeal or application shall be made in accordance with the Industrial Tribunals (Scotland) Regulations 1965(c) as amended by the Industrial Tribunals (Scotland) (Amendment) Regulations 1967(d).

(6) The powers of an appeal tribunal under paragraph (3) of this Article may be exercised by the President of the Industrial Tribunals (England and Wales) or by the President of the Industrial Tribunals (Scotland) as the case may be.

(a) S.I. 1965/1101 (1965 II, p. 2805).   (b) S.I. 1967/301 (1967 I, p. 1040).
(c) S.I. 1965/1157 (1965 II, p. 3266).   (d) S.I. 1967/302 (1967 I, p. 1050).

Evidence

8.—(1) Upon the discharge by a person assessed to the levy of his liability under an assessment the Board shall if so requested issue to him a certificate to that effect.

(2) The production in any proceedings of a document purporting to be certified by the Secretary of the Board to be a true copy of an assessment or other notice issued by the Board or purporting to be a certificate such as is mentioned in the foregoing paragraph of this Article shall, unless the contrary is proved, be sufficient evidence of the document and of the facts stated therein.

Signed by order of the Secretary of State.

25th July 1977.

John Golding,
Joint Parliamentary Under Secretary of State,
Department of Employment.

Article 3

SCHEDULE

1. The provisions of this Schedule shall have effect for the purpose of calculating the appropriate sum under Article 3 of this Order.

2. For the purposes of this Schedule—

   (*a*) references to an establishment are references to a cotton and allied textiles establishment;

   (*b*) subject to sub-paragraph (*c*), references to the sum of the emoluments are references to the sum of the emoluments of the persons employed by the employer at or from the establishment;

   (*c*) no regard shall be had to the emoluments of any person wholly engaged in agriculture or in the supply of food or drink for immediate consumption;

   (*d*) "A" is the sum of the emoluments in the eleventh base period;

   (*e*) "B" is the sum of the emoluments in the tenth base period.

3. Where $\frac{A}{B}$ is equal to or less than $\frac{3}{4}$ the appropriate sum shall be $\frac{A}{B}$ multiplied by A.

4. In any other case the appropriate sum shall be A.

EXPLANATORY NOTE

(This Note is not part of the Order.)

This Order gives effect to proposals of the Cotton and Allied Textiles Industry Training Board which were submitted to and approved by the Manpower Services Commission, and thereafter submitted by the Manpower Services Commission to the Secretary of State. The proposals are for the imposition of a levy upon employers in the cotton and allied textiles industry for the purpose of encouraging adequate training in the industry.

The levy is to be imposed in respect of the eleventh levy period commencing on the day upon which this Order comes into operation and ending on 31st March 1978. The levy will be assessed by the Board and there will be a right of appeal against an assessment to an industrial tribunal.

STATUTORY INSTRUMENTS

1977 No. 1229

SOCIAL SECURITY

The Mobility Allowance (Vehicle Scheme Beneficiaries) Regulations 1977

Made - - - -	26th July 1977
Laid before Parliament	27th July 1977
Coming into Operation	17th August 1977

In exercise of the powers conferred upon me by section 37A(1) and (5) and section 114(1) and (2) of the Social Security Act 1975(a), section 13 of the Social Security (Miscellaneous Provisions) Act 1977(b) and of all other powers enabling me in that behalf I hereby make the following regulations which contain only provisions made in consequence of the Social Security (Miscellaneous Provisions) Act 1977 and which accordingly, by virtue of section 24(4)(a) of that Act are not subject to the requirements of section 139(1) of the Social Security Act 1975 for prior reference to the National Insurance Advisory Committee:—

Citation, commencement and interpretation

1.—(1) These regulations may be cited as the Mobility Allowance (Vehicle Scheme Beneficiaries) Regulations 1977 and shall come into operation on 17th August 1977.

(2) In these regulations unless the context otherwise requires:—

"the Act" means the Social Security (Miscellaneous Provisions) Act 1977;

"the principal Act" means the Social Security Act 1975;

"the principal regulations" means the Mobility Allowance Regulations 1975(c);

"vehicle scheme beneficiary" means any person of the class specified in section 13(3)(a), (c) or (d) of the Act or any person of the class specified in section 13(3)(b) of the Act whose application was approved on or after 1st January 1976;

"certificate" means a certificate for the purposes of section 13(1) of the Act; and other expressions have the same meaning as in the principal Act.

(3) Except in so far as the context otherwise requires any reference in these regulations to—

(a) a numbered regulation is a reference to the regulation bearing that number in these regulations and any reference in a regulation to a numbered paragraph is a reference to the paragraph of that regulation bearing that number;

(a) 1975 c. 14. (b) 1977 c. 5.
(c) S.I. 1975/1573 (1975 III, p. 5450).

(*b*) any provision made by or contained in any enactment or instrument shall be construed as a reference to that provision as amended or extended by any enactment or instrument and as including a reference to any provision which may re-enact it or replace it with or without modifications.

(4) The rules for the construction of Acts of Parliament contained in the Interpretation Act 1889(**a**) shall apply for the purposes of the interpretation of these regulations as they apply for the purposes of the interpretation of an Act of Parliament.

Prescribed periods for purposes of section 13(3)(*c*) *of the Act*

2. For the purposes of section 13(3)(*c*) of the Act—

(*a*) the prescribed period before 1st January 1976 shall be that commencing with 1st January 1970 and ending with 31st December 1975; and

(*b*) the prescribed period after 1st January 1976 shall be that commencing with 2nd January 1976 and ending with 31st March 1978.

Issue of certificates

3.—(1) The Secretary of State shall issue a certificate in the form approved by him in respect of any person—

(*a*) who has made an application for a certificate in the form approved by the Secretary of State; and

(*b*) whom the Secretary of State considers satisfies the conditions specified in paragraph (2).

(2) The conditions referred to in paragraph (1) are—

(*a*) that he is a vehicle scheme beneficiary; and

(*b*) that his physical condition has not improved to such an extent that he no longer satisfies the conditions which it was necessary for him to satisfy in order to become a vehicle scheme beneficiary.

Duration and cancellation of certificates

4.—(1) Subject to paragraphs (2) and (3) the period during which a certificate is in force shall commence on the day specified in the certificate as being the date on which it comes into force and shall continue for the life of the person concerned.

(2) The period specified in paragraph (1) shall not commence—

(*a*) in the case of a vehicle scheme beneficiary who on or after 1st August 1977 is receiving payments in pursuance of section 33(3) of the Health Services and Public Health Act 1968(**b**) in respect of a vehicle belonging to him, before 5th July 1978; or

(*b*) in relation to any other vehicle scheme beneficiary—

(i) before 16th November 1977 if his surname begins with any of the letters from A to K in the alphabet; or

(ii) before 15th February 1978 if his surname begins with any of the letters from L to Z in the alphabet.

(3) If in any case the Secretary of State determines that the condition specified in regulation 3(2)(*b*) is not satisfied, the certificate shall cease to be in force

---

(**a**) 1889 c. 63. (**b**) 1968 c. 46.

from the date of such non-satisfaction as determined by the Secretary of State
(or such later date as appears to the Secretary of State to be reasonable in the
circumstances).

Supply of information in connection with certificates

5.—(1) Any person who is an applicant for a certificate or in respect of whom
a certificate has been issued—

(*a*) shall furnish to the Secretary of State such information and evidence
relating to his circumstances as the Secretary of State may require on
the making of the application and from time to time thereafter; and

(*b*) shall notify the Secretary of State of any change in his circumstances
which might effect the cancellation of the certificate; and

(*c*) shall comply with any notice given to him by the Secretary of State
which requires him to submit himself to medical examination for the
purposes of determining whether he satisfies the condition specified in
regulation 3(2)(*b*).

(2) The requirements of regulation 7 of the principal regulations as to
notices given for the purposes of that regulation shall apply to notices given
for the purposes of paragraph (1)(*c*).

*Application of the principal Act and principal regulations in relation to vehicle
scheme beneficiaries*

6. In relation to a person in respect of whom a certificate is in force—

(*a*) section 37A of the principal Act shall have effect as though in subsection (5) the words "or over pensionable age" were omitted; and

(*b*) the principal regulations shall have effect as though—

(i) regulation 2(1)(*c*) and (*d*) were omitted; and

(ii) in regulation 14 after paragraph (1)(*b*) there were inserted—

"or

(*c*) the issue of a certificate under the Mobility Allowance
(Vehicle Scheme Beneficiaries) Regulations 1977."; and

(iii) in regulation 20 after paragraph (3) there were added—

"(4) Where the grounds of an application under paragraph (2)
are that a certificate issued for the purposes of section 13 of the
Social Security (Miscellaneous Provisions) Act 1977 has been
cancelled, the insurance officer may himself determine any medical
question arising on review adversely to the person in question
without referring it to a medical board and the provisions of
regulation 15(3) and 16 to 19 shall apply to such determination
as though it were a determination under regulation 15(2)(*b*).".

*Entitlement to an allowance in respect of weeks before that in which a claim
is received by the Secretary of State*

7. A person in respect of whom a certificate is in force may be entitled to
mobility allowance for any week—

(*a*) falling before the week in which a claim for the allowance by or in
respect of him is received by the Secretary of State; and

(*b*) falling after the date specified in the certificate in respect of him as being the date on which such certificate comes into force.

David Ennals,
One of Her Majesty's Principal
Secretaries of State.

26th July 1977.

EXPLANATORY NOTE

(This Note is not part of the Regulations.)

These Regulations make provisions concerning the issue and cancellation of certificates whereby, by virtue of section 13 of the Social Security (Miscellaneous Provisions) Act 1977, certain classes of persons may be deemed to satisfy certain of the conditions for mobility allowance specified in section 37A of the Social Security Act 1975.

They also make provision for further defining the classes of persons concerned and for relaxing for those in respect of whom the certificates are issued requirements of the Social Security Act 1975 and the Mobility Allowance Regulations 1975 relating to the upper age limit for the allowance, the residence and presence conditions for the allowance, the period for which a person may be entitled to the allowance and the determination of claims for the allowance.

STATUTORY INSTRUMENTS

1977 No. 1230 (S.96)

AGRICULTURE

LIVESTOCK INDUSTRIES

The Artificial Insemination of Cattle (Scotland) Regulations 1977

Made - - - -	*25th July* 1977
Laid before Parliament -	*27th July* 1977
Coming into Operation -	*1st September* 1977

In exercise of the powers conferred on me by section 17 of the Agriculture (Miscellaneous Provisions) Act 1943(a), and of all other powers enabling me in that behalf, I hereby make the following regulations:—

PART I—INTRODUCTORY

Citation, extent and commencement

1. These regulations may be cited as the Artificial Insemination of Cattle (Scotland) Regulations 1977, shall apply to Scotland and shall come into operation on 1st September 1977.

Interpretation

2.—(1) In these regulations, unless the context otherwise requires—

"animal" includes a domestic fowl, turkey, goose and duck;

"approved bull" means a bull which is approved for the time being—
    (*a*) by the Secretary of State under regulation 5 of these regulations, or
    (*b*) by the Minister under regulation 5 of the Artificial Insemination of Cattle (England and Wales) Regulations 1977(b);

"artificial insemination" means the artificial insemination of a cow;

"building" includes a part of a building;

(a) 1943 c. 16.   (b) S.I. 1977/1260 (1977 II, p. 3502).

"centre storage licence" means a licence granted under regulation 7(1)(c);

"cow" includes heifer;

"embryo transfer unit" means premises wholly or mainly used for the purpose of the collection or the transference of embryos of cattle and "exempted embryo transfer unit" means an embryo transfer unit in respect of which a certificate issued by the Secretary of State is in force certifying that the unit is an exempted embryo transfer unit for the purpose of these regulations;

"evaluation" in relation to semen means the examination of semen from a bull and the assessment of its suitability for use in artificial insemination;

"farm" includes an embryo transfer unit and a research or experimental establishment;

"farm storage licence" means a licence granted under regulation 7(1)(e);

"farm storage servicing licence" means a licence granted under regulation 7(1)(f);

"flask" means a cryogenic flask;

"the Minister" means the Minister of Agriculture, Fisheries and Food;

"owner" includes a joint owner, and any person having authorised possessory use, and "ownership" shall be construed accordingly;

"process", in relation to semen, means all or any of the following—
   (a) dilute (except for the purpose of, or in the course of, the evaluation of semen);
   (b) add any substance which is calculated to prolong the natural life of the semen;
   (c) package into straws;
   (d) freeze (except for the purpose of, or in the course of, the evaluation of semen);

and "processing" shall be construed accordingly except that the processing of semen shall not be regarded as completed until all the processes listed in the next definition have been carried out;

"processed", in relation to semen, means, except where the context otherwise requires, semen which has passed through all the following processes—
   (a) dilution;
   (b) addition of any substance which is calculated to prolong the natural life of the semen;
   (c) packaging into straws;
   (d) freezing;

"processing centre" means premises specified in a processing licence;

"processing licence" means a licence granted under regulation 7(1)(a);

"prohibited area" means—

(*a*) an infected place or area within the meaning of section 10(2) of the Diseases of Animals Act 1950(**a**) declared to be infected with

  (i) foot and mouth disease; or

  (ii) any other disease in relation to which an order made under section 11 of the said Act prohibits or regulates the removal of semen into, within, or out of that infected place or area, or

(*b*) premises into or from which the movement of cattle, sheep or swine is prohibited or regulated by a notice served under any order made under the said Act which notice prohibits the movement of semen;

"qualified person" means any of the following—

  (*a*) a veterinary surgeon;

  (*b*) a veterinary practitioner; and

  (*c*) a person, not being a veterinary surgeon or a veterinary practitioner, who collects semen under the direction of a veterinary surgeon approved by the Secretary of State in this behalf;

"quarantine" means holding in isolation;

"quarantine centre" means premises specified in a quarantine licence;

"quarantine licence" means a licence granted under regulation 7(1)(*b*);

"raw semen" means semen which has not been diluted or treated in any way so as to prolong its natural life;

"research or experimental establishment" means premises on which research into or experiments with cattle-breeding is or are carried out and "exempted research or experimental establishment" means a research or experimental establishment in respect of which a certificate issued by the Secretary of State is in force certifying that the establishment is an exempted research or experimental establishment for the purposes of these regulations;

"semen" means semen collected from a bull;

"storage centre" means premises specified in a centre storage licence;

"straw" means a container holding one dose of processed semen for use in artificial insemination;

"supply licence" means a licence granted under regulation 7(1)(*d*);

"veterinary practitioner" means a person registered in the supplementary veterinary register kept under section 8 of the Veterinary Surgeons Act 1966(**b**); and

"veterinary surgeon" means a person registered in the register of veterinary surgeons kept under section 2 of the Veterinary Surgeons Act 1966.

(2) References in these regulations to any enactment or regulations are (unless the context otherwise requires) references thereto as from time to time amended or replaced.

(**a**) 1950 c. 36.   (**b**) 1966 c. 36.

(3) Any reference in these regulations to a numbered regulation or Schedule shall be construed as a reference to the regulation or Schedule so numbered in these regulations.

(4) The Interpretation Act 1889(a) shall apply for the interpretation of these regulations as it applies for the interpretation of an Act of Parliament, and as if these regulations and the regulations hereby revoked were Acts of Parliament.

Revocation

3. The Artificial Insemination of Cattle (Scotland) Regulations 1957(b) are hereby revoked.

Application of Regulations

4.—(1) These regulations shall not apply to anything done by a permitted person in the course of or for the purpose of artificial insemination of a cow with raw semen which has been collected from a bull by a permitted person when, at the time of such insemination, the cow is—

(a) in the same ownership as the bull from which the semen is collected;

(b) kept on land occupied by the owner of the bull; and

(c) comprised in the same herd as the bull.

(2) Nothing in these regulations shall apply to anything done in the course of or for the purpose of the artificial insemination of a cow—

(a) on an exempted embryo transfer unit with raw semen which has been collected from a bull by a qualified person; or

(b) on an exempted research or experimental establishment with semen which has been collected from a bull by a qualified person.

(3) In paragraph (1) of this regulation, "permitted person" means—

(a) the owner of the bull from which semen is collected;

(b) a person in the regular and sole employment of the owner of the bull;

(c) a veterinary surgeon; or

(d) a veterinary practitioner.

PART II—APPROVAL OF BULLS

Bulls for use in artificial insemination

5.—(1) For the purposes of these regulations the Secretary of State may on application made to him by or on behalf of the owner of a bull approve the bull for use in artificial insemination.

(2) The Secretary of State may require an applicant for approval of a bull for use in artificial insemination—

(a) 1889 c. 63.   (b) S.I. 1957/1954 (1957 I, p. 168).

(a) to furnish him with such information as he may deem necessary for proper consideration of the application; and

(b) to permit the bull to be subjected to such isolation and to such veterinary tests or examinations as he may deem necessary.

(3) In considering whether or not to approve a bull for use in artificial insemination the Secretary of State shall have regard to the health of the bull and may take into account the health of other cattle with which that bull may have been in contact and the genetic qualities and physical characteristics, including abnormalities or defects of any kind, of the bull and its progeny.

(4) The Secretary of State may approve a bull for use in artificial insemination without condition or subject to the following conditions or to one or more of them—

(a) that the approved bull shall be subjected to such further isolation and shall satisfy the Secretary of State with regard to such further veterinary investigations as may be specified;

(b) that only during a specified period shall semen of the approved bull be collected for use in artificial insemination;

(c) that the amount of semen of the approved bull which may be supplied for use in artificial insemination of cows comprised in a herd other than a herd in the same ownership as the approved bull shall not exceed a specified total amount;

(d) that the semen of the approved bull shall be supplied for use in the artificial insemination only of cows comprised in such herd or herds as may be specified;

(e) that semen for use in artificial insemination shall be collected from the approved bull only on specified premises.

(5) Where a bull is approved subject to one or more of the conditions set out in the preceding paragraph, those conditions shall be binding on the owner for the time being of the approved bull.

(6) Where a bull is approved subject to one or both of the conditions set out in sub-paragraphs (c) and (d) of paragraph (4) of this regulation the owner of semen from that bull shall not knowingly supply that semen for use in such a way that there is a breach of either or both of those conditions.

(7) Where the Secretary of State has approved a bull for use in artificial insemination subject to the condition set out in paragraph (4)(c) of this regulation, notice of any subsequent change of ownership of that bull or of any subsequent disposal of semen from that bull shall be given to the Secretary of State by the owner of that bull or semen.

Provided that no notice shall require to be given to the Secretary of State in respect of semen which is moved from a storage centre under regulation 22(2)(c), (d) or (e).

(8) Where the owner of an approved bull or the owner of any semen from an approved bull knows or suspects that any progeny of that bull has shown signs of any abnormality the owner shall as soon as is practicable

give notice of that knowledge or suspicion to the Secretary of State and if subsequently so directed by the Secretary of State to any person whom that owner reasonably believes to be in possession of semen from that bull.

(9) The Secretary of State may at any time by notice to such person as he considers appropriate—

(a) cancel or vary any condition subject to which the bull was approved or may subject the approval of the bull to any of the conditions specified in paragraph (4) of this regulation not previously imposed, or

(b) withdraw the approval of the bull.

(10) On the death of an approved bull, the owner shall forthwith give notice to the Secretary of State of the death and the circumstances in which it occurred.

PART III—LICENCES

General prohibition of evaluation, etc. of semen

6. The evaluation, processing, keeping in quarantine, storage or movement from a storage centre of semen, or the causing or permitting of such evaluation, processing, keeping in quarantine, storage or movement, or the delivery to farms of equipment or materials required for the storage and use of semen in artificial insemination or the servicing whilst on the farm of such equipment is hereby prohibited except under the authority of and in accordance with the conditions of a licence issued by the Secretary of State and for the time being in force.

Licences

7.—(1) For the purposes of these regulations the Secretary of State may on application made to him grant one or more of the following licences—

(a) a processing licence;

(b) a quarantine licence;

(c) a centre storage licence;

(d) a supply licence;

(e) a farm storage licence; and

(f) a farm storage servicing licence.

(2) Where the Secretary of State grants two or more licences to the same person he may, if he thinks fit, grant the licences in the form of a combined licence.

(3) A processing licence shall authorise the licensee named therein to evaluate or process semen on such premises ("a processing centre") as are specified in the licence.

(4) A quarantine licence shall authorise the licensee named therein to keep processed semen in quarantine on such premises ("a quarantine centre") as are specified in the licence.

(5) A centre storage licence shall authorise the licensee named therein to store processed semen on such premises ("a storage centre") as are specified in the licence and to move semen from those premises in accordance with regulation 22(1).

(6) A supply licence shall authorise the licensee named therein to move processed semen from a storage centre in accordance with regulation 22(2).

(7) A farm storage licence shall authorise the licensee named therein to store processed semen on a farm specified in the licence and to use or cause such semen to be used in the artificial insemination of cows, which are kept on the farm or farms specified in the licence and which are, except where the farm is an exempted embryo transfer unit or an exempted research or experimental establishment or within an area which by reason of its lack of a suitable artificial insemination service the Secretary of State considers to be a remote area, owned by the licensee.

(8) A farm storage servicing licence shall authorise the licensee named therein to deliver to farms equipment or materials (including liquid nitrogen for farm storage flasks) required for the storage and use of semen or to service such equipment in accordance with regulation 25.

PART IV—COLLECTION, EVALUATION AND PROCESSING OF SEMEN

Collection of semen

8. No person shall collect semen from a bull for evaluation or processing unless he is a qualified person.

9. No person shall collect semen from a bull for processing unless that bull is an approved bull and—

(*a*) is at a processing centre; or

(*b*) where the approval of the bull for use in artificial insemination was subject to the conditions set out in regulation 5(4)(*a*) of these regulations, has been kept in isolation on premises specified in the approval of the bull under regulation 5(4)(*e*) since the commencement of the veterinary investigations specified under regulation 5(4)(*a*).

10.—(1) Where the collection of semen is to take place on the premises specified in the approval of the bull under regulation 5(4)(*e*) a teaser animal may be used only if authorised by a qualified person.

(2) In this regulation "teaser animal" means a bovine animal which is used as an aid in the collection of semen from a bull.

Delivery of semen for evaluation or processing

11. No person shall—

(*a*) submit for processing semen collected from a bull kept on a processing centre; or

(*b*) deliver to a processing centre semen for evaluation or processing; unless he is a qualified person.

Evaluation of semen

12.—(1) No person shall accept semen for evaluation unless it is submitted to him by a qualified person on the processing centre where the semen was collected, or is delivered to him at a processing centre by a qualified person.

(2) No person shall evaluate semen or cause or permit semen to be evaluated except under the authority of and in accordance with the conditions of a processing licence for the time being in force.

Processing of semen

13.—(1) No person shall accept semen for processing unless either it is submitted to him by a qualified person on the processing centre where the semen was collected, or it is delivered to him at a processing centre and—

(*a*) is delivered by a qualified person; or

(*b*) comes from another processing centre in Great Britain for completion of processing.

(2) No person shall process semen or cause or permit semen to be processed unless he knows or reasonably believes it to be semen collected from an approved bull.

(3) No person shall process semen or cause or permit semen to be processed except under the authority of and in accordance with the conditions of a processing licence for the time being in force.

Conditions of processing licences

14. A processing licence shall be issued subject to such of the conditions set out in Schedule 1, and to such other conditions (if any), as may be specified in the licence.

Movement of semen from a processing centre

15.—(1) No person shall move semen or cause or permit semen to be moved from a processing centre except direct—

(*a*) in the case of partially processed semen to another processing centre in Great Britain or to an exempted research or experimental establishment;

(*b*) in the case of processed semen to a quarantine centre in Great Britain; or

(*c*) to a place outside Great Britain.

(2) The person to whom a processing licence is granted shall, as soon as it is reasonably practicable after processing of the semen has been completed, move the semen or cause it to be moved direct to—

(*a*) a quarantine centre in Great Britain; or

(*b*) a place outside Great Britain.

PART V—QUARANTINE OF SEMEN

Acceptance of semen to be kept in quarantine

16. No person shall accept semen to be kept in quarantine unless—

(a) it is delivered to him at a quarantine centre; and

(b) it comes from a processing centre in Great Britain or is imported into Great Britain under a licence issued under section 17(3) of the Agriculture (Miscellaneous Provisions) Act 1943(a).

Keeping of semen in quarantine

17. No person shall keep semen in quarantine or cause or permit semen to be kept in quarantine except under the authority of and in accordance with the conditions of a quarantine licence for the time being in force.

Conditions of quarantine licences.

18. A quarantine licence shall be issued subject to such of the conditions set out in Schedule 2, and to such other conditions (if any), as may be specified in the licence.

Movement of semen from a quarantine centre

19.—(1) Subject to the provisions of paragraph (4) of this regulation no person shall move semen or cause or permit semen to be moved from a quarantine centre until the semen has been kept there for a period of 28 days.

(2) No person shall move semen or cause or permit semen to be moved from a quarantine centre except direct—

(a) to a storage centre in Great Britain; or

(b) to a place outside Great Britain.

(3) Subject to the provisions of paragraph (4) of this regulation, the person to whom a quarantine licence is granted shall as soon as practicable after semen has been kept at the quarantine centre for 28 days move the semen or cause it to be moved direct—

(a) to a storage centre in Great Britain; or

(b) to a place outside Great Britain.

(4) Nothing in this regulation shall prevent the movement of semen from a quarantine centre direct to a place outside Great Britain before it has been kept there for 28 days.

(a) 1943 c. 16.

PART VI—STORAGE, SUPPLY AND USE OF SEMEN

Acceptance of semen for storage

20. No person shall accept semen for storage unless either—

(a) the semen—

(i) is delivered to him at a storage centre; and

(ii) comes from another storage centre in Great Britain or from a quarantine centre in Great Britain, or is imported into Great Britain under a licence issued under section 17(3) of the Agriculture (Miscellaneous Provisions) Act 1943; or

(b) the semen—

(i) is delivered to him at a building specified in the farm storage licence granted to him; and

(ii) comes from the storage centre specified in the farm storage licence as the storage centre from which he may obtain semen.

Storage of semen

21. No person shall store semen or cause or permit semen to be stored except—

(i) under the authority of and in accordance with the conditions of a centre storage licence for the time being in force; or

(ii) under the authority of and in accordance with the conditions of a farm storage licence for the time being in force.

Movement of semen from a storage centre

22. No person shall move semen or cause or permit semen to be moved from a storage centre, except under the authority of and in accordance with the conditions of a centre storage licence or a supply licence for the time being in force and—

(1) in the case of a storage centre in respect of which a centre storage licence only is granted in accordance with regulation 7(1)(c) direct—

(a) to another storage centre in Great Britain; or

(b) to a place outside Great Britain;

(2) in the case of a storage centre in respect of which a supply licence is also granted in accordance with regulation 7(1)(d)—

(a) direct to another storage centre in Great Britain; or

(b) direct to a place outside Great Britain; or

(c) by means of an artificial insemination service to farms situate within the area designated in the supply licence; or

(d) to any person who by virtue of a farm storage licence granted to him is entitled to obtain semen from that storage centre; or

(e) to a veterinary surgeon or a veterinary practitioner approved by the Secretary of State and practising within an area which by reason of its lack of a suitable artificial insemination service the Secretary of State considers to be a remote area.

Conditions of licences for the storage and supply of semen

23.—(1) A centre storage licence shall be issued subject to such of the conditions set out in Schedule 3, and to such other conditions (if any), as may be specified in the licence.

(2) A supply licence shall be issued subject to such of the conditions set out in Schedule 4, and to such other conditions (if any), as may be specified in the licence.

(3) A farm storage licence shall be issued subject to such of the conditions set out in Schedule 5, and to such other conditions (if any), as may be specified in the licence.

General prohibition on use of semen

24. No person shall use semen from a bull in the artificial insemination of a cow unless—

(a) that semen has been obtained from a storage centre in accordance with the provisions of these regulations, and

(b) he is—

    (i) a veterinary surgeon,

    (ii) a veterinary practitioner,

    (iii) a full-time employee of a holder of a supply licence who complies with the requirements of the conditions of the licence relating to such an employee,

    (iv) the holder of a farm storage licence or a full-time employee of such holder who complies with the requirements of any condition of the licence relating to such a holder or employee or, within an area, which, by reason of its lack of a suitable artificial insemination service the Secretary of State considers to be a remote area, such person as the Secretary of State may approve, and who complies with the requirements of the conditions of the licence relating to such a person,

    (v) a person employed as an inseminator by the holder of a supply licence.

PART VII—FARM STORAGE SERVICING

Delivery and service of equipment required for storage and use of semen

25. No person shall deliver to a farm equipment or materials (including liquid nitrogen for farm storage flasks) required for the storage and use of semen in artificial insemination or service such equipment whilst on the farm except under the authority of and in accordance with the conditions of a farm storage servicing licence for the time being in force.

Provided that nothing in this regulation shall prevent the holder of a farm storage licence from servicing equipment which belongs to him, or from collecting any materials for use on his own farm.

26. A farm storage servicing licence shall be issued subject to such of the conditions set out in Schedule 6, and to such other conditions (if any), as may be specified in the licence.

PART VIII—GENERAL

Applications etc. to be in writing

27. Any application, approval, authorisation, certificate, consent, direction, licence or notice made, given or granted for the purposes of these regulations shall be in writing.

Offences

28. No person shall—

(a) furnish any information required by regulation 5(2)(a),

(b) give any certificate required by any condition of a licence under these regulations,

(c) for the purpose of obtaining a licence under these regulations make any statement or furnish any information,

which he knows to be false or does not believe to be true.

Transitional provisions

29.—(1) Where immediately before the date of coming into operation of these regulations there was in force in respect of a bull a licence issued by the Secretary of State under the Artificial Insemination of Cattle (Scotland) Regulations 1957(**a**) or by the Minister under the Artificial Insemination of Cattle (England and Wales) Regulations 1957(**b**) permitting the distribution or sale of semen from the bull, the bull shall for the purposes of these regulations be deemed to be an approved bull, and these regulations shall apply in respect of the bull and its semen as they apply to an approved bull and its semen.

(2) Where immediately before the coming into operation of these regulations the owner of semen was entitled by virtue of regulation 3(2)(a) of the Artificial Insemination of Cattle (Scotland) Regulations 1957 or regulation 4(2)(a) of the Artificial Insemination of Cattle (England and Wales) Regulations 1957 to use that semen without a licence, that owner may continue to use that semen in the artificial insemination of cows belonging to him and the bull from which the semen was taken shall, for that purpose only, be deemed to be an approved bull.

(3) Where a bull is deemed to be an approved bull by virtue of paragraph (1) above, and the licence issued in respect of it imposed a limit on the amount of semen which could be distributed or sold, then the amount of semen which may be supplied for use in the artificial insemination of cows comprised in a herd other than a herd in the same ownership as the bull shall not exceed that limit, reduced by the amount of its semen which was distributed or sold under the licence before the coming into operation of these regulations.

(4) Where a bull is deemed to be an approved bull by virtue of paragraph (1) above, and the licence issued in respect of it provided that its semen could be distributed or sold for use only in a specified herd or specified herds, then the semen of that bull shall be supplied only for use in the artificial insemination of cows comprised in the herd or herds so specified.

(**a**) S.I. 1957/1954 (1957 I, p. 168). (**b**) S.I. 1957/1948 (1957 I, p. 165).

(5) Where a bull is deemed to be an approved bull by virtue of paragraph (1) or (2) above, then that bull—

(*a*) shall be subjected to such isolation, and undergo such veterinary investigations, as the Secretary of State may by notice direct; and

(*b*) shall, if the Secretary of State by notice so directs, cease to be so deemed.

Bruce Millan
One of Her Majesty's Principal Secretaries
of State.

New St Andrew's House,
Edinburgh.

25th July 1977.

SCHEDULE 1

Regulation 14

CONDITIONS TO WHICH PROCESSING LICENCES ARE GENERALLY SUBJECT

1. Except with the consent of the Secretary of State no bull or other animal shall be brought onto a processing centre.

2. If the Secretary of State, for reasons of disease prevention, directs that any animal be removed from a processing centre the animal shall be removed from the processing centre forthwith.

3. Except with the consent of the Secretary of State no semen of any animal other than a bull shall be brought onto a processing centre.

4. Evaluation or examination of semen from a bull which is not an approved bull shall, after appropriate hygiene precautions have been taken, be conducted as an entirely separate operation and at an entirely separate time from the processing of semen, and semen which is accepted for evaluation or examination from such a bull shall be destroyed as soon as is reasonably practicable after any part of it has been evaluated or examined.

5. All equipment, apparatus and materials of any kind used for the evaluation or examination of semen from an unapproved bull shall be either destroyed or cleansed and disinfected before being used for the evaluation or processing of semen from an approved bull.

6. If the Secretary of State, in order to prevent the risk of disease or the transmission of genetic abnormality, directs that semen be removed from a processing centre it shall be removed therefrom and if to the same end he directs that semen be destroyed on a processing centre it shall be destroyed there.

7. Where a processing centre is within a prohibited area no semen shall be delivered to or moved from that centre without the consent of the Secretary of State.

8. Except with the consent of the Secretary of State no semen shall be moved from a processing centre which is outside a prohibited area to a quarantine centre which is within such an area.

9. The licensee shall—

(a) keep such records as are set out in paragraph 10 of this Schedule;

(b) retain each entry in the records for two years after it is made;

(c) produce all such records for inspection by a duly authorised officer of the Secretary of State at any reasonable time on request; and

(d) render to the Secretary of State in such form and at such times as he may direct returns relating to such records or any part of them.

10. The records referred to in paragraph 9 above shall be kept for all semen collected or received, processed, moved, removed or destroyed and shall show: the date and place of semen collection or the date on which the semen was received from another processing centre and the name and address of that centre; the name, breed or type, earmarks or herd book number of the donor bull; the date of semen evaluation or processing; the quantity of semen obtained after processing; and the date and quantity of semen moved and the address to which it was moved or the date and quantity of semen removed or destroyed and by whom removed or destroyed.

SCHEDULE 2

Regulation 18

CONDITIONS TO WHICH QUARANTINE LICENCES ARE GENERALLY SUBJECT

1. No bull or other animal shall be brought onto a quarantine centre.

2. The licensee shall take suitable precautions to ensure that persons entering the quarantine centre have not been in recent contact with cattle, sheep, pigs or goats.

3. If the Secretary of State in order to prevent the risk of disease or the transmission of genetic abnormality directs that semen be removed from a quarantine centre it shall be removed therefrom and if to the same end he directs that semen be destroyed on a quarantine centre it shall be destroyed there.

4. Where a quarantine centre is within a prohibited area no semen shall be moved from the centre without the consent of the Secretary of State.

5. Except with the consent of the Secretary of State no semen shall be moved from a quarantine centre which is outside a prohibited area to a storage centre which is within such an area.

6. No semen shall be added to that already held in a flask at a quarantine centre for so long as that flask remains at the centre.

7. The licensee shall—

(a) keep such records as are set out in paragraph 8 of this Schedule;

(b) retain each entry in the records for two years after it is made;

(c) produce all such records for inspection by a duly authorised officer of the Secretary of State at any reasonable time on request; and

(d) render to the Secretary of State in such form and at such times as he may direct returns relating to such records or any part of them.

8. The records referred to in paragraph 7 of this Schedule shall be kept for all semen received, moved or removed or destroyed and shall show: the name and address of the processing centre from which the semen was accepted or in the case of imported semen, the name and address of the consignor as given on the import licence; the date and quantity of semen received; the name, breed or type, earmarks or herd book number of the donor bull; the date and quantity of semen moved and the address to which it was moved or the date and quantity of semen removed or destroyed and by whom removed or destroyed.

SCHEDULE 3

Regulation 23(1)

CONDITIONS TO WHICH CENTRE STORAGE LICENCES ARE GENERALLY SUBJECT

1. Except with the consent of the Secretary of State no bull or other animal shall be brought onto a storage centre.

2. If the Secretary of State in order to prevent the risk of disease or the transmission of genetic abnormality directs that semen be removed from a storage centre it shall be removed therefrom and if to the same end he directs that semen be destroyed on a storage centre it shall be destroyed there.

3. Where a storage centre is within a prohibited area no semen shall be moved from the centre without the consent of the Secretary of State.

4. Except with the consent of the Secretary of State no semen shall be moved from a storage centre which is outside a prohibited area to another storage centre which is within such an area.

5. The licensee shall—

(a) keep such records as are set out in paragraph 6 of this Schedule;

(b) retain each entry in the records for two years after it is made or for so long as any semen in respect of which the entry is made remains at the storage centre, whichever is the longer period;

(c) produce all such records for inspection by a duly authorised officer of the Secretary of State at any reasonable time on request; and (*d*) render to the Secretary of State in such form and at such times as he may direct returns relating to such records or any part of them.

6. The records referred to in paragraph 5 of this Schedule shall be kept for all semen received, moved or removed or destroyed and shall show: the name and address of the quarantine or storage centre from which the semen was received or of the consignor shown in the import licence; the date and quantity of semen received; the name, breed or type, earmarks or herd book number of the donor bull; the date and quantity of semen moved and the address to which it was moved or the date and quantity of semen removed or destroyed and by whom removed or destroyed.

SCHEDULE 4

Regulation 23(2)

CONDITIONS TO WHICH SUPPLY LICENCES ARE GENERALLY SUBJECT

1.—(1) Semen of an approved bull shall be supplied whether by means of an artificial insemination service or to holders of farm storage licences only if—

(*a*) the owner of the semen authorises the semen to be supplied; and

(*b*) a certificate is issued certifying that the amount of semen specified in the authorisation given under the preceding sub-paragraph, when aggregated with the amount or amounts of semen specified in any other authorisation or authorisations given (whether or not to the same person) under this paragraph or under paragraph 1(*a*) of Schedule 4 to the Artificial Insemination of Cattle (England and Wales) Regulations 1977, does not exceed—

(i) where the bull was approved subject to a condition under regulation 5(4)(*c*), the amount specified in that condition,

(ii) where the bull is deemed to have been approved by virtue of regulation 29(1) and the licence in force in respect of the semen from that bull before these regulations came into operation imposed a limit on the amount of semen of that bull which could be distributed or sold, that limit reduced by the amount which had been distributed or sold before these regulations came into operation, or

(iii) in the case of imported semen, where the relevant import licence was subject to a condition that the amount of semen of the bull from which the semen was taken which may be used in artificial insemination should not exceed a specified total amount, the amount specified in that condition.

(2) A certificate issued for the purpose of sub-paragraph (1)(*b*)(i) of this paragraph shall be signed by the owner for the time being of the bull referred to in the certificate.

(3) A certificate issued for the purpose of sub-paragraph (1)(*b*)(ii) of this paragraph shall be signed by the person to whom the relevant licence was granted.

(4) A certificate issued for the purpose of sub-paragraph (1)(*b*)(iii) of this paragraph shall be signed by the holder of the relevant import licence.

2. In the case of a bull which was approved subject to the condition set out in regulation 5(4)(*c*) the licensee shall at such intervals and in such form as the Secretary of State shall direct, notify the Secretary of State of the amount of semen supplied by him in accordance with paragraph 1(1)(*b*) of this Schedule.

3. Where a bull is approved subject to a condition under regulation 5(4)(*a*) specifying further veterinary investigation, its semen shall not, without the permission in writing of the Secretary of State, be supplied for use in artificial insemination.

4. For the purposes of a supply licence artificial insemination shall be carried out only by—

(*a*) a veterinary surgeon;

(*b*) a veterinary practitioner; or

(*c*) a full-time employee of the holder of the supply licence who to the licence holder's satisfaction is competent in artificial insemination and associated hygiene precautions and who is under the general direction of a veterinary surgeon specified in the licence.

5. If the Secretary of State so directs no semen shall be supplied to a specified farm and no semen shall be supplied without the consent of the Secretary of State to a farm which is within a prohibited area.

6. The licensee shall at least once every 6 months inspect or cause to be inspected any building which is specified in a farm storage licence and situate within the area designated in the supply licence, shall inspect records kept by the holder of such farm storage licence, and shall maintain records of all such inspections and shall give notice to the Secretary of State immediately of any irregularities or unsatisfactory conditions which are discovered.

7. The licensee shall—

(*a*) keep such records as are set out in paragraphs 8 and 9 of this Schedule;

(*b*) retain each entry in the records for two years after it is made;

(*c*) produce all such records for inspection by a duly authorised officer of the Secretary of State at any reasonable time on request;

(*d*) render to the Secretary of State in such form and at such times as he may direct returns relating to such records or any part of them.

8. The licensee shall maintain records of all inseminations carried out showing: the date and place of the insemination; the name and address of the owner of the cow inseminated; and the name, breed or type, earmarks or herd book number of that cow and of the donor bull. All abnormalities of progeny reported to him shall be recorded with all relevant details including: the date and place of the insemination, the semen used with details of the donor bull and the cow inseminated, the type of abnormality and the date it was reported.

9. The licensee shall maintain records of the supply of semen to farms showing: the name and address of the holder of the farm storage licence to whose farm the semen was supplied; the address of that farm; the date and

quantity of semen supplied, and the name, breed or type, earmarks or herd book number of the donor bull.

SCHEDULE 5

Regulation 23(3)

CONDITIONS TO WHICH FARM STORAGE LICENCES ARE GENERALLY SUBJECT

1. Semen shall be stored only in a flask kept in the building specified in the farm storage licence.

2. The number of straws stored on the farm shall not exceed in aggregate thrice the number of breeding cows kept on the farm or farms specified in the licence.

3. Semen shall be destroyed if the Secretary of State so directs to prevent the risk of disease or the transmission of genetic abnormality.

4. Except with the consent of the Secretary of State, semen shall not be removed from the farm on which the building specified in the licence is situated.

5. Semen shall not be used except in the artificial insemination of cows owned by the licensee and kept on the farm or farms specified in the licence.

6. The artificial insemination of cows kept on a farm shall be carried out only by the following persons or one or more of them—

(a) the licensee or a full-time employee of that person, provided that in either case he has completed a course of training in artificial insemination under the direction of a veterinary surgeon and recognised by the Agricultural Training Board or has been regularly carrying out artificial insemination during the period of 12 months immediately preceding the coming into force of these regulations;

(b) a veterinary surgeon;

(c) a veterinary practitioner; and

(d) a person employed as an inseminator by the holder of a supply licence.

7. The licensee shall—

(a) permit representatives of the storage centre specified in the licence to enter at all reasonable times and inspect the building specified in that licence;

(b) keep records in accordance with paragraph 8 of this Schedule;

(c) retain each entry in the records for two years after it is made; and

(d) produce at all reasonable times on request all such records for inspection by a duly authorised officer of the Secretary of State or by a representative of the storage centre specified in the licence.

8. The records referred to in paragraph 7 of this Schedule shall be kept in the forms specified and set out below or in such other forms as may be approved by the Secretary of State—

(*a*) as to stocks of semen held in or received for flasks on farms   Form A

(*b*) as to usage of semen from flasks on farms   Form B

(*c*) as to deliveries of equipment and materials (including liquid nitrogen for farm flasks) required for the storage and use of semen and as to servicing of such equipment   Form C

FORM A

RECORDS OF STOCKS OF SEMEN HELD IN, OR RECEIVED FOR, FARM STORAGE FLASK

1. Name and address of licensee ....

2. Name and address of farm on which flask is kept (if different from 1 above) ....

3. FS LICENCE NUMBER ....

4. Name and address of licensed storage centre authorised to supply semen

....

Date	Quantities of semen (number of doses)		Name(s) of donor bull(s)	Breed	Herd Book No. (if not known give earmarks)	Remarks
	in stock *	received †				
			1.			
			2.			
			3.			
			4.			
			5.			
			6			

Record of semen held in stock or received

* In stock column entries are required to be made annually.

† A separate entry is required for each delivery date and each bull.

FORM B

RECORD OF USAGE OF SEMEN FROM FARM STORAGE FLASK

1. Name and address of licensee ....

2. Address of farm on which flask is kept (if different from 1 above) ....

DONOR BULL (See Note below)

Name	Breed	Herd Book No. (if not known give earmarks)
1.		
2.		
3.		
4.		
5.		
6.		

Note: A separate entry is required in respect of each donor bull

COWS INSEMINATED

(1) Earmarks *	(2) Insemination Dates*		
	1st	2nd	3rd

*OR

(number) .... insemination certificates attached for period .... giving details as in to .... columns (1) and (2) above

REMARKS (See Note below)

Note: Record in this column— number of straws used in each insemination; any disposal of semen other than use in insemination, and reason for such disposal; any calving difficulties etc.

FORM C

RECORD OF DELIVERIES OF EQUIPMENT AND MATERIALS
(INCLUDING LIQUID NITROGEN FOR FARM FLASK) FOR STORAGE AND USE OF SEMEN AND
OF SERVICING OF SUCH EQUIPMENT

1. Name and address of licensee ....

2. Address of farm on which flask is kept (if different from 1 above) ....

....

3. Name and address of licensed supplier/servicer ....

....

Date of delivery or servicing	Details of Delivery or Servicing		Remarks
	Quantity, etc.	Item	

2e

SCHEDULE 6

Regulation 26

CONDITIONS TO WHICH FARM STORAGE SERVICING LICENCES ARE GENERALLY
SUBJECT

1. The licensee shall comply with the following requirements—

(a) the interior of any vehicle used to transport liquid nitrogen, supply tanks or any other equipment shall be capable of being cleansed and disinfected and shall be kept in a clean condition;

(b) employees while engaged on delivery services shall wear protective clothing and shall carry out personal disinfection, using an approved disinfectant, before leaving licensed premises at which equipment or supplies are being left;

(c) employees while engaged on delivery services shall not have contact with cattle, sheep, pigs or goats on any premises.

2. The licensee shall—

(a) keep records in accordance with paragraph 3 of this Schedule;

(b) retain each entry in the records for 2 years after it is made; and

(c) produce all such records for inspection by a duly authorised officer of the Secretary of State at any reasonable time on request.

3. The records referred to in paragraph 2 of this Schedule shall be kept by the licensee, at his normal place of business, in respect of all deliveries to farms of equipment or materials (including liquid nitrogen for farm storage flasks) required for the storage of semen or its use in artificial insemination and in respect of servicing such equipment. The records shall include details of delivery or servicing dates, the registration numbers of vehicles used for the delivery or servicing, the premises at which the delivery or servicing was carried out, the types of equipment or materials delivered or a description of the servicing carried out.

EXPLANATORY NOTE

(This Note is not part of the Regulations)

These Regulations, which revoke and supersede the Artificial Insemination of Cattle (Scotland) Regulations 1957, establish a new system for the control of the practice of artificial insemination in Scotland.

The Regulations provide for the issuing, by the Secretary of State, of approvals, conditional or unconditional, of bulls for use in artificial insemination, for the cancellation and variation of any condition imposed, and for the revoking of approvals given. They prohibit the collection of semen for processing except from an approved bull, and permit the evaluation, processing, quarantine, storage and supply of semen for use in artificial insemination only under the authority of licences granted by the Secretary of State, and set out in the Schedules the principal conditions which may be specified in each type of licence.

The Regulations also (1) provide for the quarantining of processed semen in quarantine centres, (2) permit the movement of semen (other than that being exported) from a quarantine centre only to a storage centre, and (3) lay down that from storage centres semen may only be supplied for use by means of an artificial insemination service or for use by the holder of a farm storage licence in the insemination of cows owned by the licensee and kept on the farm or farms specified in the licence.

The Regulations also lay down that artificial insemination may be carried out only by veterinary surgeons and certain other specified persons and provide for the control of the delivery of equipment and materials required for the storage and use of semen and of the servicing of such equipment. Transitional provisions are also included providing for bulls, the use of whose semen was authorised immediately before the coming into force of these Regulations, to be regarded as approved bulls.

The Regulations do not apply to the use of raw semen in cows belonging to the owner of the bull from which the semen came, or at embryo transfer units where the Secretary of State has granted a certificate of exemption. Further, the Regulations do not apply to the use of semen at research or experimental establishments which are similarly exempted.

Because of the special problems which arise in the remote areas of Scotland, the provisions of Regulations 7(7), 22(2)(e) and 24(b)(iv) have been modified to enable storage centres to supply semen to veterinary surgeons or veterinary practitioners in those areas and allow the holders of farm storage licences to carry out the artificial insemination of cows kept on their own and neighbouring farms specified in their licence. In addition, such artificial insemination of cows may be carried out by a person approved by the Secretary of State.

STATUTORY INSTRUMENTS

1977 No. 1231

DEFENCE

The Army, Air Force and Naval Discipline Acts (Continuation) Order 1977

Laid before Parliament in draft

Made - - - - *26th July* 1977

At the Court at Buckingham Palace, the 26th day of July 1977

Present,

The Queen's Most Excellent Majesty in Council

Whereas a draft of the following Order in Council has been laid before Parliament and approved by resolution of each House of Parliament:

Now, therefore, Her Majesty, in pursuance of section 1(2) of the Armed Forces Act 1976(**a**), is pleased, by and with the advice of Her Privy Council, to order, and it is hereby ordered, as follows:—

1. The Army Act 1955(**b**), the Air Force Act 1955(**c**) and the Naval Discipline Act 1957(**d**) shall continue in force for a period of twelve months beyond 31st August 1977, that date being the date on which they would otherwise expire.

2. This Order may be cited as the Army, Air Force and Naval Discipline Acts (Continuation) Order 1977.

N. E. Leigh,
Clerk of the Privy Council.

(**a**) 1976 c. 52.   (**b**) 1955 c. 18.   c) 1955 c. 19.   (**d**) 1957 c. 53.

1977 No. 1232

HEALTH AND SAFETY

The Health and Safety at Work etc. Act 1974 (Application outside Great Britain) Order 1977

Made - - -	*26th July* 1977
Laid before Parliament	*3rd August* 1977
Coming into Operation	*1st September* 1977

At the Court at Buckingham Palace, the 26th day of July 1977

Present,

The Queen's Most Excellent Majesty in Council

Her Majesty, in exercise of the powers conferred by section 84(3) and (4) of the Health and Safety at Work etc. Act 1974(a), is pleased, by and with the advice of Her Privy Council, to order, and it is hereby ordered, as follows:—

Citation and commencement

1. This Order may be cited as the Health and Safety at Work etc. Act 1974 (Application outside Great Britain) Order 1977 and shall come into operation on 1st September 1977.

Interpretation

2.—(1) In this Order, unless the context otherwise requires—

"the 1974 Act" means the Health and Safety at Work etc. Act 1974;

"designated area" means any area designated by order under section 1(7) of the Continental Shelf Act 1964(b) and "within a designated area" includes over and under it;

"the prescribed provisions of the 1974 Act" means sections 1 to 59 and 80 to 82 of the 1974 Act;

"territorial waters" means United Kingdom territorial waters adjacent to Great Britain and "within territorial waters" includes on, over and under them;

"vessel" includes a hovercraft and any floating structure which is capable of being manned.

(2) The Interpretation Act 1889(c) shall apply for the interpretation of this Order as it applies for the interpretation of an Act of Parliament.

(a) 1974 c. 37.   (b) 1964 c. 29.   (c) 1889 c. 63.

(3) For the purposes of this Order, a person shall be deemed to be engaged in diving operations throughout any period from the time when he commences to prepare for diving until the time when—

(*a*) he is no longer subjected to raised pressure;

(*b*) he has normal inert gas partial pressure in his tissues; and

(*c*) if he entered the water, he has left it;

and diving operations include the activity of any person in connection with the health and safety of a person who is, or is deemed to be, engaged in diving operations.

Application of the 1974 *Act in territorial waters and designated areas outside Great Britain*

3.—(1) The prescribed provisions of the 1974 Act shall, to the extent specified in the following Articles of this Order, apply to and in relation to the premises and activities outside Great Britain which are so specified as those provisions apply within Great Britain.

(2) The reference in paragraph (1) of this Article to premises and activities includes a reference to any person, article or substance on those premises or engaged in or, as the case may be, used or for use in connection with any such activity, but does not include a reference to an aircraft which is airborne.

Offshore installations

4.—(1) The prescribed provisions of the 1974 Act shall apply within territorial waters or a designated area to and in relation to—

(*a*) any offshore installation and any activity on it;

(*b*) any of the following activities in connection with an offshore installation, whether carried on from the installation itself, on or from a vessel or in any other manner, that is to say, inspection, testing, loading, unloading, fuelling, provisioning, construction, reconstruction, alteration, repair, maintenance, cleaning, demolition, dismantling and diving operations and any activity which is immediately preparatory to any of the said activities;

(*c*) the survey and preparation of the sea bed for an offshore installation.

(2) In this Article—

"offshore installation" means any installation or part of an installation, whether floating or not, which—

(*a*) is maintained within territorial waters or a designated area or is intended to be established there in connection with the exploitation of mineral resources or with exploration with a view to such exploitation; and

(*b*) is at, or within 500 metres of, its working station;

including any such installation in the course of construction, demolition or dismantling but not including any installation which at the relevant time is, or forms part of, a pipeline within the meaning of Article 5(2) of this Order.

Pipelines

5.—(1) The prescribed provisions of the 1974 Act shall apply within territorial waters or a designated area to and in relation to—

(*a*) any pipeline works

(*b*) the following activities in connection with pipeline works—

    (i) the loading, unloading, fuelling or provisioning of a vessel,

    (ii) the loading, unloading, fuelling, repair and maintenance of an aircraft on a vessel,

being in either case a vessel which is engaged in pipeline works.

(2) "Pipeline" means a pipe or system of pipes for the conveyance of any thing, together with—

(*a*) any apparatus for inducing or facilitating the flow of any thing through, or through a part of, the pipe or system;

(*b*) valves, valve chambers and similar works which are annexed to, or incorporated in the course of, the pipe or system;

(*c*) apparatus for supplying energy for the operation of any such apparatus or works as are mentioned in the preceding paragraphs;

(*d*) apparatus for the transmission of information for the operation of the pipe or system;

(*e*) apparatus for the cathodic protection of the pipe or system; and

(*f*) a structure used or to be used solely for the support of a part of the pipe or system;

but not including—

    (i) a pipeline of which no initial or terminal point is situated in the United Kingdom or within territorial waters or a designated area; or

    (ii) any part of a pipeline which is an offshore installation within the meaning of Article 4(2) of this Order and is capable of being manned;

"pipeline works" means—

(*a*) assembling or placing a pipeline or length of pipeline including the provision of internal or external protection for it, and any processes incidental to any of those activities;

(*b*) inspecting, testing, maintaining, adjusting, repairing, altering or renewing a pipeline or length of pipeline;

(*c*) changing the position of or dismantling or removing a pipeline or length of pipeline;

(*d*) opening the bed of the sea for the purposes of the works mentioned in sub-paragraphs (*a*) to (*c*) of this definition, tunnelling or boring for those purposes and other works needed for or incidental to those purposes;

(*e*) diving operations in connection with any of the works mentioned in sub-paragraphs (*a*) to (*d*) of this definition or for the purpose of determining whether a place is suitable as part of the site of a proposed pipeline and the carrying out of surveying operations for settling the route of a proposed pipeline.

Mines

6.—(1) The prescribed provisions of the 1974 Act shall apply to and in relation to the working of a mine, and to work for the purpose of or in connection with the working of any part of a mine, within territorial waters or extending beyond them.

(2) In this Article "mine" and "working of a mine" have the same meaning as in the Mines and Quarries Act 1954(**a**).

Other activities within territorial waters

7. The prescribed provisions of the 1974 Act shall apply within territorial waters to and in relation to—

> (*a*) the construction, reconstruction, alteration, repair, maintenance, cleaning, demolition and dismantling of any building or other structure not being a vessel, or any preparation for any such activity;
>
> (*b*) the loading, unloading, fuelling or provisioning of a vessel;
>
> (*c*) diving operations;
>
> (*d*) the construction, reconstruction, finishing, refitting, repair, maintenance, cleaning or breaking up of a vessel except when carried out by the master or any officer or member of the crew of that vessel;

except that this Article shall not apply in any case where at the relevant time Article 4, 5 or 6 of this Order applies, or to vessels which are registered outside the United Kingdom and are on passage through territorial waters.

Legal proceedings

8.—(1) Proceedings for any offence under section 33 of the Health and Safety at Work etc. Act 1974, being an offence to which that section applies by virtue of this Order, may be taken, and the offence may for all incidental purposes be treated as having been committed, in any place in Great Britain.

(2) Section 3 of the Territorial Waters Jurisdiction Act 1878(**b**) (which requires certain consents for the institution of proceedings) shall not apply to proceedings for any offence to which paragraph (1) of this Article relates.

Miscellaneous provisions

9. The prescribed provisions of the 1974 Act shall apply in accordance with this Order to individuals whether or not they are British subjects, and to bodies corporate whether or not they are incorporated under the law of any part of the United Kingdom.

10. Nothing in this Order except Article 8(2) shall be taken to limit or prejudice the operation which any Act or legislative instrument may, apart from this Order, have in territorial waters or elsewhere.

N. E. Leigh,
Clerk of the Privy Council.

(**a**) 1954 c. 70.   (**b**) 1878 c. 73.

EXPLANATORY NOTE

(This Note is not part of the Order.)

This Order applies provisions of Parts I, II and IV of the Health and Safety at Work etc. Act 1974, with appropriate exceptions, to offshore installations and pipelines within territorial waters and areas designated under the Continental Shelf Act 1964 and to certain work activities in connection with those installations and pipelines.

The Order also applies those provisions of the 1974 Act to construction works, diving operations and certain other activities within territorial waters and to mines extending under the sea.

STATUTORY INSTRUMENTS

1977 No. 1233

LOCAL GOVERNMENT, ENGLAND AND WALES

The Local Authorities (Armorial Bearings) Order 1977

Made - - - -	*26th July* 1977
Coming into Operation	1*st September* 1977

At the Court at Buckingham Palace, the 26th day of July 1977

Present,

The Queen's Most Excellent Majesty in Council

Her Majesty, by virtue and in exercise of the powers conferred on Her by section 247 of the Local Government Act 1972**(a)**, is pleased, by and with the advice of Her Privy Council, to order, and it is hereby ordered, as follows:—

1. This Order may be cited as the Local Authorities (Armorial Bearings) Order 1977 and shall come into operation on 1st September 1977.

2. The Interpretation Act 1889**(b)** shall apply for the interpretation of this Order as it applies for the interpretation of an Act of Parliament.

3. Subject to Article 4 of this Order, there is hereby authorised the bearing and use by a local authority specified in the first column of the Schedule to this Order of the armorial bearings lawfully borne and used before 1st April 1974 by the local authority specified in the second column of that Schedule in respect of the first-mentioned authority.

4. Any armorial bearings the bearing and use of which is authorised by Article 3 of this Order shall be first exemplified according to the laws of arms and recorded in the College of Arms, otherwise such authority shall be void and of no effect.

N. E. Leigh,
Clerk of the Privy Council.

(a) 1972 c. 70.   (b) 1889 c. 63.

SCHEDULE

Local authority established by or under the Local Government Act 1972	Local authority ceasing to exist by virtue of section 1 or 20 of the Local Government Act 1972
The County Council of Nottinghamshire	The county council of Nottinghamshire
The City Council of Sheffield	The corporation of the city of Sheffield
The Town Council of Bridgnorth	The corporation of the borough of Bridgnorth
The Town Council of Budleigh Salterton	The urban district council of Budleigh Salterton
The Town Council of Great Torrington	The corporation of the borough of Great Torrington
The Town Council of Harwich	The corporation of the borough of Harwich
The Town Council of Malton	The urban district council of Malton
The Town Council of Romsey	The corporation of the borough of Romsey

EXPLANATORY NOTE

(*This Note is not part of the Order.*)

This Order confers on the local authorities specified in the first column of the Schedule to the Order the right to bear and use the armorial bearings formerly borne and used by the local authorities specified in the second column.

STATUTORY INSTRUMENTS

1977 No. 1234

ANTARCTICA

The Antarctic Treaty (Contracting Parties) Order 1977

Made - - - - *26th July* 1977

At the Court at Buckingham Palace, the 26th day of July 1977

Present,

The Queen's Most Excellent Majesty in Council

Her Majesty, in exercise of the powers conferred upon Her by sections 7(1) and 10(7) of the Antarctic Treaty Act 1967(a) is pleased, by and with the advice of Her Privy Council, to order, and it is hereby ordered, as follows:—

1. The Governments of the States named in the Schedule to this Order are the Contracting Parties for the purposes of the Antarctic Treaty Act 1967.

2. This Order may be cited as the Antarctic Treaty (Contracting Parties) Order 1977.

3. The Antarctic Treaty (Contracting Parties) Order 1968(b) is hereby revoked.

N. E. Leigh,
Clerk of the Privy Council

SCHEDULE

Argentina.
Australia.
Belgium.
Brazil.
Chile.
Czechoslovakia.
Denmark.
The French Republic.
German Democratic Republic.
Japan.
The Netherlands.
New Zealand.
Norway.
Poland.
Romania.
Republic of South Africa.
Union of Soviet Socialist Republics.
United Kingdom of Great Britain and Northern Ireland.
United States of America.

(a) 1967 c. 65.   (b) S.I. 1968/887 (1968 II, p. 2351).

EXPLANATORY NOTE

(This Note is not part of the Order.)

This Order adds Brazil, the German Democratic Republic and Romania to the States the Governments of which are certified for the purposes of the Antarctic Treaty Act 1967 as the Contracting Parties to the Antarctic Treaty (Schedule 1 to the Act).

STATUTORY INSTRUMENTS

1977 No. 1235

ANTARCTICA

The Antarctic Treaty (Specially Protected Areas) Order 1977

Made - - - -	26th July 1977
Laid before Parliament	3rd August 1977
Coming into Operation	1st September 1977

At the Court at Buckingham Palace, the 26th day of July 1977

Present,

The Queen's Most Excellent Majesty in Council

Her Majesty, in exercise of the powers conferred upon Her by sections 7(2)(b) and 10(7) of the Antarctic Treaty Act 1967(a), is pleased, by and with the advice of Her Privy Council, to order, and it is hereby ordered, as follows:—

1. This Order may be cited as the Antarctic Treaty (Specially Protected Areas) Order 1977 and shall come into operation on 1st September 1977.

2. Specially Protected Area No. 6 (Cape Crozier, Ross Island) and Specially Protected Area No. 10 (Byers Peninsula, Livingston Island, South Shetland Islands) shall cease to be designated as Specially Protected Areas for the purposes of the Antarctic Treaty Act 1967 and shall be omitted from the Schedule to the Antarctic Treaty (Specially Protected Areas) Order 1968(b).

3. The Antarctic Treaty (Specially Protected Area) Order 1969(c) (designation of Fildes Peninsula, King George Island, South Shetland Islands as Specially Protected Area No. 12) is hereby revoked.

4. For the purposes of the Antarctic Treaty Act 1967, the following area, being an area which has been recommended for inclusion in Annex B to Schedule 2 to the said Act, is designated as a Specially Protected Area:

SPECIALLY PROTECTED AREA NO. 17
LITCHFIELD ISLAND, ARTHUR HARBOUR,
PALMER ARCHIPELAGO
Lat. 64° 46′S., Long. 64° 06′W.

This area, the location of which is shown on the map in the Schedule hereto, is a small island, about 2.5 km² in area.

N. E. Leigh,
Clerk of the Privy Council.

(a) 1967 c. 65.   (b) S.I. 1968/888 (1968 II, p. 2352).
(c) S.I. 1969/854 (1969 II, p. 2388).

SCHEDULE

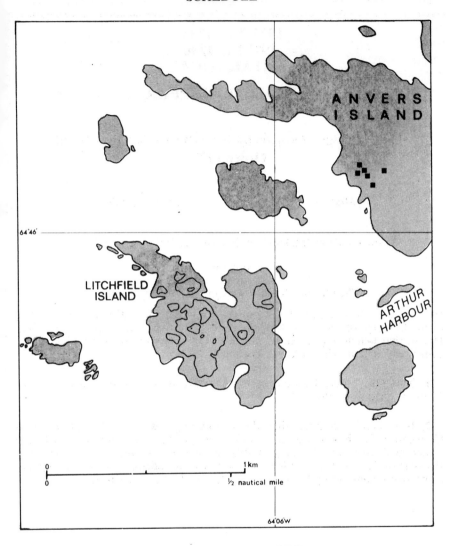

EXPLANATORY NOTE

(This Note is not part of the Order.)

This Order designates as a Specially Protected Area for the purposes of the Antarctic Treaty Act 1967 a further area in the Antarctic which has been recommended for inclusion in Annex B to the Agreed Measures for the Conservation of Antarctic Fauna and Flora (Schedule 2 to the Act) in pursuance of Article IX (1) of the Antarctic Treaty; and terminates the designation of three areas which are to be protected in future by administrative arrangements made pursuant to Recommendation VIII-4 of the Eighth Antarctic Treaty Consultative Meeting as Sites of Special Scientific Interest (Cmnd. 6786).

STATUTORY INSTRUMENTS

1977 No. 1236

MERCHANT SHIPPING

The Carriage of Goods by Sea (Parties to Convention) Order 1977

Made - - - - 26th July 1977

At the Court at Buckingham Palace, the 26th day of July 1977

Present,

The Queen's Most Excellent Majesty in Council

Her Majesty, in exercise of the powers conferred upon Her by section 2(1) of the Carriage of Goods by Sea Act 1971 (a) and of all other powers enabling Her in that behalf is pleased, by and with the advice of Her Privy Council, to order, and it is hereby ordered, as follows:—

1. This Order may be cited as the Carriage of Goods by Sea (Parties to Convention) Order 1977.

2. It is hereby certified that the contracting States to the International Convention for the unification of certain rules of law relating to bills of lading signed at Brussels on 25th August 1924, as amended by the Protocol signed at Brussels on 23rd February 1968 and the territories in respect of which they are respectively contracting States are as listed in the Schedule to this Order.

N. E. Leigh,
Clerk of the Privy Council.

(a) 1971 c. 19.

SCHEDULE

Contracting States	Territories in respect of which they are respectively parties	Dates on which the Convention as amended came into force
The United Kingdom of Great Britain and Northern Ireland	The United Kingdom of Great Britain and Northern Ireland	23rd June 1977
	The Isle of Man	23rd June 1977
The Kingdom of Denmark	Denmark	23rd June 1977
The Republic of Ecuador	Ecuador	23rd June 1977
The French Republic	France	23rd June 1977
The Lebanese Republic	Lebanon	23rd June 1977
The Kingdom of Norway	Norway	23rd June 1977
The Republic of Singapore	Singapore	23rd June 1977
The Kingdom of Sweden	Sweden	23rd June 1977
The Swiss Confederation	Switzerland	23rd June 1977
The Syrian Arab Republic	Syria	23rd June 1977

EXPLANATORY NOTE
(*This Note is not part of the Order.*)

The Carriage of Goods by Sea Act 1971 gives effect in the United Kingdom to the 1924 Brussels Convention ("the Hague Rules") as amended by the 1968 Brussels Protocol.

This Order certifies the contracting States to the 1924 Convention as amended by the 1968 Protocol and the territories in respect of which they are contracting States.

STATUTORY INSTRUMENTS

1977 No. 1237

FUGITIVE CRIMINAL

The Extradition (Hijacking) (Amendment) Order 1977

Made - - - -	26th July 1977
Laid before Parliament	3rd August 1977
Coming into Operation	1st September 1977

At the Court at Buckingham Palace, the 26th day of July 1977

Present,

The Queen's Most Excellent Majesty in Council

Whereas extradition treaties have come into force between the United Kingdom and Finland and between the United Kingdom and the United States of America which replace the treaties with these States specified in Schedule 2 to the Extradition (Hijacking) Order 1971(a) as amended by the Extradition (Hijacking) (Amendment) Order 1972(b):

And Whereas other States have become parties to the Convention for the Suppression of Unlawful Seizure of Aircraft signed at The Hague on 16th December 1970(c) requiring the further amendment of Schedules 2 and 3 to the Extradition (Hijacking) Order 1971:

And Whereas it is expedient that the amendments to Schedules 2 and 3 to the above-mentioned Order as specified in subsequent amending Orders(d) should be consolidated:

Now, therefore, Her Majesty, in exercise of the powers conferred upon Her by sections 2, 17 and 21 of the Extradition Act 1870(e) and sections 3(2), 6(1) and 6(3) of the Hijacking Act 1971(f), or otherwise in Her Majesty vested, is pleased, by and with the advice of Her Privy Council, to order, and it is hereby ordered, as follows:—

1. This Order may be cited as the Extradition (Hijacking) (Amendment) Order 1977 and shall come into operation on 1st September 1977.

2. The Interpretation Act 1889(g) shall apply for the interpretation of this Order as it applies for the interpretation of an Act of Parliament.

3. The Extradition (Hijacking) Order 1971 shall be amended by substituting in place of the entries in Schedule 2 (which names the foreign States with which the United Kingdom has extradition treaties in force and which are parties to the Convention for the Suppression of Unlawful Seizure of Aircraft signed at The Hague on 16th December 1970) the entries specified in Schedule 1 hereto.

4. The Extradition (Hijacking) Order 1971 shall be amended by substituting in place of the entries in Part I of Schedule 3 (which names the foreign States with which the United Kingdom has no extradition treaties in force and which are parties to the Convention for the Suppression of Unlawful Seizure of Aircraft signed at The Hague on 16th December 1970) the entries specified in Schedule 2 hereto.

5. The following Orders in Council are hereby revoked:—

The Extradition (Hijacking) (Amendment) Order 1972

The Extradition (Hijacking) (Amendment Order 1974

(a) S.I. 1971/2102 (1971 III, p. 6193).   (b) S.I. 1972/1102 (1972 II, p. 3291).   (c) Cmnd. 4956.
(d) The relevant amending instruments are S.I. 1972/1102, 1974/1107, 1975/803, 1976/769
.(1972 II, p. 3291; 1974 II, p. 4044; 1975 II, p. 2881; 1976 II, p. 2003).
  (e) 1870 c. 52.   (f) 1971 c. 70.   (g) 1889 c. 63.

The Extradition (Hijacking) (Amendment) Order 1975
The Extradition (Hijacking) (Amendment) Order 1976

N. E. Leigh,
Clerk of the Privy Council.

SCHEDULE 1

State	Date of Extradition Treaty	Date of Entry into Force of Convention
Argentina...	22nd May 1889	11th October 1972
Austria	9th January 1963	11th March 1974
Belgium	29th October 1901	23rd September 1973
Chile	26th January 1897	3rd March 1972
Colombia	27th October 1888	2nd August 1973
Czechoslovakia	11th November 1924	6th May 1972
Denmark	31st March 1873	16th November 1972
Ecuador	20th September 1880	14th October 1971
El Salvador	23rd June 1881	16th February 1973
Finland	30th May 1924/29th October 1975	14th January 1972
France	14th August 1876	18th October 1972
Germany, Federal Republic of...	14th May 1872 (as re-applied and amended by the Agreement of 23rd February 1960)	10th November 1974
Greece	24th September 1910	20th October 1973
Hungary	3rd December 1873	14th October 1971
Iceland	31st March 1873	29th July 1973
Iraq	2nd May 1932	29th January 1972
Israel	4th April 1960	14th October 1971
Italy	5th February 1873	21st March 1974
Mexico	7th September 1886	18th August 1972
Netherlands	26th September 1898	26th September 1973
Nicaragua	19th April 1905	6th December 1973
Norway	26th June 1873	14th October 1971
Panama	25th August 1906	9th April 1972
Paraguay	12th September 1908	5th March 1972
Poland	11th January 1932	20th April 1972
Portugal	17th October 1892	27th December 1972
Romania	21st March 1893	9th August 1972
Spain	4th June 1878	29th November 1972
Sweden	26th April 1963	14th October 1971
Switzerland	26th November 1880/19th December 1934	14th October 1971
United States of America ...	22nd December 1931/8th June 1972	14th October 1971
Yugoslavia	6th December 1900	1st November 1972

SCHEDULE 2

State	Date of Entry into Force of Convention
Benin (formerly Dahomey)	12th April 1972
Brazil	13th February 1972
Bulgaria	14th October 1971
Byelorussia	29th January 1972
Chad	11th August 1972
Costa Rica	14th October 1971
Egypt, Arab Republic of	30th March 1975
Gabon	14th October 1971
Indonesia	26th September 1976
Iran	24th February 1972
Ivory Coast	8th February 1973
Japan	14th October 1971
Jordan	16th December 1971
Korea, Republic of	17th February 1973
Lebanon	9th September 1973
Mali	14th October 1971
Mongolia	7th November 1971
Niger	14th November 1971
Pakistan	29th December 1973
Philippines	25th April 1973
Saudi Arabia	14th July 1974
South Africa	29th June 1972
Turkey	17th May 1973
Ukraine	20th March 1972
Union of Soviet Socialist Republics	24th October 1971
Vietnam, Republic of	2nd February 1974

EXPLANATORY NOTE

(This Note is not part of the Order.)

The coming into force of extradition treaties between the United Kingdom and Finland and between the United Kingdom and the United States of America which replace earlier treaties has necessitated amendments to the entries for these States in Schedule 2 to the Extradition (Hijacking) Order 1971. The opportunity has also been taken to consolidate in one Order the names of foreign States which have become parties to the Convention for the Suppression of Unlawful Seizure of Aircraft signed at The Hague on 16th December 1970.

STATUTORY INSTRUMENTS

1977 No. 1238

FUGITIVE CRIMINAL

The Extradition (Protection of Aircraft) (Amendment) Order 1977

Made - - - -	26th July 1977
Laid before Parliament	3rd August 1977
Coming into Operation	1st September 1977

At the Court at Buckingham Palace, the 26th day of July 1977

Present,

The Queen's Most Excellent Majesty in Council

Whereas extradition treaties have come into force between the United Kingdom and Finland and between the United Kingdom and the United States of America which replace the treaties with these States specified in Schedule 2 to the Extradition (Protection of Aircraft) Order 1973(a):

And Whereas other States have become parties to the Convention for the Suppression of Unlawful Acts against the Safety of Civil Aviation signed at Montreal on 23rd September 1971(b) requiring the further amendment of the above-mentioned Order:

And Whereas it is expedient that the amendments to Schedules 2 and 3 to the above-mentioned Order as specified in subsequent amending Orders(c) should be consolidated:

Now, therefore, Her Majesty, in exercise of the powers conferred upon Her by sections 2, 17 and 21 of the Extradition Act 1870(d) and sections 5(2), 27(1) and (3) of the Protection of Aircraft Act 1973(e), or otherwise in Her Majesty vested, is pleased, by and with the advice of Her Privy Council, to order, and it is hereby ordered, as follows:—

1. This Order may be cited as the Extradition (Protection of Aircraft) (Amendment) Order 1977 and shall come into operation on 1st September 1977.

2. The Interpretation Act 1889(f) shall apply for the interpretation of this Order as it applies for the interpretation of an Act of Parliament.

3. The Extradition (Protection of Aircraft) Order 1973 shall be amended by substituting in place of the entries in Schedule 2 (which names the foreign States with which the United Kingdom has extradition treaties in force and which are parties to the Convention for the Suppression of Unlawful Acts against the Safety of Civil Aviation signed at Montreal on 23rd September 1971) the entries specified in Schedule 1 hereto.

(a) S.I. 1973/1756 (1973 III, p. 5363).   (b) Cmnd. 5524.
(c) The relevant amending instruments are S.I. 1974/1108, 1975/804, 1976/770
(1974 II, p. 4046; 1975 II, p. 2883, 1976 II, p. 2005).
(d) 1870 c. 52.   (e) 1973 c. 47.   (f) 1889 c. 63.

4. The Extradition (Protection of Aircraft) Order 1973 shall be amended by substituting in place of the entries specified in Part I of Schedule 3 (which names the foreign States with which the United Kingdom has no extradition treaties in force and which are parties to the Convention for the Suppression of Unlawful Acts against the Safety of Civil Aviation signed at Montreal on 23rd September 1971) the entries specified in Schedule 2 hereto.

5. The following Orders in Council are hereby revoked:—

The Extradition (Protection of Aircraft) (Amendment) Order 1974
The Extradition (Protection of Aircraft) (Amendment) Order 1975
The Extradition (Protection of Aircraft) (Amendment) Order 1976

N. E. Leigh,
Clerk of the Privy Council.

SCHEDULE 1

State	Date of Extradition Treaty	Date of Entry into Force of Convention
Argentina...	22nd May 1889	26th December 1973
Austria	9th January 1963	11th March 1974
Belgium	29th October 1901	12th September 1976
Chile	26th January 1897	30th March 1974
Colombia	27th October 1888	3rd January 1975
Czechoslovakia	11th November 1924	9th August 1973
Denmark	31st March 1873	16th February 1973
Finland	30th May 1924/29th October 1975	12th August 1973
France	14th August 1876	30th July 1976
Greece	24th September 1910	14th February 1974
Hungary	3rd December 1873	26th January 1973
Iceland	31st March 1873	29th July 1973
Iraq	2nd May 1932	10th October 1974
Israel	4th April 1960	26th January 1973
Italy	5th February 1873	21st March 1974
Mexico	7th September 1886	12th October 1974
Netherlands	26th September 1898	26th September 1973
Nicaragua	19th April 1905	6th December 1973
Norway	26th June 1873	31st August 1973
Panama	25th August 1906	26th January 1973
Paraguay	12th September 1908	4th April 1974
Poland	11th January 1932	27th February 1975
Portugal	17th October 1892	14th February 1973
Romania	21st March 1893	14th September 1975
Spain	4th June 1878	26th January 1973
Sweden	26th April 1963	9th August 1973
United States of America ...	22nd December 1931/ 8th June 1972	26th January 1973
Yugoslavia	6th December 1900	26th January 1973

SCHEDULE 2

State	Date of Entry into Force of Convention
Brazil	26th January 1973
Bulgaria	24th March 1973
Byelorussia	2nd March 1973
Cameroon	10th August 1973
Chad	26th January 1973
Costa Rica	21st October 1973
Dominican Republic	28th December 1973
Egypt, Arab Republic of	19th June 1975
Gabon	29th July 1976
German Democratic Republic	26th January 1973
Indonesia	26th September 1976
Iran	9th August 1973
Ivory Coast	8th February 1973
Japan	12th July 1974
Jordan	15th March 1973
Korea, Republic of	31st August 1973
Libya	21st March 1974
Mali	26th January 1973
Mongolia	26th January 1973
Niger	26th January 1973
Pakistan	23rd February 1974
Philippines	25th April 1973
Saudi Arabia	14th July 1974
South Africa	26th January 1973
Ukraine	26th March 1973
Union of Soviet Socialist Republics	21st March 1973

EXPLANATORY NOTE

(This Note is not part of the Order.)

The coming into force of extradition treaties between the United Kingdom and Finland and between the United Kingdom and the United States of America which replace earlier treaties has necessitated amendments to the entries for these States in Schedule 2 to the Extradition (Protection of Aircraft) Order 1973. The opportunity has also been taken to consolidate in one Order the names of foreign States which have become parties to the Convention for the Suppression of Unlawful Acts against the Safety of Civil Aviation signed at Montreal on 23rd September 1971.

STATUTORY INSTRUMENTS

1977 No. 1239

FUGITIVE CRIMINAL

The Extradition (Tokyo Convention) (Amendment) Order 1977

Made - - - -	26th July 1977
Laid before Parliament	3rd August 1977
Coming into Operation	1st September 1977

At the Court at Buckingham Palace, the 26th day of July 1977

Present,

The Queen's Most Excellent Majesty in Council

Whereas extradition treaties have come into force between the United Kingdom and Finland and between the United Kingdom and the United States of America which replace the treaties with those States specified in Schedule 1 to the Extradition (Tokyo Convention) Order 1971(a):

And Whereas other States have become parties to the Convention on Offences and certain other Acts Committed on board Aircraft signed at Tokyo on 14th September 1963(b) requiring the further amendment of the above Order:

And Whereas it is expedient that the amendments to Schedule 1 to the above-mentioned Order as specified in subsequent amending Orders(c) should be consolidated:

Now, therefore, Her Majesty, in exercise of the powers conferred upon Her by sections 2, 17 and 21 of the Extradition Act 1870(d) and section 2(2) of the Tokyo Convention Act 1967(e), or otherwise in Her Majesty vested, is pleased, by and with the advice of Her Privy Council, to order, and it is hereby ordered, as follows:—

1. This Order may be cited as the Extradition (Tokyo Convention) (Amendment) Order 1977 and shall come into operation on 1st September 1977.

2. The Interpretation Act 1889(f) shall apply for the interpretation of this Order as it applies for the interpretation of an Act of Parliament.

3. The Extradition (Tokyo Convention) Order 1971 shall be amended by substituting in place of the entries in Schedule 1 (which names the States with which the United Kingdom has extradition treaties in force and which are parties to the Convention on Offences and certain other Acts Committed on

---

(a) S.I. 1971/2103 (1971 III, p. 6202). (b) Cmnd. 4230.
(c) The relevant amending instruments are S.I. 1972/960, 1973/762 (1972 II. p. 2983; 1973 I, p. 2423).
(d) 1870 c. 52. (e) 1967 c.52. (f) 1889 c. 63.

board Aircraft signed at Tokyo on 14th September 1963) the entries specified in Schedule 1 hereto.

4. The Extradition (Tokyo Convention) Order 1971 shall be further amended by substituting in place of the entries in Schedule 2 (which names the territories to which the application of the Tokyo Convention is extended) the entries specified in Schedule 2 hereto.

5. The Extradition (Tokyo Convention) (Amendment) Order 1972 and the Extradition (Tokyo Convention) (Amendment) Order 1973 are hereby revoked.

N. E. Leigh,
Clerk of the Privy Council.

Article 3 **SCHEDULE 1**

Sᴛᴀᴛᴇꜱ ᴡɪᴛʜ ᴡʜɪᴄʜ ᴛʜᴇ Uɴɪᴛᴇᴅ Kɪɴɢᴅᴏᴍ ʜᴀꜱ ᴇxᴛʀᴀᴅɪᴛɪᴏɴ ᴛʀᴇᴀᴛɪᴇꜱ ᴀɴᴅ
ɪɴ ʀᴇꜱᴘᴇᴄᴛ ᴏꜰ ᴡʜɪᴄʜ ᴛʜᴇ Tᴏᴋʏᴏ Cᴏɴᴠᴇɴᴛɪᴏɴ ɪꜱ ɪɴ ꜰᴏʀᴄᴇ.

State	Date of Extradition Treaty	Date of entry into force of Convention
Argentina	22nd May 1889	21st October 1971
Austria	9th January 1963	8th May 1974
Belgium	29th October 1901	4th November 1970
Chile	26th January 1897	24th April 1974
Colombia	27th October 1888	4th October 1973
Denmark	31st March 1873	4th December 1969
Ecuador	20th September 1880	3rd March 1970
Finland	30th May 1924/ 29th October 1975	1st July 1971
France	14th August 1876	10th December 1970
Germany, Federal Republic of	14th May 1872 (as re-applied and amended by the Agreement of 23rd February 1960)	16th March 1970
Greece	24th September 1910	29th August 1971
Guatemala	4th July 1885	15th February 1971
Hungary	3rd December 1873	3rd March 1971
Iceland	31st March 1873	14th June 1970
Iraq	2nd May 1932	13th August 1974
Israel	4th April 1960	18th December 1969
Italy	5th February 1873	4th December 1969
Luxembourg	24th November 1880	20th December 1972
Mexico	7th September 1886	4th December 1969
Netherlands	26th September 1898	12th February 1970
Nicaragua	19th April 1905	22nd November 1973
Norway	26th June 1873	4th December 1969
Panama	25th August 1906	14th February 1971
Paraguay	12th September 1908	7th November 1971

State	Date of Extradition Treaty	Date of entry into force of Convention
Poland	11th January 1932	17th June 1971
Portugal	17th October 1892	4th December 1969
Romania	21st March 1893	16th May 1974
Spain	4th June 1878	30th December 1969
Sweden	26th April 1963	4th December 1969
Switzerland	26th November 1880	21st March 1971
Thailand	3rd September 1883	4th June 1972
United States of America	22nd December 1931/ 8th June 1972	4th December 1969
Uruguay	26th March 1884	26th April 1977
Yugoslavia	6th December 1900	13th May 1971

Article 4 SCHEDULE 2

TERRITORIES TO WHICH THE APPLICATION OF THE TOKYO CONVENTION IS EXTENDED

Belize

Bermuda

British Antarctic Territory

British Indian Ocean Territory

British Virgin Islands

Cayman Islands

Falkland Islands and Dependencies

Gibraltar

Gilbert Islands

Hong Kong

Montserrat

Pitcairn, Henderson, Ducie and Oeno Islands

St. Helena and Dependencies

Sovereign Base Areas of Akrotiri and Dhekelia in the Island of Cyprus

Turks and Caicos Islands

Tuvalu

EXPLANATORY NOTE

(This Note is not part of the Order.)

The coming into force of extradition treaties between the United Kingdom and Finland and between the United Kingdom and the United States of America which replace earlier treaties has necessitated amendments to the entries for those States in Schedule 1 to the Extradition (Tokyo Convention) Order 1971. The opportunity has also been taken to consolidate in one Order the names of foreign States which have become parties to the Convention on Offences and certain other Acts Committed on board Aircraft signed at Tokyo on 14th September 1963.

STATUTORY INSTRUMENTS

1977 No. 1240

HEALTH VISITING AND SOCIAL WORK

The Central Council for Education and Training in Social Work Order 1977

Made - - -	*26th July* 1977
Laid before Parliament	*3rd August* 1977
Coming into Operation	*1st October* 1977

At the Court at Buckingham Palace, the 26th day of July 1977

Present,

The Queen's Most Excellent Majesty in Council

Her Majesty, in exercise of the powers conferred upon Her by section 3(3) of the Health Visiting and Social Work (Training) Act 1962(a), as amended by section 11 of the Local Authority Social Services Act 1970(b), and of all other powers enabling Her in that behalf, is pleased, by and with the advice of Her Privy Council, to order, and it is hereby ordered, as follows:—

Citation and Commencement

1. This Order may be cited as the Central Council for Education and Training in Social Work Order 1977, and shall come into operation on 1st October 1977.

Interpretation

2.—(1) In this Order, unless the context otherwise requires:—

"the Act of 1962" means the Health Visiting and Social Work (Training) Act 1962;

"the Act of 1968" means the Social Work (Scotland) Act 1968(c);

"the Council" means the Central Council for Education and Training in Social Work.

(2) The rules for the construction of Acts of Parliament contained in the Interpretation Act 1889(d) shall apply for the purposes of the interpretation of this Order as they apply for the purposes of the interpretation of an Act of Parliament.

Conferment on the Council of functions in relation to other social work

3. The functions of the Council as set out in section 3(1) and (2) of the Act of 1962 (functions of the Central Council for Education and Training in Social Work) shall be extended to include such social work as is required in the services provided under the enactments set out in Schedule 1 to this Order or any corresponding enactments in force in Northern Ireland, or similar services provided by a voluntary organisation.

(a) 1962 c. 33.	(b) 1970 c. 42.
(c) 1968 c. 49.	(d) 1889 c. 63.

Modification of the constitution of the Council

4. The First Schedule to the Act of 1962 (Constitution, etc., of Councils) shall be modified in accordance with the provisions set out in Schedule 2 to this Order.

Revocation

5. The Central Council for Education and Training in Social Work Order 1974(**a**) is hereby revoked.

N. E. Leigh,

Clerk of The Privy Council.

Article 3   SCHEDULE 1

1. *Services provided under enactments applying to England and Wales*

Enactment	Nature of functions
(*a*) Enactments specified in the Local Authority Social Services Act 1970 (c. 42). Schedule 1.	Services assigned to the social services committee in so far as such services are not included in section 3(5) of the Act of 1962.
(*b*) Sections 1, 2 and 9 of the Children and Young Persons Act 1969 (c. 54) in so far as they are not included in (*a*) above.	Function of a local authority in their capacity as a local education authority.
(*c*) Sections 47–49 of and Schedule 3 to the Powers of Criminal Courts Act 1973 (1973 c. 62).	Probation and after care services.
(*d*) Education Acts 1944–1976 (7 and 8 Geo. 6. c. 31; 9 and 10 Geo. 6. c. 50; 11 and 12 Geo. 6. c. 40; 1 and 2 Eliz. 2. c. 33; 7 and 8 Eliz. 2. c. 60; 10 and 11 Eliz. 2. c. 12; 1964 c. 82; 1965 c. 3; 1967 c. 3; 1968 c. 17; 1968 c. 37; 1970 c. 14; 1970 c. 52; 1971 c. 74; 1973 c. 16; 1973 c. 23; 1975 c. 2; 1976 c. 5; 1976 c. 81).	Functions of a local authority in their capacity as a local education authority.
(*e*) National Health Service Reorganisation Act 1973 (c. 32) as read with the National Health Service (Preservation of Boards of Governors) Order 1974 (**b**).	Services provided under section 2(2) of the said Act and administered by Regional and Area Health Authorities and Boards of Governors of Teaching Hospitals.

2. *Services provided under enactments applying to Scotland*

Services provided under the Act of 1968 (in so far as such services are not included in section 3(5) of the Act of 1962) or under the National Health Service (Scotland) Acts 1947 to 1976 (1947 c. 27; 1972 c. 58; 1973 c. 32; 1976 c. 83).

(a) S.I. 1974/1265 (1974 II, p. 4831).   (b) S.I. 1974/281 (1974 I, p. 963).

SCHEDULE 2   Article 4

Modification of the Constitution of the Council

1. In paragraph 1 of the First Schedule to the Act of 1962 for the words "thirty-two" there shall be substituted the words "sixty-four".

2. For paragraph 4 of the First Schedule to the Act of 1962 there shall be substituted the following paragraph:—

"4. The other members of the Central Council for Education and Training in Social Work shall be appointed as follows:—

(*a*) Eight to be appointed by Ministers, after consultation with voluntary organisations and others concerned with social work training.

(*b*) Four by the Association of Metropolitan Authorities.

(*c*) Five by the Association of County Councils.

(*d*) Two by the Convention of Scottish Local Authorities.

(*e*) One by the Central Council of Probation and After-Care Committees.

(*f*) One by the Regional Health Authorities.

(*g*) Two by the Committee of Vice-Chancellors and Principals of the Universities of the United Kingdom.

(*h*) One by the Council for National Academic Awards.

(*i*) One by the Committee of Directors of Polytechnics.

(*j*) One by the Association of Principals of Technical Institutions jointly with the Association of Colleges for Further and Higher Education.

(*k*) Two by the National Association of Teachers in Further and Higher Education.

(*l*) Two by the Joint University Council for Social and Public Administration.

(*m*) Two by the Association of Teachers in Social Work Education.

(*n*) One by the Local Government Training Board.

(*o*) One by the National Institute for Social Work.

(*p*) Eight by the British Association of Social Workers.

(*q*) Two by the Association of Directors of Social Services.

(*r*) One by the Association of Directors of Social Work (in Scotland).

(*s*) One by the Conference of Chief Probation Officers.

(*t*) Two by the National Association of Probation Officers.

(*u*) Two by the Residential Care Association.

(*v*) One by the National Association of Chief Education Welfare Officers acting jointly with the National Association for Social Workers in Education.

(*w*) One by the British Medical Association.

(*x*) One by the Society of Community Medicine.

(*y*) One by the Joint Committee of the Royal Colleges, the Royal Scottish Corporations and the Central Consultants and Specialists Committee (known as the Joint Consultants Committee).

(*z*) One by the General Nursing Council for England and Wales.

(*aa*) One by the Personal Social Services Council.

(*bb*) One by the Standing Committee on Probation Manpower Needs.

(*cc*) One by the Advisory Council on Social Work (in Scotland).

(*dd*) Two by the National Joint Council for Local Authorities Administrative, Professional, Technical and Clerical Services (Staff Side).

(*ee*) One by the National Union of Students.

(*ff*) One by the Association of Community Home Schools acting jointly with the National Association of Heads and Matrons of Assessment Centres.

(*gg*) One by the Association of Community Workers.

(*hh*) One by the National Association of Teachers of the Mentally Handicapped."

3. In place of paragraph 11 of the First Schedule to the Act of 1962 there shall be substituted the following paragraph:—

"11. The Ministers shall ensure that four members of the Central Council for Education and Training in Social Work are persons who at the time of their appointment are ordinarily resident in Wales; that six such members at the time of their appointment are ordinarily resident in Scotland and three members at the time of their appointment are ordinarily resident in Northern Ireland; the Health Ministers and the Secretary of State for Education and Science shall ensure that at least one member of the Council for the Education and Training of Health Visitors is a person who at the time of his appointment is ordinarily resident in Wales; and shall, if necessary, make their appointments accordingly.".

4. Paragraphs 7, 8 and 9 of the First Schedule to the Act of 1962 shall be repealed.

5. In paragraph 10 of the First Schedule to the Act of 1962 for the words "each Council" there shall be substituted the words "the Council for the Education and Training of Health Visitors".

6. After paragraph 20 of the First Schedule to the Act of 1962 there shall be inserted the following paragraph:—

"*Interpretation*

21. In this Schedule "The Ministers" means the Secretaries of State respectively for Social Services, the Home Department, Education and Science, Scotland and Wales, and the Head of the Department of Health and Social Services for Northern Ireland.".

EXPLANATORY NOTE

(*This Note is not part of the Order.*)

This Order supersedes the Central Council for Education and Training in Social Work Order 1974, which extended the functions of the Central Council for Education and Training in Social Work to include social work required in the services provided under the enactments set out in Schedule 1 or any corresponding enactments in force in Northern Ireland or similar services provided by a voluntary organisation.

The Order also, by Schedule 2, makes modifications to the constitution of the Central Council for Education and Training in Social Work.

STATUTORY INSTRUMENTS

1977 No. 1241

MERCHANT SHIPPING

The Merchant Shipping Act 1974 (Guernsey) (Amendment) Order 1977

Made - - - -	26th July 1977
Laid before Parliament	3rd August 1977
Coming into Operation	1st September 1977

At the Court at Buckingham Palace, the 26th day of July 1977

Present,

The Queen's Most Excellent Majesty in Council

Her Majesty, in exercise of the powers conferred upon Her by section 20(1) of the Merchant Shipping Act 1974(a) and section 738(1) of the Merchant Shipping Act 1894(b) (read with section 23(1) of the Act of 1974), is pleased, by and with the advice of Her Privy Council, to order, and it is hereby ordered, as follows:—

1. This Order may be cited as the Merchant Shipping Act 1974 (Guernsey) (Amendment) Order 1977 and shall come into operation on 1st September 1977.

2. In the Schedule to the Merchant Shipping Act 1974 (Guernsey) Order 1975(c) for paragraphs 5 and 6 there shall be substituted the following provisions:—

'5. In section 2(9) for the definition of "company" and "group" there shall be substituted the following definitions:—

"company" means a company registered in pursuance of—

(a) the Law of Guernsey entitled "Loi relative aux Sociétés Anonymes ou à Responsabilité Limitée" registered on the Records of the Island of Guernsey on the 21st day of March, 1908; or

(b) the Law of Alderney entitled "Loi relative aux Sociétés Anonymes ou à Responsabilité Limitée" registered on the Records of the Island of Guernsey on the 22nd day of May, 1894

or a body incorporated under the Law of the United Kingdom or of any other country;

"group" in relation to companies, means a holding company and its subsidiaries as defined by section 154 of the Companies Act 1948, an Act of Parliament (or for companies in Northern Ireland section 148 of the Companies Act (Northern Ireland)

(a) 1974 c. 43.   (b) 1894 c. 60.   (c) S.I. 1975/2182 (1975 III, p. 8212).

1960 (an Act of the Parliament of Northern Ireland)) subject, in the case of a company incorporated in Guernsey or elsewhere outside the United Kingdom, to any necessary modifications of those definitions;

6. For section 2(10) there shall be substituted the following provision:—

"(10) In this section "sea" does not include any waters on the landward side of the base-lines from which the territorial sea of the British Islands adjacent to Guernsey is measured.".'

N. E. Leigh,

Clerk of the Privy Council.

EXPLANATORY NOTE

(This Note is not part of the Order.)

This Order amends the Merchant Shipping Act 1974 (Guernsey) Order 1975 which extended certain provisions of the Merchant Shipping Act 1974 to the Bailiwick of Guernsey with exceptions, adaptations and modifications specified in the Schedule to that Order.

It substitutes in the Schedule to the Order of 1975—

(a) for paragraph 5 a new paragraph which redefines two expressions. "Company" is redefined to include a body incorporated otherwise than under the laws in force in the Bailiwick of Guernsey, whether under the law of the United Kingdom or of any other country. "Group" in relation to companies is redefined in terms which reflect the new definition of "company";

(b) for paragraph 6 a new paragraph omitting a textual transposition which had occurred in the Schedule to the Order of 1975.

STATUTORY INSTRUMENTS

1977 No. 1242

MERCHANT SHIPPING

The Merchant Shipping Act 1974 (Jersey) (Amendment) Order 1977

Made - - - -	26th July 1977
Laid before Parliament	3rd August 1977
Coming into Operation	1st September 1977

At the Court at Buckingham Palace, the 26th day of July 1977

Present,

The Queen's Most Excellent Majesty in Council

Her Majesty, in exercise of the powers conferred upon Her by section 20(1) of the Merchant Shipping Act 1974(a) and section 738(1) of the Merchant Shipping Act 1894(b) (read with section 23(1) of the said Act of 1974) is pleased, by and with the advice of Her Privy Council, to order, and it is hereby ordered, as follows:—

1. This Order may be cited as the Merchant Shipping Act 1974 (Jersey) (Amendment) Order 1977 and shall come into operation on 1st September 1977.

2. In the Schedule to the Merchant Shipping Act 1974 (Jersey) Order 1975(c) for paragraph 5 there shall be substituted the following provision:—

"5. In section 2(9) for the definitions of "company" and "group" there shall be substituted the following definitions—

' "company" means a company registered in pursuance of the Companies (Jersey) Laws 1861 to 1968 or a body incorporated under the law of the United Kingdom or of any other country;

"group" in relation to companies, means a holding company and its subsidiaries as defined by section 154 of the Companies Act 1948, an Act of Parliament (or for companies in Northern Ireland section 148 of the Companies Act (Northern Ireland) 1960, an Act of the Parliament of Northern Ireland), subject, in the case of a company incorporated in Jersey or elsewhere outside the United Kingdom, to any necessary modifications of those definitions;'."

N. E. Leigh,
Clerk of the Privy Council.

(a) 1974 c. 43.   (b) 1894 c. 60.   (c) S.I. 1975/2181 (1975 III, p. 8210).

EXPLANATORY NOTE

(This Note is not part of the Order.)

This Order amends the Merchant Shipping Act 1974 (Jersey) Order 1975 which extended certain provisions of the Merchant Shipping Act 1974 to the Bailiwick of Jersey with exceptions, adaptations and modifications specified in the Schedule to that Order.

It substitutes for paragraph 5 of the Schedule to the Order of 1975 a new paragraph which redefines two expressions. "Company" is redefined to include a body incorporated otherwise than under the law of Jersey whether under the law of the United Kingdom or of any other country. "Group" in relation to companies is redefined in terms which reflect the new definition of "company".

STATUTORY INSTRUMENTS

1977 No. 1243

DANGEROUS DRUGS

The Misuse of Drugs Act 1971 (Modification) Order 1977

Laid before Parliament in draft

Made - - - -		*26th July* 1977
Coming into Operation		*20th September* 1977

At the Court at Buckingham Palace, the 26th day of July 1977

Present,

The Queen's Most Excellent Majesty in Council

Whereas a draft of this Order has been laid before Parliament on the recommendation of the Advisory Council on the Misuse of Drugs and has been approved by a resolution of each House of Parliament:

Now, therefore, Her Majesty, in pursuance of section 2(2) of the Misuse of Drugs Act 1971(a), is pleased, by and with the advice of Her Privy Council, to order, and it is hereby ordered, as follows:—

1.—(1) This Order may be cited as the Misuse of Drugs Act 1971 (Modification) Order 1977 and shall come into operation on the expiration of the period of eight weeks beginning with the day on which it is made.

(2) The Interpretation Act 1889(b) shall apply for the interpretation of this Order as it applies for the interpretation of an Act of Parliament.

2. Schedule 2 to the Misuse of Drugs Act 1971 (which, as amended(c), specifies the drugs which are subject to control under that Act) shall be amended in accordance with the following provisions of this Order.

3. Paragraph 1 of Part I of the said Schedule 2 shall be amended as follows:—

(*a*) the list of substances and products beginning with the word "Acetorphine" and ending with the words "4-Phenylpiperidine-4-carboxylic acid ethyl ester" shall be designated sub-paragraph (*a*), and accordingly the letter "(*a*)" shall be inserted before the word "Acetorphine"; and

(*b*) there shall be added at the end the following sub-paragraphs—

"(*b*) any compound (not being a compound for the time being specified in sub-paragraph (*a*) above) structurally derived from

---

(**a**) 1971 c. 38.   (**b**) 1889 c. 63.

(**c**) S.I. 1973/771, 1975/421 (1973 I, p. 2446; 1975 I, p. 1317).

tryptamine or from a ring-hydroxy tryptamine by substitution at the nitrogen atom of the sidechain with one or more alkyl substituents but no other substituent;

(c) any compound (not being methoxyphenamine or a compound for the time being specified in sub-paragraph (a) above) structurally derived from phenethylamine, an N-alkylphenethylamine, α-methylphenethylamine, an N-alkyl-α-methylphenethylamine, α-ethylphenethylamine, or an N-alkyl-α-ethylphenethylamine by substitution in the ring to any extent with alkyl, alkoxy, alkylenedioxy or halide substituents, whether or not further substituted in the ring by one or more other univalent substituents.".

N. E. Leigh,

Clerk of the Privy Council.

EXPLANATORY NOTE

(This Note is not part of the Order.)

This Order adds to Part I of Schedule 2 to the Misuse of Drugs Act 1971 (which specifies the Class A drugs which are subject to control under the Act) two classes of compounds (other than members of those classes which are already controlled). The classes are certain tryptamine derivatives, and certain phenethylamine derivatives.

STATUTORY INSTRUMENTS

1977 No. 1244

SEA FISHERIES

BOATS AND METHODS OF FISHING

The Sea Fish (Conservation) (Isle of Man) Order 1977

Made - - - -	26th *July* 1977
Coming into Operation	1st *August* 1977

At the Court at Buckingham Palace, the 26th day of July 1977

Present,

The Queen's Most Excellent Majesty in Council

Her Majesty, in exercise of the powers conferred upon Her by section 24(2) and (3) of the Sea Fish (Conservation) Act 1967(**a**) and section 11(3) of the Fishery Limits Act 1976(**b**) is pleased, by and with the advice of Her Privy Council, to order, and it is hereby ordered, as follows:—

1. This Order may be cited as the Sea Fish (Conservation) (Isle of Man) Order 1977 and shall come into operation on 1st August 1977.

2.—(1) The Interpretation Act 1889(**c**) shall apply for the purpose of the interpretation of this Order as it applies for the interpretation of an Act of Parliament and as if this Order and the Order hereby revoked were Acts of Parliament.

(2) This Order shall be construed as one with the Sea Fish (Conservation) (Isle of Man) Order 1973(**d**).

3. The Sea Fish (Conservation) (Isle of Man) (No. 2) Order 1973(**e**) is hereby revoked.

4. Section 4 of the Sea Fish (Conservation) Act 1967, as substituted by section 3 of the Fishery Limits Act 1976 (which relates to the licensing of fishing boats), shall extend to the Isle of Man subject to the adaptations and modifications specified in the Schedule to this Order.

5. The Schedule to the Sea Fish (Conservation) (Isle of Man) Order 1973 (as originally made) shall be varied as follows:—

    (*a*) in paragraph 15 for the words "section 5" there shall be substituted the words "sections 4 and 5";

    (*b*) for paragraph 18 there shall be substituted the following paragraph:—

        'For section 11, as amended by the Fishery Limits Act 1976,

---

(**a**) 1967 c. 84.   (**b**) 1976 c. 86.
(**c**) 1889 c. 63.   (**d**) S.I. 1973/237 (1973 I, p. 890).
(**e**) S.I. 1973/1887 (1973 III, p. 6557).

(penalties for offences) there shall be substituted the following section:—

"11.—(1) Any person guilty of an offence under section 1, 3, 4 or 5 of this Act shall be liable—

(a) in the case of an offence under section 4(3) or 5(1) on summary conviction to a fine not exceeding £50,000 or on conviction on information to a fine;

(b) in the case of an offence under section 1(3), 3, 4(6) or 5(6), on summary conviction to a fine not exceeding £1,000 or on conviction on information to a fine;

(c) in the case of an offence under section 4(7) on summary conviction to a fine not exceeding £1,000.

(2) The court by which a person is convicted of an offence may—

(a) in the case of an offence under section 3, 4(3) or (6) or 5(1) or (6) order the forfeiture of the net or other fishing gear in respect of which the contravention constituting the offence occurred;

(b) in the case of an offence under section 1(3), 4(3) or (6) or 5(1) or (6) order the forfeiture of any fish in respect of which the offence was committed;

(c) in the case of an offence under section 4(3) or (6) order that the owner or the charterer (if any) of the fishing boat used to commit the offence or, as the case may be, of the boat named in the licence of which the condition is broken, be disqualified for a specified period from holding a licence under that section in respect of that boat." ';

(c) paragraph 19 shall be omitted;

(d) for paragraph 20 there shall be substituted the following paragraph:—

"20. In section 15(2) for paragraphs (b) and (c) there shall be substituted the following paragraphs:—

"(b) any fish caught in contravention of a provision imposed by an order under section 4 or 5 of this Act, where the fish are on a fishing boat used in contravention of the prohibition or are in the ownership or custody, or under the control, of the owner, the master or the charterer (if any) of the fishing boat;

(c) any net or other fishing gear used in contravention of a prohibition imposed by an order under the said section 4 or 5;

and paragraph (d) shall be omitted.";

(e) in paragraph 21 for sub-paragraph (b) and (c) there shall be substituted the following provisions:—

"(b) for the words "within the fishery limits of the British Islands" there shall be substituted the words "within British fishery limits (but outside territorial waters)";

(c) for the words after "the enforcement of" there shall be substituted the words "section 1, 3, 4 or 5 of this Act or any order made thereunder".".

N. E. Leigh,
Clerk of the Privy Council.

SCHEDULE

ADAPTATIONS AND MODIFICATIONS IN THE EXTENSION OF SECTION 4
OF THE SEA FISH (CONSERVATION) ACT 1967 TO THE ISLE OF MAN
AND WATERS ADJACENT THERETO

1. For section 4(1) there shall be substituted the following provision: —

"(1) The Ministers may by order provide—

(a) that in any specified area within waters adjacent to the Isle of
Man (but outside territorial waters) fishing by fishing boats (whether
British or foreign) is prohibited unless authorised by a licence
granted by the Isle of Man Board of Agriculture and Fisheries
(hereinafter called "the Board") and for the time being in force;

(b) that in any area specified in the order (being outside the waters
referred to in paragraph (a) above) fishing by British fishing boats
registered in the Isle of Man is prohibited unless so authorised.".

2. For section 4(4) there shall be substituted the following provision: —

"(4) The Board may, with the approval of the Finance Board, make
charges for the granting of a licence under this section and may make
different charges in relation to different classes of licence.".

3. In section 4(6) for the words "Minister granting the licence" there shall
be substituted the word "Board".

4. In section 4(7) for the words "Minister granting a licence under this
section" there shall be substituted the word "Board".

5. For section 4(8) there shall be substituted the following subsection: —

"(8) The licensing powers conferred on the Board by this section may
be exercised, in consultation with the Ministers, so as to limit the
number of fishing boats, or of any class of fishing boats, engaged in
fishing in any area, or in fishing in any area for any description of fish,
to such extent as appears to the Ministers and the Board to be necessary
or expedient for the regulation of sea fishing.".

6. In section 4(9) for the words "Minister who granted the licence" there
shall be substituted the word "Board".

7. In section 4(10) for the words "Minister who granted it" there shall be
substituted the word "Board".

8. For section 4(11) there shall be substituted the following subsection: —

"(11) The Board may make arrangements, with the consent of the
Ministers, for any of its licensing powers under this section to be
exercised by any person on its behalf.".

9. In section 4(12) after the words "United Kingdom" there shall be
inserted the words "or the Isle of Man".

10. After section 4(12) there shall be inserted the following subsections:—

"(13) For the purposes of this section "waters adjacent to the Isle of Man" means the waters extending to 12 miles from the baselines from which the breadth of the territorial sea adjacent to the Isle of Man is measured but not extending beyond a line every point of which is equidistant from the nearest points of such base lines and the corresponding base lines of the United Kingdom.

(14) The definitions set out in sections 1(7) and 3(8) of this Act shall have effect for the purposes of this section, but in the definition of "sea fish" the words following "any such fish" shall be omitted.

(15) In this section "miles" means international nautical miles of 1,852 metres.".

EXPLANATORY NOTE

(This Note is not part of the Order.)

This Order revokes a previous Order extending section 4 of the Sea Fish (Conservation) Act 1967 to the Isle of Man and extends a new section 4, as substituted by section 3 of the Fishery Limits Act 1976, with adaptations and modifications. The Order also extends to the Isle of Man the increased penalties for contraventions of the 1967 Act provided for in the 1976 Act.

STATUTORY INSTRUMENTS

1977 No. 1255

CIVIL AVIATION

The Air Navigation (Amendment) Order 1977

Made - - - - - -	*26th July* 1977
Laid before Parliament - - -	*3rd August* 1977
Coming into Operation—	
for the purposes of Article 3(15)	*30th December* 1977
for all other purposes - -	*24th August* 1977

At the Court at Buckingham Palace, the 26th day of July 1977

Present,

The Queen's Most Excellent Majesty in Council

Her Majesty, in exercise of the powers conferred upon Her by sections 8 and 57 of the Civil Aviation Act 1949(a) as amended by section 62(1) of the Civil Aviation Act 1971(b) and of all other powers enabling Her in that behalf is pleased, by and with the advice of Her Privy Council, to order, and it is hereby ordered, as follows:

Citation and commencement

1. This Order may be cited as the Air Navigation (Amendment) Order 1977 and shall come into operation for the purposes of Article 3(15) on 30th December 1977 and for all other purposes on 24th August 1977.

Interpretation

2. The Interpretation Act 1889(c) shall apply for the purpose of the interpretation of this Order as it applies for the purpose of the interpretation of an Act of Parliament.

Amendment of the Air Navigation Order 1976

3. The Air Navigation Order 1976(d) shall be amended as follows:

(1) In Article 2(2) in sub-paragraphs (b) and (c), a comma shall be inserted after the word "authority" wherever it appears;

(2) In Article 2(2) in sub-paragraph (c) after the word "direction" there shall be inserted the word "order";

(a) 1949 c. 67.	**(b)** 1971 c. 75.
(c) 1889 c. 63.	**(d)** S.I. 1976/1783 (1976 III, p. 4769).

(3) In Article 11(6), after the words "the log book", there shall be inserted "relating to the same part of the aircraft or to the same equipment or apparatus";

(4) In Article 13(6), for the words "equipment of services", there shall be substituted "equipment or services";

(5) In Article 18(6), after the words "any particular operator" there shall be inserted "of any aircraft registered in the United Kingdom";

(6) In Article 19 in sub-paragraph (b)(ii) of the proviso to paragraph (1), for the words "he is fit to so act", there shall be substituted "he is fit so to act";

(7) In Article 19 in sub-paragraph (b)(v) of the proviso to paragraph (1) after "instruction in flying" there shall be inserted "or the conducting of flying tests";

(8) In Article 19(3), after "United Kingdom" there shall be inserted "or under the law of a relevant overseas territory";

(9) In Article 19(8) in sub-paragraph (b) for the words "owned and operated" there shall be substituted the words "owned or operated";

(10) In Article 20(8)(b), for the last sentence there shall be substituted—

"The medical certificate shall be deemed to be suspended upon the occurrence of such injury or the elapse of such period of illness or the confirmation of the pregnancy, and

(aa) in the case of injury or illness the suspension shall cease upon the holder being medically examined under arrangements made by the Authority and pronounced fit to resume his functions as a member of the flight crew or upon the Authority exempting, subject to such conditions as it thinks fit, the holder from the requirement of a medical examination; and

(bb) in the case of pregnancy, the suspension may be lifted by the Authority for such period and subject to such conditions as it thinks fit and shall cease upon the holder being medically examined under arrangements made by the Authority after the pregnancy has ended and pronounced fit to resume her functions as a member of the flight crew."

(11) In Article 23(2) after the words "a flying machine", there shall be inserted "or glider";

(12) In Article 28—

(a) at the end of the proviso to paragraph (2) there shall be added—

"(c) the aircraft is a helicopter the maximum total weight authorised of which does not exceed 3000 kg, and the total seating capacity of which does not exceed five persons."

(b) at the end of paragraph (5) there shall be added—

"Provided that in the case of a helicopter, if in all the circumstances it is not reasonably practicable for the copies of the load sheet and instructions to be kept elsewhere than in the helicopter, they may be carried in the helicopter in a box approved by the Authority for that purpose.";

(13) In Article 29, at the end of paragraph (4) there shall be added—

"(5) Without prejudice to the provisions of paragraph (3) of this Article a helicopter, in respect of which there is in force under this Order a certificate of airworthiness designating the helicopter as being of performance Group B shall not fly over water for the purpose of public transport—

(a) so as to be more than 20 seconds flying time from a point from which it can make an autorotative descent to land suitable for an emergency landing unless it is equipped with apparatus approved by the Authority enabling it to land safely on water but shall not so fly on any flight for more than three minutes except with the permission in writing of the Authority and in accordance with any conditions subject to which that permission may have been given. For the purpose of this subparagraph flying time shall be calculated on the assumption that the helicopter is flying in still air at the speed specified in the certificate of airworthiness in force in respect of the helicopter as the speed for compliance with regulations governing flights over water;

(b) over that part of the bed of the River Thames which lies between the following points:

Hammersmith Bridge   (51°29′16″N) (00°13′45″W)

Greenwich Reach   (51°29′03″N) (00° 00′37″W)

between the ordinary high water marks on each of its banks, unless it is equipped with apparatus approved by the Authority enabling it to land safely on water.

(6) Without prejudice to the provisions of paragraph (3) of this Article, a helicopter in respect of which there is in force under this Order a certificate of airworthiness designating the helicopter as being of performance Group A2 shall not fly over water for the purpose of public transport for more than 15 minutes during any flight unless it is equipped with apparatus approved by the Authority enabling it to land safely on water.

(14) In Article 33, for paragraph (2) there shall be substituted—

"(2) Each pilot at the controls shall be secured in his seat by either a safety belt with or without one diagonal shoulder strap, or a safety harness except that during take-off and landing a safety harness shall be worn if it is required by Article 13 of this Order to be provided.";

(15) After Article 35, there shall be inserted the following new Article—

"*Minimum Navigation Performance*

35A. An aircraft registered in the United Kingdom shall not fly in airspace prescribed for the purposes of this Article unless—

(a) it is equipped with navigation systems which enable the aircraft to maintain the prescribed navigation performance capability; and

(b) the navigation systems required by paragraph (a) hereof are approved by the Authority and installed and maintained in a manner approved by the Authority; and

(c) the operating procedures for the navigation systems required by paragraph (a) hereof are approved by the Authority; and (*d*) the equipment is operated in accordance with the approved procedures while the aircraft is flying in the said airspace."

(16) In Article 36—

(*a*) in the heading the word "data" shall be deleted;

(*b*) in paragraph (1)—

(i) after the word "recorder" there shall be inserted the words "or a cockpit voice recorder";

(ii) for "sub-paragraph 4(5)" there shall be substituted "sub-paragraph 4(4) or (5)";

(17) In Article 38, at the end of paragraph (4) there shall be added—

"(4A) A passenger shall not be carried in a helicopter at any time when an article, person or animal is suspended therefrom, other than a passenger who has duties to perform in connection with the article, person or animal."

(18) In Article 40, for paragraph (3) there shall be substituted—

"(3) For the purposes of this Article 'munitions of war' means such weapons and ammunition as are designed for use in warfare or against the person, including parts designed for such weapons and ammunition."

(19) In Article 52, in the heading for "responsibilties", there shall be substituted "responsibilities";

(20) For Article 61(6) there shall be substituted—

"Every applicant for and holder of an air traffic controller's licence or a student air traffic controller's licence shall upon such occasions as the Authority may require—

(*a*) submit himself to medical examination by a person approved by the Authority either generally or in a particular case who shall make a report to the Authority in such form as the Authority may require; and

(*b*) submit himself to such examinations and tests and furnish such evidence as to his knowledge, experience, competence and skill, as the Authority may require.";

(21) In Article 63, for paragraph (3) there shall be substituted—

"(3) Upon the pregnancy of the holder of an air traffic controller's licence being confirmed, the licence shall be deemed to be suspended and such suspension may be lifted by the Authority subject to such conditions as it thinks fit, and shall cease upon the holder being medically examined under arrangements made by the Authority after the pregnancy has ended and pronounced fit to resume her functions under the licence."

(22) In Article 90—

(*a*) in paragraph (1),

(i) in the entry beginning "Log book" after the words "variable pitch propeller log book" there shall be inserted "or personal flying log book";

(ii) after the entry beginning "Record' 'there shall be inserted the following new entry—

" 'Relevant overseas territory' means any Colony and any country or place outside Her Majesty's dominions in which for the time being Her Majesty has jurisdiction;";

(*b*) in paragraph (6), sub-paragraph (*a*)(ii) for "in the case of the British Airways Board, the members of the Board" there shall be substituted "in the case of the British Airways Board or the Authority, the members of the Board or the Authority respectively";

(*c*) in paragraph (10), for the word "contest", there shall be substituted "context".

(23) In Schedule 1—

(*a*) in Part A, in the shoulder heading, for "23(1)" there shall be substituted "23(2)";

(*b*) in Part B, paragraph III sub-paragraph (*b*) for "constracting" there shall be substituted "contrasting";

(24) In Schedule 4 the final sentence shall be deleted.

(25) In Schedule 5—

(*a*) in paragraph 4—

(i) in sub-paragraph (6)(*a*), for "270,000 kg" there shall be substituted "27,000 kg";

(ii) in sub-paragraph (6)(*b*), for "conforms" there shall be substituted "conform";

(iii) in sub-paragraph (6)(*c*), for "or such a certificate" there shall be substituted "for such a certificate";

(iv) in sub-paragraph (7)(*a*) for "maximum total authorised" there shall be substituted "maximum total weight authorised";

(*b*) in paragraph 5—

(i) in Scale G, sub-paragraph (ii) for "illumintion" there shall be substituted "illumination";

(ii) in Scale K, Part 1, sub-paragraph (ii) for "to enable such person", there shall be substituted "to enable such persons";

(iii) at the end of Scale M, there shall be added the following proviso—

"Provided that in the case of an aircraft carrying out aerobatic manoeuvres consisting only of erect spinning, the Authority may permit a safety belt with one diagonal shoulder strap to be fitted if it is satisfied that such restraint is sufficient for the carrying out of erect spinning in that aircraft and that it is not reasonably practicable to fit a safety harness in that aircraft.";

(iv) at the end of Scale P and Scale S respectively, there shall be added the following proviso—

"Provided that an aeroplane shall not be required to carry the said equipment, if before take-off the equipment is found to be unserviceable, and the aircraft flies in accordance with arrangements approved by the Authority.";

(v) in Scale X, for "reasonable" there shall be substituted "reasonably";

(26) In Schedule 6, in paragraph 2,

(*a*) in sub-paragraph (1)(*a*) the letter "F" shall be deleted from the column headed "G" and shall be inserted in the column headed "F";

(*b*) in sub-paragraph (3)(*a*)(i) for "apprach" there shall be substituted "approach";

(27) In Schedule 8—

(a) in Area A, in the heading, for "Artic" there shall be substituted "Arctic";

(b) in Area B, for the word "areas" there shall be substituted" area";

(c) in Area K, for the point "67° north latitude 50° west longitude" there shall be substituted "67° north latitude 60° west longitude";

(28) In Schedule 9, Part A—

(a) in paragraph 1 in the entry relating to the Private Pilot's Licence (Aeroplanes), in paragraph (a) of the proviso—

(i) after "instruction in flying" there shall be inserted "or the conducting of flying tests in either case";

(ii) after "the person giving" there shall be inserted "the instruction or conducting the test";

(iii) after "the person receiving the instruction" there shall be inserted "or undergoing the test";

(b) in paragraph 2 in the entry relating to the Private Pilot's Licence (Helicopters and Gyroplanes) in paragraph (a) of the proviso—

(i) after "instruction in flying" there shall be inserted "or the conducting of flying tests in either case";

(ii) after "the person giving" there shall be inserted "the instruction or conducting the test";

(iii) after "the person receiving the instruction", there shall be inserted "or undergoing the test";

(c) in paragraph 3 in the entry relating to the Private Pilot's Licence (Balloons and Airships) in paragraph (a) of the proviso—

(i) after "instruction in flying" there shall be inserted "or the conducting of flying tests in either case";

(ii) after "the person giving" there shall be inserted "the instruction or conducting the test";

(iii) after "the person receiving the instruction", there shall be inserted "or undergoing the test";

(29) In Schedule 11, in Part B—

(a) at the end of paragraph 1(2)(b) there shall be added the following sub-paragraph—

"(c) Every pilot included in the flight crew who is seated at the flying controls during take-off or landing shall within the relevant period:—

(i) have been tested as to his proficiency in using instrument approach-to-land systems of the type in use at the aerodromes of intended landing and any alternate aerodromes, such test being carried out either in flight in instrument flight conditions or in instrument flight conditions simulated by means approved by the Authority or under the supervision of a person approved by the Authority for the purpose by means of a flight simulator approved by the Authority; and

(ii) have carried out when seated at the flying controls not less than three take-offs and three landings in aircraft of the type to be used on the flight".

(*b*) sub-paragraphs (5)(*a*)(ii), (5)(*a*)(iii) and (6) of paragraph 1 shall be deleted;

(*c*) in sub-paragraph (7)(*a*) of paragraph 1, for "sub-paragraph (5)(*a*)(iii) and (6)(*b*)" there shall be substituted "sub-paragraph (2)(*c*)(ii);";

(*d*) for sub-paragraph (7)(*b*) of paragraph 1, there shall be substituted—

"(*b*) in the case of sub-paragraphs (2)(*a*)(ii), (2)(*b*)(ii), (2)(*c*)(i) and (3)(*b*) of this paragraph, of 6 months;".

N. E. Leigh,
Clerk of the Privy Council.

EXPLANATORY NOTE

(This Note is not part of the Order.)

This Order amends the Air Navigation Order 1976.

In addition to some minor and drafting amendments the following changes are made:

(1) The holder of a flight crew licence or an air traffic controller's licence may now be permitted by the Authority to continue to exercise the privileges of her licence during pregnancy subject to such conditions as the Authority thinks fit. Previously the licence was deemed to be suspended upon confirmation of the pregnancy and remained so suspended until the pregnancy had ended and the licence holder had been examined and pronounced fit to resume the exercise of those privileges. (Article 3(10) and (22))

(2) A person who gives instruction in flying a glider to any person for the purpose of becoming qualified for the grant of a Commercial Pilot's Licence (Gliders) must now have a flying instructor's rating or an assistant flying instructor's rating included in his licence. (Article 3(11))

(3) Helicopters of less than 3000 kgs maximum total weight authorised and with a seating capacity not exceeding 5 persons may now fly on a flight for the purpose of public transport without the prior preparation of a load sheet. Additionally all helicopters may now carry both copies of the load sheet, if required to be completed in the aircraft in a container of a type approved by the Authority. Previously one copy of the load sheet was required to be kept elsewhere than in the aircraft. (Article 3(12))

(4) A helicopter designated by its certificate of airworthiness as being of performance Group B may not now fly for the purpose of public transport over water further than 20 seconds flying time from a point at which it could make an autorotative descent to land, unless it is equipped with flotation apparatus or if it is so equipped, further than 3 minutes flying time from that point. Additionally a helicopter of the same designation may not now fly for the purpose of public transport along the River Thames helicopter route without being equipped with flotation apparatus. (Article 3(13))

(5) A helicopter designated by its certificate of airworthiness as being of performance Group A2 may not now fly for the purpose of public transport over water for more than 15 minutes during any flight unless it is equipped with flotation apparatus. (Article 3(13))

(6) An aircraft may not now fly in prescribed airspace unless it is equipped with navigation systems which enable the aircraft to maintain the prescribed navigation performance capability, the equipment is installed and maintained in a manner approved by the Authority and the equipment is operated in accordance with operating procedures approved by the Authority while the aircraft is flying within the prescribed airspace. Under Article 90(1) of the Air Navigation Order 1976, "prescribed" means prescribed in regulations made by the Secretary of State under that Order. (Article 3(15))

(7) In aeroplanes which are required to be equipped with cockpit voice recorders that equipment must now be in use whenever the aircraft is in flight. Such an aeroplane may, however, now fly notwithstanding that its flight recorder has become unserviceable if it flies with the approval of the Authority. (Article 3(16)).

(8) The definition of "munitions of war", which under Article 40 of the Air Navigation Order 1976 may not be carried in aircraft, is now extended to include weapons or ammunition designed for use against the person, whether or not in warfare and parts designed for such weapons or ammunition. (Article 3(19))

(9) Only those pilots who are seated at the flying controls of public transport aircraft during take-off or landing are now required to undergo the tests and practice hitherto required by Schedule 11, Part B paragraph 1(6). (Article 3(30))

STATUTORY INSTRUMENTS

1977 No. 1256

COPYRIGHT

The Copyright (International Conventions) (Amendment No. 3) Order 1977

Made - - - -		26th July 1977
Laid before Parliament		3rd August 1977
Coming into Operation		24th August 1977

At the Court at Buckingham Palace, the 26th day of July 1977

Present,

The Queen's Most Excellent Majesty in Council

Her Majesty, by and with the advice of Her Privy Council, and by virtue of the authority conferred upon Her by sections 31, 32 and 47 of the Copyright Act 1956(a) and of all other powers enabling Her in that behalf, is pleased to order, and it is hereby ordered, as follows:

1.—(1) This Order may be cited as the Copyright (International Conventions) (Amendment No. 3) Order 1977, and shall come into operation on 24th August 1977.

(2) The Interpretation Act 1889(b) shall apply to the interpretation of this Order as it applies to the interpretation of an Act of Parliament.

2. The Copyright (International Conventions) Order 1972(c), as amended(d), shall be further amended as follows:

(a) in Schedule 3 (countries in whose case copyright in sound recordings includes the exclusive right of public performance and broadcasting) there shall be included a reference to Uruguay;

(b) in Schedules 4 and 5 (countries whose broadcasting organisations have copyright protection in relation to their sound and television broadcasts) there shall be included references to Uruguay and related references to 24th August 1977 in the list of dates in each of those two Schedules.

3.—(1) This Order except for Article 2(b) shall extend to all the countries mentioned in the Schedule hereto.

(2) Article 2(b) shall extend to Gibraltar and Bermuda.

N. E. Leigh,
Clerk of the Privy Council.

(a) 1956 c. 74.　　　(b) 1889 c. 63.　　　(c) S.I. 1972/673 (1972 I, p. 2172).
(d) The amendments are not relevant to the subject matter of this Order.

SCHEDULE

COUNTRIES TO WHICH THIS ORDER EXTENDS

Bermuda

Belize

British Virgin Islands

Cayman Islands

Falkland Islands and Dependencies

Gibraltar

Hong Kong

Isle of Man

Montserrat

St. Helena and its Dependencies

EXPLANATORY NOTE

(This Note is not part of the Order.)

This Order further amends the Copyright (International Conventions) Order 1972. It takes account of the accession of Uruguay to the International Convention for the Protection of Performers, Producers of Phonograms and Broadcasting Organisations.

The Order extends, so far as is appropriate, to dependent countries of the Commonwealth to which the 1972 Order extends.

STATUTORY INSTRUMENTS

1977 No. 1257

HOVERCRAFT

The Hovercraft (Application of Enactments) (Amendment) Order 1977

Laid before Parliament in draft

Made -   -   -   -   *26th July* 1977

Coming into Operation   *27th July* 1977

At the Court at Buckingham Palace, the 26th day of July 1977

Present,

The Queen's Most Excellent Majesty in Council

Whereas a draft of this Order has been laid before Parliament and has been approved by a resolution of each House of Parliament in accordance with section 1(4) of the Hovercraft Act 1968**(a)**:

Now, therefore, Her Majesty, in exercise of the powers conferred upon Her by section 1(1)(*h*) and (*k*) and by section 1(3) of the Hovercraft Act 1968, and of all other powers enabling Her in that behalf, is pleased, by and with the advice of Her Privy Council, to order, and it is hereby ordered, as follows:—

1. This Order may be cited as the Hovercraft (Application of Enactments) (Amendment) Order 1977 and shall come into operation on 27th July 1977.

2. The Interpretation Act 1889**(b)** shall apply for the interpretation of this Order as it applies for the interpretation of an Act of Parliament and as if this Order and the Orders hereby revoked were Acts of Parliament.

3. For the provisions relating to the Collision Regulations (Ships and Sea-planes on the Water) and Signals of Distress (Ships) Order 1965 in columns 1, 2 and 3 of Part B of Schedule 1 to the Hovercraft (Application of Enactments) Order 1972**(c)** there shall be substituted the following:—

(a) 1968 c. 59.   **(b)** 1889 c. 63.
(c) S.I. 1972/971 (1972 II, p. 3024).

"Column 1	Column 2	Column 3
Instruments applied	References	Modifications in relation to hovercraft or activities or places connected therewith (if any)
The Collision Regulations and Distress Signals Order 1977	S.I. 1977/982.	(1) For Article 3(1)(*b*) there shall be substituted "to all United Kingdom registered hovercraft and to all other hovercraft within United Kingdom territorial waters" (2) For Article 3(2) there shall be substituted "The provisions of section 21 of the 1949 Act (distress signals) shall apply to all United Kingdom registered hovercraft, and to all other hovercraft within United Kingdom territorial waters." "

4. The Collision Regulations (Ships and Seaplanes on the Water) and Signals of Distress (Ships) Order 1965(**a**), as amended(**b**), in their application to hovercraft, are hereby revoked.

N. E. Leigh,
Clerk of the Privy Council.

EXPLANATORY NOTE

(This Note is not part of the Order.)

This Order amends the Hovercraft (Application of Enactments) Order 1972 by substituting for references in Schedule 1 thereto to the Collision Regulations (Ships and Seaplanes on the Water) and Signals of Distress (Ships) Order 1965, references to the Collision Regulations and Distress Signals Order 1977. Modifications are made to the 1977 Order so as to apply the provisions of the Collision Regulations and the distress signals to United Kingdom registered hovercraft and to all other hovercraft within United Kingdom territorial waters. The Collision Regulations (Ships and Seaplanes on the Water) and Signals of Distress (Ships) Order 1965, as amended, in their application to hovercraft, are revoked.

(**a**) S.I. 1965/1525 (1965 II, p. 4411).
(**b**) S.I. 1972/809, 1974/1890 (1972 II, p. 2602; 1974 III, p. 6501).

STATUTORY INSTRUMENTS

1977 No. 1258

CIVIL AVIATION

The Tokyo Convention (Certification of Countries) Order 1977

Made - - - -   *26th July* 1977

At the Court at Buckingham Palace, the 26th day of July 1977

Present,

The Queen's Most Excellent Majesty in Council

Her Majesty, in exercise of the powers conferred upon Her by section 7(1) of the Tokyo Convention Act 1967(a) (which provides that Her Majesty may by Order in Council certify which countries are Convention countries, that is to say countries in which the Convention on Offences and certain other Acts Committed on board Aircraft signed in Tokyo on 14th September 1963 is for the time being in force) and of all other powers enabling Her in that behalf is pleased, by and with the advice of Her Privy Council, to order, and it is hereby ordered, as follows:

1. This Order may be cited as the Tokyo Convention (Certification of Countries) Order 1977.

2.—(1) The Tokyo Convention (Certification of Countries) Order 1971(b) is hereby revoked.

(2) Section 38(2) of the Interpretation Act 1889(c) (which relates to the effect of repeals) shall apply to this Order as if this Order were an Act of Parliament and as if the Order revoked by this Article were an Act of Parliament thereby repealed.

3. It is hereby certified that the countries listed in the Schedule hereto are Convention countries.

N. E. Leigh,
Clerk of the Privy Council.

(a) 1967 c. 52.   (b) S.I. 1971/2118 (1971 III, p. 6244).   (c) 1889 c. 63.

SCHEDULE

The United Kingdom of Great Britain and Northern Ireland
    The Channel Islands
    The Isle of Man
    Belize
    Bermuda
    British Antarctic Territory
    British Indian Ocean Territory
    British Virgin Islands
    Cayman Islands
    The Sovereign Base Areas of Akrotiri and Dhekelia in the island of Cyprus
    Falkland Islands and Dependencies
    Gibraltar
    Gilbert Islands
    Hong Kong
    Montserrat
    Pitcairn, Henderson, Ducie and Oeno Islands
    St. Helena and Dependencies
    Solomon Islands
    Turks and Caicos Islands
    Tuvalu
Afghanistan
Argentine Republic
Australia and all territories subject to the sovereignty or authority of Australia
Austria
Bahamas
Barbados
Belgium
Brazil
Burundi
Canada
Chad
Chile
Colombia
Costa Rica
Cyprus
Denmark and the Faroe Islands
Dominican Republic
Ecuador
Egypt
Fiji
Finland
France and all territories subject to the sovereignty or authority of France
Gabon
The Federal Republic of Germany
Ghana
Greece
Guatemala
Hungary
Iceland
India
Indonesia
Iran
Iraq
The Republic of Ireland
Israel
Italy
Ivory Coast
Japan
Jordan
Kenya

SCHEDULE—*continued*

The Republic of Korea
Laos
Lebanon
Lesotho
Libya
Luxembourg
The Democratic Republic of Madagascar
Malawi
Mali
Mexico
Morocco
The Netherlands except the Netherlands Antilles
New Zealand
Nicaragua
Niger
Nigeria
Norway and all territories subject to the sovereignty or authority of Norway
Oman
Pakistan
Panama
Papua New Guinea
Paraguay
The Philippines
Poland
Portugal and all territories subject to the sovereignty or authority of Portugal
Romania
Rwanda
Saudi Arabia
Senegal
Seychelles
Sierra Leone
Singapore
South Africa
Spain and all territories subject to the sovereignty or authority of Spain
Sweden
Switzerland
Thailand
Togo
Trinidad and Tobago
Tunisia
Turkey
The United States of America and all territories subject to the sovereignty or authority
of the United States of America
Upper Volta
Uruguay
Yugoslavia
Zambia

EXPLANATORY NOTE

(This Note is not part of the Order.)

This Order revokes and replaces the Tokyo Convention (Certification of Countries) Order 1971. It certifies in which countries the Convention on Offences and certain other Acts Committed on board Aircraft, signed in Tokyo on 14th September 1963, is for the time being in force. Under section 7(1) of the Tokyo Convention Act 1967 this Order is conclusive evidence of the matters certified.

STATUTORY INSTRUMENTS

1977 No. 1259

VALUE ADDED TAX

The Value Added Tax (Self-Supply) (Amendment) Order 1977

Made - - - - - -	*25th July* 1977
Laid before the House of Commons	*26th July* 1977
Coming into Operation - - -	*1st October* 1977

The Treasury, in exercise of the powers conferred on them by sections 6(1) and 21(2) of the Finance Act 1972(a) and of all other powers enabling them in that behalf, hereby make the following Order:—

1. This Order may be cited as the Value Added Tax (Self-Supply) (Amendment) Order 1977 and shall come into operation on 1st October 1977.

2. The Interpretation Act 1889(b) shall apply for the interpretation of this Order as it applies for the interpretation of an Act of Parliament.

3. In Article 3(2)(*b*) of the Value Added Tax (Self-Supply) (No. 2) Order 1972(c), for "£5,000" in the second line thereof there shall be substituted "£7,500".

David Stoddart,
T. M. Cox,
Two of the Lords Commissioners
of Her Majesty's Treasury.

25th July 1977.

EXPLANATORY NOTE
(This Note is not part of the Order.)

This Order increases from £5,000 to £7,500 the value of certain supplies of printed matter, as specified by the Value Added Tax (Self-Supply) (No. 2) Order 1972, which must be made by a person before that Order will apply to those supplies.

(a) 1972 c. 41.   (b) 1889 c. 63.   (c) S.I. 1972/1169 (1972 II, p. 3473).

STATUTORY INSTRUMENTS

1977 No. 1260

AGRICULTURE

LIVESTOCK INDUSTRIES

·The Artificial Insemination of Cattle (England and Wales) Regulations 1977

Made - - -	*25th July* 1977	
Laid before Parliament	*27th July* 1977	
Coming into Operation	*1st September* 1977	

The Minister of Agriculture, Fisheries and Food, in exercise of the powers conferred upon him by section 17 of the Agriculture (Miscellaneous Provisions) Act 1943(a), and of all other powers enabling him in that behalf, hereby makes the following regulations:—

PART I

INTRODUCTORY

Citation, extent and commencement

1. These regulations may be cited as the Artificial Insemination of Cattle (England and Wales) Regulations 1977, shall apply to England and Wales and shall come into operation on 1st September 1977.

Interpretation

2.—(1) In these regulations, unless the context otherwise requires—

"animal" includes a domestic fowl, turkey, goose and duck;

"approved bull" means a bull which is approved for the time being—

    (*a*) by the Minister under regulation 5, or

    (*b*) by the Secretary of State for Scotland under regulation 5 of the Artificial Insemination of Cattle (Scotland) Regulations 1977(b);

"artificial insemination" means the artificial insemination of a cow;

"building" includes part of a building;

"centre storage licence" means a licence granted pursuant to regulation 7(1)(*c*);

"cow" includes heifer;

"embryo transfer unit" means premises wholly or mainly used for the purpose of the collection or the transference of embryos of cattle and "exempted embryo transfer unit" means an embryo transfer unit in respect of which a certificate issued by the Minister is in force certifying that the unit is an exempted embryo transfer unit for the purpose of these regulations;

(a) 1943 c. 16.   (b) S.I. 1977/1230 (1977 II, p. 3422).

"evaluation" in relation to semen means the examination of semen from a bull and the assessment of its suitability for use in artificial insemination;

"farm" includes an embryo transfer unit and a research or experimental establishment;

"farm storage licence" means a licence granted pursuant to regulation 7(1)(*e*);

"farm storage servicing licence" means a licence granted pursuant to regulation 7(1)(*f*);

"flask" means a cryogenic flask;

"the Minister" means the Minister of Agriculture, Fisheries and Food;

"owner" includes a joint owner and any person having authorised possessory use, and "ownership" shall be construed accordingly;

"process", in relation to semen, means all or any of the following:—
 (*a*) dilute (except for the purpose of, or in the course of, the evaluation of semen);
 (*b*) add any substance which is calculated to prolong the natural life of the semen;
 (*c*) package into straws;
 (*d*) freeze (except for the purpose of, or in the course of, the evaluation of semen);

and "processing" shall be construed accordingly, except that the processing of semen shall not be regarded as completed until all the processes listed in the next definition have been carried out;

"processed", in relation to semen, means, except where the context otherwise requires, semen which has passed through all the following processes:—
 (*a*) dilution;
 (*b*) addition of any substance which is calculated to prolong the natural life of the semen;
 (*c*) packaging into straws;
 (*d*) freezing;

"processing centre" means premises specified in a processing licence;

"processing licence" means a licence granted pursuant to regulation 7(1)(*a*);

"prohibited area" means—
 (*a*) an infected place or area within the meaning of section 10(2) of the Diseases of Animals Act 1950(**a**) declared to be infected with—
  (i) foot and mouth disease, or
  (ii) any other disease in relation to which an order made under section 11 of the said Act prohibits or regulates the removal of semen into, within or out of that infected place or area, or

_____
(**a**) 1950 c. 36.

(*b*) premises into or from which the movement of cattle, sheep or swine is prohibited or regulated by a notice served under any order made under the said Act which notice prohibits the movement of semen;

"qualified person" means any one of the following:—

(*a*) a veterinary surgeon;

(*b*) a veterinary practitioner; and

(*c*) a person, not being a veterinary surgeon or a veterinary practitioner, who collects semen under the direction of a veterinary surgeon approved by the Minister in this behalf;

"quarantine" means holding in isolation;

"quarantine centre" means premises specified in a quarantine licence;

"quarantine licence" means a licence granted pursuant to regulation 7(1)(*b*);

"raw semen" means semen which has not been diluted or treated in any way so as to prolong its natural life;

"research or experimental establishment" means premises on which research into or experiments with cattle-breeding is or are carried out and "exempted research or experimental establishment" means a research or experimental establishment in respect of which a certificate issued by the Minister is in force certifying that the establishment is an exempted research or experimental establishment for the purposes of these regulations;

"semen" means semen collected from a bull;

"storage centre" means premises specified in a centre storage licence;

"straw" means a container holding one dose of processed semen for use in artificial insemination;

"supply licence" means a licence granted pursuant to regulation 7(1)(*d*);

"veterinary practitioner" means a person registered in the supplementary veterinary register kept under section 8 of the Veterinary Surgeons Act 1966(**a**); and

"veterinary surgeon" means a person registered in the register of veterinary surgeons kept under section 2 of the Veterinary Surgeons Act 1966.

(2) References in these regulations to any enactment or regulations are (unless the context otherwise requires) references thereto as from time to time amended or replaced.

(3) Any reference in these regulations to a numbered regulation or Schedule shall be construed as a reference to the regulation or Schedule so numbered in these regulations.

(4) The Interpretation Act 1889(**b**) shall apply for the interpretation of these regulations as it applies for the interpretation of an Act of Parliament, and as if these regulations and the regulations hereby revoked were Acts of Parliament.

(a) 1966 c. 36.　　　　　　　　　　　　　(b) 1889 c. 63.

STOKE-ON-TRENT
CITY
LIBRARIES

Revocation

3. The Artificial Insemination of Cattle (England and Wales) Regulations 1957(**a**) are hereby revoked.

Application of regulations

4.—(1) These regulations shall not apply to anything done by a permitted person in the course of or for the purpose of the artificial insemination of a cow with raw semen which has been collected from a bull by a permitted person when, at the time of such insemination, the cow is—

(*a*) in the same ownership as the bull from which the semen is collected;

(*b*) kept on land occupied by the owner of the bull; and

(*c*) comprised in the same herd as the bull.

(2) Nothing in these regulations shall apply to anything done in the course of or for the purpose of the artificial insemination of a cow—

(*a*) on an exempted embryo transfer unit with raw semen which has been collected from a bull by a qualified person, or

(*b*) on an exempted research or experimental establishment with semen which has been collected from a bull by a qualified person.

(3) In paragraph (1) of this regulation, "permitted person" means—

(*a*) the owner of the bull from which semen is collected;

(*b*) a person in the regular and sole employment of the owner of the bull;

(*c*) a veterinary surgeon; or

(*d*) a veterinary practitioner.

PART II

APPROVAL OF BULLS

Bulls for use in artificial insemination

5.—(1) For the purposes of these regulations the Minister may on application made to him by or on behalf of the owner of a bull approve the bull for use in artificial insemination.

(2) The Minister may require an applicant for approval of a bull for use in artificial insemination—

(*a*) to furnish him with such information as the Minister may deem necessary for proper consideration of the application, and

(*b*) to permit the bull to be subjected to such isolation and to such veterinary tests or examinations as the Minister may deem necessary.

(3) In considering whether or not to approve a bull for use in artificial insemination the Minister shall have regard to the health of the bull and may take into account the health of other cattle with which that bull may have been in contact and the genetic qualities and physical characteristics, including abnormalities or defects of any kind, of the bull and its progeny.

(**a**) S.I. 1957/948 (1957 I, p. 165).

(4) The Minister may approve a bull for use in artificial insemination without condition or subject to the following conditions or to one or more of them—

(*a*) that the approved bull shall be subjected to such further isolation, and shall satisfy the Minister with regard to such further veterinary investigations, as may be specified;

(*b*) that only during a specified period shall semen of the approved bull be collected for use in artificial insemination;

(*c*) that the amount of semen which may be supplied for use in the artificial insemination of cows comprised in a herd other than a herd in the same ownership as the approved bull shall not exceed a specified total amount;

(*d*) that the semen of the approved bull shall be supplied for use in the artificial insemination only of cows comprised in such herd or herds as may be specified;

(*e*) that semen for use in artificial insemination shall be collected from the approved bull only on specified premises.

(5) Where a bull is approved subject to one or more of the conditions set out in the preceding paragraph, that condition or those conditions shall be binding on the owner for the time being of the approved bull.

(6) Where a bull is approved subject to one or both of the conditions set out in sub-paragraphs (*c*) and (*d*) of paragraph (4) above, the owner of semen from that bull shall not knowingly supply that semen for use in such a way that there is a breach of either or both of those conditions.

(7) Where the Minister has approved a bull for use in artificial insemination subject to the condition set out in paragraph (4)(*c*) of this regulation, notice of any subsequent change of ownership of that bull or of any subsequent disposal of semen from that bull shall be given to the Minister by the owner of that bull or semen: Provided that no notice shall be required to be given to the Minister in respect of semen which is moved from a storage centre pursuant to regulation 22(2)(*c*) or (*d*).

(8) Where the owner of an approved bull or the owner of any semen from an approved bull knows or suspects that any progeny of that bull has shown signs of any abnormality the owner shall as soon as is practicable give notice of that knowledge or suspicion to the Minister, and if subsequently so directed by the Minister to any person whom that owner reasonably believes to be in possession of semen from that bull.

(9) The Minister may at any time by notice to such persons as the Minister shall consider appropriate—

(*a*) cancel or vary any condition subject to which a bull was approved or may subject the approval of the bull to any of the conditions specified in paragraph (4) of this regulation not previously imposed, or

(*b*) withdraw the approval of the bull.

(10) On the death of an approved bull, the owner shall forthwith give notice to the Minister of the death and the circumstances in which it occurred.

Part III

Licences

General prohibition of evaluation, etc., of semen

6. The evaluation, processing, keeping in quarantine, storage or movement from a storage centre of semen, or the causing or permitting of such evaluation, processing, keeping in quarantine, storage or movement, or the delivery to farms of equipment or materials required for the storage and use of semen in artificial insemination, or the servicing whilst on a farm of such equipment, is hereby prohibited except under the authority of and in accordance with the conditions of a licence issued by the Minister and for the time being in force.

Licences

7.—(1) For the purposes of these regulations the Minister may on application made to him grant one or more of the following licences—

(*a*) a processing licence;

(*b*) a quarantine licence;

(*c*) a centre storage licence;

(*d*) a supply licence;

(*e*) a farm storage licence;

(*f*) a farm storage servicing licence.

(2) Where the Minister grants two or more licences to the same person he may, if he thinks fit, grant the licences in the form of a combined licence.

(3) A processing licence shall authorise the licensee named therein to evaluate or process semen on such premises ("a processing centre") as are specified in the licence.

(4) A quarantine licence shall authorise the licensee named therein to keep processed semen in quarantine on such premises ("a quarantine centre") as are specified in the licence.

(5) A centre storage licence shall authorise the licensee named therein to store processed semen on such premises ("a storage centre") as are specified in the licence and to move semen from those premises in accordance with regulation 22(1).

(6) A supply licence shall authorise the licensee named therein to move processed semen from a storage centre in accordance with regulation 22(2).

(7) A farm storage licence shall authorise the licensee named therein to store processed semen on a farm specified in the licence and to use or cause such semen to be used in the artificial insemination of cows which are kept on the farm or farms specified in the licence and which are, except where the farm is an exempted embryo transfer unit or an exempted research or experimental establishment, owned by the licensee.

(8) A farm storage servicing licence shall authorise the licensee named therein to deliver to farms equipment or materials (including liquid nitrogen for farm storage flasks) required for the storage and use of semen or to service such equipment in accordance with regulation 25.

PART IV

COLLECTION, EVALUATION AND PROCESSING OF SEMEN

Collection of semen

8. No person shall collect semen from a bull for evaluation or processing unless he is a qualified person.

9. No person shall collect semen from a bull for processing unless that bull is an approved bull and—

(a) is at a processing centre, or

(b) where the approval of the bull for use in artificial insemination was subject to the conditions set out in regulation 5(4)(a) of these regulations, has been kept in isolation on premises specified in the approval of the bull under regulation 5(4)(e) since the commencement of the veterinary investigations specified under regulation 5(4)(a).

10.—(1) Where the collection of semen is to take place on the premises specified in the approval of the bull under regulation 5(4)(e), a teaser animal may be used only if authorised by a qualified person.

(2) In this regulation "teaser animal" means a bovine animal which is used as an aid in the collection of semen from a bull.

Delivery of semen for evaluation or processing

11. No person shall—

(a) submit for processing at a processing centre semen collected from a bull kept on that centre, or

(b) deliver semen to a processing centre for evaluation or processing,

unless he is a qualified person.

Evaluation of semen

12.—(1) No person shall accept semen for evaluation unless it is submitted to him by a qualified person on the processing centre where the semen was collected, or is delivered to him at a processing centre by a qualified person.

(2) No person shall evaluate semen or cause or permit semen to be evaluated except under the authority of and in accordance with the conditions of a processing licence for the time being in force.

Processing of semen

13.—(1) No person shall accept semen for processing unless either it is submitted to him by a qualified person on the processing centre where the semen was collected, or it is delivered to him at a processing centre and

(a) is delivered by a qualified person, or

(b) comes from another processing centre in Great Britain for completion of processing.

(2) No person shall process semen or cause or permit semen to be processed unless he knows or reasonably believes it to be semen collected from an approved bull.

(3) No person shall process semen or cause or permit semen to be processed except under the authority of and in accordance with the provisions of a processing licence for the time being in force.

Conditions of processing licences

14. A processing licence shall be issued subject to such of the conditions set out in Schedule 1, and to such other conditions (if any), as may be specified in the licence.

Movement of semen from a processing centre

15.—(1) No person shall move semen or cause or permit semen to be moved from a processing centre except direct—

  (*a*) in the case of partially processed semen to another processing centre in Great Britain, or to an exempted research or experimental establishment,

  (*b*) in the case of processed semen to a quarantine centre in Great Britain, or

  (*c*) to a place outside Great Britain.

(2) The person to whom a processing licence is granted shall as soon as is reasonably practicable after processing of the semen has been completed move the semen or cause it to be moved direct to—

  (*a*) a quarantine centre in Great Britain, or

  (*b*) a place outside Great Britain.

Part V

Quarantine of Semen

Acceptance of semen to be kept in quarantine

16. No person shall accept semen to be kept in quarantine unless—

  (*a*) it is delivered to him at a quarantine centre, and

  (*b*) it comes from a processing centre in Great Britain or is imported into Great Britain under a licence issued under section 17(3) of the Agriculture (Miscellaneous Provisions) Act 1943.

Keeping of semen in quarantine

17. No person shall keep semen in quarantine or cause or permit semen to be kept in quarantine except under the authority of and in accordance with the conditions of a quarantine licence for the time being in force.

Conditions of quarantine licences

18. A quarantine licence shall be issued subject to such of the conditions set out in Schedule 2, and to such other conditions (if any), as may be specified in the licence.

Movement of semen from a quarantine centre

19.—(1) Subject to the provisions of paragraph (4) of this regulation no person shall move semen or cause or permit semen to be moved from a quarantine centre until the semen has been kept there for a period of twenty-eight days.

(2) No person shall move semen or cause or permit semen to be moved from a quarantine centre except direct—

(*a*) to a storage centre in Great Britain, or

(*b*) to a place outside Great Britain.

(3) Subject to the provisions of paragraph (4) of this regulation, the person to whom a quarantine licence is granted shall as soon as practicable after semen has been kept at the quarantine centre for twenty-eight days move the semen or cause it to be moved direct—

(*a*) to a storage centre in Great Britain, or

(*b*) to a place outside Great Britain.

(4) Nothing in this regulation shall prevent the movement of semen from a quarantine centre direct to a place outside Great Britain before it has been kept there for twenty-eight days.

PART VI

STORAGE, SUPPLY AND USE OF SEMEN

Acceptance of semen for storage

20. No person shall accept semen for storage unless either—

(*a*) the semen—

(i) is delivered to him at a storage centre, and

(ii) comes from another storage centre in Great Britain or from a quarantine centre in Great Britain, or is imported into Great Britain under a licence issued under section 17(3) of the Agriculture (Miscellaneous Provisions) Act 1943; or

(*b*) the semen—

(i) is delivered to him at a building specified in the farm storage licence granted to him, and

(ii) comes from the storage centre specified in the farm storage licence as the storage centre from which he may obtain semen.

Storage of semen

21. No person shall store semen or cause or permit semen to be stored except—

(1) under the authority of and in accordance with the conditions of a centre storage licence for the time being in force, or

(2) under the authority of and in accordance with the conditions of a farm storage licence for the time being in force.

Movement of semen from a storage centre

22. No person shall move semen or cause or permit semen to be moved from a storage centre except under the authority of and in accordance with the conditions of a centre storage licence or a supply licence for the time being in force and—

(1) in the case of a storage centre in respect of which a centre storage licence only is granted in accordance with regulation 7(1)(c) direct—

    (*a*) to another storage centre in Great Britain, or

    (*b*) to a place outside Great Britain;

(2) in the case of a storage centre in respect of which a supply licence is also granted in accordance with regulation 7(1)(d)—

    (*a*) direct to another storage centre in Great Britain,

    (*b*) direct to a place outside Great Britain,

    (*c*) by means of an artificial insemination service to farms situate within the area designated in the supply licence, or

    (*d*) to any person who by virtue of a farm storage licence granted to him is entitled to obtain semen from that storage centre.

Conditions of licences for the storage and supply of semen

23.—(1) A centre storage licence shall be issued subject to such of the conditions set out in Schedule 3, and to such other conditions (if any), as may be specified in the licence.

(2) A supply licence shall be issued subject to such of the conditions set out in Schedule 4, and to such other conditions (if any), as may be specified in the licence.

(3) A farm storage licence shall be issued subject to such of the conditions set out in Schedule 5, and to such other conditions (if any), as may be specified in the licence.

General prohibition on use of semen

24. No person shall use semen from a bull in the artificial insemination of a cow unless—

(*a*) that semen has been obtained from a storage centre in accordance with the provisions of these regulations, and

(*b*) he is—

    (i) a veterinary surgeon,

    (ii) a veterinary practitioner,

    (iii) a full-time employee of the holder of a supply licence who complies with the requirements of the conditions of the licence relating to such an employee,

    (iv) the holder of a farm storage licence or a full-time employee of such holder who complies with the requirements of the conditions of the licence relating to such holder or employee as the case may be, or

    (v) a person employed as a full-time inseminator by the holder of a supply licence.

PART VII

FARM STORAGE SERVICING

Delivery and service of equipment required for storage and use of semen

25. No person shall deliver to a farm equipment or materials (including liquid nitrogen for farm storage flasks) required for the storage and use of semen in artificial insemination, or service such equipment whilst on the farm, except under the authority of and in accordance with the conditions of a farm storage servicing licence for the time being in force:

Provided that nothing in this regulation shall prevent the holder of a farm storage licence from servicing equipment which belongs to him, or from collecting any equipment or materials for use on his own farm.

Conditions of licences for farm storage servicing

26. A farm storage servicing licence shall be issued subject to such of the conditions set out in Schedule 6, and to such other conditions (if any), as may be specified in the licence.

PART VIII

GENERAL

Applications, etc., to be in writing

27. Any application, approval, authorisation, certificate, consent, direction, licence or notice made, given or granted for the purposes of these regulations, shall be in writing.

Offences

28. No person shall—

(a) furnish any information required under regulation 5(2)(a),

(b) give any certificate required by any condition of a licence under these regulations, or

(c) for the purpose of obtaining a licence under these regulations make any statement or furnish any information,

which he knows to be false or does not believe to be true.

Transitional provisions

29.—(1) Where immediately before the coming into operation of these regulations there was in force in respect of a bull a licence issued by the Minister under the Artificial Insemination of Cattle (England and Wales) Regulations 1957 or by the Secretary of State for Scotland under the Artificial Insemination of Cattle (Scotland) Regulations 1957(a) permitting the distribution or sale of semen from the bull, the bull shall for the purposes of these regulations be deemed to be an approved bull, and these regulations shall apply in respect of the bull and its semen as they apply to an approved bull and its semen.

(a) 1957/1954 (1957 I, p. 168).

(2) Where immediately before the coming into operation of these regulations the owner of semen was entitled by virtue of regulation 4(2)(*a*) of the Artificial Insemination of Cattle (England and Wales) Regulations 1957 or regulation 3(2)(*a*) of the Artificial Insemination of Cattle (Scotland) Regulations 1957 to use semen without a licence, that owner may continue to use that semen in the artificial insemination of cows belonging to him, and the bull from which the semen was taken shall, for that purpose only, be deemed to be an approved bull.

(3) Where a bull is deemed to be an approved bull by virtue of paragraph (1) above, and the licence issued in respect of it imposed a limit on the amount of semen which could be distributed or sold, then the amount of semen which may be supplied for use in the artificial insemination of cows comprised in a herd other than a herd in the same ownership as the bull shall not exceed that limit, reduced by the amount of its semen which was distributed or sold under the licence before the coming into operation of these regulations.

(4) Where a bull is deemed to be an approved bull by virtue of paragraph (1) above, and the licence issued in respect of it provided that its semen could be distributed or sold for use only in a specified herd or specified herds, then the semen of that bull shall be supplied only for use in the artificial insemination of cows comprised in the herd or herds so specified.

(5) Where a bull is deemed to be an approved bull by virtue of paragraph (1) or (2) above, then that bull—

  (*a*) shall be subjected to such isolation, and undergo such veterinary investigations, as the Minister may by notice direct; and

  (*b*) shall, if the Minister so directs, cease to be so deemed.

In Witness whereof the Official Seal of the Minister of Agriculture, Fisheries and Food is hereunto affixed on 25th July 1977.

(L.S.)

John Silkin,
Minister of Agriculture, Fisheries and Food.

SCHEDULE 1   Regulation 14

Conditions to which processing licences are generally subject

1. Except with the consent of the Minister no bull or other animal shall be brought on to a processing centre.

2. If the Minister, for reasons of disease prevention, directs that any animal be removed from a processing centre the animal shall be removed from the processing centre forthwith.

3. Except with the consent of the Minister no semen of any animal other than a bull shall be brought on to a processing centre.

4. Evaluation or examination of semen from a bull which is not an approved bull shall, after appropriate hygiene precautions have been taken, be conducted as an entirely separate operation and at an entirely separate time from the processing of semen, and semen which is accepted for evaluation or examination from such a bull shall be destroyed as soon as is reasonably practicable after any part of it has been evaluated or examined.

5. All equipment, apparatus and materials of any kind used for the evaluation or examination of semen from an unapproved bull shall be either destroyed or cleansed and disinfected before being used for the evaluation or processing of semen from an approved bull.

6. If the Minister, in order to prevent the risk of disease or the transmission of genetic abnormality, directs that semen be removed from a processing centre it shall be removed therefrom and if to the same end he directs that semen be destroyed on a processing centre it shall be destroyed there.

7. Where a processing centre is within a prohibited area no semen shall be delivered to or moved from that centre without the consent of the Minister.

8. Except with the consent of the Minister no semen shall be moved from a processing centre which is outside a prohibited area to a quarantine centre which is within such an area.

9. The licensee shall—

(a) keep such records as are set out in paragraph 10 of this Schedule;

(b) retain each entry in the records for two years after it is made;

(c) produce all such records for inspection by a duly authorised officer of the Minister at any reasonable time on request; and

(d) render to the Minister in such form and at such times as he may direct returns relating to such records or any part of them.

10. The records referred to in paragraph 9 above shall be kept for all semen collected or received, processed, moved, removed or destroyed and shall show: the date and place of semen collection or the date on which the semen was received from another processing centre and the name and address of that centre; the name, breed or type, earmarks or herd book number of the donor bull; the date of semen evaluation or processing; the quantity of semen obtained after processing; and the date and quantity of semen moved and the address to which it was moved or the date and quantity of semen removed or destroyed and by whom removed or destroyed.

Regulation 18   SCHEDULE 2

Conditions to which quarantine licences are generally subject

1. No bull or other animal shall be brought on to a quarantine centre.

2. The licensee shall take suitable precautions to ensure that persons entering the quarantine centre have not been in recent contact with cattle, sheep, pigs or goats.

3. If the Minister in order to prevent the risk of disease or the transmission of genetic abnormality directs that semen be removed from a quarantine centre it shall be removed therefrom and if to the same end he directs that semen be destroyed on a quarantine centre it shall be destroyed there.

4. Where a quarantine centre is within a prohibited area no semen shall be moved from the centre without the consent of the Minister.

5. Except with the consent of the Minister no semen shall be moved from a quarantine centre which is outside a prohibited area to a storage centre which is within such an area.

6. No semen shall be added to that already held in a flask at a quarantine centre for so long as that flask remains at the centre.

7. The licensee shall—

(a) keep such records as are set out in paragraph 8 of this Schedule;

(b) retain each entry in the records for two years after it is made;

(c) produce all such records for inspection by a duly authorised officer of the Minister at any reasonable time on request; and

(d) render to the Minister in such form and at such times as he may direct returns relating to such records or any part of them.

8. The records referred to in paragraph 7 of this Schedule shall be kept for all semen received, moved or removed or destroyed and shall show: the name and address of the processing centre from which the semen was accepted or, in the case of imported semen, the name and address of the consignor as given in the import licence; the date and quantity of semen received; the name, breed or type, earmarks or herd book number of the donor bull; the date and quantity of semen moved and the address to which it was moved or the date and quantity of semen removed or destroyed and by whom removed or destroyed.

SCHEDULE 3　　　　　Regulation 23(1)

Conditions to which centre storage licences are generally subject

1. Except with the consent of the Minister no bull or other animal shall be brought on to a storage centre.

2. If the Minister in order to prevent the risk of disease or the transmission of genetic abnormality directs that semen be removed from a storage centre it shall be removed therefrom and if to the same end he directs that semen be destroyed on a storage centre it shall be destroyed there.

3. Where a storage centre is within a prohibited area no semen shall be moved from the centre without the consent of the Minister.

4. Except with the consent of the Minister no semen shall be moved from a storage centre which is outside a prohibited area to another storage centre which is within such an area.

5. The licensee shall—

(a) keep such records as are set out in paragraph 6 of this Schedule;

(b) retain each entry in the records for two years after it is made or for so long as any semen in respect of which the entry is made remains at the storage centre, whichever is the longer period;

(c) produce all such records for inspection by a duly authorised officer of the Minister at any reasonable time on request; and

(d) render to the Minister in such form and at such time as he may direct returns relating to such records or any part of them.

6. The records referred to in paragraph 5 of this Schedule shall be kept for all semen received, moved or removed or destroyed and shall show: the name and address of the quarantine or storage centre from which the semen was received, or in the case of imported semen, the name and address of the consignor as given in the import licence; the date and quantity of semen received; the name, breed or type, earmarks or herd book number of the donor bull; the date and quantity of semen moved and the address to which it was moved or the date and quantity of semen removed or destroyed and by whom removed or destroyed.

Regulation 23(2) **SCHEDULE 4**

Conditions to which supply licences are generally subject

1.—(1) Semen of an approved bull shall be supplied whether by means of an artificial insemination service or to holders of farm storage licences only if—

(a) the owner of the semen authorises the semen to be supplied; and

(b) a certificate is issued certifying that the amount of semen specified in the authorisation given under (a) above, when aggregated with the amount or amounts of semen specified in any other authorisation or authorisations given (whether or not to the same person) under this paragraph or under paragraph 1(1)(a) of Schedule 4 to the Artificial Insemination of Cattle (Scotland) Regulations 1977, does not exceed—

(i) where the bull was approved subject to a condition under regulation 5(4)(c), the amount specified in that condition,

(ii) where the bull is deemed to have been approved by virtue of regulation 29(1) and the licence in force in respect of the semen from that bull before these regulations came into operation imposed a limit on the amount of semen of that bull which could be distributed or sold, that limit reduced by the amount which had been distributed or sold before these regulations came into operation, or

(iii) in the case of imported semen, where the relevant import licence was subject to a condition that the amount of semen of the bull from which the semen was taken which may be used in artificial insemination should not exceed a specified total amount, the amount specified in that condition.

(2) A certificate issued for the purpose of sub-paragraph (1)(b)(i) of this paragraph shall be signed by the owner for the time being of the bull referred to in the certificate.

(3) A certificate issued for the purpose of sub-paragraph (1)(b)(ii) of this paragraph shall be signed by the person to whom the relevant licence was granted.

(4) A certificate issued for the purpose of sub-paragraph (1)(b)iii) of this paragraph shall be signed by the holder of the relevant import licence.

2. In the case of a bull which was approved subject to the condition set out in regulation 5(4)(c) the licensee shall, at such intervals and in such form as the Minister shall direct, notify the Minister of the amount of semen supplied by him in accordance with paragraph 1 of this Schedule.

3. Where a bull is approved subject to a condition under regulation 5(4)(a) specifying further veterinary investigation, its semen shall not, without the permission in writing of the Minister, be supplied for use in artificial insemination.

4. For the purposes of a supply licence artificial insemination shall be carried out only by—

(a) a veterinary surgeon;

(b) a veterinary practitioner; or

(c) a full-time employee of the holder of the supply licence who to the licence holder's satisfaction is competent in artificial insemination and associated hygiene precautions and who is under the general direction of a veterinary surgeon specified in the licence.

5. If the Minister so directs, no semen shall be supplied to a specified farm nor shall semen be supplied without the Minister's consent to a farm which is within a prohibited area.

6. The licensee shall at least once every six months inspect or cause to be inspected any building which is specified in a farm storage licence and situate within the area designated in the supply licence and shall also inspect records kept by the holder of such farm storage licence and shall maintain records of all such inspections and shall give notice to the Minister immediately of any irregularities or unsatisfactory conditions which are discovered.

7. The licensee shall—

(a) keep such records as are set out in paragraphs 8 and 9 of this Schedule;

(b) retain each entry in the records for two years after it is made;

(c) produce all such records for inspection by a duly authorised officer of the Minister at any reasonable time on request;

(d) render to the Minister in such form and at such times as he may direct returns relating to such records or any part of them.

8. The licensee shall maintain records of all inseminations carried out showing: the date and place of the insemination; the name and address of the owner of the cow inseminated; and the name, breed or type, earmarks or herd book number of that cow and of the donor bull.   All abnormalities of progeny reported to him shall be recorded with all relevant details including: the date and place of the insemination, the semen used with details of the donor bull and the cow inseminated, the type of abnormality and the date it was reported.

9. The licensee shall maintain records of the supply of semen to farms showing: the name and address of the holder of the farm storage licence to whose farm the semen was supplied; the address of that farm; the date and quantity of semen supplied; and the name, breed or type, earmarks or herd book number of the donor bull.

SCHEDULE 5   Regulation 23(3)

Conditions to which farm storage licences are generally subject

1. Semen, except that required for immediate use, shall be stored in a flask kept in the building specified in the farm storage licence.

2. The number of straws stored on the farm shall not exceed in aggregate twice the number of breeding cows kept on the farm or farms specified in the licence.

3. Semen shall be destroyed if the Minister so directs to prevent the risk of disease or the transmission of genetic abnormality.

4. Except with the consent of the Minister, semen shall not be removed from the farm on which the building specified in the licence is situated.

5. Semen shall not be used except in the artificial insemination of cows owned by the licensee and kept on the farm or farms specified in the licence.

6. The artificial insemination of cows kept on a farm shall be carried out only by the following persons or one or more of them—

(a) the licensee or a full-time employee of that person, provided that in either case he has completed a course of training in artificial insemination under the direction of a veterinary surgeon and recognised by the Agricultural Training Board or has been regularly carrying out artificial insemination during the period of 12 months immediately preceding the coming into force of these regulations;

(b) a veterinary surgeon;

(c) a veterinary practitioner; and

(d) a person employed as a full-time inseminator by the holder of a supply licence.

7. The licensee shall—

(a) permit representatives of the storage centre specified in the licence to enter at all reasonable times and inspect the building specified in that licence;

(b) keep records in accordance with paragraph 8 of this Schedule;

(c) retain each entry in the records for two years after it is made; and

(d) produce at all reasonable times on request all such records for inspection by a duly authorised officer of the Minister or by a representative of the storage centre specified in the licence.

8. The records referred to in paragraph 7 of this Schedule shall be kept in the forms specified and set out below or in such other forms as may be approved by the Minister—

(a) as to stocks of semen held in or received for flasks on farms ...   Form A

(b) as to usage of semen from flasks on farms   ...   .   Form B

(c) as to deliveries of equipment and materials (including liquid nitrogen for farm flasks) required for the storage and use of semen and as to servicing of such equipment ...   .   Form C

FORM A

RECORD OF STOCKS OF SEMEN HELD IN, OR RECEIVED FOR, FARM STORAGE FLASK

1. Name and address of licensee...
2. Name and address of farm on which flask is kept (if different from 1 above)..

3. FS LICENCE NUMBER...

4. Name and address of licensed storage centre authorised to supply semen...

Record of semen held in stock or received

Date	Quantities of semen (number of doses)		Name(s) of donor bull(s)	Breed	Herd Book No. (if not known give earmarks)	Remarks
	in stock *	received †				
			1.			
			2.			
			3.			
			4.			
			5.			
			6.			

* In stock column entries are required to be made annually.

† A separate entry is required for each delivery date and each bull.

FORM B

RECORD OF USAGE OF SEMEN FROM FARM STORAGE FLASK

1. Name and address of licensee..

2. Address of farm on which flask is kept (if different from 1 above)..

....

DONOR BULL (See Note below)

Name	Breed	Herd Book No. (if not known give earmarks)
1.		
2.		
3.		
4.		
5.		
6.		

Note: A separate entry is required in respect of each donor bull.

COWS INSEMINATED

(1) Earmarks *	(2) Insemination Dates*			REMARKS (See Note below)
	1st	2nd	3rd	

* OR

................(number) insemination certificates attached for period .... to .... giving details as in columns (1) and (2) above.

Note: Record in this column—number of straws used in each insemination; any disposal of semen other than by use in insemination, and reason for such disposal; any calving difficulties etc.

FORM C

RECORD OF DELIVERIES OF EQUIPMENT AND MATERIALS (INCLUDING LIQUID NITROGEN FOR FARM FLASK) FOR STORAGE AND USE OF SEMEN AND OF SERVICING OF SUCH EQUIPMENT

1. Name and address of licensee..

2. Address of farm on which flask is kept (if different from 1 above)..

3. Name and address of licensed supplier/servicer..

Date of delivery or servicing	Details of Delivery or Servicing		Remarks
	Quantity, etc.	Item	
1.			
2.			
3.			
4.			
5.			
6.			

Regulation 26   **SCHEDULE 6**

Conditions to which farm storage servicing licences are generally subject

1. The licensee shall comply with the following requirements—

   (a) the interior of any vehicle used to transport liquid nitrogen, supply tanks or any other equipment shall be capable of being cleansed and disinfected and shall be kept in a clean condition;

   (b) employees while engaged on delivery services shall wear protective clothing and shall carry out personal disinfection, using an approved disinfectant, before leaving licensed premises at which equipment or supplies are being left;

   (c) employees while engaged on delivery services shall not have contact with cattle, sheep, pigs or goats on any premises.

2. The licensee shall—

   (a) keep records in accordance with paragraph 3 of this Schedule;

   (b) retain each entry in the records for two years after it is made; and

   (c) produce all such records for inspection by a duly authorised officer of the Minister at any reasonable time on request.

3. The records referred to in paragraph 2 of this Schedule shall be kept by the licensee, at his normal place of business, in respect of all deliveries to farms of equipment or materials (including liquid nitrogen for farm storage flasks) required for the storage of semen or its use in artificial insemination, and of servicing such equipment. The records shall include details of delivery or servicing dates, the registration numbers of vehicles used for the delivery or servicing, the premises at which the delivery or servicing was carried out, the types of equipment or materials delivered or a description of the servicing carried out.

EXPLANATORY NOTE

(This Note is not part of the Regulations.)

These Regulations, which revoke and supersede the Artificial Insemination of Cattle (England and Wales) Regulations 1957, establish a new system for the control of the practice of artificial insemination in England and Wales.

The Regulations provide for the issuing of approvals, conditional or unconditional, by the Minister, of bulls for use in artificial insemination, for the cancellation and variation of any condition imposed, and for the revoking of approvals given. They prohibit the collection of semen for processing except from an approved bull, and permit the evaluation, processing, quarantine, storage and supply of semen for use in artificial insemination only under the authority of licences granted by the Minister, and set out in the Schedules the principal conditions which may be specified in each type of licence.

Further, the Regulations provide for the quarantining of processed semen in quarantine centres, permit the movement of semen (other than that being exported) from a quarantine centre only to a storage centre and lay down that from storage centres semen may only be supplied for use by means of an artificial insemination service or for use by the holder of a farm storage licence in the insemination of cows owned by the licensee and kept on the farm or farms specified in the licence.

The Regulations also lay down that artificial insemination may be carried out only by veterinary surgeons and certain other specified persons and provide for the control of the delivery of equipment and materials required for the storage and use of semen, and of the servicing of such equipment. Transitional provisions are also included providing for bulls, the use of whose semen was authorised immediately before the coming into force of these regulations, to be regarded as approved bulls.

The Regulations do not apply to the use of raw semen in cows belonging to the owner of the bull from which the semen came, or at embryo transfer units in respect of which the Minister has granted an exemption. They also do not apply to the use of any semen at research or experimental establishments similarly exempted.

STATUTORY INSTRUMENTS

1977 No. 1261 (S. 95)

EDUCATION, SCOTLAND

The Independent Schools Tribunal (Scotland) Rules 1977

Made - - - -	*20th July* 1977
Coming into Operation	*22nd August* 1977

The Lord President of the Court of Session, in exercise of the powers conferred upon him by section 116 of the Education (Scotland) Act 1962(a) as amended by section 6(2) of and schedule 2 to the Education (Scotland) Act 1976(b) and of all other powers enabling him in that behalf, after consultation with the Council on Tribunals in accordance with section 10 of the Tribunals and Inquiries Act 1971(c) and with the concurrence of the Secretary of State, hereby makes the following Rules:—

Citation and commencement

1. These Rules may be cited as the Independent Schools Tribunal (Scotland) Rules 1977 and shall come into operation on 22nd August 1977.

Interpretation

2.—(1) The Interpretation Act 1889(d) shall apply for the interpretation of these Rules as it applies for the interpretation of an Act of Parliament.

(2) In these Rules:—

"the Act" means the Education (Scotland) Act 1962;

"the Act of 1946" means the Education (Scotland) Act 1946(e);

"notice of complaint" means a notice of complaint served by the Secretary of State under section 112 of the Act;

"the tribunal" means an Independent Schools Tribunal constituted in accordance with the provisions of section 113(1) of and schedule 7 to the Act.

Notice of Appeal

3.—(1) An appeal to the tribunal shall be instituted by sending to the Secretary of State a written notice of appeal signed by the appellant, setting out the grounds of appeal and stating an address to which all communications regarding the appeal should be sent.

(a) 1962 c. 47.	(b) 1976 c. 20.	(c) 1971 c. 62.
(d) 1889 c. 63.	(e) 1946 c. 72.	

(2) The notice shall be sent to the Secretary of State—

(*a*) in the case of an appeal under section 113 of the Act against a notice of complaint, within the time limited by that notice; or

(*b*) in the case of an appeal under section 115 of the Act against a refusal of the Secretary of State to remove a disqualification imposed by an order under Part V of the Act of 1946 or Part V of the Act, within one month after the communication of the refusal to the appellant.

(3) Where the appeal is against a notice of complaint alleging that a teacher is not a proper person to be employed as a teacher in any school, the appellant shall at the same time send a copy of the notice of appeal to the proprietor of the school or to the teacher, as the case may be.

(4) As soon as the tribunal has been constituted in accordance with the provisions of section 113(1) of and schedule 7 to the Act for the purpose of hearing the appeal, the Lord President shall appoint a person to act as secretary of the tribunal for the purposes of the appeal, and the Secretary of State shall send to the secretary of the tribunal three copies of the notice of appeal.

Date, time and place of hearing

4. The chairman of the tribunal shall fix a date, time and place for the hearing of the appeal and shall cause to be served upon the appellant, not less than twenty-eight days before the date so fixed, a notice in the form set out in the Schedule to these Rules and shall at the same time send a copy of the notice to the Secretary of State, and where the appeal is against a notice of complaint alleging that a teacher is not a proper person to be employed as a teacher in any school, to the proprietor of the school or the teacher as the case may be.

Abandonment of appeal

5. If an appellant at any time before the date fixed for the hearing gives notice in writing to the secretary of the tribunal that he desires to withdraw his appeal, the tribunal shall hear and determine the appeal in his absence.

Default of appearance

6. If an appellant or the Secretary of State fails to appear at the time and place fixed for the hearing of the appeal, the tribunal may hear and determine the appeal in his absence.

Right of audience

7.—(1) An appellant may appear and be heard in person, by counsel or solicitor or by any other person allowed by the tribunal to appear on his behalf, and if a partnership, by a partner and if a company, by a duly authorised director or officer of the company.

(2) The Secretary of State may appear and be heard by counsel or solicitor or by any officer of his department.

Hearing

8. The hearing of an appeal shall take place in public unless the tribunal determines that there are exceptional reasons which make it desirable that the hearing or some part of it should take place in private.

Procedure at hearing

9.—(1) An appellant and the Secretary of State shall have the right to address the tribunal and call witnesses, whose evidence shall be given on oath and who shall be subject to cross-examination and to re-examination.

(2) The tribunal may require the attendance of further witnesses in addition to those called by or on behalf of the appellant and the Secretary of State.

(3) The tribunal may permit evidence to be given by affidavit but may at any stage of the proceedings require the personal attendance of any deponent for examination and cross-examination.

(4) The tribunal shall not reject any evidence on the ground only that such evidence would be inadmissible in a court of law.

(5) After the evidence has been concluded, the Secretary of State and the appellant shall have the right to address the tribunal if they so desire.

Decision of tribunal

10.—(1) The decision of the tribunal on the appeal shall, in the event of disagreement, be the decision of the majority and may be given orally at the hearing or in writing as soon as may be after the hearing.

(2) The secretary of the tribunal shall send a copy of the decision given by the tribunal, together with a statement of its findings and the reasons for the decision and any order made by the tribunal to the appellant and the Secretary of State.

Stated Case to Court of Session

11. If any party to proceedings before the tribunal is dissatisfied in point of law with a decision of the tribunal, he may make application to the tribunal to state a case for the opinion of the Court of Session on any question of law arising in the proceedings and the provisions of Rules 276 to 280 of the Rules of the Court of Session**(a)** shall apply accordingly.

Extension of time

12. The time limited by these Rules for doing any act in connection with an appeal may be extended by the tribunal or by the chairman upon such terms (if any) as may seem just notwithstanding that the time limited has expired before an application for extension is made.

Power to regulate procedure

13.—(1) Subject to the provisions of the Act and these Rules, the tribunal shall have power to regulate its own procedure.

(2) Failure to comply with any requirements of these Rules shall invalidate any proceedings unless the tribunal so directs.

Revocation

14.—(1) The Independent Schools Tribunal (Scotland) Rules 1961**(b)** are hereby revoked.

(a) S.I. 1965/321 (1965 I, p. 803).　　　(b) S.I. 1961/2402 (1961 III, p. 4449).

(2) Section 38 of the Interpretation Act 1889 shall apply as if these Rules were an Act of Parliament and as if the Rules revoked by these Rules were Acts of Parliament repealed by an Act of Parliament.

G. C. Emslie,
Lord President of the Court
of Session.

Edinburgh.
15th July 1977.

I concur,

Bruce Millan,
One of Her Majesty's Principal
Secretaries of State.

New St. Andrew's House,
Edinburgh.
20th July 1977.

SCHEDULE *Rule 4*

NOTICE OF HEARING

THE EDUCATION (SCOTLAND) ACT, 1962

Take notice that your appeal under section 113 of the Education (Scotland) Act, 1962 against the Secretary of State's notice of complaint dated   day of   , alleging that (here insert short statement of grounds of complaint) [or under section 115 of the Education (Scotland) Act, 1962 against the Secretary of State's refusal to remove the disqualification imposed on (here insert description of disqualification) under Part V of the Education (Scotland) Act, 1946 or Part V of the said Act of 1962] will be heard by the Independent Schools Tribunal sitting at
on the   day of   at   . If for any reason you do not wish, or are unable, to attend at the above time and place, you should IMMEDIATELY inform me in writing at the address mentioned at the head of this notice stating the reasons for your inability to attend.

(sgd) Secretary.

EXPLANATORY NOTE

(*This Note is not part of the Rules.*)

These Rules make provision in respect of the constitution and proceedings of the Independent Schools Tribunal for Scotland.

STATUTORY INSTRUMENTS

1977 No. 1264

SEEDS

The Forest Reproductive Material (Amendment) Regulations 1977

Made - - - -	*22nd July* 1977
Laid before Parliament	*8th August* 1977
Coming into Operation	*9th August* 1977

The Minister of Agriculture, Fisheries and Food, the Secretary of State for Scotland and the Secretary of State for Wales, acting jointly, in exercise of the powers vested in them by subsections (1), (1A), (2), (3), (4) and (8) of section 16 of the Plant Varieties and Seeds Act 1964(a) as amended by section 4(1) of, and sub-paragraphs (1), (2), (3), (4) and (5) of paragraph 5 of Schedule 4 to, the European Communities Act 1972(b), and all other powers enabling them in that behalf, after consultation with representatives of such interests as appear to them to be concerned, hereby make the following regulations:—

Citation and commencement

1.—(1) These regulations may be cited as the Forest Reproductive Material (Amendment) Regulations 1977.

(2) These regulations shall come into operation on 9th August 1977.

Interpretation

2.—(1) In these regulations "the principal regulations" means the Forest Reproductive Material Regulations 1977(c).

(2) The Interpretation Act 1889(d) shall apply for the interpretation of these regulations as it applies for the interpretation of an Act of Parliament.

Amendment of the principal regulations

3. The principal regulations shall be amended by the deletion of Part C of Schedule 2 to those regulations, and the substitution therefor of the following—
> "C. *Clones*
>
> Items 3, 4, 5, 6 and 8 of Part A shall apply insofar as they are appropriate.".

(a) 1964 c. 14.	(b) 1972 c. 68.
(c) S.I. 1977/891 (1977 II, p. 2478).	(d) 1889 c. 63.

In Witness whereof the Official Seal of the Minister of Agriculture, Fisheries and Food is hereunto affixed on

(L.S.)

John Silkin,
Minister of Agriculture, Fisheries and Food.

20th July 1977.

Bruce Millan,
Secretary of State for Scotland.

22nd July 1977.

John Morris,
Secretary of State for Wales.

21st July 1977.

EXPLANATORY NOTE
(This Note is not part of the regulations.)

These regulations amend the Forest Reproductive Material Regulations 1977 by correcting the list of requirements contained in Part C of Schedule 2 to those regulations for the approval for registration in the National Register of Basic Material of clones intended for the production of selected reproductive material.

STATUTORY INSTRUMENTS

1977 No. 1265

NORTHERN IRELAND

The Northern Ireland (Emergency Provisions) Act 1973 (Amendment) Order 1977

Made - - -	*26th July* 1977
Laid before Parliament	*3rd August* 1977
Coming into Operation	*9th August* 1977

Whereas it appears to me that by reason of urgency it is necessary to make this Order without a draft thereof having been approved by resolution of each House of Parliament:

Now, therefore, in exercise of the powers conferred on me by section 27(3) of the Northern Ireland (Emergency Provisions) Act 1973(a), as substituted by paragraph 3(3) of Schedule 2 to the Criminal Jurisdiction Act 1975(b), I hereby make the following Order:—

1. This Order may be cited as the Northern Ireland (Emergency Provisions) Act 1973 (Amendment) Order 1977 and shall come into operation on 9th August 1977.

2.—(1) In this Order "the Act of 1973" means the Northern Ireland (Emergency Provisions) Act 1973, as amended by any enactment or under any enactment, including that Act.

(2) The Interpretation Act 1889(c) shall apply for the interpretation of this Order as it applies for the interpretation of an Act of Parliament.

3.—(1) Part I of Schedule 4 to the Act of 1973 (scheduled offences for the purposes of the Act) shall have effect subject to the following amendments, that is to say,—

    (*a*) in paragraph 6, after sub-paragraph (*aa*) (inserted by paragraph 4 of Schedule 2 to the Northern Ireland (Emergency Provisions) (Amendment) Act 1975(**d**)), there shall be inserted the following sub-paragraph:—

    "(*aaa*) section 16 (threats to kill), subject to note 2 below; ";

(a) 1973 c. 53.   (b) 1975 c. 59.   (c) 1889 c. 63.   (d) 1975 c. 62.

(*b*) after paragraph 13B (inserted by Article 13(5) of the Criminal Damage (Northern Ireland) Order 1977(**a**)) there shall be inserted the following paragraph:—

"*Criminal Law* (*Amendment*) (*Northern Ireland*) *Order* 1977

13C. Offences under Article 3 of the Criminal Law (Amendment) (Northern Ireland) Order 1977 (bomb hoaxes), subject to note 5 below.";

(*c*) in note 2, after "4," there shall be inserted "16,"; and

(*d*) in note 5, after "1977" there shall be inserted "or Article 3 of the Criminal Law (Amendment) (Northern Ireland) Order 1977".

(2) In Part II of the said Schedule 4, after sub-paragraph (*c*) of paragraph 13, there shall be inserted the following sub-paragraph:—

"(*d*) an offence under section 5(1) of the Criminal Law Act (Northern Ireland) 1967(**b**) of failing to give information to a constable which is likely to secure, or to be of material assistance in securing, the apprehension, prosecution or conviction of a person for a substantive offence;".

(3) Paragraphs (1)(*a*) and (*c*) and (2) above shall not have effect in relation to an offence for which a person has been committed for trial before 9th August 1977.

Roy Mason,
One of Her Majesty's Principal
Secretaries of State.

Northern Ireland Office.
26th July 1977.

EXPLANATORY NOTE

(*This Note is not part of the Order.*)

This Order adds to the list of "scheduled offences" in Schedule 4 to the Northern Ireland (Emergency Provisions) Act 1973 offences under Article 3 of the Criminal Law (Amendment) (Northern Ireland) Order 1977 (S.I. 1977/1249 N.I.16), which relate to bomb hoaxes, and section 16 of the Offences Against the Person Act 1861 (c. 100), as amended by Article 4 of that Order, which relate to threats to kill, except insofar as the Attorney General for Northern Ireland certifies that, in any particular case, the offence is not to be treated as a scheduled offence.

The Order also adds to the list of scheduled offences any offence under section 5(1) of the Criminal Law Act (Northern Ireland) 1967 of concealing from the police information relating to a person who has committed a scheduled offence.

Offences under section 16 of the 1861 Act and section 5 of the 1967 Act are not to be treated as scheduled offences where the defendant was committed for trial before 9th August 1977.

(**a**) S.I. 1977/426 (N.I.4).   (**b**) 1967 c. 18 (N.I.).

STATUTORY INSTRUMENTS

1977 No. 1266

MEDICAL PROFESSION

The General Medical Council (Registration Regulations) (Amendment) Order of Council 1977

Made - - - - *27th July* 1977

At the Council Chamber, Whitehall, the 27th day of July 1977

By the Lords of Her Majesty's Most Honourable Privy Council

Whereas in pursuance of section 4 of the Medical Act 1969(a) the General Medical Council have made regulations entitled "The Medical Practitioners Registration (No. 2) (Amendment) Regulations 1977";

And whereas by subsection (8) of the said section such regulations shall not have effect until approved by Order of the Privy Council:

Now, therefore, Their Lordships, having taken the said regulations into consideration, are hereby pleased to approve the same as set out in the Schedule to this Order.

This Order may be cited as the General Medical Council (Registration Regulations) (Amendment) Order of Council 1977.

N. E. Leigh,
Clerk of the Privy Council.

(a) 1969 c. 40.

SCHEDULE

THE MEDICAL PRACTITIONERS REGISTRATION (NO. 2) (AMENDMENT) REGULATIONS 1977

The General Medical Council in exercise of their powers under section 4(4) and (6) of the Medical Act 1969 hereby make the following Regulations:—

Citation and Commencement

1. These Regulations may be cited as the Medical Practitioners Registration (No. 2) (Amendment) Regulations 1977 and shall come into operation on 1st August, 1977.

Amendment of the 1969 Regulations

2. The Medical Practitioners Registration (No. 2) Regulations 1969(a) shall be amended as follows:—

   (*a*) In Regulation 4 the reference to "the United Kingdom, the Republic of Ireland, the Channel Islands and the Isle of Man" shall be amended to read "the United Kingdom, the Republic of Ireland, the Channel Islands, the Isle of Man, and any other Member State of the European Communities";

   (*b*) In Regulation 5 there shall be inserted in sub-paragraph (*b*) after the words "these Regulations" the words "furnishes for entry in the register an address outside the countries listed in Regulation 4";

   (*c*) In Regulation 6 there shall be inserted after the words "the Isle of Man" the words "or any other Member State of the European Communities";

   (*d*) In Regulation 9 there shall be substituted for paragraph (2) the following:

      "(2) Such an application

         (*a*) must be made in the manner set out in Form B in the Schedule to these Regulations, unless the information required by that Form has already been furnished to the satisfaction of the Registrar; and

         (*b*) must be accompanied by such fee or fees if any as is or are required by the Regulations made under section 5(1)(*a*) of the Act of 1969 for such restoration;"

   (*e*) For the Forms set out in the Schedule to the Regulations there shall be respectively substituted the following Forms:

FORM A   Regulation 5

APPLICATION FOR INCLUSION IN THE OVERSEAS LIST

I am the person now registered as a medical practitioner under the Medical Acts of the United Kingdom as follows:—

....

(full name)

....

(registered qualifications)

I am at present resident in:..

....

(country where resident overseas)

I hereby declare that it is my intention to remain resident outside the United Kingdom, the Republic of Ireland, the Channel Islands and the Isle of Man, and any other Member State of the European Economic Community, for at least one year from the date of this application.

I hereby apply for inclusion in the Overseas List of the Register of medical practitioners. I understand that entitlement to be included in the Overseas List ceases if at any

(**a**) *See* S.I. 1970/47 (1970 I, p. 315).

time I enter the United Kingdom, the Republic of Ireland, the Channel Islands or the Isle of Man, or any other Member State of the European Economic Community, and

(*a*) remain there for a period of more than three months, or

(*b*) render while there any service as a medical practitioner for gain.

I hereby undertake to inform the Registrar of the Council if any time I cease to be entitled to be included in the Overseas List.

I desire the following address, being an address outside the United Kingdom, the Republic of Ireland, the Channel Islands, the Isle of Man, or any other Member State of the European Economic Community, to be entered as my address in the Overseas List of the Register:...
....
(full address)

Signature of practitioner:...

Date:..

Regulation 9   **FORM B**

APPLICATION FOR RESTORATION TO THE PRINCIPAL LIST AFTER ERASURE OTHERWISE THAN BY DIRECTION OR ORDER OF THE DISCIPLINARY COMMITTEE

I, the undersigned..
now holding the qualification(s) of...
....

hereby declare as follows:—

1. I am the person formerly registered as a medical practitioner with the name
....
and the qualification(s) of...
....

2. I desire that my name be restored to the Principal List of the Register of medical practitioners and that the following address be entered in the Register:.....................
....

Signature of practitioner:...

Date:...

Regulation 10   **FORM C**

APPLICATION FOR RESTORATION TO THE OVERSEAS LIST AFTER ERASURE OTHERWISE THAN BY DIRECTION OR ORDER OF THE DISCIPLINARY COMMITTEE

I, the undersigned..
now holding the qualification(s) of...
hereby declare as follows:—

1. I am the person formerly included in the Register of medical practitioners with the name...
and with the qualification(s) of..

2. I am at present resident in..
(country where resident overseas)

3. It is my intention to remain resident outside the United Kingdom, the Republic of Ireland, the Channel Islands, the Isle of Man and any other State which is a member of the European Economic Community for at least one year from the date of this application.

4. I desire my name to be restored to the Overseas List of the register of medical practitioners. I understand that entitlement to be included in the Overseas List ceases if at any time I enter the United Kingdom, the Republic of Ireland, the Channel Islands or the Isle of Man, or any other State which is a member of the European Economic Community, and:

(*a*) remain there for a period of more than three months, or

(*b*) render while there any service as a medical practitioner for gain.

5. I hereby undertake to inform the Registrar of the Council if at any time I cease to be entitled to be included in the Overseas List.

6. I desire the following address, being an address outside the United Kingdom, the Republic of Ireland, the Channel Islands, the Isle of Man, or any other Member State of the European Economic Community to be entered as my address in the Overseas List of the Register ·...
....
     (full address)

       Signature of practitioner:...

           Date:...

Given under the official seal of the General Medical Council this twenty-sixth day of May, nineteen hundred and seventy seven.

L.S.   John Richardson,
                          President.

EXPLANATORY NOTE

(This Note is not part of the Order.)

The regulations approved by this Order

(1)   extend the list of countries in which residence disqualifies persons from being registered in the Overseas List of the register of medical practitioners maintained by the General Medical Council to include all Member States of the European Communities;

(2)   modify the requirements for a form to be completed on application for the inclusion of a name in the Overseas List or for a name to be restored to the Register.

STATUTORY INSTRUMENTS

1977 No. 1267

IRON AND STEEL

The Iron and Steel (Borrowing Powers) Order 1977

Laid before the House of Commons in draft

Made - - - -	*22nd July* 1977
Coming into Operation	1*st August* 1977

The Secretary of State, in exercise of his powers under subsection (2) of section 19 of the Iron and Steel Act 1975(a) (as inserted by section 2(2) of the Iron and Steel (Amendment) Act 1976(b)), and with the consent of the Treasury, hereby makes the following Order, a draft of which has been approved by a resolution of the House of Commons in accordance with subsection (3A) of section 36 of the Iron and Steel Act 1975 (as inserted by section 2(3)(*a*) of the Iron and Steel (Amendment) Act 1976):—

1. This Order may be cited as the Iron and Steel (Borrowing Powers) Order 1977 and shall come into operation on 1st August 1977.

2. The aggregate of the amounts outstanding in respect of any borrowing by the British Steel Corporation and the publicly-owned companies and of any sums paid to the British Steel Corporation by the Secretary of State, mentioned in Section 19 of the Iron and Steel Act 1975, as amended by section 2 of the Iron and Steel (Amendment) Act 1976, shall not exceed the sum of £4,000 million.

22nd July 1977

We consent to the making of this Order

G. B. Kaufman,
Minister of State
Department of Industry

22nd July 1977

Donald R. Coleman,
J. Dormand,
Two of The Lords Commissioners of
Her Majesty's Treasury

(a) 1975 c. 64.   (b) 1976 c. 41.

EXPLANATORY NOTE

(This Note is not part of the Order.)

Subsection (2) of section 19 of the Iron and Steel Act 1975 (as inserted by section 2(2) of the Iron and Steel (Amendment) Act 1976) sets an overall limit on borrowing by the British Steel Corporation and the publicly-owned companies and investment by the Secretary of State in the British Steel Corporation of £3,000 million or such greater sum not exceeding £4,000 million as the Secretary of State may specify by Order made with the consent of the Treasury.

This Order specifies the maximum permissible limit as £4,000 million.

STATUTORY INSTRUMENTS

1977 No. 1268 (C. 42)

LANDLORD AND TENANT

The Rent (Agriculture) Act 1976 (Commencement No. 2) Order 1977

Made -   - - -   *26th July* 1977

The Secretary of State and the Minister of Agriculture, Fisheries and Food acting jointly, in exercise of the powers conferred upon them by paragraph 8 of Schedule 3 to the Rent (Agriculture) Act 1976(a) and of all other powers enabling them in that behalf, hereby make the following order:—

Citation and interpretation

1.—(1) This order may be cited as the Rent (Agriculture) Act 1976 (Commencement No. 2) Order 1977.

(2) The Interpretation Act 1889(b) applies for the interpretation of this order as it applies for the interpretation of an Act of Parliament.

Commencement

2. The date appointed as "the date of operation for forestry workers" within the meaning of the Rent (Agriculture) Act 1976 shall be 1st October 1977.

Peter Shore,
One of Her Majesty's Principal
Secretaries of State.

26th July 1977.

In Witness whereof the Official Seal of the Minister of Agriculture, Fisheries and Food is hereunto affixed on 26th July 1977.

John Silkin,
Minister of Agriculture, Fisheries and Food.

(a) 1976 c. 80.   (b) 1889 c. 63.

EXPLANATORY NOTE

(This Note is not part of the Order.)

This Order appoints 1st October 1977 as the date of operation for forestry workers for the purposes of the Rent (Agriculture) Act 1976. That Act came into operation generally on 1st January 1977 (being the date appointed by the Rent (Agriculture) Act 1976 (Commencement No. 1) Order 1976. S.I. 1976/ 2124). Its operation was, however, subject to Part II of Schedule 3 to that Act, which postponed its operation in relation to workers employed, or formerly employed, in forestry, either as whole-time workers or as permit workers, and their successors until the date of operation for forestry workers.

STATUTORY INSTRUMENTS

1977 No. 1271 (C. 43)

WEIGHTS AND MEASURES

The Weights and Measures &c. Act 1976 (Schedule 4) (Commencement) Order 1977

Made - - - - *27th July* 1977

The Secretary of State, in exercise of his powers under paragraph 4 of Schedule 4 to the Weights and Measures &c. Act 1976(**a**) hereby makes the following Order:—

1. This Order may be cited as the Weights and Measures &c. Act 1976 (Schedule 4) (Commencement) Order 1977.

2.—(*a*) Paragraphs 2, 3 and 4 of Schedule 4 to the Weights and Measures &c. Act 1976 shall come into force on 1st September 1977.

(*b*) Paragraph 1 of the said Schedule shall come into force on 1st April 1978.

John Fraser,

Minister of State,
Department of Prices and Consumer Protection.

27th July 1977.

EXPLANATORY NOTE

(*This Note is not part of the Order.*)

This Order brings into force Schedule 4 to the Weights and Measures &c. Act 1976, which amends Schedule 6 (relating to solid fuel) to the Weights and Measures Act 1963, and contains provisions relating to ancillary matters.

(**a**) 1976 c. 77.

STATUTORY INSTRUMENTS

1977 No. 1272

COUNTER-INFLATION

The Counter-Inflation (Price Code) Order 1977

Made - - - -	*27th July* 1977
Laid before Parliament -	*29th July* 1977
Coming into Operation -	*1st August* 1977

The Secretary of State in exercise of the powers conferred by section 2 of the Counter-Inflation Act 1973(**a**), as amended under the Prices Act 1974(**b**) and by the Price Commission Act 1977(**c**), by section 3 of the Remuneration, Charges and Grants Act 1975(**d**) as amended(**c**) and by sections 15(2) and 21(2) of the said Act of 1977 and of all other powers enabling him in that behalf, and having consulted the Price Commission and representatives of consumers, persons experienced in the supply of goods or services, employers and employees and other persons in accordance with subsection (4) of the said section 2, hereby makes the following Order:—

1.—(1) This Order may be cited as the Counter-Inflation (Price Code) Order 1977 and shall come into operation on 1st August 1977.

(2) The Interpretation Act 1889(**e**) shall apply for the interpretation of this Order as it applies for the interpretation of an Act of Parliament, and as if for the purposes of section 38 of that Act this Order were an Act of Parliament and the orders revoked by article 3 of this Order were Acts of Parliament thereby repealed.

2. The Price Code prepared by the Secretary of State and set out in the Schedule to this Order shall be the code for the purposes of the Counter-Inflation Act 1973.

3.—(1) Subject to paragraph (2) below, the Counter-Inflation (Price Code) Order 1976(**f**) and the Counter-Inflation (Price Code) Order 1976 (Amendment) Order 1976(**g**) are hereby revoked.

(**a**) 1973 c. 9.	(**b**) *See* S.I. 1974/1218 (1974 II, p. 4631).
(**c**) 1977 c. 33.	(**d**) 1975 c. 57.　　　　　(**e**) 1889 c. 63.
(**f**) S.I. 1976/1170 (1976 II, p. 3226).	(**g**) S.I. 1976/2207 (1976 III, p. 6190).

(2) Where, in relation to any product, a certificate given by the Secretary of State under paragraph 103 of the code set out in Schedule 1 to the Counter-Inflation (Price Code) Order 1976 or a certificate referred to in article 3(3) of that order is in force when this Order comes into operation, that certificate shall continue to have effect for so long as it remains in force as if it were given under paragraph 24 of the Code set out in the Schedule to this Order and as if references therein to any provision of the first mentioned code or of the code first mentioned in the said article were references to the corresponding provision of the Code set out in the Schedule to this Order.

Roy Hattersley,

Secretary of State for Prices and Consumer Protection.

27th July 1977.

(*Article 2*)

THE SCHEDULE

THE PRICE CODE

PART I

PURPOSE, PRINCIPLES AND SCOPE

PART II

NET PROFIT MARGINS

THE PRICE CODE

PURPOSE, PRINCIPLES AND SCOPE

Purpose

Purpose of the Code

1. The Code has a dual purpose. First, the Price Commission are required to exercise their functions so as to ensure that it is implemented. Secondly, all those concerned with the determination of prices and charges should have regard to it.

Who is concerned with the Code?

2. The Code is therefore addressed both to the Commission and to all those concerned with price and charge determination.

Principles

General principles

3. The general principles are—

    (*a*) to restrain prices by controls on net profit margins and gross percentage margins while safeguarding and encouraging investment;

    (*b*) to reinforce the effects of competition, and to secure its full benefits in the general level of prices;

    (*c*) to provide a sanction against the payment of remuneration in excess of specified limits.

Scope

Scope of control

4. With the exceptions specified in paragraphs 5 to 9 below, the margin controls relate to all prices of goods and services supplied in the course of business on the home market.

Prices and charges outside control

5. The control on net profit margins does not relate to the following prices and charges—

    (*a*) prices for the sale of goods or charges for the performance of services which are supplied, whether by the person selling or performing them or another, outside the United Kingdom or to persons or in relation to property outside the United Kingdom;

    (*b*) prices for the sale of any goods—

       (i) which have been produced or manufactured outside the United Kingdom; and

       (ii) which have not been subjected to any process in the United Kingdom other than packing or repacking, cleaning and sterilising or, in the case of crude oil, stabilisation; and

       (iii) which have not been sold to any person in the United Kingdom;

    and charges for the performance of any services in the United Kingdom or in relation to any property in the United Kingdom which are performed for any person outside the United Kingdom;

    (*c*) prices of goods and services where the application of the control would be inconsistent with an international agreement or arrangement between states or organisations of states;

    (*d*) prices at sales by auction, where such sales are a normal practice in the particular trade;

(e) prices of goods at the point of sale on a commodity market in the United Kingdom such as the London Metal Exchange or prices directly determined by reference to such markets;

(f) prices for the sale of scrap metal;

(g) prices of second-hand goods (other than second-hand road vehicles sold by distributors);

(h) charges for—
    (i) the carriage of goods or passengers on international journeys;
    (ii) the carriage of goods or passengers on other journeys by sea, excluding charges which are determined by a tariff of general application;
    (iii) air navigation relating wholly or mainly to international traffic, and the provision of landing and related facilities for aircraft;
    (iv) harbour operations within the harbour area (other than charges mentioned in head (v) below) made by a harbour authority within the meaning of the Harbours Act 1964(a) or the Harbours Act (Northern Ireland) 1970(b), as the case may be;
    (v) ship, passenger and goods dues in relation to which an objection may be made to the National Ports Council under section 31 of the said Act of 1964 or to the Department of Commerce under section 7 of the said Act of 1970 and charges exigible by virtue of section 29 of the said Act of 1964 (local light dues); and
    (vi) international mail, giro, remittance and telecommunications services;

(i) charges for services provided by shipbrokers;

(j) charges for package holidays taken outside the United Kingdom;

(k) prices of ethical medicines supplied to the United Kingdom market to the extent that regulation of their prices is within the scope of any agreement relating to those prices made between the Secretary of State for Social Services and representatives of manufacturers of those medicines; but only so long as such an agreement is in force;

(l) prices in Government contracts for warlike and other stores and services which are within the agreement between Her Majesty's Government and industry governing the pricing of, and control of profit from, non-competitive contracts; these prices will be subject to the controls provided in that agreement;

(m) insurance premiums, which are subject to restriction by the Secretary of State for Trade;

(n) taxi fares, where subject to control by the Home Secretary or the Secretary of State for Scotland;

(o) charges payable to returning officers in connection with Parliamentary elections, determined under the Representation of the People Act 1949(c);

(p) bus fares which are fixed by conditions attached to a road service licence granted under section 135 of the Road Traffic Act 1960(d) or a permit granted under section 30 of the Transport Act 1968(e) and charges made in respect of the use of vehicles under authorisations granted under section 2(3)(b) of the Passenger Vehicles (Experimental Areas) Act 1977(f);

(q) charges for carriage by air transport for which an air transport licence granted by the Civil Aviation Authority is by section 21 of the Civil Aviation Act 1971(g) required to be held by the operator;

(r) subscriptions and certain prices charged by non-profit-making organisations as in paragraphs 64 to 66;

(s) charges being payments in respect of services provided under or pursuant to Part IV of the National Health Service Act 1946(h) or Part IV of the National Health Service (Scotland) Act 1947(i) to persons providing such services;

(a) 1964 c. 40.	(b) 1970 c. 1 (N.I.).	(c) 1949 c. 68.
(d) 1960 c. 16.	(e) 1968 c. 73.	(f) 1977 c. 21.
(g) 1971 c. 75.	(h) 1946 c. 81.	(i) 1947 c. 27.

(*t*) charges for services to the Post Office by sub-postmasters;

(*u*) prices for the sale of tops of wool and other fine animal hair;

(*v*) prices of tallow, meat and bone-meal processed from waste fat, bone and offal;

(*w*) charges made by the British Airports Authority and the British Railways Board for the parking of vehicles;

(*x*) charges of the Post Office for services of a description provided only to a government department; and

(*y*) charges for the services of local authorities and local authority joint boards.

Food

6. The prices of manufactured food and drink, like those of manufactured products generally, are within the scope of the control as are those of semi-processed foodstuffs such as butter, cheese and quick-frozen vegetables.

Agriculture

7.—(1) The prices paid to United Kingdom producers or producers' organisations or to overseas suppliers for fresh foods and similar products, which are subject to fluctuations on world and United Kingdom markets because of seasonal factors or changes in the relationship between supply and demand, are not controlled. This applies in particular to meat, including bacon and poultry, fish, eggs, fruit and vegetables. However, enterprises which resell these products, whether home-produced or imported, at any subsequent stage will be subject to control.

(2) The price for the sale of raw beet sugar for further refining is not controlled.

(3) The price for the sale of whole hams in cans is not controlled.

Milk for liquid consumption

8. The retail price of milk for liquid consumption and the margins of milk distributors will continue to be subject to the existing controls by the Minister of Agriculture, Fisheries and Food and the Secretary of State for Scotland. So long as these controls apply, the price of milk for liquid consumption and distributors' margins on milk for liquid consumption will not be subject to the Code.

Other animal and vegetable products

9. What is said in paragraph 7(1) in relation to prices paid for fresh foods applies also to prices of other primary products of animal or vegetable origin which are subject to similar fluctuations.

Part II
Net Profit Margins

Reference level

10.—(1) Prices should be determined so as to secure that net profit margins, as defined in paragraph 11, do not in any period of 12 months exceed the reference level.

(2) For the purposes of the Code, subject to sub-paragraph (3), the "reference level" means the simple average level of the net profit margins in either—

(*a*) the best two of the last five years of account of the unit for profit margin control ending not later than 30th April 1973, or

(*b*) the best two of the last eight years of account for that unit ending not later than 31st July 1976,

as the enterprise may choose; and where an enterprise applies a reference level determined under head (*b*) in any period, subject to the provisions of the Code apart from this sub-paragraph, it shall apply that reference level in each subsequent period.

(3) For the purposes of sub-paragraph (2)(*b*) there shall be left out of account any excess of the net profit margin over the reference level determined under the code in force at the time.

(4) For the purposes of this paragraph and paragraphs 11 to 13, 33, 35, 38 and 39, references to any period of 12 months shall, in relation to an enterprise which has an accounting period of, or periods which in the aggregate amount to, other than 12 months, be construed as a reference to the accounting period or, as the case may be, the aggregate of the accounting periods of that enterprise which is nearest to 12 months.

Net profit margin

11.—(1) "Net profit margin" means the margin of net profit expressed as a percentage of turnover. "Net profit" means the net profit, determined in accordance with generally accepted accounting principles consistently applied by the enterprise concerned, which arises from trading operations within the control after taking into account all expenses of conducting and financing them, including the additional payments mentioned in sub-paragraph (2), depreciation as provided in paragraph 26 and, in the case of enterprises applying paragraph 27, interest within that paragraph, but before deducting corporation tax or income tax.

(2) The additional payments referred to in sub-paragraph (1) are additional payments in accordance with section 26 of the Independent Broadcasting Authority Act 1973(**a**) (which relates to rental payments by television programme contractors to the Independent Broadcasting Authority) as substituted by section 1 of the Independent Broadcasting Authority Act 1974(**b**).

Stock relief

12.—(1) In determining net profit for the purposes of the Code (except paragraph 38(1)) in relation to any period of 12 months ending after 31st July 1976, an enterprise may deduct an amount in respect of increases in the value of stock ("stock value increase") determined under this paragraph; and where an enterprise has obtained relief under this paragraph or under paragraph 82 of the 1976 Code in any period—

(*a*) it shall also apply this paragraph in each similar period ending within the 13 months following the first such period; and

(*b*) after the expiry of the last period mentioned in sub-paragraph (*a*), may apply this paragraph as if it had not previously obtained relief under this paragraph or paragraph 82 of the 1976 Code;

and for that purpose references to stock value increase include references to a decrease in the value of stock and references to the deduction of stock value increase include references to the addition of such a decrease.

(2) "stock value increase", in the case of any enterprise, means 70 per cent of the excess of the value of the stock at the end of a period of 12 months chosen by the enterprise for the purpose of calculating the net profit margin under paragraph 10 over the value of stock at the beginning of that period; and decrease in the value of stock shall be determined in a similar manner; and in applying sub-paragraph (1) above no account shall be taken of—

(*a*) any decrease in the value of stock below the value of stock at the beginning of the first period by reference to which the enterprise has applied this paragraph or paragraph 82 of the 1976 Code; and

(*b*) any amount by which the sum of decreases in the value of stock exceeds the sum of increases in the value of stock, being increases in respect of which the enterprise has obtained relief under that sub-paragraph or under paragraph 82 of the 1976 Code.

(a) 1973 c. 19.   (b) 1974 c. 16.

(3) For the purposes of this paragraph, "stock" includes work in progress but does not include any description of security, and the value of stock shall be determined in accordance with generally accepted accounting principles consistently applied by the enterprise.

Action where profit margin is likely to be exceeded

13.—(1) Where, in any period of 12 months, the reference level—

(*a*) has been exceeded; or

(*b*) in the light of interim accounts or other evidence, is likely to be exceeded;

and the circumstances mentioned in sub-paragraph (2) have not arisen, price reductions should be made, provided that account has been taken of distorting factors. The reductions should be sufficient to eliminate the actual or expected excess over the reference level as soon as reasonably possible, and to offset any excess which has already arisen in a period subsequent to 30th April 1973 over the level determined from time to time under such of the orders referred to in paragraph 68 as were in force at the time in question.

(2) The circumstances referred to in sub-paragraph (1) arise where, in any period of 12 months following that mentioned in sub-paragraph (1), the reference level—

(*a*) has not been reached; or

(*b*) in the light of interim accounts or other evidence, is not likely to be reached, and the amount of the actual or expected shortfall is equal to or exceeds the amount of the actual or expected excess mentioned in sub-paragraph (1) above.

(3) Reductions under sub-paragraph (1) need not be made until an amount has been recovered which corresponds with the amount giving rise to any deficiency in any period of 12 months ending after 31st July 1976 below either of the returns mentioned in paragraph 38(3).

Unit for profit margins

14. In calculating the net profit margin under paragraph 10, the unit for profit margin control shall be either—

(*a*) the enterprise as a whole; or

(*b*) the distribution activity of the enterprise or its manufacturing activity or its activity of providing services or an activity comprising the two last-mentioned activities; or

(*c*) a unit of an enterprise, being a separate constituent company or sub-division, provided that the Commission are satisfied that:

(i) the unit constituted, before 30th April 1973, and still constitutes a separate unit immediately below the level of the main Board of the enterprise as a whole for management, operational and accounting purposes. In applying the test in this sub-paragraph the Commission may disregard an intermediate non-trading company; and

(ii) the accounts of all such units, if combined with one another, can be reconciled with those of the enterprise as a whole; and are not materially distorted by transactions conducted otherwise than on arm's length terms; or

(*d*) in a case where the Commission, having regard to any of the matters mentioned in heads (*a*), (*c*) and (*d*) of paragraph 22, are satisfied that in the circumstances of an enterprise it is appropriate that a unit of the enterprise, which would fall within sub-paragraph (*c*) above if it had constituted a separate unit before 30th April 1973, should be the unit for profit margin control, that unit.

The same unit should then be adhered to for all the purposes of the Code to which the net profit margin is relevant, except paragraph 38(1).

Meaning of 'enterprise as a whole'

15.—(1) For the purpose of paragraph 14—

(a) where the enterprise is a company, 'the enterprise as a whole' means the company or (where the company is a member of a group) all the companies in the group, carrying on business in the United Kingdom; and

(b) where the enterprise is a partnership or other unincorporated body of persons, means the partnership or body in question.

(2) In sub-paragraph (1) above—

(a) 'company' includes any body corporate; and

(b) 'group' means the person (including a company) having control of a company together with all companies directly or indirectly controlled by him.

Allocation of profits to controlled prices

16.—(1) Allocation of profits between sales to which the control on net profit margins relates and those to which it does not may be necessary where an enterprise—

(a) sells in both home and overseas markets; or

(b) makes sales at home, some of which are within and some outside the scope of the control.

(2) Where such an enterprise—

(a) has made allocations which represent a fair division of profits in its circumstances, over part or all of the field; and

(b) has done so on a consistent basis;

it should continue to use this basis for all calculations relevant to the Code. In other cases enterprises may make such allocations by dividing profits in proportion to the value of sales in each area, or on any other basis which represents good accounting practice, provided that they adhere to the chosen basis for all calculations relevant to the Code.

Transfer prices

17. Where the Commission are satisfied that prices, either of purchases or of sales which an enterprise proposes to regard as a basis for the calculation of net profit margins, differ from what they would be if the goods or services had been transferred on an arm's length basis, they may substitute modified profit margins which in their judgement fairly reflect what would be appropriate on that basis.

Enterprises not trading for five years before 1st May 1973

Modified base period for profit margin calculation

18. Where an enterprise has traded for less than five complete years of account before 1st May 1973, or has traded at a loss in one or more of those years, the reference level determined under paragraph 10(2)(a) may be calculated as follows—

(a) if there have been four years of trading before 1st May 1973, the average of the best two; if three or two years, the best year;

(b) if there have been less than two years of trading before 1st May 1973, the limitations on profit margins will not apply except where the enterprise chooses to apply paragraph 10(2)(b); and

(c) any year in which an enterprise made a loss may be treated as equivalent to a year of no trading and sub-paragraphs (a) and (b) may be applied accordingly.

Changes in membership of groups of companies etc.

New enterprises

19.—(1) Subject to paragraph (2) below, the reference level of an enterprise shall not be liable to variation by virtue only of a change in the ownership of the business carried on by the enterprise.

(2) Where a new enterprise is formed from a reconstruction or amalgamation of existing enterprises, in calculating the reference level of the new enterprise under paragraph 10, the net profit margin shall be determined in accordance with paragraph 11 by expressing the aggregate profits of the constituent enterprises as a percentage of their aggregate turnover.

Acquisitions and disposals

20. Where at any time before or after this Code comes into operation an enterprise acquires a new undertaking or disposes of an existing undertaking, then, subject to paragraph 21, in calculating net profit margins and reference levels in relation to the enterprise after the acquisition or disposal, the sales and profits or losses of the undertaking acquired (before and after the acquisition) shall be included and the sales and profits or losses of the undertaking disposed of (before and after the disposal) shall be excluded.

Acquisitions since 29th April 1973

21.—(1) Where an enterprise has acquired a new undertaking after 29th April 1973—

(a) the words "constituted, before 30th April 1973, and still" in paragraph 14(c) will not apply in relation to the new undertaking; and

(b) the new undertaking may be integrated into a unit for profit margin control which has been or could have been established under paragraph 14, so long as the conditions of paragraph 14(b) or (c) are or continue to be met where applicable.

(2) Where the new undertaking is integrated into such a unit, the unit's reference level may be adjusted to include an element reflecting any relief which the new undertaking could have obtained under paragraph 23 immediately before the acquisition (paragraph 23 being assumed, in the case of an acquisition before the date when this Code comes into operation, to have been in force at the relevant time).

(3) This paragraph will not apply unless—

(a) the acquisition of the new undertaking is the result of a transaction at arm's length; and

(b) the new undertaking existed outside the enterprise as a whole before the transaction.

Reliefs

Modification of reference levels

22.—(1) The Commission may permit a modification of the reference level if they are satisfied that, in the circumstances of the enterprise, a modification is justified.

(2) When considering whether a modification is justified the Commission shall have regard to the matters mentioned in section 2(2) of the Price Commission Act 1977 and any other matter, being matters which appear to them to be relevant, including such of the following as may apply—

(a) the enterprise was substantially reconstructed in or since the base period;

(b) the base period was not representative for the enterprise;

(c) there has been a substantial change in the character or activities of the enterprise since the base period;

(*d*) there has been a substantial change in the relationship between the unit for profit margin control concerned and the enterprise as a whole.

Relief for low profits

23.—(1) In a case where the Commission are satisfied that an enterprise cannot, without exceeding its reference level and excluding any increase arising from the application of paragraph 46, obtain the greater of—

(*a*) a return on capital of 12½ per cent, and

(*b*) a return on turnover of 3 per cent,

the reference level shall, for so long as may be necessary, be taken to be such a level as would permit such return to be obtained.

(2) In this paragraph, 'capital' means the net assets employed, excluding any part of them which is represented by borrowings on which interest is to be taken into account under paragraphs 27 to 30 and excluding goodwill. The value of the assets concerned shall be determined in accordance with generally accepted accounting principles consistently applied by the enterprise concerned but should be based on the historic costs of the assets except that where, in annual accounts for a year ended on or before 30th September 1972, the enterprise has revalued an asset, the value may be based on the value of the asset shown in those accounts.

Special cases

Shortages and balance of payments

24. Where—

(*a*) having regard to the need to alleviate the shortage or threatened shortage referred to below, the Secretary of State has certified in relation to any product or commodity that—

(i) there is a severe shortage of supplies in the domestic market or serious threat of such shortage; and

(ii) significant damage is being thereby caused or threatened to the interests of particular industries or of consumers in the United Kingdom; or

(*b*) having regard to the need to remove or reduce a significant adverse effect on the United Kingdom balance of payments or a serious threat thereof, the Secretary of State has certified, in relation to any product or commodity, that such an adverse effect or threat exists;

then, for so long as the certificate remains in force, such departures from the provisions of the Code relating to net profit margins shall be permitted by the Commission as the Secretary of State may specify in the certificate.

Mergers and acquisitions

25. Where, in relation to the acquisition of any company by any other company or of any merger between companies, the Secretary of State is of the opinion that the acquisition or merger is of special importance to a particular industry or to consumers in the United Kingdom and is satisfied that the provisions of the Code relating to net profit margins have, or might have, a significant adverse effect, the Secretary of State may so certify in relation to enterprises of any description or to any enterprise in circumstances of any description; and, for so long as the certificate remains in force, such departures from the provisions of the Code relating to net profit margins shall be permitted by the Commission as the Secretary of State may specify in the certificate.

Supplementary provisions

Depreciation

26. For the purposes of the Code, 'depreciation' means the aggregate amount of depreciation, calculated in accordance with generally accepted accounting principles

consistently applied by the enterprise, for the period to which the calculation relates in respect of assets of the enterprise which were used in the activity concerned in that period based—

(a) where the calculation of depreciation is made by reference to a period ending after 31st July 1976, on, at the option of the enterprise, either—
   (i) the historic cost of the asset or a revaluation of the asset calculated in accordance with generally accepted accounting principles and which has appeared in annual accounts for a period ending on or before 30th September 1972 increased, in either case, by a multiple of 1.4; or
   (ii) a revaluation of the asset calculated in accordance with generally accepted accounting principles, and having appeared in annual accounts; and

(b) where that calculation is made by reference to a period ending before 1st August 1976, on either—
   (i) the historic cost of the asset; or
   (ii) a revaluation of the asset calculated in accordance with generally accepted accounting principles and having appeared in annual accounts for a period ending on or before 30th September 1972.

Interest—general rule

27.—(1) Except where an enterprise as a whole within the meaning of paragraph 15 elects under paragraph 28, interest shall be taken into account for the purposes of the net profit margin control, except interest—

(a) which is a distribution of profits; or

(b) which is payable on a loan by another unit of the same enterprise and—
   (i) which is not required for the purposes of the principal activity of the unit by or for which it is paid, or
   (ii) which is at a rate higher than that which would have been charged if the transaction had been at arm's length; or

(c) which, although expressed as interest, is capital expenditure; or

(d) which relates to the acquisition after 29th April 1973 of a new member in a group of companies.

(2) In taking interest into account under sub-paragraph (1) above, interest received shall be treated as part of the turnover of the profit margin unit by or for which it is received.

Interest to be disregarded if enterprise so elects

28.—(1) Subject to the following provisions of this paragraph, where an enterprise, other than an enterprise within paragraphs 53 to 62 or an enterprise within paragraph 130(1) of the 1976 Code, so elects in accordance with paragraph 29, interest shall not be taken into account for the purposes of any provision of the Code.

(2) For the purposes of paragraphs 10(2), 23(1)(b) and 38(1) and (3)(b), interest other than interest mentioned in heads (a) to (d) of paragraph 27 shall be taken into account in determining net profit margins.

(3) Interest falling within paragraph 63(2) shall be taken into account for all purposes of the Code other than the adjustment of the reference level under sub-paragraph (4) below.

(4) Subject to sub-paragraph (3) above, the reference level determined under paragraph 10(2) for any enterprise applying this paragraph shall be adjusted, if not previously adjusted pursuant to paragraph 19(5) of the 1976 Code, by the addition or subtraction, as the case may require, of the percentage which interest relating to trading operations within the control for the latest complete year of account bears to turnover for the same period.

Time for election under paragraph 28

29.—(1) An election under paragraph 28—

(a) shall be irrevocable,

(b) shall apply to all units of the enterprise,

(c) shall be exercised in the case of an enterprise required by an order under section 15 of the Counter-Inflation Act 1973 to furnish periodical returns to the Commission not later than the earlier of the date when it first furnishes such a return after 30th September 1977 and 31st December 1977 and in the case of an enterprise not so required not later than the last-mentioned date.

(2) Where an enterprise has made an election under paragraph 19(2) of the 1976 Code, the enterprise may not later than the time specified in sub-paragraph (1)(c) above revoke that earlier election and apply paragraph 27 above.

Acquisitions and mergers

30.—(1) Where an enterprise acquires control of any undertaking, interest shall be treated for the purposes of the net profit margin control in relation to that undertaking as it fell to be treated in relation to that enterprise immediately before the acquisition of control.

(2) Where any enterprises are amalgamated or reconstructed, the enterprises resulting from the amalgamation or reconstruction may make an election under paragraph 28 as if for the requirement in sub-paragraph 29(1)(c) there were substituted a requirement to exercise the election not later than the expiry of three months beginning with the date of formation of any enterprise resulting from the amalgamation or reconstruction.

Temporary employment subsidy and regional employment premiums etc.

31. In any calculation under the Code in relation to any period ending after 31st July 1976 no account shall be taken of—

(a) grant made pursuant to arrangements under section 5(1) of the Employment and Training Act 1973(**a**);

(b) payments made under section 26(1) of the Finance Act 1967(**b**); and

(c) grant made under Part I or Part II of the Industry Act 1972(**c**).

Assistance under enactments

32. In the application of the Code to—

(a) any enterprise being a person to whom an advance by way of grant is made under the Highlands and Islands Shipping Services Act 1960(**d**); or

(b) the Civil Aviation Authority;

no account shall be taken of any grant made, in the case of (a), to the enterprise in pursuance of the said Act of 1960 or, in the case of (b), to the Authority in pursuance of section 10(1)(a) of the Civil Aviation Act 1971(**e**).

Part III

Gross Percentage Margins of Distributors

Distribution

33.—(1) In the determination of prices for sales within the United Kingdom, wholesalers, retailers and other enterprises engaged in distribution should ensure that their gross percentage margins in any period of 12 months do not exceed the proportion specified in sub-paragraph (2) of the level of the gross percentage margin in either—

(**a**) 1973 c. 50.	(**b**) 1967 c. 54.	(**c**) 1972 c. 63.
(**d**) 1960 c. 31.	(**e**) 1971 c. 75.	

(*a*) the last complete account year of the enterprise ending on or before 30th April 1973; or

(*b*) a 12-month period ending between 30th October 1972 and 30th April 1973 for which separate accounts are or can be made available;

less in either case an appropriate reduction for the abolition of SET:

Provided that where an enterprise began trading after 30th April 1972, there shall be substituted the margin for any continuous period of 12 months falling within the first two years of trading and for which separate accounts are, or can be made, available.

(2) The proportion of the gross percentage margin referred to in sub-paragraph (1) will be:

(*a*) 100 per cent. for any period before 6th May 1974;

(*b*) 90 per cent. for any period beginning on or after 6th May 1974.

(3) A figure of 100 per cent. and not 90 per cent. applies—

(*a*) for any period beginning on or after 6th May 1974 to—

(i) distributors engaged mainly in retailing with total annual sales of less than £250,000;

(ii) other distributors with total annual sales of less than £500,000; and

(iii) all sales of goods exempted from restrictions on resale price maintenance by order under section 5 of the Resale Prices Act 1964(a); and

(*b*) for any period beginning on or after 1st August 1976 to—

(i) distributors engaged mainly in retailing with total annual sales of less than £500,000; and

(ii) other distributors with total annual sales of less than £1,000,000; and

(*c*) for any period beginning on or after 1st August 1977 to—

(i) distributors engaged mainly in retailing with total annual sales of less than £600,000; and

(ii) other distributors with total annual sales of less than £1,200,000.

Safeguard for net profit margins

34. Where the net profit margin of the enterprise as defined in paragraphs 14 and 15 is reduced or is likely to be reduced to a level more than three-twentieths below the reference level, gross percentage margins may be increased (though not above 115 per cent. of the figure determined under paragraph 33(1)) to the extent necessary to restore the net profit margin to a level three-twentieths below the reference level. No increase under paragraph 46 shall be taken into account in applying this paragraph but an increase in the appropriate net profit margin reference level and level of gross percentage margin may also be made under that paragraph.

Gross percentage margin

35.—(1) For all the purposes of the Code 'gross percentage margin' in the case of an enterprise which has traded for not less than two years means the aggregate difference between the cost to the distributor of all the goods he sells in the home market in any period of 12 months and the value of his sales of those goods in that period, expressed as a percentage of the sales value. The difference should be calculated according to the normal accounting practice consistently applied by the enterprise.

(2) In determining its gross percentage margin, an enterprise may obtain relief under paragraph 12 and, in applying that paragraph—

(*a*) the amount of any increase or decrease in the value of stock determined under that paragraph for any period shall be taken into account; and

(*b*) references therein to an enterprise shall be construed as references to an enterprise as defined in paragraph 41.

(a) 1964 c. 58.

Distributors' stocks

36. In most cases prices determined by distributive enterprises will have to take account of the cost of goods used from stock for sale. Such enterprises should adhere to the practice they have followed consistently for pricing purposes in arriving at such costs and at the relevant gross percentage margins.

Repricing

37.—(1) Retailers should not increase the prices of goods that are or have been displayed for sale by reference to increases in replacement costs, even if such price increases would otherwise be permitted by the Code.

(2) This paragraph does not apply—

(*a*) to any particular description of goods on which the average rate of annual stockturn for the distribution activities of the enterprise as a whole is less than 10; or

(*b*) to price increases directly resulting from the withdrawal of special offers; or

(*c*) to goods exempted from restrictions on resale price maintenance by an order under section 5 of the Resale Prices Act 1964; or

(*d*) where the Commission are satisfied, after consulting representative bodies, that the effect on prices of applying the paragraph would be contrary to consumers' interests.

Distributors making low profits

38.—(1) An enterprise engaged in distribution may increase prices to cover its expenses, being expenses referred to in paragraph 11(1), plus a margin (excluding any increase under paragraph 46) consisting of an amount equal in any period of 12 months to 2 per cent. of turnover during that period, notwithstanding the limitation on gross percentage margins.

(2) Price increases may not be made under this paragraph if they cause the profit margin reference level referred to in paragraphs 10 to 23 to be exceeded.

(3) Where the Commission are satisfied that the net profit margin of an enterprise (excluding any increase arising from the application of paragraph 46) represents less than the greater of—

(*a*) a return of 10 per cent. on capital, and

(*b*) a return of 2 per cent. on turnover,

none of the provisions relating to the control of gross percentage margins shall be applied so as to prevent such a return from being obtained.

Action where gross or net percentage margins are likely to be exceeded

39.—(1) Where, in any period of 12 months—

(*a*) a distributor's net profit margin or gross percentage margin has exceeded the level allowed under the Code; or

(*b*) in the light of interim accounts or other evidence, that level is likely to be exceeded;

and the circumstances mentioned in sub-paragraph (2) have not arisen, price reductions should be made, provided that account is taken of distorting factors. The reduction should be sufficient to eliminate the actual or expected increase over the permitted level as soon as reasonably possible, and to offset any excess which has already arisen in a period subsequent to 30th April 1973 over the level determined from time to time under such of the orders referred to in paragraph 68 as were in force at the time in question.

(2) The circumstances mentioned in sub-paragraph (1) arise where, in any period of 12 months following that mentioned in sub-paragraph (1), the net profit margin reference level or gross percentage margin—

(*a*) has not been reached; or

(b) in the light of interim accounts or other evidence is not likely to be reached,

and the amount of the actual or expected shortfall is equal to or exceeds the amount of the actual or expected excess mentioned in sub-paragraph (1) above.

(3) Reductions under sub-paragraph (1) need not be made until an amount has been recovered which corresponds with the amount giving rise to any deficiency in any period of 12 months ending after 31st July 1976 below either of the returns mentioned in paragraph 38(3).

Modification of permitted gross percentage margins

40.—(1) The Commission may permit a modification of the gross percentage margin ascertained under paragraph 33 if they are satisfied that in the circumstances of the enterprise the modification is justified.

(2) When considering whether a modification is justified, the Commission shall have regard to the matters mentioned in section 2(2) of the Price Commission Act 1977(a) and any other matter, being matters which appear to them to be relevant, including such of the following as may apply—

(a) that the base period was not representative for the enterprise;

(b) that since the base period there has been a substantial change in—

(i) the character of the enterprise,

(ii) the description or descriptions of goods sold by it, or

(iii) the proportion which any description of such goods bears to any other description of such goods.

Definition of enterprise

41. For the purpose of this part of the Code except paragraph 38(3), an enterprise means either an enterprise as a whole of a separate constituent company or sub-division provided that in the latter case separate accounts for such sub-divisions—

(a) are or can be made available for all relevant periods,

(b) are not materially distorted by transactions conducted otherwise than on arm's length terms, and

(c) would, if combined with one another and with the accounts of all other activities or transactions of the enterprise, produce results consistent with those shown by the accounts of the enterprise taken as a whole.

Mixed enterprises

42. Where the activities of an enterprise are not confined to distribution but include manufacturing or the provision of services, distribution must be treated separately for the purposes of the gross percentage margin control unless separate accounts satisfying paragraph 41 cannot be made available for that activity. Where these activities are not treated separately, the main activity of the enterprise will determine whether the provisions of the Code relating to distribution or to manufacturing and services apply.

PART IV

INVESTMENT

Relief for investment

43. Enterprises may increase net profit margin reference levels and the levels of gross percentage margins by reference to their estimated capital expenditure on investment in assets physically located (or, in the case of road vehicles, based) in the United Kingdom, in accordance with the provisions of paragraphs 44 to 47.

(a) 1977 c. 33.

Meaning of ' expenditure on investment '

44.—(1) 'Expenditure on investment' means expenditure, approved in the case of a company by the board of directors, which it is estimated will actually become due and payable in the investment year (any estimate being revised from time to time on the basis of fact or of revised estimates, as circumstances may require) being—

> (a) in the case of the owner, capital expenditure on new and second-hand plant and machinery except—
>
>> (i) plant and machinery which is let under a leasing or hiring agreement for not less than one year and on which the benefit of relief under paragraph 46 is transferred by the owner to the lessee or hirer, and
>>
>> (ii) plant and machinery which is let under a hire-purchase agreement or sold under a conditional sale agreement;
>
> (b) in the case of a lessee or hirer under a leasing or hiring agreement for not less than one year, capital expenditure by the owner on plant and machinery in a case where the owner has transferred to him the benefit of relief within sub-paragraph (2) below;
>
> (c) in the case of a hirer under a hire-purchase agreement or the purchaser under a conditional sale agreement, an amount equal to the capital expenditure by the owner on the plant and machinery covered by the agreement;
>
> (d) capital expenditure on the construction of buildings; and
>
> (e) capital expenditure on the acquisition of buildings for occupation by the enterprise,

less, in any case, the disposal value of such plant, machinery and buildings (calculated, in the case of plant or machinery the subject of an agreement within (b) above, in accordance with sub-paragraph (2)) disposed of in the investment year by the person who would be entitled to relief under paragraph 46 if the asset were acquired by him at the time of its disposal; and, where relief has been obtained by virtue of head (b) or (c) above, the termination of the agreement in question (otherwise, in the case of a hire-purchase or conditional sale agreement, than by due performance of the agreement) shall be treated as a disposal by the lessee, hirer or purchaser as the case may be:

Provided that—

> (i) expenditure relating to trading operations outside the control (except by virtue only of paragraph 5(a)) shall be left out of account;
>
> (ii) expenditure relating to ethical medicines of which the prices are outside the control by virtue of paragraph 5(a) shall be left out of account if their prices would, if they were sold in the United Kingdom market, be outside the control by virtue of paragraph 5(k); and
>
> (iii) expenditure which cannot be appropriated to a distribution activity shall be apportioned in proportion to the turnover of all the activities concerned in the year of account ended not more than 12 months before the beginning of the investment year.

(2) In a case falling within head (b) of sub-paragraph (1) above, relief shall be calculated under paragraph 46, and it shall be assumed for the purposes of the calculation in a case where the benefit of relief under that paragraph has been transferred by the owner in respect of a leasing or hiring agreement—

> (a) that the expenditure on investment is the capital expenditure first incurred by the owner less an amount equal to the sum of the payments made to him in respect of the leasing or hiring under any previous agreement; and
>
> (b) that the disposal value of the plant or machinery for the purposes of that sub-paragraph shall be the capital expenditure first incurred by the owner less an amount equal to the sum of the payments made to him in respect of the leasing or hiring under the agreement in question and under any previous agreement.

(3) In this paragraph, 'buildings' means industrial buildings and warehouses and, in the case of an enterprise carrying on a distribution activity, buildings occupied by it

for the purpose of storing goods and retail shops occupied by it, and 'plant and machinery' does not include television sets for domestic use or mechanically propelled vehicles other than—

    (*a*) vehicles of a construction primarily suited for the conveyance of goods or burden of any description;

    (*b*) vehicles of a type not commonly used as private vehicles and unsuitable to be so used; and

    (*c*) vehicles provided wholly or mainly for hire to, or for the carriage of, members of the public in the ordinary course of a trade.

(4) Where the Commission are satisfied that expenditure within heads (*a*) to (*e*) of sub-paragraph (1) above or the disposal value of the plant, machinery and buildings mentioned in that sub-paragraph differs from what it would be if the expenditure had been incurred, or the plant, machinery and buildings had been disposed of, on an arm's length basis, they may substitute modified expenditure or a disposal value, as the case may be, which in their judgment fairly reflects what would be appropriate on that basis.

Other definitions relating to investment relief

45.—(1) 'Investment year' means a period of 12 months chosen by the enterprise—

    (*a*) in the case of an enterprise which has not obtained relief under paragraph 98 of the 1976 Code, beginning on a date not earlier than nine months before, and not later than, the beginning of the relief year, being a date after 31st December 1976; and

    (*b*) in the case of any other enterprise, beginning immediately after its investment year under the said paragraph 98;

and, in either case, any consecutive period of 12 months.

(2) 'Relief year' means a period of 12 months chosen by the enterprise—

    (*a*) in the case of an enterprise which is required to furnish periodical returns pursuant to an order under section 15 of the Counter-Inflation Act 1973 and which has not obtained relief under paragraph 98 of the 1976 Code, beginning not earlier than 56 days after the enterprise concerned has informed the Commission (whether before or after the Code comes into operation) that it intends to apply this paragraph;

    (*b*) in the case of an enterprise which is required to furnish such returns and which has obtained relief under paragraph 98 of the 1976 Code, consecutive upon the relief year under that paragraph, provided that no relief shall be taken under paragraph 46 earlier than 28 days after the enterprise concerned has informed the Commission that it intends to apply that paragraph; and

    (*c*) in any other case, beginning at any time;

and any later consecutive period of 12 months.

(3) 'Relevant expenditure' means an amount (revised from time to time to take account of revision of expenditure on investment) which is represented by 50 per cent of expenditure on investment.

(4) 'Turnover', in relation to a relief year, means the turnover on trading operations within the control which may reasonably be expected to be achieved in the year in question, revised from time to time on the basis of fact or as circumstances may require.

Calculation of relief

46.—(1) The permitted increases in net profit margin reference levels and the levels of gross percentage margins shall be calculated in accordance with the following provisions of this paragraph. An enterprise—

    (*a*) may, for a relief year, treat the net profit margin reference level as increased by the addition of a figure found by expressing the relevant expenditure as a percentage of turnover; and (*b*) in respect of its distribution activities, may, for a relief year, treat the level of the gross percentage margin from time to time ascertained under paragraph 33 as increased by the addition of a figure found by expressing the relevant expenditure as a percentage of turnover.

(2) Investment expenditure in respect of which the enterprise has benefited from a modification under paragraph 101 of the 1976 Code or any provision which it replaced may not be included in the calculation of relevant expenditure where the modification was to the provisions relating to profit margins.

(3) In this paragraph 'relief year' includes any relief year applied under the 1976 Code.

Transitional provisions relating to investment relief

47.—(1) Where the relief year of an enterprise ascertained under paragraph 97 of the 1976 Code or paragraph 79 or 79A of the 1974 Code ends after 31st July 1977 and—

(*a*) the application of sub-paragraph (1) of paragraph 98 of that Code has not caused the relevant expenditure to be recovered in sales in the part of the relief year ending with that date; or

(*b*) the application of that paragraph or paragraph 79 or 79A of the 1974 Code has not caused relevant expenditure relating to any earlier relief year of the enterprise to be recovered in sales before 1st August 1977 (which expenditure, so far as it is unrecovered, is hereinafter referred to as 'earlier unrecovered expenditure');

the permitted increase in the net profit margin reference level and, in the case of a distributor, the level of the gross percentage margin shall be calculated, for the balance of the relief year unexpired after that date, in accordance with sub-paragraph (2) below; and the enterprise may, in the period of twelve months immediately following the relief year, treat the reference level and gross percentage margin as increased respectively by the percentage points calculated under sub-paragraph (3).

(2) The permitted increase referred to in sub-paragraph (1) above shall be calculated in accordance with paragraph 46 as if in that paragraph—

(*a*) for references to the relevant expenditure there were substituted references to relevant expenditure reduced by the amount recovered before 1st August 1977 and increased by the amount of any earlier unrecovered expenditure;

(*b*) for the references in sub-paragraphs (1)(*a*) and (*b*) to a relief year there were substituted references to the balance of the relief year unexpired after 31st July 1977; and

(*c*) for references to 'turnover' there were substituted references to turnover in the said balance of the relief year.

(3) The increase in the reference level and gross percentage margin in the period of twelve months following the relief year referred to in sub-paragraph (1) shall be the amount, expressed as a percentage of turnover in that period, by which the permitted increase, as defined in sub-paragraph (2), exceeds two percentage points.

(4) Where—

(*a*) the relief year of an enterprise ascertained under paragraph 97 of the 1976 Code or paragraph 79 or 79A of the 1974 Code has ended before 1st August 1977;

(*b*) the application of sub-paragraph (1) of paragraph 98 of that Code or paragraph 79 or 79A of the 1974 Code, as the case may be, has not caused relevant expenditure for that year or earlier unrecovered expenditure to be recovered in sales before that date; and

(*c*) no relief year of the enterprise is in progress at that date,

the permitted increase in the net profit margin reference level and, in the case of a distributor, the level of the gross percentage margin shall be calculated by expressing the sum of such expenditure as a percentage of estimated turnover in the twelve months beginning with that date.

Action where relief exceeded

48.—(1) If relief under paragraph 46 has exceeded or is likely to exceed the relevant expenditure then, notwithstanding any other provisions of the Code, net profit margin reference levels and the levels of gross percentage margins shall each be reduced by an amount necessary to ensure that no more than the amount of the relevant expenditure is recovered.

(2) Where relief under paragraph 98 of the 1976 Code is likely to exceed, or has exceeded, the relevant expenditure for the purposes of the said paragraph 98, sub-paragraph (1) above shall have effect as if the references therein to paragraph 46 included a reference to paragraph 98 of the 1976 Code and references to the relevant expenditure were references to the relevant expenditure under that paragraph.

PART V

INDIRECT TAXES

Profit margins and indirect taxes

49.—(1) In making comparisons between net profit margins as a percentage of sales and the reference level, due account must be taken of the effect on margins of changes in indirect tax on goods and services sold, so that the comparison is not materially distorted. The comparison with earlier years should be made on a basis which excludes purchase tax from sales in the period up to the end of March 1973 and excludes VAT from 1st April 1973 onwards. Where customs and excise duties have been included in the sales figures, these duties should be included throughout, adjusted as necessary to take account of the partial replacement of excise duties by VAT and of other changes in those duties. Subject to the following provisions of this paragraph, where indirect taxes have been increased after 25th March 1974, a deduction should be made from the value of sales corresponding to the cash value of the extra tax borne by the goods sold; conversely where indirect taxes have been reduced after 25th March 1974, a corresponding addition should be made to the value of sales.

(2) In the case of sales of alcoholic beverages and tobacco and tobacco products, sub-paragraph (3) below applies in relation to every sale in the course of an activity which consists of distribution or the provision of services and, in relation to sales in the course of a manufacturing activity, to sales before 1st August 1977; and where the activities of an enterprise comprise more than one of those activities, paragraph 42 shall have effect for the purposes of determining in the course of which activity sales are made.

(3) In determining margins for the purposes of sub-paragraph (1), in cases where indirect taxes (other than VAT) have been paid the value of sales—

(a) before 17th January 1977 shall be taken to be—
  (i) in the case of alcoholic beverages, 85 per cent. of the value of sales, and
  (ii) in the case of tobacco and tobacco products, 80 per cent. of the value of sales;

(b) after 16th January 1977 shall be taken to be—
  (i) in the case of alcoholic beverages, 80 per cent. of the value of sales, and
  (ii) in the case of tobacco and tobacco products, 75 per cent. of the value of sales before 1st August 1977 and 73 per cent. of the value of sales on and after that date.

(4) Where the Commission are satisfied, having regard to the sales mix of the enterprise in respect of the products within sub-paragraph (3) that a higher percentage than is specified in that sub-paragraph is appropriate, they may, in the case of any enterprise, substitute that higher percentage.

Purchase tax

50. Where an enterprise does not already have accounts showing separately the purchase tax element in the turnover of previous years, or which permit the precise calculation of the amount of excise duty abatement from records of duty paid, such elements should be estimated on the basis of the best available information. Where total purchase tax can be ascertained from purchase invoices this total can be deducted from tax inclusive sales. Where such purchase invoices are not available, the purchase tax element may be estimated by applying to the value of purchases of goods charged to different rates of purchase tax appropriate factors derived from those rates.

Prices and indirect taxes

51.—(1) Where indirect taxes have been increased after 25th March 1974, an addition not exceeding the cash amount of the increase may be made to prices. Where indirect taxes are reduced, the reduction must be fully reflected in prices. The cash amount of the increase or reduction should be applied so far as practicable to the goods bearing the indirect taxes.

(2) This paragraph also applies to the effects of changes in the coverage of indirect taxes.

Calculation of gross percentage margin

52. In arriving at sales and cost of sales, indirect taxes should be treated on the same basis as for calculating net profit margins in paragraph 49.

PART VI

PARTICULAR SECTORS

Public sector

Meaning of 'nationalised industry'

53. Paragraphs 54 and 55 apply to the following nationalised industries—

National Coal Board;
Electricity Council;
Area Electricity Boards;
Central Electricity Generating Board;
North of Scotland Hydro-Electric Board;
South of Scotland Electricity Board;
Northern Ireland Electricity Service;
British Gas Corporation;
British Steel Corporation;
Post Office;
British Airways Board;
British Airports Authority;
British Railways Board;
British Transport Docks Board;
British Waterways Board.

Special provisions for nationalised industries

54. In the application of the Code to the nationalised industries mentioned in paragraph 53 no account shall be taken of Government compensation or grants taken directly to revenue account; and in paragraph 26, "depreciation" means the aggregate amount of provision for the writing off of displaced plant and deferred charges and either—

    (*a*) depreciation of each of the other assets of the industry determined in accordance with paragraph 26, or

(b) in a case where provision for supplemental depreciation is made at replacement cost by the British Transport Docks Board and the Post Office, such supplemental provision.

Financial reconstruction

55. Where a statute effects, or has since 1973 effected, a change in the finances of a nationalised industry, any resulting changes in the accounting practices of the industry or in the value of its assets and liabilities shall be taken into account in calculations under the Code.

Water undertakings

56. Water authorities and water undertakers in England and Wales must comply with their obligations under statute (including, in the case of a statutory water company, any agreement between a water authority and the company under section 12 of the Water Act 1973) but shall have regard to the principles of the Code and shall not make charges which, taken as a whole, are likely to result in a higher revenue in any accounting year than is required to comply with their duty under section 29(1) of the Water Act 1973, wherein the reference to outgoings shall include depreciation calculated in accordance with the provisions of the Code and such allocations to reserve as may be necessary to comply with any directions made under paragraph 32 of the Third Schedule to that Act.

Banks, finance houses and similar enterprises
Application of Code

57. Most banks, finance houses and similar financial enterprises are engaged partly in business for which the charge is a rate of interest and partly in business for which the charge is of a different nature. Interest charges are not within the control. The other charges of these enterprises are subject to control. It will therefore be necessary to allocate profits between the two classes of business for the purpose of the control on non-interest charges. Paragraph 16 applies.

Extension of meaning of exports

58. For the purposes of the Code the enterprises described in paragraph 57 may treat as goods and services exported—

(a) transactions in sterling with any person or body corporate resident outside the United Kingdom; and

(b) dealings in foreign currencies.

Non-interest charges

59. The provisions of the Code relating to the limitation on net profit margins, defined in the case of these enterprises as in paragraph 61, apply to their non-interest charges. These include commissions, fees and all similar charges.

Hire purchase etc.

60.—(1) In the case of hire-purchase, credit sale and conditional sale agreements, the net profit margin control applies in relation to all separately identifiable fees and charges payable by the debtor to the creditor, other than repayments of credit and charges for credit.

(2) In the case of charges under plant and machinery leasing agreements, the provisions of the Code apply in full.

Special definition of net profit margin

61. For the purposes of the Code 'net profit margin' means—

(a) in the case of enterprises within paragraph 57 undertaking plant and machinery leasing contracts, where either the greater part of the business of the enterprise consists of such contracts, or separate accounts can be produced for such contracts, net income from charges for this business less associated costs, including overheads, expressed as a proportion of average resources employed;

(b) in the case of enterprises undertaking hire-purchase, credit sale and conditional sale business where either the greater part of the business of the enterprise consists of such business or separate accounts can be produced for such business, net income from separately identifiable fees and charges payable by the debtor to the creditor, other than repayments of credit and charges for credit, expressed as a percentage of gross income from the transactions concerned;

(c) in the case of all other enterprises within paragraph 57, net income from charges (that is, gross income less costs, including associated overheads) expressed as a percentage of gross income (that is, total income from the transactions concerned); and in this sub-paragraph, gross and net income includes interest earned on customers' current account credit balances held in the course of controlled (that is, non-interest) business.

National Giro

62.—(1) In the case of the banking services of the Post Office, the reference level for the purposes of paragraph 10 means the average level of the years of account ending in 1975 and 1976, the level for the year of account ending in 1975 being determined on the following assumptions—

(a) that the reduction of the liability of the Post Office under section 4 of the Post Office (Banking Services) Act 1976(a) should be deemed to have been effected on 1st April 1974 instead of on 1st April 1975; and

(b) that from the amount of such reduction there were deducted any part of the liability of the Post Office to which the said section 4 applies which was incurred during the year to 31st March 1975.

(2) Paragraph 55 applies to the banking services of the Post Office.

Services

Application of Code

63.—(1) The limitation on net profit margins will apply to profit of firms or individuals providing professional or other services irrespective of the method by which fees are determined.

(2) For the purpose of paragraph 11, turnover and net profit include interest on money belonging to another person retained by solicitors and estate agents and other enterprises which retain such interest in the ordinary course of business.

(3) Where the number of partners in a firm has changed as a result of the substitution of a partner for an employee, or of an employee for a partner, the reference level may be recalculated by reference to the changed number of partners. Paragraph 19 applies to amalgamations of and successions to partnerships.

Non-profit-making organisations

Charges outside control

64. The controls on margins do not apply in relation to subscriptions charged by organisations which—

(a) exist for religious, charitable, educational, representational or recreational purposes; and

(b) are non-profit-making; and

(c) do not carry on a trade or business as their main activity.

Provisions supplemental to paragraph 64.

65. The Code will not apply to prices charged in the course of its activities by an organisation satisfying the tests in paragraph 64 or by any properly authorised person

(a) 1976 c. 10.

acting on behalf of that organisation, if they are charged in order to raise funds for the purposes of the organisation, and those activities involve no substantial or continuing competition with trading enterprises.

Charges within control

66. Except where they are outside the control under paragraph 65, prices charged in any trading activity carried on by an organisation which meets the requirements of paragraph 64 are governed by the Code, unless—

(*a*) the customers of the trading activity are confined to members of the organisation; or

(*b*) in the case of the control on net profit margins, separate accounts cannot be made available for the trading activity.

PART VII

GENERAL

Modification etc of particular provisions of the Code

67. Where the particular provisions of the Code cannot be directly applied to particular cases or sectors without modification, the Commission will, in exercising their functions, apply those provisions with such adaptations or modifications as appear to them to be necessary to give effect to the principles and objectives of the Code.

Transitional provisions

68.—(1) Where an increase in a price or charge was implemented while the Code set out in any of the following Orders, that is to say—

(*a*) the Counter-Inflation (Price and Pay Code) Order 1973(**a**);

(*b*) the Counter-Inflation (Price and Pay Code) (No. 2) Order 1973(**b**) as amended;

(*c*) the Counter-Inflation (Price Code) Order 1974(**c**) as amended; and

(*d*) the Counter-Inflation (Price Code) Order 1976(**d**);

was in force and was not permissible under whichever of those Codes was for the time being in force, the price or charge in question should be reduced to the level that would have been permitted under the appropriate Code.

(2) Where in any particular case an increase in a price or charge was impermissible under the Code in force at the time, the revocation of that Code does not of itself make the increase permissible.

(3) In relation to labour cost increases after 6th November 1972 in respect of work executed before 1st August 1976, paragraph 71 (contracts containing escalation or variation of price clauses) and paragraph 73 (contracts subject to prime cost or cost reimbursement arrangements) of the 1976 Code shall have effect subject to paragraphs 74 and 76 of that Code as if they formed part of the Code, and paragraph 75 of the 1976 Code shall have effect for the purpose of applying those paragraphs.

(4) A person shall not by virtue only of the revocation of any of the Orders referred to in sub-paragraph (1) above be entitled to recover under any contract any sum forgone by way of a productivity deduction required to be made under any Code set out in a Schedule to any of those Orders.

(5) In the Code, 'the 1974 Code' means the code set out in the Counter-Inflation (Price Code) Order 1974 and 'the 1976 Code' means the code set out in the Counter-Inflation (Price Code) Order 1976 as amended from time to time in each case.

(**a**) S.I. 1973/658 (1973 I, p. 2106).   (**b**) S.I. 1973/1785 (1973 III, p. 5445).
(**c**) S.I. 1974/2113 (1974 III, p. 8253).   (**d**) S.I. 1976/1170 (1976 II, p. 3226).

Charges

69. References in the Code to prices include references to charges, unless there is explicit provision to the contrary.

Goods and services

70. References in the Code to goods or products include references to services, unless there is explicit provision to the contrary.

Co-operatives, etc.

71. A reference to an enterprise includes a reference to a co-operative, a partnership or to an individual carrying on a business.

Food subsidies included in price

72. A subsidy received or to be received by an enterprise on any food under section 1 of the Prices Act 1974(a) shall for all the purposes of this Code be treated as part of the price received by the enterprise for that food or for any product of which that food is an ingredient.

PART VIII

PAY SANCTION

Sanction against payment of remuneration in excess of pay limits

73. For the purpose of providing a sanction against the payment of remuneration in excess of the limits ("the pay limits") at any time mentioned in section 1 of the Remuneration, Charges and Grants Act 1975(b) as extended by or under section 17 of the Price Commission Act 1977(c), the provisions of the Code relating to net profit margins and gross percentage margins shall have effect subject to paragraphs 74 and 75.

Disallowance of excessive remuneration

74.—(1) In determining net profit for the purposes of paragraph 10(1), the expenses mentioned in paragraph 11 and the labour costs mentioned in sub-paragraph (2) below shall, during the period of 12 months beginning with the date on which the person in question first pays any part of such increase, be taken not to include an increase in remuneration any part of which arises after 11th July 1975, being an increase which is, at the date when he first pays it or any part of it, in excess of the pay limits then in force.

(2) Where the share of labour costs expressed as a percentage of the related expenses within the meaning of paragraph 11 is less than 15 per cent., the amount disallowed under sub-paragraph (1) above shall be increased by the proportion which 15 per cent. bears to that share; and in this sub-paragraph "labour costs" means wages, salaries, other remuneration within the meaning of section 7 of the Remuneration, Charges and Grants Act 1975, employers' national insurance contributions and training costs.

Modification of safeguard provisions

75. In determining expenses for the purpose of calculating the net profit margin under paragraphs 23, 34 and 38 no account shall be taken of any increase in remuneration to the extent that it is disallowed under paragraph 74.

Duty of Commission to refer questions about remuneration to Secretary of State

76. Before taking steps to enforce paragraph 74, the Commission shall refer any question whether increased remuneration exceeds the pay limits to the Secretary of State for Employment and shall accept his determination as certified to them.

(a) 1974 c. 24.   (b) 1975 c. 57.   (c) 1977 c. 33.

EXPLANATORY NOTE

(This Note is not part of the Order.)

This Order substitutes a new Price Code for the Code which has been in operation since 1st August 1976 under the Counter-Inflation (Price Code) Order 1976 as amended.

The principal change is the removal of provisions imposing cost-related controls on manufacturing and service firms. Controls on net profit margins and, in the case of distributors, gross margins remain.

Other changes are—

(a) the minimum profit margin reference level of the greater of 12½ per cent. on capital and 2½ per cent. on turnover is modified by increasing the percentage figure on turnover to 3 per cent. (paragraph 23);

(b) firms are permitted to change any election they have made under the 1976 Code as to whether or not interest should be left out of account for the purposes of the Code (paragraphs 28 and 29);

(c) the net profit margin safeguard for distributors is modified by raising the level of gross margins in order to allow an increased percentage of net profit margin reference levels to be obtained (paragraph 34);

(d) certain prices and charges are added to those exempt from the Price Code (paragraph 5(f), (i) and (v));

(e) investment relief is extended to the acquisition of existing industrial buildings, warehouses and shops which are for occupation by the enterprise claiming relief (paragraph 44(1)(e)).

STATUTORY INSTRUMENTS

1977 No. 1280

AGRICULTURE

The Hops Marketing Scheme (Amendment) Order 1977

Made -   -   -   -   *26th July* 1977

Whereas the Hops Marketing Board duly submitted to the Minister of Agriculture, Fisheries and Food (hereinafter called "the Minister") certain amendments of the Hops Marketing Scheme 1932(a), as amended (b), which amendments, as subsequently modified by the Minister, are set forth in the Schedule hereto:

And Whereas the Minister laid before each House of Parliament the amendments set forth in the said Schedule and the House of Commons resolved on 19th July 1977 and the House of Lords resolved on 22nd July 1977 that they should be approved:

Now, therefore, the Minister in pursuance of section 2 of the Agricultural Marketing Act 1958(c) and Schedule 1 to that Act, hereby makes the following order:—

1. This order may be cited as the Hops Marketing Scheme (Amendment) Order 1977.

2. The amendments of the Hops Marketing Scheme 1932, as amended, which are set forth in the Schedule hereto are hereby approved and shall come into operation on 15th August 1977.

In Witness whereof the Official Seal of the Minister of Agriculture, Fisheries and Food is hereunto affixed on 26th July 1977.

(L.S.)

John Silkin,
Minister of Agriculture, Fisheries and Food.

(a) S.R. & O. 1932/505 (Rev. I, p. 203: 1932, p. 24).
(b) S.R. & O. 1934/841, 1939/444, 1945/1486, S.I. 1948/642 (Rev. I, p. 204: 1934 I.p. 14; 1939 I, p. 24; 1945 I, p. 1; 1948 I, p. 23), S.I. 1949/2456, 1950/655, 1955/464, 1965/406, 1972/1427, 1974/2030 (1949 I, p. 54; 1950 I, p. 38; 1955 I, p. 124; 1965 I, p. 1113; 1972 III, p. 4295; 1974 III, p. 7857).
(c) 1958 c. 47.

SCHEDULE

The Hops Marketing Scheme 1932, as amended, shall be further amended as follows:—

1. By inserting in sub-paragraph (*b*) of paragraph 35 thereof after the words "hop plants", in both places where those words occur, the words "and hop baling presses";

2. By inserting immediately after paragraph 38 thereof the following paragraph:—

"38A.—(1) The provisions of paragraphs 39, 40, 41 and 42 of this Scheme shall have no effect in respect of hops harvested after 31st December 1976.

(2) The provisions of the Fourth Schedule to this Scheme shall have effect only in respect of hops harvested after 31st December 1976.";

3. By substituting in sub-paragraph (2) of paragraph 54 thereof for the words "the Permanent Joint Hops Committee or with such other" the word "such";

4. By substituting for paragraph 75 thereof the following paragraph:—

"75. Any producer who is aggrieved by any act or omission of the Board may refer the matter to the arbitration of a single arbitrator to be agreed between him and the Board or in default of agreement to be nominated by the Minister, and the arbitrator may make such order in the matter as he thinks just:

Provided that for the purposes of any arbitration under this paragraph, every notice purporting to be given under paragraph 39 of, or paragraphs 2, 3 or 4 of the Fourth Schedule to, this Scheme and every allotment of a Basic Quota purporting to be made under Part VII of this Scheme, shall be conclusively presumed to have been correct, unless the claim to refer the matter to arbitration was received by the Board on or before the twenty-eighth day after the day on which the claimant first had notice of the weight, grading or valuation or the allotment.

The Arbitration Act 1950(a), or any amendment or re-enactment thereof for the time being in force shall apply in relation to the reference.";

5. By inserting at the end thereof the following Schedule:—

"The Fourth Schedule

1.—(1) The Board may at any time sell or otherwise deal with any hops accepted by the Board notwithstanding that they have not been weighed, graded or valued, or that notices have not been sent, in accordance with any provision of this Scheme.

(2) If the total quantity of hops of any season accepted by the Board from a registered producer does not exceed his annual quota for that season as ascertained under Part VII of this Scheme, all the hops of that season accepted by the Board from him shall (except as otherwise provided in the Scheme as respects insufficiently cured hops) be treated as for 'quota account'.

(3) If the total quantity of hops of any season accepted by the Board from a registered producer exceeds his annual quota for that season as ascertained as aforesaid, then, of the hops so accepted, a quantity equal to the amount of that annual quota shall (except as otherwise provided in the Scheme as respects insufficiently cured hops) be treated as for 'quota account' and the remainder shall be treated as for 'non-quota account'.

Payment for hops on a category pool basis:

2.—(1) The following definitions shall apply for the purposes of this and the two immediately following paragraphs of this Schedule:

"available sum" in relation to any season, means the sum realised by the Board in respect of the sale of hops harvested in that season after deducting any sum set aside in accordance with sub-paragraph (3) of paragraph 5 of this Schedule or payable in accordance with paragraph 8 of this Schedule;

(a) 1950 c. 27.

"category" means any category of hops prescribed by the Board by reference to variety, grade, description (which term shall include description by reference to the area, district, locality or place in which they were harvested), alpha acid content, seed content, or any other factor or factors which shall be specified in the prescription;

"Forward Contract Plan" has the meaning ascribed to it in sub-paragraph (4)(b) of paragraph 3 of this Schedule;

"hops to be treated as for non-quota account" in relation to any season shall include any hops harvested in that season which are in the opinion of the Board insufficiently cured:

Provided that, if the Board by resolution so determine, such hops may be treated as for 'quota account' in any season when, in the opinion of the Board, the supply of hops accepted by the Board is less than the demand;

"provisional valuation" means any valuation determined by the Board in accordance with sub-paragraph (6) of this paragraph or sub-paragraph (1) of paragraph 4 of this Schedule;

"relevant sum" means that part of the available sum which is realised by the Board in respect of the sale of hops of a particular category;

"revised valuation" means any valuation arrived at in accordance with sub-paragraph (9) of this paragraph or sub-paragraph (2) of paragraph 4 of this Schedule.

(2) If the Board shall, not later than 31st August 1977 and not later than 1st April in any subsequent calendar year, send notice to registered producers that the Board will pay on a category pool basis for hops harvested in the forthcoming season, then sub-paragraphs (3) to (9) of this paragraph, and the whole of the next following paragraph, shall apply to such hops.

(3) The Board shall, not later than 1st September in the year in which the hops are to be harvested, prescribe categories of hops and send notice to registered producers accordingly:
Provided that:
(i) the Board may, not later than the 31st March of the year next following the said year, vary any such prescription by reference to alpha acid content, seed content, market requirement or any other factor which could not, in the opinion of the Board, reasonably have been prescribed by 1st September in the year in which the hops were to be harvested;
(ii) the categories shall be so prescribed that any hops which are accepted by the Board (other than seedless hops in respect of which the Board decide to make payments in accordance with paragraph 8 of this Schedule) shall be capable of being allocated to one, but not more than one, of the categories.

(4) The Board shall cause all hops accepted from any registered producer to be weighed and graded and shall, as soon as the relevant matters have been determined, allocate them to the appropriate category or categories and shall send notice of these matters to the registered producer.

(5) The Board shall, for each grade of hops included in any category, determine a provisional price per 50 kilograms on such basis as shall ensure, in the opinion of the Board, that the relationship among provisional prices reflects the relative market values of the grades of hops concerned:
Provided that the Board may fix provisional prices for lower grade hops falling within any category according to their estimate of the quality of such hops.

(6) The Board shall use the provisional prices determined in accordance with sub-paragraph (5) of this paragraph to establish a separate provisional valuation for the total quantity of each registered producer's hops which has been allocated by the Board to each category.

(7) The Board shall send to each registered producer concerned notice of the provisional prices and any provisional valuations determined in accordance with the foregoing provisions of this paragraph.

(8) When sales by the Board of hops allocated to any category are, in the opinion of the Board, substantially complete, the Board shall reduce or increase the provisional prices determined in accordance with sub-paragraph (5) of this paragraph having regard to the provisions of any Forward Contract Plan for the time being in force and in the light of the actual prices realised by the Board for hops in that category.

(9) The Board shall use the revised prices arrived at in accordance with sub-paragraph (8) of this paragraph to establish a separate revised valuation for the total quantity of each registered producer's hops which has been allocated to each category.

3.—(1) The Board shall determine for each registered producer which of the hops valued in accordance with sub-paragraph (9) of the foregoing paragraph are to be treated as for quota and non-quota account respectively, subject to exercise by the registered producer of any rights under sub-paragraph (ii) of the proviso to paragraph 52 of this Scheme, and shall send notice to the registered producer concerned of this determination, and of the revised valuations of all such hops.

(2) Subject to the provisions of any Forward Contract Plan for the time being in force, the Board shall exercise their power under sub-paragraph (1) of this paragraph in such a way as will in the opinion of the Board maximise the payment made to any registered producer.

(3) The Board shall modify any determination made in accordance with sub-paragraph (1) of this paragraph to take account of any exercise by any registered producer concerned of his rights under sub-paragraph (ii) of the proviso to paragraph 52 of this Scheme:

Provided that this sub-paragraph shall apply only where particulars of such exercise of rights are notified to the Board by such date as the Board shall prescribe.

(4) (a) If the Board shall have established a Forward Contract Plan for any season, in accordance with the next following sub-paragraph 3(4)(b), applicable to any category, then the Board shall first divide the relevant sum in respect of that category among registered producers who have contracted with the Board under such Plan until there has been appropriated to each of them an amount equal to the entitlement (if any) of such producer under the terms of such Plan in respect of that category.

(b) For the purposes of this paragraph a Forward Contract Plan is a Plan established by resolution of the Board, primarily in order the better to secure that the Board will be in a position to fulfil their own commitments to sell hops under forward contracts and which shall define in respect of any season:

(i) the terms and conditions upon which the Board may enter into an agreement with any registered producer under which that producer would undertake specified obligations as to the quantity of hops of specified categories produced by him (being hops of a specified season which are to be treated as for quota account) which he will consign to the Board and the Board would undertake specified obligations as to the payments to be made to such producer in respect of the actual consignment of all or part of such hops to the Board;

(ii) a date (not being later than 31st December immediately preceding the season (or the earliest season) in respect of which the said agreements are to operate) before which notice giving particulars of the Plan for that season shall have been sent by the Board to each registered producer.

(5) If any balance of the relevant sum for any category then remains, then (after taking any action affecting the same which they consider appropriate under sub-paragraph (6) of this paragraph) the Board shall divide such sum among registered producers in proportion to their respective revised valuations for hops in that category which are to be treated as for quota account, other than those hops in respect of which an appropriation has been made under sub-paragraph (4)(*a*) above until there has been appropriated to each of them an amount equal to such valuation, or, if the relevant sum is insufficient for that purpose, until it has been exhausted.

(6) Where, in the opinion of the Board, the relevant sum relating to a category of hops comprising varieties of hops which the Board regard as trial varieties is insufficient to encourage the continued supply of such varieties, the Board may, if and to the extent that they think fit, supplement the relevant sum out of the balance of the relevant sum for any other category remaining after the appropriations provided for in sub-paragraphs (4) and (5) of this paragraph have been made, or (if for special reasons the Board consider it desirable to do so) then out of such last-mentioned relevant sum before such appropriations have been made.

(7) If, after the Board have acted in accordance with sub-paragraphs (4) and (5) of this paragraph, and taken any action which they consider appropriate under sub-paragraph (6) of this paragraph, in respect of any category, and a balance still remains of the relevant sum for that category, the Board shall divide such balance, on such basis as they think fit, among registered producers having revised valuations for hops in the category to which the relevant sum relates which are to be treated as for non-quota account, but so that the Board shall be under no obligation to pay for such hops for non-quota account as are not sold by the Board.

(8) When the Board have determined, under sub-paragraphs (4), (5), (6) and (7) of this paragraph, the sums which, apart from this sub-paragraph, would be payable to any registered producer, the Board shall deduct from the aggregate of such sums such amounts as are provided for under paragraph 6 of this Schedule and shall pay the balance of such aggregate sum to the registered producer concerned.

Payment for hops not on a category pool basis:

4.—(1) If in relation to the hops harvested in any season the Board shall not have sent notice to registered producers as provided in sub-paragraph (2) of paragraph 2 of this Schedule the Board shall weigh all such hops tendered to them by any registered producer and accepted by them, shall provisionally value such hops having regard to the principles set out in sub-paragraph (5) of paragraph 2 of this Schedule as the Board consider appropriate and shall send notice to the producer of the weights so found, and of the provisional valuation.

(2) When sales of hops harvested in that season are, in the opinion of the Board, substantially complete, the Board shall reduce or increase the provisional valuations made in accordance with sub-paragraph (1) of this paragraph in the light of the prices realised by the Board for hops so harvested and the proportion of such hops which have been sold, to arrive at revised valuations.

(3) The Board shall determine for each registered producer which of the hops valued in accordance with sub-paragraph (1) of this paragraph are to be treated as for quota and non-quota account respectively, subject to exercise by the registered producer of any rights under sub-paragraph (ii) of the proviso to paragraph 52 of this Scheme, and shall send notice to the registered producers concerned of this determination and of the revised valuations of all such hops:

Provided that:

    (i) the Board shall exercise their power under this sub-paragraph in such a way as will in the opinion of the Board maximise the payment made to any registered producer in respect of hops treated as for quota account;

   (ii) the Board shall modify any determination made in accordance with this sub-paragraph to take account of any exercise by any registered producer concerned of his rights under sub-paragraph (ii) of the proviso to paragraph 52 of this Scheme:

      Provided that this sub-paragraph (ii) shall apply only where particulars of such exercise of rights are notified to the Board by such date as the Board shall prescribe.

(4) If all hops valued in accordance with sub-paragraph (1) of this paragraph are sold by the Board, then the Board shall divide the available sum among registered producers in proportion to their respective revised valuations determined in accordance with sub-paragraph (2) of this paragraph.

(5) If some part of the hops referred to in sub-paragraph (1) of this paragraph remain unsold when sales are, in the opinion of the Board, substantially complete, then the Board shall divide the available sum among registered producers:

   (a) in proportion to their respective revised valuations, determined in accordance with sub-paragraph (2) of this paragraph, of hops to be treated as for quota account, until there has been divided among them an amount equal to the total of such valuations;

   (b) as respects any balance, on such basis as the Board consider appropriate but so that the Board shall be under no obligation to pay for such hops for non-quota account as are not sold by the Board.

(6) When the Board have determined, under sub-paragraphs (4) and (5) of this paragraph, the sums which, apart from this sub-paragraph, would be payable to any registered producer, the Board shall deduct from the aggregate of such sums such amounts as are provided for under paragraph 6 of this Schedule and shall pay the balance of such aggregate sum to the registered producer concerned.

Incentive Fund:

5.—(1) The following definitions shall apply for the purposes of this paragraph:

"designated amount" means the amount or maximum amount of the incentive payment for each 50 kilograms of hops designated by the Board;

"designated hops" means hops of the season and description designated by the Board in accordance with sub-paragraph (2) of this paragraph;

"Incentive Fund" means the total sum set aside by the Board in accordance wih sub-paragraph (3) of this paragraph.

(2) The Board may, not later than 30th November in any calendar year, send to each registered producer a notice designating hops of the forthcoming season, by reference to variety, place of harvesting, grade or any other description which may be designated in the notice as hops for which an incentive payment of a designated amount shall be paid by the Board:

Provided that, where hops are designated wholly, or partly, by reference to alpha acid content or seed content, the Board need not designate the qualifying content until, in the opinion of the Board, the relevant facts have been established after harvesting.

(3) If the Board have exercised their power under sub-paragraph (2) of this paragraph in relation to hops of any season, then the Board shall set aside, out of the sum realised by the Board in respect of hops harvested in that season, such sum as shall, in the opinion of the Board, suffice to enable the Board to pay the designated amounts on all designated hops accepted by the Board from registered producers, whether for quota account only or for quota account and non-quota account, as the Board may prescribe.

(4) The Board shall pay to each registered producer the appropriate designated amount or, if the appropriate designated amount is a maximum amount, such part thereof as the Board shall think fit, for each 50 kilograms of designated hops accepted from him by the Board:

Provided that if the Incentive Fund proves insufficient to make payments as provided for in this sub-paragraph, the Board may draw from their reserves such further sum as may be required for this purpose.

(5) If any balance of the Incentive Fund then remains the Board may retain it for similar use in a subsequent season or may treat it as part of the general funds of the Board, as they shall think fit.

Deductions to be made by the Board:

6. The deductions to which reference is made in sub-paragraph (8) of paragraph 3, and sub-paragraph (6) of paragraph 4 of this Schedule shall be such sums as the Board shall determine:

> (*a*) as commission on such basis as the Board consider appropriate in the light of charges made to the Board for relevant services;

> (*b*) in order to provide:

>> (i) for the expenses of the Board (other than commission) in respect of hops of the relevant season;

>> (ii) a contribution to the fund required to enable the Board to meet their general expenses and liabilities (including any liability to pay compensation under this Scheme) and, if they think fit, provide reserves:

Provided that any deduction under sub-paragraph (*b*) of this paragraph shall be determined, in either case, at the same rate for each 50 kilograms of hops accepted by the Board;

> (*c*) as a deduction which shall in the opinion of the Board be just, having regard to the circumstances of any case where hops are found to be contaminated after acceptance by the Board:

Provided always that the amount to be deducted as aforesaid from any sum payable to a registered producer shall under no circumstances exceed the sum payable.

Notices:

7.—(1) The information contained in any notice of weight, grading or valuation sent in accordance with paragraphs 2, 3 or 4 of this Schedule shall be final and conclusive unless and until varied by agreement between the Board and the producer concerned or by an award under Part X of this Scheme.

(2) Neither the accidental omission by the Board to send to or serve on any registered producer any notice or notification as required by any provision of this Scheme (except paragraph 48), nor the non-receipt thereof by any registered producer, shall invalidate any act of the Board.

Seedless Hops:

8. Notwithstanding any other provision in this Scheme, where in the opinion of the Board it would be impracticable or inappropriate for registered producers of seedless hops to receive payment in respect thereof in accordance with the provisions of this Scheme, other than this paragraph, then the Board shall out of the available sum (as defined in sub-paragraph (1) of paragraph 2 of this Schedule), make such payments as they consider appropriate in respect of such hops. In this paragraph the expression "seedless hops" includes hops of which the seed content does not exceed a maximum prescribed by the Board and which are grown on sites specified and approved by the Board."

EXPLANATORY NOTE

(This Note is not part of the Order.)

This Order approves the amendments to the Hops Marketing Scheme 1932, as amended, which are set forth in the Schedule. The amendments provide, in respect of hops harvested after 31st December 1976, for Varietal Pools and a Forward Contract Plan and bring up to date the existing provisions relating to the Incentive Fund. The amendments make also minor and consequential changes to the Scheme.

STATUTORY INSTRUMENTS

1977 No. 1281

COUNTER-INFLATION

The Prices and Charges (Notification of Increases and Information) Order 1977

Made - - - - -	*27th July* 1977
Laid before Parliament -	*29th July* 1977
Coming into Operation -	*1st August* 1977

ARRANGEMENT OF ARTICLES

PART I

PRELIMINARY

The Secretary of State, in exercise of powers conferred on him by sections 5 and 15 of, and paragraphs 1(1) and 2(*a*) and (*b*), 2(4) and 3 of Schedule 2 and paragraphs 1(1), (2), (4) and (6) and 2(2) of Schedule 3 to, the Counter-Inflation Act 1973(**a**) as amended under the Prices Act 1974(**b**) and by sections 14 and 15(4) of the Price Commission Act 1977(**c**), and of all other powers enabling him in that behalf, hereby makes the following Order:—

PART I

PRELIMINARY

Citation, commencement and interpretation

1.—(1) This Order may be cited as the Prices and Charges (Notification of Increases and Information) Order 1977 and shall come into operation on 1st August 1977.

(2) In this Order—
"the 1973 Act" means the Counter-Inflation Act 1973;

"the 1977 Act" means the Price Commission Act 1977;

"bank, finance house or similar enterprise" means a person (other than a building society incorporated under the Building Societies Act 1962(**d**) or under the enactments repealed by that Act) whose ordinary business includes the business of banking, the business of lending money, the letting of goods under hire purchase agreements, or the selling of goods under conditional sale agreements;

"base period" has the meaning assigned to it by article 3(6);

"coal or steel undertaking" means an undertaking as defined in article 80 of the Treaty establishing the European Coal and Steel Community, signed at Paris on 18th April 1951, otherwise than for the special purposes therein mentioned;

"the code" means the code for the time being contained in an order (**e**) under section 2 of the 1973 Act as amended by section 15(1) of the 1977 Act;

"the 1976 code" means the code set out in the Counter-Inflation (Price Code) Order 1976 (**f**) as amended (**g**);

"the Commission" means the Price Commission established by section 1(1) of the 1973 Act;

"distributor" means a person who carries on in the course of business activities falling within Order XXIII (other than the wholesale slaughtering of animals for human consumption, leasing industrial or office machinery, the hiring of furniture, radio and television sets and other domestic appli-

---

(**a**) 1973 c. 9.
(**c**) 1977 c. 33.
(**e**) S.I. 1977/1272 (1977 II, p. 3541).
(**g**) S.I. 1976/2207 (1976 III, p. 6190).

(**b**) *See* S.I. 1974/1218 (1974 II, p. 4631).
(**d**) 1962 c. 37.
(**f**) S.I. 1976/1170 (1976 II, p. 3226).

ances or the activities of bakers or processors of scrap metals) or falling within minimum list heading 894 of Order XXVI (other than the repairing of motor vehicles) of the Standard Industrial Classification;

"gross percentage margin" has the meaning assigned to it by paragraph 35 of the code;

"local authority" means, in England and Wales, a county council, the Greater London Council, the Common Council of the City of London, a district council or a London borough council and, in Scotland, a regional council, an islands council and a district council;

"manufacturer" means a person other than a local authority who carries on in the course of business activities falling within Orders II, III (other than the quick freezing of meat, poultry or fish, the curing of bacon or ham and the preparation of oven-ready poultry), IV to XIX, XXI (other than minimum list heading 603) and XXII (other than a travel ticket agent) of the Standard Industrial Classification and bakers;

"net profit margin" has the meaning assigned to it by paragraph 11 of the code;

"provider of construction services" means a person who carries on in the course of business activities falling within Order XX of the Standard Industrial Classification (other than the hiring of contractors' plant and scaffolding);

"provider of professional services" means a person who carries on in the course of business activities falling within Order XXV (other than the provision of school meals) of the Standard Industrial Classification or the activity of a house or estate agent;

"provider of services" means a person other than a local authority who carries on in the course of business activities falling within minimum list headings 864 and 865 of Order XXIV or within Order XXVI (other than minimum list heading 894) of the Stardard Industrial Classification or the hiring of furniture, radio and television sets and other domestic appliances, or the hiring of contractors' plant and scaffolding or the leasing of industrial and office machinery or the repairing of motor vehicles or the activities of a travel ticket agent;

"the Standard Industrial Classification" means the edition thereof published by Her Majesty's Stationery Office in 1968, as amended by Amendment List No. 1 so published in 1977 together with the alphabetical list of industries so published in 1968 as amended by Amendment Lists Nos. 1 and 2 so published in 1970 and 1977 respectively;

"water authority" includes a statutory water company and, in the Isles of Scilly only, a local authority and, in Scotland, a water authority within the meaning of section 148 of the Local Government (Scotland) Act 1973(a),

and all other expressions have the same respective meanings as they have for the purposes of the 1973 Act and the 1977 Act.

(a) 1973 c. 65.

(3) Where a person satisfies more than one of the definitions of the following expressions contained in paragraph (2) above, that is to say, "bank, finance house or similar enterprise", "distributor", "manufacturer", "provider of construction services", "provider of professional services" and "provider of services", the provisions of this Order shall apply to him in relation to each of the expressions he satisfies.

(4) Except as provided in articles 5(3) and 11, paragraph 2(1) of Schedule 3 to the 1973 Act (which relates to the identification of two or more different persons) shall apply for the purposes of this Order as it applies for the purposes of sections 5 and 6 of that Act but—

(a) in relation to article 7 only so as to require a person to notify an increased price or charge which he himself intends to implement; and

(b) in relation to articles 14, 16 to 19 and 21 only so as to require a person to furnish returns or to keep records relating to the activities which he himself carries on:

Provided that any of the several persons who are by virtue of this paragraph to be treated as one may, in the case of (a), serve a notification under article 7 on behalf of himself and of any other such person and, in the case of (b), may furnish returns or keep records on behalf of any other such person.

(5) In relation to persons mentioned in paragraphs 1 to 4 of Schedule 2, articles 3 to 12 of this Order shall apply only to banking and any other activity carried on by those persons which falls within the definition of "manufacturer" or "provider of services" in paragraph (2) above.

(6) Nothing in this Order applies to any person who is a body established for religious, charitable, educational, representational or recreational purposes, which is non-profit making and does not carry on a trade or business as its main activity.

(7) The Interpretation Act 1889 (a) shall apply for the interpretation of this Order as it applies for the interpretation of an Act of Parliament and as if this Order and the Orders hereby revoked were Acts of Parliament.

Revocation and saving

2.—(1) Subject to paragraphs (2) and (3) below the Orders set out in Schedule 1 to this Order are hereby revoked.

(2) Article 7 shall not impose any obligation on any person in respect of any increase in a price or charge of which notice has been given to the Commission in pursuance of an order under section 5 of the 1973 Act referred to in paragraph (1) above so far as that increase is implemented before 1st October 1977; but any such increase or part thereof not implemented before that date is subject to section 21(4) of the 1977 Act.

(3) Anything done under the Counter-Inflation (Notification of Increases in Prices and Charges) Order 1976 (b), being a thing mentioned in paragraph (4), and anything done under the Counter-Inflation (Prices and Charges)

(a) 1889 c. 63.   (b) S.I. 1976/1171 (1976 II, p. 3280).

(Information) Order 1976 (**a**) (both of which orders are revoked by paragraph (1) above) or under any provision in any earlier order under section 5 or 15 of the 1973 Act, being in the former case a provision corresponding to any one of those mentioned in paragraph (4), shall, for the purposes of this Order, be treated as if it had been done under the corresponding provision of this Order and as if this Order had then been in operation.

(4) The things done under the Counter-Inflation (Notification of Increases in Prices and Charges) Order 1976 which are referred to in paragraph (3) above and to which that paragraph applies are—

> (*a*) any certificate made by the Commission under article 7;

> (*b*) any notice given by the Commission under article 9; and

> (*c*) anything done or required to be done under article 12.

Application of Order

3.—(1) This article shall have effect only for the purpose of ascertaining whether any provision of this Order applies to a person by reason of sales exceeding a certain amount.

(2) Subject to paragraphs (3), (4) and (5) of this article, there shall be taken into account in determining sales, in relation to goods, the total amount (excluding excise duties) of prices charged for their sale in the course of business in the base period and, in relation to services, the total amount of charges made in the base period for their performance, there being left out of account in either case trade discounts, rebates and other allowances.

(3) There shall be left out of account—

> (*a*) any price or charge to which, by virtue of paragraph 1 of Schedule 3, this Order does not apply and, in the case of transport, charges for carriage between terminals of which one or both are outside the United Kingdom and charges for carriage between points in the United Kingdom where the tariff applicable to those charges is one for the whole of the first-mentioned carriage;

> (b) in the case of a person who is a manufacturer, the price for the sale of goods manufactured by another person and the price for the sale of goods or the charge for the performance of services in the course of any activity not mentioned in the definition of "manufacturer" in article 1(2);

> (c) in the case of a provider of services, the price for the sale of goods or the charge for the performance of services in the course of any activity not mentioned in the definition of "provider of services" in article 1(2);

> (*d*) in the case of a person who has ceased to carry on an activity in the course of business since the beginning of the base period, any price or charge in respect of that activity.

(4) There shall also be left out of account car tax payable by the person in question and value added tax which is, under Part I of the Finance Act 1972(**b**), chargeable by the person in question on the supply by him of goods

---

(a) S.I. 1976/1172 (1976 II, p. 3298).   (b) 1972 c. 41.

and services (including goods and services specified in an order under section 6 of that Act) other than on the supply of any goods of which the price, or any services for which the charge, is under paragraph (3) above to be left out of account.

(5) Where a person has not carried on any activity in the course of business throughout the whole of the base period—

> (*a*) in the case of a person who commenced to carry on that activity in the course of business (not being an activity to which sub-paragraph (*b*) of this paragraph applies) during the base period, the amounts determined under this article apart from this paragraph shall be increased by the proportion which 12 months bears to the period falling within the base period during which the person carried on that activity;

> (*b*) in the case of a person who commenced to carry on that activity in the base period in succession to another person (whether upon purchase, amalgamation or reconstruction, or otherwise) the amounts determined under this article apart from this paragraph both in respect of the person and of that other person shall be aggregated and—

>> (i) if the aggregate of the periods during which the person and that other person carried on that activity during the base period exceeds 12 months, the aggregated amounts shall be reduced; or

>> (ii) if the aggregate of those periods is less than 12 months, the aggregated amounts shall be increased;

> by the proportion which 12 months bears to the aggregate of those periods;

> (*c*) in the case of a person who commenced to carry on an activity after the end of the base period in succession to another person (whether upon purchase, amalgamation or reconstruction, or otherwise) this article shall apply to the person as it would have applied to that other person had he carried on no other activity in the course of business in the base period.

(6) In this Order, "base period" in relation to any person means his latest completed year of account; and the amounts referred to in paragraph (2) above shall, where the accounting period is longer than 12 months, be reduced or, where the accounting period is shorter than 12 months, be increased by the proportion which 12 months bears to the length of the accounting period.

(7) In ascertaining the amount of sales in relation to any person, whether as a manufacturer or as a provider of services, account shall be taken of all transactions effected by the persons (of whom he is one) who are, under the provisions of paragraph 2(1) of Schedule 3 to the 1973 Act, to be treated as one, including any transaction between such persons except where both parties to the transaction are acting as manufacturers or as providers of services, as the case may be.

Meaning of increase

4.—(1) In ascertaining for the purposes of this Order whether a price or charge represents an increase, the following provisions of this article shall have effect.

(2) The price or charge shall be compared with those charged or made by a

person in the course of business for comparable transactions as regards goods or services of the same description and, as between earlier and later transactions, account shall only be taken of the latest.

(3) If there are no prices or charges which can be taken for comparison under paragraph (2) above, the comparison may be with prices or charges charged or made by that person in the course of business for transactions which are not in all respects comparable and, as regards goods or services which are not of precisely the same description, with a fair adjustment to take account of the differences; and as between different transactions or different descriptions of goods or services, those taken for comparison under this paragraph shall be those which are most closely comparable.

(4) Where a person charges or makes different prices or charges for the same goods or services in relation to different persons or to persons of different descriptions or to the same persons or descriptions of persons in different circumstances, a price or charge shall be treated as an increased price or charge in relation to any person only if it exceeds the price or charge charged or made in relation to the same person, persons of the same description or persons of the same description in the same circumstances, as the case may be.

(5) A price or charge shall not be treated for the purposes of this Order as an increased price or charge only because it exceeds an earlier price or charge if the increase does not exceed the cash amount of—

(a) any increase (including a change from a nil amount) in—

    (i) excise duties, customs duties or car tax on, or on anything comprised in, the goods in question which, whether by virtue of a contract or otherwise, is, or is to be, borne in the particular case by the person intending to implement the increase; or

    (ii) value added tax chargeable by that person on the supply of the goods or services in question; or

    (iii) any fee prescribed (a) under sub-section (3) of section 11 of the Weights and Measures Act 1963 (b) or sub-section (3) of section 5 of the Weights and Measures Act (Northern Ireland) 1967 (c) (both of which provisions relate to the passing and stamping as fit for use for trade of weighing or measuring equipment) which is payable in respect of, or of anything comprised in, the goods in question by the person intending to implement the increase; or

(b) except for the purposes of article 19 any reduction in subsidy under section 1 of the Prices Act 1974 (d) on any food, or on any ingredient in a food product, received by the person intending to implement the increase.

Provisions supplemental to article 4 relating to cost adjustment provisions

5.—(1) Subject to article 4, an increased price or charge shall be treated for the purposes of this Order as an increased price or charge because it exceeds an earlier price or charge unless the condition specified in paragraph (2) below is satisfied.

(a) *See* S.I. 1975/1381 (1975 II, p. 4737).   (b) 1963 c. 31.
(c) 1967 c. 6 (N.I.).   (d) 1974 c. 24.

(2) The condition referred to in the preceding paragraph is a condition that the increased price or charge is made in accordance with any formula, which provides for the price or charge to be varied because of changes in costs specified in a provision of the contract under which the increased price or charge is proposed to be charged or made and that either—

(a) that provision was subsisting at 25th March 1974; or

(b) it was the established practice at that date of the person proposing to implement the increased price or charge to be party, as seller of the goods or as provider of the services, to contracts containing a provision specifying the same formula as, or a formula similar to, the above-mentioned formula whereby that person sold or agreed to sell goods or to perform services (being, in either case, of the same description as those to which the increased price or charge relates) to persons in the capacity of distributors or in the capacity of domestic consumers; or

(c) the contract provides for the goods to be sold to, or for the service to be performed for, any person except in the capacity of a distributor or in the capacity of a domestic consumer.

(3) For the purposes of this article paragraph 2(1)(b) of Schedule 3 to the 1973 Act shall not have effect.

Ranges of products

6.—In a case where a person has for the purposes of any order under section 5 of the 1973 Act hereby revoked or of any previous order under that section treated any product as forming part of a particular range of related products, he shall, for the purposes of this Order, continue to treat that product as forming part of that range, being, in a case where the product has on different occasions been treated for the first-mentioned purposes as forming part of different ranges, the range of which the product was treated as forming part on the last occasion before 1st August 1977, unless the Commission certify, having regard to changes in the person's practice of determining prices and charges, that this article shall not apply to the product in question.

PART II

NOTIFICATION OF INCREASES

Obligation to notify increased prices and charges

7.—(1) Subject to the provisions of articles 8 to 11 before a person specified in paragraph (3) below implements in the course of any business carried on by him in the United Kingdom—

(*a*) an increased price for the sale of goods or an increased charge for the performance of services previously sold or provided; or

(*b*) in respect of goods or services which are not identical with goods or services previously sold or performed, a price or charge in excess of that in respect of goods or services of substantially the same description as the goods or services in respect of which the price or charge is proposed to be implemented;

(not being, in either case, goods or services of a kind referred to in Schedule 3) he shall give notice of the proposed price or charge, as the case may be, to the Commission in accordance with article 12:

Provided that no notice need be given under this article—

(i) (except in a case where (ii) below applies) if the increase taken with any earlier increase implemented during the period of 12 months immediately preceding the date of implementation of the increase is not more than 2 per cent of the latest price or charge before the commencement of that period; and

(ii) in the case of an increase relating to a range of related products or services, if the increase (weighted by value of sales in a period of not less than 12 weeks and not more than 14 weeks ending not more than 14 weeks before the date of implementation of the increase), taken with any increase in respect of such goods or services implemented during the period of 12 months immediately preceding that date, does not exceed 2 per cent of the average price (weighted by value of sales in a period of not less than 12 weeks ending not more than 14 weeks before the commencement of that period);

and article 4 shall, with necessary modifications, have effect for determining whether an increase exceeds the limits specified in this proviso.

(2) If, notwithstanding the proviso to paragraph (1) above, notice of an increase not exceeding the limits therein specified is given to the Commission, this order has effect as if the notice were a notice required to be given under that paragraph.

(3) The persons referred to in paragraph (1) above are—

(*a*) any person who is a manufacturer and has sales exceeding £12,000,000;

(*b*) any person who is a provider of services and has sales exceeding £9,000,000;

(*c*) any person specified in Schedule 2 and subject to the provisions of that Schedule;

(*d*) a water authority in England and Wales having sales exceeding £9,000,000.

(4) This article applies—

(a) in the case of a manufacturer, only to the price for goods sold and to the charge for services performed in the course of an activity referred to in the definition of "manufacturer" in article 1(2); and

(b) in the case of a provider of services, only to the price for goods sold and to the charge for services performed in the course of an activity referred to in the definition of "provider of services" in article 1(2).

(5) A price or charge in respect of which an increase is required to be notified to the Commission shall be restricted by the exclusion of the increase for the period of 28 days beginning with the date of service of the notification on the Commission; and a person shall contravene the Order if he implements the increase before the end of that period.

Provisions supplemental to article 7

Small activities

8.—(1) Article 7 shall not apply, in relation to any person referred to in paragraph (3)(a) or (b) of that article, to the price or charge for any goods or services—

(a) manufactured or performed in the course of any activity falling within any of the minimum list headings of the Standard Industrial Classification; or

(b) manufactured or performed in the course of any one or more activities falling within one minimum list heading of the Standard Industrial Classification, which the Commission certify, having regard to the person's established practice of determining prices or charges, may be treated as an activity or activities separate from other activities falling within the minimum list heading:

Provided that the sales of the person in question in respect of all his activities within the minimum list heading in question or, in the case of (b) above, in respect of any of his activities treated as a separate activity, do not exceed the lesser of 10 per cent of his sales and—

(i) in the case of a manufacturer, £10,000,000; and

(ii) in the case of a provider of services, £7,500,000.

(2) In ascertaining whether sales exceed the amounts referred to in paragraph (1) above the provisions of article 3 shall apply, but no account shall be taken of any goods or services referred to in Schedule 3.

Resale of goods by provider of services

9. A person referred to in paragraph (3)(b) of article 7 shall not be required by that article to give notice to the Commission of an increased price for the sale of any goods if those goods are manufactured by another person (not being a person who, under paragraph 2(1) of Schedule 3 to the 1973 Act is to be treated as one with that person) and that increased price does not exceed the price for the sale of identical goods charged by the person who manufactured them.

Goods comprising more than one component

10.—(1) Where—

(*a*) in a notification of an intended increase in the price of any goods, a person states that goods of that description may or will be comprised (with or without change) in other goods specified in the notification; and

(*b*) the price for the sale of the former goods may be charged—

(i) in accordance with this Order or in accordance with the consent of the Commission or of the Minister; and

(ii) without contravening any restriction imposed by or under the provisions of the 1977 Act mentioned in paragraph (2) below and without breaching any undertaking given pursuant to section 7 or 12 of that Act; and

(*c*) the former goods are comprised (with or without change) in any other goods so specified and manufactured by that person;

article 7 shall not apply to the implementation of an increase in the price for the sale of those other goods if—

(i) that increase is no greater than the cash amount of the increase in the price for the sale of the former goods; and

(ii) before the implementation of the increase in the price for the sale of the former goods, the Commission have not given notice to that person that article 7 shall apply to the implementation of an increase in the price for sale of those other goods.

(2) The provisions of the 1977 Act referred to in sub-paragraph (*b*)(i) of paragraph (1) above are—

(*a*) section 4(2)(*b*) (which modifies and extends the restrictions on implementation of price increases imposed by section 5 of the 1973 Act where the Commission give notification of their intention to investigate a price increase);

(*b*) section 7(1) (which gives temporary effect to recommendations of the Commission in consequence of reports on investigations); and

(*c*) sections 7(5)(*a*) and 12(3)(*b*) (which enable the Secretary of State to make orders in consequence of investigations of price increases and of examinations of questions relating to prices and charges respectively) but not including any provisions made under section 12(4) (which provides that orders under section 12(3)(*b*) may include provisions relating to recommended prices).

Sales within groups of companies

11. Where—

(*a*) a person or a company controlled by him sells goods to another company controlled by him or a company controlled by a person sells goods to him; and

(*b*) the seller sells and the purchaser purchases in the capacity of a manufacturer or of a provider of services;

then, notwithstanding the provisions of paragraph (4) of article 1, article 7 shall not have effect in relation to the price for that sale.

Method of notification

12. A notification required to be made under article 7—

(*a*) shall be in writing signed by the person or one of the persons required to make the notification or his authorised agent or, in the case of a body corporate, signed by an officer of the body corporate serving the notification, and shall be dated;

(*b*) shall contain particulars of the matters specified in Schedule 4 to this Order; and

(*c*) shall be accompanied by true copies—

(i) of all appropriate accounts containing particulars of sales ascertained under article 3 unless these have already been furnished; and

(ii) of such other documents (other than published documents generally available) which the person required to make the notification wishes to be taken into account by the Commission in exercising their functions under the 1973 Act and the 1977 Act in relation to the increase.

Approval of increases in special cases

13.—(1) Where a notification of a proposed increased price or charge served on the Commission under article 12 relates to an increase which would not be in accordance with the provisions of the code unless the Commission exercised their powers under—

(*a*) paragraph 22 (which relates to modifications of the reference level);

(*b*) paragraph 23 (which relates to relief for low profits);

(*c*) paragraph 49(4) (which relates to profit margins of goods subject to certain indirect taxes);

and contains a request that the notification shall be treated as a request for approval of the proposed increase under any of those powers, the Commission shall entertain the proposal and shall, within the period of 56 days beginning when the notification is served on them, give notice to the applicant either—

(i) that they approve the proposed increase; or

(ii) that they approve the proposed increase subject to the conditions, limitations or qualifications (if any) specified in the notice; or

(iii) that they do not approve the proposed increase:

Provided that the approval of an increase in a price or charge under this article shall not permit the increase to be implemented before the end of the period referred to in article 7(5).

(2) Except in the case of a proposed increase under paragraph 22 of the code, where the Commission have not, within the period of 56 days beginning with the date of service on them of the notification, served on the person giving the notification a notice under paragraph (1) above, they shall be deemed for the purposes of any provision of Schedule 2 to the 1973 Act to have given their approval to the proposed increase; and any approval which is deemed to have been given by virtue of this paragraph shall be subject to the condition that, if it appears to the Commission that the net profit

margin relating to the price or charge to which the approval relates exceeds the appropriate reference level under the code, they may at any time exercise their powers under section 6 of the 1973 Act.

PART III

INFORMATION RELATING TO PRICES AND CHARGES

Periodical returns

Obligation to furnish periodical returns

14. Subject to article 23, each person, not being a local authority or a water authority—

(*a*) who is a manufacturer and has sales exceeding £12,000,000;

(*b*) who is a distributor and has sales exceeding £18,000,000;

(*c*) who is a provider of services and has sales exceeding £9,000,000;

(*d*) who is a provider of construction services and has sales exceeding £9,000,000;

(*e*) who is a provider of professional services and has sales exceeding £900,000; or

(*f*) who is a bank, finance house, or similar enterprise and had on 30th March 1973 gross sterling deposits exceeding £200,000,000 or, in the case of one or more companies which are banks, finance houses or similar enterprises and are controlled by the same person, together with that person, had on that date gross sterling deposits exceeding that amount;

shall furnish to the Commission returns in accordance with article 15 relating to each activity carried on by him in the course of business being an activity referred to in the relevant definition in article 1(2).

Time for and contents of returns under article 14

15.—(1) Returns under article 14 (reconcilable with annual accounts)—

(*a*) may be related to management accounting periods but shall not be less than 4 nor more than 5 in number in each year and all, or all but one, of them shall relate to periods of approximately the same length not being less than 12 weeks save that, for the purposes of paragraphs 2, 5, 7 and 10 of Schedule 5, the returns shall relate to an exact 12 month period or to the periods mentioned in paragraph 10(4) of the code;

(*b*) shall relate to all times after 28th April 1973;

and each return shall be furnished to the Commission within 42 days after the end of the period to which it relates.

(2) No return shall be required to be furnished in relation to any period of 12 weeks during the whole of which article 14 does not apply to the person in question, or in respect of any matter of which particulars have not changed since the preceding return.

(3) A return under article 14—

(*a*) shall specify the period to which it relates and shall contain particulars of the matters specified in Part I of Schedule 5 to this Order:

Provided that a return shall not contain particulars, pursuant to paragraph 8 of that Schedule, of any settlement relating to remuneration where the settlement does not apply to more than 100 employees as defined in sub-paragraph (3) of that paragraph; and

(b) shall contain a declaration in the form and containing the particulars specified in Part II of Schedule 5 to this Order signed by the person or one of the persons required to make the return or, in the case of a body corporate, by an officer of the body corporate.

Special returns relating to investment relief

16.—(1) Where paragraph 46 (investment relief) of the code—

(a) is to be applied by a person referred to in article 14; or

(b) has been applied by such a person,

he shall furnish to the Commission—

(i) in the case of (a) above, a return giving particulars of the matters specified in paragraphs 1, 2, 5, 11 and 12 of Schedule 5; and

(ii) in the case of (b) above, within 42 days after the first six months of the relief year and after the second six months of that year, a return giving particulars of the matters specified in paragraphs 1, 2, 5, 13 and 14 of that Schedule.

(2) A return under paragraph (1) above shall be made in respect of each unit for profit margin control determined under paragraph 14 of the code in which paragraph 46 of the code is to be or has been applied.

(3) In paragraph (1) above, "the relief year" and in paragraphs 9 to 12 of Schedule 5, "expenditure on investment", "the investment year", "the relief year", "relevant expenditure" and "turnover" have the meanings assigned to them respectively in paragraphs 44 and 45 of the code.

Special returns relating to investment relief under the 1976 code

17.—(1) In a case where relief has been obtained under paragraph 98 of the 1976 code, article 16 and paragraphs 11, 12 and 13 of Schedule 5 have effect.

(2) For the purposes of sub-paragraph (1) of this article, references to "the investment year", "the relief year" and "turnover" are references to those expressions as defined in paragraph 98 of the 1976 code and references to "relevant expenditure" shall be construed in accordance with paragraph 97(3) of that code.

Special returns relating to small increases

18.—(1) A person who implements an increased price for the sale of goods or an increased charge for the performance of services which he would but for the proviso to article 7(1) be required to notify to the Commission under this Order shall, not later than 14 days after he implements the increased price or charge, furnish to the Commission a return containing particulars of the matters referred to in paragraph (2).

(2) The matters mentioned in paragraph (1) are—

(*a*) those specified in paragraphs 1, 2 and 16 of Schedule 4;

(*b*) the price or charge to which the return relates;

(*c*) the increase in the price or charge; and

(*d*) in respect of goods or services—

    (i) within head (i) of the proviso to article 7(1), the latest price or charge before the commencement of the period therein referred to;

    (ii) within head (ii) of that proviso, the average price (weighted by value of sales in a period of not less than 12 weeks ending not more than 14 weeks before the commencement of the period therein referred to).

Increases in food prices

19. A person who implements an increased price for the sale of—

(*a*) any food or food product which he would, but for the provisions of paragraph 5(*b*) of article 4, be required to notify to the Commission; or

(*b*) any product within paragraph 8 of Schedule 3,

shall, not later than seven days after he implements the increased price, furnish to the Commission a return containing the same particulars as he would be required to notify to the Commission but for those provisions; and Schedule 4 shall have effect accordingly.

Provisions supplementary to articles 16 to 19

20. A return under any of articles 16 to 19—

(*a*) shall be in writing signed by the person or one of the persons required to make the return or his authorised agent or, in the case of a body corporate, signed by an officer of the body corporate making the return;

(*b*) shall contain a declaration that to the best of the knowledge, information and belief of the person signing the return, the particulars stated in it are correct and complete; and

(*c*) shall be dated.

Records

Obligation to keep records

21. Subject to article 23 each person (other than a person referred to in article 14)—

  (*a*) who is a manufacturer and has sales exceeding £2,400,000;

  (*b*) who is a distributor and has sales exceeding £600,000;

  (*c*) who is a provider of services and has sales exceeding £600,000;

  (*d*) who is a provider of construction services and has sales exceeding £2,400,000;

  (*e*) who is a provider of professional services and has sales exceeding £240,000;

(*f*) who is a bank, finance house or similar enterprise and on 30th March 1973 had outstanding lending balances owed to him and balances outstanding under hire purchase or conditional sale agreements, repayable or payable in sterling, exceeding in total £10,000,000 or, in the case of one or more companies which are banks, finance houses or similar enterprises and are controlled by the same person, together with that person, had such balances, exceeding in total £10,000,000;

(*g*) which is a local authority or a water authority,

shall keep the records specified in article 22.

Contents of records

22.—(1) The records referred to in article 21 are records of the particulars specified in Part I of Schedule 5, but those records may be comprised in or combined with other records from which those particulars may readily be derived.

(2) The records referred to in article 21 shall be maintained—

(*a*) by a person other than a local authority and a water authority in respect of the whole of the period commencing on 29th April 1973;

(*b*) by a local authority or water authority in England and Wales, in respect of the whole of the period commencing on 1st April 1974; and

(*c*) by a local authority or water authority in Scotland, in respect of the whole of the period commencing on 15th May 1975.

Provisions supplemental to articles 14 and 21

23.—(1) Unless the Commission so request, a return under article 14 or a record under article 21 shall not contain—

(*a*) in the case of a person referred to in paragraphs (*a*) or (*c*) to (*f*) of article 14 or in paragraphs (*a*) or (*c*) to (*g*) of article 21 particulars relating to any goods or services in respect of which no notice of an intended increased price or charge is, by virtue of Schedule 3 (except paragraph 18(*c*)) to this Order, required to be given to the Commission or relating to the provision of accommodation in aircraft;

(b) in the case of any person, any particulars (other than those referred to in paragraph 1(1) of Schedule 5) which have been contained in a previous return under this Order or any earlier order under section 15 of the 1973 Act, a notification of an intended increased price or charge under this Order or any earlier order under section 5 of that Act, a proposal under an Order under paragraph 1 of Schedule 2 to that Act, or any particulars which have been furnished to the Commission pursuant to a notice under section 15(1) of that Act.

(2) A return under article 14 shall indicate which amounts (if any) contained in it are estimated amounts and a corrected amount shall be contained in the first return required to be made after corrected amounts are prepared or, where no such return is required to be made, shall be furnished in a special return within 21 days after those accounts are prepared.

Roy Hattersley,

27th July 1977. Secretary of State for Prices and Consumer Protection.

SCHEDULE 1

(Article 2(1))

Orders revoked	*References*
The Counter-Inflation (Notification of Increases in Prices and Charges) Order 1976	S.I. 1976/1171 (1976 II, p. 3280)
The Counter-Inflation (Prices and Charges) (Information) Order 1976	S.I. 1976/1172 (1976 II, p. 3298)
The Counter-Inflation (Prices and Charges) (Information) Order 1976 (Amendment) Order 1976	S.I. 1976/1377 (1976 II, p. 3782)
The Counter-Inflation (Notification of Increases in Prices and Charges) Order 1976 (Amendment) Order 1976	S.I. 1976/1378 (1976 II, p. 3783)

SCHEDULE 2

(Article 7(3)(c))

Persons required to notify increases in the price for the sale of goods or the charge for the performance of services.

1. Barclays Bank Limited.
2. Lloyds Bank Limited.
3. Midland Bank Limited.
4. National Westminster Bank Limited.
5. British Waterways Board.
6. Milk Marketing Boards, but in respect only of milk not referred to in paragraph 7 of Schedule 3.

SCHEDULE 3

(Article 3(3)(*a*) and 7(1))

Prices and charges in respect of which no notice of an intended increase is required to be made to the Price Commission.

1. The price for the sale of goods or the charge for the performance of services which are supplied, whether by the person selling or performing them or another, outside the United Kingdom or to persons or in relation to property outside the United Kingdom.

2. The price for the sale of any goods—

(*a*) which have been produced or manufactured outside the United Kingdom; and

(*b*) which have not been subjected to any process in the United Kingdom other than packing or repacking, cleaning and sterilizing or, in the case of crude oil, stabilisation; and

(*c*) which have not been sold to any person in the United Kingdom;

and the charge for the performance of any services in the United Kingdom or in relation to any property in the United Kingdom which are performed for any person outside the United Kingdom.

3. The price for the sale, whether alive or dead, of any goods produced in the course of agriculture, horticulture or fishing including—

(*a*) (except in the case of a Milk Marketing Board) liquid milk not referred to in paragraph 7 below; and

(*b*) by-products for animal feeding which arise in the milling of grain, the processing of sugar beet or oilseeds or in the manufacture of alcoholic drinks;

which have not been incorporated in any processed product and to which no process has been applied except—

(i) cleaning, sterilizing, breaking down of bulk supplies or packaging; and

(ii) in the case of any carcasses or parts of carcasses of livestock or poultry or of any product of fishing, chilling, freezing, curing, cutting up or boning, in the case only of bacon and ham, cooking and, in the case only of whole hams, canning.

4. The price for the sale before 30th August 1977 of canned, chilled, chipped, dehydrated and frozen potatoes, crisps and other snacks consisting wholly or mainly of potato and other similar potato products.

5. The price for the sale of blended butter.

6. The price for the sale of raw beet sugar for further refining.

7. The price for the sale of liquid milk of which the maximum price is for the time being controlled by an order (**a**) under section 6 of the Emergency

---

(**a**) S.I. 1971/1037, 1038; 1974/1548, 1549; 1975/1664; 1977/858, 859 (1971 II, pp. 3105, 3108; 1974 III, pp. 5867, 5869; 1975 III, p. 5720; 1977 II, pp. 2366, 2368).

Laws (Re-enactments and Repeals) Act 1964 (a).

8. The price for the sale, otherwise than in cans, of sausages, meat pies, sausage rolls and other manufactured meat products.

9. The price for the sale of—

(a) unseasoned timber in logs;

(b) raw wool which has not undergone any process of combing, spinning or felting and tops of wool and other fine animal hair;

(c) untanned hides.

10. The price for the sale of coal and steel (as defined in Annex 1 to the Treaty establishing the European Coal and Steel Community, signed at Paris on 18th April 1951, together with any additions to the lists in that Annex made by the Special Council of Ministers under article 81 of that Treaty) charged by an undertaking as defined in article 80 of that Treaty (otherwise than for the special purposes therein mentioned) except for sales to domestic consumers.

11. The price for the sale of scrap metal.

12. The charge for carriage by sea transport between terminals—

(a) of which one or both are outside the United Kingdom including charges for carriage between points in the United Kingdom, where the tariff applicable to those charges is one for the whole of the first-mentioned carriage; or

(b) of which both are within the United Kingdom, whether or not the charge relates to a voyage during which a call is made at any other place, other than a charge which is in accordance with a tariff of general application.

13. The charge for carriage by air transport for which an air transport licence granted by the Civil Aviation Authority is by section 21 of the Civil Aviation Act 1971 (b) required to be held by the operator.

14. The charge for a package holiday taken outside the United Kingdom.

15. (a) Bus fares which are fixed by conditions attached to a road service licence granted under section 135 of the Road Traffic Act 1960 (c) or a permit granted under section 30 of the Transport Act 1968 (d) and charges made in respect of the use of vehicles under authorisations granted under section 2(3)(b) of the Passenger Vehicles (Experimental Areas) Act 1977 (e);

(b) bus fares which are charged in pursuance of an agreement with the London Transport Executive under section 23 of the Transport (London) Act 1969 (f) or a consent continued in force or granted under Schedule 4 to that Act;

(a) 1964 c. 60.   (b) 1971 c. 75.
(c) 1960 c. 16.   (d) 1968 c. 73.
(e) 1977 c. 21.   (f) 1969 c. 35.

(c) taxi fares fixed by regulations made by, or by byelaws confirmed by, the Secretary of State;

(d) charges made by the British Airports Authority and the British Railways Board for the parking of vehicles.

16. (a) Charges or dues for the provision of aids for air navigation where that provision is made principally in connection with transport between terminals of which one or both are outside the United Kingdom;

(b) charges for the provision of landing and related facilities for aircraft;

(c) pilotage dues within the meaning of the Pilotage Act 1913(a);

(d) charges for harbour operations within the harbour area (other than charges mentioned in head (e) below) made by a harbour authority within the meaning of the Harbours Act 1964(b) or the Harbours Act (Northern Ireland) 1970(c) as the case may require;

(e) ship, passenger and goods dues in relation to which an objection may be made to the National Ports Council under the said Act of 1964 or to the Department of Commerce under section 7 of the said Act of 1970 and charges exigible by virtue of section 29 of the said Act of 1964 (local light dues).

17. Charges made by the Post Office in accordance with any international agreement in respect of the carriage of postal packets or the provision of telecommunications, giro or remittance services to or from any place in the United Kingdom to or from any other place.

18. (a) The price of any goods on any sale by auction;

(b) the price of any goods determined on a commodity market in the United Kingdom (including any price to the extent to which it is determined by reference to a price determined on any such market);

(c) the price for the sale of any goods or the charge for the performance of any services under any contract formed by acceptance of a competitive tender.

19. The price for the sale of goods to or the charge for the performance of services for a government department to which the profit formula for non-competitive contracts as recorded in the Report by the Review Board for Government Contracts published by Her Majesty's Stationery Office in 1974 relates.

20. The price for the sale of manufactured goods (other than the price for the sale of motor vehicles by a person who ordinarily sells motor vehicles in the course of business)—

(a) which have been used to a material extent otherwise than solely for the purpose of testing, examination or adjustment and, in the case of a ship, aircraft or hovercraft, in the course of its delivery to a person who ordinarily sells ships, aircraft or hovercraft in the course of business; and

---

(a) 1913 c. 31 (2&3 Geo. 5).   (b) 1964 c. 40.   (c) 1970 c. 1 (N.I.).

(b) which have not been substantially changed after completion of their manufacture.

21. Insurance premiums.

22. Charges by way of interest.

23. Charges for services to the Post Office by sub-postmasters.

24. Charges being payments in respect of services provided under or pursuant to Part IV of the National Health Service Act 1946(a) or Part IV of the National Health Service (Scotland) Act 1947(b) to persons providing such services.

25. The price for the sale of any human pharmaceutical which may be prescribed under the National Health Service but is not advertised to the general public.

26. The price for the sale of goods or the charge for the performance of services to the extent that any increase made therein is required for the purpose of implementing, and only to the extent required for that purpose, any obligation created or arising by or under any international agreement or arrangement (being an agreement or arrangement between states or organisations of states and not any other) or is made as a direct consequence of any such increase already made.

27. Charges for services provided by shipbrokers.

28. The price for the sale of tallow, meat and bonemeal processed from waste fat, bone and offal.

29. The price for the sale of any product where more than one half of the total costs of that product immediately before the date of any proposed increase in the price represents the cost of milk, but only by an amount corresponding to an increase in the intervention prices of butter and skimmed milk powder.

30. The price for the sale of any goods during a period not exceeding 12 months in which the goods are sold principally for the purpose of testing their acceptability to prospective users, being goods—

(a) which are during that period for sale only in a certain area of the United Kingdom; and

(b) which have not been sold anywhere in the United Kingdom before that period.

(a) 1946 c. 81.   (b) 1947 c. 27.

SCHEDULE 4

(Article 12(*b*))

Matters relating to an increase in the price of goods or the charge for the performance of a service of which particulars are required to be notified to the Price Commission.

Only paragraphs 16 and 18 apply to water authorities.

1. The name of the person required to make the notification, his address or, in the case of a body corporate, its registered or principal office in the United Kingdom and the address for service of notices by the Commission, if different.

2. The name of an individual (not being the person mentioned in paragraph 1) to whom any enquiry concerning the notification may be made by the Commission and the office or employment held by him.

Profit margin control

3. The unit for profit margin control, determined in accordance with paragraph 14 of the code, to which the notification relates; and its title and address.

4.—(1) The reference level of the net profit margin of the unit for net profit margin control in relation to the price or charge specified pursuant to paragraph 7, ascertained in accordance with the code and, unless already notified to the Commission, particulars of the manner in which it is calculated.

(2) The net profit margin of the unit for net profit margin control in relation to the price or charge specified pursuant to paragraph 7, calculated in accordance with the code—

(*a*) on the assumption that only the increase to which the notification relates is made; and

(*b*) on the assumption that the increase and other specified increases in prices and charges are made:

Provided that the particulars referred to in this paragraph may, where the Commission so inform the person in question, be furnished in the form of an estimate.

Particulars of the price increase

5. Intended date for implementation of the proposed increase.

6. The goods or services to which the notification relates.

7. The price or charge for the sale of goods or the performance of services to which the notification relates at the date of the notification.

8. The increase in the price or charge ascertained in accordance with articles 4 and 5 and, in a case where the increase is an average increase relating to a range of related products or services, particulars of the increases proposed for each product or service within the range.

9. Where the goods or services to which the notification relates—

(a) are identical with goods or services previously sold or performed, particulars of the amount of sales in respect of those goods or services; or

(b) are not identical with goods or services previously sold or performed, particulars of the amount of sales in respect of goods or services of substantially the same description;

during a period ending not more than 42 days before the date when the notification is made, being a representative period (which shall be specified) of not less than three months, the amount being increased by the proportion which that period bears to 12 months: Provided that the particulars referred to in paragraphs (a) and (b) may, where the Commission so inform the person required to make the notification, be furnished in the form of an estimate.

10. The increase pursuant to implementation of the increased price in receipts from sales of goods or the provision of services to which the notification relates calculated over a period of 12 months beginning with the date of implementation of the increased price; and in a case where in determining such receipts a change in turnover is assumed, particulars of that assumed change.

11. The percentage margin over total costs per unit of output or per £ of sales—

(a) either at the date of implementation of the last price increase before the date of the notification or during a representative period (which shall be specified) following that last increase; and

(b) either immediately following the date of the increase to which the notification relates or during a representative period (which shall be specified) after that date.

12. Total costs per unit of output or per £ of sales either at the date or during the period stated pursuant to paragraph 11 above.

13. In the case of the first notification after 31st July 1977 relating to a particular range of related products or services, the method of allocating costs which are not incurred exclusively in respect of that range to the prices of particular products or services within the range and particulars of the accounting principles employed in the calculation of depreciation and the cost of sales; and in the case of any subsequent notification relating to the range in question, particulars of any change in the method of allocating costs or in the accounting principles employed of which notice has been given to the Commission pursuant to the preceding provisions of this paragraph.

Grounds for price increase

14. Particulars of the application of those matters mentioned in section 2(2)(a) to (h) of the 1977 Act which the person giving the notification considers relevant to the increase to which the notification relates including, in the case of subsection (2)(a) of that section, sufficient information concerning the costs incurred in supplying the goods or services to which the notification relates to enable the Commission to ascertain what are the principal costs incurred and whether there have been changes in those costs which the Commission should take into account.

15. Particulars of any matter not mentioned in section 2(2)(*a*) to (*h*) of the 1977 Act which the person making the notification considers the Commission should have regard to in exercising any of the functions mentioned in section 2(3) of the 1977 Act.

Pay settlements

16.—(1) In a case where the person required to make the notification has made a settlement involving an increase after 11th July 1975 in the remuneration of his employees, particulars of—

(*a*) in each case—

    (i) the date of each such settlement, the persons to whom it applies and the date of its implementation;

    (ii) the number and description of employees to which each such settlement relates; and

    (iii) in relation to each employee, the date of the previous settlement relating to his remuneration; and

(*b*) in a case where such a settlement applies to more than 100 employees and provides for any payment of remuneration in respect of any period before 1st August 1977—

    (i) remuneration of employees under the settlement, being remuneration to which it appears to the person making the notification that the pay limits apply;

    (ii) remuneration of employees under the settlement, being remuneration to which it appears to that person that the pay limits do not apply;

    (iii) where the increase in remuneration of any individual employee arising after 11th July 1975 and before 1st August 1976 exceeds £6 a week, particulars of how that increase is made up; and

    (iv) where the increase in remuneration of any individual employee arising after 31st July 1976 and before 1st August 1977 may in any week exceed £4 or the greater of £2.50 and 5 per cent of total earnings for all hours worked, particulars of how that increase is made up; and

(*c*) a statement that remuneration of employees under each such settlement complies with the pay limits.

(2) In this paragraph—

"employee" means an employee of the person required to make the notification;

"pay limits" means the limits on remuneration mentioned in section 1 of the Remuneration, Charges and Grants Act 1975 (**a**);

"remuneration", in relation to any employee, includes any benefit, facility or advantage, whether in money or otherwise, provided by the employer or by some other person under arrangements with the employer, whether for the employee or otherwise, by reason of the fact that the employer employs him;

(**c**) 1975 c. 57.

"settlement" includes any agreement, arrangement, award or decision relating to remuneration, by whomsoever made and whether binding or not.

Market share

17.—(1) Either—

(a) a statement that, in the opinion of the person required to make the notification, he supplies at least 15 per cent of all the goods or services supplied in the United Kingdom of the description to which the notification relates, and of the percentage amount supplied by him; or

(b) a statement that, in the opinion of that person, he does not supply 15 per cent or more of such goods or services; or

(c) a statement that, in the opinion of that person, information given pursuant to (a) or (b) above in a previous notification remains substantially the same.

(2) Where a percentage amount is stated pursuant to sub-paragraph (1) above, particulars of the criteria employed in determining that percentage amount.

Water authorities

18. In the case of a water authority—

(a) estimates of its income and expenditure during the accounting year in which the proposed increased price or charge is to be implemented;

(b) particulars, where available, of or estimates of such income and expenditure during the preceding accounting year;

(c) the provisions of any direction given to it by a Minister and, in the case of a statutory water company, of any arrangements between the company and any other water authority relevant to the calculation of any increase specified pursuant to paragraph 8 above;

(d) its proposals for restructuring of charges.

SCHEDULE 5

Articles 15(3)(*a*) and 22(1))

PART I

PERIODICAL RETURNS AND RECORDS

Paragraphs 1(2) *to* (4), 2, 5, 7 *and* 9 *to* 14 *do not apply to water authorities.*

In this Schedule

(*a*) "indirect taxes" means

    (i) customs and excise duties;

    (ii) value added tax which is, under Part I of the Finance Act 1972(**a**) chargeab!e to or by (as the case may be) the person required to make the return or to keep the record; and

    (iii) car tax; and

(*b*) "change" means any increase (including a change from a nil amount) and any decrease taking effect, in either case, after 25th March 1974.

Persons required to furnish the return or to keep the record

1.—(1) The name of the person required to furnish the return or to keep the record, his address or, in the case of a body corporate, its registered or principal office in the United Kingdom, and the address for service of notices by the Commission, if different.

(2) In the case of a company which is controlled by any person, his name and the names of all other companies controlled by him and carrying on business in the United Kingdom.

(3) In the case of a company, any change in its structure or in the identity of any company controlled by the same person (including any such change since the period to which the reference level relates).

(4) Except in the case of a local authority, the unit for profit margin control, determined in accordance with the code, to which the return or record relates; and its title and address.

Gross percentage margin

2.—(1) In the case of a distributor, particulars of the level of the gross percentage margin ascertained under paragraphs 33 and 34 of the code.

(2) The gross percentage margin as a distributor of the person required to make the return or to keep the record, the total value of sales to which it relates and—

(**a**) 1972 c. 41.

(a) in respect of the total value of sales, particulars of the amount of, and of any change in, indirect taxes comprised in that value and charged to or assessed on him; and

(b) in respect of the amount, employed in the calculation of the gross percentage margin, of the cost to him of the goods concerned, particulars of the amount of, and of any change in, indirect taxes comprised in that amount.

Profits, sales and costs
(Paragraphs 3, 4, 6 and 7 do not apply to distributors.)

3. The nature of the activity or activities to which the return or record relates and the goods or services to which each activity relates.

4. Except in the case of a local authority, the total value of sales (including charges for the performance of services), the total value of such sales including indirect taxes, the total value of such sales excluding indirect taxes and any changes in the amount of indirect taxes.

5. Except in the case of a local authority—

(a) particulars of the reference level of the net profit margin determined in accordance with the code;

(b) particulars of the net profit margin corresponding to the reference level and the manner in which it is caculated including particulars of any change in indirect taxes comprised in any amount used in the calculation.

6. Particulars of any increase or decrease in any price or charge, specifying the goods or services concerned, the date when the price or charge was implemented and the date when the increase or decrease in the price or charge was implemented.

7.—(1) The return on capital, which shall be determined by expressing net profit, ascertained in accordance with paragraph 11(1) of the code, for the period to which the return relates, as a percentage of the amount of capital, ascertained in accordance with paragraph 23 of the code, employed in the unit for profit margin control.

(2) If, in the opinion of the person required to make the return, the return on capital ascertained by reference to the matters mentioned in sub-section (2)(c) and (d) of section 2 of the 1977 Act differs from the amount stated under sub-paragraph (1) above by 5 percentage points or more, an estimate of the return on capital ascertained by reference to those matters, the amount of which shall be calculated in a manner which is consistent with any calculation made pursuant to this sub-paragraph in any previous return under this Order.

8.—(1) Where any change takes place in the remuneration of employees of the person required to make the return or to keep the record, particulars of the matters specified in sub-paragraph (2) below.

(2) The particulars referred to in sub-paragraph (1) above are particulars of—

(*a*) the date of making of each settlement ("relevant settlement") relating to remuneration mentioned in that sub-paragraph, or to any such remuneration and other remuneration, the persons by whom the settlement was made, the persons to whom it applies and the date of its implementation;

(*b*) the number and description of employees to which each relevant settlement relates;

(*c*) in the case of any settlement which provides for any payment of remuneration in respect of any period before 1st August 1977, remuneration of employees under each relevant settlement, being remuneration to which it appears to the person required to make the return or to keep the record that the pay limits apply;

(*d*) in the case of any settlement which provides for any payment of remuneration in respect of any period before 1st August 1977, remuneration of employees under each relevant settlement, being remuneration to which it appears to that person that the pay limits do not apply; and

(*e*) in relation to each employee, the date of implementation of the previous settlement relating to his remuneration;

and expressions used in this paragraph and in paragraph 16 of Schedule 4 have the meanings assigned to them by sub-paragraph (2) of that paragraph.

Special provisions relating to banks, finance houses or similar enterprises

9. In the case of enterprises mentioned in (*a*) to (*c*) of paragraph 61 of the code, the following particulars in respect of the period to which the return relates, that is to say—

(*a*) in the case of enterprises falling within sub-paragraph (*a*) of that paragraph (enterprises undertaking plant and machinery leasing contracts) particulars of—

    (i) net income from charges, ascertained in accordance with that sub-paragraph, for business of the description referred to therein; and

    (ii) average resources employed;

(*b*) in the case of enterprises falling within sub-paragraph (*b*) of that paragraph (enterprises undertaking hire-purchase etc. business), particulars of—

    (i) net income from separately identifiable fees and charges falling within that sub-paragraph; and

    (ii) gross income from the transactions to which those fees and charges relate; and

(*c*) in the case of enterprises falling within sub-paragraph (*c*) of that paragraph (banks, finance houses and similar financial enterprises not falling within (*a*) or (*b*) of that paragraph), gross and net income as therein defined.

Stock relief

10.—(1) Where, in determining net profit margins or gross percentage margins, a person has applied paragraph 12 of the code (which makes provision for relief on account of increase in the value of stocks), particulars of and an indication of the reason for any increase or decrease in the value of stocks to be taken into account under that paragraph and of how net profit margins or gross percentage margins have been adjusted.

(2) In relation to the first period in which a person has obtained relief under paragraph 12 of the code or paragraph 82 of the 1976 code, particulars of—

(a) the value of stock at the beginning of each of the two periods to which annual accounts relate last ended before the beginning of the period in which relief is obtained, as shown in those accounts, together with any necessary appropriation of such values to each activity in respect of which net profit margins fall to be separately determined for the purpose of the code and to other activities; and

(b) the like information in respect of each period in relation to which the person in question is required to furnish a return to the Commission and which falls within the two periods referred to in (a) above:

Provided that where particulars of any matter to be specified pursuant to this paragraph are not readily available, it shall be sufficient compliance with this paragraph to furnish particulars thereof in the form of an estimate together with a description of the manner in which the estimate is made.

(3) In this paragraph "stock" has the meaning assigned to it by paragraph 12(3) of the code.

Special provisions relating to investment relief under paragraph 46 of the code

11. Particulars of—

(a) the beginning of the investment year;

(b) the beginning of the relief year;

(c) expenditure on investment in the investment year and the manner in which it is calculated;

(d) the amount of expenditure on investment in relation to the first six months of the investment year and in relation to the second six months of the investment year;

(e) the amount of the relevant expenditure;

(f) an estimate of turnover in the relief year;

(g) the intended modification to the net profit margin reference level for the relief year specified pursuant to paragraph 5(a) above, being a figure found by expressing the relevant expenditure as a percentage of turnover for the relief year; and

(h) in the case of a distributor, the intended modification to the level of the gross percentage margin for the relief year specified pursuant to paragraph 2(1) above, being a figure found by expressing the relevant expenditure as a percentage of turnover for the relief year.

Particulars relating to earlier years

12. In respect of each of the three latest complete years of account—

(*a*) turnover;

(*b*) the amount (and the manner in which it is calculated) which would be the expenditure on investment if, in the definition of "expenditure on investment" in paragraph 44(1) of the code, for the reference to the investment year, there were substituted references to each of those years respectively:

Provided that where particulars of any matter to be specified pursuant to this paragraph are not readily available, it shall be sufficient compliance with this paragraph to furnish particulars thereof in the form of an estimate together with a description of the manner in which the estimate is made.

Further particulars relating to the investment year and to the relief year

13. Particulars of—

(*a*) each of the matters specified in paragraph 11 above on the basis of fact or of revised estimates, as the case may require;

(*b*) the amount recovered in sales on account of relevant expenditure;

(*c*) in a case where the enterprise has applied paragraph 47 of the code (which relates to the increasing of net profit margin reference levels and gross margins where an enterprise has unused investment relief), calculations under that paragraph; and

(*d*) the amount (if any) recovered in sales on account of relevant expenditure in excess of the relevant expenditure.

14. If relief under paragraph 46 of the code has exceeded the relevant expenditure, particulars of the steps to be taken under paragraph 48 of the code.

Water authorities

15. Particulars of—

(*a*) income and expenditure of a water authority during the period to which the record relates;

(*b*) the provision of any direction given to it by a Minister and, in the case of a statutory water company, of any arrangement between the company and any other water authority relevant to the calculation of prices; and

(*c*) steps taken in restructuring of prices.

PART II

DECLARATION

I, [name of person making the return and the capacity in which he makes it] of [address] on behalf of [myself or name of person required to make the return if different] pursuant to article 14 of the Prices and Charges (Notification of Increases and Information) Order 1977 make this return to the Price Commission in respect of the period beginning on [date] and ending on [date] and declare that, to the best of my knowledge, information and belief, the particulars specified herein are correct and complete.

Signed: [signature of person making the return]

Date: [date of signature]

EXPLANATORY NOTE

(This Note is not part of the Order.)

This Order consolidates, with amendments, the Counter-Inflation (Notification of Increases in Prices and Charges) Order 1976 and the Counter-Inflation (Prices and Charges) (Information) Order 1976 as amended.

The Order makes provision for notification to the Price Commission of proposed increases in prices and charges, for the furnishing of periodic returns and for the keeping of records. These obligations apply primarily to firms whose sales exceed the limits specified in article 7 (notification), article 14 (periodic returns) and article 21 (record-keeping). These limits have been increased and are as follows—

Sector	Notification	Periodic returns	Record-keeping
Manufacture	£12,000,000	£12,000,000	£2,400,000
Distribution	—	£18,000,000	£ 600,000
Commercial Services	£ 9,000,000	£ 9,000,000	£ 600,000
Construction	—	£ 9,000,000	£2,400,000
Professional Services	—	£ 900,000	£ 240,000

The other principal changes are—

(*a*) The information which is required to be furnished to the Price Commission with notifications of proposed increases in prices and charges is substantially changed to take account of new functions of the Price Commission under the Price Commission Act 1977 (Schedule 4).

(*b*) Exemption from the obligation to notify proposed increases to the Price Commission is given in respect of certain prices and charges which were not previously exempt (Schedule 3, paragraphs 8, 15, 27–30).

STATUTORY INSTRUMENTS

1977 No. 1282

PRICES

The Prices and Charges (Safeguard for basic profits) Regulations 1977

Made - - - -	*27th July* 1977
Laid before Parliament	*29th July* 1977
Coming into Operation	*1st August* 1977

Arrangement of regulations

The Secretary of State, after consulting in accordance with subsection (2) of section 9 of the Price Commission Act 1977(a) with the Price Commission and representatives of persons therein referred to, in exercise of his powers under subsection (1) of that section and section 22(3) of that Act and of all other powers enabling him in that behalf, hereby makes the following Regulations:—

Preliminary

Citation, commencement and interpretation

1.—(1) These Regulations may be cited as the Prices and Charges (Safeguard for basic profits) Regulations 1977 and shall come into operation on 1st August 1977.

(2) In these Regulations—

'the 1973 Act' means the Counter-Inflation Act 1973(b);

'the 1977 Act' means the Price Commission Act 1977;

'bank, finance house or similar enterprise' means a person (other than a building society incorporated under the Building Societies Act 1962(c) or under the enactments repealed by that Act) whose ordinary business includes the business of banking, the business of lending money, the letting of goods under hire purchase agreements, or the selling of goods under conditional sale agreements;

'base profit margin' has the meaning given by regulation 8;

'the 1976 code' means the code set out in Schedule 1 to the Counter-Inflation (Price Code) Order 1976(d) as amended (e);

'the 1977 code' means the code set out in the Schedule to the Counter-Inflation (Price Code) Order 1977(f);

'current profit margin' has the meaning given by regulation 9;

'depreciation' has the meaning given by regulation 14;

'distributor' means a person who carries on in the course of business activities falling within Order XXIII (other than the wholesale slaughtering of animals for human consumption, leasing industrial or office machinery, the hiring of furniture, radio and television sets and other domestic appliances or the activity of bakers or processors of scrap metals) or falling within minimum list heading 894 of Order XXVI (other than the repairing of motor vehicles) of the Standard Industrial Classification;

'goods' includes services;

'investigation safeguard' has the meaning given by regulation 2(3);

'manufacturer' means a person who carries on in the course of business activities falling within Orders II, III (other than the quick freezing of meat, poultry or fish, the curing of bacon or ham and the preparation of oven-ready poultry), IV to XXI and XXII (other than travel ticket agents) of the Standard Industrial Classification and bakers;

(a) 1977 c. 33. (b) 1973 c. 9. (c) 1962 c. 37.
(d) S.I. 1976/1170 (1976 II, p. 3226). (e) S.I. 1976/2207 (1976 III, p. 6190).
(f) S.I. 1977/1272 (1977 II, p. 3541).

'the notification order' means the Prices and Charges (Notification of Increases and Information) Order 1977(a);

'price' includes charge;

'principal safeguard' has the meaning given by regulation 2(3);

'product' has the meaning given by regulation 3(2);

'provider of services' means a person who carries on in the course of business activities falling within minimum list headings 864 and 865 of Order XXIV or within Order XXV (other than the provision of school meals) or within Order XXVI (other than minimum list heading 894) of the Standard Industrial Classification or the hiring of furniture, radio and television sets and other domestic appliances, or the leasing of industrial and office machinery or the repairing of motor vehicles or the activities of a travel ticket agent;

'the Standard Industrial Classification' means the edition thereof published by Her Majesty's Stationery Office in 1968, as amended by Amendment List No. 1 so published in 1977, together with the alphabetical list of industries so published in 1968 as amended by Amendment Lists Nos. 1 and 2 so published in 1970 and 1977 respectively;

'total costs' has the meaning given by regulation 13;

'turnover' has the meaning given by regulation 15;

'turnover/capital ratio' means the proportion which the amount of turnover of a unit of an enterprise bears to the amount of capital, determined in accordance with regulation 16, employed in it; and

'unit' means an undertaking or part of it described in paragraph (1) of regulation 12.

(3) For the purposes of these Regulations, the amount of any price shall be the net amount of that price.

(4) The Interpretation Act 1889(b) shall apply for the interpretation of these Regulations as it applies for the interpretation of an Act of Parliament.

Application of Regulations

2.—(1) The investigation safeguard is relevant to the considerations of the Commission concerning a manufacturer, a provider of services, a bank, finance house or similar institution and any person in respect of a contract within article 5 of the notification order, under paragraph (*b*) of section 4(5) of the 1977 Act and of that paragraph as applied by section 5(4) of that Act.

(2) The principal safeguard is relevant to any person who is a distributor or a person mentioned in paragraph (1) above and who is subject to any restriction under section 7 or 13 of the 1977 Act.

(3) In these Regulations—

'the investigation safeguard' means a safeguard for basic profits which is relevant for the purposes of paragraph (*b*) of sub-section (5) of section 4 of the 1977 Act and that paragraph as applied by sub-section (4) of section 5 of that Act, being a safeguard which has effect for the period

---

(a) S.I. 1977/1281 (1977 II, p. 3577).   (b) 1889 c. 63.

beginning with the giving by the Commission pursuant to sub-section (1) of the said section 4 of a notification relating to an increase or the giving by them pursuant to sub-section (1) of the said section 5 of a notification relating to a price, as the case may be, and ending with the effective date of the report by the Commission relating to the increase or the price or the giving by the Secretary of State of notice to the Commission pursuant to sub-section (3) of the said section 4 or sub-section (5) of the said section 5 or the giving by the Commission to the Secretary of State of notice pursuant to sub-section (4) of the said section 4; and

'the principal safeguard' means a safeguard for basic profits which persons are not to be prevented from earning by virtue of any provision of section 7 of the 1977 Act or of such a notice as is mentioned in section 13(1) of that Act.

(4) Nothing in these Regulations affords a safeguard for the profits of any unit other than the unit in the course of the business of which the increase or price in question is proposed or is charged, as the case may be, or to which the margin in question relates.

The Safeguards

Investigation safeguard for manufacturers and providers of services

3.—(1) The investigation safeguard in relation to a manufacturer or a provider of services is, in relation to a product, the greatest of—

(a) except as otherwise provided by regulation 7, a current profit margin of 3 per cent; and

(b) a current profit margin of 80 per cent of the base margin; and

(c) a current profit margin equal to the base profit margin—

(i) in the case of a person who is required under section 15 of the 1973 Act to furnish periodical returns to the Commission, if, at the date when the investigation safeguard is to be applied, the margin of the unit in which the product is supplied in the period to which the most recent such return is required to relate is not more than 3 per cent of turnover in that period or $12\frac{1}{2}$ per cent of capital employed in the unit at the end of that period, and

(ii) in any other case, if the margin of the unit in which the product is supplied in the year of account of that unit completed last before the date on which the investigation safeguard falls to be applied is not more than 3 per cent of turnover in that year or $12\frac{1}{2}$ per cent of capital employed in the unit at the end of that year.

(2) Subject to paragraph (3) below, in these Regulations 'product' means—

(a) a single description of goods; or

(b) more than one description of goods.

(3) In the case—

(a) of a person who is required under section 5 of the 1973 Act to give notice to the Commission of an increase, sub-paragraph (a) of the preceding paragraph shall not have effect in relation to any goods for the sale of which he is required to give notice of a single increase and accordingly in paragraph (1) above 'product' means all the goods to which such an increase relates; and

(b) of any other person, 'product' means the goods to which the price specified in a notification pursuant to sub-section (1) of section 5 of the 1977 Act, or a direction pursuant to sub-section (1) of section 10 of that Act, relates.

(4) In heads (i) and (ii) of paragraph (1)(c), 'margin' means a margin on turnover after deduction of expenses; and subject to regulation 7 'expenses' shall be ascertained in the like manner as total costs but as if sub-paragraph (d) of paragraph (1) of regulation 13 and paragraphs (2) and (3) of that regulation were omitted.

Modification of investigation safeguard for capital intensive units

4. In relation to a product supplied in a unit of which the turnover/capital ratio for the period or year of account referred to in head (i) or head (ii) of regulation 3(1)(c), as the case may be, does not exceed 3.75 : 1, for the reference in regulation 3(1)(a) to 3 per cent there shall be substituted a reference to the percentage specified in column 2 of the following table as applicable to the range of ratios specified in column 1 of that table within which the turnover/capital ratio of the unit falls.

TABLE

Column 1 Range of turnover/capital ratios	Column 2 Margin over total costs
Under 3.75 : 1 and not under 3.25 : 1	3.5 per cent
Under 3.25 : 1 and not under 2.75 : 1	4 per cent
Under 2.75 : 1 and not under 2.25 : 1	5 per cent
Under 2.25 : 1 and not under 1.875 : 1	6 per cent
Under 1.875 : 1 and not under 1.625 : 1	7 per cent
Under 1.625 : 1 and not under 1.375 : 1	8 per cent
Under 1.375 : 1 and not under 1.125 : 1	10 per cent
Under 1.125 : 1	12.5 per cent

Principal safeguard for manufacturers and providers of services

5. The principal safeguard in the case of a manufacturer or provider of services is, in relation to a product, the greater of—

(a) except as provided by regulation 7, a current profit margin of 3 per cent; and

(b) a current profit margin of 50 per cent of the base profit margin.

Safeguard for distributors

6.—(1) The principal safeguard in the case of a distributor is the greater of—

(a) a margin of 2 per cent of turnover; and

(*b*) a margin of 80 per cent of the following margin, that is to say—

(i) in the case of a person who is required under section 15 of the 1973 Act to furnish periodical returns to the Commission, the margin for the latest period of 12 months ending before 1st June 1977 for which such a report relating to the relevant unit was required to be furnished, and

(ii) in the case of any other person, the margin for the latest year of account ending before 1st June 1977.

(2) If at any time a person's profit affords a margin in the then latest period of 12 months or year of account, as the case may be, which is less than the margin referred to in sub-paragraph (*a*) or sub-paragraph (*b*) of paragraph (1) above, as the case may be, nothing in, or done under, section 7 or section 13 of the 1977 Act shall have effect so as to restrict the prices or margins of that person.

(3) In this regulation, except as provided by regulation 7, 'margin' means a margin on turnover after deduction of expenses; and subject to regulation 7 'expenses' shall be ascertained in the like manner as total costs but as if sub-paragraph (*d*) of paragraph (1) of regulation 13 and paragraph (2) and (3) of that regulation were omitted.

(4) In the case of a distributor of whom the proportion which his sales in the relevant unit in the period or year of account referred to in head (i) or (ii) of paragraph (1)(*b*), as the case may require, bears to the average of the stock of that unit at the beginning of that period or year and at the end of that period or year does not exceed 10 : 1, for the reference in paragraph (1)(*a*) above to 2 per cent there shall be substituted a reference to the percentage specified in column 2 of the following table as applicable to the range of proportions specified in column 1 of that table within which that proportion falls.

TABLE

Column 1 Proportion of sales to stock	Column 2 Margin of turnover
Under 10 : 1 and not under 9 : 1	2.5 per cent
Under 9 : 1 and not under 8 : 1	3 per cent
Under 8 : 1 and not under 7 : 1	3.5 per cent
Under 7 : 1 and not under 6 : 1	4 per cent
Under 6 : 1 and not under 5 : 1	4.5 per cent
Under 5 : 1	5 per cent

Adaptation of regulations 3 to 6 for unincorporated enterprises

7.—(1) Except in their application to a body corporate, regulations 3 to 6 shall have effect as if—

(*a*) total costs for the purposes of determining the current profit margin referred to in regulations 3(1)(*a*) and 5(*a*) and expenses for the purpose of determining the margin referred to in regulation 6(1)(*a*) included the amount determined under paragraph (2) below in respect of the year of account last ended before the date when the safeguard in question falls to be applied; and

(b) expenses for the purpose of determining the margins referred to in heads (i) and (ii) of regulation 3(1)(c) included the amount determined under paragraph (2) below in respect of the period or year of account in question.

(2) The amount referred to in paragraph (1) above is 50 per cent of the greater of—

(a) the amount shown in audited accounts as available for distribution as net profit in respect of a period or year of account; and

(b) the amount withdrawn in that period or year of account on account of net profit in respect of that or any previous period or year of account,

apportioned as necessary; and for the purposes of this paragraph, net profit includes any sum (other than a contribution to a pension fund) paid for the benefit of any person entitled to participate in profits or to any other person at his request or to the wife or husband of any such person and the value of any benefit provided for any such person or the wife or husband of any such person otherwise than in money.

Base profit margin

8.—(1) The base profit margin shall be the excess of the price ascertained under paragraph (2) below over the total costs ascertained in accordance with paragraph (3) below expressed as a percentage of those costs.

(2) For the purposes of paragraph (1) above, a price shall be ascertained immediately after the implementation of the last increase in it—

(a) before 1st July 1977 in the case of a person required under section 5 of the 1973 Act to give notice to the Commission of an increase in that price; and

(b) before 1st June 1977 in the case of any other person.

(3) For the purposes of paragraph (1) above, total costs—

(a) in the case of a person referred to in sub-paragraph (a) of paragraph (2) above, shall be the total costs specified in relation to the increase in a notice in accordance with the section there mentioned; and

(b) in any other case, shall be ascertained at the date of implementation of such increase.

(4) Article 4 of the notification order shall have effect for ascertaining whether a price has been increased.

Current profit margin

9. For the purposes of these Regulations, the current profit margin at any time is the excess of the price in question over the total costs expressed as a percentage of those costs.

Loading of increases

10.—(1) In a case where an investigation under section 6 of the 1977 Act, a restriction under section 7 of that Act or a notice under section 13(1) of that Act relates to more than one price, a person may, subject to paragraph (2) below, under the investigation safeguard and, in any case, under the principal safeguard apply different increases to different prices.

(2) The Commission may in a variation notice specify such limitations as they consider appropriate on the operation of paragraph (1) above; and accordingly the investigation safeguard shall have effect subject to such limitation.

Escalation and variation of price clauses

11.—(1) In relation to any person in respect of a contract falling within article 5 of the notification order, the investigation safeguard and the principal safeguard are the greater of the safeguards provided by regulation 6; and that regulation shall have effect accordingly but as if for references to a distributor there were substituted references to such a person and as if for the reference in sub-paragraph (1)(a) to 2 per cent of turnover there were substituted a reference to 3 per cent of turnover and paragraph (4) were omitted.

(2) Regulations 3 to 5 shall not have effect in relation to a contract falling within the said article 5.

Calculation of safeguards

Meaning of 'unit'

12.—(1) For the purposes of these Regulations, 'unit' means—

(a) either—

(i) the undertaking of the person in question taken as a whole, or

(ii) his undertaking as a manufacturer, his undertaking as a provider of services, his undertaking as a distributor, his undertaking as a bank, finance house or similar institution or his undertaking as a manufacturer and as a provider of services,

as he may decide; or

(b) a part of his undertaking taken as a whole or of an undertaking within sub-paragraph (a)(ii) above if he so desires and the Commission are satisfied that the part constitutes an undertaking separate from other undertakings of the person and that the accounts of the parts can be reconciled with those of the person's undertaking taken as a whole and are not materially distorted by transactions conducted otherwise than at arm's length,

being, for so long as the Price Code set out in the Schedule to the Counter-Inflation (Price Code) Order 1977(a) is in operation, the unit ascertained under paragraph 14 of that Code.

(a) S.I. 1977/1272 (1977 II, p. 3541).

(2) For the purposes of this regulation, references to a person include all other persons with whom he is for the purposes of sections 5 and 6 of the 1973 Act to be treated as one by virtue of paragraph 2(1) of Schedule 3 to that Act : Provided that if a person ceases to be so treated as one with another person, no account shall be taken of any profits or costs of that other person.

Meaning of 'total costs'

13.—(1) In these Regulations, 'total costs' means all costs relating to a product including depreciation but not—

(a) disbursements or expenses not wholly and exclusively laid out or expended for the purposes of the business in the course of which they are incurred;

(b) any capital withdrawn from or any sum employed or intended to be employed as capital in that business;

(c) save as provided by regulation 18 below, interest; and

(d) additional payments in accordance with section 26 of the Independent Broadcasting Authority Act 1973(a), as substituted by section 1 of the Independent Broadcasting Authority Act 1974(b) (which relates to rental payments by television programme contractors to the Independent Broadcasting Authority).

(2) The calculation of total costs shall be made by reference to costs per unit of volume of output or, where the investigation safeguard or the principal safeguard is to be applied in the case of more than one description of goods, may be made by reference to costs per £ of sales value and, where the calculation has been made by reference to costs per unit of volume of output or by reference to costs per £ of sales value, it shall be so made for all purposes of these Regulations in relation to the same increase or price.

(3) Total costs shall be calculated at the date when the investigation safeguard or the principal safeguard is to be applied and shall be determined by reference to the volume of output or value of sales, as the case may require—

(a) where that date falls within the first half of an accounting year, over the preceding accounting year; and

(b) where that date falls within the second half of an accounting year, over the period comprising the second half of the preceding accounting year and the first half of the current accounting year.

Meaning of 'depreciation'

14. In these Regulations, 'depreciation' means the aggregate amount of depreciation, calculated in accordance with generally accepted accounting principles consistently applied by the person concerned, for the period to which

(a) 1973 c. 19.   (b) 1974 c. 16.

the calculation relates in respect of each asset used in the relevant unit in that period based—

(a) where the calculation of depreciation is made by reference to a period ending after 31st July 1976, on, at the option of that person, either—

(i) the historic cost of the asset or a revaluation of the asset, determined in accordance with generally accepted accounting principles, which has appeared in annual accounts for a period ending on or before 30th September 1972 increased, in either case, by a multiple of 1.4, or

(ii) a revaluation of the asset, determined in accordance with generally accepted accounting principles, which has appeared in annual accounts; and

(b) where that calculation is made by reference to a period ending before 1st August 1976, on either—

(i) the historic cost of the asset, or

(ii) a revaluation of the asset, determined in accordance with generally accepted accounting principles, which has appeared in annual accounts for a period ending on or before 30th September 1972.

Ascertainment of 'turnover'

15. For the purposes of these Regulations, 'turnover' is the turnover of the relevant unit during the period or year of account in question, no account being taken of any revenue arising from transactions at prices to which by virtue of Section 22(2) of the 1977 Act section 10(1) or 12(3) of that Act does not apply.

Ascertainment of amount of capital

16.—(1) The amount of capital for the purposes of regulations 3 and 4 shall be ascertained at the end of the period referred to in head (i) or in head (ii) of regulation 3(1)(c), as the case may be, and shall, in any such case, be the value of net assets (excluding the value of goodwill and after deducting borrowings in respect of which interest is to be taken into account under regulation 18) and shall be based on the historic cost of assets save that where, in annual accounts for a year ended on or before 30th September 1972, an asset has been re-valued, the value of that asset may be based on such value.

(2) In ascertaining the amount of capital, there shall be left out of account any capital relating to goods revenue relating to which is to be left out of account under regulation 15.

Treatment of stocks

17.—(1) In determining total costs for the purposes of regulations 8 and 9, the cost of materials (that is to say, materials, components, consumable stores and supplies) may, at the option of the person to or by whom the safeguard is to be applied, be taken to be the cost of the materials in question or the cost of similar materials at the date by reference to which the calculation is made, that is to say, the price paid or to be paid by that person for materials last delivered to him before that date in a quantity customarily purchased by him for the purposes of the unit concerned, being a price negotiated at arm's length and representative of the current level of prices under similar transactions.

(2) In determining a margin under regulations 3 and 6, in relation to any period of 12 months ending after 31st July 1976, a person may deduct an amount in respect of increases in the value of stock ('stock value increase') determined under this regulation; and if he does so—

(a) he shall apply this paragraph in each similar period ending within the 13 months following the first such period; and

(b) after the expiry of the last period mentioned in (a) above, he may apply this paragraph as if he had not previously done so;

and for that purpose, references to stock value increase include references to a decrease in the value of stock and references to the deduction of stock value increase include references to the addition of such a decrease.

(3) In the preceding paragraph, 'stock value increase', in the case of any unit, means 70 per cent of the excess of the value of the stock at the end of a period of 12 months over the value of stock at the beginning of that period and a decrease in the value of stock shall be an amount determined in a similar manner; and for the purposes of paragraph (2) above no account shall be taken of—

(a) any decrease in the value of stock below the value of stock at the beginning of the first period by reference to which the said paragraph (2) is applied in respect of that unit; and

(b) any amount by which the sum of decreases in the value of stock exceeds the sum of increases in the value of stock, being increases in respect of which the said paragraph (2) has been so applied to that unit.

(4) In the two preceding paragraphs, 'stock' includes work in progress but does not include any description of security; and for the purposes of these Regulations the value of stock shall be determined in accordance with generally accepted accounting principles consistently applied by the person concerned.

(5) A person who has exercised an option—

(a) under paragraph (1) above in relation to a price shall apply it in all calculations under these Regulations in relation to that price; and

(b) under paragraph (2) above in relation to a margin shall apply it in all calculations under these Regulations but without prejudice to sub-paragraph (b) of that paragraph.

Treatment of interest

18.—(1) Subject to paragraph (2) below, for the purposes of these Regulations—

(a) interest paid by a person shall be treated as part of total costs and of expenses within the meaning of regulations 3(4) and 6(3); and (*b*) interest received by a person shall be treated as part of the turnover of the unit by or for which it is received.

(2) In a case where a person has under paragraph 19(2) of the 1976 Code or paragraph 28 of the 1977 Code elected that interest shall not be taken into account for certain purposes, interest paid and interest received shall not be taken into account in ascertaining current profit margin for the purposes of regulations 3(1)(*b*) and (*c*) and 5(*b*), a return on capital for the purposes of regulation 3(1)(*c*), base profit margin for the purposes of regulation 8 and any calculation under regulation 6(1)(*b*) until, under paragraph 29(2) of the 1977 Code, he revokes any such election under the said paragraph 19(2); and the revocation of any provision of the 1976 Code or the 1977 Code shall not affect the operation of this regulation.

(3) There shall be left out of account, for the purposes of this regulation, any interest—

(*a*) which is a distribution of profits; or

(*b*) which is payable on a loan by another unit of the same enterprise and—

    (i) which is not required for the purposes of the principal activity of the unit by or for which it is paid, or

    (ii) which is at a rate higher than that which would have been charged if the transaction had been at arm's length; or

(*c*) which, although expressed as interest, is capital expenditure; or

(*d*) which relates to the acquisition after 29th April 1973 of a new member in a group of companies.

(4) Notwithstanding the provisions of the two preceding paragraphs, interest received by a person on money belonging to another and retained by him in the ordinary course of business shall be treated as interest received within paragraph (1)(*b*) above.

Treatment of indirect taxes

19.—(1) In any calculation under these Regulations, there shall be left out of account the cash value of value added tax borne by the person to or by whom the safeguard is to be applied and, except as provided in paragraph (2) below, the effect of any change in other indirect taxes after 25th March 1974.

(2) In cases where indirect taxes other than value added tax would otherwise fall to be included in a calculation under this regulation, the value of sales—

(*a*) before 17th January 1977 shall be taken to be—

    (i) in the case of alcoholic beverages, 85 per cent of the value of sales, and

    (ii) in the case of tobacco and tobacco products, 80 per cent of the value of sales; and

(*b*) after 16th January 1977 shall be taken to be—

    (i) in the case of alcoholic beverages, 80 per cent of the value of sales, **and**

(ii) in the case of tobacco and tobacco products, 75 per cent of the value of sales before 1st August 1977 and 73 per cent of the value of sales on and after that date:

Provided that, in relation to the investigation safeguard and the principal safeguard, if the Commission are satisfied, having regard to the proportion which the volume or value of a person's sales of goods to which sub-paragraph (*a*) or (*b*) above applies, as the case may require, bears to the volume or value of all sales of the unit as compared with the proportions which appear to them to be those which ordinarily obtain, that a percentage higher than that specified in head (i) or (ii) of the sub-paragraph in question is appropriate, they may specify that higher percentage and, in relation to the calculation in question, such sub-paragraph shall have effect accordingly.

Matters to be left out of account

20.—(1) For the purposes—

(*a*) of regulation 3(1)(*a*) and (*b*) and 5 and of the current profit margin mentioned in regulation 3(1)(*c*), there shall be left out of account any revenue arising from transactions at prices to which by virtue of section 22(2) of the 1977 Act section 5(1)(*d*) of that Act does not apply, and

(*b*) of the margins mentioned in regulations 3(1)(*c*)(i) and (ii) and 6, there shall be left out of account any revenue which is to be left out of account under regulation 15.

(2) For any purpose of these Regulations, there shall be left out of account in ascertaining any amount or value—

(*a*) an advance by way of grant under the Highlands and Islands Shipping Services Act 1960(**a**);

(*b*) payments made under section 26(1) of the Finance Act 1967(**b**);

(*c*) grant made under Part I or Part II of the Industry Act 1972(**c**); and

(*d*) grant made pursuant to arrangements under section 5(1) of the Employment and Training Act 1973(**d**).

Treatment of food subsidies

21. A subsidy received or to be received by a person on any food under section 1 of the Prices Act 1974(**e**) shall for all purposes of these Regulations be treated as part of the price received by the unit in question for that food or for any product of which that food is an ingredient.

General provisions as to calculations

22. Save as otherwise expressly provided in these Regulations, any amount or value shall be determined and any apportionment shall be made in accordance with generally accepted accounting principles consistently applied by the person in question and shall be consistent with annual or management accounts and practices employed by that person in relation to the relevant unit.

(**a**) 1960 c. 31.	(**b**) 1967 c. 54.	(**c**) 1972 c. 63.
(**d**) 1973 c. 50.	(**e**) 1974 c. 24.	

Special cases

Banks, finance houses and similar institutions

23.—(1) In relation to a bank, finance house or similar institution, the investigation safeguard and the principal safeguard are the greater of the safeguards provided by regulation 6 (except paragraph (4)); and that regulation shall have effect accordingly but as if for references to a distributor there were substituted references to a bank, finance house or similar institution and as if for the reference in sub-paragraph (1)(a) to 2 per cent of turnover there were substituted a reference to 3 per cent of turnover.

(2) Notwithstanding the foregoing provisions of these Regulations, the margin referred to in regulation 6 as applied by this regulation—

(a) in the case of a unit of which the principal business is plant and machinery leasing transactions, shall in respect of such transactions be the net income from charges received in the period in question less associated costs, including overheads, expressed as a percentage of average resources employed for the purposes of such transactions;

(b) in the case of a unit of which the principal business is hire purchase, credit sale and conditional sale transactions, shall in respect of such transactions be net income from separately identifiable fees and charges (other than interest) expressed as a percentage of gross income; and

(c) in the case of any other unit and, in the case of a unit within either of the two preceding paragraphs in respect of any other transaction, shall be the excess of total income (including interest on customers' current account credit balances) received in the period in question over costs, including associated overheads, expressed as a percentage of total income, no account being taken of any interest relating to such transactions as are mentioned in the two preceding sub-paragraphs;

and in any determination under this regulation no account shall be taken of transactions in sterling with any person resident outside the United Kingdom or any dealings in a currency other than sterling.

Public sector

24.—(1) In any calculations under these regulations, no account shall be taken of any Government compensation or grant taken directly to revenue account by any Area Electricity Board, the British Airports Authority, the British Airways Board, the British Gas Corporation, the British Railways Board, the British Steel Corporation, the British Transport Docks Board, the British Waterways Board, the Central Electricity Generating Board, the Electricity Council, the National Coal Board, the North of Scotland Hydro-Electric Board, the Northern Ireland Electricity Service, the Post Office and the South of Scotland Electricity Board.

(2) No account shall be taken under these Regulations of any grant made to the Civil Aviation Authority in pursuance of section 10(1)(a) of the Civil Aviation Act 1971**(a)**.

(a) 1971 c. 75.

(3) In the case of the British Transport Docks Board and the Post Office, 'depreciation' means depreciation within regulation 14 together with, in the case of an asset to which it relates, supplemental depreciation at replacement cost.

Roy Hattersley,
Secretary of State for
Prices and Consumer Protection.

27th July 1977.

EXPLANATORY NOTE

(This Note is not part of the Regulations.)

These Regulations provide safeguards for the profits of enterprises whose proposals for price increases or whose prices are under investigation by the Price Commission or which are subject to restriction following a report on an investigation or on an examination carried out by the Price Commission under a direction by the Secretary of State.

The profit safeguard for manufacturers and providers of services during an investigation is a current profit margin in relation to a product or range of products of 3 per cent or, if higher, a current profit margin of 80 per cent of the profit margin at a base date (regulation 3), except where a higher safeguard is provided (regulations 3(1)(c) and 4). The Price Commission are under a duty under the Price Commission Act 1977 to allow price increases to permit such a profit to be obtained. The safeguard during the period of any restriction following a report is the same with the substitution of 50 per cent of the margin in a base period for 80 per cent (regulation 5).

Distributors are not subject to any restriction during an investigation. The profit safeguard during any subsequent period of restriction is the greater of a margin of 2 per cent of turnover, modified in certain circumstances by reference to the ratio between sales and stocks, or of 80 per cent of a margin a base period (regulation 6).

STATUTORY INSTRUMENTS

1977 No. 1284

ANIMALS

DISEASES OF ANIMALS

The Brucellosis (England and Wales) Order 1977

Made	*27th July* 1977
Coming into Operation	*1st August* 1977

The Minister of Agriculture, Fisheries and Food, in pursuance of the powers conferred on him by sections 1, 5, 17(2), 19(7) and 85(1) of the Diseases of Animals Act 1950(a), as read with the Diseases of Animals (Extension of Definitions) Order 1971(b), and as extended by section 106(3) of the Agriculture Act 1970 (c), and of all his other enabling powers, hereby makes the following order:—

Citation and commencement

1. This order, which may be cited as the Brucellosis (England and Wales) Order 1977, shall come into operation on 1st August 1977.

Interpretation

2.—(1) In this order, unless the context otherwise requires, the following expressions shall have the meanings hereby respectively assigned to them—

"abortion or premature calving" means an abortion or a calving which takes place less than 271 days after service or insemination, whether the calf is born alive or dead;

"attested area" means an area declared to be an attested area under Article 3(2) of this order;

"bovine animal" means a bull, cow, heifer or calf, but does not include a steer;

"brucellosis" means the disease caused by brucella abortus, otherwise known as epizootic abortion or contagious abortion;

"dealer in bovine animals" means any person whose trade or business regularly includes the selling of bovine animals purchased by him for the purpose of resale within 28 days, and not for the purpose of rearing, fattening or breeding;

(a) 1950 c. 36. For change of title of the Minister see S.I. 1955/554 (1955 I, p. 1200).
(b) S.I. 1971/531 (1971 I, p. 1530). (c) 1970 c. 40.

"eradication area" means an area declared to be an eradication area under Article 3(1) of this order;

"full-term calving" means a calving which take place 271 days or more after service or insemination, whether the calf is born alive or dead;

"licence" means any licence issued under this order by a veterinary inspector or other officer of the Ministry or by an officer of the Secretary of State, and includes any permit, approval, or other form of authorisation;

"the Minister" and "the Ministry" means respectively the Minister and the Ministry of Agriculture, Fisheries and Food;

"premises" includes land, with or without buildings, and where any person occupies together land which comprises two or more non-adjacent areas, each of those areas shall be deemed to be separate premises for the purposes of this order;

"reactor" means a bovine animal which gives rise to a reaction consistent with its being affected with brucellosis when tested for that disease either by or on behalf of the Minister or the Secretary of State or otherwise, as the case may be, provided that in the case of a test otherwise so carried out the result thereof has been reported to the Minister or the Secretary of State;

"slaughterhouse" means a slaughterhouse or knacker's yard, as defined in section 34 of the Slaughterhouses Act 1974(a);

"steer" means a castrated bull or male calf aged six months or over;

"veterinary inspector" means a veterinary inspector appointed by the Minister.

(2) Other expressions used in this order have, so far as the context admits, the same meanings as in the Diseases of Animals Act 1950.

(3) References in this order to any enactment. or order are (unless the context otherwise requires) references thereto as from time to time amended or replaced.

(4) The Interpretation Act 1889(b) applies to the interpretation of this order as it applies to the interpretation of an Act of Parliament and as if this order and the orders revoked by it were Acts of Parliament.

Declaration of brucellosis eradication and attested areas

3.—(1) The areas described in Schedule 1 hereto, being areas as respects which the Minister is satisfied that a substantial majority of the cattle therein are free from brucellosis, are hereby declared to be eradication areas for purposes connected with the control of brucellosis.

(2) The areas described in Schedule 2 hereto, being areas as respects which the Minister is satisfied that brucellosis in cattle is for practical purposes non-existent therein, are hereby declared to be attested areas for purposes connected with the control of brucellosis.

(a) 1974 c. 3.   (b) 1889 c. 63.

Application of Articles 6 to 27

4.—(1) The provisions of Articles 6 to 27 shall not apply to or have effect in the eradication areas which are described in Part II of Schedule 1 hereto until 1st November 1977.

(2) The provisions of this order shall not apply to an export quarantine station, within the meaning of section 36(1) of the Diseases of Animals Act 1950, which is situated within an eradication area or attested area unless that station is referred to in the description of that area.

(3) The provisions of this order shall not apply in relation to approved premises, within the meaning of the Importation of Animals Order 1977(a), and shall apply in relation to imported animals only—

(*a*) from the time specified in the licence issued in respect of those animals under Article 11(5) of that order; or

(*b*) where the existence or suspected existence of disease in any part of Great Britain makes it expedient that no such licence should be issued for the time being, from the time when those animals have completed the period of detention in quarantine required under the provisions of that order or, as the case may be, have been rested at an approved reception centre for the period so required.

(4) For the purposes of this order, premises which—

(*a*) are situated partly within an area to which this order applies, and partly outside any such area, shall be deemed to be wholly within that area,

(*b*) are situated partly within an attested area or areas and partly within an eradication area or areas, shall be deemed to be wholly within that attested area within which the greater or greatest part of the premises is situated,

(*c*) are situated wholly or partly within two or more attested areas or two or more eradication areas, shall be deemed to be within that area within which the greater or greatest part of the premises is situated.

Restriction on vaccination

5. No person other than—

(*a*) a veterinary inspector,

(*b*) a veterinary surgeon authorised for the purpose by the Minister, or

(*c*) a person acting under the authority of a licence issued for the purpose by a veterinary inspector employed by the Minister, who complies with the conditions (if any) subject to which the licence is issued,

shall vaccinate bovine animals against brucellosis in an area declared by this order to be an eradication area or an attested area.

(**a**) S.I. 1977/994 (1977 II, p. 2631).

Movement of bovine animals into or through eradication areas or attested areas

6.—(1) No bovine animal shall be moved into an eradication area or attested area, except under the authority of a licence issued by an officer of the Ministry or, in the case of bovine animals being moved from a place in Scotland, an officer of the Secretary of State, and in accordance with the terms and conditions (if any) subject to which the licence is issued.

(2) The provisions of paragraph (1) above shall not apply to the movement, otherwise than on foot, of bovine animals—

(*a*) through an eradication area or attested area from a place outside that area direct to another place outside that area;

(*b*) into an eradication area or attested area direct to a slaughterhouse in that area (from which they shall not be removed alive) for the purpose of unloading and slaughter there;

(*c*) (other than reactors) into an eradication area direct to premises in that area for the purpose of unloading and sale there, being premises used for the time being in connection with the holding of a market under the authority of a licence issued under Article 21 of this order imposing a condition that cattle in the premises may only be sold there for immediate slaughter;

(*d*) under the age of 6 months into an eradication area or attested area direct to premises in that area for the purpose of unloading and sale there, being premises used for the time being in connection with the holding of a market under the authority of a licence issued under Article 21 of this order; or

(*e*) from one attested area to another attested area by a route which, disregarding any part thereof which involves the carriage of such animals by sea or air, is entirely over land comprised in an attested area.

(3) The exemption from the provisions of paragraph (1) of this Article conferred by paragraph (2)(c) above shall not apply in respect of the movement into an attested area of bovine animals which—

(*a*) are lactating,

(*b*) have calved within the preceding 14 days, or

(*c*) are showing signs of vaginal discharge.

(4) When bovine animals are moved into or through an eradication area or attested area in the circumstances referred to in any of sub-paragraphs (*a*) to (*d*) of paragraph (2) above, the person in charge of those animals shall ensure that they do not come into contact with any other bovine animals, other than those with which they were in contact immediately before they entered the area, and that they are not (except in case of emergency) unloaded within the area from the vehicle by means of which they are transported otherwise than as provided for in the relevant sub-paragraph.

Movement of bovine animals on to premises within an eradication area

7. No bovine animals shall be moved on to premises within an eradication area, except under the authority of a licence issued by an officer of the

Ministry or, in the case of such animals being moved on to those premises from a place in Scotland, an officer of the Secretary of State, and in accordance with the terms and conditions (if any) subject to which the licence is issued: provided that the provisions of this paragraph shall not apply to—

(a) bovine animals to which the provisions of sub-paragraphs (b) to (d) of paragraph (2) of the preceding Article apply, or

(b) bovine animals being moved (otherwise than on foot) from a place within an eradication area direct to a slaughterhouse or market within that area.

Movement of bovine animals within an eradication area or attested area

8.—(1) A veterinary inspector or other officer of the Ministry may, by notice in writing served at any time on the occupier of any premises situated within an eradication area or attested area, prohibit the movement of bovine animals on to or off those premises except under the authority of a licence or, where a licence has been issued under the preceding Article, of a further licence, and in accordance with the terms and conditions (if any) of that licence or further licence.

(2) A notice served in accordance with the preceding provisions of this paragraph shall remain in force until withdrawn by a further notice in writing signed by a veterinary inspector or other officer of the Ministry, and served as aforesaid.

Movement of cattle to temporary accommodation for cattle intended for export

9.—(1) Nothing in Articles 6(1) and 7 of this order shall apply to bovine animals being moved otherwise than on foot into an eradication area or attested area direct to approved premises within that area.

(2) In this Article, "approved premises" means premises which have been approved under Article 3(1) of the Exported Animals Protection Order 1964(a) for the resting of animals immediately before their exportation from Great Britain, and also approved in writing for the purposes of this order by an officer of the Ministry.

Control of slaughterhouses in attested areas

10. No slaughterhouse in an attested area, other than a slaughterhouse which has been approved for the purposes of this order by a veterinary inspector, shall admit, or be used for the purpose of slaughtering, a reactor from within the attested area or any bovine animals from any place outside the attested area.

Supplementary provision as to approvals

11.—(1) An approval of premises under Article 9 or of a slaughterhouse under Article 10 of this order may be given subject to compliance by the

---

(a) S.I. 1964/704 (1964 II, p. 1352).

owner or occupier of the premises or, as the case may be, the slaughterhouse to which it relates with such conditions as may be specified in the approval.

(2) Such an approval may, by notice in writing served on such owner or occupier, be withdrawn or varied at any time by a veterinary inspector, but without prejudice to anything lawfully done pursuant to such approval before such withdrawal or variation has taken effect.

Testing of bovine animals for brucellosis

12.—(1) The owner or other person in charge of bovine animals kept on premises within an eradication area or attested area shall comply with all reasonable requirements of a veterinary inspector or other officer of the Ministry with a view to facilitating the examination of any such animals by a veterinary inspector, or the application thereto of any diagnostic test for brucellosis, and in particular, shall arrange for the collection, penning and securing of any such animals if so required.

(2) If any person fails to comply with any reasonable requirement of a veterinary inspector or other officer of the Ministry made in accordance with the provisions of the preceding paragraph, the Minister may, without prejudice to any proceedings for an offence arising out of such default, take or cause to be taken all such steps as may be necessary to facilitate the examination of such cattle, or the application thereto of any diagnostic test for brucellosis, and the amount of any expenses reasonably incurred by the Minister for the purpose of making good the default shall (without prejudice to any proceedings which may be taken for the default) be recoverable by him as a civil debt from the person in default.

(3) Where the owner or other person in charge of bovine animals kept on premises within an eradication area or attested area arranges for, or permits any diagnostic test for brucellosis to be carried out on any such animals (other than any such diagnostic test which is carried out by or on behalf of the Ministry) he shall, after receipt thereof, forthwith communicate the results of such test to the Ministry.

(4) The owner or other person in charge of bovine animals kept on premises within an eradicated area or attested area shall not do, or cause or permit to be done, anything which is likely to affect in any way the result of any diagnostic test for brucellosis carried out, or to be carried out, on any such animals by or on behalf of the Ministry.

Marking of bovine animals

13.—(1) If so required in writing by a veterinary inspector or other officer of the Ministry, the owner or other person in charge or bovine animals kept on premises within an eradication area or attested area shall mark such animals in the manner required by the veterinary inspector or other officer of the Ministry.

(2) A veterinary inspector or other officer of the Ministry may paint, stamp, clip, tag, or otherwise mark bovine animals kept on premises within an eradication area or attested area.

(3) No person shall alter, remove, obliterate or deface, or attempt to alter, remove, obliterate or deface any mark made under either of the foregoing provisions of this Article.

Notification of abortion or premature calving

14.—(1) Where the owner or other person in charge of bovine animals kept on premises within an eradication area or attested area has reason to believe that any abortion or premature calving has occurred among such animals, he shall forthwith—

(a) give notice of the fact to a veterinary inspector or other officer of the Ministry, and

(b) arrange for the isolation, as far as practicable, of the animal concerned, and its calf and placenta, from all other animals in his ownership, or under his charge.

(2) An animal to which the preceding paragraph applies shall remain in isolation, and its calf and placenta shall be retained by the owner or other person in charge of the said animal, until such time as a veterinary inspector or other officer of the Ministry otherwise directs in writing.

Precautions against spread of infection

15.—(1) Where a veterinary inspector or other officer of the Ministry has certified that any animal kept on premises within an eradication area or attested area has reacted to a diagnostic test for brucellosis, the occupier of the premises shall, on being notified of such certification, take such steps as may be reasonably practicable to prevent the infection of bovine animals kept on adjoining premises by contact with bovine animals kept on his premises.

(2) Where a veterinary inspector or other officer of the Ministry has reason to believe that any bovine animal kept on premises within an eradication area or attested area may be infected with brucellosis, or has been exposed to such infection, he may serve on the owner or other person in charge of such animal, or on the occupier of the premises, a notice in writing requiring him to isolate any bovine animals specified in the notice from any other such animals.

(3) A notice served in accordance with the provisions of the preceding paragraph may provide that any cow or heifer on the premises which is about to calve should, as far as is practicable, be isolated from all other bovine animals on the premises during the period of calving.

(4) Where a veterinary inspector or other officer of the Ministry has reason to believe that any bovine animal kept, or formerly kept, on premises within an eradication area or attested area may be infected with brucellosis, he may, by separate notice in writing served on the owner or other person in charge of such animal, or on the occupier of the premises, require him—

(a) to arrange for the isolation of any animal or animals which may be specified in the notice on any part or parts of the premises so specified;

(b) to ensure that any part or parts of the premises specified in the notice shall not be used by any animal on the premises, or by such animal or animals as may be so specified;

(c) at his own expense, and within a period specified in the notice, to cleanse and disinfect such part or parts of the premises as may be so specified, in the manner (if any) indicated in the notice;

(d) to restrict the spreading of manure or the spraying of slurry, in accordance with the requirements of the notice.

(5) If any person on whom a notice is served in accordance with the provisions of the preceding paragraph fails to comply with the requirements thereof in so far as they relate to any of the matters referred to in sub-paragraph (c) of that paragraph, the Minister may, without prejudice to any proceedings for an offence arising out of such default, carry out, or cause to be carried out, the works specified in the notice, and the amount of any expenses reasonably incurred by the Minister for the purpose of making good the default shall (without prejudice to any proceedings which may be taken for the default) be recoverable by him as a civil debt from the person in default.

(6) Where a veterinary inspector or other officer of the Ministry has reason to believe that any bovine animal present at, or which has been present at, any slaughterhouse or other premises within an eradication area or attested area which are used for any show, exhibition, market, sale or fair, may be infected with brucellosis, he may serve on the occupier of such slaughterhouse or other premises a notice in writing prescribing the manner in which any manure, slurry or other animal waste shall be disposed of.

Disinfecting of vehicles, plant or equipment on infected premises

16.—(1) Where a veterinary inspector or other officer of the Ministry has reason to believe that any bovine animal kept, or formerly kept, on premises within an eradication area or attested area may be infected with brucellosis, he may serve on the occupier of the premises a notice in writing requiring him to arrange for the cleansing and disinfection of any vehicle, plant or equipment before it leaves the premises.

(2) If any person on whom a notice is served under the provisions of the preceding paragraph fails to comply with any of the requirements thereof, the Minister may, without prejudice to any proceedings for an offence arising out of such default, carry out, or cause to be carried out, the works specified in the notice, and the amount of any expenses reasonably incurred by the Minister for the purpose of making good the default shall (without prejudice to any proceedings which may be taken for the default) be recoverable by him as a civil debt from the person in default.

Notification of full-term calvings in herds affected with brucellosis

17. Where an animal kept, or formerly kept, on premises within an eradication area or attested area has reacted to a diagnostic test for brucellosis, or where a veterinary inspector or other officer of the Ministry has reason to believe that brucellosis infection exists on such premises, he may serve on the owner or other person in charge of any bovine animal thereon a notice in writing requiring him to notify the Ministry, within such period as may be specified therein, of any full-term calving which may occur among such bovine animals.

Control of milk and milk products

18.—(1) No milk or dairy by-product (other than milk or a dairy by-product produced by an accredited herd) shall be brought on to any premises within an eradication area or attested area on which bovine animals are kept, for the purpose of processing or bottling on such premises, or of feeding to animals thereon, unless such milk or dairy by-product has been—

(a) converted into powdered form, boiled or otherwise heat treated, or

(b) brought on to the premises under the authority of a licence issued by a veterinary inspector or other officer of the Ministry, and in accordance with the terms and conditions (if any) subject to which the licence is issued.

(2) Notwithstanding the provisions of the preceding paragraph, where a veterinary inspector or other officer of the Ministry has reason to believe that any milk or dairy by-product produced by an accredited herd may be infected with brucellosis, he may serve on the occupier of any premises within an eradication area or attested area a notice in writing prohibiting any such milk or dairy by-product from being brought on to such premises.

(3) For the purposes of this Article—

(a) "accredited herd" means a herd of bovine animals in Great Britain which, to the satisfaction of the Minister (in relation to England and Wales) or of the Secretary of State (in relation to Scotland), either—

(i) has been found to be free from brucellosis by means of a series of diagnostic tests carried out by him or on his behalf and has been, since the date of commencement of such tests, the subject of adequate precautions against the introduction or re-introduction and consequent spreading of brucellosis, or

(ii) has been wholly constituted by the transfer of animals from other accredited herds in Great Britain or from such similar herds outside Great Britain as the Minister or the Secretary of State (as the case may be) may either generally, or in any special case, allow, and has been, since being so constituted, the subject of such precautions as aforesaid; and

(b) "heat treated" means pasteurised, sterilised or ultra-heat treated.

Manure, slurry, etc.

19. No manure, slurry or slaughterhouse or other animal waste shall be brought on to premises within an eradication area or attested area on which bovine animals are kept, except under the authority of a licence issued by a veterinary inspector or other officer of the Ministry, and in accordance with the terms and conditions (if any) subject to which the licence is issued.

Restriction on use of semen

20. A veterinary inspector or other officer of the Ministry may, by notice in writing served on the owner or other person in charge of bovine animals kept on premises within an eradication area or attested area, prohibit the use of semen among such animals, or restrict its use to the extent specified in the notice.

Shows, exhibitions, etc.

21.—(1) No premises within an eradication area or attested area shall be used in connection with the holding of any show, exhibition, market, sale or fair at which bovine animals are to be present, except under the authority of a licence issued by an officer of the Ministry, and in accordance with the terms and conditions (if any) subject to which the licence is issued.

(2) Where a veterinary inspector or other officer of the Ministry has reason to suspect that any bovine animal on premises within an eradication area or attested area at which a show, exhibition, market, sale or fair is being held, is infected with, or has been exposed to the infection of, brucellosis, he may require the animal to be removed from those premises, and (as the owner or other person in charge of the animal may elect) taken either—

(a) to a slaughterhouse for immediate slaughter, or

(b) back to the premises from which the animal was brought to the show, exhibition, market, sale or fair, or

(c) to such other premises as may be approved by him for the purpose.

(3) If the premises to which an animal is to be removed in accordance with the provisions of sub-paragraphs (b) or (c) of the preceding paragraph are situated within an eradication area or attested area, the animal shall only be removed thereto on condition that it is immediately put into isolation for a period to be terminated by a notice in writing served on the owner or other person in charge of the said animal by a veterinary inspector or other officer of the Ministry.

Control of premises used by dealers in bovine animals

22.—(1) No premises within an eradication area or attested area shall be used by a dealer in bovine animals for the keeping of such animals in connection with his business as a dealer, other than premises which have been approved for the purpose by an officer of the Ministry.

(2) Any such approval as is referred to in the preceding paragraph may be given subject to compliance by the owner or occupier of the premises to which it relates with such conditions as may be specified therein.

Animals other than bovine animals

23. A veterinary inspector or other officer of the Ministry may, by notice in writing served on the owner or other person in charge of bovine animals kept on premises within an eradication area or attested area, or on the occupier of such premises, require him to take such steps as may be specified in the notice to ensure that such animals do not come into contact with any other animals kept on the premises.

Power to slaughter on account of brucellosis

24. Section 17 of the Diseases of Animals Act 1950 (which enables the

Minister to slaughter animals on account of disease, on payment of compensation) shall apply to brucellosis.

Notice of intended slaughter

25.—(1) Where the Minister proposes to cause a bovine animal kept on any premises within an eradication area or attested area to be slaughtered under the powers conferred by section 17 of the Act in its application to brucellosis, a veterinary inspector may serve a notice of intended slaughter on the owner or other person in charge of the animal informing him of the proposed slaughter and requiring him to detain the animal pending its slaughter (or pending its surrender and removal for such slaughter) on such part of the premises as is specified in the notice and to isolate it as far as practicable from such other animals as are so specified.

(2) The person on whom such a notice has been served—

(a) shall comply with the notice, and

(b) shall not move the animal, or cause or permit it to be moved, off the part of the premises on which it is required to be detained, except under the authority of a licence issued by an officer of the Ministry.

(3) In this article, "notice of intended slaughter" means a notice served in the form specified in Schedule 3 to this order, or in a form substantially to the like effect.

Assistance in securing animals

26.—(1) Where the Minister proposes to cause a bovine animal kept on any premises within an eradication area or attested area to be slaughtered under the powers conferred by section 17 of the Act in its application to brucellosis, the owner or other person in charge of the animal shall comply with all reasonable requirements of a veterinary inspector or other officer of the Ministry as to the collection, penning and securing of the animal for identification and inspection in connection with the ascertainment of its value.

(2) If the owner or other person in charge of an animal fails to comply with such a requirement as is mentioned in paragraph (1) above, the Minister may carry out the requirement, without prejudice to any proceedings for an offence arising out of the default, and may on demand recover from the person in default as a civil debt the reasonable expense of doing so.

(3) Nothing in this article shall affect the powers of entry and other powers conferred by sections 6 and 73 of the Diseases of Animals Act 1950.

Production of licences

27. Where, under the provisions of this order, a licence is required for the movement of a bovine animal, the person in charge of any such animal being so moved shall, on demand made under this order by a veterinary inspector or other officer of the Ministry, or by an inspector of a local authority or police constable, produce the licence, and allow a copy thereof or extract therefrom to be taken, and shall also if required, furnish his name and address.

Offences

28. The contravention of any provision of this order, or of any notice served or licence issued thereunder, or the failure to comply with any condition of any such notice or licence, or the causing or permitting of any such contravention or non-compliance, or, in the case of a dealer in bovine animals, the use of any premises contrary to Article 22(1) of this order, or contrary to any condition subject to which such premises are approved, shall be an offence against the Diseases of Animals Act 1950.

Local authority to enforce order

29. This order shall, except where otherwise expressly provided, be executed and enforced by the local authority.

Revocation

30. The orders listed in Schedule 4 are hereby revoked.

Transitional provisions

31. Where at the date of coming into operation of this order there is in force a notice or licence issued under the Brucellosis (Area Eradication) (England and Wales) Order 1971 (a), as amended (b), and extended (c), that notice or licence shall be deemed for the purposes of this order to have been issued under this order.

In Witness whereof the Official Seal of the Minister of Agriculture, Fisheries and Food is hereunto affixed on 27th July 1977.

(L.S.)

John Silkin,
Minister of Agriculture, Fisheries and Food.

(a) S.I. 1971/1717 (1971 III, p. 4673).
(b) S.I. 1972/1173, 1976/244, 1977/949 (1972 II, p. 3486; 1976 I, p. 615; 1977 II, p. 2666).
(c) 1972/1174 (1972 II, p. 3488).

Article 3(1)

SCHEDULE 1

PART I

ERADICATION AREAS

In England

Eradication Area No. 1

An area comprising—

The counties of Lincolnshire, Cambridgeshire, Bedfordshire, Berkshire (excluding Reading livestock market), Hertfordshire, Essex, Surrey, Kent, West Sussex, East Sussex, the City and Boroughs of Greater London.

So much of the county of Buckinghamshire as lies to the south of the road M40.

In the county of Leicestershire
      The district of Rutland.

In the county of Oxfordshire
      The district of Vale of White Horse.

So much of the district of South Oxfordshire and of Oxford Borough which lies to the south of the road M40 and its continuation as the road A40 to the junction with the road A4142 and east of the road A4142 (eastern Oxford by-pass) and south of the road A423 from its junction with the road A4142 westwards until it crosses the River Thames. Also that part of the district as lies to the west and south of the River Thames.

Eradication Area No. 2

An area comprising—

In the county of Hampshire
   In the district of Test Valley
      The parishes of Melchett Park and Plaitford and Wellow.

The district of New Forest excluding the parishes of Whitsbury, Rockbourne, Breamore, Martin and Damerham and so much of the parishes of Fordingbridge and Harbridge and Ibsley as lies to the west of the River Avon.

In the county of Dorset
   In the district of Christchurch
      The parish of Burton.

      So much of the parish of Christchurch as lies to the east of the River Avon.

In the county of Wiltshire

   In the district of Salisbury

      The parishes of Whiteparish, Redlynch and Landford.

      So much of the parish of Downton as lies to the east of the River Avon.

All the said river is excluded from the eradication area where it forms part of its boundary.

Eradication Area No. 3

An area comprising—

The county of Devon.

In the county of Cornwall

   In the district of North Cornwall

      The parishes to the north of, and including St Gennys, Otterham, Warbstow, Trenglos, Tresmeer, Egloskerry and St Stephens by Launceston Rural.

In the county of Somerset

   The district of West Somerset.

   The district of Taunton Deane excluding Taunton livestock market.

   The district of Sedgemoor excluding the parishes of Shipham, Cheddar and Wedmore.

   In the district of Mendip

      The parishes of Sharpham and Walton.

   In the district of Yeovil

      The parishes of High Ham, Somerton, Compton Dundon, Aller, Pitney, Langport, Long Sutton, Kingsdon, Curry Rivel, Drayton, Muchelney, Huish Episcopi, Long Load, Ash, Tintinhull, Ilchester, Fivehead, Curry Mallet, Isle Abbots, Isle Brewers, Beercombe, Ashill, Ilton, Puckington, Barrington, Kingsbury Episcopi, Martock, Stoke-sub-Hamdon, Norton-sub-Hamdon, East Chinnock, West Chinnock, Hazlebury Plucknett, Chiselborough, Broadway, Buckland St Mary, Combe St Nicholas, Whitestaunton, Wambrook, Chard, Winsham, Wayford, Cricket St Thomas, Chaffcombe, Ilminster, Ilminster Without, Ilminster Without Detached, Knowle St Giles, Dowlish Wake, Kingstone, Donyatt, White Lackington, Seavington St Mary, Seavington St Michael, Lopen, Hinton St George, Merriott, Crewkerne, West Crewkerne, Misterton, North Perrott, Dinnington, Cudworth, Chillington, South Petherton, Shepton Beauchamp and Stocklinch.

Eradication Area No. 4

An area comprising—

In the county of Salop

That part of the county to the west of the road A49–A41–A49 (excluding Shrewsbury and Whitchurch livestock markets).

In the county of Hereford and Worcester

That part of the county as lies to the west of the road A49 from Ludlow to Kingsthorne and to the west of the road A466 from Kingsthorne to Monmouth.

All the said roads are excluded from the eradication area where they form part of its boundary.

Eradication Area No. 5

An area comprising—

The county of Cumbria *excluding:*

The districts of Barrow-in-Furness and South Lakeland.

In the district of Copeland

The parishes of Bootle, Millom, Millom Without, Waberthwaite, and Whicham, so much of the parish of Eskdale as lies south and east of the River Esk to its intersection with the unclassified road near Penny Hill and south of the said road running to Hard Knott Pass. So much of the parish of Muncaster as lies south and east of the River Esk and so much of the parish of Ulpha as lies south of the unclassified road (Hard Knott Pass).

In the district of Eden

The parishes of Patterdale, Martindale, Bampton, Barton, Askham, Sockbridge and Tirril, Yanwath and Eamont Bridge, Clifton Lowther, Thrimby, Little Strickland, Great Strickland, Newby, Sleagill, Morland, Cliburn, Brougham, Temple Sowerby, Newbiggin, Kirkby Thore, Bolton, Kings Meaburn, Milburn, Long Marton, Dufton, Murton, Appleby, Crackenthorpe, Colby, Shap, Shap Rural, Crosby Ravensworth, Hoff, Ormside, Asby, Warcop, Musgrave, Helbeck, Brough, Brough Sowerby, Stainmore, Kaber, Winton, Hartley, Nateby, Mallerstang, Wharton, Kirkby Stephen, Waitby, Soulby, Crosby Garrett, Ravenstonedale, Orton, Tebay.

In the county of Lancashire

The Borough of Burnley and the districts of Hyndburn and Pendle.

In the Borough of Ribble Valley

The parishes of Balderstone, Billington, Chatburn, Clayton-le-Dale, Clitheroe, Dinckley, Downham, Gisburn, Horton, Little Mitton,

ANIMALS

Mearley, Mellor, Middop, Newsholme, Osbaldeston, Pendleton, Ramsgreave, Read, Rimington, Sabden, Salesbury, Twiston, Worston, Whalley, Wilpshire, Wiswell and so much of the parishes of Grindleton and Sawley as lies to the south and east of the River Ribble.

In the county of North Yorkshire
In the district of Craven

The parishes of Airton, Appletreewick, Arncliffe, Bank Newton, Barden, Bordley, Beamsley, Bolton Abbey, Bradleys Both, Broughton, Buckden, Burnsall, Calton, Carleton, Cononley, Coniston Cold, Conistone with Kilnsey, Cowling, Cracoe, Draughton, Elslack, Embsay with Eastby, Eshton, Farnhill, Flasby with Winterburn, Gargrave, Grassington, Glusburn, Halton East, Halton Gill, Hanlith, Hartlington, Hawkswick, Hazlewood with Storiths, Hebden, Hellifield, Hetton, Kettlewell with Starbotton, Kirkby Malham, Langcliffe, Linton, Litton, Long Preston, Lothersdale, Malham, Malham Moor, Martons Both, Nappa, Otterburn, Rylstone, Scosthrop, Skipton, Stirton with Thorlby, Sutton, Swinden, Thornton-in-Craven, Thorpe, Threshfield and so much of the parishes of Horton-in-Ribblesdale, Rathmell, Settle, and Stainforth as lie to the east of the River Ribble.

In the county of Humberside

The districts of Scunthorpe, Glanford, Cleethorpes and Grimsby.

All the said river is excluded from the eradication area where it forms part of its boundary.

In Wales
Eradication Area No. 6

An area comprising—
In the county of Clwyd

The Borough of Colwyn

The district of Glyndwr (excluding the community areas of Llandrillo, Llangar, Gwyddelwern, Corwen, Bettws Gwerfyl Goch and Llansantffraid Glynyfrdwy).

The Borough of Wrexham-Maelor (excluding Wrexham livestock market).

The county of West Glamorgan excluding—
In the Borough of Neath

The community areas of Dylais Higher and Glyneath.

In the Borough of Lliw Valley

The community areas of Llanguicke, Rhyndwyclybach and Mawr and that part of the community area of Llwchwr which was formerly the parishes of Llandeilo, Tal-y-bont and Llangyfelach.

The county of Mid Glamorgan *excluding—*
    In the Borough of Cynon Valley
        The community area of Penderyn.

    In the Borough of Merthyr Tydfil
        The community area of Vaynor.

The county of South Glamorgan

The county of Gwent *excluding—*
    In the Borough of Blaenau Gwent
      The community areas of Brynmawr and Llanelli.

Articles 3(1) and 4(1)

SCHEDULE 1

PART II

ERADICATION AREAS TO WHICH ARTICLES 6–27 ARE NOT APPLICABLE UNTIL 1 NOVEMBER 1977

In England

In the county of Buckinghamshire

So much of the county as lies to the north of the road M40, including the said road.

In the county of Cheshire

So much of the county as lies to the west of the River Dee.

All the said river is excluded from the eradication area where it forms part of its boundary.

The county of Dorset *excluding*

In the district of Christchurch

The parish of Burton and so much of the parish of Christchurch as lies east of the River Avon.

The county of Durham

In the metropolitan county of Tyne and Wear

So much of the county as lies to the south of the River Tyne.

In the county of North Yorkshire

The district of Harrogate and so much of the districts of Richmondshire and Hambleton as lies to the west of the road A1.

The county of Hampshire *excluding*

The parishes of Melchett Park and Plaitford and Wellow in the district of Test Valley and the parishes of Whitsbury, Rockbourne, Breamore, Martin and Damerham and so much of the parishes of Fordingbridge and Harbridge and Ibsley as lies to the west of the River Avon in the district of New Forest.

In the county of Lancashire

The Boroughs of Blackburn, Chorley, South Ribble and Rossendale, excluding Haslingden livestock market, and the district of West Lancashire.

Preston livestock market.

In the metropolitan county of Merseyside
  The district of Sefton.

The county of Leicestershire *excluding*
  The district of Rutland.

The county of Salop *excluding*
  That part of the county to the west of the road A49–A41–A49 and Market Drayton livestock market.

In the county of Hereford and Worcester
  That part of the former county of Hereford as lies to the east of the road A49 from Ludlow to Kingsthorne and to the east of the road A466 from Kingsthorne to Monmouth.

The county of Oxford *excluding*
  Banbury livestock market, field OS nos. 8400 and 9200 in the parish of Banbury and all that part of the county described in eradication area No. 1 in Part I of this Schedule.

In the county of Somerset
  The district of Mendip excluding the parishes of Sharpham and Walton.

  In the district of Sedgemoor
    The parishes of Shipham, Cheddar and Wedmore.

  In the district of Yeovil
    The parishes of Barton St. David, Keinton Mandeville, Kingweston, Charlton Mackrell, Babcary, Lovington, Alford, Castle Cary, Ansford, Pitcombe, Bruton, Brewham, North Barrow, South Barrow, North Cadbury, Yarlington, Shepton Montague, Bratton Seymour, Charlton Musgrove, Cucklington, Penselwood, Yeovilton, West Camel, Queen Camel, Sparkford, South Cadbury, Compton Paunce-foot, Maperton, Wincanton, Stoke Trister, Limington, Chilton Cantelo, Marston Magna, Rimpton, Corton Denham, Charlton Horethorn, Holton, North Cheriton, Abbas and Templecombe, Milborne Port, Horsington, Henstridge, Chilthorne Domer, Yeovil Without, Yeovil, Mudford, Montacute, Odcombe, Brympton, West Coker, East Coker, Barwick, Hardington Mandeville and Closworth.

In the district of Taunton Deane
  Taunton livestock market.

In Wales

In the county of Clwyd
  The Boroughs of Rhuddlan and Delyn.
  The district of Alyn and Deeside (excluding that part of the district which lies to the north of the River Dee).

  All the said river is excluded from the eradication area where it forms part of its boundary.

Article 3(2)

SCHEDULE 2

ATTESTED AREAS

In England

Attested Area No. 1

An area comprising—

The counties of Norfolk, Suffolk, the Isle of Wight and the Isles of Scilly.

Attested Area No. 2

An area comprising—

In the county of Lancashire
> The Boroughs of Lancaster, Blackpool, Fylde, Preston (excluding Preston livestock market) and Wyre.

In the Borough of Ribble Valley
> So much of the Borough as lies north and west of the River Ribble.

In the county of North Yorkshire
In the district of Craven
> The parishes of Burton in Lonsdale, Ingleton, Thornton-in-Lonsdale, Austwick, Bentham, Clapham cum Newby, Giggleswick, Halton West, Lawkland, Wigglesworth and so much of the parishes of Horton in Ribblesdale, Rathmell, Settle and Stainforth as lies west of the River Ribble.

In the county of Cumbria
> The districts of Barrow-in-Furness and South Lakeland.

In the district of Copeland
> The parishes of Bootle, Millom, Millom Without, Waberthwaite, and Whicham, so much of the parish of Eskdale as lies south and east of the River Esk to its intersection with the unclassified road near Penny Hill and south of the said road running to Hard Knott Pass. So much of the parish of Muncaster as lies south and east of the River Esk and so much of the parish of Ulpha as lies south of the unclassified road (Hard Knott Pass).

In the district of Eden

The parishes of Patterdale, Martindale, Bampton, Barton, Askham, Sockbridge and Tirril, Yanwath and Eamont Bridge, Clifton Lowther, Thrimby, Little Strickland, Great Strickland, Newby, Sleagill, Morland, Cliburn, Brougham, Temple Sowerby, Newbiggin, Kirkby Thore, Bolton, Kings Meaburn, Milburn, Long Marton, Dufton, Murton, Appleby, Crackenthorpe, Colby, Shap, Shap Rural, Crosby Ravensworth, Hoff, Ormside, Asby, Warcop, Musgrave, Helbeck, Brough, Brough Sowerby, Stainmore, Kaber, Winton, Hartley, Nateby, Mallerstang, Wharton, Kirkby Stephen, Waitby, Soulby, Crosby Garrett, Ravenstonedale, Orton, Tebay.

In Wales

Attested Area No. 3

An area comprising—

The counties of Dyfed, Gwynedd and Powys.

In the county of Clwyd
In the district of Glyndwr

The community areas of Llandrillo, Llangar, Gwyddelwern, Corwen, Bettws Gwerfyl Goch and Llansantffraid Glyndyfrdwy.

In the county of West Glamorgan
In the Borough of Neath

The community areas of Dylais Higher and Glyneath.

In the Borough of Lliw Valley

The community areas of Llanguicke, Rhyndwyclydach and Mawr and that part of the community area of Lwchwr which was formerly the parishes of Llandeilo, Taly-y-Bont and Llangyfelach.

In the county of Mid Glamorgan
In the district of Cynon Valley

The community area of Penderyn.

In the Borough of Merthyr Tydfil

The community area of Vaynor.

In the county of Gwent
In the Borough of Blaenau Gwent

The community areas of Brynmawr and Llanelli.

Article 25

SCHEDULE 3

DISEASES OF ANIMALS ACT 1950

Ministry of Agriculture, Fisheries and Food	Department of Agriculture and Fisheries for Scotland
The Brucellosis (England and Wales) Order 1977	The Brucellosis (Scotland) Order 1972

Notice of Intended Slaughter

Herd Ref. No. ....

To ....

of ....

....

....

I, the undersigned, being a Veterinary Inspector appointed by the Minister of Agriculture, Fisheries and Food, hereby give notice that the Minister proposes to cause the following bovine animals to be slaughtered with all convenient speed under the powers conferred by section 17 of the above Act in its application to brucellosis, namely:

(a) *affected animals and reactors* (see Note 2 below)

kept at ....

....

(b) *other animals* (see Note 2 below)

kept at ....

....

I require you, pending such slaughter (or pending surrender and removal for such slaughter), to detain the animal(s) specified above in

....

....

being part of the premises where it is/they are now kept, and to keep it/them isolated as far as practicable from other bovine animals.

Dated.. 19...

Signed..
Veterinary Inspector of the Ministry of
Agriculture, Fisheries and Food.

Note 1: In accordance with article 15(1) of the Brucellosis (England and Wales) Order 1977 and Article 9(1) of the Brucellosis (Area Eradication) (Scotland) Order 1971 (as amended) you are required to take such steps as may be reasonably practicable to prevent the infection of cattle kept on adjoining premises by contact with cattle kept on your premises.

Note 2: The Brucellosis (England and Wales) Compensation Order 1972 (as amended) and the Brucellosis Compensation (Scotland) Order 1972 (as amended) define affected animals and reactors and fix rates of compensation for them and for other bovine animals which are slaughtered as a result of being exposed to the infection of brucellosis.

Article 30

SCHEDULE 4

Orders revoked	*Reference*
The Brucellosis (Eradication Areas) (England and Wales) Order 1971	S.I. 1971/533
The Brucellosis (Eradication Areas) (England and Wales) (Amendment) Order 1971	S.I. 1971/1716
The Brucellosis (Area Eradication) (England and Wales) Order 1971	S.I. 1971/1717 (1971 III, p. 4673)
The Brucellosis (Eradication Areas) (Norfolk and Suffolk) Order 1972	S.I. 1972/161
The Brucellosis (Area Eradication) (England and Wales) (Amendment) Order 1972	S.I. 1972/1173 (1972 II, p. 3486)
The Brucellosis (Area Eradication) (England and Wales) (Extension) Order 1972	S.I. 1972/1174 (1972 II, p. 3488)
The Brucellosis (Eradication Areas) (West Sussex and Cambridgeshire and Essex) Order 1972	S.I. 1972/1175
The Brucellosis (England and Wales) Order 1972	S.I. 1972/1521 (1972 III, p. 4473)
The Brucellosis (Eradication Areas) (Norfolk and Suffolk) (Amendment) Order 1973	S.I. 1973/590
The Brucellosis (Eradication Areas) (West Sussex and Cambridgeshire and Essex) (Amendment) Order 1973	S.I. 1973/987
The Brucellosis (Eradication Areas) (Wales) Order 1973	S.I. 1973/988 (1973 II, p. 3017)
The Brucellosis (Eradication Areas) (England and Wales) Order 1974	S.I. 1974/1151
The Brucellosis (Berkshire, South-West Oxfordshire, Surrey, etc. Eradication Area) Order 1975	S.I. 1975/143
The Brucellosis (Area Eradication) (England and Wales) (Amendment) Order 1976	S.I. 1976/244 (1976 I, p. 615)

Orders revoked	*Reference*
The Brucellosis (Eradication Areas) (England and Wales) Order 1976	S.I. 1976/245
The Brucellosis (Eradication Areas) (England and Wales) (Amendment) Order 1976	S.I. 1976/614
The Brucellosis (Eradication Areas) (England and Wales) (Amendment) (No. 2) Order 1976	S.I. 1976/1403
The Brucellosis (Eradication Areas) (England and Wales) (No. 2) Order 1976	S.I. 1976/1640
The Brucellosis (Eradication Areas) (England and Wales) (Amendment) (No. 3) Order 1976	S.I. 1976/1853
The Brucellosis (Eradication Areas) (South-West England No. 5 and North Buckinghamshire) Order 1977	S.I. 1977/692
The Brucellosis (Area Eradication) (England and Wales) (Amendment) Order 1977	S.I. 1977/949 (1977 II, p. 2666)

EXPLANATORY NOTE

(This Note is not part of the Order.)

Under section 5 of the Diseases of Animals Act 1950, the Minister of Agriculture, Fisheries and Food may make an order declaring an area to be an eradication area for purposes connected with the control of any particular disease, if he is satisfied that a substantial majority of the cattle in that area are free from that disease, and, for similar purposes, he may declare an area to be an attested area if he is satisfied that that disease is for practical purposes non-existent therein. In relation to brucellosis, the provisions of section 5 of the 1950 Act have been extended by section 106(3) of the Agriculture Act 1970, so as to give the Minister (in addition to the powers conferred on him by the earlier section) power to impose in respect of cattle in a brucellosis eradication or attested area such other prohibitions or requirements as he may consider necessary or desirable for the purpose of eradicating that disease.

This Order, which supersedes various existing orders—

(a) consolidates existing eradication areas and revises the descriptions of areas in the light of local government boundary changes.

(b) declares the first attested areas;

(c) consolidates existing provisions which apply in eradication or attested areas. These include a prohibition against the movement of bovine animals into such areas (except under licence or on certain journeys), a power to prohibit the movement of such animals on to or off particular premises in such areas, a restriction on the vaccination of bovine animals in such areas against brucellosis, and ancillary prohibitions designed to prevent the introduction or spreading of brucellosis;

(d) incorporates three changes to the consolidated general provisions referred to above. Firstly, it prohibits slaughterhouses in an attested area from admitting, or being used for the purpose of slaughtering, bovine animals from outside that area unless that slaughterhouse has been approved by a veterinary inspector for that purpose. Secondly, the movement of such animals into an attested area direct to a slaughter market is prohibited except under licence; and thirdly the movement into an attested area direct to a market licensed under this Order of bovine animals under the age of six months is now permitted without a licence;

(e) enables the Minister to cause animals which are affected or suspected of being affected with brucellosis or which have been exposed to the infection of that disease to be slaughtered on payment of compensation, and, where such animals are kept at premises situated in an eradication or attested area, to require them to be detained and isolated until removed for slaughter.

STATUTORY INSTRUMENTS

1977 No. 1285

PRICES

The Price Investigation and Examination (Exceptions) Order 1977

Laid before Parliament in draft

Made	- - -	*28th July* 1977
Coming into Operation		*1st August* 1977

The Secretary of State, in pursuance of the powers conferred by section 22(2) of the Price Commission Act 1977(a) and of all other powers enabling him in that behalf, hereby makes the following Order, a draft whereof has been approved by resolution of each House of Parliament:—

Citation, commencement and interpretation

1.—(1) This Order may be cited as the Price Investigation and Examination (Exceptions) Order 1977 and shall come into operation on 1st August 1977.

(2) In this Order, "the Act" means the Price Commission Act 1977 and all other expressions have the same respective meanings as they have for the purposes of the Act.

(3) The Interpretation Act 1889(b) shall apply for the interpretation of this Order as it applies for the interpretation of an Act of Parliament.

Exceptions from certain provisions of the Price Comission Act 1977

2.—(1) The provisions of subsection (1)(*a*) of section 5 and of subsection (5)(*b*) of section 7 of the Act (which relate, among other things, respectively to the giving by the Price Commission to the Secretary of State of a notification that a price or charge should be the subject of an investigation in pursuance of section 6 of the Act and to the acceptance by the Secretary of State of an undertaking offered by a person by reference to a report made to him by the Price Commission pursuant to the said section 6) shall not apply in the case of a price or charge of a description specified in Part I, II or III of the Schedule.

(2) The provisions of subsection (1) of section 10 of the Act (which relates to a direction by the Secretary of State to the Price Commission to examine any question relating to prices or charges) shall not apply in the case of a price or a charge of a description specified in Part I of the Schedule.

(3) The provisions of heads (*b*) to (*d*) of subsection (2) of section 11 and of subsection (3) of section 12 of the Act (which relate respectively to matters to be included in a report of the Price Commission in pursuance of subsection (1) of the said section 11, to the acceptance by the Secretary of State of an undertaking offered by a person by reference to a report made to him by the

---

(a) 1977 c. 33.   (b) 1889 c. 63.

Price Commission in pursuance of the said section 11 and to the making of orders by the Secretary of State in consequence of such a report) shall not apply in the case of a price or charge of a description specified in Part II of the Schedule, but nothing in this paragraph shall preclude any such report from containing indications or advice relating to a margin of a distributor (whether a margin described in regulations under section 5(6)(*b*) of the Act or another) or any such undertaking or order from containing provisions relating to such a margin.

Roy Hattersley
Secretary of State for Prices and
Consumer Protection.

28th July 1977.

(*Article 2*)

THE SCHEDULE
PART I

Exceptions from sections 5(1)(*a*), 7(5)(*b*) *and* 10(1) *of the Price Commission Act* 1977.

1. Charges for carriage by air transport for which an air transport licence granted by the Civil Aviation Authority is by section 21 of the Civil Aviation Act 1971(**a**) required to be held by the operator.

2. Bus fares which are fixed by conditions attached to a road service licence granted under section 135 of the Road Traffic Act 1960(**b**) or a permit granted under section 30 of the Transport Act 1968(**c**) and charges made in respect of the use of vehicles under authorisations granted under section 2(3)(*b*) of the Passenger Vehicles (Experimental Areas) Act 1977(**d**).

3. Insurance premiums.

4. Charges for services to the Post Office by sub-postmasters.

5. Charges being payments in respect of services provided under or pursuant to Part IV of the National Health Service Act 1946(**e**) or Part IV of the National Health Service (Scotland) Act 1947(**f**) to persons providing such services.

6. Charges payable to returning officers in connection with Parliamentary elections, determined under the Representation of the People Act 1949(**g**).

7. Subscriptions charged by organisations which—

   (*a*) exist for religious, charitable, educational, representational or recreational purposes; and

   (*b*) are non-profit-making; and

   (*c*) do not carry on a trade or business as their main activity,

and any price charged or charge made in the course of its activities where the purchaser or the person for whom the services are performed is a member of the organisation.

(**a**) 1971 c. 75.	(**b**) 1960 c. 16.	(**c**) 1968 c. 73.	(**d**) 1977 c. 21
(**e**) 1946 c. 81.	(**f**) 1947 c. 27.	(**g**) 1949 c. 68.	

8. Prices for the sale of liquid milk of which the maximum price is for the time being controlled by an order(a) under section 6 of the Emergency Laws (Re-enactments and Repeals) Act 1964(b).

PART II

Exceptions from sections 5(1)(a), 7(5)(b), 11(2)(b) to (d) and 12(3) of the Price Commission Act 1977.

1. Prices for the sale of goods or charges for the performance of services which are supplied, whether by the person selling or performing them or another, outside the United Kingdom or to persons or in relation to property outside the United Kingdom.

2. Prices for the sale of any goods—

    (a) which have been produced or manufactured outside the United Kingdom; and

    (b) which have not been subjected to any process in the United Kingdom other than packing or re-packing, cleaning and sterilising or, in the case of crude oil, stabilisation; and

    (c) which have not been sold to any person in the United Kingdom,

and charges for the performance of any services in the United Kingdom or in relation to any property in the United Kingdom which are performed for any person outside the United Kingdom.

3. Prices for the sale, whether alive or dead, of any goods produced in the course of agriculture, horticulture or fishing including—

    (a) (except in the case of a Milk Marketing Board) liquid milk not referred to in paragraph 8 of Part I of this Schedule; and

    (b) by-products for animal feeding which arise in the milling of grain, the processing of sugar beet or oilseeds or in the manufacture of alcoholic drinks,

which have not been incorporated in any processed product and to which no process has been applied except—

    (i) cleaning, sterilising, breaking down of bulk supplies or packaging; and

    (ii) in the case of any carcasses or parts of carcasses of livestock or poultry or of any product of fishing, chilling, freezing, curing, cutting up or boning, in the case only of bacon and ham, cooking and, in the case only of whole hams, canning.

4. Prices for the sale of raw beet sugar for further refining.

5. Prices for the sale of tallow, meat and bone meal processed from waste fat, bone and offal.

6. Prices for the sale of—

    (a) unseasoned timber in logs;

    (b) raw wool which has not undergone any process of combing, spinning or felting and tops of wool and other fine animal hair; and

    (c) untanned hides.

7. Prices for the sale of coal and steel (as defined in Annex I to the Treaty establishing the European Coal and Steel Community, signed at Paris on 18th April 1951, together with any additions to the list in that Annex made by the Special Council of Ministers under Article 81 of that Treaty) charged by an undertaking as defined in Article 80 of that Treaty (other than for the special purposes therein mentioned) except for sales to domestic consumers.

8. Prices for the sale of scrap metal.

(a) S.I. 1971/1037, 1038, 1974/1548, 1549, 1975/1664, 1977/858, 859 (1971 II, pp. 3105, 3108; 1974 III, pp. 5867, 5869; 1975 III, p. 5720; 1977 II, pp. 2366, 2368).

(b) 1964 c. 60.

9. Charges for carriage by sea transport between terminals of which one or both are outside the United Kingdom including charges for carriage between points in the United Kingdom, where the tariff applicable to those charges is one for the whole of the first-mentioned carriage.

10. Charges for a package holiday taken outside the United Kingdom.

11. (*a*) Charges or dues for the provision of aids for air navigation where that provision is made principally in connection with transport between terminals of which one or both are outside the United Kingdom;

(*b*) charges for the provision of landing and related facilities for aircraft;

(*c*) pilotage dues within the meaning of the Pilotage Act 1913(a);

(*d*) charges for harbour operations within the harbour area made by a harbour authority within the meaning of the Harbours Act 1964(b) or the Harbours Act (Northern Ireland) 1970(c) as the case may be, in so far as they relate to transport of a description referred to in paragraph 9 above; and

(*e*) ship, passenger and goods dues in relation to which an objection may be made to the National Ports Council under the said Act of 1964 or to the Department of Commerce under section 7 of the said Act of 1970 and charges exigible by virtue of section 29 of the said Act of 1964 (local light dues).

12. (*a*) Prices of any goods on any sale by auction; and

(*b*) prices for the sale of any goods determined on a commodity market in the United Kingdom (including any price to the extent to which it is determined by reference to a price determined on any such market).

13. Prices for the sale of manufactured goods—

(*a*) which have been used to a material extent otherwise than solely for the purpose of testing, examination or adjustment and, in the case of a ship, aircraft, hovercraft or motor vehicle in the course of its delivery to a person who ordinarily sells ships, aircraft, hovercraft or motor vehicles in the course of business; and

(*b*) which have not been substantially changed after completion of their manufacture.

14. Prices for the sale of goods to, or charges for the performance of services for, a Government Department to which the profit formula for non-competitive contracts as recorded in the Report by the Review Board for Government Contracts published by Her Majesty's Stationery Office in 1974 relates.

15. Charges by the Post Office for services of a description provided only to a Government Department.

16. Prices for the sale of any human pharmaceutical which may be prescribed under the National Health Service but is not advertised to the general public.

17. Prices for the sale of goods or charges for the performance of services to the extent that any increases made therein are required for the purpose of implementing, and only to the extent required for that purpose, any obligation created or arising by or under any international agreement or arrangement (being an agreement or arrangement between states or organisations of states and not any other) or are made as a direct consequence of any such increase already made.

18. Charges made by the Post Office in accordance with any international agreement in respect of the carriage of postal packets or the provision of telecommunications, giro or remittance services to or from any place in the United Kingdom to or from any other place.

19. Charges by way of interest.

(a) 1913 (2 & 3 Geo. 5) c. 31.   (b) 1964 c. 40.   (c) 1970 c. 1. (N. I.).

PART III

Exceptions from sections 5(1)(a) and 7(5)(b) of the Price Commission Act 1977

1. Charges for services provided by ship brokers.

2. Taxi fares fixed by regulations made by, or by byelaws confirmed by, the Secretary of State.

3. Charges for carriage by sea transport between terminals of which both are within the United Kingdom, whether or not any such charge relates to a voyage during which a call is made at any other place, other than charges which are in accordance with a tariff of general application.

4. Charges for harbour operations within the harbour area made by a harbour authority within the meaning of the Harbours Act 1964 or the Harbours Act (Northern Ireland) 1970 as the case may be (other than charges falling within paragraph 11(*d*) of Part II of this Schedule).

EXPLANATORY NOTE

(This Note is not part of the Order.)

This Order specifies prices and charges to which an investigation by the Price Commission under section 5 of the Price Commission Act 1977 may not relate. These prices and charges are largely the same as those of which no notice of a proposed increase has to be given to the Commission pursuant to an Order under section 5 of the Counter-Inflation Act 1973 and which are for that reason excepted from the Commission's power to investigate price increases following a notification by them under section 4 of the 1977 Act (Article 2 and Parts I, II and III of the Schedule).

The Order also specifies prices and charges which may not be the subject of an examination by the Price Commission following a direction by the Secretary of State under section 10 of the 1977 Act (and, consequently, an Order or undertaking under section 12 following a report under section 11) (Article 2 and Part I of the Schedule).

In addition, the Order specifies further prices and charges which may not be the subject of such an Order or undertaking under section 12 of the Act (Article 2 and Part II of the Schedule).

STATUTORY INSTRUMENTS

1977 No. 1286

TELEGRAPHS

The Wireless Telegraphy (Broadcast Licence Charges & Exemption) (Amendment) Regulations 1977

Made - - - -	28th July 1977
Laid before Parliament	29th July 1977
Coming into Operation	30th July 1977

The Secretary of State, in exercise.of the powers conferred by section 2(1) of the Wireless Telegraphy Act 1949(a) as enacted, and also as extended by the Wireless Telegraphy (Channel Islands) Order 1952(b) and the Wireless Telegraphy (Isle of Man) Order 1952(c) and now vested in him(d), and of all other powers enabling him in that behalf, hereby, with the consent of the Treasury, makes the following regulations:—

1. These Regulations may be cited as the Wireless Telegraphy (Broadcast Licence Charges & Exemption) (Amendment) Regulations 1977 and shall come into operation on 30th July 1977.

2.—(1) In these Regulations, " the principal Regulations " means the Wireless Telegraphy (Broadcast Licence Charges & Exemption) Regulations 1970(e), as amended(f).

(2) The Interpretation Act 1889(g) applies for the interpretation of these Regulations as it applies for the interpretation of an Act of Parliament.

·3. The principal Regulations shall be amended by substituting in the third column of Schedule 3 to those Regulations:—

(a) for " £8 ", in all four places, " £9 "; and

(b) for " £18 ", in all four places, " £21 ".

(a) 1949 c. 54.　　(b) S.I. 1952/1900 (1952 III, p. 3414).
(c) S.I. 1952/1899 (1952 III, p. 3418).
(d) 1969 c. 48.　S.I. 1969/1369, 1371, 1974/691 (1969 III, pp. 4085, 4087; 1974 I, p. 2708).
(e) S.I. 1970/548 (1970 I, p. 1753).
(f) The relevant amending instruments are: S.I. 1971/295, 1975/212 (1971 I, p. 1013; 1975 I, p. 558).
(g) 1889 c. 63.

4. The Wireless Telegraphy (Broadcast Licence Charges & Exemption) (Amendment) Regulations 1975(a) are hereby revoked.

Merlyn Rees,

One of Her Majesty's Principal
Secretaries of State.

Home Office.
28th July 1977.

We consent to these Regulations.

James Callaghan,
Denis W. Healey,

Two of the Commissioners of
Her Majesty's Treasury.

28th July 1977.

EXPLANATORY NOTE

(*This Note is not part of the Regulations.*)

These Regulations raise the amount of the basic fee for television licences from £8 to £9 in the case of monochrome and from £18 to £21 in the case of colour.

(a) S.I. 1975/212 (1975 I, p. 558).

STATUTORY INSTRUMENTS

1977 No. 1287

AGRICULTURE

The Common Agricultural Policy (Protection of Community Arrangements) (Amendment) Regulations 1977

Made - - -	*27th July* 1977
Laid before Parliament	*5th August* 1977
Coming into Operation	*26th August* 1977

The Minister of Agriculture, Fisheries and Food and the Secretary of State, being Ministers designated(**a**) in that behalf under section 2(2) of the European Communities Act 1972(**b**), in exercise of the powers conferred upon them by the said section 2(2) and of all other powers enabling them in that behalf, hereby make the following regulations:—

Citation, commencement and interpretation

1.—(1) These regulations may be cited as the Common Agricultural Policy (Protection of Community Arrangements) (Amendment) Regulations 1977, and shall come into operation on 26th August 1977.

(2) The Interpretation Act 1889(**c**) shall apply to the interpretation of these regulations as it applies to the interpretation of an Act of Parliament.

Amendment

2. The Common Agricultural Policy (Protection of Community Arrangements) Regulations 1973(**d**) as amended(**e**) are hereby further amended by inserting in the first column of the Schedule thereto immediately above the words "Milk Products" the word "Isoglucose".

In Witness whereof the Official Seal of the Minister of Agriculture, Fisheries and Food is hereunto affixed on 25th July 1977.

(L.S.)

John Silkin,
Minister of Agriculture, Fisheries and Food

27th July 1977.

Bruce Millan,
One of Her Majesty's Principal Secretaries of State.

(**a**) S.I. 1972/1811 (1972 III, p. 5216).   (**b**) 1972 c. 68.   (**c**) 1889 c. 63.
(**d**) S.I. 1973/424 (1973 I, p. 1388).   (**e**) S.I. 1974/980 (1974 II, p. 3671).

EXPLANATORY NOTE

(This Note is not part of the Regulations.)

These Regulations amend the Common Agricultural Policy (Protection of Community Arrangements) Regulations 1973 by extending the powers for the protection of the Community support system to cover the common regime for isoglucose set up by Council Regulation (EEC) No. 1111/77 of 17th May 1977 (O.J. No. L134, 28.5.77, p. 4).

STATUTORY INSTRUMENTS

1977 No. 1288

SOCIAL SECURITY

The Social Security (Claims and Payments) Amendment Regulations 1977

Made - - - -	*28th July* 1977
Laid before Parliament	*5th August* 1977
Coming into Operation	*5th September* 1977

The Secretary of State for Social Services, in exercise of the powers conferred upon him by section 79(1) and (3) of the Social Security Act 1975(a) and of all other powers enabling him in that behalf, after reference to the National Insurance Advisory Committee, hereby makes the following regulations:—

Citation, interpretation and commencement

1. These regulations, which may be cited as the Social Security (Claims and Payments) Amendment Regulations 1977, shall be read as one with the Social Security (Claims and Payments) Regulations 1975(b), as amended(c), (hereinafter referred to as "the principal regulations") and shall come into operation on 5th September 1977.

Amendment of regulation 12 of the principal regulations

2.—(1) In regulation 12 of the principal regulations (forward allowance and disallowance of unemployment benefit) paragraph (2) shall be amended in accordance with the following provisions of this regulation and shall accordingly have effect as set out in the Schedule hereto.

(2) In sub-paragraph (*a*) of the said paragraph (2) after the words "a claim for unemployment benefit" there shall be inserted the following:—

"made—

(i) while such certificate has effect; or

(ii) within 28 days before the date upon which the certificate is issued, whether or not benefit has already been allowed on such claim; or

(iii) while a previous certificate under this regulation had effect so as to allow that claim to be treated as made for a period after the date on which it was made,".

(3) At the end of sub-paragraph (*b*) of the said paragraph (2) there shall be added the words "other than, in the case of a claim made before the certificate is issued, any part of the period for which benefit has already been allowed".

(a) 1975 c. 14.   (b) S.I. 1975/560 (1975 I, p. 2014).
(c) The relevant amending instrument is S.I. 1976/1736 (1976 III, p. 4596).

New regulation to be inserted in the principal regulations

3. After regulation 12 of the principal regulations there shall be inserted the following regulation:—

"*Special provisions relating to claims for unemployment benefit made during periods connected with public holidays*

12A.—(1) In this regulation:—

  (a) "public holiday" means, as the case may be, Christmas Day, Good Friday or a Bank Holiday under the Banking and Financial Dealings Act 1971(**a**); and "Christmas and New Year holidays" and "Good Friday and Easter Monday" shall be construed accordingly and shall in each case be treated as one period;

  (b) "office closure" means a period during which an unemployment benefit office is closed in connection with a public holiday;

  (c) in computing any period of time Sundays shall not be disregarded.

(2) Where any claim for unemployment benefit, other than a claim to which regulation 12(2) applies, is made during one of the periods set out in paragraph (3), the following provisions shall apply—

  (a) a claim for unemployment benefit may be treated by an insurance officer as a claim for that benefit for a period, to be specified in his decision, not exceeding 21 days after the date of the claim;

  (b) on any claim so treated, benefit may be awarded as if the provisions of sub-paragraphs (b) and (c) of paragraph (2) and the provisions of paragraph (3) of regulation 12 applied.

(3) For the purposes of paragraph (2) the periods are—

  (a) in the case of Christmas and New Year holidays, a period beginning with the start of the twenty-first day before the first day of office closure and ending at midnight between the last day of office closure and the following day;

  (b) in the case of Good Friday and Easter Monday and in the case of any other public holiday, a period beginning with the start of the fourteenth day before the first day of office closure and ending at midnight between the last day of office closure and the following day.".

Signed by authority of the Secretary of State for Social Services.

Stanley Orme,
Minister for Social Security,
Department of Health and Social Security.

28th July 1977.

SCHEDULE

Regulation 2(1)

Regulation 12(2) of the principal regulations as amended by these Regulations

(2) While such a certificate has effect, the following provisions of this paragraph shall apply as respects claims for unemployment benefit (being, if the certificate is not of general effect, claims made in the case, class of case, area or areas, as the case may be, to which the certificate relates)—

(**a**) 1971 c. 80.

(*a*) a claim for unemployment benefit *made*—

(*i*) *while such certificate has effect; or*

(*ii*) *within* 28 *days before the date upon which the certificate is issued, whether or not benefit has already been allowed on such claim; or*

(*iii*) *while a previous certificate under this regulation had effect so as to allow that claim to be treated as made for a period after the date on which it was made,*

may be treated by an insurance officer as a claim for that benefit for a period, to be specified in his decision, not exceeding 13 weeks after the date of the claim;

(*b*) on any claim so treated benefit may be awarded for the whole or part of the specified period *other than, in the case of a claim made before the certificate is issued, any part of the period for which benefit has already been allowed*;

(*c*) if on any claim so treated benefit is awarded for part only of the specified period, further decisions awarding benefit for the remainder of that period, or any part of it may be given on the same claim.

EXPLANATORY NOTE

(*This Note is not part of the Regulations.*)

These Regulations amend the Social Security (Claims and Payments) Regulations 1975 so as to add to the claims for unemployment benefit which may be treated as made for a period after the date of the claim where the Secretary of State has certified normal administration of benefit to be impracticable or unduly difficult and so as to allow such claims made in the periods immediately before public and bank holidays to be treated as claims made to cover periods associated with such holidays falling after the date on which the claims are made.

A provision of the Social Security (Claims and Payments) Regulations 1975 as amended by these Regulations is set out in a Schedule to this instrument and the words added by these Regulations are shown in italics.

The Report of the National Insurance Advisory Committee dated 11th July 1977 on the draft of these Regulations referred to them is contained in Command Paper (Cmnd No. 6897) published by Her Majesty's Stationery Office.

STATUTORY INSTRUMENTS

1977 No. 1289

SOCIAL SECURITY

The Social Security (Claims and Payments) (Unemployment Benefit Transitory Provisions) Regulations 1977

Made - - -		*28th July* 1977
Laid before Parliament		*5th August,* 1977
Coming into Operation		*5th September* 1977

The Secretary of State for Social Services, in exercise of the powers conferred upon him by section 79(1) and (3) of the Social Security Act 1975(a) and of all other powers enabling him in that behalf, after reference to the National Insurance Advisory Committee, hereby makes the following regulations:—

Citation, commencement and interpretation

1.—(1) These regulations, which may be cited as the Social Security (Claims and Payments) (Unemployment Benefit Transitory Provisions) Regulations 1977, shall come into operation on 5th September 1977.

(2) In these regulations—

  (*a*) "spell of unemployment" means any period of one or more days on which a person is unemployed and any two or more such periods, not separated by a period of more than 3 consecutive days which in relation to that person are not days of unemployment, shall be treated as one spell of unemployment;

  (*b*) "unemployment benefit office" means any office or place appointed by the Secretary of State for the purpose of claiming unemployment benefit;

  (*c*) in computing any period of time Sundays shall not be disregarded.

(3) The rules for the construction of Acts of Parliament contained in the Interpretation Act 1889(b) shall apply for the purposes of the interpretation of these regulations as they apply for the purposes of the interpretation of an Act of Parliament.

Limited transitory provision for claims for unemployment benefit in advance

2.—(1) The provisions of this regulation shall apply for the purposes of a claim for unemployment benefit, made within a period of one year commencing with the coming into operation of this regulation at an unemployment benefit office specified in the Schedule to these regulations, where that claim is made by a person who has, during the spell of unemployment in which such claim is made, already made a claim for unemployment benefit at that unemployment benefit office.

(a) 1975 c. 14.   (b) 1889 c. 63.

(2) A claim for unemployment benefit to which this regulation applies may, unless in any case the Secretary of State otherwise directs, be made, on the form approved by the Secretary of State for the purpose, for a period falling in part before the date of the claim and in part, by not more than 7 days, after the date of the claim and, on any such claim, benefit may be awarded for the period to which the claim relates.

(3) Any decision under paragraph (2) of this regulation awarding unemployment benefit in respect of any period falling after the date of the claim shall be subject to the condition that the claimant continues to satisfy the requirements for payment thereof during the period to which the award relates and, if the said requirements are found not to have been satisfied at some time during the said period, the award shall be reviewed.

Signed by authority of the Secretary of State for Social Services.

Stanley Orme,
Minister for Social Security,
Department of Health and Social Security.

28th July 1977.

SCHEDULE

Regulation 2(1)

Unemployment Benefit Offices Specified for the Purposes of these Regulations

21 Raby Road, Hartlepool, Cleveland TS24 8AX.

High Street, Newburn, Newcastle-upon-Tyne NE15 8LN.

5 Widnes Road, Widnes, Cheshire WA8 6AB.

Church Road, Walton, Liverpool L4 5TX.

The Presbyterian Church Hall, Larchwood Avenue, Maghull, Liverpool L31 7BS.

Portland Place, Halifax, West Yorks HX1 2JH.

23 Marker Street, Hebden Bridge, West Yorks HX7 6EU.

1 Regent Parade, Wharf Street, Sowerby Bridge, West Yorks HX6 2BR.

Adelaide Street, Todmorden, Lancs OL14 5HU.

Station House, Station Road, Scunthorpe, South Humberside DN15 6RJ.

Oddfellows Hall, High Street, Barton-on-Humber, South Humberside DN18 5PB.

43A Cross Street, Burton-on-Trent, Staffs DE14 1EH.

New Street, Oakengates, Telford, Salop TF2 6JD.

Government Buildings, Glebe Street, Wellington, Telford, Salop TF1 1LF.

Herschell Street, Glasgow G13 1HT.

5/7 Allander Walk, Town Centre South, Cumbernauld, Glasgow G67 1EA.

22 Nelson Street, Bristol BS1 2LD.

The Youth Centre, Harbour Road, Portishead, Bristol BS20 9BJ.

Carlyon House, 20 Carlyon Road, St. Austell, Cornwall PL25 4BU.

Working Men's Institute, Par, Cornwall.

Provincial House, Keninck Road, Barry, South Glam CF6 6DJ.

Hayes Rooms, Town Hall Square, Llantwit Major CF6 9SD.
1 Stanwell Road, Penarth CF6 2YZ.
Government Buildings, North Penrallt, Caernarvon, Gwynedd LL55 1PR.
Masonic Chambers, Margaret Street, Beaumaris, Gwynedd LL58 8DW.
Old Town Hall, Penygroes, Caernarvon, Gwynedd, LL54 6NL.
Ty Glyder, rear of 339 High Street, Bangor, Gwynedd LL57 1YA.
9 Ogwen Terrace, Bethesda, Bangor, Gwynedd LL57 3AY.
Collyer Place, Peckham, London SE15 5DS.
Settles Street, Commercial Road, London E1 1JW.
23 Priory Street, Hastings, East Sussex TN34 1EG.
41 St. Leonards Road, Bexhill, East Sussex TN40 1HS.
68 The Broadway, Southall, Middlesex UB1 1QD.
235 Viveash Close, Nestles Avenue, Hayes, Middlesex UB3 4RW.
41/55 Windmill Road, Ruislip Manor, Middlesex HA4 80B.
Colham House, Bakers Road, Uxbridge, Middlesex UB8 1SQ.

EXPLANATORY NOTE

(This Note is not part of the Regulations.)

These Regulations make transitory provision to allow certain claims to unemployment benefit, made at certain specified unemployment benefit offices within a period of one year commencing with the coming into operation of the Regulations, to be made for a period falling partly after the date on which the claim is made.

The Report of the National Insurance Advisory Committee dated 11th July 1977 on the draft of these Regulations referred to them is contained in Command Paper (Cmnd. No. 6897) published by Her Majesty's Stationery Office.

STATUTORY INSTRUMENTS

1977 No. 1290

HOUSING, ENGLAND AND WALES

The Rent Rebates and Rent Allowances (Students) (England and Wales) Regulations 1977

Made - - - -	*27th July* 1977
Laid before Parliament	*5th August* 1977
Coming into Operation	*1st September* 1977

The Secretary of State for the Environment as respects England and the Secretary of State for Wales as respects Wales, in exercise of the powers conferred on them by section 25(3)(*c*) of the Housing Finance Act 1972(**a**) (added by section 11(7)(*b*) of the Rent Act 1974(**b**)) and of all other powers enabling them in that behalf, hereby make the following regulations: —

Citation, commencement and interpretation

1.—(1) These regulations may be cited as the Rent Rebates and Rent Allowances (Students) (England and Wales) Regulations 1977 and shall come into operation on 1st September 1977.

(2) The Interpretation Act 1889(**c**) shall apply for the interpretation of these regulations as it applies for the interpretation of an Act of Parliament.

(3) In these regulations "the principal regulations" means the Rent Rebates and Rent Allowances (Students) (England and Wales) Regulations 1976(**d**).

Amendments of the principal regulations

2.—(1) In regulation 2(1) of the principal regulations there shall be substituted for the figure "£6" the figure "£7".

(2) In regulation 3 of the principal regulations there shall be substituted for the date "31st August 1976" the date "31st August 1977".

Peter Shore,
Secretary of State for the Environment.

22nd July 1977.

John Morris,
Secretary of State for Wales.

27th July 1977.

(**a**) 1972 c. 47.　　　　　　　　　　(**b**) 1974 c. 51.
(**c**) 1889 c. 63.　　　　　　　　　　(**d**) S.I. 1976/1242 (1976 II, p. 3518).

EXPLANATORY NOTE

(This Note is not part of the Regulations.)

These Regulations, which apply to England and Wales, amend the Rent Rebates and Rent Allowances (Students) (England and Wales) Regulations 1976 (referred to as "the principal regulations"). They raise from £6 to £7 the amount prescribed as the deduction to be made in calculating the rent which is eligible to be met by a rent rebate or a rent allowance under Part II (rent rebates and rent allowances) of the Housing Finance Act 1972, as amended by the Rent Act 1974 and the Housing Rents and Subsidies Act 1975 (c. 6) in the case of tenants who are students in receipt of certain awards or grants from public funds for the purpose of their further full-time education. They come into operation on 1st September 1977.

STATUTORY INSTRUMENTS

1977 No. 1291

SEA FISHERIES

BOATS AND METHODS OF FISHING

The Norway Pout (Prohibition of Fishing) (No. 2) Order 1977

Made - - - -	28*th July* 1977
Laid before Parliament	29*th July* 1977
Coming into Operation	1*st August* 1977

The Minister of Agriculture, Fisheries and Food and the Secretaries of State respectively concerned with the sea fishing industry in Scotland and Northern Ireland, in exercise of the powers conferred on them by the following sections of the Sea Fish (Conservation) Act 1967(a) namely, sections 5(1) and (2), 15 and 20 (as section 15 is amended by section 22(1) of and paragraph 38(3) of Schedule 1 to the Sea Fisheries Act 1968(b) and as sections 5(2) and 15 are amended by section 9(1) of and paragraph 16(1) of Schedule 2 to the Fishery Limits Act 1976(c)) and of all other powers enabling them in that behalf, hereby make the following order:—

Citation and commencement

1. This Order may be cited as the Norway Pout (Prohibition of Fishing) (No. 2) Order 1977 and shall come into operation on 1st August 1977.

Interpretation

2. The Interpretation Act 1889(e) shall apply for the interpretation of this order as it applies for the interpretation of an Act of Parliament.

Revocation of previous order

3. The Norway Pout (Prohibition of Fishing) (Order) 1977(d) is hereby revoked.

Prohibition

4. As from 1st September 1977, the fishing for Norway pout (Trisopterus esmarkii) within the area of the North Sea specified in the Schedule to this order is hereby prohibited.

5. In accordance with section 5(3) of the Sea Fish (Conservation) Act 1967, it is hereby declared that this order is not made for the sole purpose of giving effect to such a convention or agreement as is mentioned in section 5(1) of that Act.

Enforcement

6. For the purpose of the enforcement of this order, there are hereby conferred on every British sea fishery officer the powers of a British sea

---

(a) 1967 c. 84.   (b) 1968 c. 77.   (c) 1976 c. 86.
(d) S.I. 1977/200 (1977 I, p. 562).   (e) 1889 c. 63.

fishery officer under section 8(2) to (4) of the Sea Fisheries Act 1968 as subsection (4) is amended by section 9(1) of and paragraph 17(1) of Schedule 2 to the Fishery Limits Act 1976.

In witness whereof the Official Seal of the Minister of Agriculture, Fisheries and Food is hereunto affixed on 26th July 1977.

John Silkin,
Minister of Agriculture, Fisheries and Food.

Bruce Millan,
Secretary of State for Scotland.

25th July 1977.

Roy Mason,
Secretary of State for Northern Ireland.

28th July 1977.

SCHEDULE

The area of the North Sea bounded on the south by a line running due east from a point on the coast of Scotland at 56°00′ north latitude to the Greenwich meridian; thence due north to the parallel of 60°00′ north latitude; thence due west to the meridian of 04°00′ west longitude; thence due south to the coast of Scotland.

EXPLANATORY NOTE

(This Note is not part of the Order.)

This Order, which is designed to protect stocks of fish for human consumption which are taken as a by catch in the Norway pout fishery provides that from 1st September 1977 the fishing for Norway pout in an area of the North Sea adjoining the east and north coasts of Scotland is prohibited. By virtue of section 5(8) of the Sea Fish (Conservation) Act 1967, the Order applies to all fishing boats including foreign vessels.

This Order revokes the Norway Pout (Prohibition of Fishing) Order 1977.

STATUTORY INSTRUMENTS

1977 No. 1292

SEA FISHERIES

FISHERY LIMITS

The Fishing Boats (Specified Countries) Designation (No. 3) (Variation) Order 1977

Made - - - -	28th July 1977
Laid before Parliament	29th July 1977
Coming into Operation	30th July 1977

The Minister of Agriculture, Fisheries and Food and the Secretaries of State concerned with sea fishing in Scotland and Northern Ireland respectively, in exercise of the powers conferred on them by sections 2(1) and 6(2) of the Fishery Limits Act 1976(**a**) and of all other powers enabling them in that behalf, hereby make the following order:—

Citation and commencement

1. This order may be cited as the Fishing Boats (Specified Countries) Designation (No. 3) (Variation) Order 1977 and shall come into operation on 30th July 1977.

Interpretation

2. The Interpretation Act 1889(**b**) shall apply to the interpretation of this order as it applies to the interpretation of an Act of Parliament.

Variation of principal order

3. The Fishing Boats (Specified Countries) Designation (No. 3) Order 1977(**c**) shall be varied as follows:—

(i) For article 4 there shall be substituted the following article—

"4.—(1) The Faroe Islands and Norway are hereby designated for the purposes of section 2(1) of the Act.

(2) In relation to the Faroe Islands and Norway there is hereby designated the area within British fishery limits other than that part of that area which is within 12 miles from the baselines from which the breadth of the territorial sea is measured.

(3) The descriptions of sea fish for which the fishing boats registered in Norway may fish in the area referred to in paragraph (2) of this article shall be all descriptions of sea fish.

(4) The descriptions of sea fish for which the fishing boats registered in the Faroe Islands may fish in the area referred to in paragraph (2) of this article shall be all descriptions of sea fish except herring."

(**a**) 1976 c. 86.   (**b**) 1889 c. 63.   (**c**) S.I. 1977/1084 (1977 II, p. 3068).

(ii) For article 5 there shall be substituted the following article:—

"5. The provisions of this order so far as they relate to the Faroe Islands shall cease to have effect on 15th September 1977."

In Witness whereof the Official Seal of the Minister of Agriculture, Fisheries and Food is hereunto affixed on 27th July 1977.

(L.S.)

John Silkin,
Minister of Agriculture, Fisheries and Food.

Bruce Millan,
Secretary of State for Scotland.

28th July 1977.

Roy Mason,
Secretary of State for Northern Ireland.

28th July 1977.

EXPLANATORY NOTE

(This Note is not part of the Order.)

This Order varies the Fishing Boats (Specified Countries) Designation (No. 3) Order 1977 (the principal order) as follows:—

1. Herring are excluded from the descriptions of sea fish for which fishing boats registered in the Faroe Islands may fish.

2. The time during which the provisions of the principal order (as varied by this order) relating to the Faroe Islands are to have effect is extended until 15th September 1977.

STATUTORY INSTRUMENTS

1977 No. 1293

LEGAL AID AND ADVICE, ENGLAND

The Legal Aid (General) (Amendment) Regulations 1977

Made - - - -	*27th July* 1977
Laid before Parliament	*5th August* 1977
Coming into Operation	*1st October* 1977

The Lord Chancellor, in exercise of the powers conferred on him by sections 9 and 20 of the Legal Aid Act 1974(a), hereby makes the following Regulations:—

1.—(1) These Regulations may be cited as the Legal Aid (General) (Amendment) Regulations 1977 and shall come into operation on 1st October 1977.

(2) The Interpretation Act 1889(b) shall apply to the interpretation of these Regulations as it applies to the interpretation of an Act of Parliament.

(3) In these Regulations a regulation referred to by number means a regulation so numbered in the Legal Aid (General) Regulations 1971(c), as amended (d).

2. In regulation 1(3), for the definition of "matrimonial proceedings" there shall be substituted the following:—

" "matrimonial proceedings" means—

(*a*) any proceedings with respect to which rules may be made under section 50 of the Matrimonial Causes Act 1973(e), or

(*b*) any proceedings in a county court under section 17 of the Married Women's Property Act 1882(f) or section 1 of the Matrimonial Homes Act 1967(g); or

(*c*) any proceedings under the Domestic Violence and Matrimonial Proceedings Act 1976(h);".

3. In regulation 3(8), after the words "in English" there shall be inserted the words "or in French".

(a) 1974 c. 4.   (b) 1889 c. 63.
(c) S.I. 1971/62 (1971 I, p. 75).
(d) The relevant amending instruments are S.I. 1971/1877, 1972/1749, 1976/628 (1971 III p. 5114; 1972 III, p, 5076; 1976 I, p. 1775).
(e) 1973 c. 18.   (f) 1882 c. 75.
(g) 1967 c. 75.   (h) 1976 c. 50.

4. In regulation 5, the following paragraph shall be substituted for paragraph (1):—

"(1) An application for a certificate in respect of—

(*a*) matrimonial proceedings, or

(*b*) authorised summary proceedings,

shall be considered by the secretary, who, after having had regard to the determination made by the Commission of the disposable income and disposable capital of the applicant and the maximum contribution payable by him or the terms of any undertaking lodged by him under regulation 3(4), may (save in the circumstances mentioned in paragraph (11)) approve the application on behalf of the appropriate committee; and in every case in which he does not approve the application he shall refer it to the committee for their consideration and approval or refusal."

5. In regulation 6, the following shall be added at the end of paragraph (2):—

"or (*d*) proceedings in the Court of Justice of the European Communities on a reference to that Court for a preliminary ruling."

6. In regulation 15, the following shall be substituted for paragraphs (2) and (3):—

"(2) Where it appears to an assisted person's solicitor that the proper conduct of the proceedings so requires, counsel may be instructed; but, unless authority has been given in the certificate, a Queen's Counsel or more than one counsel shall not be instructed without the authority of the appropriate area committee.

(3) Every set of papers delivered to counsel instructed by virtue of paragraph (2) shall include a copy of the certificate and shall be endorsed in the manner set out in Schedule 3 with such variations as circumstances may require; and no fees shall be marked thereon.";

and in paragraph (7), for "paragraph (1) or (3)" there shall be substituted "paragraph (1) or (2)".

7. In regulation 18, the following shall be substituted for paragraph (10)(*c*) and (*d*):—

"(*c*) the first £2,500 of any money, or the value of any property, recovered or preserved by virtue of—

    (i) an order made, or deemed to be made, under the provisions of section 23(1)(*c*), 23(2), 24, 27(6)(*c*), or 35 of the Matrimonial Causes Act 1973; or

    (ii) an order made, or deemed to be made, under the provisions of sections 2 and 6 of the Inheritance (Provision for Family and Dependants) Act 1975**(a)** or any provision repealed by that Act; or

    (iii) an order made, or deemed to be made, after 30th September 1977 under section 17 of the Married Women's Property Act 1882; or

    (iv) an agreement made after 30th September 1977 which has the same effect as an order made, or deemed to be made, under any of the provisions specified in this sub-paragraph; or

---

(a) 1975 c. 63.

(*d*) where the certificate was issued before 3rd May 1976, any money or property, of whatever amount or value, recovered or preserved by virtue of an order made, or deemed to be made, under any of the provisions specified in sub-paragraph (*c*)(i) or (ii) before 1st August 1976 or which, if made on or after that date, gives effect to a settlement entered into before that date;".

8. In regulation 22, for the figure of £75 specified in paragraph (2)(*a*) there shall be substituted the figure of £200.

Dated 27th July 1977.

Elwyn-Jones, C.

EXPLANATORY NOTE

(*This Note is not part of the Regulations.*)

These Regulations further amend the Legal Aid (General) Regulations 1971 so as to:—

 (i) allow an application for legal aid to be in French if the applicant is resident outside the United Kingdom and unable to be there while his application is being considered;

 (ii) extend the delegated power of the local secretary to approve applications for legal aid in matrimonial proceedings;

 (iii) require the authority of the area committee before a legal aid certificate can extend to proceedings on a reference to the Court of Justice of the European Communities;

 (iv) require a solicitor to apply to the area committee for authority to instruct either a Queen's Counsel alone or (as at present) more than one counsel;

 (v) extend the benefit of the £2,500 exemption from the statutory charge under regulation 18(10)(*c*) to money or property comprised in an order under section 17 of the Married Women's Property Act 1882 and to certain agreements made between the parties to proceedings; and

 (vi) raise the limit of the power of an area committee to assess a bill under regulation 22(2)(*a*) from £75 to £200.

STATUTORY INSTRUMENTS

1977 No. 1294

COUNTER-INFLATION

The Limits on Remuneration Order 1977

Laid before Parliament in draft

Made - . -   -   -   *28th July* 1977

Coming into Operation   1st *August* 1977

Whereas the document laid before Parliament by command of Her Majesty in July 1975 (Cmnd. 6151) and mentioned in section 1(1) of the Remuneration, Charges and Grants Act 1975(**a**) ("the 1975 Act") provided limits on remuneration up to and including 31st July 1976:

And whereas a reference to the limits on remuneration set out in the document laid before Parliament by command of Her Majesty in June 1976 (Cmnd. 6507) (which provides limits on remuneration for the period beginning on 1st August 1976 and ending with 31st July 1977) was added to the reference to the limits mentioned in section 1(1) of the 1975 Act by the Limits on Remuneration Order 1976(**b**):

And whereas the period for which section 1 of the 1975 Act has effect has been extended by section 17(2) of the Price Commission Act 1977(**c**) to 31st July 1978:

And whereas Her Majesty has caused to be laid before Parliament a document (Cmnd. 6882) which sets out limits on remuneration for the period beginning on 1st August 1977 and ending with 31st July 1978 or twelve months after the date of the last pay settlement under Cmnd. 6507, whichever is the earlier:

And whereas a draft of the following Order was laid before Parliament in accordance with section 1(3) of the 1975 Act and approved by resolution of each House of Parliament:

Now, therefore, the Secretary of State, in exercise of the powers conferred on him by section 1(2) of the 1975 Act and of all other powers enabling him in that behalf, hereby makes the following Order:—

Citation, commencement and interpretation

1.—(1) This Order may be cited as the Limits on Remuneration Order 1977 and shall come into operation on 1st August 1977.

(2) The Interpretation Act 1889(**d**) shall apply to the interpretation of this Order as it applies to the interpretation of an Act of Parliament.

(**a**) 1975 c. 57.　　　　　　(**b**) S.I. 1976/1097 (1976 II, p. 2920).
(**c**) 1977 c. 33.　　　　　　(**d**) 1889 c. 63.

Limits on Remuneration

2. In subsection (1) of section 1 of the 1975 Act, to the reference to the limits mentioned in that subsection there shall be further added a reference to the limits set out in the document laid before Parliament by command of Her Majesty in July 1977 (Cmnd. 6882).

28th July 1977.

Albert Booth,
Secretary of State for Employment.

EXPLANATORY NOTE

(This Note is not part of the Order.)

Section 1(1) of the Remuneration, Charges and Grants Act 1975, as originally enacted, referred to the White Paper, The Attack on Inflation (Cmnd. 6151), which provided limits on remuneration up to and including 31st July 1976. The Limits on Remuneration Order 1976 added to the reference to those limits in section 1(1) a reference to the limits on remuneration set out in the White Paper, The Attack on Inflation: The Second Year (Cmnd. 6507) which are for the period 1st August 1976 up to and including 31st July 1977. This Order, which comes into operation on 1st August 1977, further adds to the reference to those limits a reference to the limits set out in the White Paper, The Attack on Inflation after 31st July 1977 (Cmnd. 6882) which are for the period 1st August 1977 up to and including 31st July 1978 or twelve months after the date of the last pay settlement under Cmnd. 6507, whichever is the earlier.

STATUTORY INSTRUMENTS

1977 No. 1295

PARLIAMENT

The Ministerial and other Salaries Order 1977

Laid before Parliament in draft

| Made - - - - | *29th July* 1977 |
| Coming into Operation | 30th July 1977 |

At the Court at Windsor Castle, the 29th day of July 1977

Present,

The Queen's Most Excellent Majesty in Council

Whereas a draft of this Order has been approved by resolution of each House of Parliament in pursuance of subsection (4) of section 1 of the Ministerial and other Salaries Act 1975(**a**):

Now therefore Her Majesty, in pursuance of that subsection, is pleased, by and with the advice of Her Privy Council, to order, and it is hereby ordered, as follows:—

Citation, commencement and revocation

1.—(1) This Order may be cited as the Ministerial and other Salaries Order 1977.

(2) This Order shall come into operation on 30th July 1977.

(3) The Junior Ministers' and other Salaries Order 1976(**b**) is hereby revoked.

Increase by £208 a year of salaries of certain Ministers

2.—(1) For the amount specified in subsection (2) of section 1 of the Ministerial and other Salaries Act 1975 as the aggregate amount of the salary payable to the Lord Chancellor under that subsection and the salary payable to him as Speaker of the House of Lords there shall be substituted £20,208.

(2) For the amount specified in Part I of Schedule 1 to the Act of 1975 as the amount of salary payable to the holder of any office listed at (*a*) to (*g*) in that Part so long as he is a member of the Cabinet there shall be substituted £13,208.

(3) For the amount specified in Part II of that Schedule as the maximum amount of salary payable to the holder of any office listed at (*a*) to (*g*) in Part I so long as he is not a member of the Cabinet there shall be substituted £9,708.

(4) For the amount of salary specified in Part III or IV of that Schedule in relation to each of the offices specified in the first column of the following Table there shall be substituted the amount of salary specified in relation to that office in the second column of that Table.

(**a**) 1975 c. 27.   (**b**) S.I. 1976/1215 (1976 II, p. 3440).

TABLE

Office	Salary
Solicitor General for Scotland	£8,270
Captain of the Honourable Corps of Gentlemen-at-Arms ...	£7,020
Parliamentary Secretary other than Parliamentary Secretary to the Treasury	£6,020
Captain of the Queen's Bodyguard of the Yeomen of the Guard	£5,520
Lord in Waiting	£5,020

Increase by 5 per cent. of salaries of Leader of the Opposition and Chief Opposition Whip in the House of Lords

3. For the amount of salary specified in Part I of Schedule 2 to the Act of 1975 in relation to each of the positions in the House of Lords which are specified in the first column of the following Table there shall be substituted the amount of salary specified in relation to that position in the second column of that Table.

TABLE

Position	Salary
Leader of the Opposition	£4,003
Chief Opposition Whip	£2,953

N. E. Leigh,
Clerk of the Privy Council.

EXPLANATORY NOTE

(This Note is not part of the Order.)

The Order increases by £208 the annual salaries payable under the Ministerial and other Salaries Act 1975 to certain Ministers and by 5 per cent. those payable to the Leader of the Opposition and the Chief Opposition Whip in the House of Lords.

STATUTORY INSTRUMENTS

1977 No. 1296

TOWN AND COUNTRY PLANNING, ENGLAND AND WALES

The Location of Offices Bureau (Amendment) Order 1977

Laid before Parliament in draft

Made - - - -	*29th July* 1977
Coming into Operation	*8th August* 1977

At the Court at Windsor Castle, the 29th day of July 1977

Present,

The Queen's Most Excellent Majesty in Council

Whereas in pursuance of section 8(2) of the Minister of Town and Country Planning Act 1943(a) an Address has been presented to Her Majesty by both Houses of Parliament praying that an Order be made in the following terms:

Now, therefore, Her Majesty, in exercise of the powers conferred on Her by the said section 8 and by section 10 of the said Act, is pleased, by and with the advice of Her Privy Council, to order and it is hereby ordered, as follows:—

1.—(1) This Order may be cited as the Location of Offices Bureau (Amendment) Order 1977, and the Location of Offices Bureau Order 1963(b) and this Order may be cited together as the Location of Offices Bureau Orders 1963 and 1977.

(2) This Order shall come into operation ten days after the date hereof.

(3) The Interpretation Act 1889(c) shall apply for the interpretation of this Order as it applies for the interpretation of an Act of Parliament.

2. The Location of Offices Bureau Order 1963 shall be amended as follows:—

(*a*) For article 3 there shall be substituted the following article: —

" **3.**—(1) It shall be the general duty of the Bureau to promote the better distribution of office employment in England and Wales and to take such steps as may be necessary for this purpose including, without prejudice to the generality of the foregoing, the provision of information and publicity and the promotion of research.

(2) In discharging its functions the Bureau shall comply with such directions of a general character as may be given by the Secretary of State.";

(a) 1943 c. 5.   (b) S.I. 1963/792 (1963 I, p. 1176).   (c) 1889 c. 63.

(*b*) In the Schedule to the Order, for paragraph 1 there shall be substituted the following paragraph: —

" 1.—(1) The members of the Bureau, of whom there shall be not more than five, shall be appointed by the Secretary of State, and he shall appoint one of them to be chairman and may appoint one to be deputy chairman.

(2) Subject to the following provisions of this Schedule, a member of the Bureau and the chairman and deputy chairman (if any) shall hold office for a period of three years and otherwise in accordance with the terms of his appointment.".

N. E. Leigh,
Clerk of the Privy Council.

EXPLANATORY NOTE

(*This Note is not part of the Order.*)

This Order amends the Location of Offices Bureau Order 1963, which established, under section 8 of the Minister of Town and Country Planning Act 1943, the Location of Offices Bureau to assist the former Minister of Housing and Local Government (now the Secretary of State) in the exercise of functions in relation to the use and development of land in England and Wales. The Order of 1963 provided that the Bureau should give such assistance by encouraging the decentralisation and diversion of office employment from congested areas in central London to suitable centres elsewhere: by the provisions of this Order, that duty has been replaced by a duty to promote the better distribution of office employment in England and Wales.

This Order also increases the maximum number of members of the Bureau from four to five and increases the period for which members hold office from two years to three years.

1977 No. 1297

INCOME TAX

The Double Taxation Relief (Air Transport Profits) (Ethiopia) Order 1977

Laid before the House of Commons in draft

Made - - - - *29th July* 1977

At the Court at Windsor Castle, the 29th day of July 1977

Present,

The Queen's Most Excellent Majesty in Council

Whereas a draft of this Order was laid before the House of Commons in accordance with the provisions of section 497(8) of the Income and Corporation Taxes Act 1970(a) and an Address has been presented to Her Majesty by that House praying that an Order may be made in the terms of this Order:

Now, therefore, Her Majesty, in exercise of the poweis conferred upon Her by section 497 of the said Income and Corporation Taxes Act 1970 and section 39 of the Finance Act 1965(b), as amended, and of all other powers enabling Her in that behalf, is pleased, by and with the advice of Her Privy Council, to order, and it is hereby ordered, as follows:—

1. This Order may be cited as the Double Taxation Relief (Air Transport Profits) (Ethiopia) Order 1977.

2. It is hereby declared—

(*a*) that the arrangements specified in the Schedule to this Order have been made with the Provisional Military Government of Socialist Ethiopia with a view to affording relief from double taxation in relation to income tax, corporation tax, or capital gains tax and taxes of a similar character imposed by the laws of Ethiopia; and

(*b*) it is expedient that those arrangements should have effect.

N. E. Leigh,
Clerk of the Privy Council.

(**a**) 1970 c. 10.   (**b**) 1965 c. 25.

SCHEDULE

(1) The Provisional Military Government of Socialist Ethiopia shall exempt from income tax and from any other tax on profits or income which is, or may become, chargeable in Ethiopia all profits and income derived from all air transport operations by a United Kingdom undertaking operating authorised scheduled air services between the United Kingdom and Ethopia.

(2) The Government of the United Kingdom shall exempt from income tax, corporation tax, capital gains tax and from any other tax on profits or income which is, or may become, chargeable in the United Kingdom all profits and income derived from all air transport operations by an Ethiopian undertaking operating authorised scheduled air services between Ethiopia and the United Kingdom.

(3) The expression "air transport operations" means the transport of persons, animals, goods or mail by the owner or charterer of an aircraft including the sale of travel tickets and documents relating to such transport.

(4) The expression "authorised scheduled air services" means scheduled services authorised by the aeronautical authorities of Ethiopia and the United Kingdom.

(5) The expression "a United Kingdom undertaking" means the Government of the United Kingdom, physical persons resident in the United Kingdom and not resident in Ethiopia and corporations and partnerships constituted under the laws in force in the United Kingdom whose place of effective management is in the United Kingdom.

(6) The expression "an Ethiopian undertaking" means the Provisional Military Government of Socialist Ethiopia, physical persons resident in Ethiopia and not resident in the United Kingdom, and corporations and partnerships constituted under the laws in force in Ethiopia whose place of effective management is in Ethiopia.

(7) Each Government shall notify the other in writing through the diplomatic channel of the completion of the procedures required by its law to bring this Agreement into force. The Agreement shall enter into force on the date of the later of these notifications and shall thereupon have effect as regards profits, income or capital gains arising on or after 1 April 1973.

(8) This Agreement may be terminated by either Government by giving six months notice in writing to the other Government.

EXPLANATORY NOTE
(This Note is not part of the Order.)

The Schedule to this Order sets out the arrangements made with Ethiopia, in Notes exchanged between the Contracting Governments on 1 February 1977, under which the profits, income and capital gains derived from all air transport operations, by an undertaking of one of the countries operating authorised scheduled air services between that and the other country are to be exempt from tax in that other country.

The arrangements apply to profits, income or capital gains arising on or after 1 April 1973.

STATUTORY INSTRUMENTS

1977 No. 1298

INCOME TAX

The Double Taxation Relief (Shipping and Air Transport Profits) (Zaire) Order 1977

Laid before the House of Commons in draft

Made -   -   -   -   29th July 1977

At the Court at Windsor Castle, the 29th day of July 1977

Present,

The Queen's Most Excellent Majesty in Council

Whereas a draft of this Order was laid before the House of Commons in accordance with the provisions of section 497(8) of the Income and Corporation Taxes Act 1970(a) and an Address has been presented to Her Majesty by that House praying that an Order may be made in the terms of this Order:

Now, therefore, Her Majesty, in exercise of the powers conferred upon Her by section 497 of the said Income and Corporation Taxes Act 1970 and section 39 of the Finance Act 1965(b), as amended, and of all other powers enabling Her in that behalf, is pleased, by and with the advice of Her Privy Council, to order, and it is hereby ordered, as follows:—

1. This Order may be cited as the Double Taxation Relief (Shipping and Air Transport Profits) (Zaire) Order 1977.

2. It is hereby declared—

(*a*) that the arrangements specified in the Schedule to this Order have been made with the Government of the Republic of Zaire with a view to affording relief from double taxation in relation to income tax, corporation tax, or capital gains tax and taxes of a similar character imposed by the laws of Zaire; and

(*b*) it is expedient that those arrangements should have effect.

Clerk of the Privy Council.

(**a**) 1970 c. 10.   (**b**) 1965 c. 25.

SCHEDULE

AGREEMENT BETWEEN THE UNITED KINGDOM OF GREAT BRITAIN
AND NORTHERN IRELAND AND THE REPUBLIC OF ZAIRE
FOR THE AVOIDANCE OF DOUBLE TAXATION ON REVENUES
ARISING FROM THE BUSINESS OF SHIPPING AND AIR
TRANSPORT IN INTERNATIONAL TRAFFIC

The United Kingdom of Great Britain and Northern Ireland and the Republic of Zaire;

Anxious to strengthen their links of friendship and to conclude an agreement for the avoidance of double taxation on revenues arising from the business of shipping and air transport in international traffic;

Have agreed as follows:

Article 1

(1) The terms "one of the Contracting States" and "the other Contracting State" mean the United Kingdom of Great Britain and Northern Ireland or the Republic of Zaire, as the context requires.

(2) The term "the business of shipping or air transport" means the business of transporting by air and/or sea persons, animals, goods or mail including the sale of travel tickets connected with such transport by sea and/or air transport undertakings.

(3) The term "international traffic" means any transport by a ship or aircraft operated by an undertaking of one of the Contracting States, except when the ship or aircraft is operated solely between places in the other Contracting State.

(4) The term "United Kingdom undertakings" means public, semi-public or private sea and/or air transport undertakings constituted under the laws in force in the United Kingdom and managed and controlled in the United Kingdom.

(5) The term "Zairian undertakings" means public, semi-public or private sea and/or air transport undertakings constituted under the laws in force in the Republic of Zaire and managed and controlled in the Republic of Zaire.

Article 2

(1) The United Kingdom undertakes to exempt Zairian undertakings from all taxes on income, profits or capital gains arising from the business of shipping and/or air transport in international traffic carried on in the United Kingdom and taxable in the Republic of Zaire.

(2) The Republic of Zaire undertakes to exempt United Kingdom undertakings from all taxes on income, profits or capital gains arising from the business of shipping and/or air transport in international traffic carried on in the Republic of Zaire and taxable in the United Kingdom.

(3) The provisions of this Article shall likewise apply to income, profits or capital gains derived by such an undertaking from the participation in a pool, a joint business or an international operating agency.

Article 3

This Agreement shall continue in force indefinitely but may be terminated by either Contracting State by giving six months' notice in writing to the other Contracting State.

Article 4

This Agreement shall be approved in conformity with the constitutional procedures applicable in each of the two Contracting States. It shall enter into force on the first day of the month following the exchange of Notes through the diplomatic channel confirming that on both sides these constitutional procedures have been completed, and shall thereupon have effect as regards income, profits or capital gains arising on or after the date of signature.

Done in duplicate at London this 11th day of October 1976, in the English and French languages, both texts being equally authoritative.

For the Republic of Zaire:

For the Government
of the United Kingdom
of Great Britain and
Northern Ireland:

ANTHONY CROSLAND   NGUZA

EXPLANATORY NOTE

(This Note is not part of the Order.)

The arrangements with Zaire which are scheduled to this Order, provide that shipping and air transport profits derived from one country by a resident of the other country are (subject to certain conditions) to be exempt from tax in the former country.

The arrangements apply to profits, income or capital gains arising on or after 11 October 1976.

STATUTORY INSTRUMENTS

1977 No. 1299
INCOME TAX
The Double Taxation Relief (Taxes on Income) (Kenya) Order 1977

Laid before the House of Commons in draft

Made - - - - *29th July* 1977

At the Court at Windsor Castle, the 29th day of July 1977

Present,

The Queen's Most Excellent Majesty in Council

Whereas a draft of this Order was laid before the House of Commons in accordance with the provisions of section 497(8) of the Income and Corporation Taxes Act 1970(a), and an Address has been presented to Her Majesty by that House praying that an Order may be made in the terms of this Order:

Now, therefore, Her Majesty, in exercise of the powers conferred upon Her by section 497 of the said Income and Corporation Taxes Act 1970, section 98(2) of the Finance Act 1972(b) and section 39 of the Finance Act 1965(c), as amended, and of all other powers enabling Her in that behalf, is pleased, by and with the advice of Her Privy Council, to order, and it is hereby ordered, as follows:—

1. This Order may be cited as the Double Taxation Relief (Taxes on Income) (Kenya) Order 1977.

2. It is hereby declared—

(*a*) that the arrangements specified in the Agreement set out in Part I of the Schedule to this Order and in the Protocol set out in Part II of that Schedule have been made with the Government of Kenya with a view to affording relief from double taxation in relation to income tax, corporation tax or capital gains tax and taxes of a similar character imposed by the laws of Kenya; and

(*b*) that it is expedient that those arrangements should have effect.

N. E. Leigh,
Clerk of the Privy Council.

(a)1970 c.10. (b) 1972 c.41. (c) 1965 c.25.

SCHEDULE

Part I

AGREEMENT BETWEEN THE GOVERNMENT OF THE UNITED KINGDOM OF GREAT BRITAIN AND NORTHERN IRELAND AND THE GOVERNMENT OF THE REPUBLIC OF KENYA FOR THE AVOIDANCE OF DOUBLE TAXATION AND THE PREVENTION OF FISCAL EVASION WITH RESPECT TO TAXES ON INCOME AND CAPITAL GAINS

The Government of the United Kingdom of Great Britain and Northern Ireland and the Government of the Republic of Kenya;

Desiring to conclude an agreement for the avoidance of double taxation and the prevention of fiscal evasion with respect to taxes on income and capital gains;

Have agreed as follows:

ARTICLE 1

Personal scope

This Agreement shall apply to persons who are residents of one or both of the Contracting States.

ARTICLE 2

Taxes covered

(1) The taxes which are the subject of this Agreement are:

(*a*) in the United Kingdom of Great Britain and Northern Ireland:

(i) the income tax;

(ii) the corporation tax; and

(iii) the capital gains tax;

(*b*) in Kenya:

(i) the income tax; and

(ii) the graduated personal tax.

(2) This Agreement shall also apply to any identical or substantially similar taxes which are imposed by either Contracting State after the date of signature of this Agreement in addition to, or in place of, the existing taxes. The competent authorities of the Contracting States shall notify to each other any changes which are made in their respective taxation laws.

ARTICLE 3

General definitions

(1) In this Agreement, unless the context otherwise requires:

(*a*) the term "United Kingdom" means Great Britain and Northern Ireland, including any area outside the territorial sea of the United Kingdom which in accordance with international law has been or may hereafter be designated, under the laws of the United Kingdom concerning the Continental Shelf, as an area within which the rights of the United Kingdom with respect to the sea bed and sub-soil and their natural resources may be exercised;

(*b*) the term "Kenya" means the Republic of Kenya, including any area adjacent to the territorial waters of Kenya designated, in accordance with international law, as an area within which Kenya may exercise rights with respect to the sea bed and sub-soil and their natural resources;

(*c*) the term "nationals" means:

(i) in relation to the United Kingdom, all citizens of the United Kingdom and Colonies who derive their status as such from their connection with the United Kingdom and all legal persons, partnerships and associations deriving their status as such from the law in force in the United Kingdom;

    (ii) in relation to Kenya, all citizens of the Republic of Kenya and all legal persons, partnerships and associations deriving their status as such from the law in force in Kenya;

(d) the term "United Kingdom tax" means tax imposed by the United Kingdom being tax to which this Agreement applies by virtue of the provisions of Article 2; the term "Kenya tax" means tax imposed by Kenya being tax to which this Agreement applies by virtue of the provisions of Article 2; but neither of these terms are to include any tax payable in the United Kingdom or Kenya which is payable in respect of any default or omission in relation to the taxes which are the subject of this Agreement or which represents a penalty imposed under the law of the United Kingdom or Kenya relating to those taxes;

(e) the term "tax" means United Kingdom tax or Kenya tax, as the context requires;

(f) the terms "a Contracting State" and "the other Contracting State" mean the United Kingdom or Kenya, as the context requires;

(g) the term "persons" means
    (i) in relation to the United Kingdom an individual, a company and any other body of persons;
    (ii) in relation to Kenya an individual, a company and any other body of persons treated as an entity for tax purposes;

(h) the term "company" means any body corporate or any entity which is treated as a body corporate for tax purposes;

(i) the terms "enterprise of a Contracting State" and "enterprise of the other Contracting State" mean respectively an enterprise carried on by a resident of a Contracting State and an enterprise carried on by a resident of the other Contracting State;

(j) the term "competent authority" means, in the case of the United Kingdom the Commissioners of Inland Revenue or their authorised representative, and in the case of Kenya the Minister for Finance or his authorised representative.

(2) As regards the application of this Agreement by a Contracting State any term not otherwise defined shall, unless the context otherwise requires, have the meaning which it has under the laws of that Contracting State relating to the taxes which are the subject of this Agreement.

ARTICLE 4

Fiscal domicile

(1) For the purpose of this Agreement, the term "resident of a Contracting State" means, subject to the provisions of paragraphs (2) and (3) of this Article, any person who, under the law of that State, is liable to taxation therein by reason of his domicile, residence, place of management or any other criterion of a similar nature. The terms 'resident of the United Kingdom" and "resident of Kenya" shall be construed accordingly.

(2) Where by reason of the provisions of paragraph (1) of this Article an individual is a resident of both Contracting States, then his status shall be determined in accordance with the following rules:

(a) he shall be deemed to be a resident of the Contracting State in which he has a permanent home available to him. If he has a permanent home available to him in both Contracting States, he shall be deemed to be a resident of the Contracting State with which his personal and economic relations are closest (hereinafter referred to as his centre of vital interests);

(b) if the Contracting State in which he has his centre of vital interests cannot be determined, or if he has not a permanent home available to him in either Contracting State, he shall be deemed to be a resident of the Contracting State in which he has an habitual abode;

(c) if he has an habitual abode in both Contracting States or in neither of them, he shall be deemed to be a resident of the Contracting State of which he is a national;

(*d*) if he is a national of both Contracting States or of neither of them, the competent authorities of the Contracting States shall settle the question by mutual agreement.

(3) Where by reason of the provisions of paragraph (1) of this Article a person other than an individual is a resident of both Contracting States, then it shall be deemed to be a resident of the Contracting State in which its place of effective management is situated.

ARTICLE 5

Permanent establishment

(1) For the purposes of this Agreement, the term "permanent establishment" means a fixed place of business in which the business of the enterprise is wholly or partly carried on.

(2) The term "permanent establishment" shall include especially:

(*a*) a place of management;

(*b*) a branch;

(*c*) an office;

(*d*) a factory;

(*e*) a workshop;

(*f*) a mine, oil well, quarry or other place of extraction of natural resources;

(*g*) a farm, plantation or other place where agricultural, forestry, plantation or related activities are carried on;

(*h*) a building site or construction or assembly project which exists for more than six months;

(*i*) the provision of supervisory activities for more than six months on a building site or construction or assembly project.

(3) The term "permanent establishment" shall not be deemed to include:

(*a*) the use of facilities solely for the purpose of storage, display or delivery of goods or merchandise belonging to the enterprise;

(*b*) the maintenance of a stock of goods or merchandise belonging to the enterprise solely for the purpose of storage, display or delivery;

(*c*) the maintenance of a stock of goods or merchandise belonging to the enterprise solely for the purpose of processing by another enterprise;

(*d*) the maintenance of a fixed place of business solely for the purpose of purchasing goods or merchandise, or for collecting information, for the enterprise;

(*e*) the maintenance of a fixed place of business solely for the purpose of advertising, for the supply of information, for scientific research or for similar activities which have a preparatory or auxiliary character, for the enterprise.

(4) An enterprise of a Contracting State shall be deemed to have a permanent establishment in the other Contracting State if it carries on the activity of providing the services within that other Contracting State of public entertainers or athletes referred to in Article 19.

(5) A person acting in a Contracting State on behalf of an enterprise of the other Contracting State—other than an agent of an independent status to whom the provisions of paragraph (7) of this Article apply—shall be deemed to be a permanent establishment in the first-mentioned State if:

(*a*) he has, and habitually exercises in that State, an authority to conclude contracts in the name of the enterprise, unless his activities are limited to the purchase of goods or merchandise for the enterprise; or

(*b*) he maintains in that former State a stock of goods or merchandise belonging to the enterprise from which he regularly fulfils orders on behalf of that enterprise.

(6) An insurance enterprise of a Contracting State shall be deemed to have a permanent establishment in the other Contracting State if it collects premiums in that other State or insures risks therein through an employee or through a representative who is not an agent of independent status within the meaning of paragraph (7).

(7) An enterprise of a Contracting State shall not be deemed to have a permanent establishment in the other Contracting State merely because it carries on business in that other State through a broker, general commission agent or any other agent of an independent status, where such persons are acting in the ordinary course of their business. An agent shall not, however, be deemed to be an agent of an independent status within the meaning of this paragraph if his activities are devoted wholly or almost wholly to the business of that enterprise.

(8) The fact that a company which is a resident of a Contracting State controls or is controlled by a company which is a resident of the other Contracting State, or which carries on business in that other State (whether through a permanent establishment or otherwise), shall not of itself constitute either company a permanent establishment of the other.

ARTICLE 6

Limitation of relief

Where under any provision of this Agreement any person is relieved from tax in a Contracting State on certain income if (with or without other conditions) that person is subject to tax in the other Contracting State in respect of that income and that person is subject to tax in respect of that income in that other State by reference to the amount thereof which is remitted to or received in that other State, the relief from tax to be allowed under this Agreement in the first-mentioned Contracting State shall apply only to the amounts so remitted or received.

ARTICLE 7

Income from immovable property

(1) Income from immovable property may be taxed in the Contracting State in which such property is situated.

(2)(a) The term "immovable property" shall, subject to the provisions of subparagraph (b) below be defined in accordance with the law of the Contracting State in which the property in question is situated.

(b) The term "immovable property" shall in any case include property accessory to immovable property, livestock and equipment used in agriculture and forestry, rights to which the provisions of general law respecting landed property apply, usufruct of immovable property and rights to variable or fixed payments as consideration for the working of, or the right to work, mineral deposits, sources and other natural resources; ships, boats and aircraft shall not be regarded as immovable property.

(3) The provisions of paragraph (1) of this Article shall apply to income derived from the direct use, letting, or use in any other form of immovable property.

(4) The provisions of paragraphs (1) and (3) of this Article shall also apply to the income from immovable property of an enterprise and to income from immovable property used for the performance of professional services.

(5) Notwithstanding the preceding provisions of this Article profits derived by an agricultural, forestry or plantation enterprise shall be dealt with in accordance with the provisions of Article 8.

ARTICLE 8

Business profits

(1) The profits of an enterprise of a Contracting State shall be taxable only in that State unless the enterprise carries on business in the other Contracting State through a permanent establishment situated therein. If the enterprise carries on business as aforesaid, the profits of the enterprise may be taxed in the other State but only so much of them as is attributable to that permanent establishment.

(2) Where an enterprise of a Contracting State carries on business in the other Contracting State through a permanent establishment situated therein, there shall in each Contracting State be attributed to that permanent establishment the profits which it might be expected to make if it were a distinct and separate enterprise engaged in the same or similar activities under the same or similar conditions and dealing at arm's length with the enterprise of which it is a permanent establishment.

(3) In the determination of the profits of a permanent establishment situated in a Contracting State, there shall be allowed as deductions expenses of the enterprise (other than expenses which would not be deductible under the law of that State if the permanent establishment were a separate enterprise) which are incurred for the purposes of the permanent establishment including executive and general administrative expenses so incurred whether in the State in which the permanent establishment is situated or elsewhere.

(4) In so far as it has been customary in a Contracting State, according to its law, to determine the profits to be attributed to a permanent establishment on the basis of an apportionment of the total profits of the enterprise to its various parts, nothing in paragraph (2) of this Article shall preclude that Contracting State from determining the profits to be taxed by such an apportionment as may be customary; the method of apportionment adopted shall, however, be such that the result shall be in accordance with the principles of this Article.

(5) No profits shall be attributed to a permanent establishment by reason of the mere purchase by that permanent establishment of goods or merchandise for the enterprise.

(6) For the purposes of the preceding paragraphs, the profits to be attributed to the permanent establishment shall be determined by the same method year by year unless there is good and sufficient reason to the contrary.

(7) Where profits include items which are dealt with separately in other Articles of this Agreement, then the provisions of those Articles shall not be affected by the provisions of this Article.

ARTICLE 9

Shipping and air transport

A resident of a Contracting State shall be exempt from tax in the other Contracting State on profits from the operation of ships or aircraft other than profits from voyages of ships or aircraft confined solely to places in the other Contracting State.

ARTICLE 10

Associated enterprises

Where—

(a) an enterprise of a Contracting State participates directly or indirectly in the management, control or capital of an enterprise of the other Contracting State; or

(b) the same persons participate directly or indirectly in the management, control or capital of an enterprise of a Contracting State and an enterprise of the other Contracting State;

and in either case conditions are made or imposed between the two enterprises in their commercial or financial relations which differ from those which would be made between independent enterprises, then any profits which would, but for those conditions, have accrued to one of the enterprises, but, by reason of those conditions, have not so accrued, may be included in the profits of that enterprise and taxed accordingly.

ARTICLE 11

Dividends

(1)(*a*) Dividends derived from a company which is a resident of the United Kingdom by a resident of Kenya may be taxed in Kenya.

(*b*) Where a resident of Kenya is entitled to a tax credit in respect of such a dividend under paragraph (2) of this Article tax may also be charged in the United Kingdom and according to the laws of the United Kingdom, on the aggregate of the amount or value of that dividend and the amount of that tax credit at a rate not exceeding 15 per cent.

(*c*) Except as aforesaid dividends derived from a company which is a resident of the United Kingdom by a resident of Kenya who is subject to tax in Kenya on them shall be exempt from any tax in the United Kingdom which is chargeable on dividends.

(2) A resident of Kenya who receives dividends from a company which is a resident of the United Kingdom shall, subject to the provisions of paragraph (3) of this Article and provided he is subject to tax in Kenya on the dividends, be entitled to the tax credit in respect thereof to which an individual resident in the United Kingdom would have been entitled had he received those dividends, and to the payment of any excess of such credit over his liability to United Kingdom tax.

(3) Paragraph (2) of this Article shall not apply where the recipient of the dividend is a company which either alone or together with one or more associated companies controls directly or indirectly at least 10 per cent of the voting power in the company paying the dividend. For the purpose of this paragraph two companies shall be deemed to be associated if one is controlled directly or indirectly by the other, or both are controlled directly or indirectly by a third company.

(4) Dividends derived from a company which is a resident of Kenya by a resident of the United Kingdom may be taxed in the United Kingdom. Such dividends may also be taxed in Kenya but the tax so charged shall not exceed 15 per cent of the gross amount of the dividends if the recipient of the dividends is subject to tax on them in the United Kingdom.

(5) The term "dividends" as used in this Article means income from shares or other rights, not being debt-claims, participating in profits, as well as income from other corporate rights assimilated to income from shares by the taxation law of the State of which the company making the distribution is a resident and also includes any other item (other than interest or royalties relieved from tax under the provisions of Article 12 or Article 13 of this Agreement) which, under the law of the Contracting State of which the company paying the dividend is a resident, is treated as a dividend or distribution of a company.

(6) If the recipient of the dividends being a resident of a Contracting State owns 10 per cent or more of the class of shares in respect of which the dividends are paid then paragraphs (1) and (2) or as the case may be paragraph (4) of this Article shall not apply to the dividends to the extent that they can have been paid only out of profits which the company paying the dividends earned or other income which it received in a period ending 12 months or more before the relevant date. For the purposes of this paragraph the term "relevant date" means the date on which the recipient of the dividends became the owner of 10 per cent or more of the class of shares in question.

Provided that this paragraph shall apply only if the shares were acquired primarily for the purpose of securing the benefit of this Article and not for bona fide commercial reasons.

(7) The provisions of paragraphs (1) and (2), or as the case may be paragraph (4) of this Article shall not apply where a resident of a Contracting State has in the other Contracting State a permanent establishment and the holding by virtue of which the dividends are paid is effectively connected with the business carried on through such permanent establishment. In such a case the provisions of Article 8 shall apply.

(8) Where a company which is a resident of a Contracting State derives profits or income from the other Contracting State that other State may not impose any tax on the dividends paid by the company to persons who are not residents of that other State or subject the company's undistributed profits to a tax on undistributed profits, even if the dividends paid or the undistributed profits consist wholly or partly of profits or income arising in that other State.

ARTICLE 12

Interest

(1) Interest arising in a Contracting State and paid to a resident of the other Contracting State may be taxed in that other State.

(2) However, such interest may be taxed in the Contracting State in which it arises, and according to the law of that State; but where such interest is paid to a resident of the other Contracting State who is subject to tax there in respect thereof the tax so charged in the Contracting State in which the interest arises shall not exceed 15 per cent of the gross amount of the interest.

(3) Notwithstanding the provisions of paragraph (2), interest arising in a Contracting State and paid to the Government of the other Contracting State or a local authority thereof, the Central Bank of that other Contracting State, or any agency wholly owned by that Government or local authority shall be exempt from tax in the first-mentioned Contracting State. The competent authorities of the Contracting States may determine by mutual agreement any other governmental institution to which this paragraph shall apply.

(4) The term "interest" as used in this Article means income from Government securities, bonds or debentures, whether or not secured by mortgage and whether or not carrying a right to participate in profits, and other debt-claims of every kind as well as all other income assimilated to income from money lent by the taxation law of the State in which the income arises.

(5) The provisions of paragraphs (1) and (2) of this Article shall not apply if the recipient of the interest, being a resident of a Contracting State, has in the other Contracting State in which the interest arises a permanent establishment and the debt-claim from which the interest arises is effectively connected with a business carried on through that permanent establishment. In such a case, the provisions of Article 8 shall apply.

(6) Interest shall be deemed to arise in a Contracting State when the payer is that State itself, a political subdivision, a local authority or a resident of that State. Where, however, the person paying the interest, whether he is a resident of a Contracting State or not, has in a Contracting State a permanent establishment in connection with which the indebtedness on which the interest is paid was incurred, and such interest is borne by that permanent establishment, then such interest shall be deemed to arise in the Contracting State in which the permanent establishment is situated.

(7) Any provision of the law of one of the Contracting States which relates only to interest paid to a non-resident company with or without any further requirement, shall not operate so as to require such interest paid to a company which is a resident of the other Contracting State to be left out of account as a deduction in computing the taxable profits of the company paying the interest as being a dividend or distribution. The preceding sentence shall not however apply to interest received by a company which is a resident of one of the Contracting States in which more than 50 per cent of the voting power is controlled, directly or indirectly by a person or persons resident in the other Contracting State.

(8) Where, owing to a special relationship between the payer and the recipient or between both of them and some other person, the amount of the interest paid, having regard to the debt-claim for which it is paid, exceeds the amount which would have been agreed upon by the payer and the recipient in the absence of such relationship, the provisions of this Article shall apply only to the last-mentioned amount. In that case, the excess part of the payments shall remain taxable according to the law of each Contracting State, due regard being had to the other provisions of this Agreement.

ARTICLE 13

Royalties

(1) Royalties arising in a Contracting State and paid to a resident of the other Contracting State may be taxed in that other State.

(2) However, such royalties may be taxed in the Contracting State in which they arise, and according to the law of that State; but where such royalties are paid to a resident of the other Contracting State who is subject to tax there in respect thereof the tax so charged in the Contracting State in which the royalties arise shall not exceed 15 per cent of the gross amount of the royalties.

(3) The term "royalties" as used in this Article means payments of any kind received as a consideration for the use of, or the right to use, any copyright of literary, artistic or scientific work (including cinematograph films, and films or tapes for radio or television broadcasting), any patent, trade mark, design or model, plan, secret formula or process, or for the use of, or the right to use, industrial, commercial or scientific equipment, or for information concerning industrial, commercial or scientific experience.

(4) The provisions of paragraphs (1) and (2) of this Article shall not apply if the recipient of the royalties, being a resident of a Contracting State, has in the other Contracting State a permanent establishment and the right or property giving rise to the royalties is effectively connected with a business carried on through that permanent establishment. In such a case, the provisions of Article 8 shall apply.

(5) Royalties shall be deemed to arise in a Contracting State when the payer is that State itself, a political subdivision, a local authority or a resident of that State. Where, however, the person paying the royalties, whether he is a resident of a Contracting State or not, has in a Contracting State a permanent establishment in connection with which the obligation to pay the royalties was incurred, and such royalties are borne by that permanent establishment, then such royalties shall be deemed to arise in the Contracting State in which the permanent establishment is situated.

(6) Where, owing to a special relationship between the payer and the recipient or between both of them and some other person, the amount of the royalties paid, having regard to the use, right or information for which they are paid, exceeds the amount which would have been agreed upon by the payer and the recipient in the absence of such relationship, the provisions of this Article shall apply only to the last-mentioned amount. In that case, the excess part of the payments shall remain taxable according to the law of each Contracting State, due regard being had to the other provisions of this Agreement.

ARTICLE 14

Management fees

(1) Management fees arising in a Contracting State and paid to a resident of the other Contracting State may be taxed in that other State.

(2) Notwithstanding Article 8, management fees may also be taxed in the State in which they arise and according to the law of that State; but where such management fees are paid to a resident of the other Contracting State who is subject to tax there in respect thereof the tax so charged in the Contracting State in which the management fees arise shall not exceed 15 per cent of the gross amount of the management fees arising there.

(3) The term "management fees" as used in this Article means payments of any kind to any person, other than to an employee of the person making the payments, in consideration for any services of a managerial, technical or consultancy nature.

(4) The provisions of paragraphs (1) and (2) of this Article shall not apply if the recipient of the management fees, being a resident of a Contracting State, has in the other Contracting State in which the management fees arise a permanent establishment with which the management fees are effectively connected. In such a case the provisions of Article 8 shall apply.

(5) If a resident of one of the Contracting States who receives management fees which arise in the other Contracting State and who is subject to tax in respect thereof in the first-mentioned Contracting State so elects for any year of assessment, financial year or year of income, the tax chargeable in respect of those management fees in the Contracting State in which they arise shall be calculated as if he had a permanent establishment in the last-mentioned Contracting State and as if those management fees were taxable in accordance with Article 8 as profits attributable to that permanent establishment.

(6) Management fees shall be deemed to arise in a Contracting State when the payer is the government of that State or a political subdivision thereof, a local authority or a resident of that State, and to the extent that they are attributable to services rendered in that State. Where, however, the person paying the management fees whether he is a resident of a Contracting State or not, has in a Contracting State a permanent establishment in connection with which the obligation to pay the management fees was incurred and the management fees are borne by that permanent establishment, then the management fees shall be deemed to arise in that Contracting State to the extent that they are attributable to services rendered in that State.

ARTICLE 15

Capital gains

(1) Capital gains from the alienation of immovable property, as defined in paragraph (2) of Article 7, may be taxed in the Contracting State in which such property is situated.

(2) Capital gains from the alienation of movable property forming part of the business property of a permanent establishment which an enterprise of a Contracting State has in the other Contracting State or of movable property pertaining to a fixed base available to a resident of a Contracting State in the other Contracting State for the purpose of performing professional services, including such gains from the alienation of such a permanent establishment (alone or together with the whole enterprise) or of such a fixed base, may be taxed in the other State.

(3) Notwithstanding the provisions of paragraph (2) of this Article, capital gains derived by a resident of a Contracting State from the alienation of ships and aircraft operated in international traffic and movable property pertaining to the operation of such ships and aircraft shall be taxable only in that Contracting State.

(4) Capital gains from the alienation of any property other than those mentioned in paragraphs (1), (2) and (3) of this Article shall be taxable only in the Contracting State of which the alienator is a resident.

(5) The provisions of paragraph (4) of this Article shall not affect the right of a Contracting State to levy according to its own law a tax on capital gains from the alienation of any property derived by a person who is a resident of the other Contracting State and has been a resident of the first-mentioned Contracting State at any time during the ten years immediately preceding the alienation of the property.

ARTICLE 16

Independent personal services

(1) Income derived by a resident of a Contracting State in respect of professional services or other independent activities of a similar character other than management fees as defined in paragraph (3) of Article 14 shall be taxable only in that State unless:

(a) he has a fixed base regularly available to him in the other Contracting State for the purpose of performing his activities, in which case so much of the income may be taxed in that other Contracting State as is attributable to that fixed base; or

(b) he is present in that other Contracting State for a period or periods exceeding in the aggregate 183 days in the fiscal year concerned, in which case so much of the income may be taxed in that other Contracting State as is attributable to the activities performed in that other Contracting State.

(2) The term "professional services" includes especially independent scientific, literary, artistic, educational or teaching activities as well as the independent activities of physicians, lawyers, engineers, architects, dentists and accountants.

ARTICLE 17

Employments

(1) Subject to the provisions of Articles 18, 20, 21, 22 and 23, salaries, wages and other similar remuneration derived by a resident of a Contracting State in respect of an employment shall be taxable only in that State unless the employment is exercised in the other Contracting State. If the employment is so exercised, such remuneration as is derived therefrom may be taxed in that other State.

(2) Notwithstanding the provisions of paragraph (1) of this Article, remuneration derived by a resident of a Contracting State in respect of an employment exercised in the other Contracting State shall be taxable only in the first-mentioned State if:

(a) the recipient is present in the other State for a period or periods not exceeding in the aggregate 183 days in the fiscal year concerned; and

(b) the remuneration is paid by, or on behalf of, an employer who is not a resident of the other State; and

(c) the remuneration is not borne by a permanent establishment or a fixed base which the employer has in the other State.

(3) Notwithstanding the preceding provisions of this Article, remuneration in respect of an employment exercised aboard a ship or aircraft in international traffic may be taxed in the Contracting State of which the person deriving the profits from the operation of the ship or aircraft is a resident.

ARTICLE 18

Directors' fees

Directors' fees and similar payments derived by a resident of a Contracting State in his capacity as a member of the board of directors of a company which is a resident of the other Contracting State may be taxed in that other State.

ARTICLE 19

Artistes and athletes

Notwithstanding the provisions of Articles 16 and 17, income derived by public entertainers, such as theatre, motion picture, radio or television artistes, and musicians, and by athletes, from their personal activities as such may be taxed in the Contracting State in which those activities are exercised. Provided that this Article shall not apply to public entertainers and athletes whose visit to a Contracting State is supported wholly or substantially from the public funds of the other Contracting State.

ARTICLE 20

Pensions

(1) Any pension (other than a pension of the kind referred to in paragraph (2) of this Article) and any annuity, derived from sources within a Contracting State by an individual who is a resident of the other Contracting State may be taxed in the first-mentioned Contracting State, but if the individual is subject to tax in the other Contracting State in respect of the pension the tax so charged in the first-mentioned Contracting State shall not exceed the lower of

(a) 5 per cent of the pension, or

(b) the amount of the tax chargeable on the pension in the other Contracting State.

(2) Pensions paid by, or out of funds created by, a Contracting State to an individual for services rendered to that Contracting State in the discharge of governmental functions may be taxed in that Contracting State.

(3) The term "annuity" means a stated sum payable periodically at stated times, during life or during a specified or ascertainable period of time, under an obligation to make the payments in return for adequate and full consideration in money or money's worth.

ARTICLE 21

Governmental functions

(1) Remuneration paid by, or out of funds created by, a Contracting State to an individual for services rendered to that Contracting State in the discharge of governmental functions shall be exempt from tax in the other Contracting State if the individual is not a resident of that other Contracting State or is resident there solely for the purpose of rendering those services.

(2) The provisions of this Article shall not apply to payments in respect of services rendered in connection with any trade or business carried on by either of the Contracting States for purposes of profit.

ARTICLE 22

Students

(1) A student or business apprentice who is or was immediately before visiting a Contracting State a resident of the other Contracting State and who is present in the first-mentioned Contracting State solely for the purpose of his education or training shall be exempt from tax in that first-mentioned Contracting State on:

(a) payments made to him by persons residing outside that first-mentioned Contracting State for the purposes of his maintenance, education or training; and

(b) remuneration from employment in that first-mentioned Contracting State, provided that the remuneration constitutes earnings reasonably necessary for his maintenance and education.

(2) The benefits of this Article shall extend only for such period of time as may be reasonably or customarily required to complete the education or training undertaken, but in no event shall any individual have the benefits of this Article for more than three consecutive years.

ARTICLE 23

Teachers

A professor or teacher who visits a Contracting State for a period not exceeding two years for the purpose of teaching at a university, college, school or other educational institution in that Contracting State and who is, or was immediately before that visit, a resident of the other Contracting State shall be exempt from tax in the first-mentioned Contracting State on any remuneration for such teaching in respect of which he is subject to tax in the other Contracting State.

ARTICLE 24

Income not expressly mentioned

Items of income of a resident of a Contracting State being income of a class or from sources not expressly mentioned in the foregoing Articles of this Agreement in respect of which he is subject to tax in that State shall be taxable only in that State. Provided that this Article shall not be construed as affecting the taxation of income attributable to a permanent establishment which a resident of one Contracting State has in the other Contracting State.

ARTICLE 25

Capital

(1) Capital represented by immovable property, as defined in paragraph (2) of Article 7, may be taxed in the Contracting State in which such property is situated.

(2) Capital represented by movable property forming part of the business property of a permanent establishment of an enterprise, or by movable property pertaining to a fixed base used for the performance of professional services, may be taxed in the Contracting State in which the permanent establishment or fixed base is situated.

(3) Notwithstanding the provisions of paragraph (2) of this Article, ships and aircraft operated in international traffic and movable property pertaining to the operation of such ships and aircraft shall be taxable only in the Contracting State of which the operator is a resident.

(4) All other elements of capital of a resident of a Contracting State shall be taxable only in that State.

ARTICLE 26

Elimination of double taxation

(1) Subject to the provisions of the law of the United Kingdom regarding the allowance as a credit against United Kingdom tax of tax payable in a territory outside the United Kingdom (which shall not affect the general principle hereof), Kenya tax payable under the laws of Kenya and in accordance with this Agreement, whether directly or by deduction, on profits, income or chargeable gains from sources within Kenya shall be allowed as a credit against any United Kingdom tax computed by reference to the same profits, income or chargeable gains by reference to which the Kenya tax is computed. Provided that in the case of a dividend the credit shall take into account only such tax in respect thereof as is additional to any tax payable by the company on the profits out of which the dividend is paid and is ultimately borne by the recipient without reference to any tax so payable.

(2) For the purpose of paragraph (1) of this Article, the term "Kenya tax payable" shall be deemed to include any amount which would have been payable as Kenya tax for any year but for—

    (a) a reduction of tax granted for that year or any part thereof under paragraph (2)(b) of the Second Schedule to the Income Tax (Allowances and Rates) (No. 2) Act 1971, so far as it was in force on, and has not been modified since, the date when this Agreement was signed, or has been modified only in minor respects so as not to affect its general character; or

    (b) any other provision which may subsequently be made granting an exemption or reduction of tax which is agreed by the competent authorities of the United Kingdom and Kenya to be of a substantially similar character, if it has not been modified thereafter or has been modified only in minor respects so as not to affect its general character.

Provided that relief from United Kingdom tax shall not be given by virtue of this paragraph in respect of income from any source if the income arises in a period starting more than ten years after the exemption from, or reduction of, Kenya tax was first granted in respect of that source.

(3) Where a resident of Kenya:

(*a*) derives income from sources within the United Kingdom which, in accordance with the provisions of this Agreement, is exempt from Kenya tax but may be taxed in the United Kingdom, then Kenya may, in calculating the tax on the remaining income of that person, apply the rate of tax which would have been applicable if the income derived from sources within the United Kingdom had not been exempted;

(*b*) derives income from sources within the United Kingdom which may be taxed in both Contracting States, then Kenya shall allow as a deduction from the tax on the income of that person an amount equal to the tax paid in the United Kingdom. Such deduction, however, shall not exceed that part of the Kenya tax as computed before the deduction is given, which is appropriate to the income derived from the United Kingdom.

(4) For the purposes of paragraphs (1) and (3) of this Article income, profits and capital gains owned by a resident of a Contracting State which may be taxed in the other Contracting State in accordance with this Agreement shall be deemed to arise from sources in that other Contracting State.

ARTICLE 27

Personal allowances

(1) Subject to the provisions of paragraph (3) of this Article, individuals who are residents of Kenya shall be entitled to the same personal allowances, reliefs and reductions for the purpose of United Kingdom tax as British subjects not resident in the United Kingdom.

(2) Subject to the provisions of paragraph (3) of this Article, individuals who are residents of the United Kingdom shall be entitled to the same personal allowances, reliefs and reductions for the purposes of Kenya tax as Kenya citizens not resident in Kenya.

(3) Nothing in this Agreement shall entitle an individual who is a resident of a Contracting State and whose income from the other Contracting State consists solely of dividends, interest or royalties (or solely of a combination thereof) to the personal allowances, reliefs and reductions of the kind referred to in this Article for the purpose of taxation in that other Contracting State.

ARTICLE 28

Non-discrimination

(1) The nationals of a Contracting State shall not be subjected in the other Contracting State to any taxation or any requirement connected therewith which is other or more burdensome than the taxation and connected requirements to which nationals of that other State in the same circumstances are or may be subjected.

(2) The taxation on a permanent establishment which an enterprise of a Contracting State has in the other Contracting State shall not be less favourably levied in that other State than the taxation levied on enterprises of that other State carrying on the same activities.

(3) Enterprises of a Contracting State, the capital of which is wholly or partly owned or controlled directly or indirectly, by one or more residents of the other Contracting State, shall not be subjected in the first-mentioned Contracting State to any taxation or any requirement connected therewith which is other or more burdensome than the taxation and connected requirements to which other similar enterprises of that first-mentioned State are or may be subjected.

(4) Nothing contained in this Article shall be construed as obliging either Contracting State to grant to individuals not resident in that State any of the personal allowances, reliefs and reductions for tax purposes which are granted to individuals so resident.

(5) In this Article the term "taxation" means taxes of every kind and description.

ARTICLE 29

Mutual agreement procedure

(1) Where a resident of a Contracting State considers that the actions of one or both of the Contracting States result or will result for him in taxation not in accordance with this Agreement, he may, notwithstanding the remedies provided by the national laws of those States, present his case to the competent authority of the Contracting State of which he is a resident.

(2) The competent authority shall endeavour, if the objection appears to it to be justified and if it is not itself able to arrive at an appropriate solution, to resolve the case by mutual agreement with the competent authority of the other Contracting State, with a view to the avoidance of taxation not in accordance with the Agreement.

(3) The competent authorities of the Contracting States shall endeavour to resolve by mutual agreement any difficulties or doubts arising as to the interpretation or application of the Agreement.

(4) The competent authorities of the Contracting States may communicate with each other directly for the purpose of reaching an agreement in the sense of the preceding paragraphs.

ARTICLE 30

Exchange of information

The competent authorities of the Contracting States shall exchange such information (being information which is at their disposal under their respective taxation laws in the normal course of administration) as is necessary for carrying out the provisions of this Agreement or for the prevention of fraud or the administration of statutory provisions against legal avoidance in relation to the taxes which are the subject of this Agreement. Any information so exchanged shall be treated as secret but may be disclosed to persons (including a court or administrative body) concerned with assessment, collection, enforcement or prosecution in respect of taxes which are the subject of this Agreement. No information shall be exchanged which would disclose any trade, business, industrial or professional secret or any trade process.

ARTICLE 31

Territorial extension

(1) This Agreement may be extended, either in its entirety or with modifications, to any territory for whose international relations the United Kingdom is responsible and which imposes taxes substantially similar in character to those to which this Agreement applies. Any such extension shall take effect from such date and subject to such modifications and conditions, including conditions as to termination, as may be specified and agreed between the Contracting States in notes to be exchanged for this purpose.

(2) Unless otherwise agreed by both Contracting States, the termination of this Agreement shall terminate the application of this Agreement to any territory to which it has been extended under the provisions of this Article.

ARTICLE 32

Entry into force

This Agreement shall come into force on the date when the last of all such things shall have been done in the United Kingdom and Kenya as are necessary to give the Agreement the force of law in the United Kingdom and Kenya respectively, and shall thereupon have effect:

(a) in the United Kingdom:
   (i) as respects income tax and capital gains tax, for any year of assessment beginning on or after 6 April 1973;
   (ii) as respects corporation tax, for any financial year beginning on or after 1 April 1973;

(b) in Kenya:
   as respects income arising for the year of income 1973 and subsequent years.

ARTICLE 33

Termination

This Agreement shall continue in effect indefinitely but either of the Contracting Governments may, on or before the thirtieth day of June in any calendar year after the year 1978, give notice of termination to the other Contracting Government and, in such event, the Agreement shall cease to be effective:

(a) in the United Kingdom:
   (i) as respects income tax, surtax and capital gains tax, for any year of assessment beginning on or after 6 April in the calendar year next following that in which the notice is given;
   (ii) as respects corporation tax, for any financial year beginning on or after 1 April in the calendar year next following that in which the notice is given;

(b) In Kenya:
   as respects income arising for the year of income next following that in which the notice is given and subsequent years.

In witness whereof the undersigned, duly authorised thereto, have signed this Agreement.

Done in duplicate at Nairobi this Thirty First day of July one thousand nine hundred and seventy three.

FOR THE GOVERNMENT OF THE UNITED KINGDOM OF GREAT BRITAIN AND NORTHERN IRELAND:

FOR THE GOVERNMENT OF THE REPUBLIC OF KENYA:

ANTONY DUFF.

MWAI KIBAKI.

PART II

PROTOCOL AMENDING THE AGREEMENT SIGNED AT NAIROBI ON 31 JULY 1973 BETWEEN THE GOVERNMENT OF THE UNITED KINGDOM OF GREAT BRITAIN AND NORTHERN IRELAND AND THE GOVERNMENT OF THE REPUBLIC OF KENYA FOR THE AVOIDANCE OF DOUBLE TAXATION AND THE PREVENTION OF FISCAL EVASION WITH RESPECT TO TAXES ON INCOME AND CAPITAL GAINS, SIGNED AT LONDON ON 20 JANUARY 1976, AS AMENDED BY NOTES EXCHANGED AT NAIROBI ON 8 FEBRUARY 1977

The Government of the United Kingdom of Great Britain and Northern Ireland and the Government of the Republic of Kenya;

Desiring to conclude a Protocol to amend the Agreement between the Contracting Governments for the avoidance of double taxation and the prevention of fiscal evasion with respect to taxes on income and capital gains, signed at Nairobi on 31 July 1973 (hereinafter referred to as "the Agreement");

Have agreed as follows:

ARTICLE I

Paragraph (3) of Article 12 of the Agreement shall be deleted and replaced by the following:

"(3) Notwithstanding the provisions of paragraph (2):

(a) interest arising in a Contracting State, and paid to the Government of the other Contracting State or a local authority thereof, the Central Bank of that other Contracting State, or any agency wholly owned by that Government or local authority shall be exempt from tax in the first-mentioned Contracting State. The competent authorities of the Contracting States may determine by mutual agreement any other governmental institution to which this paragraph shall apply;

(b) interest arising in Kenya which is paid to a resident of the United Kingdom, other than to a person mentioned in sub-paragraph (a) of this paragraph, may be exempt from Kenya tax at the discretion of the competent authority of Kenya."

ARTICLE II

Paragraph (2) of Article 14 of the Agreement shall be deleted and replaced by the following:

"(2) Notwithstanding Article 8, management fees may also be taxed in the State in which they arise and according to the law of that State; but where such management fees are paid to a resident of the other Contracting State who is subject to tax there in respect thereof the tax so charged in the Contracting State in which the management fees arise shall not exceed 12½ per cent of the gross amount of the management fees arising there."

ARTICLE III

Paragraph (5) of Article 14 of the Agreement shall be deleted and replaced by the following:

"(5) If a resident of one of the Contracting States who receives management fees which arise in the other Contracting State and who is subject to tax in respect thereof in the first-mentioned Contracting State so elects for any year of assessment, financial year or year of income, the tax chargeable in respect of those management fees in the Contracting State in which they arise shall be calculated as if he had a permanent establishment in the last-mentioned Contracting State and as if those management fees were taxable in accordance with Article 8 as profits attributable to that permanent establishment. Provided that in no such case shall the expenses deductible in calculating the tax chargeable in respect of those management fees exceed 75 per cent of the gross amount of those management fees arising in the last-mentioned Contracting State."

ARTICLE IV

Paragraph (1) of Article 20 of the Agreement shall be deleted and replaced by the following:

"(1) Any pension (other than a pension of the kind referred to in paragraph (2) of this Article) and any annuity, derived from sources within a Contracting State by an individual who is a resident of the other Contracting State may be taxed in the first-mentioned Contracting State, but if the individual is subject to tax in the other Contracting State in respect of the pension or annuity the tax so charged in the first-mentioned Contracting State shall not exceed the lower of:

(*a*) 5 per cent of the pension or annuity, or

(*b*) the amount of tax chargeable on the pension or annuity in the other Contracting State."

ARTICLE V

Paragraph (1) of Article 26 of the Agreement shall be deleted and replaced by the following:

"(1) Subject to the provisions of the law of the United Kingdom regarding the allowance as a credit against United Kingdom tax of tax payable in a territory outside the United Kingdom (which shall not affect the general principle hereof):

(*a*) Kenya tax payable under the laws of Kenya and in accordance with this Agreement, whether directly or by deduction, on profits, income or chargeable gains from sources within Kenya shall be allowed as a credit against any United Kingdom tax computed by reference to the same profits, income or chargeable gains by reference to which the Kenya tax is computed. Provided that in the case of a dividend the credit shall take into account only such tax in respect thereof as is additional to any tax payable by the company on the profits out of which the dividend is paid and is ultimately borne by the recipient without reference to any tax so payable.

(*b*) In the case of a dividend paid by a company which is a resident of Kenya to a company which is a resident of the United Kingdom and which controls directly or indirectly at least 10 per cent of the voting power in the company paying the dividend the credit shall take into account (in addition to any Kenya tax for which credit may be allowed under the provisions of sub-paragraph (*a*) of this paragraph) the Kenya tax payable by the company in respect of the profits out of which such dividend is paid."

ARTICLE VI

Paragraph (2) of Article 28 of the Agreement shall be deleted and replaced by the following:

"(2) The taxation on a permanent establishment which an enterprise of one of the Contracting States has in the other Contracting State shall not be less favourably levied in that other Contracting State than the taxation levied on an enterprise of that other Contracting State carrying on the same activities. Provided that this paragraph shall not prevent the Government of one of the Contracting States from imposing on the profits attributable to a permanent establishment in that Contracting State of a company which is a resident of the other Contracting State a tax not exceeding $7\frac{1}{2}$ per cent of those profits in addition to the tax which would be chargeable on those profits if they were the profits of a company which was a resident of that Contracting State."

ARTICLE VII

Article 32 of the Agreement shall be deleted and replaced by the following:

"ARTICLE 32

Entry into force

This Agreement shall come into force on the date when the last of all such things shall have been done in the United Kingdom and Kenya as are necessary to give the Agreement the force of law in the United Kingdom and Kenya respectively, and shall thereupon have effect:

(*a*) in the United Kingdom:

    (i) in respect of income tax and capital gains tax, for any year of assessment beginning on or after 6 April 1976;

    (ii) in respect of corporation tax, for any financial year beginning on or after 1 April 1976;

(*b*) in Kenya:

    in respect of income arising for the year of income 1976 and subsequent years."

ARTICLE VIII

This Protocol, which shall form an integral part of the Agreement, shall come into force when the last of all such things shall have been done in the United Kingdom and Kenya as are necessary to give the Protocol the force of law in the United Kingdom and Kenya respectively, and shall thereupon have effect:

(*a*) in the United Kingdom:

    (i) in respect of income tax and capital gains tax, for any year of assessment beginning on or after 6 April 1976;

    (ii) in respect of corporation tax, for any financial year beginning on or after 1 April 1976;

(*b*) in Kenya:

    in respect of income arising for the year of income 1976 and subsequent years.

In witness whereof the undersigned, duly authorised thereto, have signed this Protocol.

Done in duplicate at London this 20th day of January 1976.

FOR THE GOVERNMENT
OF THE UNITED KINGDOM
OF GREAT BRITAIN AND
NORTHERN IRELAND:

FOR THE GOVERNMENT
OF THE REPUBLIC OF
KENYA:

D. ENNALS.

NG'ETHE NJOROGE.

EXPLANATORY NOTE

(This Note is not part of the Order.)

The Agreement (as amended by the Protocol) with Kenya scheduled to this Order contains a number of provisions similar to those included in the previous Arrangement which was made in 1952 and terminated by Kenya with effect from 6 April 1973. The most important are those relating to the taxation of shipping and air transport profits, certain trading profits not arising through a permanent establishment and earnings from employment. Where income continues to be taxable in both countries credit will, as in the earlier Arrangement, be given by the country of the taxpayer's residence for the tax payable in the country of origin of the income. Under the new Agreement the United Kingdom will also give credit for tax spared under certain provisions of Kenyan law.

There are significant changes in the treatment provided for dividends, interest, royalties, management fees and pensions.

The treatment of dividends takes account of the introduction of the imputation system of company taxation in the United Kingdom. Where a United Kingdom company pays a dividend to a resident of Kenya (other than to a company which controls 10 per cent or more of the voting power in the paying company), the recipient will, subject to certain conditions, receive the tax credit to which an individual resident in the United Kingdom and in receipt of such a dividend would be entitled, less a deduction at a rate not exceeding 15 per cent on the aggregate of the dividend and the tax credit. Dividends paid by Kenyan companies to residents of the United Kingdom will, in general, be subject to tax in Kenya at a rate not exceeding 15 per cent.

The rate of tax in the country of source on interest and royalties flowing to the other country will, in general, not exceed 15 per cent; interest received by the Government (or a governmental institution) will be exempt from tax in the country of source.

The rate of tax in the country of source on management fees flowing to the other country will, subject to certain conditions, not exceed $12\frac{1}{2}$ per cent of the fees.

The tax chargeable by the country of source on pensions (other than Government service pensions) is limited to the lower of 5 per cent of the pension or the amount of tax chargeable on the pension in the country of the pensioner's residence.

Governmental remuneration will normally be taxed by the paying Government only. The remuneration of visiting teachers and certain payments made to students will (subject to certain conditions) be exempt in the country visited.

There is provision for the taxation of capital gains on immovable property by the country in which the property is situated. Capital gains arising from the disposal of movable property will normally be taxed only in the country of the taxpayer's residence unless they arise from the disposal of assets of a permanent establishment or fixed base which the taxpayer has in the other country.

There are also provisions for the exchange of information, for consultation between the taxation authorities of the two countries and for the safeguarding of nationals and enterprises of one country against discriminatory taxation in the other country; an additional tax—not exceeding $7\frac{1}{2}$ per cent—may however be charged on profits earned in one country by a permanent establishment of a company which is a resident of the other.

The Agreement is to take effect in the United Kingdom as respects income tax and capital gains tax for the tax year 1976-77 and subsequent years and as respects corporation tax for the financial year commencing on 1 April 1976 and subsequent years.

STATUTORY INSTRUMENTS

1977 No. 1300

INCOME TAX

The Double Taxation Relief (Taxes on Income) (Netherlands) Order 1977

Laid before the House of Commons in draft

Made - - - - 29th July 1977

At the Court at Windsor Castle, the 29th day of July 1977

Present,

The Queen's Most Excellent Majesty in Council

Whereas a draft of this Order was laid before the House of Commons in accordance with the provisions of section 497(8) of the Income and Corporation Taxes Act 1970(a), and an Address has been presented to Her Majesty by that House praying that an Order may be made in the terms of this Order:

Now, therefore, Her Majesty, in exercise of the powers conferred upon Her by section 497 of the said Income and Corporation Taxes Act 1970, section 98(2) of the Finance Act 1972(b) and section 39 of the Finance Act 1965(c), as amended, and of all other powers enabling Her in that behalf, is pleased, by and with the advice of Her Privy Council, to order, and it is hereby ordered, as follows:—

1. This Order may be cited as the Double Taxation Relief (Taxes on Income) (Netherlands) Order 1977.

2. It is hereby declared—

(a) that the arrangements specified in the Protocol set out in the Schedule to this Order, which vary the arrangements set out in the Schedule to the Double Taxation Relief (Taxes on Income) (Netherlands) Order 1968(d), have been made with the Government of the Kingdom of the Netherlands with a view to affording relief from double taxation in relation to income tax, corporation tax, petroleum revenue tax or capital gains tax and taxes of a similar character imposed by the laws of the Netherlands; and

(b) that it is expedient that these arrangements should have effect.

Clerk of the Privy Council.

(a) 1970 c. 10. (b) 1972 c. 41. (c) 1965 c. 25. (d) S.I. 1968/577 (1968 I, p. 1326).

SCHEDULE

PROTOCOL AMENDING THE CONVENTION BETWEEN THE GOVERNMENT OF THE UNITED KINGDOM OF GREAT BRITAIN AND NORTHERN IRELAND AND THE GOVERNMENT OF THE KINGDOM OF THE NETHERLANDS FOR THE AVOIDANCE OF DOUBLE TAXATION AND THE PREVENTION OF FISCAL EVASION WITH RESPECT TO TAXES ON INCOME AND CAPITAL, SIGNED AT LONDON ON 31 OCTOBER 1967

The Government of the United Kingdom of Great Britain and Northern Ireland and the Government of the Kingdom of the Netherlands:

Desiring to conclude a Protocol to amend the Convention between the Government of the United Kingdom of Great Britain and Northern Ireland and the Government of the Kingdom of the Netherlands for the avoidance of double taxation and the prevention of fiscal evasion with respect to taxes on income and capital, signed at London on 31 October 1967, (hereinafter referred to as "the Convention");

Have agreed as follows:

ARTICLE I

Paragraph (1) of Article 2 of the Convention shall be deleted and replaced by the following:

"(1) The taxes which are the subject of this Convention are:

(a) In the United Kingdom of Great Britain and Northern Ireland:

(i) the income tax;

(ii) the corporation tax;

(iii) the petroleum revenue tax; and

(iv) the capital gains tax;
(hereinafter referred to as "United Kingdom tax");

(b) In the Netherlands:

(i) the income tax (inkomstenbelasting);

(ii) the wages tax (loonbelasting);

(iii) the company tax (vennootschapsbelasting);

(iv) the dividend tax (dividendbelasting); and

(v) the capital tax (vermogensbelasting);
(hereinafter referred to as "Netherlands tax")."

ARTICLE II

Article 11 of the Convention shall be deleted and replaced by the following:

"ARTICLE 11

Dividends

(1) Dividends derived from a company which is a resident of one of the States by a resident of the other State may be taxed in that other State.

(2) However, such dividends may be taxed in the State of which the company paying the dividends is a resident, and according to the law of that State, but where such dividends are beneficially owned by a resident of the other State the tax so charged shall not exceed:

(a) 5 per cent of the gross amount of the dividends if the beneficial owner is a company the capital of which is wholly or partly divided into shares and it controls directly or indirectly at least 25 per cent of the voting power in the company paying the dividends;

(b) in all other cases 15 per cent of the gross amount of the dividends.

This paragraph shall not affect the taxation of the company in respect of the profits out of which the dividends are paid.

(3) As long as an individual resident in the United Kingdom is entitled under United Kingdom law to a tax credit in respect of dividends paid by a company which is resident in the United Kingdom, paragraph (2) of this Article shall not apply to dividends derived from a company which is a resident of the United Kingdom by a resident of the Netherlands. In these circumstances the following provisions of this paragraph shall apply:

(a) (i) Where a resident of the Netherlands is entitled to a tax credit in respect of such a dividend under sub-paragraph (b) of this paragraph tax may also be charged in the United Kingdom and according to the laws of the United Kingdom on the aggregate of the amount or value of that dividend and the amount of that tax credit at a rate not exceeding 15 per cent.

(ii) Where a resident of the Netherlands is entitled to a tax credit in respect of such a dividend under sub-paragraph (c) of this paragraph tax may also be charged in the United Kingdom and according to the laws of the United Kingdom on the aggregate of the amount or value of that dividend and the amount of that tax credit at a rate not exceeding 5 per cent.

(iii) Except as provided in sub-paragraphs (a)(i) and (a)(ii) of this paragraph dividends derived from a company which is a resident of the United Kingdom and which are beneficially owned by a resident of the Netherlands shall be exempt from any tax in the United Kingdom which is chargeable on dividends.

(b) A resident of the Netherlands who receives dividends from a company which is a resident of the United Kingdom shall, subject to the provisions of sub-paragraph (c) of this paragraph and provided he is the beneficial owner of the dividends, be entitled to the tax credit in respect thereof to which an individual resident in the United Kingdom would have been entitled had he received those dividends, and to the payment of any excess of that tax credit over his liability to tax in the United Kingdom.

(c) The provisions of sub-paragraph (b) of this paragraph shall not apply where the beneficial owner of the dividend is a company which either alone or together with one or more associated companies controls directly or indirectly 10 per cent or more of the voting power in the company paying the dividend. In these circumstances a company which is a resident of the Netherlands and receives dividends from a company which is a resident of the United Kingdom shall, provided it is the beneficial owner of the dividends, be entitled to a tax credit equal to one half of the tax credit to which an individual resident in the United Kingdom would have been entitled had he received those dividends, and to the payment of any excess of that tax credit over its liability to tax in the United Kingdom. For the purposes of this sub-paragraph, two companies shall be deemed to be associated if one controls directly or indirectly more than 50 per cent of the voting power in the other company, or a third company controls more than 50 per cent of the voting power in both of them.

(4) The term "dividends" for United Kingdom tax purposes includes any item which under the law of the United Kingdom is treated as a distribution and for Netherlands tax purposes includes any item which under the law of the Netherlands is subject to dividend tax.

(5) If the beneficial owner of the dividends being a resident of one of the States owns 10 per cent or more of the class of shares in respect of which the dividends are paid and does not suffer tax thereon in that State then paragraph (2), or as the case may be paragraph (3), of this Article shall not apply to the dividends to the extent that they can have been paid only out of profits which the company paying the dividends earned or other income which it received in a period ending twelve months or more before the relevant date. For the purposes of this paragraph the term "relevant date" means the date on which the beneficial owner of the dividends became the owner of 10 per cent or more of the class of shares in question. Provided that this paragraph shall apply only if the shares were acquired primarily for the purpose of securing the benefit of this Article and not for *bona fide* commercial reasons.

(6) The provisions of paragraph (1) and of paragraph (2) or (3), as the case may be, shall not apply if the recipient of the dividends, being a resident of one of the States, has in the other State, of which the company paying the dividends is a resident, a permanent establishment and the holding by virtue of which the dividends are paid is effectively connected with the business carried on through such permanent establishment. In such a case the provisions of Article 8 shall apply.

(7) Where a company which is a resident of one of the States derives profits or income from the other State, that other State may not impose any tax on the dividends paid by the company to persons who are not residents of that other State, or subject the company's undistributed profits to a tax on undistributed profits, even if the dividends paid or the undistributed profits consist wholly or partly of profits or income arising in such other State, except insofar as the holding in respect of which the dividends are paid is effectively connected with a permanent establishment or a fixed base situated in that other State."

ARTICLE III

Paragraphs (2) and (5) of Article 12 of the Convention shall be deleted and replaced by the following:

"(2) The term "interest" for United Kingdom tax purposes includes any item which under the law of the United Kingdom is treated as interest and for Netherlands tax purposes includes any item which under the law of the Netherlands is treated as interest, but subject to the provisions of paragraph (4) of this Article shall not include any item which is treated as a dividend under the provisions of Article 11.

(5) Where, owing to a special relationship between the payer and the recipient or between both of them and some other person the amount of the interest paid exceeds the amount which would have been determined, taking into consideration the terms and amount of the debt-claim which would have been agreed upon, by the payer and the recipient in the absence of such relationship, the provisions of this Article shall apply only to the last-mentioned amount. In that case, the excess part of the payment shall remain taxable according to the law of each State, due regard being had to the other provisions of this Convention."

ARTICLE IV

Article 14 of the Convention shall be deleted and replaced by the following:

"ARTICLE 14

Application of Articles 11, 12 and 13

(1) The reductions and exemptions from tax in the State of source given by Articles 11, 12 and 13 as well as the payment of the United Kingdom tax credit referred to in paragraph (3) of Article 11 shall be effected in accordance with the mode of application determined (having due regard to the taxation laws of that State) by the taxation authorities of the States.

(2) Where tax has been deducted at the source in excess of the amount of tax chargeable under the provisions of Articles 11, 12 or 13 the excess amount of tax shall be refunded upon application to the taxation authorities concerned, provided that the application is made within a period of six years after the end of the calendar year in which the tax was deducted.

(3) The provisions of paragraph (2) or, as the case may be, paragraph (3) of Article 11, paragraph (1) of Article 12 and paragraph (1) of Article 13 shall not apply if:

(a) the holding, security or asset giving rise to the income in question was obtained in virtue of any contract, option or any arrangement under which the beneficial owner agreed, or might be obliged, to sell again or to transfer again the holding, security or asset or to sell or transfer a similar holding, security or asset, or

(b) the beneficial owner of the holding, security or asset giving rise to the income in question sells the holding, security or asset within three months from the date on which he acquired it."

Article V

Paragraph (2)(*b*) of Article 26 of the Convention shall be deleted and replaced by the following:

"(2)(*b*) Without prejudice to the application of the provisions concerning the compensation of losses in the unilateral regulations for the avoidance of double taxation the Netherlands shall allow a deduction from the amount of tax computed in conformity with paragraph (2)(*a*) of this Article equal to such part of that tax which bears the same proportion to the aforesaid tax, as the part of the income or capital which is included in the basis mentioned in paragraph (2)(*a*) of this Article and may be taxed in the United Kingdom according to Articles 7, 8, 11 (paragraph (6)), 12 paragraph (3)), 13 (paragraph (3)), 15 (paragraph (1)), 16, 17 (paragraphs (1) and (3)), 18 (paragraph (1)), 19, 21 (paragraphs (2) and (3)), and 24 (paragraphs (1) and (2)) of this Convention bears to the total income or capital which forms the basis mentioned in paragraph (2)(*a*) of this Article.

Further, the Netherlands shall allow a deduction from the Netherlands tax so computed for such items of income, as may be taxed in the United Kingdom according to Articles 11 (paragraphs (2) or (3), as the case may be) and 15 (paragraph (4)) and are included in the basis mentioned in paragraph (2)(*a*) of this Article. The amount of this deduction shall be the lesser of the following amounts:

　(i) the amount equal to the United Kingdom tax;

　(ii) the amount of the Netherlands tax which bears the same proportion to the amount of tax computed in conformity with paragraph (2)(*a*) of this Article, as the amount of the said items of income bears to the amount of income which forms the basis mentioned in paragraph (2)(*a*) of this Article."

Article VI

As respects the Kingdom of the Netherlands this Protocol shall only apply to the Part of the Kingdom of the Netherlands that is situated in Europe.

Article VII

Each of the Contracting Parties shall notify to the other the completion of the procedure required by its law for the bringing into force of this Protocol. This Protocol shall enter into force on the date of the later of these notifications and shall thereupon have effect:

　(*a*) in the United Kingdom:

　　(i) for any chargeable period beginning on or after 1 January 1975; and

　　(ii) in relation to dividends paid on or after 6 April 1975;

　(*b*) in the Netherlands:

　　(i) for taxable years and periods beginning on or after 1 January 1975; and

　　(ii) in relation to dividends paid on or after 6 April 1975.

In witness whereof the undersigned, duly authorised thereto, have signed this Protocol.

Done in duplicate at London this 22nd day of March 1977 in the English and Dutch languages, both texts being equally authoritative.

For the Government of the United Kingdom of Great Britain and Northern Ireland

For the Government of the Kingdom of the Netherlands

FRANK A. JUDD

R. FACK

EXPLANATORY NOTE

(This Note is not part of the Order.)

The Protocol scheduled to this Order makes certain alterations to the Convention set out in the Schedule to the Double Taxation Relief (Taxes on Income) (Netherlands) Order 1968. These alterations follow mainly from the introduction of the new United Kingdom corporation tax system which, so far as it relates to the tax treatment of dividends paid by United Kingdom companies to overseas shareholders, came into operation on 6 April 1973.

The Protocol provides rules for the taxation of dividends which are to apply as long as under United Kingdom law an individual resident in the United Kingdom is entitled to a tax credit in respect of dividends paid by a company resident in the United Kingdom.

Where a United Kingdom company pays a dividend to a Netherlands company controlling 10 per cent or more of its voting power, the Netherlands company receiving the dividend will be entitled to a tax credit equal to one half of the tax credit which would be payable to a United Kingdom resident individual less a sum of not more than 5 per cent of the aggregate amount of the dividend and the tax credit paid. Where the recipient is an individual resident of the Netherlands or a Netherlands company controlling less than 10 per cent of the voting power of the United Kingdom company, the tax credit payable will be equal to the tax credit which would be payable to a United Kingdom resident individual less a sum not exceeding 15 per cent of the aggregate of the dividend and the tax credit.

Certain consequential changes have been made to the provisions under which residents of the Netherlands receiving dividends from United Kingdom companies are given double taxation relief in the Netherlands. The Protocol also provides that the rate of Netherlands withholding tax on dividends paid to a United Kingdom company controlling at least 25 per cent of the voting power of the Netherlands company paying the dividend will be limited to a maximum of 5 per cent. In all other cases the Netherlands withholding tax will be not more than 15 per cent.

The Protocol also amends the list of taxes covered by the Convention and removes from the definition of interest any item of interest which is treated in the Netherlands or the United Kingdom as a dividend. It provides for refunds to be made where excessive tax has been withheld at source.

The Protocol is expressed to take effect in relation to dividends paid on or after 6 April 1975.

STATUTORY · INSTRUMENTS

1977 No. 1301

MERCHANT SHIPPING

SAFETY

CIVIL AVIATION

The Collision Regulations and Distress Signals (Amendment) Order 1977

Made - - - -	*29th July* 1977
Laid before Parliament	1*st August* 1977
Coming into Operation	2*nd August* 1977

At the Court at Windsor Castle the 29th day of July 1977

Present,

The Queen's Most Excellent Majesty in Council

Her Majesty, in exercise of the powers conferred upon Her by sections 418, 424 and 738 of the Merchant Shipping Act 1894(a) and all other powers enabling Her in that behalf, on the joint recommendation of the Secretary of State for Defence and the Secretary of State for Trade, is pleased, by and with the advice of Her Privy Council, to order, and it is hereby ordered, as follows:—

1. This Order may be cited as the Collision Regulations and Distress Signals (Amendment) Order 1977 and shall come into operation on 2nd August 1977.

2. The Collision Regulations and Distress Signals Order 1977(b) shall be amended as follows:

(1) At the end of Article 3(1) there shall be added the following proviso:
"Provided that nothing in this Order shall be taken to require compliance by any vessel or class of vessels which, by virtue of Rule 38 of the Collision Regulations, may be exempted from compliance therewith, with any of the provisions of the said Regulations specified in paragraphs (*a*) to (*g*) inclusive of that Rule, at any time when, by virtue of that Rule, that vessel or class of vessels may be exempted from that provision."

(2) In Schedule 2 there shall be inserted in the list of foreign countries, in the appropriate alphabetical order, the following:

Argentina	Israel
Austria	Japan

N. E. Leigh,
Clerk of the Privy Council.

(a) 1894 c. 60.   (b) S.I. 1977/982 (1977 II, p. 2728).

EXPLANATORY NOTE

(This Note is not part of the Order.)

This Order amends the Collision Regulations and Distress Signals Order 1977:

(1) by making it clear that vessels falling within the provisions of Rule 38 (Exemptions) of the Collision Regulations are, without more, exempt from the requirements therein specified (installation and repositioning of lights, and requirements as to sound signal appliances) for the periods of time therein specified;

(2) by adding to the list in Schedule 2 to the Order, further foreign countries to whose vessels the Collision Regulations and Distress Signals Rules apply.

STATUTORY INSTRUMENTS

1977 No. 1302

COUNTER-INFLATION

The Counter-Inflation (Continuation of Enactments) Order 1977

Laid before Parliament in draft

Made - - - -	29*th July* 1977
Coming into Operation	31*st July* 1977

At the Court at Windsor Castle, the 29th day of July 1977

Present,

The Queen's Most Excellent Majesty in Council

Whereas section 2(4) of the Remuneration, Charges and Grants Act 1975(**a**) ("the 1975 Act") empowers Her Majesty by Order in Council to continue in force sections 8 and 10 (as amended) of the Counter-Inflation Act 1973(**b**) for any period during which section 1 of the 1975 Act is in force:

And whereas the period for which the said section 1 has effect has been extended by section 17(2) of the Price Commission Act 1977(**c**) to 31st July 1978:

And whereas a draft of the following Order was laid before Parliament in accordance with section 2(5) of the 1975 Act and approved by resolution of each House of Parliament:

Now, therefore, Her Majesty, in exercise of the powers conferred upon Her by section 2(4) of the 1975 Act, is pleased, by and with the advice of Her Privy Council, to order, and it is hereby ordered, as follows:—

1.—(1) This Order may be cited as the Counter-Inflation (Continuation of Enactments) Order 1977.

(2) The Interpretation Act 1889(**d**) shall apply for the interpretation of this Order as it applies for the interpretation of an Act of Parliament.

(3) This Order shall come into operation on 31st July 1977.

2. The following provisions (as amended)(**e**) of Part II of the Counter-Inflation Act 1973(**f**), namely sections 8 and 10, shall continue in force until the expiration of the period ending with 31st July 1978.

N. E. Leigh,
Clerk of the Privy Council.

(**a**) 1975 c. 57.   (**b**) 1973 c. 9.   (**c**) 1977 c. 33.   (**d**) 1889 c. 63.
(**e**) S.I. 1974/1218 (1974 II, p. 4631); sections 14(2) and 15(4) of, and paragraph 2 of Schedule 2 to, the Price Commission Act 1977.
(**f**) Provisions of Part II continued in force to 31st July 1976 by S.I. 1976/228 (1976 I, p. 581) and to 31st July 1977 by S.I. 1976/1161 (1976 II, p. 3212).

EXPLANATORY NOTE

(This Note is not part of the Order.)

This Order, made under section 2 of the Remuneration, Charges and Grants Act 1975, as amended by section 17(2) of the Price Commission Act 1977, continues in force until the end of July 1978 certain provisions of Part II of the Counter-Inflation Act 1973 which would otherwise have ceased to be in force at the end of July 1977. Those provisions are section 8 (power to modify Acts about prices) and section 10 (restrictions on dividends).

STATUTORY INSTRUMENTS

1977 No. 1303

ANIMALS

DISEASES OF ANIMALS

The Brucellosis Incentive Payments Scheme 1977

Made - - - -	28th July 1977
Laid before Parliament	5th August 1977
Coming into Operation	26th August 1977

The Minister of Agriculture, Fisheries and Food, the Secretary of State for Scotland and the Secretary of State for Wales, acting jointly, in exercise of the powers conferred upon them by section 106(1), (9) and (10) of the Agriculture Act 1970(a) and of all other powers enabling them in that behalf, with the consent of the Treasury, hereby make the following scheme:—

Citation, commencement and extent

1. This scheme, which may be cited as the Brucellosis Incentive Payments Scheme 1977, shall come into operation on 26th August 1977 and shall apply to Great Britain.

Interpretation

2.—(1) In this scheme, unless the context otherwise requires:—

"accredited herd" means a herd of cattle in Great Britain which to the satisfaction of the appropriate Minister either—

(a) has been found to be free from brucellosis by means of a series of diagnostic tests carried out by him or on his behalf, and has been, since the date of the commencement of such tests, the subject of adequate precautions against the introduction or reintroduction and consequent spreading of brucellosis, or

(b) has been wholly constituted by the transfer of animals from other accredited herds in Great Britain or from such similar herds outside Great Britain as the Minister of Agriculture, Fisheries and Food, in relation to herds in England and Wales, or the Secretary of State, in relation to herds in Scotland, may either generally or in any special case allow, and has been, since being so constituted, the subject of such precautions as aforesaid;

"accreditation date" means the date on which samples were first taken for use in the final test as a result of which a herd becomes an accredited herd, or, in the case of an accredited herd wholly constituted by the transfer of animals from other accredited herds, the date on which the herd is constituted;

"the appropriate Minister" means the Minister of Agriculture, Fisheries and Food or, in relation to herds kept in Scotland, the Secretary of State for Scotland;

"brucellosis" means the disease caused by brucella abortus;

(a) 1970 c. 40.

"brucellosis incentives agreement" means a voluntary arrangement between the appropriate Minister and the owner of a herd providing for the eradication of brucellosis from the herd upon terms which include, for the duration of the incentive period relating to the herd, the slaughter by the owner of any reactors found in the herd without compensation, the making of incentive payments to the owner, and the taking by him of precautions against the introduction or reintroduction and consequent spreading of brucellosis;

"cow" means a female bovine animal which in the opinion of the appropriate Minister is suitable for breeding;

"eligible cow" means a cow which has borne a calf or is a replacement cow;

"eligible herd" means an accredited herd which is the subject of, and the owner of which is party to, a brucellosis incentives agreement;

"incentive period", in relation to a herd, means the period of five years beginning with the accreditation date of the herd;

"incentive payment" means a payment made under this scheme to the owner of a herd in pursuance of a brucellosis incentives agreement;

"Milk Marketing Board" means a board constituted by a scheme relating to the marketing of milk made, or having effect as if made, under the Agricultural Marketing Act 1958(a);

"operative date" means the date on which this scheme comes into operation;

"period of qualification" means—

    (a) in relation to a herd accredited on or after the operative date, the incentive period relating to the herd, and

    (b) in relation to a herd accredited before the operative date, the period beginning with that date and ending with the last day of the incentive period relating to the herd;

"replacement cow" means a cow which has in the opinion of the appropriate Minister been brought into a herd to replace a cow which, having borne a calf, has died or been disposed of.

(2) The Interpretation Act 1889(b) shall apply for the interpretation of this scheme as it applies for the interpretation of an Act of Parliament.

Qualifying days

3.—(1) As regards England and Wales the qualifying days for the purposes of this scheme shall be—

    (a) in the case of any eligible herd—

        (i) the last day (hereinafter referred to as the relevant day) of the period of six months beginning with the day after the herd's accreditation date;

        (ii) any anniversary of the relevant day; and

    (b) in the case of an eligible herd in relation to which the relevant day, or an anniversary thereof, falls within the period beginning with 1st July 1977 and ending with the operative date, the operative date.

(2) As regards Scotland the qualifying days for the purposes of this scheme shall be the 1st January in the year 1978 and in any following year.

(a) 1958 c. 47.   (b) 1889 c. 63.

Incentive payments in respect of eligible cows

4.—(1) Incentive payments may be made by the appropriate Minister in accordance with the provisions of this scheme in connection with the eradication of brucellosis from herds of cattle.

(2) Subject to the provisions of sub-paragraph (4) below the appropriate Minister may make to the owner of an eligible herd one incentive payment in respect of each eligible cow which is in the herd on a qualifying day falling within the period of qualification relating to that herd, and which has been comprised in that herd throughout the six months immediately preceding that qualifying day, or, in the case of a replacement cow, throughout such shorter period as the appropriate Minister, having regard to the time in the herd of the cow replaced, may allow.

(3) The amount of each incentive payment shall be £5.

(4) No payment shall be made under this scheme—

(a) in respect of a herd which for the time being qualifies under the Brucellosis (Beef Incentives) Payments Scheme 1972(**a**), as amended(**b**), for incentive payments, as defined in that scheme; or

(b) in respect of a herd which for the time being qualifies under the Brucellosis (Payments for Cows in Accredited Herds) (Scotland) Scheme 1970(**c**), as amended(**d**), for incentive payments, as defined in that scheme;

(c) as regards any one herd, in respect of more than five qualifying days.

Assessment of numbers after slaughter in brucellosis eradication

5. In assessing for the purposes of paragraph 4(2) above the number of eligible cows in an eligible herd on a qualifying day, the appropriate Minister may disregard any temporary reduction in numbers on that day when he is satisfied that such reduction has been caused by the slaughter of cows in the course of brucellosis eradication, and that those cows have been or will be replaced as soon as is reasonably practicable by the owner of the herd with cows which the appropriate Minister is satisfied are eligible cows, and may make incentive payments in respect of such number of eligible cows as would, in his opinion, have been comprised in that herd on that qualifying day had its numbers not been reduced by reason of such slaughter.

Reduction for milk production

6. If during the 12 months immediately preceding a qualifying day an eligible herd has produced a quantity of milk in respect of which a Milk Marketing Board has made payments under paragraph 4 of the Milk (Eradication of Brucellosis) Scheme 1970(**e**) as amended(**f**), the number of cows in that herd for which incentive payments may be made in respect of that qualifying day shall be reduced by such number as may be determined by the Minister.

Application for payments

7. Applications for incentive payments shall be made in such manner and at such time as the appropriate Minister may direct, and no payments may

(**a**) S.I. 1972/1329 (1972 II, p. 4010).   (**b**) S.I. 1975/2211 (1975 III, p. 8320).
(**c**) S.I. 1970/1469 (1970 III, p. 4789).
(**d**) S.I. 1971/1072, 1973/644 (1971 II, p. 3204; 1973 I, p. 2007).
(**e**) S.I. 1970/1277 (1970 II, p. 4162).
(**f**) S.I. 1971/532, 1972/1645, 1976/387 (1971 I, p. 1532; 1972 III, p. 4845; 1976 I, p. 1043).

be made to a herd owner until he has applied to the appropriate Minister in the manner and at the time directed.

Recovery

8. Where, in the opinion of the appropriate Minister, any incentive payments made to any person in respect of cows comprised in a herd on a qualifying day were wrongly made because the provisions of this scheme or of a brucellosis incentives scheme have not been complied with, because payments were made in respect of more cows than in fact qualified for payment, or because some of the cows in respect of which payment was made are found to have been ineligible, the appropriate Minister shall be entitled to recover on demand from that person as a civil debt the incentive payments so wrongly made.

In Witness whereof the Official Seal of the Minister of Agriculture, Fisheries and Food is hereunto affixed this 22nd day of July 1977.

(L.S.)

John Silkin,
Minister of Agriculture, Fisheries and Food.

26th July 1977.

Bruce Millan,
Secretary of State for Scotland.

27th July 1977.

John Morris,
Secretary of State for Wales.

We approve,

Donald R. Coleman,
T. E. Graham,
Two of the Lords Commissioners
of Her Majesty's Treasury.

28th July 1977.

EXPLANATORY NOTE
(This Note is not part of the Scheme.)

This Scheme, made under section 106(1) of the Agriculture Act 1970, empowers the Minister of Agriculture, Fisheries and Food, and the Secretary of State for Scotland in relation to herds kept in Scotland, to make incentive payments in connection with the eradication of brucellosis to the owners of eligible herds (that is, of herds accredited as free from brucellosis which are the subject of a voluntary brucellosis incentives agreement).

The Scheme enables incentive payments to continue to be made in respect of herds which until 2nd January 1977, when beef cow subsidy ceased to be payable, could qualify for brucellosis incentive payments made under the Brucellosis (Beef Incentives) Payment Scheme 1972, as amended, as a supplement to that subsidy.

It also enables incentive payments to be made in respect of certain eligible herds which hitherto have not qualified for such payments, but does not provide for any retrospective payment.

The Scheme does not apply to herds which are eligible for such incentive payments under the Brucellosis (Beef Incentives) Payments Scheme 1972 as are payable as a supplement to compensatory allowances under the Hill Livestock (Compensatory Allowances) Regulations 1975 (S.I. 1975/2210), or for incentive payments under the Brucellosis (Payments for Cows in Accredited Herds) (Scotland) Scheme 1970, as amended.

Under the Scheme, a payment of £5 may be made for each eligible cow which is in an eligible herd on a qualifying day and which has been comprised in that herd throughout the six months immediately before that qualifying day. In England and Wales a herd's qualifying days are the day six months after its date of accreditation as a brucellosis-free herd and the anniversaries of that day (in a few cases the qualifying day in 1977 is the operative date of the scheme). In Scotland, the qualifying days are the first day of January in the year 1978 and succeeding years. No incentive payments can, however, be made in respect of any qualifying day which falls outside a herd's incentive period (that is, the period of five years commencing with its date of accreditation) or which occurs before the operative date. Further, as regards any one herd, payments may be made in respect of no more than five qualifying days.

The Scheme also provides for—

(a) the reduction of the number of eligible cows in a herd in respect of milk produced by that herd for which milk incentive payments have been made under the Milk (Eradication of Brucellosis) Scheme 1970, and

(b) the disregarding of a temporary reduction, caused by slaughter in the course of brucellosis eradication, in the number of eligible cows in a herd on a qualifying day, and

contains provisions relating to applications for incentive payments and the recovery of payments wrongly made.

STATUTORY INSTRUMENTS

1977 No. 1304

AGRICULTURE

The Non-Marketing of Milk and Milk Products and the Dairy Herd Conversion Premiums Regulations 1977

Made - - - -	*27th July* 1977
Laid before Parliament	*5th August* 1977
Coming into Operation	*26th August* 1977

The Minister of Agriculture, Fisheries and Food, the Secretary of State for Scotland and the Secretary of State for Wales, being Ministers designated **(a)** for the purposes of section 2(2) of the European Communities Act 1972**(b)** in relation to the Common Agricultural Policy of the European Economic Community, acting jointly, in exercise of the powers conferred on them by the said section 2(2) and of all their other enabling powers, hereby make the following regulations:—

Citation, extent and commencement

1. These regulations, which may be cited as the Non-Marketing of Milk and Milk Products and the Dairy Herd Conversion Premiums Regulations 1977, shall apply throughout the United Kingdom, and shall come into operation on 26th August 1977.

Interpretation

2.—(1) In these regulations, unless the context otherwise requires—

"authorised officer" means—

  (*a*) in relation to England and Wales, an authorised officer of the Minister,

  (*b*) in relation to Scotland, an authorised officer of the Secretary of State for Scotland, and

  (*c*) in relation to Northern Ireland, an authorised officer of the Department of Agriculture for Northern Ireland,

acting in each case on behalf of the competent authority in connection with the discharge of the authority's functions under the Regulation of the Council, the Regulation of the Commission and these regulations;

"the competent authority" has the meaning assigned to it by regulation 3 of these regulations;

"the Minister" means the Minister of Agriculture, Fisheries and Food;

"the Regulation of the Council" means Regulation (EEC) No. 1078/77 of the Council of 17th May 1977**(c)**;

(**a**) S.I. 1972/1811 (1972 III, p. 5216). (**b**) 1972 c. 68.
(**c**) O.J. No. L131, 26.5.77, p. 1.

"the Regulation of the Commission" means Regulation (EEC) No. 1307/77 of the Commission of 15th June 1977(a).

(2) Other expressions used in these regulations have, in so far as the context admits, the same meanings as in the Regulation of the Council and in the Regulation of the Commission.

(3) The Interpretation Act 1889(b) applies to the interpretation of these regulations as it applies to the interpretation of an Act of Parliament.

Appointment of competent authority

3. For the purposes of the Regulation of the Council and of the Regulation of the Commission (which together lay down schemes for the payment of premiums to producers for the non-marketing of milk and milk products and the conversion of dairy herds to meat production), the competent authority shall be—

    (a) in relation to England and Northern Ireland, and in relation to Wales for the purpose of the making, receipt or recovery of any payment, the Minister;

    (b) in relation to Wales, save for the purpose of the making, receipt or recovery of any payment, the Minister and the Secretary of State for Wales acting jointly;

    (c) in relation to Scotland, the Secretary of State for Scotland.

Powers of inspection

4.—(1) Where a producer has applied for the payment of a premium under Article 1 of the Regulation of the Council, or has given an undertaking under Article 2(2) or Article 3(2) thereof, or where the successor of a producer has given an undertaking under Article 6 of that Regulation, an authorised officer may enter on any land occupied by that producer or successor, or otherwise used by him for the keeping of cattle or sheep, and may—

    (a) verify and register the total area of land farmed by the applicant;

    (b) mark and register the dairy herd on such land;

    (c) inspect and count any cattle or sheep kept by the producer or successor on such land; and

    (d) require the producer or successor to furnish for inspection any bill, account, voucher or record in his possession or under his control relating to the numbers of cattle or sheep kept, or formerly kept, by him, or relating to transactions carried out by him, or in respect of which he has or has had an interest, concerning cattle or sheep, or milk or milk products.

(2) In exercising the power conferred on him by the preceding paragraph, an authorised officer may be accompanied by such other persons acting under his instructions as appear to him to be necessary for the purpose of inspecting and counting animals, and in relation to the inspection of documents he shall be entitled to make such copies thereof, or take such extracts therefrom, as he may think fit.

(3) The producer or successor, and any other person in charge of animals on the land, shall render all reasonable assistance to an authorised officer to enable him to exercise the powers conferred on him by paragraph (1) of this regulation.

(a) O.J. No. L150, 18 6 77, p. 24.   (b)1889 c. 63.

Recovery of premiums

5.—(1) Subject to paragraph (2) of this regulation, where any person—

(*a*) with a view to obtaining the payment to himself or to any other person of a premium payable under the Regulation of the Council—

(i) makes any statement which is untrue or misleading in a material respect, or

(ii) furnishes to the competent authority any inaccurate information, or

(*b*) having given an undertaking under Article 2(2), Article 3(2) or Article 6 of the Regulation of the Council, fails in any way to comply therewith, or

(*c*) in an appropriate case, fails to satisfy the competent authority with regard to the matters referred to in Article 2(1) and Article 3(1) of the Regulation of the Council,

the competent authority shall be entitled to recover on demand as a civil debt the whole or any part of any premium paid to him or to any other person.

(2) Sub-paragraphs (*b*) and (*c*) above shall not apply to a producer who has been released from the obligations laid down in Article 2(2) of the Regulation of the Council by virtue of Article 2(3) or 2(4) of that Regulation.

Offences

6. Any person who—

(*a*) knowingly or recklessly makes a false statement for the purpose of obtaining the payment to himself or to any other person of a premium payable under the Regulation of the Council, or

(*b*) obstructs an authorised officer in the exercise of the powers conferred on him by regulation 4 of these regulations, or fails to furnish to such an officer on request any document referred to in paragraph (1)(*d*) of that regulation,

shall be liable on summary conviction to a fine not exceeding £400.

In Witness whereof the Official Seal of the Minister of Agriculture, Fisheries and Food is hereunto affixed on 21st July 1977.

(L.S.)   *John Silkin,*
Minister of Agriculture, Fisheries and Food.

25th July 1977.   *Bruce Millan,*
Secretary of State for Scotland.

27th July 1977.   *John Morris,*
Secretary of State for Wales.

EXPLANATORY NOTE

(This Note is not part of the Regulations.)

Under Regulation (EEC) No. 1078/77 of the Council of Ministers of the European Communities dated 17th May 1977, as supplemented by Regulation (EEC) No. 1307/77 of the Commission dated 15th June 1977 the details of two schemes are laid down. The purpose of one of these schemes is to encourage farmers at present engaged in producing and supplying milk or milk products to cease from supplying these commodities, and the other is to encourage farmers to change from the production of milk and milk products to the production of meat.

The present Regulations make provision for those matters which are left to Member States by the schemes and which are necessary for their proper implementation in the United Kingdom. They accordingly appoint the "competent authority" which will be responsible for administering the schemes in the various parts of the United Kingdom, and provide for powers of entry on to land by authorised officers acting on behalf of the competent authority for the purposes of marking, registering, inspecting and counting animals, verifying and registering the area farmed by the applicant and of examining relevant documents.

The Regulations give to the competent authority power to recover premiums paid in certain circumstances, and they also create a number of offences which are punishable on summary conviction by a fine not exceeding £400.

STATUTORY INSTRUMENTS

1977 No. 1306

CINEMATOGRAPHS AND CINEMATOGRAPH FILMS
EXHIBITION OF FILMS

The Films (Exemption from Quota) Order 1977

Made - - - -	14*th July* 1977
Laid before Parliament	14*th July* 1977
Coming into Operation	4*th August* 1977

The Secretary of State, in exercise of powers conferred by section 4(4) of the Films Act 1960(a), as amended by section 5 of the Films Act 1966(b), and now vested in him(c), and of all other powers enabling him in that behalf, and after consulting the Cinematograph Films Council, hereby makes the following Order:—

1. This Order may be cited as the Films (Exemption from Quota) Order 1977 and shall come into operation seven days after it has been approved by resolution of each House of Parliament.

2. The Secretary of State hereby directs that section 4(3) of the Films Act 1960 (which, as amended(d), provides for exemption from the quota requirements of that Act in respect of the exhibition of films at a cinema whose weekly average net box office receipts do not, during a specified period, exceed £150) shall have effect as if for the reference to £150 there were substituted a reference to £350.

Michael Meacher,
Parliamentary Under-Secretary of State,
Department of Trade.

4th July 1977.

---

a) 1960 c. 57.   **(b)** 1966 c. 48.   **(c)** S.I. 1970/1537 (1970 III, p. 5293).
d) *See* Films Act 1966 (c. 48), s. 5, and Films Act 1970 (c. 26), s. 12.

EXPLANATORY NOTE

(This Note is not part of the Order.)

The Films Act 1960, section 4(3) (as amended), provides for exemption from the quota requirements of that Act for any cinema whose weekly average net box office receipts do not exceed £150. This Order increases that amount to £350.

STATUTORY INSTRUMENTS

1977 No. 1307

EDUCATION, ENGLAND AND WALES

The Local Education Authority Awards Regulations 1977

Made - - - -	28th July 1977
Laid before Parliament	10th August 1977
Coming into Operation	1st September 1977

ARRANGEMENT OF REGULATIONS

PART I

GENERAL

PART II

AWARDS

PART III

PAYMENTS

SCHEDULES

Schedule 1.   Fees.
Schedule 2.   Requirements.
Schedule 3.   Resources.
Schedule 4.   Widows, widowers, divorced persons, etc.
Schedule 5.   Educational qualifications.
Schedule 6.   Sandwich courses.

The Secretary of State for Education and Science, in exercise of the powers conferred by sections 1 and 4(2) of, and paragraphs 3 and 4 of Schedule 1 to, the Education Act 1962(a) (as amended by section 1 of the Education Act 1975(b) and section 8 of the Education Act 1976(c), and vested in her(d), hereby makes the following Regulations:—

PART I

GENERAL

Citation, commencement and interpretation

1.—(1) These Regulations may be cited as the Local Education Authority Awards Regulations 1977 and shall come into operation on 1st September 1977.

(2) The Interpretation Act 1889(e) shall apply for the interpretation of these Regulations as it applies for the interpretation of an Act of Parliament.

(3) Without prejudice to paragraph (2) above, section 37 (exercise of powers before commencement) of the Interpretation Act 1889 shall apply in relation to these Regulations as it applies in relation to an Act; and section 38(2) (effect of repeals) of that Act shall have effect in relation to the Regulations revoked by these Regulations as if they were enactments repealed by an Act.

Definitions

2.—(1) In these Regulations, unless the context otherwise requires—

"academic authority" means, in relation to an establishment, the governing body, or other body having the functions of a governing body;

"authority" means local education authority;

"award" includes an award bestowed under previous Awards Regulations;

"Certificate in Education" includes Teacher's Certificate;

"course", in relation to any designated course except one prescribed under Regulation 7(1)(*d*)(ii) or (iii), includes a course of full-time study and a sandwich course;

"establishment" means a university or establishment of further education, and "establishment of further education" includes a college of education;

"high-cost country" means Austria, Belgium, Denmark, Federal Republic of Germany, France, Japan, Luxembourg, Netherlands, Norway, Sweden, Switzerland or the United States of America;

"independent student" means a student who either—

(*a*) attained the age of 25 before the beginning of the year for which payments in pursuance of his award fall to be made, or

---

(a) 1962 c. 12.   (b) 1975 c. 2.   (c) 1976 c 81.
(d) S.I. 1964/490 (1964 I, p. 800).   (e) 1889 c. 63.

(*b*) supported himself out of his earnings for any three years preceding the first year of his course, there being treated for the purposes of this provision as a period during which he so supported himself (subject to paragraph (2) below)—

(i) any period not exceeding six months during which the student was registered for employment as mentioned in section 5 of the Supplementary Benefits Act 1976(**a**) or in receipt of unemployment benefit under section 14(1)(*a*) of the Social Security Act 1975(**b**);

(ii) any period during which the student held a State Studentship or comparable award;

(iii) any period during which the student received sickness benefit, invalidity pension or maternity allowance under section 14(1)(*b*), 15(1)(*b*), 22(1) or 36(1) of the Social Security Act 1975; or

(iv) in the case of a student who is or has been married, any period during which he could not reasonably have been expected to support himself out of his earnings because he had the care of his dependent children;

"maintenance grant", "full maintenance grant" and "minimum maintenance payment" have the meanings respectively assigned to them by Regulation 14 below;

"previous Awards Regulations" means the Regulations revoked by Regulation 3 below and any Regulations superseded by those Regulations;

"sandwich course" and, in relation to such a course, "prescribed proportion" and "sandwich year" have the meanings respectively assigned to them by paragraph 1 of Schedule 6;

"statutory award" means any award bestowed or grant paid under the Education Act 1962, as amended by the Education Act 1975 and the Education Act 1976, or any comparable grant which is paid out of moneys provided by Parliament;

"student" means a person upon whom an award has been bestowed under these Regulations or previous Awards Regulations;

"university" means a university in the United Kingdom and includes a university college and a constituent college, school or hall of a university;

"year", in relation to a course, means the period of twelve months beginning on 1st January, 1st April or 1st September according as the academic year of the course in question begins in the spring, the summer or the autumn respectively; and references to the first year of a designated course shall be construed accordingly.

(2) The definition of "independent student" in paragraph (1) above shall have effect as if any reference therein to an enactment contained in the Supplementary Benefits Act 1976 or the Social Security Act 1975 included, in relation to a period before the coming into force of the enactment in question, a reference to the corresponding enactment then in force.

(3) In these Regulations "designated course" means a course prescribed by or under Regulation 7 and any reference otherwise unqualified to such a course

---

(**a**) 1976 c. 71.　　　　　　(**b**) 1975 c. 14.

shall, as the context requires, be construed as a reference to a designated course which the person in question attends or has applied to attend; and any reference to a first degree course, a Dip HE course, a course for the Higher Diploma, a course of initial training for teachers or a course comparable to a first degree course shall be construed in accordance with Regulation 7.

(4) In these Regulations references to payments made to a student include references to payments made to the academic authority in respect of a student by virtue of Regulation 22(2).

(5) In calculating a person's income for any year any reduction for income tax is to be made by calculating the tax payable on the income received in that year as if the year were a year of assessment within the meaning of the Income Tax Acts (the necessary apportionment being made in any case where the relevant provisions of those Acts change during the year).

(6) For the purposes of these Regulations a person's marriage is to be treated as having been terminated, not only by the death of the other spouse or the annulment or dissolution of the marriage by an order of a court of competent jurisdiction, but also by virtue of the parties to the marriage ceasing to live together, whether or not an order for their separation has been made by any court.

Revocations

3.—(1) The Local Education Authorities Awards Regulations 1975(a), the Local Education Authorities Awards (Amendment) Regulations 1975(b) and, subject to paragraph (2) below, the Local Education Authorities Awards (Amendment) Regulations 1976(c) are hereby revoked.

(2) Nothing in this Regulation shall affect the said Regulations of 1976 so far as they amend the Students' Dependants' Allowances Regulations 1975(d).

(a) S.I. 1975/1207 (1975 II, p. 4142). (b) S.I. 1975/1697 (1975 III, p. 5810).
(c) S.I. 1976/1087 (1976 II, p. 2896). (d) S.I. 1975/1225 (1975 II, p. 4213).

PART II
AWARDS

Duty to bestow awards

4. Subject to and in accordance with these Regulations, it shall be the duty of an authority to bestow an award in respect of a person's attendance at a designated course during an academic year beginning after 31st August 1977 if—

(*a*) the person is ordinarily resident in the authority's area (within the meaning of section 1 of the Education Act 1962), and

(*b*) an award has not already been bestowed upon him under the previous Awards Regulations, by that or another authority, in respect of the course in question.

Modification of provisions for determining ordinary residence

5.—(1) This Regulation shall have effect for modifying paragraph 2 of Schedule 1 to the Education Act 1962 in the case of a person who, apart from this Regulation, would be treated by virtue of that paragraph as having been ordinarily resident in the area of more than one authority within the period of twelve months ending with the date, subject to paragraph (3) below, of the beginning of the course.

(2) Any such person as is described in paragraph (1) above shall be treated as being ordinarily resident in the area of the authority in which he was so resident on the last day of the month of October, February, or June (according as the academic year of the course begins in the spring, the summer or the autumn respectively) preceding, subject to paragraph (3) below, the beginning of the course.

(3) Where the course began before 1st September 1977, paragraphs (1) and (2) above shall have effect as if each reference to the beginning of the course were a reference to the beginning of the academic year of the course first starting after that date.

No area students

6.—(1) A person who apart from this Regulation would by virtue of paragraph 2 of Schedule 1 to the Education Act 1962, fall to be treated for the purposes of section 1 of that Act as not being ordinarily resident in any area shall for those purposes be treated as being so resident—

(*a*) in the area in which he was resident on the relevant day;

(*b*) if he was not resident in the area of any authority on the relevant day but at any time during the two years preceding that day would have fallen to be treated as belonging to an area for the purposes of section 7 of the Education (Miscellaneous Provisions) Act 1953(**a**), in the last such area;

(*c*) in any other case, in the area in which the establishment is situated.

(2) In this Regulation "relevant day" means the last day of the month of October, February or June (according as the academic year of the course begins in the spring, the summer or the autumn, respectively) preceding the beginning of the course or, where it began before 1st September 1977, preceding the beginning of the academic year of the course first starting after that date; and "area" means area of an authority.

(**a**) 1953 c. 33.

Designated courses

7.—(1) The following are prescribed as designated courses—

(a) a first degree course, that is to say—

(i) a course provided by an establishment for a first degree of a university or for the degree of Bachelor of Medicine or an equivalent degree;

(ii) a course provided by an establishment of further aducation for a first degree of the Council for National Academic Awards;

(b) a Dip HE course, that is to say—

(i) a course provided by an establishment for the Diploma of Higher Education;

(ii) a course provided by an establishment for the Diploma of Higher Education or a first degree as the student may elect after the commencement of the course;

(c) a course for the Higher Diploma, that is to say, a course provided by an establishment of further education for the Higher National Diploma, the Higher Diploma of the Technician Education Council ("TEC") or the Higher National Diploma of the Business Education Council ("BEC");

(d) a course of initial training for teachers, that is to say—

(i) a course for the initial training of teachers (other than a course for the degree of Bachelor of Education) provided by an establishment;

(ii) a part-time day course of teacher training, involving not less than 3 days attendance a week during the course, for the time being prescribed for the purposes of this provision by the Secretary of State;

(iii) any other course of teacher training, whether part-time or partly full-time and partly part-time, for the time being so prescribed;

(e) a course comparable to a first degree course, that is to say—

(i) a course of at least 3 academic years duration provided by a university for a certificate (except the University of Oxford Certificate in Fine Art) or diploma;

(ii) a course for the time being prescribed for the purposes of this provision by the Secretary of State.

(2) In this Regulation references to an establishment and an establishment of further education do not include references to establishments of further education which are neither maintained, nor assisted by recurrent grants, out of public funds.

Conditions

8.—(1) Subject to paragraph (2), the duty of an authority to bestow an award shall be subject to the conditions that—

(a) an application in writing for the award reaches the authority before the end of the term in which the student commences to attend the course or, where it began before 1st September 1977, before the end of the first term beginning on or after that date; and (*b*) the applicant gives the authority a written undertaking that, where any sum is paid, whether as a provisional payment or not, in pursuance of the award before the end of the year in respect of which the sum is payable, he will if called upon to do so repay the amount by which the sums paid during the year exceed (for whatever reason) the grant payable in respect of that year.

(2) If the applicant is a minor, paragraph (1)(*b*) shall have effect, with the necessary modifications, as if the references to the applicant were references to the applicant or his parent.

Exceptions relating to attendance at previous courses

9.—(1) An authority shall not bestow an award on a person in respect of his attendance at a course if it is their duty to transfer an award already bestowed on him so that it is held in respect of his attendance at that course.

(2) Subject to paragraphs (5) and (6) below, an authority shall not be under a duty to bestow an award on a person in respect of his attendance at a course if—

(*a*) (in the case of a person who has not attained the age of 25 before the first year) he has previously attended a full-time course of further education of not less than two academic years' duration or successfully completed a part-time course of such education of equivalent duration or attended or, as the case may be, successfully completed a comparable course outside the United Kingdom; or

(*b*) (in the case of a person who has attained the age of 25 before the first year) he has previously attended a full-time course of not less than two academic years' duration to which Schedule 1 to the Further Education Regulations 1975(**a**) applies or successfully completed a part-time course of equivalent duration to which that Schedule applies or attended or, as the case may be successfully completed a comparable course outside the United Kingdom—

unless (in either case) the course which he previously attended or, as the case may be, completed—

(i) was a course of not more than two academic years' duration or a part-time course of equivalent duration, being one to which Schedule 1 to the Further Education Regulations 1975 applies; or

(ii) was a course for a qualification prescribed by Schedule 5; or

(iii) was provided by a college designated by the Schedule to the State Awards Regulations 1963(**b**), as amended(**c**), (colleges providing long term residential courses of full-time education for adults).

(3) Subject to paragraphs (5) and (6) below, an authority shall not be under a duty to bestow an award on a person in respect of his attendance at a course prescribed by or under Regulation 7(1)(*a*), (*d*) or (*e*) if he has previously—

(*a*) attended a course prescribed by or under Regulation 7(1)(*a*), (*d*)(i) or (*e*) or successfully completed a course prescribed under Regulation 7(1)(*d*)(ii) or (iii); or

(**a**) S.I. 1975/1054 (1975 II, p. 3676).
(**b**) S.I. 1963/1223 (1963 II, p. 2035).
(**c**) The relevant amending instrument is S.I. 1975/940 (1975 II, p. 3284).

(b) attended a course prescribed by Regulation 7(1)(b)(ii) in a case where after the commencement of the course he elected to study for a first degree.

(4) Subject to paragraph (6) below, an authority shall not be under a duty to bestow an award on any person in respect of his attendance at any course prescribed by Regulation 7(1)(b) or (c) if he has previously—

(a) successfully completed a part-time course of teacher training prescribed under sub-paragraph (d)(ii) or (iii) of Regulation 7(1), or

(b) attended any other course prescribed by or under Regulation 7(1).

(5) Nothing in paragraphs (2) and (3) above shall affect the duty of an authority to bestow an award on a person—

(a) in respect of his attendance at a course for the post-graduate Certificate in Education (or a comparable qualification) or for the Art Teacher's Certificate or Diploma (or a comparable qualification);

(b) in respect of his attendance at any full-time course of initial training as a teacher of one academic year's duration, or a comparable part-time course, not within sub-paragraph (a) above, unless he has for more than three years held a statutory award in respect of his attendance at a full-time course to which Schedule 1 to the Further Education Regulations 1975 applies or a comparable course outside England and Wales.

(6) In the case of any course which began before 1st September 1977, the duty of an authority to bestow an award on a person in respect thereof shall not be affected by paragraph (2), (3) or (4) above by reason only of his having attended the course from its beginning.

(7) For the purposes of this Regulation a person shall only be treated as having attended a course if he has attended that course for more than one term; and it is hereby declared that any reference to a person having attended or completed a course shall be construed as a reference to his having done so before or after the coming into operation of these Regulations.

Other exceptions

10. An authority shall not be under a duty to bestow an award in respect of a person's attendance at a course—

(a) upon a person who has not been ordinarily resident in the United Kingdom for the three years immediately preceding the first year of the course in question unless the authority are satisfied that he has not been so resident only because he, his wife (or, in the case of a woman student, her husband) or his parent was for the time being employed outside the United Kingdom;

(b) upon a person who has, in the opinion of the authority, shown himself by his conduct to be unfitted to receive an award;

(c) in the case of a course comparable to a first degree course, upon a person who does not possess a qualification prescribed by Schedule 5.

Transfer of awards

11.—(1) An award shall be transferred by the authority so as to be held in respect of attendance at a course other than that in respect of which it is held in any case where—

(a) subject to paragraph (2) below, on the recommendation of the academic authority the student commences to attend another course at the establishment;

(b) subject to paragraph (2) below, with the consent of the academic authority of both establishments concerned, given on educational grounds, the student commences to attend a course at another establishment;

(c) with the consent of the academic authority of both establishments concerned, the student completes his course at another establishment by attending a course which began in the same year as the course at the first establishment concerned and is of the same duration as, and in other respects comparable with, that course;

(d) on the completion of a Dip HE course the student is admitted to a course prescribed by or under Regulation 7(1)(a), (d) or (e);

(e) after commencing a course for the Certificate in Education, the student is, on or before the completion of that course, admitted to a course for the degree of Bachelor of Education;

(f) on the completion of a course for the Certificate in Education or the degree of Bachelor of Education, the student is admitted to a course of initial training for teachers of the deaf.

(2) For the purposes of sub-paragraphs (a) and (b) of paragraph (1) above, a recommendation or consent shall be given before the expiry of two months after the end of the first year of the course in respect of which the award was originally bestowed and, notwithstanding anything in the said sub-paragraphs, the authority may, after consultation with the academic authority, refuse to transfer the award thereunder if they are satisfied that when the student applied for it he did not intend to complete the course to which the application related.

(3) It shall be the duty of the authority to transfer the award under sub-paragraphs (d), (e) or (f) of paragraph (1) whether or not the two courses are provided by the same establishment.

Termination of awards

12.—(1) The award shall terminate on the expiry of the period ordinarily required for the completion of the course:

Provided that—

(a) if the academic authority refuse to allow the student to complete the course, the authority shall terminate the award forthwith;

(b) if the student does not complete the course within the period ordinarily required, the authority—

(i) may extend the award until the student has completed the course; and

(ii) shall extend it for a period equivalent to any period in respect of which they have made any payment under Regulation 23(1) below.

(2) The authority may, after consultation with the academic authority, terminate the award if they are satisfied that the student has shown himself by his conduct to be unfitted to hold it.

Supplementary provisions

13. The authority may require the student to provide from time to time such information as they consider necessary for the exercise of their functions under this Part; and if in the case of any student the authority are satisfied that he has wilfully failed to comply with any such requirement or has provided information which he knows to be false in a material particular or has recklessly provided information which is so false in a material particular, they may terminate the award or withhold any payments due under it as they see fit.

PART III

PAYMENTS

Payments

14. Subject to Regulation 13 above and Regulations 20, 23 and 24 below, the authority shall in respect of each year pay in pursuance of the award—

(*a*) in respect of fees, a sum equal to the aggregate of any such fees payable in respect of the student as are described in Schedule 1;

(*b*) in respect of maintenance—

(i) except in a case in which Regulation 17, 18, 19 or 21 below applies, either the sum of £80 (in these Regulations called "the minimum maintenance payment") or a grant calculated in accordance with Regulation 15 below (in these Regulations called "the maintenance grant" or "the full maintenance grant"), whichever is the greater;

(ii) in a case in which one of those Regulations applies (subject to Regulation 17(3) a sum or grant determined in accordance with the Regulation in question.

Calculation of maintenance grant

15.—(1) The maintenance grant in respect of any year shall be the amount by which the student's resources fall short of his requirements and for the purpose of ascertaining that amount—

(*a*) the requirements of the student shall be taken to be the aggregate of such of the amounts specified in Schedule 2 as are applicable in his case;

(*b*) the resources of the student shall be taken to be the aggregate of his income for the year calculated in accordance with Part 1 of Schedule 3 and any contribution applicable in his case by virtue of Part 2 or 3 of that Schedule.

(2) This Regulation and Schedules 2 and 3 shall have effect—

(*a*) in such a case as is mentioned in Schedule 4, subject to the provisions thereof;

(*b*) in such a case as is mentioned in the proviso to Regulation 17(2), subject as therein provided.

Assessment of requirements and resources

16. The requirements and resources of a student shall be assessed by the authority, and for the purpose of the exercise of their functions under this Regulation the authority shall require the student to provide from time to time such information as they consider necessary as to the resources of any person whose means are relevant to the assessment of his requirements and resources.

Sandwich courses

17.—(1) This Regulation shall apply where the course is a sandwich course unless the student is a member of a religious order and Regulation 18 below applies.

(2) The payment in respect of maintenance under Regulation 14(*b*) above shall be the minimum maintenance payment or a maintenance grant, whichever is the greater:

Provided that, for the purpose of calculating the maintenance grant in respect of a sandwich year, Schedules 2 and 3 shall have effect subject to the provisions of Schedule 6.

(3) No payment in respect of maintenance under Regulation 14(*b*) above shall be made in respect of a year in which there are no periods of full-time study.

Members of religious orders

18.—(1) This Regulation shall apply where the student is a member of a religious order ("the Order") unless the course is a part-time course of teacher training prescribed under Regulation 7(1)(*d*)(iii) above and Regulation 19 below applies.

(2) Subject to paragraph (5), the payment in respect of maintenance under Regulation 14(*b*) above shall be the sum specified as appropriate in the case of the student in paragraph (3) or (4) below:

Provided that—

  (*a*) where the course is a sandwich course, the payment in respect of a sandwich year shall be the prescribed proportion of the sum so specified;

  (*b*) where the course is a part-time course of teacher training prescribed under Regulation 7(1)(*d*)(ii) above, the payment shall be three-quarters of the sum so specified.

(3) In the case of a student who resides at his parent's home or in a house of the Order, the appropriate sum shall be £430.

(4) In the case of any other student, the appropriate sum shall be £555 except that, where he is attending a course—

  (*a*) at the University of London,

  (*b*) at an establishment within the area comprising the City of London and the metropolitan police district, or

  (*c*) at an institution in a country outside the United Kingdom which is not a high-cost country,

it shall be £630 and, where he is attending a course at an institution in a high-cost country, it shall be £725.

(5) The payment in respect of maintenance, determined as aforesaid, shall, in the case of any student who is attending such a course as is mentioned in paragraph 13(1) of Part 2 of Schedule 2 and for the purposes thereof necessarily incurs expenditure in the purchase of special equipment, be increased by so much of that expenditure as does not during the course exceed £40.

Part-time courses of teacher training

19.—(1) This Regulation shall apply where the course is a part-time course of teacher training prescribed under sub-paragraph (*d*)(ii) or (*d*)(iii) of Regulation 7(1) above unless, in the case of a course prescribed under the said sub-paragraph (*d*)(ii), the student is a member of a religious order and Regulation 18 above applies.

(2) Where the course is prescribed under the said sub-paragraph (*d*)(ii), the payment in respect of maintenance under Regulation 14(*b*) shall be the minimum maintenance payment or a grant equal to three-quarters of the full maintenance grant, whichever is the greater.

(3) Where the course is prescribed under the said sub-paragraph (*d*)(iii), the said payment under Regulation 14(*b*) shall be—

(*a*) in the case of a student employed full-time as a teacher, a sum equal to any such expenditure which he is obliged to incur as is mentioned in sub-paragraph (1)(*a*), (*b*) or (*c*) of paragraph 10 of Part 2 of Schedule 2.

(*b*) in the case of any other student, a sum equal to the aggregate of the amount by which such expenditure exceeds £32 and the amount of £245.

Assisted students

20.—(1) Notwithstanding anything in the preceding provisions of these Regulations, no payment under Regulation 14(*a*) or (*b*) shall be made to a student in respect of any year in respect whereof he receives such payments as are mentioned in paragraph (2) below amounting to not less than the aggregate of—

(*a*) such fees payable in respect of him as are described in Schedule 1, and

(*b*) his requirements for ordinary maintenance ascertained in accordance with Part 1 of Schedule 2.

(2) The payments referred to in paragraph (1) above are the aggregate payments received by the student—

(*a*) by way of remuneration paid in respect of any period for which he had leave of absence from his employment to attend the course, and

(*b*) in pursuance of any scholarship, studentship, exhibition or award of similar description bestowed on him in respect of the course (otherwise than in pursuance of section 1 of the Education Act 1962);

except that, if the student's course is a part-time course of teacher training prescribed under Regulation 7(1)(*d*)(iii) above, any payments by way of remuneration shall be disregarded.

Students provided with free board and lodging

21.—(1) This Regulation shall apply where the student is provided with free board and lodging by the academic authority in accordance with arrangements whereunder fees for board and lodging are charged only to those students whose resources exceed their requirements (ascertained as provided in Regulation 15).

(2) The payment in respect of maintenance under Regulation 14(*b*) above shall be a maintenance grant calculated in accordance with Regulation 15.

Method of payment

22.—(1) The authority shall make any payment due under these Regulations in such instalments (if any) and at such times as they consider appropriate; and in the exercise of their functions under this paragraph the authority may in particular make provisional payments pending the final calculation of the grant.

(2) Any payment in respect of such fees as are described in Schedule 1 may be made to the academic authority but subject thereto all payments shall be made to the student.

Discretionary payments

23.—(1) In respect of any period during which the student repeats any part of his course, the authority shall not be required to make any payments under Regulation 14(a) or (b) above but may pay in pursuance of the award such sums (if any) as they consider appropriate, being sums not exceeding the amount of any payments that would, apart from this Regulation, be payable to that student in respect of that period.

(2)(a) This paragraph shall apply in the case of a student who—

(i) has previously attended a course of more than one, but not more than two, academic years' duration to which Schedule 1 to the Further Education Regulations 1975 applies or successfully completed a part-time course corresponding to such a course ("the previous course"), and

(ii) holds an award bestowed, or transferred in pursuance of Regulation 11(1)(d) above so as to be held, in respect of a course prescribed by or under Regulation 7(a), (d) or (e), not being a course for the degree of Bachelor of Education or of initial training for teachers, in either case, of one academic year's duration ("the current course").

(b) If the academic authority do not treat the student's attendance at the previous course as excusing him from attending the whole of the first two academic years of the current course, then, in respect of so much of those first two years as he is not excused from attending, the authority shall not be required to make any payments under Regulation 14(a) or (b) above but may pay in pursuance of the award such sums (if any) as they consider appropriate, being sums not exceeding the amount of any payments that would, apart from this Regulation, be payable to that student in respect of that period.

Suspension, etc. of payments

24.—(1) Without prejudice to Regulation 13, in the case of any student who is for the time being in default of any requirement to provide such information as is described in Regulation 16, the authority may withhold, in whole or in part, any payment due to him by way of maintenance grant:

Provided that, in the case of a student in respect of whom apart from this paragraph such a grant would be payable (other than a student to whom Regulation 21 above applies), the authority shall in respect of any year in which he remains in default pay a sum not less than the minimum maintenance payment.

(2) Any payment otherwise due under these Regulations shall be reduced by an amount equal to the sum specified by paragraph (3) below in respect of—

(a) any period after the termination of the award; and

(b) any period during which the student is excluded from attendance at the course by the academic authority or is absent without leave;

and in respect of any other period during which the student does not attend the course (other than a period of not more than 28 days due to his illness) they may reduce the payment by such amount not exceeding that sum, as having regard to all relevant circumstances, they consider appropriate.

(3) The sum referred to in paragraph (2) above is the aggregate of—

(*a*) fees otherwise due that are not payable by reason of the student not attending the course; and

(*b*) the appropriate proportion of the balance of any maintenance grant payable to him.

Regulations 14, 20(1) and 22(2)

SCHEDULE 1

Fees

The fees referred to in Regulation 14(*a*) are—

(*a*) the aggregate of any fees for admission, registration or matriculation (including matriculation exemption), any sessional or tuition fees, any composition fee and any graduation fee (in each case excluding any element thereof representing or attributable to any such fee as is mentioned in the following sub-paragraphs, or to maintenance) subject to a maximum of £750 in the case of a course which is a post-graduate one or £500 in the case of any other course:

Provided that the said maximum shall not apply in the case of a course at the Guildhall School of Music, the London School of Music, the Royal Academy of Music, the Royal Academy Schools, the Royal College of Music or the Trinity College of Music;

(*b*) college fees or dues at the universities of Cambridge, Durham, Kent, Lancaster, Oxford and York (excluding any element thereof representing or attributable to any such fee as is mentioned in the following sub-paragraphs or to maintenance);

(*c*) any fees charged by an external body in respect of examinations or the validation of the course or otherwise charged by such a body whose requirements must (for the purposes of the course) be satisfied, or any fees attributable to fees so charged;

(*d*) any fee (howsoever described) by way of subscription to a students' union, junior common room or similar body where either—

    (i) membership is obligatory by virtue of any requirement contained in, or having effect under, the instruments regulating the conduct of the establishment, or

    (ii) the fee is an element of a composition fee.

SCHEDULE 2   Regulations 15(1)(*a*), 18(5)
19(3) and 20(1)

REQUIREMENTS

PART 1

ORDINARY MAINTENANCE

1. The requirements of the student referred to in Regulation 15(1)(*a*) shall include his requirement for ordinary maintenance during—

(*a*) any period while he is attending the course, and

(*b*) the Christmas and Easter vacations;

and the amount of such requirement ("ordinary maintenance requirement") shall be determined in accordance with this Part of this Schedule.

2.—(1) Subject to paragraph 4 below, this paragraph shall apply in the case of—

(*a*) any student who, on the recommendation of the academic authority, resides in the establishment or in a hostel or other accommodation administered by the academic authority;

(*b*) any independent or married student who does not reside at his parents' home;

(*c*) any other student who does not reside at his parents' home, except where he can in the opinion of the authority conveniently attend the course from his parents' home and the authority, after consultation with the academic authority, consider that in all the circumstances the ordinary maintenance requirement specified in paragraph 3(2) below would be appropriate; and

(*d*) any student residing at his parents' home whose parents by reason of age, incapacity or otherwise cannot reasonably be expected to support him and in respect of whom the authority are satisfied that in all the circumstances the ordinary maintenance requirement specified herein would be appropriate.

(2) In the case of such a student the ordinary maintenance requirement shall be £1,010 except that where he is attending—

(*a*) a course at the University of London;

(*b*) a course at an establishment within the area comprising the City of London and the metropolitan police district;

(*c*) as part of his course, at an institution in a country outside the United Kingdom which is not a high cost country,

it shall be £1,145 and, where he is attending, as part of his course, at an institution in a high-cost country it shall be £1,315.

3.—(1) Subject to paragraph 4 below, this paragraph shall apply in the case of any other student, that is to say, in the case of—

(*a*) a student residing at his parents' home, except where the conditions specified in paragraph 2(1)(*d*) are satisfied;

(*b*) a student whose case falls within the exception to paragraph 2(1)(*c*).

(2) In the case of such a student the ordinary maintenance requirement shall be £785.

4.—(1) This paragraph shall apply, to the exclusion of paragraph 2 or 3 above, in the case of a student who is provided with board and lodging by the academic authority in accordance with arrangements under which fees for board and lodging are charged only to those students whose resources exceed their requirements (ascertained as provided in Regulation 15).

(2) In the case of such a student the ordinary maintenance requirement shall be £430.

PART 2

SUPPLEMENTARY MAINTENANCE ETC.

5. The requirements of the student referred to in Regulation 15(1)(a) shall include his requirements—

(a) for supplementary maintenance in the cases and for the periods mentioned in paragraphs 6, 7, 8 and 14 below, and

(b) in respect of such expenditure as is mentioned in paragraphs 9 to 13 and 15 below;

and the amount of any such requirement ("supplementary requirement") shall be determined in accordance with this Part of this Schedule.

6.—(1) This paragraph shall apply in the case of a student who attends at his course for a period ("excess period") in any academic year in excess of—

(a) in the case of the University of Oxford or Cambridge, 25 weeks 3 days;

(b) in any other case, 30 weeks 3 days;

except that this paragraph shall not apply where the student is provided with board and lodging as mentioned in paragraph 4 above.

(2) In respect of each week and any part of a week comprised in the excess period the supplementary requirement shall be in the case of—

(a) a student residing at his parents' home, £10.80;

(b) a student not so residing, £18.30 except that where he is attending—

(i) a course at the University of London;

(ii) a course at an establishment within the area comprising the City of London and the metropolitan police district;

(iii) as part of his course, at an institution in a country outside the United Kingdom which is not a high-cost country,

it shall be £22.80 and, where he is attending, as part of his course, at an institution in a high-cost country it shall be £28.50.

7. (1) This paragraph shall apply in the case of a student who attends at his course for a period of not less than 45 weeks in any year.

(2) In respect of each complete week comprised in the period in that year for which he is not attending his course, the student's supplementary requirement shall be determined in accordance with paragraph 6(2) above.

8.—(1) This paragraph shall apply, unless paragraph 7 above applies, in the case of a student at an establishment of further education which is not wholly maintained out of public funds, or at a service establishment mentioned in sub-paragraph (3), who undertakes a period of vacation study on the recommendation of the academic authority—

(a) under the guidance of that authority, or

(b) where he is studying modern languages either—

(i) under such guidance, or

(ii) with a family, approved for the purposes hereof by that authority, in a country whose language is a main language of the course.

(2) In respect of each day of such vacation study the supplementary requirement shall be such amount, if any, as the authority consider appropriate not exceeding the amount hereinafter specified, that is to say—

(a) in the case of a student residing at his parents' home, not exceeding £2.20;

(b) in the case of a student not so residing, not exceeding £3.30 or, where he is studying—

(i) at the University of London;

(ii) at an establishment within the area comprising the City of London and the metropolitan police district;

(iii) at an institution, or as mentioned in sub-paragraph (1)(b)(ii) above, in a country outside the United Kingdom which is not a high-cost country,

not exceeding £3.90 or, where he is studying at an institution, or as mentioned in sub-paragraph (1)(b)(ii) above, in a high-cost country, not exceeding £4.70.

(3) The service establishments referred to in paragraph (1) are the Royal Military College of Science, Shrivenham and the Royal Naval Engineering College, Manadon.

9.—(1) This paragraph shall apply in the case of a student at an establishment of further education which is not wholly maintained out of public funds, or at a service establishment mentioned in paragraph 8(3) above, who incurs additional expenditure on his maintenance for the purpose of attending, as part of his course, a period of term-time residential study away from the establishment, being study within the United Kingdom unless (apart from the said period) he is attending, as part of his course, at an institution in a country outside the United Kingdom and the study is away from that institution.

(2) Subject to paragraph 16 below, in respect of each day for which the student incurs such additional expenditure his supplementary requirement shall be £3.20 or the daily additional expenditure, whichever is the less.

10.—(1) This paragraph shall apply in the case of a student who is obliged to incur expenditure—

(a) within the United Kingdom for the purpose of attending the establishment;

(b) within or outside the United Kingdom, for the purpose of attending, as part of his course, any period of study at an institution in a country outside the United Kingdom;

(c) in the case of a student at an establishment of further education which is not wholly maintained out of public funds, or at a service establishment mentioned in paragraph 8(3) above—

    (i) within or outside the United Kingdom, for the purpose of attending a period of vacation study or of term-time residential study in respect of which he has a supplementary requirement under paragraph 8 or 9 above, and

    (ii) without prejudice to the preceding provisions of this paragraph, on any other term-time travel within the United Kingdom in connection with his course.

(2) Subject to paragraph 16 below, the student's supplementary requirement in respect of such expenditure shall be the amount by which, in the aggregate, it exceeds £32.

(3) In the case of an establishment which is a constituent college, school or hall of a university, or is a university with such constituent establishments, the reference in sub-paragraph (1)(a) above to the student attending the establishment shall be construed as including a reference to his attending, in connection with his course, any constituent establishment of the university in question.

11.—(1) This paragraph shall apply in the case of a student whose home is for the time being outside the United Kingdom and who incurs expenditure travelling between his home and the establishment at the beginning and end of term.

(2) The student's supplementary requirement in respect of such expenditure shall be of such amount as the authority consider appropriate, not exceeding the expenditure necessarily incurred.

12.—(1) This paragraph shall apply in the case of a student who reasonably incurs any expenditure in insuring against liability for the cost of medical treatment provided outside the United Kingdom for any illness or bodily injury contracted or suffered during a period of study outside the United Kingdom.

(2) Subject to paragraph 16 below, the student's supplementary requirement in respect of such expenditure shall be the amount reasonably incurred.

13.—(1) This paragraph shall apply in the case of a student who—

    (a) is attending a course in architecture, art and design, domestic science, landscape architecture, medicine, music, ophthalmic optics, physical education, town and country planning or veterinary science (or medicine) or a course comprising any of those subjects as a principal subject, and

    (b) for the purposes thereof necessarily incurs expenditure in the purchase of special equipment.

(2) The student's supplementary requirement in respect of such expenditure shall be so much of the expenditure as does not during the course exceed £40.

14.—(1) This paragraph shall apply in the case of a student who, in any week during a vacation (not being a week in respect of which a supplementary requirement falls to be determined under paragraph 7 or 8) would, in the opinion of the authority, suffer undue hardship but for this paragraph.

(2) The student's supplementary requirement in respect of each such week shall be such amount as the authority consider appropriate having regard to his means, not exceeding £21.85.

15.—(1) This paragraph shall apply in the case of a disabled student where the authority are satisfied that, by reason of his disability, he is obliged to incur additional expenditure in respect of his attendance at the course.

(2) The student's supplementary requirement in respect of such expenditure shall be such amount as the authority consider appropriate, not exceeding £160.

16.—(1) The following provisions, that is to say—

(*a*) paragraph 9;

(*b*) paragraph 10, in its application to expenditure incurred outside the United Kingdom, and

(*c*) paragraph 12,

shall have effect subject to sub-paragraph (2) below.

(2) A student's supplementary requirement under any of the said paragraphs (in the case of paragraph 10 in its application as aforesaid)—

(*a*) must be the amount specified in sub-paragraph (2) of the paragraph in question only where the academic authority certify that if the student did not undertake the relevant period of study he would not be eligible to complete his course;

(*b*) where the academic authority do not so certify, shall be such amount as the authority consider appropriate, not exceeding the amount so specified.

PART 3

MAINTENANCE OF DEPENDANTS

17.—(1) The requirements of the student referred to in Regulation 15(1)(*a*) shall include his requirements for the maintenance of dependants and the amount of any such requirement ("dependants requirement") shall be determined in accordance with this Part of this Schedule.

(2) In this Part of this Schedule a reference to the 1971 Regulations is a reference to the Awards (First Degree, etc. Courses) Regulations 1971(**a**), as from time to time amended(**b**); and a reference to any provision of those Regulations includes a reference to a provision to the like effect contained in arrangements made under section 2(3) of the Education Act 1962 and "award" shall be construed accordingly.

(3) In this Part of this Schedule—

"child" includes a person adopted in pursuance of adoption proceedings and a step-child;

"dependant" means, subject to sub-paragraphs (4) and (5) below, the student's spouse or a person dependent on the student, not being a person living with him as his spouse;

(**a**) S.I. 1971/1297 (1971 II, p. 3722).
(**b**) S.I. 1972/1124; 1973/1233, 1298, 1644; 1974/1231, 1540 (1972 II, p. 3326; 1973 II, pp. 3683; 3916; III, p. 5094; 1974 II, p. 4665; III, p. 5831).

"income" means income for the year from all sources less income tax, social security contributions and child benefit and, in the case of the spouse, the amount of any payment made by the student or his spouse and previously made by the student in pursuance of an obligation reasonably incurred before the first year.

(4) A person, including the student's spouse, shall not be treated as a dependant of a student during any period for which the person holds a statutory award in respect of his attendance at a full-time course to which Schedule 1 to the Further Education Regulations 1975 applies, at a comparable course outside England and Wales or at a course prescribed under Regulation 7(1)(*d*)(ii).

(5) A person, other than the student's spouse, shall not be treated as a dependant of a student if the person's income exceeds by £215 or more—

(*a*) in the case of an adult dependant or, if the student has neither a dependent spouse nor such a dependant, in the case of the eldest dependent child, the sum specified in paragraph 18(4)(*a*) below,

(*b*) subject as aforesaid, in the case of a dependent child, the appropriate sum specified in paragraph 18(4)(*b*) below.

18.—(1) This paragraph shall apply in the case of a student who married before the first year of his course where he has dependants and either—

(*a*) is an independent student; or

(*b*) held an award bestowed in respect of attendance at a course beginning before 1st September 1975 and is a person to whom paragraph 10 of Schedule 1 to the 1971 Regulations applied by virtue of sub-paragraph 2(*c*) of that paragraph;

except that for the purpose of determining a student's dependants requirement for an adult dependant other than his spouse it shall be immaterial whether or not he married as aforesaid.

(2) The dependants requirement of the student shall, subject to paragraphs 20 and 21 below, be—

(*a*) if the student's spouse holds a statutory award and in calculating payments under it account is taken of the spouse's dependants requirement, one half of the amount determined in accordance with sub-paragraphs (3) and (4) below;

(*b*) in any other case, subject to paragraph 19 below, the whole of the amount so determined.

(3) The amount referred to in sub-paragraph (2) above shall be the amount which is $X - (Y - Z)$ where—

(*a*) X is the aggregate of the relevant sums specified in sub-paragraph (4) below;

(*b*) Y is the aggregate of the income of the student's dependants;

(*c*) Z is so much of the sum ascertained by multiplying £215 by the number of his dependants as does not exceed Y.

(4) The relevant sums referred to in sub-paragraph (3) above are—

(*a*) £480, and

(*b*) in respect of each dependent child—

    (i) under the age of 11 immediately before the beginning of the academic year, £185,

    (ii) then aged 11 or over, but under 17, £325,

    (iii) then aged 17 or over, £480;

except that the eldest dependent child shall be disregarded for the purposes hereof if the student has neither a dependent spouse nor other adult dependant.

19.—(1) This paragraph shall apply in the case of a student upon whom an award was bestowed in respect of his attendance at a course which began before 1st September 1975 whose dependants requirement falls to be determined in accordance with paragraph 18(2)(*b*) above.

(2) While he holds the award, the student's dependants requirement shall be determined in accordance with Part 4 of Schedule 1 to the 1971 Regulations where that amount is greater than the amount specified in paragraph 18(2)(*b*).

20.—(1) This paragraph shall apply in the case of a student with dependants who—

(*a*) satisfies either of the conditions in paragraph 18(1)(*a*) and (*b*) above, and

(*b*) maintains a home for himself and a dependant at a place other than that at which he resides while attending the course.

(2) The dependants requirement of the student (determined in accordance with paragraph 18(2)(*a*) or (*b*) and, where applicable, paragraph 19) shall be increased by £225.

21.—(1) This paragraph shall apply in the case of a student, in whose case paragraph 18 above applies, who maintains any dependant outside the United Kingdom.

(2) Notwithstanding anything in the foregoing paragraphs of this Part of this Schedule, the dependants requirement of the student shall be of such amount as the authority consider reasonable in all the circumstances, not exceeding the amount determined in accordance with those paragraphs.

PART 4

OLDER STUDENTS

22. This Part of this Schedule shall apply in the case of a student who attained the age of 26 before the first year of his course and either—

(*a*) was in full-time employment for a total of three of the six years immediately preceding that year; or

(*b*) held an award (or was in receipt of a grant under arrangements made under section 2(3) of the Education Act 1962) in respect of his attendance at a previous course and either was in full-time employment as aforesaid immediately preceding the first year of that course or was a person to whom paragraph 14 of Schedule 1 to the 1971 Regulations applied (or any provision to the like effect in such arrangements as aforesaid).

23. The requirements of the student referred to in Regulation 15(1)(*a*) shall include the sum of £100 for every complete year not exceeding four by which his age at the beginning of the first year of his course exceeds 25.

PART 5

CONSTRUCTION OF PARTS 1 TO 4

24. In this Schedule any reference to the home of the student's parents shall be construed, in the case of a student whose spouse attends a full-time course at any establishment, as including a reference to the home of the parents of the student's spouse.

25. In this Schedule any reference to a requirement, expenditure or attendance in respect of which no period of time is specified shall be construed as a reference to a requirement, expenditure or attendance for the year.

SCHEDULE 3 Regulation 15(1)

RESOURCES

PART 1

STUDENT'S INCOME

Calculation of student's income

1. In calculating the student's income for the purposes of Regulation 15(1)(*b*) there shall be taken into account his income (reduced by income tax and social security contributions) from all sources, but there shall be disregarded the following resources—

(*a*) the first £215 of the aggregate of—

    (i) any income other than such as is mentioned in any of the following sub-paragraphs, and

    (ii) so much of any income mentioned in sub-paragraph (*b*) below as is not disregarded under that sub-paragraph;

(*b*) the first £500 of any income by way of—

    (i) scholarship, studentship, exhibition or award of a similar description bestowed on the student in respect of the course (in pursuance of a sponsorship scheme or otherwise) not being an award bestowed in pursuance of section 1 of the Education Act 1962, and

    (ii) in the case of a student released by his employer to attend the course, any payments made by that employer;

(*c*) in the case of a student who—

    (i) has no parent living, and

    (ii) is not such a person as is mentioned in paragraph 3(*a*) or (*b*) below,

so much of any income as is described and applied for his benefit as mentioned in paragraph 5(2) below as, when aggregated with any amount disregarded under sub-paragraph (*a*) above, does not exceed £430;

(*d*) any disability pension not subject to income tax;

(*e*) any bounty received as a reservist with the armed forces;

(*f*) remuneration for work done in vacations;

(*g*) in the case of a student in respect of whom a parental contribution is by virtue of Part 2 of this Schedule treated as forming part of his resources, any payment made under covenant by his parent;

(*h*) any payment made for a specific educational purpose otherwise than to meet such fees and such requirements for maintenance as are specified in Schedules 1 and 2;

(*i*) child benefit;

(*j*) any benefit under the Supplementary Benefits Act 1976;

(*k*) any attendance allowance under section 35 of the Social Security Act 1975;

(*l*) any allowance granted to him in pursuance of a scheme under section 19 of the Housing Finance Act 1972(**a**);

(**a**) 1972 c. 47.

and in the case of any such student as is described in paragraph 3(*a*) or (*b*) below there shall be deducted the amount of any payment made in pursuance of an obligation reasonably incurred by him before the first year of his course unless his spouse is a dependant for the purposes of Part 3 of Schedule 2 and in pursuance of paragraph 17(3) thereof, the payment is taken into account in determining her income.

PART 2

PARENTAL CONTRIBUTION

Definitions

2.—(1) In this Part of this Schedule—

"child" includes a person adopted in pursuance of adoption proceedings but, except in paragraph 4 below, does not include a child who holds a statutory award nor, except in paragraph 6(1) and (3) below, a step-child; and "parent" shall be construed accordingly;

"gross income" has the meaning assigned to it by paragraph 5 below;

"income of the student's parent" means the total income of the parent from all sources computed as for income tax purposes, except that no deduction shall be made which is in respect of personal reliefs under Chapter II of Part I of the Income and Corporation Taxes Act 1970(**a**) or which is otherwise of a kind for which provision is made by paragraph 6 below;

"residual income" means, subject to sub-paragraph (2) below, the balance of gross income remaining in any year after the deductions specified in paragraph 6 below have been made.

(2) Where, in a case not falling within the proviso to paragraph 5(1) below, the authority are satisfied that the income of the parent in any financial year is as a result of some event beyond his control likely to be and to continue after that year to be not more than four-fifths of his income in the financial year preceding that year, they may for the purpose of enabling the student to attend the course without hardship, ascertain the parental contribution for the academic year in which that event occurred by taking as the residual income the average of the residual income for each of the financial years in which that academic year falls.

Application of Part 2

3. 9 parental contribution ascertained in accordance with this Part shall be applicable in the case of every student except any of the following—

(*a*) an independent student;

(*b*) a student who held an award bestowed, or was in receipt of a grant under arrangements made under section 2(3) of the Education Act 1962(**b**), in respect of his attendance at a course beginning before 1st September 1975, and in whose case no contribution was applicable by virtue of previous Awards Regulations or such arrangements;

(*c*) a student in respect of whom the authority are satisfied that his parents cannot be found.

(**a**) 1970 c. 10.   (**b**) 1962 c. 12.

Parental contribution

4.—(1) Subject to sub-paragraph (2) below, the parental contribution shall be—

(*a*) in any case in which the residual income is more than £3,199 but less than £4,800, £20 with the addition of £1 for every complete £5 by which it exceeds £3,200; and

(*b*) in any case in which the residual income is more than £4,799 but less than £6,000, £340 with the addition of £1 for every complete £10 by which it exceeds £4,800; and

(*c*) in any case in which the residual income is not less than £6,000, £460 with the addition of £1 for every complete £11 by which it exceeds £6,000;

reduced in each case by £45 in respect of every other child of the parent who holds a statutory award; and in any case in which the residual income is less than £3,200 the parental contribution shall be nil.

(2) For any year in which a statutory award is held by—

(*a*) more than one child of the parent;

(*b*) the parent; or

(*c*) the student's step-parent—

the parental contribution for the student shall be such proportion of any contribution ascertained in accordance with this Part as the authority (after consultation with any other authority concerned) consider just.

Gross Income

5.—(1) Subject to the provisions of this paragraph "gross income" means the income of the student's parent in the financial year preceding the year in respect of which the resources of the student fall to be assessed:

Provided that, where the authority are satisfied that the income of the parent in the next succeeding financial year is likely to be not more than four-fifths of that income, they may for the purpose of calculating the parental contribution ascertain the gross income by reference to that next succeeding financial year; and in that case the above definition shall have effect accordingly both in relation to that year and, if the authority so determine, the year following that year and any subsequent year.

(2) Where trustees of property held in trust for a student or for any other person dependent on the parent pay, by virtue either of section 31(1) of the Trustee Act 1925(**a**) or of the trust instrument, any income of that property to the parent or otherwise apply it for or towards the maintenance, education or other benefit of the beneficiary the amount so paid or applied shall be treated as part of the gross income of the parent.

(3) Any dividends or interest paid or credited to the parent by a building society which has entered into arrangements with the Commissioners of Inland Revenue under section 343(1) of the Income and Corporation Taxes Act 1970 shall be deemed to have been received by him after deduction of income tax at the reduced rate determined under those arrangements for the year of assessment in which the dividends or interest are paid or credited; and the amount deemed to have been so deducted shall be treated as part of his gross income.

(**a**) 1925 c. 19.

(4) There shall be treated as part of the gross income all income arising from an office or employment which by virtue of any enactment is as such exempt from tax.

(5) Where the parents do not ordinarily live together the parental contribution shall be ascertained by reference to the income of whichever parent the authority consider the more appropriate in the circumstances.

Deductions

6.—(1) For the purpose of determining a parent's residual income there shall be deducted from his gross income, in respect of any child dependent on him during the year for which the contribution falls to be ascertained, the amount by which the relevant sum specified below exceeds the child's income in that year:—

Age of child immediately before beginning of academic year	Sum
Under 11	£425
11 or over but under 17	£435
17 or over	£545

(2) For the purpose aforesaid there shall also be deducted from the parent's gross income—

(a) in respect of any person, other than a spouse or child, dependent on the parent during the year for which the contribution falls to be ascertained, the amount by which £545 exceeds the income of that person in that year;

(b) the amount of any sums paid as interest (including interest on a mortgage) in respect of which relief is given under the Income Tax Acts, or as interest under the option mortgage scheme;

(c) the amount of any contributions to a dependants' pension scheme (being a contribution in respect of which relief is given under the Income Tax Acts);

(d) the aggregate amount of any other contributions to a pension or superannuation fund or scheme and of any premiums on a policy of life assurance (being a contribution or premium in respect of which relief is given under the Income Tax Acts) or so much of that amount as does not exceed 15% of the parent's gross income;

(e) where the parents are living together and are gainfully employed, the cost in wages of domestic assistance not exceeding whichever is the less of £435 and the emoluments of the parent who earns the less;

(f) where the parents ordinarily live together and one of them is incapacitated, so much of the cost in wages of domestic assistance as does not exceed £435;

(g) where a parent whose marriage has terminated either is gainfully employed or is incapacitated, so much of the cost in wages of domestic assistance as does not exceed £435;

(*h*) in respect of additional expenditure incurred by reason of the fact that the parent lives in a place where the cost of living is higher than that cost in the United Kingdom, such sum (if any) as the authority consider reasonable in all the circumstances;

(*i*) in the case of a parent who holds a statutory award, the amount by which the aggregate of his requirements for his ordinary maintenance (ascertained in accordance with Part 1 of Schedule 2) and £215 exceeds the sum payable in pursuance of that award.

(3) Where the student holds an award bestowed in respect of his attendance at a course beginning before September 1975, for the purpose aforesaid there shall also be deducted from the parent's gross income so much of any expenditure in respect of a child or payments under covenant as—

(*a*) would have been deductible by virtue of sub-paragraph (10), (11) or (12) of paragraph 6 of Schedule 2 to the Awards (First Degree etc. Courses) Regulations 1971 (or provisions to the like effect contained in arrangements made under section 2(3) of the Education Act 1962); and

(*b*) does not exceed the amounts respectively deducted in respect of that child, or payments under that covenant, in ascertaining the parental contribution for the year ending last before 1st September 1975.

PART 3

SPOUSE'S CONTRIBUTION

Application of Part 3

7. A spouse's contribution ascertained in accordance with this Part shall be applicable in the case of every man student living with his wife and every woman student living with her husband if (in either case) no parental contribution is applicable by virtue of paragraph 3(*a*), (*b*) or (*c*) above.

Spouse's contribution

8.—(1) Subject to sub-paragraphs (3) and (4) below, Part 2 above, except paragraphs 3, 4(1) and (2)(*a*), 5(5) and 6(2)(*g*), shall apply with the necessary modifications for the ascertainment of the spouse's contribution as it applies for the ascertainment of the parental contribution, references to the parent being construed except where the context otherwise requires as references to the student's spouse and the references to the parent and step-parent in paragraph 4(2)(*b*) and (*c*) being construed as references to the student's child and step-child respectively.

(2) The spouse's contribution shall be—

(*a*) in any case in which the residual income is more than £2,999 but less than £4,800, £20 with the addition of £1 for every complete £5 by which it exceeds £3,000; and

(*b*) in any case in which the residual income is not less than £4,800, £380 with the addition of £1 for every complete £10 by which it exceeds £4,800;

and in any case in which the residual income is less than £3,000 the spouse's contribution shall be nil.

(3) If the student marries during any year for which the contribution falls to be ascertained the contribution for that year shall be the fraction of the sum ascertained in accordance with the provisions of sub-paragraphs (1) and (2) above of which the denominator is 52 and the numerator is the number of complete weeks between the date of the marriage and whichever is the earlier of the end of that year and the end of the course.

(4) If the student's marriage terminates during any year for which the contribution falls to be ascertained the contribution for that year shall be the fraction of the sum ascertained in accordance with the provisions of sub-paragraphs (1) and (2) above of which the denominator is 52 and the numerator is the number of complete weeks between the beginning of that year and the termination of the marriage.

SCHEDULE 4   Regulation 15(2)

WIDOWS, WIDOWERS, DIVORCED PERSONS, ETC.

1. In its application to a student whose marriage terminates during the course, Regulation 15 shall have effect subject to the proviso that the grant shall be payable to him after the termination of his marriage at a rate not lower than that at which it was payable before its termination.

2. If the student has dependants within the meaning of Part 3 of Schedule 2 and paragraph 18 thereof applies to him, then, whether his marriage terminated before or during the course—

(a) the sum to be disregarded under paragraph 1(a) of Schedule 3 shall be £565 instead of £215, or

(b) his requirements under paragraph 18 of Part 3 of Schedule 2 shall be treated as increased by the sum of £350, or

(c) in the case of a student to whom Part 4 of Schedule 2 applies, his requirements shall be treated as including the sum specified in paragraph 23 thereof,

whichever is the most favourable to him.

3. A student whose marriage has terminated may elect that the sum specified as his requirements in Part 3 of Schedule 2 shall be disregarded and that instead there shall in calculating his income be disregarded £720 in respect of his eldest dependent child and £350 in respect of every other dependent child.

Regulations 9(2) and 10   SCHEDULE 5

EDUCATIONAL QUALIFICATIONS

1. A foundation credit of the Open University obtained by a student who had attained the age of 21 at the beginning of the Open University course in question.

2. A pass at advanced level in two subjects in the examination for the General Certificate of Education.

3. An Ordinary National Certificate or Diploma.

4. A Certificate or Diploma of TEC.

5. A National Certificate or National Diploma of BEC.

6. A pass in two principal subjects in the examination for the Higher School Certificate.

7. An Attestation of Fitness of the Scottish Universities Entrance Board.

8. A pass in three subjects in the higher grade gained at not more than two sittings of the Scottish Universities Preliminary Examination, the Scottish Certificate of Education Examination or the examination for the Scottish Leaving Certificate.

9. A pass at advanced level in two subjects in the Northern Ireland General Certificate or Senior Certificate of Education Examination.

10. The European Baccalaureate awarded by any establishment to which the European Communities (European Schools) Order 1972(a) applied at the time when it was awarded.

11. The International Baccalaureate Diploma awarded by the International Baccalaureate Office, Geneva.

12. Any other qualification for the time being prescribed by the Secretary of State for the purposes of these Regulations.

(a) S.I. 1972/1582 (1972 III, p. 4586).

SCHEDULE 6 Regulations 2(1) and 17

SANDWICH COURSES

1. In this Schedule—

(a) "sandwich course" means a course consisting of alternate periods of full-time study in an establishment and associated industrial, professional or commercial experience (in this Schedule called "periods of experience") at a place outside the establishment so organised that, taking the course as a whole, the student attends the periods of full-time study for an average of not less than 19 weeks in each year; and for the purpose of calculating his attendance the course shall be treated as beginning with the first period of full-time study and ending with the last such period;

"periods of experience" does not include unpaid service in a hospital, with a local authority acting in the exercise of their functions relating to health, welfare or the care of children and young persons or with a voluntary organisation providing facilities or carrying out activities of a like nature, teaching practice or unpaid research in an establishment;

"sandwich year" means, as respects any student, any year of a sandwich course which includes periods of both such study and such experience as are described above;

"prescribed proportion" means the proportion which the number of weeks in the year for which the student in question attends the establishment bears to 30, except that where that proportion is greater than the whole it means the whole;

"modified proportion" means the proportion which the number of weeks in the year in which there are no periods of experience for the student in question bears to 52; and

(b) in the application of this Schedule to a student whose marriage has terminated, references to Schedules 2 and 3 are to be construed as references to those Schedules as modified in accordance with Schedule 4.

2. The provisions of Schedule 2 shall, as respects any sandwich year, have effect subject to the following modifications—

(a) where the period of full-time study does not exceed 30 weeks 3 days, the student's requirements for his ordinary maintenance shall be the prescribed proportion of the appropriate amount specified in Part 1;

(b) where the period of full-time study exceeds 30 weeks 3 days, the student's requirements for his ordinary and supplementary maintenance shall be the aggregate of the appropriate amount specified in Part 1 and the appropriate amount specified in paragraph 6 of Part 2;

(c) the student's requirements in respect of such expenditure as is referred to in paragraph 5(b) of Part 2 shall be determined in accordance with that Part except that his requirements in respect of such expenditure as is mentioned in paragraph 10 shall be the amount by which the expenditure exceeds the prescribed proportion of £32;

(d) the student's requirement for the maintenance of a dependant shall be the modified proportion of the sum specified in Part 3 except that

2o

where such a requirement falls to be increased under paragraph 20 it shall be increased by the prescribed proportion of the sum there specified; and

(e) if the student is a person to whom Part 4 applies, his requirements under that Part shall be the prescribed proportion of the amount there specified.

3. The provisions of Schedule 3 shall, as respects any sandwich year, have effect subject to the following modifications—

(a) the sum to be disregarded under paragraph 1(a) of Part 1 shall be the prescribed proportion of £215 and the reference in paragraph 1(c) to £430 shall be construed as a reference to the aggregate of £215 and the prescribed proportion of £215;

(b) in calculating the student's income there shall be disregarded any payment made to him by his employer in respect of any period of experience;

(c) the amount of the parental contribution applicable to his case shall be the prescribed proportion of the contribution ascertained in accordance with Part 2; and

(d) the amount of the spouse's contribution applicable to his case shall be the prescribed proportion of the contribution ascertained in accordance with Part 3.

Given under the Official Seal of the Secretary of State for Education and Science on 28th July 1977.

(L.S.)

Shirley Williams,

Secretary of State for Education and Science.

EXPLANATORY NOTE

(This Note is not part of the Regulations.)

These Regulations consolidate, with amendments, the Local Education Authorities Awards Regulations 1975. The principal amendments are described below.

Provision is made whereunder an application for an award may be made notwithstanding that the student has begun his course *(Regulation (8)(1)(a))*.

Courses leading to the Higher Diploma of the Technician Education Council or the Higher National Diploma of the Business Education Council qualify for awards *(Regulation 7(1)(c))*.

The element in an award in respect of fees is not subject to a means test *(Regulation 14(a))* and the means test applicable to the maintenance element is relaxed *(paragraphs 1, 4 and 8 of Schedule 3)*.That element is increased and, save in special cases, is always at least £80 *(Regulations 14(b) and 15)*.

STATUTORY INSTRUMENTS

1977 No. 1308

EDUCATION, ENGLAND AND WALES

The Students' Dependants' Allowances Regulations 1977

Made - - - -	28th July 1977
Laid before Parliament	10th August 1977
Coming into Operation	1st September 1977

The Secretary of State for Education and Science, in exercise of the powers conferred by section 3(a) of the Education Act 1962(a) and section 3 of the Education Act 1973(b) and vested in her(c), hereby makes the following Regulations:—

Citation and commencement

1. These Regulations may be cited as the Students' Dependants' Allowances Regulations 1977 and shall come into operation on 1st September 1977.

Interpretation

2.—(1) In these Regulations, except where the context otherwise requires—

"eligible dependant" has the meaning assigned thereto by Regulation 4;

"the principal Regulations" means the Local Education Authority Awards Regulations 1977(d);

"spouse" includes a woman who cohabits with a man as his wife and a man who cohabits with a woman as her husband but nothing in this definition shall affect the meaning of "wife" or "husband";

other expressions have the same meanings as in the principal Regulations.

(2) In these Regulations, except where the context otherwise requires, a reference to a Regulation is a reference to a Regulation of these Regulations and a reference in a Regulation to a paragraph is a reference to a paragraph of that Regulation.

(3) The Interpretation Act 1889(e) shall apply for the interpretation of these Regulations as it applies for the interpretation of an Act of Parliament; and section 38(2) (effect of repeals) of that Act shall apply in relation to the Regulations revoked by these Regulations as if they were enactments repealed by an Act.

Revocations

3. The Students' Dependants' Allowances Regulations 1975(f) and the Local Education Authorities Awards (Amendment) Regulations 1976(g) (so

---

(a) 1962 c. 12.
(b) 1973 c. 16.
(c) S.I. 1964/490 (1964 I, p. 800).
(d) S.I. 1977/1307 (1977 II, p. 3731).
(e) 1889 c. 63.
(f) S.I. 1975/1225 (1975 II, p. 4213).
(g) S.I. 1976/1087 (1976 II, p. 2896).

far as they are not revoked by the Local Education Authority Awards Regulations 1977(**a**)) are hereby revoked.

Power to pay allowances

4.—(1) Subject to Regulation 5, the Secretary of State may pay an allowance to a student in respect of any eligible dependant within the meaning of paragraph (2) where his requirements in respect of that dependant are not taken into account for the purposes of his award in pursuance of Part 3 of Schedule 2 to the principal Regulations.

(2) The eligible dependants of a student shall be—

(*a*) the student's wife or husband, where they are living together, if—

(i) the wife or husband does not hold a statutory award and they have a dependent child, or

(ii) it is for the time being certified by a registered medical practitioner that the wife or husband is incapable of being gainfully employed for a period of at least eight weeks;

(*b*) a child dependent on the student unless—

(i) the parents do not live together and the child resides with the other parent, or

(ii) the student's spouse holds a statutory award in the calculation of which account is taken of the child.

Exceptions

5.   No allowance shall be payable to a student if—

(*a*) no payment in respect of fees or maintenance falls to be made to him under Regulation 14(*a*) or (*b*) of the principal Regulations by reason of Regulation 20 thereof (assisted students), or

(*b*) no payment in respect of maintenance falls to be made to him under Regulation 14(*b*) of the principal Regulations, other than such as is mentioned in the proviso to Regulation 24(1) thereof (withholding of payments), by reason of the said Regulation 24(1).

Amount of allowance

6.—(1) Subject to paragraph (4), an allowance shall be payable to a student with an eligible dependant in any week in a year at the weekly rate determined in accordance with paragraphs (2) and (3)—

(*a*) where he lives with his spouse, for any week or part of a week for which—

(i) the student attends his course at the establishment, or

(ii) he is pursuing a period of vacation study undertaken as mentioned in paragraph 8(1) of Part 2 of Schedule 2 to the principal Regulations or a period of term-time residential study such as is mentioned in paragraph 9(1) of the said Part 2 (whether or not the establishment is such as is mentioned in the said paragraphs);

(*b*) where he does not so live, irrespective of whether he is attending his course, or pursuing a period of study, as aforesaid.

(2) The weekly amount of the allowance shall, subject to paragraph (3), be the amount by which the aggregate of—

(**a**) S.I. 1977/1307 (1977 II, p. 3731).

(a) one fifty-second of the relevant sums mentioned in paragraph 18(4) of Part 3 of Schedule 2 to the principal Regulations so, however, that for the purposes hereof no account shall be taken of a dependent child who is not an eligible dependant, and

(b) where the student maintains a home for himself and an eligible dependant at a place within the United Kingdom, other than that at which he resides while attending the course, the sum specified in paragraph 20 of the said Part 3 divided by the number of weeks in the year for which he attends his course,

exceeds one fifty-second of the annual income of the student's family (within the meaning of Regulation 7) for the year in question.

(3) If an allowance is payable by virtue of these Regulations to both the student and the student's spouse the weekly amount shall be half the amount ascertained in accordance with paragraph (2).

(4) No allowance shall be paid for any week in which the capital resources of the student's household (assessed in accordance with Part III of Schedule 1 to the Supplementary Benefits Act 1976(a)) amount to £1,200 or more.

(5) For the purposes of this Regulation a student shall be treated as having attended at an establishment, or as having pursued a period of study, for a part of a week if and only if he attends at an establishment, or pursues a period of study, on four consecutive days; and, in determining whether he has attended the establishment or pursued a period of study, any period during which he is absent on account of illness shall be ignored.

Income of student's family

7.—(1) For the purposes of these Regulations the income of the student's family in any year shall be taken to be the aggregate of—

(a) any sums disregarded under Part 1 of Schedule 3 to the principal Regulations in calculating a student's income for the purposes there mentioned except—

(i) the first £715 of any such income as is mentioned in paragraph 1(b) thereof (awards and payments by employer);

(ii) such income as is mentioned in paragraph 1(f), (j), (i), (k) or (l) thereof (vacation earnings, supplementary benefit, child benefit, attendance allowance and rent allowance);

(iii) where the student's course is a sandwich course, such income as is mentioned in paragraph 3(b) of Schedule 6 to the principal Regulations (payments in respect of periods of experience);

(b) income (reduced by income tax, family allowances and social security contributions and disregarding the income specified in paragraph (2)) of a spouse or child who is a member of the same household; and

(c) in the case of a student to whom the minimum maintenance payment is paid under the principal Regulations, the amount (if any) by which his resources exceed his requirements (ascertained as provided in Regulation 15 of those Regulations).

(2) The income to be disregarded under paragraph (1)(b) is—

(a) except in a case falling within sub-paragraph (c) below, in respect of the earned income of the spouse whichever is the less of £215 and half that income;

(a) 1976 c. 71.

(*b*) any payment under a statutory award; and

(*c*) all income of a person who attends—

(i) a designated course other than one prescribed under sub-paragraph (*d*)(iii) of Regulation 7(1) of the principal Regulations (certain courses of teacher training), or

(ii) a full-time course of further education which is not prescribed by or under the said Regulation 7(1) as a designated course.

Supplementary

8.—(1) An allowance may be paid in instalments.

(2) An allowance, and an instalment of an allowance, may be paid before the end of the year by reference to which, in accordance with Regulation 6, it falls to be assessed; and any overpayment in any year may, and any under payment in a year shall, be corrected by way of deduction from or addition to any allowance payable in the next following year or, if no such allowance is payable, by repayment to or payment by the Secretary of State.

Given under the Official Seal of the Secretary of State for Education and Science on 28th July 1977.

(L.S.)

Shirley Williams,
Secretary of State for Education
and Science.

EXPLANATORY NOTE

(This Note is not part of the Regulations.)

These Regulations consolidate the Students' Dependants' Allowances Regulations 1975, with amendments. The principal changes are described below.

Regulation 7 of the 1975 Regulations is not reproduced (there are no longer persons in receipt of grant as there mentioned).

The present Regulations are drafted by reference to the Local Education Authority Awards Regulations 1977 ("the principal Regulations"), which supersede the Local Education Authorities Awards Regulations 1975 (S.I. 1975/1207) and, *inter alia*, increase the amount prescribed as a student's requirements. An allowance under the present Regulations is payable at a rate determined in part by reference to the principal Regulations (*Regulation 6(2)(a)*) and, accordingly, is payable at an increased rate.

The means-test for an allowance is relaxed so far as concerns the student's scholarship and similar income and the earned income of his spouse or a person living with him as his spouse (*Regulation 7(1)(a)(i) and (2)(a)*).

STATUTORY INSTRUMENTS

1977 No. 1309

ROAD TRAFFIC

The Heavy Goods Vehicles (Drivers' Licences) Regulations 1977

Made - - - -	*28th July* 1977
Laid before Parliament	*9th August* 1977
Coming into Operation	*30th August* 1977

ARRANGEMENT OF REGULATIONS

PART IV—SUPPLEMENTARY

SCHEDULES

The Secretary of State for Transport, in exercise of the powers conferred by
sections 114(1) and (3), 115(1A), 119, 120(1), 121, 124, 125(3) and (4) and 188(7)

of the Road Traffic Act 1972**(a)**, as amended by section 15 of the Road Traffic Act 1974**(b)** and by section 1(2) of, and paragraphs 10 and 11 of Schedule 1 to, the Road Traffic (Drivers' Ages and Hours of Work) Act 1976**(c)**, and of the powers conferred by section 1(4) of, and paragraph 3(4) to (6) of Schedule 2 to, the said Act of 1976, and of all other enabling powers, and after consultation with representative organisations in accordance with the provisions of section 199(2) of the said Act of 1972, hereby makes the following Regulations:—

PART I—PRELIMINARY

Commencement, citation and revocation

1.—(1) These Regulations shall come into operation on 30th August 1977 and may be cited as the Heavy Goods Vehicles (Drivers' Licences) Regulations 1977.

(2) The Regulations specified in Schedule 1 are hereby revoked.

(3) In so far as any application, appointment or requirement made, notice or approval given, licence, certificate or other document granted or issued or other thing done under the Regulations revoked by paragraph (2) above could have been made, given, granted, issued or done under a corresponding provision of these Regulations, it shall not be invalidated by the said revocation but shall have effect as if made, given, granted, issued or done under that corresponding provision.

(4) Any reference in·any such application, appointment, requirement, notice, approval, licence, certificate or other document as is mentioned in paragraph (3) above to any provision of the Regulations revoked by these Regulations, whether specifically or by means of a general description, shall, unless the context otherwise requires, be construed as a reference to the corresponding provision of these Regulations.

(5) Paragraphs (3) and (4) above shall have effect without prejudice to the operation of section 38 of the Interpretation Act 1889**(d)** (which relates to the effect of repeals) as it applies for the purposes of these Regulations by virtue of Regulation 2(5) below.

Interpretation

2.—(1) In these Regulations, unless the context otherwise requires, the following expressions have the meanings hereby respectively assigned to them, that is to say—

"the Act of 1972" means the Road Traffic Act 1972;

"the Act of 1976" means the Road Traffic (Drivers' Ages and Hours of Work) Act 1976;

"articulated vehicle combination" means a motor vehicle which is so constructed that a trailer designed to carry goods may by partial super-imposition be attached thereto in such a manner as to cause a substantial part of the weight of the trailer to be borne by the motor vehicle and to which a trailer is so attached;

"clerk to the traffic commissioners" means the clerk to the traffic commissioners for any traffic area constituted for the purposes of Part III of the Road Traffic Act 1960**(e)**;

(a) 1972 c. 20. (b) 1974 c. 50. (c) 1976 c. 3.
(d) 1889 c. 63. (e) 1960 c. 16.

"full licence" means a hgv driver's licence other than a provisional hgv driver's licence;

"hgv driver's licence" means a heavy goods vehicle driver's licence;

"hgv trainee driver's licence" means a hgv driver's licence which—

  (i) is a licence to drive heavy goods vehicles of class 1, 1A, 2, 2A, 3 or 3A,

  (ii) is applied for by a person under the age of 21 on the date of the application,

  (iii) has effect for a period during the whole or a part of which the holder is under the age of 21, and

  (iv) is not a restricted standard licence;

and "hgv trainee driver's full licence" and "hgv trainee driver's provisional licence" shall be construed accordingly;

"licensing authority" has the same meaning as in section 113(1) of the Act of 1972;

"Northern Ireland (ordinary) driving licence" means a licence to drive a motor vehicle granted under the law for the time being in force in Northern Ireland that corresponds to Part III of the Act of 1972, not being a licence granted under any Order in Council under section 1(3) of and Schedule 1 to the Northern Ireland Act 1974(a), a Measure of the Northern Ireland Assembly, or any enactment passed by the Parliament of Northern Ireland, in consequence of a dispensation from passing a test of competence to drive by reason of the applicant's residence outside the United Kingdom;

"Northern Ireland hgv driver's licence" means a licence to drive heavy goods vehicles granted under the law for the time being in force in Northern Ireland that corresponds to Part IV of the Act of 1972, not being a licence granted under any Order in Council under section 1(3) of, and Schedule 1 to, the Northern Ireland Act 1974, a Measure of the Northern Ireland Assembly, or any enactment passed by the Parliament of Northern Ireland, in consequence of a dispensation from passing a test of competence to drive by reason of the applicant's residence outside the United Kingdom;

"Northern Ireland restricted licence" means a Northern Ireland hgv driver's licence which, by virtue of provisions of the law of Northern Ireland corresponding to paragraphs 2 and 3 of Schedule 2 to the Act of 1976, restricts the person to whom it is granted to the driving of heavy goods vehicles of a permissible maximum weight not exceeding 10 tonnes falling within class 3 or 3A;

"ordinary driving licence" means a licence to drive a motor vehicle granted under Part III of the Act of 1972;

"registered", in relation to, or to matters arising in connection with, the training scheme, a hgv trainee driver's licence, or an application for such a licence, means registered for the time being by the Training Committee in accordance with the relevant provisions of the training scheme;

"relevant maximum weight" has the same meaning as in section 110 of the Act of 1972;

"restricted standard licence" means a hgv driver's licence for vehicles of class 3 or 3A which is restricted by virtue of—

  (i) paragraph 3(3) and (5) of Schedule 2 to the Act of 1976, or

  (ii) paragraph (1) or (2) of Regulation 31,

to vehicles having a maximum permissible weight not exceeding 10 tonnes;

(a) 1974 c. 28.

"standard hgv driver's licence" means a hgv driver's licence which is not a hgv trainee driver's licence, and "standard" in relation to a full licence or a provisional licence, shall be construed accordingly;

"test" means a test of competence to drive heavy goods vehicles of any class, being a test for which provision is made under section 119(1) of the Act of 1972;

"training agreement", in relation to an individual who is undergoing, or is to undergo, hgv driver training, means his agreement therefor with his registered employer in pursuance of the training scheme;

"the Training Committee" means the Committee which has been established by the employers' associations and the trade unions in the road goods transport industry with a constitution approved by the Secretary of State and which is known as the National Joint Training Committee for Young HGV Drivers in the Road Goods Transport Industry;

"the training scheme" means the scheme which has been established by the Training Committee with the approval of the Secretary of State (given for the purpose of regulations under section 119 of the Act of 1972) for training young drivers of heavy goods vehicles and which provides for—

(i) the registration by the Training Committee of employers who are willing and able to provide hgv driver training for persons employed by them,

(ii) the registration by the Training Committee of persons operating establishments for providing hgv driver training,

(iii) a syllabus for hgv driver training, and

(iv) the registration by the Training Committee of individual employees who are undergoing, or are to undergo, hgv driver training in the service of a registered employer in accordance with a form of agreement approved by the Training Committee;

"vehicle with automatic transmission" means a vehicle in which the driver is not provided with any means whereby he may, independently of the use of the accelerator or the brakes, vary gradually the proportion of the power being produced by the engine which is transmitted to the road wheels of the vehicle.

(2) In these Regulations, unless the context otherwise requires—

(a) any reference to a class or classes of heavy goods vehicles is a reference to one of the classes or to the classes of heavy goods vehicles specified in Schedule 2;

(b) any reference to a numbered class of such vehicles is a reference to a class of that number specified in that Schedule; and

(c) any reference to an additional class, in relation to a class of heavy goods vehicles, is a reference to a class specified in the column in that Schedule headed "Additional Classes" in relation to that class.

(3) Any reference in these Regulations to any enactment or instrument shall be construed, unless the context otherwise requires, as a reference to that enactment or instrument as amended, re-enacted or replaced by any subsequent enactment or instrument.

(4) Any reference in these Regulations to a numbered Regulation or Schedule is a reference to the Regulation or Schedule bearing that number in these Regulations except where otherwise expressly provided.

(5) The Interpretation Act 1889 shall apply for the interpretation of these Regulations as it applies for the interpretation of an Act of Parliament, and as if for the purpose of section 38 of that Act these Regulations were an Act of Parliament and the Regulations revoked by Regulation 1(2) were Acts of Parliament thereby repealed.

PART II—LICENCES

Applications for licences

3.—(1) A person who desires to obtain the grant of a hgv driver's licence shall—

(*a*) furnish to the appropriate licensing authority all relevant particulars and make any relevant declaration specified in such form as the Secretary of State may require;

(*b*) submit his application not more than two months before the date on which the licence is to have effect; and

(*c*) send with his application—

    (i) if required by the licensing authority, a certificate in such form as the Secretary of State may require signed by a registered medical practitioner (as that expression is construed by section 52(2) of the Medical Act 1956(**a**)) not more than three months prior to the date on which the licence is to have effect,

    (ii) his ordinary driving licence or his Northern Ireland (ordinary) driving licence,

    (iii) the fee for the hgv driver's licence,

    (iv) a pass certificate showing that he has passed the test within the relevant period for the class of heavy goods vehicles which the hgv driver's licence applied for will authorise him to drive, except in the case of an application for a provisional licence or where he has held a full hgv driver's licence authorising him to drive such vehicles within the relevant period, that is to say, the period specified in section 114(1) of the Act of 1972 ending on the date of the coming into force of the hgv driver's licence applied for,

    (v) if the application is an application for a hgv trainee driver's licence, the Training Committee's certificate as to his registration as a trainee hgv driver, as to his employer's registration under the training scheme, as to the class of heavy goods vehicles for which he is, or is to undergo, training and as to any registered hgv driver training establishment whose vehicles he may drive, and

    (vi) if the application is an application for a standard hgv driver's licence or a hgv trainee driver's licence by a person who holds a current hgv trainee driver's licence, that licence.

(2) Any application for a hgv driver's licence which does not comply with paragraph (1) above may be treated by the licensing authority as of no effect, but where the licensing authority so treats such an application or refuses the grant of a licence any fee and any documents required by sub-paragraph (*c*) of that paragraph to be sent with the application shall be returned to the applicant.

(**a**) 1956 c. 76.

(3) A person shall not apply for a hgv driver's licence if—

(a) he holds a hgv driver's licence which has been suspended or a Northern Ireland hgv driver's licence which has been suspended, whether (in either case) the suspension has effect under section 115 of the Act of 1972 or under the provision of the law for the time being in force in Northern Ireland that corresponds to that section;

(b) he is disqualified for holding or obtaining a hgv driver's licence or a Northern Ireland hgv driver's licence, whether (in either case) the disqualification has effect under section 116(1)(a) of the Act of 1972 or under the provision of the law for the time being in force in Northern Ireland that corresponds to that section;

(c) he is disqualified by a court for holding or obtaining an ordinary driving licence or by a court in Northern Ireland for holding or obtaining a Northern Ireland (ordinary) licence;

(d) he is disqualified by reason of his age for holding or obtaining an ordinary driving licence to drive any of the vehicles in the class of heavy goods vehicles to which the hgv driver's licence is to relate; or

(e) in the event of the application being granted he would hold more than one hgv driver's licence or would hold a hgv driver's licence and a Northern Ireland hgv driver's licence.

(4) In this Regulation "appropriate licensing authority" means the licensing authority to whom the application for a licence is required to be made in accordance with section 113 of the Act of 1972 or, as the case may be, Regulation 26.

Qualifications of applicants

4. An applicant for a hgv driver's licence shall have the following qualifications, experience and knowledge:—

(a) he must not be a person to whom paragraph (3) of Regulation 3 applies;

(b) he shall not—

(i) at any time since he attained the age of three years, have had an epileptic attack, or

(ii) suffer from any disease or disability likely to cause the driving by him of a heavy goods vehicle to be a source of danger to the public;

(c) he shall hold an ordinary driving licence or a Northern Ireland (ordinary) driving licence in either case authorising him to drive a vehicle or vehicles in the class of heavy goods vehicles in respect of which he desires to obtain the grant of a licence;

(d) in the case of an applicant for a hgv trainee driver's licence—

(i) the licence referred to in sub-paragraph (c) above shall be free from the endorsement, under section 101 of the Act of 1972 or under that provision of the law for the time being in force in Northern Ireland that corresponds to that section, of particulars of any conviction, and

(ii) he shall be a person who is a registered employee of a registered employer; and

(e) in the case of an applicant for a hgv trainee driver's licence to drive heavy goods vehicles of a class shown in column (1) of the Table in this sub-paragraph, a period of one year shall have expired since the date on which he passed the test to drive heavy goods vehicles of the class or classes specified in relation thereto in column (2) of that Table.

TABLE

(1) Class for which licence applied for	(2) Class for which applicant has passed the test
Class 2	Class 3
Class 2A	Class 3 or 3A
Class 1	Class 2
Class 1A	Class 2 or 2A

Grant of licences subject to a limitation

5. Where an applicant for a hgv driver's licence—

(*a*) holds an ordinary driving licence which contains a provision under section 87(4) or 88(2)(*bb*) of the Act of 1972 limiting the applicant to the driving of vehicles of a particular construction or design only; or

(*b*) holds a Northern Ireland (ordinary) licence which contains a similar provision under the law for the time being in force in Northern Ireland that corresponds to the said section 87(4), or 88(2)(*bb*)

any full licence granted to the applicant to drive a heavy goods vehicle shall contain a corresponding limitation.

Form of licences

6.—(1) Standard hgv drivers' licences shall be issued in the form of a book containing—

(*a*) in the case of a full licence, particulars in the form set out in Part I of Schedule 3; and

(*b*) in the case of a provisional licence, particulars in the form set out in Part II of that Schedule.

(2) Hgv trainee drivers' licences shall contain—

(*a*) in the case of a full licence, particulars in the form set out in Part I of Schedule 4; and

(*b*) in the case of a provisional licence, particulars in the form set out in Part II of Schedule 4.

(3) Where an applicant for a hgv driver's licence is already a holder of a hgv driver's licence the licensing authority may, instead of issuing him with a new book, issue the appropriate hgv driver's licence by affixing in the book already held a page or pages containing such particulars as would fall to be included in any new book issued to the applicant.

Signature of licences

7. Every person to whom a hgv driver's licence is granted shall forthwith sign it in ink with his usual signature.

Fees for licences

8. The fee for the grant of a full licence shall be £3 and the fee for the grant of a provisional licence shall be £1·50.

Provisional standard licences

9.—(1) A full standard licence to drive heavy goods vehicles of any class shall also be treated for the purposes of Part IV of the Act of 1972 as a provisional standard licence to drive heavy goods vehicles of any other class in respect of which the holder is not by reason of his age disqualified under section 96(1) of the Act of 1972 for holding or obtaining an ordinary driving licence.

(2) In applying the provisions of paragraph (1) above the effect of Regulation 4(1)(*d*) of the Motor Vehicles (Driving Licences) Regulations 1976(**a**) shall be disregarded.

(3) Subject to paragraph (4) below, a provisional standard licence, including a full standard licence which is treated as a provisional standard licence under paragraph (1) above, shall be subject to the following conditions, that is to say, the holder shall not drive a heavy goods vehicle of any class which he may drive by virtue of the provisional standard licence—

   (*a*) otherwise than under the supervision of a person who is present with him in the vehicle and who holds a full standard licence to drive a vehicle of that class;

   (*b*) unless there is clearly displayed in a conspicuous manner on the front and on the back of the vehicle a distinguishing mark in the form set out in Schedule 5;

   (*c*) if the vehicle is one to which a trailer is attached, except where the trailer is part of an articulated vehicle combination being driven by the holder, or where the relevant maximum weight of the drawing vehicle does not exceed 7·5 tonnes.

(4) The condition specified in paragraph (3)(*a*) above shall not apply whilst the holder of a provisional standard licence is undergoing a test and none of the conditions specified in the said paragraph (3) shall apply in relation to the driving of a heavy goods vehicle of any class where the holder of the standard licence has passed a test for a vehicle of that class.

Hgv trainee drivers' licences

10.—(1) Subject to paragraph (8) below, every hgv trainee driver's licence shall be subject to the following condition, namely, that the holder shall not drive a heavy goods vehicle of any class for which the licence is issued (other than a vehicle of class 4 or 4A), or for which by virtue of paragraph (3) below the licence is treated as a provisional licence, unless—

   (*a*) the holder is the registered employee of a registered employer named in the licence;

   (*b*) the vehicle is a heavy goods vehicle of a class to which his training agreement applies and which is stated in the licence; and

   (*c*) the vehicle is owned by that registered employer or by a registered hgv driver training establishment named in the licence.

(2) Insofar as a hgv trainee driver's full licence is not at the same time a full licence to drive heavy goods vehicles of classes 4 and 4A, it shall also be treated

(**a**) S.I. 1976/1076 (1976 II, p. 2852).

for the purposes of Part IV of the Act of 1972 as a hgv driver's provisional licence to drive heavy goods vehicles of those classes.

(3) The holder of a hgv trainee driver's full licence to drive heavy goods vehicles of a class shown in column (1) of the Table in this paragraph may, on or after the expiration of one year from the date on which he passed the test to drive heavy goods vehicles of that class and on surrendering that licence in accordance with Regulation 14(3) and paying the fee prescribed thereby, be granted a hgv trainee driver's licence which will be a full licence to drive heavy goods vehicles of the class to which the surrendered licence relates and will also be treated for the purposes of Part IV of the Act of 1972 as a hgv trainee driver's provisional licence to drive heavy goods vehicles of the class or classes specified in relation thereto in column (2) of that Table.

TABLE

(1) Class for which full licence is held	(2) Class for which licence is to be treated as a provisional licence
Class 3	Classes 2 and 2A
Class 3A	Class 2A
Class 2	Classes 1 and 1A
Class 2A	Class 1A

(4) Subject to paragraphs (5), (6) and (8) below, a hgv trainee driver's provisional licence, including a hgv trainee driver's full licence which is treated as a hgv trainee driver's provisional licence under paragraph (2) or (3) above, shall be subject to the following conditions (additional to that required by paragraph (1) above), that is to say, that the holder shall not drive a heavy goods vehicle of any class which he may drive by virtue of the provisional licence—

(a) otherwise than under the supervision of a person who is present with him in the vehicle and who holds a full standard licence to drive a vehicle of that class;

(b) unless there is clearly displayed in a conspicuous manner on the front and on the back of the vehicle a distinguishing mark in the form set out in Schedule 5;

(c) if the vehicle is being used to draw a trailer, unless the trailer is part of an articulated vehicle combination being driven by the holder.

(5) The condition specified in paragraph (4)(a) above shall not apply while the holder of a hgv trainee driver's provisional licence is undergoing a test.

(6) Where the holder of a hgv trainee driver's provisional licence (including a full licence which is treated as a provisional licence as mentioned above) has passed a test for a heavy goods vehicle of a class for which the licence is a provisional licence—

(a) the condition specified in paragraph (4)(a) above—

(i) shall not apply in any case so far as regards the driving of a vehicle of class 4 or 4A if the test is, or by virtue of Regulation 20 has effect as, a test for a vehicle of that class,

(ii) shall not apply so far as regards the driving of a vehicle of class 2, 2A, 3 or 3A if the test is, or by virtue of Regulation 20 has effect as, a test for a vehicle of that class, except in a case where the vehicle is being used to draw a trailer which is not part of an articulated vehicle combination being driven by the holder and the holder is under the age of 21,

(iii) shall not apply so far as regards the driving of a vehicle of class 1 or 1A, if the test is, or by virtue of Regulation 20 has effect as, a test for a vehicle of that class, except in a case where the holder is under the age of 21,

but shall remain applicable in the excepted cases mentioned in (ii) and (iii) above; and

(b) the conditions specified in paragraph (4)(b) and (c) above shall not apply so far as regards the driving of any vehicle of a class for which the test has been, or is by virtue of Regulation 20 deemed to have been, passed.

(7) Subject to paragraph (8) below, a hgv trainee driver's full licence to drive heavy goods vehicles—

(a) of class 1 or 1A, shall be subject to the condition that the holder, when under the age of 21, shall not drive any such vehicle otherwise than under the supervision of a person who is present with him in the vehicle and who holds a full standard licence to drive a vehicle of that class;

(b) of class 2, 2A, 3 or 3A, shall be subject to the condition that the holder, when under the age of 21 and when the vehicle is being used to draw a trailer which is not a part of an articulated vehicle combination being driven by the holder, shall not drive any such vehicle otherwise than under the supervision of a person who is present with him in the vehicle and who holds a full standard licence to drive a vehicle of that class.

(8) Paragraphs (1), (4) and (7) above shall have effect subject to Regulation 31(5) in a case where the holder of a hgv trainee driver's full or provisional licence to drive heavy goods vehicles of class 3 or 3A has held a restricted standard licence or a Northern Ireland restricted licence.

Suspension or revocation

11.—(1) The holder of a hgv driver's licence which has been suspended or revoked by a licensing authority shall, on receipt of notice, either delivered to the holder personally or sent by the recorded delivery service to the holder's last known address, of the decision of the licensing authority to suspend or revoke the licence, forthwith deliver it to the licensing authority for endorsement or cancellation.

(2) A licensing authority who suspends a hgv driver's licence shall endorse particulars of the suspension on the hgv driver's licence and shall return it to the holder at the end of the period of suspension on a demand in writing being made by that person.

(3) The holder of a Northern Ireland hgv driver's licence which has been suspended or revoked by a licensing authority shall, on receipt of notice, delivered or sent to the holder as mentioned in paragraph (1) above, of the decision of the licensing authority to suspend or revoke the licence, forthwith deliver the licence to the licensing authority who shall send it to the authority in Northern Ireland by whom it was issued together with particulars of the suspension or, as the case may be, of the revocation.

(4) The circumstances referred to in section 115(1A) of the Act of 1972 (obligatory revocation of hgv driver's licence when the holder is under the age of 21) are that the holder's ordinary driving licence or Northern Ireland (ordinary) driving licence bears more than one relevant endorsement. In this paragraph "relevant endorsement" means endorsement of particulars of a conviction in pursuance either of section 101 of the Act of 1972 (endorsement of licences) or of that provision of the law for the time being in force in Northern Ireland that corresponds to the said section 101.

Removal of disqualification

12.—(1) A licensing authority may remove a disqualification under paragraph (*a*) of section 116(1) of the Act of 1972 if the application for the removal of the disqualification is made after the expiration of whichever is relevant of the following periods from the commencement of the disqualification, that is to say—

    (*a*) two years, if the disqualification is for less than four years;

    (*b*) one half of the period of the disqualification, if it is for less than ten years, but not less than four years;

    (*c*) five years in any other case, including disqualification for an indefinite period.

(2) Where an application under paragraph (1) above for the removal, under section 116(2) of the Act of 1972, of a disqualification is refused, a further such application in respect of the same person shall not be entertained if made within three months after the date of refusal.

Withdrawal of ordinary driving licence or of Northern Ireland (ordinary) driving licence

13.—(1) If the holder of a hgv driver's licence is disqualified for holding or obtaining an ordinary driving licence, or if such a licence is refused or revoked under section 87 of the Act of 1972, or if he is disqualified under the law for the time being in force in Northern Ireland for holding or obtaining a Northern Ireland (ordinary) driving licence, or if such a licence is refused or revoked under any provision of that law that corresponds to the said section 87, he shall forthwith—

    (*a*) notify the licensing authority in whose area he resides of the particulars of the disqualification, refusal or revocation; and

    (*b*) deliver his hgv driver's licence to that licensing authority.

(2) Where a person who has delivered his hgv driver's licence to a licensing authority in accordance with paragraph (1) above ceases to be disqualified, unless the hgv driver's licence has been revoked or a period of suspension is still current, the licensing authority on production of that person's ordinary driving licence or, as the case may be, of his Northern Ireland (ordinary) driving licence, shall return the hgv driver's licence to him if it has not expired.

Lost, defaced and exchanged licences

14.—(1) If the holder of a hgv driver's licence satisfies the licensing authority by whom it was granted that the hgv driver's licence has been lost or defaced the licensing authority shall, on payment of a fee of 75p and in the case of a defaced hgv driver's licence on surrender to the licensing authority of the licence, issue to him a duplicate hgv driver's licence and shall endorse thereon particulars of any suspension endorsed upon the original hgv driver's licence, and the duplicate so issued shall have the same effect as the original.

(2) If at any time while a duplicate hgv driver's licence (being a licence issued in the place of a lost hgv driver's licence) is in force the original licence is found and the person to whom the original licence was granted becomes aware of that fact he shall forthwith inform the licensing authority and, if the original licence is not in his possession, he shall forthwith take all reasonable steps to obtain possession of it, and if it is in his possession or if he obtains possession of it, he shall forthwith return it as soon as may be to the licensing authority by whom it was granted.

(3) If the holder of a hgv driver's licence surrenders it and applies for a new hgv driver's licence he shall, if he so requires and on payment of a fee of 75p, be granted a hgv driver's licence to continue in force only for the period for which the surrendered licence would have continued if it had not been surrendered.

Production of licences

15.—(1) Subject to paragraph (6) below, any such person as follows, that is to say,—

    (*a*) the driver of a heavy goods vehicle on a road; or

    (*b*) a person who supervises the holder of a provisional licence (including a full licence which is treated as a provisional licence under Regulation 9(1) or 10(2) or (3)) or the holder of a hgv trainee driver's full licence to drive heavy goods vehicles of class 1 or 1A, or heavy goods vehicles of class 2, 2A, 3 or 3A (when being used to draw a trailer which is not part of an articulated vehicle combination), while the holder is driving a heavy goods vehicle on a road,

shall, on being so required by a constable or an examiner, produce his hgv driver's licence or, as the case may be, his Northern Ireland hgv driver's licence for examination so as to enable the constable or examiner to ascertain the name and address of the holder of the licence, the date of its issue, and the authority by whom it was granted, and shall, on being so required by an examiner as aforesaid, give his name and address and acknowledge that such information as may be recorded by the examiner on the examiner's record sheet is correct by signing the said record sheet.

(2) Subject to paragraph (6) below, any such person as follows, that is to say—

    (*a*) a person whom a constable has reasonable cause to believe to have been the driver of a heavy goods vehicle at a time when an accident occurred owing to its presence on a road; or

    (*b*) a person whom a constable has reasonable cause to believe to have committed an offence in relation to the use of a heavy goods vehicle on a road; or

    (*c*) a person whom a constable has reasonable cause to believe was supervising the holder of a provisional licence (including a full licence which is treated as a provisional licence under Regulation 9(1) or 10(2) or (3)) or the holder of a hgv trainee driver's full licence to drive heavy goods vehicles of class 1 or 1A, or heavy goods vehicles of class 2, 2A, 3 or 3A (when being used to draw a trailer which is not part of an articulated vehicle combination), while driving a heavy goods vehicle at a time when an accident occurred owing to the presence of the vehicle on a road or at a time when an offence is suspected of having been committed by the said holder in relation to the use of the vehicle on a road, shall, on being so required by a constable, produce his hgv driver's licence or, as the case may be, his Northern Ireland hgv driver's licence for examination so as to enable the constable to ascertain the name and address of the holder of the licence, the date of its issue, and the authority by whom it was issued.

(3) Subject to paragraph (6) below, where a hgv driver's licence has been suspended or revoked by a licensing authority, then if the holder of the licence fails to deliver it to that authority for endorsement or cancellation as required by Regulation 11(1), a constable or an examiner may require him to produce it, and upon its being produced may seize it and deliver it for endorsement or cancellation to that authority.

(4) Subject to paragraph (6) below, where a Northern Ireland hgv driver's licence has been suspended or revoked by a licensing authority, then if the holder of the licence fails to deliver it to that authority as required by Regulation 11(3), a constable or an examiner may require him to produce it and, upon its being produced may seize it and deliver it to that authority.

(5) Subject to paragraph (6) below, where a constable or an examiner has reasonable cause to believe that the person to whom a licence has been granted, or any other person, has knowingly made a false statement for the purpose of obtaining the grant of the hgv driver's licence, the constable or examiner may require the holder of the hgv driver's licence to produce it to him.

(6) If any person is unable to produce his hgv driver's licence or, as the case may be, his Northern Ireland hgv driver's licence when required to do so in accordance with any of the foregoing paragraphs of this Regulation, it shall be a sufficient compliance with that paragraph if—

(*a*) in a case where the licence was required by a constable to be produced, within five days after the production of the licence was so required he produces it in person for examination for the same purposes at such police station as may have been specified by him at the time its production was required; or

(*b*) in a case where the licence was required by an examiner to be produced, within ten days after the production of the licence was so required it is produced for examination for the same purposes at the office of such examiner or such licensing authority as may have been specified by him at the time its production was required.

(7) The holder of a hgv driver's licence or of a Northern Ireland hgv driver's licence shall, upon being required to do so by a licensing authority, cause the licence or his ordinary driving licence or, as the case may be, his Northern Ireland (ordinary) driving licence to be produced to that authority within ten days after the day on which the requirement was made.

(8) In this Regulation, "examiner" means an examiner appointed under section 56 of the Act of 1972.

PART III—TESTS OF COMPETENCE

Application for tests

16.—(1) A person who desires to take a test to be conducted by an examiner appointed under Regulation 18(1)(*a*) shall apply for an appointment for a test to the clerk to the traffic commissioners for the traffic area in which the driving test centre at which the applicant wishes to be tested is situated.

(2) An applicant for such an appointment shall, when making the application, specify the class of heavy goods vehicles in respect of which he desires to take the test and pay to the said clerk the fee prescribed by Regulation 23.

(3) Upon receipt of an application and fee in accordance with this Regulation from a person qualified in accordance with Regulation 17 to take the test for which the application is made the said clerk shall make arrangements for the taking of the test and offer the applicant an appointment therefor.

Qualifications of applicants for tests

17.—(1) An applicant for a test shall be a person who is—

(a) entitled to drive a vehicle or vehicles in the class of heavy goods vehicles in respect of which he desires to take the test by holding an ordinary driving licence or a Northern Ireland (ordinary) driving licence and a hgv driver's licence or a Northern Ireland hgv driver's licence, or

(b) entitled to drive such a vehicle or vehicles by virtue of section 84(4) of the Act of 1972 or by virtue of regulations under section 107(1)(g) of the Act of 1972 and by holding a hgv driver's licence or a Northern Ireland hgv driver's licence.

(2) Subject to paragraph (3) below, an applicant for a test in respect of a heavy goods vehicle of class 3 or 3A who is under the age of 21 when the test is taken shall, in addition to complying with the requirements of paragraph (1) above, be a person who—

(a) has held a hgv trainee driver's provisional licence for, and has been regularly driving heavy goods vehicles of that class for at least the 3 months immediately preceding the taking of the test; or

(b) has held an ordinary driving licence or a Northern Ireland (ordinary) driving licence authorising him to drive, and has been regularly driving, motor cars, small goods vehicles or small passenger vehicles for at least one year immediately preceding the taking of the test.

(3) Paragraph (2) above shall not apply to an applicant for a test who holds a restricted standard licence or a Northern Ireland restricted licence.

(4) In this Regulation "small goods vehicle" and "small passenger vehicle" have the same meaning as in section 110 of the Act of 1972.

Persons who may conduct tests

18.—(1) Tests may be conducted—

(a) by examiners appointed for that purpose by the Secretary of State;

(b) by examiners appointed for that purpose by the Secretary of State, insofar as concerns the testing of persons subject to the Naval Discipline Act 1957(a), to military law or to air force law, or of persons employed in the driving of motor vehicles for the purposes of the naval, military or air forces of Her Majesty raised in the United Kingdom;

(c) in England and Wales, by the chief officer of any fire brigade maintained in pursuance of the Fire Services Act 1947(b), or, in Scotland by the fire-master of such a brigade, insofar as concerns the testing of members of any such brigade or of persons employed in the driving of motor vehicles for the purposes of any such brigade;

(d) by any chief officer of police in so far as concerns the testing—
  (i) of members of a police force, or

(a) 1957 c. 53.   (b) 1947 c. 41.

(ii) of persons employed in the driving of motor vehicles for police purposes by a police authority, or by the Receiver for the Metropolitan Police District or by the Commissioner of Police for the Metropolis.

(2) Any person authorised by virtue of paragraph (1)(*c*) or (*d*) above to conduct tests may, subject to the approval of the Secretary of State, authorise suitable persons to act as examiners of those who submit themselves for a test.

Nature of tests

19. The test which a person is required to pass before a full licence can be granted to him authorising him to drive a heavy goods vehicle of a particular class shall be a test carried out on a vehicle of that class, being a test which satisfies the examiner—

(*a*) that the candidate is fully conversant with the contents of the Highway Code;

(*b*) that he has sufficient knowledge of the mechanical operation of the vehicle on which he is tested, including at the discretion of the examiner the effect of distribution of load on the performance of the vehicle, to enable him to drive it safely;

(*c*) that he is competent to drive without danger to, and with due consideration for, other users of the road, the vehicle on which he is tested; and

(*d*) that he is able to perform safely and competently the operations specified in Schedule 6.

Additional classes of vehicles covered by tests

20. A person who has passed a test to drive heavy goods vehicles of a particular class shall be deemed for the purposes of Part IV of the Act of 1972 also to have passed the test to drive heavy goods vehicles of any additional class.

Evidence of results of tests

21.—(1) A person who passes a test shall be furnished with a certificate to that effect in the form (adapted as the case may require) set out in Part I of Schedule 7.

(2) A person who fails to pass a test shall be furnished with a statement to that effect in the form (adapted as the case may require) set out in Part II of Schedule 7.

Production of vehicle for test, etc.

22.—(1) A person submitting himself for a test shall—

(*a*) provide for the purpose of the test a vehicle which—

(i) is suitable for the purpose of the test and, in the case of a test in respect of a vehicle of class 2, 2A, 3 or 3A, is not an articulated vehicle combination or the tractive unit thereof,

(ii) is not carrying goods or burden of any description,

(iii) is fitted with a seat which is firmly secured to the vehicle and in such a position that the examiner is able properly to conduct the test from it and is afforded adequate protection from bad weather when conducting the test,

(iv) is not a vehicle in respect of which any person is required to be employed as a driver or attendant in addition to the applicant by virtue of section 34 of the Act of 1972, and

(v) is not fitted with a device designed to permit a person other than the driver to operate the accelerator, unless any pedal or lever by which the device is operated and any other parts which it may be necessary to remove to make the device inoperable by such a person during the test have been removed; and

(b) sign the examiner's attendance record.

(2) Where a person submitting himself for a test provides a vehicle which does not comply with paragraph (1) above or fails to sign the examiner's attendance record the examiner may refuse to conduct the test.

Fees for tests

23. The fee payable by a person who applies for a test to be conducted by an examiner appointed under Regulation 18(1)(*a*) shall be £24.

Refund of fees

24. The fee paid in pursuance of Regulations 16 and 23 on application for an appointment for a test may be repaid in the following cases and not otherwise, that is to say—

(*a*) if no such appointment is made, or an appointment made is subsequently cancelled by or on behalf of the Secretary of State;

(*b*) if the person for whom the appointment is made gives notice cancelling the appointment to the clerk to the traffic commissioners by whom the appointment was made of not less than three clear days (excluding Saturdays, Sundays, any bank holidays, Christmas Day or Good Friday) before the date of the appointment;

(*c*) if the person for whom the appointment is made keeps the appointment but the test does not take place, or is not completed, for reasons attributable neither to him nor to any vehicle provided by him for the purposes of the test; or

(*d*) if an order for repayment of the fee is made by a court or sheriff under section 117 of the Act of 1972 pursuant to a finding that the test was not properly conducted in accordance with these Regulations.

For the purposes of this Regulation "bank holiday" means a day which is a bank holiday by or under the Banking and Financial Dealings Act 1971(a) either generally or in the locality in which is situated the office of the clerk to the traffic commissioners to whom notice cancelling an appointment for a test falls to be given.

Additional qualification

25.—(1) Subject to paragraph (3) below, a person who passes a test prescribed by these Regulations shall be treated as having passed a test of competence to drive prescribed under section 85(2) of the Act of 1972—

(*a*) for vehicles of any class comprised in Group A of the groups set out in the relevant version of Schedule 3 to the Motor Vehicles (Driving Licences) Regulations, if the vehicle on which he passes the test is not a vehicle with automatic transmission, or

(*b*) for vehicles of any class comprised in group B of the groups set out in the relevant version of that Schedule, if the vehicle on which he passes the test is a vehicle with automatic transmission,

---

(a) 1971 c. 80.

if at the time he takes the test he is the holder of an ordinary driving licence (being a provisional licence within the meaning of Part III of the Act of 1972) or of a Northern Ireland (ordinary) driving licence (being a licence corresponding to such a provisional licence), or is entitled to drive by virtue of section 84(4) of the Act of 1972 or by virtue of regulations under section 107(1)(g) of the Act of 1972, and at that time he does not hold and is not entitled to be granted an ordinary driving licence (other than such a provisional licence) or a Northern Ireland (ordinary) driving licence (other than a licence corresponding to such a provisional licence) authorising him to drive any such vehicle:

Provided that if the test prescribed by these Regulations proves his competence to drive vehicles of a particular construction or design only he shall be treated for the purposes of this Regulation as having passed the test of competence to drive prescribed under the said section 85(2) only so far as relates to vehicles of that construction or design.

(2) In paragraph (1) above the reference to the relevant version of Schedule 3 to the Motor Vehicles (Driving Licences) Regulations is—

(a) where the test was passed before 1st January 1976, a reference to that Schedule to the Motor Vehicles (Driving Licences) Regulations 1971(a) as it stood before amendment by the Motor Vehicles (Driving Licences (Amendment) (No. 4) Regulations 1975(b),

(b) where the test was passed on or after 1st January 1976 but before 1st August 1976, a reference to that Schedule to the said Regulations of 1971 as amended by the said (No. 4) Regulations of 1975, and

(c) where the test is passed on or after the 1st August 1976, a reference to that Schedule to the Motor Vehicles (Driving Licences) Regulations 1976(c).

(3) A person who is treated as having passed the test of competence prescribed under the said section 85(2) by virtue of paragraph (1) above shall be furnished with a certificate to that effect in the form (adapted as the case may require) set out in Part III of Schedule 7.

PART IV—SUPPLEMENTARY

Service personnel

26. The licensing authority for the South Eastern Traffic Area is hereby prescribed for the purposes of section 188(7) of the Act of 1972 (issuing, suspension and revocation of hgv drivers' licences for service personnel).

Northern Ireland licences

27.—(1) The licensing authority for the North Western Traffic Area is hereby prescribed for the purposes of section 125(3) and (4) of the Act of 1972 (suspension, revocation and disqualification in respect of Northern Ireland licences as respects Great Britain).

(2) The magistrates' court or sheriff to whom an appeal shall lie by the holder of a Northern Ireland licence, being a person who is not resident in Great Britain and who is aggrieved by the suspension or revocation of the licence or by

---

(a) S.I. 1971/451 (1971 I, p. 1338).

(b) S.I. 1975/2037 (1975 III, p. 7478).   (c) S.I. 1976/1076 (1976 II, p. 2852).

the ordering of disqualification for holding or obtaining a hgv driver's licence, shall be—

> (i) such a magistrates' court or sheriff as he may nominate at the time he puts down his appeal, or
>
> (ii) in the absence of a nomination of a particular court under sub-paragraph (i) above, the magistrates' court in whose area the office of the licensing authority for the North Western Traffic Area is situated.

Offences

28. It is hereby declared that a contravention of or failure to comply with any provision of Regulation 3(3), 7, 11(1), 13(1), 14(2) or 15 is an offence.

Exemptions

29.—(1) Part IV of the Act of 1972 shall not apply to heavy goods vehicles of the following classes, that is to say—

(*a*) track laying vehicles;

(*b*) vehicles propelled by steam;

(*c*) road rollers;

(*d*) road construction vehicles used or kept on the road solely for the conveyance of built-in road construction machinery (with or without articles or materials used for the purpose of that machinery);

(*e*) engineering plant;

(*f*) works trucks;

(*g*) any industrial tractor, that is to say a tractor, not being a land tractor, which has an unladen weight not exceeding 3½ tons, is designed and used primarily for work off roads, or for work on roads in connection only with road construction or maintenance (including any such tractor when fitted with an implement or implements designed primarily for use in connection with such work, whether or not any such implement is of itself designed to carry a load) and is so constructed as to be incapable of exceeding a speed of 20 miles per hour on the level under its own power;

(*h*) land locomotives and land tractors;

(*i*) digging machines;

(*j*) vehicles exempted from excise duty by virtue of section 7(1) of the Vehicle (Excise) Act 1971(**a**) (vehicles used less than a certain distance on public roads);

(*k*) any motor car as defined in section 190(2) of the Act of 1972 which is so constructed that a trailer designed to carry goods may by partial superimposition be attached thereto in such a manner as to cause a substantial part of the weight of the trailer to be borne thereby, but to which no trailer is attached;

(*l*) vehicles used as public service vehicles as defined in sections 117 and 118 of the Road Traffic Act 1960;

(*m*) vehicles used for no other purpose than the haulage of lifeboats and the conveyance of the necessary gear of the lifeboats which are being hauled;

(**a**) 1971 c. 10.

(*n*) vehicles manufactured before 1st January 1940 used unladen and not drawing a laden trailer;

(*o*) vehicles in the service of a visiting force or headquarters;

(*p*) wheeled armoured vehicles being the property of, or for the time being under the control of, the Secretary of State for Defence;

(*q*) any vehicle driven by a constable for the purpose of removing or avoiding obstruction to other road users or danger to other road users or members of the public, for the purpose of safe-guarding property (including the heavy goods vehicle and its load) or for other similar purposes;

(*r*) any articulated vehicle combination which has a permissible maximum weight not exceeding 7·5 tonnes, or the tractive unit of which does not exceed 15 cwt unladen weight;

(*s*) any vehicle having a relevant maximum weight not exceeding 3·5 tonnes to which a trailer is attached, not being an articulated vehicle combination;

(*t*) any vehicle (not being an articulated vehicle combination) having an unladen weight not exceeding 10 tons, being a vehicle which belongs to the holder of public service vehicle licence granted under section 127 of the Road Traffic Act 1960 or is in his possession under an agreement for hire purchase, hire or loan, when driven on his behalf by a person who holds a licence to drive public service vehicles granted under section 144 of that Act for the purpose of—

(i) proceeding to or returning from a place where assistance is to be, or has been, rendered to a disabled vehicle, being a vehicle in respect of which, at the time when it became disabled, a public service vehicle licence granted under the said section 127 was in force, or

(ii) moving such a disabled vehicle so as to prevent its causing an obstruction or towing it from the place where it has become disabled to a place where it is to be repaired, stored or broken up;

(*u*) any vehicle fitted with apparatus designed for raising a disabled vehicle partly from the ground and for drawing a disabled vehicle when so raised (whether by partial superimposition or otherwise) being a vehicle which—

(i) is used solely for dealing with disabled vehicles,

(ii) is not used for the conveyance of any load other than a disabled vehicle when so raised, water, fuel and accumulators and articles required for the operation of, or in connection with, such apparatus as aforesaid or otherwise for dealing with disabled vehicles, and

(iii) has an unladen weight not exceeding 3 tons; and

(*v*) play-buses.

(2) In this Regulation—

"digging machine" has the meaning given thereto in Schedule 3 to the Vehicles (Excise) Act 1971;

"engineering plant", "land locomotive" and "land tractor" have the meanings given thereto in Regulation 3(1) of the Motor Vehicles (Construction and Use) Regulations 1973(**a**);

"play-bus" means a vehicle—

(*a*) which was originally constructed to carry passengers but has been adapted to carry goods or burden of any description, and

---

(**a**) S.I. 1973/24 (1973 I, p. 93).

(b) which is owned by a person or body of persons who carry on, otherwise than in the course of a trade or business conducted with a view to profit, activities which consist of, or include, the provision of play equipment for children by making it available at different places,

when being driven on a road—

(i) by or on behalf of the owner of the vehicle for the carriage of such equipment, or of such equipment together with not more than two passengers of full age appointed by such owner to supervise the use of the equipment by children, to or from the place where the equipment is to be, or has been, made available for such use, or

(ii) for the purpose of proceeding to or from the place where a mechanical defect in the vehicle itself is to be, or has been, remedied, or

(iii) in such circumstances that by virtue of section 5 of the Vehicles (Excise) Act 1971 the vehicle is not chargeable with duty in respect of its use on public roads;

"play equipment for children" includes articles required in connection with the use of such equipment by children;

"road construction vehicle" and "road construction machinery" have the meanings given thereto by section 4(2) of the Vehicles (Excise) Act 1971;

"track laying", in relation to a vehicle, means that the vehicle is so designed and constructed that the weight thereof is transmitted to the road surface either by means of continuous tracks or by a combination of wheels and continuous tracks in such circumstances that the weight transmitted to the road surface by the tracks is not less than half the weight of the vehicle;

"works truck" has the meaning given thereto in Schedule 2 to the Goods Vehicles (Plating and Testing) Regulations 1971(a); and

expressions used in sub-paragraph (o) of paragraph (1) above have the same meaning as in the Visiting Forces and International Headquarters (Application of Law) Order 1965(b).

Effect on existing hgv drivers' licences of changes in definitions

30. The validity of a hgv driver's licence granted before 15th April 1976 shall not be affected by the coming into operation on that date of paragraph 11 of Schedule 1 to the Act of 1976 (which amends the definition of heavy goods vehicle in the Act of 1972), and for the purpose of determining the vehicles which the holder of the licence is thereby authorised to drive on or after that date, or on or after the date of the commencement of the licence, if later, the references in the licence to heavy goods vehicles, or to the classes of such vehicles, or to any one or more numbered classes of such vehicles, shall be construed as embracing (and only embracing) the vehicles which fall within the definition of heavy goods vehicle or, as the case may be, the definition of the vehicles comprised in the classes or the particular numbered class or classes of heavy goods vehicles, as such definitions have effect in these Regulations.

Special provisions with respect to standard licences affected by the transitional savings in Schedule 2 to the Act of 1976

31.—(1) A full or provisional standard licence for heavy goods vehicles of class 3 or 3A granted to a person—

(a) S.I. 1971/352 (1971 I, p. 1098).   (b) S.I. 1965/1536 (1965 II, p. 4462).

(a) to whom paragraph 2 of Schedule 2 to the Act of 1976 applies,

(b) who is under the age of 21 when the licence is granted, and

(c) whose ordinary driving licence is, by reason of sub-paragraph (3) of that paragraph, restricted as mentioned in that sub-paragraph,

shall be restricted to heavy goods vehicles of class 3 or 3A having a permissible maximum weight not exceeding 10 tonnes, and for the purpose of Regulation 3(3)(d) the class of heavy goods vehicles for which the licence is granted shall be class 3 or 3A (as the case may be) restricted as aforesaid, but this restriction, insofar as it is imposed solely by reason of this paragraph, shall cease when the holder of the standard licence attains 21.

(2) Where a full standard licence for heavy goods vehicles of class 3 or 3A, which has been granted, on an application made during 1976, to a person to whom paragraph 3 of Schedule 2 to the Act of 1976 applies, restricts that person, by virtue of sub-paragraphs (3) and (5) of that paragraph, to the driving of heavy goods vehicles having a permissible maximum weight not exceeding 10 tonnes, then the class of vehicle the driving of which is authorised by that licence (as a full licence) shall, for the purpose of these Regulations, be class 3 or 3A (as the case may be) restricted as aforesaid, and accordingly any subsequent full standard licence for heavy goods vehicles of class 3 or 3A granted to that person shall, unless he has in the meantime passed a test which is, or by virtue of Regulation 20 has effect as, a test for a vehicle of class 3 or 3A, be subject to the same restriction.

(3) A restricted standard licence which is a full licence shall (without prejudice to the effect of Regulation 9(1)) be treated for the purposes of Part IV of the Act of 1972 as a provisional standard licence to drive heavy goods vehicles of class 3 or 3A having a permissible maximum weight exceeding 10 tonnes if the holder has attained the age of 21.

(4) The holder of a restricted standard licence which is a full licence shall not, for the purposes of Regulation 9(3)(a), or 10(4)(a) or (7)(b), be regarded as the holder of a full standard licence for heavy goods vehicles of class 3 or 3A, if the vehicle being driven has a permissible maximum weight exceding 10 tonnes.

(5) Where a person under the age of 21 holds a restricted standard licence and applies for a hgv trainee driver's licence, or holds an hgv trainee driver's licence and applies for a restricted standard licence, he shall send to the licensing authority with his application his restricted standard licence, or hgv trainee driver's licence, as the case may be, and, if his application is granted—

(a) the licensing authority shall issue to him an hgv trainee driver's licence which (without prejudice to its nature as such a licence) shall authorise him to drive heavy goods vehicles of the restricted class 3 or 3A which a restricted standard licence would authorise him to drive, but without complying with the conditions specified in Regulation 10(1)(a), (b) and (c) and, if the restricted standard licence which he held or to which he is entitled is a full licence, also without complying with the conditions specified in Regulation 10(4) and (7)(b), and

(b) any subsequent hgv trainee driver's licence granted to him before he attains the age of 21 shall authorise him similarly.

(6) In paragraph (5) above the expression "restricted standard licence" includes a Northern Ireland restricted licence.

William Rodgers,
Secretary of State for Transport.

28th July 1977.

SCHEDULE 1

Regulations revoked by Regulation 1(2)

Title	Year and Number
The Heavy Goods Vehicles (Drivers' Licences) Regulations 1975.	S.I. 1975/739 (1975 II, p. 2733)
The Heavy Goods Vehicles (Drivers' Licences) (Amendment) Regulations 1975	S.I. 1975/1731 (1975 III, p. 5880)
The Heavy Goods Vehicles (Drivers' Licences) (Amendment) Regulations 1976	S.I. 1976/473 (1976 I, p. 1374)
The Heavy Goods Vehicles (Drivers' Licences) (Amendment) (No. 2) Regulations 1976	S.I. 1976/1075 (1976 II, p. 2850)

STOKE-ON-TRENT
CITY
LIBRARIES

(See Regulation 2)

SCHEDULE 2

CLASSES OF HEAVY GOODS VEHICLES

1 Class	2 Definition	3 Additional Classes
Class 1	An articulated vehicle combination not with automatic transmission, other than a vehicle combination coming within class 4	Classes 1A, 2, 2A, 3, 3A, 4 and 4A
Class 1A	An articulated vehicle combination with automatic transmission, other than a vehicle combination coming within class 4A	Classes 2A, 3A and 4A
Class 2	A heavy goods vehicle not with automatic transmission, other than an articulated vehicle combination, designed and constructed to have more than four wheels in contact with the road surface	Classes 2A, 3 and 3A
Class 2A	A heavy goods vehicle with automatic transmission, other than an articulated vehicle combination, designed and constructed to have more than four wheels in contact with the road surface	Class 3A
Class 3	A heavy goods vehicle not with automatic transmission, other than an articulated vehicle combination, designed and constructed to have not more than four wheels in contact with the road surface.	Class 3A
Class 3A	A heavy goods vehicle with automatic transmission, other than an articulated vehicle combination, designed and constructed to have not more than four wheels in contact with the road surface	
Class 4	An articulated vehicle combination not with automatic transmission, the tractive unit of which does not exceed 2 tons unladen weight	Class 4A
Class 4A	An articulated vehicle combination with automatic transmission, the tractive unit of which does not exceed 2 tons unladen weight	

For the purposes of the above definitions where a vehicle is fitted with two wheels in line transversely and the distance between the centres of their respective areas of contact with the road is less than 18 inches they shall be regarded as only one wheel.

(See Regulation 6)

SCHEDULE 3

PART I

FORM OF HEAVY GOODS VEHICLE FULL DRIVER'S LICENCE

Road Traffic Act 1972 and Road Traffic (Drivers' Ages and Hours of Work) Act 1976

HEAVY GOODS VEHICLE

DRIVER'S LICENCE

Issued by the Licensing Authority for

[

Space for name and address
of holder   ]

is hereby authorised to drive heavy goods vehicles of Classes 1, 1A, 2, 2A, 3, 3A, 4, 4A

....

....

....

from .... until .... inclusive.

PROVISIONAL LICENCE

This licence has effect as a provisional licence in respect of the classes of heavy goods vehicles for which it is not a full licence. Such heavy goods vehicles may be driven subject to the conditions applying to provisional licence holders and the minimum age requirements being satisfied.

Usual signature of licensee...

PART II

FORM OF HEAVY GOODS VEHICLE PROVISIONAL DRIVER'S LICENCE

Road Traffic Act 1972 and Road Traffic (Drivers' Ages and Hours of Work) Act 1976

HEAVY GOODS VEHICLE

PROVISIONAL DRIVER'S LICENCE

Issued by the Licensing Authority for

[Space for name and address
of holder

                                                              ]

is hereby authorised to drive heavy goods vehicles of [all Classes] [Classes 4 and 4A] subject to the conditions prescribed in Regulation 9 of the Heavy Goods Vehicles (Drivers' Licences) Regulations 1977.

from .... until .... inclusive.

Usual signature of licensee...

(See Regulation 6)

SCHEDULE 4

PART I

FORM OF HEAVY GOODS VEHICLE TRAINEE DRIVER'S FULL LICENCE

Road Traffic Acts 1972 and 1974 and Road Traffic (Drivers' Ages and Hours of Work) Act 1976

HEAVY GOODS VEHICLE

TRAINEE DRIVER'S LICENCE

Issued by the Licensing Authority for

Space for name and address of holder

[   ]

is hereby authorised, subject to the conditions set out or referred to below, to drive heavy goods vehicles of Classes

[here specify classes]

from .... until .... inclusive.

CONDITIONS

Name and address of holder's registered employer   ....

....

Name and address of registered hgv driver   ....

training establishment whose vehicles the holder   ....

may drive   ....

....

Class of heavy goods vehicle to which holder's   ....

training agreement applies   ....

1. The holder shall not by virtue of this licence (including the provisional licence below) drive a heavy goods vehicle of class 1, 1A, 2, 2A, 3 or 3A unless—

   (*a*) he is a registered employee of the registered employer named above,

   (*b*) the vehicle is owned by that registered employer or by a registered hgv driver training establishment named above, and

   (*c*) the vehicle is a heavy goods vehicle of a class which is stated above as being a class to which the holder's training agreement applies.

In this Condition "registered" means registered for the time being by the National Joint Committee for Young HGV Drivers in the Road Goods Transport Industry in accordance with the relevant provisions of their training scheme.

2p

2. The holder shall not by virtue of this licence, while under the age of 21, drive otherwise than under the supervision of a person who is present with him in the vehicle and who holds a full licence (not being a trainee driver's licence) to drive a vehicle of that class—

    (*a*) a heavy goods vehicle of class 1 or 1A, or

    (*b*) a heavy goods vehicle of class 2, 2A, 3 or 3A when the vehicle is being used to draw a trailer which is not part of an articulated vehicle combination.

PROVISIONAL LICENCE

This licence has effect as a provisional licence in respect of heavy goods vehicles of class [here specify]. Such heavy goods vehicles may be driven subject to the conditions applying to provisional licence holders.

Usual signature of licensee...

PART II

FORM OF HEAVY GOODS VEHICLE TRAINEE DRIVER'S PROVISIONAL LICENCE

Road Traffic Acts 1972 and 1974 and Road Traffic (Drivers' Ages and Hours of Work) Act 1976

HEAVY GOODS VEHICLE

TRAINEE DRIVER'S PROVISIONAL LICENCE

Issued by the Licensing Authority for

Space for name and address of holder

[   ]

is hereby authorised, subject to the conditions set out or referred to below, to drive heavy goods vehicles of Classes

[here specify classes]

from .... until .... inclusive.

CONDITIONS

Name and address of holder's registered employer   ....
....

Name and address of registered hgv driver   ....
training establishment whose vehicles the holder   ....
may drive   ....
....

Class of heavy goods vehicle to which holder's   ....
training agreement applies   ....

1. The holder shall not by virtue of this licence drive a heavy goods vehicle of class 1, 1A, 2, 2A, 3 or 3A unless—

    (*a*) he is a registered employee of the registered employer named above,

    (*b*) the vehicle is owned by that registered employer or by a registered hgv driver training establishment named above, and

    (*c*) the vehicle is a heavy goods vehicle of a class which is stated above as being a class to which the holder's training agreement applies.

In this Condition "registered" means registered for the time being by the National Joint Training Committee for Young HGV Drivers in the Road Goods Transport Industry in accordance with the relevant provisions of their training scheme.

2. This licence is subject also to the special conditions applying to hgv trainee drivers' provisional licences set out in Regulation 10 of the Heavy Goods Vehicles (Drivers' Licences) Regulations 1977.

Usual signature of licensee...

(See Regulations 9 and 10)

SCHEDULE 5

Diagram of distinguishing mark to be displayed on a vehicle driven under a provisional licence.

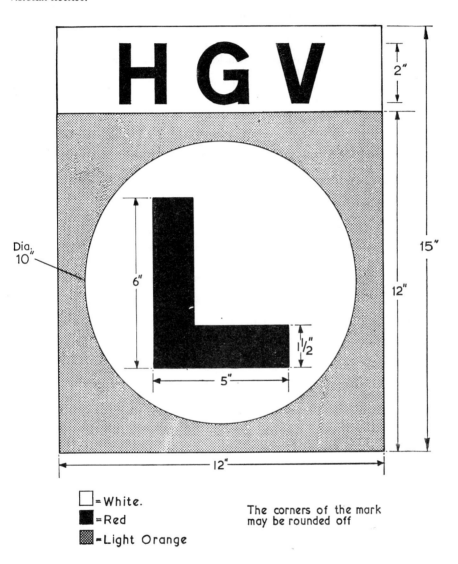

☐ = White.
■ = Red
▨ = Light Orange

The corners of the mark
may be rounded off

(See Regulation 19)

SCHEDULE 6

Nature of Tests—Operations

A. Start the engine of the vehicle.

B. Move off straight ahead and at an angle.

C. Maintain a proper position in relation to a vehicle immediately in front.

D. Overtake and take an appropriate course in relation to other vehicles.

E. Turn right and left.

F. Make an emergency stop.

G. Manoeuvre the vehicle both forwards and backwards, including steering the vehicle along a predetermined course; make it enter a narrow opening and bring it to rest at a predetermined position.

H. Indicate his intended actions by appropriate signals at appropriate times in a clear and unmistakeable manner.

I. Act correctly and promptly in response to all signals given by traffic signs and persons regulating road traffic and take appropriate action on signs given by other road users.

(See Regulations 21 and 25)

SCHEDULE 7

Part I

Form of Certificate of passing a test of competence to drive a Heavy Goods Vehicle

Road Traffic Act 1972 and Road Traffic (Drivers' Ages and Hours of Work) Act 1976
HEAVY GOODS VEHICLE DRIVING TEST

Pass Certificate

I certify that...

....

....

has been examined and has passed the test of competence to drive a heavy goods vehicle of class

as prescribed for the purposes of section 114(1) of the Road Traffic Act 1972.

....

....

....

PART II

FORM OF STATEMENT OF FAILURE TO PASS A TEST OF
COMPETENCE TO DRIVE A HEAVY GOODS VEHICLE

Road Traffic Act 1972 and Road Traffic (Drivers' Ages and Hours of Work) Act 1976
HEAVY GOODS VEHICLE DRIVING TEST

Statement of Failure

Name ....

Address ....

....

has this day been examined on a heavy goods vehicle of Class .... and has failed
to pass the test of competence to drive prescribed for the purposes of section 114(1)
of the Road Traffic Act 1972.

PART III

FORM OF CERTIFICATE OF BEING TREATED AS HAVING PASSED
AN ORDINARY DRIVING TEST

Road Traffic Act 1972 and Road Traffic (Drivers' Ages and Hours of Work) Act 1976
HEAVY GOODS VEHICLE DRIVING TEST

Pass certificate for ordinary driving test

....

has been examined and has passed a test of competence for the purposes of section
114(1) of the Road Traffic Act 1972, and shall be treated under Regulation 25 of the
Heavy Goods Vehicles (Drivers' Licences) Regulations 197 as having passed the
test of competence prescribed under section 85(2) of that Act to drive ....

....

....

....

EXPLANATORY NOTE

(This Note is not part of the Regulations.)

These Regulations consolidate, with further amendments, the Heavy Goods
Vehicles (Drivers' Licences) Regulations 1975 ("the 1975 Regulations") as
amended by the other Regulations specified in Schedule 1 to these Regulations.
The effect of the principal further amendments is as follows.

The provision in Regulation 4(c) of the Regulations of 1975, as amended, for
minimum ages for qualifying to apply for hgv drivers' licences, is removed.
That provision duplicated section 96(1) of the Act of 1972, as amended by
section 1 of the Road Traffic (Drivers' Ages and Hours of Work) Act 1976
and Regulation 4 of the Motor Vehicles (Driving Licences) Regulations 1976

(S.I. No. 1076). The Requirements as to minimum ages of the said section 96 as amended or the corresponding Northern Ireland provision are applied to applicants for hgv drivers' licences in these Regulations by the requirement in Regulation 3(3)(*d*) that the applicant must not be disqualified by reason of his age in respect of any vehicle in the class of heavy goods vehicles to which the licence is to relate and in Regulation 4(*c*) that the applicant must hold an ordinary driving licence or the equivalent Northern Ireland licence authorising him to drive a vehicle or vehicles in the class of heavy goods vehicles to which the licence is to relate.

New provision is made in Regulation 31, together with the new definition of "restricted standard licence" in Regulation 2(1) and amendments in Regulations 10 and 17, to take account of the issue of hgv drivers' licences which, in consequence of paragraph 3 of Schedule 2 to the Road Traffic (Drivers' Ages and Hours of Work) Act 1976, are restricted to vehicles not exceeding 10 metric tons permissible maximum weight (as defined in section 110 of the Act of 1972 as amended by paragraph 5 of Schedule 1 to the Act of 1976) in class 3 or 3A, and to apply a similar restriction to renewals of such licences (Regulation 31(2)) and to hgv drivers' licences issued to holders of ordinary driving licences which are restricted to vehicles not exceeding 10 metric tons permissible maximum weight under paragraph 2 of Schedule 2 to that Act, while they are under 21 years of age (Regulation 31(1)).

The requirement in Regulation 21(2)(*b*) of the 1975 Regulations that a person submitting himself for a test shall produce to the examiner his ordinary driving licence, Northern Ireland (ordinary) driving licence or evidence that he has applied for but not received such a licence and his hgv driver's licence or Northern Ireland hgv driver's licence, is removed.

Two exemptions from heavy goods vehicle licensing are introduced in Regulation 29(1)(*r*) and (*s*). They preserve the exemption in Regulation 28(1)(*r*) of the 1975 Regulations for any articulated vehicle combination (as defined in Regulation 2(1)) the tractive unit of which does not exceed 15 cwt. unladen weight, and also exempt:—

    (i) any articulated vehicle combination which has a permissible weight not exceeding 7·5 metric tons (Regulation 29(1)(*r*)), and

    (ii) any vehicle having a relevant maximum weight (as defined in section 110 of the Act of 1972 as amended by paragraph 5 of Schedule 1 to the Act of 1976) not exceeding 3·5 metric tons to which a trailer is attached, which is not an articulated vehicle combination (Regulation 29(1)(*s*)).

STATUTORY INSTRUMENTS

1977 No. 1310 (S. 97)

HOUSING, SCOTLAND

The Rent Rebate and Rent Allowance Schemes (Students) (Scotland) Amendment Regulations 1977

Made - - - -	*27th July* 1977
Laid before Parliament	*9th August* 1977
Coming into Operation	*1st September* 1977

In exercise of the powers conferred on me by paragraph 17(3) of Schedule 2 to the Housing (Financial Provisions) (Scotland) Act 1972(**a**) (a paragraph added to that Act by section 12(5) (*b*) of the Rent Act 1974(**b**)) and of all other powers enabling me in that behalf, I hereby make the following regulations:—

Citation and Commencement

1. These regulations, which may be cited as the Rent Rebate and Rent Allowance Schemes (Students) (Scotland) Amendment Regulations 1977, shall come into operation on 1st September 1977.

Interpretation

2.—(1) The Interpretation Act 1889(**c**) shall apply for the interpretation of these regulations as it applies for the interpretation of an Act of Parliament and as if for the purposes of section 38 of that Act these regulations were an Act of Parliament and the regulations revoked by regulation 5 hereof were an Act of Parliament thereby repealed.

(2) In these regulations "the principal regulations" means the Rent Rebate and Rent Allowance Schemes (Students) (Scotland) Regulations 1975(**d**).

Amendment of Principal Regulations

3. In regulation 3 of the principal regulations as amended(**e**) there shall be substituted for the figure "£6" the figure "£7".

4. The Rent Rebate and Rent Allowance Schemes (Students) (Scotland) Amendment Regulations 1976(**e**) shall cease to have effect for the purposes of any application for a rebate or allowance relating to any week commencing after 31st August 1977.

Revocation

5. The Rent Rebate and Rent Allowance Schemes (Students) (Scotland) Amendment Regulations 1976 are hereby revoked.

> *Bruce Millan,*
> One of Her Majesty's Principal
> Secretaries of State.

New St. Andrew's House,
Edinburgh.
27th July 1977.

(**a**) 1972 c. 46.	(**b**) 1974 c. 51.	(**c**) 1889 c. 63.	
(**d**) S.I. 1975/1322 (1975 II, p. 4470).		(**e**) S.I. 1976/1288 (1976 II, p. 3667).	

EXPLANATORY NOTE
(This Note is not part of the Regulations.)

These Regulations amend the Rent Rebate and Rent Allowance Schemes (Students) (Scotland) Regulations 1975 previously amended by the Rent Rebate and Rent Allowance Schemes (Students) (Scotland) Amendment Regulations 1976 to provide for the increase to £7 of the deduction which they prescribe. They also revoke the Amendment Regulations referred to. This deduction is made in calculating the rent on the basis of which any rent rebate or rent allowance under Part II (rent rebates and rent allowances) of the Housing (Financial Provisions) (Scotland) Act 1972 may be payable in the case of tenants who are students in receipt of awards or grants in respect of their attendance at full-time courses at universities, colleges of education or other establishments of further education in Scotland.

The Regulations come into operation on 1st September 1977.

STATUTORY INSTRUMENTS

1977 No. 1311 (C. 44)

SOCIAL SECURITY

The Social Security Act 1975 (Commencement No. 3) Order 1977

Made - - - -	*29th July* 1977
Laid before Parliament	*8th August* 1977
Coming into Operation	*30th August* 1977

The Secretary of State for Social Services, in exercise of the powers conferred upon him by paragraph 1 of Schedule 5 to the Social Security Benefits Act 1975(a) as continued by paragraph 27(3) of Schedule 3 to the Social Security (Consequential Provisions) Act 1975(b), and of all other powers enabling him in that behalf, hereby makes the following order: —

Citation and commencement

1. This order may be cited as the Social Security Act 1975 (Commencement No. 3) Order 1977 and shall come into operation on 30th August 1977.

Appointed day

2. In the case of a woman who under section 36(2) of the Social Security Act 1975(c) is not entitled to a non-contributory invalidity pension except where she is incapable of performing normal household duties, the provisions of that Act relating to non-contributory invalidity pension shall come into operation on 30th August 1977 but not so as to confer entitlement to that pension (hereafter in this order referred to as a "a housewife's non-contributory invalidity pension") in respect of any period before 17th November 1977.

Transitional provision relating to claims for a housewife's non-contributory invalidity pension made before 17th November 1977

3.—(1) A claim for a housewife's non-contributory invalidity pension made in the period beginning on 30th August 1977 and ending immediately before 17th November 1977 shall be treated as a claim for that pension made for a period beginning on 17th November 1977.

(2) A decision awarding a housewife's non-contributory invalidity pension on such a claim as is referred to in paragraph (1) of this article which is given before 17th November 1977—

    (a) may, if it appears that the conditions for entitlement will not be satisfied on 17th November 1977, award benefit from the date on which it appears that they will be satisfied, being a date not later than 16th December 1977;

(a) 1975 c. 11.   (b) 1975 c. 18.   (c) 1975 c. 14.

(b) shall be subject to the condition that the requirements for entitlement to that pension are satisfied when that pension becomes payable under the award; and

(c) may be reviewed if those requirements are found not to have been satisfied.

David Ennals,
Secretary of State for Social Services.

29th July 1977.

EXPLANATORY NOTE

(This Note is not part of the Order.)

This Order brings into operation the provisions of the Social Security Act 1975 relating to non-contributory invalidity pension for those women who under section 36(2) of that Act are not entitled to that pension unless they are incapable of performing normal household duties.

The Order provides for entitlement to the pension to commence from 17th November 1977 but enables claims for it to be made and decided from 30th August 1977.

STATUTORY INSTRUMENTS

1977 No. 1312

SOCIAL SECURITY

The Social Security (Non-Contributory Invalidity Pension) Amendment Regulations 1977

Made - - - -	*29th July* 1977
Laid before Parliament	*8th August* 1977
Coming into Operation	*30th August* 1977

The Secretary of State for Social Services, in exercise of the powers conferred upon him by sections 36(6) and (7), 79(1) and 82(1) of the Social Security Act 1975(**a**), and of all other powers enabling him in that behalf, and after reference to the National Insurance Advisory Committee, hereby makes the following regulations:—

Citation, commencement and interpretation

1.—(1) These regulations may be cited as the Social Security (Non-Contributory Invalidity Pension) Amendment Regulations 1977 and shall come into operation on 30th August 1977.

(2) In these regulations "the principal regulations" means the Social Security (Non-Contributory Invalidity Pension) Regulations 1975(**b**) as amended(**c**); and the rules for the construction of Acts of Parliament contained in the Interpretation Act 1889(**d**) shall apply in relation to this instrument and to the revocation effected by it as if this instrument and the regulation revoked by it were Acts of Parliament and as if the revocation were a repeal.

Amendment of the principal regulations

2. Regulation 13 of the principal regulations (transitional provision relating to claims for non-contributory invalidity pension in respect of certain hospital in-patients) is hereby revoked and in the place of that regulation there shall be inserted the following regulations:—

"*Application of the Act and regulations to a woman not entitled to non-contributory invalidity pension unless she is incapable both of work and of performing normal household duties*

13.—(1) For the purpose of determining whether a woman in whose case paragraph (*a*) or (*b*) of section 36(2) of the Act applies (woman residing with her husband or whose husband is contributing to her maintenance at a weekly rate not less than that of non-contributory invalidity pension, or living together as husband and wife with a man to whom she is not married) is entitled to non-contributory invalidity pension for any day, but for that purpose only—

(**a**) 1975 c. 14.
(**c**) S.I. 1975/1166 (1975 II, p. 4031).
(**b**) S.I. 1975/1058 (1975 II, p. 3691).
(**d**) 1889 c. 63.

(*a*) she shall not under the provisions of the Act or of regulations made under it be treated as being or as having been incapable of work on any day unless on that day she is or was incapable both of work and of performing normal household duties; and

(*b*) a day shall not be treated as having been a day of interruption of employment in her case for the purposes of regulation 6 of these regulations (modification of section 36(1) of the Act in the case of a person who has previously been entitled to non-contributory invalidity pension) unless it was a day on which she was incapable both of work and of performing normal household duties.

(2) Paragraph (1)(*a*) of this regulation shall not apply for the purposes of regulation 3(3) of these regulations.

Circumstances in which a woman is or is not to be treated as incapable of performing normal household duties

13A.—(1) A woman shall not be treated as incapable of performing normal household duties unless she is so incapable by reason of some specific disease or bodily or mental disablement.

(2) Where as a result of such a disease or disablement a woman—

(*a*) is unable to perform to any substantial extent, or cannot reasonably be expected to perform to any substantial extent, normal household duties; or

(*b*) in the absence of substantial assistance from or supervision by another person, is unable to perform to any substantial extent, or cannot reasonably be expected to perform to any substantial extent, such duties,

she may be treated as incapable of performing such duties.

(3) Where a woman is living as a member of a household in circumstances in which, were she capable of performing normal household duties, she might ordinarily be expected to be responsible for performing such duties in that household—

(*a*) if in the circumstances existing in that household as they relate to the performance of normal household duties therein she would fall to be regarded as incapable of performing such duties, she may be so regarded notwithstanding that she would not be so regarded in substantially different household circumstances; and

(*b*) if in the circumstances existing in that household as they relate to the performance of normal household duties therein she would not fall to be regarded as incapable of performing normal household duties, she may be treated as not so incapable notwithstanding that she would be or fall to be treated as incapable of performing such duties in substantially different household circumstances.

(4) In determining whether a woman who is entitled to non-contributory invalidity pension immediately before she attains retiring age is thereafter entitled to that pension, she shall on and after attaining that age be treated as incapable of performing normal household duties.".

David Ennals,
Secretary of State for Social Services.

29th July 1977.

EXPLANATORY NOTE
(This Note is not part of the Regulations.)

These Regulations further amend the Social Security (Non-Contributory Invalidity Pension) Regulations 1975 ("the Principal Regulations").

Regulation 1 is formal. Regulation 2 revokes regulation 13 of the Principal Regulations (a transitional provision which is spent) and adds in its place two new regulations containing provisions relating to women who are entitled to non-contributory invalidity pension only if they are incapable both of work and of performing normal household duties.

The Report of the National Insurance Advisory Committee dated 25th April 1977 on the draft of these Regulations referred to them is contained in Command Paper (Cmnd. 6900) published by Her Majesty's Stationery Office.

STATUTORY INSTRUMENTS

1977 No. 1315

CUSTOMS AND EXCISE

The Customs Duties and Drawbacks (Tobacco) (No. 3) Order 1977

Made - - - -	*29th July* 1977
Laid before the House of Commons - -	*1st August* 1977
Coming into Operation	*2nd August* 1977

The Treasury, by virtue of the powers conferred upon them by section 1(4), (5) and (6) of the Finance Act 1973(a), as amended(b), and of all other powers enabling them in that behalf, hereby make the following Order:—

1.—(1) This Order may be cited as the Customs Duties and Drawbacks (Tobacco) (No. 3) Order 1977 and shall come into operation on 2nd August 1977.

(2) The Interpretation Act 1889(c) shall apply for the interpretation of this Order as it applies for the interpretation of an Act of Parliament.

2. The Customs Duties and Drawbacks (Tobacco) Order 1977(d), as amended(e), shall be further amended by:—

(*a*) substituting in Article 4 for the figures "5 or 6" the figures "5, 6 or 6A"; and

(*b*) inserting after Article 6 the following article—

" 6A. The rates of customs duty chargeable on tobacco of heading 24.02 which is an originating product of Cyprus(f) or Malta(g) shall be the rates provided under Article 4 of this Order, reduced, in the case of the rates in Column B, to 30 per cent. thereof.".

T. E. Graham,
J. Dormand,
Two of the Lords Commissioners of
Her Majesty's Treasury.

29th July 1977.

(**a**) 1973 c. 51.

(**b**) See section 8(3) of the Finance Act 1976 (c. 40) and section 1(7) of the Finance Act 1977 (c. 36).

(**c**) 1889 c. 63.

(**d**) S.I. 1977/921 (1977 II, p. 2563).

(**e**) The amendment is not relevant to the subject matter of this Order.

(**f**) *See* the Agreement between the Community and Cyprus and the Protocol thereto signed on 19th December 1972 (annexed to Regulation (EEC) No. 1246/73 O.J. No. L133, 21.5.73, p. 1); the Protocol signed on 19th December 1972 (annexed to Regulation (EEC) No. 1247/73 O.J. No. L133, 21.5.73, p. 87); and Regulation (EEC) No. 1641/77 O.J. No. L183, 22.7.77, p. 6.

(**g**) *See* the Agreement between the Community and Malta and the Protocol thereto signed on 5th December 1970 (annexed to Regulation (EEC) No. 492/71 O.J. No. L61, 14.3.71, p. 1); the Protocol signed on 4th March 1976 (annexed to Regulation (EEC) No. 939/76 O.J. No. L111, 28.4.76, p. 1); and Regulation (EEC) No. 1693/77 O.J. No. L188, 28.7.77, p. 12.

EXPLANATORY NOTE

(This Note is not part of the Order.)

1. This Order, which comes into operation on 2nd August 1977, amends the Customs Duties and Drawbacks (Tobacco) Order 1977 which establishes the rates of customs revenue duties and drawbacks on tobacco.

2. It implements Regulations of the Council of Ministers of the EEC, by allowing a preferential rate of 30 per cent. of the normal protective element in the duties on manufactured tobacco of Cyprus and Malta.

1977 No. 1316

ROAD TRAFFIC

The Vehicle and Driving Licences (Compensation to Officers) Regulations 1977

Made - - - -	*28th July* 1977
Laid before Parliament	*12th August* 1977
Coming into Operation	*2nd September* 1977

ARRANGEMENT OF REGULATIONS

PART I—PRELIMINARY

PART II—ENTITLEMENT TO COMPENSATION

PART III—RESETTLEMENT COMPENSATION

PART IV—LONG-TERM COMPENSATION

The Secretary of State for Transport in exercise of the powers conferred by section 2(3) of the Vehicle and Driving Licences Act 1969(a) and now vested in him (b) and of all other enabling powers, hereby makes the following regulations:—

(a) 1969 c. 27.   (b) S.I. 1970/1681 (1970 III, p. 5551).

Part I—Preliminary

Citation, commencement and revocation

1.—(1) These regulations may be cited as the Vehicle and Driving Licences (Compensation to Officers) Regulations 1977 and shall come into operation on 2nd September 1977.

(2) Subject to the following paragraphs of this regulation, the Vehicle and Driving Licences (Compensation to Officers) Regulations 1970(**a**) are hereby revoked.

(3) Nothing in these regulations shall have effect, in relation to a person to whom the 1970 Regulations applied, so as to invalidate or otherwise affect the operation of those regulations or anything duly done or suffered under them before these regulations first applied to that person and thereafter anything so done or suffered as well as any payments for loss or diminution of emoluments made by or on behalf of the Secretary of State to or in respect of that person before the commencement of these regulations shall be taken into account by the Secretary of State in considering that person's case for the payment of compensation under these regulations, and any compensation to which that person becomes entitled under these regulations shall be reduced or where appropriate otherwise adjusted accordingly.

(4) Without prejudice and subject to paragraph (3) any claim made, review begun or decision notified under the 1970 Regulations before the commencement of these regulations shall be continued and have effect under these regulations as if it were made, begun or notified under the corresponding provisions of these regulations subject, however, to such adjustments or alterations as are appropriate to take account of the provisions of these regulations; and in particular where any person has become entitled to payment of any compensation under the 1970 Regulations, the Secretary of State shall under regulation 32(1)(*b*) carry out a review of his decision, or where the decision has been the subject of an appeal, the decision of the tribunal relating to that person as if the coming into operation of these regulations were an occurrence of a material change in the circumstances of the case, whether that person has required such a review under regulation 32(2) or not, and whether the said occurrence took place before or after the expiry of 6 months from the decision date within the meaning of regulation 32(4).

Interpretation

2.—(1) In these regulations, unless the context otherwise requires, the following expressions have the meanings hereby respectively assigned to them, that is to say—

"accrued pension" in relation to a pensionable officer who has suffered loss of employment, means—

   (*a*) if his last relevant pension scheme provided benefits in which he had a right to participate, the pension to which he would have become entitled under that scheme according to the method of calculation, modified where necessary for the purpose of giving effect to these regulations, prescribed by that scheme, if, at the date on which he ceased to be subject to that scheme, he had attained normal retiring age and complied with any requirement of that scheme as to a minimum

(**a**) S.I. 1970/301 (1970 I, p. 1125).

period of qualifying service or contribution and completed any additional contributory payments or payments in respect of added years which he was in the course of making; and

(b) in any other case, such portion of the pension (if any) of which he had reasonable expectations as the Secretary of State considers equitable, having regard to any practice of the authority or body by whom he was employed on the day immediately preceding the loss, the officer's age, the length of his employment at the date of loss and all the other circumstances of the case;

"accrued retiring allowance", in relation to a pensionable officer who has suffered loss of employment, means—

(a) if his last relevant pension scheme provided benefits in which he has a right to participate, any lump sum payment to which he would have become entitled under that scheme according to the method of calculation (modified where necessary for the purpose of giving effect to these regulations) prescribed by that scheme if, at the date on which he ceased to be subject to that scheme, he had attained normal retiring age and complied with any requirement of that scheme as to a minimum period of qualifying service or contribution and completed any additional contributory payments or payments in respect of added years which he was in the course of making; and

(b) in any other case, such portion of the lump sum payment (if any) of which he had reasonable expectations as the Secretary of State considers equitable, having regard to any practice of the authority or body by whom he was employed on the day immediately preceding the loss, the officer's age, the length of his employment at the date of loss and all the other circumstances of the case;

"accrued incapacity pension" and "accrued incapacity retiring allowance" have the same respective meanings as "accrued pension" and "accrued retiring allowance" except that the reference to a person's attaining normal retiring age shall be construed as a reference to his becoming incapable of discharging efficiently the duties of his employment by reason of permanent ill-health or infirmity of mind or body;

"added years", in relation to a person who suffers loss of employment, means—

(a) in the case of a pensionable employee, any additional years of service being purchased by him in his employment immediately prior to the loss in question under regulation D10 or D11 of the Local Government Superannuation Regulations 1974(a) or, in Scotland, of the Local Government Superannuation (Scotland) Regulations 1974(b) or under any of the former regulations within the meaning of regulation A4 of either of the said sets of superannuation regulations of 1974 and includes any additional years of service which having been granted under any provision similar to that referred to in either of the said regulations D10 or D11 were being so purchased under or by virtue of interchange rules, and

(b) in the case of any other person, any additional years of service, similar to those mentioned in paragraph (a) of this definition, being purchased by him under the last relevant pension scheme,

---

(a) S.I. 1974/520 (1974 I, p. 1986).   (b) S.I. 1974/812 (1974 II, p. 3093).

being in either case additional years which were being purchased partly at the expense of the employer and partly at the expense of the person under arrangements which were entered into before the employer either informed him in writing that his employment was to be terminated or was likely to be terminated or gave him written notice of termination of his employment;

"additional contributory payments" means—

(*a*) additional contributory payments of the kind referred to in regulation D6, D7 or D8 of the Local Government Superannuation Regulations 1974 or, in Scotland, in the correspondingly numbered regulations of the Local Government Superannuation (Scotland) Regulations 1974, or under any of the former regulations within the meaning of the said regulation A4, or

(*b*) any similar payments made under the last relevant pension scheme as a condition of—

(i) reckoning any period of employment as service or as a period of contribution for the purposes of the scheme, or

(ii) reckoning non-contributing service as contributing service (which expressions have the same meaning as in the scheme) for the purposes of the scheme, or

(iii) increasing the length at which any period of service or of contribution would be reckonable for the purpose of calculating a benefit under the scheme, or

(*c*) any payments similar to any of those mentioned in the foregoing paragraphs made in pursuance of interchange rules;

"compensation question" means a question arising under these regulations—

(*a*) as to a person's entitlement to compensation for loss of employment or for loss or diminution of emoluments, or

(*b*) as to the manner of a person's employment or the comparability of his duties;

"emoluments" has the meaning given by regulation 38(1), and "annual rate of emoluments" has the meaning given by regulation 38(3);

"enactment" includes any instrument made under an Act;

"fund authority" in relation to any person, means the authority maintaining the superannuation fund or account in relation to that person;

"interchange rules" means rules made under section 2 of the Superannuation (Miscellaneous Provisions) Act 1948(a) (which provides for the pensions of persons transferring to different employment) and includes any similar instrument made, or having effect as if made, under any other Act which makes similar provision;

"local authority" means in England and Wales, any of the authorities listed in Part I of Schedule 2 to these regulations, and in Scotland, any of the authorities listed in Part II of that Schedule;

"long-term compensation" means compensation payable in accordance with the provisions of Part IV of these regulations for loss of employment or loss or diminution of emoluments;

(a) 1948 c. 33.

"material date", in relation to any person who has suffered loss of employment or loss or diminution of emoluments, means the date of the coming
into operation of these regulations or the date on which the loss or diminution
occurred, whichever is the earlier;

"minimum pensionable age" means, in relation to a pensionable officer,
the earliest age at which under his last relevant pension scheme he could
have become entitled to receive payment of an unreduced pension solely by
virtue of his having attained a specified age and completed a specified period
of service;

"national service" means, in relation to any person, service which is
compulsory national service or relevant service within the meaning of the
Reserve and Auxiliary Forces (Protection of Civil Interests) Act 1951(a)
and any similar service immediately following such service entered into with
the consent of the authority or person under whom an officer held his last
relevant employment, or, where appropriate, the authority by whom such
an officer was appointed;

"normal retiring age" means in the case of a pensionable officer to whom an
age of compulsory retirement applied by virtue of any enactment to which he
was subject in the employment which he has lost or the emoluments of which
have been diminished or by virtue of the conditions of that employment,
that age, and in any other case the age of sixty-five years if the officer is a
male, or sixty years if the officer is a female;

"officer" includes the holder of any place, situation or employment and
the expression "office" shall be construed accordingly;

"pensionable employee" has the same meaning as in the Local Government
Superannuation Regulations 1974, and, in Scotland, as in the Local Government Superannuation (Scotland) Regulations 1974;

"pensionable officer", in relation to a person who has suffered loss of
employment or loss or diminution of emoluments, means a person who
immediately before such loss or diminution was subject to a pension scheme
associated with the employment he has lost or, as the case may be, the employment in which his emoluments have been diminished;

"pension scheme", in relation to a pensionable officer, means any form of
arrangement associated with his employment for the payment of superannuation benefits, whether subsisting by virtue of Act of Parliament, trust,
contract or otherwise; and "last relevant pension scheme", in relation to a
pensionable officer, means a pension scheme to which he was subject immediately before suffering loss of employment or loss or diminution of emoluments;

"reckonable service", in relation to a person, means any period of whole-
time or part-time employment in any relevant employment and includes any
period of national service or war service undertaken on his ceasing to hold
such an employment, but does not include employment in respect of which he
has become entitled to receive a benefit from a pension scheme other than
his last relevant pension scheme;

"the 1970 Regulations" means the Vehicle and Driving Licences (Compensation to Officers) Regulations 1970(b);

(a) 1951 c. 65.   (b) S.I. 1970/301 (1970 I, p. 1125).

"relevant employment" means employment—

(a) under the Crown or in the service of a local authority; or

(b) by any authority or body for the purposes of the Crown or of local government in Great Britain; or

(c) under any officer employed as mentioned in paragraph (a) or (b) of this definition for the purposes of the functions of the employing authority or body; or

(d) preceding any of the foregoing employments which was reckonable for the purposes of the last relevant pension scheme;

but, except for national service and war service, does not include service in the armed forces of the Crown;

"resettlement compensation" means compensation payable in accordance with Part III of these regulations for loss of employment;

"retirement compensation" means compensation payable in accordance with the provisions of regulation 18, 19 or 20;

"the Secretary of State", except in paragraph 8 of Schedule 2, means the Secretary of State for Transport;

"tribunal" means a tribunal established under section 12 of the Industrial Training Act 1964(a);

"war service" means war service within the meaning of the Local Government Staffs (War Service) Act 1939(b), the Teachers Superannuation (War Service) Act 1939(c) or, in Scotland, the Education (Scotland) (War Service Superannuation) Act 1939(d)), the Police and Firemen (War Service) Act 1939(e) or employment for war purposes within the meaning of the Superannuation Schemes (War Service) Act 1940(f) and includes any period of service in the First World War in the armed forces of the Crown or in the forces of the Allied or Associated Powers if such service immediately followed a period of relevant employment and was undertaken either compulsorily or with the permission of the employer in that employment.

(2) Where under any provision of these regulations an annual value is to be assigned to a capital sum or a capital value to an annual amount—

(a) the annual or capital value shall be ascertained in accordance with the tables set out in Schedule 1 insofar as they provide for the particular case;

(b) where the said tables do not provide for a case in which an annual value is to be assigned to a capital sum or a capital value to an annual amount, the annual or capital value shall be the value as may be agreed between the Secretary of State and the person to whom the capital sum or annual amount is payable; and

(c) for the purpose of determining the application of the said tables, the headings and the note to each table shall be treated as part of the table.

(3) In these regulations, unless the context otherwise requires, references to any enactment shall be construed as references thereto as amended, re-enacted, applied or modified by any subsequent enactment.

(a) 1964 c. 16.	(b) 1939 c. 94.	(c) 1939 c. 95.
(d) 1939 c. 96.	(e) 1939 c. 103.	(f) 1940 c. 26.

(4) References in these regulations to a numbered regulation or Schedule shall, unless the reference is to a regulation of or a Schedule to specified regulations, be construed as references to the regulation or Schedule bearing that number in these regulations.

(5) References in any of these regulations to a numbered paragraph shall, unless the reference is to a paragraph of a specified regulation, be construed as references to the paragraph bearing that number in the first mentioned regulation.

(6) The Interpretation Act 1889(a) shall apply for the interpretation of these regulations as it applies for the interpretation of an Act of Parliament, and, subject to regulation 1(3) and (4), as if for the purposes of section 38 of that Act those regulations were an Act of Parliament and the Regulations revoked by regulation 1(2) were Acts of Parliament thereby repealed.

PART II—ENTITLEMENT TO COMPENSATION

Persons to whom the regulations apply

3.—(1) These Regulations shall apply to any person who—

(a) was employed immediately before the 25th June 1969 for the whole or for part only of his time—

(i) as an officer of a county council or under such an officer for the purposes of the functions conferred on county councils by the Vehicles (Excise) Act 1962(b) or Part II of the Road Traffic Act 1960(c) (which provide for the levying of excise duty on vehicles, the licensing and registration of vehicles and the licensing of drivers); or

(ii) as an officer of the Council of the Isles of Scilly or under such an officer for the purposes of the functions relating to the licensing of drivers which are conferred on that council by virtue of the Isles of Scilly Order 1937(d), or

(b) would have been so employed at that time but for any national service on which he was then engaged.

(2) In this Regulation "county council" means the council of a county, the Greater London Council, the council of a county borough and the council of a burgh within the meaning of the Local Government Scotland Act 1947(e) containing a population, according to the census for the time being last taken, of or exceeding fifty thousand.

Grounds of entitlement to compensation

4. Subject to the provisions of these regulations, any person to whom these regulations apply and who suffers loss of employment or loss or diminution of emoluments which is attributable to section 1 of the Vehicle and Driving Licences Act 1969 shall be entitled to have his case considered for the payment of compensation under these regulations, and such compensation shall be determined in accordance with these regulations.

(a) 1889 c. 63.
(b) 1962 c. 13.
(c) 1960 c. 16.
(d) S.R. & O. 1937/783 (Rev. XII, p. 554: 1937 p. 1550).
(e) 1947 c. 43.

National service

5.—(1) Any person to whom these regulations apply because he satisfies the provisions of regulation 3(1)(*b*) and who before the expiry of two months after ceasing to be engaged on his national service, or if prevented by sickness or other reasonable cause, as soon as practicable thereafter, gives notice to the Secretary of State that he is available for employment, shall be entitled to have his case considered for the payment of compensation on the ground—

(*a*) if he is not given or offered re-employment in his former office or in any reasonably comparable office (whether in the same or in a different service), of loss of employment; or

(*b*) if he is so re-employed with diminished emoluments as compared with the emoluments which he would have enjoyed had he continued in his former employment, of diminution of emoluments.

(2) The loss of employment which is the cause of a claim for compensation under paragraph (1)(*a*) shall be treated as having occurred on the earlier of the two following dates, that is to say, the date of the refusal of re-employment or a date one month after the date on which the person gave notice that he was available for employment; and the person shall be deemed to have been entitled to the emoluments which he would have enjoyed at such earlier date had he continued in his former employment.

PART III—RESETTLEMENT COMPENSATION

Resettlement compensation for loss of employment

6. The Secretary of State shall, subject to the provisions of these regulations, pay resettlement compensation to any person to whom these regulations apply and who satisfies the conditions set out in Regulation 7.

Conditions for payment of resettlement compensation

7.—(1) Without prejudice to any other requirement of these regulations, the conditions for the payment of resettlement compensation to any person are that—

(*a*) he has, not later than ten years after the material date, suffered loss of employment attributable to section 1 of the Vehicle and Driving Licences Act 1969;

(*b*) he shall not, at the date of the loss, have attained normal retiring age;

(*c*) he shall have been for a period beginning 2 years immediately before the material date continuously engaged (disregarding breaks not exceeding in the aggregate 6 months) for the whole or part of his time in relevant employment;

(*d*) he shall have made a claim for such compensation in accordance with the provisions of Part VII of these regulations not later than 13 weeks after the loss of employment which is the cause of his claim, or 13 weeks after the coming into operation of these regulations, whichever is the later, or within any longer period which the Secretary of State allows in any particular case where he is satisfied that the delay in making the claim was due to ill health or other circumstances beyond the claimant's control;

(e) the loss of employment which is the cause of his claim shall have occurred for some reason other than misconduct or incapacity to perform such duties as, immediately before the loss, he was performing or might reasonably have been required to perform; and

(f) he shall not, subject to paragraphs (2) and (3) after his employer either informed him in writing that his employment was to be terminated or was likely to be terminated or gave him written notice of termination of his employment, have been offered in writing

(i) any relevant employment which is reasonably comparable with the employment which he has lost, or

(ii) any employment suitable for him under the Crown or by a local authority in the same locality as that in which he had been employed immediately before he suffered the loss.

(2) In ascertaining for the purposes of this regulation whether a person has been offered employment which is reasonably comparable with the employment which he has lost, no account shall be taken of the fact that the duties of the employment offered are in relation to a different service from that in connection with which his employment was held or are duties which involve a transfer of his employment from one place to another within Great Britain.

(3) For the purposes of this regulation, where the Secretary of State is satisfied—

(a) that acceptance of an offer would have involved undue hardship to the person,

(b) that he was prevented from accepting an offer by reason of ill-health or other circumstances beyond his control, or

(c) that, before the commencement of these regulations, an offer—

(i) has not been accepted by him, and

(ii) has lapsed or otherwise terminated,

no account shall be taken of that offer.

Amount of resettlement compensation

8.—(1) The amount of resettlement compensation which may be paid to a person shall, subject to the provisions of paragraphs (2) to (6), be the amount described in sub-paragraph (a) or (b) whichever is the greater, namely—

(a) an amount equal to 13 weeks emoluments and, in the case of a person who has attained the age of 45 one additional week's emoluments for every year of his age after attaining the age of 45 and before the loss of employment, subject to a maximum addition of 13 such weeks; or

(b) an amount equal to—

(i) one and one half week's emoluments for each completed year of reckonable service in which the person was not below the age of 41,

(ii) one week's emoluments for each completed year of reckonable service (not falling within sub-paragraph (i) above) in which the person was not below the age of 22, and

(iii) one half week's emoluments for each completed year of reckonable service not falling within sub-paragraph (i) or (ii) above.

(2) For the purposes of paragraph (1)(*a*), if the loss of employment takes place within three years of the date on which the person would have attained normal retiring age, the amount shall be reduced by the fraction of which—

(*a*) the numerator is the number of complete periods of 6 months in the period beginning on the date 3 years before that on which he would have attained normal retiring age and ending on the date of loss of employment, and

(*b*) the denominator is 6;

but the amount payable to a person who, on the material date, has not been so continuously engaged in relevant employment as described in regulation 11(1)(*c*) shall not by this paragraph be reduced to less than the equivalent of 13 weeks' emoluments.

(3) For the purpose of paragraph (1)(*b*), in the case of a person who has completed more than 20 years reckonable service, only the period of 20 years immediately prior to the loss of employment shall be taken into account.

(4) For the purpose of paragraph (1)(*b*), if the loss of a person's employment takes place after he has attained the age described in paragraph (5), the amount shall be reduced by the fraction of which the numerator is the number of whole months in the period beginning on the date on which he attained that age and ending on the date of loss of employment and of which the denominator is 12.

(5) The age mentioned in paragraph (4) is—

(*a*) the age of compulsory retirement applied to the person by virtue of any enactment to which he was subject in the employment which he has lost or by virtue of the conditions of that employment, less 12 months, or

(*b*) if no age of compulsory retirement is applied to the person as described in sub-paragraph (*a*) above, the age of 64.

(6) For the purpose of this regulation, the weekly rate of emoluments shall be deemed to be seven 365ths of the annual rate of emoluments.

Adjustment of resettlement compensation

9. A person who is entitled to—

(*a*) a redundancy payment under the Redundancy Payments Act 1965(**a**), or

(*b*) any similar payment in consequence of the loss of his employment under any other enactment or under any contract or arrangement with the authority by whom he was employed (other than payments by way of a return of contributions under a pension scheme), or

(*c*) any payment under or by virtue of the provisions of any enactment relating to the reinstatement in civil employment of persons who have been in the service of the Crown,

shall—

(i) if the amount of any resettlement compensation that would, apart from this regulation, be payable exceeds the payment or payments specified in (*a*), (*b*) and (*c*) above, be entitled to resettlement compensation equal to that excess, or

---

(**a**) 1965 c. 62.

(ii) if the amount of any resettlement compensation that would, apart from this regulation, be payable is equal to or less than the payment or payments specified in (*a*), (*b*) and (*c*) above, not be entitled to resettlement compensation.

PART IV—LONG-TERM COMPENSATION

Long-term compensation for loss of employment or loss or diminution of emoluments

10. The Secretary of State shall, subject to the provisions of these regulations, pay long-term compensation to any person to whom these regulations apply and who satisfies the conditions set out in regulation 11.

Conditions for payment of long-term compensation

11.—(1) Without prejudice to any other requirement of these regulations, the conditions for the payment of long-term compensation to any person are that—

(*a*) he has, not later than 10 years after the material date, suffered loss of employment or loss or diminution of emoluments attributable to section 1 of the Vehicle and Driving Licences Act 1969;

(*b*) he shall not, save as is provided in regulation 26, at the date of the loss or diminution have attained normal retiring age;

(*c*) he shall have been for a period beginning not less than 5 years immediately before the material date continuously engaged (without a break of more than 12 months at any one time) for the whole or part of his time in relevant employment;

(*d*) he shall have made a claim for such compensation in accordance with the provisions of Part VII of these regulations not later than 2 years after the loss or diminution which is the cause of the claim or 2 years after the coming into operation of these regulations whichever is the later; and

(*e*) if the cause of the claim for compensation is loss of employment—

(i) the loss shall have occurred for some reason other than misconduct or incapacity to perform the duties that, immediately before the loss, he was performing or might reasonably have been required to perform; and

(ii) he shall not, subject to paragraph (2), after the employer either informed him in writing that his employment was to be terminated or was likely to be terminated or gave him written notice of termination of his employment, have been offered in writing any relevant employment which is reasonably comparable with the employment which he has lost.

(2) Regulation 7(2) and (3) (which relate to offers of employment) shall apply for the purposes of this regulation in ascertaining whether a person has been offered reasonably comparable employment.

(3) Claims for long-term compensation for loss of employment shall in all respects be treated as claims for such compensation for the loss of emoluments occasioned thereby and the provisions of these regulations shall apply to all such claims accordingly.

Factors to be considered in determining payment of long-term compensation

12.—(1) For the purpose of determining whether long-term compensation for loss or diminution of emoluments should be paid to any person, and if so, the amount of the compensation (subject to the limits set out in these regulations) the Secretary of State shall, subject to the provisions of paragraphs (2) and (3), have regard to such of the following factors as may be relevant, that is to say—

(*a*) the conditions upon which the person held the employment which he has lost, including in particular its security of tenure, whether by law or practice;

(*b*) the emoluments and other conditions, including security of tenure, whether by law or practice, of any work or employment undertaken by the person as a result of the loss of employment;

(*c*) the extent to which he has sought suitable employment and the emoluments which he might have acquired by accepting other suitable employment which, after his employer either informed him in writing that his employment was to be terminated, or was likely to be terminated or gave him written notice of termination of his employment, has been offered to him in writing; and

(*d*) all the other circumstances of his case;

but, subject to the provisions of regulation 40, no account shall be taken of the fact that he entered the employment which he has lost or of which the emoluments have been diminished after 13 November 1968.

(2) In ascertaining for the purposes of paragraph (1)(*b*) and (1)(*c*) the emoluments in respect of any work or employment that gives the employee or his widow child or other dependant the right to benefit under a pension scheme under which the employee is not under an obligation to pay contributions, the amount of emoluments shall be increased by the amount of contributions which the employee would have to pay to secure equivalent benefits under a pension scheme in respect of which both the employer and the employee are under an obligation to pay equal contributions.

(3) Regulation 7(3) shall apply for the purposes of this regulation in ascertaining whether a person has been offered suitable employment.

Amount of long-term compensation payable for loss of emoluments

13.—(1) Long-term compensation for loss of emoluments shall, subject to the provisions of these regulations, be payable until the normal retiring age or death of a person to whom it is payable, whichever first occurs, and shall not exceed a maximum annual sum calculated in accordance with the provisions of paragraphs (2) to (4).

(2) The said maximum annual sum shall, subject as hereinafter provided, be the aggregate of the following sums, namely—

(*a*) for every year of a person's reckonable service, one-sixtieth of the emoluments which he has lost; and

(*b*) in the case of a person who has attained the age of 40 at the date of the loss, a sum calculated in accordance with the provisions of paragraph (3) appropriate to his age at that date,

but the said maximum annual sum shall in no case exceed two-thirds of the emoluments which the person has lost.

(3) The sum referred to in paragraph (2)(*b*) shall be—

(*a*) in the case of a person who has attained the age of 40 but has not attained the age of 50 at the date of the loss, the following fraction of the emoluments which he has lost—

(i) where his reckonable service is less than 10 years, one sixtieth for each year of that service after attaining the age of 40; or

(ii) where his reckonable service amounts to 10 years but is less than 15 years, one sixtieth for each year of that service after attaining the age of 40 and one additional sixtieth; or

(iii) where his reckonable service amounts to 15 years but is less than 20 years, one sixtieth for each year of that service after attaining the age of 40 and two additional sixtieths; or

(iv) where his reckonable service amounts to 20 years or more, one sixtieth for each year of that service after attaining the age of 40 and three additional sixtieths;

but the sum so calculated shall not in any case exceed one sixth of the said emoluments;

(*b*) in the case of a person who has attained the age of 50 but has not attained the age of 60 at the date of the loss, one sixtieth of the said emoluments for each year of his reckonable service after attaining the age of 40, up to a maximum of 15 years; and

(*c*) in the case of a person who has attained the age of 60 at the date of the loss, one sixtieth of the said emoluments for each year of his reckonable service after attaining the age of 45.

(4) The amount of long-term compensation calculated in accordance with paragraphs (2) and (3) shall be reduced by the amount by which the aggregate of—

(*a*) the emoluments of any work or other employment undertaken by him as a result of the loss of employment, and

(*b*) the long-term compensation which apart from this paragraph and any reduction under regulation 30(3) and (4) would be payable to him,

exceeds the emoluments of the employment which has been lost.

(5) Long-term compensation shall be payable to a person at intervals equivalent to those at which the emoluments of his employment were previously paid or at such other intervals as may be agreed between the person and the Secretary of State.

Long-term compensation for diminution of emoluments

14.—(1) Long-term compensation for diminution of emoluments in respect of any employment shall, subject to the provisions of these regulations, consist of an annual sum calculated in accordance with the provisions of paragraph (2).

(2) The said annual sum shall not exceed the sum that would be the annual sum under the provisions of regulations 13(1) to (4) calculated on the assumptions—

(*a*) that there was a loss of employment, and

(*b*) that emoluments after diminution were emoluments of any work or employment undertaken as a result of the loss of employment.

(3) Long-term compensation for diminution of emoluments shall be payable to a person at intervals equivalent to those at which the emoluments of his employment are or were previously paid or at such other intervals as may be agreed between the person and the Secretary of State.

Period during which long-term compensation is to be payable

15.—(1) Long-term compensation shall be payable with effect from the date of the claim or from any earlier date permitted by the succeeding provisions of this regulation.

(2) Where a claim for long-term compensation is duly made within 13 weeks of the commencement of these regulations or the occurrence of the loss or diminution which is the cause of the claim (whichever is the later), the award shall be made effective from the date on which the loss or diminution occurred.

(2) Where a claim for long-term compensation is made after the expiry of the period mentioned in paragraph (2), the award may, at the discretion of the Secretary of State, be made retrospective to a date not earlier than 13 weeks prior to the date on which the claim was made:

Provided that if the Secretary of State is satisfied that the failure to make the claim within the period mentioned in paragraph (2) was due to ill-health or other circumstances beyond the claimant's control, the award may be made retrospective to a date not earlier than that on which the loss or diminution occurred.

(4) Long-term compensation shall not be payable to a person for any period in respect of which compensation under Part V of these regulations is payable to him.

PART V—RETIREMENT COMPENSATION AND PAYMENTS ON DEATH

Entitlement to retirement compensation and other payments

16.—(1) The Secretary of State shall, subject to the provisions of these regulations, pay retirement compensation to any person to whom this Part of these regulations applies, and shall make the other payments for which provision is made in regulations 23 to 27.

(2) Save as is provided in regulation 26, this Part of these regulations applies to a pensionable officer who satisfies the conditions set out in regulation 11.

(3) Regulation 12 shall apply in relation to compensation under this Part of these regulations as it applies in relation to compensation under Part IV.

Additional factors governing payment of retirement compensation

17.—(1) Where retirement compensation is payable under any one of regulations 18, 19 or 20, such compensation shall not be payable under any other of those regulations.

(2) If a person has attained the age of 40 at the date on which he lost his employment or suffered a diminution of his emoluments, the Secretary of State,

in calculating the amount of the retirement compensation payable to him, shall credit him with an additional period of service on the following basis, namely—

(a) 2 years, whether or not he has completed any years of service after attaining the age of 40,

(b) 2 years for each of the first 4 years of his reckonable service between the date when he attained the age of 40 and the date of the loss or diminution, and

(c) one year for each year of that reckonable service after the fourth,

but the additional period so credited shall not exceed the shortest of the following periods, namely—

(i) the number of years that, when added to his pensionable service, would amount to the maximum period of service which would have been reckonable by him had he continued in his employment until attaining normal retiring age,

(ii) the period of his reckonable service, or

(iii) 15 years;

and in calculating the amount of any retirement compensation payable to him, any period so added shall be aggregated with any period entailing reduction of the relevant pension or retiring allowance because of a retirement pension payable under section 28 of the Social Security Act 1975**(a)**.

(3) The benefit in respect of the additional period described in paragraph (2) shall be calculated at the same rate as is applicable for the day immediately preceding the loss or diminution.

(4) When retirement compensation is awarded, or when an award is reviewed under regulation 32, the additional compensation payable in consequence of any period credited to a person under paragraph (2) may be reduced or withheld to the extent that the Secretary of State may think reasonable having regard to the pension scheme (if any) associated with any further employment obtained by him.

(5) If under his last relevant pension scheme the amount of any benefit to which a person might have become entitled could have been increased at the discretion of the authority administering the pension scheme or of any other body, the Secretary of State may increase, to an extent not exceeding that to which his accrued pension, accrued retiring allowance, accrued incapacity pension or accrued incapacity retiring allowance might have been increased or supplemented, the corresponding component of any retirement compensation payable to him; and in this connection the Secretary of State shall have regard to the terms of any relevant resolutions of the authority or body with regard to the increase of benefits and to the provisions of any enactment protecting the interests of that person.

(6) If under his last relevant pension scheme a person would have been entitled to surrender a proportion of any pension which might have become payable in favour of his spouse or any dependant, then, if he so desires and informs the Secretary of State by notice in writing accordingly within one month after becoming entitled to retirement compensation under these regulations, he may surrender a proportion of so much of the said compensation as is payable by way of an annual sum on the like terms and conditions and in consideration of the like payments by the Secretary of State as if the said annual sum were a pension to which he had become entitled under the said pension scheme.

(a) 1975 c. 14.

(7) In calculating for the purpose of regulation 18 or 19 the amount of the annual sum which is equal to the person's accrued pension, no account shall be taken of any reduction falling to be made in the pension by reason of the provisions of any enactment relating to National Insurance or Social Security until the person reaches the age at which under his last relevant pension scheme the pension would have been so reduced.

Retirement compensation for loss of emoluments payable to pensionable officer on attainment of normal retiring age

18.—(1) Subject to the provisions of these regulations, when a person to whom this Part of these regulations applies reaches normal retiring age, the retirement compensation payable to him for loss of emoluments shall be—

(a) an annual sum equal to the amount of his accrued pension, and

(b) a lump sum equal to the amount of his accrued retiring allowance (if any).

(2) No compensation shall be payable under this regulation if the person has continued to pay superannuation contributions as if he had suffered no loss of emoluments.

Retirement compensation payable to pensionable officer on his becoming incapacited or reaching minimum pensionable age

19.—(1) Where a person to whom this Part of these regulations applies and who has suffered loss of employment before attaining what would have been his normal retiring age—

(a) becomes incapacitated in circumstances in which, if he had continued in the employment which he has lost, he would have become entitled to a pension under his last relevant pension scheme, or

(b) attains the age which, had he continued to serve in the employment which he has lost, would have been his minimum pensionable age,

he shall be entitled on the happening of either event to claim—

(i) in the case mentioned in sub-paragraph (a) above an annual sum equal to the amount of his accrued incapacity pension and a lump sum equal to the amount of his accrued incapacity retiring allowance (if any) and

(ii) in the case mentioned in sub-paragraph (b) above, an annual sum equal to the amount of his accrued pension and a lump sum equal to the amount of his accrued retiring allowance (if any),

subject however to the conditions specified in paragraph (5).

(2) On receipt of a claim under paragraph (1), the Secretary of State shall consider whether the claimant is a person to whom that paragraph applies, and

(a) if the Secretary of State is satisfied that he is not such a person, the claimant shall be notified in writing accordingly; or

(b) if the Secretary of State is satisfied that he is such a person, he shall assess the amount of compensation payable to the claimant and notify him in writing accordingly;

and notification in accordance with sub-paragraph (a) or (b) above shall, for the purpose of these regulations, be deemed to be a notification by the Secretary of State of a decision on a claim for compensation.

(3) The Secretary of State may require any person who makes a claim under paragraph (1)(*a*) to submit himself to a medical examination by a registered medical practitioner selected by the Secretary of State, and if he does so, he shall also offer the person an opportunity of submitting a report from his own medical adviser as a result of an examination by him, and the Secretary of State shall take that report into consideration together with the report of the medical practitioner selected by him.

(4) If a person wishes to receive compensation under this regulation, he shall so inform the Secretary of State in writing within one month from the receipt of the notification under paragraph (2) or, where the claim has been the subject of an appeal, from the decision of the tribunal thereon, and the compensation shall be payable as from the date on which the Secretary of State received the claim.

(5) The calculation of compensation under this regulation shall be subject to the following conditions—

(*a*) where the Secretary of State, by virtue of.regulation 17, has credited the person with an additional period of service, no account shall be taken of any additional period beyond the period which he could have served, had he not lost his employment, before the date on which the claim was received by the Secretary of State; and

(*b*) if, by reason of any provision of the relevant pension scheme for a minimum benefit, the amount of any such pension or retiring allowance is in excess of that attributable to the person's actual service, no account shall be taken of any such additional period of service except to the extent (if any) by which it exceeds the number of years represented by the difference between his actual service and the period by reference to which the minimum benefit has been calculated; and

(*c*) if the number of years by reference to which an accrued incapacity pension or accrued incapacity retiring allowance is to be calculated is less than any minimum number of years of qualifying service prescribed by the relevant pension scheme, the amount of such pension or retiring allowance shall, notwithstanding any minimum benefit prescribed by the pension scheme, not exceed the proportion of the minimum benefit which the number of years of pensionable service bears to the minimum number of years of qualifying service.

Retirement compensation for diminution of emoluments

20.—(1) A person to whom this Part of these regulations applies and who has suffered a diminution of his emoluments shall be entitled to receive retirement compensation in accordance with the provisions of this regulation.

(2) The provisions of regulations 18 and 19 shall apply to any such person as if he had suffered loss of employment immediately before the diminution occurred; but the amount of retirement compensation payable shall be the amount which would have been payable in respect of loss of employment multiplied by a fraction of which—

(*a*) the numerator is the amount by which his pensionable emoluments have been diminished, and

(*b*) the denominator is the amount of his pensionable emoluments immediately before they were diminished;

and for the purposes of this calculation no account shall be taken of any reduction which might otherwise fall to be made in the accrued pension or accrued incapacity pension because of a retirement pension payable under section 28 of the Social Security Act 1975.

(3) No compensation shall be payable under this regulation—

(*a*) if the person has continued to pay superannuation contributions as if his emoluments had not been diminished, or

(*b*) where by virtue of the provisions of his last relevant pension scheme the person's superannuation benefits are calculated by reference to remuneration for a period prior to the date on which his emoluments were diminished.

Superannuation contributions

21.—(1) A person entitled to retirement compensation under regulation 18 or 19 shall pay an amount equal to any sum which was paid to him by way of return of superannuation contributions (including any interest) after ceasing to be employed—

(*a*) if the provisions of his last relevant pension scheme enable him to be credited with benefits attributable to that sum, to the fund authority, and

(*b*) in any other case, to the Secretary of State.

(2) If the person does not pay as specified in paragraph (1), his retirement compensation shall be reduced by an annual amount the capital value of which is equal to the amount of the said superannuation contributions.

(3) For the purposes of this regulation the expression "superannuation contributions" shall include payments made by the person in respect of added years, any additional contributory payments made by him and any other payments made by him for the purpose of increasing the benefits to which he would have become entitled under his last relevant pension scheme.

Retirement compensation of a person who obtains further pensionable employment

22.—(1) Where a person to whom this Part of these regulations applies, after suffering loss of employment or diminution of emoluments, enters employment in which he is subject to a pension scheme and thereafter becomes entitled to reckon for the purposes of that scheme any service or period of contribution which falls to be taken into account for the purpose of assessing the amount of any retirement compensation payable to him, his entitlement to retirement compensation shall be reviewed, and, subject to the provisions of this regulation, no retirement compensation shall be payable in respect of that service or period unless the annual rate of the emoluments to which he was entitled immediately before the loss or diminution exceeds the annual rate on entry of the emoluments of the new employment, and any retirement compensation so payable to him shall, insofar as it is calculated by reference to remuneration, be calculated by reference to the difference between the said annual rates.

(2) The provisions of this regulation shall not operate to increase the amount of any retirement compensation payable in respect of diminution of emoluments beyond the amount which would have been payable if the person had attained

normal retiring age immediately before he ceased to hold the employment in which he suffered the diminution of emoluments.

(3) No retirement compensation shall be payable in the circumstances mentioned in this regulation if the person has continued to pay superannuation contributions as if his emoluments had not been diminished.

Compensation payable to widow or dependants of a claimant

23.—(1) Where a person to whom this Part of these regulation applies dies, payments in accordance with this regulation and regulations 24 and 25 shall be made to or for the benefit of his widow, child or other dependant or to his personal representatives or, as the case maybe, to trustees empowered by him to stand possessed of any benefit under his last relevant pension scheme.

(2) Where the widow, child or other dependant has become, or but for the person's loss of employment would have become, entitled to benefits under his last relevant pension scheme, the widow, child or other dependant, as the case may be, shall (subject to the provisions of this regulation) be entitled to compensation calculated from time to time in accordance with the methods prescribed by the last relevant pension scheme modified as follows:—

(a) where the person dies before becoming entitled to receive retirement compensation and the last relevant pension scheme provides that when he dies in service his widow, child or other dependant shall be entitled for any period to a benefit equal to his pensionable remuneration, the annual rate of compensation for that period shall be equal to the annual amount of his long-term compensation calculated in accordance with paragraphs (1) to (3) of regulation 13;

(b) where the person dies before becoming entitled to receive retirement compensation and the last relevant pension scheme provides that when he dies in service his widow, child or other dependant shall be entitled for any period to a benefit calculated by reference to the pension or incapacity pension which would have been payable to him if he had retired immediately before his death, the compensation for that period shall be calculated by reference to the retirement compensation to which he would have been entitled under regulation 19 if that regulation had been applied to him immediately before his death;

(c) where a person dies after becoming entitled to receive retirement compensation and the last relevant pension scheme provides that when he dies after having retired his widow, child or other dependant shall be entitled for any period to a benefit equal to his pension, the annual rate of compensation for that period shall be equal to the annual amount of retirement compensation;

(d) where a person dies after he had become entitled to receive retirement compensation and the last relevant pension scheme provides that when he dies after having retired his widow, child or other dependant shall be entitled for any period to a benefit calculated by reference to his pension, the annual rate of compensation for that period shall be calculated by reference to the annual amount of retirement compensation that would have been payable to him but for any reduction or suspension under regulation 30(1);

(e) for the purposes of calculating compensation in accordance with the foregoing provisions, each year added to a person's reckonable service under regulation 17 (or which would have been added if retirement under regulation 19 were assumed) shall be deemed to have been service rendered immediately before the loss of employment.

(3) Calculation of the amounts described in paragraph (2) shall be subject to the following adjustments:—

(a) where any retirement compensation has been surrendered under regulation 17(6) or compounded under regulation 33, any sum payable under paragraph (2)(b) and (d) shall be calculated as if such surrender or compounding had not taken place;

(b) it shall be assumed the retirement compensation payable, or which would have been payable, had been such sum as would have been payable if the accrued pension or accrued incapacity pension had not been reduced by reason of the provisions of any enactment relating to National Insurance or Social Security; and

(c) if immediately before his death the person's long-term compensation was reduced under regulation 13(4) or 32(7) or his retirement compensation was reduced or suspended under regulation 30(1) by reason of employment in which he was subject to a pension scheme and the widow, child or other dependant is entitled under that scheme for any period to a benefit equal to his pensionable remuneration, regard shall be had to any such reduction or suspension for the purposes of paragraph (2)(a) and (c).

(4) Where the widow, child or other dependant has become, or but for the person's loss of employment would have become, entitled to a benefit other than a benefit mentioned in paragraph (2)(a) to (d), the widow, child or other dependant, as the case may be, shall be entitled, (subject to the provisions of paragraph (5)), to an annual sum equal to the annual amount of the pension which would have been payable if he had died immediately before the date on which he suffered the loss of employment, having then complied with any requirements of the last relevant pension scheme as to a minimum period of qualifying service or contribution and completed any additional contributory payments or payments in respect of added years which he was then in the course of making.

(5) The calculation referred to in paragraph (4) shall be made on the basis of the method prescribed by the last relevant pension scheme of the person in question for the calculation of benefits for a widow, child or other dependant, and insofar as the age at which he died is relevant for the purposes of the said calculation, the calculation shall be made by reference to his age at the date of death.

(6) Any sums payable to or for the benefit of a widow, child or other dependant under this regulation shall cease to be payable when a corresponding pension under the last relevant pension scheme would have ceased to be payable; and where that scheme provides for payment of the pension to any person on behalf of a child or other dependant, any sum payable under this regulation to a child or other dependant shall be paid to that person on behalf of the child or dependant in the like manner and for the like period as is provided in the pension scheme.

(7) Except where the compensation has been reduced under regulation 21, compensation payable under this regulation and regulation 24 shall in the aggregate be reduced by an amount the capital value whereof is equal to the amount of any superannuation contributions as defined in regulation 21(3) returned to the person in respect of whom the compensation is payable and not paid to the Secretary of State, the compensation under each of those regulations being reduced in proportion to the capital value of each amount.

(8) If the person in question suffered a diminution of emoluments, then—

    (*a*) where his last relevant pension scheme provides benefits of a kind described in pararaph (2), the provisions of that paragraph shall apply with the substitution of references to diminution of emoluments for reference to loss of employment, and the sums payable to his widow, child or other dependant shall be calculated as if he had suffered loss of employment and as if the loss of emoluments occasioned thereby had been equivalent to the amount of the diminution; but no sum shall be payable under this sub-paragraph—

        (i) where the person has continued to pay superannuation contributions as if his emoluments had not been diminished, or

        (ii) where, by virtue of the provisions of his last relevant pension scheme, the person's superannuation benefits are calculated by reference to remuneration for a period prior to the date on which his emoluments were diminished; and

    (*b*) where his last relevant pension scheme provides benefits of a kind described in paragraph (4), the provisions of that paragraph shall apply with the substitution of references to diminution of emoluments for the references to loss of employment.

Compensation where death grant would have been payable

24.—(1) If the widow, the personal representatives of a person to whom this Part of these regulations applies or trustees empowered by that person to stand possessed of any benefit under his last relevant pension scheme might have become entitled to a death grant under that scheme, she or they, as the case may be, shall be entitled to receive a sum calculated in accordance with the provisions of regulation 23(7) and paragraph (2) of this regulation.

(2) The amount of the sum referred to in paragraph (1) shall be ascertained in accordance with the method of calculation prescribed by the last relevant pension scheme for the ascertainment of death grant as if the person had died immediately before losing his employment, subject to the following modifications—

    (*a*) account shall be taken of any additional period of service credited to him under regulation 17(2)—

        (i) in the case of a person who has been in receipt of retirement compensation under regulation 19, to the extent of the period between the loss of employment and the date of the claim made under that regulation, and

        (ii) in any other case, to the extent of the period between the loss of employment and the person's death:

    (*b*) if the aggregate of the person's pensionable service and the additional period under regulation 17(2) is less than any minimum period of qualifying service prescribed by the pension scheme for the receipt of a death grant, the said sum shall not exceed that proportion of the death grant, calculated as aforesaid which is equal to the proportion which the aggregate service bears to the minimum period of qualifying service prescribed by the pension scheme; and

    (*c*) there shall be deducted from the sum described above the amount of any retirement compensation paid to the person under regulation 18 or 19, or where any part of the compensation has been surrendered under regulation 17(6), the amount which would have been so paid but for such a surrender.

(3) In calculating a death grant under this regulation, any sum payable under regulation 23(2) or (8)(*a*) to or for the benefit of the widow, child or dependant, shall be deemed to be a pension payable to or for the benefit of the widow, child or dependant, as the case may be.

(4) This regulation shall apply in the case of a person who has suffered a diminution of emoluments with the substitution of references to diminution of emoluments for references to loss of employment, and the sum payable to the widow, personal representatives or trustees of such a person shall be calculated as if he had lost emoluments equivalent to the amount of the diminution; but no sum shall be payable under this paragraph—

(*a*) where the person has continued to pay superannuation contributions as if his emoluments had not been diminished, or

(*b*) where, by virtue of the provisions of his last relevant pension scheme, the person's superannuation benefits are calculated by reference to remuneration for a period prior to the date on which his emoluments were diminished.

Balance payable to claimant's widow or personal representatives

25.—(1) If no sum is payable to the widow, child or other dependant of any person under regulation 23(2) or (8)(*a*) and no sum is payable under regulation 24 and the person dies before he has received in the aggregate by way of retirement compensation a sum equivalent to the aggregate of—

(i) any superannuation contributions as defined in regulation 21(3) paid by him which have not been returned to him, and

(ii) any amount paid by him in accordance with regulation 21(1) together with compound interest thereon calculated—

(*a*) at the rate of 3 per cent per annum with half yearly rests up to the date of his death as from 1st April or 1st October following the half year in which the amount was paid, or

(*b*) in such other manner as may be provided by the last relevant pension scheme

(whichever calculation gives the greater amount), there shall be paid to his personal representatives the difference between the aggregate amount received by way of retirement compensation as aforesaid and the said equivalent sum.

(2) If any annual sum which became payable to a widow under regulation 23(2) or (8)(*a*) has ceased to be payable on her remarriage or death, and any sum payable to a child or other dependant under either of those paragraphs has ceased to be payable, and if the aggregate amount of the payments which were made as aforesaid to her husband by way of retirement compensation and to the widow or personal representatives or trustees under regulation 24 is less than a sum equivalent to the amount which would have been payable to the personal representatives under that regulation if no sum had been payable under either of the said paragraphs (2) or (8)(*a*), there shall be paid to her or her personal representatives the difference between such aggregate amount and the said equivalent sum.

(3) For the purpose of this regulation, a person who has surrendered any part of his retirement compensation under regulation 17(6), or whose retirement

compensation has been reduced in accordance with regulation 30(3), shall be deemed to have received during any period the amount of compensation for that period which he would have received but for such a surrender or such a reduction.

Compensation payable to non-pensionable officer on reaching normal retiring age

26.—(1) Where a person who is not a pensionable officer is receiving long-term compensation for loss of employment and attains normal retiring age, the Secretary of State shall, if satisfied that the person would, but for the loss, have continued in the employment he has lost for a substantial period beyond that age, continue to pay compensation to him for the remainder of his life at half its former rate.

(2) Where a person who is not a pensionable officer suffers loss of employment on or after attaining normal retiring age, the Secretary of State shall, if satisfied that the person would in the normal course have continued in the employment he has lost for a further substantial period, pay compensation to him for the remainder of his life at half the rate to which he would have been entitled under regulation 13 had he not attained normal retiring age at the date on which he lost his employment.

Persons subject to policy schemes

27.—(1) Regulations 18, 19, 20 and 24 shall not apply to a person (in this regulation referred to as a "policy scheme participant") who had been participating in a scheme associated with his employment for providing superannuation benefits by means of contracts or policies of insurance, and who, after the loss of his employment or the diminution of his emoluments, continued to participate in that scheme, or became entitled to a benefit or prospective benefit thereunder other than a return of contributions.

(2) If a policy scheme participant has lost his employment, the Secretary of State, may, if the relevant scheme so permits, make such payments to or in respect of him, whether by way of the payment of premiums or otherwise, as are actuarially equivalent to the amounts by which his retirement compensation might have been increased under regulation 17(2) or (5) had he been a person to whom regulation 18 or 19 applied.

(3) If a policy scheme participant has suffered a diminution of his emoluments, the Secretary of State may, if the relevant scheme so permits, make such payments to or in respect of him, whether by way of the payment of premiums or otherwise, as will secure to him the like benefits as if his emoluments had not been diminished.

(4) If a policy scheme participant becomes entitled to a benefit under such a scheme as is mentioned in paragraph (1) before reaching normal retiring age, the Secretary of State may reduce any long-term compensation payable to him by the amount of such benefit.

Intervals for payment of compensation under Part V

28. Any compensation awarded under this Part of these regulations to or in respect of any person shall be payable at intervals equivalent to those at which the corresponding benefit would have been payable under the person's last relevant pension scheme or at such other intervals as may be agreed between the person entitled to receive the compensation and the Secretary of State.

PART VI—ADJUSTMENT, REVIEW AND COMPOUNDING OF COMPENSATION

Adjustment of compensation where superannuation benefit is also payable

29.—(1) Where any period of service of which account was taken in calculating the amount of any compensation payable under Part IV or V of these regulations is subsequently taken into account for the purpose of calculating the amount of any superannuation benefit payable to or in respect of any person in accordance with a pension scheme associated with any employment undertaken subsequent to the loss of employment or diminution of emoluments which was the subject of the claim for compensation, the Secretary of State may in accordance with this regulation withhold or reduce the compensation payable.

(2) If the part of any superannuation benefit which is attributable to a period of service mentioned in paragraph (1) equals or exceeds the part of any compensation which is attributable to the same period, that part of the compensation may be withheld, or, if the part of the superannuation benefit is less than the part of the compensation, the compensation may be reduced by an amount not exceeding that part of the superannuation benefit.

(3) In the case of a death benefit payable in respect of any person, the sum payable under regulation 24 may be reduced by an amount not greater than the proportion of the death benefit which the period of service mentioned in paragraph (1) bears to the total period of service of which account was taken in the calculation of the death benefit.

(4) In addition to any reduction authorised by paragraph (2) or (3), if, in the circumstances mentioned in paragraph (1), compensation is attributable in part to any provision of the last relevant pension scheme for a minimum benefit, the compensation may be reduced by an amount not exceeding that part.

(5) Where any additional period of service has been credited to a person under regulation 17(2) and that period is equal to or less than the period reckonable in respect of the subsequent employment mentioned in paragraph (1), the compensation may be reduced (in addition to any other reduction authorised by this regulation) by an amount not exceeding that attributable to the additional period of service so credited or, if the period is greater than the period reckonable in respect of the subsequent employment, by the proportion of that amount which the period reckonable in respect of the subsequent employment bears to the additional period so credited.

(6) In making any reduction under paragraphs (2) to (5), the amount of pension or, as the case may be, lump sum to be taken into account relating to the subsequent employment shall be the amount of such pension or lump sum reduced by a fraction of that pension or lump sum, where—

(a) the numerator is equivalent to the aggregate of the amount of increases which would have been awarded under the provisions of the Pensions (Increase) Act 1971(a), during the period beginning with the day following loss of the employment for which compensation is payable and ending on

---

(a) 1971 c. 56.

the day the subsequent employment terminated, on an official pension (within the meaning of that Act) of £100 a year which commenced from the first mentioned day, and

(b) the denominator is equivalent to the aggregate of an official pension of £100 a year and the amount of the increases so determined.

(7) Where compensation has been calculated in accordance with regulation 22, the provisions of this regulation shall only apply in relation to the part (if any) of the superannuation benefit which is attributable to annual emoluments in excess of those to which the person was entitled on entering the new employment referred to in regulation 22.

(8) Where compensation is payable in respect of diminution of emoluments, the provisions of this regulation shall apply only in relation to the part (if any) of the superannuation benefit which is attributable to annual emoluments in excess of those to which the person was entitled immediately prior to the diminution.

Reduction of compensation in certain cases

30.—(1) If under a person's last relevant pension scheme any benefit for which the scheme provided would have been subject to reduction or suspension on his taking up other specified employment, any retirement compensation to which he is entitled for loss of employment or diminution of emoluments shall, where such an employment is taken up, be reduced or suspended in the like manner and to the like extent; but in calculating the amount of the reduction there shall be aggregated with the emoluments of the employment taken up the amount of any superannuation benefit by way of annual amounts payable to the person under a pension scheme associated with the employment which he has lost, or, as the case may be, the employment in which the emoluments were diminished.

(2) There shall be deducted from the retirement compensation payable to any person any additional contributory payments remaining unpaid at the date when he suffered loss of employment that are not recovered in accordance with the provisions of the last relevant pension scheme; and any such payments not recovered at the date of his death shall be deducted from any compensation payable in respect of that person under regulation 23, 24 or 25(2).

(3) Where compensation under these regulations is payable otherwise than for diminution of emoluments to or in respect of any person, and that person or his widow, child or other dependant or his personal representatives or trustees as are mentioned in regulation 24(1) is or are also entitled (whether immediately or on the person's attaining some greater age) to a superannuation benefit under his last relevant pension scheme in respect of any service of which account was taken in calculating the compensation,

(a) any instalment of that compensation which is payable in respect of any period shall be reduced by the amount of the instalment of such superannuation benefit which is payable in respect of the same period, and

(b) any of that compensation which is payable under Part IV or Part V of these regulations and which is payable as a lump sum, shall be reduced by the amount of any lump sum superannuation benefit.

(4) Where compensation is payable under Part IV of these regulations to any person and that person is or becomes entitled to receive a superannuation benefit under a pension scheme other than his last relevant pension scheme in respect of service of which account was taken in calculating the compensation,

any instalment of the compensation which is payable in respect of any period shall be reduced by the amount of the instalment of the superannuation benefit which is payable in respect of the same period.

(5) For the purpose of paragraphs (3) and (4), no account shall be taken of any sum payable in consequence of the surrender by any person of part of his superannuation benefit under any provision in that behalf in the relevant pension scheme with a view to obtaining or increasing allowances for his widow, child or other dependant; and the person shall be deemed to have received during any period the amount of superannuation benefit which he would have received but for such a surrender.

(6) Where in any week a person entitled to long-term compensation for loss or diminution of emoluments is also entitled to a National Insurance benefit, there shall be deducted from the long-term compensation payable in respect of that week a sum equal to the amount by which the aggregate of—

(a) the National Insurance benefit that would be payable in respect of that week if calculated at the rate applicable at the date of loss or diminution, and

(b) the weekly rate at which the long-term compensation would be payable but for this regulation,

exceeds two-thirds of the weekly rate of the emoluments of the employment which he has lost or in which the emoluments have been diminished.

(7) No reduction shall be made under paragraph (6) insofar as—

(a) an equivalent sum is deducted from the emoluments of his current employment, and

(b) that deduction from those emoluments has not occasioned an increase in his long-term compensation.

(8) In paragraph (6) the expression "weekly rate" means seven 365ths of the relevant annual rate, and the expression "National Insurance benefit" means any unemployment, sickness, invalidity or injury benefit or retirement pension payable under any enactment relating to National Insurance or Social Security, other than a benefit claimable by him in respect of a dependant.

Notification of change of circumstances

31. Where—

(a) a pensionable officer after suffering loss of employment or diminution of emoluments enters any employment referred to in regulation 22 or becomes entitled to any superannuation benefit on ceasing to hold such an employment,

(b) a person entitled to long-term compensation, whilst that compensation is liable to review in accordance with the provisions of regulation 32 enters any employment, or ceases to hold an employment, or receives any increase in his emoluments in an employment,

(c) a person entitled to retirement compensation enters employment in which the compensation is subject to reduction or suspension under regulation 30 or ceases to hold such an employment, or receives any increase in his remuneration in such an employment, or (*d*) a person entitled to long-term compensation starts to receive any benefit, any increase in benefit or any further benefit, under any enactment relating to National Insurance or Social Security,

he shall forthwith in writing inform the Secretary of State of that fact.

Review of awards of long-term or retirement compensation

32.—(1) The Secretary of State shall—

(*a*) on the expiry of 6 months from the decision date, or

(*b*) on the occurrence of any material change in the circumstances of the case,

whichever shall first occur, and thereafter within a period of 2 years after the decision date, or within any longer period specified in the subsequent provisions of this regulation, and at intervals of not more than 6 months, review his decision or, where the claim has been the subject of an appeal, the decision of the tribunal, and (subject to paragraph (7) these regulations shall apply in relation to such a review as they apply in relation to the initial determination of the claim; and on such a review, in the light of any material change in the circumstances of the case, compensation may be awarded, or compensation previously awarded may be increased, reduced or discontinued, subject to the limits set out in these regulations.

(2) The person to whom the decision relates may require the Secretary of State to carry out the review mentioned in paragraph (1) at any time within 2 years after the decision if he considers that there has been a change in the circumstances of his case which is material for the purposes of these regulations.

(3) The Secretary of State shall carry out a review in accordance with paragraph (1), notwithstanding the expiration of the period of 2 years mentioned in that paragraph, if—

(*a*) the emoluments of employment or work undertaken as a result of the loss of employment had been taken into account in determining the amount of any compensation awarded,

(*b*) that employment or work has been lost or the emoluments thereof reduced, otherwise than by reason of misconduct or incapacity to perform the duties which the person might reasonably have been required to perform, and

(*c*) the Secretary of State is satisfied that the loss or reduction is causing him hardship,

and where any decision is so reviewed, the decision shall be subject to further review in accordance with paragraph (1) as if the review carried out under this paragraph had been the initial determination of the claim.

(4) Paragraphs (1) and (2) shall apply in relation to any decision on a claim for long-term or retirement compensation in respect of diminution of emoluments as they apply in relation to any decision mentioned in paragraph (1) and as if in paragraph (1) "decision date" means the date on which any decision on a claim for long-term compensation for diminution of emoluments is notified to the claimant, but—

(*a*) where the person to whom the decision relates ceases to hold the employment in which his emoluments were diminished, a review shall be held within three months after that date, but no further review shall be held after the expiry of that period, and

(b) while that person continues to hold that employment, there shall be no limit to the period within which a review may take place.

(5) Notwithstanding anything contained in the foregoing provisions of this regulation, the Secretary of State shall review a decision (whether his or the tribunal's) on a claim for long-term compensation for loss of employment or diminution of emoluments after the expiration of any period within which a review is required to be made if at any time—

(a) the person to whom the decision relates becomes engaged in any employment (hereinafter referred to as "his current employment") the emoluments of which are payable out of public funds and which he has undertaken subsequent to the loss or diminution, and

(b) the aggregate of the emoluments of his current employment, any superannuation benefit by way of annual amounts payable to him in respect of the employment which he has lost or the employment in which his emoluments have been diminished and the long-term compensation payable to him exceeds the emoluments of the employment which he has lost, or as the case may be, in which the emoluments have been diminished.

(6) The Secretary of State shall further review any decision reviewed under paragraph (5) whenever the emoluments of the person's current employment are increased.

(7) On any review under this regulation, the amount of long-term compensation which, apart from this paragraph and any reduction under regulation 30(3) and (4), would be payable to the person may be reduced by an amount not exceeding the amount by which the aggregate of the compensation and the annual rate of emoluments of his current employment exceeds the annual rate of emoluments of the employment which he has lost or, as the case may be, in which the emoluments have been diminished.

(8) The Secretary of State shall give to a person to whom a decision relates not less than 14 days' notice of any review of that decision to be carried out under this regulation unless the review is carried out at his request.

(9) In this regulation the expression "decision date" means that date on which any decision on a claim for long-term or retirement compensation for loss of employment is notified to a claimant under regulation 34.

(10) For the purposes of regulations 13(4), 22(1) and 29(7) and (8) and on any review under this regulation, no account shall be taken of any increase in the emoluments of any work or employment undertaken as a result of the loss of employment or diminution of emoluments, or of any superannuation benefit attributable to such an increase, if such an increase is effective from any date after the date of the loss or diminution and is attributable to a rise in the cost of living.

(11) Nothing in this regulation shall preclude the making of any adjustment of compensation required by regulation 29 or 30.

Compounding of awards

33.—(1) In the case where an annual sum which has been or might be awarded under these regulations does not exceed £35, the Secretary of State may, at his discretion, compound his liability in respect thereof by paying a lump sum equivalent to the capital value of the annual sum, and, if any lump sum payable has been or might be awarded in addition to such annual sum under regulation 18, 19 or 20, the Secretary of State may likewise discharge his liability in respect thereof by an immediate payment.

(2) In any other case, if the person who has been awarded long-term or retirement compensation requests him to do so, the Secretary of State may, after having regard to the state of health of that person and the other circumstances of the case, compound up to one quarter of his liability to make payments under the award (other than payments to a widow, child or other dependant under Regulation 23) by the payment of an equivalent amount as a lump sum or, where any compensation has been awarded as a lump sum, by increasing that compensation to such equivalent amount, and in calculating for this purpose the liability of the Secretary of State to make such payments, account shall be taken of the annual value of lump sum payments of compensation other than payments of compensation under Part III of these regulations.

(3) The making of a composition under paragraph (2) in relation to an award of long-term or retirement compensation shall not prevent the subsequent making of compensation under paragraph (1) in relation to that award but, subject as aforesaid, not more than one composition may be made in relation to any award.

Part VII—Procedure and Miscellaneous

Procedure on making claims

34.—(1) Every claim for compensation under these regulations and every request for review of an award of long-term or retirement compensation shall be made in accordance with this regulation.

(2) Every such claim and request shall be made to the Secretary of State in writing and shall state whether any other claim for compensation has been made by the claimant under these regulations.

(3) Resettlement compensation shall be claimed separately from any other form of compensation claimable under these regulations.

(4) The Secretary of State shall consider any such claim or request in accordance with the relevant provisions of these regulations and shall notify the person making the claim or request in writing of his decision—

> (*a*) in the case of a claim for resettlement compensation, not later than one month after the receipt of the claim and
>
> (*b*) in the case of a claim for, or request for the review of an award of compensation under Part IV or V of these regulations, not later than thirteen weeks after the receipt of the claim or request, and
>
> (*c*) in any other case, as soon as possible after the decision;

but the decision of the Secretary of State shall not be invalidated by reason of the fact that notice of the decision is given after the expiry of the period mentioned in this paragraph.

(5) Every notification of a decision by the Secretary of State (whether granting or refusing compensation or reviewing an award, or otherwise affecting any compensation under these regulations) shall contain a statement—

> (*a*) giving reasons for the decision;

(b) showing how any compensation has been calculated and, in particular, if the amount is less than the maximum which could have been awarded under these regulations, showing the factors taken into account, in awarding that amount;

and

(c) directing the attention of the claimant to his right under regulation 42, if he is aggrieved by the decision to institute proceedings before a tribunal and giving him the address to which the application instituting such proceedings should be sent.

Claimants to furnish information

35.—(1) Any person claiming or receiving compensation or whose award of compensation is being reviewed shall furnish all such information as the Secretary of State may at any time reasonably require; and he shall verify that information in such manner, including the production of books or of original documents in his possession or control, as may be reasonably so required.

(2) Such a person shall, on receipt of reasonable notice, present himself for interview at such place as the Secretary of State may reasonably require; and any person who attends for interview may, if he so desires, be represented by his adviser.

Procedure on death of clamaint

36.—(1) In the event of the death of a claimant or of a person who, if he had survived, could have been a claimant, a claim for compensation under these regulations may be continued or made, as the case may be, by his personal representatives.

(2) Where any such claim is continued or made as aforesaid by personal representatives, the personal representatives shall, as respects any steps to be taken or thing to be done by them in order to continue or make the claim, be deemed for the purposes of these regulations to be the person entitled to claim, but save as aforesaid, the person in whose right they continue or make the claim shall be deemed for the purposes of these regulations to be that person, and the relevant provisions of these regulations shall be construed accordingly.

(3) The Secretary of State may in any case where a person who, if he had survived, could have been a claimant has died, extend the period within which a claim under regulation 7 or 11 is to be made by his personal representatives.

Calculation of service

37.—(1) For the purpose of determining the amount of any compensation payable in respect of the loss of an office to which, or of any two or more offices to which in the aggregate, a person devoted substantially the whole of his time, any previous period of part-time employment shall be treated as though it were whole-time employment for a proportionately reduced period.

(2) For the purpose of making any calculation under these regulations in respect of a person's reckonable service, all periods of that service shall be aggregated by reference to completed years and completed days; and any provision in these regulations requiring compensation to be calculated by reference to a year of reckonable service shall (unless the provision specifically states that

compensation is payable in respect of completed years) be construed as including completed days, each completed day over and above a completed year being expressed as one 365th of a year.

General provisions as to emoluments

38.—(1) In these regulations, subject to the provisions of paragraph (2) and regulations 39 and 40 the expression "emoluments" means all salary, wages, fees and other payments paid or made to an officer as such for his own use, and also the money value of any accommodation or other allowances in kind appertaining to his employment, but does not include payments for overtime which are not a usual incident of his employment, or any allowances payable to him to cover the cost of providing office accommodation or clerical or other assistance, or any travelling or subsistence allowance or other moneys to be spent, or to cover expenses incurred, by him for the purposes of his employment.

(2) Where fees or other variable payments were paid to an officer as part of his emoluments during any period immediately preceding the loss or diminution, the amount in respect of fees or other variable payments to be included in the annual rate of emoluments shall be the annual average of the fees or other payments paid to him during the period of 5 years immediately preceding the loss or diminution, or such other period as the Secretary of State may think reasonable in the circumstances.

(3) For the purposes of these regulations, the annual rate of emoluments, in relation to any employment which has been lost or the emoluments whereof have been lost or diminished, shall be the amount described in (*a*), (*b*) or (*c*) of this paragraph, whichever is the greater—

(*a*) the emoluments received by him in the period of 12 months immediately preceding the loss or diminution;

(*b*) in the case of emoluments payable monthly, the emoluments payable in respect of the last complete month immediately preceding the loss or diminution multiplied by 12; or

(*c*) in the case of emoluments payable weekly, the emoluments payable in respect of the last complete week immediately preceding the loss or diminution multiplied by 52.

Emoluments of part-time employment

39. In ascertaining for the purposes of these regulations whether, and how far, the emoluments of alternative employment fall short of emoluments which have been lost where those emoluments were payable in respect of two or more part-time employments, the emoluments of the alternative employment or of the aggregate of two or more alternative employments shall be apportioned in the proportion which the emoluments of the part-time employments bore to each other.

Temporary variation of emoluments

40. In calculating for the purpose of these regulations the amount of any emoluments lost, or the amount by which any emoluments have been diminished and in determining the resettlement and long-term compensation of any person who has suffered such a loss or diminution, no account shall be taken of any temporary increase or decrease in the amount of the person's emoluments which is attributable to section 1 of the Vehicle and Driving Licences Act 1969 and which occurs otherwise than in the ordinary course of his employment.

Compensation not assignable

41.—(1) Subject to the provisions of any enactment in that behalf, any compensation to which a person becomes entitled under these regulations shall be paid by the Secretary of State and shall be payable to, or in trust for, the person who is entitled to receive it, and shall not be assignable.

(2) Without prejudice to any other right of recovery, any compensation paid in error may be recovered by the Secretary of State by deduction from any compensation payable under these regulations.

Right of appeal from decision of Secretary of State

42.—(1) Every person who is aggrieved by any decision of the Secretary of State with respect to a compensation question or by any failure on the part of the Secretary of State to notify him of any such decision within the appropriate time prescribed by these regulations, may within 13 weeks of the notification to him of the decision or the expiry of the prescribed time, as the case may be, institute proceedings for the determination of the question by a tribunal in accordance with—

  (a) in England and Wales, the Industrial Tribunals (Labour Relations) Regulations 1974**(a)**; or

  (b) in Scotland, the Industrial Tribunals (Labour Relations) (Scotland) Regulations 1974**(b)**

and these regulations; and the tribunal shall determine the question accordingly.

(2) For the purpose of any proceedings instituted in pursuance of this regulation, a person or persons may be appointed to sit with the tribunal as assessor or assessors.

(3) The Secretary of State shall give effect to the decision of a tribunal subject to any modifications that may be required in consequence of any appeal from that decision on a point of law.

William Rodgers,
Secretary of State for Transport

28th July 1977.

(a) S.I. 1974/1386 (1974 II, p. 5330).   (b) S.I. 1974/1387 (1974 II, p. 5342).

SCHEDULE 1　　　　　　Regulation 2(2)

TABLES AS TO CAPITAL VALUES AND ANNUAL AMOUNTS

TABLE I(a)

The capital value of an annual amount of £1 per annum, payable for life, which attracts pensions increase when the officer attains age 55, or immediately on retirement if age 55 has already been attained.

Age last birthday	Capital value of £1 per annum, with pensions increase attaching from age 55	
	Female	Male
	£ p	£ p
30	14·82	14·34
31	14·86	14·37
32	14·91	14·39
33	14·95	14·41
34	14·99	14·42
35	15·03	14·43
36	15·06	14·44
37	15·09	14·44
38	15·12	14·43
39	15·14	14·42
40	15·15	14·40
41	15·16	14·37
42	15·15	14·33
43	15·14	14·29
44	15·12	14·23
45	15·09	14·16
46	15·05	14·08
47	14·99	13·99
48	14·92	13·88
49	14·83	13·75
50	14·72	13·61
51	14·59	13·45
52	14·43	13·26
53	14·25	13·04
54	14·04	12·79
55	13·79	12·52
56	13·54	12·24
57	13·28	11·95
58	13·01	11·66
59	12·74	11·36
60	12·46	11·06
61	12·17	10·76
62	11·87	10·45
63	11·57	10·14
64	11·27	9·82
65	10·96	9·51
66	10·64	9·19
67	10·32	8·87
68	10·00	8·56
69	9·68	8·25

TABLE I(*a*)—*contd.*

Age last birthday	Capital value of £1 per annum, with pensions increase attaching from age 55	
	Female	Male
	£ p	£ p
70	9·36	7·94
71	9·03	7·63
72	8·70	7·32
73	8·38	7·02
74	8·05	6·72
75	7·73	6·43
76	7·41	6·14
77	7·09	5·86
78	6·78	5·59
79	6·47	5·32

NOTE:—This table is for use in connection with regulation 33(1) and (2) of the regulations for the compounding of annual retirement compensation which a person is currently entitled to receive under regulation 18, 19 or 20. Where the compensation is payable before age 60 (in the case of females) or 65 (in the case of males) but will be reduced on the attainment of that age to take account of a National Insurance pension the table should be used in conjunction with Table II(*a*) i.e. Table II(*a*) should be used for valuing that part of the compensation which ceases to be payable at 60(65) and this table should be used for valuing the remainder. This table is not applicable for—

(i) compounding an annual sum payable to a widow under regulation 23 of the regulations (Table III should be used).

(ii) compounding annual retirement compensation which will not begin to be paid until some future date.

TABLE I(*b*)

The capital value of an annual payment of £1, payable for life, and attracting pensions increase from the outset.

Age last birthday	Capital value of £1 per annum, attracting pensions increase throughout life	
	Female	Male
	£ p	£ p
23	18·59	18·24
24	18·52	18·15
25	18·44	18·05
26	18·36	17·95
27	18·28	17·85
28	18·19	17·74
29	18·10	17·63
30	18·00	17·51
31	17·90	17·38
32	17·79	17·25
33	17·68	17·12
34	17·57	16·98
35	17·45	16·83
36	17·32	16·68
37	17·19	16·52
38	17·05	16·35
39	16·91	16·18
40	16·76	16·00
41	16·61	15·81
42	16·45	15·62
43	16·29	15·42
44	16·12	15·21
45	15·94	15·00
46	15·76	14·78
47	15·57	14·56
48	15·37	14·33
49	15·17	14·09
50	14·96	13·84
51	14·74	13·59
52	14·51	13·33
53	14·28	13·07
54	14·04	12·80

TABLE I(*b*)—*contd.*

| Age last birthday | Capital value of £1 per annum, attracting pensions increase throughout life | |
	Female	Male
	£ p	£ p
55	13·79	12·52
56	13·54	12·24
57		
58		
59		
	as for Table I(*a*) from age 55	
60		
—		
—		
—		

NOTE:—This table is for use in connection with regulation 33(1) and (2) for the compounding of annual retirement compensation which a person is currently entitled to receive under regulation 19 if he becomes incapacitated before normal retiring age. Where the compensation is payable before age 60 (in the case of females) or 65 (in the case of males) but will be reduced on the attainment of that age to take account of a National Insurance pension, the table should be used in conjunction with Table II(*b*) i.e. Table II(*b*) should be used for valuing that part of the compensation which ceases to be payable at 60(65) and this table should be used for valuing the remainder.

This table is not applicable for—

 (i) compounding an annual payable sum to a widow under regulation 23 of the regulations (Table III should be used).

(ii) compounding annual retirement compensation which will not begin to be paid until some future date.

TABLE II(a)

Capital value of £1 per annum, ceasing at age 60 (females), 65 (males), which attracts pensions increase from age 55 or retirement if greater.

Age last birthday	Capital value	
	Female	Male
	£ p	£ p
30	12·11	12·92
31	12·01	12·87
32	11·91	12·81
33	11·80	12·75
34	11·68	12·68
35	11·55	12·60
36	11·40	12·51
37	11·24	12·41
38	11·07	12·30
39	10·88	12·18
40	10·67	12·04
41	10·44	11·89
42	10·19	11·72
43	9·92	11·53
44	9·63	11·33
45	9·31	11·11
46	8·96	10·86
47	8·58	10·59
48	8·16	10·30
49	7·71	9·98
50	7·22	9·62
51	6·68	9·23
52	6·09	8·80
53	5·45	8·33
54	4·75	7·81
55	3·99	7·24
56	3·18	6·64
57	2·33	6·01
58	1·43	5·35
59	·49	4·65
60	—	3·91
61	—	3·13
62	—	2·30
63	—	1·42
64	—	·48

NOTE:—This table is for use in connection with regulation 33(1) and (2) for the compounding of any part of annual retirement compensation which will cease to be payable on the attainment of age 60 (in the case of females) or 65 (in the case of males). Table I(a) should be used in relation to the remainder of such compensation, i.e. the part which is payable for life—see note on that table.

TABLE II(*b*)

Capital value of £1 per annum, ceasing at age 60 (females), 65 (males), which attracts pensions increase from the outset of the pension.

Age last birthday	Capital value	
	Female	Male
	£ p	£ p
23	16·68	17·24
24	16·51	17·10
25	16·33	16·95
26	16·14	16·79
27	15·94	16·63
28	15·74	16·46
29	15·52	16·28
30	15·29	16·09
31	15·05	15·89
32	14·80	15·68
33	14·54	15·46
34	14·26	15·23
35	13·97	15·00
36	13·66	14·75
37	13·34	14·49
38	13·01	14·22
39	12·66	13·94
40	12·29	13·64
41	11·90	13·33
42	11·49	13·01
43	11·07	12·67
44	10·63	12·31
45	10·16	11·94
46	9·67	11·56
47	9·15	11·16
48	8·61	10·74
49	8·04	10·30
50	7·45	9·85
51	6·83	9·38
52	6·17	8·88
53	5·48	8·36
54	4·75	7·81
55	3·99	7·24
56	3·18	6·64
57	2·33	6·01
58	1·43	5·35
59	·49	4·65

TABLE II(*b*)—*contd.*

Age last birthday	Capital value	
	Female	Male
	£ p	£ p
60	—	3·91
61	—	3·13
62	—	2·30
63	—	1·42
64	—	·48

NOTE:—This table is for use in connection with regulation 33(1) and (2) for the compounding of any part of annual retirement compensation which will cease to be payable on the attainment of age 60 (in the case of females) or 65 (in the case of males). Table I(*b*) should be used in relation to the remainder of such compensation, i.e. the part which is payable for life—see note on that table.

TABLE III

Capital value of an annual amount of £1, which attracts pensions increase from the outset, payable to a widow until death or remarriage.

Age of widow at date of widowhood	Capital value	Age of widow at date of widowhood	Capital value
	£ p		£ p
20	6·00	45	13·14
21	6·00	46	13·25
22	6·00	47	13·34
23	6·00	48	13·40
24	6·13	49	13·44
25	6·58	50	13·46
26	7·01	51	13·46
27	7·41	52	13·43
28	7·78	53	13·38
29	8·11	54	13·31
30	8·41	55	13·22
31	8·72	56	13·10
32	9·06	57	12·96
33	9·42	58	12·80
34	9·82	59	12·61
35	10·24	60	12·39
36	10·65	61	12·14
37	11·04	62	11·87
38	11·40	63	11·57
39	11·73	64	11·27
40	12·04	65	10·96
41	12·33	66	10·64
42	12·59	67	10·32
43	12·81	68	10·00
44	12·99	69	9·68
		70	9·35

NOTE:—This table is for use in connection with Regulation 33(1) for compounding annual compensation payable to a widow under regulation 23. It should also be used, where a reduction of compensation under regulation 23(7) of the regulations falls to be apportioned between the compensation payable under that regulation and under regulation 24, for ascertaining the capital value of annual compensation to a widow.

TABLE IV(*a*)

The annual amount, payable for life, which attracts pensions increase from age 55, or from retirement if age 55 has already been attained, equivalent in value to a lump sum of £100.

Age last birthday	Annual amount, attracting pensions increase from age 55, and payable for life, equal in value to a lump sum of £100	
	Female	Male
	£ p	£ p
30	6·75	6·97
31	6·73	6·96
32	6·71	6·95
33	6·69	6·94
34	6·67	6·93
35	6·65	6·93
36	6·64	6·93
37	6·63	6·93
38	6·61	6·93
39	6·61	6·93
40	6·60	6·94
41	6·60	6·96
42	6·60	6·98
43	6·61	7·00
44	6·61	7·03
45	6·63	7·06
46	6·64	7·10
47	6·67	7·15
48	6·70	7·20
49	6·74	7·27
50	6·79	7·35
51	6·85	7·43
52	6·93	7·54
53	7·02	7·67
54	7·12	7·82
55	7·25	7·99
56	7·39	8·17
57	7·53	8·37
58	7·69	8·58
59	7·85	8·80
60	8·03	9·04
61	8·22	9·29
62	8·42	9·57
63	8·64	9·86
64	8·87	10·18
65	9·12	10·52
66	9·40	10·88
67	9·69	11·27
68	10·00	11·68
69	10·33	12·12

TABLE IV(*a*)—*contd.*

Age last birthday	Annual amount, attracting pensions increase from age 55, and payable for life, equal in value to a lump sum of £100	
	Female	Male
	£ p	£ p
70	10·68	12·59
71	11·07	13·11
72	11·49	13·66
73	11·93	14·25
74	12·42	14·88
75	12·94	15·55
76	13·50	16·29
77	14·10	17·06
78	14·75	17·89
79	15·46	18·80

NOTE:—This table is for use in connection with regulation 21 for ascertaining the annual amount by which retirement compensation under regulation 18, 19 or 20 is to be reduced where a claimant has not paid to the compensating authority an amount equal to any sum paid to him by way of superannuation contributions. It should also be used in connection with regulation 33(2) of the regulations for calculating for the purposes of that paragraph the annual value of retirement compensation awarded as a lump sum.

TABLE IV(*b*)

The annual amount, which attracts pensions increase throughout life, equivalent in value to a lump sum of £100.

Age last birthday	Annual sum, attracting pensions increase throughout life, equal in value to a lump sum of £100	
	Female	Male
	£ p	£ p
23	5·38	5·48
24	5·40	5·51
25	5·42	5·54
26	5·45	5·57
27	5·47	5·60
28	5·50	5·64
29	5·52	5·67
30	5·56	5·71
31	5·59	5·75
32	5·62	5·80
33	5·66	5·84
34	5·69	5·89
35	5·73	5·94
36	5·77	6·00
37	5·82	6·05
38	5·87	6·12
39	5·91	6·18
40	5·97	6·25
41	6·02	6·33
42	6·08	6·40
43	6·14	6·49
44	6·20	6·57
45	6·27	6·67
46	6·35	6·77
47	6·42	6·87
48	6·51	6·98
49	6·59	7·10
50	6·68	7·23
51	6·78	7·36
52	6·89	7·50
53	7·00	7·65
54	7·12	7·81

TABLE IV(*b*)—*contd.*

Age last birthday	Annual sum, attracting pensions increase throughout life, equal in value to a lump sum of £100	
	Female	Male
	£ p	£ p
55	7·25	7·99
56	7·39	8·17
57		
58		
59		
60	as for Table IV(*a*) from age 55	
—		
—		

NOTE:—This table is for use in connection with regulation 21 for ascertaining the annual amount by which retirement compensation under regulation 19 is to be reduced where a claimant has become incapacitated before normal retiring age and has not paid to the compensating authority an amount equal to any sum paid to him by way of superannuation contributions. It should also be used in connection with regulation 33(2) of the regulations for calculating for the purposes of that paragraph the annual value of retirement compensation awarded as a lump sum.

TABLE V

The annual amount, which attracts pensions increase from the outset, payable to a widow until death or remarriage, equivalent in value to a lump sum of £100.

Age of widow at date of widowhood	Annual amount	Age of widow at date of widowhood	Annual amount
	£ p		£ p
20	16·67	45	7·61
21	16·67	46	7·55
22	16·67	47	7·50
23	16·67	48	7·46
24	16·31	49	7·44
25	15·20	50	7·43
26	14·27	51	7·43
27	13·50	52	7·45
28	12·85	53	7·47
29	12·33	54	7·51
30	11·89	55	7·56
31	11·47	56	7·63
32	11·04	57	7·72
33	10·62	58	7·81
34	10·18	59	7·93
35	9·77	60	8·07
36	9·39	61	8·24
37	9·06	62	8·42
38	8·77	63	8·64
39	8·53	64	8·87
40	8·31	65	9·12
41	8·11	66	9·40
42	7·94	67	9·69
43	7·81	68	10·00
44	7·70	69	10·33
		70	10·70

NOTE:—This table is for use in connection with regulation 23(7) for ascertaining the annual amount by which compensation to a widow is to be reduced in the circumstances described in that paragraph. If a reduction is required to be apportioned between compensation payable under regulations 23 and 24, the capital value of annual compensation to a widow should be ascertained by reference to Table III.

TABLE VI(*a*)

The capital value of each £100 of the total amount of long-term compensation, payable to age 65, in which the annual payments attract pensions increase from age 55, according to the outstanding period of long-term compensation.

Outstanding number of complete years of long-term compensation	Capital value	
	Female	Male
	£ p	£ p
0	98·65	98·50
1	95·95	95·50
2	93·25	92·60
3	90·65	89·80
4	88·20	87·15
5	85·90	84·70
6	83·70	82·40
7	81·60	80·25
8	79·60	78·20
9	77·70	76·30
10	75·80	74·40
11	73·85	72·45
12	71·80	70·45
13	69·75	68·40
14	67·70	66·40
15	65·65	64·40
16	63·65	62·45
17	61·70	60·55
18	59·80	58·75
19	58·00	57·00
20	56·25	55·30
21	54·55	53·65
22	52·95	52·10
23	51·40	50·60
24	49·90	49·15
25	48·45	47·75
26	47·05	46·40
27	45·75	45·10
28	44·45	43·90
29	43·20	42·75
30	42·05	41·60

NOTE:—This table is for use in connection with regulation 33(1) and (2) for compounding awards of long-term compensation under Part IV of the regulations. The total amount of the annual long-term compensation which is to be compounded must first be calculated, i.e. the amount which the person would receive on account of that compensation, or the part of it which is to be compounded, if it were paid until age 65. For each £100 so calculated, the lump sum payment will be the amount shown in the table according to the number of complete years in the period between the date of compounding and age 65.

TABLE VI(b)

The capital value of each £100 of the total amount of long-term compensation, payable to age 70, in which the annual payments attract pensions increase from age 55, according to the outstanding period of long-term compensation.

Outstanding number of complete years of long-term compensation	Capital value	
	Female	Male
	£ p	£ p
0	98·50	98·30
1	95·50	94·90
2	92·60	91·60
3	89·80	88·40
4	87·20	85·45
5	84·75	82·80
6	82·45	80·35
7	80·30	78·10
8	78·25	76·00
9	76·35	74·05
10	74·50	72·20
11	72·75	70·45
12	71·10	68·85
13	69·55	67·30
14	68·00	65·85
15	65·50	64·40
16	64·95	62·90
17	63·35	61·40
18	61·70	59·85
19	60·05	58·25
20	58·40	56·70
21	56·80	55·20
22	55·20	53·70
23	53·65	52·25
24	52·15	50·80
25	50·70	49·40
26	49·25	48·05
27	47·90	46·75
28	46·55	45·50
29	45·25	44·30
30	44·05	43·10

NOTE:—This table is for use in connection with regulation 33(1) and (2) for compounding awards of long-term compensation under Part IV of the regulations. The total amount of the annual long-term compensation which is to be compounded must first be calculated, i.e. the amount which the person would receive on account of that compensation, or the part of it which is to be compounded, if it were paid until age 70. For each £100 so calculated, the lump sum payable will be the amount shown in the table according to the number of complete years in the period between the date of compounding and age 70.

Regulation 2(1)   SCHEDULE 2

LOCAL AUTHORITIES

PART I

In England and Wales

1. (*a*) The council of an administrative county, county borough or county district,
         or the representative body of a parish (ceasing to exist after 31st March 1974),

   (*b*) the council of a county or district (established by or under the Local Govern-
         ment Act 1972(**a**)),

   (*c*) in England, any parish council, common parish council or parish meeting,

   (*d*) in Wales, a parish council, common parish council or parish meeting (ceasing
         to exist after 31st March 1974), or

   (*e*) in Wales, a community council (established by or under the said Act of 1972).

2. the council of a metropolitan borough or London borough, the Common Council
   of the City of London, the Greater London Council and the Council of the
   Isles of Scilly;

3. any burial board or joint burial board established under the Burial Acts 1852 to
   1906;

4. any joint board or joint body constituted by or under any enactment for the
   purpose of exercising the functions of two or more authorities described in paragraphs 1, 2 or 3 above, and any special planning board within the meaning of
   paragraph 3 of Schedule 17 to the said Act of 1972;

5. any other authority or body, not specified in paragraphs 1, 2, 3 or 4 above,
   established by or under any enactment for the purpose of exercising the functions
   of or advising one or more of the authorities specified in paragraphs 1, 2, 3 or
   4 above;

6. any committee (including a joint committee) established by or under any enactment for the purpose of exercising the functions of, or advising, one or more
   authorities described in paragraphs 1, 2, 3, 4 or 5 above;

7. any two or more authorities described in paragraphs 1, 2, 3, 4, 5 or 6 above acting
   jointly or as a combined authority; or

8. a police authority (other than the Secretary of State) within the meaning of
   section 62 of the Police Act 1964(**b**) both as originally enacted and as subsequently
   amended and any previous police authority for whom Schedule 11 (Transitional
   Provisions) to that Act had effect or who was the police authority for an area or
   district which was before 1st April 1947 or after 31st March 1946 a separate
   police area.

PART II

In Scotland

9. (*a*) the council of a county, county of city, large burgh, small burgh or district
         referred to in section 1(5) of the Local Government (Scotland) Act 1973(**c**),
         or

   (*b*) a regional, islands or district council established by or under the said Act of
         1973;

(**a**) 1972 c. 70.   (**b**) 1964 c. 48.   (**c**) 1973 c. 65.

10. any joint board or joint body constituted by or under any enactment for the purpose of exercising any of the functions of two or more authorities described in paragraph 9 above;

11. any other authority or body, not specified in paragraphs 9 or 10 above, established by or under any enactment for the purpose of exercising any of the functions of, or advising, one or more of the authorities specified in paragraphs 9 or 10 above;

12. any committee (including a joint committee) established by or under any enactment for the purpose of exercising any of the functions of, or advising, one or more authorities described in paragraphs 9, 10 or 11 above, or

13. any two or more authorities described in paragraphs 9, 10, 11, or 12 above acting jointly or as a combined authority.

EXPLANATORY NOTE

(This Note is not part of the Regulations.)

1. These **Regulations** revoke and re-enact, with amendments, the Vehicle and Driving Licences (Compensation to Officers) Regulations 1970 made under section 2 of the Vehicle and Driving Licences Act 1969. The principal changes are outlined in the following paragraphs.

2. Transitional provisions and savings have been made for persons entitled or in payment under the revoked regulations (regulation 1(3) and (4)).

3. The qualifying service for resettlement compensation has been reduced from 3 to 2 years (regulation 7). Compensation is payable as a lump sum, with the maximum award raised from 26 weeks net emoluments to 30 weeks gross emoluments (regulation 8). It is subject to adjustment only in respect of redundancy or similar payments which the claimant may be awarded (regulation 9). No reductions such as were formerly provided are to be made in respect of superannuation or National Insurance Benefits, or earnings from alternative employment.

4. The qualifying service for long-term compensation has been reduced from 8 to 5 years (regulation 11). The award is no longer to be reduced to take account of resettlement compensation payments. Awards for diminution of emoluments are no longer to be restricted to two-thirds of the amount of the diminution (regulation 14). The basis of calculation has been altered from net to gross emoluments.

5. The qualifying service for retirement compensation has been reduced from 8 to 5 years (regulation 16). The award is no longer to be reduced to take account of re-settlement compensation payment. It is not payable if the person has continued to pay superannuation contributions as if he had suffered no loss of emoluments (regulation 18).

6. The bar to compensation where emoluments have been diminished by less than $2\frac{1}{2}\%$ has been removed.

7. A person is required to pay either to the fund authority (as defined by regulation 2(1)) or to the Secretary of State an amount equivalent to any sum paid to him by way of return of contributions when he lost his employment (regulation 21).

8. The provisions relating to compensation payable to a personal representative, widow or dependent have been revised to provide short term benefits at higher rates than previously (regulation 23).

9. In reviewing and making adjustments to long-term and retirement compensation to take account of superannuation benefits payable and earnings from alternative employment, provision is made to disregard the effect of certain increases in those benefits and earnings (regulation 32).

STATUTORY INSTRUMENTS

1977 No. 1317

LONDON GOVERNMENT

The Control of Off-Street Parking in Greater London (Appeals Procedure) Regulations 1977

Made	-	-	-	*28th July* 1977
Laid before Parliament				*9th August* 1977
Coming into Operation				*30th August* 1977

The Secretary of State for Transport in exercise of the powers conferred by paragraph 17 of Schedule 5 to the Transport (London) Act 1969(a) and now vested in him(b), and of all other enabling powers, hereby makes the following Regulations:—

Commencement and citation

1. These Regulations shall come into operation on 30th August 1977, and may be cited as the Control of Off-Street Parking in Greater London (Appeals Procedure) Regulations 1977.

Interpretation

2.—(1) In these Regulations, unless the context otherwise requires—
"the Act" means the Transport (London) Act 1969;
"appeal" means an appeal to which these Regulations apply and "the appellant" shall be construed accordingly;
"appointed person" means the person appointed by the Secretary of State to hold the hearing or inquiry in connection with the appeal;
"the Council" means the Greater London Council;
"hearing" means a hearing by a person appointed by the Secretary of State for the purposes of the appeal;
"interested person" means any person (other than the appellant) who is entitled to any interest in the premises or who is the licence holder or the applicant for, or for a variation of the terms and conditions of, the licence or who, in a case involving an appeal against the revocation of, or the refusal to renew, a licence under section 36 of the Act in relation to the premises, was the holder of that licence;
"the licence" means the licence under section 36 of the Act to which the appeal relates, and "applicant for a licence", "proposed licence" and "licence holder" shall be construed accordingly;
"the local authority", in relation to an appeal, means the local authority whose decision is under appeal; and
"the premises" means the premises to which the licence or proposed licence (as the case may be) relates.

(a) 1969 c. 35.   (b) S.I. 1970/1681 (1970 III, p. 5551).

(2) References in these Regulations to the decision of the local authority include references to any decision of which the local authority are deemed by paragraph 14(2) of Schedule 5 to the Act to have given notification, and references to notification of the decision of the local authority include references to any notification so deemed to have been given.

(3) Any reference in these Regulations to a numbered Regulation is a reference to the Regulation bearing that number in these Regulations.

(4) The Interpretation Act 1889(a) shall apply for the interpretation of these Regulations as it applies for the interpretation of an Act of Parliament.

Application of Regulations

3. These Regulations apply to appeals under paragraph 14 of Schedule 5 to the Act against decisions of a local authority relating to licences for the operation of public off-street parking places in Greater London and prescribe the procedure to be followed in connection with such appeals.

Notice of appeal and supporting documents

4.—(1) Any person who desires to appeal under the provisions of paragraph 14 of Schedule 5 to the Act against a decision of the local authority referred to in that paragraph shall serve notice of his appeal on the Secretary of State within 42 days from the date of notification of the decision to which it relates or within such longer period from that date as the Secretary of State may (whether before or after the expiration of the said 42 days) allow.

(2) The notice of appeal shall be in writing and shall contain such of the particulars specified in Schedule 1 to these Regulations as are appropriate having regard to the nature of the case.

(3) The appellant shall furnish to the Secretary of State with his notice of appeal copies of such of the documents specified in Schedule 2 to these Regulations as are appropriate having regard to the nature of the case.

(4) At the same time as the appellant serves notice of appeal on the Secretary of State and furnishes to the Secretary of State copies of the documents which he is required by the foregoing provisions of this Regulation to furnish, he shall serve a copy of that notice on, and furnish copies of those documents to—

(*a*) the local authority,

(*b*) the Council, and

(*c*) all interested persons known to the appellant.

Representations by local authority and Council

5.—(1) Not later than 42 days after the receipt by them of the copy of the notice of appeal and of all the documents of which the appellant is required by Regulation 4(4) to furnish copies to them the local authority and the Council shall each submit to the Secretary of State in writing such written representations as they may wish to submit to him in relation to the appeal.

(2) Where the local authority desire to appear before and be heard by a person appointed by the Secretary of State, the local authority shall include in their representations aforesaid a request to this effect, and where the Council desire to appear at any hearing which may be held they shall include in their representations aforesaid a statement of that desire.

(a) 1889 c. 63.

(3) At the same time as the local authority or the Council (as the case may be) submit representations to the Secretary of State under paragraph (1) of this Regulation they shall serve a copy of those representations on—

(a) the appellant,

(b) where the representations are those of the local authority, the Council,

(c) where the representations are those of the Council, the local authority, and

(d) any other person upon whom a copy of the notice of appeal has been served in accordance with Regulation 4(4).

Request for a hearing

6.—(1) The appellant may include in the notice of appeal a request for an opportunity to appear before, and be heard by, a person appointed by the Secretary of State.

(2) In any case where the appellant has not included such a request in the notice of appeal but does desire such an opportunity, he shall make his request to the Secretary of State in writing within 28 days of being asked by the Secretary of State whether he does so desire.

(3) A copy of the appellant's request as aforesaid shall at the same time be served by the appellant upon the persons on whom copies of the notice of appeal were served.

(4) Any interested person may notify the Secretary of State in writing of his desire to appear at any hearing which may be held in connection with the appeal (such notification stating the name and address for service of the person in question and indicating the nature and extent of his interest (if any) in the premises) and if any such person does so notify the Secretary of State he shall at the same time serve a copy of the notification upon the appellant, the local authority and the Council.

(5) Where a copy of the notice of appeal has been served on an interested person under Regulation 4(4), any notification by that person under paragraph (4) above shall be given within 28 days of the service of that notice.

Deciding an appeal on written evidence only

7.—(1) Where neither the appellant nor the local authority have requested the Secretary of State to afford to each of them an opportunity of appearing before and being heard by a person appointed by the Secretary of State, or where any such request has been withdrawn, the Secretary of State may decide the appeal on the basis of the documents and written representations submitted to him, but before so deciding—

(a) the Secretary of State may by notice in writing require any one or more of the following, that is to say—

(i) the appellant,

(ii) the local authority,

(iii) the Council,

(iv) any interested person,

to furnish such further documents or information (being documents or information in the possession or control of the person or body in question) as the Secretary of State may specify, and

(b) the Secretary of State shall in all cases (whether he requires further documents or information to be furnished as aforesaid or not) give the appellant an opportunity to comment on any representations made by the local authority or the Council under Regulation 5(1).

(2) In its application to an appeal which has been decided by the Secretary of State on the basis of documents and written representations, Regulation 15 shall have effect as if in paragraph (1) for the words "the interested persons who appeared at the hearing" there were substituted the words "any interested person named in the notice of appeal as a person upon whom the appellant was serving a copy of that notice" and all the words after "and the Council" were omitted, and as if paragraphs (2) and (3) were omitted.

Notice of refusal to entertain appeal

8.—(1) At any time before—

(a) deciding an appeal on the basis of documents and written representations submitted to him in a case where Regulation 7 applies, or

(b) fixing the date, time and place for the hearing in any other case,

the Secretary of State may give notice in writing to the appellant, the local authority, the Council and any interested persons on whom the appellant has served a copy of the notice of appeal, that it appears to the Secretary of State that the appeal is one which, by virtue of paragraph 15 of Schedule 5 to the Act (appeals against necessary decisions), he is not required to entertain in whole or in part.

(2) Upon giving by the Secretary of State of a notice under paragraph (1) above—

(a) relating to the whole of the appeal, no further steps shall be taken in connection with the appeal, or

(b) relating to a part only of the appeal, no further steps shall be taken in connection with that part, but the other part of the appeal shall thereafter be treated as the appeal for the purposes of these Regulations.

(3) If in any case, before giving notice under paragraph (1) above, the Secretary of State has received any representations from the local authority or the Council under Regulation 5(1), the Secretary of State shall either allow the appellant an opportunity to comment on those representations before he decides to give the notice under paragraph (1) above or shall completely disregard those representations in coming to a decision to give such notice.

Notification of hearing

9.—(1) Where a hearing by a person appointed by the Secretary of State is required by virtue of paragraph 16(1) of Schedule 5 to the Act, a date, time and place for the hearing shall be fixed and may be varied by the Secretary of State, who shall (except as hereinafter provided) give not less than 42 days notice in writing of such date, time and place to—

(a) the appellant,

(b) the local authority,

(c) the Council, if they have notified the Secretary of State of their desire to appear at any hearing,

(d) every interested person who has notified the Secretary of State of his desire to appear at any hearing, and

(e) any other person upon whom a copy of the notice of appeal has been served in accordance with Regulation 4(4).

(2) With the consent of the appellant, the local authority and (if they have notified the Secretary of State of their desire to appear) the Council, the Secretary

of State may give such lesser period of notice as may be agreed with all of them, and in that event he may specify a date for the service of the statements referred to in Regulation 10(1) later than the date therein prescribed.

(3) Where it becomes necessary or advisable to vary the time or place fixed for the hearing, the Secretary of State shall give such notice of the variation as may appear to him to be reasonable in the circumstances.

Statements to be served before the hearing

10.—(1) Not later than 28 days before the date of the hearing (or such later date as the Secretary of State may specify under Regulation 9(2)) each of the persons and bodies specified in paragraph (2) of this Regulation shall serve upon all the other persons and bodies so specified and upon the Secretary of State—

(*a*) a written statement of any submission which the person or body in question proposes to put forward at the hearing, and

(*b*) a list of any documents (including maps and plans) which the person or body in question intends to refer to or put in evidence at the hearing,

and shall also afford to all the other persons and bodies aforesaid a reasonable opportunity to inspect and, where practicable, to take copies of such documents.

(2) The persons and bodies referred to in paragraph (1) above are—

(*a*) the appellant,

(*b*) the local authority,

(*c*) if they have notified the Secretary of State of their desire to appear at any hearing, the Council, and

(*d*) every interested person who has notified the Secretary of State of his desire to appear at any hearing.

Appearances at hearing

11.—(1) The persons entitled to appear at the hearing shall be—

(*a*) the appellant,

(*b*) the local authority,

(*c*) if they have notified the Secretary of State of their desire to appear, the Council,

(*d*) the interested persons who have notified the Secretary of State of their desire to appear.

(2) Any other person may appear at the hearing at the discretion of the appointed person.

(3) The local authority and the Council may appear by their clerk or by any other officer appointed for the purpose, or by counsel or solicitor; and any other person may appear on his own behalf or be represented by counsel, solicitor or any other person.

(4) Where there are two or more persons having a similar interest in the matter under inquiry at the hearing, the appointed person may allow one or more persons to appear for the benefit of some or all persons so interested.

Procedure at the hearing

12.—(1) Except as otherwise provided in these Regulations, the procedure at the hearing shall be such as the appointed person shall in his discretion determine.

(2) Unless in any particular case the appointed person with the consent of the appellant otherwise determines, the appellant shall begin and shall have the right of final reply; and the other persons entitled or permitted to appear shall be heard in such order as the appointed person may determine:

(3) The appellant, the interested persons who have notified the Secretary of State of their desire to appear, the local authority and the Council shall be entitled to call evidence and cross-examine persons giving evidence, but any other person appearing at the hearing may do so only to the extent permitted by the appointed person.

(4) The appointed person shall not require or permit the giving or production of any evidence, whether written or oral, which would be contrary to the public interest; but save as aforesaid any evidence may be admitted at the discretion of the appointed person, who may direct that documents tendered in evidence may be inspected by any person entitled or permitted to appear at the hearing and that facilities be afforded him to take or obtain copies thereof.

(5) The appointed person may allow the local authority, the Council, the appellant, an interested person, or all or any of them, to alter or add to the submissions contained in any statement served under Regulation 10(1), or to any list of documents which accompanied such statement, so far as may be necessary for the purpose of determining the questions in controversy between the parties, but shall (if necessary by adjourning the hearing) give the appellant, the local authority or the Council, as the case may be, and the interested persons who are appearing at the hearing, an adequate opportunity of considering any such fresh submission or document.

(6) If any person entitled to appear at the hearing fails to do so, the appointed person may proceed with the hearing at his discretion.

(7) The appointed person shall be entitled (subject to disclosure thereof at the hearing) to take into account any written representations or statements received by him before the hearing from any person.

(8) The appointed person may from time to time adjourn the hearing and, if the date, time and place of the adjourned hearing are announced before the adjournment, no further notice shall be required.

Site inspections

13.—(1) The appointed person may make an unaccompanied inspection of the premises before or during the hearing without giving notice of his intention to the persons entitled to appear at the hearing.

(2) The appointed person may, and shall if so requested by the appellant, the local authority or the Council before or during the hearing, inspect the premises after the close of the hearing and shall, in all cases where he intends to make such an inspection, announce during the hearing the date and time at which he proposes to do so.

(3) The appellant, the local authority, the Council and the interested persons who are appearing at the hearing shall be entitled to accompany the appointed person on any inspection after the close of the hearing; but the appointed person shall not be bound to defer his inspection if any person entitled to accompany him is not present at the time appointed.

Procedure after hearing

14.—(1) The appointed person shall after the close of the hearing make a report in writing to the Secretary of State which shall include the appointed person's findings of fact and his recommendations, if any, or his reason for not making any recommendations.

(2) Where the Secretary of State—

(*a*) differs from the appointed person on a finding of fact, or

(*b*) after the close of the hearing takes into consideration any new evidence (including expert opinion on a matter of fact) or any new issue of fact (not being a matter of government policy) which was not raised at the hearing,

and by reason thereof is disposed to disagree with a recommendation made by the appointed person, he shall not come to a decision which is at variance with any such recommendation without first notifying the appellant, the local authority, the Council (if they appeared at the hearing), and any interested person who appeared at the hearing, of his disagreement and the reasons for it and affording them an opportunity of making representations in writing within 21 days or (if the Secretary of State has taken into consideration any new evidence or any new issue of fact, not being a matter of government policy) of asking within 21 days for the re-opening of the hearing.

(3) The Secretary of State may in any case if he thinks fit cause the hearing to be re-opened, and shall cause it to be re-opened if asked to do so in accordance with the last foregoing paragraph; and, if the hearing is re-opened, Regulation 9 shall apply as it applied to the original hearing, but with the substitution in paragraph (1) of "28" for "42".

Notification of decision

15.—(1) The Secretary of State shall notify his decision, and his reasons therefor, in writing to the appellant, the interested persons who appeared at the hearing, the local authority and the Council and to any person who, having appeared at the hearing, has asked to be notified of the decision; and, where a copy of the appointed person's report is not sent with the notification of the decision, the notification shall be accompanied by a summary of the appointed person's conclusions and recommendations.

(2) If any person entitled to be notified of the Secretary of State's decision under the last foregoing paragraph has not received a copy of the appointed person's report, he shall be supplied with a copy thereof on written application made to the Secretary of State within 28 days from the date of his decision.

(3) For the purposes of this Regulation "report" does not include documents, photographs or plans appended to the report, but any person entitled to be supplied with a copy of the report under paragraph (2) above may apply to the Secretary of State in writing within 42 days of the notification to him of the decision or the supply to him of the report, whichever is the later, for an opportunity of inspecting such documents, photographs, and plans, and the Secretary of State shall afford him an opportunity accordingly.

Service of notices by post

16. Notices or documents required or authorised to be served or sent under the provisions of any of these Regulations may be sent by post.

Inquiries

17.—(1) Where the Secretary of State in exercise of his powers under paragraph 16(2) of Schedule 5 to the Act, appoints a person to hold an inquiry in connection with the appeal—

(*a*) the provisions of Regulations 9 to 16 shall apply to any such inquiry as they apply to a hearing and for that purpose references in those Regulations to a hearing shall be construed as references to such inquiry, and

(*b*) in addition, the provisions of the subsequent paragraphs of this Regulation shall apply to any such inquiry.

(2) Without prejudice to the provisions of Regulation 9 (applied as aforesaid) the Secretary of State may require the local authority to take one or more of the following steps, namely—

(*a*) to publish in one or more newspapers circulating in the locality in which the premises are situated such notices of the inquiry as he may direct;

(*b*) to serve notice of the inquiry in such form and on such persons or classes of persons as he may specify;

(*c*) to post such notices of the inquiry as he may direct in a conspicuous place or places near to the premises;

but the requirements as to the period of notice contained in Regulation 9(1) shall not apply to any such notices.

(3) Where the premises are under the control of the appellant, he shall, if so required by the Secretary of State, affix firmly to some object on the premises, in such a manner as to be readily visible to and legible by the public, such notice of the inquiry as the Secretary of State may specify, and thereafter for such period before the inquiry as the Secretary of State may specify the appellant shall not remove the notice or cause or permit it to be removed.

(4) Any persons on whom the Secretary of State has required notice of the inquiry to be served under paragraph (2)(*b*) of this Regulation shall be entitled to appear at the inquiry.

(5) Where in pursuance of Regulation 14 the Secretary of State decides to re-open the inquiry the provisions of paragraph (2) of this Regulation shall apply as they applied to the original inquiry.

William Rodgers,
Secretary of State for Transport.

28th July 1977.

SCHEDULE 1

PARTICULARS TO BE INCLUDED IN A NOTICE OF APPEAL

1. The name and address of the appellant.

2. The name and address of any solicitor or other person acting on behalf of the appellant.

3. The appellant's address for service of documents, if different from that stated in 1 above.

4. The address and a brief description of the premises.

5. A brief statement of the decision of the local authority under appeal (including the date on which that decision was notified to the appellant) and of the appellant's interest in that decision.

6. A statement of the grounds of appeal.

7. A statement of the decision which the appellant desires the Secretary of State to make.

8. A statement of the names and addresses of all persons upon whom the appellant is serving a copy of the notice and, in the case of any interested person, a statement of the interest of that person (so far as known to the appellant).

SCHEDULE 2

DOCUMENTS OF WHICH COPIES ARE TO BE FURNISHED TO THE SECRETARY OF STATE
BY THE APPELLANT

1. Where there is a licence in existence, the licence.

2. Where the appeal relates to an application for a licence or for a variation of the terms and conditions of the licence, the application and all relevant documents submitted to the local authority with the application.

3. Except where the case is one to which paragraph 14(2) of Schedule 5 to the Act applies, the local authority's notification of their decision and of their reasons therefor.

4. All other relevant correspondence with the local authority.

EXPLANATORY NOTE

(This Note is not part of the Regulations.)

These Regulations prescribe the procedure for appeals to the Secretary of State against decisions of local authorities in Greater London in connection with licences for the operation of public off-street parking places in those areas where such operation is controlled under the provisions of section 36 of, and Schedule 5 to, the Transport (London) Act 1969.

The requirements with respect to the notice of appeal and supporting documents are set out in Regulation 4 and Schedules 1 and 2. Regulations 5 and 6 provide for written representations, and for requests for a hearing of the appeal by a person appointed by the Secretary of State, and Regulation 7 deals with the case where an appeal is decided on written representations. Regulation 8 lays down the procedure to be followed in cases where, by virtue of paragraph 15 of Schedule 5 to the 1969 Act, the Secretary of State is entitled to refuse to entertain the appeal.

The provisions with respect to hearings of appeals are contained in Regulation 9 (notification), Regulation 10 (statements to be served), Regulation 11 (appearances), Regulation 12 (procedure at the hearing), Regulation 13 (site inspections) and Regulation 14 (procedure after the hearing).

Regulation 15 provides for the notification of the decision consequent on a hearing of an appeal and for the giving of reasons for the decision.

Regulation 17 adapts the provisions of the Regulations for the cases where, in exercise of his power under paragraph 16(2) of Schedule 5 to the 1969 Act, the Secretary of State decides to hold an inquiry in connection with an appeal, instead of a hearing by a person appointed by him. The Regulation also makes provision for requiring public notice of the inquiry to be given.

STATUTORY INSTRUMENTS

1977 No. 1321

TERMS AND CONDITIONS OF EMPLOYMENT

The Redundancy Payments (Variation of Rebates) Order 1977

Laid before Parliament in draft

Made -	-	-	-	31*st July* 1977
Coming into Operation				14*th August* 1977

The Secretary of State in exercise of powers conferred on him by section 1(1) and (3) of the Redundancy Rebates Act 1977(**a**) and of all other powers enabling him in that behalf, hereby makes the following Order a draft of which has been laid before Parliament and approved by resolution of each House of Parliament.

Citation and commencement

1. This Order may be cited as the Redundancy Payments (Variation of Rebates) Order 1977 and shall come into operation at the end of the period of fourteen days beginning with the day on which it is made.

Interpretation

2.—(1) The Interpretation Act 1889(**b**) shall apply to the interpretation of this Order as it applies to the interpretation of an Act of Parliament.

(2) In this Order, unless the context otherwise requires—

"employee" has the same meaning as in section 25 of the Redundancy Payments Act 1965;

"rebate" has the same meaning as in section 30 of that Act;

"redundancy payment" has the same meaning as in section 1 of that Act;

"the relevant date", in relation to a redundancy payment, means the date which is the relevant date for the purpose of calculating the amount of that payment under Schedule 1 to that Act; and

"the 1965 Act" means the Redundancy Payments Act 1965(**c**) as amended by the Redundancy Rebates Act 1969(**d**), the Trade Union and Labour Relations Act 1974(**e**) and the Employment Protection Act 1975(**f**).

Modification of Schedule 5 of the 1965 Act

3. Schedule 5 to the 1965 Act shall have effect as if—

(*a*) in paragraphs 2 and 9 (which provide for a rebate to be calculated by reference to certain fractions of a week's pay) for the words "three-

---

(**a**) 1977 c. 22.	(**b**) 1889 c. 63.
(**c**) 1965 c. 62.	(**d**) 1969 c. 8.
(**e**) 1974 c. 52.	(**f**) 1975 c. 71.

quarters", "one-half" and "one-quarter" there were substituted respectively the words "123/200", "41/100" and "41/200"; and

(*b*) in paragraphs 3 and 12 (which provide for a rebate payable in respect of a reduced payment to be one-half of the amount of the payment) for the words "one-half" there were substituted the words "41/100".

Transitional and consequential provisions

4.—(1) Article 3 above shall not have effect in relation to any rebate payable in respect of the whole or part of a redundancy payment if—

(*a*) the relevant date is a date earlier than that on which this Order comes into operation; or

(*b*) the condition in paragraph (*a*) above would be fulfilled but for the operation of subsection (10) of section 3 of the 1965 Act (which postpones the relevant date, as determined under subsection (9) of that section, in certain cases of dismissal where less than the statutory minimum period of notice is given).

(2) Article 3 above shall not have effect in relation to any rebate payable in respect of a payment to an employee on the termination of his contract of employment which is paid—

(*a*) in pursuance of an agreement in respect of which an order under section 11 of the 1965 Act is in operation; or

(*b*) in pursuance of an award made as mentioned in section 12 of that Act in connection with such an agreement,

where, under the agreement in question, the employee's contract is treated for the purposes of the agreement as having been terminated on a date earlier than the date on which this Order comes into operation.

Signed by order of the Secretary of State.

31st July 1977.

Harold Walker,
Minister of State,
Department of Employment.

EXPLANATORY NOTE

(*This Note is not part of the Order.*)

This Order reduces the amount of rebate payable to an employer from the Redundancy Fund in respect of redundancy and equivalent payments under the Redundancy Payments Act 1965 as amended. The rebate is reduced from 50% to 41% of the corresponding redundancy and equivalent payments.

STATUTORY INSTRUMENTS

1977 No. 1322

TERMS AND CONDITIONS OF EMPLOYMENT

The Guarantee Payments (Exemption) (No. 8) Order 1977

Made - - - -	*30th July* 1977
Coming into Operation	*5th September* 1977

Whereas the four Agreements between the Smiths Food Group (a division of Toms Foods Ltd.) and the Transport and General Workers' Union relating respectively to the division's establishments at—

19 Copse Road, Fleetwood;

Caistor Road, Great Yarmouth;

224 Southampton Road, Paulsgrove, Portsmouth;

Stockport Road, Cheadle Heath, Stockport

are collective agreements each of which makes provision whereby employees to whom the said agreement relates have a right to guaranteed remuneration:

And whereas the parties to each of the said collective agreements (whose descriptions are set out in Schedule 1 to this Order) have all made application to the Secretary of State under section 28(1) of the Employment Protection Act 1975(a) ("the Act"):

And whereas the Secretary of State having regard to the provisions of each of the agreements (which so far as are material are set out in Schedule 2 to this Order) is satisfied that section 22 of the Act should not apply to those employees:

And whereas each of the said agreements complies with section 28(4) of the Act:

Now, therefore, the Secretary of State in exercise of the powers conferred on him as the appropriate Minister under section 28(1) of the Act and of all other powers enabling him in that behalf, hereby makes the following Order:—

Citation and commencement

1. This Order may be cited as the Guarantee Payments (Exemption) (No. 8) Order 1977 and shall come into operation on 5th September 1977.

Interpretation

2.—(1) The Interpretation Act 1889(b) shall apply to the interpretation of this Order as it applies to the interpretation of an Act of Parliament.

(2) The "exempted agreements" are the agreements referred to in the preamble above.

(a) 1975 c. 71.   (b) 1889 c. 63.

Exemption

3. Section 22 of the Act shall not apply to any person who is an employee to whom an exempted agreement relates.

Signed by order of the Secretary of State.
30th July 1977.

Harold Walker,
Minister of State,
Department of Employment.

SCHEDULE 1
PARTIES TO THE COLLECTIVE AGREEMENTS

1. *Representing Employers:*
   the Smiths Food Group, a division of Toms Foods Ltd., a subsidiary of General Mills Inc. (USA).

2. *Representing Employees:*
   the Transport and General Workers' Union.

SCHEDULE 2
Material Provisions of Exempted Agreements

A. THE FLEETWOOD AGREEMENT
Short Time Working Agreement

STAGE 1

The Company will seek to avoid lay off, short time working or redundancy by allowing normal wastage to reduce production capacity.

The Company will inform the stewards at an establishment where this "run down" is taking place and will provide them with such information as to anticipated time scale and size of run down as is reasonable in the circumstances.

The Company will expect the remaining employees to work flexibly so as to maintain a balanced work force. When this results in an employee being required to accept work of a lower grade (e.g. machine minder to work as a packer) the higher rate of pay will be maintained for up to six weeks and thereafter will be reduced to that appropriate to the lower grade. Selection of people for work at a lower grade will be on a basis of length of service in the higher grade.

STAGE 2

Should reduction in production capacity effected by Stage 1 be insufficient to meet the reduced production requirement, the Company will give notice of its intention to work a short week or operate a lay off. Selection for lay off being on a basis of length of service whilst maintaining a balanced workforce. Consideration being given to short time or lay off of part time employees before full time employees are affected.

To protect the earnings of employees affected by this stage the Company will pay a basic day's wages for up to a total of five days of short time or lay off cumulative in any calendar quarter (1st January to 31st March, 1st April to 30th June, 1st July to 30th September, 1st October to 31st December). Before implementing short time working or lay off at an establishment the Company will discuss the matter with the shop stewards at least one week before it is intended to operate the short week or lay off.

QUALIFICATIONS FOR AND CALCULATION OF PAYMENT UNDER STAGE 2

Payment in respect of short time, that is to say where a short working week of less than five days is to be operated, or lay off, that is to say when employees are laid off for a period in excess of five consecutive days' duration will be made to employees who would normally have been at work on the day or days in question provided that the employee has a minimum of four weeks' service at the time of the start of the period of short time working or lay off.

No payment will be due to an employee who refuses reasonable alternative work within their competence for the day or days in question, selection for alternative work being at the discretion of management.

Any person absent from the establishment during a period of short time working or lay off due to certified sickness, holiday or prior permission without pay shall be excluded from benefit under this agreement.

No payment will be due if the short time or lay off results from Industrial Action at any of the Group's establishments. A basic day's wages shall be eight hours wages inclusive of any shift premium. The wage rate being that which would have been paid had the employee been at work. In the case of part time employees working less than a normal eight hour shift a day's work shall be the hours that they are normally contracted to work on that day.

APPEAL

Any employee who feels that he/she has been treated unfairly under the terms of this agreement shall have the right of appeal in accordance with the Company's grievance procedure. In addition, the employee has, in every case, the right to present a case to an industrial tribunal that the Company has failed to make a payment, or part of a payment, to which the employee is entitled under this agreement.

B. THE GREAT YARMOUTH AGREEMENT
SHORT TIME WORKING AGREEMENT

STAGE 1

The Company will seek to avoid lay off, short time working or redundancy by allowing normal wastage to reduce production capacity.

The Company will inform the stewards at an establishment where this "run down" is taking place and will provide them with such information as to anticipated time scale and size of run down as is reasonable in the circumstances.

The Company will expect the remaining employees to work flexibly so as to maintain a balanced work force. When this results in an employee being required to accept work of a lower grade (e.g. machine minder to work as a packer) the higher rate of pay will be maintained for up to six weeks and thereafter will be reduced to that appropriate to the lower grade. Selection of people for work at a lower grade will be on a basis of length of service in the higher grade.

STAGE 2

Should reduction in production capacity effected by stage 1 be insufficient to meet the reduced production requirement, the Company will give notice of its intention to work a short week or operate a lay off. Selection for lay off being on a basis of length of service whilst maintaining a balanced workforce.

To protect the earnings of employees affected by this stage the Company will pay a basic day's wages for up to a total of five days of short time or lay off cumulative in any calendar quarter (1st January to 31st March, 1st April to 30th June, 1st July to 30th September, 1st October to 31st December). Before implementing short time working or lay off at Gt. Yarmouth the Company will discuss the matter with the shop stewards at least one week before it is intended to operate the short week or lay off.

QUALIFICATIONS FOR AND CALCULATION OF PAYMENT UNDER STAGE 2

Payment in respect of short time, that is to say where a short working week of less than five days is to be operated, or lay off, that is to say when employees are laid off for a period in excess of five consecutive days' duration will be made to employees who would normally have been at work on the day or days in question provided that the employee has a minimum of four weeks' service at the time of the start of the period of short time working or lay off.

No payment will be due to an employee who refuses reasonable alternative work within their competence for the day or days in question, selection for alternative work being at the discretion of management.

Any person absent from the establishment during a period of short time working or lay off due to certified sickness, holiday or prior permission without pay shall be excluded from this agreement.

No payment will be due if the short time or lay off results from Industrial Action at any of the Group's establishments. A basic day's wages shall be eight hours' wages inclusive of any shift premium. The wage rate being that which would have been paid had the employee been at work. In the case of part time employees working less than a normal eight hour shift a day's work shall be the hours that they are normally contracted to work on that day.

APPEAL

Any employee who feels that he/she has been treated unfairly under the terms of this agreement shall have the right of appeal in accordance with the Company's grievance procedure. In addition, the employee has, in every case, the right to present a case to an industrial tribunal that the Company has failed to make a payment, or part of a payment, to which the employee is entitled under this agreement.

C. THE PAULSGROVE AGREEMENT
SHORT TIME WORKING AGREEMENT

STAGE 1

The Company will seek to avoid lay off, short time working or redundancy by allowing normal wastage to reduce production capacity.

The Company will inform the stewards at an establishment where this "run down" is taking place and will provide them with such information as to anticipated time scale and size of run down as is reasonable in the circumstances.

The Company will expect the remaining employees to work flexibly so as to maintain a balanced work force. When this results in an employee being required to accept work of a lower grade (e.g. machine minder to work as a packer) the higher rate of pay will be maintained for up to six weeks and thereafter will be reduced to that appropriate to the lower grade. Selection of people for work at a lower grade will be on a basis of length of service in the higher grade.

STAGE 2

Should the policy of "run down" be inadequate to meet the reduced production requirements the Company will reduce the working week, or lay off, all or part of the part time labour force in the latter case selection will be on the basis of length of service.

The shop stewards being kept fully informed of the situation prior to any action being taken to implement cuts in accordance with this stage.

STAGE 3

Should reduction in production capacity effected by stages 1 and 2 be insufficient to meet the reduced production requirement, the Company will give notice of its intention to work a short week or operate a lay off of its full time permanent employees.

To protect the earnings of employees affected by either stages 2 or 3 the Company will pay a basic day's wages for up to a total of five days of short time or lay off cumulative in any calendar quarter (1st January to 31st March, 1st April to 30th June, 1st July to 30th September, 1st October to 31st December). Before implementing short time working or lay off at any establishment the Company will discuss the matter with the shop stewards at least one week before it is intended to operate the short week or lay off.

QUALIFICATIONS FOR AND CALCULATION OF PAYMENT UNDER STAGES 2 AND 3

Payment in respect of short time, that is to say where a short working week of less than five days is to be operated, or lay off, that is to say when employees are laid off for a period in excess of five consecutive days' duration will be made to employees who would normally have been at work on the day or days in question provided that the employee has a minimum of four weeks' service at the time of the start of the period of short time working or lay off.

No payment will be due to an employee who refuses reasonable alternative work within their competence for the day or days in question, selection for alternative work being at the discretion of management.

Any person absent from the establishment during a period of short time working or lay off due to certified sickness, holiday or prior permission without pay shall be excluded from this agreement.

No payment will be due if the short time or lay off results from Industrial Action at any of the Group's establishments. A basic day's wages shall be eight hours wages inclusive of any shift premium. The wage rate being that which would have been paid had the employee been at work. In the case of part time employees working less than a normal eight hour shift a day's work shall be the hours that they are normally contracted to work on that day.

APPEAL

Any employee who feels that he/she has been treated unfairly under the terms of this agreement shall have the right of appeal in accordance with the Company's grievance procedure. In addition, the employee has, in every case, the right to present a case to an industrial tribunal that the Company has failed to make a payment, or part of a payment, to which the employee is entitled under this agreement.

D.   THE STOCKPORT AGREEMENT
SHORT TIME WORKING AGREEMENT

STAGE 1

The Company will seek to avoid lay off, short time working or redundancy by allowing normal wastage to reduce production capacity.

The Company will inform the stewards at an establishment where this "run down" is taking place and will provide them with such information as to anticipated time scale and size of run down as is reasonable in the circumstances.

The Company will expect the remaining employees to work flexibly so as to maintain a balanced work force. When this results in an employee being required to accept work of a lower grade (e.g. machine minder to work as a packer) the higher rate of pay will be maintained for up to six weeks and thereafter will be reduced to that appropriate to the lower grade. Selection of people for work at a lower grade will be on a basis of length of service in the higher grade.

STAGE 2

Should reduction in production capacity effected by stage 1 be insufficient to meet the reduced production requirement, the Company will give notice of its intention to work a short week or operate a lay off. Selection for lay off being on a basis of length of service whilst maintaining a balanced workforce.

To protect the earnings of employees affected by this stage the Company will pay a basic day's wages for up to a total of five days of short time or lay off cumulative in any calendar quarter (1st January to 31st March, 1st April to 30th June, 1st July to 30th September, 1st October to 31st December). Before implementing short time working or lay off at an establishment the Company will discuss the matter with the shop stewards at least one week before it is intended to operate the short week or lay off.

QUALIFICATIONS FOR AND CALCULATION OF PAYMENT UNDER STAGE 2

Payment in respect of short time, that is to say where a short working week of less than five days is to be operated, or lay off, that is to say when employees are laid off for a period in excess of five consecutive days' duration will be made to employees who would normally have been at work on the day or days in question provided that the employee has a minimum of four weeks' service at the time of the start of the period of short time working or lay off.

No payment will be due to an employee who refuses reasonable alternative work within their competence for the day or days in question, selection for alternative work being at the discretion of management.

Any person absent from the establishment during a period of short time working or lay off due to certified sickness, holiday or prior permission without pay shall be excluded from this agreement.

No payment will be due if the short time or lay off results from Industrial Action at any of the Group's establishments. A basic day's wages shall be eight hours' wages inclusive of any shift premium. The wage rate being that which would have been paid had the employee been at work. In the case of part time employees working less than a normal eight hour shift a day's work shall be the hours that they are normally contracted to work on that day.

APPEAL

Any employee who feels that he/she has been treated unfairly under the terms of this agreement shall have the right of appeal in accordance with the Company's grievance procedure. In addition, the employee has, in every case, the right to present a case to an industrial tribunal that the Company has failed to make a payment, or part of a payment, to which the employee is entitled under this agreement.

EXPLANATORY NOTE
(This Note is not part of the Order.)

This Order excludes from the operation of section 22 of the Employment Protection Act 1975 employees at four establishments of the Smiths Foods Group (a division of Toms Foods Ltd.) being employees to whom collective agreements with the Transport and General Workers' Union relate.

Copies of the Agreements are available for inspection between 10.0 a.m. and noon and between 2 p.m. and 5 p.m. (Monday to Friday) at the offices of the Department of Employment, 8 St. James's Square, London SW1Y 4JB.

STATUTORY INSTRUMENTS

1977 No. 1323

SPORTS GROUNDS

The Safety of Sports Grounds (Designation) Order 1977

Made - - - -	*29th July* 1977
Laid before Parliament	*9th August* 1977
Coming into Operation	*1st January* 1978

In exercise of the powers conferred upon me by section 1(1) of the Safety of Sports Grounds Act 1975(a), and after such consultation as is mentioned in section 18(4) thereof, I hereby make the following Order:—

1. This Order may be cited as the Safety of Sports Grounds (Designation) Order 1977 and shall come into operation on 1st January 1978.

2. The sports stadia specified in the Schedule to this Order (being stadia each of which in the opinion of the Secretary of State has accommodation for more than 10,000 spectators) are hereby designated as stadia requiring safety certificates under the Safety of Sports Grounds Act 1975.

Merlyn Rees,
One of Her Majesty's Principal
Secretaries of State.

Home Office.
29th July 1977.

Article 2.   SCHEDULE

Address of Stadium	Occupier of Stadium
Stamford Bridge Grounds Fulham Road London	Chelsea Football and Athletic Co. Ltd.
City Ground Nottingham	Nottingham Forest Football Club
Molineux Grounds Waterloo Road Wolverhampton	Wolverhampton Wanderers Football Club (1923) Ltd.

(a) 1975 c. 52.

EXPLANATORY NOTE

(This Note is not part of the Order.)

By this Order the Secretary of State designates certain sports stadia as stadia requiring safety certificates under the Safety of Sports Grounds Act 1975.

STATUTORY INSTRUMENTS

1977 No. 1324

SOCIAL SECURITY

The Family Income Supplements (Computation) (No. 2) Regulations 1977

Laid before Parliament in draft

Made	-	-	-	29*th July* 1977
Coming into Operation			15*th November* 1977	

Whereas a draft of the following regulations was laid before Parliament and approved by a resolution of each House of Parliament:

Now, therefore, the Secretary of State for Social Services, in exercise of the powers conferred upon him by sections 2(1), 3(1), 3(1A), 3(4) and 10(3) of the Family Income Supplements Act 1970(a) (as amended by paragraphs 3 and 4 of Schedule 4 to the Child Benefit Act 1975(b)), and of all other powers enabling him in that behalf, hereby makes the following regulations:—

Citation, commencement and interpretation

1.—(1) These regulations may be cited as the Family Income Supplements (Computation) (No. 2) Regulations 1977 and shall come into operation on 15th November 1977.

(2) In these regulations, unless the context otherwise requires—

"the Act" means the Family Income Supplements Act 1970;

"benefit" means a family income supplement under the Act;

and other expressions have the same meanings as in the Act.

(3) The rules for the construction of Acts of Parliament contained in the Interpretation Act 1889(c) shall apply in relation to this instrument and in relation to the revocation effected by it as if this instrument and the regulations revoked by it were Acts of Parliament, and as if the revocation were a repeal.

Prescribed amount

2. The prescribed amount for any family for the purposes of section 2 of the Act shall be—

(a) if the family includes only one child, £43·80; and

(b) if the family includes more than one child, £43·80 plus £4·00 for each child additional to the first.

(a) 1970 c. 55.   (b) 1975 c. 61.   (c) 1889 c. 63.

Maximum amount of benefit

3. The weekly rate of benefit shall not exceed—

(*a*) if the family includes only one child, £9·50; and

(*b*) if the family includes more than one child, £9·50 plus £1·00 for each child additional to the first.

Revocation

4.—(1) The Family Income Supplements (Computation) Regulations 1977(a) are hereby revoked.

(2) Without prejudice to the general application by regulation 1(3) of these regulations of the rules for the construction of Acts of Parliament contained in section 38 of the Interpretation Act 1889 (effect of repeal) with regard to the effect of revocations, nothing in paragraph (1) of this regulation shall be taken as affecting the application of the regulations revoked by the said paragraph (1) in relation to any period for which benefit is payable falling before 15th November 1977.

David Ennals,

Secretary of State for Social Services.

29th July 1977.

EXPLANATORY NOTE

(This Note is not part of the Regulations.)

These Regulations specify the prescribed amount for any family and the weekly rate of benefit under the Family Income Supplements Act 1970 in accordance with the amendments made to the 1970 Act by the Child Benefit Act 1975 which require that the prescribed amount and the weekly rate of benefit which had been included in sections 2 and 3 of the 1970 Act should be specified in regulations.

Regulation 1 relates to the citation, commencement and interpretation of the regulations; regulation 2 specifies the prescribed amount from 15th November 1977; regulation 3 specifies the maximum weekly amount of benefit; and regulation 4 revokes previous regulations.

(a) S.I. 1977/586 (1977 I, p. 1879).

STATUTORY INSTRUMENTS

1977 No. 1325

SOCIAL SECURITY

The Social Security Benefits Up-rating Order 1977

Laid before Parliament in draft

Made - - -		*29th July* 1977
Coming into Operation		14*th November* 1977

Whereas, consequent upon a review under section 125 of the Social Security Act 1975(**a**) as amended by sections 23(1), 23(4) and 65(1) of, and Part I of Schedule 4 to, the Social Security Pensions Act 1975(**b**) and section 7(1) and (2) of the Social Security (Miscellaneous Provisions) Act 1977(**c**), a draft of the following order was laid before Parliament and approved by resolution of each House of Parliament;

Now, therefore, the Secretary of State for Social Services, in conjunction with the Treasury(**d**), in exercise of the powers conferred upon him by section 124 of the first mentioned Act, and of all other powers enabling him in that behalf, hereby makes the following order:—

Citation, commencement and interpretation

1.—(1) This order may be cited as the Social Security Benefits Up-rating Order 1977 and shall come into operation on 14th November 1977.

(2) In this order, unless the context otherwise requires, "the Act" means the Social Security Act 1975.

(3) The rules for the construction of Acts of Parliament contained in the Interpretation Act 1889(**e**) shall apply in relation to this instrument and in relation to the revocation effected by it as if this instrument and the order revoked by it were Acts of Parliament and as if the revocation were a repeal.

Increase in rates or amounts of certain benefits under the Act and the Industrial Injuries and Diseases (Old Cases) Act

2.—(1) In Schedule 4 to the Act as amended by section 21(1) and (2) of, and Schedules 4 and 5 to, the Child Benefit Act 1975(**f**) and by the Social Security Benefits Up-rating Order 1976(**g**), the sums, reduced where appropriate by the Child Benefit and Social Security (Fixing and Adjustment of Rates) Regulations 1976(**h**) and, subject to such reduction, as specified in Parts I (contributory

---

(**a**) 1975 c. 14. (**b**) 1975 c. 60. (**c**) 1977 c. 5.
(**d**) See section 166(5) of the Social Security Act 1975. (**e**) 1889 c. 63.
(**f**) 1975 c. 61. (**g**) S.I. 1976/1029 (1976 II, p. 2705).
(**h**) S.I. 1976/1267 (1976 II, p. 3576).

periodical benefits), III (non-contributory periodical benefits), IV (increase of benefits for dependants) and V (rate or amount of industrial injuries benefit), except the sum specified in the said Part III for age addition, shall be further increased from and including the respective dates specified in Article 3 below; and the said Schedule 4 shall accordingly have effect as set out in the Schedule to this order.

(2) In the Industrial Injuries and Diseases (Old Cases) Act 1975(a) as amended by the Social Security Benefits Up-rating Order 1976 the sum of £9·20 referred to in section 2(6)(c) (maximum weekly rate of lesser incapacity allowance supplementing workmen's compensation) and section 7(2)(b) (industrial diseases benefit schemes: weekly rate of allowance payable where disablement is not total) shall be further increased; and from and including 16th November 1977 the references in those provisions to that sum shall accordingly have effect as references to £10·50.

Dates on which benefits under the Act are increased by this order

3. The increases of benefit under the Act effected by this order shall take effect in the case of—

(a) maternity allowance, widow's and widowed mother's allowance, widow's pension, Category A, B, C and D retirement pension, child's special allowance, attendance allowance, invalid care allowance (except in a case where the Secretary of State has made arrangements for it to be paid on a Wednesday), guardian's allowance and industrial death benefit by way of widow's and widower's pension and allowance in respect of children of deceased's family (including where appropriate increases for dependants), on 14th November 1977;

(b) invalid care allowance (in a case where the Secretary of State has made arrangements for it to be paid on a Wednesday), mobility allowance, disablement benefit (including increases of disablement pension), maximum disablement gratuity under section 57(5) of the Act, increase of unemployability supplement under section 59 of the Act and maximum under section 91(1) of the Act of aggregate of weekly benefit payable for successive accidents, on 16th November 1977; and

(c) unemployment and sickness benefit, invalidity pension and allowance, non-contributory invalidity pension and injury benefit (including where appropriate increases for dependants), on 17th November 1977.

Increase of amount specified in sections 30(1), 45(3) and 66(4) of the Act

4. The amount specified in sections 30(1), 45(3) and 66(4) of the Act, excluding paragraphs (a) and (b) of those provisions (amount of weekly earnings which must be exceeded before certain benefits are reduced by reference to earnings) shall be increased to £40.

Increase of sum specified in section 6(1)(a) of the Social Security Pensions Act 1975

5. With effect from 16th November 1977, the sum specified in section 6(1)(a) of the Social Security Pensions Act 1975 (weekly rate of basic component of Category A retirement pension) shall be increased to the sum of £17·50.

(a) 1975 c. 16.

Revocation

6. The Social Security Benefits Up-rating Order 1976 is hereby revoked.

David Ennals,
Secretary of State for Social Services.

29th July 1977.

T. M. Cox,
T. E. Graham,
Two of the Lords Commissioners of
Her Majesty's Treasury.

29th July 1977.

SCHEDULE 1

Article 2(1)

SCHEDULE 4 TO THE ACT AS AMENDED BY THIS ORDER

SCHEDULE 4

RATES OF BENEFITS, GRANTS AND INCREASES FOR DEPENDANTS

PART I

CONTRIBUTORY PERIODICAL BENEFITS (SS. 14–31)

Description of benefit	Weekly rate
1. Unemployment or sickness benefit (section 14).	(a) higher rate ... ... £14·70 (b) lower rate ... ... £10·50 (the appropriate rate being determined in accordance with section 14(4)).
2. Invalidity pension (section 15).	£17·50
3. Invalidity allowance (section 16).	(a) higher rate ... ... £3·70 (b) middle rate ... ... £2·30 (c) lower rate ... ... £1·15 (the appropriate rate being determined in accordance with section 16(2)).
4. Maternity allowance (section 22).	£14·70
5. Widow's allowance (section 24).	£24·50
6. Widowed mother's allowance (section 25).	£17·50
7. Widow's pension (section 26).	£17·50
8. Category A retirement pension (section 28).	£17·50
9. Category B retirement pension (section 29).	(a) lower rate ... ... £10·50 (b) higher rate ... ... £17·50 (the appropriate rate being determined in accordance with section 29(7)).
10. Child's special allowance (section 31).	£7·40

PART II

MATERNITY GRANT AND DEATH GRANT

Description of Grant	Amount
	£
1. Maternity grant (section 21).	25·00
2. Death grant (section 32), where the deceased was at his death—	
(a) under the age of 3	9·00
(b) between the ages of 3 and 6	15·00
(c) between the ages of 6 and 18	22·50
(d) over the age of 18—	
(i) if on 5th July 1948 that person had attained the age of 55 in the case of a man or 50 in the case of a woman ...	15·00
(ii) in any other case	30·00

PART III
NON-CONTRIBUTORY PERIODICAL BENEFITS (SS. 34–40)

Description of benefit	Weekly rate
1. Attendance allowance (section 35).	(a) higher rate ... ... £14·00 (b) lower rate ... ... £9·30 (the appropriate rate being determined in accordance with section 35(3)).
2. Non-contributory invalidity pension (section 36).	£10·50.
3. Invalid care allowance (section 37).	£10·50.
3A. Mobility allowance (section 37A).	£7·00.
4. Guardian's allowance (section 38).	(a) where entitlement in respect of only, elder or eldest child ... ... £7·40 (b) where entitlement in respect of each additional child ... ... £6·90
5. Category C or Category D retirement pension (section 39).	(a) lower rate ... ... £6·30 (b) higher rate ... ... £10·50 (the appropriate rate being determined in accordance with section 39(2)).
6. Age addition (to a pension of any category, and otherwise under section 40).	£0·25

PART IV
INCREASES FOR DEPENDANTS (SS. 41–49)

Benefit to which increase applies	Increase for qualifying child (2)		Increase for adult dependent
	only, elder or eldest (a)	each additional such child (b)	(3)
(1)			
	£	£	£
1. Unemployment or sickness benefit— (a) where the beneficiary is under pensionable age	3·50	3·00	9·10
(b) where the beneficiary is over pensionable age	7·40	6·90	10·50
2. Invalidity pension	7·40	6·90	10·50
3. Maternity allowance	3·50	3·00	9·10
4. Widow's allowance	7·40	6·90	—
5. Widowed mother's allowance	7·40	6·90	—
6. Category A or B retirement pension ...	7·40	6·90	10·50
7. Category C retirement pension	7·40	6·90	6·30
8. Child's special allowance	—	6·90	—
9. Non-contributory invalidity pension ...	7·40	6·90	6·30
10. Invalid care allowance	7·40	6·90	6·30

Where unemployment or sickness benefit is payable at a weekly rate determined under section 14(6) of this Act, column (3) of this Part of this Schedule shall have effect subject to section 44(5)(b); and where an invalidity pension is payable at a weekly rate determined under section 15(4) of this Act, column (3) shall have effect subject to section 47(2)(b).

Part V

Rate or Amount of Industrial Injuries Benefit

Description of benefit, etc.	Rate or amount
1. Injury benefit under section 56 (weekly rates).	(a) for any period during which the beneficiary is over the age of 18 or is entitled to an increase of benefit in respect of a child or adult dependant ... ... £17·45 (b) for any period during which the beneficiary is not over the age of 18 and not so entitled ... £14·70
2. Maximum disablement gratuity under section 57(5).	£1,900.
3. Disablement pension under section 57(6) (weekly rates).	For the several degrees of disablement set out in column 1 of the following Table, the respective amounts in that Table, using— (a) column 2 for any period during which the beneficiary is over the age of 18 or is entitled to an increase of benefit in respect of a child or adult dependant; (b) column 3 for any period during which the beneficiary is not over the age of 18 and not so entitled:

TABLE

Degree of disablement	Amount	
(1) Per cent.	(2) £	(3) £
100	28·60	17·50
90	25·74	15·75
80	22·88	14·00
70	20·02	12·25
60	17·16	10·50
50	14·30	8·75
40	11·44	7·00
30	8·58	5·25
20	5·72	3·50

Description of benefit, etc.	Rate or amount
4. Unemployability supplement under section 58 (increase of weekly rate of disablement pension).	£17·50
5. Increase under section 59 of weekly rate of unemployability supplement (early onset of incapacity for work).	(a) if on the qualifying date the beneficiary was under the age of 35, or if that date fell before 5th July 1948 £3·70 (b) if head (a) above does not apply and on the qualifying date the beneficiary was under the age of 45 ... £2·30 (c) if heads (a) and (b) above do not apply, and on the qualifying date the beneficiary was a man under the age of 60, or a woman under the age of 55 ... ... £1·15

Description of benefit, etc.	Rate or amount
6. Maximum increase under section 60 of weekly rate of disablement pension in cases of special hardship.	£11·44 or the amount (if any) by which the weekly rate of the pension, apart from any increase under section 61, 63, 64 or 66, falls short of £28·60 whichever is the less.
7. Maximum increase under section 61 of weekly rate of disablement pension where constant attendance needed.	(a) except in cases of exceptionally severe disablement ... ... £11·40 (b) in any case ... ... £22·80
8. Increase under section 63 of weekly rate of disablement pension (exceptionally severe disablement).	£11·40
9. Increase under section 64 of weekly rate of injury benefit (dependent children).	(a) in respect of only, elder or eldest qualifying child ... £3·50 (b) in respect of each additional qualifying child ... ... £3·00
10. Increase under section 64 of weekly rate of disablement pension (dependent children).	(a) in respect of only, elder or eldest qualifying child ... £7·40 (b) in respect of each additional qualifying child ... ... £6·90
11. Increase under section 66(2) of weekly rate of injury benefit (adult dependant).	£9·10
12. Increase under section 66(2) of weekly rate of disablement pension (adult dependant).	£10·50

13. Widow's pension under section 68 (weekly rates)—
  (a) initial rate   ...   .
  (b) higher permanent rate   ...
  (c) lower permanent rate ...   ...
	
	£24·50
	£18·05
	30 per cent of the weekly rate for the time being of a widow's pension as specified in Part I of this Schedule, paragraph 7.

14. Widower's pension under section 69 (weekly rate).	£18·05

15. Allowance under section 70 in respect of children—
  (a) weekly rate of allowance at higher rate
 	
  (b) weekly rate of allowance at lower rate
	
	(i) in respect of only, elder or eldest qualifying child ... £7·40
	(ii) in respect of each additional qualifying child ... ... £6·90
	(i) in respect of only, elder or eldest qualifying child ... £3·50
	(ii) in respect of each additional qualifying child ... ... £3·00

Description of benefit, etc.	Rate or amount	
16. Maximum under section 91(1) of aggregate of weekly benefit payable for successive accidents.	(a) for any period during which the beneficiary is over the age of 18 or is entitled to an increase of benefit in respect of a child or adult dependant	£28·60
	(b) for any period during which the beneficiary is not over the age of 18 and not so entitled	£17·50

EXPLANATORY NOTE

(This Note is not part of the Order.)

This Order, a draft of which has been laid before and approved by a resolution of each House of Parliament, is made consequent upon a review under section 125 of the Social Security Act 1975 and after consideration, in accordance with section 37A of that Act, of whether the rate of mobility allowance should be increased, and it increases with effect from specified dates in the week beginning 14th November 1977 the rates and amounts of the benefits and increases of benefit (except age addition) specified in Parts I, III, IV and V of Schedule 4 to that Act. The Order also increases the rates laid down in the Industrial Injuries and Diseases (Old Cases) Act 1975 for the maximum weekly rate of lesser incapacity allowance supplementing workmen's compensation and the weekly rate of allowance under the Industrial Diseases Benefit Schemes where disablement is not total. Further the Order increases the amount, specified in the Social Security Act 1975, of weekly earnings which must be exceeded before certain benefits are reduced by reference to earnings and it increases the sum specified in the Social Security Pensions Act 1975 for the basic component of a Category A retirement pension.

In accordance with section 124(3) of the Social Security Act 1975, a copy of a report by the Government Actuary (Cmnd. 6848) giving his opinion on the likely effect on the National Insurance Fund of the making of this Order was laid before Parliament with the draft Order.

STATUTORY INSTRUMENTS

1977 No. 1326

SOCIAL SECURITY

The Supplementary Benefits (Determination of Requirements) Regulations 1977

Laid before Parliament in draft

Made - - - -	*29th July* 1977
Coming into Operation	*14th November* 1977

Whereas a draft of the following regulations was laid before Parliament and approved by resolution of each House of Parliament:

Now, therefore, the Secretary of State for Social Services, with the consent of the Treasury, in exercise of the powers conferred by section 2(2), as amended (a) and (3), of the Supplementary Benefits Act 1976(b) and of all other powers enabling him in that behalf, hereby makes the following regulations:—

Citation, commencement and interpretation

1.—(1) These regulations may be cited as the Supplementary Benefits (Determination of Requirements) Regulations 1977 and shall come into operation on 14th November 1977.

(2) In these regulations, unless the context otherwise requires, "the Act" means the Supplementary Benefits Act 1976(b) and other expressions have the same meaning as in the Act.

(3) The rules for the construction of Acts of Parliament contained in the Interpretation Act 1889(c) shall apply for the purpose of the interpretation of these regulations as they apply for the purposes of the interpretation of an Act of Parliament.

Amendment of provisions for calculating requirements

2.—(1) Part II (calculation of requirements) of Schedule 1 to the Act (provisions for determining right to and amount of supplementary benefits) shall be varied in accordance with the following provisions of this regulation.

(2) For paragraph 7 (normal requirements) and paragraph 8 (blind persons) there shall be substituted the following paragraphs—

"Normal requirements

7. Requirements of persons, other than blind persons—

				£
(*a*) husband and wife or other persons falling within paragraph 3(1) of this Schedule ..	A	..		23.55
	B	..		28.35
	C	..		28.60

(a) See section 14(4) of the Social Security (Miscellaneous Provisions) Act 1977 c. 5.
(b) 1976 c. 71.   (c) 1889 c. 63.

(b) person living alone or householder not
falling within sub-paragraph (a) above
who is directly responsible for household
necessities and rent (if any)   ..   ..   A   .. 14.50

     B   .. 17.90

     C   .. 18.15

(c) any other person aged—

     (i) not less than 18 years   ..   ..   A   .. 11.60

     B   .. 14.35

     C   .. 14.60

     (ii) less than 18 but not less than 16 years 8.90

     (iii) less than 16 but not less than 13 years 7.40

     (iv) less than 13 but not less than 11 years 6.10

     (v) less than 11 but not less than 5 years 4.95

     (vi) less than 5 years 4.10

Blind persons

8. Requirements of persons who are or include blind persons—

(a) husband and wife or other persons falling
within paragraph 3(1) of this Schedule—

     (i) if one of them is blind   ..   ..   A   .. 24.80

     B   .. 29.60

     C   .. 29.85

     (ii) if both of them are blind ..   ..   A   .. 25.60

     B   .. 30.40

     C   .. 30.65

(b) any other blind person aged—

     (i) not less than 18 years   ..   ..   A   .. 15.75

     B   .. 19.15

     C   .. 19.40

     (ii) less than 18 but not less than 16 years 9.80

     (iii) less than 16 but not less than 13 years 7.40

     (iv) less than 13 but not less than 11 years 6.10

     (v) less than 11 but not less than 5 years 4.95

     (vi) less than 5 years   ..   .. 4.10"

(3) In paragraph 10 (attendance requirements)—

(a) in sub-paragraph (1)(a), for "£12.20" there shall be substituted
"£14.00";

(b) in sub-paragraph (1)(b), for "£8.15" there shall be substituted
"£9.30".

(4) In paragraph 11 (rent) in sub-paragraph (1)(*b*), for "£1.20" there shall be substituted "£1.45".

David Ennals,
Secretary of State for Social Services.

29th July 1977.

We consent,

T. M. Cox,
T. E. Graham,
Two of the Lords Commissioners of
Her Majesty's Treasury.

29th July 1977.

EXPLANATORY NOTE
(*This Note is not part of the Regulations.*)

These Regulations vary the provisions of Part II (calculation of requirements) of Schedule 1 (determination of right to and amount of supplementary benefits) to the Supplementary Benefits Act 1976. Regulation 2 increases certain weekly amounts allowed for requirements; paragraph (2) relates to normal and blind persons' requirements; paragraph (3) relates to the attendance requirements of severely disabled persons and paragraph (4) to the rent addition for non-householders. These Regulations come into operation on 14th November 1977.

STATUTORY INSTRUMENTS

1977 No. 1327

SOCIAL SECURITY

The Child Benefit and Social Security (Fixing and Adjustment of Rates) Amendment Regulations 1977

Laid before Parliament in draft

Made - - - - *29th July* 1977

Coming into Operation *14th November* 1977

Whereas a draft of the following regulations was laid before and approved by resolution of each House of Parliament:

Now, therefore, the Secretary of State for Social Services, in exercise of the powers conferred upon him by section 17(1) of the Child Benefit Act 1975(a) and of all other powers enabling him in that behalf, hereby makes the following regulations:—

Citation, commencement and interpretation

1.—(1) These regulations may be cited as the Child Benefit and Social Security (Fixing and Adjustment of Rates) Amendment Regulations 1977 and shall come into operation on 14th November 1977.

(2) In this instrument "the Social Security Act" means the Social Security Act 1975(b); and the rules for the construction of Acts of Parliament contained in the Interpretation Act 1889(c) shall apply in relation to this instrument and in relation to the regulation revoked by it as if this instrument and that regulation were Acts of Parliament and as if the revocation were a repeal.

Revocation of regulation 3 of the Child Benefit and Social Security (Fixing and Adjustment of Rates) Regulations 1976

2. Regulation 3 of the Child Benefit and Social Security (Fixing and Adjustment of Rates) Regulations 1976(d) (reduction of weekly rates of benefits and increases of benefits under the Social Security Act in respect of children) shall be revoked—

(*a*) paragraphs (*a*) and (*b*) thereof (child's special allowance and guardian's allowance under the Social Security Act) on 14th November 1977;

(*b*) paragraphs (*c*) and (*d*) thereof (increase under Chapter III of Part II of the Social Security Act of benefits for child dependants)—

(i) in relation to an increase of maternity allowance, widow's allowance, widowed mother's allowance, Category A, B or C retirement pension, child's special allowance or (where the Secretary of State

---

(a) 1975 c. 61.   (b) 1975 c. 14.   (c) 1889 c. 63.
(d) S.I. 1976/1267 (1976 II, p. 3576).

has not made arrangements for invalid care allowance to be paid on a Wednesday) invalid care allowance, on 14th November 1977;

(ii) in relation to an increase of invalid care allowance where the Secretary of State has made arrangements for that allowance to be paid on a Wednesday, on 16th November 1977;

(iii) in relation to an increase of unemployment benefit, sickness benefit, invalidity pension or non-contributory invalidity pension, on 17th November 1977;

(c) paragraph (e) thereof (increase of injury benefit under the Social Security Act in respect of dependent children) on 17th November 1977;

(d) paragraph (f) thereof (increase of disablement pension under the Social Security Act in respect of dependent children) on 16th November 1977; and

(e) paragraphs (g) and (h) thereof (allowance under section 70 of the Social Security Act in respect of children) on 14th November 1977.

David Ennals,
Secretary of State for Social Services.

29th July 1977.

EXPLANATORY NOTE

(*This Note is not part of the Regulations.*)

These Regulations amend the Child Benefit and Social Security (Fixing and Adjustment of Rates) Regulations 1976 ("the 1976 Regulations") by revoking regulation 3 thereof.

Regulation 3 of the 1976 Regulations reduced the weekly rates of benefits and increases of benefits under the Social Security Act 1975 ("the 1975 Act") in respect of children to take account of the introduction on 4th April 1977 of child benefit under the Child Benefit Act 1975.

The Social Security Benefits Up-rating Order 1977 (S.I. 1977/1325), which increases the weekly rates of various benefits and increases of benefits under the 1975 Act, takes account of the reductions provided for in regulation 3 of the 1976 Regulations and accordingly that regulation is revoked by these Regulations.

STATUTORY INSTRUMENTS

1977 No. 1328

SOCIAL SECURITY

The Child Benefit and Social Security (Fixing and Adjustment of Rates) Amendment (No. 2) Regulations 1977

Laid before Parliament in draft

Made - - - -	*29th July* 1977
Coming into Operation	*3rd April* 1978

Whereas a draft of the following regulations was laid before and approved by a resolution of each House of Parliament:

Now, therefore, the Secretary of State for Social Services, in conjunction with the Treasury(a), in exercise of the powers conferred upon him by sections 5 and 17(1) of the Child Benefit Act 1975(b), and of all other powers enabling him in that behalf, hereby makes the following regulations:—

Citation, interpretation and commencement

1. These regulations, which may be cited as the Child Benefit and Social Security (Fixing and Adjustment of Rates) Amendment (No. 2) Regulations 1977, shall be read as one with the Child Benefit and Social Security (Fixing and Adjustment of Rates) Regulations 1976(c) (hereinafter referred to as "the principal regulations") and shall come into operation on 3rd April 1978.

Amendment of regulation 2 of the principal regulations

2.—(1) Regulation 2 of the principal regulations (weekly rates of child benefit) shall be amended in accordance with the following provisions of this regulation.

(2) For paragraph (1) of the said regulation 2 there shall be substituted the following paragraph:—

"2.—(1) Subject to paragraph (2) of this regulation and regulation 20(1) of the General Regulations (transitional provision relating to apprentices in respect of whom a family allowance was payable under the Family Allowances Acts 1965 to 1975) the weekly rate of child benefit payable in respect of a child shall be £2·30.".

(3) In paragraph (2) of the said regulation 2, for the reference to £0·50 there shall be substituted a reference to £1·00.

(4) Paragraph (3) of the said regulation 2 is hereby revoked.

(a) See s. 22(1)(a) of the Child Benefit Act 1975 (c. 61).   (b) 1975 c. 61.
(c) S.I. 1976/1267 (1976 II, p. 3576).

(5) In sub-paragraph (*b*) of paragraph (4) of the said regulation 2, the words "or (2)" shall be omitted.

Insertion of a regulation 3 into the principal regulations

3. After regulation 2 of the principal regulations there shall be inserted the following regulation:—

"*Reduction of weekly rates of benefits and increases of benefits under the Social Security Act in respect of children*

3. The sums specified in any of the provisions mentioned in section 17(2) of the Act shall be reduced—

(*a*) in the case of the sum specified in the second column of paragraph 10 of Part I of Schedule 4 to the Social Security Act (child's special allowance), by £1·30;

(*b*) in the case of the sums specified in the second column of paragraph 4 of Part III of that Schedule (guardian's allowance)—

(i) where the child is the only, elder or eldest qualifying child, by £1·30;

(ii) where the child is an additional qualifying child, by £0·80;

(*c*) in the case of the sums specified in column (2) of Part IV of that Schedule (increase under Chapter III of Part II of the Social Security Act of certain benefits for child dependants)—

(i) where the child is the only, elder or eldest qualifying child, by £1·30;

(ii) where the child is an additional qualifying child, by £0·80;

(*d*) in the case of the sums specified in the second column of paragraph 9 of Part V of the said Schedule (increase of injury benefit in respect of dependent children)—

(i) where the child is the only, elder or eldest qualifying child, by £1·30;

(ii) where the child is an additional qualifying child, by £0·80;

(*e*) in the case of the sums specified in the second column of paragraph 10 of the said Part V (increase of disablement pension in respect of dependent children)—

(i) where the child is the only, elder or eldest qualifying child, by £1·30;

(ii) where the child is an additional qualifying child, by £0·80;

(*f*) in the case of the sums specified in the second column of paragraph 15(*a*) of the said Part V (allowance at higher rate in respect of children of certain deceased persons)—

(i) where the child is the only, elder or eldest qualifying child, by £1·30;

(ii) where the child is an additional qualifying child, by £0·80;

(*g*) in the case of the sums specified in the second column of paragraph 15(*b*) of the said Part V (allowance at lower rate in respect of children of certain deceased persons)—

(i) where the child is the only, elder or eldest qualifying child, by £1·30;

(ii) where the child is an additional qualifying child, by £0·80.".

David Ennals,
Secretary of State for Social Services.

29th July 1977.

T. M. Cox,
T. E. Graham,
Two of the Lords Commissioners
of Her Majesty's Treasury.

29th July 1977.

EXPLANATORY NOTE

(*This Note is not part of the Regulations.*)

These Regulations amend the Child Benefit and Social Security (Fixing and Adjustment of Rates) Regulations 1976 ("the 1976 Regulations") by providing (except in relation to certain apprentices in respect of whom an allowance was payable under the Family Allowances Acts 1965 to 1975) for higher rates of child benefit under the Child Benefit Act 1975 with effect from Monday 3rd April 1978. With effect from that date they also reduce the weekly rates of benefits and increases of benefits under the Social Security Act 1975 payable in respect of children ("child dependency benefit").

Regulation 1 is formal; regulation 2 amends regulation 2 of the 1976 Regulations to give effect to the increases in the weekly rates of child benefit; and regulation 3 provides for the reduction of child dependency benefit.

STATUTORY INSTRUMENTS

1977 No. 1329

AIRCRAFT AND SHIPBUILDING INDUSTRIES

The Aircraft Industry (Pension Schemes) Regulations 1977

Made - - - -	*2nd August* 1977
Laid before Parliament	*10th August* 1977
Coming into Operation	*1st September* 1977

The Secretary of State, in exercise of the powers conferred on him by section 49(4) and (11) of the Aircraft and Shipbuilding Industries Act 1977**(a)**, hereby makes the following Regulations:—

Citation, commencement and interpretation

1.—(1) These Regulations may be cited as the Aircraft Industry (Pension Schemes) Regulations 1977 and shall come into operation on 1st September 1977.

(2) In these Regulations—

"the Act" means the Aircraft and Shipbuilding Industries Act 1977;

"actuary" has the meaning assigned to it by regulation 3 below;

"the Corporation" means British Aerospace;

"the Corporation's part", "divided pension scheme" and "the holding company's part" have the meanings respectively assigned to them by regulation 3 below;

"undivided pension scheme" has the meaning assigned to it by regulation 2 below;

"wholly owned subsidiary's pension scheme" means a pension scheme of a wholly owned subsidiary of the Corporation established or administered by that subsidiary for the purpose of providing pensions exclusively to or in respect of persons who are or have been employees of it.

(3) The Interpretation Act 1889**(b)** shall apply for the interpretation of these Regulations as it applies for the interpretation of an Act of Parliament.

Undivided pension scheme

2.—(1) The following provision of this regulation shall apply to a pension scheme (hereinafter called "an undivided pension scheme") established or administered by a holding company not being a wholly owned subsidiary of the Corporation for providing pensions exclusively to or in respect of persons who are or have been employees of a wholly owned subsidiary of that company which became a wholly owned subsidiary of the Corporation on 29th April 1977.

(2) An undivided pension scheme shall have effect as if references therein to the holding company were references to the wholly owned subsidiary.

(a) 1977 c. 3.   **(b)** 1889 c. 63.

Divided pension scheme

3.—(1) The following provisions of this regulation shall apply to a pension scheme (hereinafter called "a divided pension scheme") to which both the conditions specified in paragraph (2) below apply.

(2) The conditions referred to in paragraph (1) above are—

(*a*) that the scheme is a scheme established or administered by a holding company for providing pensions to or in respect of persons who are or have been employees of the holding company or of wholly owned subsidiaries of the holding company, some but not all of which subsidiaries became wholly owned subsidiaries of the Corporation on 29th April 1977; and

(*b*) that the assets of the scheme are vested in trustees appointed in accordance with its provisions.

(3) A divided pension scheme shall be deemed in all respects to be, and shall be administered as, two separate pension schemes, being as to one part a scheme for providing pensions to or in respect of persons who are or have been employees of the wholly owned subsidiaries of the holding company which became wholly owned subsidiaries of the Corporation on 29th April 1977 (hereinafter called "the Corporation's part"), and as to the other part a scheme for providing pensions to or in respect of persons who are or have been employees of the holding company or of the other wholly owned subsidiaries of the holding company (hereinafter called "the holding company's part").

(4) As soon as practicable the assets and liabilities as at 29th April 1977 of every divided pension scheme shall be apportioned between the Corporation's part and the holding company's part, and every such apportionment shall, in default of agreement between the parties, be determined by an actuary appointed by the Secretary of State.

(5) For the purposes of this regulation the expression "actuary" means a person who holds the diploma of Fellowship of the Institute of Actuaries or of the Faculty of Actuaries in Scotland.

(6) The part of such assets as aforesaid apportioned to the Corporation's part shall be transferred to the trustees of that part appointed as mentioned in paragraph (7) below, and the part of such liabilities as aforesaid apportioned to that part shall have effect as against the trustees of it.

(7) Trustees of the Corporation's part shall be appointed in accordance with the provisions of the scheme as soon as practicable; the existing trustees shall, until such agreement, continue to act in respect of both the Corporation's part and the holding company's part.

(8) Where any policy of assurance forms part of the assets of the scheme and the benefits and liabilities thereunder have been apportioned as aforesaid the assurer shall amend the policy so that it will relate solely to the benefits and liabilities apportioned to the holding company's part and shall issue in favour of the trustees of the Corporation's part another policy to provide for the benefits and liabilities apportioned to that part.

(9) In relation to the Corporation's part the provisions of a divided pension scheme shall have effect as if references to the Corporation were substituted for references to the holding company.

Modification of pension schemes

4.—(1) The pension schemes to which this regulation applies shall have effect as if any references in them to service as an employee of a wholly owned subsidiary of the Corporation included a reference to service after 29th April 1977 with any other such wholly owned subsidiary or with the Corporation.

(2) For the purposes of any pension scheme to which this regulation applies the service of any person as a full-time member of the Corporation, being a person who was subject to such a scheme when he became such a member, may be treated as if it were service as an employee of the Corporation.

(3) Where a pension scheme to which this regulation applies provides that any description of benefit may, or may in particular circumstances, be conferred on a person only at the request or with the consent of the wholly owned subsidiary concerned, or the Corporation as the case may be, no such request shall be entertained or consent given in the case of a benefit for or in respect of a member of the Corporation without the prior approval of the Minister for the Civil Service and the Secretary of State.

(4) This regulation applies to—

(*a*) a wholly owned subsidiary's pension scheme;

(*b*) an undivided pension scheme;

(*c*) the Corporation's part of a divided pension scheme.

G. B. Kaufman,
Minister of State,
Department of Industry.

2nd August 1977.

EXPLANATORY NOTE

(This Note is not part of the Regulations.)

These Regulations make provision with respect to the pension rights of employees of companies which have vested in British Aerospace under the Aircraft and Shipbuilding Industries Act 1977, and to those of employees and members of British Aerospace.

Pension schemes run by the pre-vesting holding companies of companies which have vested in British Aerospace to provide pensions exclusively for employees of such vesting companies will continue with British Aerospace performing the functions of the pre-vesting holding companies in relation to them (Regulation 2).

Pension schemes which related partly to employees of vesting companies and partly to employees of non-vesting companies are split (Regulation 3). The assets and liabilities of such pension schemes referable to employees of vesting companies are transferred to trustees.

All pension schemes providing pensions for employees of companies within the British Aerospace group are modified so as to cause service as an employee of any company in the group, or of British Aerospace, to count as pensionable service for the purposes of any such scheme. Such pension schemes are also modified to allow employees who are appointed whole-time members of British Aerospace to count their service as service for the purposes of the relevant scheme, subject to any employer's discretionary benefits being conferred on such persons only with the approval of the Secretary of State and the Minister for the Civil Service (Regulation 4).

STATUTORY INSTRUMENTS

1977 No. 1330

CINEMATOGRAPHS AND CINEMATOGRAPH FILMS

The Cinematograph Films (Collection of Levy) (Amendment No. 5) Regulations 1977

Laid before Parliament in draft

Made - - - -	*2nd August* 1977
Coming into Operation	25th September 1977

Whereas a draft of these Regulations has been laid before Parliament and approved by Resolution of each House pursuant to section 2(7) of the Cinematograph Films Act 1957(**a**):

Now, therefore, the Secretary of State in exercise of the powers conferred by section 2 of the said Act, as amended and extended by the Films Act 1970(**b**), and now vested in him(**c**), and after consultation with the Cinematograph Films Council, hereby makes the following Regulations:—

1. These Regulations may be cited as the Cinematograph Films (Collection of Levy) (Amendment No. 5) Regulations 1977 and shall come into operation on 25th September 1977.

2. The Interpretation Act 1889(**d**) shall apply to the interpretation of these Regulations as it applies to the interpretation of an Act of Parliament.

3. The Cinematograph Films (Collection of Levy) Regulations 1968(**e**), as amended(**f**), shall have effect as if in regulation 3—

(*a*) for the reference to 7½p there were substituted a reference to 12½p, and

(*b*) for the reference to £700 in the two places in which it occurs there were substituted a reference to £900.

Michael Meacher,
Parliamentary Under-Secretary of State,
Department of Trade.

2nd August 1977.

(a) 1957 c. 21.   (b) 1970 c. 26.   (c) S.I. 1970/1537 (1970 III, p. 5293).
(d) 1889 c. 63.   (e) S.I. 1968/1077 (1968 II, p. 2905).
(f) The relevant amending instrument is S.I. 1975/1885 (1975 III, p. 7085).

EXPLANATORY NOTE

(This Note is not part of the Regulations.)

These Regulations further amend the Cinematograph Films (Collection of Levy) Regulations 1968 by—

(i) increasing from 7½p to 12½p the portion of the payment for admission (net of VAT) which is not liable to levy, and

(ii) increasing from £700 to £900 the amount by reference to which total or partial exemption from payment of levy is allowed in respect of cinemas at which takings or average takings are small.

STATUTORY INSTRUMENTS

1977 No. 1331

CIVIL AVIATION

The Civil Aviation (Air Travel Organisers' Licensing) (Reserve Fund) (Amendment) Regulations 1977

Laid before Parliament in draft

Made - - - -   2nd August 1977
Coming into Operation   3rd August 1977

Whereas a draft of these Regulations has been laid before Parliament and approved by Resolution of each House pursuant to section 4(3) of the Air Travel Reserve Fund Act 1975(**a**):

Now, therefore, the Secretary of State, in exercise of his powers under section 26 of the Civil Aviation Act 1971(**b**) and section 4 of the Air Travel Reserve Fund Act 1975 and of all other powers enabling him in that behalf and after consultation with the Civil Aviation Authority as required by those Acts hereby makes the following Regulations:—

1. These Regulations may be cited as the Civil Aviation (Air Travel Organisers' Licensing) (Reserve Fund) (Amendment) Regulations 1977 and shall come into operation on the day after they are made.

2. The Interpretation Act 1889(**c**) shall apply for the purpose of the interpretation of these Regulations as it applies for the purpose of the interpretation of an Act of Parliament.

3. The Civil Aviation (Air Travel Organisers' Licensing) (Reserve Fund) Regulations 1975(**d**) shall be amended as follows:—

After Regulation 4, there shall be inserted the following Regulation:—

"4A. Notwithstanding anything in Regulation 4 of these Regulations, no contribution shall be payable under paragraph (1) of that Regulation in respect of any contribution period beginning on or after 1st October 1977 and accordingly the requirements in paragraph (2) of that Regulation shall not apply in relation to any such contribution period."

Michael Meacher,
Parliamentary Under-Secretary of State,
2nd August 1977.   Department of Trade.

(**a**) 1975 c. 36.   (**b**) 1971 c. 75.   (**c**) 1889 c. 63.
(**d**) S.I. 1975/1196 (1975 II, p. 4106).

EXPLANATORY NOTE

(This Note is not part of the Regulations.)

These Regulations amend The Civil Aviation (Air Travel Organisers' Licensing) (Reserve Fund) Regulations 1975 by suspending the obligation on the holders of air travel organisers' licences to make contributions to The Air Travel Reserve Fund established pursuant to The Air Travel Reserve Fund Act 1975 in respect of any contribution period beginning on or after 1st October 1977.

STATUTORY INSTRUMENTS

1977 No. 1332

WEIGHTS AND MEASURES

The Weights and Measures Act 1963 (Cocoa and Chocolate Products) Order 1977

Laid before Parliament in draft

Made - - -		*2nd August* 1977
Coming into Operation		*8th August* 1977

Whereas the Secretary of State pursuant to section 54(2) of the Weights and Measures Act 1963(a) (hereinafter referred to as "the Act") has consulted with organisations appearing to him to be representative of interests substantially affected by this Order and considered the representations made to him by such organisations with respect to the subject matter of this Order:

And whereas a draft of this Order has been laid before Parliament and approved by resolution of each House of Parliament pursuant to section 54(3) of the Act:

Now, therefore, the Secretary of State in exercise of the powers conferred by section 21(2), (3) and (5) of the Act and now vested in him (b) and of all other powers enabling him in that behalf, hereby makes the following Order:—

1. This Order may be cited as the Weights and Measures Act 1963 (Cocoa and Chocolate Products) Order 1977 and shall come into operation on 8th August 1977.

2.—(1) In this Order—

"cocoa product", "chocolate product", "container", "fancy chocolate product" and "reserved description" have the same meanings as they have in the Cocoa and Chocolate Products Regulations 1976(c); except that "cocoa product" and "chocolate product" shall include a product specially prepared for diabetics or to which a slimming claim (as defined in the said Regulations) is lawfully applied and which has been specially prepared in connection with that claim by the addition of any ingredient other than an edible substance as so defined.

(2) The Interpretation Act 1889(d) shall apply for the interpretation of this Order as it applies for the interpretation of an Act of Parliament.

(a) 1963 c. 31.
(c) S.I. 1976/541 (1976 I, p. 1586).

(b) S.I. 1970/1537 (1970 III, p. 5293).
(d) 1889 c. 63.

3.—(1) Subject to Article 4 below—

(*a*) Part VIII, other than paragraph 3(*a*) and the exemption thereto in paragraph 4(*b*), and Part XI of Schedule 4 to the Act shall cease to apply to cocoa products and chocolate products after 31st December 1977; and

(*b*) the said paragraph 3(*a*) and the exemption shall cease to apply to cocoa products after 31st August 1978.

(2) Subject to Article 4 below—

(i) in the case of products as respects which there are no requirements in the said Parts with which the products have to comply, they need not comply with the requirements of this Order until 31st December 1977;

(ii) in any other case, the products must, until 31st December 1977 or, as the case may be, 31st August 1978, comply either with the requirements of those Parts or with the requirements of this Order,

and subject as aforesaid, after the relevant date products must comply with the provisions of this Order.

4.—(1) The application of section 22(2) of the Act, as it applies for the purposes of section 21(2)(*c*) in relation to cocoa products and chocolate products which do not comply with the provisions of this Order, but which in the case of products falling within subparagraph (ii) above do comply with the provisions of the said Parts, shall be excluded in the cases and in respect of the persons specified in paragraphs (2) and (3) below.

(2) In the case of products made for sale, pre-packed or otherwise made up in a container for sale in Great Britain on or before 31st December 1977 or, as the case may be, 31st August 1978 and products imported into Great Britain on or before the relevant date and made for sale, pre-packed or otherwise so made up before importation, the exclusion shall be in respect of all persons.

(3) In the case of products made for sale, pre-packed or otherwise so made up in Great Britain after the relevant date and products imported into Great Britain after that date and made for sale, pre-packed or otherwise so made up before importation, the exclusion shall be in respect of any person other than—

(*a*) where the products were made for sale, pre-packed or otherwise so made up in Great Britain, the person who made the products for sale, pre-packed them or otherwise so made them up and if he made them for sale, pre-packed them or otherwise so made them up on behalf of another person, that other person;

(*b*) where the products were imported into Great Britain, the person who imported them and if he imported them on behalf of another person, that other person.

(4) The foregoing provisions of this Article shall cease to have effect, in a case in which the relevant date is 31st December 1977, after 30th April 1978, and in a case in which the relevant date is 31st August 1978, after 31st August 1979.

5. Except in the case of an article whose net weight is less than 50g, cocoa products and chocolate products which are not pre-packed shall, when sold by retail, be sold only by net weight.

6.—(1) Cocoa products of the reserved descriptions specified in paragraph (2) below shall, except where made up in a quantity of less than 50g or exceeding 1kg, be pre-packed only if they are made up in one of the following quantities by net weight, that is to say—

50g, 75g, 125g, 250g, 500g, 750g and 1kg.

(2) Products of the reserved descriptions referred to in paragraph (1) above are cocoa, cocoa powder, fat-reduced cocoa, fat-reduced cocoa powder, sweetened cocoa, sweetened cocoa powder, sweetened fat-reduced cocoa, sweetened fat-reduced cocoa powder, drinking chocolate and fat-reduced drinking chocolate.

7.—(1) Chocolate products in bar or tablet form of the reserved descriptions specified in paragraph (2) below being a bar or tablet weighing not less than 85g and not more than 500g, shall be made for sale only in one of the following weights, that is to say—

85g, 100g, 125g, 150g, 200g, 250g, 300g, 400g, or 500g.

(2) The reserved descriptions referred to in paragraph (1) above are chocolate, plain chocolate, gianduja nut chocolate, milk chocolate, gianduja nut milk chocolate, white chocolate, filled chocolate, cream chocolate and skimmed milk chocolate.

8.—(1) Except where the net weight is less than 50g and subject to the following provisions of this Article, cocoa products and chocolate products shall be pre-packed or otherwise made up in a container for sale only if the container is marked with an indication of quantity by net weight.

(2) In a case where the net weight of the products made up in a container is 10kg or more, the container need not be marked with an indication of quantity by net weight if the products are not sold by retail and, at the time when they are sold, a document including such an indication accompanies the container.

This paragraph applies only to products of the following reserved descriptions, that is to say, cocoa bean, cocoa nib, cocoa dust, cocoa fines, cocoa mass, cocoa press cake, fat-reduced cocoa press cake and expeller cocoa press cake.

(3) Where the contents of a container on a sale otherwise than by retail consists of products (whether pre-packed or not) of a kind sold by retail singly or consists of inner packs in which products are pre-packed, the container need not be marked with an indication of quantity by net weight if the net weight of—

(a) each individual item or the products in each inner pack is 50g or more, and the net weight of an individual item or products in an inner pack and the number of such items or inner packs are marked on the container;

(b) each individual item is less than 50g, and the number of items is marked on the container;

and, where the contents of the container consist of more than one description of products, the information is given for each description.

(4) A container need not be marked with an indication of quantity by net weight if it is an outer container in which products are pre-packed and the inner container or, if there is more than one, each inner container is marked with an indication of quantity by net weight which is clearly legible from outside the outer container.

(5) A container need not be marked with an indication of quantity by net weight if it is a container in which fancy chocolate products are pre-packed, except that when the products are on sale by retail the exemption provided by this paragraph shall apply only if an indication of quantity by net weight is given on a ticket or notice displayed on or in immediate proximity to the products.

(6) Where the provisions of both paragraph (2) and paragraph (3) apply in a particular case, the information permitted by paragraph (3) to be marked on the container may be given in a document accompanying the container.

9. Section 22(2) of the Act, in so far as it applies for the purposes of section 21(2)(*b*) of the Act in relation to a contravention of Article 8 above in a case mentioned in paragraph (2), or paragraph (3) as extended by paragraph (6), of that Article, shall have effect subject to the modification that the following provisions be omitted, that is to say—

(*a*) in paragraph (*a*), the words "has in his possession for sale,";

(*b*) paragraph (*b*);

(*c*) in paragraph (*c*), the words "have in his possession for sale or for delivery after sale,"; and

(*d*) the words "whether the sale is, or is to be, by retail or otherwise".

John Fraser,
Minister of State.

2nd August 1977.   Department of Prices and Consumer Protection.

EXPLANATORY NOTE

(This Note is not part of the Order.)

This Order implements the weight provisions of Council Directive No. 73/241/EEC (O.J. No. L228. 16.8.73, p.23) as amended by Council Directives No. 74/411/EEC (O.J. No.L221. 12.8.74, p.17), No. 74/644/EEC

(O.J. No. L349. 28.12.74, p.63), No. 75/155/EEC (O.J. No.L64. 11.3.75, p.21) and No. 76/628/EEC (O.J. No. L223. 16.8.76, p.1) relating to Cocoa and Chocolate Products intended for human consumption, and provides that Parts VIII and XI of Schedule 4 to the Weights and Measures Act 1963 will cease to have effect as respects cocoa and chocolate products.

The principal changes are as follows:

(a) weight marking is extended to cover all cocoa and chocolate products weighing 50g (approximately 1¾oz) or more after 31st December 1977, and alternative information is permitted in the case of sales otherwise than by retail, which may be marked on the outer container or given in an accompanying document (Article 8);

(b) chocolate bars or tablets of the reserved descriptions specified, weighing not less than 85g (3oz) and not more than 500g (1lb 1½oz), are to be made for sale only in a prescribed range of metric weights after 31st December 1977 (Article 7);

(c) after 31st August 1978 cocoa and chocolate powders of the reserved descriptions specified may be pre-packed only in a prescribed range of metric quantities (Articles 3 and 6);

(d) transitional provisions are included in the Order to allow time for cocoa and chocolate products as respects which there have hitherto been no statutory requirements, and products which comply with the provisions of the Act to be sold by manufacturers, importers, wholesalers and retailers, notwithstanding that the products do not comply with the Order (Article 4);

(e) section 22 of the Act is also modified to take account of the case where the information required by the Order may be given in an accompanying document instead of on the container (Article 9).

STATUTORY INSTRUMENTS

1977 No. 1333

WEIGHTS AND MEASURES

The Weights and Measures Act 1963 (Sugar) (Amendment) Order 1977

Laid before Parliament in draft

Made - - -	*2nd August* 1977
Coming into Operation	*1st September* 1977

Whereas the Secretary of State pursuant to section 54(2) of the Weights and Measures Act 1963(**a**) (hereinafter referred to as "the Act") has consulted with organisations appearing to him to be representative of interests substantially affected by this Order and considered the representations made to him by such organisations with respect to the subject matter of this Order:

And whereas a draft of this Order has been laid before Parliament and approved by resolution of each House of Parliament pursuant to section 54(3) of the Act:

Now, therefore, the Secretary of State, in exercise of powers conferred by sections 21(2), (3) and (5), and 54(1) and (4) of the Act and now vested in him(**b**) and of all other powers enabling him in that behalf, hereby makes the following Order:—

1.—(1) This Order may be cited as the Weights and Measures Act 1963 (Sugar) (Amendment) Order 1977 and shall come into operation on 1st September 1977.

(2) The Interpretation Act 1889(**c**) shall apply for the interpretation of this Order as it applies for the interpretation of an Act of Parliament.

2. The Weights and Measures Act 1963 (Sugar) Order 1974(**d**) shall have effect subject to the following amendments:—

(*a*) for Article 4 there shall be substituted the following two Articles:—

"**4.**—(1) Subject to paragraphs (2) and (3) of this Article and to Article 5 below, sugar shall be pre-packed or otherwise made up in a container for sale, only if it is made up in one of the following quantities by net weight, that is to say—

(*a*) 12 oz, 1lb, 1½lb, or a multiple of 1lb; or

(*b*) 125g, 250g, 500g, 750g, 1kg, 1.5kg, 2kg, 2.5kg, 3kg, 4kg or 5kg.

(**a**) 1963 c. 31.   (**b**) S.I. 1970/1537 (1970 III, p. 5293).
(**c**) 1889 c. 63.   (**d**) S.I. 1974/1166 (1974 II, p. 4450).

(2) After 21st April 1978, paragraph (1) shall have effect as if subparagraph (a) thereof were omitted:

Provided that the application of section 22(2) of the Act, as it applies for the purposes of section 21(2)(c) in relation to sugar pre-packed or otherwise made up in a container for sale in imperial quantities specified in the said subparagraph (a) shall be excluded—

(a) in the case of sugar pre-packed or otherwise so made up in Great Britain on or before that date and sugar imported into Great Britain on or before that date and pre-packed or otherwise so made up before importation, in relation to all persons; and

(b) in the case of sugar pre-packed or otherwise so made up in Great Britain after that date and sugar imported into Great Britain after that date and pre-packed or otherwise so made up before importation, in relation to any person other than—

(i) where the sugar was pre-packed or otherwise so made up in Great Britain, the person who pre-packed it or otherwise so made it up and if he pre-packed it or otherwise so made it up on behalf of another person, that other person;

(ii) where the sugar was imported into Great Britain, the person who imported it and if he imported it on behalf of another person, that other person.

(3) After 2nd July 1978 the proviso in paragraph (2) above shall cease to have effect.

4A. Subject to Article 5 sugar shall be pre-packed or otherwise made up in a container for sale, only if the container is marked with an indication of quantity by net weight.";

(b) in Article 5, for the words "Article 4(a)" and "Article 4(b)" there shall be substituted respectively the words "Article 4" and "Article 4A".

John Fraser,
Minister of State
Department of Prices and Consumer Protection.

2nd August 1977.

EXPLANATORY NOTE

(*This Note is not part of the Order.*)

The provisions of this Order amend on 1st September 1977 those of the Weights and Measures Act 1963 (Sugar) Order 1974.

The amendment provides that after the 21st April 1978 the prescribed range of imperial weights in which sugar may be pre-packed or otherwise made up in a container for sale, is withdrawn.

During the period 22nd April to 2nd July 1978 exclusion is nevertheless provided for all persons from the offences connected with selling, agreeing to sell, or being in possession for sale of, sugar pre-packed in Great Britain or otherwise made up in a container for sale in Great Britain, or to sugar imported into Great Britain, in imperial quantities on or before the 21st April 1978. Furthermore, these offences when connected with sugar pre-packed in Great Britain or otherwise made up in a container for sale in Great Britain, or sugar imported into Great Britain, in imperial quantities after the 21st April 1978, are restricted until 2nd July 1978, to pre-packers, persons who otherwise so made it up and importers into Great Britain and those on whose behalf the goods were pre-packed, otherwise so made up or imported.

The requirement to weight mark containers is continued in this Order.

STATUTORY INSTRUMENTS

1977 No. 1334

CONSUMER PROTECTION

PRICES

The Price Marking (Cheese) Order 1977

Made - - - -	*1st August* 1977
Laid before Parliament	*10th August* 1977
Coming into Operation	*1st March* 1978

Whereas the Secretary of State, in accordance with the provisions of section 4(3) of the Prices Act 1974(**a**), has consulted in such manner as appeared to him to be appropriate having regard to the subject-matter and urgency of this Order, with such organisations representative of interests substantially affected by this Order as appeared to him, having regard to those matters, to be appropriate:

Now, therefore, the Secretary of State, in exercise of his powers under section 4 of that Act, hereby makes the following Order:—

1.—(1) This Order may be cited as the Price Marking (Cheese) Order 1977 and shall come into operation on 1st March 1978.

(2) In this Order "cheese" means cheese, whether or not containing flavouring or colouring matter, and whether or not coated with or mixed with other food for the purpose of giving the cheese a distinctive appearance or flavour; and includes processed cheese and cheese spread.

(3) The Interpretation Act 1889(**b**) shall apply for the interpretation of this Order as it applies for the interpretation of an Act of Parliament.

2.—(1) Subject to paragraph (2) below, no person shall, in Great Britain offer or expose cheese for sale by retail unless an indication of the price of the cheese is given, being an indication complying with the appropriate requirements the Schedule hereto.

(2) Paragraph (1) above shall not apply to—

(*a*) cheese in a quantity not exceeding 25g; or

(*b*) cheese offered or exposed for sale only for consumption at the premise of the seller; or

---

(**a**) 1974 c. 24.   (**b**) 1889 c. 63.

(*c*) cheese forming part of an assortment of articles of food pre-packed together for consumption together as a meal and ready for such consumption without being cooked, heated or otherwise prepared.

Robert Maclennan,
Paliamentary Under-Secretary of State,
Department of Prices and Consumer Protection.

1st August 1977.

SCHEDULE

1. In this Schedule—

"container" includes any form of packaging of cheese for sale as a single item, whether by way of wholly or partly enclosing the cheese or by way of attaching the cheese to some other article, and in particular a wrapper;

"gross weight", in relation to any cheese, means the aggregate weight of the cheese and any container in which it is made up;

"pre-packed" means made up in advance ready for retail sale in or on a container;

"selling price", in relation to any cheese, means the price at which the cheese is offered or exposed for sale, not being a price expressed by reference to a unit of measurement;

"unit price", in relation to any cheese, means the price per pound weight of the cheese.

2.—(1) In the case of pre-packed cheese the indication of price shall consist of—

(*a*) the selling price; and

(*b*) subject to sub-paragraph (2) below the unit price calculated by reference to the selling price and to the weight marked on the container.

(2) Sub-paragraph (1)(*b*) above shall not apply in the case of—

(*a*) a whole cheese the net weight of which is not more than 500g;

(*b*) cheese pre-packed in a container made wholly or mainly of ceramic or other rigid material;

(*c*) processed cheese, cheese spread or natural cheese of a type other than one referred to in sub-paragraph (3) below, being processed cheese, cheese spread or natural cheese made up in a container marked with an indication of quantity by weight which was so marked, or which bears a label which was so marked, before the cheese to fill the container was selected.

(3) The types of natural cheese which are not excepted by sub-paragraph (2)(*c*) above from the requirement that the unit price is to be given are Caerphilly, Cheddar, Cheshire, Derby, Double Gloucester, Dunlop, Edam, Gouda, Lancashire, Leicestershire and Wensleydale.

3. In the case of cheese which is not pre-packed, the indication shall be an indication of the unit price.

4. An indication of the price, if it is not marked on the cheese or on the container, shall be easily recognisable by an intending purchaser under normal conditions of purchase as referring to the cheese in question; but the indication need not be adjacent to the cheese and may be grouped with other indications of the prices of other cheese to which this Order applies in the form of a list or otherwise.

5. Where the indication of the price is not adjacent to the cheese to which it refers it shall be in such a position that it is readily discernible by an intending purchaser from the place where he would under normal conditions of purchase select the cheese, or, if he would not select the cheese himself, where he would, under those conditions, ask for the cheese. If there is more than one such indication in relation to any cheese it shall be sufficient if one such indication complies with this paragraph.

6. If the indications of the selling price and the unit price are both marked on the container they shall be in close proximity to one another but sufficiently distinct as not to confuse an intending purchaser under normal conditions of purchase.

7. Any indication shall be clear and legible, and easily read by an intending purchaser under normal conditions of purchase.

8. Where the indication of a unit price has been calculated by reference to the gross weight of the cheese, that fact shall be clearly indicated.

EXPLANATORY NOTE

(*This Note is not part of the Order.*)

This Order requires the price of cheese offered or exposed for retail sale to be indicated. The requirements to be fulfilled in indicating the prices are set out in the Schedule.

The unit price (price per lb weight of the goods) is to be indicated for all cheese which is not pre-packed.

In the case of pre-packed cheese the selling price is to be indicated, and the unit price is additionally to be indicated for—

    (*a*) pre-packed natural cheese of the following types—

        Caerphilly, Cheddar, Cheshire, Derby, Double Gloucester, Dunlop, Edam, Gouda, Lancashire, Leicestershire and Wensleydale;

    (*b*) other pre-packed natural cheese, processed cheese and cheese spread which is pre-packed in varying quantities rather than to a predetermined fixed weight pattern and is marked with an indication of quantity by weight.

Exemptions are given from the requirement to indicate the unit price for pre-packed whole cheese weighing not more than 500g and cheese pre-packed in a rigid container such as a ceramic jar.

Exemptions from all the requirements of the Order are made for cheese in a quantity not exceeding 25g (approximately $9/_{10}$oz), cheese offered or exposed for retail sale only for consumption on the premises of the seller, and cheese forming part of an assortment of articles of food pre-packed together for consumption as a meal without needing to be cooked, heated or otherwise prepared.

STATUTORY INSTRUMENTS

1977 No. 1335

WEIGHTS AND MEASURES
The Weights and Measures Act 1963 (Cheese) Order 1977

Laid before Parliament in draft

Made - - - -   *1st August* 1977

Coming into Operation   *1st March* 1978

Whereas the Secretary of State pursuant to section 54(2) of the Weights and Measures Act 1963(**a**) (hereinafter referred to as "the Act") has consulted with organisations appearing to him to be representative of interests substantially affected by this Order and considered the representations made to him by such organisations with respect to the subject matter of this Order:

And whereas a draft of this Order has been laid before Parliament and approved by resolution of each House of Parliament pursuant to section 54(3) of the Act:

Now, therefore, the Secretary of State, in exercise of powers conferred by section 21(2), (3) and (5) of the Act and now vested in him(**b**) and of all other powers enabling him in that behalf, hereby makes the following Order:—

1.—(1) This Order may be cited as the Weights and Measures Act 1963 (Cheese) Order 1977 and shall come into operation on 1st March 1978.

(2) In this Order "cheese" means cheese, whether or not containing flavouring or colouring matter, and whether or not coated with or mixed with other food for the purpose of giving the cheese a distinctive appearance or flavour; and includes processed cheese and cheese spread.

(3) The Interpretation Act 1889(**c**) shall apply for the interpretation of this Order as it applies for the interpretation of an Act of Parliament.

2.—(1) Part III of Schedule 4 to the Act shall cease to have effect.

(2) In paragraph 3 of Part XI of the said Schedule after subparagraph (2) there shall be inserted "(2A) cheese as defined in the Weights and Measures Act 1963 (Cheese) Order 1977;".

3. Subject to Article 5 below, cheese which is not pre-packed shall, when sold by retail, be sold only—

(*a*) by net weight; or

(*b*) if the cheese is sold in a container which does not exceed the appropriate weight specified in Table A of Part XII of Schedule 4 to the Act, either by net weight or by gross weight.

(**a**) 1963 c. 31.   (**b**) S.I. 1970/1537 (1970 III, p. 5293).   (**c**) 1889 c. 63.

4.—(1) Subject to Article 5 below—

    (*a*) processed cheese;

    (*b*) cheese spread; and

    (*c*) natural cheese of any of the types specified in paragraph (2) below, shall be pre-packed only if the container is marked with an indication of quantity by net weight.

(2) The types of cheese referred to in paragraph (1) above are Caerphilly, Cheddar, Cheshire, Derby, Double Gloucester, Dunlop, Edam, Gouda, Lancashire, Leicestershire and Wensleydale.

5. There shall be exempted from all the requirements of Articles 3 and 4 of this Order any cheese in a quantity not exceeding 25g.

Robert Maclennan,

Parliamentary Under-Secretary of State,

Department of Prices and Consumer Protection.

1st August 1977.

EXPLANATORY NOTE

(*This Note is not part of the Order.*)

This Order provides that Part III (which relates only to cheese) of Schedule 4 to the Weights and Measures Act 1963 shall cease to have effect on 1st March 1978 when the provisions of that Part are replaced by those of this Order.

It requires that cheese which is not pre-packed may, when sold by retail, only be sold by net weight, or under certain circumstances, by gross weight. The permitted weight of the containers in which cheese may be sold by gross weight is lowered. Cheese is defined as including cheese containing flavouring or colouring matter or coated or mixed with other food for the purpose of giving the cheese a distinctive appearance or flavour.

The number of varieties of cheese which may only be pre-packed if the container is marked with the quantity by net weight is increased to include all the cheeses covered by Article 4. The provision which required the weight of some pre-packed cheese to be made known to the purchaser at the time of sale is abolished. The exemption from the requirements of the Schedule for sales of cheese under 1oz is replaced by an exemption for sale of cheese not exceeding 25g (approximately 9/10oz).

STATUTORY INSTRUMENTS

1977 No. 1336

HOUSING, ENGLAND AND WALES
HOUSING, SCOTLAND

The Assistance for House Purchase and Improvement (Variation of Subsidy) Order 1977

Laid before the House of Commons in draft

Made - - - -	*29th July* 1977
Coming into Operation	*7th August* 1977

The Secretary of State for the Environment, the Secretary of State for Wales and the Secretary of State for Scotland, acting jointly in exercise of their powers under subsections (3), (4) and (5) of section 28 of the Housing Subsidies Act 1967(a) (added to that section by section 78 of the Housing Act 1969(b))(c) and of all other powers enabling them in that behalf, with the approval of the Treasury, hereby make the following order in the terms of a draft which has been laid before the Commons House of Parliament and has been approved by a resolution of that House:—

Citation and commencement

1. This order may be cited as the Assistance for House Purchase and Improvement (Variation of Subsidy) Order 1977 and shall come into operation at the expiration of a period of ten days beginning with the date on which it is made.

Interpretation

2.—(1) In this order—

"the Act" means the Housing Subsidies Act 1967;

"the 1969 Order" means the Assistance for House Purchase and Improvement (Increase of Subsidy) Order 1969(d);

"the 1973 Order" means the Assistance for House Purchase and Improvement (Increase of Subsidy) Order 1973(e);

"the 1974 Order" means the Assistance for House Purchase and Improvement (Increase of Subsidy) Order 1974(f); and

"the 1975 Order" means the Assistance for House Purchase and Improvement (Increase of Subsidy) Order 1975(g).

(2) The Interpretation Act 1889(h) applies for the interpretation of this order as it applies for the interpretation of an Act of Parliament.

(a) 1967 c. 29.   (b) 1969 c. 33.

(c) The powers conferred on the Minister of Housing and Local Government are now exercisable by the Secretary of State for the Environment under S.I. 1970/1681 (1970 III, p. 5551).

(d) S.I. 1969/1626 (1969 III, p. 5120).   (e) S.I. 1973/1928 (1973 III, p. 6671).
(f) S.I. 1974/1005 (1974 II, p. 3785).   (g) S.I. 1975/1240 (1975 II, p. 4231).
(h) 1889 c. 63.

[DET 28911]

(3) References in this order to any enactment shall be construed as references to that enactment as amended, and as including references thereto as applied, by or under any enactment.

3. With respect to interest payable for any period beginning on or after 1st October 1977 under a contract requiring repayment of a loan subsidised under Part II of the Act, the 1969 Order (as varied by the 1973 Order, the 1974 Order and the 1975 Order) shall be further varied and have effect as follows:—

(a) in article 4, for the date "1st September 1975" there shall be substituted the date "1st October 1977", and

(b) for the Schedule, there shall be substituted the following Schedule—

"SCHEDULE

(1) Rate of Interest	(2) Higher Percentage	(3) Higher Percentage
Exceeding 6.4 per cent. per annum but not exceeding 7.0 per cent. per annum ..	2.3 per cent.	2.05 per cent.
Exceeding 7.0 per cent. per annum but not exceeding 7.6 per cent. per annum ..	2.5 per cent.	2.25 per cent.
Exceeding 7.6 per cent. per annum but not exceeding 8.2 per cent. per annum ..	2.7 per cent.	2.45 per cent.
Exceeding 8.2 per cent. per annum but not exceeding 8.8 per cent. per annum ..	2.9 per cent.	2.65 per cent.
Exceeding 8.8 per cent. per annum but not exceeding 9.4 per cent. per annum ..	3.1 per cent.	2.85 per cent.
Exceeding 9.4 per cent. per annum but not exceeding 10.0 per cent. per annum ..	3.3 per cent.	3.05 per cent.
Exceeding 10.0 per cent. per annum but not exceeding 10.6 per cent. per annum ..	3.5 per cent.	3.25 per cent.
Exceeding 10.6 per cent. per annum but not exceeding 11.2 per cent. per annum ..	3.7 per cent.	3.45 per cent.
Exceeding 11.2 per cent. per annum but not exceeding 11.8 per cent. per annum ..	3.9 per cent.	3.65 per cent.
Exceeding 11.8 per cent. per annum but not exceeding 12.4 per cent. per annum ..	4.1 per cent.	3.85 per cent.
Exceeding 12.4 per cent. per annum but not exceeding 13.0 per cent. per annum ..	4.3 per cent.	4.05 per cent.
Exceeding 13.0 per cent. per annum but not exceeding 13.6 per cent. per annum ..	4.5 per cent.	4.25 per cent.

(1) Rate of Interest	(2) Higher Percentage	(3) Higher Percentage
Exceeding 13.6 per cent. per annum but not exceeding 14.2 per cent. per annum ..	4.7 per cent.	4.45 per cent.
Exceeding 14.2 per cent. per annum but not exceeding 14.8 per cent. per annum ..	4.9 per cent.	4.65 per cent.
Exceeding 14.8 per cent. per annum ..	5.1 per cent.	4.85 per cent."

29th July 1977.

Peter Shore,
Secretary of State for the Environment.

29th July 1977.

John Morris,
Secretary of State for Wales.

29th July 1977.

Bruce Millan,
Secretary of State for Scotland.

We approve,

29th July 1977.

J. Dormand,
T. E. Graham,
Two of the Lords Commissioners
of Her Majesty's Treasury.

EXPLANATORY NOTE

(This Note is not part of the Order.)

This Order varies option mortgage subsidy payable under Part II of the Housing Subsidies Act 1967 in respect of interest payable under option mortgages for any period beginning on or after 1st October 1977 where the rate of interest for the time being exceeds 6.4 per cent. per annum.

The Order substitutes new scales of percentages for the existing scales set out in the Schedule to the Assistance for House Purchase and Improvement (Increase of Subsidy) Order 1969, as varied by the Assistance for House Purchase and Improvement (Increase of Subsidy) Order 1973, the Assistance for House Purchase and Improvement (Increase of Subsidy) Order 1974 and the Assistance for House Purchase and Improvement (Increase of Subsidy) Order 1975. The rates of subsidy are revised by subtracting 0.1 per cent. from the existing rates.

The new scale of percentages in column (2) of the Schedule applies in the case of annuity mortgages and fixed instalment mortgages and the new scale of percentages in column (3) of the Schedule applies in the case of endowment mortgages and standing mortgages.

STATUTORY INSTRUMENTS

1977 No. 1341

PENSIONS

The Local Government Superannuation (City of London) Regulations 1977

Made - - - -	*1st August* 1977
Laid before Parliament	*12th August* 1977
Coming into Operation	*1st October* 1977

The Secretary of State for the Environment, in exercise of the powers conferred upon him by section 110(1)(**a**) of the National Insurance Act 1965(**b**), having been determined by the Minister for the Civil Service to be the appropriate Minister of the Crown under that section, and in exercise of the powers conferred upon him by sections 7, 8 and 12 of the Superannuation Act 1972(**c**), as read with paragraph 5(1) of Schedule 7 to that Act, and of all other powers enabling him in that behalf, after consultation with such associations of local authorities as appeared to him to be concerned, the local authorities with whom consultation appeared to him to be desirable, the local Act authority concerned and such representatives of other persons likely to be affected by the regulations as appeared to him to be appropriate, hereby makes the following regulations:—

Citation and commencement

1. These regulations may be cited as the Local Government Superannuation (City of London) Regulations 1977 and shall come into operation on 1st October 1977.

Interpretation

2.—(1) In these regulations, unless the context otherwise requires—

"City of London employing body" means the Common Council, the magistrates' courts committee for the City of London, the probation and after-care committee for the City of London probation and after-care area or the Board of Governors of the Museum of London;

(**a**) Continued in force by regulation 3 of and Schedule 1 to the National Insurance (Non-participation—Transitional Provisions) Regulations 1974 (S.I. 1974/2057 (1974 III, p. 8011)).
(**b**) 1965 c. 51.　　　　　　　　　　　(**c**) 1972 c. 11.

"existing contributor" means—

(a) a person who, having been a contributor to the local Act superannuation fund immediately before the operative date, becomes on that date a pensionable employee under a City of London employing body; or

(b) a person who, having been in the employment of a City of London employing body immediately before the operative date but immediately before that date not having been a contributor to the local Act superannuation fund by virtue of article 17(c) of the Corporation of London (Superannuation) Scheme 1938 (which provides that a person who has attained the age of 55 years and has not completed, and cannot before attaining the age of compulsory retirement applicable in his case complete, 10 years of service, shall not be entitled to participate in the benefits of the local Act superannuation fund), becomes on that date a pensionable employee under a City of London employing body;

"former contributor" means a person who, having ceased to be a contributor to the local Act superannuation fund within a period of 12 months before the operative date, becomes a pensionable employee under a City of London employing body within 12 months of so ceasing;

"the local Act superannuation provisions" means the provisions of the enactments, and of the schemes and other instruments in force thereunder immediately before the operative date, which relate to the superannuation of employees of a City of London employing body;

"the local Act superannuation fund" means the fund maintained by the Common Council under the local Act superannuation provisions;

"the new superannuation fund" means the superannuation fund to be established and administered by the Common Council under the principal regulations;

"the operative date" means 1st October 1977;

"the principal regulations" means the Local Government Superannuation Regulations 1974(a),

and other words and expressions to which meanings are assigned by the principal regulations have the same respective meanings.

(2) For the purposes of—

(a) the reference in regulation 7(i) of these regulations to a person continuing in the employment there referred to and the reference in regulation 12 of these regulations to a person continuing in the employment of the City of London employing body under whom he first became a pensionable employee, the employment shall be regarded as continuing if employment by a City of London employing body is followed immediately by employment by another City of London employing body;

(b) the reference in regulation 10 of these regulations to a person continuing in the employment of the City of London employing body under whom he first became a pensionable employee, the employment

---

(a) S.I. 1974/520 (1974 I, p. 1986).

shall be regarded as continuing if employment by a City of London employing body is followed, within 12 months and without any intervening period of employment by any scheduled body, not being a City of London employing body, by employment by the same or another City of London employing body.

(3) In these regulations, unless the context otherwise requires—

(a) any reference to any enactment or instrument shall be construed as a reference to that enactment or instrument as amended, modified, extended or applied by or under any other enactment or instrument (including these regulations); and

(b) any reference to any enactment applying to England and Wales listed in the table in paragraph 5 of Schedule 7 to the Act of 1972, or any instrument (including a scheme) made under any enactment so listed or any provision of any such enactment or instrument shall, additionally, be construed as a reference to that enactment, instrument or provision as having effect by virtue of sub-paragraph (1) of that paragraph.

(4) The Interpretation Act 1889(a) shall apply for the interpretation of these regulations as it applies for the interpretation of an Act of Parliament and as if these regulations and the instruments revoked by regulation 23 below were Acts of Parliament.

General application of the principal regulations

3.—(1) As from the operative date—

(a) the Common Council shall be included among the bodies required to establish and administer superannuation funds for the purposes of the principal regulations; and, accordingly, in regulation B1 of the principal regulations (superannuation funds), after paragraph (b) there shall be inserted the following paragraph—

"(bb)   the Common Council;";

(b) the Common Council and the probation and after-care committee for the City of London probation and after-care area shall be included among the bodies whose whole-time employees are to be compulsorily superannuable under the principal regulations; and, accordingly, in column (1) of Part I of Schedule 1 to the principal regulations (which Part describes the bodies whose whole-time employees are to be compulsorily superannuable)—

(i) in the entry beginning "A county council", after the word "Council," there shall be inserted the words "the Common Council,"; and

(ii) in the entry beginning "A probation", the words from "other than" to the end shall be omitted; and

(c) the employees of the Board of Governors of the Museum of London shall be included among the persons who may be superannuable under the principal regulations; and, accordingly, in column (3)

(a) 1889 c. 63.

of Part II of Schedule 1 to the principal regulations (which Part describes the persons who may be superannuable), at the end of the penultimate entry there shall be added the words ", the Board of Governors of the Museum of London",

and, subject to the modifications contained in regulations 8 to 15, 17 and 18 of these regulations, the provisions of the principal regulations shall apply accordingly.

(2) Any reference in any of the provisions of the principal regulations to another provision of those regulations which is modified by any of the provisions of regulations 8 to 15, 17 and 18 of these regulations shall, in relation to any person to whom, or to any body or to the new superannuation fund to which, the modification relates, be construed, whenever the modification applies in relation to that person, body or fund, as a reference to that other provision as so modified.

Closure of the local Act superannuation fund, etc.

4.—(1) With effect from the operative date the Common Council shall close the local Act superannuation fund and transfer the balance standing to the credit thereof to the new superannuation fund, and all liabilities of, or liabilities of any body or individual to, the local Act superannuation fund shall become liabilities of or to the new superannuation fund.

(2) All invested moneys belonging to the local Act superannuation fund and the income from such moneys which immediately before the operative date were under or by virtue of section 16 of the City of London (Various Powers) Act 1946(a) held in the names of official trustees of the Corporation within the meaning of that section or in the names of such trustees individually and collectively shall by virtue of these regulations be transferred to and vest in the Corporation and, where any securities in which any such moneys are invested are standing in the books of a company in the names of official trustees of the Corporation within the meaning aforesaid or in the names of such trustees individually and collectively, a certificate of the town clerk of the City of London shall be a sufficient authority to the company to transfer the securities into the name of the Corporation and to pay the dividends or interest to the Corporation.

In this paragraph—

"company" includes the Bank of England and any company or person keeping books in which any securities are registered or inscribed;

"the Corporation" means the mayor and commonalty and citizens of the City of London;

"securities" has the same meaning as in the Prevention of Fraud (Investments) Act 1958(b).

(3) Where a person ceased to contribute to the local Act superannuation fund before the operative date and did not, or does not, become before that date a contributor to any other superannuation fund maintained under Part I of the Act of 1937, or the principal regulations or a local Act, the new

---

(a) 9 & 10 Geo. 6. c. xxix. (b) 1958 c. 45.

superannuation fund shall on and after that date be deemed to be the fund to which he was last a contributor.

Valuation of the local Act superannuation fund

5. The Common Council shall obtain an actuarial valuation of, and report on, the assets and liabilities of the local Act superannuation fund as at 1st April 1974.

Preservation of pensionable status

6. Every person who—

(*a*) on the operative date is in the employment of a City of London employing body;

(*b*) immediately before the operative date was a contributor to the local Act superannuation fund; and

(*c*) does not otherwise on the operative date become a pensionable employee,

shall become a pensionable employee in that employment on the operative date.

Option to certain persons not to become pensionable employees

7. Any person who on the operative date was in the employment of a City of London employing body and who immediately before that date was not in that employment a contributor to the local Act superannuation fund either—

(*a*) by virtue of article 17(*c*) of the Corporation of London (Superannuation) Scheme 1938; or

(*b*) because, being employed as a whole-time manual worker, he had not been placed on the establishment staff in relation to that employment,

being a person who in that employment would otherwise become a pensionable employee, may, by notice in writing given to the Common Council within 3 months after the operative date, elect that he shall not become a pensionable employee—

(i) where immediately before the operative date he was not in that employment a contributor to the local Act superannuation fund by virtue of the said article 17(*c*), so long as he continues in the employment of that body;

(ii) where immediately before the operative date he was not in that employment such a contributor because he was such a person as is mentioned in paragraph (*b*) above, so long as he continues as a whole-time manual worker in the employment of that body.

General modification of the principal regulations in their application to existing contributors and to former contributors

8.—(1) In relation to an existing contributor and to a former contributor, the provisions of the principal regulations, other than regulation K1 thereof (retrospective application) and any of those provisions as applied by paragraph (2) of that regulation, shall, unless the context otherwise requires, have effect as if for any reference therein to an expression in column (1) of Schedule 1 to these regulations (which lists certain expressions used in the principal regulations), except any such reference in regulation E15(2) of the principal regulations (reduction of retirement pension, etc., in the case of certain re-employed local government pensioners), there were substituted a reference to the expression appearing opposite thereto in column (2).

(2) In relation to an existing contributor who is such a person as is mentioned in paragraph (*b*) of the definition of "existing contributor" in regulation 2(1) of these regulations, the principal regulations shall apply as if—

(*a*) he had become a contributor to the local Act superannuation fund on the day immediately before the operative date; and

(*b*) immediately before that date he had been entitled to reckon as service reckonable for the purpose of calculating the amount of any benefit under the local Act superannuation provisions at half its length any service, employment or period which he would have been entitled so to reckon if on the day immediately before that date he had been such a contributor.

Modification of the principal regulations relating to use and investment of the new superannuation fund's moneys, periodical valuation of that fund and actuary's certificates

9. In relation to the Common Council and to the new superannuation fund—

(*a*) regulation B6(2)(*a*) of the principal regulations (use and investment of superannuation fund's moneys) shall have effect as if the references therein to the appointed day were references to the operative date;

(*b*) regulation B7(1) of the principal regulations (periodical valuation of superannuation fund) shall have effect as if sub-paragraph (*a*) were omitted; and

(*c*) regulation B8 of the principal regulations (actuary's certificates) shall have effect as if—

(i) in paragraph (1)—

(A) the reference in sub-paragraph (*a*) to the appointed day were a reference to the operative date;

(B) the reference in sub-paragraph (*b*) to obtaining under regulation B7 an actuarial valuation of, and report on, the assets and liabilities of a superannuation fund maintained under Part B of the principal regulations included a reference to obtaining the actuarial valuation of, and report on, the assets and liabilities of the local Act superannuation fund required under regulation 5 of these regulations as at 1st April 1974;

(C) in sub-paragraph (i), for the words from ", taking" to "during" there were substituted the words "the amount of the employer's contribution payable, where the certificate is required to be obtained under sub-paragraph (*a*), in the period beginning on 1st October 1977 and ending with 31st March 1978 (in this regulation referred to as "the first period") and, where the certificate is required to be obtained under sub-paragraph (*b*), in each year of the relevant period, should bear to the total remuneration on which contributions will during the first period or. as the case may be,";

(D) in sub-paragraph (ii), for the words from "taking" to "sub-paragraph (i)" there were substituted the words "the amount of the employer's contribution should in the first period or, as the case may be, in any such year of the relevant period"; and

(E) at the end of the paragraph there were inserted the following—

"In this paragraph "relevant period" means—

(*a*) where the actuarial valuation mentioned in sub-paragraph (*b*) was made as at 1st April 1974, the period of 3 years beginning with 1st April 1978; and

(*b*) where the actuarial valuation was made as at a date subsequent to 1st April 1974, the period of 5 years beginning with 1st April third following the date as at which that valuation was made.";

and

(ii) paragraphs (2) and (3) were omitted.

Modification of the principal regulations relating to contributions of certain existing contributors and former contributors

10. In relation to—

(*a*) an existing contributor who was immediately before the operative date required under the local Act superannuation provisions to make contributions at a rate lower than the rate applicable in his case specified in regulation C1 of the principal regulations (payment and amount of employee's contributions); and

(*b*) a former contributor who was immediately before he last ceased to be a contributor to the local Act superannuation fund required as aforesaid to make contributions at such a rate as aforesaid,

the said regulation C1 shall have effect, so long as he continues in the employment of the City of London employing body under whom he first became a pensionable employee, as if it required him to make contributions to the new superannuation fund at the like rate as he was liable to make to the local Act superannuation fund when he was last a contributor to that fund before the operative date.

Modification of the principal regulations relating to employer's contributions

11. In relation to a City of London employing body, regulation C5 of the principal regulations (employer's contributions) shall have effect as if—

    (*a*) in paragraph (1)—

        (i) in sub-paragraph (*a*)—

            (A) for the words from the beginning to "regulation B8" there were substituted the words "in the period beginning with 1st October 1977 and ending with 31st March 1978";

            (B) the words "each year of" were omitted;

            (C) for the words "paragraph (1)(*a*) of that regulation" there were substituted the words "regulation B8(1)(*a*)"; and

            (D) for the word "year", in the last place where it occurs, there were substituted the word "period"; and

        (ii) in sub-paragraph (*b*)—

            (A) for the words from "period", in the first place where it occurs, to "regulation B8" there were substituted the words "relevant period";

            (B) for the words "paragraph (1)(*b*) of that regulation" there were substituted the words "regulation B8(1)(*b*)"; and

            (C) at the end of that sub-paragraph there were inserted the following—

                "In this sub-paragraph "relevant period" has the same meaning as in regulation B8(1).";

    and

    (*b*) in paragraph (2), the reference to the appointed day were a reference to the operative date.

Modification of the principal regulations relating to interest on return of contributions to existing contributors

12. Notwithstanding anything in regulation C8 of the principal regulations (return of contributions in certain cases), an existing contributor shall, so long as he continues in the employment of the City of London employing body under whom he first became a pensionable employee, be entitled on ceasing to be employed by reason of his voluntary resignation and becoming entitled to a return of contributions under that regulation to receive compound interest, calculated to the date on which he ceased to hold his employment, at the rate of 4% per annum with half-yearly rests, on such part of the sum payable to him under that regulation as is equal to the amount of his contributions payable before 1st April 1972 to any superannuation fund under Part I of the Act of 1937, or under the Act of 1922 or under a local Act scheme.

Modification of the principal regulations relating to service

13. In relation to a City of London employing body, to existing contributors and to former contributors, Part D of the principal regulations (service) and Schedules 3 to 8 to those regulations, other than as applied by regulation K1(2) thereof, shall be modified as follows:—

(*a*) regulation D1(1) (reckonable service) shall have effect as if sub-paragraph (*e*) were omitted;

(*b*) regulation D2 (qualifying service) shall have effect as if paragraph (*c*) were omitted;

(*c*) any reference in the said Part D or in the said schedules to the appointed day, except the reference in regulation D1(1)(*a*), shall be read as a reference to the operative date;

(*d*) regulation D6(1) (non-contributing service treated as contributing service on payment of additional contributory payments) shall have effect as if for sub-paragraph (*a*) there were substituted the following sub-paragraph—

"(*a*) became a contributory employee after 5th July 1954;";

(*e*) regulation D10(1) (added years reckonable on payment as reckonable service) shall have effect as if in sub-paragraph (*b*) after the words "designated employee" there were inserted the words ", contributory employee";

(*f*) regulation D12(2) (increase of reckonable service on lump sum payment) shall have effect as if—

(i) in sub-paragraph (*a*), for the words "on first becoming a pensionable employee," there were substituted the words "on 1st April 1974 or on the date on which he last became a contributor to the superannuation fund maintained by the Common Council under their local Act scheme, whichever is the later,"; and

(ii) for sub-paragraph (*b*) there were substituted the following sub-paragraph—

"(*b*) a pensionable employee who—

(i) is a person to whom regulation E19 applies; and

(ii) has not made an election under paragraph (2) of that regulation.";

(*g*) in relation to an existing contributor or former contributor who before the operative date had attained the age of 59 years, regulation D13 (increase of reckonable service on the making of periodical payments) shall have effect as if—

(i) in paragraph (1), after the words "administering authority" there were inserted the words "within 12 months after the date on which he first became a pensionable employee"; and

(ii) in paragraph (5)(*a*), for the word "has" there were substituted the words ", on 1st April 1974 or on the date on which he last became a contributor to the superannuation fund maintained by the Common Council under their local Act scheme, whichever is the later, had"; and (*h*) in relation to such an existing contributor or former contributor as is mentioned in paragraph (*g*) above, Schedule 8 (amount to be paid for additional period) shall have effect as if in the table in Part I and in Table I and Table II in Part II there were added the appropriate entries set out in Schedule 2 to these regulations.

Modification of the principal regulations relating to benefits

14. In relation to a City of London employing body, to existing contributors and to former contributors, Part E of the principal regulations (benefits) and Schedules 9 to 12 to those regulations, other than as applied by regulation K1(2) thereof, shall be modified as follows:—

(*a*) any reference in that Part or in those schedules to the appointed day shall be read as a reference to the operative date;

(*b*) regulation E19 (benefits of persons with no entitlement under the former regulations to a retiring allowance and widow's pension or to a widow's pension) shall have effect as if—

(i) in the heading, for the words "or to a widow's pension" there were substituted the words "or to a retiring allowance";

(ii) in paragraph (1)(*b*)(ii), for the words "a pension payable to his widow" there were substituted the words "a lump sum retiring allowance"; and

(iii) at the end of the regulation there were added the following paragraph—

"(4) Where any such person as is mentioned in paragraph (1)(*b*)(i)—

(*a*) was not married immediately before 1st October 1977; 1977;

(*b*) has first married on or after that date;

(*c*) has not made an election under paragraph (2);

(*d*) from the day on which he first became a pensionable employee has continued without a break of 12 months or more to contribute to the superannuation fund maintained by the Common Council under Part B; and

(*e*) is at any time during the period of 3 months after the date of first marrying a pensionable employee under any City of London employing body;

then, if at any time when he is such a pensionable employee during that period he elects, by notice in writing given to the Common Council, that this paragraph shall apply in his case, he shall be treated for the purposes of paragraph (2) as if he were not such a person as is mentioned in paragraph (1)(*b*)(i) but were such a person as is mentioned in paragraph (1)(*b*)(ii).";

and

(*c*) Schedule 12 to the principal regulations (modifications to Part E in its application to persons with no entitlement under the former regulations to a retiring allowance and widow's pension or to a widow's pension) shall have effect as if for that schedule there were substituted the schedule set out in Schedule 3 to these regulations.

Modification of the principal regulations relating to National Insurance modification

15. In relation to persons who are pensionable employees of a City of London employing body, Part F of the principal regulations (National Insurance modification) shall have effect as if any reference in that Part to the commencement of the regulations or to the appointed day were a reference to the operative date.

Increase of reckonable service at discretion of a City of London employing body on retirement of certain of their employees

16. For regulation G8 of the principal regulations there shall be substituted the following regulation—

"Increase of reckonable service at discretion of the Common Council, etc., on retirement of certain pensionable employees

G8.—(1) Where a pensionable employee of a City of London employing body—

> (a) who was a contributor immediately before 1st October 1977 to the superannuation fund maintained by the Common Council under their local Act scheme; and
>
> (b) who became a pensionable employee on 1st October 1977,

becomes entitled on ceasing to be employed by them to a retirement pension, other than by virtue of regulation E2(1)(c), the City of London employing body may, in consideration of special circumstances, resolve to add a number of years, not exceeding 10 years, to his reckonable service.

(2) Upon the exercise by a City of London employing body, other than the Common Council, of the discretion vested in them under paragraph (1)—

> (a) that body shall forthwith give notice thereof in writing to the Common Council; and
>
> (b) if the Common Council are dissatisfied with the decision of that body they may within 1 month of receiving the notice appeal to the Secretary of State, whose determination shall be final, and if the Common Council appeal the decision of the body shall not be effective until the appeal is determined.

(3) In this regulation "City of London employing body" means the Common Council, the magistrates' courts committee for the City of London, the probation and after-care committee for the City of London probation and after-care area or the Board of Governors of the Museum of London.".

Application and modification of provisions of the principal regulations relating to persons ceasing to be employed after 30th March 1972

17.—(1) Regulation K1 of the principal regulations (retrospective application) shall apply to a person who—

> (a) ceased on or after 31st March 1972 but before the operative date to hold an employment in which he was a contributor to the local Act superannuation fund; or

(b)   dies on or after 31st March 1972 but before the operative date while still in such an employment.

(2) In relation to such a person as is mentioned in paragraph (1) above and to a City of London employing body—

(a)   unless the context otherwise requires, the said regulation K1 shall have effect, and the provisions of the principal regulations applied by paragraph (2) of that regulation, subject to the modifications therein mentioned, shall have effect for the purposes therein mentioned, as if for any reference therein to an expression in column (1) of Schedule 1 to these regulations, except any such reference in regulation E15(2) of the principal regulations, there were substituted a reference to the expression appearing opposite thereto in column (2);

(b)   regulation E19 of the principal regulations and Schedule 12 thereto shall have effect for the purposes referred to in sub-paragraph (a) above as modified by regulation 14(b) (i) and (ii) and (c) of these regulations;

(c)   paragraph (2)(a) of the said regulation K1 shall have effect as if in the exceptions therein mentioned any reference to the appointed day were a reference to the operative date;

(d)   paragraphs (3) and (4) of the said regulation K1 shall have effect as if the references therein to the appointed day were references to the operative date; and

(e)   regulation K2 of the principal regulations (right to opt out) shall have effect as if—

(i)   the reference therein to 31st March 1974 were a reference to 30th September 1977; and

(ii)   the reference therein to the appointed day were a reference to the operative date.

Modification of the principal regulations relating to miscellaneous and supplemental matters

18. In relation to a City of London employing body and to their employees, Part L of the principal regulations (miscellaneous and supplemental) shall have effect as if any reference in that Part to the commencement of the regulations or to the appointed day, and the reference in regulation L3(3)(a) (decisions to be taken by administering authorities as to status of employees) to 1st April 1975, were a reference to the operative date.

Persons transferred to the Common Council under section 18(4)(a) of the National Health Service Reorganisation Act 1973

19.—(1) This regulation shall apply to a person who—

(a)   was by or under an order made under section 18(4)(a) of the National Health Service Reorganisation Act 1973(a) transferred to the employment of the Common Council;

(a) 1973 c. 32.

(b) immediately before he was so transferred was in an employment in which he was an officer within the meaning of the Health Service regulations;

(c) on the date on which he was so transferred became a contributor to the local Act superannuation fund in the employment to which he was so transferred; and

(d) became a pensionable employee in that employment on the operative date.

(2) Subject to paragraph (3) below, a person to whom this regulation applies shall be entitled to reckon—

(a) as reckonable service any service which for the purposes of the Health Service regulations he was entitled to reckon in relation to the employment mentioned in paragraph (1)(b) above as, or as a period of, contributing service; and

(b) as qualifying service any service which for the purposes of those regulations he was entitled to reckon in relation to that employment for the purposes of determining whether he was entitled to a benefit under those regulations, but for no other purpose:

Provided that for the purposes of this paragraph any period of part-time service shall be treated as though it were whole-time service for a proportionately reduced period and, except for the purposes referred to in paragraph (3) of regulation D18 of the principal regulations (counting of non-contributing service), any service which was reckonable under the Health Service regulations for all purposes, other than for the purpose of determining whether any benefit was payable, as a period of contributing service at half its length shall be counted at half its length.

(3) A person to whom this regulation applies who on the operative date was in the employment to which he was transferred as mentioned in paragraph (1)(a) above engaged on duties reasonably comparable to those on which he was engaged immediately before he was so transferred may, within 6 months after the operative date, give notice in writing to the Common Council that he does not wish to avail himself of the benefits provided under the principal regulations and in that event the principal regulations shall have effect in relation to him as if they conferred on him rights corresponding with those which he would have enjoyed if he had remained subject to the Health Service regulations, and the principal regulations shall continue so to apply so long as he is employed without a disqualifying break of service by the Common Council on duties reasonably comparable as mentioned above.

(4) The provisions of Part H of the principal regulations (determination of questions and appeals) shall apply in relation to any question concerning the rights of a person under this regulation.

(5) In this regulation "the Health Service regulations" means the National Health Service (Superannuation) Regulations 1961(a) to 1974(b).

(a) S.I. 1961/1441 (1961 II, p. 2824).   (b) S.I. 1974/223 (1974 I, p. 765).

Preservation of rights and liabilities under the principal regulations of persons who were pensionable employees of the Common Council before the operative date

20.—(1) This regulation shall apply to a person who—

(*a*) immediately before the operative date was a pensionable employee under the Common Council by virtue of regulation B2(1)(*j*) of the principal regulations; and

(*b*) was in the employment of the Common Council on the operative date.

(2) Nothing in these regulations shall prejudice or affect any right enjoyed under the principal regulations immediately before the operative date by a person to whom this regulation applies or any liability to which that person was subject immediately before that date and any such person shall continue to enjoy or, as the case may be, be subject to any such right or liability in the like manner and for the like period as if these regulations had not been made.

Minor and consequential amendments of the principal regulations

21. The provisions of the principal regulations mentioned in Schedule 4 to these regulations shall have effect subject to the amendments there specified, being minor amendments and amendments consequential on the provisions of these regulations.

Consequential amendments of other instruments and of enactments

22. The provisions of the instruments and enactments mentioned in Schedule 5 to these regulations shall have effect subject to the consequential amendments there specified.

Repeals and revocations

23.—(1) The enactments mentioned in column (2) of Part I of Schedule 6 to these regulations shall cease to have effect to the extent specified in column (3).

(2) The instruments mentioned in column (2) of Part II of that schedule are hereby revoked to the extent specified in column (3).

SCHEDULE 1   Regulations 8 and 17

GENERAL MODIFICATION OF THE PRINCIPAL REGULATIONS

(1)	(2)
1. the Acts of 1937 to 1953, or the regulations made thereunder the Acts of 1937 to 1953, or the regulations made thereunder, applying as amended or extended by the provisions of any local Act or scheme or together with any such provisions	the local Act superannuation provisions
2. the appropriate superannuation fund within the meaning of the Act of 1937 a superannuation fund maintained under Part I of the Act of 1937	the local Act superannuation fund
3. contributory employee	contributor to the local Act superannua-fund
4. contributing service for the purposes of the former regulations	service reckonable for all the purposes of the local Act superannuation provisions at its full length
5. non-contributing service for the purposes of the former regulations	service reckonable for the purpose of calculating the amount of a benefit under the local Act superannuation provisions at half its length
6. the former regulations	the local Act superannuation provisions
7. a provision in the former regulations	the corresponding or similar provision in the local Act superannuation provisions
8. revocation of the former regulations by the principal regulations	repeal and revocation of the local Act superannuation provisions by these regulations

Regulation 13(g)   **SCHEDULE 2**

PART I

Entries to be added to the Table in Part I of Schedule 8 to the principal regulations

(1) Age	(2) Men	(3) Women
60	16.90	17.60
61	17.60	18.10
62	17.70	18.20
63	17.80	18.30
64	17.90	18.30

PART II

Entries to be added to Table I in Part II of Schedule 8 to the principal regulations

Figure to be used by reference to the under-mentioned pensionable age

Age on birthday next following election	Employees to whom on retirement regulation E3(2) would apply 65	60	Over 60 and under 61	61 and under 62	62 and under 63	63 and under 64	64 and under 65	65
60	3.75	—	—	18.98	9.37	6.17	4.58	3.69
61	4.70	—	—	—	18.77	9.27	6.12	4.63
62	6.27	—	—	—	—	18.57	9.19	6.18
63	9.43	—	—	—	—	—	18.39	9.27
64	18.89	—	—	—	—	—	—	18.55

PART III

ENTRIES TO BE ADDED TO TABLE II IN PART II OF
SCHEDULE 8 TO THE PRINCIPAL REGULATIONS

Figure to be used by reference to the under-mentioned pensionable age

Age on birthday next following election	Employees to whom on retirement regulation E3(2) would apply	60	Over 60 and under 61	61 and under 62	62 and under 63	63 and under 64	64 and under 65	65
	65							
60	3.93	—	—	19.34	9.48	6.21	4.59	3.69
61	4.93	—	—	—	19.00	9.33	6.13	4.62
62	6.58	—	—	—	—	18.68	9.20	6.17
63	9.88	—	—	—	—	—	18.40	9.26
64	19.79	—	—	—	—	—	—	18.52

SCHEDULE 3   Regulation 14

SCHEDULE SUBSTITUTED FOR SCHEDULE 12 TO THE PRINCIPAL REGULATIONS

SCHEDULE 12   Regulation E19

MODIFICATIONS TO PART E IN ITS APPLICATION TO
PERSONS WITH NO ENTITLEMENT UNDER THE FORMER
REGULATIONS TO A RETIRING ALLOWANCE AND
WIDOW'S PENSION OR TO A RETIRING ALLOWANCE

PART I

1. In regulation E3(1), for the words "one eightieth" there shall be substituted the words "one sixtieth".

2. For regulation E6(2) there shall be substituted the following—

"(2) Subject to paragraphs (3) and (4) and as hereafter in this Part provided, the amount of a widow's long-term pension shall be the aggregate of—

(a) the amount ascertained by multiplying one four hundred and eightieth of the pensionable remuneration of the husband of the widow by the length in years of his reckonable service before 1st April 1972; and

(b) the amount ascertained by multiplying one one hundred and sixtieth of the pensionable remuneration of the husband of the widow by the length in years of his reckonable service after 31st March 1972.".

3. In regulation E8—

(a) In paragraph (1)—

(i) in sub-paragraph (c) and the word "or" immediately preceding it shall be omitted;

(ii) for sub-paragraphs (i) and (ii) there shall be substituted the words "a children's short-term pension in respect of the period of 3 months after the day of his death"; and

(iii) proviso (b) and the word "and" immediately preceding it shall be omitted; and

(b) in paragraph (2)—

(i) the words "and a children's long-term pension"; and

(ii) in the proviso, the words from "or, as" to "pension";

shall be omitted.

PART II

1. For regulation E3(1) there shall be substituted the following—

"(1) Subject to paragraphs (9) and (10) and as hereafter in this Part provided, the rate of the retirement pension to be paid to a person shall be the aggregate of—

(a) the amount ascertained by multiplying one seventieth of his pensionable remuneration by the length in years of his reckonable service before 1st April 1972; and

(b) the amount ascertained by multiplying one sixtieth of his pensionable remuneration by the length in years of his reckonable service after 31st March 1972.".

2. In regulation E6—

(a) for paragraph (2) there shall be substituted the following paragraph—

"(2) Subject to paragraphs (2A) to (4) and as hereafter in this Part provided, the amount of a widow's long-term pension shall be the aggregate of—

(a) three tenths of the retirement pension to which the husband of the widow was or would have been entitled at the time of his death in respect of his reckonable service before 1st April 1972;

(b) the amount ascertained by multiplying one four hundred and eightieth of the pensionable remuneration of the husband of the widow by the length in years of his reckonable service before 1st April 1972; and (*c*) the amount ascertained by multiplying one one hundred and sixtieth of the pensionable remuneration of the husband of the widow by the length in years of his reckonable service after 31st March 1972.";

and

(*b*) after paragraph (2) there shall be inserted the following paragraph—

"(2A) Where—

(*a*) the age of the widow at the date of the death of her husband was less than that of her husband and she has no eligible children; or

(*b*) the age of the widow at the date of the death of her husband was greater than that of her husband,

the amount calculated under paragraph (2)(*a*) shall be reduced or increased by such amount as shall be certified to be just by an actuary.".

3. In regulation E8(1)—

(*a*) in proviso (*b*), at the end there shall be added the word "and"; and

(*b*) after that proviso there shall be added the following proviso—

"(*c*) in any case where a widow's long-term pension is payable to the widow of the deceased person, the children's long-term pension shall not be payable until the day following the widow's death.".

4. In regulation E9—

(*a*) for paragraph (2) there shall be substituted the following paragraphs—

"(2) Subject to paragraphs (2A) to (4), the amount of a children's long-term pension shall be the aggregate of—

(*a*) three tenths of the retirement pension to which the deceased person was or would have been entitled at the time of his death in respect of his reckonable service before 1st April 1972;

(*b*) the amount ascertained by multiplying one four hundred and eightieth of the pensionable remuneration of the deceased person by the length in years of his reckonable service before 1st April 1972; and

(*c*) the amount ascertained by multiplying one one hundred and sixtieth of the pensionable remuneration of the deceased person by the length in years of his reckonable service after 31st March 1972.

(2A) For the purpose of calculating the amount of a children's long-term pension under paragraph (2) no account shall be taken of reckonable service before the age of 60 years beyond a total of 40 years and any reckonable service to be disregarded by virtue of this paragraph shall be taken from the beginning of the period of the reckonable service.";

and

(*b*) in paragraph (4), the words from "or, if" to the end of that paragraph shall be omitted.

PART III

1. In regulation E2(1), the words "and a lump sum retiring allowance" shall be omitted.

2. In regulation E3—

(a) paragraphs (2) to (6), (12) and (13) shall be omitted; and

(b) in paragraph (10), for the words "Subject to paragraphs (11) to (13)" there shall be substituted the words "Subject to paragraph (11)".

3. For regulation E6(3) there shall be substituted the following—

"(3) In the case of the widow of a person who was at the time of his death employed in an employment in which he was a pensionable employee, for the purpose of calculating the amount of a widow's long-term pension under paragraph (2) the husband of the widow shall be treated as having been entitled immediately before his death to reckon as reckonable service such an additional period as he would have been entitled to reckon under regulation E3(7) if he had been at the time of his death entitled to benefits under these regulations by virtue of regulation E2(1)(b)(i).

(4) For the purpose of calculating the amount of a widow's long-term pension under paragraph (2) no account shall be taken of reckonable service before the age of 60 years beyond a total of 40 years and any reckonable service to be disregarded by virtue of this paragraph shall be taken from the beginning of the period of the reckonable service.".

4. In regulation E11—

(a) in paragraph (1)(b), the words "and retiring allowance" shall be omitted and for the words from "and either" to the end there shall be substituted the word "; or";

(b) in paragraph (1)(c), the words "and retiring allowance" and the words "or payment of that allowance" shall be omitted;

(c) in paragraph (2)(a)—

(i) for the words "or (b)(ii)" there shall be substituted the words "or (b)"; and

(ii) for the words "paragraph (1)(b)(ii)" there shall be substituted the words "paragraph (1)(b)";

(d) paragraphs (2)(b), (3), (6) and (8) shall be omitted;

(e) in paragraph (5), for the words "paragraph (1)(b)(i)" there shall be substituted the words "paragraph (1)(b)"; and

(f) in paragraph (7), the words "Subject to paragraph (8)," shall be omitted.

5. In regulation E12, the words "a married male employee" shall be omitted.

SCHEDULE 4 Regulation 21

MINOR AND CONSEQUENTIAL AMENDMENTS OF THE PRINCIPAL REGULATIONS

1. In Part A of the principal regulations (preliminary)—

(*a*) in regulation A3(1) (definitions)—

(i) in the definition of "justices' clerk (outside the inner London area)", the words from "other" to the end shall be omitted;

(ii) in the definition of "local Act contributor", for the words "is or has been," there shall be substituted the word "was"; and

(iii) in the definition of "rent officer" and "deputy rent officer", the words from "other" to the end shall be omitted; and

(*b*) after regulation A6 there shall be inserted the following regulation—

"*Secretary and treasurer of the Board of Governors of the Museum of London*

A6A. For the purposes of these regulations a person appointed under section 9(2) of the Museum of London Act 1965(a) (employment of staff) to act as secretary or treasurer of the Board of Governors of the Museum of London shall be treated as not being an employee of that Board.".

2. In regulation B3 of the principal regulations (appropriate superannuation fund)—

(*a*) in paragraph (1), for the words "paragraph (2)" there shall be substituted the words "paragraphs (2) and (4A)";

(*b*) after paragraph (4) there shall be inserted the following paragraph—

"(4A) The appropriate superannuation fund in relation to any pensionable employee of the Common Council who immediately before the appointed day was by virtue of article 15 of the London Authorities (Superannuation) Order 1965(b) entitled to participate in the benefits of the superannuation fund maintained under Part I of the Act of 1937 by the Greater London Council, and who became a pensionable employee on the appointed day and during the period beginning with the appointed day and ending with 30th September 1977 continued without a break in the employment of the Common Council, shall be the superannuation fund maintained by the Greater London Council, so long as he continues without a break in the employment of the Common Council.";

(*c*) in paragraph (5), for the words "regulation B2(1)(*j*) or (*l*)" there shall be substituted the words "regulation B2(1)(*l*)" and after the words "in Greater London" there shall be inserted the words "(other than the City of London probation and after-care area)"; and

(*d*) in paragraph (6), after the words "county council" there shall be inserted the words ", the Common Council".

(a) 1965 c. 17.   (b) S.I. 1965/621 (1965 I, p. 1970).

3. In regulation C7(*b*) of the principal regulations (employer's further payments) for the words "D9 or D14" there shall be substituted the words "D9, D14 or G8".

4. In Part D of the principal regulations—

(*a*) in regulation D1(1)(*g*) (reckonable service) for the words from "regulation" to "D14" there shall be substituted the words "these regulations or the Local Government Superannuation (City of London) Regulations 1977"; and

(*b*) in regulation D2(*d*) (qualifying service) for the words "regulation D15 or D16" there shall be substituted the words "these regulations or the Local Government Superannuation (City of London) Regulations 1977".

5. In regulation E3(8) of the principal regulations (amount of retirement pension and retiring allowance) after the word "under" there shall be inserted the words "paragraph (2) of".

Regulation 22   SCHEDULE 5

CONSEQUENTIAL AMENDMENTS OF OTHER INSTRUMENTS AND OF ENACTMENTS

1. In the Local Government Superannuation Act 1937(**a**), in section 40(1) (definitions), as having effect as provisions of regulations under section 7 of the Act of 1972, in the definition of "local authority", at the end there shall be added the words "and the Board of Governors of the Museum of London".

2. In the Local Government Superannuation Act 1953(**b**)—

(*a*) in section 1(6) (regulations as to superannuation benefits), as set out in paragraph 4(*c*) of Part I of Schedule 18 to the principal regulations, at the end there shall be added the words ", as amended by the Local Government Superannuation (City of London) Regulations 1977"; and

(*b*) in section 18(5) (gratuities), as set out in paragraph 5(*c*) of that part of that schedule, at the end there shall be added the words ", as amended by the Local Government Superannuation (City of London) Regulations 1977".

3. In the Local Government Superannuation (Benefits) Regulations 1954(**c**), in regulation 7(6) (injury allowance), as set out in paragraph 1(*d*) of Part II of Schedule 18 to the principal regulations, at the end there shall be added the words ", as amended by the Local Government Superannuation (City of London) Regulations 1977".

4. In the Local Government Act 1972(**d**), in section 154(1) (accounts to be audited by district or approved auditor), for paragraph (*b*) there shall be substituted the following—

"(*b*) the accounts relating to the superannuation fund established and administered by the Common Council under the Local Government Superannuation Regulations 1974, as amended by the Local Government Superannuation (City of London) Regulations 1977;".

(a) 1937 c. 68.
(c) S.I. 1954/1048 (1954 II, p. 1595).
(b) 1953 c. 25.
(d) 1972 c. 70.

SCHEDULE 6 Regulation 23

REPEALS AND REVOCATIONS

PART I

ENACTMENTS

(1) Chapter	(2) Short title	(3) Extent of repeal
21 & 22 Geo. 5. c. xiv.	The City of London (Various Powers) Act 1931.	Part II.
23 & 24 Geo. 5. c. xxiii.	The City of London (Various Powers) Act 1933.	Section 12.
1 Edw. 8. & 1 Geo. 6. c. 68.	The Local Government Superannuation Act 1937.	The whole Act, except sections 28, 29, 30(3), 35, 36(6), 38, 40(1) and 42 and Part V of Schedule 2 as those sections and that part have effect as provisions of regulations under section 7 of the Superannuation Act 1972.
2 & 3 Geo. 6. c. 94.	The Local Government Staffs (War Service) Act 1939.	Sections 3 and 9, so far as they apply to England and Wales.
7 & 8 Geo. 6. c. iv.	The City of London (Various Powers) Act 1944.	Section 9(1).
9 & 10 Geo. 6. c. xxix.	The City of London (Various Powers) Act 1946.	Sections 15 and 16.
11 & 12 Geo. 6. c. 33.	The Superannuation (Miscellaneous Provisions) Act 1948.	Sections 6 and 7 and the definitions in section 17(1) of "contributory employee", "local Act scheme", "local Act contributor" and "local authority", so far as the said sections 6 and 7 and those definitions apply to England and Wales.

(1) Chapter	(2) Short title	(3) Extent of repeal
11 & 12 Geo. 6. c. 65.	The Representation of the People Act 1948.	Section 72, so far as it applies to England and Wales.
14 Geo. 6. c. v.	The City of London (Various Powers) Act 1950.	Part II.
1 & 2 Eliz. 2. c. 25.	The Local Government Superannuation Act 1953.	The whole Act, so far as it applies to England and Wales, except sections 1(1), (3)(c) and (d), (4)(c) and (5), 18, 21, 27 and 29 and Schedule 4 as those sections and that schedule have effect as provisions of regulations under section 7 of the Superannuation Act 1972.
2 & 3 Eliz. 2. c. xxvii.	The City of London (Various Powers) Act 1954.	Part IV.
4 & 5 Eliz. 2. c. l.	The City of London (Various Powers) Act 1956.	Part II.
8 & 9 Eliz. 2. c. xxxvi.	The City of London (Various Powers) Act 1960.	Section 38.
1964 c. 48.	The Police Act 1964.	In Schedule 4, paragraphs 5(1) to (3), (6) and (7) and, in Schedule 11, paragraph 3, except so far as those paragraphs apply to a person who by virtue of a scheme made under Part I of the Act was transferred before 1st April 1974.

(1) Chapter	(2) Short title	(3) Extent of repeal
1964 c. 75.	The Public Libraries and Museums Act 1964.	In Schedule 1, paragraphs 1(1) to (3) and 3 and the definition of "pensions" in paragraph 5, except so far as the said paragraphs 1(1) to (3) and 3 and that definition apply to a person who by the operation of the Act was transferred before 1st April 1974.
1965 c. 17.	The Museum of London Act 1965.	Section 10.
1968 c. xxxvii.	The City of London (Various Powers) Act 1968.	Sections 6 and 7.
1970 c. lxix.	The City of London (Various Powers) Act 1970.	Part II.
1972 c. 11.	The Superannuation Act 1972.	In Schedule 6, paragraphs 49 and 50.

PART II

INSTRUMENTS

(1) References	(2) Short title	(3) Extent of revocation
—	The Corporation of London (Super-annuation) Scheme 1938 approved by the Minister of Health on 15th December 1938.	The whole scheme.
S.R. & O. 1939/56 (Rev. XVII p. 824: 1939 II, p. 2655).	The Local Government (Mental Hospital, etc., Employment) Regulations 1939.	The whole regulations, so far as they have effect as provisions of regulations under section 8(2) of the Superannuation Act 1972.
S.R. & O. 1939/57 (Rev. XVII p. 834: 1939 II, p. 2667).	The Local Government (Service of Registration Officers) Regulations 1939.	The whole regulations.
S.I. 1949/628 (1949 I, p. 3054).	The Local Government (Break of Service) Regulations 1949.	The whole regulations.
S.I. 1954/1048 (1954 II, p. 1595).	The Local Government Superannuation (Benefits) Regulations 1954.	The whole regulations, except regulations 1 and 7 as they have effect as provisions of regulations under section 7 of the Superannuation Act 1972.
S.I. 1954/1192 (1954 II, p. 1570).	The Local Government Superannuation (Administration) Regulations 1954.	The whole regulations.
S.I. 1954/1211 (1954 II, p. 1676).	The Local Government Superannuation (Reckoning of Service on Transfer) Regulations 1954.	The whole regulations.

(1) References	(2) Short title	(3) Extent of revocation
S.I. 1954/1212 (1954 II, p. 1723).	The Local Government Superannuation (Transfer Value) Regulations 1954.	The whole regulations, so far as they have effect as provisions of regulations under section 8(2) of the Superannuation Act 1972.
S.I. 1954/1227 (1954 II, p. 1674).	The Local Government Superannuation (Mental Hospital, etc., Employment) (Amendment) Regulations 1954.	The whole regulations, so far as they have effect as provisions of regulations under the said section 8 (2).
S.I. 1954/1237 (1954 II, p. 1672).	The Local Government Superannuation (Limitation of Service) Regulations 1954.	The whole regulations.
S.I. 1955/476.	The City of London Superannuation Scheme Approval Instrument 1955.	The whole instrument together with the scheme approved thereby.
S.I. 1955/1041 (1955 II, p. 1825).	The Local Government Superannuation (Benefits) (Amendment) Regulations 1955.	The whole regulations, except regulations 1 and 15 as they have effect as provisions of regulations under section 7 of the Superannuation Act 1972.
S.I. 1965/621 (1965 I, p. 1970).	The London Authorities (Superannuation) Order 1965.	The whole order, except articles 1 to 3 and 26.
S.I. 1967/1330 (1967 III, p. 3975).	The London Authorities (Superannuation) (Amendment) Order 1967.	The whole order, except articles 1 to 3.
S.I. 1969/413 (1969 I, p. 1163).	The London Authorities (Superannuation) (Amendment) Order 1969.	The whole order.
S.I. 1969/793 (1969 II, p. 2227).	The National Insurance (Modification of Local Government Superannuation Schemes) Regulations 1969.	The whole regulations.

(1) References	(2) Short title	(3) Extent of revocation
S.I. 1969/1563.	The Justices' Clerks and Assistants (Superannuation) (City of London) Regulations 1969.	The whole regulations.
—	The Corporation of London (Super-annuation) (No. 1) Scheme 1970 approved by the Corporation of London (Super-annuation) (No. 1) Scheme 1970 Approval Instrument 1970 (a).	The whole scheme, except articles 1, 2 and 4.
—	The Corporation of London (Super-annuation) Scheme 1971 approved by the Secretary of State for the Environment on 30th April 1971.	The whole scheme.
S.I. 1974/520 (1974 I, p. 1986).	The Local Government Superannuation Regulations 1974.	Regulation B2(1) (j). In regulation E15, in paragraph (1), the words "or local Act authority", in the second place where they occur; in paragraph (3), in paragraphs (a) and (b) of the proviso, the words "or local Act authority", in the second place where they occur in each paragraph; and, in paragraph (4), the words "or local Act authority".

Peter Shore,
Secretary of State for the Environment

1st August 1977.

(a) S.I. 1970/1666.

EXPLANATORY NOTE

(This Note is not part of the Regulations.)

The Common Council of the City of London administer a superannuation scheme under local Acts; this scheme is the last remaining "local Act scheme" (defined in section 8(5) of the Superannuation Act 1972). Outside the City of London the superannuation of local government employees in England and Wales (and of certain other persons) is provided for by regulations under section 7 of the Act of 1972 ("the national scheme"), the principal of which are the Local Government Superannuation Regulations 1974 which came into operation on 1st April 1974.

These Regulations revoke the City's local Act scheme and replace it by the national scheme.

In particular—

(1) Regulation 3 amends the regulations of 1974 by including the Common Council among the bodies which are under a duty to maintain a superannuation fund for the purposes of the regulations of 1974 and by including among the bodies whose employees are to be or may be superannuable under those regulations the Common Council, the probation and after-care committee for the City of London probation and after-care area and the Board of Governors of the Museum of London.

(2) Regulation 4 makes provision for the winding-up of the fund maintained under the City's local Act scheme, which is required to be valued as at 1st April 1974 (regulation 5), and for the transfer of its assets and liabilities to the fund to be maintained by the Common Council under the regulations of 1974.

(3) Regulation 6 ensures that no employee who immediately before the date of coming into operation of these regulations was a contributor to the City's local Act superannuation fund fails to become superannuable on that date under the national scheme.

(4) Regulation 7 enables certain employees who were not contributors to the City's local Act superannuation fund, but would by virtue of these regulations become superannuable under the national scheme, to opt out of the last-mentioned scheme.

(5) Regulations 8 to 15 and 18 modify the regulations of 1974 in their application in the City. The principal modifications are directed to two matters—(i) conferring on, or in respect of, certain persons who, at any time within the 12 months before the coming into operation of these regulations, have been contributors to the City's local Act superannuation fund the like rights and powers as respects the reckoning under the regulations of 1974 of periods of service reckonable under the City's local Act scheme and other periods as would have been conferred by those regulations had that scheme been replaced by the national scheme on 1st April 1974, and (ii) preserving special rights enjoyed under the City's local Act scheme by, and in respect of, those persons.

(6) Regulation 16 preserves, by way of amendment to the regulations of 1974, a local Act discretion to increase service.

(7) Regulation 17 applies, with modifications, Part K of the regulations of 1974 (which gave rights to benefits under those regulations, but with power to opt out, to, and in respect of, persons who retired or died in their employment between 30th March 1972 and 1st April 1974) to, and in respect of, persons who, having been contributors to the City's local Act superannuation fund, retired or died in their employment between 30th March 1972 and the coming into operation of these regulations. Express power for this retrospective operation is contained in section 12 of the Act of 1972.

(8) Regulation 19 provides for the reckoning by persons transferred to the employment of the Common Council under the National Health Service Reorganisation Act 1973 of service reckonable by them under the National Health Service superannuation scheme; alternatively they can opt to retain rights corresponding to those which they enjoyed under that scheme. Similar provisions, applicable to persons to whom the regulations of 1974 applied on 1st April 1974, are contained in regulation J17(3) of those regulations.

(9) Regulation 20 preserves the existing rights and liabilities under the regulations of 1974 of a small number of employees of the Common Council who were not contributors to the City's local Act superannuation fund, but were superannuable under the national scheme before the coming into operation of these regulations.

(10) Regulations 21 and 22 make minor and consequential amendments.

(11) Regulation 23 provides for repeals and revocations; in particular it revokes the City's local Act scheme.

STATUTORY INSTRUMENTS

1977 No. 1342

LOCAL GOVERNMENT, ENGLAND AND WALES

The Rate Support Grants (Adjustment of Needs Element) (Amendment) Regulations 1977

Made - - -	*1st August* 1977
Laid before Parliament	*10th August* 1977
Coming into Operation	*1st September* 1977

The Secretary of State for Education and Science, in exercise of the powers conferred upon her by section 10(3) of the Local Government Act 1974(**a**) and paragraph 3 of Schedule 2 thereto after consulting with such associations of local authorities as appeared to her to be concerned and with the local authority with whom consultation appeared to her to be desirable in accordance with section 10(5) of the said Act, hereby makes the following regulations:—

1.—(1) These regulations may be cited as the Rate Support Grants (Adjustment of Needs Element) (Amendment) Regulations 1977 and shall come into operation on 1st September 1977.

(2) In these regulations "the principal regulations" means the Rate Support Grants (Adjustment of Needs Element) Regulations 1976(**b**).

2. For sub-paragraph (*f*) of regulation 2 of the principal regulations (expenditure to which those regulations apply) there shall be substituted the following provisions:—

"(*f*) in making payments to or in respect of accountants seconded to a Cost Investigation Unit administered by the Secretary of State for the purpose of research into any of the functions of authorities;

(*g*) in the maintenance of the Hereward College of Further Education for the Physically Handicapped and being—

(i) expenditure by way of the payment of ground rent in respect of the site of the said College or of loan charges in respect of capital expenditure incurred or contracted for before 1st September 1977 in connection with the provision of the site, buildings, car parks, furniture and equipment of the said College, or

(ii) other expenditure incurred in the maintenance of the College before 1st September 1977;

(*h*) in making payments to persons who cease to be employed as teachers in colleges of education and become employed either by a local authority in a different capacity or as teachers in voluntary schools."

(**a**) 1974 c. 7.   (**b**) S.I. 1976/1939 (1976 III, p. 5200).

3. In regulation 4(1) of the principal regulations (apportionment of expenditure)—

    (*a*) for the words "regulation 2(*d*) to (*f*)" there shall be substituted the words "regulation 2(*d*) to (*g*)";

    (*b*) for the words "regulation 2(*a*) to (*c*)" in both places where they occur there shall be substituted the words "regulation 2(*a*), (*b*), (*c*) and (*h*)".

4. Nothing in regulation 3 above shall affect the principal regulations in their application to a financial year (within the meaning thereof) beginning before 1st April 1978.

Given under the Official Seal of the Secretary of State for Education and Science on 1st August 1977.

(L.S.)

Shirley Williams,
Secretary of State for Education and Science.

EXPLANATORY NOTE

(This Note is not part of the Regulations.)

These Regulations amend the Rate Support Grants (Adjustment of Needs Element) Regulations 1976.

First, they provide that maintenance expenditure on the Hereward College of Further Education for the Physically Handicapped shall not on 1st September 1977 cease to be expenditure to which the regulations of 1976 apply insofar as it relates to the payment of ground rent and loan charges.

Secondly, they alter the apportionment between authorities of certain expenditure. They provide that expenditure in making payments in certain cases to persons who cease to be employed as teachers in colleges of education shall be apportioned in like manner as expenditure in maintaining such colleges.

STATUTORY INSTRUMENTS

1977 No. 1344

OFFSHORE INSTALLATIONS

The Continental Shelf (Protection of Installations) (No. 4) Order 1977

Made - - - -	*2nd August* 1977
Laid before Parliament	*3rd August* 1977
Coming into Operation	*3rd August* 1977

The Secretary of State, in exercise of powers conferred by section 2(1) of the Continental Shelf Act 1964(a) (hereinafter referred to as "the Act") and now vested in him(b), hereby orders as follows:—

1.—(1) This Order may be cited as the Continental Shelf (Protection of Installations) (No. 4) Order 1977 and shall come into operation on 3rd August 1977.

(2) The Interpretation Act 1889(c) shall apply to the interpretation of this Order as it applies to the interpretation of an Act of Parliament.

2.—(1) Subject to paragraph (2) of this Article, for the purpose of protecting the offshore installation designated in the Schedule hereto, ships are hereby prohibited from entering, without the consent of the Secretary of State, that area (hereinafter referred to as a "safety zone") specified in the said Schedule (being a part of an area designated by an Order in Council made under section 1(7) of the Act).

(2) Nothing in paragraph (1) of this Article shall apply to prohibit a ship from entering the safety zone:
- (*a*) in connection with the laying, inspection, testing, repair, alteration, renewal or removal of any submarine cable or pipe-line in or near that safety zone;
- (*b*) to provide services for, to transport persons or goods to or from, or under the authority of a government department to inspect, an installation in that safety zone;
- (*c*) if it is a ship belonging to a general lighthouse authority and it enters to perform duties relating to the safety of navigation;
- (*d*) when carrying out movements with a view to saving or attempting to save life or property;
- (*e*) owing to stress of weather; or
- (*f*) when in distress.

John Cunningham,
Parliamentary Under Secretary of State,
2nd August 1977.   Department of Energy.

(**a**) 1964 c. 29.
(**b**) S.I. 1969/1498, 1970/1537 (1969 III, p. 4797; 1970 III, p. 5293).
(**c**) 1889 c. 63.

SCHEDULE

SAFETY ZONE

The area within a radius of 500 metres of the point having the co-ordinates of latitude and longitude according to European Datum (1950) set out in columns 1 and 2 of the table below in respect of the offshore installation the name or other designation of which is set opposite those co-ordinates in column 3 of the said table.

TABLE

1	2	3
Latitude North	Longitude East	Name or other designation of offshore installation
53° 17′ 55″	02° 37′ 11″	49/24–L

EXPLANATORY NOTE

(This Note is not part of the Order.)

This Order specifies as a safety zone a certain sea area (being an area within a radius of 500 metres of an offshore installation) and prohibits ships from entering the zone except with the permission of the Secretary of State or in the circumstances provided for in Article 2(2).

STATUTORY INSTRUMENTS

1977 No. 1345 (S. 99)

SPORTS GROUNDS

The Safety of Sports Grounds (Designation) (Scotland) Order 1977

Made - - -	*29th July* 1977
Laid before Parliament	*9th August* 1977
Coming into Operation	*1st January* 1978

In exercise of the powers conferred on me by section 1(1) of the Safety of Sports Grounds Act 1975(**a**), and of all other powers enabling me in that behalf, and after consultation with such persons or bodies of persons as appear to me requisite, I hereby make the following order:—

1.—(1) This order, which extends to Scotland only, may be cited as the Safety of Sports Grounds (Designation) (Scotland) Order 1977 and shall come into operation on 1st January 1978.

(2) The Interpretation Act 1889(**b**) shall apply for the interpretation of this order as it applies for the interpretation of an Act of Parliament.

2. Each stadium specified in the Schedule to this order, being a sports stadium which in the opinion of the Secretary of State has accommodation for more than 10,000 spectators, is hereby designated as a stadium requiring a safety certificate under the Safety of Sports Grounds Act 1975.

Bruce Millan,
One of Her Majesty's Principal
Secretaries of State.

New St. Andrew's House,
Edinburgh.
29th July 1977.

SCHEDULE   *Article* 2

STADIA IN SCOTLAND DESIGNATED AS REQUIRING SAFETY CERTIFICATES UNDER THE
SAFETY OF SPORTS GROUNDS ACT 1975

Kilbowie Park, Clydebank.
Love Street Park, Paisley.

(**a**) 1975 c. 52.   (**b**) 1889 c. 63.

EXPLANATORY NOTE

(This Note is not part of the Order.)

This Order designates Kilbowie Park, Clydebank and Love Street Park, Paisley as stadia which require safety certificates under the Safety of Sports Grounds Act 1975. Other sports stadia in Scotland which require safety certificates are designated under the Safety of Sports Grounds (Designation) (Scotland) Order 1976 (S.I. 1976/1285).

STATUTORY INSTRUMENTS

1977 No. 1348 (C.45)

COMPANIES

The Companies Act 1976 (Commencement No. 5) Order 1977

Made - - - *2nd August* 1977

The Secretary of State, in exercise of his powers under section 45(3) of the Companies Act 1976(**a**), hereby makes the following Order:—

1. This Order may be cited as the Companies Act 1976 (Commencement No. 5) Order 1977.

2.—(1) Subject to paragraph (2) below and to the limitations mentioned in the first column of the Schedule hereto, the provisions of the Companies Act 1976 specified in that Schedule shall come into operation on 1 October 1977.

(2) Paragraph (1) of this article shall not apply to sections 1(9), 1(10), 8, 12(12), 42(1) and 42(2) of, and Schedules 2 and 3 to, the Companies Act 1976 insofar as they relate to the repeal or amendment of any provision of the Companies Acts as that provision is applied to unregistered companies by virtue of section 435 of the Companies Act 1948(**b**).

Stanley Clinton Davis,

Parliamentary Under-Secretary of State,
Department of Trade.

2nd August, 1977.

(**a**) 1976 c. 69.   (**b**) 1948 c. 38.

SCHEDULE

PROVISIONS COMING INTO OPERATION ON 1 OCTOBER 1977

Provisions of the Act	Subject matter of provisions
Section 1.	Duty to prepare, lay and deliver accounts by reference to accounting reference periods.
Section 2, so far as it is not already in operation.	Accounting reference period of a company.
Section 3.	Alteration of accounting reference period.
Section 4(1), (2) and (5).	Penalties for not complying with section 1 within the period allowed for laying and delivering accounts.
Section 5.	Default order in case of continued failure to comply with section 1(7) after the end of the period allowed for laying and delivering accounts.
Section 6.	The period allowed for laying and delivering accounts.
Section 7(1) to (6).	Transitional provisions and savings.
Section 7(7), except in relation to proceedings for an offence under section 148 of the Companies Act 1948 against an unregistered company to which the said section 148 is applied by virtue of section 435 of that Act.	
Section 7(8).	
Section 8.	Group accounts.
Section 9.	Duty to prepare and deliver accounts in the case of oversea companies.
Section 10, so far as it is not already in operation.	Accounting reference period of oversea company.
Section 11.	Penalty for not complying with section 9 within the period allowed for delivering accounts.
Section 12.	Accounting records.

Provisions of the Act	Subject matter of provisions
Section 34(1), except insofar as it amends section 52(1)(a) of the Companies Act 1948.	Use of prescribed forms for notices under the Companies Act 1967(a).
Section 42(1), insofar as it relates to the amendment of the statutory provisions mentioned below in relation to Schedule 2.	Minor and consequential amendments.
Section 42(2), insofar as it relates to the repeal of, or of words in, the statutory provisions mentioned below in relation to Schedule 3.	Repeals.
Schedule 1, except insofar as it relates to the amendment of section 52(1)(a) of the Companies Act 1948.	Prescribed forms for the Companies Act 1967.
Schedule 2, insofar as it amends— (a) the following provisions of the Companies Act 1948, namely—sections 149(6), 151(1), 152(1), 155, 156(1), 157(1), 158(1), 415 and 436; in Schedule 1, regulation 123 in Part I of Table A and article 60 of Table C, regulation 124 in Part I of Table A and article 61 of Table C, regulation 126 in Part I of Table A and article 63 of Table C and regulation 127 in Part I of Table A and article 64 of Table C; (b) paragraph 24(1) of Schedule 2 to the Betting, Gaming and Lotteries Act 1963(b), except in relation to unregistered companies to which section 148 of the Companies Act 1948 is applied by virtue of section 435 of that Act;	Minor and consequential amendments.

(a) 1967 c.81.   (b) 1963 c. 2.

Provisions of the Act	Subject matter of provisions
(c) the following provisions of the Protection of Depositors Act 1963(**a**) namely— section 13(4), except in relation to unregistered companies to which any provision in Part IV of the Companies Act 1948 is applied by virtue of section 435 of that Act; and section 16(1)(*d*), except in relation to unregistered companies to which section 147 of the Companies Act 1948 is applied by virtue of section 435 of that Act.	
(*d*) the following provisions of the Companies Act 1967, namely—sections 14, 15(1) and 23 and Schedule 3;	
(*e*) section 46(1)(c) of the Insurance Companies Act 1974(**b**), except in relation to unregistered companies to which section 147 of the Companies Act 1948 is applied by virtue of section 435 of that Act.	
Schedule 3 insofar as it provides for the repeal of, or of words in, the following provisions:—	Repeals.
(*d*) sections 127, 147, 148, 153(2), 331 and 410 of the Companies Act 1948 and in Schedule 15 to that Act the entry relating to section 410;	
(*b*) section 13(7) of the Protection of Depositors Act 1963, except in relation to unregistered companies to which section 127 of the Companies Act 1948 is applied by virtue of section 435 of that Act;	

Provisions of the Act	Subject matter of provisions
(c) in section 21 of the Companies Act 1967, the words "laid before it in general meeting"; section 47 of that Act; in section 56(2) of that Act, the words from "and in subsection (3)" to "that subsection"; in Schedule 4 to that Act, the entry relating to section 410.	
(d) in section 24(5) of the Iron and Steel Act 1975(a), at the end, the words "laid before it in general meeting", except insofar as that subsection relates to the report of the directors of unregistered companies to which section 157 of the Companies Act 1948 is applied by virtue of section 435 of that Act.	

EXPLANATORY NOTE

(This Note is not part of the Order.)

This Order brings into force on 1 October 1977 the provisions of the Companies Act 1976 specified in the Schedule to the Order. These provisions relate to the duty to prepare, lay and deliver accounts by reference to accounting reference periods and to keep and preserve proper accounting records. The Order also brings into operation on the same date certain minor and consequential amendments and repeals, except in relation to unregistered companies within the meaning of section 435 of the Companies Act 1948.

(a) 1975 c. 64.

STATUTORY INSTRUMENTS

1977 No. 1349

TERMS AND CONDITIONS OF EMPLOYMENT

The Guarantee Payments (Exemption) (No. 9) Order 1977

Made - - - - 2nd August 1977

Coming into Operation 8th September 1977

Whereas the National Agreement between the Cut Sole Associates—British Leather Federation and the National Union of the Footwear, Leather and Allied Trades is a collective agreement which makes provision whereby employees to whom the said agreement relates have a right to guaranteed remuneration:

And whereas the parties to the said collective agreement (whose descriptions are set out in Schedule 1 to this Order) all made application to the Secretary of State under section 28(1) of the Employment Protection Act 1975(a) ("the Act"):

And whereas the Secretary of State, having regard to the provisions of the agreement (which so far as are material are set out in Schedule 2 to this Order), is satisfied that section 22 of the Act should not apply to those employees:

And whereas the said agreement complies with section 28(4) of the Act:

Now, therefore, the Secretary of State in exercise of the powers conferred on him as the appropriate Minister under section 28(1) of the Act and of all other powers enabling him in that behalf, hereby makes the following Order:—

Citation and commencement

1. This Order may be cited as the Guarantee Payments (Exemption) (No. 9) Order 1977 and shall come into operation on 8th September 1977.

Interpretation

2.—(1) The Interpretation Act 1889(b) shall apply to the interpretation of this Order as it applies to the interpretation of an Act of Parliament.

(2) The "exempted agreement" means the National Agreement between the Cut Sole Associates—British Leather Federation and the National Union of the Footwear, Leather and Allied Trades.

Exemption

3. Section 22 of the Act shall not apply to any person who is an employee to whom the exempted agreement relates.

Signed by order of the Secretary of State.

Harold Walker,
2nd August 1977. Minister of State,
Department of Employment.

(a) 1975 c. 71. (b) 1889 c. 63.

SCHEDULE 1

PARTIES TO THE COLLECTIVE AGREEMENT

1. *Representing Employers:*
   the Cut Sole Associates—British Leather Federation.

2. *Representing Employees:*
   the National Union of the Footwear, Leather and Allied Trades.

SCHEDULE 2

MATERIAL PROVISIONS OF THE EXEMPTED AGREEMENT

A. *Guaranteed Wages Agreement (Schedule B to the Agreement)*

1. The Agreement provides that each employee under contract of service with an employer in the Cut Sole industry, who is subject to the provisions of the National Agreement, 1974, shall, for each week when the employee is available for and willing to work, be guaranteed a wage in accordance with the Provisions of this Agreement.

It shall be obligatory on the part of the employer to pay the guaranteed wage when due, without claim to be made by the operative.

2. Each employee must be capable of, available for and willing to perform the work associated with his usual occupation, or reasonable alternative work where his usual work is not available.

In case of any difficulty in interpretation of what is reasonable alternative work, it shall be settled, if possible, by consultation between the local officer(s) of the Union and representatives of the firm concerned.

3. The normal working week of 40 hours consisting of the days for which payment is made up shall, during the currency of this Agreement, unless otherwise amended, be regarded as the week under the guarantee for dayworkers and pieceworkers,
except that
the week under the guarantee for part-time employees who by agreement with their employers are not employed for the full normal working week of 40 hours, shall be the subject of agreement between the employer and the employee(a).

4. Subject to Clauses 7 and 8, the weekly wages of all employees, both dayworkers and pieceworkers, shall be guaranteed as follows:

To the Dayworker

75 per cent of the Contract Weekly Wage Rates.

To the Pieceworker

75 per cent of the Basic Weekly Wage, calculated in accordance with Clause 5.

5. The basic weekly wage for pieceworkers shall be assessed subject to the following conditions:

(a) The basic weekly wage shall be calculated according to the piece-worker's average earnings for a 40 hour week, exclusive of overtime and all time lost by the employee on account of bad timekeeping, during a period of four full consecutive weeks of normal productive employment.

(b) Where either the employer or the employee consider the average weekly earnings, assessed in accordance with paragraph (a) above to be inappropriate or unfair, an alternative period of four full weeks of

---

(a) It has been agreed between the parties to the exempted agreement that, in calculating the guarantee to which part-time workers are entitled, the same principles apply as apply to the calculation of the guarantee for employees working the normal working week of forty hours. In all cases, the guarantee represents 75% of the employee's average earnings as assessed under Clauses 4 and 5 and related to the number of hours for which he has contracted to work.

normal productive employment shall be agreed. Where such alternative period is not available an agreed figure shall be established by negotiation. If the employer and employee fail to agree upon an alternative period or figure the usual procedure of negotiation shall be used to settle the dispute.

(c) The basic weekly wage of all new piecework employees shall be assessed in accordance with paragraph (a) above within a period of 9 weeks from the date of taking up employment.

(d) The employer shall inform each pieceworker of the basic weekly wage assessed in accordance with (a) above.

6. At quarterly intervals, in order to take account of a change in an employee's earning capacity arising from any cause, the employer or the employee may give notice to the other of reassessment of the basic average wage. For the purpose of such reassessment there shall be calculated the employee's rate of average earnings for a 40 hour week, exclusive of overtime and all time lost by the employee on account of bad timekeeping, during an agreed period of four full weeks of normal productive employment.

> (NOTE: When a change takes place in the percentage additions to piecework rates in March and/or September, the pieceworker's basic weekly wage shall be adjusted by a percentage equal to the difference between the old and the new piecework percentage additions in force with effect from the beginning of the working week in which the change takes place.)

7. The guarantees prescribed in Clause 4 shall not apply:

(a) in respect of all time lost by the employee on his own responsibility, through sickness or any other cause, and the week under the guarantee shall be reduced correspondingly.

(b) in the event of a breakdown of machinery, fire, flood, or stoppage of fuel or power supply, affecting the whole of a department, or more, the week under the guarantee shall be reduced correspondingly in respect of each employee affected by such occurrence.

(c) at holiday times and stocktaking, at which times the days of holiday or stocktaking exempt from the guarantee shall not exceed:

		Days paid under the Holidays with Pay Agreement
Easter	3 working days	Good Friday, Easter Monday and Easter Tuesday, or Easter Monday, Easter Tuesday and Easter Wednesday.
Spring Bank Holiday (or alternative)	2 working days	Spring Bank Holiday Monday and Tuesday.
Late Summer Bank Holiday (or alternative)	1 working day	Late Summer Bank Holiday (or alternative).
Annual Holiday	15 working days	3 working weeks.
Christmas	3 working days	Christmas Eve, Christmas Day and Boxing Day when any of these fall on working days of the week.
New Year's Day	1 working day	New Year's Day, when this falls on a working day of the week.

(NOTE: When Christmas Eve, Christmas Day, Boxing Day or New Year's Day do not fall on working days of the week, they are not reckoned within the 3 days, or 1 day as the case may be, but are still required to be paid for under the Holidays with Pay Agreement.)

Stocktaking   2 working days

provided that

  (i) one additional day may be added at the instance of the employer to the above mentioned number of days at any holiday period by agreement between the employer and his employees, and to ascertain the views of the employees, a ballot shall be taken of either the whole factory, if it is intended to close the whole factory, or of the individual departments affected. In each case the majority of the votes cast shall be decisive.

 (ii) for the purposes of stocktaking only, at the direction of the employer, one additional day only may be added to any holiday period, or the two days may be taken other than at a holiday period provided that not more than two such days are added or taken in one year;

and the week under the guarantee shall be reduced by the actual days of holiday and stocktaking.

> NOTE: a stocktaking day is defined as a day on which, for the purpose of taking stock, it is not possible to process work in progress. This would normally involve a physical check of stock, including work which is being processed through a factory, and which further involves the necessity of stopping the whole factory or department on the day in question.

8. In the event of any employees in a department or a factory taking part in a strike, the guarantee shall cease to apply to all employees employed in the factory immediately upon notification of the strike to the General Secretary of the National Union and to the Union Branch Secretary where the strike takes place.

9. The respective parties to this Agreement, namely the Cut Sole Associates—British Leather Federation and the National Union of the Footwear, Leather and Allied Trades, undertake to use their best endeavours to promote good time-keeping and regular attendance on the part of the employees in the interests of regularity of working, efficiency of organisation and full output, and further, they re-affirm the statement of reciprocal obligations in Clause 10 of the National Agreement 1974 namely:

It shall be obligatory:

  (i) On the part of the Employer to pay the full rate of wages for all output.

 (ii) On the part of the Employees to use their trade skill and productive ability to the best advantage and fullest capacity and with no restriction of output following a change of organisation or machinery.

10. This Agreement is an integral part of the National Agreement between the Cut Sole Associates and the Union, and any question which may arise as to the interpretation of this Guaranteed Wages Agreement shall be interpreted by a Joint Sub-Committee of the Associates and the Union to be appointed for this purpose.

11. Nothing in this Agreement is intended to override or supersede Clause 6 of the National Agreement, 1974.

12. This Agreement, as amended, takes effect as and from the 28th February or 1st March 1974 and shall continue in operation concurrently with, and shall become part of the National Agreement, 1974 and its operation and ratification shall be in accordance with Clause 27 of the National Agreement.

B. *Additional provisions added by an Addendum dated 14th October 1976*

13. It shall be permissible for the Cut Sole Associates of the British Leather Federation and the National Union to agree jointly to a temporary suspension of this Guaranteed Wages Agreement in exceptional circumstances.

14. This Guaranteed Wages Agreement shall remain in force so long as exemption from the relevant provisions of the Employment Protection Act 1975 shall be allowed by the Government.

C. *Disputes Procedure (Clause 24 of the Agreement)*

24. In case of any dispute as to the interpretation and application of this Agreement an Arbitration Board shall be appointed, consisting of two Union representatives and two members of the Cut Sole Associates—British Leather Federation, with an independent chairman. The findings of this Board to be final and binding.

EXPLANATORY NOTE

(This Note is not part of the Order.)

This Order excludes from the operation of section 22 of the Employment Protection Act 1975 employees to whom the National Agreement between the Cut Sole Associates—British Leather Federation and the National Union of the Footwear, Leather and Allied Trades relates.

Copies of the Agreement are available for inspection between 10 a.m. and noon and between 2 p.m. and 5 p.m. on any week-day (except Saturdays) at the offices of the Department of Employment, 8 St. James's Square, London SW1Y 4JB.

STATUTORY INSTRUMENTS

1977 No. 1353

INDUSTRIAL ASSURANCE

The Industrial Assurance (Premium Receipt Books) (Amendment) Regulations 1977

Made - - - -	*29th July* 1977
Laid before Parliament	*11th August* 1977
Coming into Operation	*1st September* 1977

The Industrial Assurance Commissioner, with the approval of the Treasury, in pursuance of subsection (2) of section 8 of the Industrial Assurance and Friendly Societies Act 1948(**a**), and of all other powers enabling him in that behalf, hereby makes the following Regulations:—

1.—(1) These Regulations may be cited as the Industrial Assurance (Premium Receipt Books) (Amendment) Regulations 1977 and shall come into operation on 1st September 1977.

(2) The rules for the construction of Acts of Parliament contained in the Interpretation Act 1889(**b**) shall apply for the purpose of the interpretation of these Regulations.

2. The Industrial Assurance (Premium Receipt Books) Regulations 1948(**c**), as amended by the Industrial Assurance (Premium Receipt Books) (Amendment) Regulations 1961(**d**), shall be amended by the addition after sub-paragraph (*e*) of paragraph (2) of regulation 6 of the following sub-paragraphs:

"(*f*) "the amount of the premium" in relation to a policy to which the prescribed scheme, or an approved scheme which provides for payment of net premiums, applies, means the amount of the net premium; and

(*g*) "the prescribed scheme", "an approved scheme" and "net premium" have the meanings assigned in paragraph (1) of regulation 2 of the Industrial Assurance (Life Assurance Premium Relief) Regulations 1977(**e**)."

K. Brading,
Industrial Assurance Commissioner

Date: 20th July 1977

We approve these Regulations

T. E. Graham,
J. Dormand,
Two of the Lords Commissioners
of Her Majesty's Treasury

Date: 29th July 1977

(**a**) 1948 c. 39. (**c**) S.I. 1948/2770 (Rev. VIII, p. 915; 1948 I, p. 1619).
(**b**) 1889 c. 63. (**d**) S.I. 1961/597 (1961 I, p. 1312).
(**e**)S.I. 1977/1144 (1977 II, p. 3216).

EXPLANATORY NOTE

(This Note is not part of the Regulations.)

The Industrial Assurance (Premium Receipt Books) Regulations 1948, as amended by these Regulations, will require that where, after 6th April 1979, tax relief on premiums paid on policies of industrial assurance is effected by the premium payer retaining $17\frac{1}{2}$ per cent of the premium, the particulars included in premium receipt books shall include the net amount of the premium after deduction of the amount retained.

STATUTORY INSTRUMENTS

1977 No. 1356 (S.101)

EDUCATION, SCOTLAND

The Education Authority Bursaries (Scotland) Amendment (No. 2) Regulations 1977

Made - - - -	*2nd August* 1977
Laid before Parliament	*8th August* 1977
Coming into Operation	*9th August* 1977

In exercise of the powers conferred upon me by sections 49(3) and 144(5) of the Education (Scotland) Act 1962(a) and of all other powers enabling me in that behalf, I hereby make the following regulations:—

Citation and commencement

1. These regulations, which may be cited as the Education Authority Bursaries (Scotland) Amendment (No. 2) Regulations 1977, shall come into operation on 9th August 1977.

Amendment of regulations

2. In the Education Authority Bursaries (Scotland) Amendment Regulations 1977(b), for sub-paragraph (iv) of Regulation 3(c) the following sub-paragraph is hereby substituted—

"(iv) for sub-paragraph 1(8) there shall be substituted the following sub-paragraph—

'An allowance of £6 a week towards the personal expenses of the holder, after he has attained the age of 18 years, during periods other than vacations.' "

Bruce Millan,
One of Her Majesty's Principal
Secretaries of State.

New St. Andrew's House,
Edinburgh.

2nd August 1977.

(a) 1962 c. 47.

(b) S.I. 1977/1150 (1977 II, p. 3235)

EXPLANATORY NOTE

(This Note is not part of the Regulations.)

These Regulations make an amendment to Schedule 2 part 1 paragraph 1(8) of the Education Authority Bursaries (Scotland) Regulations 1969 in substitution for the amendment of that sub-paragraph made in Regulation 3(*c*)(iv) of the Education Authority Bursaries (Scotland) Amendment Regulations 1977. These Regulations make clear that an allowance towards personal expenses shall be payable only to the holder of a category B Bursary during term-time.

STATUTORY INSTRUMENTS

1977 No. 1358 (S. 102)

ELECTRICITY

The North of Scotland Hydro-Electric Board (Compensation for Smelter Deficits) (No. 2) Order 1977

Laid before the House of Commons in draft

Made - - - -	28*th July* 1977
Coming into Operation	29*th July* 1977

In exercise of the powers conferred upon me by section 2(1) of the Electricity (Financial Provisions) (Scotland) Act 1976(a) and of all other powers enabling me in that behalf, and after consultation with the North of Scotland Hydro-Electric Board (hereinafter referred to as the Board), I hereby, with the consent of the Treasury, make the following order, a draft of which has been laid before the House of Commons and has been approved by resolution of that House in accordance with section 3(1) of the said Act:—

1. This order may be cited as the North of Scotland Hydro-Electric Board (Compensation for Smelter Deficits) (No. 2) Order 1977 and shall come into operation on 29th July 1977.

2. The Interpretation Act 1889(b) shall apply for the interpretation of this order as it applies for the interpretation of an Act of Parliament.

3. The sum of £11,112,061 shall be paid by me to the Board in compensation for the deficit incurred by the Board, including interest charges on monies necessarily borrowed to finance that deficit, during the year ended 31st March 1977 under the contract entered into in 1968 between the Board and the British Aluminium Company Limited for the supply of electricity to that Company's aluminium reduction plant at Invergordon.

4. The sum of £130,008 shall be paid by me to the Board in reimbursement of the capital contributions paid by the Board to the South of Scotland Electricity Board between 19th February and 31st March 1977, including interest charges on monies necessarily borrowed to finance those contributions, to maintain entitlement to that part of the generating capacity of Hunterston "B" nuclear power station assigned to the Board for the purpose of supplying electricity to the British Aluminium Company Limited for the operation of that Company's aluminium reduction plant at Invergordon.

(a) 1976 c. 61.   (b) 1889 c. 63.

Bruce Millan,
One of Her Majesty's Principal
Secretaries of State.

New St. Andrew's House,
Edinburgh.
25th July 1977.

We consent.
28th July 1977.

Donald R. Coleman,
T. E. Graham,
Two of the Lords Commissioners
of Her Majesty's Treasury.

EXPLANATORY NOTE

(This Note is not part of the Order.)

This Order specifies the payments to be made to the North of Scotland Hydro-Electric Board in compensation for the deficit and interest thereon incurred by the Board during the year ended 31st March 1977 in supplying electricity to the aluminium reduction plant of the British Aluminium Company Limited at Invergordon, and in reimbursement of the capital contributions paid by the Board to the South of Scotland Electricity Board between 19th February and 31st March 1977 to maintain entitlement to that part of the generating capacity of Hunterston "B" nuclear power station assigned to the Board for the purpose of supplying electricity to the Invergordon aluminium reduction plant, and interest thereon.

STATUTORY INSTRUMENTS

1977 No. 1359 (S.103)

NATIONAL ASSISTANCE SERVICES

The National Assistance (Charges for Accommodation) (Scotland) Regulations 1977

Made - - - -	1st *August* 1977
Laid before Parliament	11th *August* 1977
Coming into Operation	14th *November* 1977

In exercise of the powers conferred on me by section 22 of the National Assistance Act 1948(a) as read with section 87(3) and (4) of the Social Work (Scotland) Act 1968(b), and of all other powers enabling me in that behalf, I hereby make the following regulations:—

Citation and commencement

1. These regulations may be cited as the National Assistance (Charges for Accommodation) (Scotland) Regulations 1977, and shall come into operation on 14th November 1977.

Interpretation

2.—(1) In these regulations, unless the context otherwise requires—

"the Act of 1948" means the National Assistance Act 1948;

"the Act of 1975" means the Social Security Act 1975(c);

"Personal Injuries Scheme", "Service Pensions Instrument" and "1914–18 War Injuries Scheme" have the same meanings as in the Social Security (Overlapping Benefits) Regulations 1975(d).

(2) Any reference in these regulations to the provisions of an enactment or instrument shall be construed, unless the context otherwise requires, as a reference to that enactment or instrument as amended, varied, extended or applied by or under any other enactment or instrument.

(3) The Interpretation Act 1889(e) shall apply for the interpretation of these regulations as it applies for the interpretation of an Act of Parliament, and as if these regulations and the regulations hereby revoked were Acts of Parliament.

Revocation of existing regulations

3. The National Assistance (Charges for Accommodation) (Scotland) Regulations 1976(f) are hereby revoked.

Prescription of minimum charges

4. For the purposes of section 22(3) of the Act of 1948 (which relates to charges to be made for accommodation provided under Part III of the Act) the liability of a person to pay for accommodation provided in premises managed by a local authority shall in no case be reduced below the sum of £14.00 per week.

(a) 1948 c. 29.   (b) 1968 c. 49.   (c) 1975 c. 14.
(d) S.I. 1975/554 (1975 I, p. 1918).   (e) 1889 c. 63.
(f) S.I. 1976/1670 (1976 III, p. 4203).

5. Where accommodation is provided for a child accompanied by a person over the age of 16, the liability of that person under section 22(7) of the Act of 1948 to pay for the accommodation of that child shall in no case be reduced below such of the following sums as is appropriate, that is to say—

(a) in respect of a child under 5 years of age, the sum of £4.10 per week;

(b) in respect of a child aged 5 years or over but less than 11 years, the sum of £4.95 per week;

(c) in respect of a child aged 11 years or over but less than 13 years, the sum of £6.10 per week;

(d) in respect of a child aged 13 years or over but less than 16 years, the sum of £7.40 per week.

Prescription of sum needed for personal requirements

6. For the purposes of section 22(4) of the Act of 1948 a local authority shall assume that a person to whom subsection (3) of that section applies will need for his personal requirements the sum of £3.50 per week:

Provided that if that person is someone to whom there is payable attendance allowance under the provisions of section 35 of the Act of 1975 or constant attendance allowance under any Personal Injuries Scheme, Service Pensions Instrument or any 1914–18 War Injuries Scheme, the aforementioned sum assumed to be needed for his personal requirements shall be increased by the amount of such attendance allowance or constant attendance allowance.

Bruce Millan
One of Her Majesty's Principal
Secretaries of State.

New St. Andrew's House,
Edinburgh.
1st August 1977.

EXPLANATORY NOTE
(This Note is not part of the Regulations.)

These Regulations replace the National Assistance (Charges for Accommodation) (Scotland) Regulations 1976. The minimum weekly amount which a person is required to pay for accommodation provided for him under the Social Work (Scotland) Act 1968 (which by virtue of section 87(3) of that Act is to be regarded for purposes of charges as accommodation provided under Part III of the National Assistance Act 1948) is increased from £12.25 to £14.00 per week. In the case of a person accompanied by a child, the weekly amounts payable in respect of the child are increased from £3.60 to £4.10 when the child is under 5 years, from £4.35 to £4.95 when the child is aged 5 years or over but less than 11 years, from £5.35 to £6.10 when the child is 11 years or over but less than 13 years, and from £6.50 to £7.40 when the child is 13 years or over but less than 16 years. The weekly sum for personal requirements which (unless in special circumstances the local authority considers a different sum appropriate) the local authority shall allow in assessing a person's ability to pay for accommodation is increased from £3.05 to £3.50 but if the person is one to whom there is payable attendance allowance under the Social Security Act 1975 or constant attendance allowance under any Personal Injuries Scheme, Service Pensions Instrument or any 1914–18 War Injuries Scheme, the weekly sum for personal requirements shall be increased by that amount.

STATUTORY INSTRUMENTS

1977 No. 1360 (S. 104)

EDUCATION, SCOTLAND

The Teachers' Superannuation (Scotland) Regulations 1977

Made - - - -	*1st August* 1977
Laid before Parliament	*17th August* 1977
Coming into Operation	*7th September* 1977

ARRANGEMENT OF REGULATIONS

PART I

GENERAL

PART II

CONTRIBUTIONS

Part III

Added Years

Part IV

Contributions for Pre-April 1972 Family Pensions

Part V

Return of Contributions

Part X

Financial Provisions

Part XI

Supplementary Provisions

Schedules

In exercise of the powers conferred on me by sections 9 and 12(1) of the Superannuation Act 1972**(a)**, and of all other powers enabling me in that behalf, after consultation with representatives of education authorities and of teachers and with such representatives of other persons likely to be affected as appear to me to be appropriate, and with the consent of the Minister for the Civil Service, I hereby make the following regulations:—

PART I

GENERAL

Citation and commencement

1.—(1) These regulations may be cited as the Teachers' Superannuation (Scotland) Regulations 1977, shall come into operation on 7th September 1977 and, except as otherwise expressly provided, shall have effect from 1st August 1977.

(2) These regulations extend to Scotland only.

Interpretation

2.—(1) The Interpretation Act 1889**(b)** shall apply for the interpretation of these regulations as it applies for the interpretation of an Act of Parliament.

(2) Any reference in these regulations to any provision of any enactment or instrument shall, except in so far as the context otherwise requires, be construed as a reference to that provision as amended, modified or extended by any enactment or instrument and as including a reference to any provision which it re-enacts or replaces, or which may re-enact or replace it.

(3) Any reference to a regulation, Part or Schedule not otherwise identified is a reference to a regulation or Part of, or a Schedule to, these regulations; and any reference to a paragraph or a sub-paragraph is a reference to a paragraph of the regulation or of the Schedule, as the case may be, or to a sub-paragraph of the paragraph, in which the reference occurs.

Definitions

3.—(1) Unless the context otherwise requires—

"Act of 1922" means the Education (Scotland) (Superannuation) Act 1922**(c)**;

"Act of 1939" means the Education (Scotland) (War Service Superannuation) Act 1939**(d)**;

"the 1969 regulations" means the Teachers Superannuation (Scotland) Regulations 1969**(e)**;

"the 1971 family benefits regulations" means the Teachers Superannuation (Family Benefits) (Scotland) Regulations 1971**(f)**;

"actuarial" in relation to any sum or value (however described) means the sum or value determined by the Government Actuary;

"agreed" means agreed between the Secretary of State and the teacher or other person concerned;

"British Isles" means the United Kingdom, the Channel Islands and the Isle of Man;

(a) 1972 c. 11.   (b) 1889 c. 63.
(c) 1922 c. 48.   (d) 1939 c. 96.
(e) S.I. 1969/77 (1969 I, p. 133).   (f) S.I. 1971/1775 (1971 III, p. 4813).

"child" includes an illegitimate child or a child accepted as a member of the teacher's family, who is wholly or mainly dependent on the teacher, and has not attained the age of 17 or, having attained the age of 17, is receiving full-time education or attending a course of not less than 2 years' full-time training for a trade, profession or calling but does not include a person who is married nor a person who is for the time being in receipt of a disqualifying income; and a person who is incapacitated on the date when by virtue of this definition he would otherwise cease to be a child shall be treated as being a child for so long as that incapacity persists;

"comparable British service" means service which is pensionable under a public service superannuation scheme for teachers in any part of the British Isles other than Scotland;

"disqualifying income" means remuneration payable to a person attending a course of full-time training at a rate not less than the annual rate for the time being payable of an official pension (within the meaning of the Pensions (Increase) Act 1971(a)) which began on 1st April 1972 at the annual rate of £250;·

"employer" means the employer of a teacher and includes a local authority, governing body or other body of managers;

"financial year" means a period of 12 months beginning on 1st April;

"full-time service" means service as a teacher under a contract providing for regular service for the whole of the working week;

"full-time teacher" means a teacher employed in full-time service;

"further education centre" has the meaning assigned to it by the Further Education (Scotland) Regulations 1959(b);

"incapacitated" means incapacitated during any period in which—

(a) in the case of a teacher, he is in the opinion of the Secretary of State incapable through infirmity of mind or body of serving efficiently as a teacher in reckonable service; and

(b) in the case of any other person, he is in the opinion of the Secretary of State incapable by reason of infirmity of mind or body of earning his livelihood and he is not maintained out of moneys provided by Parliament or raised by the rates levied by local authorities;

"incapacity gratuity" means a gratuity payable by virtue of regulation 56, or where the context so requires, a short service gratuity paid or payable by virtue of previous provisions;

"interchange provisions" means Part IX or any previous provisions to the like effect;

"local authority" has the meaning assigned to it by the Local Government (Scotland) Act 1973(c);

"nominated beneficiary" means a person nominated by a teacher under regulation 65 but does not include an incapacitated child on his ceasing to be a child;

"organiser" means a person in employment which involves the performance of duties in connection with the provision of education or services ancilliary to education;

"part-time service" means—

(a) service as a teacher under a contract providing for regular service which is less than full-time; or

(a) 1971 c. 56.
(b) S.I. 1959/477 (1959 I, p. 1068).
(c) 1973 c. 65.

(b) service under a contract terminable without notice as a teacher employed temporarily in place of a regularly employed teacher but does not include—

    (i) service which is remunerated at an hourly rate or by capitation fees; or

    (ii) service of a person who is, or is deemed to be, a pensionable employee within the meaning of the Local Government Superannuation (Scotland) Regulations 1974 to 1975(a);

"part-time teacher" means a teacher employed in part-time service;

"pensionable salary" has the meaning assigned to it by regulation 8;

"previous provisions" means schemes or regulations or rules relating to the superannuation of teachers in Scotland in force at any time before the commencement of these regulations;

"reckonable service", subject to regulation 6, has the meaning assigned to it by regulation 4;

"re-employed teacher" means a teacher who enters reckonable service after a retiring allowance has become payable to him;

"retiring allowance" means a yearly pension payable for life (hereinafter referred to as an 'annual pension') and a lump sum calculated and paid or payable in accordance with Part VI;

"salary" has the meaning assigned to it by regulation 7;

"Salaries Memorandum" means a memorandum setting out the scales and other provisions required for determining the relevant remuneration of teachers being a memorandum referred to in an order made by the Secretary of State under section 2 of the Remuneration of Teachers (Scotland) Act 1967(b) or that section as applied by section 4 of that Act;

"service", in relation to reckonable service, means salaried employment under a contract of service with an employer of a person who at the date of the employment is over 18 and under 70 years of age;

"service counting for benefit" has the meaning assigned to it by Schedule 9;

"supervisor" means a person employed in a capacity connected with education which to a substantial extent involves the supervision or control of teachers;

"teacher" includes a person who has ceased to be a teacher and, except in Schedule 1, an organiser and a supervisor;

"terminal sum" includes

    (a) a lump sum;

    (b) an incapacity gratuity;

    (c) any sum payable on the death of the teacher; and

    (d) any sum payable under Part V;

"war service" has the meaning assigned to it by regulation 68(1);

"widow" means the wife of a deceased teacher but does not include a woman who married him after the date on which he was last employed in reckonable service;

"widower" except in Part VI means the husband of a deceased woman teacher who at the time of her death was her nominated beneficiary.

(a) S.I. 1975/638 (1975 I, p. 2284).   (b) 1967 c. 36.

(2) References to an annual pension, a lump sum, a gratuity or a family pension are references to an annual pension, lump sum, gratuity or family pension payable under Parts VI and VII and "benefit", when used without qualification, is a reference to any or every such annual pension, lump sum, gratuity or family pension as the context requires but, except in regulation 86, does not include a return of contributions.

(3) References to the purchase of added years are, in relation to previous provisions, to be construed as including references to the payment of contributions by a teacher in respect of a period during which he was not employed in reckonable service.

(4) Unless the context otherwise requires, references to contributions and benefits payable in respect of a teacher are to be construed as including references to contributions paid by, and to benefits paid to, teachers.

(5) Other expressions used in these regulations to which meanings are assigned by the Education (Scotland) Acts 1939 to 1976(a) shall, unless the context otherwise requires, have the same respective meanings in these regulations as in those Acts.

Reckonable service

4.—(1) "Reckonable service" means—
  (a) any period during which a teacher is or was employed in reckonable service;
  (b) added years purchased;
  (c) service credited to the teacher by virtue of interchange provisions;
  (d) any period which is deemed to be service under the Act of 1939;
  (e) war service;
  (f) national service which is treated as teaching service by virtue of the Teachers' Pensions (National Service) (Scotland) Rules 1952(b).

(2) A teacher is in reckonable service at any time when he is—
  (a) in full-time service in an employment specified in Schedule 1; or
  (b) in part-time service in an employment specified in Schedule 1 which the teacher has elected, or is deemed to have elected, by virtue of regulation 5, to have recorded as reckonable service; or
  (c) in employment which is in continuation of employment treated as reckonable service under previous provisions—

and a teacher is referred to as having been employed in such service before the commencement of these regulations in respect of any period during which he was employed in comparable service under previous provisions.

(3) A teacher shall be treated as being in reckonable service during any period in which—
  (a) he is on ordinary leave (including leave pending the termination of his contract of service) on full pay;
  (b) he is on sick leave (recorded as such by his employer) unless either—
    (i) he has been continuously so absent for more than 12 months or, in the case of absence on account of pulmonary tuberculosis, for more than 18 months; or

(a) 1976 c. 20.　　　　(b) S.I. 1952/518 (1952 I, p. 928).

(ii) he is not entitled to at least half pay, disregarding any reduction provided for by the terms of his employment;

(c) he is on special leave on full pay—

(i) to attend a course of instruction;

(ii) to serve as a teacher outside the British Isles under arrangements approved by the Secretary of State for the interchange of teachers;

(iii) for any other reason connected with his service as a teacher approved by the Secretary of State;

(iv) for any reason (other than sickness) not connected with his service as a teacher for any period not exceeding 30 working days in any financial year;

(d) he is suspended from duty on full pay.

(4) In aggregating the total reckonable service recorded in respect of any teacher—

(a) the amount in any financial year shall not exceed 365 days;

(b) all periods of reckonable service shall be aggregated and where 2 or more periods total 365 days or more each period of 365 days shall be reckoned as 1 year, service on the 29th February in a leap year being disregarded; and

(c) a half or greater fraction of a day shall be reckoned as a day and a smaller fraction shall be disregarded.

Part-time service

5.—(1) There shall be recorded as reckonable service the part-time employment of a teacher in any employment specified in Schedule 1 who elects by notice in writing to the Secretary of State to have his employment so recorded.

(2) An election for the purposes of this regulation shall be irrevocable and shall have effect from the first day of the month following that in which the Secretary of State notifies the teacher of its receipt or such earlier date as the Secretary of State may with the agreement of the employer direct.

(3) Any part-time teacher who was in reckonable service before 1st August 1977 by virtue of previous provisions shall be deemed to have made an election under paragraph (1) unless he notifies the Secretary of State to the contrary by 30th November 1977 or in the case of a teacher who is not in service on that date within 3 months of his re-entry into teaching service.

(4) For the purposes of entitlement to benefit under regulations 46 and 47 part-time service to which this regulation applies shall be treated as if it were full-time service; and for all other purposes of these regulations there shall be recorded as service in any financial year such number of days which bears to 365 the same proportion as the amount of salary paid to the teacher (or in a case of a teacher paying for current added years under Part III the salary which, in the opinion of the Secretary of State, he could have expected to receive) during the year bears to the amount of salary which would have been payable to him if he had been employed throughout the year in the same service at the annual rate of salary appropriate thereto.

(5) For the purposes of paragraph (4) any reduction of salary during any period of absence from reckonable service on sick leave as mentioned in regulation 4(3)(b) shall be disregarded.

Service not reckonable

6.—(1) A period of service is not reckonable if—

(a) it is in continuation of service which was treated as not being reckonable service under previous provisions; or

(b) contributions are payable in respect of it by virtue of regulations under section 10(1) of the Superannuation Act 1972(a).

(2)(a) The service to which this paragraph applies of a teacher who immediately before 1st August 1977 was in service which was treated as not being reckonable service by virtue of previous provisions shall not be reckonable service unless he elects under sub-paragraph (c) that it shall be reckonable service;

(b) this paragraph applies to service in any employment specified in Schedule 1 by virtue of which the teacher is entitled to participate in benefits under section 7 or 8 of the Superannuation Act 1972 ("further employment") beginning within 1 year of his ceasing to be employed as mentioned in sub-paragraph (a), and to subsequent further employment beginning within 1 year of his ceasing to be employed in further employment;

(c) an election for the purposes of this paragraph shall be made (within 3 months of the commencement of the employment to which this paragraph applies) by notice in writing to the Secretary of State and to the person administering the superannuation scheme under which the benefits mentioned in sub-paragraph (b) are provided.

(3) The service of a teacher is not reckonable—

(a) in the case of a teacher who before becoming employed was ordinarily resident outside the British Isles if and for so long as the Secretary of State is satisfied both that the employment will not exceed 2 years and that, when it is completed, he will cease to be resident within the British Isles;

(b) if having entered reckonable service for the first time after attaining the age of 55—

(i) without having been employed in comparable British service; or

(ii) having been employed in comparable British service in respect of which the Secretary of State did not receive a transfer value under interchange provisions—

he so elects by notice in writing to the Secretary of State within 3 months of his becoming so employed.

Salary

7.—(1) Subject to paragraphs (2) and (3), the salary of a teacher shall for the purposes of these regulations, be taken to be the aggregate of the emoluments, whether in money or in kind, receivable by the teacher in respect of his employment in reckonable service excluding—

(a) payments in respect of overtime, special services or extra duties;

(b) any emoluments receivable from or out of an educational endowment or bequest;

(c) any additional allowance paid to a teacher serving outside the British Isles under arrangements approved by the Secretary of State for the interchange of teachers;

(a) 1972 c. 11.

(*d*) any special allowance paid to a teacher by the Secretary of State under the Teachers (Special Allowances) (Scotland) Provisional Regulations 1959**(a)**;

(*e*) payments by way of travelling or expense allowances;

(*f*) additional payments which under the Salaries Memorandum are not deemed to be part of the teacher's salary for superannuation purposes;

(*g*) any payments made in respect of the period from 1st September 1939 to 31st March 1944 by way of bonus or allowance in respect of increased cost of living.

(2) The Secretary of State may make a direction, in such cases as he thinks appropriate, disapplying any exclusion under paragraph (1) from the salary of a teacher.

(3) In determining the salary to which a teacher is entitled for the purposes of abatement of annual pension under regulation 60, the following payments to him shall be disregarded—

(*a*) any payments in respect of employment in connection with education which, while employed in reckonable or comparable British service, the teacher undertook in addition to such service and which he continues after ceasing such service, not exceeding, when expressed as an annual rate, the average annual rate of such payments for the last 3 years of his employment in reckonable service or comparable British service;

(*b*) any payments in respect of employment in connection with education outside the British Isles, being employment in which, in the opinion of the Secretary of State, it is expedient to facilitate the employment of teachers from Scotland; and

(*c*) any fees in respect of employment for the purposes of the Scottish Certificate of Education or the General Certificate of Education.

Pensionable salary

8.—(1) Pensionable salary means—

(*a*) as regards a teacher who has been employed in reckonable service for 1 year or more—

   (i) if he has been continuously employed in reckonable service throughout his terminal service, the highest amount of his salary for any year in that period;

   (ii) if he has not been so continuously employed, the highest amount of his salary for any 365 successive days of reckonable service in the period;

(*b*) as regards a teacher who has been employed in reckonable service for less than 1 year, the average annual rate of his salary during that service.

(2) For the purposes of this regulation—

(*a*) a teacher shall be treated as having received during any period in respect of which he has paid contributions for current added years under Part III the salary by reference to which those contributions were calculated;

(*b*) a teacher's pensionable salary shall include any increment which would have been payable after 1st August 1975 and which has been withheld or deferred in the national interest and in this context "increment" means an increase in pay for which provision is made in a pay scale; and

----

(**a**) S.I. 1959/1270 (1959 I, p. 1108).

(*c*) the salary of a teacher between 1st October 1974 and 30th September 1975 in respect of any such service as is specified in paragraph 1 of Schedule 5 shall be deemed to be the salary which is treated as his pensionable salary in respect of that period for the purposes of calculating any benefit payable in respect of him under a superannuation scheme operated under the Federated Superannuation System for Universities.

(3) If the Secretary of State is satisfied that the salary of a teacher has been unreasonably increased in respect of any period which is in the opinion of the Secretary of State relevant for the purposes of this regulation, his pensionable salary shall be calculated by reference to such a salary in respect of that period as the Secretary of State considers reasonable.

(4) In the case of a teacher who becomes entitled to retiring allowances by virtue only of regulation 46(1)(*c*), then unless either—

(*a*) he attained or, as the case may be, attains the age of 60 after 31st March 1972; or

(*b*) he attained the age of 60 before 1st April 1972 and was or, as the case may be, is employed in reckonable service on or after that date—

his pensionable salary shall be construed as a reference to the pensionable salary during his terminal service with the omission of the words "but has been employed for 1 year or more".

(5) In this regulation—

"reckonable service" includes employment of any kind specified in paragraphs 1 to 4 of Schedule 5, unless the teacher otherwise elects by notice in writing to the Secretary of State before any retiring allowances become payable to him;

"salary", in relation to a teacher who has made an election under regulation 12(2), means the salary by reference to which the contributions payable in respect of him were calculated (or, if by reason of regulation 16 contributions have ceased after 45 years, the salary by reference to which apart from that regulation contributions would be payable);

"terminal service" means—

(i) as regards any teacher who has been employed in reckonable service for 3 years or more, the 3 years of such service (whether continuous or not) next preceding the commencement of any pension or the accrual of any right to a lump sum or gratuity; and

(ii) as regards any teacher who has not been employed in reckonable service for 3 years or more but has been employed for 1 year or more, the period of that service.

Modification for national insurance

9. Schedule 12 has effect for modifying these regulations in consequence of the enactments relating to national insurance.

Savings, transitional provisions and revocations

10.—(1) Section 38(1) (repeals) of the Interpretation Act 1889(**a**) shall apply in respect of the regulations revoked by these regulations as if they were enactments repealed by an Act of Parliament.

(**a**) 1889 c. 63.

(2)(*a*) Anything done under any provision of the regulations hereby revoked, or any provision of previous provisions shall, if in force immediately before 1st August 1977 continue in force notwithstanding such revocation in like manner as if it had been done under these regulations, and in so far as it could have been done under a particular provision of these regulations, shall be deemed to have been done under that provision;

(*b*) without prejudice to the generality of sub-paragraph (*a*), references therein to anything done shall include—

(i) the determination of a question;

(ii) the exercise of a discretion;

(iii) the making of a payment (whether it relates to contributions or benefits);

(iv) the giving of a notice; and

(v) the making of an election.

(3) The provisions of the 1971 family benefits regulations specified in column 1 of Schedule 13 shall apply subject to the modifications specified in column 2 of that Schedule to any contributor within the meaning of those regulations who has not been employed in reckonable service since 31st March 1972 for so long as he continues not to be so employed.

(4) Subject to paragraph (3) and regulation 26 (which relates to pre-1973 contributors), the regulations specified in Schedule 14 shall cease to have effect and those regulations are hereby revoked.

PART II

CONTRIBUTIONS

Financing of benefits by contributions

11.—(1) For the purpose of defraying the cost of benefits contributions shall be paid to the Secretary of State by teachers and their employers.

(2) As regards any teacher—

(*a*) the teacher's contributions shall be the aggregate of:—

(i) 6 per cent of his salary for the time being; and

(ii) any contributions which he has elected or is required to pay under Parts III or IV; and

(*b*) the employer's contributions shall be the aggregate of:—

(i) a sum equal to the rate per cent of the teacher's salary for the time being calculated by deducting the rate determined by paragraph (2)(*a*)(i) from the rate determined under regulation 82(4); and

(ii) any supplementary contributions for the time being specified under regulation 82(3).

(3) The total contributions paid by a teacher under these regulations shall not exceed 15 per cent of his salary.

Contributions in respect of teacher on reduced salary

12.—(1) Subject to paragraph (3) the contributions payable in respect of a teacher whose salary is reduced during absence on sick (including maternity) leave shall be calculated by reference to the salary before the deduction of sickness or maternity benefit under the enactments relating to those benefits.

(2) The contributions payable in respect of a full-time teacher who before a retiring allowance becomes payable to him suffers a reduction in salary while continuing to be employed in reckonable service shall, if with the approval of the Secretary of State he so elects within 6 months of that reduction taking effect, be calculated by reference to the salary at which he was employed immediately before the reduction ("previous salary") until the salary at which he is currently employed ceases to be lower than his previous salary or he elects by notice in writing to the Secretary of State that the contributions shall cease to be calculated by reference to his previous salary.

(3) The contributions payable in pursuance of an election under paragraph (2) in respect of a teacher whose salary is reduced because of sickness shall be calculated by reference to a proportionate price of his previous salary.

(4) Nothing in this regulation shall affect an election made by a re-employed teacher under previous provisions.

Payment of teacher's contributions

13.—(1) The employer of a teacher employed in reckonable service shall deduct and pay to the Secretary of State—

(a) from every payment of salary to the teacher, the contributions payable by the teacher in respect of that salary; and

(b) from any payment or payments of salary to the teacher, any contributions payable by the teacher in respect of previous payments of salary which were not deducted from those payments.

(2) A teacher who has ceased to be employed by any employer shall pay to the Secretary of State any contributions payable in respect of salary paid by that employer which were not deducted from that salary together with any interest payable under regulation 15(3); and any such payment shall be made within 6 weeks of the serving on the teacher by the Secretary of State of a notice specifying the amount due to be paid.

(3) Any contributions not paid to the Secretary of State in accordance with paragraph (1) or (2) shall, together with any interest payable under regulation 15(2) or (3) be deducted from any benefit payable in respect of the teacher.

Time for making payments to the Secretary of State

14.—(1) Every teacher's contribution payable by deduction from salary shall be remitted and every employer's contribution shall be paid by the employer to the Secretary of State by the 15th day of each calendar month following the end of the month to which the salary relates.

(2) For the purposes of this regulation the annual salary of a teacher is to be deemed to be payable in 12 equal instalments; and any arrears of salary due by virtue of any retrospective increase in his remuneration shall be treated as payable in the month in which they are paid.

Interest on contributions

15.—(1) Unless the Secretary of State in any particular case otherwise directs, compound interest at the rate of 12 per cent per annum with monthly rests shall be payable by the employer on so much of the contributions due to be remitted by the employer to the Secretary of State in terms of regulation 13(1) and not received by the Secretary of State by the 15th day of the calendar month following the month to which the contributions relate and interest payable by virtue of this paragraph shall accrue from the 16th day of the month and shall be paid and remitted by the employer to the Secretary of State.

(2) Except in a case to which regulation 13(2) applies compound interest at the rate of 4 per cent per annum with yearly rests shall be paid from the day following the expiry of 6 months following the period to which a contribution payable by a teacher direct to the Secretary of State relates on so much of that contribution as is not paid before that day.

(3) Compound interest at the rate of 4 per cent per annum with yearly rests shall be paid from the day following the expiry of 6 weeks after the serving of a notice under regulation 13(2) on so much of the contributions specified in that notice as is not paid before that day.

Cessation of contributions after 45 years of service

16. No contributions shall be payable in respect of any reckonable service beyond a total of 45 years.

Repayment of returned contributions

17.—(1) A re-employed teacher to whom contributions have been returned under regulation 45 may, if he is subsequently employed in reckonable service, repay those contributions to the Secretary of State at any time while he is so employed together with compound interest at the rate of $3\frac{1}{2}$ per cent per annum with yearly rests from the date of the return of the contributions until the date of their repayment to the Secretary of State.

(2) A teacher to whom contributions were returned before 1st June 1973 under a provision other than paragraph (1) may, if he becomes again employed in reckonable service, repay those contributions to the Secretary of State at any time while he is so employed together with compound interest at the rate of $3\frac{1}{2}$ per cent per annum with yearly rests from the date of the return of the contributions until the date of their repayment to the Secretary of State, provided that nothing in this paragraph shall apply in respect of contributions repaid to the Secretary of State after 31st May 1973 and subsequently returned by him to the teacher.

(3) Paragraph (1) and (2) shall apply with the necessary modifications to a teacher who is subsequently employed in comparable British service as they apply to a teacher who is subsequently employed in reckonable service, but only if the Secretary of State has not paid a transfer value in respect of him to the person responsible for the management of the superannuation scheme to which he becomes subject by virtue of that service.

(4) Paragraph (1) shall not apply to a re-employed teacher if he is by reason of his subsequent employment in reckonable service entitled to further benefits under regulation 59, unless he has not attained the age of 60 and payment to him of a pension is for the time being suspended under regulation 62.

Method of repayment of contributions returned under regulation 17

18.—(1) A teacher to whom regulation 17 applies shall if he so elects repay to the Secretary of State the sum specified by that regulation in accordance with this regulation.

(2) The payments under this regulation shall be made in uniform instalments of such amount and at such intervals as may be agreed while the teacher is employed in reckonable service and shall continue to be paid until the sum referred to in paragraph (1), together with the interest payable on it by virtue of paragraph (4) has been paid.

(3) The annual amount of any instalments paid under this regulation shall not exceed whichever is the lesser of—

(a) 9 per cent of the teacher's annual salary at the rate payable on the date the Secretary of State receives his election; and

(b) 1/5th of the sum specified in regulation 17(2) or such greater fraction of that sum as is represented by the reciprocal of the number of years by which his age on that date is less than 60—

reduced (in either case) by the amount by which any contributions payable by the teacher by way of deductions from salary under any provision of these regulations exceeds 6 per cent of his salary.

(4) Where a teacher elects to repay any contributions returned to him in accordance with the provisions of this regulation, there shall be payable, in addition to the sum specified by regulation 17(2), compound interest on the amount of that sum for the time being outstanding calculated at $3\frac{1}{2}$ per cent per annum with yearly rests from 31st March in each year from the payment of the first instalment under this regulation until the last payment of the sum specified by regulation 17(2); and any interest payable by virtue of this paragraph shall be paid in an instalment or instalments, of the amount and at the intervals agreed under paragraph (2), after the payment of the sum so specified has been completed.

(5) If a teacher who has commenced to pay instalments in accordance with this regulation becomes entitled to the award of a retiring allowance, or a death gratuity becomes payable in respect of him, before he has completed repayment, then—

(a) any retiring allowance payable in respect of him shall be calculated on the basis that he had completed repayment; and

(b) the amount outstanding shall be deducted from the lump sum or gratuity payable in respect of him.

(6) If, in a case not falling within paragraph (5), a teacher who has commenced to pay instalments in accordance with this regulation ceases to be employed in reckonable service before he has completed payment, he shall pay the amount outstanding in a single payment.

PART III

ADDED YEARS

Maximum purchase of added years

19.—(1) A teacher may purchase added years in accordance with this Part; but, subject to regulation 29, may not purchase added years, whether past or current or past and current, in excess of the permitted maximum, that is to say, subject to regulation 20, the number of years specified by the relevant entry in the following table—

TABLE

Age on first entry	Permitted maximum
. Under 50	30
50	23
51	16
52	9
53	2
54	Twice the period remaining before the 55th birthday

(2) A teacher who ceases (otherwise than on death or becoming eligible for a retiring allowance under regulation 46(2)(c) or 47) to be employed in reckonable service before attaining the age of 60 without having completed the payment of his contributions under this Part may not purchase, and shall not be treated as having purchased, added years in excess of the number which bears to the greatest number of years which he could have purchased in accordance with these regulations the same proportion as his reckonable service bears to the reckonable service which he would have completed if he had been continuously employed in such service from the day when those contributions first became payable until he attained the age of 60.

(3) A teacher whose employment in reckonable service before he purchases added years has not been continuous shall for the purposes of these regulations be treated as having become first employed in such service at the age determined by adding to his actual age when he first became employed in reckonable service—

(a) any period after he was first employed in reckonable service during which he was not employed in such service; and

(b) any period which is treated as reckonable service by virtue of contributions paid under regulation 28 or a previous provision to the like effect.

Modification of regulation 19 in certain cases

20.—(1) This regulation modifies the provisions of regulation 19(1) in its application to the purchase of past added years by a teacher who on last becoming employed in reckonable service was entitled in respect of any former employment, trade, profession, vocation or office to superannuation benefits (including any immediate or deferred pension or lump sum and any gratuity or refund of contributions).

(2) The permitted maximum in respect of such a teacher as is described in paragraph (1) shall be such a number of years as will secure that the aggregate annual amount of the following sums does not exceed 2/3rds of his pensionable salary—

(a) (except where the total value of the superannuation benefits does not exceed a lump sum of £2,000 or a deferred pension of £52) the actuarial value, expressed as an annuity payable to him, of any such superannuation benefits as are referred to in that paragraph;

(b) so much of the annual pension payable to him as is attributable to his reckonable service before attaining the age of 60; and

(c) the actuarial value, expressed as an annuity payable to him, of so much of the lump sum payable to him as is attributable to such service.

(3) For the purposes of paragraph (2) it is to be assumed that the teacher will continue to be employed in reckonable service until he attains the age of 60 on the same salary scale on which he is employed on the date when the calculation of the permitted maximum in his case falls to be made.

Purchase of past added years

21.—(1) Subject to regulation 22 a teacher employed in reckonable service except service which is reckonable under regulation 4(3)(*b*), who is, or as the case may be, was first employed in such service before attaining the age of 55 may elect to purchase the number of years, or any number of complete years, before the date of purchase during which he has not been employed in reckonable service—

(*a*) after attaining the age of 20; and

(*b*) before attaining the age of 60, or if on 1st April 1974 he had attained the age of 60, 65.

(2) Paragraph (1) applies to a teacher who is, or as the case may be, was first employed in comparable British service before attaining the age of 55 as it applies to a teacher so employed in reckonable service if, on the day he elects to purchase past added years that comparable British service is reckonable by virtue of a transfer value received under regulation 73.

(3) A teacher may not by virtue of this regulation purchase any added years which he has purchased as current added years by virtue of regulation 27.

(4) A part-time teacher to whom regulation 5(1) or (3) applies shall purchase added years by Method 2 in accordance with regulation 24; and any other teacher shall purchase such years by Method 1, 2 or 3 in accordance with regulations 23, 24 or 25 or partly by Method 2 and partly by either Method 1 or Method 3.

(5) In its application to any years following the discontinuance of the teacher's employment in reckonable service paragraph (1) shall have effect with the substitution of the word "those" for the word "complete".

Elections to purchase past added years

22.—(1) A first election for the purposes of regulation 21 shall be made by the teacher not later than his 55th birthday, unless either—

(*a*) having been employed in reckonable service before (but not after) 1st April 1974 he becomes again employed in such service after attaining the age of 55; or

(*b*) he first becomes employed in reckonable service after attaining the age of 55 having previously been employed in comparable British service in respect of which—

(i) he paid contributions under a provision corresponding to this Part in force elsewhere in the British Isles; and

(ii) a transfer value was paid to the Secretary of State;

and in those cases the election shall be made not later than the expiry of 6 months after the day on which he first becomes again employed, or as the case may be, first becomes employed in such service.

(2) Subject to regulation 19 a subsequent election for the purposes of regulation 21 may be made by a teacher—

(a) within 6 months of his becoming again employed in reckonable service in respect of any period after he has made an election under paragraph (1) or this sub-paragraph during which he has not been employed in reckonable service; or

(b) at any time after he has made an election under paragraph (1) for which he specified that purchase shall be made under regulation 23 by Method 1 provided that:—

    (i) he is under 58 years of age at the time of the subsequent election;

    (ii) he again elects to purchase by Method 1; and

    (iii) the 15 per cent limitation specified in regulation 11(3) is not exceeded.

(3) A first election under this regulation by a teacher employed in full-time service shall specify the method or combination of methods by which the contributions payable by the teacher shall be paid; and, if he elects to pay contributions by Method 1, the rate at which he elects to pay those contributions.

(4) An election shall be made by notice in writing to the Secretary of State and shall be effective from the date of its receipt.

(5) An election may be varied in accordance with the provisions of paragraph (2), or paragraph 4 of Schedule 3, but subject thereto shall be irrevocable.

Method 1 contributions

23.—(1) Method 1 contributions shall be paid at the rate for the time being specified by the teacher in accordance with Schedule 3 from the first day of the month following the acceptance of his election until the actuarial cost (as determined by reference to table 1 of Schedule 3) of purchasing the added years which he elected to purchase has been met.

(2) If the teacher becomes employed in reckonable part-time service, or in circumstances to which regulation 39 does not apply ceases to pay contributions by Method 1 before the actuarial cost referred to in paragraph (1) has been met, then, subject in either case to regulation 19(2), either—

(a) if he so elects by notice in writing to the Secretary of State within 3 months of his ceasing to pay those contributions, he shall pay to the Secretary of State the actuarial equivalent of the balance of contributions outstanding, and he shall be treated as having purchased the added years which he elected to purchase; or

(b) if he does not so elect, he shall be treated as having purchased only that number of added years as bears to the number which he elected to purchase the same proportion as the period during which he paid contributions bears to the period during which those contributions would have been paid if he had continued to pay them until the actuarial cost had been met.

(3) If a teacher to whom paragraph (2) applies by virtue of his ceasing to be employed in full-time reckonable service again becomes employed in such service without having made an election as is mentioned in paragraph (2)(a), contributions shall be paid by him in accordance with paragraph (1) in respect of so many of the added years which he elected to purchase as he is treated by virtue of paragraph (2)(b) as not having purchased.

(4) In the case of any teacher in respect of whom the period referred to in paragraph (1) ends after whichever is the later of his 60th birthday and the date upon which retiring allowances first become payable to him under regulation 46(2)(a) or (b)—

(*a*) if the amount of his contributions determined in accordance with table 2 of Schedule 3 as outstanding for payment does not exceed the terminal sum payable in respect of him, that amount shall be deducted from that sum; and

(*b*) if that amount exceeds that sum, then no terminàl sum shall be payable in respect of him and either—

    (i) the teacher shall be treated as having purchased that number of added years which bears to the number he elected to purchase the same proportion as the aggregate of the number of years during which he paid contributions and the number during which he is deemed in accordance with this paragraph to have paid contributions bears to the total period during which those contributions would have been paid if he had continued to pay them until the actuarial cost of purchasing the added years had been met; or

    (ii) if he so elects the teacher may pay the excess to the Secretary of State by a single payment:

provided that, unless he elects that it shall apply to him, this paragraph shall not apply to a teacher to whom paragraph (2)(*b*) applies in any case where the period required to meet the actuarial cost referred to ends without his again becoming employed in reckonable service.

(5) For the purposes of paragraph (4)(*b*)(i) a teacher to whom that paragraph applies is deemed to have paid contributions during the number of years shown in the entry in column A of table 2 of Schedule 3 against the entry in column B specifying the highest factor in column B which does not exceed the sum ascertained by dividing the terminal sum payable in respect of him by the annual amount of his contributions at the last rate payable.

(6) Paragraph (4) (except the proviso) shall apply with the necessary modifications in the case of any teacher in respect of whom a terminal sum becomes payable before his 60th birthday other than by virtue of regulation 46(2)(*c*), the reference in paragraph (4)(*b*)(i) to the number of yeaŕs during which he paid contributions being read as a reference to the number of years during which he would have paid contributions if he had remained in reckonable service until he attained the age of 60 and the reference to the number of years during which he is deemed to have paid contributions being read as a reference to the number which is the actuarial equivalent of the terminal sum that would apart from that paragraph have been payable to him.

(7) Method 1 contributions shall be paid direct to the Secretary of State during any period in which the teacher is paying contributions for current added years in accordance with regulation 28 and in any other circumstances by deduction from salary.

Method 2 contributions

24. Method 2 contributions shall be made by payment direct to the Secretary of State not later than 1 month after the acceptance of the teacher's election of an amount ascertained by multiplying the number of added years which the teacher elects to purchase by the factor determined in accordance with table 3 of Schedule **3**.

Method 3 *contributions*

25.—(1) Method 3 contributions shall be paid—

(*a*) in the case of a teacher who has not attained the age of 55, in accordance with the formula:

$$\text{annual instalment} = \frac{S \times (1 + \cdot 05N)}{N}$$

where S = the amount ascertained in accordance with regulation 24; and

N = the number of years over which payment is to extend; and

(*b*) in any other case, by the payment of the actuarial equivalent of the contributions payable by that teacher by Method 2.

(2) Method 3 contributions shall be payable monthly in uniform instalments by deduction from salary during any period in which the teacher is employed in reckonable service or direct to the Secretary of State if he is paying contributions for current added years in accordance with regulation 28—

(*a*) in the case of a teacher who is not over 55, for such a period of not less than 5 nor more than 10 years expiring not later than his 60th birthday as may be agreed; and

(*b*) in the case of a teacher who is over 55 for a period of 5 years.

(3) The annual amount of Method 3 contributions shall not exceed whichever is the lesser of—

(*a*) 9 per cent of the annual rate of the teacher's salary at the date of the acceptance of his election to pay them; and

(*b*) such lower percentage as may be determined by deducting from 9 per cent the percentage rate of any contributions which on the date of that acceptance the teacher is paying in addition to the contributions payable as the teacher's contribution by virtue of regulation 11.

(4) In a case where the teacher becomes incapacitated before attaining the age of 60 or dies without having completed the payment of his contributions—

(*a*) if he has paid contributions for not less than 1 year, he shall be treated as having purchased the number of years which he elected to purchase;

(*b*) if he has not paid contributions for 1 year, he shall be treated as not having purchased added years and the amount of contributions paid by him shall be returned to him or, as the case may be, paid to his personal representatives.

(5) If the teacher ceases to pay contributions before the amount determined under paragraph (1) has been paid either—

(*a*) on a retiring allowance becoming payable to him by virtue of regulation 46; or

(*b*) on his ceasing to be employed in reckonable full-time service in circumstances to which neither paragraph (4) nor sub-paragraph (*a*) apply,

then subject in either case to regulation 19(2), either—

(i) if he so elects by notice in writing to the Secretary of State within 3 months of the occurrence of the event specified in sub-paragraph (*a*) or, as the case may be, this sub-paragraph, the amount outstanding shall be paid by deduction from the terminal sum payable in respect of him or in such other manner as may be agreed; or

(ii) if he does not so elect, he shall be treated as having purchased that number of added years which bears to the number which he elected to purchase the same proportion as the number of instalments which he has paid bears to the number of instalments which he would have paid if payment of contributions under this regulation had not been discontinued.

Pre-1973 *contributors*

26.—(1) "Pre-1973 contributor" means a teacher who on 1st August 1977 was paying contributions under regulation 31 of the 1969 regulations which he commenced to pay before 1973.

(2) A pre-1973 contributor who does not elect to purchase added years under regulation 21 within the time specified by regulation 22 shall continue to pay contributions in accordance with the said regulation 31 and accordingly regulation 15(3) of the 1969 regulations shall continue to apply to him.

(3) If a pre-1973 contributor who by virtue of paragraph (2) continues to pay contributions in accordance with the said regulation 31 ceases to be employed in reckonable service before attaining the age of 60 without becoming entitled to retiring allowances under regulation 46, 47 or 56 he shall be treated as having purchased that number of added years which bears to the period of previous employment in respect of which he gave notice to the Secretary of State under regulation 15(3)(*a*) of the 1969 regulations the same proportion as the period during which he paid additional contributions under the said regulation 31 bears to the period between the date when he began to pay those contributions and his 60th birthday.

(4) A pre-1973 contributor who elects to purchase added years under regulation 21 shall, on commencing to pay contributions under these regulations, cease to pay contributions under regulation 31 of the 1969 regulations and shall be treated as having purchased such a number of added years as is specified by paragraph (3).

Purchase of *current added years*

27.—(1) Subject to paragraphs (2) and (3) a teacher, not being a teacher who is entitled to a retiring allowance under regulation 46(2)(*c*), whose employment in reckonable service is discontinued shall purchase so many as he may elect of any years before he attains the age of 60 during the period following that discontinuance—

(*a*) not exceeding 6 years during which he is employed—

(i) as a teacher in any school outside the British Isles in which, in the opinion of the Secretary of State, it is expedient to facilitate the employment of teachers from Scotland;

(ii) in an educational service outside the British Isles in employment which to a substantial extent involves the control or supervision of teachers in such schools;

(*b*) not exceeding 3 years during which he is not so employed as is mentioned in sub-paragraph (*a*).

(2) If in the case of any teacher who has purchased added years under paragraph (1)—

(*a*) his employment in reckonable service is discontinued within 1 year of his becoming again employed in reckonable service; or (*b*) on the expiry of those years he continues not to be employed in reckonable service,

he may purchase only so many (if any) added years during the further period in which he is not employed in reckonable service as, when added to the number previously purchased by him under this regulation, do not exceed the maximum prescribed by the sub-paragraph of paragraph (1) which is applicable to that further period.

(3) Paragraph (1) shall not, unless the Secretary of State so directs in respect of any teacher, apply in any case where the employment of a teacher in reckonable service is discontinued within 1 year of the expiry of any period in respect of which he has previously paid contributions for current added years.

(4) An election for the purposes of this regulation shall be made by notice in writing to the Secretary of State—

(*a*) in a case falling within paragraph (1)(*a*), within 6 months; or

(*b*) in a case falling within paragraph (1)(*b*), within 3 months

of the relevant sub-paragraph becoming applicable to the teacher.

(5) Added years shall be purchased for the purposes of this regulation in accordance with regulation 28.

(6) Regulation 88 shall not apply in relation to this regulation.

Contributions for current added years

28.—(1) The contributions payable by a teacher in respect of current added years shall be a sum equal to the aggregate of the contributions which would have been payable in respect of those years if he had continued throughout those years to be employed in reckonable service at the salary which in the opinion of the Secretary of State he could have expected to receive if he had been so employed.

(2) So much of the contributions paid by a teacher under this regulation as is equal to the contributions which would have been payable by him if he had continued to be employed in reckonable service shall be treated as having been paid by way of teacher's contributions and the remainder shall be treated as having been paid by way of employer's contributions.

Special provision relating to period 1st December 1973—31st March 1974

29.—(1) Notwithstanding regulation 19(1), a teacher who at any time between 1st December 1973 and 31st March 1974 inclusive was employed in reckonable service for any number of days specified in the 1st column below, shall be treated as having purchased the number of days specified in the corresponding entry in the 2nd column.

Column 1						Column 2
Less than 12	...	...	...	...	...	... 0
12—35	...	...	...	...	...	... 1
36—59	...	...	...	...	...	... 2
60—83	...	...	...	...	...	... 3
84—107	...	...	...	...	...	... 4
more than 107	...	...	...	...	...	... 5

(2) In any case where, by reason of the operation of paragraph (1), the reckonable service of a teacher before he attains the age of 60 exceeds 40 years, the provisions for the payment of contributions contained in regulation 23, 24 or 25 (as the case may be) shall be modified accordingly.

(3) Paragraph (1) shall not apply to any teacher who paid contributions at the rate of 6½ per cent instead of at 6 per cent in respect of any period of reckonable service between 1st December 1973 and 31st March 1974 inclusive and who, before 11th September 1975, received a return of his excess contributions.

PART IV

CONTRIBUTIONS FOR PRE-APRIL 1972 FAMILY PENSIONS

Interpretation of Part IV

30. In this Part—

"member" means a teacher employed in reckonable service on or after 1st April 1972 who immediately before that date had service counting for benefit within the meaning of regulation 37 of the 1971 family benefits regulations;

"non-member" means a teacher employed in reckonable service on or after 1st April 1972 who immediately before that date had no such service counting for benefit as is referred to in the definition of "member";

"deemed normal service" means 2/3rds of any service as at 31st March 1972 in respect of which the full amount of normal contributions was held in the Teachers' Family Benefits Fund on that date;

"deemed additional service" means the number of years determined in accordance with table 1 of Schedule 4 as the actuarial value of any additional contributions held in that fund on 31st March 1972 in respect of reckonable service as at that date;

"notional service" means the number of years determined as the actuarial value of the interest of the member concerned in the balance (so determined) of that fund as at 31st March 1972.

Member's contributions

31.—(1) A member shall pay contributions in accordance with these regulations in respect of so much (if any) as he elects of his reckonable service before 1st April 1972 as exceeds the aggregate of his deemed normal service, his notional service, his deemed additional service (if any) and 1/6th of the period of previous service in respect of which prior to that date he paid or elected to pay contributions for family pensions.

(2) A member who elected to pay additional contributions in respect of his previous service by Method III within the meaning of the 1971 family benefits regulations may, by notice in writing delivered to the Secretary of State within the time specified for an election by regulation 35, revoke his election to pay such contributions; and any such member who does not so revoke that election shall be liable to a deduction from the terminal sum in accordance with regulation 38(1).

Non-member's contributions

32. A non-member shall, if he so elects, pay contributions in respect of the whole of his reckonable service before 1st April 1972 or, if that service amounts to 5 years or more, 5 or more complete years of that service as he may elect.

Retired teacher's contributions

33. A teacher who, having been employed in reckonable service on or after 1st April 1972, retired from such service without having made an election shall, if a retiring allowance becomes payable to him and he then so elects, pay contributions in the form of a lump sum equal to the actuarial equivalent of the contributions which he could have elected to pay under regulation 31(1) or (2) if he had again become employed in reckonable service before that allowance became payable to him.

Election to pay contributions

34. —(1) The first election by any teacher for the purposes of this Part shall specify—

(a) the number of years in respect of which he elects to pay contributions; and

(b) the rate at which he elects to pay contributions expressed as a percentage, being a whole number not exceeding 9, of the salary in respect of which contributions fall to be paid.

(2) An election shall be made in writing and delivered to the Secretary of State and shall be effective from the date of its receipt by him.

(3) In so far as it specifies the number of years in respect of which contributions are to be paid an election shall be irrevocable; but in so far as it specifies the rate at which contributions are to be paid it may from time to time be varied by a subsequent election to pay contributions at a higher rate (expressed as is specified in paragraph (1)(b)) taking effect from 1st April following the end of the calendar year in which that subsequent election is received by the Secretary of State.

Time for making elections

35.—(1) A man teacher may make a first election within the 6 months next following the first to occur of any of the following events—

(a) his marriage, if he is then employed in reckonable service;

(b) his becoming again employed in reckonable service after his marriage while not so employed;

(c) his becoming again employed in reckonable service after ceasing to be so employed within the period specified by paragraph (3) for the making of an election;

(d) the acceptance of a nomination by him of an adult dependant under regulation 65.

(2) A woman teacher may make a first election within the 6 months next following the acceptance of a nomination by her of an adult dependant under regulation 65.

(3) Subject to paragraphs (1) and (2), a first election for the purposes of this Part shall be made by—

(a) a member who was not employed in reckonable service for a continuous period of 6 months between 1st November 1974 and 31st July 1977; and

(b) a non-member who was not employed for such a period after 8th January 1974 and before 1st August 1977,

within 6 months of the teacher again becoming employed in reckonable service.

Determination by Secretary of State

36.—(1) The Secretary of State shall as soon as may be after the receipt of an election determine in accordance with table 2 of Schedule 4 the period for which contributions are required to be paid by the teacher.

(2) A determination under paragraph (1) may be varied by a subsequent determination, and shall be so varied if—

> (*a*) payment of contributions is interrupted by a break in reckonable service; or

> (*b*) the amount of his contributions is reduced by reason of the teacher being for the time being employed in part-time service or (in the case of a teacher already so employed) being so employed for a smaller proportion of his time; or

> (*c*) a contribution is not paid.

(3) The Secretary of State shall as soon as may be after making a determination serve a notice in writing on the teacher specifying as may be appropriate—

> (*a*) the day on which, in accordance with regulation 37, the payment of contributions is to begin;

> (*b*) the period for which contributions are required to be paid; and

> (*c*) any liability of the teacher to a deduction by virtue of regulation 38 from the terminal sum payable in respect of him.

Rate and duration of contributions

37.—(1) Contributions shall be paid, at the rate for the time being specified by the teacher in an election under this Part, for so long as he continues to be employed, or is treated as if he were employed, in reckonable service (any period in respect of which he pays contributions for current added years under Part III being treated as a period of employment in reckonable service).

(2) Contributions shall begin to be paid by a teacher on the 1st day of the month next following the date of the notice served on him by the Secretary of State under regulation 36(3) and shall cease to be paid on whichever is the earlier of the day he retires from reckonable service and the day specified in that notice as the last day on which contributions are required to be paid by him.

Deduction from terminal sum

38.—(1) If a member who elected to pay contributions by Method III (within the meaning of the 1971 family benefits regulations) and did not revoke his election to pay such contributions either—

> (*a*) does not elect to pay contributions under regulation 31(1); or

> (*b*) elects to pay such contributions in respect of a period which is less than 2/3rds of the period in respect of which he elected to pay contributions by the said Method III—

there shall be deducted from the terminal sum payable in respect of him the actuarial cost of defraying the benefits payable in respect of him in so far as they relate to his reckonable service before 1st April 1972.

(2) If, as regards any teacher, the period determined under regulation 36(1) ends after whichever is the later of his 60th birthday and the date on which retiring allowances first become payable to him under regulation 46(2)(*a*) or (*b*) there shall be deducted from the terminal sum payable in respect of him the amount determined in accordance with table 2 of Schedule 3 as outstanding for payment.

(3) There shall be deducted from any terminal sum payable in respect of a teacher before his 60th birthday by virtue of regulation 46(2)(*c*) or 47 the actuarial equivalent of the amount which would have been outstanding for payment on that birthday if he had continued to pay contributions under this Part at the last rate specified by him until he attained the age of 60; and if any such teacher becomes again employed in reckonable service he shall be treated as having paid those contributions.

(4) There shall be deducted from the terminal sum payable in respect of a teacher who was a former external contributor, (within the meaning of the 1971 family benefits regulations) or paid to the Secretary of State in such manner as may be agreed, the actuarial equivalent of the cost of defraying such part of any pension payable in respect of that teacher as is attributable to outstanding contributions under the provisions of an external scheme within the meaning of those regulations.

(5) If a married man teacher to whom regulation 35 applies dies within 6 months of becoming employed in reckonable service without having made an election under the preceding provisions of this Part then unless his widow elects that regulation 66 shall not apply, the amount determined under paragraph (6) shall be deducted from so much of the terminal sum payable in respect of him as is applicable for her benefit, or paid to the Secretary of State in such manner as may be agreed.

(6) The amount mentioned in paragraph (5) is the amount by which the cost of defraying so much of the widow's pension payable under regulation 66 as relates to the teacher's reckonable service before 1st April 1972 exceeds the actuarial equivalent of the contributions which would have been payable by him under this Part if he had remained in reckonable service until he attained the age of 60.

(7) There shall be deducted from so much of the terminal sum payable in respect of a teacher as is applicable for the benefit of his widow or paid to the Secretary of State in such manner as may be agreed, the actuarial equivalent of the long-term pension payable to her under regulation 67.

(8) References to sums applicable for the benefit of a widow are references to sums which may be so applied in accordance with the teacher's will, or if he died intestate, in accordance with the law relating to intestacy.

(9) If, in the case of a teacher in respect of whom a deduction has been made from the terminal sum under paragraph (2) or (3) or (5) or (7), a retrospective increase (whether authorised before or after the commencement of these regulations) in the salary payable in respect of his reckonable service would result in a further sum being payable by way of lump sum benefit but the further deduction required by that paragraph would be greater than that sum, the teacher, or as the case may be the teacher's widow, may elect not to pay those contributions; and in that event no further deduction shall be made from the terminal sum.

Part V

Return of Contributions

Return of contributions on cessation of employment

39.—(1) A teacher shall be entitled on the expiry of the period specified in sub-paragraph (*d*) to have returned the balance of his contributions calculated as at the date of return in accordance with regulation 42, reduced by a sum equal to the tax chargeable on that balance under paragraph 2 of Part II of

Schedule 5 to the Finance Act 1970(a) (charge to tax on repayment of employee's contributions), if before attaining the age of 70 he has ceased or ceases to be employed in reckonable service and the following conditions apply:—

    (a) he is not entitled to any benefit;

    (b) in the case of a teacher whose reckonable service ends after 31st March 1977 he is not qualified by service since 1st April 1972 for any such benefit;

    (c) since he ceased to be employed in reckonable service a transfer value in respect of him has neither been paid, nor is payable, by the Secretary of State under interchange provisions;

    (d) he continues not to be employed in reckonable service for at least 3 months or such shorter period as (in special circumstances) may be approved by the Secretary of State; and

    (e) the period mentioned in sub-paragraph (d) is not a period of absence in respect of which contributions for current added years are being paid under Part III.

(2) Unless the Secretary of State otherwise directs in pursuance of paragraph (3), paragraph (1) shall not apply to a teacher whose salary in any financial year has exceeded £5,000 but any such teacher shall, if he has attained the age of 60 and would apart from this paragraph be entitled to have returned any sum under paragraph (1), be entitled to be paid by the Secretary of State an annuity equal to the actuarial equivalent of the balance of his contributions.

(3) The Secretary of State, after consultation with the Board of Inland Revenue, may direct that paragraph (1) shall apply to a teacher notwithstanding that his salary in any financial year has exceeded £5,000 in any case where the Secretary of State is satisfied that the teacher's salary exceeded that amount by virtue only of a general increase in the remuneration of teachers authorised after he ceased to be employed in reckonable service.

Return of contributions at 70

40.—(1) A teacher who has at any time since 31st March 1926 been employed in reckonable service and on attaining the age of 70 is not (or as the case may be was not) entitled to benefit under these regulations or previous provisions, shall be entitled to have returned the balance of his contributions calculated in accordance with regulation 42 as at the date on which he attains (or as the case may be attained) the age of 70, reduced by a sum equal to the tax chargeable under paragraph 2 of Part II of Schedule 5 to the Finance Act 1970.

(2) Unless the Secretary of State otherwise directs in pursuance of paragraph (3), paragraph (1) shall not apply to a teacher whose salary in any financial year has exceeded £5,000; but any such teacher shall, if he would apart from this paragraph be entitled to have returned any sum under paragraph (1), be entitled to be paid by the Secretary of State an annuity equal to the actuarial equivalent of the balance of his contributions.

(3) The Secretary of State, after consultation with the Board of Inland Revenue, may direct that paragraph (1) shall apply to a teacher notwithstanding that his salary in any financial year has exceeded £5,000 in any case where the Secretary of State is satisfied that the teacher's salary exceeded that amount by virtue only of a general increase in the remuneration of teachers authorised after he ceased to be employed in reckonable service.

(a) 1970 c. 24.

Payment to personal representatives

41. The personal representatives of a teacher who had at any time since 31st March 1926 been employed in reckonable service may be entitled to be paid a sum equal to the balance of his contributions (except a member's contributions to which regulation 43 applies) calculated as at the date of his death where either—

    (*a*) the teacher was such a person as is mentioned in regulation 43(1); or

    (*b*) a death gratuity would but for regulation 57(3) be payable in respect of him and no pension is payable in respect of his widow or an adult nominated beneficiary under Part VII—

together with the amount which would have been payable to him under regulation 43 if on the day of his death he had become entitled to be paid under that regulation (no reduction being made in respect of tax chargeable under paragraph 2 of Part II of Schedule 5 to the Finance Act 1970).

Calculation for purposes of regulations 39 to 41

42.—(1) For the purposes of this Part the balance of a teacher's contributions as at any date at which it is to be calculated ("the date of calculation") shall be the amount by which the aggregate of the contributions paid by the teacher specified in paragraph (2) exceeds the aggregate of the payments to the teacher specified in paragraph (3).

(2) The contributions referred to are any contributions paid or treated as paid as teacher's contributions, together with compound interest at 3 per cent per annum with yearly rests from the first day of the financial year following that to which they were or are attributable under the superannuation provisions in force at the time they were paid to the date of calculation.

(3) The payments referred to are the aggregate of any sums (including any previous return of contributions) and any amount added to a death gratuity by virtue of the Pensions (Increase) Act 1971**(a)** paid or payable to the teacher or his personal representatives under statutory provisions for the superannuation of teachers in the British Isles, together with compound interest at 3 per cent per annum with yearly rests from the date of payment to the date of calculation.

(4) The contributions specified in paragraph (2), and mentioned in paragraph (3) as returned, include contributions paid or treated as paid as teacher's contributions in respect of comparable British service or class A external service (within the meaning of the 1969 regulations as originally made) of any teacher in respect of whom the Secretary of State has received a transfer value in respect of that service under interchange provisions.

(5) No account shall be taken of any contributions paid in respect of a period of service which, having been reckoned under section 15 of the Local Government Superannuation (Scotland) Act 1937**(b)** or a corresponding provision contained in a local Act scheme within the meaning of that Act, is reckonable as service under regulations made under section 10 of the Superannuation Act 1972**(c)**.

(6) In any case where a payment in lieu of contributions has been made by the Secretary of State under the National Insurance Act 1965**(d)**, the amount recoverable by the Secretary of State shall be deemed to have been deducted from the teacher's contributions on the date on which the payment in lieu of contributions became due.

    (a) 1971 c. 56.   **(b)** 1937 c. 69.
    (c) 1972 c. 11.   **(d)** 1965 c. 51.

(7) In calculating for the purposes of paragraph (2) of this regulation the aggregate of the contributions paid by the teacher, the aggregate of any contributions returned to the teacher and not repaid by him to the Secretary of State shall be left out of account, and in calculating the aggregate of any sums paid to the teacher or his personal representatives the aggregate of any sums paid in returning contributions to the teacher other than contributions for past added years under Part III shall be left out of account.

(8) A teacher to whom paragraph 13 of Schedule 12 applies shall be entitled to be paid by the Secretary of State a sum equal to the balance of his contributions calculated as at the date of return and for that purpose the provisions of this Part shall apply subject to the modification that the balance of his contributions as determined thereunder shall be reduced by an amount equal to half of the actuarial value of the annual pension payable to him.

(9) For the purposes of paragaph (3) there shall be disregarded any allocation of an annual pension under regulation 53 or deduction from a lump sum benefit under regulation 38.

Return of member's contributions

43.—(1) A member (within the meaning of regulation 30) who could have elected, but did not elect before ceasing to be employed in reckonable service to pay contributions under regulation 31, shall be entitled to be paid the sum applicable to his case in accordance with paragraph (2), reduced by a sum equal to the tax chargeable on the return under paragraph 2 of Part II of Schedule 5 to the Finance Act 1970, if one of the following conditions is satisfied—

(a) he is entitled to have returned the balance of his contributions under regulation 39; or

(b) he is entitled to have returned the balance of his contributions under regulation 40; or

(c) he becomes eligible for retiring allowances and on his death no pension other than an allocated pension under regulation 53 will be payable to his widow or an adult nominated beneficiary.

(2) The sum to be paid under paragraph (1) is—

(a) in the case of a teacher in respect of whom, had he died at any time between 1st April 1965 and 31st March 1972 no benefit would have been payable under the family pensions provisions in force at that time, the aggregate of the normal and additional contributions paid under those provisions; or

(b) in any other case, the aggregate of—

(i) half the normal contributions paid by him in respect of any period ending before the date on which he ceased to have a wife to whom in the event of his death a pension would have been payable;

(ii) the normal contributions paid by him in respect of any other period; and

(iii) the additional contributions paid by him

together, in any case, with compound interest calculated at 3 per cent per annum with yearly rests from the 1st day of the financial year next following the date of payment by the teacher to the date of return to him.

Return of contributions paid under 1922 *Act*

44. A teacher who paid contributions under the Act of 1922 and who did not subsequently become employed in reckonable service, or the personal representatives of such a teacher, shall be entitled to be paid by the Secretary of State a sum equal to the amount of those contributions reduced by the amount of any sums paid to him by way of benefit under a previous provision.

Return to pensioners after further service—

45. A teacher—

(*a*) to whom an annual pension, lump sum or incapacity gratuity was granted or paid under previous provisions or has become payable under these regulations;

(*b*) who after a retiring allowance or gratuity was granted, paid or became payable to him on or after the commencement of these regulations, is employed in reckonable service; and

(*c*) who since any such retiring allowance or gratuity was granted, paid or became payable to him is not qualified by reason of his service for a subsequent annual pension in respect of his further service—

shall be entitled on ceasing to be employed in reckonable service to have returned by the Secretary of State a sum equal to the contributions paid by him in respect of the service mentioned in paragraph (*c*) together with compound interest at 3 per cent per annum with yearly rests from the date of payment to the date of calculation, reduced by a sum equal to the tax chargeable on that return under paragraph 2 of Part II of Schedule 5 to the Finance Act 1970.

Part VI

Personal Benefits

Entitlement to retiring allowances on grounds of age or redundancy

46.—(1) Subject to paragraph (2) a retiring allowance shall be paid to any teacher who being under the age of 65 has left reckonable service, or being under the age of 70 service which is defined as reckonable in regulation 8(5), and who—

(*a*) was on 1st April 1972 employed in reckonable service and has been employed in such service, whether before or after that date, for at least 5 years; or

(*b*) has been employed in reckonable service after 31st March 1972 for at least 5 years; or

(*c*) served in reckonable service before 23rd April 1973 and has been employed for at least 10 years in reckonable service or partly in reckonable service and partly in employment which commenced before the said date of a description specified in Schedule 5.

(2) Subject to paragraph (1) and regulation 47 a retiring allowance shall be paid to a teacher—

(*a*) who has attained the age of 60 or such earlier age as is applicable to the teacher by virtue of regulation 48; or

(*b*) who has retired under the Retirement of Teachers (Scotland) Act 1976**(a)**; or

---

(a) 1976 c. 65.

(c) whose employer has certified that on or after 1st April 1976 the teacher ceased, or is ceasing, after attaining the age of 50, to hold his employment by reason of redundancy or in the interests of the efficient exercise of the employer's functions.

(3) For all purposes of this regulation paragraph (1) shall be read without the words "for at least 5 years" (in both places where they occur) in their application to a teacher in respect of whom either—

(a) after his accrued entitlement to benefits had been transferred by payment of a transfer value to the superannuation scheme of the Commission of the European Community, the Secretary of State has received on his return to reckonable service a transfer value from the person responsible for the management of that scheme; or

(b) the Secretary of State has received a transfer value from the person responsible for the management of any other superannuation scheme under which the teacher had, immediately before that transfer value was paid, been credited with service qualifying for benefits which, taken with his reckonable service, amounts to at least 5 years.

Entitlement to retiring allowance on grounds of incapacity

47.—(1) A retiring allowance shall be paid to any teacher who becomes incapacitated before the age of 60 and who, except on grounds of age or redundancy, satisfies the conditions for entitlement to retiring allowances as set out in regulation 46.

(2) A retiring allowance payable under this regulation shall begin to accrue on the day following that on which the teacher ceases to be employed in reckonable service, or if application has been made at a later date, on the date of application or such other date as the Secretary of State, having regard to all the circumstances, thinks appropriate.

(3) Any retiring allowance payable by virtue of this regulation shall, from the day on which the teacher attains the age of 60, be deemed to be paid by virtue of regulation 46.

Early retirement of services civilian teachers

48.—(1) In the application of these regulations to a teacher with reckonable service who has at any time been in reckonable service as a services civilian teacher under Part IX of the Teachers' Superannuation Regulations 1967(a) for any reference to the age of 60 in this Part there shall be substituted a reference to such age as is ascertained by deducting from 60 years a period of 3 months for each completed year of such service not exceeding 20 (other than as a locally entered teacher) in a specified country.

(2) For the purposes of this regulation—

(a) a "services civilian teacher" means a person employed by the Secretary of State for Defence in full-time civilian service with the Royal Navy, the Army or the Royal Air Force either in the capacity of a teacher or lecturer or in a capacity which to a substantial extent involves the control or supervision of teachers;

(b) "specified country" means a country or place to which section 25 of the Superannuation Act 1965(b) for the time being applied; and

(c) "locally entered teacher" means a services civilian teacher who was engaged elsewhere than in the United Kingdom.

(a) S.I. 1967/489 (1967 I, p. 1562).   (b) 1965 c. 74.

Reckonable service for entitlement and for benefit

49.—(1) For the purposes of entitlement to benefit under this Part—

(*a*) a teacher shall be treated as having been employed in reckonable service during any period which is treated as reckonable service by virtue of payment of contributions for current added years under Part III;

(*b*) references to reckonable service do not include service treated as reckonable by virtue of the payment of contributions for past added years under Part III;

(*c*) any period in respect of which contributions paid by the teacher have been returned and not repaid to the Secretary of State in pursuance of regulation 17 shall be disregarded.

(2) In calculating any benefit payable under this Part—

(*a*) war service shall count as half;

(*b*) any period of reckonable service in respect of which a proportion only of the contributions due has been paid shall count as that proportion of the period; and

(*c*) there shall be disregarded any period of service in respect of which either—

(i) contributions have not been paid by the teacher unless the Secretary of State directs otherwise; or

(ii) contributions paid by the teacher have been returned and not repaid to the Secretary of State in pursuance of regulation 17; or

(iii) an annuity has been paid to the teacher under regulation 39(2) or 40(2);

(*d*) no account shall be taken of—

(i) any reckonable service in excess of 45 years; or

(ii) reckonable service in excess of 40 years before the teacher attains the age of 60; and

(*e*) for the purposes of calculating the lump sum under regulation 54 in the case of a teacher who has reckonable service before 1st October 1956—

(i) any service to be disregarded by virtue of sub-paragraph (*d*)(i) shall be taken from the beginning of his reckonable service; and

(ii) sub-paragraph (*d*)(ii) shall not apply.

Calculation where reckonable service is less than 20 years

50. In calculating the retiring allowance of a teacher whose employment in reckonable service amounts to less than 20 years—

(*a*) any annual pension shall be increased by 1/350th of his pensionable salary in respect of each past added year (if any) purchased by him under Part III which is in excess of the number applicable to him by virtue of sub-paragraph (*b*); and

(*b*) in the case of the lump sum there shall be disregarded any past added years purchased by him under Part III in excess of the number of column (2) of the table below which appears against the entry in column (1) specifying the number of years of such employment.

TABLE

(1)	(2)
Number of completed years of employment in reckonable service	Past added years
19	17
18	15
17	13
16	11
15	9
14	7
less than 14	8 less than the number of years of actual reckonable service

(c) For the purpose of paragraph (b) a teacher who becomes incapacitated before attaining the age of 60 shall be treated as having continued in actual reckonable service until the date on which he attains that age.

Enhancement of reckonable service

51.—(1) If while he is employed in reckonable service a teacher becomes incapacitated, his reckonable service shall be enhanced in accordance with the table below.

(2) The table below applies only if the application for the retiring allowance under regulation 47 is made within 12 months after the teacher was last employed in reckonable service or, where the Secretary of State is satisfied that the teacher could not reasonably have been expected to make the application within 12 months, such longer period as may be approved by him.

TABLE

(1) Actual reckonable service	(2) Service counting for allowances (subject to column (3))	(3) Limitation on column (2)
5 years to 9 years 364 days	Twice the number of years of the actual reckonable service	Not exceeding the amount of service which could have been completed by 65th birthday
10 years to 13 years 122 days	20 years	ditto
More than 13 years 122 days	*either* 20 years *or* actual reckonable service plus 6 years 243 days whichever is more favourable	ditto Not exceeding the amount of service which could have been completed by 60th birthday

(3) For the purposes of this regulation a teacher shall be treated as having been employed in reckonable service during any period which is treated as reckonable service by virtue of the payment of contributions for current added years under Part III, but subject thereto references to reckonable service do not include service treated as reckonable by virtue of the payment of contributions for past added years under Part III.

Amount of annual pension

52. Subject to regulations 50 and 55 the annual pension payable to a teacher shall be calculated by multiplying 1/80th of his pensionable salary by the number of years of his reckonable service which may be taken into account in accordance with regulations 49 and 51.

Allocation of annual pension

53.—(1) A teacher may in accordance with Schedule 6 by declaration or declarations allocate not more than 1/3rd of the annual pension payable to him for the provision as he may elect of either—

(*a*) a pension commencing on his death to his widow, or a person dependent on him, for the life of that widow or dependant (Option A); or

(*b*) an annuity to him and his wife for their joint lives and, on his death, a pension for life to his widow (Option B).

(2) In paragraph (1) the reference to a teacher's wife is a reference to his wife at the time of the declaration and "widow" shall be construed accordingly; and in its application to a woman teacher the paragraph shall have effect with the substitution of references to the teacher's husband and widower for the references to the teacher's wife and widow.

(3) No declaration shall take effect before a teacher is entitled to a retiring allowance by virtue of regulation 46; but notice of intention to make a declaration may be given at any time within, and shall not be given before, the 4 months preceding the date of entitlement to those allowances.

(4) Subject to the provisions of Schedule 6 relating to the revocation and voidance of declarations, a declaration shall take effect on its delivery to the Secretary of State and thereupon—

(*a*) as from the date upon which the annual pension begins to accrue—

    (i) the amount of the annual pension calculated under regulation 52 shall be reduced by the amount allocated by the teacher; and

    (ii) in a case falling within paragraph (1)(*b*), the annuity there mentioned shall be paid at the rate determined by the Secretary of State in accordance with actuarial tables;

(*b*) on the subsequent death of the teacher, a pension shall be payable in accordance with his declaration at the rate so determined.

(5) Where a teacher whose declaration is made otherwise than in pursuance of a notice of his intention to retire within 4 months of the serving of that notice dies while employed in reckonable service after his declaration takes effect, he shall, for the purposes of paragraph (4), be deemed to have died immediately after the annual pension which would have been payable to him began to accrue.

(6) Where an annual pension has begun to accrue after the teacher has notified the Secretary of State of his intention to make an allocation but before the declaration referred to in paragraph (1) has been delivered to the Secretary of State, the annual pension may be paid at a rate not exceeding 2/3rds of the rate calculated under regulation 52 until the delivery of that declaration; and any overpayment or underpayment of the annual pension shall be deducted from or, as the case may be, added to subsequent payments of the annual pension.

(7) A teacher who has made an allocation under this regulation and to whom a retiring allowance has not at any time been payable may make a further allocation in favour of the same beneficiary and in accordance with the same

option as his previous allocation, unless the previous allocation becomes void upon the death of the beneficiary, in which case the further allocation shall be in favour of another beneficiary and may be in accordance with another option.

Amount of lump sum

54.—(1) Subject to paragraph (2) the lump sum payable to a teacher shall be the aggregate of—

(a) the amount ascertained by multiplying 1/30th of his pensionable salary by the number of years of his reckonable service before 1st October 1956; and

(b) the amount ascertained by multiplying 3/80ths of his pensionable salary by the aggregate of the number of years of his reckonable service after 30th September 1956 and any number of past added years which he purchased under Part III.

(2) As regards a teacher who has reckonable service before 1st October 1956 the amount of lump sum attributable to service before he attained the age of 60 shall not exceed $1\frac{1}{2}$ times his pensionable salary.

(3)(a) Where a lump sum benefit has been paid under regulations made under section 220 of the Local Government (Scotland) Act 1973(a) (early retirement of certain officers) to a teacher who was not entitled to be paid a retiring allowance under previous provisions, an amount equal to so much of the lump sum benefit as is related to the reckonable service then credited to him shall be deducted from—

(i) any lump sum, balance of contributions or death gratuity payable by virtue of regulations 46, 42 or 57 in respect of that teacher or;

(ii) any transfer value in respect of reckonable service of that teacher which falls to be paid by the Secretary of State by virtue of regulation 72 or previous provisions after that lump sum benefit was paid but before any such retiring allowance becomes payable.

(b) Any amount deducted in pursuance of sub-paragraph (a) shall be paid by the Secretary of State to the local authority by whom the lump sum benefit was paid as soon as may be after—

(i) (in a case falling within sub-paragraph (a)(i), the lump sum, balance of contributions or death gratuity becomes or would, apart from sub-paragraph (a) have become payable in respect of the teacher; or

(ii) (in a case falling within sub-paragraph (a)(ii)) the payment of the transfer value in question.

(c) A teacher to whom a lump sum benefit has been paid under regulations made under section 220 of the Local Government (Scotland) Act 1973 shall be treated for the purposes of regulation 39 (return of contributions on cessation of employment) and 40 (return of contributions at 70) as being qualified for a retiring allowance or gratuity under these regulations and accordingly shall not be entitled to be repaid any sum under regulations 39 or 40.

Modifications for teachers on reduced salary

55.—(1) The retiring allowance payable to a teacher retiring at 60 of a description specified in column A of the table below whose pensionable salary falls by virtue of an election made under regulation 12(2) to be calculated by

(a) 1973 c. 65.

reference to his salary within the meaning of regulation 8(5) shall not exceed the fraction prescribed in column B of that table of whichever is the greater of the 2 sums specified in paragraph (2).

TABLE

A	B	
Description of teacher	Fraction of specified sum	
	For pension	For lump sum
(i) First entered reckonable service before age 40 and has service falling within regulation 4(1)(a) or (c) of at least 20 years	1/2	120/80
(ii) First entered reckonable service at age 40	1/2	108/80
(iii) age 41	1/2	99/80
(iv) age 42	1/2	90/80
(v) age 43	1/2	81/80
(vi) age 44	1/2	72/80
(vii) age 45	1/2	63/80
(viii) age 46	1/2	54/80
(ix) age 47	1/2	48/80
(x) age 48	1/2	42/80
(xi) age 49	1/2	36/80
(xii) age 50	2/5	30/80
(xiii) age 51	3/10	24/80
(xiv) age 52	1/5	21/80
(xv) age 53	1/10	18/80
(xvi) age 54	1/14	15/80

NOTE: This paragraph does not apply to a teacher if the aggregate of his reckonable service before the date on which his pensionable salary falls to be calculated and the period between that date and his 60th birthday amounts to less than 5 years.

(2) The 2 sums mentioned in paragraph (1) are—

(a) the highest salary of the teacher for any 1 of the last 5 years of reckonable service; or

(b) the annual average of the teacher's total remuneration for any period of 3 consecutive years during which he was employed in reckonable service ending not more than 10 years before the date when he ceased to so employed.

Gratuities on grounds of incapacity

56.—(1) An incapacity gratuity shall be paid to a teacher who ceases to be employed in reckonable service and who—

(a) is not entitled to any retiring allowance by virtue of regulation 46 or 47; and

(b) before attaining the age of 70 has become incapacitated; and

(c) has been employed in reckonable service for not less than 1 year; and

(d) has been so employed within the 12 months immediately preceding an application for a gratuity under this regulation.

(2) The amount of an incapacity gratuity shall be calculated by multiplying 1/12th of the teacher's pensionable salary by the number of years of his reckonable service.

(3) In the case of a teacher who subsequently becomes entitled to a retiring allowance by virtue of regulation 46 or 47 the amount of the lump sum payable under regulation 54 shall be reduced by the amount of the incapacity gratuity paid under this regulation.

Death gratuities

57.—(1) There may be paid to the personal representatives of a teacher who dies while employed in reckonable service, or within 1 year of ceasing by reason of incapacity to be so employed, a gratuity of an amount equal to whichever is the greater of—

(a) the amount of the pensionable salary less the amount of any lump sum or incapacity gratuity previously paid to him; or

(b) the lump sum which would have been payable to him if he had at the date of his death become incapacitated and his service had been enhanced under regulation 51.

(2) There may be paid to the personal representatives of a teacher who—

(a) after 31st March 1972 ceased or ceases to be employed in reckonable service or service which would be reckonable if he had not attained the age of 70; and

(b) was immediately before his death credited with not less than 5 years' reckonable service; and

(c) is not a teacher in respect of whom a gratuity is payable under paragraph (1)—

a gratuity of an amount equal to the lump sum which would have been payable to him by virtue of regulation 54(1) if he had been entitled to a lump sum in accordance with those provisions.

(3) No gratuity shall be payable under this regulation in respect of a teacher to whose personal representatives is payable the balance of his contributions under regulation 41 or to whom retiring allowances were paid on grounds of incapacity by virtue of regulation 47 after he last ceased to be employed in reckonable service.

Deficiency payments

58.—(1) If, on the death of a teacher to whom retiring allowances have become payable in respect of reckonable service amounting to 10 years or more, the aggregate amount of the sums paid to him by way of annual pension and lump sum is less than his pensionable salary (no account being taken, in a case to which regulation 59(2) applies, of the salary referred to there as the pensionable salary determined at the end of further service) there may be paid to his personal representatives an amount equal to the deficiency.

(2) If, on the death of a teacher to whom retiring allowances have become payable in respect of reckonable service amounting to less than 10 years, the amount of the annual pension paid to him is less than 5 times the annual rate of that pension, there may be paid to his personal representatives an amount equal to the deficiency.

(3) There may be paid to the personal representatives of a teacher who dies in circumstances in which, if he had ceased to be employed for reasons other than death, he might have been entitled under regulation 59 in respect of further service to an annual pension and a lump sum, a deficiency payment not exceeding the amount whereby the lump sum which might have been so payable to the teacher exceeds the lump sum last paid to him.

(4) Notwithstanding paragraphs (1) and (2) a deficiency payment shall not be paid in respect of a teacher who was last employed in service of a kind specified in Schedule 5 which has been taken into account for the purposes of regulation 46(1)(c).

(5) For the purposes of this regulation there shall be disregarded any allocation of an annual pension or any deduction from a lump sum benefit.

Benefits after further service

59.—(1) If a teacher to whom a retiring allowance has become payable is again employed in reckonable service for not less than 365 days ("further service"), any annual pension previously paid shall cease to be paid on the discontinuance of that further service and, subject to paragraph (2), there shall be payable—

(a) an annual pension in respect of the whole of his reckonable service calculated in accordance with this Part; and

(b) a lump sum in respect of the service so calculated, reduced by the amount of any lump sum previously paid (any deduction under regulation 38 being disregarded).

(2) Where the pensionable salary of the teacher as determined at the end of his further service is less than his pensionable salary as determined for the purpose of calculating the retiring allowance previously payable, there shall be payable—

(a) an annual pension of an amount equal to the annual pension previously payable; and

(b) an annual pension in respect of his further service calculated in accordance with regulation 52; and

(c) a lump sum in respect of that service calculated in accordance with regulation 54.

(3) For the purposes of paragraphs (1)(a) and (2)(a) the amount of any annual pension shall be taken to be the amount thereof apart from any allocation under regulation 53.

(4) If a teacher to whom an incapacity allowance has become payable by virtue of regulation 47 is again employed in reckonable service for not less than 365 days, there shall be payable on the discontinuance of that further service—

(a) an annual pension calculated—

(i) in respect of his reckonable service before he attained the age of 60, in accordance with regulation 51 (his further service being deemed for this purpose to have begun on the day on which he became entitled to his previous annual pension); and

(ii) in respect of his reckonable service after he attained the age of 60, in accordance with regulation 52;

(b) a lump sum calculated in accordance with regulations 51 and 54 respectively, reduced by the amount of any lump sum previously paid;

(5) Paragraph (4) shall apply to a teacher whose further service is discontinued before he attains the age of 60 only if it is discontinued on his incapacity.

2 w

(6) In the application of paragraph (4) to any teacher in respect of whom the previous retiring allowance payable fell to be calculated under column (3) of the table in regulation 51 the references to the age of 60 shall be read as references to the age of 65.

Abatement of annual pension

60.—(1) This regulation shall apply to any teacher who, after a retiring allowance has become payable to him is employed as a teacher in—

(*a*) reckonable or comparable British service or service which would be reckonable or comparable British service if he had not attained the age of 70 or had 45 years' reckonable service;

(*b*) subject to paragraph (2), service which would be reckonable if he had not before 1st July 1976 elected that his annual pension should be dealt with under "Method B" as set out in previous provisions; or

(*c*) employment which is paid out of the Consolidated Fund or out of moneys provided by Parliament; or

(*d*) employment by a local authority, or other body which receives grant from the Secretary of State or a local authority for the purposes of employing him.

(2) A teacher who before 1st July 1976 elected that his annual pension should be dealt with under the said "Method B" may elect to be in reckonable service by giving notice in writing to the Secretary of State and such an election shall have effect from the commencement of these regulations or from the date of the election, whichever shall be the later.

(3) In the case of a teacher to whom this regulation applies, the annual pension payable to him shall—

(*a*) whilst he holds any employment to which paragraph (1) applies, being employment which is expressed to be regular employment, be so reduced or suspended (if necessary) as to ensure that his earnings together with his annual pension (including any increase under the Pensions (Increase) Act 1971)**(a)** shall not exceed his salary of reference;

(*b*) whilst he holds any employment to which paragraph (1) applies, being employment which is not expressed to be regular employment, be so reduced or suspended (if necessary) for any quarter as to ensure that his earnings during that quarter together with his annual pension (including any increase under the Pensions (Increase) Act 1971) shall not exceed 1/4 of his salary of reference.

(4) For the purposes of paragraph (3) where, under previous provisions or under any corresponding provisions for the time being in force in any statutory superannuation scheme applicable to teachers in comparable British service, a teacher has surrendered the whole or part of his lump sum in return for additional annual pension, no account shall be taken of the said additional pension.

(5) For the purposes of paragraph (3) the rate of earnings at the commencement of the period of employment shall be deemed to remain constant throughout the period of employment, provided that where there is a change of grade,

---

(a) 1971 c. 56.

or any other change in the conditions or terms of the employment which in the opinion of the Secretary of State constitutes a variation in the employment, the rate of earnings shall be taken to be that payable on the commencement of such change.

(6) For the purposes of this regulation the salary of reference of a re-employed teacher shall be the highest salary rate received during the last 3 years of reckonable or comparable British service, whether continuous or not, before retiring allowances last became payable to him, provided that—

  (i) if during that period the teacher has paid contributions on a previous higher salary under previous provisions and that salary is more favourable, it shall be the salary of reference;

  (ii) the salary of reference shall be reduced by the amount of any part of the annual pension which the teacher has allocated under regulation 53 or previous provisions or under any corresponding provisions applicable to teachers in comparable British service;

  (iii) the salary of reference so reduced by the amount (if any) specified in sub-paragraph (ii) shall be increased by the amount (if any) which would have been due to the teacher under the Pensions (Increase) Act 1971 if the salary of reference before being so reduced had been an annual pension coming into payment on the day following his last day of reckonable or comparable British service.

Avoidance of duplicate benefits

61.—(1) Subject to paragraph (3), if a period of reckonable service in respect of which retiring allowances are payable under these regulations is also reckoned for the purpose of any other pension payable to a teacher directly or indirectly out of moneys provided by Parliament or the rates levied by local authorities the Secretary of State shall, subject as hereafter in this regulation provided, reduce those retiring allowances by such a sum as will secure that the actuarial value in respect of that period shall be reduced by an amount equal to the actuarial value thereof of the other pension in respect of that period.

(2) For the purposes of this regulation any years of service added to reckonable service for the purpose of calculating a pension shall be deemed to be service, and any sum payable, whether as a continuing allowance or as a lump sum, by way of pension, superannuation allowance, compensation for loss or abolition of office or otherwise in respect of retirement, shall be deemed to be pension.

(3) A retiring allowance shall not be reduced under this regulation as to make it less than the actuarial value of the contributions paid by the teacher in respect of that period, and for this purpose the amount of those contributions shall be taken to include—

  (a) all contributions paid for current added years under Part III;

  (b) compound interest on those contributions calculated at the rate of 3 per cent per annum with yearly rests from 1st October in the financial year in which they are received to the date on which the annual pension begins to accrue.

(4) No reduction of annual pension shall be made which would result in the amount of that annual pension attributable to any period of reckonable service between 2nd April 1961 and 5th April 1975 (both dates inclusive) which was

non-participating employment within the meaning of the National Insurance Act 1965(a) being less than the amount of annual pension required to constitute equivalent pension benefits for the purposes of that Act.

(5) This regulation shall not apply in relation to a retirement pension granted to such an employee as is mentioned in regulation E14 of the Local Government Superannuation (Scotland) Regulations 1974 to 1975(b), under Part 1 of the Local Government Superannuation (Scotland) Act 1937(c) or under regulations under section 7 of the Superannuation Act 1972(d).

Suspension and resumption of incapacity pensions

62.—(1) If the Secretary of State is satisfied that a teacher under 60 in respect of whom an annual pension is payable by virtue of regulation 47 has ceased to be incapacitated payment of that annual pension may be suspended from such day as the Secretary of State thinks appropriate.

(2) Subject to paragraph (3), the payment of an annual pension suspended under paragraph (1) shall be resumed, if the Secretary of State is satisfied that the teacher has again become incapacitated, from the date on which application for the resumption of payment is received.

(3) Payment of an annual pension shall not be resumed—

(*a*) in the case of a teacher under 60, if he has been employed in reckonable service since the annual pension first became payable to him unless he has also been so employed within the period of 12 months immediately preceding the date of the application for the resumption of payment mentioned in paragraph (2);

(*b*) in the case of any teacher, if, since the annual pension was suspended, the Secretary of State has paid a transfer value in respect of him under interchange provisions;

(*c*) in the case of any teacher, if an annual pension has become payable to him in respect of further service by virtue of regulation 59(4).

(4) If, in a case where payment of an annual pension is resumed by reason of the Secretary of State being satisfied that the teacher has again become incapacitated, the Secretary of State is satisfied that the teacher was incapacitated during any part of the period during which the payment of the annual pension was suspended, the annual pension appropriate to that period shall be paid to the teacher.

(5) For the purposes of these regulations an annual pension whose payment has been resumed under paragraph (2) by reason of the teacher having attained the age of 60, and any further annual pension payable to that teacher, shall be deemed to be paid by virtue of regulation 46.

(6) Notwithstanding the preceding provisions of this regulation there shall in relation to any period of reckonable service between 2nd April 1961 and 5th April 1975 (both dates inclusive) which was non-participating employment within the meaning of the National Insurance Act 1965 be payable to a teacher to whom this regulation applies by way of annual pension an amount not less than that required to constitute equivalent pension benefits for the purposes of that Act.

(a) 1965 c. 51. (b) S.I. 1975/638 (1975 I, p. 2284).
(c) 1937 c. 69. (d) 1972 c. 11.

PART VII

FAMILY PENSIONS

Short-term pensions

63.—(1) On the death of a teacher in reckonable service or within 1 year of ceasing by reason of incapacity to be so employed a short-term pension shall be paid in accordance with table 1 or 2, as the case may be, of Schedule 7.

(2) A short-term pension shall be paid in accordance with table 3 of Schedule 7 on the death of every retired teacher who—

(a) has been in reckonable service since 1st April 1972;

(b) has 5 years' reckonable service counting for benefit; and

(c) at the time of death is in receipt of a pension under any provision (except an allocation provision) of these regulations.

(3) In the case of a retired teacher who was a re-employed teacher at the time of his death a short-term pension shall be paid in accordance with either table 2 or table 3 of Schedule 7, whichever is more favourable.

Long-term pensions

64.—(1) A long-term pension shall be paid in accordance with table 1 and where applicable, table 2 of Schedule 8 on the death of any teacher who was employed in reckonable service on or after 1st April 1972 and whose service counting for benefit amounts to at least 5 years.

(2) A long-term pension shall commence on the termination of any short-term pension or on the day following the death of the teacher if no short-term pension is payable.

(3) Only one pension (whether short-term or long-term) shall be payable at any one time in respect of the children of any teacher; and where apart from this paragraph more than one such pension would be payable the greater of those pensions shall be paid.

(4) If the annual rate of the long-term pension payable to a widow or adult nominated beneficiary or child exceeds the annual rate of the short-term pension the long-term pension shall be in substitution for the short-term pension.

(5) Any pension payable under this Part shall cease to be paid, unless the Secretary of State otherwise directs, upon that person marrying or commencing to cohabit with a person to whom he or she is not married; but any such pension which has ceased to be payable by reason of marriage or cohabitation may, if the Secretary of State so decides, be paid upon the person again becoming a widow or widower or on the termination of the last marriage, or as the case may be, the cohabitation.

(6) Any pension payable to or for the benefit of a child shall cease, subject to regulation 3, when the child ceases to be a child within the meaning of these regulations.

Nomination of beneficiaries

65.—(1) A man teacher who is unmarried and any woman teacher may at any time when—

(*a*) employed in reckonable service; and

(*b*) there is not in force a nomination made by the teacher for the purposes of previous provisions relating to family pensions—

nominate to receive a pension under this Part a person who at the time of the nomination is wholly or mainly dependent on the teacher and is—

(i) the teacher's parent; or

(ii) the teacher's husband; or

(iii) the teacher's widowed stepmother or stepfather; or

(iv) an unmarried descendant of either of the teacher's parents; or

(v) any unmarried descendant of the deceased wife of a teacher.

(2) The nomination of a beneficiary under this regulation shall become void—

(*a*) on the receipt by the Secretary of State of a written notice of revocation by the teacher;

(*b*) on the death or marriage of the nominated beneficiary;

(*c*) if the teacher is a man, on his marriage;

(*d*) if the beneficiary is a child, on his ceasing to be a child.

Special pension for widow

66. Unless she elects that this regulation shall not apply to her, there shall be paid to the widow of a teacher to whom regulation 38(5) applies who dies within 6 months of becoming employed in reckonable service without having made an election under Part IV a long-term pension of either—

(*a*) 1/2 of the annual pension which would have been payable to the teacher if on the day of his death such an annual pension had been an incapacity pension; or

(*b*) such lesser amount (but not less than 5/160ths of the teacher's pensionable salary) as she may elect within such time as is specified in a notice served on her by the Secretary of State specifying the deduction from the terminal sum in respect of that pension under regulation 38.

Special provision for widows of certain non-members

67.—(1) A long-term pension shall, if she elects by notice in writing to the Secretary of State within 3 months of the teacher's death, be paid to the widow of any non-member who dies without having been employed in reckonable service since 7th January 1974 if a death gratuity is payable in respect of him in terms of regulation 57(2).

(2) A long-term pension under this regulation shall be calculated by multiplying 1/160th of the teacher's pensionable salary by the number of years by reference to which the death gratuity falls to be calculated.

Part VIII

Special Provisions Relating to War Service

Application to teachers

68.—(1) "War service" means such service over the age of 18 as is mentioned in Section 1 of the Superannuation Act 1946(a) at any time between 1st September 1939 and 31st March 1949 (both dates inclusive), but does not include any service which was or is reckonable service or was or is comparable British service or in respect of which a naval pension, a service pension (within the meaning of the Recall of Army and Air Force Pensioners Act 1948(b)) or retired pay is payable.

(2) Paragraph (1) applies to any teacher who, after war service and without having first been employed in comparable British service, was first employed in reckonable service—

(a) before 1st July 1950; or

(b) after 30th June 1950 on the satisfactory completion of a period of probationary teaching service which under previous provisions the Secretary of State required the teacher to undertake; or

(c) after 30th June 1950 on the completion of a course leading to certification as a teacher under the Regulations for the Preliminary Education, Training and Certification of Teachers for Various Grades of Schools (Scotland) 1931(c), being—

    (i) a course provided under the Supply of Teachers (Emergency Arrangements) (Scotland) Regulations 1947(d); or the scheme for the emergency recruitment and training of teachers established by the Ministry of Education; or any scheme to like effect established by the Ministry of Education, Northern Ireland; or

    (ii) a course in respect of which grants were paid to him under the Further Education and Training Scheme for the purposes of training him for a teaching career; or

    (iii) a course which he began before 1st July 1950; or

    (iv) if he began the final year of the course before 1st November 1950, any such course as is mentioned in regulation 30(1) (4 year first degree and teacher training courses) of the Training of Teachers Grant Regulations 1948(e).

(3) This Part does not apply to a teacher if the first period of his reckonable service referred to in paragraph (2) is not treated as reckonable service for the purpose of calculating any benefit.

Contributions in respect of war service

69.—(1) For the purpose of defraying so much of the cost of any benefits as is attributable to war service there shall be deducted from the lump sum or gratuity payable in respect of the teacher an amount equal to the aggregate of—

(a) $3\frac{3}{4}$ per cent of the aggregate remuneration in respect of war service which would have been received by a teacher in receipt of a salary at an annual rate of £200 (if the teacher is a man) or £175 (if the teacher is a woman) during that period; and

---

(a) 1946 c. 60.   **(b)** 12, 13 & 14 Geo. 6 c. 8.
(c) S.R. & O. 1931/180 (Rev. VI, p. 758: 1931 p. 363).
(d) S.I. 1947/127 (1947 I, p. 631).
(e) S.I. 1948/1704 (Rev. VI, p. 570: 1948 I, p. 736).

(b) compound interest on that sum at the rate of 3½ per cent per annum with yearly rests from 1st July 1950 until either—

(i) the date of payment of the lump sum or gratuity from which the deduction falls to be made; or

(ii) where a transfer value is payable by virtue of regulation 72, the date on which the teacher becomes subject to the approved superannuation scheme.

(2) Unless he makes an election under regulation 70, paragraph (1) shall not apply to any war service of a teacher if, apart from this paragraph, the pension payable to or in respect of him would not be more, or the death gratuity would be less, than would have been the case if paragraph (1) had not applied to that service.

Contributions for family pensions in respect of war service

70.—(1) A teacher in whose case the whole of his reckonable service would in the event of his death count for benefit for the purposes of Schedule 9, shall if he so elects pay additional contributions in respect of his war service.

(2) Where a teacher makes an election for the purposes of this regulation the lump sum or gratuity payable in respect of him shall be reduced by the amount determined as the actuarial cost of the increase in the amount of any pension which is payable by virtue of this regulation.

(3) An election for the purposes of this regulation shall be made in writing and delivered to the Secretary of State so as to be received by him before the payment of the lump sum or gratuity from which the reduction falls to be made.

(4) If the teacher dies without having made an election, the election may be made by his widow and paragraphs (2) and (3) shall apply with the necessary modifications accordingly.

PART IX

INTERCHANGES

Superannuation schemes

71.—(1) For the purposes of this Part "superannuation scheme" means—

(a) a scheme established under—

(i) section 1 of the Superannuation Act 1972(a) or the Superannuation (Northern Ireland) Order 1972(b) or other arrangements for superannuation maintained in pursuance of regulations made, or having effect as if made, under that Act or Order; or

(ii) section 1 of the Police Pensions Act 1976(c) or section 25 of the Police Act (Northern Ireland) 1970(d); or

(iii) a Fireman's Pension Scheme made under section 26 of the Fire Services Act 1947(e) or a scheme made under section 17 of the Fire Service Act (Northern Ireland) 1969(f); or

---

(a) 1972 c. 11.　　　　　　　　　　(b) S.I. 1972/1073 (N.I. 10).
(c) 1976 c. 35.　　　　　　　　　　(d) 1970 c. 9 (N.I.).
(e) 1947 c. 41.　　　　　　　　　　(f) 1969 c. 13 (N.I.).

(iv) a scheme made under the Parliamentary and Other Pensions Act 1972(**a**) or the scheme established by Part II of the Ministerial Salaries and Members Pensions Act (Northern Ireland) 1965(**b**) or arrangements for superannuation maintained in pursuance of an order in Council under section 9 or 26 of the Northern Ireland Constitution Act 1973(**c**) ("a statutory scheme"); or

(*b*) the trusts of a fund approved by the Board of Inland Revenue under section 208 of the Income and Corporation Taxes Act 1970(**d**) or a scheme (other than a statutory scheme) approved by the Board of Inland Revenue under section 222 of that Act or under Chapter II of Part II of the Finance Act 1970(**e**) or approved by the Board for the purposes of this Part in the case of any teacher ("a non-statutory scheme"); and reference to a non-statutory scheme in regulation 72 is a reference to a scheme approved by the Board of Inland Revenue on the day when the teacher first becomes subject to the scheme.

(2) In their application to a statutory scheme references to the person responsible for the management of the scheme are to be construed as references to the Minister of the Crown, local authority or police or fire authority administering the scheme.

Payment of transfer values

72.—(1) On an application being made in writing by the person responsible for the management of a superannuation scheme approved by the Board of Inland Revenue the Secretary of State may pay to that person a transfer value (calculated in accordance with Part I of Schedule 10) in respect of a former teacher who, after being employed in reckonable service, becomes subject to that scheme and any such application shall be made within 6 months from the day when the former teacher became subject to the scheme.

(2) When the payment of any such transfer value is made the reckonable service of the teacher to whom it relates shall cease to be treated as such for all purposes of these regulations.

Receipt of transfer values

73.—(1) The Secretary of State may receive a transfer value from the person responsible for the management of a superannuation scheme in respect of a teacher who, after being subject to that scheme, elects within 6 months of his becoming employed in reckonable service that such a transfer value shall be paid in respect of him.

(2) A teacher in respect of whom a transfer value is received by virtue of paragraph (1) shall be credited with reckonable service in accordance with Part 2 of Schedule 10.

Modifications relating to teachers in comparable British service

74. In their application to teachers in comparable British service—

(*a*) regulation 72 shall have effect with the insertion of "or has at any time become" after "becomes"; and

---

(**a**) 1972 c. 48.   (**b**) 1965 c. 18 (N.I.)
(**c**) 1973 c. 36.   (**d**) 1970 c. 10.
(**e**) 1970 c. 24.

(b) regulation 73 shall have effect with the substitution of the words "or has at any time elected" for the words "within 6 months of his becoming employed in reckonable service".

Exceptions

75.—(1) No transfer value shall be paid under regulation 72 in respect of a teacher who, when the application relating to him was received by the Secretary of State, was in receipt of an annual pension by virtue of regulation 46.

(2) No transfer value shall be received under these regulations in respect of a re-employed teacher to whom regulation 60(1)(*a*) or (*b*) applies or a person who is in receipt of an annual pension under a provision in a statutory scheme corresponding to regulation 46.

PART X

FINANCIAL PROVISIONS

Teachers' superannuation account

76. An account of the receipts and payments under these regulations in continuation of the account kept under regulation 6 of the Teachers Superannuation (Financial Provisions) (Scotland) Regulations 1972(**a**) shall be kept by the Secretary of State for every financial year ("the accounting period") commencing with the accounting period which ended on 31st March 1972 in the form specified in Part 1 of Schedule 11.

Receipts

77. There shall be treated as receipts into the account for each accounting period—

(*a*) the contributions paid by teachers and employers under regulations 11(2)(*a*) and (*b*) and received by the Secretary of State during the period;

(*b*) a sum equal to the amount determined in accordance with Part III of Schedule 11 as payments during the period upon retiring allowances and gratuities attributable to service before 1st June 1922;

(*c*) any transfer value received during the period by the Secretary of State under regulation 73(1) from the Minister for the Civil Service, the Secretary of State for Social Services or the Secretary of State for Education and Science;

(*d*) a sum representing interest calculated in accordance with regulation 79;

(*e*) the amount of any balance of receipts over payments remaining at the end of the last preceding accounting period; and

(*f*) any other receipts in the period including payments of interest under regulation 15.

(a) S.I. 1972/551 (1972 I, p. 1855).

Payments

78. There shall be treated as payments from the account for each accounting period—

(*a*) any payments during the period of benefits;

(*b*) any transfer value paid during the period by the Secretary of State under regulation 72(1) to the Minister for the Civil Service, the Secretary of State for Social Services or the Secretary of State for Education and Science; and

(*c*) any other payments during the period by the Secretary of State under these regulations.

Interest

79.—(1) The sum representing interest which is to be treated as a receipt to the account under regulation 77(*d*) shall be calculated in accordance with this regulation.

(2) The interest on the balance of receipts (excluding interest calculated in accordance with this regulation) over payments in an accounting period shall for that period be one half, and for the next succeeding and subsequent accounting periods the whole, of the interest that would have accrued on the investment of a sum equal to that balance if it had been invested at the beginning of that accounting period in a security selected by the Secretary of State, after consultation with the Government Actuary, at the price determined in accordance with paragraph (4) increased for any period by any sum added for that period by virtue of regulation 80(1)(*a*).

(3) For the period up to and including the accounting period beginning on 1st April 1970 the accumulated balance of revenue over expenditure shall be deemed to have been invested in the manner set out in Part II of Schedule 11.

(4) The price of a security shall be the price halfway between the highest and lowest prices shown in the Official Daily List of the London Stock Exchange for 1st October in the period in question or, if that Exchange is or was closed on that day, the last day before that day on which it is or was open.

Accounting on redemption of securities

80.—(1) On the date of redemption of a security in which an investment is deemed to have been made for the purposes of regulation 79—

(*a*) the sum representing interest which, in accordance with that regulation, is treated as having been received into the account in respect of that investment shall be increased by the amount by which the notional proceeds of its redemption exceeds the sum deemed to have been invested in it or, as the case may be, reduced by the amount by which those proceeds fall short of that sum; and

(*b*) a sum equivalent to the sum deemed to have been invested in the security shall be deemed to be re-invested on that date in a security selected by the Secretary of State after consultation with the Government Actuary.

(2) The notional proceeds of redemption referred to in paragraph (1) shall be the amount which would be received in respect of an investment on the redemption of the security in which it is deemed to have been made, reduced by any capital gains tax deemed to be payable in accordance with regulation 81.

(3) For the purposes of this regulation the date of redemption of a security is the last date on which it may be redeemed in accordance with the terms on which it was issued.

Notional deductions for tax

81.—(1) In relation to any investment deemed to have been made for the purposes of this Part—

(a) income tax in respect of interest; and

(b) capital gains tax in respect of any capital gains accruing on the redemption of the security in which it was made,

shall be deemed to be payable to the same extent as they would be payable if the investment were held for the purposes of a retirement benefits scheme approved under Chapter II of Part II of the Finance Act 1970 and providing benefits comparable to those provided under these regulations.

(2) The rates of income tax and capital gains tax, deemed to be payable in any year under paragraph (1) shall be the rates of those taxes charged for that year.

(3) Any question arising under this regulation as to the extent to which income tax and capital gains tax shall be deemed to be payable under paragraph (1) shall be determined by the Secretary of State and his decision shall be final.

Actuarial inquiries

82.—(1) The Government Actuary shall make an actuarial inquiry with respect to the teachers' superannuation account at the end of the accounting period which ended on 31st March 1976 and at the end of every 5th subsequent accounting period.

(2) An inquiry made in pursuance of paragraph (1) shall determine whether the value at the end of the accounting period ("the terminal date") of the payments attributable to service after 1st June 1922 included in the account after the terminal date in respect of teachers who were then employed or had previously been employed in reckonable service exceeds or falls short of the aggregate of—

(a) the value at the terminal date of—

(i) all contributions payable in respect of such teachers after that date (except supplementary contributions payable after the accounting period in which the report required by paragraph (5) is made); and

(ii) the sums falling to be credited to the account after that date in accordance with sub-paragraphs (d) and (f) of regulation 77; and

(b) the actuarial value of the notional investments by reference to which the sum representing interest is calculated in accordance with regulation 79.

(3) Where an actuarial inquiry reveals a deficiency the report of the inquiry shall specify the rate per cent. (being a rate of a multiple of one quarter of 1 per cent) at which supplementary contributions paid by employers of teachers employed in reckonable service would remove the deficiency by the expiry of a period of 40 years beginning with the accounting period next after that in which the report is made.

(4) An inquiry under this regulation shall determine the rate per cent of the salaries of teachers who became employed in reckonable service on the first day of the period following the period for which the inquiry is made at which contributions paid to the Secretary of State would in the opinion of the Government Actuary defray the costs of the benefits likely to be payable in respect of their service.

(5) The report on each actuarial inquiry under this regulation shall be made to the Secretary of State and shall be laid by him before each House of Parliament.

PART XI

SUPPLEMENTARY PROVISIONS

Records and information

83.—(1) Employers of persons to whom by reason of their employment these regulations apply shall record for each such person for each financial year—

(*a*) the rate of salary;

(*b*) the amount of salary paid, distinguishing payments which are subject to contributions from other payments;

(*c*) the value of any emoluments in kind treated as forming part of the salary of the teacher by virtue of regulation 7;

(*d*) the contributions deducted;

(*e*) the period of employment in reckonable service;

(*f*) the dates of absence on sick leave and special leave, with reasons for the latter leave, and the proportion of salary during such absence—

and shall make to the Secretary of State such reports and returns, and give him such information relating to such persons, as he may require for the purposes of his functions under these regulations.

(2) Every person to whom by reason of his employment these regulations apply or, as the case may be, the personal representatives of every person to whom by that reason they applied, shall give such information and produce such documents to the Secretary of State as he may require for the purposes of his functions under these regulations.

Payment of benefits

84.—(1) Every pension, annuity or other sum payable under these regulations which does not consist of a single payment—

(*a*) shall normally be payable monthly; but

(*b*) may, on the application of the person entitled thereto, be paid by quarterly instalments; or

(*c*) may be paid in such instalments and at such intervals as the Secretary of State may think appropriate.

(2) Where payment of any such sum is due in respect of a period which is less than the interval at which it is payable—

(*a*) the amount payable in respect of each complete month of the period shall be 1/12th of the annual rate of the sum; and (*b*) the amount payable in respect of a period of less than 1 complete month shall bear the same proportion to 1/12th of the annual rate of the sum as the number of days in respect of which it is payable bears to the total number of days in the month in which those days fall.

(3) If a person in respect of whom a benefit is payable is a minor, or is in the opinion of the Secretary of State incapable by reason of infirmity of mind or body of managing his affairs, the Secretary of State may pay the benefit to any person having the care of that person or apply it in such manner as he thinks appropriate for the benefit of that person or his dependants.

Payments in respect of deceased persons

85. On the death of a person to whom or to whose estate any sum not exceeding £1,500 is due under these regulations the Secretary of State may, without confirmation or other proof of the title of the personal representatives of that person, pay that sum to the personal representatives or to the person, or to or among any 1 or more of any persons, appearing to him to be beneficially entitled to the personal estate of the deceased.

Benefits not assignable

86.—(1) Every assignation of or charge on, and every agreement to assign or charge, any benefit payable under these regulations, shall be void and no such benefit shall be liable to arrestment.

(2) On the bankruptcy of a person entitled to any such benefit, no part of the benefit shall pass to any trustee or other person acting on behalf of his creditors.

(3) Nothing in these regulations shall affect the powers of the court under section 148 of the Bankruptcy (Scotland) Act 1913**(a)** (under which the court may order the payment of the whole or part of these benefits to the trustees in bankruptcy).

(4) In this regulation—

    (*a*) "benefit" includes any right to a return of contributions under Part V;

    (*b*) "assignation" does not include allocation under regulation 53 or any disposition made in pursuance of an agreement with the Secretary of State relating to the recovery of overpayment of benefit.

Forfeiture of benefits

87. The Secretary of State may withhold, or pay at such reduced rate as he may determine, the payment of any retiring allowance or gratuity payable apart from this regulation to or in respect of a teacher who is convicted of any offence committed before or after the benefit becomes payable which is—

    (*a*) an offence of treason; or

    (*b*) one or more offences under the Official Secret Acts 1911 to 1939**(b)** for which he has been sentenced on the same occasion to a term of imprisonment of, or for 2 or more consecutive terms amounting in the aggregate to, at least 10 years; or

    (*c*) any other offence in connection with his employment as a teacher which is certified by the Secretary of State either to have been gravely injurious to the State or to be liable to lead to serious loss of confidence in the public service.

(a) 1913 c. 20.   (b) 1911 c. 28; 1920 c. 75; 1939 c. 121.

Extension of time

88. Subject to regulation 27(6), the Secretary of State may in any particular case extend the time within which anything is required or authorised to be done under these regulations.

Power to determine questions

89. Subject to section 11(2) of the Superannuation Act 1972**(a)** any question which arises under these regulations as to the rights and liabilities of or in respect of any person shall be decided by the Secretary of State, whose decision shall be final.

Consequential amendment of enactments

90.—(1) The references in regulation E14 of the Local Government Superannuation (Scotland) Regulations 1974 to 1975**(b)** to the Teachers Superannuation (Scotland) Regulations 1969 to 1976**(c)** and to regulation 51 of the Teachers Superannuation (Scotland) Regulations 1969**(d)** shall include references to these regulations and regulation 61 respectively.

(2) Section 8(2)(*a*) (date of accrual of earnings related pension) of the Pensions (Increase) Act 1971**(e)** shall not apply in respect of any person payable under these regulations based on the pensionable salary of the teacher.

Bruce Millan,
One of Her Majesty's Principal
Secretaries of State.

New St. Andrew's House,
Edinburgh.

28th July 1977.

Consent of the Minister for the Civil Service given under his Official Seal on 1st August 1977.

(L.S.)

W. G. Bristow,
Authorised by the Minister for
the Civil Service.

(a) 1972 c. 11.   **(b)** S.I. 1975/638 (1975 I, p. 2284).
(c) S.I. 1976/910 (1976 II, p. 2346).   **(d)** S.I. 1969/77 (1969 I, p. 133).
(e) 1971 c. 56.

Regulations 4 and 5

SCHEDULE 1

SPECIFIED EMPLOYMENTS WHICH ARE RECKONABLE SERVICE

1. Employment as a teacher in a public or grant-aided school, or in a college of education, central institution, or other establishment which is maintained or grant-aided out of moneys either provided by Parliament or raised by the rates levied by local authorities, except a teacher in employment on or after 1st April 1975 with the East of Scotland College of Agriculture, the North of Scotland College of Agriculture or the West of Scotland Agricultural College who is subject to the Department of Agriculture and Fisheries for Scotland Superannuation Scheme 1975 as a consequence of that employment.

2. Employment as a teacher in a school which is an accepted school within the meaning of Schedule 2 and whose employment therein is reckonable service by virtue of that Schedule.

3. Employment as a teacher in a university or part of a university, which before becoming a university or part of a university was a central institution, being a teacher whose employment therein immediately before 1st August 1977 was reckonable service.

4. Employment as a teacher of a kind other than in this Schedule before specified if—

   (a) he is employed by an education authority otherwise than in a public school; or

   (b) his employer receives grant either from the Secretary of State or a local authority for the purposes of employing him and he elects by notice in writing to the Secretary of State within 3 months of the commencement of his employment, with the agreement of his employer, that his service shall be reckonable service and the Secretary of State agrees; or

   (c) his employment is approved by the Secretary of State for the purposes of this Schedule and he elects by notice in writing to the Secretary of State within 3 months of the commencement of his employment, with the agreement of his employer, that his service shall be reckonable service and the Secretary of State so agrees.

5. Continuation in employment after 1st August 1977 as a supervisor or organiser or in another capacity which was treated as reckonable service under previous provisions.

Schedule 1, paragraph 2

SCHEDULE 2

ACCEPTED SCHOOLS

1. For the purposes of this Schedule—

   (a) "accepted school" means an independent school which—

      (i) immediately before 1st August 1977 was accepted under previous provisions; or

      (ii) being registered, is accepted by the Secretary of State under the provisions of this Schedule upon the application of the governing body or proprietor;

   (b) "registered" means registered in the register of independent schools in accordance with Part V of the Education (Scotland) Act 1962(a);

   (c) "proprietor" has the meaning assigned to it by section 145 of the Education (Scotland) Act 1962 and includes a person who, by reason of holding any office or having any interest in a company by which the school is conducted, is substantially in the position of a proprietor.

(a) 1962 c. 47.

2. Notwithstanding the provisions of paragraph 1 the Secretary of State shall have power in such case as he thinks appropriate to accept under the provisions of this Schedule an independent school which is for the time being only provisionally registered.

3. The date on which an independent school becomes an accepted school under paragraph 1(*a*)(ii) shall, unless an alternative date is agreed by the Secretary of State and the governing body or proprietor thereof, be the 1st September preceding acceptance of the application.

4. An accepted school shall cease to be an accepted school on such a day as is specified in a notice in writing sent by the Secretary of State to the governing body or proprietor of the school on or after any of the following events—

(*a*) the receipt by the Secretary of State of an application by the governing body or proprietor that the school shall cease to be an accepted school;

(*b*) the school ceasing to be on the register of independent schools in Scotland;

(*c*) any default by the governing body or proprietor in the payment of contributions;

(*d*) failure by the governing body or proprietor to comply within 1 month with any requirement of the Secretary of State to make any report or return, give any information or produce any document, under regulation 83;

(*e*) failure by the governing body or proprietor to comply with any other provision of the regulations relating to the employment of teachers in reckonable service;

(*f*) the closure of the school.

5. Subject as hereafter in this Schedule provided, service as a teacher in an accepted school shall be reckonable service.

6. The service of a teacher in an accepted school shall not be reckonable service if—

(*a*) the teacher is a proprietor thereof; or

(*b*) paragraph (1)(*a*)(i) applies to the school and the teacher's employment therein immediately before 1st August 1977 was not reckonable service; or

(*c*) being employed in the school immediately before the date on which the Secretary of State notifies the governing body or proprietor thereof that he has accepted it, the teacher so elects within 3 months of that date by notice in writing to the Secretary of State.

7. A teacher, not being a person to whom paragraph 6(*a*) applies, employed in an accepted school whose service therein is not reckonable service may elect by notice in writing to the Secretary of State that his service therein shall be reckonable service and, on his so electing, it shall be such service from a date determined by the Secretary of State.

Regulations 23 and 38

SCHEDULE 3

ADDED YEARS

METHOD 1 ELECTIONS

1. The rate at which Method 1 contributions shall be payable shall be expressed as a percentage, being a whole number not exceeding 9, of the rate of the salary in respect of which the contributions fall to be paid.

2. The rate shall be such that the actuarial cost of purchasing added years will not be met within less than 5 years or (in the case of a teacher who is aged 55 or over when he begins to pay contributions) before the teacher attains the age of 60.

3. In the case of a teacher who is paying additional contributions under Parts III or IV otherwise than under regulation 23 the maximum rate of contributions under these regulations shall be determined by deducting from 9 per cent the percentage rate of those additional contributions.

4. An election under these regulations may be varied by a subsequent election to pay contributions at a higher rate in accordance with the provisions of this Schedule, taking effect,

(a) in the case of contributions payable by virtue of regulation 23(4), on the teacher again becoming employed in reckonable service; and

(b) in any other case, from 1st April in the year following the year in which the varying election is received by the Secretary of State.

Regulation 23(1)

METHOD 1 CONTRIBUTIONS AND DEDUCTIONS

TABLE 1

CONTRIBUTIONS

A	B								
Age on the date from which the teacher's election is effective (regulation 22(4))	Period in years for which contributions are required to be paid in respect of each added year (regulation 21)								
	Rate of contributions elected (regulation 22)								
	1%	2%	3%	4%	5%	6%	7%	8%	9%
31 and under	16·00	8·00	5·33	4·00	3·20	2·67	2·29	2·00	1·78
32	16·10	8·05	5·37	4·02	3·22	2·68	2·30	2·01	1·79
33	16·20	8·10	5·40	4·05	3·24	2·70	2·31	2·02	1·80
34	16·30	8·15	5·43	4·07	3·26	2·72	2·33	2·04	1·81
35	16·40	8·20	5·47	4·10	3·28	2·73	2·34	2·05	1·82
36	16·50	8·25	5·50	4·12	3·30	2·75	2·36	2·06	1·83
37	16·60	8·30	5·53	4·15	3·32	2·77	2·37	2·07	1·84
38	16·70	8·35	5·57	4·17	3·34	2·78	2·39	2·09	1·86
39	16·80	8·40	5·60	4·20	3·36	2·80	2·40	2·10	1·87
40	16·90	8·45	5·63	4·22	3·38	2·82	2·41	2·11	1·88
41	17·00	8·50	5·67	4·25	3·40	2·83	2·43	2·12	1·89
42	17·15	8·58	5·72	4·29	3·43	2·86	2·45	2·14	1·91
43	17·30	8·65	5·77	4·32	3·46	2·88	2·47	2·16	1·92
44	17·45	8·72	5·82	4·36	3·49	2·91	2·49	2·18	1·94
45	17·60	8·80	5·87	4·40	3·52	2·93	2·51	2·20	1·96
46	17·75	8·87	5·92	4·44	3·55	2·96	2·54	2·22	1·97
47	17·95	8·97	5·98	4·49	3·59	2·99	2·56	2·24	1·99
48	18·15	9·07	6·05	4·54	3·63	3·02	2·59	2·27	2·02
49	18·35	9·17	6·12	4·59	3·67	3·06	2·62	2·29	2·04
50	18·55	9·27	6·18	4·64	3·71	3·09	2·65	2·32	2·06
51	18·80	9·40	6·27	4·70	3·76	3·13	2·69	2·35	2·09
52	19·05	9·52	6·35	4·76	3·81	3·17	2·72	2·38	2·12
53	19·30	9·65	6·43	4·82	3·86	3·22	2·76	2·41	2·14
54	19·55	9·77	6·52	4·89	3·91	3·26	2·79	2·44	2·17
55	19·80	9·90	6·60	4·95	3·96	3·30	2·83	2·47	2·20
56	20·05	10·02	6·68	5·01	4·01	3·34	2·86	2·51	2·23
57	20·25	10·12	6·75	5·06	4·05	3·37	2·89	2·53	2·25
58	20·40	10·20	6·80	5·10	4·08	3·40	2·91	2·55	2·27
59	20·50	10·25	6·83	5·12	4·10	3·42	2·93	2·56	2·28
60	20·55	10·27	6·85	5·14	4·11	3·42	2·94	2·57	2·28
61	20·50	10·25	6·83	5·12	4·10	3·42	2·93	2·56	2·28
62	20·45	10·22	6·82	5·11	4·09	3·41	2·92	2·56	2·27
63	20·35	10·18	6·78	5·09	4·07	3·39	2·91	2·54	2·26
64	20·25	10·12	6·75	5·06	4·05	3·37	2·89	2·53	2·25
65	20·10	10·05	6·70	5·02	4·02	3·35	2·87	2·51	2·23
66	19·90	9·95	6·63	4·97	3·98	3·32	2·84	2·49	2·21
67	19·65	9·82	6·55	4·91	3·93	3·27	2·81	2·46	2·18
68	19·35	9·67	6·45	4·84	3·87	3·22	2·76	2·42	2·15
69	19·00	9·50	6·33	4·75	3·80	3·17	2·71	2·38	2·11

NOTE: The necessary interpolations are to be made where the period elected under regulation 21 is not an exact number of years.

Regulations 23(4) and 38(2)

TABLE 2

DEDUCTIONS

As regards any teacher the deduction to be made is the annual amount of his contributions at the last rate payable multiplied by the factor shown in column B against the entry in column A which specifies the number of further years during which contributions would have been payable, reduced where necessary in accordance with the provisions of regulation 19(2).

A Number of further years during which contributions would have been payable	B Factor
1	·990
2	1·961
3	2·913
4	3·846
5	4·760
6	5·657
7	6·536
8	7·398
9	8·244
10	9·072
11	9·884
12	10·681
13	11·461
14	12·227
15	12·977
16	13·713
17	14·434
18	15·141
19	15·835
20	16·514

NOTE: The necessary interpolations are to be made where the further period for which contributions would have been payable is not an exact number of years.

Regulation 24

TABLE 3

METHOD 2 CONTRIBUTIONS

The factor for the purposes of regulation 24 is the percentage of the full salary of the teacher at the rate payable to him on the date on which the Secretary of State receives his election which appears in the table below against the entry relating to his age on that date.

Age	Percentage
under 23	11·15
23	11·25
24	11·35
25	11·45
26	11·50
27	11·55
28	11·65
29	11·75
30	11·85
31	11·95
32	12·05
33	12·15
34	12·25
35	12·35
36	12·45
37	12·55
38	12·65
39	12·75
40	12·85
41	12·95
42	13·05
43	13·15
44	13·25
45	13·40
46	13·55
47	13·70
48	13·85
49	14·00
50	14·15
51	14·30
52	14·45
53	14·65
54	14·90
55	15·15
56	15·45
57	15·80
58	16·20
59	16·70
60	17·30
61	17·40
62	17·50
63	17·55
64 and over	17·60

Notes:

1. If the teacher has, within 1 year (or, in the case of a teacher who has attained the age of 57, 3 years) immediately preceding the receipt by the Secretary of State of an election to pay contributions, suffered a reduction in salary or taken up a new post in reckonable service at a lower rate of salary than the rate of his previous post in that service, his salary for the purposes of regulation 24 shall be the amount of the salary which, in the opinion of the Secretary of State, would have been payable to him if he had continued to be employed on terms and conditions comparable to those on which he was employed immediately before his salary was reduced or, as the case may be, his post was changed.

2. In the case of any teacher whose election is received during the period by reference to which his pensionable salary falls to be determined, the factor for the purposes of regulation 24 is the percentage of such a salary not exceeding his pensionable salary as the Secretary of State may, after consulting the Government Actuary, determine.

Regulation 30

SCHEDULE 4

TABLE 1

DEEMED ADDITIONAL SERVICE

The deemed additional service of any teacher shall be determined in accordance with the formula $\dfrac{ab}{c}$ where—

a is the factor shown in the appropriate entry of column B of the table below;

b is the amount (in pounds) of his additional contributions held in the Teachers' Family Benefits Fund at 31st March 1972; and

c is the amount (in pounds) of his annual salary at that date.

A Age of teacher at last birthday before 1st April 1972	B Factor	A Age of teacher at last birthday before 1st April 1972	B Factor
18	21·4	40	50·3
19	23·9	41	50·2
20	26·2	42	50·0
21	28·4	43	49·8
22	30·6	44	49·6
23	32·6		
24	34·5	45	49·4
		46	49·3
25	36·3	47	49·2
26	38·0	48	49·1
27	39·6	49	49·0
28	41·1		
29	42·6	50	49·0
		51	49·0
30	43·9	52	49·0
31	45·2	53	48·9
32	46·4	54	48·9
33	47·4		
34	48·4	55	48·8
		56	48·8
35	49·2	57	48·7
36	49·8	58	48·7
37	50·0	59	48·6
38	50·2		
39	50·3	60 and over	48·6

Regulation 36

TABLE 2

DETERMINATION OF CONTRIBUTIONS FOR PRE-APRIL 1972 FAMILY PENSIONS

A	B
Age on the date 6 months before the date from which additional contributions begin to be paid	Period in years for which contributions are required to be paid in respect of each year of service (regulations 34(1)(*a*) and 36(1))

	Rate of contributions elected (regulation 34(1)(*b*))								
	1%	2%	3%	4%	5%	6%	7%	8%	9%
32 and under ...	3·15	1·58	1·05	·79	·63	·525	·45	·395	·35
33–37	3·20	1·60	1·07	·80	·64	·535	·46	·40	·355
38–42	3·30	1·65	1·10	·82	·66	·55	·47	·41	·365
43–47	3·35	1·68	1·12	·84	·67	·56	·48	·42	·37
48 and over ...	3·40	1·70	1·13	·85	·68	·565	·485	·425	·375

NOTES:

1. A teacher who before the day specified in relation to him under regulation 36(3)(*a*) paid in accordance with previous provisions additional contributions so payable after 31st March 1972 shall be taken to have paid contributions in accordance with regulation 34 at the rate specified by him in accordance with regulation 34(1)(*b*) for the number of years equal to the fraction of which the denominator is that rate and the numerator is the amount of those contributions expressed as a percentage of his annual salary on the day specified; and, as regards any such teacher, that number shall accordingly be deducted from the period determined in accordance with table 2 above.

2. The necessary interpolations are to be made where the period elected under regulation 34(1)(*a*) is not an exact number of years.

Regulation 46(1)(*c*)

SCHEDULE 5

EMPLOYMENTS COUNTING TOWARDS ENTITLEMENT TO RETIRING ALLOWANCES

1. Employment in the British Isles in a university, university college or college of a university or as a full-time teacher—

(*a*) in respect of which contributions were payable under the Federated System of Superannuation for Universities before 1st April 1975; or

(*b*) whose accrued rights under that system in respect of his previous such employment were transferred to the Universities Superannuation Scheme established on 1st April 1975.

2. Employment as an inspector appointed under section 77(2) of the Education Act 1944(a) of a person whose previous teaching service had before 23rd April 1973 been approved by the Secretary of State for Education and Science for the purpose of paragraph 9 of Schedule 2 to the Teachers' Superannuation Regulations 1967(b).

3. Employment of any person as a civil servant before 23rd April 1973 in a post in which teaching experience was certified by the Secretary of State to have been of value at the date of appointment thereto, having been preceded by employment for not less than 3 years in service as a teacher in a capacity approved by the Secretary of State.

4. Pensionable employment as an educational officer or in some other educational capacity in the service of the British Broadcasting Corporation.

5. Membership of the House of Commons which is reckonable service within the meaning of the Parliamentary and Other Pensions Act 1972(c).

6. Employment as a civil servant in Scotland, England or Wales which is not covered by paragraph 3.

7. Pensionable employment as a civil servant in Northern Ireland, the Isle of Man or the Channel Islands.

8. Employment which is contributory service for the purpose of the Overseas Service Pensions (Scheme and Fund) Regulations 1966(d).

9. Employment in a country specified in section 1(3) of the British Nationality Act 1948(e) or any colony within the meaning of that Act which is or was pensionable under any law for the time being in force in that country or which is employment by the Government or a public authority of that country in respect of which contributions are or were payable to a provident fund, being employment—

(a) as a full-time teacher;

(b) involving to a substantial extent the control or supervision of teachers; or

(c) as a civil servant.

10. Pensionable employment in a university, university college or college of a university in any country specified in section 1(3) of the British Nationality Act 1948 or in any colony within the meaning of that Act.

11. Employment in the Republic of South Africa or in the mandated territory of South West Africa of a kind specified in paragraph 9 or 10 of a person who at any time during the 3 months immediately preceding 31st May 1962 was employed in that Republic or in that territory in service which was 2nd class service for the purpose of regulation 6 of the Teachers (Superannuation) (Scotland) Regulations 1957(f).

12. Employment as a full-time teacher of a person holding a commission in the naval, military or air forces of the Crown or of any of the women's services mentioned in Schedule 4 to the Superannuation Act 1965(g), being employment in respect of which retired pay is being earned.

13. Employment in respect of which contributions are payable to the Social Workers' Pension Fund.

14. Employment, other than employment to which paragraph 1 applies, in respect of which contributions are payable under the Federated System of Superannuation for Universities.

(a) 1944 c. 31. (b) S.I. 1967/489 (1967 I, p. 1562).
(c) 1972 c. 48. (d) S.I. 1966/1629 (1966 III, p. 5076).
(e) 1948 c. 56. (f) S.I. 1957/356 (1957 I, p. 733).
(g) 1965 c. 74.

15. Employment in the service of the British Council in respect of which contributions are payable under the British Council Overseas Service Pensions Scheme.

16. Employment as an officer of an employing authority within the meaning of the National Health Service (Superannuation) (Scotland) Regulations 1961 to 1975(a) or the National Health Service (Superannuation) Regulations 1961 to 1975(b).

17. Employment in respect of which contributions are payable under the Federated Superannuation Scheme for Nurses and Hospital Officers—

(a) to which either the National Health Service (Superannuation) (Scotland) Regulations 1961 to 1975 or the National Health Service (Superannuation) Regulations 1961 to 1975 apply;

(b) by an employing authority or a local Act authority within the meaning of the Local Government Superannuation (Scotland) Act 1937(c) or the Local Government Superannuation Act 1937(d);

(c) to which are applicable any regulations or scheme made under section 2 or section 5A of the Local Government (Superannuation) Act (Northern Ireland) 1950(e), as amended by the Local Government (Superannuation) (Amendment) Act (Northern Ireland) 1951(f), or under section 61 of the Health Services Act (Northern Ireland) 1948(g); or

(d) in a civil service in the British Isles.

18. Employment after reckonable service in employment to which interchange provisions for the time being apply.

19. Service before 1st May 1975 which was reckonable for the purposes of Part VIII of the Teachers' Superannuation Regulations 1967(h).

20. Pensionable employment by a body representing teachers.

21. Pensionable service as a regular minister of any religious denomination or as a clerk in holy orders.

Regulation 53

SCHEDULE 6

ALLOCATION DECLARATIONS

1. A declaration for the purposes of regulation 53 shall allocate an amount, expressed as a whole number of pounds, not exceeding any of—

(a) 1/3rd of the gross amount of the annual pension;

(b) the amount which would render the balance of the gross annual pension less than the amount of the pension payable to the beneficiary under regulation 53(1); and

(c) the amount which would result in the amount of the annual pension attributable to any period of reckonable service between 2nd April 1961 and 5th April 1975 (both dates inclusive) which was non-participating employment within the meaning of the National Insurance Act 1965(i) being less than the amount required to constitute so much of the annual pension as is payable in respect of that period equivalent pension benefits for the purposes of that Act.

The references in this paragraph to the gross amount of an annual pension are references to the amount of an annual pension before any deductions are made from it under Schedule 12.

(a) S.I. 1975/1376 (1975 II, p. 4693).   (b) S.I. 1975/1292 (1975 II, p. 4362).
(c) 1937 c. 69.   (d) 1937 c. 68.
(e) 1950 c. 10 (N.I.).   (f) 1951 c. 9 (N.I.).
(g) 1948 c. 3 (N.I.).   (h) S.I. 1967/489 (1967 I, p. 1562).
(i) 1965 c. 51.

2. The validity of a declaration shall not be affected by reason of the fact that, in consequence of any decrease in the amount of the annual pension after the declaration has taken effect, the amount allocated exceeds any amount specified in paragraph 1; but subject thereto, the amount allocated shall not exceed those amounts.

3. A declaration shall be made in the form approved by the Secretary of State within 3 months (or, in the case of a teacher resident outwith Scotland 4 months) of the despatch to the teacher of the declaration form mentioned in paragraph 5 after the teacher has—

(a) within the time so specified in the table below, given the Secretary of State notice of his intention to make the allocation;

(b) satisfied the Secretary of State as to his health; and

(c) provided the Secretary of State with such information (verified in such manner) as the Secretary of State may require relating to the beneficiary.

4.—(1) For the purposes of paragraph 3(b) the teacher shall submit himself for examination by a medical practitioner nominated by the Secretary of State; and the teacher may, if as a result of such an examination he does not satisfy the Secretary of State as to his health, submit himself for examination by another medical practitioner so nominated.

(2) Any fees or other expenses which may be incurred by a teacher in connection with a medical examination or otherwise in satisfying the Secretary of State as is mentioned in paragraph 3 shall be paid by the teacher.

5. As soon as may be after the teacher has notified the Secretary of State of his intention to allocate the Secretary of State shall send the teacher a declaration form and particulars of the following:—

(a) the actuarial equivalents of allocations in terms of pension and annuities payable under regulation 53;

(b) the amount, or as the case may be estimated amount, of any annual pension payable in respect of him;

(c) information about the medical examination required for the purposes of paragraph 4(1); and

(d) the time specified by paragraph 3 for the making of the declaration.

6.—(1) Subject to regulation 53(7) a declaration may be varied or revoked by a further declaration made before the day specified in the table.

(2) A declaration shall become void on the death before the day specified in the table of either the teacher or the beneficiary.

TABLE

Paragraph	Subject matter	Retiring teacher	Continuing teacher
3(a)	Notice of intention to allocate	Not later than application for payment of pension or such later date as may be approved by the Secretary of State	Not earlier than 4 months before the date on which the teacher will become entitled to a retiring allowance under regulation 46 (assuming he continues service to that date)
6(1)	Revocation or variation of declaration	Commencement of payment of pension	The day on which the declaration takes effect
6(2)	Voidance of declaration	Whichever is the later of the day before the commencement of payment of the pension and the expiration of the day on which the declaration is delivered to the Secretary of State	Whichever is the later of the day on which the declaration takes effect and the day on which it is delivered to the Secretary of State

NOTES:

1. Any declaration or other document which is sent by registered post or recorded delivery service shall be deemed to have been delivered at the time at which it would have been delivered in the ordinary course of post.

2. The reference in the table to a retiring teacher is to a teacher whose declaration is made in pursuance of notice of his intention to retire within 4 months of the serving of the notice; and the reference to a continuing teacher is to a teacher who is not a retiring teacher.

Regulation 63

SCHEDULE 7

SHORT-TERM PENSIONS

TABLE 1

Less than 5 years' service counting for benefit under Schedule 9

Category	Where teacher is married at date of death or there is an adult nominated beneficiary	Where teacher is not married at date of death and there is no adult nominated beneficiary	Duration of pension (months)	Rate of pension (all categories)
1	Widow or widower or other adult nominated beneficiary but no child.		3	
2	Widow or widower or other adult nominated beneficiary with one child.		4½	Annual rate of salary of teacher on last day of reckonable service
3	Widow or widower or other adult nominated beneficiary with 2 or more children.		6	
4	—	1 child	2	
5	—	2 or more children	4	

TABLE 2

5 or more years' service counting for benefit under Schedule 9

Where teacher is married at date of death or there is an adult nominated beneficiary	Where teacher is not married at date of death and there is no adult nominated beneficiary	Duration of pension (months)	Rate of pension
Categories 1–5 in table 1		3	Annual rate of salary of teacher on last day of reckonable service

TABLE 3

Retired teachers with 5 or more years' service counting for benefit under Schedule 9

Where teacher is married at date of death or there is an adult nominated beneficiary	Where teacher is not married at date of death and there is no adult nominated beneficiary	Duration of pension (months)	Rate of pension
Categories 1–5 in table 1		3	Rate of annual pension received by teacher immediately before death

NOTES:

1. In all cases the widower must be a nominated beneficiary as defined in regulation 3.

2. Where a child's pension is payable it shall be payable to or for the benefit of the child or, as the case may be, jointly to or for the benefit of any children dependent on the teacher at the time of death.

3. On the death of a widow, widower or other adult nominated beneficiary before the termination of short-term pension payable under categories 2 or 3 of table 1, the balance of pension is payable to the child or children, as the case may be.

Regulations 64 and 65

SCHEDULE 8

TABLE 1

AMOUNT OF ADULT'S LONG-TERM PENSION

(1) Beneficiary	(2) Fraction of teacher's pensionable salary for each year of service	(3) Service
Widow	1/160th	Reckonable service counting for benefit
Adult nominated beneficiary	1/160th	ditto

NOTE: Where an election has been made by a teacher or the teacher's widow under regulation 38(9) the retrospective increase in the teacher's salary referred to in that regulation shall be ignored in calculating the teacher's pensionable salary in column (2).

Regulations 64 and 65

TABLE 2

AMOUNT OF CHILD'S LONG-TERM PENSION

(1) Widow or adult nominated beneficiary in receipt of a pension	(2) No widow or adult nominated beneficiary in receipt of a pension	(3) Fraction of teacher's pensionable salary for each year of service	(4) Service
1 child		1/320th	Reckonable service counting for benefit
2 or more children	.	1/160th	ditto
	1 child	1/240th	Teacher's total reckonable service
	2 or more children	1/120th	ditto

NOTES:

1. Where a child's pension is payable it shall be payable to or for the benefit of the child or, as the case may be, jointly to or for the benefit of any children dependent on the teacher at the time of death.

2. If the teacher dies while employed in reckonable service or while in receipt of an incapacity pension by virtue of regulation 47:—

   (a) the reckonable service counting for benefit in column (4) above shall be enhanced in accordance with paragraph 2(i) of Schedule 9 and

   (b) the teacher's total reckonable service in column (4) above shall be enhanced by such number of years as could have been added to his reckonable service by virtue of regulation 51, any past added years which he could have elected to purchase under Part III being disregarded.

3. On the death of a widow or adult nominated beneficiary, a child's pension payable under column (1) becomes payable under column (2) as from the date of death.

Regulations 63 and 64

SCHEDULE 9

SERVICE COUNTING FOR BENEFIT

1. For the purposes of this Schedule the service counting for benefit shall be the aggregate of the reckonable service of a teacher since 1st April 1972 and so much of his service to which paragraph 2 applies as does not exceed the aggregate of—

   (a) his reckonable service between 1st April 1965 and 31st March 1972; and

   (b) any service (whether reckonable or not) before 1st April 1965 in respect of which he could have elected to pay contributions under regulation 34—

any past added years which the teacher has since 1st April 1972 elected to purchase under Part III being treated for the purposes of sub-paragraphs (a) and (b) as reckonable service since 1st April 1972.

2. As regards any teacher, this paragraph applies to—

   (a) any reckonable service before 1st April 1972 in respect of which the teacher elects or, as the case may be, elected to pay contributions under regulation 32;

   (b) his deemed normal service within the meaning of Part IV;

(c) his deemed additional service within the meaning of Part IV;

(d) twice his notional service within the meaning of Part IV;

(e) any period of service as is specified in an election by him to pay contributions under regulation 31 or regulation 33;

(f) (i) where the teacher has elected to pay contributions under regulation 31 1/5th of the period of service in respect of which the teacher has so elected but not exceeding 1/5th of the maximum period for which the teacher could have elected to pay under regulation 31 if his reckonable service prior to 1st April 1972 had not exceeded the period of the previous service in respect of which prior to that date he paid, or elected to pay, family pensions contributions; or

   (ii) where the teacher has elected to pay contributions under regulation 33, a period equal to the period of service in respect of which the teacher has elected to pay such contributions;

(g) any service in respect of which contributions have been deducted from the terminal sum payable in respect of him by virtue of regulation 38(1);

(h) any war service in respect of which the teacher paid contributions under regulation 70;

(i) if the teacher died while employed in reckonable service or while in receipt of an annual pension to which he became entitled by virtue of regulation 47, such number of years as bears to any period which (disregarding any past added years which he elected to purchase) was or could have been added to his reckonable service by virtue of regulation 51 the same proportion as the aggregate number of years of his reckonable service under paragraphs 1(a) and sub-paragraphs (a), (b), (c), (d), (e), (f), (g) and (h) bears to his total reckonable service;

(j) any past added years which the teacher has since 1st April 1972 elected to purchase under Part III;

(k) any previous service within the meaning of previous provisions for family pensions in respect of which he paid contributions by Method I or II (within the meaning of those provisions) after 31st March 1972 if these contributions have not been returned to him or he has not elected to pay contributions under regulation 31.

Regulations 72(1) and 73(2)

SCHEDULE 10

TRANSFER VALUES

PART I

Transfer values

1. The transfer value payable in respect of any teacher shall be—

   (a) the aggregate of the sums calculated in accordance with paragraph 2 in respect of accrued gross annual pension (reduced by a sum in respect of national insurance modification calculated in accordance with paragraph 4), lump sum and widow's pension, together with—

   (b) compound interest at 6 per cent with yearly rests in respect of each complete year beginning with the day upon which the teacher ceases to be employed in reckonable service and ending with the day on which the transfer value is paid.

2.—(1) The sums in respect of gross annual pension and lump sum shall be calculated by multiplying the accrued entitlement (within the meaning of paragraph 3) of the teacher to that benefit by the appropriate factor.

(2) The sum in respect of widow's pension shall be calculated by multiplying by 4 the accrued entitlement of the teacher to that pension.

(3) The accrued entitlement of a teacher to a benefit is the amount expressed in pounds calculated by multiplying his pensionable salary immediately before the date when he ceased to be employed in reckonable service by the fraction of which the numerator and denominator are shown in columns (2) and (3) respectively of the table below in the entry relating to that benefit.

TABLE

(1) Benefit	(2) Numerator	(3) Denominator
1. Gross annual pension	Years of service	80
2. Lump sum	(a) years of service before 1st October 1956	30
	(b) 3 times years of service after 30th September 1956	80
3. Widow's pension	Years of service counting for benefit	160

4. The amount by which the sum in respect of the teacher's gross annual pension is to be reduced shall be calculated by multiplying by the appropriate factor such of the following sums as fall to be applied in his case:—

(a) if paragraph 4 of Schedule 12 applies to him, £1·70 for each year of his service;

(b) if paragraph 5 of that Schedule applies to him, the sum determined as applicable to him by virtue of the table in the appendix to that Schedule;

(c) if his reckonable service includes any such period of employment as is described in paragraphs 7, 8 or 9 of that Schedule, the amount by which by virtue of those provisions the annual pension payable to him would have been reduced.

NOTES:

1. "The appropriate factor" means the factor appearing in the appropriate column of the appropriate part of the table in the appendix to this Schedule against the entry relating to the age of the teacher at the date when he ceased to be employed in reckonable service.

2. "Service" means reckonable service and as regards any teacher includes the number of past added years calculated in accordance with regulations 23(2)(b), 25(5)(b)(ii) and 26(3), but does not include any period in respect of which any contributions under these regulations or previous provisions payable while the teacher was employed in reckonable service have not been paid by him when he ceases to be so employed.

3. War service counts as half.

PART II

Reckonable service

5. The reckonable service of a teacher in respect of whom the Secretary of State receives a transfer value relating to his comparable British service shall be the service certified by the person responsible for the management of the superannuation scheme to which he was subject as the service which stood to his credit under that scheme when it ceased to apply to him.

6. A teacher who was previously subject to any other superannuation scheme shall be credited with reckonable service equal to the reckonable service which would enable the Secretary of State to pay, in respect of a former teacher of his age, a transfer value of the amount which the Secretary of State received in respect of the teacher.

7. For the purposes of paragraph 6—

(*a*) the former teacher referred to in that paragraph is to be treated as not being an existing teacher within the meaning of Schedule 12 unless the teacher referred to either—

(i) is entitled to that classification by virtue of paragraph 2(1)(*a*) of that Schedule; or

(ii) was formerly subject to a statutory superannuation scheme under which he was not subject to modification of superannuation benefits on account of flat-rate national insurance;

(*b*) in the case of a teacher who was formerly subject to a statutory superannuation scheme or to a non-statutory superannuation scheme which is for the time being treated by the Secretary of State with the agreement of the Minister for the Civil Service as a statutory scheme for the purposes of this Schedule—

(i) the calculation of the reckonable service to be credited to him is to be made by reference to his age, and to the salary notified to the Secretary of State by the person responsible for the management of the scheme as the salary payable to him, on the last day on which he was a member of that scheme; and

(ii) any sum representing interest included in the transfer value paid to the Secretary of State is to be ignored;

(*c*) in the case of a teacher who was formerly subject to any other non-statutory scheme—

(i) the calculation of the reckonable service to be credited to him is to be made by reference to his age, and to the full salary at the rate payable to him, on the day on which he became employed in reckonable service or, if the transfer value in respect of him is received by the Secretary of State more than 1 year after he becomes employed in reckonable service, the day on which that transfer value is received; and

(ii) any sum representing interest which is included in the transfer value is to be taken into account.

8. If in the case of any teacher the reckonable service credited to him by virtue of paragraph 6 is less than his pensionable service under the scheme to which he was formerly subject, that pensionable service (and not the service so credited to him) shall be treated as reckonable service for the purposes of any provision of the regulations relating to entitlement to benefit.

APPENDIX

PART A—MEN

Age for paragraph 2(1), 4, 7(b)(1) or 7(c)(1) as the case may be	Gross pension £	Lump sum £	Deduction for national insurance modification £
Less than 20	5·00	·60	·25
20	5·05	·60	·25
21	5·10	·61	·25
22	5·15	·61	·30
23	5·20	·61	·30
24	5·25	·62	·30
25	5·30	·62	·35
26	5·35	·63	·40
27	5·40	·63	·40
28	5·45	·63	·45
29	5·50	·64	·50
30	5·55	·64	·50
31	5·60	·65	·55
32	5·65	·66	·60
33	5·70	·66	·65
34	5·75	·67	·70
35	5·80	·67	·80
36	5·85	·68	·90
37	5·90	·68	1·00
38	5·95	·68	1·10
39	6·00	·69	1·20
40	6·05	·69	1·30
41	6·10	·70	1·40
42	6·15	·70	1·50
43	6·20	·71	1·60
44	6·25	·72	1·70
45	6·30	·72	1·80
46	6·40	·73	1·90
47	6·50	·74	2·00
48	6·60	·74	2·20
49	6·70	·75	2·40
50	6·80	·75	2·60
51	6·90	·76	2·90
52	7·10	·76	3·20
53	7·30	·77	3·50
54	7·50	·78	3·80
55	7·70	·79	4·20
56	8·00	·80	4·60
57	8·30	·81	5·00
58	8·60	·82	5·40
59	9·00	·84	5·80
60	9·50	·86	6·30
61	9·50	·88	6·80
62	9·50	·91	7·40
63	9·50	·94	8·10
64	9·50	·98	9·00
65	9·50	1·00	9·50

APPENDIX

PART D—WOMEN

Age for paragraph 2(1), 4, 7(*b*)(1) or 7(*c*)(1) as the case may be	Gross pension £	Lump sum £	Deduction for national insurance modification £
Less than 20	7·00	·60	·50
20	7·05	·60	·50
21	7·10	·61	·55
22	7·15	·61	·60
23	7·20	·61	·65
24	7·25	·62	·70
25	7·35	·62	·75
26	7·40	·63	·80
27	7·45	·63	·85
28	7·50	·63	·90
29	7·55	·64	·95
30	7·65	·64	1·05
31	7·70	·65	1·15
32	7·80	·66	1·25
33	7·90	·66	1·35
34	7·95	·67	1·45
35	8·05	·67	1·55
36	8·15	·68	1·65
37	8·25	·68	1·75
38	8·35	·68	1·85
39	8·45	·69	1·95
40	8·55	·69	2·10
41	8·65	·70	2·25
42	8·75	·70	2·45
43	8·85	·71	2·65
44	8·95	·72	2·90
45	9·05	·73	3·15
46	9·15	·74	3·40
47	9·25	·75	3·70
48	9·35	·76	4·00
49	9·45	·77	4·35
50	9·55	·78	4·75
51	9·65	·79	5·15
52	9·80	·80	5·60
53	9·95	·81	6·10
54	10·10	·82	6·65
55	10·30	·83	7·25
56	10·50	·84	7·95
57	10·75	·85	8·75
58	11·05	·87	9·65
59	11·40	·89	10·65
60	11·75	·91	11·75
61	11·75	·93	11·75
62	11·75	·95	11·75
63	11·75	·97	11·75
64	11·75	·99	11·75
65	11·75	1·00	11·75

STOKE-ON-TRENT
CITY
LIBRARIES

Regulation 76

SCHEDULE 11

TEACHERS' SUPERANNUATION ACCOUNT

PART I

FORM OF ACCOUNT

THE TEACHERS' SUPERANNUATION (SCOTLAND) REGULATIONS 1977

Account of receipts and payments from 1st April 19   to 31st March 19

A Receipts	B Payments
£000's	£000's
I. To balance on (end of period of previous account)	I. By retiring allowances and gratuities
II. To contributions—	(i) annual pensions attributable to service on or after 1st June 1922 ... ...
(i) from teachers and other persons eligible	
(ii) from employers ...	(ii) lump sums, deficiency payments and incapacity gratuities ...
III. To moneys provided by Parliament, equal to the payments under heading II of the payments side of this account	(iii) death gratuities ...
	(iv) widows' pensions ...
IV. to payments on re-entry into employment in reckonable service	(v) children's pensions ...
	(vi) other beneficiaries' pensions ... ...
V. To amounts recovered from returns of contributions in accordance with section 60(1) of the National Insurance Act 1965 ...	(vii) short-term family pensions ... ...
	(viii) returns of contributions ... ...
VI. To transfer values and other receipts	II. By annual pensions attributable to service before 1st June 1922 ... ...
VII. To interest on balance of receipts over payments calculated in accordance with regulation 79 ...	III. By payments in lieu of graduated contributions ...
	IV. By transfer values and other payments ... ...
	V. Balance on 31st March 19

PART II

NOTIONAL INVESTMENT AS AT 31ST MARCH 1971 OF BALANCE OF REVENUE OVER EXPENDITURE

1. For the purpose of determining the sum representing interest to be paid into the account prescribed by regulation 76 and this Schedule the accumulated balance of revenue over expenditure as at 31st March 1971 (being the balance remaining at the end of the accounting period beginning on 1st April 1955 and the balances in respect of subsequent accounting periods up to and including that beginning on 1st April 1970) shall be deemed at that date to have been invested in the investments and in the manner following:—

£ 33,136,000   Funding 3½ per cent stock 1999–2004
£209,462,000   Treasury 5½ per cent stock 2008–2012
£ 6,856,000   Bearing interest at the rate of 3½ per cent per annum

2. (a) The sum of £6,856,000 specified in paragraph 1 above shall be treated as having been reduced to £2,532,000 on 31st March 1972 and to nil on 31st March 1973; and

(b) The amount deemed to have been invested in pursuance of regulation 79(2) shall be increased for the accounting period beginning on 1st April 1971 by £4,324,000 and for the accounting period beginning on 1st April 1972 by £2,532,000.

PART III
APPORTIONMENT OF PAYMENTS

1. The amount of payments by way of annual pensions attributable to service after 1st June 1922 is the amount calculated by multiplying the total payments on such pensions by half the net sums of apportioned pensions in payment at the end of the last preceding accounting period; and the balance of that total shall be attributable to service before 1st June 1922.

2. The amount of payments by way of gratuities and other lump sums attributable to service after 1st June 1922 shall be calculated by multiplying the whole of such payments by the net sum of apportioned lump sums and gratuities awarded during the accounting period; and the balance of that expenditure shall be attributable to service before 1st June 1922.

3. In this Part—

(a) an apportioned retiring allowance shall be calculated by multiplying the amount of the retiring allowance by a fraction of which the numerator is the period (to the nearest year) of the reckonable service of the teacher since 1st June 1922 and the denominator is the total (to the nearest year) of his reckonable service;

(b) the net sum of apportioned retiring allowances shall be calculated by multiplying the sum of apportioned pensions in payment or lump sums or gratuities awarded during the period in question by the total number of pensions in payment or lump sums or gratuities awarded;

(c) in calculating the net sum of apportioned retiring allowances the amount of any retiring allowance, or the sum of any retiring allowances, shall be taken to the nearest pound and other amounts shall be taken to the nearest £1,000;

(d) an annual pension shall be taken to be in payment at any time after it has been put into payment and has not ceased to be payable.

Regulation 9
SCHEDULE 12
MODIFICATIONS RELATING TO NATIONAL INSURANCE

Interpretation

1. In this Schedule, unless the context otherwise requires—

"the Act" means the National Insurance Act 1965(a);

"existing teacher" has the meaning assigned to it by this Schedule;

"national insurance modifications" means the modifications made to these regulations and to previous provisions whereby the superannuation benefits provided thereunder are modified in relation to insured persons for the purposes of the Act;

"new entrant teacher" has the meaning assigned to it by this Schedule;

"non-participating employment" has the meaning assigned to it by section 56(1) of the Act;

"participating employment" means employment other than non-participating employment;

"retired teacher" means a teacher who has ceased to be employed in reckonable service and who, if a man, has attained the age of 65 or, if a woman, has attained the age of 60.

(a) 1965 c. 51.

Classification of teachers

2.—(1) For the purposes of this Schedule—

(a) "existing teacher" means—

(i) a teacher who was employed in reckonable service at any time before 1st July 1948 whether or not his contributions in respect of that service were returned to him; or

(ii) a teacher who before 1st March 1948 had completed a course approved for the purposes of this Schedule by the Secretary of State ("an approved course") or was engaged on an approved course, or had been accepted or provisionally accepted for an approved course, or had applied to be accepted for and had as a result of that application subsequently become engaged on an approved course and had entered reckonable service within 6 months of completing the said approved course.

(b) "new entrant teacher" means either—

(i) a teacher who enters upon reckonable service for the first time on or after 1st July 1948; or

(ii) a teacher to whom sub-paragraph (a) applies and who makes an election under sub-paragraph (3).

(2) (a) An existing teacher shall be unmodified, that is to say, shall be a teacher to whom the national insurance modifications do not apply; and

(b) a new entrant teacher shall be modified, that is to say, shall be a teacher to whom the national insurance modifications apply.

(3) An existing teacher in reckonable service on 1st July 1948 shall remain unmodified unless he elected on or before 30th September 1948 to be modified or, if he was not in reckonable service on 1st July 1948, so elects within 3 months after the date on which he first enters or re-enters reckonable service. Notice so given is irrevocable.

(4) Where a teacher was employed in comparable British service, or in other employment to which interchange provisions apply, he shall on entering reckonable service retain the classification which in the opinion of the Secretary of State corresponds to his classification in his former superannuation scheme, and where his classification has not been so determined the provisions of sub-paragraph (3) shall apply to him as they apply to a teacher who was not in reckonable service on 1st July 1948.

Reduction of contributions

3. In relation to teachers who are modified regulations 11(2)(a)(i) and 11(2)(b)(i) shall have effect subject to the modification that the contributions payable thereunder both by the teacher and by his employer shall be reduced, in the case of a woman, by £2·95 a year and, in the case of a man, by £2·40 a year.

Reduction of annual pension

4.—(1) An annual pension payable under these regulations to a retired teacher to whom paragraph 2(1)(b)(i) or 2(4) applied shall be reduced by whichever is the lesser of £67·75 and the amount calculated by multiplying £1·70 for each completed year, and by a proportionate amount in respect of part of a year, of reckonable service after 1st July 1948.

(2) For the purposes of this paragraph any enhancement of reckonable service under regulation 51 or any past added years purchased under Part III shall be deemed to be service after 1st July 1948.

(3) Sub-paragraph (1) shall apply in the case of any retired teacher to whom paragraph 3 does not apply if the Secretary of State is satisfied that the contributions paid by him were modified on the assumption that that paragraph did apply in his case; and regulation 49(2)(b) shall not apply in respect of those contributions.

5.—(1) An annual pension payable under these regulations to a retired teacher who is modified by virtue of an election made in terms of paragraph 2(3) shall be reduced for each completed year, and proportionately for part of a year, of reckonable service after the date of modification by the sum specified in either column (2) or column (3), whichever is appropriate, of the table in the appendix to this Schedule which appears against his age at the date of modification specified in column (1).

(2) In the case of a retired teacher who is modified by virtue of an election made in terms of paragraph 2(3) the date of modification shall be, for the purposes of this paragraph, 1st July 1948 where notice has been given before the said date and the 1st day of the month following the date of the election in any other case.

(3) For the purposes of this paragraph any enhancement of reckonable service under regulation 51 and any past added years purchased under Part III shall be deemed to be service after the date of modification.

6. For the purposes of paragraphs 4 and 5 the reckonable service of a retired teacher shall be the amount of service not exceeding 40 years which may be taken into account for the purpose of calculating the amount of the annual pension payable to him.

7. If, in calculating the amount of annual pension payable to a retired teacher under these regulations, there is taken into account any period of employment between 2nd April 1961 and 5th April 1975 (both dates inclusive) which is participating employment the annual pension shall, except as provided in paragraphs 9 and 10, be reduced for each year of such period and proportionately for part of a year, by the appropriate amount specified in the following table:—

TABLE

Annual rate of salary during period	Reduction in annual pension for each whole year of period			
	From 3rd April 1961 to 5th January 1964		From 6th January 1964 to 5th April 1975	
	Men	Women	Men	Women
	£	£	£	£
Not exceeding £468	nil	nil	nil	nil
Over £468 but not exceeding £520	.19	·16	·19	·16
Over £520 but not exceeding £572	·58	·48	·58	·48
Over £572 but not exceeding £624	·96	·80	·96	·80
Over £624 but not exceeding £676	1·35	1·12	1·35	1·12
Over £676 but not exceeding £728	1·73	1·44	1·73	1·44
Over £728 but not exceeding £780	2·12	1·76	2·12	1·76
Over £780 but not exceeding £832	2·31	1·92	2·51	2·09
Over £832 but not exceeding £884	2·31	1·92	2·90	2·42
Over £884 but not exceeding £936	2·31	1·92	3·29	2·74
Over £936...	2·31	1·92	3·48	2·90

8. If, in calculating the amount of an annual pension there is taken into account any period of employment between 2nd April 1961 and 5th April 1975 (both dates inclusive) in respect of which a payment in lieu of contributions has been made under the Act the annual pension shall, except as provided in paragraphs 9 and 10 be reduced—

(a) by £2·31 in the case of a man and by £1·92 in the case of a woman for each year, and proportionately for part of a year, of any period from 3rd April 1961 to 5th January 1964; and

(b) by £3·48 in the case of a man and by £2·90 in the case of a woman for each year, and proportionately for part of a year, of any period from 6th January 1964 to 5th April 1975.

9. Where—

(a) a period of employment of a retired teacher which was participating employment or in respect of which a payment in lieu of contributions had been made is treated as reckonable service by virtue of interchange provisions; and

(b) the Secretary of State is informed of the amount by which the pension of a retired teacher under the pension scheme applicable to him before interchange provisions applied to him would have been reduced in respect of that period by reason of graduated retirement benefit payable under the Act or of the method of calculating such reduction,

the annual pension in respect of that period shall be reduced by that amount or by an amount calculated in accordance with that method, as the case may be, and no reduction shall be made under paragraph 7 or 8 in respect of that period.

10. No reduction in the amount of an annual pension shall be made under paragraph 7 or 8 in respect of any added years or period of national service which is reckonable service by virtue of regulation 4(1)(b) or 4(1)(f) respectively.

The account

11. There shall be treated as payments out of the account kept under regulation 76 payments in lieu of contributions made under the Act by the Secretary of State during the accounting period and as receipts amounts recovered by him under section 60 of the Act during the accounting period.

Equivalent pension benefits

12. An annual pension payable to a teacher shall, so far as attributable to any teaching service which is non-participating employment (exclusive of any period of such employment in respect of which a payment in lieu has been made under the Act), be not less than the amount required to constitute the benefits in respect of that service equivalent pension benefits for the purposes of that Act.

13. A teacher who—

(a) if a man, on the 65th anniversary of his birth, or, if a woman, on the 60th anniversary of her birth, is employed in reckonable service; and

(b) is not otherwise entitled to the payment of retiring allowances under regulation 46 or to the resumption of an annual pension under regulation 62

shall be paid in respect of any such service as aforesaid between 2nd April 1961 and 5th April 1975 (both dates inclusive) which is non-participating employment (exclusive of any period of such employment in respect of which a payment in lieu of contributions has been made under the Act) an annual pension not less than that required to constitute the benefits in respect of that service equivalent pension benefits for the purposes of that Act.

APPENDIX

TABLE

Age at date of modification	Yearly reduction of pension for each completed year of reckonable service after date of modification	
	Men	Women
(1)	(2)	(3)
	£	£
20 or under	1·70	1·70
21	1·65	1·60
22	1·60	1·53
23	1·55	1·45
24	1·50	1·37
25	1·47	1·30
26	1·45	1·23
27	1·43	1·17
28	1·40	1·13
29	1·35	1·07
30	1·33	1·03
31	1·30	0·97
32	1·27	0·95
33	1·25	0·93
34	1·23	0·90
35	1·20	0·87
36	1·17	0·85
37	1·15	0·83
38	1·13	0·80
39	1·10	0·77
40	1·07	0·75
41	1·07	0·73
42	1·05	0·73
43	1·03	0·70
44	1·00	0·70
45	0·97	0·67
46	0·95	0·65
47	0·95	0·65
48	0·93	0·63
49	0·93	0·63
50 and over	0·93	0·60

Regulation 10(3)

SCHEDULE 13

TRANSITORY PROVISIONS RELATING TO FAMILY PENSIONS

Provision of the 1971 family benefits regulations	Modification
34	Paragraph (1)(*d*) shall be omitted.
43	Paragraph (1)(*c*) shall be omitted.
44(2)	—
44(4), (5), (5A) and (6)	The reference in paragraph (4)(*c*) to class B external service is to be construed as a reference to service specified in paragraphs 1, 2 and 3 of Schedule 4 and sub-paragraph (*d*) shall be omitted.
45	—
49	Paragraph (*b*) shall be omitted.
50	The references to regulation 52 as amended shall be omitted.
51	Paragraph (2)(*b*) shall be omitted.
59–69	The regulations shall apply only in relation to nominations made under regulation 57 before, and still effective at, 1st April 1972.

Regulation 10(4)

SCHEDULE 14

REVOCATIONS

Regulations revoked	References
The Teachers Superannuation (Scotland) Regulations 1969	S.I. 1969/77 (1969 I, p. 133)
The Teachers Superannuation (Scotland) (Amendment) Regulations 1969	S.I. 1969/659 (1969 II, p. 1820)
The Teachers Superannation Account (Rates of Interest) (Scotland) Regulations 1969	S.I. 1969/785 (1969 II, p. 2203)
The Teachers Superannuation (Family Benefits) (Scotland) Regulations 1971	S.I. 1971/1775 (1971 III, 4813)
The Teachers Superannuation (Scotland) Amendment Regulations 1971	S.I. 1971/1995 (1971 III, p. 5683)
The Teachers Superannuation (Family Benefits) (Scotland) Amendment Regulations 1972	S.I. 1972/442 (1972 I, p. 1644)
The Teachers Superannuation (Financial Provisions) (Scotland) Regulations 1972	S.I. 1972/551 (1972 I, p. 1855)
The Teachers Superannuation (Financial Provisions and Family Benefits) (Scotland) Regulations 1972	S.I. 1972/1239 (1972 II, p. 3738)
The Superannuation (Teachers and Teachers' Families) (Scotland) Regulations 1973	S.I. 1973/547 (1973 I, p. 1738)
The Teachers Superannuation (Family Benefits) (Scotland) Amendment Regulations 1973	S.I. 1973/2078 (1973 III, p. 7164)
The Teachers Superannuation (Miscellaneous Amendments) (Scotland) Regulations 1974	S.I. 1974/376 (1974 I, p. 1198)
The Teachers Superannuation (Added Years and Interchange) (Scotland) Regulations 1974	S.I. 1974/1135 (1974 II, p. 4315)
The Teachers Superannuation (Miscellaneous Amendments) (Scotland) (No. 2) Regulations 1974	S.I. 1974/1993 (1974 III, p. 6981)
The Teachers Superannuation (Contributions) (Scotland) (No. 2) Regulations 1974	S.I.1974/1994 (1974 III, p. 6985)
The Teachers Superannuation (Family Benefits) (Scotland) Amendment Regulations 1975	S.I. 1975/98 (1975 I, p. 292)
The Teachers Superannuation (War Service) (Scotland) Regulations 1975	S.I. 1975/872 (1975 II, p. 3085)
The Teachers Superannuation (Family Benefits) (Scotland) Regulations 1975	S.I. 1975/931 (1975 II, p. 3249)
The Teachers Superannuation (Service Credit) (Scotland) Regulations 1975	S.I. 1975/1352 (1975 III, p. 4603)
The Teachers Superannuation (Miscellaneous) Provisions) (Scotland) Regulations 1976	S.I. 1976/910 (1976 II, p. 2346)

EXPLANATORY NOTE

(This Note is not part of the Regulations.)

These Regulations consolidate, with a few minor changes, all the regulations relating to the superannuation of teachers (including the payment of pensions and other benefits to their dependants).

Apart from minor corrections and drafting improvements the only changes are:—

(*a*) the provision of superannuation benefits to teachers who have attained the age of 50 and who have to retire early because of redundancy or in the interests of the efficiency of the service (regulation 46);

(*b*) an alternative method of calculating benefits payable to retired teachers who resume service for a year or more (regulation 59);

(*c*) the provision of short-term pensions for adult nominated beneficiaries (other than widows who were already provided for) and in all cases where a teacher dies within a year of ceasing to be on the payroll because of prolonged sick-leave (regulation 63 and Schedule 7); and

(*d*) the alteration of the accounting arrangements from an income and expenditure basis to a receipts and payments basis (regulations 76-78) and the setting-out in regulations of the Form of Account (Schedule 11).

As authorised by section 12(1) of the Superannuation Act 1972 the Regulations have retrospective effect to 1st August 1977 except as otherwise expressly provided in regulations 38(9) and 46(2)(*c*).

STATUTORY INSTRUMENTS

1977 No. 1361

SOCIAL SECURITY

The Social Security (Attendance Allowance) Amendment Regulations 1977

Made - - - -	*3rd August* 1977
Laid before Parliament	*8th August* 1977
Coming into Operation	*29th August* 1977

The Secretary of State for Social Services, in exercise of the powers conferred upon him by sections 35 and 81 of the Social Security Act 1975(a) and section 80(2) of that Act as amended by section 17(2) of the Social Security (Miscellaneous Provisions) Act 1977(b) and of all other powers enabling him in that behalf, hereby makes the following regulations which relate only to matters which have been referred to the Attendance Allowance Board for advice under section 140 of the first mentioned Act and, by section 139(2) of, and paragraph 16 of Schedule 15 to, that Act, do not have to be referred to the National Insurance Advisory Committee:—

Citation, commencement and interpretation

1.—(1) These regulations may be cited as the Social Security (Attendance Allowance) Amendment Regulations 1977 and shall come into operation on 29th August 1977.

(2) In these regulations the Social Security (Attendance Allowance) (No. 2) Regulations 1975(c) as amended(d) are referred to as "the principal regulations" and the Social Security (Claims and Payments) Regulations 1975(e) as amended(f) are referred to as "the Claims and Payments Regulations".

(3) The rules for the construction of Acts of Parliament contained in the Interpretation Act 1889(g) shall apply in relation to this instrument and in relation to any revocation effected by it as if this instrument and any regulations revoked by it were Acts of Parliament and as if each revocation were a repeal.

Amendment of regulation 2 of the principal regulations

2. Regulation 2 of the principal regulations (entitlement conditions relating to residence and presence in Great Britain) shall be amended by the substitution in paragraph (3)(*a*) for the reference to "paragraph (2)(*a*)" of a reference to "paragraph (2)(*a*), (*b*) or (*c*)".

Amendment of regulation 4 of the principal regulations

3. Regulation 4 of the principal regulations (adults in certain accommodation other than hospitals) shall be amended by the addition, at the end of that regulation, of the words—

> "and not being, in a case of a person who has not attained the age of 18 where accommodation is provided in pursuance of section 12 of the Health Services and Public Health Act 1968(h), accommodation in a private dwelling.".

(a) 1975 c. 14.   (b) 1977 c. 5.   (c) S.I. 1975/598 (1975 I, p. 2179).
(d) The relevant amending instrument is S.I. 1977/342 (1977 I, p. 1033).
(e) S.I. 1975/560 (1975 I, p. 2014).
(f) There is no amendment relevant to the subject of these regulations.
(g) 1889 c. 63.   (h) 1968 c. 46.

Amendment of regulation 6 of the principal regulations

4. Regulation 6 of the principal regulations (modification of section 35(1) to (4) of the Social Security Act 1975 in its application to children) shall be amended by the substitution for paragraph (5) of that regulation (provisions relating to person entitled to attendance allowance in respect of a child) of the following paragraph:

"(5) Paragraph (4) shall have effect subject to the following provisions—

(a) in a case to which sub-paragraph (c) of paragraph (4) applies, where, but for this sub-paragraph more than one person would be entitled to an attendance allowance in respect of a child for any period, the person so entitled shall be such one of those persons as the Secretary of State may determine; and

(b) where a sum has been paid to any person on account of attendance allowance in respect of a child for any period and has not been repaid or recovered, attendance allowance in respect of that child for that period shall not be payable to any other person who may establish title to it except to the extent that it may be payable at a higher rate than that already paid; and

(c) where a woman is living with her husband, attendance allowance to which she is entitled by virtue of paragraph (4) shall be payable to her or to her husband; and

(d) except where some other person would, but for this sub-paragraph, be awarded the allowance, if a child has been living with any person that child shall be treated as continuing to live with him during any period—

(i) throughout which the child is not living with him which has not lasted for more than 28 days continuously; and

(ii) where that person is one of spouses living together and the other spouse would have become entitled to the allowance had he claimed it, during such further period as the Secretary of State may determine to be reasonable in all the circumstances of the case;

and, where a child would otherwise be regarded as living with a person although absent from that person he shall, subject to the provisions of this sub-paragraph, be deemed, for the purposes of attendance allowance, to have ceased so to live; and

(e) a person, who has been contributing to the cost of providing for a child, shall be treated as continuing so to contribute during any period, in which he is not so contributing, which has not lasted for more than 28 days continuously; so however that this sub-paragraph shall not apply where some other person would, without the application of this sub-paragraph, be awarded the allowance; and

(f) a person shall be treated as contributing to the cost of providing for a child if that person is one of spouses living together and the other of them is so contributing.".

Amendment of regulation 7 of the principal regulations

5. Regulation 7 of the principal regulations (children in hospital and certain other accommodation) shall be amended by the insertion in paragraph (1)(b) of that regulation, immediately after the words "Schedule to these regulations", of the words:—

"not being, in a case where accommodation is provided in pursuance of section 12 of the Health Services and Public Health Act 1968, accommodation in a private dwelling.".

Amendment of the Schedule to the principal regulations

6.—(1) The Schedule to the principal regulations (attendance allowance not payable to persons living in accommodation provided in pursuance of, or provided wholly or partly at public expense in pursuance of, any of the enactments specified) shall be amended in accordance with the following provisions of this regulation.

(2) In column 3 of the said Schedule there shall be inserted after the reference to section 13 of the Children Act 1948(a) and after the reference to section 21 of the Social Work (Scotland) Act 1968(b) the words "(except subsection (1)(a))".

(3) Also in column 3 of the said Schedule for the reference to section 37(2) and (3) of the Social Work (Scotland) Act 1968 there shall be substituted a reference to section 37(2), (3), (4), (5), (5A) and (5B) of that Act and for the reference to section 40(4) and (7) of the same Act there shall be substituted a reference to section 40(4), (7), (8). (8A) and (8B) of that Act.

Amendment of regulation 9 of the Claims and Payments Regulations

7. Regulation 9 of the Claims and Payments Regulations (interchange with claims for other benefits) shall be amended by the substitution, for paragraph (5) of that regulation, of the following paragraph:—

"(5) A claim for benefit under the Supplementary Benefits Act 1976(c) may be treated as a claim also for attendance allowance.".

Amendment of regulation 16 of the Claims and Payments Regulations

8. Regulation 16 of the Claims and Payments Regulations (special provision relating to payment of attendance allowance and constant attendance allowance for persons out of hospital for short periods) shall be amended by the deletion of all references to attendance allowance and to this end there shall be substituted for the said regulation 16 the following regulation:—

"*Special provision relating to payment of constant attendance allowance for persons out of hospital for short periods.*

16. Notwithstanding anything contained in the foregoing provisions of these regulations an increase of disablement pension under section 61 where constant attendance is needed ("constant attendance allowance") shall be paid at a daily rate of one-seventh of the weekly rate in any case where it becomes payable for a period of less than a week which is immediately preceded and immediately succeeded by periods during which the constant attendance allowance was not payable because regulation 13(1) of the Social Security (Industrial Injuries) (Benefit) Regulations 1975(d) applied.".

New regulation to be inserted in the Claims and Payments Regulations

9. After regulation 16 of the Claims and Payments Regulations there shall be inserted the following regulation:—

(a) 1948 c. 43.   (b) 1968 c. 49.   (c) 1976 c. 71.
(d) S.I. 1975/559 (1975 I, p. 1979).

"Special provision relating to payment of attendance allowance for persons out of hospital for periods not expected to exceed 13 weeks.

16A.—(1) In any case where an attendance allowance becomes payable for a period commencing on or after 29th August 1977 which is immediately preceded by, and which at its commencement is expected to be followed in not more than 13 weeks by periods during which—

(a) the person in respect of whom it is payable is in a hospital or in a similar institution in circumstances to which regulation 3 or 7(1)(c) of the Social Security (Attendance Allowance) (No. 2) Regulations 1975 applies; or

(b) the allowance is not payable because regulation 4 or 7(1)(b) of the Social Security (Attendance Allowance) (No. 2) Regulations 1975 applies,

the allowance payable for such period shall, so long as the period does not continue for more than 13 weeks, be paid at a daily rate of one-seventh of the weekly rate and shall be paid in arrears at weekly intervals or at such other intervals as the Secretary of State may in any case direct.

(2) In this regulation the expression "13 weeks" means a period of 91 consecutive days.

3rd August 1977.

David Ennals,
Secretary of State for Social Services.

EXPLANATORY NOTE

(This Note is not part of the Regulations.)

These Regulations amend the Social Security (Attendance Allowance) (No. 2) Regulations 1975 so as to allow attendance allowance to be payable in respect of a child who is boarded out with foster parents by a local authority and so as to make certain other minor corrections and amendments to those regulations. The Regulations also amend the Social Security (Claims and Payments) Regulations 1975 so as to enable claims for benefit under the Supplementary Benefits Act 1976 to be treated also as claims for attendance allowance and to vary the special provisions relating to payment of attendance allowance for persons out of hospital for short periods.

STATUTORY INSTRUMENTS

1977 No. 1362

SOCIAL SECURITY

The Social Security Benefits Up-rating Regulations 1977

Made - - - -	3rd August 1977
Laid before Parliament	11th August 1977
Coming into Operation	14th November 1977

The Secretary of State for Social Services, in exercise of the powers conferred upon him by sections 17(2)(*a*), 33, 36(9)(*b*), 58(3) and 131 of, and paragraph 2(1) of Schedule 14 to, the Social Security Act 1975(a) and of all other powers enabling him in that behalf, by this instrument, which contains only provisions in consequence of the Social Security Benefits Up-rating Order 1977(b), hereby makes the following regulations which, by virtue of section 139(2) of, and paragraph 17 of Schedule 15 to, that Act, are not subject to the requirements of section 139(1) of that Act for prior reference to the National Insurance Advisory Committee:—

Citation, commencement and interpretation

1.—(1) These regulations may be cited as the Social Security Benefits Up-rating Regulations 1977 and shall come into operation on 14th November 1977.

(2) In these regulations, unless the context otherwise requires:—

"the Act" means the Social Security Act 1975;

"the up-rating order" means the Social Security Benefits Up-rating Order 1977.

(3) Any reference in these regulations to any provision made by or contained in any enactment or instrument shall, except so far as the context otherwise requires, be construed as a reference to that provision as amended or extended by any enactment or instrument and as including a reference to any provision which may re-enact it or replace it with or without modification.

(4) The rules for the construction of Acts of Parliament contained in the Interpretation Act 1889(c) shall apply in relation to this instrument and in relation to the revocations effected by it as if this instrument and the regulations revoked were Acts of Parliament and as if each revocation were a repeal.

Conditions relating to payment of additional benefit under awards made before the appointed or prescribed day

2. Where an award of any benefit under Chapters I to III of Part II of the Act has been made before the day appointed or prescribed for the payment of the benefit in question at the rate provided in or by virtue of the up-rating order (hereafter in this regulation referred to as "the increased rate"), paragraphs 1 and 2 of Schedule 14 to the Act (effect of any such award) shall, unless the period to which the award relates has ended before that day or the award, in

---

(a) 1975 c. 14.   (b) S.I. 1977/1325 (1977 II, p. 3884).   (c) 1889 c. 63.

accordance with the provisions of sub-paragraph (2) of the said paragraph 2, provides for the payment of the benefit at the increased rate as from that day, have effect subject to the condition that if a question arises as to:—

(a) the weekly rate at which the benefit is payable by virtue of the up-rating order; or

(b) whether the conditions for the receipt of the benefit at the increased rate are satisfied,

the benefit shall be or continue to be payable at the weekly rate specified in the award until that question shall have been determined in accordance with the provisions of the Act.

Amendment of the Social Security (Unemployment, Sickness and Invalidity Benefit) Regulations 1975

3. Regulation 7 of the Social Security (Unemployment, Sickness and Invalidity Benefit) Regulations 1975**(a)**, as amended**(b)** (days not to be treated as days of unemployment or incapacity for work) shall be further amended by the substitution in paragraph (i)(g) for "£9·00" of "£10·00".

Amendment of the Social Security (Non-Contributory Invalidity Pension) Regulations 1975

4. Regulation 12 of the Social Security (Non-Contributory Invalidity Pension) Regulations 1975**(c)**, as amended**(b)**, (disqualification for non-contributory invalidity pension) shall be further amended by the substitution in paragraph (d)(iii) for "£9·00" of "£10·00".

Amendment of the Social Security (Industrial Injuries) (Benefit) Regulations 1975

5. Regulation 8 of the Social Security (Industrial Injuries) (Benefit) Regulations 1975**(d)**, as amended**(b)**, (earnings level for the purposes of unemployability supplement under section 58 of the Act) shall be further amended by the substitution for "£468" of "£520".

Persons not ordinarily resident in Great Britain

6. Regulation 5 of the Social Security Benefit (Persons Abroad) Regulations 1975**(e)** (application of disqualification in respect of up-rating of benefit) shall apply to any additional benefit payable by virtue of the up-rating order.

Revocation

7. The Social Security Benefits Up-rating Regulations 1976**(f)** and the Social Security Benefits Up-rating (No. 2) Regulations 1976**(g)** are hereby revoked, without prejudice to their previous operation or to anything duly done or suffered under them; and anything begun or purported to have been begun under them may be continued under these regulations as if duly begun under these regulations.

David Ennals,
Secretary of State for Social Services.

3rd August 1977.

(a) S.I. 1975/564 (1975 I, p. 2062).   (b) The relevant amending instrument is
(c) S.I. 1975/1058 (1975 II, p. 3691).   S.I. 1976/1245 (1976 II, p. 3522).
(d) S.I. 1975/559 (1975 I, p. 1979).   (e) S.I. 1975/563 (1975 I, p. 2052).
(f) S.I. 1976/1069 (1976 II, p. 2792).   (g) S.I. 1976/1245 (1976 II, p. 3522).

EXPLANATORY NOTE

(This Note is not part of the Regulations.)

These Regulations, which are made in consequence of the Social Security Benefits Up-rating Order 1977, specify circumstances in which the amount of benefit, awarded before the date from which increased rates become payable, is not automatically altered and apply the provisions of the Social Security Benefit (Persons Abroad) Regulations 1975, relating to the position of persons who are absent from and not ordinarily resident in Great Britain when the weekly rate of certain benefits is increased, to the increases of benefit provided by virtue of the Up-rating Order. The Regulations also amend the Social Security (Unemployment, Sickness and Invalidity Benefit) Regulations 1975, the Social Security (Non-Contributory Invalidity Pension) Regulations 1975 and the Social Security (Industrial Injuries) (Benefit) Regulations 1975 so as to raise to £10 a week and £520 a year respectively the earnings limits in respect of work which a person in receipt of benefit to which those regulations apply may do in certain circumstances.

STATUTORY INSTRUMENTS

1977 No. 1363 (C. 46)

TOWN AND COUNTRY PLANNING, ENGLAND AND WALES

The Town and Country Planning Act 1971 (Commencement No. 37) (Gwynedd) Order 1977

Made - - - - - - - - *29th July* 1977

The Secretary of State for Wales, in exercise of the powers conferred on him by sections 21 and 287 of the Town and Country Planning Act 1971(a), hereby makes the following order:—

1.—(1) This order may be cited as the Town and Country Planning Act 1971 (Commencement No. 37) (Gwynedd) Order 1977.

(2) In this order—

"the Act" means the Town and Country Planning Act 1971;

"the Order area" means the area described in Schedule 1 to this order.

2. The provisions of the Act which are specified in the first column of Schedule 2 to this order (which relate to the matters specified in the second column of the said Schedule) shall come into operation in the Order area on 9th September 1977.

3. Notwithstanding the bringing into operation of those provisions of Part I of Schedule 23 of the Act specified in Schedule 2 to this order, any reference in the Land Compensation Act 1961(b) to an area defined in the current development plan as an area of comprehensive development shall continue to be construed as including a reference to an area so defined in any development plan currently in force.

(a) 1971 c. 78.   (b) 1961 c. 33.

SCHEDULE 1

THE ORDER AREA

The County of Gwynedd

SCHEDULE 2

PROVISIONS COMING INTO OPERATION IN THE ORDER AREA ON 9TH SEPTEMBER 1977

Provisions of the Act	Subject matter of provisions
Section 20	Meaning of " development plan " for the purposes of the Act and of certain other enactments.
In Schedule 23 that paragraph in Part I which relates to the Land Compensation Act 1961	Meaning of " area of comprehensive development " in the Land Compensation Act 1961.

John Morris,

29th July 1977   Secretary of State for Wales

EXPLANATORY NOTE

(*This Note is not part of the Order.*)

This Order brings into force for the County of Gwynedd section 20, of, and certain of the provisions of Part I of Schedule 23 to, the Town and Country Planning Act 1971 specified in Schedule 2 to the order. Section 20 provides, for the purposes of the Act of 1971, any other enactment relating to town and country planning, the Land Compensation Act 1961 and the Highways Act 1959 (c. 25), that the development plan for any district shall consist of the structure and local plans for that area. The provision in Part I of Schedule 23 which is specified in Schedule 2 to this order provides for references in the Land Compensation Act 1961 to areas defined in the current development plan as areas of comprehensive development to be construed as references to action areas for which a local plan is in force.

The Order contains a transitional provision relating to old-style development plans (which remain in existence alongside structure plans until revoked by order of the Secretary of State). The provision secures that references to areas of comprehensive development in the Land Compensation Act 1961 are continued to be construed as including references to areas so defined in any old-style development plan.

STATUTORY INSTRUMENTS

1977 No. 1364

TOWN AND COUNTRY PLANNING, ENGLAND AND WALES

The Town and Country Planning (Repeal of Provisions No. 9) (Gwynedd) Order 1977

Made - - - -	*29th July* 1977
Coming into Operation	*9th September* 1977

The Secretary of State for Wales, in exercise of the powers conferred on him by sections 21(2) and 287 of the Town and Country Planning Act 1971(a), hereby makes the following order:—

1.—(1) This order may be cited as the Town and Country Planning (Repeal of Provisions No. 9) (Gwynedd) Order 1977 and shall come into operation on 9th September 1977.

(2) In this order "the Act" means the Town and Country Planning Act 1971; and "the Order area" means the area described in the Schedule to this order.

2. The provisions of the Act contained in Part I of Schedule 5 and in Schedule 6 to the Act are hereby repealed as respects the Order area.

SCHEDULE

THE ORDER AREA

The County of Gwynedd

John Morris,
Secretary of State for Wales.

29th July 1977.

(a) 1971 c. 78.

EXPLANATORY NOTE

(This Note is not part of the Order.)

This Order is made in consequence of the approval of the three structure plans which together cover the whole of the County of Gwynedd.

The three structure plans are: —

(a) the structure plan for the District of Ynys Mon–Isle of Anglesey (formerly the administrative county of Anglesey);

(b) the structure plan for the Districts of Arfon and Dwyfor and certain parts of the District of Aberconwy (formerly the administrative county of Caernarvon);

(c) the structure plan for the District of Meirionnydd (formerly part of the administrative county of Merioneth) and the remainder of the District of Aberconwy (referred to in the structure plan as Dyffryn Conwy and comprising those parts of the District of Aberconwy which were formerly included in the administrative county of Denbigh).

This Order repeals for the County of Gwynedd the provisions of the Town and Country Planning Act 1971 relating to development plans which are contained in Part I of Schedule 5 and in Schedule 6 to that Act. Those provisions which substantially re-enacted the provisions of the former Town and Country Planning Act 1962 (c. 38) relating to development plans are now superseded, in the area to which this order relates, by the provisions relating to structure and local plans contained in Part II of the Act of 1971.

Following this repeal, the development plan for any district (or part of a district) within the area to which this order relates is, by virtue of the provisions of paragraph 2 of Schedule 7 to the Act, the structure plan for that district (or that part of that district, as the case may be) read together with the development plan (within the meaning of Schedule 5) which is in force in that district (or that part of that district, as the case may be) at the date when this order comes into operation. The structure plan prevails in any case of conflict between the provisions of the two plans.

STATUTORY INSTRUMENTS

1977 No. 1365 (C. 47)

CRIMINAL LAW, ENGLAND AND WALES

CRIMINAL LAW, SCOTLAND

CRIMINAL LAW, NORTHERN IRELAND

The Criminal Law Act 1977 (Commencement No. 1) Order 1977

Made - - - - *4th August* 1977

In exercise of the powers conferred on me by section 65(7) of the Criminal Law Act 1977(a), I hereby make the following Order:—

1. This Order may be cited as the Criminal Law Act 1977 (Commencement No. 1) Order 1977.

2. The provisions of the Criminal Law Act 1977 specified in column 1 of the Schedule to this Order (which relate to the matters specified in column 2 thereof) shall come into force on 8th September 1977.

Merlyn Rees,

One of Her Majesty's Principal Secretaries of State.

Home Office.
4th August 1977.

(a) 1977 c. 45.

SCHEDULE

PROVISIONS OF THE CRIMINAL LAW ACT 1977 COMING
INTO FORCE ON 8TH SEPTEMBER 1977

Provisions of the Act	Subject matter of provisions
Section 5(10)(*b*)	Amendment to section 4 of the Offences Against the Person Act 1861.
Section 31(1).	Increase of fines for certain summary offences.
Section 33.	Penalty for offences under section 3 of Explosive Substances Act 1883.
Section 43.	Peremptory challenge of jurors.
Section 51.	Bomb hoaxes.
Section 52.	Misuse of Drugs Act 1971: redefinition of cannabis.
Section 54.	Inciting girl under sixteen to have incestuous sexual intercourse.
Section 55.	Amendment of Rabies Act 1974 and Diseases of Animals (N.I.) Order 1975.
Section 57.	Probation and conditional discharge; power to vary statutory minimum or maximum period.
Section 63(1) and so much of section 63(2) as relates to any provisions specified in this Schedule, or in Appendix A or B hereto.	Provisions applying to Scotland.
Section 65.	Citation, etc.
Schedule 6	Increase of fines for certain summary offences.
In Schedule 11– so much of paragraph 5 as relates to section 289C(1) of the Criminal Procedure (Scotland) Act 1975; paragraph 13.	Amendments of Criminal Procedure (Scotland) Act 1975.
So much of Schedule 12 as is specified in Appendix A hereto.	Minor and consequential amendments.
So much of Schedule 13 as is specified in Appendix B hereto.	Repeals.
Schedule 14.	Transitional provisions.

APPENDIX A

PROVISIONS OF SCHEDULE 12 TO THE CRIMINAL LAW ACT 1977
COMING INTO FORCE ON 8TH SEPTEMBER 1977

So much of Schedule 12 as amends the following enactments:—

The Offences Against the Person Act 1861 (c. 100).

The Explosive Substances Act 1883 (c. 3).

The Criminal Justice Act 1948 (c. 58).

Paragraphs 14 and 15 of Part II of Schedule 2 to the Sexual Offences Act 1956 (c. 69).

The Adoption Act 1958 (c. 5).

Section 169 of the Licensing Act 1964 (c. 26).

The Housing Act 1964 (c. 56).

The Housing (Scotland) Act 1966 (c. 49).

Section 8(7) of the Gaming Act 1968 (c. 65).

Section 13(3) of the Children and Young Persons Act 1969 (c. 54).

Sections 15(2) and 17(3) of and paragraph 9 of Schedule 3 to the Powers of Criminal Courts Act 1973 (c. 62).

The Adoption Act 1976 (c. 36).

Sections 3(8) and 5 of the Bail Act 1976 (c. 63).

APPENDIX B

REPEALS TAKING EFFECT ON 8TH SEPTEMBER 1977

Chapter	Short Title	Extent of repeal
11 & 12 Geo. 6		
1948 c. 58	Criminal Justice Act 1948.	In section 19(3), the words "or justice".
1969 c. 54	Children and Young Persons Act 1969.	In section 13(3), the words from "or if" to "place".
1967 c. 80	Criminal Justice Act 1967.	The entry relating to Part I of Schedule 3.
1973 c. 62	Powers of Criminal Courts Act 1973.	In Schedule 3, in paragraph 9, the words from "or if" to "place".
1976 c. 63	Bail Act 1976.	In Schedule 2, in paragraph 38 the words "in paragraph (a)".

EXPLANATORY NOTE

(This Note is not part of the Order.)

This Order brings into force on 8th September 1977 the provisions of the Criminal Law Act 1977 set out in the Schedule to the Order.

STATUTORY INSTRUMENTS

1977 No. 1367

COMPANIES

The Companies (Forms No. 3) Order 1977

Made - - - -	*4th August* 1977
Coming into Operation	*1st October* 1977

The Secretary of State, in exercise of the powers conferred by section 455(1) of the Companies Act 1948 (**a**), section 415 of the Companies Act 1948 (as amended by section 42(1) of, and Schedule 2 to, the Companies Act 1976(**b**)) and sections 26(3) and 29(8) of the Companies Act 1967(**c**) (as amended by section 34 of and Schedule 1 to the Companies Act 1976), and now vested in him(**d**), and sections 1(7), 3(1), 3(2), 6(3), 9(2) and 10(1) of the Companies Act 1976, and of all other powers enabling him in that behalf, hereby makes the following Order:—

1.—(1) This Order may be cited as the Companies (Forms No. 3) Order 1977 and shall come into operation on 1st October 1977.

(2) The Interpretation Act 1889(**e**) shall apply for the interpretation of this Order as it applies for the interpretation of an Act of Parliament.

2. The forms set out in the Schedule hereto with such variations as circumstances require are the forms prescribed for the purposes of the provisions of the Companies Act 1967 (as amended by the Companies Act 1976) and the Companies Act 1976 referred to therein.

3. A translation into English of any document required to be delivered to the Registrar of Companies in pursuance of section 1(7) or section 9(2) of the Companies Act 1976 shall be certified to be a correct translation if it is so certified

(*a*) where made in the United Kingdom, by—

    (i) a notary public in any part of the United Kingdom;

    (ii) a solicitor of the Supreme Court of Judicature of England and Wales or of Northern Ireland or, if made in Scotland, a solicitor; or

    (iii) any person whom a person mentioned in sub-paragraph (i) or (ii) above certifies is known to him as competent to translate the document into the English language;

(*b*) where made outside the United Kingdom, by—

    (i) any person for the time being authorised by law in the place where the translation is made to administer an oath for any judicial or other legal purpose;

    (ii) any of the British officials mentioned in section 6 of the Commissioners for Oaths Act 1889(**f**), as amended by section 2 of the Commissioners for Oaths Act 1891 (**g**) and section 3 of the Oaths and Evidence (Overseas Authorities and Countries) Act 1963(**h**);

(**a**) 1948 c. 38.   (**b**) 1976 c. 69.   (**c**) 1967 c. 81.
(**d**) S.I. 1970/1537 (1970 III, p. 5293).   (**e**) 1889 c. 63.
(**f**) 1889 c. 10.   (**g**) 1891 c. 50.   (**h**) 1963 c. 27.

(iii) a notary public; or

(iv) any person whom a person mentioned in sub-paragraph (i), (ii) or (iii) of this paragraph certifies is known to him as competent to translate the document into the English language.

4th August 1977

Derek Eagers,
An Under-Secretary,
Department of Trade.

SCHEDULE

THE COMPANIES ACTS 1948 TO 1976

G

26

Notice of place where copies of directors' service contracts or memorandums thereof are kept or of any change in that place

Pursuant to section 26(3) of the Companies Act 1967 as amended by the Companies Act 1976

Please do not write in this binding margin

To the Registrar of companies   Company number   For official use

Please complete legibly, prefer- able in black type, or bold black lettering

Name of company

*delete if inappropriate

Limited*

hereby gives you notice, in accordance with section 26(3) of the Companies A 1967 as amended by the Companies Act 1976, that such copies of the directo service contracts, or where they are not in writing such written memorandu setting out the terms of those contracts, as are required to be kept by the co pany and to be open to the inspection of the members of the company, are ke at:

†delete as appropriate

Signed   [Director] [Secretary]†   Date

Presentor's name, address and reference: (if any)

For official use
General section

Post room

Form No. 27

THE COMPANIES ACTS 1948 TO 1976

G

27

Notice of place where register of directors' interests in shares etc. is kept or of any change in that place

ase do not
te in this
ding margin

Pursuant to section 29(8) of the Companies Act 1967 as amended by the Companies Act 1976

To the Registrar of Companies   Company number   For official use

ase complete
bly, prefer-
y in black
e, or bold
ck lettering

Name of company

lete if
ppropriate

Limited*

hereby gives you notice, in accordance with section 29(8) of the Companies Act 1967 as amended by the Companies Act 1976, that the register of directors' interests in shares in, or debentures of, the company or any other body corporate, being the company's subsidiary or holding company or a subsidiary of the company's holding company, is kept at:

lete as
ropriate

Signed   [Director] [Secretary]† Date

| Presentor's name, address and reference: (if any) | For official use General section | Post room |

Form No.

THE COMPANIES ACTS 1948 TO 1976

A   **3**

Notice of new accounting reference date given during the course of an accounting reference period

Please do not write in this binding margin

Pursuant to section 3(1) of the Companies Act 1976

↓   To the Registrar of Companies   For official u~

Please complete legibly, preferably in black type or bold black lettering

Name of company

*delete if inappropriate

Limited*

hereby gives you notice in accordance with section 3(1) of the Companies A~

Note
Please read notes 1 to 5 overleaf before completing this form.

1976 that the company's new accounting reference date on which the curre~ accounting reference period and each subsequent accounting reference period the company is to be treated as coming, or as having come, to an end is as sho~ below:

Company number   Day   Month

†delete as appropriate

The current accounting reference period of the company is to be treated [shortened] [extended]* and [is to be treated as having come to an end] [will co~ to an end]† on

Day   Month   Year

1   9

See note 4(c) and complete if appropriate

If this notice states that the current accounting reference period of the compa~ is to be extended, and reliance is being placed on section 3(6)(c) of the Compar~ Act 1976, the following statement should be completed:

‡delete as appropriate

The company is a [subsidiary] [holding company]‡ of _____

_____

_____, company number _____

§delete as appropriate

the accounting reference date of which is _____
Signed   [Director] [Secretary]§   Date

Presentor's name, address and reference: (if any)	For official use Data punch	General section	Post room

NOTES

1. At any time during the course of a period which is an accounting reference period of a company by virtue of section 2 or section 3 of the Companies Act 1976 the company may give notice in the prescribed form to the Registrar of Companies, under section 3(1), specifying a date in the calendar year ("the new accounting reference date") on which that accounting reference period ("the current accounting reference period") and each subsequent accounting reference period of the company is to be treated as coming or (as the case may require) as having come to an end.

2. A notice under section 3(1) must state whether the current accounting reference period of the company—

   (*a*) is to be treated as shortened, so as to come to an end, or (as the case may require) to be treated as having come to an end, on the new accounting reference date on the first occasion on which that date falls or fell after the beginning of that accounting reference period; or

   (*b*) is to be treated as extended, so as to come to an end on the new accounting reference date on the second occasion on which that date falls after the beginning of that accounting reference period.

[Section 3(4)]

3. A notice under section 3(1) which states that the current accounting reference period of the company is to be extended shall not have effect if the current accounting reference period as extended in accordance with the notice would exceed eighteen months.

[Section 3(5)]

4. Subject to any direction given by the Secretary of State under section 3(7) of the Companies Act 1976 a notice under section 3(1) which states that the current accounting reference period of the company is to be extended shall not have effect unless—

   (*a*) no earlier accounting reference period of the company has been extended by virtue of a previous notice given by the company under section 3; or

   (*b*) the notice is given not less than five years after the date on which any earlier accounting reference period of the company which was so extended came to an end; or

   (*c*) the company is a subsidiary or holding company of another company and the new accounting reference date coincides with the accounting reference date of that other company.

[Section 3(6)]

5. The dates in the boxes on the form should be completed in the manner illustrated below:

Company number Day Month

		0	5	0	4	

Day		Month		Year		
0	5	0	4	1	9	7	9

2y

Form No. 3

THE COMPANIES ACTS 1948 TO 1976

A

3a

Notice of new accounting reference date given after the end of an accounting reference period

Pursuant to section 3(2) of the Companies Act 1976

To the Registrar of Companies

For official use

Please do not write in this binding margin ↓

Please complete legibly, preferably in black type, or bold black lettering

Name of company

*delete if inappropriate

Limited*

hereby gives you notice in accordance with section 3(2) of the Companies Act 1976 that the company's new accounting reference date on which the previous accounting reference period and each subsequent accounting reference period of the company is to be treated as coming, or as having come, to an end is as shown below:

Note
Please read notes 1 to 5 overleaf before completing this form

Company number   Day   Month

The previous accounting reference period of the company is to be treated as [shortened] [extended]† and [is to be treated as having come to an end] [will come to an end]† on

†delete as appropriate

Day   Month   year

1 9

‡delete as appropriate

The company is a [subsidiary] [holding company]‡ of _____

_____ , company number _____

the accounting reference date of which is _____

§delete as appropriate

Signed   [Director] [Secretary]§   Date

Presentor's name, address and reference: (if any)	For official use Data punch	General section	Post room

NOTES

1. Subject to the provision referred to in note 2 below, at any time after the end of a period which was an accounting reference period of a company by virtue of section 2 or section 3 of the Companies Act 1976 the company may give notice in the prescribed form to the Registrar of Companies, under section 3(2), specifying a date in the calendar year ("the new accounting reference date") on which that accounting reference period ("the previous accounting reference period") and each subsequent accounting reference period of the company is to be treated as coming or (as the case may require) as having come to an end.

2. Such notice

(a) shall not have effect unless the company is a subsidiary or holding company of another company and the new accounting reference date coincides with the accounting reference date of that other company; and

(b) shall not have effect if the period allowed for laying and delivering accounts in relation to the previous accounting reference period has already expired at the time when the notice is given.

[Section 3(3)]

3. A notice under section 3(2) must state whether the previous accounting reference period of the company—

(a) is to be treated as shortened, so as to be treated as having come to an end on the new accounting reference date on the first occasion on which that date fell after the beginning of that accounting reference period; or

(b) is to be treated as extended, so as to come to an end, or (as the case may require) to be treated as having come to an end, on the new accounting reference date on the second occasion on which that date falls or fell after the beginning of that accounting reference period.

[Section 3(4)]

4. A notice under section 3(2) which states that the previous accounting reference period of the company is to be extended shall not have effect if the previous accounting reference period as extended in accordance with the notice would exceed eighteen months.

5. The dates in the boxes on this form should be completed in the manner illustrated below:

Company number	Day		Month	
	0	5	0	4

Day		Month		Year			
0	5	0	4	1	9	7	9

Form No. F7A

THE COMPANIES ACTS 1948 TO 1976

A

F7a

Notice by an oversea company of new accounting reference date given during the course of an accounting reference period

Pursuant to sections 3(1) and 10(1) of the Companies Act 1976

Please do not write in this binding margin

To the Registrar of Companies   For office use

Please complete legibly, prefer-ably in black type, or bold black lettering

Name of company

*Country of origin

Incorporated in*

Place of business in Great Britain established at

Note
Please read notes 1 to 5 overleaf before completing this form

hereby gives you notice in accordance with sections 3(1) and 10(1) of the Com-panies Act 1976 that the company's new accounting reference date on which the current accounting reference period and each subsequent accounting reference period of the company is to be treated as coming, or as having come, to an end is as shown below:

Company number   Day   Month

F

†delete as appropriate

The current accounting reference period of the company is to be treated as [shortened] [extended]† and [is to be treated as having come to an end] [will come to an end]† on

Day   Month   Year

1 9

Signature(s) of the persons(s)
authorised under section 407(1)(c) of
the Companies Act 1948, or of some
other person in Great Britain duly
authorised by the company

....
....
....
....
....
....
....

Date

Presentor's name, address and reference: (if any)

For official use Data punch	General section	Post room

NOTES

1. In their application to oversea companies sections 2 and 3 of the Companies Act 1976 are to be read subject to the modifications contained in sub-sections (2) to (7) of section 10 of the Act.

[Section 10(1)]

2. At any time during the course of a period which is an accounting reference period of a company by virtue of section 2, 3 or 10 of the Act the company may give notice in the prescribed form to the Registrar of Companies, under section 3(1), specifying a date in the calendar year ("the new accounting reference date") on which that accounting reference period ("the current accounting reference period") and each subsequent accounting reference period of the company is to be treated as coming or (as the case may require) as having come to an end.

3. A notice under section 3(1) must state whether the current accounting reference period of the company—

(a) is to be treated as shortened, so as to come to an end, or (as the case may require) to be treated as having come to an end, on the new accounting reference date on the first occasion on which that date falls or fell after the beginning of that accounting reference period; or

(b) is to be treated as extended, so as to come to an end on the new accounting reference date on the second occasion on which that date falls or fell after the beginning of that accounting reference period.

[Section 3(4)]

4. A notice under section 3(1) which states that the current accounting reference period of the company is to be extended shall not have effect if the current accounting reference period as extended in accordance with the notice would exceed eighteen months.

[Section 3(5)]

5. The dates in the boxes on the forms should be completed in the manner illustrated below.

Company number		Day	Month
F	0	5	0	4

Day		Month		Year			
0	5	0	4	1	9	7	9

Form No. F7b

THE COMPANIES ACTS 1948 TO 1976

A

F7b

Please do not write in this binding margin ↓

Notice by an oversea company of new accounting reference date given after the end of an accounting reference period

Pursuant to sections 3(2) and 10(1) of the Companies Act 1976
To the Registrar of Companies

For official use

Please complete legibly, preferably in black type, or bold black lettering

Name of company

*Country of origin

Incorporated in*

Place of business in Great Britain established at

Note
Please read notes 1 to 6 overleaf before completing this form

hereby gives you notice in accordance with sections 3(2) and 10(1) of the Companies Act 1976 that the company's new accounting reference date on which the previous accounting reference period and each subsequent accounting reference period of the company is to be treated as coming, or as having come, to an end is as shown below:

Company number   Day   Month

F

†delete as appropriate

The previous accounting reference period of the company is to be treated as [shortened] [extended]† and [is to be treated as having come to an end] [will come to an end]† on

Day   Month   Year

1   9

‡delete as appropriate

The company is a [subsidiary] [holding company]‡ of.................................
....
...., company number...............................
the accounting reference date of which is...

Signature(s) of the person(s) authorised under section 407(1)(c) of the Companies Act 1948, or of some other person in Great Britain duly authorised by the company

....
....
....
....
....
....

Date   ....

Presentor's name, address and reference (if any)	For official use Data punch	General section	Post room

NOTES

1. In their application to oversea companies sections 2 and 3 of the Companies Act 1976 are to be read subject to the modifications contained in sub-sections (2) to (7) of section 10 of the Act.

[Section 10(1)]

2. Subject to the provision referred to in note 3 below, at any time after the end of a period which was an accounting reference period of a company by virtue of section 2, 3 or 10 of the Act the company may give notice in the prescribed form to the Registrar of Companies, under section 3(2), specifying a date in the calendar year ("the new accounting reference date") on which that accounting reference period ("the previous accounting reference period") and each subsequent accounting reference period of the company is to be treated as coming or (as the case may require) as having come to an end.

3. Such notice

(a) shall not have effect unless the company is a subsidiary or holding company of another company and the new accounting reference date coincides with the accounting reference date of that other company; and

(b) shall not have effect if the period allowed for laying and delivering accounts in relation to the previous accounting reference period has already expired at the time when the notice is given.

[Section 3(3)]

4. A notice under section 3(2) must state whether the previous accounting reference period of the company—

(a) is to be treated as shortened, so as to be treated as having come to an end on the new accounting reference date on the first occasion on which that date fell after the beginning of that accounting reference period; or

(b) is to be treated as extended, so as to come to an end, or (as the case may require) to be treated as having come to an end, on the new accounting reference date on the second occasion on which that date falls or fell after the beginning of that accounting reference period.

[Section 3(4)]

5. A notice under section 3(2) which states that the previous accounting reference period of the company is to be extended shall not have effect if the previous accounting reference period as extended in accordance with the notice would exceed eighteen months.

[Section 3(5)]

6. The dates in the boxes on this form should be completed in the manner illustrated below:

Company number Day Month

| F | | 0 | 5 | 0 | 4 |

Day Month Year

| 0 | 5 | 0 | 4 | 1 | 9 | 7 | 9 |

Form No. 5

THE COMPANIES ACTS 1948 TO 1976

A

5

Notice of overseas interests

Please do not write in this binding margin ↓

Pursuant to section 6(3) of the Companies Acts 1976

To the Registrar of Companies | Company number | For official use

Please complete legibly, prefer-ably in black type, or bold black lettering

Name of company

*delete if inappropriate

Limited*

Note Please read the notes overleaf before completing this form

The directors of the above-named company hereby give you notice in accordance

with section 6(3) of the Companies Act 1976 that the company is carrying on

business, or has interests, outside the United Kingdom, the Channel Islands and

the Isle of Man and hereby claim an extension of three months to the period

allowed under section 6 of the Companies Act 1976 for laying and delivering

accounts in relation to the accounting reference period †[ending] [which ended on]

Day   Month   Year

1   9

†delete as appropriate

Signed   [Director] [Secretary]†   Date

Presentor's name, address and reference: (if any)	For official use Data punch	General section	Post room

NOTES

1. A company which carries on business or has interests outside the United Kingdom, the Channel Islands and the Isle of Man may, by giving notice in the prescribed form to the Registrar of Companies under section 6(3) of the Companies Act 1976, claim an extension of three months in the period which otherwise would be allowed for the laying and delivery of accounts under section 6(2).

2. Notice must be given before the expiry of the period which would otherwise be allowed under section 6(2).

3. A separate notice will be required for each period for which the claim is made.

4. The date in the box on the form should be completed in the manner illustrated below:

Day		Month		Year			
0	5	0	4	1	9	7	9

EXPLANATORY NOTE

(This Note does not form part of the Order.)

This Order prescribes the forms to be used when giving notice to the registrar of companies in pursuance of those provisions of the Companies Act 1967 (as amended by the Companies Act 1976) and the Companies Act 1976 which are referred to in the forms set out in the Schedule to the Order. It also prescribes the manner in which the translation of accounts and related documents delivered to the registrar under section 1(7) or 9(2) of the Companies Act 1976 must be certified as being correct.

STATUTORY INSTRUMENTS

1977 No. 1368

COMPANIES

The Companies (Annual Return) Regulations 1977

Made - - - -	*4th August* 1977
Laid before Parliament	*15th August* 1977
Coming into Operation	*1st October* 1977

The Secretary of State, in exercise of the powers conferred by section 454(2)(*b*) of the Companies Act 1948(a), and now vested in him(**b**), and of all other powers enabling him in that behalf, hereby makes the following Regulations:—

1.—(1) These Regulations may be cited as the Companies (Annual Return) Regulations 1977 and shall come into operation on 1st October 1977.

(2) The Interpretation Act 1889(c) shall apply for the interpretation of these Regulations as it applies for the interpretation of an Act of Parliament.

2.—(1) Except as provided in paragraph (2) below, there shall be substituted for the form in Part II of Schedule 6 to the Companies Act 1948 (being the form of annual return to be made by a company having a share capital) the form set out in the Schedule to these Regulations.

(2) Paragraph (1) of this Regulation shall not apply in relation to an annual return made by a company on or after 1st October 1977 in the case of which there is a duty by virtue of section 7(3) of the Companies Act 1976(**d**) to annex to the return a copy of any balance sheet laid before the company in general meeting before that date.

Derek Eagers,
An Under-Secretary,
Department of Trade.

4th August 1977

(a) 1948 c. 38.
(c) 1889 c. 63.
(b) S.I. 1970/1537 (1970 III, p. 5293).
(d) 1976 c. 69.

Regulation 2(1) **SCHEDULE**

Form 6a

No. of Company..................

THE COMPANIES ACTS 1948 TO 1976

Annual return of a company having a share capital

Pursuant to Sections 124 *and* 126 *of the Companies Act* 1948

Annual return of...Limited*,
made up to the.........................19.........(being the fourteenth day after the date of the
annual general meeting for the year 19.........).

Delete "Limited" *if not applicable*

---

1. Address of the
    registered office of the
    company.

---

2. Summary of share capital and debentures

(a) Nominal Share Capital

(1)   Nominal share capital £..............................divided into:

                         No. of Shares   Class   Value of each share

(b) Issued Share Capital and Debentures

                                            Number   Class

(2)   Number of shares of each class taken up to the date of
      this return (which number must agree with the total
      shown in the list as held by existing members) ... ...

(3)   Number of shares of each class issued subject to pay-
      ment wholly in cash ...   .

(4)   Number of shares of each class issued as fully paid up
      for a consideration other than cash   ...   ...

(5)   Number of shares of each class   Amount per share
      issued as partly paid up for a
      consideration other than cash   £
      and extent to which each such
      share is so paid up   ...   ...

(6)   Number of shares (if any) of each class issued at a dis-
      count ...   .

(7)   Amount of discount on the issue of shares which has
      not been written off at the date of this return   ...   £ ....

                                 Amount per share   Number   Class

(8)   Amount called up on number of
      shares of each class ...   ... £

(9)   Total amount of calls received (Note 1)   ...   ...   £ ....

Number   Class

(10) Total amount (if any) agreed to be ⎧
      considered as paid on number of │
      shares of each class issued as ⎨ £ ....on ⎨
      fully paid up for a considera- │
      tion other than cash ...   ... ⎩

(11) Total amount (if any) agreed to be ⎧
      considered as paid on number │
      of shares of each class issued as ⎨ £ ....on ⎨
      partly paid up for a considera- │
      tion other than cash ...   ... ⎩

(12) Total amount of calls unpaid   ...   . £ ....

(13) Total amount of sums (if any) paid by way of com-
      mission in respect of any shares or debentures   ... £ ....

(14) Total amount of the sums (if any) allowed by way of
      discount for any debentures since the date of the
      last return   ...   . £ ....

                            Number   Class

(15) Total number of shares of each ⎰
      class forfeited ...   . ⎱

(16) Total amount paid (if any) on shares forfeited   ... £ ....

(17) Total amount of shares for which share warrants to
      bearer are outstanding   ...   . £ ....

(18) Total amount of share warrants ⎧
      to bearer issued and surrend- ⎰ Issued   ...   ... £ ....
      ered respectively since the date ⎱ Surrendered   ... £ ....
      of the last return   ...   ... ⎩

(19) Number of shares comprised in each share warrant to ⎧
      bearer, specifying in the case of warrants of different ⎨
      kinds, particulars of each kind   ...   . ⎩

---

3. Total amount of indebtedness of the company in respect
   of all mortgages and charges which are required to be
   registered with the Registrar of Companies (Note 2)   ... £ ....

Presented by:

Presentor's reference:

4. LIST OF PAST AND PRESENT

Folio in register ledger containing particulars	Names and addresses

MEMBERS (NOTES 3, 4 and 5).

	Account of shares			
Number of shares or amount of stock held by existing members at date of return (Notes 6 and 7)	Particulars of shares transferred since the date of the last return, or, in the case of the first return, of the incorporation of the company, by (a) persons who are still members, and (b) persons who have ceased to be members (Note 8)			Remarks
	Number (Note 7)	Date of registration of transfer		
		(a)	(b)	

5. Situation of the registers of members and debenture holders, if kept at an address other than the registered office.

(*a*) Register of
members (Note 9) ....

(*b*) Register of
debenture holders (Note 10) ....

6. Particulars of directors of the company at the date of this return (Note 11)

Name, nationality and date of birth (where applicable) (Notes 12, 13 and 14)	Address (Note 15)	Business occupation and particulars of other director-ships (Note 16)

Particulars of the secretary of the company at the date of this return

Name (Notes 12, 13, 17 and 18)	Address (Notes 18 and 19)

CERTIFICATION

DELETE ANY CERTIFICATE WHICH DOES NOT APPLY

Delete if not a Private Company

A. We certify that the Company has not since the date of the last Annual Return (or, if this is the first Return made, since the date of incorporation of the Company) issued any invitation to the public to subscribe for any shares or debentures of the Company.

Delete if not a Private Company or, if a Private Company, if the number of members of the Company does not exceed fifty.

B. We certify that the excess of the number of members of the Company over fifty consists wholly of persons who under Section 28(1)(*b*) of the Companies Act 1948, are not to be included in the reckoning of fifty.

Signed .... Director

.... Secretary

Banking companies: please see Note 20.

NOTES

1. Include payments on application and allotment and any sums received on shares forfeited.

2. Include also any mortgages and charges which would have been required to be so registered if created after 1st July 1908.

3. Give list of persons holding shares or stock in the company on the fourteenth day after the holding of the annual general meeting. Show also those persons who have held shares or stock in the company at any time since the date of the last return, or if this is the company's first return, since the date of incorporation.

4. If the names in the list are not arranged in alphabetical order, an index sufficient to enable the name of any person to be readily found must be annexed.

5. If the return for either of the two immediately preceding years has given as at the date of that return the full particulars required as to past and present members and the shares and stock held and transferred by them, only such of the particulars need to be given as relate to persons ceasing to be or becoming members since the date of the last return and to shares transferred since that date or to changes as compared with that date in the amount of stock held by a member.

6. The aggregate number of shares held by each member must be stated, and the aggregates must be added up so as to agree with the number of shares stated in the "summary of share capital and debentures" (paragraph 2) to have been taken up.

7. When the shares are of different classes these columns should be sub-divided, so that the number of each class held, or transferred, may be shown separately. Where any shares have been converted into stock the amount of stock held by each member must be shown.

8. The date of registration of each transfer should be given as well as the number of shares transferred on each date. The particulars should be placed opposite the name of the transferor and not opposite that of the transferee, but the name of the transferee may be inserted in the "remarks" column immediately opposite the particulars of each transfer.

9. Section 110 of the Companies Act 1948 refers.

10. If any such register or part of any such register is kept outside Great Britain, insert the address in Great Britain where any duplicate thereof is kept.

11. If the columns give insufficient space the particulars must be continued on a separate sheet. "Director" includes any person who occupies the position of a director by whatsoever name called, and any person in accordance with whose directions or instructions the directors of the company are accustomed to act.

12. Full names must be given. In the case of an individual, his present Christian name or names and surname must be given. "Christian name" includes a forename and "surname" in the case of a peer or person usually known by a title different from his surname means that title. In the case of a corporation, its corporate name must be given.

13. In the case of an individual, any former Christian names and surname must be given in addition.

"Former Christian name" and "former surname" do not include:—

(a) in the case of a peer or a person usually known by a British title different from his surname, the name by which he was known previous to the adoption of or succession to the title; or

(b) in the case of any person, a former Christian name or surname where that name or surname was changed or disused before the person bearing the name attained the age of eighteen years or has been changed or disused for a period of not less than twenty years; or

(c) in the case of a married woman, the name or surname by which she was known previous to the marriage.

14. Dates of birth need only be given in the case of directors of a company which is subject to section 185 of the Companies Act, 1948, namely a company which is not a private company or which, being a private company, is the subsidiary of a body corporate incorporated in the United Kingdom which is neither a private company nor a company registered under the law relating to companies for the time being in force in Northern Ireland and having provisions in its constitution which would, if it had been registered in Great Britain, entitle it to rank as a private company.

15. Usual residential address should be given or, in the case of a corporation, the registered or principal office.

16. The names of all bodies corporate incorporated in Great Britain of which the director is also a director should be given, except bodies corporate of which the company making the return is the wholly-owned subsidiary or bodies corporate which are the wholly-owned subsidiaries either of the company or of another company of which the company is the wholly-owned subsidiary. A body corporate is deemed to be the wholly-owned subsidiary of another if it has no members except that other and that other's wholly-owned subsidiaries and its or their nominess.

17. In the case of a Scottish firm, the firm name should be shown.

18. Where all the partners in a firm are joint secretaries, the name and principal office address of the firm alone may be stated.

19. Usual residential address should be given, or, in the case of a corporation or Scottish firm, the registered or principal office.

20. Banking companies. A banking company, in order to avail itself of the benefit of section 432 of the Companies Act 1948, must add to the annual return a statement of the names of the several places where it carries on business (on Form 24).

EXPLANATORY NOTE

(This Note is not part of the Regulations.)

These Regulations alter the form of the annual return required to be made by a company having a share capital which is set out in Part II of Schedule 6 to the Companies Act 1948. The alterations take account of the fact that from 1st October 1977, a company will no longer be required to annex copies of accounts to the annual return, subject to certain transitional arrangements.

STATUTORY INSTRUMENTS

1977 No. 1369

COMPANIES

The Companies (Forms) (Amendment No. 6) Order 1977

Made - - - -	*4th August* 1977
Coming into Operation	*1st October* 1977

The Secretary of State, in exercise of the powers conferred by section 455(1) of the Companies Act 1948(a) and section 125(1) of the Companies Act 1948 as amended by section 34 of, and Schedule 1 to, the Companies Act 1976(b), and now vested in him(c), and of all other powers enabling him in that behalf, hereby makes the following Order:—

1.—(1) This Order may be cited as the Companies (Forms) (Amendment No. 6) Order 1977 and shall come into operation on 1st October 1977.

(2) The Interpretation Act 1889(d) shall apply for the interpretation of this Order as it applies for the interpretation of an Act of Parliament.

2.—(1) Except as provided in paragraph (2) below, the Companies (Forms) Order 1949(e) as amended(f), shall have effect as if for form No. 7 set out in the Schedule thereto (being the form of annual return to be made by a company not having a share capital) there were substituted the form set out in the Schedule to this Order.

(2) Paragraph (1) of this article shall not apply in relation to an annual return made by a company on or after 1st October 1977 in the case of which there is a duty by virtue of section 7(3) of the Companies Act 1976 to annex to the return a copy of any balance sheet laid before the company in general meeting before that date.

Derek Eagers,

An Under-Secretary,
Department of Trade.

4th August 1977.

(a) 1948 c. 38.   (b) 1976 c. 69.   (c) S.I. 1970/1537 (1970 III, p. 5293).   (d) 1889 c. 63.
(e) S.I. 1949/382 (1949 I, p. 714).
(f) S.I. 1957/606, 1962/1302, 1972/1636, 1977/530 (1957 I, p. 462; 1962 II, p. 1394; 1972 III, p. 4786; 1977 I, p. 1737).

Article 2(1)   SCHEDULE
   Form 7

No. of Company ....

THE COMPANIES ACTS 1948 TO 1976

Annual return of a company not having a share capital

Pursuant to Section 125 of the Companies Act 1948
(as amended by the Companies Act 1976) and section
126 of the Companies Act 1948.

Annual return of .... Limited*

made up to the .... 19......... (being the fourteenth

day after the date of the annual general meeting for the year 19......).
                    *Delete "Limited" if not applicable.

Address of the registered office of the company

Situation of the registers of members and debenture holders, if kept at an
address other than the registered office
   (a) Register of
       members (Note 1) ....
   (b) Register of
       debenture holders (Note 2) ....

Total amount of indebtedness of the company in respect of all mortgages
and charges which are required to be registered with the Registrar of
Companies (Note 3) £......................

Particulars of directors of the company at the date of this return (Note 4)

Name, nationality and date of birth (where applicable) (Notes 5, 6 and 7)	Address (Note 8)	Business occupation and particulars of other directorships (Note 9)

Particulars of the secretary of the company at the date of this return

Name (Notes 5, 6, 10 and 11)	Address (Notes 11 and 12)

Signed .... Director   Signed .... Secretary
Banking Companies: please see Note 13.

Presented by:

Presentor's reference:

NOTES

1. Section 110 of the Companies Act 1948 refers.

2. If any such register or part of any such register is kept outside Great Britain, insert the address in Great Britain where any duplicate thereof is kept.

3. Include also any mortgages and charges which would have been required to be so registered if created after 1 July 1908.

4. If the columns give insufficient space the particulars should be continued on a separate sheet. "Director" includes any person who occupies the position of a director by whatsoever name called and any person in accordance with whose directions or instructions the directors of the company are accustomed to act.

5. Full names must be given. In the case of an individual, his present Christian name or names and surname must be given; "Christian name" includes a forename and "surname" in the case of a peer or person usually known by a title different from his surname means that title. In the case of a corporation, its corporate name must be given.

6. In the case of an individual, any former Christian names and surname must be given in addition. "Former Christian name" and "former surname" do not include: —

    (a) in the case of a peer or a person usually known by a British title different from his surname, the name by which he was known previous to the adoption of or succession to the title; or

    (b) in the case of any person, a former Christian name or surname where that name or surname was changed or disused before the person bearing the name attained the age of eighteen years or has been changed or disused for a period of not less than twenty years; or

    (c) in the case of a married woman, the name or surname by which she was known previous to the marriage.

7. Dates of birth need only be given in the case of directors of a company which is subject to section 185 of the Companies Act 1948, namely a company which is not a private company or which, being a private company, is the subsidiary of a body corporate incorporated in the United Kingdom which is neither a private company nor a company registered under the law relating to companies for the time being in force in Northern Ireland and having provisions in its constitution which would, if it had been registered in Great Britain, entitle it to rank as a private company.

8. Usual residential address should be given or, in the case of a corporation, the registered or principal office.

9. The names of all bodies corporate incorporated in Great Britain of which the director is also a director should be given, except bodies corporate of which the company making the return is the wholly-owned subsidiary or bodies corporate which are the wholly-owned subsidiaries either of the company or of another company of which the company is the wholly-owned subsidiary. A body corporate is deemed to be the wholly-owned subsidiary of another if it has no members except that other and that other's wholly-owned subsidiaries and its or their nominees.

10. In the case of a Scottish firm, the firm name should be shown.

11. Where all the partners in a firm are joint secretaries, the name and principal office address of the firm alone may be stated.

12. Usual residential address should be given or, in the case of a corporation or Scottish firm, the registered or principal office.

13. Banking companies. A banking company in order to avail itself of the benefit of section 432 of the Companies Act 1948 must add to the annual return a statement of the names of the several places at which it carries on business (on form 24).

EXPLANATORY NOTE

(This Note is not part of the Order.)

This Order amends the Companies (Forms) Order 1949, as amended. It prescribes a new form 7 (form of the annual return required to be made by a company not having a share capital) for the purpose of section 125 of the Companies Act 1948, as amended by the Companies Act 1976. The new form takes account of the fact that from 1st October 1977 a company will no longer be required to annex copies of accounts to the annual return subject to certain transitional arrangements.

STATUTORY INSTRUMENTS

1977 No. 1370

COMPANIES

The Oversea Companies (Accounts) (Exceptions) Order 1977

Made - - - -		*4th August* 1977
Coming into Operation		*1st October* 1977

The Secretary of State, in exercise of the powers conferred by section 455(1) of the Companies Act 1948(a), and now vested in him(b), and section 9(1) of the Companies Act 1976(c), and of all other powers enabling him in that behalf, hereby makes the following Order:—

1.—(1) This Order may be cited as the Oversea Companies (Accounts) (Exceptions) Order 1977 and shall come into operation on 1st October 1977.

(2) The Oversea Companies (Accounts) (Exceptions) Order 1968(d) is hereby revoked.

(3) The Interpretation Act 1889(e) shall apply for the interpretation of this Order as it applies for the interpretation of an Act of Parliament and as if this Order and the Order hereby revoked were Acts of Parliament.

2. The provisions of the Companies Act 1948 and of the Companies Act 1967(f) specified in the Schedule hereto shall be prescribed exceptions for the purposes of section 9 of the Companies Act 1976 (duty to prepare and deliver accounts in the case of oversea companies).

4th August 1977.

Derek Eagers,
An Under-Secretary,
Department of Trade.

Article 2   SCHEDULE

1. Section 156(1) of the Act of 1948, as amended by the Companies Act 1976, insofar as that subsection requires the auditors' report to be attached to the balance sheet.

2. Section 157(1) of the Act of 1948, as amended by the Companies Act 1976.

3. Paragraphs 11(10), 12(1)(c), 13A and 14(3) of Schedule 8 to the Act of 1948, as amended by the Act of 1967 and, in the case of paragraph 13A, by the Companies (Accounts) Regulations 1971(g).

4. Sections 3 to 8 (both inclusive) and sections 16 to 20 (both inclusive) of the Act of 1967.

(a) 1948 c. 38.   (b) S.I. 1970/1537 (1970 III, p. 5293).   (c) 1976 c. 69.
(d) S.I. 1968/69 (1968 I, p. 171).   (e) 1889 c. 63.   (f) 1967 c. 81.
(g) S.I. 1971/2044 (1971 III, p. 5852).

EXPLANATORY NOTE

(This Note is not part of the Order.)

This Order supersedes the Oversea Companies (Accounts) (Exceptions) Order 1968.

Oversea companies are excepted from compliance with the provisions of the Companies Acts 1948 and 1967 specified in the Schedule to the Order concerning the accounts and other documents to be prepared and delivered to the registrar of companies.

STATUTORY INSTRUMENTS

1977 No. 1374

MEDICINES

The Medicines (Fees) Amendment (No. 2) Regulations 1977

Made - - - -	5th August 1977
Laid before Parliament	11th August 1977
Coming into Operation	1st September 1977

The Secretaries of State respectively concerned with health in England and in Wales, the Secretary of State concerned with health and with agriculture in Scotland, the Minister of Agriculture, Fisheries and Food, the Department of Health and Social Services for Northern Ireland and the Department of Agriculture for Northern Ireland, acting jointly, with the consent of the Treasury, in exercise of powers conferred by section 1 (1) and (2) of the Medicines Act 1971(a) and now vested in them(b), and of all other powers enabling them in that behalf, after consulting such organisations as appear to them to be representative of interests likely to be substantially affected by the following regulations, hereby make the following regulations:—

Citation, commencement and interpretation

1.—(1) These regulations may be cited as the Medicines (Fees) Amendment (No. 2) Regulations 1977 and shall come into operation on 1st September 1977.

(2) These regulations shall be read as one with the Medicines (Fees) Regulations 1976(c) as amended(d), (hereinafter referred to as "the principal regulations").

Amendment of regulation 3 of the principal regulations

2. After paragraph (5) of regulation 3 of the principal regulations (product licences) there shall be inserted the following additional paragraphs—

"(6) Where an application for the grant of a product licence is in respect of two or more medicinal products having the same pharmaceutical form which consist of the same active ingredient in different strengths there shall be payable by the applicant a fee of £120 in respect of each different strength of the active ingredient in excess of one, in addition to any initial fee or review fee payable in accordance with the provisions of these regulations.

(7) Where, in connection with an application for the grant of a product licence, before the application is determined by the licensing authority the applicant notifies the authority that he desires to make a change in the particulars of the qualitative or quantitative composition of the medicinal product contained in the application or to make a

(a) 1971 c. 69.
(b) In the case of the Northern Ireland Departments by virtue of section 40 of, and Schedule 5 to, the Northern Ireland Constitution Act 1973 (c. 36) and section 1(3) of, and paragraph 2(1)(b) of Schedule 1 to, the Northern Ireland Act 1974 (c. 28).
(c) S.I. 1976/347 (1976 I, p. 968).
(d) S.I. 1976/1145. 1977/1056 (1976. II. p. 3123; 1977 II. p. 3012).

further change in such particulars there shall be payable by the applicant a fee of £120, in addition to any initial fee and any other fee payable by him in accordance with the provisions of these regulations."

Amendment of regulation 3A of the principal regulations

3. In regulation 3A of the principal regulations (renewal of licences of right)—

(*a*) in paragraph (1) for "£60" there shall be substituted "£120";

(*b*) in paragraph (2)(*a*) after the words "less than 5 years" there shall be inserted the words "there shall be payable by the applicant a renewal fee of £25";

(*c*) in paragraph (2)(*b*) after the words "respectively which have been renewed" there shall be inserted the words "there shall be payable by the applicant—

(i) where the licence was first renewed for the period of one year, a renewal fee of £5,

(ii) where the licence was first renewed for the period of two years, a renewal fee of £10,

(iii) where the licence was first renewed for the period of three years, a renewal fee of £15,

(iv) where the licence was first renewed for the period of four years, a renewal fee of £20,";

(*d*) after paragraph 2(*b*) there shall be omitted the words from "the renewal fee of £60 mentioned in paragraph (1)" to "a renewal fee of £25"; ·

(*e*) after paragraph (3) there shall be inserted an additional paragraph—

(4) The Minister may waive payment of or reduce any renewal fee otherwise payable in accordance with the provisions of this regulation or, if such fee has been paid, refund it in whole or in part where an application for the renewal of a product licence relates to a medicinal product which falls within a class specified in Part II of Schedule 2.".

Amendment of regulation 6 of the principal regulations

4. In regulation 6 of the principal regulations (fees in respect of variations)—

(*a*) in paragraph (2), after the words "the active ingredients" there shall be inserted the words "strength of the active ingredients," and for "£25" there shall be substituted "£120";

(*b*) after paragraph (2) there shall be inserted an additional paragraph—

"(2A) in the preceding paragraph "change in strength" means—

(*a*) in relation to a medicinal product in the form of a tablet, capsule or other discrete article, an increase or decrease in the amount of the active ingredient in such tablet, capsule or other discrete article, (*b*) in relation to a medicinal product in any form other than a tablet, capsule or other discrete article, a change in the proportion of the active ingredient in the medicinal product.".

(*c*) after paragraph (7) there shall be inserted the following paragraph—

"(8) The Minister may waive payment of or reduce any fee otherwise payable in accordance with the provisions of this regulation in relation to an application for the variation of a product licence or, if such fee has been paid, refund it in whole or in part—

(*a*) in a case where the Minister is satisfied that the gross value of the sales of the medicinal product to which the application relates during any calendar year does not exceed a sum specified for that purpose by the Minister at the time of the grant or variation of the licence to which the application relates, or

(*b*) in a case where the medicinal product to which the application relates falls within a class specified in Part II of Schedule 1, or

(*c*) in a case where the application for variation is in respect of a change in the ingredients of the medicinal product by reason of—

(i) shortage of materials or

(ii) any requirement imposed by any provision of any enactment coming into force after the grant of the product licence.".

Additions to the principal regulations

5.—(1) The principal regulations shall be amended by the addition of the following regulation after regulation 6 thereof—

"Fees in respect of product licences of right which have been subject to review

6A.—(1) Subject to the provisions of paragraph (2) below, where, in connection with the review by the licensing authority of the safety, quality and efficacy of substances or articles in respect of which product licences granted under Part II of the Act are in force, advice has been given to the licensing authority by a Committee established under section 4 of the Act in relation to a medicinal product of a description to which a product licence (in this regulation referred to as a " relevant licence") relates, an application is made—

(*a*) for the grant of a product licence relating to a medicinal product of the same description, and

(i) the relevant licence has expired under the provisions of section 24(1A)(**a**) of the Act, or

(a) Section 24(1A) was added by regulation 4(4) of the Medicines (Medicines Act 1968 Amendment) Regulations 1977 (S.I. 1977/1050 and regulation 4(4) of the Medicines Act 1968 Amendment) Regulations (Northern Ireland) 1977.

(ii) the applicant has requested the licensing authority to grant him a product licence in substitution for the relevant licence, or

(b) for the variation of the provisions of the relevant licence under section 30 of the Act in such manner that the provisions of the licence shall correspond with such advice given to the licensing authority in relation to the medicinal product, or

(c) for the first renewal of the relevant licence following the giving of such advice, except in relation to the renewal of a licence which has been granted or varied in the circumstances mentioned in sub-paragraph (a) or sub-paragraph (b) above,

there shall be payable by the applicant a fee of £120 (in this regulation referred to as "a review fee") in respect of—

(i) each description of a medicinal product to which the licence is to relate, and

(ii) where the application is in respect of two or more medicinal products which consist of the same active ingredient in different strengths, each different strength of the active ingredient

and, where any initial fee or any fee in connection with an application for variation would otherwise be payable by him in accordance with the provisions of these regulations, in substitution for such fee, provided that only one review fee shall be payable in respect of any application in respect of two or more medicinal products described in the same paragraph of Schedule 2.

(2) Where the applicant has previously paid an initial fee of £120 in accordance with the provisions of these regulations he shall not be liable to pay a review fee in accordance with the provisions of paragraph (1) above.

(3) Where the applicant has paid an initial fee of an amount less than £120, in accordance with these regulations or in accordance with regulations in force at the time when such fee became payable, the fee payable by him shall be an amount equal to the difference between £120 and the amount of the initial fee paid by him.

(4) The provisions of regulation 18(c) and paragraph 3 of Part VII of Schedule 1 shall have effect in relation to a review fee as if in that regulation and that paragraph any reference to an initial fee were a reference to a review fee.".

(2) The principal regulations shall be amended by the addition of the following regulation after regulation 15 thereof—

"Late payment of annual fees

15A.—(1) Where an annual fee has not been paid by the holder of the licence by the end of the period of three months from the due date a further fee, calculated in accordance with the provisions of the following paragraphs, shall be payable.

(2) The further fee referred to in the preceding paragraph shall be an amount equivalent to 1 per cent of the annual fee payable multiplied by the number of complete months contained in the period from the day

after the end of the period of three months from the due date until the date when the annual fee is paid, rounded down to the nearest £10. Where the annual fee payable is less than £10, no such fee shall be payable.

(3) Where the holder of a licence has not furnished evidence of his annual turnover in accordance with the provisions of Part V of Schedule 1 so that the annual fee payable in respect of a licence year cannot be determined before the due date, he may make a payment of any amount on account of the annual fee payable by him (in this regulation referred to as a "payment on account").

(4) Where the holder of a licence has made a payment on account in the circumstances mentioned in the preceding paragraph or a provisional payment in the circumstances mentioned in regulation 15, the further fee payable by him shall be calculated as if in paragraph (2) above the reference to the annual fee payable were to the difference between the payment on account, or the provisional payment, as the case may be, and the amount of the annual fee as subsequently determined.

(5) In this regulation—

(a) "due date" means the date upon which an annual fee became payable in accordance with the provisions of these regulations;

(b) references to a period calculated from a day are references to the period inclusive of that day."

Amendment of regulation 11 of the principal regulations

6. For paragraphs (1) and (2) of regulation 11 there shall be substituted the following paragraphs—

"(1) Any person who is the holder of a product licence may during the licence year ending on 31st August 1979 notify the licensing authority of his intention to apply for the renewal of that licence and at the time of such notification pay an amount equivalent to the annual fee which would have been payable if he had made an application for the renewal of that licence at that time.

(2) Where the holder of a product licence has made such a payment as is mentioned in paragraph (1) of this regulation he shall be treated for the purposes of paragraph 5 of Part IV of Schedule 1 and paragraphs 4 and 5 of Part VI of that Schedule as if he had made an application for the renewal of that licence at the time of such notification as is mentioned in paragraph (1) above and as if such payment had been the payment of an annual fee in respect of that application in the licence year ending on 31st August 1979.".

Amendment of regulation 18 of the principal regulations

7. In regulation 18 of the principal regulations (initial fees)—

(a) in paragraph (a) for "£1,800" there shall be substituted "£2,000";

(b) at the end of paragraph (c) for the full stop there shall be substituted a comma, and there shall be inserted the word "or";

(c) after paragraph (c) there shall be inserted the following additional paragraphs—

"(d) in a case where the medicinal product in respect of which the application is made consists of active ingredients each of which is an active ingredient of a particular medicinal product (in this paragraph and the following paragraphs referred to as "the existing preparation") which is for human use or animal use and—

    (i) at the time of the application for the grant of a product licence a person other than the applicant was the holder of, or an applicant for the grant of, a product licence in respect of the existing preparation and the particulars relating to the medicinal product contained in the application are the same in all respects as the corresponding particulars contained in the application in respect of the existing preparation, provided that the higher initial fee was paid in respect of the existing preparation, or

    (ii) the existing preparation is for human use and the application is in respect of a medicinal product for animal use and the conditions set out in paragraph 1 of Part III of Schedule 1 are satisfied, or

    (iii) where, as regards both the existing preparation and the medicinal product in respect of which the application is made, the conditions set out in paragraphs 1 and 2 (a) of Part III of Schedule 1 are satisfied,

and the licensing authority are satisfied that the difference between the product in respect of which the application is made and the existing preparation is not sufficiently great to make it necessary to undertake the extent of scrutiny which would be appropriate for a product containing ingredients not present in any product already on the market and that the purpose for which the existing preparation may be recommended does not differ substantially from that of the product for which the application is made, or

(e) in a case where the medicinal product in respect of which the application is made consists of a mixture of two or more active ingredients, one of which is contained as an active ingredient in a medicinal product of a different description which satisfies the provisions contained in paragraphs 1 and 2 of Part III of Schedule 1, and the purpose for which such medicinal product may be recommended does not differ substantially from that of the product in respect of which the application is made and the licensing authority are satisfied that the difference between the products is not sufficiently great to make it necessary to undertake the extent of scrutiny which would be appropriate for a product containing ingredients not present in any product already on the market".

Amendment of Schedule 1 to the principal regulations

8.—(1) Part I of Schedule 1 to the principal regulations shall be amended in accordance with the following paragraph and shall accordingly have effect as set out in the Schedule to these regulations.

(2) In Part I of Schedule 1 to the principal regulations—

(a) in paragraphs 1(a) and 2(a) of column 2 for "£1,800" there shall be substituted "£2,000";

(b) in paragraphs 1(b) and 2(b) of column 2 for "£60" there shall be substituted "£120";

(c) in paragraphs 1 and 2 of column 3 the words "£50, or" and "whichever is the greater" shall be omitted;

(d) in paragraphs 3 and 4 of column 2 for "£50" there shall be substituted "£120",

(e) in paragraph 5(c) of column 2 after the words "terms of the licence" there shall be inserted the words "except in respect of premises in which manufacturing or assembly operations are also to be carried out under the terms of the licence".

(3) In Part III of Schedule 1—

(a) in paragraph 1 the word "either" shall be omitted, and for sub-paragraph (b) there shall be substituted the following sub-paragraphs—

"(b) that any patent granted in respect of the existing preparation under the Patents Act 1949(a) has expired or has ceased to have effect for the period of one year ending on the date of the application for the grant of the product licence, and

(c) that the existing preparation has been effectively on the market for a period commencing on a date before 1st September 1971 and ending on the date of the application.";

(b) in paragraph 4 the word "or" at the end of sub-paragraph (a) and the whole of sub-paragraph (b) shall be omitted.

(4) In Part VI of Schedule 1—

(a) at the beginning of paragraph 1 there shall be inserted the words "Subject to the provisions of paragraph 2A below,";

(b) for Tables 1, 2 and 3 in paragraph 1 there shall be substituted the following tables—

(a) 1949 c. 87.

TABLE 1

PRODUCT LICENCES FOR MEDICINAL PRODUCTS FOR HUMAN USE

Where application is made in the licence year ending on 31st August of the year:	Rate of annual fee for licence year ending 31st August of the year:				
	1976	1977	1978	1979	1980 or later
1976	0.25%	0.5%	0.5%	0.5%	0.5%
1977	—	0.5%	0.5%	0.5%	0.5%
1978	—	—	0.75%	1.0%	1.25%
1979	—	—	—	1.0%	1.25%
1980 or later	—	—	—	—	1.25%

TABLE 2

PRODUCT LICENCES FOR MEDICINAL PRODUCTS FOR VETERINARY USE

Where application is made in the licence year ending on 31st August of the year:	Rate of annual fee for licence year ending on 31st August of the year:				
	1976	1977	1978	1979	1980 or later
1976	0.25%	0.5%	0.5%	0.5%	0.5%
1977	—	0.5%	0.5%	0.5%	0.5%
1978	—	—	0.75%	1.0%	1.25%
1979	—	—	—	1.0%	1.25%
1980 or later	—	—	—	—	1.25%

TABLE 3

MANUFACTURER'S LICENCES AND WHOLESALE DEALER'S LICENCES

Where application is made in the licence year ending on 31st August of the year:	Rate of annual fee for licence year ending on 31st August of the year:			
	1976 or 1977	1978	1979	1980 or later
1976	0.025%	0.05%	0.05%	0.05%
1977	0.025%	0.05%	0.05%	0.05%
1978	—	0.075%	0.1%	0.1%
1979	—	—	0.1%	0.1%
1980 or later	—	—	—	0.1%

(c) after paragraph 2 there shall be inserted an additional paragraph—

"2A— (a) Where in the licence year ending on 31st August 1978 the licence holder submits evidence to the satisfaction of the Minister that his turnover in relation to the calendar year which ended on 31st December 1976 is—

(i) less than £100,000 the annual fee payable in respect of that licence year shall be £100,

(ii) £100,000 or more but less than £200,000, the annual fee payable in respect of that licence year shall be the sum of £100 and 0·4 per cent of that part of his turnover which is more than £100,000.".

(d) for paragraph 4 there shall be substituted the following paragraph—

"4. Where an applicant has paid an annual fee which became payable by virtue of these regulations or an amount equivalent to an annual fee in accordance with the provisions of regulation 11(1) and the application is made before 1st September 1977 the annual fee payable for the licence year ending 31st August 1978, or where the application is made after 1st September 1977 the annual fee payable in respect of the licence year in which the application is made, as the case may be, shall be—

(a) where the licence is a product licence for a medicinal product for human use, at the rate of 0·25 per cent in substitution for the rate specified in Table 1 of this Part of this Schedule, or

(b) where the licence is a product licence for a medicinal product for animal use, at the rate of 0·25 per cent in substitution for the rate specified in Table 2 of this Part of this Schedule, or

(c) where the licence is a manufacturer's licence or a wholesale dealer's licence, at the rate of 0·025 per cent in substitution for the rate specified in Table 3 of this Part of this Schedule,"

(e) after paragraph 4 there shall be inserted the following paragraphs—

"5. Where an annual fee has been paid in accordance with these regulations and the application is made before 1st September 1977 the annual fee payable for the licence year ending 31st August 1978, or where the application is made after 1st September 1977 the annual fee payable in respect of the licence year in which the application is made shall not exceed—

(a) where the product licences relate to medicinal products for human use, £50,000, or

(b) where the product licences relate to medicinal products for animal use, £16,500.

6. (a) Where the Minister is satisfied that during the period from 1st September 1975 until the end of the licensing year which immediately precedes the beginning of the licence year in which an application is made—

(i) an applicant for the grant of a product licence has not, in the course of a business carried on by him, sold or supplied any medicinal product which is subject to the restrictions imposed by section 7 of the Act; or

(ii) an applicant for the grant of a manufacturer's licence has not, in the course of a business carried on by him, manufactured or assembled any medicinal product which is subject to the restrictions imposed by section 8(2) of the Act; or

(iii) an applicant for the grant of a wholesale dealer's licence has not, in the course of a business carried on by him, sold, or offered for sale, any medicinal product by way of wholesale dealing or distributed, otherwise than by way of sale, any proprietary medicinal product which is subject to the restrictions imposed by section 8(2) of the Act;

that applicant shall be treated, for the purpose of paragraph 4 of this Part of this Schedule as if he had paid an annual fee in respect of the licence year immediately preceding the year in which the application is made.

(b) Where the Minister is satisfied that such sale or supply, manufacture or assembly, or sale or offer for sale by way of wholesale dealing or distribution otherwise than by way of sale as is mentioned in sub-paragraph (a) above was exempt from the restrictions imposed by section 7, section 8(2) or section 8(3) of the Act by virtue of an exemption granted by sections 9 to 12 of the Act or by an order made under section 15 of the Act the provisions of sub-paragraph (a) shall apply as if no such sale or supply, or manufacture or assembly, or sale or offer for sale by way of wholesale dealing or distribution otherwise than by way of sale had taken place during the relevant period.

7. Notwithstanding the provisions of the preceding paragraphs of this Part of this Schedule the minimum annual fee payable by an applicant for a licence shall be—

(1) in the case of a product licence—

(a) where the application was made between 6th March 1976 and 31st August 1977 the sum of £100 or 0·5 per cent of turnover, whichever is the lower, but in no case shall the fee be less than £50, or

(b) where the application was made on or after 1st September 1977 the sum of £200, except where the applicant has paid an annual fee under these regulations for the licence year ending 31st August 1977, when the fee shall be £100;

(2) in the case of a manufacturer's licence or wholesale dealer's licence, where the application is made after 1st September 1977, twice the amount of the minimum flat rate fee specified in Part I of this Schedule unless—

(a) the applicant has paid an annual fee under these regulations for the licence year ending 31st August 1977, or

(b) the Minister is satisfied that the provisions of paragraph 6 of this Part of this Schedule apply."

(5) In Part VII of Schedule 1—

(a) in paragraphs 1 and 2 for "£10,000" there shall be substituted "£20,000",

(b) for paragraph 3 there shall be substituted the following—

"3. Where the circumstances described in paragraphs 1 and 2 of this Part of this Schedule apply any initial fees or variation fees payable shall be reduced so that the total amount of such fees in any one licence year—

(a) where the gross value of goods sold or supplied or services rendered during such a period as is mentioned in paragraphs 1 and 2 was less than £10,000, shall not exceed £50;

(b) where the gross value of goods sold or supplied or services rendered during such a period as is mentioned in paragraphs 1 and 2 was £10,000 or more but less than £20,000, shall not exceed £100.".

David Ennals,
Secretary of State for Social Services.

26th July 1977.

John Morris,
Secretary of State for Wales.

27th July 1977.

Bruce Millan,
Secretary of State for Scotland.

27th July 1977.

In witness whereof the official seal of the Minister of Agriculture, Fisheries and Food is hereunto affixed on 28th July 1977.

John Silkin,
Minister of Agriculture, Fisheries
and Food.

(L.S.)

Sealed with the official seal of the Department of Health and Social Services for Northern Ireland this 1st day of August 1977.

N. Dugdale,
Permanent Secretary.

(L.S.)

Sealed with the official seal of the Department of Agriculture for Northern Ireland this 2nd day of August 1977.

W. H. Jack,
Deputy Secretary.

(L.S.)

We consent.

T. E. Graham,
David Stoddart,
Two of the Lords Commissioners of
Her Majesty's Treasury.

5th August 1977.

Regulation 8(1)   SCHEDULE

Containing Part I of Schedule 1 to the principal regulations as amended by these regulations (a)

PART I

FEES

Column 1 Kind of licence or certificate	Column 2 Initial fee	Column 3 Annual fees
1. Product licence (products for human use)	1. (a) £2,000, or (b) £120, if the product to which the application relates is a product specified in Part II or satisfies the conditions of Part III of this Schedule. (Subject to the provisions of paragraph 3 of Part VII of this Schedule.)	1. An amount calculated in accordance with Parts IV, V and VI of this Schedule, except in relation to an application to which paragraphs 1 or 2 of Part VII of this Schedule applies.
2. Product licence (products for veterinary use)	2. (a) £2,000 or (b) £120, if the product to which the application relates is a product specified in Part II or satisfies the conditions of Part III of this Schedule. (Subject to the provisions of paragraph 3 of Part VII of this Schedule).	2. An amount calculated in accordance with Parts IV, V and VI of this Schedule, except in relation to an application to which paragraphs 1 or 2 of Part VII of this Schedule applies.
3. Clinical trial certificate	3. £120, except in relation to an application to which paragraph 4 of Part VII of this Schedule applies.	3. Nil.
4. Animal test certificate	4. £120, except in relation to an application to which paragraph 5 of Part VII of this Schedule applies.	4. Nil.
5. Manufacturer's licence	5. (a) £100 for each set of premises in which manufacturing operations are to be carried out under the terms of the licence, and (b) £50 for each set of premises in which assembly (but not manufacturing)	5. The amounts specified in paragraphs 5 (a), (b) and (c) of column 2, or an amount calculated in accordance with Parts IV, V and VI of this Schedule whichever is the greater, except in relation to an

(a) The words substituted or added by these regulations are shown in italics.

Column 1 Kind of licence or certificate	Column 2 Initial fee	Column 3 Annual fees
	operations are to be carried out under the terms of the licence, and (c) £10 for each set of premises in which medicinal products are to be stored for distribution under the terms of the licence *except in respect of premises in which manufacturing or assembly operations are also to be carried out under the terms of the licence.* (Subject to the provisions of paragraph 3 of Part VII of this Schedule).	application to which paragraphs 1, 2 or 6 of Part VII of this Schedule applies.
6. Wholesale dealer's licence not being a licence to which the following paragraph applies.	6. £10 for each separate set of premises in which medicinal products to which the licence relates are or are to be stored.	6. £10 for each separate set of premises in which medicinal products to which the licence relates are or are to be stored.
7. Wholesale dealer's licence which relates to imported proprietary products and is subject to the provisions of paragraph 8 of Schedule 3 to the Standard Provisions Regulations.	7. £50 for each separate set of premises in which any functions specified in paragraph 8(3) of Schedule 3 to the Standard Provisions Regulations are to be carried out in relation to imported proprietary products to which the licence relates or £10 for each separate set of premises in which medicinal products to which the licence relates are or are to be stored, whichever amount is the greater.	7. The amount specified in paragraph 7 of column 2, or an amount calculated in accordance with Parts IV, V or VI of this Schedule, whichever is the greater, except in relation to an application to which paragraph (1) or (2) of Part VII of this Schedule applies.

EXPLANATORY NOTE

(This Note is not part of the Regulations.)

These Regulations further amend the Medicines (Fees) Regulations 1976 (the "principal Regulations").

The main changes are—

(a) increases in both the higher and lower initial fees payable for product licences;

(b) increases in the fees payable upon the variation of a product licence, a manufacturer's licence and a wholesale dealer's licence;

(c) increases in the fees payable for a clinical trial certificate and an animal test certificate;

(d) the introduction, by the addition of regulation 6A to the principal Regulations, of fees payable by the holder of a licence of right where an application is made for a product licence;

(e) the introduction, by the addition of regulation 15A to the principal Regulations, of further fees payable where the holder of a licence has not paid the annual fee by the due date;

(f) provisions for the reduction of the higher initial fee payable where certain conditions are satisfied (regulation 7); and

(g) the substitution of new tables for the calculation of annual fees for product licences and manufacturer's and wholesale dealer's licences (regulation 8(3)).

STATUTORY INSTRUMENTS

1977 No. 1375 (C. 48)

BANKRUPTCY, ENGLAND
BANKRUPTCY, SCOTLAND

COMPANIES
WINDING-UP

The Insolvency Act 1976 (Commencement No. 3) Order 1977

Made -   -   -   -   *8th August* 1977

The Secretary of State, in exercise of the powers conferred on him by section 14(5) of the Insolvency Act 1976(a), hereby makes the following Order:—

1. This Order may be cited as the Insolvency Act 1976 (Commencement No. 3) Order 1977.

2. The provisions of the Insolvency Act 1976 set out in the first column of the Schedule hereto which relate to the matters specified in the second column of the Schedule shall come into force on 1st October 1977.

8th August 1977.

Edmund Dell,
Secretary of State for Trade.

(a) 1976 c. 60.

SCHEDULE

Provisions of the Act	Subject Matter of Provisions
Section 2	Audit of accounts of trustees in bankruptcy and liquidators.
Section 5	Proof of debts in bankruptcy.
Section 6	Power to dispense with public examination of debtor.
Section 7	Automatic discharge of bankrupt.
Section 8	Discharge of bankrupt on application of official receiver.
Section 9	Disqualification of directors of insolvent companies.

Section 14
  Subsection (3).
  Subsection (4) so far as it relates to the provisions of Schedule 3 hereafter specified.
	Supplementary provisions.

In Schedule 3 the entries relating to section 92(3) of the Bankruptcy Act 1914(a) and section 249(3) of the Companies Act 1948(b).	Repeals.

EXPLANATORY NOTE

(This Note is not part of the Order.)

This Order brings into force on 1st October 1977 the provisions of the Insolvency Act 1976 set out in the Schedule to the Order.

(a) 1914 c. 59.   (b) 1948 c. 38.

STATUTORY INSTRUMENTS

1977 No. 1377

SEA FISHERIES

BOATS AND METHODS OF FISHING

The Herring (Specified Western Waters) (Prohibition of Fishing) Order 1977

Made - - - -	*5th August* 1977
Laid before Parliament	*9th August* 1977
Coming into Operation	*10th August* 1977

The Minister of Agriculture, Fisheries and Food and the Secretaries of State respectively concerned with the sea fishing industry in Scotland and Northern Ireland, in exercise of the powers conferred on them by sections 5(1) and (2) and 15 of the Sea Fish (Conservation) Act 1967(a) (as section 15 is amended by section 22(1) of, and paragraph 38 of Schedule 1 to, the Sea Fisheries Act 1968(b) and as sections 5(2) and 15 are amended by section 9(1) of, and paragraph 16(1) of Schedule 2 to, the Fishery Limits Act 1976(c)) and of all other powers enabling them in that behalf, hereby make the following order:—

Citation, commencement and interpretation

1.—(1) This order may be cited as the Herring (Specified Western Waters) (Prohibition of Fishing) Order 1977 and shall come into operation on 10th August 1977.

(2) The Interpretation Act 1889(d) shall apply to the interpretation of this order as it applies to the interpretation of an Act of Parliament and as if this order and the order hereby revoked were Acts of Parliament.

Revocation

2. The Herring (Celtic Sea) (Prohibition of Fishing) Order 1977(e) is hereby revoked.

Prohibition

3. During the period 10th August 1977 to 31st December 1977, both dates inclusive, fishing for herring (*Clupea harengus*) within the area specified in the Schedule to this order is hereby prohibited.

4. In accordance with section 5(3) of the Sea Fish (Conservation) Act 1967, it is hereby declared that this order is not made for the sole purpose of giving effect to such a convention or agreement as is mentioned in the section 5(1) of that Act.

Enforcement

5. For the purpose of the enforcement of this order, there are hereby conferred on every British sea-fishery officer the powers of a British sea-fishery

---

(a) 1967 c. 84.   (b) 1968 c. 77.   (c) 1976 c. 86.   (d) 1889 c. 63.
(e) S.I. 1977/290 (1977 I, p. 790).

officer under section 8(2) to (4) of the Sea Fisheries Act 1968 as subsection (4) is amended by section 9(1) of, and paragraph 17(1) of Schedule 2 to, the Fishery Limits Act 1976(a).

In Witness whereof the Official Seal of the Minister of Agriculture, Fisheries and Food is hereunto affixed on 29th July 1977.

(L.S.)

John Silkin,
Minister of Agriculture, Fisheries and Food.

2nd August 1977.   *Bruce Millan,*
                                      Secretary of State for Scotland.

5th August 1977.   *Roy Mason,*
                              Secretary of State for Northern Ireland.

_____

(a) 1976 c. 86.

SCHEDULE   Article 3

AREA TO WHICH THE ORDER APPLIES

The area lying within British fishery limits bounded in the north by 52° 30' north latitude; in the east by 2° west longitude and the coasts of England and Wales; in the south by 48° north latitude; and in the west by 9° west longitude.

EXPLANATORY NOTE

(*This Note is not part of the Order.*)

This Order, which supersedes the Herring (Celtic Sea) (Prohibition of Fishing) Order 1977, prohibits fishing for herring in those parts of the Celtic Sea, the western English Channel and the Bristol Channel which lie inside British fishery limits, from 10th August to 31st December 1977, both dates inclusive.

By virtue of section 5(8) of the Sea Fish (Conservation) Act 1967, the order applies to all fishing boats including foreign vessels.

STATUTORY INSTRUMENTS

1977 No. 1378

NEW TOWNS

The New Towns in Rural Wales (Compulsory Purchase of Land) Regulations 1977

Made - - - -	*27th July* 1977
Laid before Parliament	*17th August* 1977
Coming into Operation	*7th September* 1977

The Secretary of State for Wales, in exercise of the powers conferred on him by sections 5 and 29 of and paragraphs 3, 4, 7, 15, 16, 17, 18, 21, 54 and 56(1) of Schedule 3 to the Development of Rural Wales Act 1976(a), and of all other powers enabling him in that behalf, hereby makes the following regulations:—

Application, commencement and citation

1. These regulations apply to Wales, come into operation on 7th September 1977 and may be cited as the New Towns in Rural Wales (Compulsory Purchase of Land) Regulations 1977.

Interpretation

2.—(1) In these regulations, unless the context otherwise requires:—

"the Act" means the Development of Rural Wales Act 1976;
"the Board" means the Development Board for Rural Wales, established by section 1 of the Act.

(2) In these regulations, any reference to a numbered form is a reference to the form bearing that number in the Schedule hereto, or a form substantially to the like effect.

(3) In these regulations, unless the context otherwise requires, references to any enactment shall be construed as references to that enactment as amended, extended, or applied by or under any other enactment.

(4) The Interpretation Act 1889(b) shall apply for the interpretation of these regulations as it applies for the interpretation of an Act of Parliament.

Prescribed forms

3. The prescribed forms for the under-mentioned provisions of Schedule 3 to the Act shall be as follows:—

(*a*) for the purposes of paragraph 3(1), the form of compulsory purchase order shall be form 1, or if the order provides for the vesting of land given in exchange pursuant to paragraph 15 of Schedule 3, form 2;

(*b*) for the purposes of paragraph 4(1), the form of notice to be published or, where applicable, personal notice to be served, concerning a compulsory purchase order, shall be form 3;

(a) 1976 c. 75.
(b) 1889 c. 63.

(c) for the purposes of paragraph 7, the form of notice of confirmation of a compulsory purchase order shall be form 4;

(d) for the purposes of paragraph 15(4), the form of newspaper notice stating that a certificate has been given under paragraph 15 of Schedule 3, shall be form 5;

(e) for the purposes of paragraph 16(3), the form of representation by statutory undertakers that land is operational land and request for that land to be excluded from a compulsory purchase order, shall be form 6;

(f) for the purposes of paragraph 17, the form of application by the Board or a local highway authority for a compulsory purchase order relating to operational land of statutory undertakers, shall be form 7;

(g) for the purposes of paragraph 18, the form of notice to owners, lessees and occupiers of an application for a compulsory purchase order in respect of operational land of statutory undertakers, shall be form 8;

(h) for the purposes of paragraph 21, the form of notice to owners, lessees and occupiers of the making of a compulsory purchase order in respect of operational land of statutory undertakers, shall be form 9.

Prescribed particulars

4. The particulars of the interest of an owner or occupier for the purposes of paragraph 7 (*a*) of Schedule 3 to the Act shall be the name and postal address of the owner or occupier, a statement of the nature of the interest of the owner or occupier, and particulars sufficient to enable the acquiring authority to identify the extent and boundaries of the land in respect of which the person giving the particulars is owner or occupier.

Marking of documents

5. Any document which is to be served on a person as having an interest in premises, or on a person as an occupier of premises, in the manner provided by paragraph 54(2)(*b*) of Schedule 3 to the Act shall, at the beginning of that document, have clearly and legibly marked upon it, in the following form, the words:

IMPORTANT—THIS COMMUNICATION AFFECTS YOUR PROPERTY

and where such document is not sent in a pre-paid registered letter or by the recorded delivery service but is delivered under cover to some person on the premises (in accordance with the said paragraph) the cover shall also be marked in like manner.

SCHEDULE
CONTENTS

FORM 1

COMPULSORY PURCHASE ORDER

Development of Rural Wales Act 1976

The   hereby make(s) the following order:—

1. Subject to the provisions of this order the said   [is,] [are,] under   (a) [of] [to] the Development of Rural Wales Act 1976), hereby authorised to purchase [to] compulsorily for the purpose of   (b) the land which is described in the Schedule hereto and is delineated and shown .... (c) on the map prepared in duplicate, sealed with the common seal of the said   and marked "Map referred to in the Compulsory Purchase Order 19   ". One duplicate of the map is deposited in the offices of the said   and the other is deposited in the offices of the Secretary of State for Wales.

[2. (d) In relation to the foregoing purchase, section 77 of the Railways Clauses Consolidation Act 1845 [and sections 78 to 85 of that Act excluding any amendment thereof by section 15 of the Mines (Working Facilities and Support) Act 1923] [is] [are] hereby incorporated with the Development of Rural Wales Act 1976, subject to the modifications that   (e).]

3. This order may be cited as the   Compulsory Purchase Order 19 .

SCHEDULE

Number on Map	Extent, description and situation of the land (g)	Owners or reputed owners
(1)	(2)	(3)

(h)

[(j) The order includes land falling within special categories to which paragraphs 14 and 15 of Schedule 3 to the Development of Rural Wales Act 1976 apply, namely—

| Number on map | Description |] |

Date (k)

For notes see after Form 2.

FORM 2

COMPULSORY PURCHASE ORDER

(Providing for the vesting of exchange land)

Development of Rural Wales Act 1976

The   hereby make(s) the following order:—

1. Subject to the provisions of this order the said   [is,] [are,] under   (a) [of] [to] the Development of Rural Wales Act 1976, hereby authorised to purchase compulsorily for the purpose of   (b) the land which is described in the Schedule hereto and is delineated and shown   (c) on the map prepared in duplicate, sealed with the common seal of the said   and marked "Map referred to in the   Compulsory Purchase Order 19 ". One duplicate of the map is deposited in the offices of the said   and the other is deposited in the offices of the Secretary of State for Wales.

[2. (d) In relation to the foregoing purchase, section 77 of the Railways Clauses Consolidation Act 1845 [and sections 78 to 85 of that Act excluding any amendment thereof by section 15 of the Mines (Working Facilities and Support) Act 1923] [is] [are] hereby incorporated with the Development of Rural Wales Act 1976, subject to the modifications that   (e).]

3.—(1) In this article "the order land" means (f) [the land referred to in article 1 hereof] [the land described as   in Schedule 1 hereto] and "the exchange land" means the land which is described in Schedule 2 hereto and is delineated and shown   (c) on the said map.

(2) As from the date on which this order becomes operative or the date on which the order land, or any of it, is vested in the said   (whichever is the later), the exchange land shall vest in the persons in whom the order land was vested immediately before that date, subject to the like rights, trusts and incidents as attached thereto; and the order land shall thereupon be discharged from all rights, trusts and incidents to which it was previously subject.

4. This order may be cited as the   Compulsory Purchase Order 19 .

SCHEDULE 1

Land to be Purchased

Number on Map	Extent, description and situation of the land (g)	Owners or reputed owners
(1)	(2)	(3)

(h)

[(j) The order includes land falling within special categories to which paragraphs 14 and 15 of Schedule 3 to the Development of Rural Wales Act 1976 apply, namely:—

Number on Map	Description	]

SCHEDULE 2

Exchange land

Date (k)

NOTES TO FORMS 1 AND 2

(a) Insert the section, sub-section and paragraph of (e.g. 6(1)(b)) or paragraph and Schedule to the Development of Rural Wales Act 1976 conferring power to acquire the land compulsorily.

(b) Describe the purpose by reference to the words of the relevant sub-section of section 1 or sub-paragraph of paragraph 2(1) of Schedule 3 to the Development of Rural Wales Act 1976. Where those words are in general terms covering a range of purposes, the particular purpose for which the land is required should be stated if possible.

(c) Describe the colouring or other method used to identify the land on the map. The boundaries of each parcel of land separately numbered in the Schedule to the order should be clearly delineated. Also the map itself should contain sufficient detail to enable the situation of the land to be readily identified and related to the description given in the Schedule. Maps should normally be on a scale of 1/500 or 1/1250.

(d) This article may be omitted or may be inserted with or without reference to sections 78 to 85.

(e) Insert any consequential modifications required—e.g. "references in the said [section] [sections] to the company shall be construed as references to the said and references to the [railway or] works shall be construed as references to the land authorised to be purchased and any buildings or works constructed or to be constructed thereon".

(f) Use the first alternative if the whole of the land referred to in article 1 falls within paragraph 15 of Schedule 3 to the Development of Rural Wales Act 1976. Otherwise use the second alternative and specify the parcel number(s) of the land which does fall within paragraph 15.

(g) This column should contain sufficient detail to tell the reader approximately where the land is situated, without reference to the map. In describing the land regard should be had (where appropriate) to Note (k) below.

(h) Column (1) need not be completed where the order relates only to one parcel of land. Where there are two or more parcels they should be numbered 1, 2 etc. on the map and referred to accordingly in column (1). Column (3) should be completed even where the acquiring authority has not been required to serve owners personally. If the name of an owner is not known, column 3 should be endorsed "unknown".

(j) The compulsory acquisition of land—

    (i) which is the property of a local authority,

    (ii) held inalienably by the National Trust, or

    (iii) forming part of a common, open space or fuel or field garden allotment,

is subject to paragraphs 14 or 15 of Schedule 3 to the Development of Rural Wales Act 1976 and consequently may be subject to special parliamentary procedure in certain circumstances.

The column "description" need only refer to the special category into which the relevant parcel of land falls.

(k) The order should be made under seal, duly authenticated and dated.

FORM 3

PUBLISHED NOTICE OR PERSONAL NOTICE THAT A COMPULSORY PURCHASE ORDER HAS BEEN SUBMITTED FOR CONFIRMATION

Development of Rural Wales Act 1976

Compulsory Purchase of Land in   (a)

[To: (b)]

1. The   on   made the   Compulsory Purchase Order 19   under   (c) of the Development of Rural Wales Act 1976. The said   [has] [have] submitted this order to the Secretary of State for confirmation, and if confirmed, the order will authorise the said to purchase compulsorily the land described below for the purpose of   (d).

2. A copy of the order and of the accompanying map may be seen at all reasonable hours at   (e).

3. Any objection to the order must be made in writing to the Secretary, Welsh Office, Cathays Park, Cardiff CF1 3NQ before   (f). The objection should state the title of the order, and must include or be accompanied by a statement of the grounds of the objection.

4. The Secretary of State is not required in every case to arrange for a public local inquiry to be held or for objectors to be heard by a person appointed by him for that purpose. It is important, therefore, that the statement included in or accompanying an objection should set out the grounds of the objection as fully as possible, since the objector may have no opportunity to present his case at an inquiry or hearing or to make a further statement in writing.

5. Any owner or occupier of any of the land to which the order relates may (whether or not he makes an objection to the order) send to (g) a request in writing that, in the event of the order being confirmed by the Secretary of State, he be served with a notice stating that the order has been confirmed and naming a place where a copy of the order and of the map or maps and any descriptive matter annexed thereto may be seen. Any such request must state the name and postal address of the owner or occupier making it, must state the nature of his interest in the land and must include sufficient particulars to enable the extent and boundaries of his land to be identified.

Description of Land

(h)

[Date and signature]

NOTES

(a) Insert the name of the area in which the land concerned is situated.

(b) Omit when the Form is used for a published notice. When the Form is used for a personal notice served on an owner of the land, insert the name and address of the person on whom the notice is to be served.

(c) Insert the section, sub-section and paragraph of or paragraph and Schedule to the Act as these are cited in the order.

(d) Insert the purpose as cited in the order.

(e) State the place where the order has been deposited for inspection. This should be within reasonably easy reach of persons living in the area affected.

(f) Insert a date at least 28 days from the date of first publication of the notice in a newspaper circulating in the locality (i.e. 28 days excluding the date of first publication).

(g) Insert name and address of the acquiring authority.

(h) Insert description of all the land described in the order. This need not repeat the Schedule to the order, but must be in terms which enable the reader to appreciate what land is included.

FORM 4

PUBLISHED NOTICE OR PERSONAL NOTICE OF CONFIRMATION OF A COMPULSORY PURCHASE ORDER

Development of Rural Wales Act 1976

[To: (a)]

1. Notice is hereby given that the Secretary of State, in exercise of his powers under the above Act, on confirmed [with modifications] the Compulsory Purchase Order 19 submitted by the .

2. The order as confirmed provides for the purchase for the purpose of (b) of the land described in the Schedule hereto.

3. A copy of the order as confirmed by the Secretary of State and of the map referred to therein have been deposited at (c) and may be seen there at all reasonable hours.

4. (d) The order as confirmed becomes operative on the date on which this notice is first published; but a person aggrieved by the order may, by application to the High Court within six weeks from that date, question its validity on the grounds (i) that the order is not within the powers of the Act or (ii) that his interests have been substantially prejudiced by failure to comply with any statutory requirement relating to the order.

OR

4. The order as confirmed is subject to special parliamentary procedure and will become operative as provided by the Statutory Orders (Special Procedure) Act 1945. Unless the order is confirmed by Act of Parliament under section 6 of that Act, a

person aggrieved by the order may, by application to the High Court within six weeks from the operative date, question its validity on the grounds (i) that the order is not within the powers of the Act, or (ii) that his interests have been substantially prejudiced by failure to comply with any statutory requirement relating to the order.

SCHEDULE

Land Comprised in the Order as Confirmed

(e)

[Date and signature]

NOTES

(a) Omit when the Form is used for a published notice. When the Form is used for a personal notice served on the owner etc. of the land, insert the name and address of the person on whom the notice is served.

(b) Insert the purpose as stated in the order.

(c) State the place where the order has been deposited for inspection. This should be within reasonably easy reach of persons living within the area affected.

(d) Leave standing whichever alternative is appropriate.

(e) Where this Form is to include the statement concerning general vesting declarations, the statement should be included at this point.

FORM 5

NOTICE OF GIVING OF CERTIFICATE UNDER PARAGRAPH 15 OF SCHEDULE 3 TO THE DEVELOPMENT OF RURAL WALES ACT 1976

Development of Rural Wales Act 1976

1. The   Compulsory Purchase Order 19   which has been [submitted by   (a) to the Secretary of State for confirmation] [prepared in draft by the Secretary of State] includes the land described in the Schedule hereto.

2. This land [is] [forms part of] [a common] [an open space] [a fuel or field garden allotment].

3. Notice is hereby given that the Secretary of State in exercise of his powers under paragraph 15 of Schedule 3 to the Development of Rural Wales Act 1976 has certified (b).

4. A map showing the land to which the certificate relates (and the land proposed to be given in exchange) may be inspected at   (c) at all reasonable hours.

5. The certificate becomes operative on the date on which this notice is first published; but a person aggrieved by the certificate may, by application to the High Court within six weeks from that date, question its validity on the grounds (i) that the certificate is not within the powers of the Act, or (ii) that his interests have been substantially prejudiced by failure to comply with any statutory requirement relating to the certificate.

SCHEDULE

(d)

[Date and Signature]

NOTES

(a) Insert the name of the Development Board for Rural Wales or local highway authority making the compulsory purchase order, as appropriate.

(b) Insert the terms of the certificate.

(c) State where a copy of the certificate has been deposited for inspection. This should be within reasonably easy reach of persons living in the area affected.

(d) Insert description of the land to which the certificate relates.

FORM 6

REPRESENTATION BY STATUTORY UNDERTAKERS WITH RESPECT
TO A COMPULSORY PURCHASE ORDER

Development of Rural Wales Act 1976

[Title of Compulsory Purchase Order]

To: (a)

The   (b), being statutory undertakers hereby make—

(i) a representation in accordance with paragraph 16(3) of Schedule 3 to the Development of Rural Wales Act 1976 that land, particulars of which are set out in the Schedule hereto, being the whole or part of land to which the above Compulsory Purchase Order relates, is operational land, and

(ii) a request for that land to be excluded from the order.

SCHEDULE

Extent, description and situation of the land	Interest of undertakers in the land	Purpose for which the land is held by the undertakers and (if different) present use of the land
(1)	(2)	(3)

[Date and Signature]

NOTES

(a) Insert the name and address of the appropriate Minister as respects the statutory undertakers concerned.

(b) Insert the name and address of the statutory undertakers.

FORM 7

APPLICATION FOR A COMPULSORY PURCHASE ORDER RELATING TO OPERATIONAL
LAND OF STATUTORY UNDERTAKERS

Development of Rural Wales Act 1976

The   (a) hereby make(s) an application in accordance with paragraph 16(1) of Schedule 3 to the Development of Rural Wales Act 1976 to the Secretary of State [and   (b)] for an order to be made by [them] [him] authorising the said   to purchase compulsorily for the purpose of   (c) the land which is operational land (as defined in section 34(1) of the said Act) of the   (d) and which is described in the Schedule hereto and is delineated and shown   (e) on the map annexed hereto and marked "Map referred to in an application for a Compulsory Purchase Order dated
".

SCHEDULE

Number on Map	Extent, description and situation of the land (f)	Owners or reputed owners	Lessees or reputed lessees	Occupiers
(1)	(2)	(3)	(4)	(5)

(g)

[Date and signature]

NOTES

(a) Insert the name and address of the Development Board for Rural Wales or local highway authority making the application.

(b) Insert the name of the appropriate Minister as respects the statutory under-takers, where the appropriate Minister is not the Secretary of State for Wales.

(c) Describe the purpose by reference to the words of the relevant sub-section of section 1 or sub-paragraph of paragraph 2(1) of Schedule 3 to the Development of Rural Wales Act 1976. Where those words are in general terms covering a range of purposes, the particular purpose for which the land is required should be stated if possible.

(d) Insert name of statutory undertakers.

(e) Describe the colouring or other method used to identify the land on the map. The map should contain sufficient detail to enable the situation of the land to be readily identified and related to the description given in the Schedule. Maps should normally be on a scale of 1/500 or 1/1250.

(f) This column should contain sufficient detail to tell the reader approximately where the land is situated, without reference to the map.

(g) Column (1) need not be completed where the order relates only to one parcel of land. Where there are two or more parcels they should be numbered 1, 2 etc. on the map and referred to accordingly in column (1).

FORM 8

PERSONAL NOTICE OF APPLICATION FOR COMPULSORY PURCHASE ORDER OF

OPERATIONAL LAND OF STATUTORY UNDERTAKERS

Development of Rural Wales Act 1976

To:

1. The   in exercise of [its] [their] powers under paragraph 16(1) of Schedule 3 to the above Act on   19   applied to the Secretary of State [and   (a)] for an order to be made authorising the said to purchase compulsorily for the purpose of   (b) the land described below which is operational land (as defined in section 34(1) of the said Act) of the   (c).

2. A copy of the application and of the map referred to therein have been deposited at   (d) and may be seen there at all reasonable hours.

3. If no objection is duly made by an owner, lessee or occupier of any land to which the application relates, or if all objections so made are withdrawn the Secretary of State [and   (a)] may, if [they think] [he thinks] fit make a compulsory purchase order in accordance with the application, with or without modifications.

4. If any objection is duly made by any such owner, lessee or occupier and is not withdrawn the Secretary of State [and   (a)] [are] [is] required before making an order on the application to consider the objection and if either the person by whom the objection was made or the acquiring authority so desire, to afford that person and the acquiring authority an opportunity of appearing before and being heard by a person appointed by the said Secretary of State [and   (a)].

5. Any objection to the application must be made in writing to the Secretary, Welsh Office, Cathays Park, Cardiff, CF1 3NQ before   (e). The objection should state the title of the order and must include or be accompanied by a statement of the grounds of the objection.

Description of Land

(f)

[Date and signature]

NOTES

(a) Insert the name of the appropriate Minister as respects the statutory undertakers, where the appropriate Minister is not the Secretary of State for Wales.

(b) State purpose as set out in the application for the order.

(c) State name of statutory undertakers.

(d) State the place where the application has been deposited for inspection. This should be within reasonably easy reach of persons living in the area affected.

(e) Insert a date at least 28 days from the service of the notice (i.e. 28 days excluding the date of service).

(f) Insert description of all the land comprised in the application. This need not repeat the Schedule to the application, but must be in terms from which persons interested can readily see how their land is affected.

FORM 9

PERSONAL NOTICE OF THE MAKING OF A COMPULSORY PURCHASE ORDER

FOR OPERATIONAL LAND OF STATUTORY UNDERTAKERS

Development of Rural Wales Act 1976

[Title of Compulsory Purchase Order]

To:

1. Notice is hereby given that the Secretary of State [and   (a)]
in exercise of [their] [his] powers under paragraph 16(1) of Schedule 3 to the above
Act on   19   made an order [generally] (b) in accordance with an application submitted to [them] [him] by the   authorising the said
to purchase compulsorily for the purpose of   (c) the land in the Schedule
hereto.

2. A copy of the order and of the map referred to therein have been deposited
at   (d) and may be seen there at all reasonable hours.

3. (e) The order as made becomes operative on the date on which service of [this notice is effected] [this notice and any other notices required by paragraph 21 of Schedule 3 to the above Act is completed] (f); but a person aggrieved by the order may, by application to the High Court within six weeks from that date, question its validity on the grounds (i) that the order is not within the powers of the Act, or (ii) that his interests have been substantially prejudiced by failure to comply with any statutory requirement relating to the order.

OR

3. The order as made is subject to special parliamentary procedure and will become operative as provided by the Statutory Orders (Special Procedure) Act 1945. Unless the order is confirmed by Act of Parliament under section 6 of that Act, a person aggrieved by the order may, by application to the High Court within six weeks from the operative date, question its validity on the grounds (i) that the order is not within the powers of the Act, or (ii) that his interests have been substantially prejudiced by failure to comply with any statutory requirement relating to the order.

SCHEDULE

Land Comprised in the Order as Made

[Date and Signature]

NOTES

(a) Insert the name of the appropriate Minister as respects the statutory undertakers, where the appropriate Minister is not the Secretary of State for Wales.

(b) Omit if the order was made in accordance with the application without modification.

(c) Insert the purpose as stated in the application.

(d) State the place where the order has been deposited for inspection. This should be within reasonably easy reach of persons living in the area affected.

(e) Leave standing whichever alternative is appropriate.

(f) If all the land is vested in a single owner-occupier, delete the second sentence in square brackets; otherwise delete the first sentence.

John Morris,

27th July 1977.

Secretary of State for Wales.

EXPLANATORY NOTE

(*This Note is not part of the Regulations.*)

The functions of the Development Board for Rural Wales, established by the Development of Rural Wales Act 1976 (c. 75), include the development of any area duly designated as the site of a new town which falls within the area for which the Board is responsible under that Act. The 1976 Act confers upon the Board, on local highway authorities and on the Secretary of State powers of compulsory purchase in relation to land required in connection with the development of any such new town, which have to be exercised in accordance with Part III of Schedule 3 to the 1976 Act.

These Regulations prescribe:—

(*a*) the forms of orders to be used by the Board and by local highway authorities and of notices to be used by the Board, local highway authorities and the Secretary of State when exercising their powers of compulsory purchase in accordance with Part III of Schedule 3;

(*b*) the form to be used by statutory undertakers when making representations in accordance with the provisions of paragraph 16(3) of Schedule 3 in relation to a compulsory purchase order made in accordance with Part III of Schedule 3;

(*c*) the form of application by the Board or a local highway authority for a compulsory purchase order relating to operational land of statutory undertakers;

(*d*) the particulars which an owner or occupier of land is required to give to the acquiring authority where he wishes to be served with notice of the confirmation of a compulsory purchase order affecting his land;

(*e*) the manner of marking any document served on a person of unknown identity under the provisions of Schedule 3, which ensures that the document should be identifiable as a communication of importance.

Equivalent forms, particulars and marking are prescribed by the New Towns (Compulsory Purchase of Land) Regulations 1977 (S.I. 1977/549) in connection with the making and confirmation of compulsory purchase orders under the provisions of the New Towns Act 1965 (c. 59).

STATUTORY INSTRUMENTS

1977 No. 1379

DANGEROUS DRUGS

The Misuse of Drugs (Designation) Order 1977

Made - - - -	8th August 1977
Laid before Parliament	16th August 1977
Coming into Operation—	
Articles 1 and 2	8th September 1977
Remainder	20th September 1977

In pursuance of section 7(4), (5) and (7) of the Misuse of Drugs Act 1971(a), on the recommendation of the Advisory Council on the Misuse of Drugs, I hereby make the following Order:—

1.—(1) This Order may be cited as the Misuse of Drugs (Designation) Order 1977, and (with the exception of Articles 3 and 4 and the Schedule which shall come into operation on 20th September 1977) shall come into operation on 8th September 1977.

(2) The Interpretation Act 1889(b) shall apply for the interpretation of this Order as it applies for the interpretation of an Act of Parliament, and as if any Orders revoked by this Order were Acts of Parliament repealed by an Act of Parliament.

2. During the period beginning with 8th September 1977 and ending with 19th September 1977, the Misuse of Drugs (Designation) Order 1973(c), as amended (d), shall have effect as if in Article 2 thereof there were added at the end the following paragraph:—

'(2) In that Schedule, "cannabis" has the same meaning as in the Misuse of Drugs Act 1971 as amended by section 52 of the Criminal Law Act 1977(e).'

3.—(1) The controlled drugs specified in the Schedule hereto are hereby designated as drugs to which section 7(4) of the Misuse of Drugs Act 1971 applies.

(2) In that Schedule, "cannabis" has the same meaning as in the Misuse of Drugs Act 1971 as amended by section 52 of the Criminal Law Act 1977.

4. The Misuse of Drugs (Designation) Order 1973 and the Misuse of Drugs (Designation) (Amendment) Order 1975(d) are hereby revoked.

Merlyn Rees,
One of Her Majesty's Principal
Secretaries of State.

Home Office.
8th August 1977.

(a) 1971 c. 38.	**(b)** 1889 c. 63.
(c) S.I. 1973/796 (1973 I, p. 2547).	**(d)** S.I. 1975/498 (1975 I, p. 1652).
(e) 1977 c. 45.	

SCHEDULE   Article 3.

1. The following substances and products, namely:—

(a) Bufotenine   Lysergide and other N-alkyl derivatives of lyser-
    Cannabinol   gamide
    Cannabinol derivatives   Mescaline
    Cannabis   Psilocin
    Cannabis resin   Raw opium
    Coca leaf   4-Bromo-2,5-dimethoxy-α-methylphenethylamine
    Concentrate of   N,N-Diethyltryptamine
        poppy-straw   N,N-Dimethyltryptamine
    Lysergamide   2,5-Dimethoxy-α,4-dimethylphenethylamine

(b) any compound (not being a compound for the time being specified in sub-
    paragraph (a) above) structurally derived from tryptamine or from a ring-
    hydroxy tryptamine by substitution at the nitrogen atom of the sidechain with
    one or more alkyl substituents but no other substituent;

(c) any compound (not being methoxyphenamine or a compound for the time
    being specified in sub-paragraph (a) above) structurally derived from phenethyl-
    amine, an N-alkylphenethylamine, α-methylphenethylamine, an N-alkyl-α-
    methylphenethylamine, α-ethylphenethylamine, or an N-alkyl-α-ethylphenethyl-
    amine by substitution in the ring to any extent with alkyl, alkoxy, alkylenedioxy
    or halide substituents, whether or not further substituted in the ring by one or
    more other univalent substituents.

2. Any stereoisomeric form of a substance specified in paragraph 1 above.

3. Any ester or ether of a substance specified in paragraph 1 or 2 above.

4. Any salt of a substance specified in any of paragraphs 1 to 3 above.

5. Any preparation or other product containing a substance or product specified
in any of paragraphs 1 to 4 above.

EXPLANATORY NOTE

(*This Note is not part of the Order.*)

Section 7(3) of the Misuse of Drugs Act 1971 requires regulations to be made
to allow the use for medical purposes of the drugs which are subject to control
under the Act. Section 7(3) does not however apply to any drug designated by
order under section 7(4) as a drug to which section 7(4) is to apply. This Order,
which replaces the Misuse of Drugs (Designation) Order 1973, as amended,
designates for this purpose the drugs specified in the Schedule to the Order.
It differs from the previous Order by the addition, in paragraph 1 of the Schedule,
of two new sub-paragraphs (b) and (c), which relate, respectively, to certain
tryptamine derivatives and certain phenethylamine derivatives.

Provision is made (Article 3(2)) to adopt in this Order the amendment to
the definition of cannabis in the Misuse of Drugs Act 1971 which is made by
section 52 of the Criminal Law Act 1977. An amendment to that effect is also
made (Article 2) to the 1973 Order for the purposes of the period until the
other provisions of this Order come into operation.

STATUTORY INSTRUMENTS

1977 No. 1380

DANGEROUS DRUGS

The Misuse of Drugs (Amendment) Regulations 1977

Made - - - -	8th August 1977
Laid before Parliament	16th August 1977
Coming into Operation—	
Regulations 1, 2 and 3	8th September 1977
Remainder	20th September 1977

In pursuance of sections 10, 22(*a*) and 31 of the Misuse of Drugs Act 1971(**a**) and after consultation with the Advisory Council on the Misuse of Drugs, I hereby make the following Regulations:—

1. These Regulations may be cited as the Misuse of Drugs (Amendment) Regulations 1977, and (with the exception of Regulations 4 and 5 and the Schedule which shall come into operation on 20th September 1977) shall come into operation on 8th September 1977.

2.—(1) In these Regulations, "the principal Regulations" means the Misuse of Drugs Regulations 1973(**b**) as amended by the Misuse of Drugs (Amendment) Regulations 1974(**c**), the Misuse of Drugs (Amendment) Regulations 1975(**d**) and the Misuse of Drugs (Amendment) (No. 2) Regulations 1975(**e**).

(2) The Interpretation Act 1889(**f**) shall apply for the interpretation of these Regulations as it applies for the interpretation of an Act of Parliament, and as if any Regulation revoked by these Regulations were an Act of Parliament repealed by an Act of Parliament.

3. The principal Regulations shall be amended by inserting in Regulation 2(1) thereof, after the definition of "authorised as a member of a group", the following definition:—

'"cannabis" has the same meaning as in the Act as amended by section 52 of the Criminal Law Act 1977(**g**); '.

4. The principal Regulations shall be amended by the substitution for Schedule 4 of the Schedule 4 set out in the Schedule to these Regulations.

5. Regulation 3(*d*) of the Misuse of Drugs (Amendment) Regulations 1975 is hereby revoked.

Merlyn Rees,
One of Her Majesty's Principal
Secretaries of State.

Home Office.
8th August 1977.

(**a**) 1971 c. 38.	(**b**) S.I. 1973/797 (1973 I, p. 2549).
(**c**) S.I. 1974/402 (1974 I, p. 1257).	(**d**) S.I. 1975/499 (1975 I, p. 1653).
(**e**) S.I. 1975/1623 (1975 III, p. 5620).	(**f**) 1889 c. 63.
(**g**) 1977 c. 45.	

SCHEDULE   Regulation 4.

NEW SCHEDULE TO BE INSERTED AS SCHEDULE 4 TO THE

MISUSE OF DRUGS REGULATIONS 1973

Regulations 19 and 24.   SCHEDULE 4

CONTROLLED DRUGS SUBJECT TO THE REQUIREMENTS OF

REGULATIONS 14, 15, 16, 18, 19, 20 and 24

1. The following substances and products, namely:—

(a) Bufotenine
    Cannabinol
    Cannabinol derivatives
    Cannabis and cannabis resin
    Coca leaf
    Concentrate of poppy-straw
    Lysergamide
    Lysergide and other N-alkyl derivatives of lysergamide
    Mescaline
    Psilocin
    Raw opium
    4-Bromo-2,5-dimethoxy-α-methylphenethylamine
    N,N-Diethyltryptamine
    N,N-Dimethyltryptamine
    2,5-Dimethoxy-α,4-dimethylphenethylamine

(b) any compound (not being a compound for the time being specified in sub-paragraph (a) above) structurally derived from tryptamine or from a ring-hydroxy tryptamine by substitution at the nitrogen atom of the sidechain with one or more alkyl substituents but no other substituent;

(c) any compound (not being methoxyphenamine or a compound for the time being specified in sub-paragraph (a) above) structurally derived from phenethyl-amine, an N-alkylphenethylamine, α-methylphenethylamine, an N-alkyl-α-methylphenethylamine,α-ethylphenethylamine, or an N-alkyl-α-ethylphenethyl-amine by substitution in the ring to any extent with alkyl, alkoxy, alkylenedioxy or halide substituents, whether or not further substituted in the ring by one or more other univalent substituents.

2. Any stereoisomeric form of a substance specified in paragraph 1.

3. Any ester or ether of a substance specified in paragraph 1 or 2.

4. Any salt of a substance specified in any of paragraphs 1 to 3.

5. Any preparation or other product containing a substance or product specified in any of paragraphs 1 to 4, not being a preparation specified in Schedule 1.

EXPLANATORY NOTE

(This Note is not part of the Regulations.)

These Regulations amend the Misuse of Drugs Regulations 1973, as amended, by substituting a new Schedule for Schedule 4 to those Regulations. The new Schedule differs from the old one by the addition of two classes of substances— see paragraph 1(*b*) and (*c*) of the Schedule; the classes consist of certain tryptamine derivatives, and certain phenethylamine derivatives. The amendment in Regulation 5 is consequential.

The Regulations also add (Regulation 3) a definition of cannabis to the 1973 Regulations; the effect is to adopt in those Regulations the amendment to the definition of cannabis in the Misuse of Drugs Act 1971 which is made by section 52 of the Criminal Law Act 1977.

STATUTORY INSTRUMENTS

1977 No. 1381

OVERSEAS AID

The International Fund for Agricultural Development (Initial Contribution) Order 1977

Laid before the House of Commons in draft

Made -   -   -   -   *4th August* 1977

Coming into Operation   On a date to be notified in the London, Edinburgh and Belfast Gazettes

Whereas it is provided in section 2(1) of the Overseas Aid Act 1968(a) as amended by section 7(2) of the International Finance, Trade and Aid Act 1977(b) that if Her Majesty's Government in the United Kingdom becomes bound by any arrangements for the making of an initial contribution to an international development bank the Minister of Overseas Development may with the approval of the Treasury by order made by Statutory Instrument make provision for the payment out of moneys provided by Parliament of any sums required by him for any of the purposes specified in that subsection:

Now, therefore, the Minister of Overseas Development in exercise of the powers conferred upon him by section 2 of the Overseas Aid Act 1968 as amended by section 7(2) of the International Finance, Trade and Aid Act 1977 and with the approval of the Treasury, hereby makes the following Order:

1.—(1) This Order may be cited as the International Fund for Agricultural Development (Initial Contribution) Order 1977 and shall come into operation on the date on which the Agreement establishing the International Fund for Agricultural Development dated 13 June 1976(c) enters into force in respect of the United Kingdom. This date shall be notified in the London, Edinburgh and Belfast Gazettes.

(2) In this Order—

"the Fund" means the International Fund for Agricultural Development established by the Agreement;

"the Agreement" means the Agreement establishing the International Fund for Agricultural Development dated 13 June 1976;

"the Minister" means the Minister of Overseas Development.

(3) The Interpretation Act 1889(d) shall apply to the interpretation of, and otherwise in relation to, this Order as it applies to the interpretation of, and otherwise in relation to, an Act of Parliament.

2. The Minister may, on behalf of Her Majesty's Government in the United Kingdom, out of moneys provided by Parliament—

    (*a*) make payment of an initial contribution to the initial resources of the Fund of a sum of eighteen million pounds sterling (£18,000,000) in accordance with section 2 of Article 4 of the Agreement;

(a) 1968 c. 57.   (b) 1977 c. 6.
(c) Cmnd. 6787.   (d) 1889 c. 63.

(*b*) make payment of sums required to redeem any non-interest-bearing non-negotiable notes or other obligations which may be issued or created by the Minister and accepted by the Fund in accordance with paragraph (*c*) of section 5 of Article 4 of the Agreement in place of any amount due in cash from Her Majesty's Government by way of initial contribution to the Fund.

3. Any sums received by Her Majesty's said Government from the Fund in pursuance of the Agreement shall be paid into the Consolidated Fund.

David Owen,
The Minister of

29th July 1977.   Overseas Development.

We approve,

T. E. Graham,
David Stoddart,
Two of the Lords Commissioners

4th August 1977.   of Her Majesty's Treasury.

EXPLANATORY NOTE
(*This Note is not part of the Order.*)

The Overseas Aid Act 1968 section 2(1) as amended by the International Finance, Trade and Aid Act 1977 section 7(2) provides that if the Government of the United Kingdom becomes bound by arrangements for the making of an initial contribution to an international development bank, the Minister of Overseas Development may, with the approval of the Treasury, provide by Order for the payment out of moneys provided by Parliament of sums required by him for any of the purposes specified in that subsection.

2. The Order provides for payments from time to time in accordance with arrangements made with the International Fund for Agricultural Development of sums not exceeding in total £18 million, which is the initial contribution pledged by Her Majesty's Government to that Fund and for redemption of non-interest-bearing and non-negotiable notes issued by the Minister of Overseas Development in place of any amounts due by way of the initial contribution in cash. The Order further provides that certain sums which may be received by the Government of the United Kingdom from the Fund shall be paid into the Consolidated Fund.

1977 No. 1386

COMPANIES

The Industrial Common Ownership (Loans) Regulations 1977

Made - - - -	9th August 1977
Laid before Parliament	17th August 1977
Coming into Operation	1st October 1977

The Secretary of State, in exercise of his powers under section 1(3) of the Industrial Common Ownership Act 1976(a) and of all other powers enabling him in that behalf, hereby makes the following Regulations:—

Citation, commencement and interpretation

1.—(1) These Regulations may be cited as the Industrial Common Ownership (Loans) Regulations 1977 and shall come into operation on 1st October 1977.

(2) The Interpretation Act 1889(b) shall apply for the interpretation of these Regulations as it applies for the interpretation of an Act of Parliament.

(3) In these Regulations:

"the Act" means the Industrial Common Ownership Act 1976;

"grant assisted loan" means a loan made by a relevant body in whole or in part out of moneys lent or granted to it by the Secretary of State under section 1(2) of the Act;

"independent trade union" has the meaning assigned to it by section 30(1) of the Trade Union and Labour Relations Act 1974(c);

"manufacturing industry" means, subject to paragraph (5) below, activities which are described in any of the minimum list headings in Orders III to XIX (inclusive) of the Standard Industrial Classification;

"relevant trade union" means an independent trade union which the common ownership enterprise, or as the case may be, the co-operative enterprise concerned recognises for the purposes of negotiations relating to or connected with one or more of the matters specified in section 29(1) of the Trade Union and Labour Relations Act 1974, or as to which the Advisory Conciliation and Arbitration Service has made a recommendation for such recognition under the Employment Protection Act 1975(d) which is operative within the meaning of section 15 of that Act;

"representative" means an official or other person who is authorised by a relevant trade union or, as the case may be, an independent trade union to carry on negotiations relating to or connected with one or more of the matters specified in section 29(1) of the Trade Union and Labour Relations Act 1974; and

---

(a) 1976 c. 78.　　(b) 1889 c. 63.　　(c) 1974 c. 52.　　(d) 1975 c. 71.

2aa

"Standard Industrial Classification" means, subject to paragraph (4) below, the revised edition published by Her Majesty's Stationery Office in 1968 of the publication of that name prepared by the Central Statistical Office.

(4) Where in the case of any minimum list heading in Orders III to XIX of the Standard Industrial Classification the title of the heading is not accompanied by a description of the industries or services included therein, the heading shall be construed as referring only to the manufacture of the goods specified in that title.

(5) In determining the extent to which an enterprise is engaged in manufacturing industry, the following activities shall be treated as manufacturing industry in so far as they relate to products manufactured or to be manufactured by the enterprise:—

research,
transport,
distribution,
repair and maintenance of machinery,
sales and marketing,
storage,
mining and quarrying,
production and distribution of energy and heating,
administration,
training of staff,
packaging.

Persons to whom Grant Assisted Loans may be made

2.—The persons to whom a relevant body may make grant assisted loans are:—

(*a*) a common ownership enterprise which is wholly or mainly engaged in manufacturing industry; and

(*b*) a co-operative enterprise which is so engaged.

Purpose for which Grant Assisted Loans may be made

3.—(1) A relevant body may not make grant assisted loans except for the purpose of satisfying, in whole or in part, the fixed and working capital requirements of the recipient of the loan in respect of an identified project of that recipient.

(2) Before making a grant assisted loan in respect of any such project, a relevant body shall satisfy itself that that project has a reasonable prospect of success, and if is not so satisfied, it shall make no grant assisted loan in respect of that project.

Limit on Grant Assisted Loans

4.—(1) A relevant body shall not make a grant assisted loan in a sum exceeding £7,500 without the prior written approval of the Secretary of State.

(2) The Secretary of State may give his approval subject to such conditions as he sees fit.

Security for Grant Assisted Loans

5.—(1) Subject to paragraph (2) below, a relevant body shall not make a grant assisted loan otherwise than on security adequate to secure repayment thereof.

(2) If a relevant body is satisfied that the prospects of success of a project in respect of which a grant assisted loan is sought would be seriously jeopardized if the body were to insist upon adequate security for the loan, the body may dispense, in whole or in part, with security for that loan.

Interest on and Repayment of Grant Assisted Loans

6.—(1) A relevant body shall charge interest on a grant assisted loan at a rate not lower than such rate as the Secretary of State may from time to time with the consent of Treasury specify.

(2) A relevant body shall impose the following conditions on a grant assisted loan:—

(*a*) interest on a grant assisted loan and repayments of the principal thereof shall be payable at equal intervals of not longer than twelve months;

(*b*) the first payment of interest on, and the first repayment of the principal of a grant assisted loan shall become payable not more than twelve months from the date of making of the loan, or, where the loan is made by instalments, from the date of payment of the last instalment;

(*c*) all principal moneys of a grant assisted loan shall be repaid not more than five years from the date of making of the loan or, where the loan is made by instalments, from the date of payment of the first instalment.

(3) In a case where a relevant body is satisfied, having regard to the nature of the project in respect of which a grant assisted loan is made, to the circumstances of the recipient of that loan and to all other circumstances of the case, that that project's prospects of success would be seriously jeopardized if payment of interest were required as it became payable, it may, subject to paragraph (4) below, make the loan on terms that interest thereon for a term not exceeding three years from the making of the loan, or, as the case may be, from the payment of the first instalment, shall be treated as an accretion to the principal of the loan.

(4) Where a relevant body makes a grant assisted loan on terms permitting the accretion of interest to principal in accordance with paragraph (3) above. it shall, subject to paragraph (2) of Regulation 5 above, ensure that the security obtained for that loan is adequate to secure the repayment of the principal thereof as augmented by such accretion, and the payment of interest thereon.

Trade Union Consultation

7.—Before making a grant assisted loan, a relevant body shall consult—

(*a*) a representative of each relevant trade union; and

(*b*) a representative of each other independent trade union appearing to the body to represent workers whose interests appear to the body likely to be affected by the making of a grant assisted loan

with a view to ascertaining the views of that union as to the grant assisted loan.

Bob Cryer,
Parliamentary Under-Secretary of State.
9th August 1977. Department of Industry.

EXPLANATORY NOTE

(This Note is not part of the Regulations.)

These Regulations make provision with respect to the circumstances in which, the purposes for which and the terms upon which a relevant body, as defined in section 1(5) of the Industrial Common Ownership Act 1976, may lend money granted or lent to it by the Secretary of State under section 1(2) of that Act.

STATUTORY INSTRUMENTS

1977 No. 1387

PENSIONS

The Pensions Increase (Annual Review) Order 1977

Made - - - -	*9th August* 1977
Laid before Parliament	*26th August* 1977
Coming into Operation	*1st December* 1977

Whereas the Minister for the Civil Service has, in accordance with the provisions of section 2 of the Pensions (Increase) Act 1971(**a**), as amended by section 25(1) of the Superannuation Act 1972(**b**), reviewed the rates of official pensions against the rise in the cost of living during the review period, that is to say, the period of twelve months ending with 30th June 1977, and it has been found that in that period the cost of living has risen by 17·7 per cent.:

Now therefore the Minister for the Civil Service, in exercise of the powers conferred on him by section 2 of the Pensions (Increase) Act 1971 (as amended by section 25(1) of the Superannuation Act 1972 and sections 3(1) and 3(3)(*a*) of the Pensions (Increase) Act 1974(**c**)) and section 9(4) of the said Act of 1971 and of all other powers enabling him in that behalf, hereby makes the following Order:—

Citation and commencement

1. This Order may be cited as the Pensions Increase (Annual Review) Order 1977, and shall come into operation on 1st December 1977.

Interpretation

2.—(1) In this Order—

"the 1971 Act" means the Pensions (Increase) Act 1971;

"the 1974 Act" means the Pensions (Increase) Act 1974;

"basic rate" has the meaning given by section 17(1) of the 1971 Act, as amended by section 1(3) of the 1974 Act;

"the existing Orders" means the Pensions Increase (Annual Review) Order 1972(**d**), the Pensions Increase (Annual Review) Order 1973(**e**), the Pensions Increase (Annual Review) Order 1974(**f**), the Pensions Increase (Annual Review) Order 1975(**g**) and the Pensions Increase (Annual Review) Order 1976(**h**);

(**a**) 1971 c. 56.
(**c**) 1974 c. 9.
(**e**) S.I. 1977/1370 (1973 II, p. 4234).
(**g**) S.I. 1975/1384 (1975 II, p. 4745).

(**b**) 1972 c. 11.
(**d**) S.I. 1972/1298 (1972 II, p. 3910).
(**f**) S.I. 1974/1373 (1974 II, p. 5267).
(**h**) S.I. 1976/1356 (1976 II, p. 3774).

"official pension" has the meaning given by section 5(1) of the 1971 Act; "pension authority" has the meaning given by section 7(1) of the 1971 Act; "qualifying condition" means one of the conditions laid down in section 3 of the 1971 Act, as amended by section 3(2) and (3) of the 1974 Act; "widow's pension" means a pension payable in respect of the services of the pensioner's deceased husband.

(2) For the purposes of this Order the time when a pension "begins" is that stated in section 8(2) of the 1971 Act, and the "beginning date" shall be construed accordingly.

(3) The Interpretation Act 1889(a) shall apply for the interpretation of this Order as it applies for the interpretation of an Act of Parliament.

Pension increases

3.—(1) The annual rate of an official pension may, if any qualifying condition is satisfied or the pension is a widow's pension, be increased by the pension authority in respect of any period beginning on or after 1st December 1977 as follows:—

  (a) a pension beginning on or before 1st July 1976 may be increased by 17·7 per cent. of the basic rate as increased by the amount of any increase under section 1 of the 1971 Act or under the existing Orders;

  (b) a pension beginning in the six months following 1st July 1976 may be increased by 19·5 per cent. of the basic rate.

  (c) a pension beginning in the six months following 1st January 1977 may be increased by 11·4 per cent. of the basic rate.

(2) For the purpose of showing the cumulative effect of the increases payable under section 1 of the 1971 Act, under the existing Orders and under paragraph (1) above, that section (as amended by section 3(3)(a) of the 1974 Act), with the effect of the existing Orders and paragraph (1) above incorporated in it, is set out in the Schedule to this Order.

Increases of certain lump sums

4. In respect of any lump sum or instalment of a lump sum which became payable in the six months ending with 1st July 1977, but for which the beginning date fell before 2nd January 1977, there may be paid an increase of 9·8 per cent. of the amount of the lump sum or instalment as increased by any increase under section 1 of the 1971 Act or under the existing Orders.

Given under the official seal of the Minister for the Civil Service on 9th August 1977.

(L.S.)

C. R. Morris,
Minister of State,
Civil Service Department.

(a) 1889 c. 63.

SCHEDULE

Section 1 of the Pensions (Increase) Act 1971 reproduced with the effect of the existing Orders and article 3(1) of this Order incorporated in it

1.—(1) Subject to the provisions of this Act, the annual rate of an official pension may, if any qualifying condition is satisfied or the pension is a widow's pension, be increased by the pension authority in respect of any period on or after 1st December 1977, as follows:—

(a) a pension beginning before the year 1969 may be increased by the amount necessary to bring the rate up to the 1969 standard, that is to say to the rate arrived at by applying to the basic rate of pension the multiplier given in Schedule 1 for the year in which the pension began, and by a further 178·9071 per cent. of the rate so increased;

(b) a pension beginning on or before 1st April 1969 but not earlier than that year may be increased by 178·9071 per cent. of the basic rate;

(c) a pension beginning in the six months following 1st April 1969 may be increased by 174·1799 per cent. of the basic rate;

(d) a pension beginning in the six months following 1st October 1969 may be increased by 169·4526 per cent. of the basic rate;

(e) a pension beginning in the six months following 1st April 1970 may be increased by 159·9982 per cent. of the basic rate;

(f) a pension beginning in the six months following 1st October 1970 may be increased by 150·5437 per cent. of the basic rate;

(g) a pension beginning in the six months following 1st April 1971 may be increased by 138·7277 per cent. of the basic rate;

(h) a pension beginning in the six months following 1st October 1971 may be increased by 127·1140 per cent. of the basic rate;

(i) a pension beginning in the three months following 1st April 1972 may be increased by 122·5975 per cent. of the basic rate;

(j) a pension beginning in the six months following 1st July 1972 may be increased by 117·2345 per cent. of the basic rate;

(k) a pension beginning in the six months following 1st January 1973 may be increased by 108·7734 per cent. of the basic rate;

(l) a pension beginning in the six months following 1st July 1973 may be increased by 99·4728 per cent. of the basic rate;

(m) a pension beginning in the six months following 1st January 1974 may be increased by 89·6765 per cent. of the basic rate;

(n) a pension beginning in the six months following 1st July 1974 may be increased by 73·1878 per cent. of the basic rate;

(o) a pension beginning in the six months following 1st January 1975 may be increased by 60·5972 per cent. of the basic rate.

(p) a pension beginning in the six months following 1st July 1975 may be increased by 40·2984 per cent. of the basic rate;

(q) a pension beginning in the six months following 1st January 1976 may be increased by 28·0576 per cent. of the basic rate;

(r) a pension beginning in the six months following 1st July 1976 may be increased by 19·5 per cent. of the basic rate;

(s) a pension beginning in the six months following 1st January 1977 may be increased by 11·4 per cent of the basic rate.

(2) In the case of a pension beginning before the year 1969 the increase authorised by subsection (1)(a) above shall take the place of those authorised by the Pensions (Increase) Acts 1920 to 1969, but in the cases provided for by section 6 below shall be

of the larger amount there specified by reference to increases that might have been made under those Acts together with a further increase of 178·9071 per cent. of the pension as so increased.

EXPLANATORY NOTE

(This Note is not part of the Order.)

Under section 2 of the Pensions (Increase) Act 1971 (as amended by section 25(1) of the Superannuation Act 1972) the Minister for the Civil Service is required to conduct a review of rates of public service pensions against any rise in the cost of living during the review period. The Order provides for the payment, with effect from 1st December 1977, of the pension increases resulting from the 1977 review and based on the rise in the cost of living during the review period of twelve months ending with 30th June 1977. To qualify for increase a person in receipt of a pension must satisfy one of the qualifying conditions specified in section 3 of the 1971 Act (as amended by section 3(2) and (3) of the Pensions (Increase) Act 1974) or the pension must be a widow's pension.

For pensions (or deferred lump sums) which began on or before 1st July 1976 the increase (17·7 per cent.) is of the percentage by which the cost of living rose during the review period. For pensions (or deferred lump sums) which began in the six months following 1st July 1976, or in the six months following 1st January 1977, the increases (19·5 per cent. and 11·4 per cent. respectively) are of the percentage by which the cost of living at the end of the review period exceeded its mean level during the periods of six months ending 31st July 1976 and 31st January 1977 respectively.

The Order reproduces, in the Schedule, section 1 of the 1971 Act with the effect of the earlier Orders and this Order incorporated in it, so as to indicate the cumulative increases payable under the Act and the annual Orders.

The Order also provides, in article 4, for the payment, as a result of the review, of a supplementary increase of 9·8 per cent. on deferred lump sums which became payable in the six months ending 1st July 1977, but whose beginning date fell before 2nd January 1977. This increase is based, in accordance with section 9(4) of the 1971 Act, on the difference between the mean monthly figures for the cost of living for the six months ending 1st January 1977 and those for the six months ending 1st July 1977.

1977 No. 1388

SEA FISHERIES

BOATS AND METHODS OF FISHING

The Herring (Irish Sea) Licensing Order 1977

Made - - - -	8th August 1977
Laid before Parliament	12th August 1977
Coming into Operation	15th August 1977

The Minister of Agriculture, Fisheries and Food and the Secretaries of State respectively concerned with the sea fishing industry in Scotland and Northern Ireland, in exercise of the powers conferred on them by sections 4 and 15 of the Sea Fish (Conservation) Act 1967(a) (as section 15 is amended by section 22(1) of, and paragraph 38 of Schedule 1 to, the Sea Fisheries Act 1968(b) and as sections 4 and 15 are amended by sections 3 and 9(1) of, and paragraph 16(1) of Schedule 2 to, the Fishery Limits Act 1976(c)) and of all other powers enabling them in that behalf, hereby make the following order:—

Citation, commencement and interpretation

1.—(1) This order may be cited as the Herring (Irish Sea) Licensing Order 1977 and shall come into operation on 15th August 1977.

(2) In this order "mile" means a nautical mile of 1,852 metres.

(3) The Interpretation Act 1889(d) shall apply to the interpretation of this order as it applies to the interpretation of an Act of Parliament and as if this order and the order hereby revoked were Acts of Parliament.

Revocation

2. The Herring (North Irish Sea) Licensing Order 1976(e) is hereby revoked.

Prohibition of fishing without a licence

3. Fishing for herring *(Clupea harengus)* by British fishing boats in the area specified in the Schedule to this order is hereby prohibited unless such fishing is authorised by a licence granted by one of the Ministers.

Enforcement

4. For the purpose of the enforcement of this order, there are hereby conferred on every British sea-fishery officer the powers of a British sea-fishery officer under section 8(2) to (4) of the Sea Fisheries Act 1968 as subsection (4) is amended by section 9(1) of, and paragraph 17(1) of Schedule 2 to, the Fishery Limits Act 1976.

(a) 1967 c. 84.   (b) 1968 c. 77.   (c) 1976 c. 86.   (d) 1889 c. 63.
(e) S.I. 1976/1322 (1976 II, p. 3715).

In Witness whereof the Official Seal of the Minister of Agriculture, Fisheries and Food is hereunto affixed on 8th August 1977.

(L.S.)

John Silkin,
Minister of Agriculture, Fisheries
and Food.

2nd August 1977.

Bruce Millan,
Secretary of State for Scotland.

4th August 1977.

Roy Mason,
Secretary of State for Northern
Ireland.

Article 3.   SCHEDULE

The area bounded in the north by the parallel of 55° north latitude and the south west coast of Scotland; in the east by the coasts of England and Wales; in the south by the parallel of 52° 30′ north latitude; and in the west by the coasts of the Republic of Ireland and Northern Ireland; but excluding those parts of the area which lie within twelve miles of the baselines from which are measured the breadth of the territorial seas adjacent respectively to the Isle of Man, Northern Ireland and the Republic of Ireland.

EXPLANATORY NOTE

(This Note is not part of the Order.)

This Order prohibits fishing for herring in the specified area of the Irish Sea by British fishing boats unless authorised by a licence granted by one of the Fisheries Ministers.

STATUTORY INSTRUMENTS

1977 No. 1389

SEA FISHERIES

BOATS AND METHODS OF FISHING

The Herring (Isle of Man) Licensing Order 1977

Made	- - -	*8th August* 1977
Laid before Parliament		*12th August* 1977
Coming into Operation		*15th August* 1977

The Minister of Agriculture, Fisheries and Food and the Secretaries of State respectively concerned with the sea fishing industry in Scotland and Northern Ireland, in exercise of the powers conferred on them by sections 4 and 15 of the Sea Fish (Conservation) Act 1967(a) as extended to the Isle of Man by the Sea Fish (Conservation) (Isle of Man) Order 1977(b) and the Sea Fish (Conservation) (Isle of Man) Order 1973(c) as varied by the first mentioned order and of all other powers enabling them in that behalf, hereby make the following order:—

Citation, commencement and interpretation

1.—(1) This order may be cited as the Herring (Isle of Man) Licensing Order 1977 and shall come into operation on 15th August 1977.

(2) In this order "Irish fishing boat" means a fishing boat registered in the Republic of Ireland.

(3) The Interpretation Act 1889(d) shall apply to the interpretation of this order as it applies to the interpretation of an Act of Parliament and as if this order and the order hereby revoked were Acts of Parliament.

Revocation

2. The Herring (Isle of Man) Licensing Order 1976(e) is hereby revoked.

Prohibition of fishing without a licence

3. Fishing for herring (*Clupea harengus*)—

(*a*) by British fishing boats registered in the Isle of Man in the area specified in Part 1 of the Schedule to this order; or

(*b*) by British fishing boats in the area specified in Part 2 of the Schedule to this order; or

(*c*) by Irish fishing boats in the area specified in Part 3 of the Schedule to this order

is hereby prohibited unless such fishing is authorised by a licence granted by the Isle of Man Board of Agriculture and Fisheries.

(a) 1967 c. 84. (b) S.I. 1977/1244 (1977 II, p.3481). (c) S.I. 1973/237 (1973 I, p. 890).
(d) 1889 c. 63.   (e) S.I. 1976/1323 (1976 II, p. 3717).

Enforcement

4. For the purpose of the enforcement of this order, there are hereby conferred on every British sea-fishery officer the powers of a British sea-fishery officer under section 8(2) to (4) of the Sea Fisheries Act 1968.

In Witness whereof the Official Seal of the Minister of Agriculture, Fisheries and Food is hereunto affixed on 8th August 1977.

(L.S.)

John Silkin,
Minister of Agriculture, Fisheries and Food.

                                            Bruce Millan,
2nd August 1977.   Secretary of State for Scotland.

                                            Roy Mason,
4th August 1977.   Secretary of State for Northern Ireland.

SCHEDULE

Article 3

Part 1

The area bounded in the north by the parallel of 55° north latitude and the south west coast of Scotland ; in the east by the coasts of England and Wales ; in the south by the parallel of 52°30′ north latitude; and in the west by the coasts of the Republic of Ireland and Northern Ireland; but excluding those parts of the area which lie within twelve miles of the baselines from which are measured the breadth of the territorial seas adjacent respectively to Northern Ireland and the Republic of Ireland and excluding the territorial waters around the Isle of Man.

Part 2

The area within twelve miles of the baselines from which the breadth of the territorial sea adjacent to the Isle of Man is measured but outside territorial waters.

Part 3

The area lying between six and twelve miles from the baselines from which the breadth of the territorial sea adjacent to the Isle of Man is measured, bounded in the east by a line drawn due south from Chicken Rock Lighthouse, and in the north by a line drawn due west from Jurby Head Church.

EXPLANATORY NOTE

(This Note is not part of the Order.)

This Order prohibits fishing for herring within the twelve-mile belt around the Isle of Man outside territorial waters by all British or Irish fishing boats unless such fishing is authorised by a licence granted by the Isle of Man Board of Agriculture and Fisheries. As regards British fishing boats registered in the Isle of Man the prohibition applies in the larger area described in Part 1 of the Schedule to the order.

STATUTORY INSTRUMENTS

1977 No. 1394

BANKRUPTCY, ENGLAND

The Bankruptcy (Amendment No. 2) Rules 1977

Made - - - -	5*th August* 1977
Laid before Parliament	19*th August* 1977
Coming into Operation	1*st October* 1977

The Lord Chancellor, in exercise of the powers conferred on him by section 132 of the Bankruptcy Act 1914**(a)**, with the concurrence of the Secretary of State for Trade, and after consulting the committee appointed under section 10 of the Insolvency Act 1976**(b)**, hereby makes the following Rules:—

1.—(1) These Rules may be cited as the Bankruptcy (Amendment No. 2) Rules 1977 and shall come into operation on 1st October 1977.

(2) The Interpretation Act 1889**(c)** shall apply to the interpretation of these Rules as it applies to the interpretation of an Act of Parliament.

(3) The amendments set out in these Rules shall be made to the Bankruptcy Rules 1952**(d)**, as amended **(e)**.

2. At the end of rule 8(1) there shall be added the following sub-paragraph:—

"(*k*) Applications under section 6 of the Insolvency Act 1976 for an order dispensing with the public examination of the debtor."

3. At the end of rule 188(1) there shall be added the words:—

"and the Official Receiver shall not delay the application by reason only that the case is one to which rule 196A may apply."

4. After rule 196 there shall be inserted the following rule:—

"*Order dispensing with public examination under the Insolvency Act 1976, section 6* [**Form** 75A]

196A.—(1) When a receiving order has been made against a debtor it shall be the duty of the Official Receiver to consider whether, having regard to the matters specified in section 6(1) of the Insolvency Act 1976, reasonable grounds exist to warrant an application by him under the said section for an order to dispense with the holding of a public examination.

(2) Not later than 21 days before the day appointed for the hearing of the application, the Official Receiver shall give notice of the time and place thereof to the debtor and the creditors and such notice shall inform the

---

(a) 1914 c. 59.
(c) 1889 c. 63.
(b) 1976 c. 60.
(d) S.I. 1952/2113 (1952 I, p. 213).
(e) The relevant amending instrument is S.I. 1962/295 (1962 I, p. 283).

creditors that any objections to the making of an order under the said section must be received by the Official Receiver not later than 14 days before the day so appointed.

(3) Any such application by the Official Receiver shall be made *ex parte* and shall be supported by evidence in the form of a report by the Official Receiver to the court to be filed not less than seven days before the day appointed for the hearing of the application and the report shall include a statement as to whether the Official Receiver has received from any creditor any objection to the making of an order under the said section 6 and the substance of such objection.

(4) The application may, if the court thinks fit, be heard in the absence of the debtor and if the hearing takes place on a day other than that appointed for the public examination the Official Receiver shall give notice of the outcome of the application to the debtor and to the creditors.

(5) When the court rescinds an order made under the said section 6 the Official Receiver shall apply to the court for the appointment of a time and place for the public examination of the debtor and upon the application the court shall make an order appointing a time and place for the examination and order the debtor to attend thereat."

5. After rule 237 there shall be inserted the following rules:—

"AUTOMATIC DISCHARGE

Consideration by the court

237A.—(1) When the court makes an order which concludes or, under section 6 of the Insolvency Act 1976, dispenses with the public examination of a debtor, the court shall proceed to consider whether or not to make an order under section 7(1) of that Act directing that sub-section (2) of that section shall have effect if the debtor has been or is subsequently adjudged bankrupt in the proceedings.

(2) When the court dispenses with the public examination of a debtor under section 15(10) of the Act it shall proceed to consider whether to make an order under section 7(1) of the Insolvency Act 1976 but may, if it thinks fit, adjourn such consideration for the purpose of receiving from the Official Receiver a report as to the conduct and affairs of the debtor, including his conduct during the proceedings, and such report shall be *prima facie* evidence of the matters contained therein.

Service of order by Official Receiver [**Form** 114A]

237B. If the court thinks fit to make an order under the said section 7(1) not less than two sealed copies of the order shall forthwith be sent by the Registrar to the Official Receiver who shall cause one of the copies to be served on the debtor.

Gazetting of discharge [**Form** 200(9A)]

237C. Where an order made under the said section 7(1) has not been rescinded and the circumstances set out in sub-section (2) of that section apply, the Registrar shall on the fifth anniversary of the date of the adjudication forthwith give notice to the Secretary of State to be gazetted that the debtor has been discharged under the provisions of sub-section (2) of that section.

Application by trustee to rescind order

237D. Unless the court otherwise directs, no application by a trustee to rescind an order made under the said section 7(1) shall be heard unless notice of the intended application and a copy of the affidavits in support of it have been served upon the Official Receiver and the debtor not less than eight days before the hearing of the application.

Application by Official Receiver to rescind order

237E. The Official Receiver shall apply to rescind an order made under the said section 7(1) if—

(*a*) he becomes aware of any misconduct on the part of the debtor which occurred before the making of the order and which was not known to the Official Receiver when the order was made but which, if it had been disclosed to the court, would, in the opinion of the Official Receiver, have been likely to result in the order not being made; or

(*b*) the debtor is guilty of any misconduct which, if it had occurred before the making of the order and had then been known to the court would, in the opinion of the Official Receiver, have been likely to result in the order not being made; or

(*c*) the court so directs when an application by the debtor for his discharge has been refused; or

(*d*) an application by the debtor for his discharge has been granted subject to a suspension or condition such that the debtor may still be an undischarged bankrupt on the fifth anniversary of the date of the adjudication; or

(*e*) the debtor has failed to co-operate with the Official Receiver or trustee; or

(*f*) the debtor has again been adjudged bankrupt; or

(*g*) the debtor has been convicted of any offence under the Act or any other offence connected with his bankruptcy;

and any application by the Official Receiver under paragraph (*c*) or (*d*) above may be made without notice or formality immediately following the making of the order to which the said paragraph (*c*) or (*d*) relates.

DISCHARGE ON APPLICATION OF OFFICIAL RECEIVER

Notice of hearing [**Form** 200(8A)]

237F. Not less than 14 days before the day appointed for the hearing of an application by the Official Receiver under section 8 of the Insolvency Act 1976 in respect of the adjudication of the bankrupt, notice of the time and place appointed for the hearing shall be given by the Official Receiver to the trustee and the bankrupt and to the Secretary of State to be gazetted.

Consequential provisions

237G. Rules 228, 229 and 231 to 237 shall apply to proceedings under the said section 8 as they apply to proceedings under section 26 of the Act except that it shall not be necessary to give notice to creditors of an application by the bankrupt under sub-section (8) of the said section 8."

6. In rule 251 the words "affidavit of" shall be deleted.

7. In rule 321 at the end of paragraph (*e*) the word "or" shall be deleted and after paragraph (*f*) there shall be inserted the following paragraphs:—

"(*g*) to rescind an order made under section 6 of the Insolvency Act 1976 dispensing with the public examination of a debtor, or

(*h*) to rescind an order made under section 7(1) of the Insolvency Act 1976 in relation to automatic discharge."

8. In rule 322 after paragraph (*f*) there shall be inserted the following paragraph:—

"(*g*) to dispense with the public examination of a debtor under section 6 of the Insolvency Act 1976."

9. In Appendix I there shall be inserted at the appropriate places in numerical order the forms set out in the Schedule to these Rules.

Dated 27th July 1977.

Elwyn-Jones, C.

I concur,

Dated 5th August 1977.

Edmund Dell,

Secretary of State
for Trade.

SCHEDULE

Rule 9

<small>FORMS</small>

No. 60A

<small>PROOF OF DEBT (UNSWORN) GENERAL FORM</small>

(*Title*)

No.

Date of Receiving Order

Name of Creditor	
Address of Creditor	
Total Amount of Claim as at Date of Receiving Order	£
Particulars of how Debt(s) arose and Date(s) incurred (use space overleaf if necessary)	
Particulars of any Security held	
Value of Security	£

Please attach any documentary evidence of claim.

N.B.—Bills or other negotiable securities must be produced before the proof can be admitted.

Signature of creditor or person signing on his behalf................................

Name in block letters ....

Position with or relationship to creditor ....

Admitted to vote for	Admitted to rank for dividend for
£	£
the day of 19 .	this day of 19 .
Official Receiver	Trustee

No. 75A (Rule 196A)

ORDER MADE UNDER SECTION 6 OF THE INSOLVENCY ACT 1976 DISPENSING WITH
THE PUBLIC EXAMINATION OF THE DEBTOR

(*Title*)

UPON the application of the Official Receiver in the above matter and upon
reading

and upon hearing

AND IT APPEARING to the Court that this is a suitable matter in which to
dispense with a public examination having regard to the provisions of section
6(1) of the Insolvency Act 1976

IT IS ORDERED that the public examination of the debtor be dispensed with.

Dated this   day of   19   .

By the Court,

Registrar

No. 114A (Rule 237B)

ORDER FOR AUTOMATIC DISCHARGE UNDER SECTION 7 OF THE INSOLVENCY
ACT 1976

(*Title*)

WHEREAS the public examination of the above-named
                    was [concluded] [dispensed with] by Order dated

[AND WHEREAS the said   was adjudged bankrupt by
Order dated   ]

AND IT APPEARING to the Court that this is a suitable matter in which to
make an Order under the provisions of section 7(1) of the Insolvency Act 1976
IT IS ORDERED that [if the said   is adjudged bankrupt
in these proceedings] the same results shall ensue as if this Court had on the fifth
anniversary of the adjudication granted to the bankrupt an absolute order of
discharge under section 26 of the Bankruptcy Act 1914 But this Order shall
cease to have effect if before that anniversary the bankrupt has been discharged
in respect of the adjudication within the meaning of section 7(5) of the said Act
of 1976 or the adjudication has been annulled under section 21(2) or 29 of the
said Act of 1914.

Dated this   day of   19   .

By the Court,

Registrar

No. 114B (Rules 231, 232 and 237G)

ORDER OF DISCHARGE ON APPLICATION BY THE OFFICIAL RECEIVER UNDER SECTION 8 OF THE INSOLVENCY ACT 1976

(*Title*)

UPON the application of the Official Receiver, and upon taking into consideration his Report filed on.............................as to the bankrupt's conduct and affairs, including the bankrupt's conduct during the proceedings under the bankruptcy [and upon reading   ] and upon hearing the Official Receiver and C.D., E.F., &c., creditors, and G.H., the trustee [*as the case may be*]

IT IS ORDERED that the bankrupt be and he is hereby discharged.

OR

IT IS ORDERED that the bankrupt's discharge be and it is hereby refused.

OR

IT IS ORDERED that the bankrupt's discharge be suspended until a dividend of not less than 50p in the £ has been paid to the creditors, with liberty to the bankrupt at any time after the expiration of two years from the date of this Order to apply for a modification thereof, pursuant to section 8(8) of the Insolvency Act 1976.

OR

IT IS ORDERED that the bankrupt's discharge be suspended for   and that he be discharged as from the   day of   19 .

OR

IT IS ORDERED that the bankrupt be discharged subject to the following condition to be fulfilled before his discharge takes effect, namely, he shall before the signing of this Order, consent to judgment being entered against him in the (*a*) Insert name of (*a*)   Court Court having by the Official Receiver [*or* trustee] for the sum of £   , being the jurisdiction balance [*or* part of the balance] of the debts provable in the bankruptcy which is in the bank- not satisfied at the date of this Order, and for   costs of judg-ruptcy. ment.

AND IT IS FURTHER ORDERED, without prejudice and subject to any execution which may be issued on the said judgment with the leave of the Court, that the said sum of £   be paid out of the future earnings or after-acquired property of the bankrupt in manner following, that is to say, after setting aside out of the bankrupt's earnings, and after-acquired property a yearly sum of £   for the support of himself and his family, the bankrupt shall pay the surplus, if any [*or such portion of such surplus as the Court may determine*], to the Official Receiver [*or* trustee] for distribution among the creditors in the bankruptcy. An account shall on the 1st day of January in each year, or within fourteen days thereafter, be filed in these proceedings by the bankrupt, setting forth a statement of his receipts from earnings, after-acquired property, and income during the year immediately preceding the said date, and the surplus payable under this Order shall be paid by the bankrupt to the Official Receiver [*or* trustee] within fourteen days of the filing of the said account.

(*b*) Insert name of Court. AND IT IS FURTHER ORDERED that upon the required consent being given judgment may be entered against the bankrupt in the (*b*)   · Court for the said sum of £   together with £   for costs of judgment.

Dated this   day of   19 .

By the Court,

Registrar

No. 200(8A) (Rule 237F)

APPLICATION BY OFFICIAL RECEIVER TO CONSIDER DISCHARGE OF BANKRUPT

Debtor's Name (*Surname first*)　　　　　　Address

Description　　　　　　Court　　　　　　Number of Matter

Day fixed for hearing　　　　　　Hour　　　.　　Place

No. 200(9A) (Rule 237C)

ORDER FOR AUTOMATIC DISCHARGE

Debtor's Name (*Surname first*)　　　　　　Address

Description　　　　　　Court　　　　　　Number of Matter

Date of Order

Date of operation of Order of Discharge

No. 200(9B) (Rules 233 and 237G)

ORDER MADE ON APPLICATION BY OFFICIAL RECEIVER TO CONSIDER DISCHARGE
OF BANKRUPT

Debtor's Name (*Surname first*)　　　　　　Address

Description　　　　　　Court　　　　　　Number of Matter

Date of Order　　　　　　Nature of Order made

EXPLANATORY NOTE

(*This Note is not part of the Rules.*)

These Rules amend the Bankruptcy Rules 1952 for the purpose of implementing sections 5, 6, 7 and 8 of the Insolvency Act 1976. They prescribe in particular the appropriate new procedures and forms for the following matters:—

(i) proof of debt by unsworn claim under section 5 (rules 6 and Form 60A);

(ii) applications (to be heard in open court) by the Official Receiver under section 6 to dispense with the public examination of a debtor (rules 2, 3, 4, 7 and 8 and Form 75A);

(iii) orders under section 7 relating to the automatic discharge of a bankrupt five years after adjudication (rules 5 and 7 and Forms 114A and 200(9A)); and

(iv) applications by the Official Receiver under section 8 for the court to consider the discharge of a bankrupt (rule 5 and Forms 114B, 200(8A) and 200(9B)).

STATUTORY INSTRUMENTS

1977 No. 1395

COMPANIES

The Companies (Winding-up) (Amendment No. 2) Rules 1977

Made - - - -	*5th August* 1977
Laid before Parliament	*19th August* 1977
Coming into Operation	*1st October* 1977

The Lord Chancellor, in exercise of the powers conferred on him by section 365(1) of the Companies Act 1948(**a**), with the concurrence of the Secretary of State for Trade, and after consulting the committee appointed under section 10 of the Insolvency Act 1976(**b**), hereby makes the following Rules:—

1. These Rules may be cited as the Companies (Winding-up) (Amendment No. 2) Rules 1977 and shall come into operation on 1st October 1977.

2. The amendments set out in these Rules shall be made to the Companies (Winding-up) Rules 1949(**c**), as amended(**d**).

3. At the end of rule 6(1) there shall be added the following sub-paragraph:—

"(*p*) Applications under section 9 of the Insolvency Act 1976."

4. In rule 68(1) after sub-paragraph (*d*) there shall be inserted the following words: —

"or under section 9 of the Insolvency Act 1976".

5. For rule 70 there shall be substituted the following rule:—

Hearing of application.

"**70.**—(1) Where any application under section 188 of the Act or under section 9 of the Insolvency Act 1976 is made or heard after a public examination under section 270 of the Act has been held before the Registrar or any of the persons mentioned in sub-section (9) of the said section 270, then such application shall be heard and determined by such Registrar or other person unless—

(*a*) the Judge shall otherwise direct, or

(*b*) in the case of an application by the Secretary of State under the said section 9 the public examination was directed to be held by a Court other than the High Court.

(**a**) 1948 c. 38.   (**b**) 1976 c. 60.   (**c**) S.I. 1949/330 (1949 I, p. 789).
(**d**) There are no relevant amendments.

The Judge shall personally hear all other applications under the said section 188 or the said section 9:
Provided that in the High Court the Judge may direct that such applications or any of them shall be heard and determined by the Registrar.

(2) Where any order has been made under the said section 188, any application for leave arising out of such order shall be made to the Court having jurisdiction to wind up the company as respects which leave is sought.

(3) An application for leave arising out of an order made under the said section 9 shall be made to the Court by which the order was made."

6. For rule 92 there shall be substituted the following rule:—

"92.—(1) A debt may be proved in a winding-up by the Court by delivering or sending through the post in a pre-paid letter to the Official Receiver or, if a Liquidator has been appointed, to the Liquidator— Mode of proof.

(*a*) in any case in which the Official Receiver or Liquidator so requires, an affidavit verifying the debt; and

(*b*) in any other case, an unsworn claim to the debt.

(2) In any other winding-up the Liquidator may require a debt to be proved by delivering or sending to him through the post in a pre-paid letter either an unsworn claim to the debt or an affidavit verifying the debt, as he may direct."

7. In rules 93, 94 and 95 for the words "An affidavit proving a" there shall be substituted the words "A proof of".

8. In rule 179 for the words "the last audit of" there shall be substituted the words "he last filed".

9. In the Appendix after Form 59 there shall be inserted new Form 59A as set out in the Schedule to these Rules.

Dated 27th July 1977.

Elwyn-Jones, C.

I concur,
Dated 5th August 1977.

Edmund Dell,

Secretary of State
for Trade.

SCHEDULE

Rule 9

No. 59A (Rule 94)

PROOF OF DEBT (UNSWORN) GENERAL FORM

(*Title*)

Date of Winding-up Order

Name of Creditor	
Address of Creditor	
Total Amount of Claim as at Date of Winding-up Order	£
Particulars of how Debt(s) arose and Date(s) incurred (use space overleaf if necessary)	
Particulars of any Security held	
Value of Security	£

Please attach any documentary evidence of claim.	Signature of creditor or person signing on his behalf
N.B.—Bills or other negotiable securities must be produced before the proof can be admitted.	Name in block letters
	Position with or relationship to creditor

Admitted to vote for	Admitted to rank for dividend for
£	£
the day of 19 .	this day of 19
Official Receiver	Liquidator

EXPLANATORY NOTE

(This Note is not part of the Rules.)

These Rules amend the Companies (Winding-up) Rules 1949—

(i) by applying them to applications made under section 9 of the Insolvency Act 1976 for the disqualification of directors of insolvent companies (rules 3, 4 and 5);

(ii) by making provision for unsworn proofs of debt in a winding-up by the court (rules 6, 7 and 9); and

(iii) in consequence of the coming into force of section 2 of the Insolvency Act 1976, whereunder not all filed accounts need be subject to audit (rule 8).

STATUTORY INSTRUMENTS

1977 No. 1397

SHOPS AND OFFICES

The Airports Shops Order 1977

Made - - - -	*9th August* 1977
Coming into Operation	1*st October* 1977

Whereas it appears to the Secretary of State that the airports specified in Schedule 1 hereto are airports at which there is a substantial amount of international passenger traffic:

Now therefore the Secretary of State, in exercise of powers conferred by section 1(2) of the Shops (Airports) Act 1962(a), and now vested in him (b), and of all other powers enabling him in that behalf, hereby makes the following Order:

1. This Order may be cited as the Airports Shops Order 1977 and shall come into operation on 1st October 1977.

2. The Interpretation Act 1889(c) shall apply for the interpretation of this Order as it applies for the interpretation of an Act of Parliament and as if this Order and the Orders hereby revoked were Acts of Parliament.

3. The airports specified in Schedule 1 hereto are hereby designated for the purposes of the Shops (Airports) Act 1962 as being airports at which there appears to the Secretary of State to be a substantial amount of international passenger traffic.

4. The Orders specified in Schedule 2 hereto are hereby revoked.

N. F. Ledsome,
An Assistant Secretary,
9th August 1977.   Department of Trade.

(a) 1962 c. 35.   (b) *See* S.I. 1970/1537 (1970 III, p. 5293).   (c) 1889 c. 63.

SCHEDULE 1

Aberdeen	London—Heathrow
Birmingham	Manchester International
Edinburgh	Prestwick
Glasgow	Southend
Liverpool	London—Stansted
London—Gatwick	

SCHEDULE 2

ORDERS REVOKED

Order	Reference
The London (Heathrow) Airport Shops Order 1962	S.I. 1962/2159
The London (Gatwick) Airport Shops Order 1962	S.I. 1962/2160
The Manchester Airport Shops Order 1962	S.I. 1962/2161
The Prestwick Airport Shops Order 1962	S.I. 1962/2162
The Liverpool Airport Shops Order 1963	S.I. 1963/301
The Birmingham Airport Shops Order 1963	S.I. 1963/398
The Stansted Airport Shops Order 1963	S.I. 1963/1418
The Southend Airport Shops Order 1964	S.I. 1964/5
The Glasgow Airport Shops Order 1966	S.I. 1966/963
The Edinburgh Airport Shops Order 1974	S.I. 1974/1124

EXPLANATORY NOTE

(This Note is not part of the Order.)

The Shops (Airports) Act 1962 exempts traders at airports designated for the purposes of the Act as being airports at which there appears to the Secretary of State to be a substantial amount of international passenger traffic from the provisions of Part I of the Shops Act 1950 (1950 c. 28), which relate to hours of closing, at any shop in such airport which is situated in a part of the airport to which the Act applies. By this Order the Secretary of State designates Aberdeen Airport as such an airport and revokes and consolidates the various Orders which have been made under the section designating such airports.

STATUTORY INSTRUMENTS

1977 No. 1399

MEDICINES

The Medicines (Certificates of Analysis) Regulations 1977

Made - - - -	10*th August* 1977
Laid before Parliament	22*nd August* 1977
Coming into Operation	12*th September* 1977

The Secretaries of State respectively concerned with health in England and in Wales, the Secretary of State concerned with health and with agriculture in Scotland, the Minister of Agriculture, Fisheries and Food, the Department of Health and Social Services for Northern Ireland and the Department of Agriculture for Northern Ireland, acting jointly, in exercise of powers conferred by subsection (9) of section 112 and subsection (7) of section 115 of, and paragraphs 19(3) and 20(1) and (2) of Schedule 3 to, the Medicines Act 1968(a) and now vested in them(b) and of all other powers enabling them in that behalf, after consulting such organisations as appear to them to be representative of interests likely to be substantially affected by the following regulations, hereby make the following regulations:—

Citation, commencement and interpretation

1.—(1) These regulations may be cited as the Medicines (Certificates of Analysis) Regulations 1977 and shall come into operation on 12th September 1977.

(2) In these regulations, unless the context otherwise requires, "the Act" means the Medicines Act 1968 and other expressions have the same meanings as in the Act.

(3) Except in so far as the context otherwise requires, any reference in these regulations to any provision of any enactment or instrument shall be construed as a reference to that provision as amended or extended by any enactment or instrument and as including a reference to any provision which may re-enact or replace it.

(4) The rules for the construction of Acts of Parliament contained in the Interpretation Act 1889(c) shall apply for the purposes of the interpretation of these regulations as they apply for the purposes of the interpretation of an Act of Parliament.

Revocation

2. The Medicines (Certificates of Analysis) Regulations 1976(d) are hereby revoked.

(a) 1968 c. 67.

(b) In the case of the Secretaries of State concerned with health in England and in Wales by virtue of Article 2(2) of, and Schedule 1 to, the Transfer of Functions (Wales) Order 1969 (S.I. 1969/388) 1969 I, p. 1070)),and in the case of the Northern Ireland Departments by virtue of section 40 of, and Schedule 5 to, the Northern Ireland Constitution Act 1973 (c. 36), and section 1(3) of, and paragraph 2(1)(b) of Schedule 1 to, the Northern Ireland Act 1974 (c. 28).

(c) 1889 c. 63.

(d) S.I. 1976/1970 (1976 III, p. 5241).

Form of certificates of analysis or examination

3.—(1) Every certificate of analysis issued under section 115(6) of the Act shall be in the form set out in Part I of the Schedule to these regulations.

(2) Every certificate of analysis issued under paragraph 19(1) of Schedule 3 to the Act shall be in the form set out in Part II of the Schedule to these regulations.

(3) Every certificate of analysis or examination issued under paragraph 19(2) of Schedule 3 to the Act shall be in the form set out in Part III of the Schedule to these regulations.

Fees

4. For the purposes of paragraph 20 of Schedule 3 to the Act the prescribed fee shall be 5 pence.

David Ennals,
Secretary of State for Social Services.

1st August 1977.

S. B. Jones,
Parliamentary Under-Secretary of State for Wales.

2nd August 1977.

Bruce Millan,
Secretary of State for Scotland.

3rd August 1977.

In witness whereof the official seal of the Minister of Agriculture, Fisheries and Food is hereunto affixed on 9th August 1977.

(L.S.)

John Silkin,
Minister of Agriculture, Fisheries and Food.

Sealed with the official seal of the Department of Health and Social Services for Northern Ireland this 10th day of August 1977.

(L.S.)

J. H. Copeland,
Deputy Secretary.

Sealed with the official seal of the Department of Agriculture for Northern Ireland this 10th day of August 1977.

(L.S.)

W. H. Jack,
Deputy Secretary.

SCHEDULE   Regulation 3

FORMS OF CERTIFICATE OF ANALYSIS OR EXAMINATION

PART I

CERTIFICATE OF ANALYSIS OF SAMPLE

This certificate is issued under section 115(6) of the Medicines Act 1968 by me, the undersigned, public analyst for the [1]

I hereby certify that I received on the   day of   19 , from [2]
                                               , *[to whom the sample had been
submitted by [3]   ,] one part of a sample of [4]
                    for analysis; which was undamaged, duly sealed and
fastened up and marked [5]   ; and
that the said part has been analysed by me or under my direction. I further certify
the results of analysis to be as follows:— [6]

and I am of the opinion that [7]

     day of   19 .

                              (Signature and address of analyst)

* Delete words in square brackets if not required.

_____

NOTES

These notes and the numbers referring to them are for guidance only and do not form part of and need not appear on the certificate.

(1) Here insert the name of the local authority.

(2) Here insert, as appropriate, the name of the person who submitted the sample for analysis or the name of the public analyst to whom the sample was originally submitted.

(3) Here insert the name of the person who originally submitted the sample for analysis.

(4) Here insert the name or description of the substance or article.

(5) Here insert the distinguishing mark on the sample and the date of sampling shown thereon.

(6) Here insert relevant results as appropriate, eg physical characteristics, impurities microbial or chemical, cross-contamination with other medicines, uniformity of dosage, conformance with specification or label claims.

(7) Here enter whether the sample complies with the appropriate monograph standard (if any), or other appropriate interpretation of the results.

PART II

CERTIFICATE OF ANALYSIS OF SAMPLE

This certificate is issued under paragraph 19(1) of Schedule 3 to the Medicines Act 1968 by me, the undersigned, public analyst for the [1]

I hereby certify that I received on the   day of   19 , from [2]
, *[to whom the sample had been
submitted by [3]   ,] one part of a sample of [4]
for analysis; which was undamaged, duly sealed and
fastened up and marked [5]   ; and
that the said part has been analysed by me or under my direction. I further certify
the results of analysis to be as follows:— [6]

and I am of the opinion that [7]

day of   19 .

(Signature and address of analyst)

* Delete words in square brackets if not required.

NOTES

These notes and the numbers referring to them are for guidance only and do not form part of and need not appear on the certificate.

(1) Here insert the name of the local authority.

(2) Here insert the name of the sampling officer who submitted the sample for analysis, or the name of the public analyst to whom the sample was originally submitted.

(3) Here insert the name of the sampling officer who submitted the sample for analysis.

(4) Here insert the name or description of the substance or article.

(5) Here insert the distinguishing mark on the sample and the date of sampling shown thereon.

(6) Here insert relevant results as appropriate, eg physical characteristics, impurities microbial or chemical, cross-contamination with other medicines, uniformity of dosage, conformance with specifications or label claims.

(7) Here enter whether the sample complies with the appropriate monograph standard (if any), or other appropriate interpretation of the results.

PART III

CERTIFICATE OF ANALYSIS OR EXAMINATION OF SAMPLE

This certificate is issued under paragraph 19(2) of Schedule 3 to the Medicines Act 1968 by me, the undersigned, *[having the management or control] [being a person appointed for the purpose of issuing this certificate by [1] ,
the person having the management or control] of the [2]
with which arrangements have been made in pursuance of the provisions of the Medicines Act 1968. I hereby certify that *[I] [the said [1]]
received on the   day of   19 , from [3]
one part of a sample of [4]   for *[analysis]
[examination]; which was undamaged, duly sealed and fastened up and marked [5]
     and that the said part has been *[analysed]
[examined] *[by me] [by the said [1]] [under the direction
of the said [1]]. I further certify the results of *[analysis]
[examination] to be as follows:— [6]

and I am of the opinion that [7]

     day of   19 .

(Signature and address of the person
who issues the certificate)

* Delete words in square brackets as necessary.

NOTES

These notes and the numbers referring to them are for guidance only and do not form part of and need not appear on the certificate.

(1) Here insert the name of the person having the management or control of the laboratory.

(2) Here insert the name of the laboratory.

(3) Here insert the name of the sampling officer who submitted the sample.

(4) Here insert the name or description of the substance or article.

(5) Here insert the distinguishing mark on the sample and the date of sampling shown thereon.

(6) Here insert relevant results as appropriate, eg physical characteristics, impurities microbial or chemical, cross-contamination with other medicines, uniformity of dosage, conformance with specification or label claims.

(7) Here enter whether the sample complies with the appropriate monograph standard (if any), or other appropriate interpretation of the results.

EXPLANATORY NOTE

(This Note is not part of the Regulations.)

These Regulations revoke the Medicines (Certificates of Analysis) Regulations 1976. They prescribe fresh forms of certificates of analysis and examination of samples by public analysts and certain other persons in accordance with provisions in section 115 of, and Schedule 3 to, the Medicines Act 1968. These Regulations re-enact the provision as to fees contained in the Regulations now revoked.

STATUTORY INSTRUMENTS

1977 No. 1400

MERCHANDISE MARKS

The Motor Vehicles (Designation of Approval Marks) (Amendment) Regulations 1977

Made	- - -	*8th August* 1977
Laid before Parliament		*22nd August* 1977
Coming into Operation		*1st October* 1977

The Secretary of State for Transport, in exercise of his powers under section 63(1) of the Road Traffic Act 1972(a), as amended by the Designation of Approval Marks (European Communities) Regulations 1973(b), and of all other enabling powers, and after consultation with representative organisations in accordance with the provisions of section 199(2) of that Act, hereby makes the following Regulations:—

1. These Regulations shall come into operation on 1st October 1977, and may be cited as the Motor Vehicles (Designation of Approval Marks) (Amendment) Regulations 1977.

2. The Motor Vehicles (Designation of Approval Marks) Regulations 1976(c) shall be amended so as to have effect in accordance with the following provisions of these Regulations.

3. In Schedule 2—

(*a*) in column 5(*b*) at item 42, for the words "11th March 1970" there shall be substituted the words "14th August 1970 for the Regulation and 22nd April 1971 for the Corrigendum";

(*b*) after items 39, 41, 48, 49, 50, 51, 52, 53 and 54 there shall be inserted respectively items 39A, 41A, 48A, 49A, 50A, 51A, 52A, 53A and 54A in Schedule 1 to these Regulations; and

(*c*) in column 3 at item 53, for the words "with a filament lamp" there shall be substituted the words "with a halogen filament lamp".

4. In Schedule 3, in paragraph 6, for the words "relating to the items numbered 25, 27, 29, 34, 48, 49, 50, 54, 66, 67 and 70 in Schedule 2" there shall be substituted the words "relating to the items numbered 25, 27, 29, 34, 48, 48A, 49, 49A, 50, 50A, 54, 54A, 66, 67 and 70 in Schedule 2".

(a) 1972 c. 20.
(c) S.I. 1976/2226 (1976 III, p. 6233).

(b) S.I. 1973/1193 (1973 II, p. 3571).

5. For Schedule 4 there shall be substituted the new Schedule 4 specified in Schedule 2 to these Regulations.

6. In Schedule 5—
(a) in paragraph 3, for the words "item No. 2" there shall be substituted the words "items No. 2 and 4"; and

(b) after paragraph 4 there shall be added the following paragraphs:—

"5. The arrow shown outside and immediately below the rectangle in the markings relating to item Nos. 5 and 8 in Schedule 4 indicate the side on which the photometric specifications are satisfied up to an angle of 80°H on front position (side) lamps or rear position (side) lamps whose geometric angles of visibility are asymmetrical in relation to the reference axis in a horizontal direction. The absence of an arrow means that, both left and right, the photometric specifications are satisfied up to an angle of 80°H on such lamps.

6. The absence of an arrow immediately below the rectangle in the marking relating to item No. 6 in Schedule 4 indicates that, both left and right, the photometric specifications are satisfied up to an angle of 80°H on rear position (side) lamps whose geometric angles of visibility are asymmetrical in relation to the reference axis in a horizontal direction. In cases where such lamps satisfy the said specifications up to an angle of 80°H only to the left or only to the right an arrow indicating the side to which the said specifications are so satisfied shall be added immediately below the rectangle in the said marking.

7. The number shown outside and immediately above the rectangle in the marking relating to item 9 in Schedule 4 will be varied, where appropriate, to be the numbers 1 or 2 where the direction indicator to which the marking relates belongs to category 1 or category 2, as the case may be, specified in the Community Instrument referred to in column (5) in relation to that item. The arrow shown outside and immediately below the said rectangle indicates in what position such of the direction indicators to which the said marking relates as can be mounted on one side of the vehicle shall be placed. The arrow shall be directed outwards from the vehicle in the case of a direction indicator in category 1 or category 2 specified in the said Community Instrument, and towards the front of the vehicle in the case of a direction indicator in category 5 specified in the said Community Instrument.".

8th August 1977.

William Rodgers,
Secretary of State for Transport.

SCHEDULE 1

(1) Item number	(2) Diagram showing marking	(3) Motor vehicle or motor vehicle part to which the marking relates	(4) Place where the marking is applied	(5) ECE Regulation		(6) Paragraphs in Schedule 3 relating to requirements or variations with respect to the markings
				(a) Number	(b) Date of ECE Regulation or of ECE Regulation as amended in respect of the marking requirements	
39A	(E11) 14	Motor vehicle approved in respect of the safety-belt anchorages.	The vehicle	14	(as amended) 19th August 1976	1 and 2
41A	(E11) 15–022439	Motor vehicle with a spark-ignition engine approved in respect of the emission of gaseous pollutants by the engine.	The vehicle	15	(as amended) 1st March 1977	1
48A	HCR (E11) 30 2439	Halogen (H_4) headlamp emitting both a driving beam and an asymmetrical passing beam and fitted with a halogen filament lamp (H_4) designed for right-hand traffic only.	The headlamp	20	(as amended) 1st September 1976	1, 2 and 6
49A	HCR (E11) 30 ↑ 2439	Halogen (H_4) headlamp emitting both a driving beam and an asymmetrical passing beam and fitted with a halogen filament lamp (H_4) designed for left-hand traffic only.	The headlamp	20	(as amended) 1st September 1976	1, 2 and 6

(1) Item number	(2) Diagram showing marking	(3) Motor vehicle or motor vehicle part to which the marking relates	(4) Place where the marking is applied	(5) ECE Regulation		(6) Paragraphs in Schedule 3 relating to requirements or variations with respect to the markings
				(a) Number	(b) Date of ECE Regulation, or of ECE Regulation as amended in respect of the marking requirements	
50A	HCR $\begin{array}{c}\text{E}11\end{array}$ 30 $\updownarrow$ 2439	Halogen (H$_4$) headlamp emitting both a driving beam and an asymmetrical passing beam and fitted with a halogen filament lamp (H$_4$) designed for left- or right-hand traffic.	The headlamp	20	(as amended) 1st September 1976	1, 2 and 6
51A	HC $\begin{array}{c}\text{E}11\end{array}$ $\updownarrow$ 2439	Headlamp emitting an asymmetrical passing beam and fitted with a halogen filament lamp (H$_4$) designed for left- or right-hand traffic.	The headlamp	20	(as amended) 1st September 1976	1 and 2
52A	HC $\begin{array}{c}\text{E}11\end{array}$ 2439	Headlamp emitting an asymmetrical passing beam and fitted with a halogen filament lamp (H$_4$) designed for right-hand traffic only.	The headlamp	20	(as amended) 1st September 1976	1 and 2
53A	HC $\begin{array}{c}\text{E}11\end{array}$ $\uparrow$ 2439	Headlamp emitting an asymmetrical passing beam and fitted with a halogen filament lamp (H$_4$) designed for left-hand traffic only.	The headlamp	20	(as amended) 1st September 1976	1 and 2

| 54A | HR (E 11) 30 2439 | Headlamp emitting a driving beam and fitted with a halogen filament lamp (H_4). | The headlamp | 20 (as amended) 1st September 1976 | 1, 2 and 6 |

SCHEDULE 2
"SCHEDULE 4"

APPROVAL MARKS REQUIRED BY COMMUNITY INSTRUMENTS—LIST

(1) Item number	(2) Diagram showing marking	(3) Motor vehicle part to which the marking relates	(4) Place where the marking is applied	(5) Community Instrument		(6) Paragraphs in Schedule 5 relating to requirements or variations with respect to the marking
				(a) Description	(b) Official Journal reference	
1	e11 1479	Audible warning device.	The audible warning device	Council Directive 70/388/EEC of 27th July 1970	O.J. L176, 10.8.70, p. 12 (S.E. 1970 (II), p. 571)	1 and 2
2	e11 1471	Rear-view mirror.	The rear-view mirror	Council Directive 71/127/EEC of 1st March 1971	O.J. L68, 22.3.71, p. 1 (S.E. 1971 (I), p. 136)	1, 2, 3 and 4

(1) Item number	(2) Diagram showing marking	(3) Motor vehicle part to which the marking relates	(4) Place where the marking is applied	(5) Community Instrument		(6) Paragraphs in Schedule 5 relating to requirements or variations with respect to the marking
				(a) Description	(b) Official Journal reference	
3	e 11 1471	Road transport recording equipment and the model record sheet.	The road transport recording equipment and the model record sheet	Council Regulation (EEC) No. 1463/70 of 20th July 1970	O.J. L164, 22.7.70, p. 102	1 and 2
4	e 11 1471	Reflex reflector.	The reflex reflector	Council Directive 76/757/EEC of 27th July 1976	O.J. L262, 27.9.76, p. 32	1, 2, 3 and 4
5	A e 11 1471	Front position (side) lamp.	The lamp	Council Directive 76/758/EEC of 27th July 1976	O.J. L262, 27.9.76, p. 54	1, 2 and 5
6	R e 11 1471	Rear position (side) lamp.	The lamp	Council Directive 76/758/EEC of 27th July 1976	O.J. L262, 27.9.76, p. 54	1, 2 and 6

No.	Marking	Description	Name	Council Directive	O.J. Reference	Numbers
7	S e11 1471	Stop lamp.	The lamp	Council Directive 76/758/EEC of 27th July 1976	O.J. L262, 27.9.76, p. 54	1 and 2
8	R-S e11 ↑1471	Both rear position (side) lamp and stop lamp.	The lamps	Council Directive 76/758/EEC of 27th July 1976	O.J. L262, 27.9.76, p. 54	1, 2 and 5
9	5 e11 ↑1471	Direction indicator for motor vehicles (except motor cycles) and their trailers.	The direction indicator	Council Directive 76/759/EEC of 27th July 1976	O.J. L262, 27.9.76, p. 71	1, 2 and 7
10	e11 1471	Device for the illumination of rear registration plates of motor vehicles (except motor cycles) and their trailers.	The device	Council Directive 76/760/EEC of 27th July 1976	O.J. L262, 27.9.76, p. 85	1 and 2
11	CR e11 1471	Headlamp emitting both a dipped beam and a main beam and designed for right-hand traffic only.	The headlamp	Council Directive 76/761/EEC of 27th July 1976	O.J. L262, 27.9.76, p. 96	1 and 2
12	CR e11 ↑1471	Headlamp emitting both a dipped beam and a main beam and designed for left-hand traffic only.	The headlamp	Council Directive 76/761/EEC of 27th July 1976	O.J. L262, 27.9.76, p. 96	1 and 2

(1) Item number	(2) Diagram showing marking	(3) Motor vehicle part to which the marking relates	(4) Place where the marking is applied	(5) Community Instrument (a) Description	(5) Community Instrument (b) Official Journal reference	(6) Paragraphs in Schedule 5 relating to requirements or variations with respect to the marking
13	CR e11 ↕ 1471	Headlamp emitting both a dipped beam and a main beam and designed for both left-hand traffic and right-hand traffic.	The headlamp	Council Directive 76/761/ EEC of 27th July 1976	O.J. L262, 27.9.76, p. 96	1 and 2
14	C e11 ↕ 1471	Headlamp emitting a dipped beam only and designed for both left-hand traffic and right-hand traffic.	The headlamp	Council Directive 76/761/ EEC of 27th July 1976	O.J. L262, 27.9.76, p. 96	1 and 2
15	C e11 1471	Headlamp emitting a dipped beam only and designed for right-hand traffic only.	The headlamp	Council Directive 76/761/ EEC of 27th July 1976	O.J. L262, 27.9.76, p. 96	1 and 2
16	C e11 ↑ 1471	Headlamp emitting a dipped beam only and designed for left-hand traffic only.	The headlamp	Council Directive 76/761/ EEC of 27th July 1976	O.J. L262, 27.9.76, p. 96	1 and 2

17	R e11 1471	Headlamp emitting a main beam only.	The headlamp'	Council Directive 76/761/ EEC of 27th July 1976	O.J. L262, 27.9.76, p. 96	1 and 2
18	e11 1471	Filament lamp for a headlamp emitting either a dipped beam only, or a main beam only, or both a dipped beam and a main beam.	The filament lamp	Council Directive 76/761/ EEC of 27th July 1976	O.J. L262, 27.9.76, p. 96	1 and 2
19	B e11 1471	Front fog lamp.	The lamp	Council Directive 76/762/ EEC of 27th July 1976	O.J. L262, 27.9.76, p. 122	1 and 2"

EXPLANATORY NOTE

(This Note is not part of the Regulations.)

These Regulations amend the Motor Vehicles (Designation of Approval Marks) Regulations 1976—

(1) by correcting minor errors in Schedule 2 (Regulation 3(*a*) and (*c*));

(2) by adding to the markings which are designated as approval marks by virtue of Regulation 4 of the Regulations of 1976 (Regulation 3(*b*)) and by making an amendment to Schedule 3 of those Regulations as a result of that addition (Regulation 4);

(3) by substituting a new Schedule 4 to the Regulations of 1976 which contains new markings which are designated as approval marks by virtue of Regulation 5 of those Regulations (Regulation 5); and

(4) by adding to the requirements or permitted variations specified in Schedule 5 to the Regulations of 1976 (Regulation 6).

Copies of the ECE Regulations referred to in the Regulations of 1976 and in these amending Regulations, may be obtained from Her Majesty's Stationery Office.

STATUTORY INSTRUMENTS

1977 No. 1401

ROAD TRAFFIC

The Motor Vehicles (Construction and Use) (Amendment) (No. 6) Regulations 1977

Made - - - -	*8th August* 1977	
Laid before Parliament	*22nd August* 1977	
Coming into Operation	*1st October* 1977	

The Secretary of State for Transport, in exercise of his powers under section 40(1) and (3) of the Road Traffic Act 1972(a) and of all other enabling powers, and after consultation with representative organisations in accordance with the provisions of section 199(2) of that Act, hereby makes the following Regulations:

1. These Regulations shall come into operation on 1st October 1977, and may be cited as the Motor Vehicles (Construction and Use) (Amendment) (No. 6) Regulations 1977.

2. The Motor Vehicles (Construction and Use) Regulations 1973(b), as amended (c), shall be further amended so as to have effect in accordance with the following provisions of these Regulations.

3. In Regulation 4A, in the Table—

(*a*) after item 7A there shall be inserted the following item—

"7B	Council Directive 70/157/EEC of 6th February 1970 (relating to the permissible sound level and exhaust system of motor vehicles) as amended by Commission Directive 73/350/EEC of 7th November 1973 and by Commission Directive 77/212/EEC of 8th March 1977(d).	1st July 1977		29
				", and

(*b*) after item 9A there shall be inserted the following item—

"9B	Council Directive 70/220/EEC of 20th March 1970 (relating to the measures to be taken against air pollution by gasses from spark-ignition engines of motor vehicles) as amended by Council Directive 74/290/EEC of 28thMay 1974 and by Council Directive 77/102/EEC of 30th November 1976(e).	1st April 1977		33A
				" .

(a) 1972 c. 20.   (b) S.I. 1973/24 (1973 I, p. 93).
(c) The relevant amending Instruments are S.I. 1976/528, 1507 (1976 I, p. 1558; III, p. 4010).
(d) O.J. L66, 12.3.1977, p. 33.   (e) O.J. L32, 3.2.1977, p. 32.

4. In Regulation 17 (Seat belts and anchorage points), in paragraph (8)—

(a) in sub-paragraph (a), for the words "Every motor car" there shall be substituted the words "Except as provided in sub-paragraph (cc) of this paragraph, every motor car";

(b) in sub-paragraph (b), for the words "Where in the case of " there shall be substituted the words "Except as provided in sub-paragraph (cc) of this paragraph, where in the case of";

(c) in sub-paragraph (c), for the words "If any seat" there shall be substituted the words "Except as provided in sub-paragraph (cc) of this paragraph, if any seat"; and

(d) after sub-paragraph (c) there shall be inserted the following sub-paragraph:—

"(cc) The requirements of sub-paragraphs (a), (b) and (c) of this paragraph shall not apply to a motor vehicle to which there is affixed the marking designated as an approval mark by Regulation 4 of the Motor Vehicles (Designation of Approval Marks) Regulations 1976(a) as amended (b) and shown in column 2 at item 39A of Schedule 2 to those Regulations (such marking indicating that the vehicle has been approved in respect of the safety-belt anchorages).".

William Rodgers,
Secretary of State for Transport.

8th August 1977.

EXPLANATORY NOTE

(This Note is not part of the Regulations.)

These Regulations further amend the Motor Vehicles (Construction and Use) Regulations 1973 so as—

(1) to amend, as a result of further Community Directives, the type approval requirements to which a motor vehicle must conform in order to gain exemption from the requirements of—

(a) Regulation 29 (which deals with certain construction requirements relating to noise), and

(b) Regulation 33A (which deals with the marking of certain vehicles propelled by a spark-ignition engine): and

(2) to exempt from certain requirements relating to seat belt anchorages motor vehicles to which there is affixed a marking designated as an approval mark by the Motor Vehicles (Designation of Approval Marks) Regulations 1976 (such marking indicating that the vehicle has been approved in respect of the safety belt anchorages).

(a) S.I. 1976/2226 (1976 III, p. 6233).   (b) S.I. 1977/1400 (1977 II, p. 4181).

STATUTORY INSTRUMENTS

1977 No. 1402

ROAD TRAFFIC

The Motor Vehicles (Type Approval) (Amendment) Regulations 1977

Made - - - -	8th August 1977
Laid before Parliament	22nd August 1977
Coming into Operation	1st October 1977

The Secretary of State for Transport, being a Minister designated (a) for the purposes of section 2(2) of the European Communities Act 1972(b) in relation to the regulation of the type, description, construction or equipment of vehicles, and of components of vehicles, and in particular any vehicle type approval scheme, in exercise of the powers conferred on him by the said section 2(2) and of all other enabling powers, hereby makes the following Regulations:—

1. These Regulations may be cited as the Motor Vehicles (Type Approval) (Amendment) Regulations 1977 and shall come into operation on 1st October 1977.

2. The Motor Vehicles (Type Approval) Regulations 1973(c) as amended (d) shall have effect in accordance with the following provisions of these Regulations.

3. In Part I of Schedule 2—

(a) for item 1 there shall be substituted the following item:—

"1A	70/157/EEC	6th February 1970	O.J. L42, 23.2.1970, p.16 (S.E. 1970 (I), p. 111)	The permissible sound level and the exhaust system of motor vehicles.
	as amended by 73/350/EEC	7th November 1973	O.J. L321, 22.11.1973, p. 33	
	as amended by 77/212/EEC	8th March 1977	O.J. L66, 12.3.1977, p. 33	";

(a) S.I. 1972/1811 (1972 III, p. 5216).   (b) 1972 c. 68.
(c) S.I. 1973/1199 (1973 II, p. 3610).
(d) The relevant amending Instruments are S.I. 1976/316, 1890 (1976 I, p. 852; III, p. 5061).

(*b*) for item 2 there shall be substituted the following item:—

"2	70/220/EEC	20th March 1970	O.J. L76, 6.4.1970, p. 1 (S.E. 1970 (I), p. 171)	Measures to be taken against air pollution by gases from positive ignition engines of motor vehicles.
	as amended by 74/290/EEC	28th May 1974	O.J. L159, 15.6.1974, p. 61	
	as amended by 77/102/EEC	30th November 1976	O.J. L32, 3.2.1977, p. 32	";

(*c*) after item 19 there shall be added the following items:—

"20	76/756/EEC	27th July 1976	O.J. L262, 27.9.1976, p. 1	Installation of lighting and light signalling devices.
21	76/757/EEC	27th July 1976	O.J. L262, 27.9.1976, p. 32	Reflex reflectors.
22	76/758/EEC	27th July 1976	O.J. L262, 27.9.1976, p. 54	End-outline marker lamps, front position (side) lamps, rear position (side) lamps and stop lamps.
23	76/759/EEC	27th July 1976	O.J. L262, 27.9.1976, p. 71	Direction indicator lamps
24	76/760/EEC	27th July 1976	O.J. L262, 27.9.1976, p. 85	Rear registration plate lamps.
25	76/761/EEC	27th July 1976	O.J. L262, 27.9.1976, p. 96	Headlamps which function as main beam and/or dipped beam headlamps and incandescent electric filament lamps for such headlamps.
26	76/762/EEC	27th July 1976	O.J. L262, 27.9.1976, p. 122	Front fog amps.
27	77/389/EEC	17th May 1977	O.J. L145, 13.6.1977, p. 41	Towing devices.".

William Rodgers,
Secretary of State for Transport.

8th August 1977.

EXPLANATORY NOTE

(This Note is not part of the Regulations.)

1. These Regulations amend the Motor Vehicles (Type Approval) Regulations 1973 (which provide for the type approval of certain motor vehicles and trailers and their components which conform to the requirements of certain Community Directives with respect to design, construction, equipment and marking of vehicles and their components, being the Directives specified in Part I of Schedule 2 to those Regulations).

2. These amendments extend the provisions of the Regulations of 1973 as a result of further Community Directives which are specified in these Regulations.

STATUTORY INSTRUMENTS

1977 No. 1403 (C. 49)

SOCIAL SECURITY

The Social Security Pensions Act 1975 (Commencement No. 9) Order 1977

Made - - -	*12th August* 1977
Laid before Parliament	*16th August* 1977
Coming into Operation	*6th September* 1977

The Secretary of State for Social Services, in exercise of the powers conferred upon him by section 67(1), (2) and (3) of the Social Security Pensions Act 1975(a) and of all other powers enabling him in that behalf, hereby makes the following order:—

Citation and commencement

1. This Order may be cited as the Social Security Pensions Act 1975 (Commencement No. 9) Order 1977 and shall come into operation on 6th September 1977.

Appointed days

2. The dates appointed for the coming into force of section 22 of the Social Security Pensions Act 1975, of section 65(1) of that Act as it relates to paragraphs 47, 49 and 51 to 53 of Schedule 4 to that Act and of those paragraphs in the case of a person born before 25th August 1923 who is a vehicle scheme beneficiary as defined in regulation 1(2) of the Mobility Allowance (Vehicle Scheme Beneficiaries) Regulations 1977(b) shall be—

(*a*) if on or after 1st August 1977 that person is receiving payments in pursuance of section 33 of the Health Services and Public Health Act 1968 (c) in respect of a vehicle belonging to him—

    (i) 5th April 1978 for the purposes of the making of claims for, and the determination of claims and questions relating to, mobility allowance; and

    (ii) 5th July 1978 for all other purposes relating to mobility allowance;

(*b*) if that person is not one to whom paragraph (*a*) above applies but his surname begins with any of the letters from A to K in the alphabet, 6th September 1977 for the purposes referred to in paragraph (*a*)(i) above and 16th November 1977 for the purposes referred to in paragraph (*a*)(ii) above; and

---

(a) 1975 c. 60.   (b) 1977/1229 (1977 II, p. 3418).   (c) 1968 c. 46.

(c) if that person is not one to whom paragraph (a) above applies but his surname begins with any of the letters from L to Z in the alphabet, 16th November 1977 for the purposes referred to in paragraph (a)(i) above and 15th February 1978 for the purposes referred to in paragraph (a)(ii) above.

Signed by authority of the Secretary of State for Social Services.

Eric Deakins,
Parliamentary Under-Secretary of State,
Department of Health and Social Security.

12th August 1977.

EXPLANATORY NOTE

(This Note is not part of the Order.)

This Order brings into force provisions of the Social Security Pensions Act 1975 relating to mobility allowance in relation to vehicle scheme beneficiaries within the meaning of the Mobility Allowance (Vehicle Scheme Beneficiaries) Regulations 1977.

STATUTORY INSTRUMENTS

1977 No. 1404

CUSTOMS AND EXCISE

The Customs Duties and Agricultural Levies (Goods for Free Circulation) Regulations 1977

Made - - - -	12th August 1977
Laid before Parliament	22nd August 1977
Coming into Operation	12th September 1977

The Commissioners of Customs and Excise, in pursuance of the powers conferred upon them by section 10 of the Finance Act 1977 (a) and of all other powers enabling them in that behalf, hereby make the following Regulations:—

1. These Regulations may be cited as the Customs Duties and Agricultural Levies (Goods for Free Circulation) Regulations 1977. They shall come into operation on 12th September 1977 and have effect in relation to goods imported into the United Kingdom on or after 1st July 1977.

2.—(1) In these Regulations—

"Community transit external procedure" means the procedure for external Community transit laid down by Regulation (EEC) 222/77 (b);

"outside the Community" means outside the Customs territory of the European Economic Community (c), or in the case of goods covered by the ECSC Treaty or the Euratom Treaty, outside the territories to which the Treaty constituting the Community in question applies (d), as the case may be.

(2) The Interpretation Act 1889 (e) shall apply for the interpretation of these Regulations as it applies for the interpretation of an Act of Parliament.

3. These Regulations shall apply to goods not in free circulation and in respect of which inward processing relief had been granted by the competent authorities of another member State, and which were imported into the United Kingdom from that or another member State with a view to exportation outside the Community, whether or not any further processing was to take place in the United Kingdom, and which

(a) were entered in the United Kingdom for—

(i) inward processing, or

(a) 1977 c. 36.   (b) O.J. No. L38, 9.2.1977, p. 1.
(c) *See* Regulation (EEC) 1496/68 (O.J. No. L238, 28.9.68, p. 1 (O.J./SE 1968 (II), p. 436)), and Annex I to the Treaty concerning United Kingdom accession to the Community, as adjusted by Council Decision of 1.1.73 (O.J. No. L2, 1.1.73, p. 1).
(d) *See* Article 79 (ECSC Treaty) and 198 (Euratom Treaty).
(e) 1889 c. 63.

(ii) warehousing, or

(iii) transit or transhipment, or

(b) remained under the Community transit external procedure,

and which are subsequently allowed by the Commissioners to be put on the market in the United Kingdom or destroyed, or otherwise cease to be subject to special arrangements involving the suspension of, or the giving of relief from, customs duties or agricultural levies in another member State.

4. Duties of customs and levies shall be chargeable on goods to which these Regulations apply and the amounts thereof shall be calculated by reference to either—

(a) the duties and levies from which inward processing relief was granted in another member State; or

(b) in the case of goods specified in Regulation 3(a)(ii), (iii) and (b) and which are removed from warehouse in the United Kingdom or withdrawn from exportation, the rates applicable to those goods at the time they are put on the market or destroyed, provided that the Commissioners are satisfied that the amount thereof is at least equal to the amount ascertained in accordance with paragraph (a) hereof.

5. In the case of goods described in Regulation 3(a)(i) the provisions of the Inward Processing Relief Regulations 1977 **(a)** shall apply, except that for the basis of calculation set out in Regulation 5(2) of those Regulations and any references thereto there shall be substituted the basis set out in Regulation 4(a) of these Regulations.

6. Where at any time any goods to which these Regulations apply are not produced or accounted for to the Commissioners on request, duties of customs and levies in respect of the goods shall be payable in accordance with these Regulations as if they had been put on the market.

7. Notwithstanding the previous provisions of these Regulations, where goods to which these Regulations apply are destroyed with the permission of the Commissioners, or are in their opinion destroyed accidentally or by force majeure, and are deprived of all value, no duties of customs or levies shall be charged.

H. F. Christopherson,

Commissioner of Customs and Excise.

12th August 1977.

King's Beam House,
Mark Lane,
London EC3R 7HE.

(a) S.I. 1977/910 (1977 II, p. 2539).

EXPLANATORY NOTE

(This Note is not part of the Regulations.)

These Regulations come into operation on 12th September 1977. They apply to goods, not in free circulation in another member State, on which the customs duties and agricultural levies had been suspended under inward processing relief arrangements. When such goods are imported into the United Kingdom and are intended for exportation outside the Community, but instead of being exported are put on the market within the United Kingdom or destroyed, the suspended duty becomes payable in the United Kingdom.

The Regulations implement in United Kingdom law Articles 14, 15 and 16 of Council Directive No. 69/73/EEC on "the harmonisation of provisions laid down by law, regulation or administrative action in respect of inward processing" (O.J. No. L58, 8.3.69, p. 1 (O.J./SE 1969 (1) p. 75)) and Directive 73/95/EEC (O.J. No. L120, 7.5.73, p. 17) as last amended by Directive 75/681/EEC (O.J. No. L301, 20.11.75, p. 1).

Regulation 1 provides for the Regulations to apply to goods imported into the United Kingdom on or after 1st July 1977.

Regulation 2 defines terms used in these Regulations.

Regulation 3 sets out the goods to which the Regulations apply.

Regulation 4 is the charging provision and sets out the basis for calculating duties of customs and levies on the goods as *either* the duties or levies originally suspended in another member State, *or,* for goods entered for warehousing, or in transit or transhipment, the duties or levies applicable to those goods at the time of diversion to the market within the United Kingdom, provided that the amount thereof is at least equal to the suspended duties or levies.

Regulation 5 applies the provisions of the Inward Processing Relief Regulations 1977 to goods covered by these Regulations which are entered for inward processing in the United Kingdom with the modification that the basis for calculating the amount chargeable shall be the duties or levies relieved in another member State instead of the duties or levies relieved in the United Kingdom.

Regulation 6 provides that where the goods are not accounted for, duties and levies are payable as if they had been put on the market.

Regulation 7 enables the Commissioners to remit duties or levies when goods are destroyed with their permission, accidentally or by force majeure and have no value.

STATUTORY INSTRUMENTS

1977 No. 1405 (C. 50)

MAINTENANCE OF DEPENDANTS

The Administration of Justice Act 1977 (Commencement No. 1) Order 1977

Made -   -   -   -   11*th August* 1977

The Lord Chancellor, in exercise of the powers conferred on him by section 32(6) of the Administration of Justice Act 1977(a), hereby makes the following Order:—

1. This Order may be cited as the Administration of Justice Act 1977 (Commencement No. 1) Order 1977.

2. Section 3 of the Administration of Justice Act 1977 shall come into operation on 1st September 1977 for the purposes of paragraphs 11 and 12 of Schedule 3 to that Act only.

Dated 11th August 1977.

Elwyn-Jones, C.

EXPLANATORY NOTE

(*This Note is not part of the Order.*)

This Order brings into operation paragraphs 11 and 12 of Schedule 3 to the Administration of Justice Act 1977, which provide for the amendment of sections 15 and 16 of the Maintenance Orders Act 1950 relating respectively to the service of process in Scotland and Northern Ireland and the enforcement of awards in England and Wales of capital sums awarded on divorce in Scotland.

(a) 1977 c. 38.

STATUTORY INSTRUMENTS

1977 No. 1409

EDUCATION, ENGLAND AND WALES

The Local Education Authority Awards (Amendment) Regulations 1977

Made - - - -	*11th August* 1977
Laid before Parliament	*17th August* 1977
Coming into Operation	*1st September* 1977

The Secretary of State for Education and Science, in exercise of the powers conferred by sections 1 and 4(2) of the Education Act 1962(a) (as amended by section 1 of the Education ·Act 1975(b)) and vested in her(c), hereby makes the following Regulations:—

1. These Regulations may be cited as the Local Education Authority Awards (Amendment) Regulations 1977 and shall come into operation on 1st September 1977.

2.—(1) At the end of sub-paragraph (4) of paragraph 17 of Part 3 of Schedule 2 to the Local Education Authority Awards Regulations 1977(d) (persons holding statutory awards) there shall be added the words "and in this Part of this Schedule a spouse|who so holds a statutory award is referred to as an award holder."

(2) In sub-paragraph (5)(a) of the said paragraph 17 for the words "a dependent spouse nor such a dependant" there shall be substituted the words "such a dependant nor a spouse who is either a dependant or an award holder".

3.—(1) For sub-paragraph (4)(a) of paragraph 18 of the said Part 3 there shall be substituted the following provision:—

"(a) except where the student has a spouse who is an award holder, £480, and".

(2) In sub-paragraph (4)(b) of the said paragraph 18 for the words "a dependent spouse nor other adult dependant" there shall be substituted the words "an adult dependant nor a spouse who is either a dependant or an award holder".

Given under the Official Seal of the Secretary of State for Education and Science on 11th August 1977.

(L.S.)

Gordon Oakes,
Minister of State,
Authorised by the Secretary of State for Education and Science.

(a) 1962 c. 12.
(c) S.I. 1964/490 (1964 I, p.800).

(b) 1975 c. 2.
(d) S.I. 1977/1307 (1977 II, p. 3731).

EXPLANATORY NOTE

(This Note is not part of the Regulations.)

These Regulations amend the Local Education Authority Awards Regulations 1977 and come into operation on the same date as those Regulations, namely, 1st September 1977.

The dependants requirement of a student falls to be calculated under Part 3 of Schedule 2 to the 1977 Regulations by reference to the sums mentioned in paragraph 18(4) thereof, namely, the basic sum of £480 and sums in respect of dependent children. Regulation 3(1) of the present Regulations provides that the basic sum shall not be taken into account where the student has a spouse who is herself the holder of an award (which takes account of her maintenance requirements). Regulations 2 and 3(2) define the expression "award holder" and make incidental and consequential amendments.

STATUTORY INSTRUMENTS

1977 No. 1410

NEW TOWNS

The New Town Transfer Schemes (Compensation) Regulations 1977

Made	- - -	*12th August* 1977
Laid before Parliament		*17th August* 1977
Coming into Operation		*7th September* 1977

ARRANGEMENT OF REGULATIONS

The Secretary of State for the Environment, in relation to England, and the Secretary of State for Wales, in relation to Wales, in exercise of the powers conferred upon them by section 24 of the Superannuation Act 1972(a) and of all other powers enabling them in that behalf hereby make the following regulations:—

PART I

PRELIMINARY

Title and commencement

1. These regulations may be cited as the New Town Transfer Schemes (Compensation) Regulations 1977 and shall come into operation on 7th September 1977.

Interpretation

2.—(1) In these regulations, unless the context otherwise requires—

"accrued pension", in relation to a pensionable officer who has suffered loss of employment, means—

    (a) if his last relevant pension scheme provided benefits in which he had a right to participate, the pension to which he would have become entitled under that scheme according to the method of calculation (modified where necessary for the purpose of giving effect to these regulations) prescribed by that scheme if, at the date on which he ceased to be subject to that scheme, he had attained normal retiring age and complied with any requirement of that scheme as to a minimum period of qualifying service or contribution and completed any additional contributory payments or payments in respect of added years which he was in the course of making, and

    (b) in any other case, such portion of the pension (if any) of which he had reasonable expectations as the compensating authority consider equitable, having regard to any practice of the authority or body by whom he was employed on the day immediately preceding the loss, his age, the length of his employment at the date of loss and all the other circumstances of the case;

"accrued retiring allowance", in relation to a pensionable officer who has suffered loss of employment, means—

    (a) if his last relevant pension scheme provided benefits in which he had a right to participate, any lump sum payment to which he would have become entitled under that scheme according to the method of calculation (modified where necessary for the purpose of giving effect to these regulations) prescribed by that scheme if, at the date on which he ceased to be subject to that scheme, he had attained normal retiring age and complied with any requirement of that scheme as to a minimum period of qualifying service or contribution and completed any additional contributory payments or payments in respect of added years which he was in the course of making, and

(a) 1972 c. 11.

(*b*) in any other case, such portion of the lump sum payment (if any) of which he had reasonable expectations as the compensating authority consider equitable, having regard to any practice of the authority or body by whom he was employed on the day immediately preceding the loss, his age, the length of his employment at the date of loss and all the other circumstances of the case;

"accrued incapacity pension" and "accrued incapacity retiring allowance" have the same respective meanings as "accrued pension" and "accrued retiring allowance" except that the reference to a person's attaining normal retiring age shall be construed as a reference to his becoming incapable of discharging efficiently the duties of his employment by reason of permanent ill-health or infirmity of mind or body;

"added years", in relation to a person who suffers loss of employment, means—

(*a*) in the case of a pensionable employee, any additional years of service being purchased by him in his employment immediately prior to the loss in question under regulation D10 or D11 of the Local Government Superannuation Regulations 1974(a) and includes any additional years of service which having been granted under any provision similar to that referred to in the said regulation D10 or D11 were being so purchased under or by virtue of interchange rules, and

(*b*) in the case of any other person, any additional years of service, similar to those mentioned in paragraph (*a*) of this definition, reckonable by him under the last relevant pension scheme,

being in either case additional years which were being purchased partly at the expense of the employer and partly at the expense of the person under arrangements which were entered into before the employer either gave him notice in writing that his employment was to be terminated or gave him written notice of termination of his employment;

"additional contributory payments" means—

(*a*) additional contributory payments of the kind referred to in regulation D6, D7 or D8 of the Local Government Superannuation Regulations 1974; or

(*b*) any similar payments made under the last relevant pension scheme as a condition of—

(i) reckoning any period of employment as service or as a period of contribution for the purposes of the scheme, or

(ii) reckoning non-contributing service as contributing service (which expressions have the same meaning as in the scheme) for the purposes of the scheme, or

(iii) increasing the length at which any period of service or of contribution would be reckonable for the purpose of calculating a benefit under the scheme, or

(*c*) any payments similar to any of those mentioned in the foregoing paragraphs made in pursuance of interchange rules;

(a) S.I. 1974/520 (1974 I, p. 1986).

"compensating authority", as respects a person who suffers loss of employment or loss or diminution of emoluments as a result of a transfer scheme, means—

(a) if such loss or diminution occurred on or before the expiry of a period of 6 months beginning with the transfer date, the new town corporation or district council by whom the person was employed, or the emoluments were paid, as the case may be, immediately prior to that date, or

(b) if such loss or diminution occurred after the expiry of a period of 6 months beginning with the transfer date, the new town corporation or district council by whom the person was last employed or the emoluments were last paid, as the case may be, prior to the loss or diminution,

or if that authority have ceased to exist, the authority to whom the residue of their property and liabilities has been transferred;

"compensation question" means a question arising under these regulations—

(a) as to a person's entitlement to compensation for loss of employment, or for loss or diminution of emoluments, or

(b) as to the manner of a person's employment or the comparability of his duties;

"emoluments" has the meaning given by regulation 38(1) and "annual rate of emoluments" has the meaning given by regulation 38(3);

"enactment" includes any instrument made under an Act;

"fund authority" in relation to any person, means the authority maintaining the superannuation fund or account in relation to that person;

"instrument" includes an Order in Council, regulation, order, rule, scheme, direction or agreement;

"interchange rules" means rules made under section 2 of the Superannuation (Miscellaneous Provisions) Act 1948(a) (which provides for the pensions of persons transferring to different employments) and includes any similar instrument made, or having effect as if made, under any other Act which makes similar provision;

"last relevant pension scheme", in relation to a pensionable officer, means the pension scheme to which he was subject immediately before suffering loss of employment or loss or diminution of emoluments;

"local authority" means—

(a) (i) the council of an administrative county, county borough or county district, or the representative body of a parish (ceasing to exist after 31st March 1974),

(ii) the council of a county or district (established by or under the Local Government Act 1972(b)),

(iii) in England, any parish council, common parish council or parish meeting,

(iv) in Wales, a parish council, common parish council or parish meeting (ceasing to exist after 31st March 1974), or

---

(a) 1948 c. 33.   (b) 1972 c. 70.

(v) in Wales, a community council (established by or under the Local Government Act 1972),

(vi) in Scotland, the council of a county, council of city, large burgh, small burgh or district referred to in section 1(5) of the Local Government (Scotland) Act 1973(a) or a regional, islands or district council established under that Act,

(b) the council of a metropolitan borough or London borough, the Common Council of the City of London, the Greater London Council and the Council of the Isles of Scilly,

(c) any burial board or joint burial board established under the Burial Acts 1852 to 1906(b),

(d) any joint board or joint body constituted by or under any enactment for the purpose of exercising the functions of two or more authorities described in paragraph (a), (b) or (c) above, and any special planning board within the meaning of paragraph 3 of Schedule 17 to the Local Government Act 1972,

(e) any other authority or body, not specified in paragraphs (a), (b), (c) or (d) above, established by or under any enactment for the purpose of exercising the functions of or advising one or more of the authorities specified in paragraphs (a), (b), (c) or (d) above,

(f) any committee (including a joint committee) established by or under any enactment for the purpose of exercising the functions of, or advising, one or more authorities described in paragraphs (a), (b), (c), (d) or (e) above,

(g) any two or more authorities described in paragraphs (a), (b), (c), (d), (e) or (f) above acting jointly or as a combined authority, or

(h) a police authority (other than the Secretary of State) within the meaning of section 62 of the Police Act 1964(c) both as originally enacted and as subsequently amended and any previous police authority for whom Schedule 11 (Transitional Provisions) to that Act had effect or who was the police authority for an area or district which was before 1st April 1947 or after 31st March 1946 a separate police area;

"long-term compensation" means compensation payable in accordance with the provisions of Part IV of these regulations for loss of employment or loss or diminution of emoluments;

"material date", in relation to a person who has suffered loss of employment or loss or diminution of emoluments as a result of a transfer scheme, means the transfer date or, if earlier, and if not before the date on which the transfer scheme is approved or, as the case may be, made by the Secretary of State under section 5 of the New Towns (Amendment) Act 1976(d) the date of such loss or diminution;

"minimum pensionable age" means, in relation to a pensionable officer, the earliest age at which, under his last relevant pension scheme, he could have become entitled to receive payment of an unreduced pension solely by virtue of his having attained a specified age and completed a specified period of service;

(a) 1973 c. 65   (b) 1852 c. 85; 1906 c. 44.
(c) 1964 c. 4   (d) 1976 c. 68.

"national service" means, in relation to any person, service which is compulsory national service or relevant service within the meaning of the Reserve and Auxiliary Forces (Protection of Civil Interests) Act 1951(a) and any similar service immediately following such service entered into with the consent of the authority or person under whom an officer held his last relevant employment, or, where appropriate the authority by whom such an officer was appointed;

"new town corporation" has the same meaning as in the New Towns (Amendment) Act 1976;

"normal retiring age" means in the case of a pensionable officer to whom an age of compulsory retirement applied by virtue of any enactment to which he was subject in the employment which he has lost or the emoluments of which have been diminished or by virtue of the conditions of that employment, that age, and in any other case, the age of 65 if the officer is a male, or 60 if the officer is a female;

"pensionable employee" has the same meaning as in the Local Government Superannuation Regulations 1974;

"pensionable officer", in relation to a person who has suffered loss of employment or loss or diminution of emoluments, means a person who immediately before such loss or diminution was subject to a pension scheme associated with the employment he has lost or, as the case may be, the employment in which his emoluments have been diminished;

"pensionable remuneration" and "relevant period" shall have the same meanings as in regulation E1 of the Local Government Superannuation Regulations 1974, or if those Regulations do not apply to the pension scheme concerned, shall mean the remuneration and the period which correspond in that scheme to the pensionable remuneration and the relevant period in regulation E1;

"pension scheme", in relation to a pensionable officer, means any form of arrangement associated with his employment for the payment of superannuation benefits, whether subsisting by virtue of any enactment, trust, contract or otherwise;

"reckonable service", in relation to a person, means any period of whole-time or part-time employment in any relevant employment and includes any period of national service or war service undertaken on his ceasing to hold such an employment, but does not include employment in respect of which he has become entitled to receive a benefit from a pension scheme other than his last relevant pension scheme;

"relevant employment" means employment—

(a) under the Crown or by any other person, authority or body for the purposes of the Crown, or

(b) by a local authority, or

(c) by a new town corporation, or

(d) for the purposes of the functions of a local authority or new town corporation, by a person employed as mentioned in paragraphs (b) or (c), or

(e) for the purposes of any statutory provision in the United Kingdom, being employment preceding any of the foregoing employments, or

---

(a) 1951 c. 65.

(*f*) by a body which provides a public service in the United Kingdom otherwise than for the purposes of gain or to whose funds any local authority or new town corporation contribute or to whom any grant is made out of money provided by Parliament, being employment preceding any of the employments described in paragraphs (*a*) (*b*) (*c*) or (d), or

(*g*) in such other service as the Secretary of State may, in the case of any named officer, approve,

but, except for national service and war service, does not include service in the armed forces of the Crown;

"resettlement compensation" means compensation payable in accordance with Part III of these regulations for loss of employment;

"retirement compensation" means compensation payable in accordance with the provisions of regulation 18, 19 or 20;

"transfer date" as respects a transfer scheme means the date specified in that scheme for the purposes of section 6(1) of the New Towns (Amendment) Act 1976;

"transfer scheme" means a scheme under section 1 of the New Towns (Amendment) Act 1976;

"tribunal" means a tribunal established under section 12 of the Industrial Training Act 1964(a);

"war service" means war service within the meaning of the Local Government Staffs (War Service) Act 1939(b), the Police and Firemen (War Service) Act 1939(c), the Teachers Superannuation (War Service) Act 1939(d), the Education (Scotland) (War Service Superannuation) Act 1939(e) or employment for war purposes within the meaning of the Superannuation Schemes (War Service) Act 1940(f), if such service or employment immediately followed a period of relevant employment and was rendered either compulsorily or with the permission of the employer in that employment.

(2) The holder of any office, appointment, place, situation or employment shall, for the purposes of these regulations, be regarded as an officer employed in that office, appointment, place, situation or employment, and the expressions "officer" and "employment" shall be construed accordingly.

(3) Where under any provision of these regulations an annual value is to be assigned to a capital sum or a capital value to an annual amount—

(*a*) the annual or capital value shall be ascertained in accordance with the tables set out in the Schedule to these regulations insofar as they provide for the particular case,

(*b*) where the said tables do not provide for a case in which an annual value is to be assigned to a capital sum or a capital value to an annual amount, the annual or capital value shall be the value as may be agreed between the compensating authority and the person to whom the capital sum or annual amount is payable, and

(*c*) for the purpose of determining the application of the said tables, the headings and the note to each table shall be treated as part of the table.

(a) 1964 c. 16.	(b) 1939 c. 94.	(c) 1939 c. 103.
(d) 1939 c. 95.	(e) 1939 c. 96.	(f) 1940 c. 26.

(4) In these regulations, unless the context otherwise requires, references to any enactment shall be construed as references thereto as amended, re-enacted, applied or modified by any subsequent enactment.

(5) References in these regulations to a numbered regulation shall, unless the reference is to a regulation of specified regulations, be construed as references to the regulation bearing that number in these regulations.

(6) References in any of these regulations to a numbered paragraph shall, unless the reference is to a paragraph of a specified regulation, be construed as references to the paragraph bearing that number in the first mentioned regulation.

(7) The Interpretation Act 1889(a) shall apply for the interpretation of these regulations as it applies for the interpretation of an Act of Parliament.

PART II

ENTITLEMENT TO COMPENSATION

Persons to whom the regulations apply

3. These regulations shall apply to any person who—

(a) was employed immediately before the material date for the whole or for part only of his time by a new town corporation or a district council, or

(b) would have been so employed but for any national service on which he was then engaged.

Grounds of entitlement to compensation

4. Subject to the provisions of these regulations, any person to whom these regulations apply and who suffers loss of employment or loss or diminution of emoluments as a result of a transfer scheme shall be entitled to have his case considered for the payment of compensation under these regulations, and such compensation shall be determined in accordance with these regulations.

National Service

5.—(1) Where any person to whom these regulations apply would have been employed immediately before the material date in any capacity referred to in paragraph (a) of regulation 3 but for any national service on which he was then engaged, then if before the expiry of two months after ceasing to be so engaged, or if prevented by sickness or other reasonable cause, as soon as practicable thereafter, he gives notice to the compensating authority that he is available for employment, that person shall be entitled to have his case considered for the payment of compensation on the ground—

(a) if he is not given or offered re-employment in his former office or in any reasonably comparable office (whether in the same or in a different service), of loss of employment, or

(b) if he is so re-employed with diminished emoluments as compared with the emoluments which he would have enjoyed had he continued in his former employment, of diminution of emoluments.

(a) 1889 c. 63.

(2) The loss of employment which is the cause of a claim for compensation under paragraph (1)(*a*) shall be treated as having occurred on the earlier of the two following dates, that is to say, the date of the refusal of re-employment or a date one month after the date on which the person gave notice that he was available for employment; and the person shall be deemed to have been entitled to the emoluments which he would have enjoyed at such earlier date had he continued in his former employment.

PART III

RESETTLEMENT COMPENSATION

Resettlement compensation for loss of employment

6. The compensating authority shall, subject to the provisions of these regulations, pay resettlement compensation to any person to whom these regulations apply and who satisfies the conditions set out in regulation 7.

Conditions for payment of resettlement compensation

7.—(1) Without prejudice to any other requirement of these regulations, the conditions for the payment of resettlement compensation to any person are that—

(*a*) he has suffered loss of employment as a result of a transfer scheme on, or not later than 10 years after, the material date,

(*b*) he had not at the date of the loss attained normal retiring age,

(*c*) he had been for a period of 2 years immediately before the material date continuously engaged (disregarding breaks not exceeding in the aggregate 6 months) for the whole or part of his time in relevant employment,

(*d*) he has made a claim for such compensation in accordance with the provisions of Part VII of these regulations not later than 13 weeks after the loss of employment which is the cause of his claim or 13 weeks after the coming into operation of these regulations, whichever is the later, or within any longer period which the compensating authority allow in any particular case where they are satisfied that the delay in making the claim was due to ill health or other circumstances beyond the claimant's control,

(*e*) the loss of employment which is the cause of his claim has occurred for some reason other than misconduct or incapacity to perform the duties that, immediately before the loss, he was performing or might reasonably have been required to perform, and

(*f*) he has not, subject to paragraphs (2) and (3), after the employer either gave him notice in writing that his employment was to be terminated or gave him written notice of termination of his employment, been offered in writing—

(i) any relevant employment which is reasonably comparable with the employment which he has lost, or

(ii) any employment which is suitable for him in the service of any new town corporation or any local authority at the same place or in the same locality as that where he was employed immediately before the loss.

(2) In ascertaining for the purposes of this regulation whether a person has been offered employment which is reasonably comparable with the employment which he has lost, no account shall be taken of the fact that the duties of the employment offered are in relation to a different service from that in connection with which his employment was held or are duties which involve a transfer of his employment from one place to another within England and Wales.

(3) For the purposes of this regulation, where the compensating authority are satisfied—

(a) that acceptance of an offer would have involved undue hardship to the person, or

(b) that he was prevented from accepting an offer by reason of ill-health or other circumstances beyond his control, or

(c) that, before the coming into operation of these regulations, an offer—

(i) has not been accepted by him, and

(ii) has lapsed or otherwise terminated,

no account shall be taken of that offer.

Amount of resettlement compensation

8.—(1) The amount of resettlement compensation which may be paid to a person shall, subject to the provisions of paragraphs (2) to (6), be the amount described in sub-paragraph (a) or (b) whichever is the greater, namely—

(a) an amount equal to 13 weeks' emoluments and, in the case of a person who has attained the age of 45 one additional week's emoluments for every year of his age after attaining the age of 45 and before the loss of employment, subject to a maximum addition of 13 such weeks, or

(b) an amount equal to—

(i) one and one half week's emoluments for each completed year of reckonable service in which the person was not below the age of 41,

(ii) one week's emoluments for each completed year of reckonable service (not falling within sub-paragraph (i) above) in which the person was not below the age of 22, and

(iii) one half week's emoluments for each completed year of reckonable service not falling within sub-paragraph (i) or (ii) above.

(2) For the purposes of paragraph (1)(a), if the loss of employment takes place within three years of the date on which the person would have attained normal retiring age, the amount shall be reduced by the fraction of which—

(a) the numerator is the number of complete periods of 6 months in the period beginning on the date 3 years before that on which he would have attained normal retiring age and ending on the date of loss of employment, and

(b) the denominator is 6,

but the amount payable to a person who, on the material date, has not been continuously engaged in relevant employment as described in regulation 11(1)(c) shall not by this paragraph be reduced to less than the equivalent of 13 weeks' emoluments.

(3) For the purpose of paragraph (1)(*b*), in the case of a person who has completed more than 20 years' reckonable service, only the period of 20 years immediately prior to the loss of employment shall be taken into account.

(4) For the purpose of paragraph (1)(*b*), if the loss of a person's employment takes place after he has attained the age described in paragraph (5), the amount shall be reduced by the fraction of which the numerator is the number of whole months in the period beginning on the date on which he attained that age and ending on the date of loss of employment and of which the denominator is 12.

(5) The age mentioned in paragraph (4) is—

(*a*) the age of compulsory retirement applied to the person by virtue of any enactment to which he was subject in the employment which he has lost or by virtue of the conditions of that employment, less 12 months, or

(*b*) if no age of compulsory retirement is applied to the person as described in sub-paragraph (*a*) above, the age of 64.

(6) For the purposes of this regulation, the weekly rate of emoluments shall be deemed to be seven 365ths of the annual rate of emoluments.

Adjustment of resettlement compensation

9. A person who is entitled to—

(*a*) a redundancy payment under the Redundancy Payments Act 1965(**a**), or

(*b*) any similar payment in consequence of the loss of his employment under any other enactment or under any contract or arrangement with the person, body or authority by whom he was employed (other than payments by way of a return of contributions under a pension scheme), or

(*c*) any payment under or by virtue of the provisions of any enactment relating to the reinstatement in civil employment of persons who have been in the service of the Crown,

shall—

(i) if the amount of any resettlement compensation that would, apart from this regulation, be payable exceeds the payment or the aggregate of the payments specified in (*a*), (*b*), and (*c*) above, be entitled to resettlement compensation equal to that excess, or

(ii) if the amount of any resettlement compensation that would apart from this regulation be payable is equal to or less than the payment or the aggregate of the payments specified in (*a*), (*b*), and (*c*), not be entitled to resettlement compensation.

PART IV

LONG-TERM COMPENSATION

Long-term compensation for loss of employment or loss or diminution of emoluments

10. The compensating authority shall, subject to the provisions of these regulations, pay long-term compensation to any person to whom these regulations apply and who satisfies the conditions set out in regulation 11.

(**a**) 1965 c. 62.

Conditions for payment of long-term compensation

11.—(1) Without prejudice to any other requirement of these regulations, the conditions for the payment of long-term compensation to any person are that—

(*a*) he has suffered loss of employment or loss or diminution of emoluments as a result of a transfer scheme on, or not later than 10 years after the material date,

(*b*) he had not, save as is provided in regulation 26, at the date of the loss or diminution attained normal retiring age,

(*c*) he had been, for a period of not less than 5 years immediately before the material date, continuously engaged (without a break of more than 12 months at any one time) for the whole or part of his time in relevant employment,

(*d*) he has made a claim for such compensation in accordance with the provisions of Part VII of these regulations not later than 2 years after the loss or diminution which is the cause of the claim or 2 years after the coming into operation of these regulations whichever is the later,

(*e*) if the cause of the claim for compensation is loss of employment—

(i) the loss has occurred for some reason other than misconduct or incapacity to perform the duties that, immediately before the loss he was performing or might reasonably have been required to perform, and

(ii) he has not, subject to paragraph (2), after the employer either gave him notice in writing that his employment was to be terminated or gave him written notice of termination of his employment, been offered in writing any relevant employment which is reasonably comparable with the employment which he has lost, and

(*f*) he is not in receipt of benefits payable in accordance with regulations made under section 260 of the Local Government Act 1972(**a**) or any corresponding regulation.

(2) Regulation 7(2) and (3) (which relate to offers of employment) shall apply for the purposes of this regulation in ascertaining whether a person has been offered reasonably comparable employment.

(3) Claims for long-term compensation for loss of employment shall in all respects be treated as claims for such compensation for the loss of emoluments occasioned thereby and the provisions of these regulations shall apply to all such claims accordingly.

Factors to be considered in determining payment of long-term compensation

12.—(1) For the purpose of determining whether long-term compensation for loss or diminution of emoluments should be paid to any person and, if so, the amount of the compensation (subject to the limits set out in these regulations) the compensating authority shall, subject to the provisions of paragraph (2) and (3), have regard to such of the following factors as may be relevant, that is to say—

(*a*) the conditions upon which the person held the employment which he has lost, including in particular its security of tenure, whether by law or practice,

(**a**) 1972 c. 70.

(b) the emoluments and other conditions, including security of tenure, whether by law or practice, of any work or employment undertaken by the person as a result of the loss of employment,

(c) the extent to which he has sought suitable employment and the emoluments which he might have acquired by accepting other suitable employment which, after the employer either gave him notice in writing that his employment was to be terminated or gave him written notice of termination of his employment, has been offered to him in writing,

(d) the amount of any retirement compensation or any compensation equivalent thereto which the person is receiving under regulations made under section 24 of the Superannuation Act 1972 or under any provision to the like effect in any other enactment (whenever enacted) if—

   (i) the service by reference to which that compensation is calculated is reckonable service for the purpose of these regulations, and

   (ii) the loss of employment or diminution of emoluments giving rise to that compensation occurred before the loss or diminution as respects these regulations, and

(e) all the other circumstances of his case,

but, subject to the provisions of regulation 40, no account shall be taken of the fact that he entered the employment which he has lost or the emoluments of which have been diminished after the material date; and any condition of either the employment which he has lost or any work or employment undertaken as a result of the loss requiring (either generally or in any particular case) the giving of notice of more than three months to terminate the employment shall for the purpose mentioned above be deemed to be a condition requiring the giving of three months' such notice.

(2) In ascertaining for the purposes of paragraph (1)(b) and (1)(c) the emoluments in respect of any work or employment that gives the employee or his widow, child or other dependant the right to benefit under a pension scheme under which the employee is not under an obligation to pay contributions, the amount of emoluments shall be increased by the amount of contributions which the employee would have to pay to secure equivalent benefits under a pension scheme in respect of which both the employer and the employee are under an obligation to pay equal contributions.

(3) Regulation 7(3) shall apply for the purposes of this regulation in ascertaining whether a person has been offered suitable employment.

Amount of long-term compensation payable for loss of emoluments

13.—(1) Long-term compensation for loss of emoluments shall, subject to the provisions of these regulations, be payable until the normal retiring age or death of a person to whom it is payable, whichever first occurs, and shall not exceed a maximum annual sum calculated in accordance with the provisions of paragraphs (2) to (4).

(2) The said, maximum annual sum shall, subject as hereinafter provided, be the aggregate of the following sums, namely—

(a) for each year of the person's reckonable service up to a maximum of 40 such years, one sixtieth of the emoluments which he has lost, and

(b) in the case of a person who has attained the age of 40 at the date of the loss, a sum calculated in accordance with the provisions of paragraph (3) appropriate to his age at that date.

(3) Subject to the said maximum annual sum in no case exceeding two-thirds of the emoluments which the person has lost, the sum referred to in paragraph (2)(b) shall be—

(a) in the case of a person who has attained the age of 40 but has not attained the age of 50 at the date of the loss, the following fraction of the emoluments which he has lost—

(i) where his reckonable service is less than 10 years, one-sixtieth for each year of that service after attaining the age of 40, or

(ii) where his reckonable service amounts to 10 years but is less than 15 years, one-sixtieth for each year of that service after attaining the age of 40 and one additional sixtieth, or

(iii) where his reckonable service amounts to 15 years but is less than 20 years, one-sixtieth for each year of that service after attaining the age of 40 and two additional sixtieths, or

(iv) where his reckonable service amounts to 20 years or more, one-sixtieth for each year of that service after attaining the age of 40 and three additional sixtieths,

but the sum so calculated shall not in any case exceed one-sixth of the said emoluments,

(b) in the case of a person who has attained the age of 50 but has not attained the age of 60 at the date of the loss, one-sixtieth of the said emoluments for each year of his reckonable service after attaining the age of 40, up to a maximum of 15 years, and

(c) in the case of a person who has attained the age of 60 at the date of the loss, one-sixtieth of the said emoluments for each year of his reckonable service after attaining the age of 45,

and for the purpose of applying regulation 29(5) or 30(3) to long term compensation, a period of years made up of one year for each sixtieth of the said emoluments comprised in the sum referred to in paragraph 2(b) shall be deemed to be an additional period of service credited under regulation 17(2).

(4) The amounts of long-term compensation calculated in accordance with paragraphs (2) and (3), shall be reduced by the amount by which the aggregate of—

(a) the emoluments of any work or employment undertaken by him as a result of the loss of employment, and

(b) the long-term compensation which apart from this paragraph and any reduction under regulation 30(3) and (4) would be payable to him,

STOKE-ON-TRENT
CITY
LIBRARIES

exceeds the emoluments of the employment which has been lost; and where at any time a person is receiving long term compensation or compensation equivalent thereto under any statutory or other provision and—

(i) the service by reference to which that compensation is calculated is reckonable service for the purpose of these regulations, and

(ii) the date of the loss of employment or diminution of emoluments giving rise to that compensation occurred before the loss or diminution as respects these regulations,

the amount of long term compensation calculated in accordance with paragraphs (2) and (3) shall be reduced, or further reduced, as the case may be, by the amount of that compensation.

(5) Long-term compensation shall be payable to a person at intervals equivalent to those at which the emoluments of his employment were previously paid or at such other intervals as may be agreed between the person and the compensating authority.

Long-term compensation for diminution of emoluments

14.—(1) Long-term compensation for diminution of emoluments in respect of any employment shall, subject to the provisions of these regulations, consist of an annual sum calculated in accordance with the provisions of paragraph (2).

(2) The said annual sum shall not exceed the sum that would be the annual sum under the provisions of regulations 13(1) to (4) calculated on the assumptions—

(*a*) that there was a loss of employment, and

(*b*) that emoluments after diminution were emoluments of any work or employment undertaken as a result of a loss of employment within the meaning of regulations 12(1)(*b*) and 13(4).

(3) Long-term compensation for diminution of emoluments shall be payable to a person at intervals equivalent to those at which the emoluments of his employment are or were previously paid or at such other intervals as may be agreed between the person and the compensating authority.

Period during which long-term compensation is to be payable

15.—(1) Long-term compensation shall be payable with effect from the date of the claim or from any earlier date permitted by the succeeding provisions of this regulation.

(2) Where a claim for long-term compensation is duly made within 13 weeks of the commencement of these regulations or of the occurrence of the loss or diminution which is the cause of the claim (whichever is the later), the award shall be made effective from the date on which the loss or diminution occurred.

(3) Where a claim for long-term compensation is made after the expiry of the period mentioned in paragraph (2), the compensating authority may—

(*a*) at their discretion make the award effective from a date not earlier than thirteen weeks prior to the date on which the claim was made, or

(*b*) if they are satisfied that the failure to make the claim within the period mentioned in paragraph (2) was due to ill-health or other circumstances beyond the claimant's control, make the award effective from a date not earlier than that on which the loss or diminution occurred

(4) Long-term compensation shall not be payable to a person for any period in respect of which compensation under Part V of these regulations is payable to him.

PART V

RETIREMENT COMPENSATION AND PAYMENTS ON DEATH

Entitlement to retirement compensation and other payments

16.—(1) The compensating authority shall, subject to the provisions of these regulations, pay retirement compensation to any person to whom this Part of these regulations applies and shall make the other payments for which provision is made in regulations 23 to 27.

(2) Save as is provided in regulation 26, this part of these regulations apply to a pensionable officer who satisfies the conditions set out in regulation 11.

(3) Regulation 12 shall apply in relation to compensation under this part of these regulations as it applies in relation to compensation under Part IV.

Additional factors governing payment of retirement compensation

17.—(1) Where retirement compensation is payable under any one of regulations 18, 19 or 20, compensation shall not be payable under any other of those regulations.

(2) If a person has attained the age of 40 at the date on which he lost his employment or suffered a diminution of his emoluments, the compensating authority, in calculating the amount of the retirement compensation payable to him, shall credit him with an additional period of service on the following basis, namely—

    (*a*) 2 years, whether or not he has completed any years of service after attaining the age of 40,

    (*b*) 2 years for each of the first 4 years of his reckonable service between the date when he attained the age of 40 and the date of the loss or diminution, and

    (*c*) one year for each year of that reckonable service after the fourth,

but the additional period so credited shall not exceed the shortest of the following periods, namely

    (i) the number of years that, when added to his pensionable service, would amount to the maximum period of service which would have been reckonable by him had he continued in his employment until attaining normal retiring age,

    (ii) the period of his reckonable service, or

    (iii) 15 years,

and in calculating the amount of any retirement compensation payable to him, any period so added shall be aggregated with any period entailing reduction of the relevant pension or retiring allowance because of a retirement pension payable under section 28 of the Social Security Act 1975(a).

(3) The benefit in respect of the additional period described in paragraph (2) shall be calculated at the same rate as is applicable for the day immediately preceding the loss or diminution.

(a) 1975 c. 14.

(4) When retirement compensation is awarded, or when an award is reviewed under regulation 32, the additional compensation payable in consequence of any period credited to a person under paragraph (2) may be reduced or withheld to the extent that the compensating authority may think reasonable having regard to the pension scheme (if any) associated with any further employment obtained by him.

(5) If under his last relevant pension scheme the amount of any benefit to which a person might have become entitled could have been increased at the discretion of the authority administering the pension scheme or of any other body, the compensating authority may increase, to an extent not exceeding that to which his accrued pension, accrued retiring allowance, accrued incapacity pension or accrued incapacity retiring allowance might have been increased or supplemented, the corresponding component of any retirement compensation payable to him; and in this connection the compensating authority shall have regard to the terms of any relevant resolutions of the authority or body with regard to the increase of benefits and to the provisions of any enactment protecting the interests of that person.

(6) If under his last relevant pension scheme a person would have been entitled to surrender a proportion of any pension which might have become payable to him in favour of his spouse or any dependant, then, if he so desires and informs the compensating authority by notice in writing accordingly within one month after becoming entitled to retirement compensation under these regulations, he may surrender a proportion of so much of the said compensation as is payable by way of an annual sum on the like terms and conditions and in consideration of the like payments by the compensating authority as if the said annual sum were a pension to which he had become entitled under the said pension scheme.

(7) In calculating for the purpose of regulation 18 or 19 the amount of the annual sum which is equal to a person's accrued pension, no account shall be taken of any reduction falling to be made in that pension by reason of the provisions of any enactment relating to National Insurance or Social Security until the person reaches the age at which under his last relevant pension scheme the pension would have been so reduced.

Retirement compensation for loss of employment payable to pensionable officer on attainment of normal retiring age

18.—(1) Subject to the provisions of these regulations, when a person to whom this Part of these regulations applies reaches normal retiring age, the retirement compensation payable to him for loss of employment shall be—

> (*a*) an annual sum equal to the amount of his accrued pension, and

> (*b*) a lump sum equal to the amount of his accrued retiring allowance (if any).

(2) No compensation shall be payable under this regulation if the person has continued to pay superannuation contributions as if he had suffered no loss of employment.

Retirement compensation payable to pensionable officer on his becoming incapacitated or reaching minimum pensionable age

19.—(1) Where a person to whom this Part of these regulations applies and who has suffered loss of employment before attaining what would have been his normal retiring age—

> (*a*) becomes incapacitated in circumstances in which, if he had continued

in the employment which he has lost, he would have become entitled
to a pension under his last relevant pension scheme, or

(b) attains the age which, had he continued to serve in the employment
which he has lost, would have been his minimum pensionable age,

he shall be entitled on the happening of either event to claim—

(i) in the case mentioned in sub-paragraph (a) above, an annual sum
equal to the amount of his accrued incapacity pension and a lump
sum equal to the amount of his accrued incapacity retiring allowance
(if any), and

(ii) in the case mentioned in sub-paragraph (b) above, an annual sum equal
to the amount of his accrued pension and a lump sum equal to the
amount of his accrued retiring allowance (if any),

subject however to the conditions specified in paragraph (5).

(2) On receipt of a claim under paragraph (1), the compensating authority
shall consider whether the claimant is a person to whom that paragraph applies,
and—

(a) if they are satisfied that he is not such a person, they shall notify him
in writing accordingly, or

(b) if they are satisfied that he is such a person, they shall assess the amount
of compensation payable to him and notify him in writing accordingly,

and notification as described in sub-paragraph (a) or (b) above shall, for the
purposes of these regulations, be deemed to be a notification by the authority
of a decision on a claim for compensation.

(3) A compensating authority may require any person who makes a claim
under paragraph (1)(a) to submit himself to a medical examination by a registered medical practitioner selected by that authority, and if they do so, they
shall also offer the person an opportunity of submitting a report from his own
medical adviser as a result of an examination by him, and the authority shall
take that report into consideration together with the report of a medical practitioner selected by them.

(4) If a person wishes to receive compensation under this regulation, he shall
so inform the compensating authority in writing within one month from the
receipt of a notification under paragraph (2) or, where the claim has been the
subject of an appeal, from the decision of the tribunal thereon; and the compensation shall be payable as from the date on which the compensating authority
received the claim.

(5) The calculation of compensation under this regulation shall be subject
to the following conditions—

(a) where the compensating authority, by virtue of regulation 17, have
credited the person with an additional period of service, no account shall
be taken of any additional period beyond the period which he could
have served, had he not lost his employment, before the date on which
the claim was received by the compensating authority,

(b) if, by reason of any provision of the last relevant pension scheme for
a minimum benefit, the amount of any such pension or retiring allowance is in excess of that attributable to the person's actual service,
no account shall be taken of any such additional period of service

except to the extent (if any) by which it exceeds the number of years represented by the difference between his actual service and the period by reference to which the minimum benefit has been calculated, and

(c) if the number of years by reference to which an accrued incapacity pension or accrued incapacity retiring allowance is to be calculated is less then any minimum number of years of qualifying service prescribed by the last relevant pension scheme, the amount of the pension or retiring allowance shall, notwithstanding any minimum benefit prescribed by the pension scheme, not exceed the proportion of the minimum benefit which the number of years of pensionable service bears to the minimum number of years of qualifying service.

Retirement compensation for diminution of emoluments

20.—(1) A person to whom this Part of these regulations applies and who has suffered a diminution of his emolmuents shall be entitled to receive retirement compensation in accordance with the provisions of this regulation.

(2) The provisions of regulations 18 and 19 shall apply to any such person as if he had suffered loss of employment immediately before the diminution occurred; but the amount of retirement compensation payable shall be the amount which would have been payable in respect of loss of employment multiplied by a fraction of which—

(a) the numerator is the amount by which his pensionable emoluments have been diminished, and

(b) the denominator is the amount of his pensionable emoluments immediately before they were diminished,

and for the purposes of this calculation no account shall be taken of any reduction which might otherwise fall to be made in the accrued pension or accrued incapacity pension because of a retirement pension payable under section 28 of the Social Security Act 1975.

(3) No compensation shall be payable under this regulation—

(a) if the person has continued to pay superannuation contributions as if his emoluments had not been diminished, or

(b) as respects any period in respect of which the person is entitled to retirement pension and retirement allowance under his last relevant pension scheme if, as respects that scheme, the whole of the relevant period for calculating the pensionable remuneration of that person falls before he suffered the dimunution in his emoluments.

Superannuation contributions

21.—(1) A person entitled to retirement compensation under regulation 18 or 19 shall pay an amount equal to any sum which was paid to him by way of return of superannuation contributions (including any interest) after ceasing to be employed—

(a) if the provisions of his last relevant pension scheme enable him to be credited with benefits attributable to that sum, to the fund authority, and

(b) in any other case, to the compensating authority.

(2) If the person does not pay as specified in paragraph (1), his retirement compensation shall be reduced by an annual amount the capital value of which is equal to the amount of the said superannuation contributions.

(3) For the purposes of this regulation the expression "superannuation contributions" shall include payments made by the person in respect of added years, any additional contributory payments made by him and any other payments made by him for the purpose of increasing the benefits to which he would have become entitled under his last relevant pension scheme.

(4) Any sums paid to a compensating authority under this regulation in respect of returned contributions shall be applied for the payment of compensation which the authority is liable to pay under this Part of these regulations.

Retirement compensation of a person who obtains further pensionable employment

22.—(1) Where a person to whom this Part of these regulations applies, after suffering loss of employment or diminution of emoluments, enters employment in which he is subject to a pension scheme and thereafter becomes entitled to reckon for the purposes of that scheme any service or period of contribution which falls to be taken into account for the purpose of assessing the amount of any retirement compensation payable to him, his entitlement to retirement compensation shall be reviewed, and, subject to the provisions of this regulation, no retirement compensation shall be payable in respect of that service or period unless the annual rate of the emoluments to which he was entitled immediately before the loss or diminution exceeds the annual rate on entry of the emoluments of the new employment, and any retirement compensation so payable to him shall, insofar as it is calculated by reference to remuneration, be calculated by reference to the difference between the said annual rates.

(2) The provisions of this regulation shall not operate to increase the amount of any retirement compensation payable in respect of diminution of emoluments beyond the amount which would have been payable if the person had attained normal retiring age immediately before he ceased to hold the employment in which he suffered the diminution of emoluments.

(3) No retirement compensation shall be payable in the circumstances mentioned in this regulation if the person has continued to pay superannuation contributions as if his emoluments had not been diminished.

Compensation payable to widow or dependants of a claimant

23.—(1) Where a person to whom this part of these regulations applies dies, payments in accordance with this regulation and regulations 24 and 25 shall be made to or for the benefit of his widow, child or other dependant or to his personal representatives or, as the case may be, to trustees empowered by him to stand possessed of any benefit under his last relevant pension scheme.

(2) Where the widow, child or other dependant has become, or but for the persons' loss of employment would have become, entitled to benefit under his last relevant pension scheme, the widow, child or other dependant, as the case may be, shall (subject to the provisions of this regulation) be entitled to compensation calculated from time to time in accordance with the methods prescribed by the last relevant pension scheme modified as follows:—

(a) where the person dies before becoming entitled to receive retirement compensation and the last relevant pension scheme provides that when he dies in service his widow, child or other dependant shall be entitled for any period to a benefit equal to his pensionable remuneration, the annual rate of compensation for that period shall be equal to the annual amount of his long-term compensation calculated in accordance with paragraphs (1) to (3) of regulation 13,

(b) where the person dies before becoming entitled to receive retirement compensation and the last relevant pension scheme provides that when he dies in service his widow, child or other dependant shall be entitled for any period to a benefit calculated by reference to the pension or incapacity pension which would have been payable to him if he had retired immediately before his death, the compensation for that period shall be calculated by reference to the retirement compensation to which he would have been entitled under regulation 19 if that regulation had been applied to him immediately before his death,

(c) where a person dies after becoming entitled to receive retirement compensation and the last relevant pension scheme provides that when he dies after having retired his widow, child or other dependant shall be entitled for any period to a benefit equal to his pension, the annual rate of compensation for that period shall be equal to the annual amount of retirement compensation,

(d) where a person dies after he has become entitled to receive retirement compensation and the last relevant pension scheme provides that when he dies after having retired his widow, child or other dependant shall be entitled for any period to a benefit calculated by reference to his pension, the annual rate of compensation for that period shall be calculated by reference to the annual amount of retirement compensation that would have been payable to him but for any reduction or suspension under regulation 30(1),

(e) for the purposes of calculating compensation in accordance with the foregoing provisions, each year added to a person's reckonable service under regulation 17 (or which would have been added if retirement under regulation 19 were assumed) shall be deemed to have been service rendered immediately before the loss of employment.

(3) Calculation of the amounts described in paragraph (2) shall be subject to the following adjustments—

(a) where any retirement compensation has been surrendered under regulation 17(6) or compounded under regulation 33, any sum payable under paragraph 2(b) and (d) shall be calculated as if such surrender or compounding had not taken place.

(b) it shall be assumed that retirement compensation payable, or which would have been payable, had such sum as would have been payable if the accrued pension or accrued incapacity pension had not been reduced by reason of the provisions of any enactment relating to National Insurance or Social Security, and

(c) if immediately before his death the person's long-term compensation was reduced under regulation 13(4) or 32(7) or his retirement compensation was reduced or suspended under regulation 30(1) by reason of employment in which he was subject to a pension scheme and the widow, child or other dependant is entitled under that scheme for any period to a benefit equal to his pensionable remuneration, regard shall be had to any such reduction or suspension for the purposes of paragraph 2(*a*) and (*c*).

(4) Where the widow, child or other dependant has become, or but for the person's loss of employment would have become, entitled to a benefit other than a benefit mentioned in paragraph (2)(*a*) to (*d*), the widow, child or other dependant, as the case may be, shall be entitled (subject to the provisions of paragraph (5)), to an annual sum equal to the annual amount of the pension which would have been payable if he had died immediately before the date on which he suffered the loss of employment, having then complied with any requirements of the last relevant pension scheme as to a minimum period of qualifying service or contribution and completed any additional contributory payments or payments in respect of added years which he was then in the course of making.

(5) The calculation referred to in paragraph (4) shall be made on the basis of the method prescribed by the last relevant pension scheme of the person in question for the calculation of benefits for a widow, child or other dependant, and insofar as the age at which he died is relevant for the purposes of the said calculation, the calculation shall be made by reference to his age at the date of death.

(6) Any sums payable to or for the benefit of a widow, child or other dependant under this regulation shall cease to be payable when a corresponding pension under the last relevant pension scheme would have ceased to be payable; and where that scheme provides for payment of the pension to any person on behalf of a child or other dependant, any sum payable under this regulation to a child or other dependant shall be paid to that person on behalf of the child or dependant in the like manner and for the like period as is provided in the pension scheme.

(7) Except where the compensation has been reduced under regulation 21, compensation payable under this regulation and regulation 24 shall in the aggregate be reduced by an amount the capital value whereof is equal to the amount of any superannuation contributions as defined in regulation 21(3) returned to the person in respect of whom the compensation is payable and not paid to the fund authority or the compensating authority, the compensation under each of those regulations being reduced in proportion to the capital value of each amount.

(8) If the person in question suffered a diminution of emoluments, then—

(*a*) where his last relevant pension scheme provides benefits of a kind described in paragraph (2), the provisions of that paragraph shall apply with the substitution of references to diminution of emoluments for references to loss of employment, and the sums payable to his widow, child or other dependant shall be calculated as if he had suffered loss of employment and as if the loss of emoluments occasioned thereby had been equivalent to the amount of the diminution; but no sum shall be payable under this sub-paragraph—

(i) if the person has continued to pay superannuation contributions as if his emoluments had not been diminished, or

(ii) as respects any period in respect of which benefits are payable to the widow, child or other dependant of any person under his last relevant pension scheme if, as respects that scheme, the whole of the relevant period for calculating the pensionable remuneration of that person falls before he suffered the diminution of his emoluments,

(b) where his last relevant pension scheme provides benefits of a kind described in paragraph (4), the provisions of that paragraph and of regulation 30(3)(a) shall apply with the substitution of references to diminution of emoluments for the references to loss of employment and of a reference to employment in which he has suffered such a diminution for the reference to employment which he has lost.

Compensation where death grant would have been payable

24.—(1) If the widow, the personal representatives of a person to whom this Part of these regulations applies or trustees empowered by that person to stand possessed of any benefit under his last relevant pension scheme might have become entitled to a death grant under that scheme, she or they, as the case may be, shall be entitled to receive a sum calculated in accordance with the provisions of regulation 23(7) and paragraph (2) of this regulation.

(2) The amount of the sum referred to in paragraph (1) shall be ascertained in accordance with the method of calculation prescribed by the last relevant pension scheme for the ascertainment of death grant as if the person had died immediately before losing his employment, subject to the following modifications—

(a) account shall be taken of any additional period of service credited to him under regulation 17(2)—

(i) in the case of a person who had been in receipt of retirement compensation under regulation 19, to the extent of the period between the loss of employment and the date of the claim made under that regulation, and

(ii) in any other case, to the extent of the period between the loss of employment and the person's death,

(b) if the aggregate of the person's pensionable service and the additional period under regulation 17(2) is less than any minimum period of qualifying service prescribed by the pension scheme for the receipt of a death grant, the said sum shall not exceed that proportion of the death grant calculated as aforesaid which is equal to the proportion which the aggregate service bears to the minimum period of qualifying service prescribed by the pension scheme, and

(c) there shall be deducted from the sum described above the amount of any retirement compensation paid to the person under regulation 18 or 19, or where any part of the compensation has been surrendered under regulation 17(6), the amount which would have been so paid but for such a surrender.

(3) In calculating a death grant under this regulation, any sum payable under regulation 23(2) or (8)(a) to or for the benefit of the widow, child or other dependant shall be deemed to be a pension payable to or for the benefit of the widow, child or dependant, as the case may be.

(4) This regulation shall apply in the case of a person who has suffered a diminution of emoluments with the substitution of references to diminution of emoluments for references to loss of employment, and the sum payable to

the widow, personal representatives or trustees of such a person shall be calculated as if he had lost emoluments equivalent to the amount of the diminution; but no such sum shall be payable under this paragraph—

(a) if the person has continued to pay superannuation contributions as if his emoluments had not been diminished, or

(b) where under the person's last relevant pension scheme a death gratuity is payable if, as respects that scheme, the whole of the relevant period for calculating the pensionable remuneration of that person falls before he suffered the diminution in his emoluments.

Balance payable to claimant's widow or personal representatives

25.—(1) If no sum is payable to the widow, child or other dependant of any person under regulation 23(2) or (8)(a) and no sum is payable under regulation 24 and the person dies before he has received in the aggregate by way of retirement compensation a sum equivalent to the aggregate of—

(i) any superannuation contributions paid by him which have not been returned to him, and

(ii) any amount paid by him in accordance with regulation 21(1),

together with compound interest thereon calculated—

(a) at the rate of 3 per cent. per annum with half yearly rests up to the date of his death as from 1st April or 1st October following the half year in which the amount was paid, or

(b) in such other manner as may be provided by the last relevant pension scheme,

(whichever calculation gives the greater amount) there shall be paid to his personal representatives the difference between the aggregate amount received by way of retirement compensation as aforesaid and the said equivalent sum.

(2) If any annual sum which became payable to a widow under regulation 23(2) or (8)(a) has ceased to be payable on her remarriage or death, and any sum payable to a child or other dependant under either of these paragraphs has ceased to be payable, and if the aggregate amount of the payments which were made as aforesaid to her husband by way of retirement compensation and to the widow or personal representatives or trustees under regulation 24 is less than a sum equivalent to the amount which would have been payable to the personal representatives under that regulation if no sum had been payable under either of the said paragraphs (2) or (8)(a), there shall be paid to her or her personal representatives the difference between such aggregate amount and the said equivalent sum.

(3) For the purpose of this regulation, a person who has surrendered any part of his retirement compensation under regulation 17(6), or whose retirement compensation has been reduced in accordance with regulation 30(3), shall be deemed to have received during any period the amount of compensation for that period which he would have received but for such a surrender or such a reduction.

Compensation payable to non-pensionable officer on reaching normal retiring age

26.—(1) Where a person who is not a pensionable officer is receiving long-term compensation for loss of employment and attains normal retiring age, the compensating authority shall, if satisfied that the person would, but for the loss, have continued in the employment he has lost for a substantial period beyond that age, continue to pay compensation to him for the remainder of his life at half its former rate.

(2) Where a person who is not a pensionable officer suffers loss of employment on or after attaining normal retiring age, the compensating authority may, if satisfied that the person would in the normal course have continued in the employment he has lost for a further substantial period, pay compensation to him for the remainder of his life at half the rate to which he would have been entitled under regulation 13 had he not attained normal retiring age at the date on which he lost his employment.

Persons subject to policy schemes

27.—(1) Regulations 18, 19, 20 and 24 shall not apply to a person (in this regulation referred to as a "policy scheme participant") who had been participating in a scheme associated with his employment for providing superannuation benefits by means of contracts or policies of insurance, and who, after the loss of his employment or the diminution of his emoluments, continued to participate in that scheme or became entitled to a benefit or prospective benefit thereunder other than a return of contributions.

(2) If a policy scheme participant has lost his employment, the compensating authority may, if the relevant scheme so permits, make such payments to or in respect of him, whether by way of the payment of premiums or otherwise, as are actuarially equivalent to the amounts by which his retirement compensation might have been increased under regulation 17(2) or (5) had he been a person to whom regulation 18 or 19 applied.

(3) If a policy scheme participant has suffered a diminution of his emoluments the compensating authority may, if the relevant scheme so permits, make such payments to or in respect of him, whether by way of the payment of premiums or otherwise, as will secure to him the like benefits as if his emoluments had not been diminished.

(4) If a policy scheme participant becomes entitled to a benefit under such a scheme as is mentioned in paragraph (1) before reaching normal retiring age, the compensating authority may reduce any long-term compensation payable to him by the amount of such benefit.

Intervals for payment of compensation under Part V

28. Any compensation awarded under this Part of these regulations to or in respect of any person shall be payable at intervals equivalent to those at which the corresponding benefit would have been payable under the person's last relevant pension scheme or at such other intervals as may be agreed between the person entitled to receive the compensation and the compensating authority.

PART VI

ADJUSTMENT, REVIEW AND COMPOUNDING OF COMPENSATION

Adjustment of compensation where superannuation benefit is also payable

29.—(1) Where any period of service of which account was taken in calculating the amount of any compensation payable under Part IV or V of these regulations is subsequently taken into account for the purpose of calculating the amount of any superannuation benefit payable to or in respect of any person in accordance with a pension scheme associated with any employment undertaken subsequent to the loss of employment or diminution of emoluments which was the subject of the claim for compensation, the compensating authority may in accordance with this regulation withhold or reduce the compensation payable.

(2) If the part of any superannuation benefit which is attributable to a period of service mentioned in paragraph (1) equals or exceeds the part of any compensation which is attributable to the same period, that part of the compensation may be withheld, or if the part of the superannuation benefit is less than the part of the compensation, the compensation may be reduced by an amount not exceeding that part of the superannuation benefit.

(3) In the case of a death benefit payable in respect of any person, the sum payable under regulation 24 may be reduced by an amount not greater than the proportion of the death benefit which the period of service mentioned in paragraph (1) bears to the total period of service of which account was taken in the calculation of the death benefit.

(4) In addition to any reduction authorised by paragraph (2) or (3), if, in the circumstances mentioned in paragraph (1), compensation is attributable in part of any provision of the last relevant pension scheme for a minimum benefit, the compensation may be reduced by an amount not exceeding that part.

(5) Where any additional period of service has been credited to a person under regulation 17(2) or under regulation 13(3) is deemed to be so credited and that period is equal to or less than the period spent in the employment mentioned in paragraph (1) and taken into account in calculating the amount of any superannuation benefit payable in accordance with the pension scheme associated with that employment the compensation may be reduced (in addition to any other reduction authorised by this regulation) by an amount not exceeding that part of the superannuation benefit which is attributable to a period of service equal to the additional period of service credited or deemed to be credited under regulation 17(2), or, if the period so credited is greater, by an amount not exceeding the part of the superannuation benefit which is attributable to the period spent in the subsequent employment and for the purpose of this paragraph the period spent in the subsequent employment shall be deemed to be increased by any additional period of service with which the person was credited under the pension scheme associated with that employment.

(6) Where compensation has been calculated in accordance with regulation 22, any reduction that may be made under paragraphs (2) to (5) shall not exceed the amount of the pension or lump sum comprising the part (if any) of the superannuation benefit relating to the subsequent employment which is attributable to annual emoluments in excess of those to which the person was entitled on entering the new employment referred to in regulation 22.

(7) Where compensation is payable in respect of diminution of emoluments, any reduction that may be made under paragraphs (2) to (5) shall not exceed the amount of the pension or lump sum comprising the part (if any) of the superannuation benefit relating to the subsequent employment which is attributable to annual emoluments in excess of those to which the person was entitled immediately after the diminution and taken into account in calculating the compensation.

(8) In making any reduction under paragraphs (2) to (5), or in applying paragraphs (6) or (7), the amount of pension or, as the case may be, lump sum

to be taken into account relating to the subsequent employment shall be the amount of such pension or lump sum reduced by a fraction of that pension or lump sum, where—

(a) the numerator is equivalent to the aggregate of the amount of increases which would have been awarded under the provisions of the Pensions (Increase) Act 1971(a), during the period beginning with the day following loss of the employment or diminution of the emoluments, as the case may be, for which compensation is payable and ending on the day the subsequent employment terminated, on an official pension (within the meaning of that Act) of £100 a year which commenced from the first mentioned day, and

(b) the denominator is equivalent to the aggregate of an official pension of £100 a year and the amount of the increase so determined.

Reduction of compensation in certain cases

30.—(1) If under a person's last relevant pension scheme any benefit for which the scheme provided would have been subject to reduction or suspension on his taking up other specified employment, any retirement compensation to which he is entitled for loss of employment or diminution of emoluments shall, where such an employment is taken up, be reduced or suspended in the like manner and to the like extent; but in calculating the amount of the reduction there shall be aggregated with the emoluments of the employment taken up the amount of any superannuation benefit by way of annual amounts payable to the person under a pension scheme associated with the employment which he has lost or, as the case may be, the employment in which the emoluments were diminished.

(2) There shall be deducted from the retirement compensation payable to any person any additional contributory payments remaining unpaid at the date when he suffered loss of employment that are not recovered in accordance with the provisions of the last relevant pension scheme; and any additional contributory payments not recovered at the date of his death shall be deducted from any compensation payable in respect of that person under regulation 23, 24 or 25(2).

(3) Where compensation for loss of employment is payable under these regulations to or in respect of any person, and that person or his widow, child or other dependant or his personal representatives or trustees as are mentioned in regulation 24(1) is or are also entitled (whether immediately or on the person's attaining some greater age) to a superannuation benefit under his last relevant pension scheme in respect of any service of which account was taken in calculating the compensation—

(a) any instalment of that compensation which is payable in respect of any period shall be reduced by the amount of the instalment of such superannuation benefit which is payable in respect of the same period, and

(b) any of that compensation which is payable under Part IV or Part V of these regulations and which is payable as a lump sum, shall be reduced by the amount of any lump sum superannuation benefit,

and where part of the superannuation benefit is attributable to any additional period of service with which the person was credited under his last relevant pension scheme and—

(i) that period is equal to or less than any additional period credited to that person under regulation 17(2) or under regulation 13(3) deemed

(a) 1971 c. 56.

to be so credited, the amount of the compensation shall be reduced by that part of the superannuation benefit;

(ii) that period is greater than any additional period so credited, the amount of the compensation shall be reduced by an amount equal to the amount of the superannuation benefit attributable to a period equal in length to the additional period credited or deemed to be credited under regulation 17(2).

(4) Where compensation is payable under Part IV of these regulations to any person and that person is, or becomes, entitled to receive a superannuation benefit under a previous pension scheme other than his last relevant pension scheme in respect of service of which account was taken in calculating the compensation any instalment of that compensation which is payable in respect of any period shall be reduced by the amount of the instalment of such superannuation benefit which is payable in respect of the same period.

(5) For the purposes of paragraphs (3) and (4), no account shall be taken of any sum payable in consequence of the surrender by any person of part of his superannuation benefit under any provision in that behalf in the last relevant pension scheme or the previous pension scheme with a view to obtaining or increasing allowances for his widow, child or other dependant and the person shall be deemed to have received during any period the amount of superannuation benefit which he would have received but for such a surrender.

(6) Where in any week a person entitled to long-term compensation for loss or diminution of emoluments is also entitled to a National Insurance benefit, there shall be deducted from the long-term compensation payable in respect of that week a sum equal to the amount by which the aggregate of—

(a) the National Insurance benefit that would be payable in respect of that week is calculated at the rate applicable at the date of loss or diminution, and

(b) the weekly rate at which the long-term compensation would be payable but for this regulation,

exceeds two-thirds of the weekly rate of the emoluments of the employment which he has lost or in which the emoluments have been diminished.

(7) No deduction shall be made under paragraph (6) insofar as—

(a) an equivalent sum is deducted from the emoluments of his current employment, and

(b) that deduction from those emoluments has not occasioned an increase in his long-term compensation.

(8) In paragraph (6) the expression "weekly rate" means seven 365ths of the relevant annual rate, and the expression "National Insurance benefit" means any unemployment, sickness, invalidity or injury benefit or retirement pension payable under any enactment relating to National Insurance or Social Security, other than a benefit claimable by him in respect of a dependant.

Notification of change of circumstances

31. Where—

(a) a pensionable officer after suffering loss of employment or diminution of emoluments enters any employment referred to in regulation 22 or becomes entitled to any superannuation benefit on ceasing to hold such an employment,

(b) a person entitled to long-term compensation, whilst that compensation is liable to review in accordance with the provisions of regulation 32, enters any employment, or ceases to hold an employment, or receives any increase in his emoluments in an employment,

(c) a person entitled to retirement compensation enters employment in which the compensation is subject to reduction or suspension under regulation 30 or ceases to hold such an employment, or receives any increase in his emoluments in an employment, or

(d) a person entitled to long-term compensation starts to receive any benefit, any increase in benefit or any further benefit, under any enactment relating to National Insurance or Social Security,

he shall forthwith in writing inform the compensating authority of that fact.

Review of awards of long-term or retirement compensation

32.—(1) The compensating authority shall—

(a) on the expiry of 6 months from the decision date, or

(b) on the occurrence of any material change in the circumstances of the case,

whichever shall first occur, and thereafter for a period of 2 years after the decision date, or for any longer period specified in the subsequent provisions of this regulation, and at intervals of not more than 6 months review its decision or, where the claim has been the subject of an appeal, the decision of the tribunal, and (subject to paragraph (7)) these regulations shall apply in relation to such a review as they apply in relation to the initial determination of the claim; and on such a review, in the light of any material change in the circumstances of the case, compensation may be awarded, or compensation previously awarded may be increased, reduced or discontinued, subject to the limits set out in these regulations.

(2) The person to whom the decision relates may require the compensating authority to carry out the review mentioned in paragraph (1) at any time within 2 years after the decision date if he considers that there has been a change in the circumstances of his case which is material for the purposes of these regulations.

(3) The compensating authority shall carry out a review in accordance with paragraph (1), notwithstanding the expiration of the period of 2 years mentioned in that paragraph, if—

(a) the emoluments of employment or work undertaken as a result of the loss of employment has been taken into account in determining the amount of any compensation awarded,

(b) that employment or work has been lost or the emoluments thereof reduced, otherwise than by reason of misconduct or incapacity to perform the duties which the person might reasonably have been required to perform, and

(c) the compensating authority are satisfied that the loss or reduction is causing him hardship,

and where any decision is so reviewed, the decision shall be subject to further review in accordance with paragraph (1) as if the review carried out under this paragraph had been the initial determination of the claim.

(4) Paragraphs (1) and (2) shall apply in relation to any decision on a claim for long-term or retirement compensation in respect of diminution of emoluments as they apply in relation to any decision mentioned in paragraph (1)

and as if in paragraph (1) "decision date" means the date on which any decision on a claim for long-term compensation for diminution of emoluments is notified to the claimant, but—

(a) where the person to whom the decision relates ceases to hold the employment in which his emoluments were diminished, a review shall be held within three months after that date, but no further review shall be held after the expiry of that period, and

(b) while that person continues to hold that employment, there shall be no limit to the period within which a review may take place.

(5) Notwithstanding anything contained in the foregoing provisions of this regulation, the compensating authority shall review a decision, whether of the authority or the tribunal, on a claim for long-term compensation for loss of employment or diminution of emoluments after the expiration of any period within which a review is required to be made if at any time—

(a) the person to whom the decision relates becomes engaged in any employment (hereinafter referred to as "his current employment") the emoluments of which are payable out of public funds and which he has undertaken subsequent to the loss or diminution, and

(b) the aggregate of the emoluments of his current employment, any superannuation benefit by way of annual amounts payable to him in respect of the employment which he has lost or the employment in which his emoluments have been diminished and the long-term compensation payable to him exceeds the emoluments of the employment which he has lost, or, as the case may be, in which the emoluments have been diminished.

(6) The compensating authority shall further review any decision reviewed under paragraph (5) whenever the emoluments of the person's current employment are increased.

(7) On any review under this regulation, the amount of long-term compensation which, apart from this paragraph and any reduction under regulation 30(3) and (4), would be payable to the person may be reduced by an amount not exceeding the amount by which the aggregate of the compensation and the annual rate of emoluments of his current employment exceeds the annual rate of emoluments of the employment which he has lost or, as the case may be, in which the emoluments have been diminished.

(8) The compensating authority shall give to a person to whom a decision relates not less than 14 days' notice of any review of that decision to be carried out under this regulation unless the review is carried out at his request.

(9) In this regulation the expression "decision date" means the date on which any decision on a claim for long-term or retirement compensation for loss of employment is notified to a claimant under regulation 34.

(10) For the purposes of regulations 13(4), 22(1) and 29(6) and (7) and on any review under this regulation, no account shall be taken of any increase in the emoluments of any work or employment undertaken as a result of the loss of employment or diminution of emoluments, or of any superannuation

benefit attributable to such an increase, if such increase is effective from any date after the date of the loss or diminution and is attributable to a rise in the cost of living.

(11) Nothing in this regulation shall preclude the making of any adjustment of compensation required by regulation 29 or 30.

Compounding of awards

33.—(1) In the case where an annual sum which has been or might be awarded under these regulations does not exceed £35, the compensating authority may, at their discretion, compound their liability in respect thereof by paying a lump sum equivalent to the capital value of the annual sum and, if any lump sum payment has been awarded or might be awarded in addition to such sum under regulation 18, 19 or 20, the compensating authority may likewise discharge their liability in respect thereof by an immediate payment.

(2) In any other case, if the person who has been awarded long-term or retirement compensation requests them to do so, the compensating authority may, after having regard to the state of health of that person and the other circumstances of the case, compound up to one-quarter of their liability to make payments under the award (other than payments to a widow, child or other dependant under regulation 23) by the payment of an equivalent amount as a lump sum or, where any compensation has been awarded as a lump sum by increasing that compensation to such equivalent amount; and in calculating for this purpose the liability of the authority to make such payments, account shall be taken of the annual value of lump sum payments of compensation other than payments of compensation under Part III of these regulations.

(3) The making of a composition under paragraph (2) in relation to an award of long-term or retirement compensation shall not prevent the subsequent making of a composition under paragraph (1) in relation to that award but, subject as aforesaid, not more than one composition may be made in relation to any award.

PART VII

PROCEDURE AND MISCELLANEOUS

Procedure on making claims

34.—(1) Every claim for compensation under these regulations and every request for a review of an award of long-term or retirement compensation shall be made in accordance with this regulation.

(2) Every such claim or request shall be made to the compensating authority in writing and shall state whether any other claim for compensation has been made by the claimant under these regulations.

(3) Resettlement compensation shall be claimed separately from any other form of compensation claimable under these regulations.

(4) The compensating authority shall consider any such claim or request in accordance with the relevant provisions of these regulations and shall notify the claimant in writing of their decision—

(a) in the case of a claim for resettlement compensation, not later than one month after the receipt of the claim,

(b) in the case of a claim for, or request for the review of an award of, compensation under Part IV or V of these regulations, not later than one month after the receipt of the claim or request, and

(c) in any other case, as soon as possible after the decision,

but the decision of the compensating authority shall not be invalidated by reason of the fact that notice of the decision is given after the expiry of the period mentioned in this paragraph.

(5) Every notification of a decision by the compensating authority (whether granting or refusing compensation or reviewing an award, or otherwise affecting any compensation under these regulations) shall contain a statement—

(a) giving reasons for the decision,

(b) showing how any compensation has been calculated and, in particular if the amount is less than the maximum which could have been awarded under these regulations, showing the factors taken into account in awarding that amount, and

(c) directing the attention of the claimant to his right under regulation 42 if he is aggrieved by the decision, to institute proceedings before a tribunal and giving him the address to which an application instituting those proceedings should be sent.

Claimants to furnish information.

35.—(1) Any person claiming or receiving compensation or whose award of compensation is being reviewed shall furnish all such information that the compensating authority may at any time reasonably require; and he shall verify that information in such manner, including the production of documents in his possession or control, as may be reasonably so required.

(2) Such a person shall, on receipt of reasonable notice, present himself for interview at any place that the compensating authority may reasonably require; and any person who attends for interview may, if he so desires, be represented by his adviser.

Procedure on death of claimant

36.—(1) In the event of the death of a claimant or of a person who, if he had survived, could have been a claimant, a claim for compensation under these regulations may be continued or made, as the case may be, by his personal representatives.

(2) Where any such claim is continued or made as aforesaid by personal representatives, the personal representatives shall, as respects any steps to be taken or things to be done by them in order to continue to make the claim, be deemed for the purposes of these regulations to be the person entitled to claim but, save as aforesaid, the person in whose right they continue or make the claim shall be deemed for the purposes of these regulations to be that person, and the relevant provisions of the regulations shall be construed accordingly.

(3) The compensating authority may in any case where a person who, if he had survived, could have been a claimant has died, extend the period within which a claim under regulation 7 or 11 is to be made by his personal representatives.

Calculation of service

37.—(1) For the purposes of determining the amount of any compensation payable in respect of the loss of an office to which, or of any two or more offices to which in the aggregate, a person devoted substantially the whole of his time, any previous period of part-time employment shall be treated as though it were whole-time employment for a proportionately reduced period.

(2) For the purpose of making any calculation under these regulations in respect of a person's reckonable service, all periods of that service shall be aggregated by reference to completed years and completed days; and any provision in these regulations requiring compensation to be calculated by reference to a year of reckonable service shall (unless the provision specifically states that compensation is payable in respect of completed years) be construed as including completed days, each completed day over and above a completed year being expressed as one 365th of a year.

General provisions as to emoluments

38.—(1) In these regulations, subject to the provisions of paragraph (2) and regulations 39 and 40 the expression "emoluments" means all salary, wages, fees and other payments paid or made to an officer as such for his own use, and also the money value of any accommodation or other allowances in kind appertaining to his employment, but does not include payments for overtime which are not a usual incident of his employment, or any allowances payable to him to cover the cost of providing office accommodation or clerical or other assistance, or any travelling or subsistence allowance or other moneys to be spent, or to cover expenses incurred, by him for the purposes of his employment.

(2) Where fees or other variable payments were paid to an officer as part of his emoluments during any period immediately preceding the loss or diminution, the amount in respect of fees or other variable payments to be included in the annual rate of emoluments shall be the annual average of the fees or other payments paid to him during the period of 5 years immediately preceding the loss or diminution, or such other period as the compensating authority may think reasonable in the circumstances.

(3) For the purposes of these regulations the annual rate of emoluments in relation to any employment which has been lost or the emoluments whereof have been lost or diminished shall be the amount described in (a), (b) or (c) of this paragraph, whichever is the greater—

(a) the emoluments received by him in the period of 12 months immediately preceding the loss or diminution,

(b) in the case of emoluments payable monthly, the emoluments payable in respect of the last complete month immediately preceding the loss or diminution multiplied by 12, or

(c) in the case of emoluments payable weekly, the emoluments payable in respect of the last complete week immediately preceding the loss or diminution multiplied by 52.

Emoluments of part-time employments

39. In ascertaining for the purposes of these regulations whether, and how far, the emoluments of alternative employment fall short of emoluments which have been lost where those emoluments were payable in respect of two or more part-time employments, the emoluments of the alternative employment or of the aggregate of two or more alternative employments shall be apportioned in the proportion which the emoluments of the part-time employments bore to each other.

Temporary variation of emoluments

40. In calculating for the purposes of these regulations the amount of any emoluments lost, or the amount by which any emoluments have been diminished and in determining the resettlement and long-term compensation of any person who has suffered such a loss or diminution, no account shall be taken of any temporary increase or decrease in the amount of the person's emoluments which is attributable to a transfer scheme and otherwise than in the ordinary course of his employment.

Compensation not assignable

41.—(1) Subject to the provisions of any enactment in that behalf, any compensation to which a person becomes entitled under these regulations shall be paid by the compensating authority and shall be payable to, or in trust for, the person who is entitled to receive it, and shall not be assignable.

(2) Without prejudice to any other right of recovery, any compensation paid in error may be recovered by the compensating authority by deduction from any compensation payable under these regulations.

Right of appeal from decision of compensating authority

42.—(1) Every person who is aggrieved by any decision of the compensating authority with respect to a compensation question or by any failure on the part of the compensating authority to notify him of any such decision within the appropriate time prescribed by these regulations, may within 13 weeks of the notification to him of the decision or the expiry of the prescribed time, as the case may be, institute proceedings for the determination of the question by a tribunal in accordance with the Industrial Tribunals (Labour Relations) Regulations 1974(a) and these regulations; and the tribunal shall determine the question accordingly.

(2) For the purpose of any proceedings instituted in pursuance of this regulation a person or persons may be appointed to sit with the tribunal as assessor or assessors.

(3) The compensating authority shall give effect to the decision of a tribunal subject to any modifications that may be required in consequence of any appeal from that decision on a point of law.

(a) S.I. 1974/1386 (1974 II, p. 5330).

SCHEDULE   Regulation 2(3)

TABLES AS TO CAPITAL VALUES AND ANNUAL AMOUNTS

TABLE I(a)

The capital value of an annual amount of £1 per annum, payable for life, which attracts pensions increase when the officer attains age 55, or immediately on retirement if age 55 has already been attained.

Age last birthday	Capital value of £1 per annum, with pensions increase attaching from age 55	
	Female	Male
	£ p	£ p
30	14·82	14·34
31	14·86	14·37
32	14·91	14·39
33	14·95	14·41
34	14·99	14·42
35	15·03	14·43
36	15·06	14·44
37	15·09	14·44
38	15·12	14·43
39	15·14	14·42
40	15·15	14·40
41	15·16	14·37
42	15·15	14·33
43	15·14	14·29
44	15·12	14·23
45	15·09	14·16
46	15·05	14·08
47	14·99	13·99
48	14·92	13·88
49	14·83	13·75
50	14·72	13·61
51	14·59	13·45
52	14·43	13·26
53	14·25	13·04
54	14·04	12·79
55	13·79	12·52
56	13·54	12·24
57	13·28	11·95
58	13·01	11·66
59	12·74	11·36
60	12·46	11·06
61	12·17	10·76
62	11·87	10·45
63	11·57	10·14
64	11·27	9·82
65	10·96	9·51
66	10·64	9·19
67	10·32	8·87
68	10·00	8·56
69	9·68	8·25

TABLE I(a)—contd.

Age last birthday	Capital value of £1 per annum, with pensions increase attaching from age 55	
	Female	Male
	£ p	£ p
70	9·36	7·94
71	9·03	7·63
72	8·70	7·32
73	8·38	7·02
74	8·05	6·72
75	7·73	6·43
76	7·41	6·14
77	7·09	5·86
78	6·78	5·59
79	6·47	5·32

NOTE:—This table is for use in connection with regulation 33(1) and (2) of the regulations for the compounding of annual retirement compensation which a person is currently entitled to receive under regulation 18, 19 or 20. Where the compensation is payable before age 60 (in the case of females) or 65 (in the case of males) but will be reduced on the attainment of that age to take account of a National Insurance or Social Security pension the table should be used in conjunction with Table II(a) i.e. Table II(a) should be used for valuing that part of the compensation which ceases to be payable at 60 (65) and this table should be used for valuing the remainder. This table is not applicable for—

(i) compounding an annual sum payable to a widow under regulation 23 of the regulations (Table III should be used)

(ii) compounding annual retirement compensation which will not begin to be paid until some future date.

TABLE I(b)

The capital value of an annual payment of £1, payable for life, and attracting pensions increase from the outset.

Age last birthday	Capital value of £1 per annum, attracting pensions increase throughout life	
	Female	Male
	£ p	£ p
23	18·59	18·24
24	18·52	18·15
25	18·44	18·05
26	18·36	17·95
27	18·28	17·85
28	18·19	17·74
29	18·10	17·63
30	18·00	17·51
31	17·90	17·38
32	17·79	17·25
33	17·68	17·12
34	17·57	16·98

TABLE I(*b*)—*contd.*

| Age last birthday | Capital value of £1 per annum, attracting pensions increase throughout life | |
	Female	Male
	£ p	£ p
35	17·45	16·83
36	17·32	16·68
37	17·19	16·52
38	17·05	16·35
39	16·91	16·18
40	16·76	16·00
41	16·61	15·81
42	16·45	15·62
43	16·29	15·42
44	16·12	15·21
45	15·94	15·00
46	15·76	14·78
47	15·57	14·56
48	15·37	14·33
49	15·17	14·09
50	14·96	13·84
51	14·74	13·59
52	14·51	13·33
53	14·28	13·07
54	14·04	12·80
55	13·79	12·52
56	13·54	12·24
57		
58		
59		
	as for Table I(*a*) from age 55	
60		
—		
—		
—		

NOTE:—This table is for use in connection with regulation 33(1) and (2) for the compounding of annual retirement compensation which a person is currently entitled to receive under regulation 19 if he becomes incapacitated before normal retiring age. Where the compensation is payable before age 60 (in the case of females) or 65 (in the case of males) but will be reduced on the attainment of that age to take account of a National Insurance or Social Security pension, the table should be used in conjunction with Table II(*b*) i.e. Table II(*b*) should be used for valuing that part of the compensation which ceases to be payable at 60(65) and this table should be used for valuing the remainder.

This table is not applicable for—

(i) compounding an annual sum payable to a widow under regulation 23 of the regulations (Table III should be used).

(ii) compounding annual retirement compensation which will not begin to be paid until some future date.

TABLE II(a)

Capital value of £1 per annum, ceasing at age 60 (females), 65 (males), which attracts pensions increase from age 55 or retirement age if greater.

Age last birthday	Capital Value	
	Female	Male
	£ p	£ p
30	12·11	12·92
31	12·01	12·87
32	11·91	12·81
33	11·80	12·75
34	11·68	12·68
35	11·55	12·60
36	11·40	12·51
37	11·24	12·41
38	11·07	12·30
39	10·88	12·18
40	10·67	12·04
41	10·44	11·89
42	10·19	11·72
43	9·92	11·53
44	9·63	11·33
45	9·31	11·11
46	8·96	10·86
47	8·58	10·59
48	8·16	10·30
49	7·71	9·98
50	7·22	9·62
51	6·68	9·23
52	6·09	8·80
53	5·45	8·33
54	4·75	7·81
55	3·99	7·24
56	3·18	6·64
57	2·33	6·01
58	1·43	5·35
59	0·49	4·65
60	—	3·91
61	—	3·13
62	—	2·30
63	—	1·42
64	—	0·48

NOTE:—This table is for use in connection with regulation 33(1) and (2) for the compounding of any part of annual retirement compensation which will cease to be payable on the attainment of age 60 (in the case of females) or 65 (in the case of males). Table I(a) should be used in relation to the remainder of such compensation, i.e. the part which is payable for life—see note on that table.

TABLE II(*b*)

Capital value of £1 per annum, ceasing at age 60 (females), 65 (males), which attracts pensions increase from the outset of the pension.

Age last birthday	Capital value	
	Female	Male
	£ p	£ p
23	16·68	17·24
24	16·51	17·10
25	16·33	16·95
26	16·14	16·79
27	15·94	16·63
28	15·74	16·46
29	15·52	16·28
30	15·29	16·09
31	15·05	15·89
32	14·80	15·68
33	14·54	15·46
34	14·26	15·23
35	13·97	15·00
36	13·66	14·75
37	13·34	14·49
38	13·01	14·22
39	12·66	13·94
40	12·29	13·64
41	11·90	13·33
42	11·49	13·01
43	11·07	12·67
44	10·63	12·31
45	10·16	11·94
46	9·67	11·56
47	9·15	11·16
48	8·61	10·74
49	8·04	10·30
50	7·45	9·85
51	6·83	9·38
52	6·17	8·88
53	5·48	8·36
54	4·75	7·81
55	3·99	7·24
56	3·18	6·64
57	2·33	6·01
58	1·43	5·35
59	0·49	4·65

NEW TOWNS

TABLE II(*b*)—*contd.*

Age last birthday	Capital value	
	Female	Male
	£ p	£ p
60	—	3·91
61	—	3·13
62	—	2·30
63	—	1·42
64	—	0·48

NOTE—This table is for use in connection with regulation 33(1) and (2) for the compounding of any part of annual retirement compensation which will cease to be payable on the attainment of age 60 (in the case of females) or 65 (in the case of males). Table I(*b*) should be used in relation to the remainder of such compensation, i.e. the part which is payable for life—see note on that table.

TABLE III

Capital value of an annual amount of £1, which attracts pensions increase from the outset, payable to a widow until death or remarriage.

Age of widow at date of widowhood	Capital value	Age of widow at date of widowhood	Capital value
	£ p		£ p
20	6·00	45	13·14
21	6·00	46	13·25
22	6·00	47	13·34
23	6·00	48	13·40
24	6·13	49	13·44
25	6·58	50	13·46
26	7·01	51	13·46
27	7·41	52	13·43
28	7·78	53	13·38
29	8·11	54	13·31
30	8·41	55	13·22
31	8·72	56	13·10
32	9·06	57	12·96
33	9·42	58	12·80
34	9·82	56	12·61
35	10·24	60	12·39
36	10·65	61	12·14
37	11·04	62	11·87
38	11·40	63	11·57
39	11·73	64	11·27
40	12·04	65	10·96
41	12·33	66	10·64
42	12·59	67	10·32
43	12·81	68	10·00
44	12·99	69	9·68
		70	9·35

NOTE:—This table is for use in connection with Regulation 33(1) for compounding annual compensation payable to a widow under regulation 23. It should also be used, where a reduction of compensation under regulation 23(7) of the regulations falls to be apportioned between the compensation payable under that regulation and under regulation 24, for ascertaining the capital value of annual compensation to a widow.

TABLE IV(a)

The annual amount, payable for life, which attracts pensions increase from age 55, or from retirement if age 55 has already been attained, equivalent in value to a lump sum of £100.

Age last birthday	Annual amount, attracting pensions increase from age 55, and payable for life, equal in value to a lump sum of £100	
	Female	Male
	£ p	£ p
30	6·75	6·97
31	6·73	6·96
32	6·71	6·95
33	6·69	6·94
34	6·67	6·93
35	6·65	6·93
36	6·64	6·93
37	6·63	6·93
38	6·61	6·93
39	6·61	6·93
40	6·60	6·94
41	6·60	6·96
42	6·60	6·98
43	6·61	7·00
44	6·61	7·03
45	6·63	7·06
46	6·64	7·10
47	6·67	7·15
48	6·70	7·20
49	6·74	7·27
50	6·79	7·35
51	6·85	7·43
52	6·93	7·54
53	7·02	7·67
54	7·12	7·82
55	7·25	7·99
56	7·39	8·17
57	7·53	8·37
58	7·69	8·58
59	7·85	8·80
60	8·03	9·04
61	8·22	9·29
62	8·42	9·57
63	8·64	9·86
64	8·87	10·18
65	9·12	10·52
66	9·40	10·88
67	9·69	11·27
68	10·00	11·68
69	10·33	12·12

TABLE IV(a)—contd.

Age last birthday	Annual amount, attracting pensions increase from age 55, and payable for life, equal in value to a lump sum of £100	
	Female	Male
	£ p	£ p
70	10·68	12·59
71	11·07	13·11
72	11·49	13·66
73	11·93	14·25
74	12·42	14·88
75	12·94	15·55
76	13·50	16·29
77	14·10	17·06
78	14·75	17·89
79	15·46	18·80

NOTE:—This table is for use in connection with regulation 21 for ascertaining the annual amount by which retirement compensation under regulation 18, 19 or 20 is to be reduced where a claimant has not paid to the compensating authority or fund authority an amount equal to any sum paid to him by way of superannuation contributions. It should also be used in connection with regulation 33(2) of the regulations for calculating for the purposes of that paragraph the annual value of retirement compensation awarded as a lump sum.

TABLE IV(*b*)

The annual amount, which attracts pensions increase throughout life, equivalent in value to a lump sum of £100.

Age last birthday	Annual sum, attracting pensions increase throughout life, equal in value to a lump sum of £100	
	Female	Male
	£ p	£ p
23	5·38	5·48
24	5·40	5·51
25	5·42	5·54
26	5·45	5·57
27	5·47	5·60
28	5·50	5·64
29	5·52	5·67
30	5·56	5·71
31	5·59	5·75
32	5·62	5·80
33	5·66	5·84
34	5·69	5·89
35	5·73	5·94
36	5·77	6·00
37	5·82	6·05
38	5·87	6·12
39	5·91	6·18
40	5·97	6·25
41	6·02	6·33
42	6·08	6·40
43	6·14	6·49
44	6·20	6·57
45	6·27	6·67
46	6·35	6·77
47	6·42	6·87
48	6·51	6·98
49	6·59	7·10
50	6·68	7·23
51	6·78	7·36
52	6·89	7·50
53	7·00	7·65
54	7·12	7·81

TABLE IV(*b*)—*contd.*

Age last birthday	Annual sum, attracting pensions increase throughout life, equal in value to a lump sum of £100	
	Female	Male
	£ p	£ p
55	7·25	7·99
56	7·39	8·17
57		
58		
59		
60	as for Table IV(*a*) from age 55	
—		
—		

NOTE:—This table is for use in connection with regulation 21 for ascertaining the annual amount by which retirement compensation under regulation 19 is to be reduced where a claimant has become incapacitated before normal retiring age and has not paid to the compensating authority or fund authority an amount equal to any sum paid to him by way of superannuation contributions. It should also be used in connection with regulation 33(2) of the regulations for calculating for the purposes of that paragraph the annual value of retirement compensation awarded as a lump sum.

TABLE V

The annual amount, which attracts pensions increase from the outset, payable to a widow until death or remarriage, equivalent in value to a lump sum of £100.

Age of widow at date of widowhood	Annual amount	Age of widow at date of widowhood	Annual amount
	£ p		£ p
20	16·67	45	7·61
21	16·67	46	7·55
22	16·67	47	7·50
23	16·67	48	7·46
24	16·31	49	7·44
25	15·20	50	7·43
26	14·27	51	7·43
27	13·50	52	7·45
28	12·85	53	7·47
29	12·33	54	7·51
30	11·89	55	7·56
31	11·47	56	7·63
32	11·04	57	7·72
33	10·62	58	7·81
34	10·18	59	7·93
35	9·77	60	8·07
36	9·39	61	8·24
37	9·06	62	8·42
38	8·77	63	8·64
39	8·53	64	8·87
40	8·31	65	9·12
41	8·11	66	9·40
42	7·94	67	9·69
43	7·81	68	10·00
44	7·70	69	10·33
		70	10·70

NOTE:—This table is for use in connection with regulation 23(7) for ascertaining the annual amount by which compensation to a widow is to be reduced in the circumstances described in that paragraph. If a reduction is required to be apportioned between compensation payable under regulations 23 and 24, the capital value of annual compensation to a widow should be ascertained by reference to Table III.

TABLE VI(a)

The capital value of each £100 of the total amount of long-term compensation, payable to age 65, in which the annual payments attract pensions increase from age 55, according to the outstanding period of long-term compensation.

Outstanding number of complete years of long-term compensation	Capital value	
	Female	Male
	£ p	£ p
0	98·65	98·50
1	95·95	95·50
2	93·25	92·60
3	90·65	89·80
4	88·20	87·15
5	85·90	84·70
6	83·70	82·40
7	81·60	80·25
8	79·60	78·20
9	77·70	76·30
10	75·80	74·40
11	73·85	72·45
12	71·80	70·45
13	69·75	68·40
14	67·70	66·40
15	65·65	64·40
16	63·65	62·45
17	61·70	60·55
18	59·80	58·75
19	58·00	57·00
20	56·25	55·30
21	54·55	53·65
22	52·95	52·10
23	51·40	50·60
24	49·90	49·15
25	48·45	47·75
26	47·05	46·40
27	45·75	45·10
28	44·45	43·90
29	43·20	42·75
30	42·05	41·60

NOTE:—This table is for use in connection with regulation 33(1) and (2) for compounding awards of long-term compensation under Part IV of the regulations. The total amount of the annual long-term compensation which is to be compounded must first be calculated, i.e. the amount which the person would receive on account of that compensation, or the part of it which is to be compounded, if it were paid until age 65. For each £100 so calculated, the lump sum payment will be the amount shown in the table according to the number of complete years in the period between the date of compounding and age 65.

TABLE VI(b)

The capital value of each £100 of the total amount of long-term compensation, payable to age 70, in which the annual payments attract pension increase from age 55, according to the outstanding period of long-term compensation.

Outstanding number of complete years of long-term compensation	Capital value	
	Female	Male
	£ p	£ p
0	98·50	98·30
1	95·50	94·90
2	92·60	91·60
3	89·80	88·40
4	87·20	85·45
5	84·75	82·80
6	82·45	80·35
7	80·30	78·10
8	78·25	76·00
9	76·35	74·05
10	74·50	72·20
11	72·75	70·45
12	71·10	68·85
13	69·55	67·30
14	68·00	65·85
15	66·50	64·40
16	64·95	62·90
17	63·35	61·40
18	61·70	59·85
19	60·05	58·25
20	58·40	56·70
21	56·80	55·20
22	55·20	53·70
23	53·65	52·25
24	52·15	50·80
25	50·70	49·40
26	49·25	48·05
27	47·90	46·75
28	46·55	45·50
29	45·25	44·30
30	44·05	43·10

NOTE:—This table is for use in connection with regulation 33(1) and (2) for compounding awards of long-term compensation under Part IV of the regulations. The total amount of the annual long-term compensation which is to be compounded must first be calculated, i.e. the amount which the person would receive on account of that compensation, or the part of it which is to be compounded, if it were paid until age 70. For each £100 so calculated, the lump sum payable will be the amount shown in the table according to the number of complete years in the period between the date of compounding and age 70.

Peter Shore,
Secretary of State for Environment.

11th August 1977.

Signed by Authority of the
Secretary of State for Wales

T. Alec Jones,
Parliamentary Under Secretary of State,
Welsh Office.

12th August 1977.

EXPLANATORY NOTE

(This Note is not part of the Regulations.)

1. These Regulations provide for the payment of compensation to or in respect of persons who suffer loss of employment or loss or diminution of emoluments as a result of a transfer scheme under the New Towns (Amendment) Act 1976.

2. Part I of the regulations (with the Schedule) contains definitions. Part II specifies the persons to whom the regulations apply and the grounds of entitlement to compensation.

3. The compensation payable is:
   (a) resettlement compensation for loss of employment (Part III);
   (b) long-term compensation for loss of employment or loss or diminution of emoluments (Part IV);
   (c) retirement compensation for loss of employment or loss or diminution of emoluments (Part V);
   (d) compensation to the widow, child or other dependant or to the personal representatives of a claimant who was a pensionable officer (Part V).

4. Resettlement compensation is payable in a lump sum to officers with at least 2 years' service in relevant employment. The qualifying conditions and factors to be considered are set out in regulation 7, and the methods of calculation are set out in regulations 8 and 9.

5. Long-term and retirement compensation is payable to officers with at least 5 years' service in relevant employment. The qualifying conditions and factors to be considered are set out in regulations 11 and 12.

6. The method of calculating the amount of long-term compensation is laid down in regulations 13 (loss of emoluments) and 14 (diminution of emoluments). The compensation is payable from the date determined under regulation 15, but is not payable for any period in respect of which retirement compensation is payable. In the case of a non-pensionable officer, compensation not exceeding one half of the rate of long-term compensation may be paid beyond normal retiring age (regulation 26).

7. Retirement compensation payable to a pensionable officer is based upon his accrued pension rights (regulations 18 and 20) supplemented in the case of persons aged 40 or over at the date of the loss or diminution by the addition of notional years of service (regulation 17). Special provision is made for any persons whose pension arrangements are by way of policies of insurance (regulation 27). Retirement compensation is ordinarily payable from normal retiring age but in certain circumstances is payable earlier (regulation 19).

8. Compensation is payable to the widow, child or other dependant or to the personal representatives or trustees of a claimant who dies where such persons would have benefited under the relevant pension scheme (regulations 23 to 25).

9. Part VI provides for long-term and retirement compensation to be reviewed and for awards to be varied in the light of changing circumstances (regulation 32). It also contains provisions for the adjustment, suspension and compounding of compensation in certain circumstances.

10. Part VII contains provisions relating to the procedure for making claims and notifying decisions. A right is given to a claimant who is aggrieved by a decision on a compensation question or the failure of the compensating authority to notify its decision to refer the question for determination by a tribunal in accordance with the Industrial Tribunals (Labour Relations) Regulations 1974.

STATUTORY INSTRUMENTS

1977 No. 1411

NEW TOWNS

The New Town Transfer Schemes (Staff Protection) Regulations 1977

Made - - - -		12th August 1977
Laid before Parliament		17th August 1977
Coming into Operation		7th September 1977

The Secretary of State for the Environment, in relation to England, and the Secretary of State for Wales, in relation to Wales, in exercise of the powers conferred on them by section 13(1), (3) and (7) of the New Towns (Amendment) Act 1976(a), and of all other powers enabling them in that behalf, hereby make the following regulations:—

Citation and Commencement

1. These regulations may be cited as the New Town Transfer Schemes (Staff Protection) Regulations 1977 and shall come into operation on 7th September 1977.

Interpretation

2.—(1) In these regulations, unless the context otherwise requires—

"the Act" means the New Towns (Amendment) Act 1976;

"new employment" has the meaning assigned to that expression by regulation 6 below;

"old employment" has the meaning assigned to that expression by regulation 3 below;

"terms and conditions of employment" includes any restriction arising under any Act or any instrument made under any Act on the termination of the employment of any person.

(2) For the purpose of these regulations a thing shall be deemed to happen as a result of a transfer scheme if it is shown that that thing would have been unlikely to happen had the scheme not been made by the new town corporation and district council and approved or made by the Secretary of State as the case may be, but this provision shall not prevent a thing being regarded as happening as a result of a transfer scheme if it would have been so regarded in the absence of this provision.

(3) References in these regulations to any enactment shall, except where the context otherwise requires, be construed as references to that enactment as amended or extended by or under any other enactment.

(4) The Interpretation Act 1889(b) shall apply for the interpretation of these regulations as it applies for the interpretation of an Act of Parliament.

(a) 1976 c. 68.   (b) 1889 c. 63.

Application

3. These regulations apply for the protection of the interests of any person who, on or after the approval or, as the case may be, making of a transfer scheme by the Secretary of State, is in any employment with the new town corporation or district council concerned (the old employment) and is affected by the scheme.

Notice of transfer schemes

4.—(1) As soon as practicable after a new town corporation and a district council have submitted a transfer scheme to the Secretary of State in pursuance of directions under section 3 of the Act, the new town corporation and the district council shall notify every person employed by them at that time to whom these regulations are likely to apply and every body which it appears to them is representative of such persons of such submission, shall inform every such person and body of a place where a copy of the scheme as submitted can be inspected, and shall transmit to every such body a copy of that part of the scheme which contains the information and proposals required to be contained and stated therein by section 3(6)(*d*) of the Act.

(2) As soon as practicable after a new town corporation and a district council are notified by the Secretary of State that he has approved without modification a scheme submitted to him or receive from him a copy of a scheme as finally approved by him with modifications or, as the case may be, as finally made by him, the new town corporation and the district council shall notify every person employed by them at that time to whom these regulations are likely to apply and every body which it appears to them is representative of such persons of such approval or making, shall inform every such person and body of a place where a copy of the scheme as approved or made can be inspected and of the date on which the scheme comes into force, and unless the Secretary of State has approved the scheme without modifying that part of the scheme which contains the information and proposals required to be contained and stated therein by section 3(6)(*d*) of the Act, shall transmit to every such body a copy of that part of the scheme.

Protection of employees

5. A notice to terminate the contract of employment of any person, given by reason of the fact that that person has become redundant as a result of a transfer scheme, shall not, unless such person otherwise agrees—

(*a*) be given earlier than 31st December immediately following the date on which the Secretary of State approves or makes the transfer scheme concerned, and

(*b*) come into operation earlier than the expiration of 6 months from the service thereof.

6. Every person who as a result of a transfer scheme is, whether before or after the scheme comes into force, in new employment, that is to say employment (whether with another of the parties to the scheme or the same employer) which is different from his old employment, shall, so long as he continues in the new employment and until he is served with a statement in writing referring to these regulations and specifying new terms and conditions of employment, enjoy terms and conditions of employment which are not less favourable, taken as a whole, than those which he enjoyed immediately before the termination of the old employment.

7. A statement of new terms and conditions of employment may be served on the person concerned before the commencement of his new employment but shall in any event be so served not later than the expiration of 3 months from the date on which his new employment commenced.

8.—(1) If the person concerned is engaged in duties reasonably comparable to those in which he was engaged immediately before the termination of the old employment, the new terms and conditions of employment shall be such that—

(a) the scale of his salary or remuneration, and

(b) the other terms and conditions of his employment

are not less favourable, taken together, than those which he enjoyed immediately before the termination of the old employment.

(2) If the person concerned is engaged in duties which are not reasonably comparable to those in which he was engaged immediately before the termination of the old employment, the new terms and conditions of employment shall be such that the terms and conditions of his employment (other than any relating to the scale of his salary or remuneration) are not less favourable, taken together, than those which he enjoyed immediately before the termination of the old employment.

9. Where between the commencement of the new employment and the service of new terms and conditions of employment the scale of the salary or remuneration which the person concerned enjoyed immediately before the termination of the old employment is improved, regulation 8(1) above shall have effect as if the scale as improved had been so enjoyed.

10. Where the new terms and conditions of employment involve any diminution of the scale of the salary or remuneration of the person concerned they shall not come into effect until the date, not earlier than the expiration of 3 months from the service of the statement thereof, specified in that statement.

Determination of disputes

11.—(1) Any question by a person employed by a new town corporation or district council as to whether—

(a) he is a person to whom these regulations apply,

(b) any thing that has happened to him has happened as a result of a transfer scheme,

(c) the terms and conditions of his employment are in accordance with regulation 6 or, as the case may be, 8 above,

(d) any duties are reasonably comparable within the meaning of regulation 8 above, or

(e) the terms and conditions of the new employment (other than the scale of salary or remuneration) specified in a statement of such terms and conditions served on him would give rise to hardship if applied to him, or have given rise to hardship by being so applied,

shall be determined in accordance with Circular NTSC 7/77 of the New Towns Staff Commission.

(2) If a question in relation to new terms and conditions of employment specified in a statement of such terms and conditions served on a person is submitted for determination by that person under any of the provisions of paragraph (1) above, such new terms and conditions of employment shall not have effect (and shall be deemed never to have had effect) until the determination of such question, and until such determination regulation 6 above shall continue to apply as if no such statement specifying the new terms and conditions had been served.

Hardship

12.—(1) Where it is determined that a person would or has sustained hardship as mentioned in regulation 11(1)(*e*) above the employer as respects the new employment shall, in consultation with that person and representatives of their employees seek a remedy and, not later than the expiration of 2 months (or such longer period as may be agreed by the person concerned) following the notification of the determination, notify that person of any remedy which they are able to offer him or that they are unable to offer him any remedy but that an allowance will be paid to him in respect of the hardship.

(2) In either event, the person concerned shall be informed—

(*a*) that he may, subject to paragraph (5) below, request that his employment be terminated, and

(*b*) of his entitlements if it is so terminated.

(3) Any remedy offered under paragraph (1) above may be accepted by the person concerned within the 2 months following the notification thereof or within such longer period as may be agreed by the employer.

(4) An allowance in respect of hardship shall be by periodic payments of such amount as may be determined by agreement between the person concerned and the employer or failing such agreement in accordance with Circular NTSC 7/77 of the New Towns Staff Commission.

In the event of any change of circumstances the payment of the allowance or the amount thereof may be reviewed by such agreement or failing an agreement determined in accordance with such Circular.

(5) No such request as is described in paragraph (2) above shall be made after the expiration of 2 months (or such longer period as may be agreed by the employer) from the determination of the amount of the periodic payments of the allowance.

(6) Regulation 16 below shall not apply to any person to whom an allowance is payable under this regulation.

(7) If the remedy offered is, with the agreement of the employer as respects the old employment, transfer back to the employment of that employer, and that remedy is accepted by the person concerned and he is so transferred, these regulations shall cease to apply to him.

Statements of new terms and conditions

13. A written statement given in accordance with section 4(1) of the Contracts of Employment Act 1972(**a**) shall not be regarded as a statement of new terms and conditions of employment within the meaning of these regulations unless the statement refers to these regulations.

(**a**) 1972 c. 53.

Apprenticeships

14. Any contract of apprenticeship entered into between any person who as a result of a transfer scheme is, whether before or after the scheme comes into force, in new employment with a different employer (being another of the parties to the scheme) shall have effect as a contract entered into between such person and that employer.

Saving for training arrangements

15. Where any person who as a result of a transfer scheme is, whether before or after the scheme comes into force, in new employment with a different employer (being another of the parties of the scheme) undergoing training under arrangements which have not been discharged before the date the new employment commences, those arrangements shall continue to apply with the substitution for the employer as respects the old employment of the employer as respects the new employment.

Travelling and removal expenses

16. Any additional travelling expenses and any removal or incidental expenses reasonably incurred by any person in consequence of his entering into new employment as a result of a transfer scheme shall be reimbursed by the employer as respects the new employment for a period not exceeding four years from the date of commencement of such employment.

Commencing points on scales

17. Where in relation to any person who as a result of a transfer scheme is, whether before or after the scheme comes into force, in new employment—

(*a*) on the scale of salary or remuneration applicable to him immediately before the commencement of such new employment he would have become entitled to an increment on the date of such commencement, and

(*b*) by reason of such commencement any other scale of salary or remuneration becomes applicable to him as from such date,

any term of his employment as to his commencing point on such other scale shall be applicable as if his employment before, and on and after, such date were one continuous employment under one authority.

Savings for extensions of service

18. Any extension of service under regulation L15 of the Local Government Superannuation Regulations 1974(**a**) effective immediately before the person concerned commences new employment shall continue to have effect as if it had been made by the employer as respects the new employment.

Peter Shore,
Secretary of State for the Environment.

11th August 1977.

Signed by authority of the
Secretary of State for Wales
12th August 1977.

T. Alec Jones,
Parliamentary Under Secretary of State,
Welsh Office.

(**a**) S.I. 1974/520 (1974 I, p. 1986).

EXPLANATORY NOTE

(This Note is not part of the Regulations.)

Section 13(1) of the New Towns (Amendment) Act 1976 requires the Secretary of State to make regulations containing such provisions as appear to him to be appropriate for the protection of the interests of any person who, on or after the approval or, as the case may be, making of a transfer scheme under that Act is in any employment with the new town corporation or district council concerned and is affected by the scheme.

These Regulations contain such provisions.

STATUTORY INSTRUMENTS

1977 No. 1412

CONSUMER PROTECTION
PRICES

The Price Marking (Meat) Order 1977

Made - - -	*16th August* 1977
Laid before Parliament	*22nd August* 1977
Coming into Operation	*1st March* 1978

Whereas the Secretary of State, in accordance with the provisions of section 4(3) of the Prices Act 1974(**a**), has consulted, in such manner as appeared to him to be appropriate having regard to the subject-matter and urgency of this Order, with such organisations representative of interests substantially affected by this Order, as appeared to him, having regard to those matters, to be appropriate: Now, therefore, the Secretary of State, in exercise of his powers under section 4 of that Act, as amended by section 16 of the Price Commission Act 1977(**b**), hereby makes the following Order:—

1.—(1) This Order may be cited as the Price Marking (Meat) Order 1977, and shall come into operation on 1st March 1978.

(2) Subject to paragraph (3) below, goods to which this Order applies are foods of the following descriptions, whether pre-packed or not, that is to say, fresh, chilled or frozen meat.

(3) This Order does not apply to—

    (*a*) goods described in paragraph (2) above when offered or exposed for sale as a single item together with goods not so described;

    (*b*) processed meat;

    (*c*) products commonly known as beefburgers, hamburgers or porkburgers, consisting wholly or partly of meat described in paragraph (2) above;

    (*d*) heads, feet and trotters;

    (*e*) bones, waste and scrap.

(4) In this Order—

"container" includes any form of packaging of goods for sale as a single item, whether by way of wholly or partly enclosing the goods or by way of attaching the goods to some other article, and in particular includes a wrapper;

"display area" in relation to any premises on which goods to which this Order applies are offered or exposed for sale, means—

    (*a*) windows, including the beds thereof, and display rails in windows; and

    (*b*) cabinets, counters, and shelves used for the display of goods to an intending purchaser;

"meat" means any part of an animal of any of the following descriptions, that is to say, cattle, sheep and swine;

"premises" includes a stall or vehicle;

"pre-packed" means made up in advance ready for retail sale in or on a container;

"processed", in relation to meat, includes curing, smoking and any other treatments including the addition of salts, curing agents or other substances, resulting in a change in the natural state of the meat, but does not include treatment with proteolytic enzymes, boning, paring, grinding, mincing, cutting, cleaning or trimming;

"selling price" in relation to any goods, means the price at which the goods are offered or exposed for sale, not being a price expressed by reference to a unit of measurement;

"unit price" in relation to any goods, means the price per pound weight of those goods.

(5) The Interpretation Act 1889(a) shall apply for the interpretation of this Order as it applies for the interpretation of an Act of Parliament.

(6) The Price Marking (Meat and Fish) Order 1974(b) shall not apply to meat offered or exposed for sale after 28th February 1978.

2.—(1) Subject to the following provisions of this Article, no person shall, in Great Britain, offer or expose for sale by retail goods to which this Order applies in the display area of any premises unless an indication of the price of the goods is given, being an indication complying with the appropriate requirements of the Schedule hereto.

(2) Where a piece of meat is cut at the request of, and in the presence of, an intending purchaser, an indication of the unit price of that part of the meat intended for the purchaser shall not be required.

(3) An indication of the unit price of a piece of meat shall not be required if the piece of meat is offered or exposed for sale as a single item, and

(a) the weight is less than 1 ounce, or

(b) the selling price does not exceed 10p and is marked on or in relation to the meat, and

if, in either case, any indication of a unit price which might be taken as applying to that piece of meat makes it clear that it does not so apply.

Robert Maclennan,
Parliamentary Under Secretary of State,
Department of Prices and Consumer Protection.

16th August 1977.

(a) 1889 c. 63.   (b) S.I. 1974/1368 (1974 II, p. 5253).

SCHEDULE

1. In this Schedule "gross weight", in relation to any goods, means the aggregate weight of the goods and any container in or on which they are made up.

2. In the case of pre-packed goods in respect of which an indication of weight is marked on the container in or on which the goods are made up, the indication of the price shall consist of—

    (*a*) the selling price; and

    (*b*) the unit price calculated by reference to the selling price and to the indicated weight.

3. In the case of goods, whether pre-packed or not, to which paragraph 2 does not apply, the indication shall be an indication of the unit price.

4. An indication of the selling price required by paragraph 2(*a*) above shall be marked on the container.

5. An indication of the unit price, if it is not marked on the goods or on the container, shall be easily recognisable by an intending purchaser under normal conditions of purchase as referring to goods of the description in question; but the indication need not be adjacent to the goods and may be grouped with other indications of the unit prices of other goods to which this Order applies in the form of a list or otherwise.

6. Where the indication of the unit price is not adjacent to the goods to which it refers it shall be in such a position that it is readily discernible by an intending purchaser from the place where he would under normal conditions of purchase select the goods, or, if he would not select the goods himself, where he would, under those conditions, ask for the goods. If there is more than one such indication in relation to any goods it shall be sufficient if one such indication complies with this paragraph.

7. If the indications of the selling price (whether required by this Order or not) and the unit price are both marked on the container they shall be in close proximity to one another but sufficiently distinct as not to confuse an intending purchaser under normal conditions of purchase.

8. Any indication shall be clear and legible, and easily read by an intending purchaser under normal conditions of purchase.

9. Where the indication of a unit price has been calculated by reference to the gross weight of the goods, that fact shall be clearly indicated.

EXPLANATORY NOTE

(This Note is not part of the Order.)

This Order requires the price of meat offered or exposed for retail sale in a display area of any premises to be indicated.

The Order does not apply to products such as hamburgers or to meat which has been subjected to any form of processing e.g., curing, smoking and salting, or in the other circumstances described in Article 1(3). The requirements to be fulfilled when indicating the price are set out in the Schedule.

The unit price (price per lb. weight of the goods) is to be indicated in all cases on a label on or adjacent to the goods, on a price list or by other appropriate means. In addition the selling price is to be indicated on the package in the case of meat pre-packed in a container bearing an indication of the weight of the goods.

An exemption from indicating the unit price is given for meat cut at the request of, and in the presence of, an intending purchaser. Exemption from indicating the unit price is also given for meat offered or exposed for retail sale as a single item weighing less than 1 ounce or marked with a selling price of not more than 10p.

The Price Marking (Meat and Fish) Order 1974 no longer applies to meat offered or exposed for retail sale.

STATUTORY INSTRUMENTS

1977 No. 1413

ROAD TRAFFIC

The Passenger and Goods Vehicles (Recording Equipment) (Approval of fitters and workshops) (Fees) Regulations 1977

Made - - -	*15th August* 1977
Laid before Parliament	*17th August* 1977
Coming into Operation	*7th September* 1977

The Secretary of State for Transport, with the consent of the Treasury, in exercise of the powers conferred by section 56(1) and (2) of the Finance Act 1973(**a**), and of all other enabling powers, hereby makes the following Regulations:—

1.—(1) These Regulations may be cited as the Passenger and Goods Vehicles (Recording Equipment) (Approval of fitters and workshops) (Fees) Regulations 1977 and shall come into operation on 7th September 1977.

(2) In these Regulations—

"recording equipment" means equipment which is designed for recording information as to the use of a vehicle and which is installed in a vehicle for the purposes of the relevant Community instrument;

"the relevant Community instrument" means Council Regulation (EEC) No. 1463/70 of 20 July 1970(**b**).

(3) The Interpretation Act 1889(**c**) shall apply for the interpretation of these Regulations as it applies for the interpretation of an Act of Parliament.

2. The fee to be paid to the Secretary of State for granting approval of a fitter or workshop for recording equipment in accordance with Article 14 of the relevant Community instrument (which requires recording equipment to be installed and repaired by approved fitters or approved workshops) shall be £120.

William Rodgers,

8th August 1977.   Secretary of State for Transport.

We consent to the making of
these Regulations   *David Stoddart,*

J. Dormand,
Two of the Lords Commissioners of
15th August 1977.   Her Majesty's Treasury

(**a**) 1973 c. 51.   (**b**) OJ No. L164/1 of 27.7.70.   (**c**) 1889 c. 63.

EXPLANATORY NOTE

(This Note is not part of the Regulations.)

These Regulations prescribe the fee which may be charged by the Secretary of State for Transport for approving, in accordance with Council Regulation (EEC) No. 1463/70, fitters and workshops for installing and repairing recording equipment (tachographs) in road vehicles in accordance with the Council Regulation. By virtue of the Passenger and Goods Vehicles (Recording Equipment) Regulations 1977 (S.I. 1977/777) the Secretary of State is the competent authority for giving such approvals.

STATUTORY INSTRUMENTS

1977 No. 1426 (C. 51)

CRIMINAL LAW, ENGLAND AND WALES

The Criminal Law Act 1977 (Commencement No. 2) Order 1977

Made - - - - 18*th August* 1977

In exercise of the powers conferred on me by section 65(7) of the Criminal Law Act 1977(**a**), I hereby make the following Order:—

1. This Order may be cited as the Criminal Law Act 1977 (Commencement No. 2) Order 1977.

2. The provisions of the Criminal Law Act 1977 specified in column 1 of the Schedule to this Order (which relate to the matters specified in column 2 thereof) shall come into force on 8th September 1977, in addition to the provisions coming into force on that date by virtue of the Criminal Law Act (Commencement No. 1) Order 1977(**b**).

Albert Booth,
One of Her Majesty's Principal
Secretaries of State.

18th August 1977.

(**a**) 1977 c. 45.   (**b**) S.I. 1977/1365 (1977 II, p. 4074).

SCHEDULE

PROVISIONS OF THE CRIMINAL LAW ACT 1977 COMING
INTO FORCE ON 8th SEPTEMBER 1977

Provisions of the Act	Subject matter of provisions
Section 59.	Alteration of maximum periods of imprisonment in default of payment of fines etc.
So much of Schedule 13 as is specified in the Appendix hereto.	Repeals.

APPENDIX

REPEALS TAKING EFFECT ON 8th SEPTEMBER 1977

Chapter	Short Title	Extent of repeal
1947 c.14	Exchange Control Act 1947.	In Part II of Schedule 5, paragraph 3(1).
1952 c.44	Customs and Excise Act 1952.	Section 285(1).
1952 c.55	Magistrates' Courts Act 1952.	In Schedule 3, paragraph 3.
1967 c.1	Land Commission Act 1967.	Section 82(5).
1967 c.80	Criminal Justice Act 1967.	Section 93.

EXPLANATORY NOTE

(This Note is not part of the Order.)

This Order brings into force on 8th September 1977 the provisions of the Criminal Law Act 1977 set out in the Schedule to the Order.

STATUTORY INSTRUMENTS

1977 No. 1437.

CIVIL AVIATION

The Civil Aviation (Navigation Services Charges) Regulations 1977

Made - - -	*22nd August* 1977
Laid before Parliament	*30th August* 1977
Coming into Operation	*1st October* 1977

The Secretary of State in exercise of his powers under sections 4 and 7 of the Civil Aviation (Eurocontrol) Act 1962(a), as those sections are amended respectively by paragraphs 6 and 7 of Schedule 10 to the Civil Aviation Act 1971(b), and under section 15 of the Civil Aviation Act 1968(c) and of all other powers enabling him in that behalf, and with the consent of the Treasury in respect of Regulations 4 to 9 inclusive, hereby makes the following Regulations:

Citation and Operation

1. These Regulations may be cited as the Civil Aviation (Navigation Services Charges) Regulations 1977 and shall come into operation on 1st October 1977.

Interpretation

2. (1) In these Regulations:

"aircraft documents", in relation to any aircraft, means any certificate of registration, maintenance or airworthiness of that aircraft, any log book relating to the use of that aircraft or its equipment and any similar document;

"airport charges" means charges payable to a person owning or managing an aerodrome in the United Kingdom to which section 14 of the Civil Aviation Act 1968 or any enactment having the force of law in Northern Ireland containing provisions corresponding to that section for the time being applies for the use of, or for services provided at, the aerodrome but does not include charges payable by virtue of these Regulations;

"authorised person" means:

(*a*) any constable, and

(*b*) any person authorised by the Authority (whether by name or by class or description) either generally or in relation to a particular case or class of cases;

"the court" means, as respects England and Wales, the High Court, as respects Scotland, the Court of Session, and, as respects Northern Ireland, the High Court of Justice in Northern Ireland;

"international flight" means a flight to or from a place outside the United Kingdom, Channel Islands and the Isle of Man, or a flight which is part of a through journey of the aircraft to or from a place outside those countries;

(a) 1962 c. 8.   (b) 1971 c. 75.   (c) 1968 c. 61.

"maximum total weight authorised" means, in relation to an aircraft, the maximum total weight of the aircraft and its contents at which the aircraft may take off in the United Kingdom in the most favourable circumstances in accordance with the certificate of airworthiness for the time being in force in respect of the aircraft; however, if that certificate indicates a maximum total weight at which the aircraft may taxi, that weight shall be taken to be the maximum total weight authorised;

"the 1962 Act" means the Civil Aviation (Eurocontrol) Act 1962;

"operator", in relation to an aircraft, means the person who, at the relevant time, has the management of that aircraft;

"the specified amount" means, in relation to a landing or take-off, the additional cost incurred by the Authority in providing navigation services by reason of the landing or take-off, as the case may be, being made outside hours;

"the standard charge" means, for each complete metric ton of the maximum total weight authorised of the aircraft in respect of which the charge is made, and for each fraction of a metric ton, a charge—

(i) for services provided in connection with the use of any of the aerodromes specified in Column 1 of the following Table in respect of an aircraft engaged on an international flight, of the amount specified in relation to that aerodrome in Column 2 of the said Table;

(ii) for services provided in connection with the use of any of the said aerodromes in respect of an aircraft engaged on a flight other than an international flight, of the amount specified in relation to that aerodrome in Column 3 of the said Table;

TABLE

Column 1	Column 2	Column 3
Heathrow—London	£0·80	£0·60
Gatwick—London	£0·80	£0·60
Stansted—London	£0·80	£0·60
Aberdeen (Dyce)	£2·00	£1·65
Belfast (Aldergrove)	£2·40	£2·00
Birmingham	£2·10	£1·75
Bournemouth (Hurn)	£2·10	£1·75
Edinburgh	£2·40	£2·00
Glamorgan (Rhoose)	£2·10	£1·75
Glasgow	£2·10	£1·75
Liverpool	£2·10	£1·75
Prestwick	£1·65	£1·40

"United Kingdom Air Pilot" means a document published by the Authority and so entitled;

"within hours" means within the notified hours of watch of the air traffic control unit at the aerodrome, and "outside hours" shall be construed accordingly.

(2) Unless otherwise defined in this Regulation and unless the context otherwise requires, expressions used in these Regulations shall have the same respective meanings as in the Air Navigation Order 1976(a).

(3) The Interpretation Act 1889(b) shall apply for the purpose of the interpretation of these Regulations as it applies for the purpose of the interpretation of an Act of Parliament and section 38(2) of that Act (which relates to the effect of repeals) shall apply to these Regulations as if these Regulations were an Act of Parliament and as if the Regulations revoked by these Regulations were Acts of Parliament thereby repealed.

Revocation

3.—(1) Subject to the following provisions of this Regulation, the Regulations specified in Schedule 1 hereto are hereby revoked.

(2) Any authority issued or having effect under any Regulations revoked by these Regulations in force at the date of coming into operation of these Regulations shall remain in force and shall have effect for the purposes of these Regulations as if it had been granted under the corresponding provisions thereof:

Provided that any such authority which is expressed to remain in force for a definite period shall remain in force, unless renewed, only until the expiration of that period.

(3) Any power conferred on the Authority by Regulations revoked by these Regulations being a power to authorise a person to detain an aircraft for non-payment of charges incurred under any such revoked Regulations shall be exerciseable by the Authority as if it were a power conferred by the corresponding provisions of these Regulations.

Charges for Navigation Services at Aerodromes

4.—(1) Subject to the provisions of these Regulations, the operator of every aircraft for which navigation services are provided by the Authority in connection with the use of an aerodrome referred to in the Table in Regulation 2 of these Regulations (whether or not the services are actually used or could be used with the equipment installed in the aircraft) shall pay to the Authority for those services on the occasion specified in the first column of the following Table the charges specified in relation to those occasions in the second column thereof:—

TABLE

(*a*) Upon each landing of the aircraft at that aerodrome within hours ... the standard charge

(*b*) Upon each landing of the aircraft at that aerodrome outside hours ... the standard charge surcharged by 75% or by the specified amount whichever is the greater.

(*c*) Upon each take-off of the aircraft at that aerodrome outside hours, being either
   (i) a take-off which does not take place within 1 hour of landing or
   (ii) a take-off which takes place within 1 hour of a landing made within hours ... ... the specified amount or 75% of the standard charge whichever is the greater.

(a) S.I. 1976/1783 (1976 III, p. 4769).   (b) 1889 c. 63.

(2) Where on the occasion of any landing or take-off (as the case may be) the shortest distance in the case of a landing between the aerodrome of departure and the aerodrome of landing and in the case of a take-off between the aerodrome of departure and the aerodrome of intended landing does not exceed 185 kilometres measured along the great circle, for the references to "the standard charge" in the Table in paragraph (1) of this Regulation there shall be substituted references to "half the standard charge".

(3) The minimum charge payable under this Regulation shall be £2.

5. Subject to the provisions of these Regulations, the manager for the time being of Manchester International Airport shall pay to the Authority for the navigation services provided by the Authority for aircraft using the said aerodrome the sum of £155,000 per month.

Charges for Services provided in the Shanwick Oceanic Control Area

6. Subject to the provisions of these Regulations, the operator of every aircraft (whether or not registered in the United Kingdom) which flies within the Shanwick Oceanic Control Area, as described in the United Kingdom Air Pilot on the date of coming into operation of these Regulations, and in respect of which a flight plan is communicated to the appropriate air traffic control unit in relation to its flight in that Area shall pay to the Authority for the navigation services made available by it in relation to that flight a charge of thirty-six pounds.

Value Added Tax Charge

7. For the purpose of reimbursing the Authority in respect of value added tax payable on the provision of navigation services for which a charge is payable pursuant to these Regulations there shall be charged an additional charge equal to the amount of such tax and the incidence of the first-mentioned charge shall determine the incidence of the additional charge.

Services provided outside hours where the intention to land or take-off is not carried out

8. Whenever, by reason of its having received from the operator or commander of an aircraft notice of intention to make use outside hours of an aerodrome referred to in the Table in Regulation 2 of these Regulations for landing or take-off or as an alternate aerodrome, the Authority provides navigation services outside hours but the aircraft does not land or take-off there on the occasion specified in the notice, the operator of the aircraft shall pay, in respect of each such aerodrome—

    (*a*) in the case of an intended landing or intended use of the aerodrome as an alternate aerodrome, an amount equal to the surcharge payable under Regulation 4 of these Regulations on the landing of the aircraft outside hours;

    (*b*) in the case of an intended take-off, an amount equal to the charge, if any, which would have been payable under Regulation 4 of these Regulations if the aircraft had actually taken off outside hours at the intended time:

Provided that a charge shall not be payable under this Regulation if the notice of intention is cancelled not less than 30 minutes before the end of the last period of watch within hours before the time specified in the notice for landing or for the intended use of aerodrome as an alternate aerodrome or for take-off, as the case may be.

Dispensations

9. The Authority may dispense wholly or in part with any charge payable by virtue of these Regulations if it determines that it is proper to do so having regard to all the circumstances of the case.

Detention and sale of aircraft for unpaid charges

10. Where default is made in the payment of charges incurred in respect of any aircraft under these Regulations, the Authority or an authorised person may, subject to the provisions of this and the following Regulations, take such steps as are necessary to detain, pending payment, either—

(*a*) the aircraft in respect of which the charges were incurred (whether or not they were incurred by the person who is the operator of the aircraft at the time when the detention begins); or

(*b*) any other aircraft of which the person in default is the operator at the time when the detention begins;

and if the charges are not paid within 56 days of the date when the detention begins, the Authority may sell the aircraft in order to satisfy the charges.

11. The Authority or authorised person concerned shall not detain, or continue to detain, an aircraft under these Regulations by reason of any alleged default in the payment of charges payable under these Regulations if the operator of the aircraft or any other person claiming an interest therein—

(*a*) disputes that the charges, or any of them, are due or, if the aircraft is detained under Regulation 10(*a*) of these Regulations, that the charges in question were incurred in respect of that aircraft; and

(*b*) gives to the Authority, pending the determination of the dispute, sufficient security for the payment of the charges which are alleged to be due.

12. The Authority shall not sell an aircraft under these Regulations without the leave of the court; and the court shall not give leave except on proof that a sum is due to the Authority for charges under these Regulations, that default has been made in the payment thereof and that the aircraft which the Authority seeks leave to sell is liable to sale under these Regulations by reason of the default.

13. The Authority shall, before applying to the court for leave to sell an aircraft under these Regulations, take such steps for bringing the proposed application to the notice of interested persons and for affording them an opportunity of becoming a party to the proceedings as are set forth in Schedule 2 to these Regulations. If such leave is given, the Authority shall secure that the aircraft is sold for the best price that can reasonably be obtained; but failure to comply with any requirement of this Regulation or of the said Schedule in respect of any sale, while actionable as against the Authority at the suit of any person suffering loss in consequence thereof, shall not, after the sale has taken place, be a ground for impugning its validity.

14. The proceeds of any sale under these Regulations shall be applied as follows, and in the following order, that is to say:—

(*a*) in payment of any customs duty which is due in consequence of the aircraft having been brought into the United Kingdom;

(*b*) in payment of the expenses incurred by the Authority in detaining, keeping and selling the aircraft, including its expenses in connection with the application to the court;

(*c*) in payment of any airport charges incurred in respect of any aircraft which are due from the operator of the aircraft to the person owning or managing the aerodrome at which the aircraft was detained under these Regulations;

(*d*) in payment of any charge in respect of the aircraft which is due by virtue of these or any other Regulations under section 4 of the 1962 Act;

and the surplus, if any, shall be paid to or among the person or persons whose interests in the aircraft have been divested by reason of the sale.

15. The power of detention and sale conferred by these Regulations in respect of an aircraft extends to the equipment of the aircraft and any stores for use in connection with its operation (being equipment and stores carried in the aircraft) whether or not the property of the person who is its operator, and references to the aircraft in Regulations 11 to 14 of these Regulations include, except where the context otherwise requires, references to any such equipment and stores.

16. The power of detention conferred by these Regulations in respect of an aircraft extends to any aircraft documents carried in it, and any such documents may, if the aircraft is sold under these Regulations, be transferred by the Authority to the purchaser.

17. The power conferred by these Regulations to detain an aircraft may be exercised on any occasion when the aircraft is on any aerodrome referred to in the Table in Regulation 2(1) of these Regulations or to which section 14 of the Civil Aviation Act 1968 for the time being applies.

18. Nothing in these Regulations shall prejudice any right of the Authority to recover any charges, or any part thereof, by action.

Stanley Clinton Davis,
Parliamentary Under-Secretary of State,
Department of Trade.

22nd August 1977.

We consent to the making of these Regulations.

Donald R. Coleman,

J. Dormand,

Lords Commissioners of
Her Majesty's Treasury.

19th August 1977.

(*Regulation 3*)

SCHEDULE 1

Column 1 Regulations revoked	Column 2 References
The Civil Aviation (Navigation Services Charges) Regulations 1975.	S.I. 1975/1184 (1975 II, p. 4081).
The Civil Aviation (Navigation Services Charges) (Amendment) Regulations 1975.	S.I. 1975/1631 (1975 III, p. 5633).
The Civil Aviation (Navigation Services Charges) (Second Amendment) Regulations 1975.	S.I. 1975/1968 (1975 III, p. 7304).
The Civil Aviation (Navigation Services Charges) (Third Amendment) Regulations 1976.	S.I. 1976/369 (1976 I, p. 1015).
The Civil Aviation (Navigation Services Charges) (Fourth Amendment) Regulations 1976.	S.I. 1976/2084 (1976 III, p. 5761).
The Civil Aviation (Navigation Services Charges) (Fifth Amendment) Regulations 1977.	S.I. 1977/340 (1977 I, p. 1029).

(*Regulation 13*)

SCHEDULE 2

1. *Steps to be taken to bring proposed application to court to notice of interested persons and afford them an opportunity of becoming a party to the proceedings.*

The Authority, if it proposes to apply to the court for leave to sell an aircraft under these Regulations, shall take such of the following steps for bringing the proposed application to the notice of persons whose interests may be affected by the determination of the court thereon and for affording to any such person an opportunity of becoming a party to the proceedings on the application as are applicable to the aircraft:

(1) At least 21 days before applying to the court, the Authority shall publish:

    (i) in the London Gazette and also, if the aircraft is detained in Scotland, the Edinburgh Gazette, or, if it is detained in Northern Ireland, in the Belfast Gazette; and

    (ii) in one or more local newspapers circulating in the locality in which the aircraft is detained;

such a notice as is prescribed by paragraph 2 of this Schedule, and shall also, unless in that case it is impracticable to so do, serve such a notice, in the manner so prescribed, on each of the following persons:

(*a*) the person in whose name the aircraft is registered;

(*b*) the person, if any, who appears to the Authority to be the owner of the aircraft;

(*c*) any person who appears to the Authority to be a charterer of the aircraft whether or not by demise;

(*d*) any person who appears to the Authority to be the operator of the aircraft;

(*e*) HP Information Ltd., being a company incorporated under the Companies Act 1948(a);

(*f*) any person who is registered as a mortgagee of the aircraft under an Order in Council made under section 16 of the Civil Aviation Act 1968 or who appears to the Authority to be a mortgagee of the aircraft under the law of any country other than the United Kingdom;

(a) 1948 c. 38.

(g) any other person who appears to the Authority to have a proprietary interest in the aircraft.

(2) If any person who has been served with a notice in accordance with sub-paragraph (1) of this paragraph informs the Authority in writing within 14 days of the service of the notice of his desire to become a party to the proceedings the Authority shall make that person a defendant to the application.

2. *Content and service of the notice under paragraph 1.*

(1) A notice under paragraph 1 of this Schedule shall—

(a) state the nationality and registration marks of the aircraft;

(b) state the type of aircraft;

(c) state that by reason of default in the payment of a sum due to the Authority for charges imposed by these Regulations, the Authority, on a date which shall be specified in the notice, detained the aircraft under these Regulations and, unless payment of the sum so due is made within a period of 56 days from the date when the detention began, or within 21 days of the date of service of the notice, whichever shall be the later, will apply to the court for leave to sell the aircraft;

(d) invite the person to whom the notice is given to inform the Authority within 14 days of the service of the notice if he wishes to become a party to the proceedings on the application.

(2) A notice under paragraph 1 of this Schedule shall be served—

(a) by delivering it to the person to whom it is to be sent; or

(b) by leaving it at his usual or last known place of business or abode; or

(c) by sending it by post in a prepaid registered letter, or by the recorded delivery service, addressed to him at his usual or last known place of business or abode; or

(d) if the person to whom it is to be sent is an incorporated company or body, by delivering it to the secretary, clerk or other appropriate officer of the company or body at their registered or principal office, or sending it by post in a prepaid registered letter, or by the recorded delivery service, addressed to the secretary, clerk or officer of the company or body at that office.

(3) Any notice which is sent by post in accordance with the preceding paragraph to a place outside the United Kingdom shall be sent by air mail or by some other equally expeditious means.

EXPLANATORY NOTE

(This Note is not part of the Regulations.)

These Regulations revoke and replace with minor and drafting amendments the Civil Aviation (Navigation Services Charges) Regulations 1975, as amended.

1977 No. 1438

ROAD TRAFFIC

The Motor Vehicles (Type Approval) (Great Britain) (Amendment) Regulations 1977

Made - - - -		*8th August* 1977
Laid before Parliament		*6th September* 1977
Coming into Operation		*1st October* 1977

The Secretary of State for Transport, in exercise of the powers conferred upon him by sections 47(1) and 50(1) of the Road Traffic Act 1972(a), as amended and extended by section 10 of, and Schedule 2 to, the Road Traffic Act 1974(b), and of all other enabling powers, and after consultation with representative organisations in accordance with the provisions of section 199(2) of the said Act of 1972, hereby makes the following Regulations:—

1. These Regulations may be cited as the Motor Vehicles (Type Approval) (Great Britain) (Amendment) Regulations 1977, and shall come into operation on 1st October 1977.

2. The Motor Vehicles (Type Approval) (Great Britain) Regulations 1976(c) (hereinafter referred to as "the 1976 Regulations") shall be amended in accordance with the following provisions of these Regulations.

3. In Regulation 2 (interpretation), in paragraph (1), for the definition of "dual-purpose vehicle" the following shall be substituted:—

""dual-purpose vehicle" means a vehicle constructed or adapted for the carriage both of passengers and of goods or burden of any description, being a vehicle of which the unladen weight does not exceed 2040 kilogrammes, and which satisfies the following conditions as to construction, namely:—

(*a*) the vehicle must be permanently fitted with a rigid roof, with or without a sliding panel;

(*b*) the area of the vehicle to the rear of the driver's seat must—

(i) be permanently fitted with at least one row of transverse seats (fixed or folding) for two or more passengers and those seats must be properly sprung or cushioned and provided with upholstered back-rests, attached either to the seats or to a side or the floor of the vehicle; and

(ii) be lit on each side and at the rear by a window or windows of glass or other transparent material having an area or aggregate area of not less than 1850 square centimetres on each side and not less than 770 square centimetres at the rear;

(a) 1972 c. 20.   (b) 1974 c. 50.   (c) S.I. 1976/937 (1976 II, p. 2423).

(c) the distance between the rearmost part of the steering wheel and the back-rests of the row of transverse seats satisfying the requirements specified in head (i) of the foregoing sub-paragraph (b) (or, if there is more than one such row of seats, the distance between the rearmost part of the steering wheel and the back-rests of the rearmost such row) must, when the seats are ready for use, be not less than one third of the distance between the rearmost part of the steering wheel and the rearmost part of the floor of the vehicle;".

4. In Regulation 3 (Application of regulations)—

(1) in paragraph (1)(a), after the words "1st October 1977" the words "and first used on or after 1st April 1978" shall be inserted;

(2) in paragraph (3)—

(a) in sub paragraph (d) the words "has been manufactured in Great Britain and" shall be omitted;

(b) after sub paragraph (e) the following shall be inserted—

"or (f) a motor vehicle to which sections 45 to 51 and 65 of the Act have become applicable after a period of use on roads during which, by virtue of section 188(4) of the Act (which relates to vehicles in the public service of the Crown), those sections did not apply to that vehicle.".

5. In Regulation 7 (application for further type approval certificate), in paragraph (3), for the words "section 49(9)(a) of the Act" the words "section 47(9)(a) of the Act" shall be substituted.

6. In Regulation 11 (keeping and inspection of records relating to certificates of conformity), for paragraph (2) the following shall be substituted:

"(2) The record referred to in paragraph (1) of this Regulation shall be a record of—

(a) the serial number of the certificate of conformity,

(b) the serial number of the type approval certificate referred to in the certificate of conformity,

(c) in the case of a certificate of conformity in respect of a vehicle, the manufacturer's identification number assigned to that vehicle and either the date of the manufacture of the vehicle or the date of the issue of the certificate of conformity, and

(d) in the case of a certificate of conformity in respect of a vehicle part to which the manufacturer has assigned an identification number, that number.".

7.—(1) For Schedule 1 (Type Approval Requirements) there shall be substituted the revised Schedule 1 set out in the Schedule to these Regulations.

(2) In so far as the revised Schedule 1 provided for in paragraph (1) above incorporates any addition to, or alteration in, the type approval requirements applicable to any vehicle or vehicle part, that addition or alteration shall be applicable as from the date of the coming into operation of these Regulations unless a later date is specified in relation to the item in question in column (5) of that Schedule, and the references in Regulation 4(1) of the 1976 Regulations, and in the heading to column (5) of Schedule 1, to the coming into operation of these Regulations (meaning thereby the 1976 Regulations) shall in relation to such addition or alteration be construed accordingly.

8. In Schedule 2 (forms of information document), at the end of the footnote to Part I, there shall be inserted the following:—

"The information contained in this information document should be supplemented by any additional data reasonably required to enable the Secretary of State to assess the performance of the vehicle in question".

8th August 1977.

William Rodgers,
Secretary of State for Transport.

THE SCHEDULE

REVISED SCHEDULE 1 TO THE 1976 REGULATIONS

"SCHEDULE 1"

Type Approval Requirements

(1) Item No.	(2) Subject matter	(3) Particulars of instrument or other document containing requirement and of the nature of the requirement			(4) Vehicles exempted from requirement	(5) Date of application if later than the coming into operation of these Regulations	(6) Date of cessation of application
		(a) Description, reference number and date of instrument	(b) Official Journal reference of Community Instrument	(c) Nature of requirement and place in instrument where stated			
1.	Door latches and hinges	Council Directive 70/387/EEC of 27th July 1970; or ECE Regulation 11 of 8th January 1969 (as corrected 16th March 1971 and amended 29th October 1975)	O.J. L176, 10.8.70, p. 5 (SE 1970 (II), p. 564)	Design and construction requirements in Annex 1, paragraphs 1, 2 and 3. Design and construction requirements in paragraphs 5 and 6	Vehicles which have, for the exit or entry of the occupants, no doors or only sliding doors.		
2.	Radio-interference suppression	Council Directive 72/245/EEC of 20th June 1972; or	O.J. L152, 6.7.72, p. 15 (SE 1972 (II), p. 637)	Design, construction and equipment requirements in Annex 1, paragraphs 6 and 7; and in Annex 3. Marking requirements in Annex 1, paragraph 4.	Vehicles with other than spark ignition engines.		

		ECE Regulation 10 of 17th December 1968		Design, construction and equipment requirements in paragraphs 6, 7 and 9; and in Annex 4. Marking requirements in paragraph 4	
3.	Protective steering	Council Directive 74/297/EEC of 4th June 1974; or ECE Regulation 12 of 14th April 1969 (issued with revised text on 3rd November 1975)	O.J. L165, 20.6.74, p. 16	Design and construction requirements in Annex 1, paragraphs 5 and 6. Design and construction requirements in paragraphs 5 and 6.	1. Vehicles the steering control of which has been specially constructed for the use of a person suffering from some physical defect or disability. 2. Vehicles with forward control, that is to say a vehicle in which the centre of the steering wheel is in the forward quarter of the total length of the vehicle (including any bumpers and over-riders). 3. Vehicles constructed or assembled by a person who is not ordinarily engaged in the trade or business of manufacturing such vehicles.
4.	Exhaust emissions	Council Directive 70/220/EEC of 20th March 1970 (as amended by Council Directive 74/290/EEC of 28th May 1974); or	O.J. L76, 6.4.70, p. 1 (SE 1970 (I), p. 171) and O.J. L159, 15.6.74, p. 61	Design, construction and equipment requirements in Annex 1, paragraph 3.	1. Vehicles with other than spark ignition engines. 2. Vehicles over 3500 kg gross weight.

(1) Item No.	(2) Subject matter	(3) Particulars of instrument or other document containing requirement and of the nature of the requirement			(4) Vehicles exempted from requirement	(5) Date of application if later than the coming into operation of these Regulations	(6) Date of cessation of application
		(a) Description, reference number and date of instrument	(b) Official Journal reference of Community Instrument	(c) Nature of requirement and place in instrument where stated			
4. (cont)		Council Directive 70/220/EEC of 20th March 1970 (as amended by Council Directive 74/290/EEC of 28th May 1974 and Commission Directive 77/102/EEC of 30th November 1976);	O.J. L76, 6.4.70, p. 1 (SE 1970 (I), p. 171), O.J. L159, 15.6.74, p. 61 and O.J. L32, 3.2.77, p. 32	Design, construction and equipment requirements in Annex 1, paragraph 3.			
		or					
		ECE Regulation 15 of 11th March 1970 (as amended 11th December 1974);		Design, construction and equipment requirements in paragraphs 5 and 7.			
		or					
		ECE Regulation 15 of 11th March 1970 (as amended 11th December 1974 and 1st March 1976);		Design, construction and equipment requirements in paragraphs 5 and 7.			

			O.J. L190, 20.8.72, p. 1 (SE 1972 (III), p. 889)		Vehicles with other than compression ignition engines
5.	Exhaust emissions	Council Directive 72/306/EEC of 2nd August 1972; or ECE Regulation 24 of 23rd August 1971 (as amended 12th March 1974 and corrected 1st December 1972 and 15th July 1975)		Design, construction and equipment requirements in Annex 1, paragraphs 5 and 7. Marking requirements in Annex 1, paragraph 4. Design, construction and equipment requirements in paragraphs 5 and 7. Marking requirements in paragraph 4.4.2.	
6.	Lamps—headlamps and filament lamps	1. ECE Regulation 1 of 24th March 1960 (as corrected on 20th June 1960, amended on 6th June 1962 and 30th April 1963, issued with revised text on 26th October 1964 and corrected on 8th June 1965); and ECE Regulation 2 of 24th March 1960 (as corrected on 20th June 1960, amended on 6th June 1962 and 30th April 1963, issued with revised text on 26th October 1964 and corrected on 8th June 1965); or		Design and construction requirements in paragraphs 5, 6 and 10. Marking requirements in paragraph 3. Design and construction requirements in paragraphs 5, 6, 7, 8, 9, 10 and 11. Marking requirements in paragraph 3.	

(1) Item No.	(2) Subject matter	(3) Particulars of instrument or other document containing requirement and of the nature of the requirement			(4) Vehicles exempted from requirement	(5) Date of application if later than the coming into operation of these Regulations	(6) Date of cessation of application
		(a) Description, reference number and date of instrument	(b) Official Journal reference of Community Instrument	(c) Nature of requirement and place in instrument where stated			
6. (cont)		2. ECE Regulation 5 of 22nd May 1967;		Design and construction requirements in paragraphs 6, 7, 8, 9 and 10; and in Annex 4. Marking requirements in paragraph 4.			
		or					
		3. ECE Regulation 8 of 12th June 1967 (and issued with revised text on 28th May 1971 and 23rd April 1975);		Design and construction requirements in paragraphs 5, 6, 7, 9, 10, 11, 12, 13 and 14. Marking requirements in paragraph 3.			
		or					
		4. ECE Regulation 20 of 1st March 1971;		Design and construction requirements in paragraphs 5, 6, 7, 9, 10, 11, 12, 13 and 14; and in Annex 2 and Annex 6. Marking requirements in paragraph 3.			
		or					
		5. ECE Regulation 31 of 2nd June 1975;		Design and construction requirements in			

		or		paragraphs 6, 7, 8 and 9. Marking requirements in paragraph 4.
		6. British Standard Specification No. AU 40, part 4a of 1966;		Design and construction requirements in clauses 4 to 11 inclusive. Marking requirements in clause 3.
		or		
		7. Council Directive 76/761/EEC of 27th July 1976;	O.J. L262, 27.9.76, p. 96	Design, construction and equipment requirements in Annex 1, paragraphs 1, 5, 6 and 10, in Annex III, paragraphs 1, 5, 6, 7, 8, 9 and 10 and in Annex V. Marking requirements in Annex VI, paragraphs 2.1.3, 2.1.4, 2.2.3 and 2.3.
		or		
		8. ECE Regulation 20 of 1st March 1971 (issued with revised text on 1st September 1976);		Design and construction requirements in paragraphs 5, 6, 7, 9, 10, 11, 12, 13 and 14, in Annex 2 and in Annex 6. Marking requirements in paragraphs 3 and 4.3.
7.	Lamps—side, rear, stop	ECE Regulation 7 of 22nd May 1967 (as corrected 9th February 1971);		Design and construction requirements in paragraphs 5, 6, 7, 8 and 11. Marking requirements in paragraph 3.
		or		

(1) Item No.	(2) Subject matter	(3) Particulars of instrument or other document containing requirement and of the nature of the requirement			(4) Vehicles exempted from requirement	(5) Date of application if later than the coming into operation of these Regulations	(6) Date of cessation of application
		(a) Description, reference number and date of instrument	(b) Official Journal reference of Community Instrument	(c) Nature of requirement and place in instrument where stated			
7. (cont)		Council Directive 76/758/EEC of 27th July 1976	O.J. L262, 27.9.76, p. 54	Design, construction and equipment requirements in Annex O, paragraphs 1, 5, 6, 7 and 8, in Annex I, in Annex IV and in Annex V. Marking requirements in Annex III, paragraphs 2.1.1 and 2.1.2.			
8.	Rear reflectors	ECE Regulation 3 of 23rd September 1964; or British Standard Specification No. AU 40, Part 2 (reflex reflectors for vehicles, including cycles) of 1965; or		Design and construction requirements in paragraphs 6 and 7. Marking requirements in paragraph 4.1. Design and construction requirements in clauses 5 and 6. Marking requirements in clause 4.	Vehicles with rear reflectors manufactured in Italy and bearing the marks "IGM" and "C.1" or "C.2".		

		Council Directive 76/757/EEC of 27th July 1976	O.J. L262, 27.9.76, p. 32	Design, construction and equipment requirements in Annex O, paragraphs 2, 6 and 7, in Annex I, in Annex V, in Annex VI, in Annex VII, in Annex VIII, in Annex IX, in Annex X, in Annex XI and in Annex XII. Marking requirements in Annex III, paragraph 2.1.
9.	Direction indicators	ECE Regulation 6 of 22nd May 1967; or Council Directive 76/759/EEC of 27th July 1976	O.J. L262, 27.9.76, p. 71	Design and construction requirements in paragraphs 5, 6, 7, 8 and 11. Marking requirements in paragraph 3. Design, construction and equipment requirements in Annex O, paragraphs 1, 5, 6, 7 and 8, in Annex I, in Annex IV and in Annex V. Marking requirements in Annex III, paragraphs 2.1.1 and 2.1.2.
10.	Rear-view mirrors	Council Directive 71/127/EEC of 1st March 1971	O.J. L68, 22.3.71, p. 1 (SE 1971 (I), p. 136)	Design, construction and equipment requirements in Annex I, paragraphs 2 and 3.

(1) Item No.	(2) Subject matter	(3) Particulars of instrument or other document containing requirement and of the nature of the requirement			(4) Vehicles exempted from requirement	(5) Date of application if later than the coming into operation of these Regulations	(6) Date of cessation of application
		(a) Description, reference number and date of instrument	(b) Official Journal reference of Community Instrument	(c) Nature of requirement and place in instrument where stated			
11.	Anti-theft devices	Council Directive 74/61/EEC of 17th December 1973; or ECE Regulation 18 of 14th September 1970	O.J. L38, 11.2.74, p. 22	Design, construction and equipment requirements in Annex I, paragraphs 1, 5 and 6. Design and construction requirements in paragraphs 5 and 6.	Vehicles specially constructed (and not merely adapted) for the use of a person suffering from some physical defect or disability		
12.	Seat belts and anchorages for the seats specified in Regulation 17(3) of the Motor Vehicles (Construction and Use) Regulations 1973(a), and other seat belts and anchorages if fitted	1. British Standard Specification No. AU 160a (seat belt assemblies for motor vehicles) of 1971 (as amended in 1972); or British Standard Specification No. 3254 (seat belt assemblies for motor vehicles) of 1960 (as amended in 1962, 1963 (twice), 1964 (twice), 1965, 1967, 1968 (twice), 1970 and 1976); and		Design, construction and equipment requirements in clauses 3, 4, 5, 6 and 7. Marking requirements in clause 8. Design, construction and equipment requirements in clauses 3, 4, 5, 6, 7, 8, 9, 15, 16a, 18, 19, 20, 21 and 22. Marking requirements in clauses 16a and 16b (except the requirements with respect to the certification trade mark of the British Standards Institution)			

2. British Standard Specification No. AU 48a (seat belt anchorage points) of 1971;	Design and construction requirements in clauses 3, 5, 6, 7, 8 and 9. Marking requirements in clause 10; and in Regulation 17(8)(a) of the Motor Vehicles (Construction and Use) Regulations 1973
or	
British Standard Specification No. AU 48 (seat belt anchorage points) of 1965 (as amended in 1967 (twice) and 1968);	Design and construction requirements in clauses 3, 5, 6, 7, 8 and 9. Marking requirements in Regulation 17(8)(a) of the Motor Vehicles (Construction and Use) Regulations 1973
or	
British Standard Specification No. AU 140a (seats with integral seat belt anchorages) of 1971;	Design and construction requirements in clauses 3, 5, 6, 7, 8, 9 and 10. Marking requirements in clause 11.
or	
British Standard Specification No. AU 140 (seats with integral seat belt anchorages) of 1967 (as amended in 1967);	Design and construction requirements in clauses 3, 5, 6, 7, 8, 9 and 10; and in Appendices A and B. Marking requirements in clause 11.
or	

(a) S.I. 1973/24 (1973 I, p. 93).

(1) Item No.	(2) Subject matter	(3) Particulars of instrument or other document containing requirement and of the nature of the requirement			(4) Vehicles exempted from requirement	(5) Date of application if later than the coming into operation of these Regulations	(6) Date of cessation of application
		(a) Description, reference number and date of instrument	(b) Official Journal reference of Community Instrument	(c) Nature of requirement and place in instrument where stated			
12. (cont)		Council Directive 76/115/EEC of 18th December 1975; or	O.J. L24, 30.1.76, p. 6	Design and construction requirements in Annex 1, paragraphs 4 and 5.5; and in Annex 3.			
		ECE Regulation 14 of 30th January 1970 (as amended on 16th March 1971 and issued with revised text on 19th August 1976); and		Design, construction and equipment requirements in paragraphs 5, 6 and 7, in Annex 3, in Annex 4 and in Annex 5.			
		3. Regulation 17(6) of the Motor Vehicles (Construction and Use) Regulations 1973		Design and construction requirements.			
13.	Brakes	Council Directive 71/320/EEC of 26th July 1971	O.J. L202, 6.9.71, p. 37 (SE 1971 (III), p. 746)	Design, construction and equipment requirements prescribed for category M1 vehicles in Annex 1 (except paragraphs 2.2.1.4 and 2.2.1.12.2)			30.9.1978

					Date 1	Date 2
13A.	Brakes	Council Directive 71/320/EEC of 26th July 1971 (as amended by Commission Directive 74/132/EEC of 11th February 1974 and Commission Directive 75/524/EEC of 25th July 1975)	O.J. L202, 6.9.71, p. 37 (SE 1971 (III), p. 746), O.J. L74, 19.3.74, p. 7 and O.J. L236, 8.9.75, p. 3	Design, construction and equipment requirements prescribed for category M1 vehicles in Annex 1, in Annex 2 and in Annex 7. ... and in Annex 2 and Annex 7	1.10.1978	
14.	Noise and silencers	Council Directive 70/157/EEC of 6th February 1970 (as amended by Commission Directive 73/350/EEC of 7th November 1973)	O.J. L42, 23.2.70, p. 16 (SE 1970 (I), p. 111), O.J. L321, 22.11.73, p. 33	Design, construction and equipment requirements in the Annex, paragraphs I.1.1, I.2, I.3 and I.4, so however that for vehicles with compression ignition engines the requirements with respect to sound levels specified in the Table in paragraph I.1 shall have effect for the purposes of these Regulations as if the level shown for item I.1.1 in that Table were increased by 2dB(A). Marking requirements in the Annex, paragraph II.3.		30.9.1978
14A.	Noise and silencers	Council Directive 70/157/EEC of 6th February 1970 (as amended by Commission Directive	O.J. L42, 23.2.70, p. 16 (SE 1970 (I), p. 111), O.J. L321, 22.11.73, p. 33	Design, construction and equipment requirements in the Annex, paragraphs I.1.1, I.2, I.3, I.4, II.4	1.10.1978	

(1) Item No.	(2) Subject matter	(3) Particulars of instrument or other document containing requirement and of the nature of the requirement			(4) Vehicles exempted from requirement	(5) Date of application if later than the coming into operation of these Regulations	(6) Date of cessation of application
		(a) Description, reference number and date of instrument	(b) Official Journal reference of Community Instrument	(c) Nature of requirement and place in instrument where stated			
14A (cont)		73/350/EEC of 7th November 1973		and II.6, so however that for vehicles with compression ignition engines the requirements with respect to sound levels specified in the Table in paragraph I.1 shall have effect for the purposes of these Regulations as if the level shown for item I.1.1. in that Table were increased by 2dB(A). Marking requirements in the Annex, paragraph II.3.			
15.	Glass in windscreens and windows on the outside	British Standard Specification No. 857 (safety glass for land transport) of 1967 (as amended in 1973); or British Standard Specification No. 5282		Design and construction requirements in clauses 1.3, 2.1, 2.2, 2.4, 2.5, 2.6, 3.1, 3.2, 3.4, 3.5, 3.6, 3.7 and 3.8. Marking requirements in clauses 2.3 and 3.3. Design and construction requirements in			

		(specification for road vehicles safety glass) of 1975 (as amended in 1976 and in 1977)		clauses 4 and 5. Marking requirements in clause 8.		
16.	Seats and anchorages	Council Directive 74/408/EEC of 22nd July 1974; or ECE Regulation 17 of 14th August 1970 (as corrected on 22nd April 1971 and issued with revised text on 2nd January 1976)	O.J. L221, 12.8.74, p. 1	Design and construction requirements in Annex 1, paragraphs 5, 6 and 7. Design and construction requirements in paragraphs 5, 6 and 7.		
17.	Tyres with a speed rating not exceeding 200 km/h in the case of diagonal (bias-ply) tyres or not exceeding 210 km/h in the case of radial-ply tyres	ECE Regulation 30 of 1st April 1975		Design and construction requirements in paragraph 6. Marking requirements in paragraph 3 (but excluding the requirement in paragraph 3.4 about the approval mark).	1. Vehicles not fitted with the tyres mentioned in column (2). 2. Vehicles fitted with tyres which bear on their sidewalls, after the figures denoting the tyre size, the code letter 'C' and which are of a type not listed in Annex 5 to ECE Regulation 30.	
18.	Interior fittings	Council Directive 74/60/EEC of 17th December 1973 (as corrected 25th February 1977) or ECE Regulation 21 of 2nd June 1971 (as corrected in 1972)	O.J. L38, 11.2.74, p. 2, O.J. L53, 25.2.77, p. 30	Design, construction and equipment requirements in Annex 1, paragraph 5. Design, construction and equipment requirements in paragraph 5.	Vehicles for which, or for a model of which there is in force on 1 October 1978 a type approval certificate or a Minister's approval certificate, if manufactured before 1st October 1982.	1.10.1978

(1) Item No.	(2) Subject matter	(3) Particulars of instrument or other document containing requirement and of the nature of the requirement			(4) Vehicles exempted from requirement	(5) Date of application if later than the coming into operation of these Regulations	(6) Date of cessation of application
		(a) Description, reference number and date of instrument	(b) Official Journal reference of Community Instrument	(c) Nature of requirement and place in instrument where stated			
19.	External projections	Council Directive 74/483/EEC of 17th September 1974; or	O.J. L266, 2.10.74, p. 4	Design, construction and equipment requirements in Annex 1, paragraphs 1, 5 and 6.	Vehicles for which, or for a model of which there is in force on 1st October 1978 a type approval certificate or a Minister's approval certificate, if manufactured before 1st October 1982.	1.10.1978	
		ECE Regulation 26 of 28th April 1972 (as amended 12th March 1974)		Design, construction and equipment requirements in paragraphs 5 and 6.			
20.	Speedometers	Council Directive 75/443/EEC of 26th June 1975	O.J. L196, 26.7.75, p. 1	Design and construction requirements in Annex II, paragraphs 1 and 4.		1.10.1978	

NOTE: In this Schedule the references to an ECE Regulation followed by a number are references to the Regulation so numbered which is annexed to the Agreement concerning the adoption of uniform conditions of approval for motor, vehicle equipment and parts and reciprocal recognition thereof concluded at Geneva on 20th March 1958(a) as amended(b), to which the United Kingdom is a party(c).

(a) Cmnd. 2535. (b) Cmnd. 3562.

(c) By instrument of accession dated 14th January 1963 deposited with the Secretary General of the United Nations on 15th January 1963.".

EXPLANATORY NOTE

(This Note is not part of the Regulations.)

These Regulations amend the Motor Vehicles (Type Approval) (Great Britain) Regulations 1976. The principal amendments are mentioned below.

In Regulation 2 of the 1976 Regulations the definition of 'dual-purpose vehicle' is amended so as to exclude a vehicle which falls within this category solely by reason of the fact that the driving power of the engine is, or can be, transmitted to all the wheels of the vehicle. This change excludes such vehicles from the scope of the 1976 Regulations.

In Regulation 3 of the 1976 Regulations three changes are made—

(1) the vehicles to which the 1976 Regulations are to apply are limited to those first used on or after 1 April 1978;

(2) the exemptions given by paragraph (3)(*d*) to certain vehicles which are to be exported is extended to all vehicles in this category instead of being limited to those manufactured in Great Britain;

(3) an additional exemption is given for vehicles which have been used by the Crown and are to be disposed of on the market.

In Regulation 7 of the 1976 Regulations a typographical error is corrected.

Regulation 11 of the 1976 Regulations is amended so far as regards the records required to be kept in connection with certificates of conformity.

Schedule 1 to the 1976 Regulations (which sets out the type approval requirements) is replaced by a revised Schedule 1. The main changes are:—

(1) references to further EEC Council Directives are included in column (3) in connection with items 4, 6, 7, 8, and 9;

(2) references to ECE Regulations (or amendments thereto) are altered in column (3) in connection with items 1, 4, 6, 8 and 16, and a reference to an additional ECE Regulation is included in column (3) in connection with items 8 and 12;

(3) in item 3, in column (4), the description of vehicles with a forward control is amended and a further category of vehicles is exempted;

(4) in item 6, a reference to filament lamps is added in column (2), and in column (3) a reference to British Standard Specification No. AU40 is added;

(5) in item 12, the requirement in column (3)(*c*) against British Standard Specification No. 3254 is amended so as to exclude the requirement about the certification trade mark;

(6) in items 13 and 14, a date of cessation of application (30.9.1978) is inserted in column (6);

(7) in item 15, in column (3), a reference to a further amendment to British Standard Specification No. 5282 is added;

(8) in item 17, a further exemption is shown in column (4);

(9) in items 18 and 19, exemptions are shown in column (4);

(10) new items 13A (brakes), 14A (noise and silencers) and 20 (speedometers) are added.

Schedule 2 to the 1976 Regulations is amended so as to require the inclusion of additional information in the vehicle information document set out in Part I of that Schedule.

Copies of ECE Regulations (these are regulations prepared by the United Nations Economic Commission for Europe, annexed to the Agreement of 20 March 1958 as amended (Cmnd. 2535 and 3562) relating to conditions for approval for motor vehicles equipment and parts, and accepted from time to time by the Governments which are parties to that Agreement) can be obtained from Her Majesty's Stationery Office.

STATUTORY INSTRUMENTS

1977 No. 1439

ROAD TRAFFIC

The Motor Vehicles (Type Approval) (Great Britain) (Fees) (Amendment) Regulations 1977

Made - - - -	*8th August* 1977
Laid before Parliament	*6th September* 1977
Coming into Operation	*1st October* 1977

The Secretary of State for Transport, in exercise of the powers conferred by section 50(1) of the Road Traffic Act 1972(a), as amended by section 10 of, and Schedule 2 to, the Road Traffic Act 1974(b), and of all other enabling powers, and after consultation with representative organisations in accordance with the provisions of section 199(2) of the said Act of 1972, hereby makes the following Regulations:—

1. These Regulations may be cited as the Motor Vehicles (Type Approval) (Great Britain) (Fees) (Amendment) Regulations 1977, and shall come into operation on 1st October 1977.

2. The Motor Vehicles (Type Approval) (Great Britain) (Fees) Regulations 1976(c) (hereinafter referred to as "the 1976 Regulations") shall be amended as follows:—

    (1) in Regulation 2(1) (Interpretation)—

        (*a*) for the definition of "Great Britain Regulations" there shall be substituted the following—

        " "the Great Britain Regulations" means the Motor Vehicles (Type Approval) (Great Britain) Regulations 1976(d), as amended(e);";

        (*b*) for the definition of "the Type Approval and Approval Marks (Fees) Regulations" there shall be substituted the following—

        " "the Type Approval and Approval Marks (Fees) Regulations" means the Motor Vehicles (Type Approval and Approval Marks) (Fees) Regulations 1976(f), as amended(g);";

    (2) for Schedule 1 (Table of Fees for the Examination of Vehicles or Parts of Vehicles) there shall be substituted the revised Schedule 1 set out in the Schedule to these Regulations;

    (3) in Schedule 3 (Fees for the issue of documents), after the entry relating to fee number 3 there shall be added the following entry:—

        "3A Type approval certificate for modifying a type approval certificate in respect of which fee number 1, 2 or 3 above is payable.   30".

William Rodgers,
Secretary of State for Transport.

(**a**) 1972 c. 20.
(**c**) S.I. 1976/1466 (1976 III, p. 3975).
(**e**) S.I. 1977/1438 (1977 II, p.4275).
(**g**) S.I. 1977/1440 (1977 II, p.4302).

(**b**) 1974 c. 50.
(**d**) S.I. 1976/937 (1976 II, p. 2423).
(**f**) S.I. 1976/1465 (1976 III, p. 3961).

THE SCHEDULE

Revised Schedule 1 to the 1976 Regulations

(1) Fee No.	(2) Particulars of type approval requirements (subject matter and item numbers in Schedule 1 to the Great Britain Regulations)	(3) Particulars of type of examination, vehicle or vehicle part (where not uniform in relation to each type approval requirement)	(4) Amount of fee for examination (a) £	(b) £
	Door latches and hinges—item 1			
1.		Laboratory test	410	110
2.		Vehicle test	80	70
3.	Radio-interference suppression—item 2	———	100	180
	Protective steering—item 3			
4.		Steering column test	780	270
5.		Barrier test	1,900	270
6.	Exhaust emissions (spark emission engine)—item 4	———	350	190
	Exhaust emissions (compression ignition engines)—item 5			
7.		Vehicle test	600	190
8.		Engine test-bed test	900	190
9.	Lamps—headlamps and filament lamps—item 6	Headlamps emitting an asymmetrical passing beam or a driving beam or both (ECE Regulation 1 and Directive 76/761 EEC)	170	—
10.		Sealed-beam headlamps emitting a European asymmetrical passing beam or a driving beam or both (ECE Regulation 5)	170	—
11.		Headlamps emitting an asymmetrical passing beam or a driving beam or both and equipped with halogen filament lamps (H1, H2, H3 or H4 lamps) (ECE Regulations 8 and 20)	160	—
12.		Halogen sealed-beam (H4SB) headlamps emitting an asymmetrical passing beam or a driving beam or both (ECE Regulation 31)	250	—

(1) Fee No.	(2) Particulars of type approval requirements (subject matter and item numbers in Schedule 1 to the Great Britain Regulations)	(3) Particulars of type of examination, vehicle or vehicle part (where not uniform in relation to each type approval requirement)	(4) Amount of fee for examination	
			(a) £	(b) £
13.		Filament lamps for headlamps (ECE Regulations 2, 8 and 20 and Directive 76/761/EEC)	210	—
13A.		Sealed beam headlamps (BS Au40, Part 4a)—single filament units	400	—
13B.		Sealed beam headlamps (BS Au40, Part 4a)—twin filament units	460	—
14.	Lamps—side, rear, stop— item 7	———	210	—
15.	Direction indicators— item 9		210	—
	Multi-function lamps assemblies			
16.		Any two of the lamps to which fees 14 and 15 apply	250	—
17.		Any three of the lamps to which fees 14 and 15 apply	290	—
18.	Rear reflectors—item 8	———	10	—
	Rear-view mirrors— item 10			
19.		Component	100	80
20.		Vehicle	310	190
21.	Anti-theft devices— item 11	———	240	60
	Seat belts and anchorages —item 12			
27.		Seat belts manufactured under a licence issued by the BSI	—	12
23.		Component: BS3254 (a) complete test	300	—
24.		(b) static test	30	—
25.		(c) dynamic test	110	—
26.		BS Au 160a (a) complete test	680	—
27.		(b) static test	30	—
28.		(c) dynamic test	110	—

(1) Fee No.	(2) Particulars of type approval requirements (subject matter and item numbers in Schedule 1 to the Great Britain Regulations)	(3) Particulars of type of examination, vehicle or vehicle part (where not uniform in relation to each type approval requirement)	(4) Amount of fee for examination	
			(a) £	(b) £
29.		BS Au 48 or 48a	770	60
30.		Static test to BS Au 140 or 140a	770	60
31.		Static test to Council Directive 76/115/EEC of 18th December 1975(a) to ECE Regulation 14 (as amended)	920	90
32.		Dynamic test to BS Au 140 or BS Au 140a	1,400	60
33.		Vehicle: Regulation 17(6) of the Motor Vehicles (Construction and Use) Regulations 1973(b)	10	10
34.	Brakes—items 13 and 13A	———	1,440	1,000
	Noise and silencers— items 14 and 14A			
35.		Permissible sound levels	140	110
36.		Exhaust system silencer: (a) test-bed test	1,300	350
37.		(b) track test	1,990	350
38.		(c) track test, vehicle driven by driver supplied by manufacturer	150	—
39.	Safety glass—item 15	Glass manufactured under a licence issued by the BSI	—	12
40.		All other cases: BS857 (a) windscreen, toughened	100	370
41.		(b) windscreen, laminated	160	430
42.		(c) windscreen, treated	160	430
43.		(d) rear window, toughened	80	350
44.		(e) side window, toughened	70	340
45.		(f) rear or side window, laminated	100	370
46.		All other cases: BS5282 (a) windscreen, toughened	690	960

(a) O.J. L24, 30.1.76, p. 6.   (b) S.I. 1973/24 (1973 I, p. 93).

(1) Fee No.	(2) Particulars of type approval requirements (subject matter and item numbers in Schedule 1 to the Great Britain Regulations)	(3) Particulars of type of examination, vehicle or vehicle part (where not uniform in relation to each type approval requirement)	(4) Amount of fee for examination	
			(a) £	(b) £
47.		(b) windscreen, laminated	500	770
48.		(c) rear window, toughened	380	650
49.		(d) side window, toughened	380	650
50.		(e) rear or side windows, laminated	340	610
	Seats and anchorages— item 16			
51.		Static test	1,160	190
52.		Dynamic test	1,920	190
53.	Tyres—item 17	———	210	90
54.	Interior fittings—item 18	———	1,310	790
55.	External projections— item 19	———	310	270
56.	Speedometers—item 20	———	180	160

NOTE: In this Schedule the references to an ECE Regulation followed by a number are references to the Regulation so numbered which is annexed to the Agreement concerning the adoption of uniform conditions of approval for motor vehicle equipment and parts and reciprocal recognition thereof concluded at Geneva on 20th March 1958(c) as amended (d), to which the United Kingdom is a party (e).

(c) Cmnd 2535.   (d) Cmnd. 3562.
(e) By instrument of accession dated 14th January 1963 deposited with the Secretary General of the United Nations on 15th January 1963.

EXPLANATORY NOTE

(This Note is not part of the Regulations.)

These Regulations amend the Motor Vehicles (Type Approval) (Great Britain) (Fees) Regulations 1976 (S.I. No. 1466).

Their main effect is to substitute a revised Schedule for Schedule 1 to the 1976 Regulations, which sets out the fees for the examination of vehicles or parts of vehicles.

In the revised Schedule 1—

(1) references to further EEC Council Directives are included in column (3) in the entries relating to fees numbers 9 and 13;

(2) a reference to an ECE Regulation is included in column (3) in the entry relating to fee number 31;

(3) fee number 34 is extended to cover items 13A and 14A in the revised Schedule 1 to the Great Britain Regulations 1976;

(4) new fees numbers 13A, 14A and 56 are added;

(5) the following fees are altered: —

	Amount of Present fee		Amount of new fee	
	(a) £	(b) £	(a) £	(b) £
Fee No. 1	470	140	410	110
,, ,, 4	460	240	780	270
,, ,, 5	1,430	240	1,900	270
,, ,, 6	300	190	350	190
,, ,, 7	780	190	600	190
,, ,, 8	720	190	900	190
,, ,, 14	150	—	210	—
,, ,, 15	150	—	210	—
,, ,, 16	190	—	250	—
,, ,, 17	230	—	290	—
,, ,, 18	160	—	10	—
,, ,, 20	230	190	310	190
,, ,, 21	150	60	240	60
,, ,, 29	550	60	770	60
,, ,, 30	640	60	770	60
,, ,, 31	670	90	920	90
,, ,, 32	890	60	1,400	60
,, ,, 34	1,270	1,000	1,440	1,000

	Amount of Present fee		Amount of new fee	
	(a) £	(b) £	(a) £	(b) £
Fee No. 40	360	—	100	370
„ „ 41	420	—	160	430
„ „ 42	420	—	160	430
„ „ 43	330	—	80	350
„ „ 44	330	—	70	340
„ „ 45	360	—	100	370
„ „ 46	950	—	690	960
„ „ 47	750	—	500	770
„ „ 48	540	—	380	650
„ „ 49	540	—	380	650
„ „ 50	590	—	340	610
„ „ 51	470	190	1,160	190
„ „ 52	1,110	190	1,920	190

Schedule 3 to the 1976 Regulations (fees for the issue of documents) is amended by inserting a new fee (No. 3A) for a type approval certificate which modifies one previously issued.

Copies of ECE Regulations (these are regulations prepared by the United Nations Economic Commission for Europe, annexed to the Agreement of 20 March 1958 as amended (Cmnd. 2535 and 3562) relating to conditions for approval for motor vehicle equipment and parts, and accepted from time to time by the Governments which are parties to that Agreement) can be obtained from Her Majesty's Stationery Office.

STATUTORY INSTRUMENTS

1977 No. 1440

ROAD TRAFFIC

The Motor Vehicles (Type Approval and Approval Marks) (Fees) (Amendment) Regulations 1977

Made - - - -	*19th August* 1977
Laid before Parliament	*6th September* 1977
Coming into Operation	*1st October* 1977

The Secretary of State for Transport, with the consent of the Treasury, in exercise of the powers conferred by section 56(1) and (2) of the Finance Act 1973(a) and of all other enabling powers, hereby makes the following Regulations:—

1. These Regulations may be cited as the Motor Vehicles (Type Approval and Approval Marks) (Fees) (Amendment) Regulations 1977, and shall come into operation on 1st October 1977.

2. The Motor Vehicles (Type Approval and Approval Marks) (Fees) Regulations 1976(b) (hereinafter referred to as "the 1976 Regulations") shall be amended as follows:

  (1) in Regulation 2(1) (Interpretation)—

      for the definition of "the Type Approval (Great Britain) (Fees) Regulations" there shall be substituted the following:—

        " "the Type Approval (Great Britain) (Fees) Regulations" means the Motor Vehicles (Type Approval) (Great Britain) (Fees) Regulations 1976(c), as amended(d);";

  (2) for Schedule 1 (table of fees for the testing of vehicles or parts of vehicles) there shall be substituted the revised Schedule 1 set out in the Schedule to these regulations;

  (3) in Schedule 2 (fees for the issue of documents), in column (3), in respect of fee number 5, for "10" there shall be substituted "30".

8th August 1977.

William Rodgers,
Secretary of State for Transport.

We consent to the making of these Regulations.

19th August 1977.

Donald R. Coleman,
J. Dormand,
Two of the Lords Commissioners
of Her Majesty's Treasury.

(a) 1973 c. 51.
(c) S.I. 1976/1466 (1976 III, p. 3975).

(b) S.I. 1976/1465 (1976 III, p. 3961).
(d) S.I. 1977/1439 (1977 II, p.4295).

THE SCHEDULE
Revised Schedule 1 to the 1976 Regulations

"SCHEDULE 1

TABLE OF FEES FOR THE TESTING OF VEHICLES OR PARTS OF VEHICLES

(1) Fee No.	(2) Particulars of type approval requirements (subject matter and relevant Community Directive, Community Regulation or ECE Regulation)			(3) Particulars of type of test, vehicle or vehicle part (where not uniform in relation to each type approval requirement)	(4) Amount of fee for test	
	(a) Description	(b) Community Directive or Community Regulation	(c) ECE Regulation		(a) £	(b) £
1.	Headlamps emitting an asymmetrical passing beam or a driving beam or both.	Council Directive 76/761/EEC of 27th July 1976 (O.J. L262, 29.9.76, p. 96).	Regulation No. 1 of 2nd March 1960 (as corrected on 20th June 1960, amended on 8th June 1962 and 30th April 1963 issued with revised text on 26th October 1964 and corrected on 8th June 1965).	—	170	—
2.	Incandescent electric filament lamps for headlamps emitting an asymmetrical passing beam or a driving beam or both.	Council Directive 76/761/EEC of 27th July 1976 (O.J. L262, 27.9.76, p. 96).	Regulation No. 2 of 24th March 1960 (as corrected on 20th June 1960, amended on 8th June 1962 and 30th April 1963, issued with revised text on 26th October 1964 and corrected on 8th June 1965).	—	210	—
3.	Reflex reflecting devices.	Council Directive 76/757/EEC of 27th July 1976 (O.J. L262, 27.9.76, p. 32).	Regulation No. 3 of 1st November 1963.	—	160	—
4.	Devices for the illumination of rear registration plates.	Council Directive 76/760/EEC of 27th July 1976 (O.J. L262, 27.9.76, p. 85).	Regulation No. 4 of 15th April 1964.	—	150	—
5.	Sealed-beam headlamps emitting a European asymmetrical passing beam or a driving beam or both.		Regulation No. 5 of 22nd May 1967 (as corrected on 30th September 1968).	—	170	—
6.	Direction indicators.	Council Directive 76/759/EEC of 27th July 1976 (O.J. L262, 27.9.76, p. 71).	Regulation No. 6 of 22nd May 1967.	—	210	—
7.	Lamps—side, rear, stop.	Council Directive 76/758/EEC of 27th July 1976 (O.J. L262, 27.9.76, p. 54).	Regulation No. 7 of 22nd May 1967 (as amended on 9th February 1971).	—	210	—
8.	Reversing lamps.	—	Regulation No. 23 of 20th August 1971.	—	210	—
9.	Multi-function lamp assemblies.	—		Any two of the lamps listed at items 6, 7 and 8.	250	—
10.		—	Regulations Nos. 6, 7 and 23 (as mentioned above).	Any three of the lamps listed in items 6, 7 and 8.	290	—
11.		—		Any four of the lamps listed in items 6, 7 and 8.	330	—

(1) Fee No.	(2) Particulars of type approval requirements (subject matter and relevant Community Directive, Community Regulation or ECE Regulation)			(3) Particulars of type of test, vehicle or vehicle part (where not uniform in relation to each type approval requirement)	(4) Amount of fee for test	
	(a) Description	(b) Community Directive or Community Regulation)	(c) ECE Regulation		(a) £	(b) £
12.	Headlamps emitting an asymmetrical passing beam or a driving beam or both and equipped with halogen filament lamps (H1, H2 or H3 lamps) and the filament lamps.	—	Regulation No. 8 of 12th June 1967 (issued with revised text on 28th May 1971 and 23rd April 1975).	Headlamp	160	—
13.		—		Filament lamp	210	—
14.	Radio-interference suppression.	Council Directive 72/245/EEC of 20th June 1972 (O.J. L152, 6.7.72, p. 15 (SE 1972 (II), p. 637).	Regulation No. 10 of 17th December 1968.	—	100	180
15.	Door latches and hinges.	Council Directive 70/387/EEC of 27th July 1970 (O.J. L176, 10.8.70, p. 5 (SE 1970 (II), p. 564)).	Regulation No. 11 of 8th January 1969 (as corrected on 16th March 1971 and amended on 29th October 1975).	Laboratory test	410	110
16.				Vehicle test	80	70
17.	Protective steering devices.	Council Directive 74/297/EEC of 4th June 1974 (O.J. L165, 20.6.74, p. 16).	Regulation No. 12 of 14th April 1969 (issued with revised text on 3rd November 1975).	Steering column test	780	270
18.				Barrier test	1,900	270
19.	Exhaust emissions (spark ignition engines).	Council Directive 70/220/EEC of 20th March 1970 (as amended by Council Directive 74/290/EEC of 23rd May 1974) (O.J. L76, 6.4.70, p. 1 (SE 1970 (I), p. 171) and O.J. L159, 15.6.74, p. 61).	Regulation No. 15 of 11th March 1970 (as amended on 11th December 1974).	—	350	190
19A.	Exhaust emissions (spark ignition engines).	Council Directive 70/220/EEC of 20th March 1970 (as amended by Council Directive 74/290/EEC of 23rd May 1974 and Commission Directive 77/102/EEC of 30th November 1976) (O.J. L76, 6.4.70, p. 1 (SE 1970 (I), p. 171). O.J. L159, 15.6.74, p. 61 and O.J. L32, 3.2.77, p. 32).	Regulation No. 15 of 11th March 1970 (as amended on 11th December 1974 and on 1st March 1977).	—	350	190
20.	Seats and anchorages.	Council Directive 74/408/EEC of 22nd July 1974 (O.J. L221, 12.8.74, p. 1).	Regulation No. 17 of 14th August 1970 (issued with revised text on 2nd January 1976).	Static test	1,160	190
21.				Dynamic test	1,920	190
22.	Anti-theft devices.	Council Directive 74/61/EEC of 17th December 1973 (O.J. L38, 11.2.74, p. 22).	Regulation No. 18 of 14th September 1970.	—	240	60

(1) Fee No.	(2) Particulars of type approval requirements (subject matter and relevant Community Directive, Community Regulation or ECE Regulation)			(3) Particulars of type of test, vehicle or vehicle part (where not uniform in relation to each type approval requirement)	(4) Amount of fee for test	
	(a) Description	(b) Community Directive or Community Regulation	(c) ECE Regulation		(a) £	(b) £
23.	Fog lamps.	Council Directive 76/762/EEC of 27th July 1972 (O.J. L262, 27.9.76, p. 122).	Regulation No. 19 of 14th September 1970 (issued with revised text on 22nd August 1974).	—	160	—
24.	Headlamps emitting an asymmetrical passing beam or a driving beam or both and equipped with halogen filament lamps (H4 lamps) and the filament lamps).		Regulation No. 20 of 1st March 1971.	Headlamp	160	—
25.		—		Filament lamp	210	—
26.	Interior fittings.	Council Directive 74/60/EEC of 17th December 1973 (as corrected on 23rd February 1977) (O.J. L35, 11.2.74, p. 2. O.J. L53, 25.2.77, p. 2).	Regulation No. 21 of 2nd June 1971 (as corrected in 1972).	—	1.310	790
27. 28.	Exhaust emissions (compression ignition engines).	Council Directive 72/306/EEC of 2nd August 1972 (O.J. L190, 20.8.72, p. 1 (SE 1972 (III), p. 889)).	Regulation No. 24 of 23rd August 1971 (as amended on 12th March 1974).	Vehicle test Engine test-bed test	600 900	190 190
29.	Head restraints.	—	Regulation No. 25 of 30th December 1971.	—	500	230
30.	External projections.	Council Directive 74/483/EEC of 17th September 1974 (O.J. L266, 2.10.74, p. 4).	Regulation No. 26 of 28th April 1972 (as amended on 12th March 1974).	—	310	270
31. 32.	Audible warning devices.	Council Directive 70/388/EEC of 27th July 1970 (O.J. L176, 10.8.70, p. 12 (SE 1970 (II), p. 571)).	Regulation No. 28 of 31st October 1972.	Laboratory test Vehicle test	620 120	370 100
33.	Tyres.	—	Regulation No. 30 of 1st April 1975.	—	210	90
34.	Halogen sealed-beam (H4SB) headlamps emitting an asymmetrical passing beam or driving beam or both.	—	Regulation No. 31 of 2nd June 1975.	—	250	—
35. 36.	Fuel tanks.	Council Directive 70/221/EEC of 20th March 1970 (O.J. L76, 6.4.70, p. 23 (SE 1970 (I), p. 192)).	—	Vehicles of category M1 or N1 Any other vehicles	170 260	110 190
37.	Rear protective devices.	Council Directive 70/221/EEC of 20th March 1970 (O.J. L76, 6.4.70. p. 23 (SE 1970 (I), p. 192)).	—	—	120	70

(1) Fee No.	(2) Particulars of type approval requirements (subject matter and relevant Community Directive, Community Regulation or ECE Regulation)			(3) Particulars of type of test, vehicle or vehicle part (where not uniform in relation to each type approval requirement)	(4) Amount of fee for test	
	(a) Description	(b) Community Directive or Community Regulation)	(c) ECE Regulation		(a) £	(b) £
38.	Space for mounting and fixing of rear registration plates.	Council Directive 70/222/EEC of 20th March 1970 (O.J. L76, 6.4.70, p. 25 (SE 1970 (I), p. 194)).	—	—	80	70
39.	Steering equipment.	Council Directive 70/311/EEC of 8th June 1970 (O.J. L133, 18.6.70, p. 10 (SE 1970 (II), p. 375)).	—	—	310	190
40.	Rear-view mirrors.	Council Directive 71/127/EEC of 1st March 1971 (O.J. L68, 22.3.71, p. 1 (SE 1971 (I), p. 136)).	—	Component test	100	80
41.				Installation test	310	190
42.	Brakes.	Council Directive 71/320/EEC of 26th July 1971 (O.J. L202, 6.9.71, p. 37 (SE 1971 (III), p. 746)).	—	Trailers of category 01 not fitted with brakes	50	—
43.				Trailers fitted only with overrun brakes	330	—
44.				Other trailers	1,600	—
45.				Vehicles of category M1 or N1	1,310	1,000
46.				Any other vehicles	2,060	1,000
47.	Brakes.	Council Directive 71/320/EEC of 26th July 1971 (as amended by Commission Directive 74/132/ EEC of 11th February 1974 and Commission Directive 75/524/ EEC of 25th July 1975). (O.J. L202, 6.9.71, p. 37 (SE 1971 (III), p. 746) and O.J. L74, 19.3.74, p. 7 and O.J. L236, 8.9.75, p. 3).	—	Trailers of category 01 not fitted with brakes	50	—
48.				Trailers fitted only with overrun brakes	330	—
49.				Other trailers	1,740	—
50.				Vehicles of category M1 or N1	1,440	1,120
51.				Any other vehicles	2,200	1,120
52.	Distribution of braking effort.	Commission Directive 75/524/ EEC of 25th July 1975 (O.J. L236, 8.9.75, p. 3).	—	—	170	150
53.	Sound levels.	Council Directive 70/157/EEC of 6th February 1970 (O.J. L42, 23.2.70, p. 16 (SE 1970 (I), p. 111)).	—	—	140	110

(1) Fee No.	(2) Particulars of type approval requirements (subject matter and relevant Community Directive, Community Regulation or ECE Regulation)			(3) Particulars of type of test, vehicle or vehicle part (where not uniform in relation to each type approval requirement)	(4) Amount of fee for test	
	(a) Description	(b) Community Directive or Community Regulation	(c) ECE Regulation		(a) £	(b) £
53A.	Sound levels.	Council Directive 70/157/EEC of 6th February 1970 (as amended by Commission Directive 73/350/ EEC of 7th November 1973 (O.J. L42, 23.2.75, p. 16 (SE 1970 (I), p. 111 and O.J. L321, 22.11.73, p. 33)).	—	—	140	110
54.	Exhaust systems.	Council Directive 70/157/EEC of 6th February 1970 (as amended by Commission Directive 73/350/ EEC of 7th November 1973) (O.J. L42, 23.2.70, p. 16 (SE 1970 (I), p. 111) and O.J. L321, 22.11.73, p. 33).	—	Engine test-bed test	1,300	350
55.				Track test	1,990	350
56.				Track test (employing driver provided by manufacturer)	150	—
57.	Recording equipment for road transport vehicles.	Community Regulation No. 1463/70 of 20th July 1970 (O.J. L164, 27.7.70, p. 1 (SE 1970 (II), p. 482)).	—	—	780	—
58.	Seat belt anchorages.	Council Directive 76/115/EEC of 18th December 1975 (O.J. L24, 30.1.76, p. 6).	Regulation No. 14 of 30th January 1970 (as amended on 16th March 1971 and issued with revised text on 19th August 1976).	—	920	90
59.	Advance warning triangles.	—	Regulation No. 27 of 7th June 1972.	Including fluorescent material	350	—
60.				Excluding flourescent material	250	—
61.	Installation of lighting and light signalling devices.	Council Directive 76/756/EEC of 27th July 1976 (O.J. L262, 27.9.76, p. 1).	—	— Additional tests for:	300	200
62.				Vehicles with retractable headlamps	770	520
63.				Beam adjustment	80	70
64.				Vehicles requiring simulated load for beam adjustment	200	180
65.	Statutory plates.	Council Directive 76/114/EEC of 18th December 1976 (O.J. L24, 30.1.76, p. 1).	—	—	80	70
66.	Speedometers.	Council Directive 75/443/EEC of 26th June 1975 (O.J. L196, 26.7.75, p. 1).	—	—	180	160
67.	Towing hooks.	—	—	—	50	—
68.	Rear end impact.	—	Regulation No. 32 of 14th July 1975.	—	1,460	250

2ff

(1) Fee No.	(2) Particulars of type approval requirements (subject matter and relevant Community Directive, Community Regulation or ECE Regulation)			(3) Particulars of type of test, vehicle or vehicle part (where not uniform in relation to each type approval requirement)	(4) Amount of fee for test	
	(a) Description	(b) Community Directive or Community Regulation)	(c) ECE Regulation		(a) £	(b) £
69.	Head-on impact.	—	Regulation No. 33 of 25th July, 1975.	—	1,490	290
70.	Fire risks.	—	Regulation No. 34 of 25th July, 1975.	—	4,100	600
71.				If front and rear impacts consecutive	3,400	—
72.	Items 18, 68 and 69 above.			Barrier test	3,320	490
73.				If consecutive	2,970	—
74.	Items 18, 68, 69 and 70 above.	—	—	Barrier test	4,800	860
75.				If consecutive	4,440	—
76.	Items 18 and 69 above.	—	—	Barrier test	1,730	370
77.	Items 68, 69 and 70 above.	—	—	Barrier test	4,410	750
78.	—	—	—	If consecutive	3,910	—
79.	Foot controls.	—	Regulation No. 35 of 18th September 1975.	—	280	250
80.	Reverse gear.	Council Directive 75/443/EEC of 26th June 1975 (O.J. L196, 26.7.75, p. 1).	—	—	10	10
81.	Public service vehicles.	—	Regulation No. 36 of 12th November 1975.	Rigid vehicles	1,290	1,030
82.		—	—	Articulated vehicles	1,570	1,280

NOTE: The vehicle categories mentioned against items 35, 42, 45, 47 and 50 in column (3) of this Schedule are defined in Note (b) in Annex I to Council Directive 70/156/EEC of 6th February 1970 on the approximation of the laws of the Member States relating to the type approval of motor vehicles and their trailers (O.J. L42, 23.2.70, p. 1 (SE 1970 (I), p. 96)).".

EXPLANATORY NOTE

(*This Note is not part of the Regulations.*)

These Regulations amend the Motor Vehicles (Type Approval and Approval Marks) (Fees) Regulations 1976 (S.I. No. 1465).

Their main effect is to substitute a revised Schedule 1 for Schedule 1 to the 1976 Regulations, which sets out the fees for the testing of vehicles and parts of vehicles.

In the revised Schedule 1:—

(1) references to further EEC Council Directives are included in column (2) in the entries relating to fees numbers 1, 2, 3, 4, 6, 7 and 23;

(2) references to ECE Regulations (or amendments thereto) are altered in column (2) in the entries relating to fees numbers 1, 2, 15 and 19 and a reference to an ECE Regulation is inserted in that column in the entry relating to fee number 58;

(3) new fees, numbers 19A, 53A and 61 to 82, are added;

(4) the following fees are altered:—

		Amount of Present fee		Amount of New fee	
		(a)	(b)	(a)	(b)
		£	£	£	£
Fee No.	6	150	—	210	—
,, ,,	7	150	—	210	—
,, ,,	8	150	—	210	—
,, ,,	9	190	—	250	—
,, ,,	10	230	—	290	—
,, ,,	11	280	—	330	—
,, ,,	15	470	140	410	110
,, ,,	17	460	240	780	270
,, ,,	18	1,470	240	1,900	270
,, ,,	19	300	190	350	190
,, ,,	20	470	190	1,160	190
,, ,,	21	1,110	190	1,920	190
,, ,,	22	150	60	240	60
,, ,,	27	780	190	600	190
,, ,,	28	720	190	900	190
,, ,,	31	570	370	620	370
,, ,,	35	170	140	170	110
,, ,,	41	230	190	310	190
,, ,,	44	1,550	—	1,600	—
,, ,,	45	1,270	1,000	1,310	1,000
,, ,,	46	2,010	1,000	2,060	1,000
,, ,,	50	1,410	1,120	1,440	1,120
,, ,,	51	2,150	1,120	2,200	1,120
,, ,,	58	640	60	920	90

Schedule 2 to the 1976 Regulations (fees for the issue of documents) is amended by altering the fee number 5 from £10 to £30.

Copies of ECE Regulations (these are regulations prepared by the United Nations Economic Commission for Europe, annexed to the Agreement of 20th March 1958 as amended (Cmnd. 2535 and 3562) relating to conditions for approval for motor vehicle equipment and parts, and accepted from time to time by the Governments which are parties to that Agreement) can be obtained from Her Majesty's Stationery Office.

STATUTORY INSTRUMENTS

1977 No. 1441

FOOD AND DRUGS

The Milk (Great Britain) (Amendment) (No. 2) Order 1977

Made - - -	23rd August 1977
Laid before Parliament	2nd September 1977
Coming into Operation	2nd October 1977

The Minister of Agriculture, Fisheries and Food and the Secretary of State, acting jointly in exercise of the powers conferred on them by sections 6 and 7 of the Emergency Laws (Re-enactments and Repeals) Act 1964(a) and of all other powers enabling them in that behalf, hereby make the following order:—

Citation and commencement

1. This order may be cited as the Milk (Great Britain) (Amendment) (No. 2) Order 1977, and shall come into operation on 2nd October 1977.

Amendment of the principal order

2. The Milk (Great Britain) Order 1971(b) as amended(c) shall be further amended by substituting for Schedules 1 and 2 thereto respectively Schedules 1 and 2 to this order.

Revocation

3. The Milk (Great Britain) (Amendment) Order 1977(d) is hereby revoked.

In Witness whereof the Official Seal of the Minister of Agriculture, Fisheries and Food is hereunto affixed on 16th August 1977.

(L.S.)

John Silkin,
Minister of Agriculture, Fisheries and Food.

Bruce Millan,
Secretary of State for Scotland.

23rd August 1977.

(a) 1964 c. 60.   (b) S.I. 1971/1038 (1971 II, p. 3108).
(c) S.I. 1974/1549, 1975/1664, 1977/859 (1974 III, p. 5869; 1975 III, p. 5720; 1977 II, p. 2368).
(d) S.I. 1977/859 (1977 II, p. 2368).

SCHEDULE 1

MAXIMUM RETAIL PRICES OF MILK IN ENGLAND AND WALES

1. Subject to the provisions of this Schedule, the maximum price of milk on a sale by retail in England and Wales shall be a price in accordance with the following table:—

Milk	Maximum Price (Rate per Pint)
	p
Channel Island milk	13½
South Devon milk	13½
Untreated Milk Farm Bottled	12½
Ultra Heat Treated milk...	12
Sterilised milk	12
Homogenised milk	12
Untreated milk	11½
Pasteurised milk	11½
Milk, other than the above mentioned	11½

2. A reasonable charge may be made by the seller in addition to the appropriate maximum price specified in the above table for milk sold by him as Kosher milk or Kedassia milk if—

(*a*) such milk is sold in a container distinctly labelled "Kosher" or "Kedassia", as the case may be; and

(*b*) such milk has been prepared for consumption in accordance with the appropriate Jewish practice relating thereto.

SCHEDULE 2

MAXIMUM RETAIL PRICES OF MILK IN SCOTLAND

1. Subject to the provisions of this Schedule, the maximum price of milk on a sale by retail in Scotland, excluding the islands other than the islands of Arran, Bute, Coll, Gigha, Islay and The Great Cumbrae and those comprising the Islands Area of Orkney, shall be a price in accordance with the following table:—

Milk	Maximum Price (Rate per Pint)
	p
Channel Islands milk	13½
South Devon milk	13½
Premium milk	12½
Ultra Heat Treated milk	12
Sterilised milk	12
Homogenised milk	12
Standard milk	11½
Pasteurised milk	11½
Milk, other than the above mentioned	11½

2. A reasonable charge may be made by the seller in addition to the appropriate maximum price specified in the above table for milk sold by him as Kosher milk or Kedassia milk if—

(*a*) such milk is sold in a container distinctly labelled "Kosher" or "Kedassia", as the case may be; and

(*b*) such milk has been prepared for consumption in accordance with the appropriate Jewish practice relating thereto.

EXPLANATORY NOTE

(This Note is not part of the Order.)

This amending Order, which comes into operation on 2nd October 1977, increases by ½p per pint the maximum retail prices of Channel Islands and South Devon milk on sales in Great Britain.

STATUTORY INSTRUMENTS

1977 No. 1443

EDUCATION, ENGLAND AND WALES
The Scholarships and Other Benefits Regulations 1977

Made - - - -	*22nd August* 1977
Laid before Parliament	*2nd September* 1977
Coming into Operation	*1st October* 1977

The Secretary of State for Education and Science and the Secretary of State for Wales, in exercise of the powers conferred by section 81 of the Education Act 1944(a) (read with section 4 of the Education Act 1962(b) and section 5 of the Education Act 1976(c)) and vested in them(d), hereby make the following Regulations:—

Citation and commencement

1. These Regulations may be cited as the Scholarships and Other Benefits · Regulations 1977 and shall come into operation on 1st October 1977.

Interpretation

2.—(1) In these Regulations, unless the context otherwise requires—

"authority" means local education authority;

"school" includes any school within the meaning of the Education Acts 1944 to 1976 and any course of instruction forming part only of, or conducted separately from, the work of a school.

(2) The Interpretation Act 1889(e) shall apply for the interpretation of these Regulations as it applies for the interpretation of an Act of Parliament.

(3) Except where the context otherwise requires, any reference in these Regulations to a Regulation is a reference to a Regulation contained in these. Regulations and any reference in a Regulation to a paragraph is a reference to a paragraph of that Regulation.

Revocations

3. The Regulations specified in the Schedule hereto and Regulation 6 of the Direct Grant Grammar Schools (Cessation of Grant) Regulations 1975(f) are hereby revoked.

(a) 1944 c. 31.   (b) 1962 c. 12.   (c) 1976 c. 81.
(d) S.I. 1964/490, 1970/1536 (1964 I, p. 800; 1970 III, p. 5289).
(e) 1889 c. 63.   (f) S.I. 1975/1198 (1975 II, p. 4117).

Grants of scholarships and other benefits

4. Subject to Regulations 5 and 6, every authority may for the purpose of enabling pupils to take advantage without hardship to themselves or their parents of any educational facilities available to them—

(*a*) defray such expenses of children attending county schools, voluntary schools or special schools, other than expenses in respect of clothing which the authority are authorised to provide by or under section 5 of the Education (Miscellaneous Provisions) Act 1948(**a**), as may be necessary to enable such children to take part in any school activities;

(*b*) pay the whole of any approved tuition fees and the whole or part of any approved boarding or lodging fees which are related to the attendance at schools at which fees are payable of children in respect of whom grants are payable under Regulation 4 of the Direct Grant Schools Regulations 1959(**b**), as amended(**c**);

(*c*) defray the expenses payable in respect of any attendance referred to in paragraph (*b*);

(*d*) pay the whole or part of the tuition fees, boarding or lodging fees and expenses which are related to the attendance at schools at which fees are payable of children in respect of whom no grant is payable under Regulation 4 of the Direct Grant Schools Regulations 1959, as amended;

(*e*) grant scholarships, exhibitions, bursaries or other allowances in respect of—

(i) pupils over compulsory school age attending schools;

(ii) students pursuing correspondence courses in subjects of further education.

Restrictions on the making of payments

5.—(1) No payments shall be made under Regulation 4(*d*) except in accordance with arrangements which have been approved in writing by the Secretary of State:

Provided that this paragraph shall not apply to payments in respect of any child for whom a payment of a similar nature has been made before the coming into operation of these Regulations.

(2) The Secretary of State may by giving notice in writing to an authority revoke any approval given to that authority for the purpose of this Regulation.

6. No payment shall be made under these Regulations unless—

(*a*) it is required to be made in order to prevent or relieve financial hardship;

(*b*) except in the case of a payment under Regulation 4(*e*)(ii), the amount of the payment is related to the means of the parents of the pupil;

(*c*) the authority is satisfied that the course of education to which the payment relates is suitable for the pupil.

(**a**) 1948 c. 40.   (**b**) S.I. 1959/1832 (1959 I, p. 1034).
(**c**) The relevant amending instruments are S.I. 1963/1379, 1973/1535 (1963 II, p. 2385; 1973 III, p. 4788). See also S.I. 1975/1198 (1975 II, p. 4117).

Given under the Official Seal of the Secretary of State for Education and Science on 18th August 1977. ʹ

(L.S.)

Donaldson,
Minister of State,
Authorised by the Secretary of State
for Education and Science.

Signed by authority of the Secretary
of State for Wales on 22nd August 1977.

T. Alec Jones,
Parliamentary Under-Secretary of State,
Welsh Office.

SCHEDULE

REVOCATIONS

Regulations revoked	References
The Regulations for Scholarships and Other Benefits, 1945	S.R. & O. 1945/666 (1945 I, p. 340)
The Scholarships and Other Benefits Amending Regulations No. 1, 1948	S.I. 1948/688 (1948 I, p. 754)
The Scholarships and Other Benefits Amending Regulations No. 2, 1948	S.I. 1948/2223 (1948 I, p. 755)
The Scholarships and Other Benefits Amending Regulations 1964	S.I. 1964/1294 (1964 II, p. 2974)

EXPLANATORY NOTE

(This Note is not part of the Regulations.)

These Regulations consolidate with amendments the Regulations which empower local education authorities to make payments for the purpose of enabling pupils to take advantage of educational facilities without hardship.

The principal amendments are: —

(a) children attending direct grant schools and in respect of whom no grants are payable under Regulation 4 of the Direct Grant Schools Regulations 1959 are placed in the same category as children attending other non-maintained schools;

(b) payments in respect of children in this category are to be made in accordance with arrangements approved by the Secretary of State.

STATUTORY INSTRUMENTS

1977 No. 1444

SOCIAL SECURITY

The Social Security (Claims and Payments) Amendment (No. 2) Regulations 1977

Made - - - - -	24th August 1977
Laid before Parliament - -	26th August 1977
Coming into Operation - -	30th August 1977

The Secretary of State for Social Services, in exercise of the powers conferred upon him by sections 79(3) and 115(1) of, and Schedule 13 to, the Social Security Act 1975 **(a)** and of all other powers enabling him in that behalf, after reference to the National Insurance Advisory Committee, hereby makes the following regulations:—

Citation, interpretation and commencement

1. These regulations, which may be cited as the Social Security (Claims and Payments) Amendment (No. 2) Regulations 1977, shall be read as one with the Social Security (Claims and Payments) Regulations 1975 **(b)**, as amended **(c)**, (hereinafter referred to as "the principal regulations") and shall come into operation on 30th August 1977.

Amendment of regulation 11 of the principal regulations

2.—(1) Regulation 11 of the principal regulations (forward allowances and disallowances of sickness, invalidity and injury benefit and non-contributory invalidity pension) shall be amended in accordance with the following provisions of this regulation.

(2) In paragraph (1)—

    (*a*) for the words "provisions of paragraph (3)" there shall be substituted the words "following paragraphs";

    (*b*) in sub-paragraph (*b*) the words "or disallowed" shall be deleted;

    (*c*) in sub-paragraph (*c*) the words "or disallowed" and "or disallowing" shall be deleted.

(3) After paragraph (5) there shall be added the following paragraph:—

"(6) Where a claim for non-contributory invalidity pension is made by a woman who claims by virtue of the exception to section 36(2) (incapable of performing normal household duties) that claim shall, unless in any case the Secretary of State otherwise directs, be treated as if made by her for—

    (a) 1975 c. 14.   (b) S.I. 1975/560 (1975 I, p. 2014).
    (c) The relevant amending instruments are S.I. 1975/1058, 1976/615 (1975 II, p. 3691; 1976 I, p. 1747).

(*a*) the period specified by a registered medical practitioner not being the claimant, on a form approved by the Secretary of State, as being that during which it is to be expected that the claimant is likely to continue to remain as restricted in her ability to perform the normal household duties in her own home or, if shorter, during which she should refrain from work; or

(*b*) where applicable, the period of any award of—

    (i) attendance allowance payable at the higher rate specified in paragraph 1 of Part III of Schedule 4 to the Act, or

    (ii) an increase of disablement pension where constant attendance is needed payable at the higher rate specified in paragraph 7 of Part V of Schedule 4 to the Act, or

    (iii) an increase of allowance where constant attendance is needed in cases of exceptionally severe disablement payable by virtue of regulations made under section 159(3) (*b*) (payments for pre-1948 cases), or

    (iv) increase of allowance where constant attendance is needed in cases of exceptionally severe disablement payable under any scheme made under section 5 of the Industrial Injuries and Diseases (Old Cases) Act 1975 **(a)**, or

    (v) constant attendance allowance payable at the higher rate specified for exceptional cases of very severe disablement under any Personal Injuries Scheme or Service Pensions Instrument defined in regulation 2(1) of the Social Security (Overlapping Benefits) Regulations 1975 **(b)**; or

(*c*) the period specified in a certificate issued in respect of her which complies with paragraph (5) (*b*),

in any case beginning on the first day for which non-contributory invalidity pension is claimed (not being earlier than 17th November 1977), and the provisions of paragraphs (1)(*b*) and (*c*) and (2) shall apply to such a claim, so however that, where a decision awarding benefit by virtue of this paragraph is reviewed in accordance with paragraph (2) and it appears that the woman may be entitled to non-contributory invalidity pension otherwise than by virtue of the exception to section 36(2), the period for which the claim shall, notwithstanding the foregoing provisions of this paragraph, be treated as made shall be the relevant period specified in this paragraph".

Signed by authority of the Secretary of State for Social Services.

Alfred Morris,

Parliamentary Under-Secretary of State

24th August 1977.   Department of Health and Social Security.

(a) 1975 c. 16.   **(b)** S.I. 1975/554 (1975 I, p. 1918).

EXPLANATORY NOTE

(This Note is not part of the Regulations.)

These Regulations amend the provisions in the Social Security (Claims and Payments) Regulations 1975 which relate to forward allowances and disallowances of incapacity benefits under the Social Security Act 1975, in particular to extend those provisions to non-contributory invalidity pension for those women who under section 36(2) of that Act are claiming that pension on the basis that they are incapable of work and incapable of performing normal household duties.

The Report of the National Insurance Advisory Committee dated 19th August 1977 on the draft of these Regulations referred to them is contained in Command Paper (Cmnd. 6924) published by Her Majesty's Stationery Office.

STATUTORY INSTRUMENTS

1977 No. 1447

NATIONAL DEBT

The Premium Savings Bonds (Amendment) Regulations 1977

Made - - - -	15*th August* 1977
Laid before Parliament	25*th August* 1977
Coming into Operation	1*st September* 1977

The Treasury, in exercise of the powers conferred on them by section 11 of the National Debt Act 1972(a) and of all other powers enabling them in that behalf, hereby make the following Regulations:—

1.—(1) These Regulations may be cited as the Premium Savings Bonds (Amendment) Regulations 1977 and shall come into operation on 1st September 1977.

(2) The Interpretation Act 1889(b) shall apply for the interpretation of these Regulations as it applies for the interpretation of an Act of Parliament.

2. The Premium Savings Bonds Regulations 1972(c), as amended(d), shall be further amended as follows:—

(*a*) in Regulation 2(1) by inserting, after the definition of "bond", the following definition:—

"Chief Registrar of Friendly Societies", except in the application of these Regulations to Scotland, means the Chief Registrar of Friendly Societies or a deputy appointed by him,";

(*b*) by deleting Regulation 32(2)(*f*).

J. Dormand,
T. E. Graham.

Two of the Lords Commissioners
of Her Majesty's Treasury

15th August 1977

EXPLANATORY NOTE

(*This Note is not part of the Regulations.*)

These Regulations amend the Premium Savings Bonds Regulations 1972 in their application to England, Wales, the Channel Islands and the Isle of Man by making provision, similar to that which previously applied only to Northern Ireland, for a deputy to the Chief Registrar of Friendly Societies to adjudicate in disputes relating to premium savings bonds.

(a) 1972 c. 65.   (b) 1889 c. 63.   (c) S.I. 1972/765 (1972 II, p. 2449).
(d) S.I. 1975/1191, 1976/1543 (1975 II, p. 4099; 1976 III, p. 4037).

STATUTORY INSTRUMENTS

1977 No. 1448

NATIONAL DEBT

The Savings Certificates (Amendment) (No. 2) Regulations 1977

Made - - - -	*15th August* 1977
Laid before Parliament	*25th August* 1977
Coming into Operation	*1st September* 1977

The Treasury, in exercise of the powers conferred on them by section 11 of the National Debt Act 1972(**a**), and of all other powers enabling them in that behalf, hereby make the following Regulations:—

1.—(1) These Regulations may be cited as the Savings Certificates (Amendment) (No. 2) Regulations 1977, and shall come into operation on 1st September 1977.

(2) The Interpretation Act 1889(**b**) shall apply for the interpretation of these Regulations as it applies for the interpretation of an Act of Parliament.

2. The Savings Certificates Regulations 1972(**c**), as amended(**d**), shall be further amended as follows:—

   (*a*) in Regulation 2(1) by inserting after the definition of "certificate" the following definition:—

      "Chief Registrar of Friendly Societies", except in the application of these Regulations to Scotland, means the "Chief Registrar of Friendly Societies or a deputy appointed by him,";

   (*b*) by deleting Regulation 40(2)(*f*).

J. Dormand,
Donald R. Coleman,

Two of the Lords Commissioners
of Her Majesty's Treasury.

15th August 1977.

EXPLANATORY NOTE

(*This Note is not part of the Regulations.*)

These Regulations amend the Savings Certificates Regulations in their application to England, Wales, the Isle of Man and the Channel Islands by making provision, similar to that which previously applied only to Northern Ireland, for a deputy of the Chief Registrar of Friendly Societies to adjudicate in disputes relating to savings certificates.

(**a**) 1972 c. 65.   (**b**) 1889 c. 63.   (**c**) S.I. 1972/641 (1972 I, p. 2084).
(**d**) S.I. 1975/714, 1192, 1976/2111, 1977/545 (1975 I, p. 2573; II, p. 4101; 1976 III, p. 5855; 1977 I, p. 1789).

STATUTORY INSTRUMENTS

1977 No. 1451 (L. 26)

COUNTY COURTS

FEES

The County Court Fees (Amendment) Order 1977

Made - - - -	15*th August* 1977
Laid before Parliament	6*th September* 1977
Coming into Operation	3*rd October* 1977

The Lord Chancellor and the Treasury, in exercise of the powers conferred on them by section 177 of the County Courts Act 1959(**a**), section 2 of the Public Offices Fees Act 1879(**b**) and section 365(3) of the Companies Act 1948(**c**), hereby make, concur in and sanction the following Order:—

1.—(1) This Order may be cited as the County Court Fees (Amendment) Order 1977 and shall come into operation on 3rd October 1977.

(2) The Interpretation Act 1889(**d**) shall apply to the interpretation of this Order as it applies to the interpretation of an Act of Parliament.

(3) In this Order a section, paragraph or fee referred to by number means the section, paragraph or fee so numbered in Schedule 1 to the County Court Fees Order 1975(**e**), as amended(**f**).

2. In fee No. 1(1) for the words from the beginning to "£15" in column 3 there shall be substituted the following words:—

Column 2	*Column* 3
"for the recovery of a sum of money— not exceeding £200............................	10p for every £1 or part thereof claimed. Minimum fee £1.50 Maximum fee £15
exceeding £200 but not exceeding £250	£16
exceeding £250 but not exceeding £300	£17
exceeding £300 but not exceeding £350	£18
exceeding £350	£19".

(**a**) 1959 c. 22. (**b**) 1879 c. 58. (**c**) 1948 c. 38. (**d**) 1889 c. 63.
(**e**) S.I. 1975/1328 (1975 II, p. 4493). (**f**) S.I. 1976/1479 (1976 III, p. 4000).

3. For Fee No. 12(ii) there shall be substituted the following fee:—

Column 2	Column 3
"(ii) On an application for an attachment of earnings order (other than a consolidated attachment order) to secure payment of a judgment debt	10p for every £1 or part thereof claimed. Minimum fee £1 Maximum fee £10".

Dated 29th July 1977.

Elwyn-Jones, C.

Dated 15th August 1977.

David Stoddart,
J. Diamond,
Two of the Lords Commissioners
of Her Majesty's Treasury.

EXPLANATORY NOTE

(This Note is not part of the Order.)

This Order amends the County Court Fees Order 1975, as amended by the County Court Fees (Amendment) Order 1976, by—

(a) raising both the minimum and maximum fee payable on entering a plaint for the recovery of a sum of money; and

(b) replacing the table of fees paid on an application for an attachment of earnings order by a standard fee of 10%.

STATUTORY INSTRUMENTS

1977 No. 1452

COAL INDUSTRY

The Coal Industry Nationalisation (Superannuation) (Amendment) Regulations 1977

Made - - - -	*29th August* 1977
Laid before Parliament	*9th September* 1977
Coming into Operation	*30th September* 1977

The Secretary of State, in exercise of powers conferred by subsection (1A) of section 37 of the Coal Industry Nationalisation Act 1946(a), (as inserted by section 12(1) of the Coal Industry Act 1977(b)) and section 63(1) of that Act and now vested in him (c), and of all other powers enabling him in that behalf, hereby makes the following regulations:—

1. These regulations may be cited as the Coal Industry Nationalisation (Superannuation) (Amendment) Regulations 1977 and shall come into operation on 30th September 1977.

2. The Interpretation Act 1889(d) shall apply for the interpretation of these regulations as it applies for the interpretation of an Act of Parliament.

3. The Coal Industry Nationalisation (Superannuation) Regulations 1950(e), as amended (f), shall be further amended as follows—

(1) At the end of Regulation 1 there shall be inserted the following para-graph—

"(4) The Board shall have the like power as in paragraph (1) of this regulation for the purpose of providing for pensions, gratuities and other like benefits in favour of any person who has been in the employment of a subsidiary of the Board or in favour of other persons by reference to the employment of any such person.".

(2) In Regulation 9(1), after the definition of "revelant date", there shall be inserted the following definition—

"subsidiary" has the meaning given by section 154 of the Companies Act 1948(g).".

Alexander Eadie,
Parliamentary Under Secretary of State,
Department of Energy.

29th August 1977.

(a) 1946 c. 59.   (b) 1977 c. 39.
(c) S.I. 1957/48, 1969/1498, 1970/1537 ((1957 I, p.1439; 1969 III, p.4797; 1970 III, p.5293).
(d) 1889 c. 63.   (e) S.I. 1950/376 (1950 I, p.356).
(f) The amending regulations are not relevant to the subject matter of these regulations.
(g) 1948 c. 38.

EXPLANATORY NOTE

(This Note is not part of the Regulations.)

These Regulations amend the Coal Industry Nationalisation (Superannuation) Regulations 1950 so as to enable the National Coal Board to pay or provide for the payment of pensions, gratuities and other like benefits in favour of any person who has been in the employment of a subsidiary of the Board, or in favour of other persons (such as the dependants of such a person) by reference to the employment of any such person.

STATUTORY INSTRUMENTS

1977 No. 1456

NATIONAL DEBT

The Savings Contracts (Amendment) Regulations 1977

Made - - - -	*15th August* 1977
Laid before Parliament	*31st August* 1977
Coming into Operation	*1st September* 1977

The Treasury, in exercise of the powers conferred on them by section 11 of the National Debt Act 1972(**a**), and of all other powers enabling them in that behalf, hereby makes the following Regulations:—

1.—(1) These Regulations may be cited as the Savings Contracts (Amendment) Regulations 1977, and shall come into operation on 1st September 1977.

(2) The Interpretation Act 1889(**b**) shall apply for the interpretation of these Regulations as it applies for the interpretation of an Act of Parliament.

2. The Savings Contracts Regulations 1969(**c**), as amended(**d**), shall be further amended as follows:—

(*a*) in Regulation 2(1) by inserting, after the definition of "the authority", the following definition :—

"Chief Registrar of Friendly Societies", except in the application of these Regulations to Scotland, means the Chief Registrar of Friendly Societies or a deputy appointed by him;";

(*b*) by deleting Regulation 28(2)(f).

J. Dormand,
Donald R. Coleman,
Two of the Lords Commissioners
of Her Majesty's Treasury.

15th August 1977.

EXPLANATORY NOTE

(*This Note is not part of the Regulations.*)

These Regulations amend the Savings Contracts Regulations 1969 in their application to England, Wales, the Channel Islands and the Isle of Man by making provision, similar to that which previously applied only to Northern Ireland, for a deputy to the Chief Registrar of Friendly Societies to adjudicate in respect of disputes relating to savings contracts.

(a) 1972 c. 65.   (b) 1889 c. 63.
(c) S.I. 1969/1342 (1969 III, p. 3984).   (d) S.I. 1975/1193 (1975 II, p. 4103).

STATUTORY INSTRUMENTS

1977 No. 1461

ROAD TRAFFIC

The Public Service Vehicle Operators (Qualifications) Regulations 1977

Made - - - -	26*th August* 1977
Laid before Parliament	8*th September* 1977
Coming into Operation	29*th September* 1977

The Secretary of State for Transport, being a Minister designated(a) for the purposes of section 2(2) of the European Communities Act 1972(b) in relation to the regulation and supervision of qualifications of persons engaged in road transport, in exercise of powers conferred by that section, hereby makes the following Regulations:—

Commencement and citation

1. These regulations may be cited as the Public Service Vehicle Operators (Qualifications) Regulations 1977 and shall come into operation on 29th September 1977.

Interpretation

2.—(1) In these Regulations, save where the context otherwise requires—

"the Act of 1960" means the Road Traffic Act 1960(c);

"the Act of 1968" means the Transport Act 1968(d);

"the Commissioners" means the traffic commissioners for one of the traffic areas constituted for the purposes of Part III of the Act of 1960;

"the Community instrument" means Council Directive (EEC) 74/562 of the 12th November 1974(e) on admission to the occupation of road passenger transport operator in national and international transport operations;

"international transport operation" means a transport operation involving the use of a passenger service vehicle for the provision of a public passenger transport service in part in the United Kingdom and in part elsewhere;

"national transport operation" means a transport operation involving the use of a passenger service vehicle for the provision of a public passenger transport service wholly in the United Kingdom;

(a) S.I. 1975/1707 (1975 III, p. 5814). (b) 1972 c. 68.
(c) 1960 c. 16. (d) 1968 c. 73. (e) O.J. No. L308/23 of 12.11.74.

"passenger service vehicle" means a motor vehicle so constructed and equipped as to be suitable for carrying more than nine persons (including the driver) and intended for that purpose;

"permit" means a permit under Regulation 20 of the 1952 Regulations by virtue of which a person is deemed to be the holder of a public service vehicle licence;

"public passenger transport services" means passenger transport services provided for the public, or for specific categories of users, in return for payment by the persons transported or by a person who arranges for the passengers to be transported, but does not include any such service in so far as it is provided by means of a vehicle constructed or adapted for the carriage of not more than 17 persons (including the driver)—

(i) otherwise than in the course of a business of carrying passengers, or

(ii) by a person whose main occupation is not the provision of road passenger transport services,

and for the purposes of sub-paragraph (i) above the provision by a local or public authority of a passenger transport service shall not be regarded as a provision in the course of a business of carrying passengers unless the service is provided by the public service vehicle undertaking of that authority;

"the 1952 Regulations" means the Public Service Vehicles (Licences and Certificates) Regulations 1952(a), as amended by the Public Service Vehicles (Licences and Certificates) (Amendment) Regulations 1957(b) and as modified by Regulation 9;

"relevant conviction", in relation to an applicant for, or the holder of, a standard licence, or to a transport manager, means any of the following convictions (not being a spent conviction within the meaning of the Rehabilitation of Offenders Act 1974(c))—

(a) a conviction of the person in question, or of any servant or agent of his, of contravening any provision (however expressed) contained in or having effect under any enactment (including any enactment hereafter passed) relating to—

(i) the maintenance of road vehicles in a fit and serviceable condition,

(ii) limits of speed and weight laden and unladen of road vehicles,

(iii) the licensing of drivers,

(b) a conviction of the person in question of contravening any provision of Part III of the Act of 1960 or of any regulations thereunder, or of any of sections 232 to 235 and 239 of that Act so far as they relate to public service vehicles,

(c) a conviction of the person in question, or of any servant or agent of his, of contravening, in relation to a public service vehicle, any provision of Part VI of the Act of 1968 or of any regulations thereunder,

---

(d) a conviction of the person in question, or of any servant or agent of his, of contravening any provision of section 92 of the Finance Act 1965(a) (which relates to grants towards bus fuel duty) or of Schedule 8 to the Act of 1968 (which relates to new bus grants),

(e) a conviction of the person in question, or of any servant or agent of his, of contravening any provision (however expressed) which prohibits or restricts the waiting of vehicles, being a provision contained in an order made under section 1, 6, 9 or 11 of the Road Traffic Regulation Act 1967(b) or under any enactment repealed by that Act and re-enacted by any of those sections,

(f) a conviction of the person in question, or of any servant or agent of his, of contravening any provision of these Regulations;

"responsible road passenger transport employment", in relation to an individual, means employment in the service of a person who carries on a road passenger transport undertaking, and in a position where that individual has effective responsibility for the management of transport operations of the undertaking;

"road passenger transport undertaking" means an undertaking which involves the use of passenger service vehicles under public service vehicle licences;

"standard licence" and "restricted licence" have the meanings respectively given in Regulation 3;

"transport manager", in relation to an applicant for, or a holder of, a standard licence, means a person who is, or is to be, employed by the applicant or the holder, as the case may be, in a position where he is responsible for the operation of passenger service vehicles used or to be used by the applicant or holder for the provision of public passenger transport services; and

"year" means a calendar year;

and any expression not defined above which is also used in Part III of the Act of 1960 has the same meaning as in that part of that Act.

(2) For the purpose of these Regulations a person who is an applicant for, or a holder of, a standard licence, or who is a transport manager, shall be regarded as being engaged in road passenger transport operations, if the person in question is—

(a) the holder or, if an individual, one of the joint holders, of a public service vehicle licence which relates to a passenger service vehicle, or

(b) a person who, by virtue of a permit, is deemed to be the holder or, if an individual, one of the joint holders, of such a public service vehicle licence, or

(c) if an individual, in responsible road transport employment.

(3) Any reference in these Regulations to the holder of a public service vehicle licence is a reference to the person to whom the licence was granted and does not include a reference to a person who is deemed to be the holder of such a licence by virtue of a permit.

(a) 1965 c. 25.   (b) 1967 c. 76.

(4) Any reference in these Regulations to any enactment or instrument is a reference to that enactment or instrument as amended or extended by or under any subsequent enactment or instrument (including these Regulations).

(5) Any reference in these Regulations to a numbered Regulation is a reference (except where the context otherwise requires) to the Regulation having that number in these Regulations.

(6) The Interpretation Act 1889(a) shall apply for the interpretation of these Regulations as it applies for the interpretation of an Act of Parliament.

Classification of public service vehicle licences

3.—(1) For the purpose of enabling the Community instrument to be implemented in Great Britain public service vehicle licences applied for on or after 1st January 1978 shall be divided into two classes, namely—

(a) standard licences—that is to say, public service vehicle licences which relate to passenger service vehicles and which authorise such vehicles to be used on roads for the provision of services which consist of or include public passenger transport services; and

(b) restricted licences—that is to say public service vehicle licences which—

(i) relate to vehicles which are not passenger service vehicles, or

(ii) authorise passenger service vehicles to be used on roads otherwise than for the provision of public passenger transport services.

(2) A standard licence may authorise the passenger service vehicle to which it relates to be used for the provision of public passenger transport services—

(a) on both international and national transport operations, or

(b) on national transport operations only.

(3) A public service vehicle licence shall indicate whether it is a standard or restricted licence, and a standard licence shall indicate whether it covers both international and national transport operations or national transport operations only.

(4) Every application for a public service vehicle licence shall state whether the licence applied for is a standard licence or a restricted licence and every application for a standard licence shall state whether the licence applied for is to cover both international and national transport operations or national transport operations only.

(5) Subject to paragraph (7) below, a person who causes or permits a passenger service vehicle to be used on a road in Great Britain for the provision of public passenger transport services shall be guilty of an offence unless—

(a) he is the holder of a standard licence which is in force in relation to that vehicle, or

(b) he is, by virtue of a permit, deemed to be the holder of such a licence which is in force in relation to that vehicle,

and any such offence shall be punishable, on summary conviction, by a fine not exceeding £100.

(a) 1889 c. 63.

(6) Subject to paragraph (7) below, a person who causes or permits a passenger service vehicle to be used on a road in Great Britain for the provision of public passenger transport services on an international transport operation in a case where the standard licence relating to that vehicle covers national transport operations only, shall be guilty of an offence and shall be liable on summary conviction to a fine not exceeding £50.

(7) Paragraphs (5) and (6) above shall not apply to any use of a vehicle on a road which is authorised by a public service vehicle licence, or a permit, applied for before 1st January 1978.

(8) Nothing in this Regulation shall apply to a public service vehicle licence applied for before 1st January 1978.

(9) Except as provided in this Regulation and in Regulation 8, the provisions of these Regulations shall not affect the application of Part III of the Act of 1960, or of any Regulations thereunder, to restricted licences.

(10) Part III of the Act of 1960 and any regulations thereunder shall have effect in relation to standard licences subject to the provisions of these Regulations.

Applications for standard licences

4.—(1) The provisions of this Regulation shall have effect for enabling or assisting the Commissioners, to whom application is made for the grant of a standard licence, to determine whether the applicant—

(a) is of good repute,

(b) has appropriate financial standing, and

(c) is professionally competent, or employs or will employ a transport manager who is of good repute and is professionally competent.

(2) Subject to paragraph (4) below, when making to the Commissioners his first application for a standard licence in any year after 1977, the applicant shall submit to those Commissioners, together with his application for the licence, a declaration signed by him or on his behalf, containing—

(a) particulars of any relevant convictions of the applicant during the 5 years preceding the making of the application,

(b) a statement that the applicant has or will have adequate financial resources available for the purpose of operating his road passenger transport undertaking,

(c) in a case where the applicant relies on his own professional competence for satisfying the professional competence requirement, particulars of his professional competence qualifications, and

(d) in a case where the applicant does not so rely, particulars of the name, address and place of work or intended place of work of his transport manager and of the professional competence qualifications of the transport manager and of any relevant convictions of such manager during the 5 years preceding the making of the application.

(3) When making to the Commissioners any subsequent application for a standard licence in any year after 1977 the applicant shall either—

(a) include in his application a statement that there has been no change in the particulars given in his licence declaration for that year, and that no additional particulars would be required to be included in his licence declaration for that year if the application were his first application for such a licence in that year, or

(b) submit, along with his appliction, a further declaration stating the changes which have occurred in the relevant particulars in his licence declaration for that year and any additional particulars which would be required to be included in his licence declaration if the application were his first application for a standard licence in that year.

(4) Where an applicant for a standard licence is—

(a) a person who was engaged in road passenger transport operations before 1st January 1978 and has been so engaged after 31st December 1969, or

(b) a partnership firm one or more of whose members was and has been so engaged as aforesaid,

paragraph (2)(a) and (d) above shall apply in relation to the applicant, and, where appropriate, to his transport manager, with the substitution of "1 year" for "5 years".

(5) In this Regulation—

(a) any reference, in relation to an applicant, to his first application to the Commissioners for a standard licence in any year is a reference to the first or only application made by him in that year for the grant of a standard licence by the particular Commissioners to whom the application is made;

(b) any reference, in relation to an applicant, to a subsequent application by him to the Commissioners for a standard licence in any year is a reference to any application for such a licence made subsequently by him in that year to the Commissioners to whom he made his first application;

(c) "licence declaration", in relation to any year, means the declaration required by paragraph (2) above to be made by an applicant in connection with his first application for a standard licence in that year, as for the time being varied or supplemented by any further declaration required by paragraph (3) above or any further information furnished in pursuance of Regulation 5.

(6) Where an applicant applies to the Commissioners at the same time for two or more standard licences and the case is one where, if only one such licence were being applied for, his application for that licence would be his first application for a standard licence in any year, then all these applications together shall for the purpose of this Regulation be regarded as his first application for a standard licence in that year.

Licence declarations—further information

5.—(1) If at any time during the currency of a licence declaration for any year there occur any of the following events—

(a) a relevant conviction of the declarant or of the transport manager of whom particulars are given in the declaration,

(b) the bankruptcy or liquidation of the declarant, or the sequestration of his estate or the appointment of a receiver, manager or trustee of his road passenger transport undertaking,

(c) where the declarant is a firm consisting of two or more partners, any change in the membership of the firm,

(d) a change in the identity of the transport manager of the declarant's road passenger transport undertaking,

the declarant shall, within 28 days of the occurrence of such event, give notice thereof in writing to the Commissioners to whom the declaration was submitted, and if without reasonable excuse he fails to do so, he shall be guilty of an offence and liable, on summary conviction, to a fine not exceeding £100.

(2) In this Regulation "licence declaration" has the same meaning as in Regulation 4 and "the declarant", in relation to a licence declaration, means the applicant for or, as the case may be, the holder of, a standard licence who made the declaration or on whose behalf it was made, and for the purposes of this Regulation a licence declaration for any licence year shall be regarded as current from the date on which it was submitted to the Commissioners under Regulation 4(2) until the expiry of the last standard licence granted in reliance on that declaration by those Commissioners or until the date on which the declarant submits to those Commissioners under the said Regulation 4(2) a licence declaration for the next subsequent year, whichever first occurs.

Decisions on applications for standard licences

6.—(1) An application for a standard licence shall be refused by the Commissioners to whom it is made unless they are satisfied, having regard to—

(i) any information which they may have with respect to the matters specified in section 35(2) of the Act of 1968, or

(ii) any other relevant information obtained by them in pursuance of Regulation 4 or 5, or otherwise,

that—

(a) the applicant is of good repute,

(b) the applicant has appropriate financial standing, and

(c) the applicant is himself professionally competent or will at all times during the currency of the licence have a transport manager who is of good repute and is professionally competent.

(2) A refusal of a standard licence under paragraph (1) above shall be regarded as a refusal under section 127(7) of the Act of 1960.

Revocation of standard licences

7.—(1) Subject to paragraph (4) below, where, at any time during the currency of a standard licence, it appears to the Commissioners by whom the licence was granted, whether from information given to them in pursuance of Regulation 4 or 5 or otherwise obtained by them, that—

(a) the licence holder is not of good repute, or

(*b*) the licence holder does not have appropriate financial standing, or

(*c*) the licence holder is not professionally competent and does not have a transport manager who is of good repute and is professionally competent,

then those Commissioners shall, whether or not they have power to do so under section 127(7) of the Act of 1960 (as read with section 35(1) of the Act of 1968), revoke the licence.

(2) Before revoking a standard licence under paragraph (1) above the Commissioners shall give notice in writing to the holder of the licence that they are considering its revocation, and shall state in the notice the grounds upon which revocation is being considered and the time within which written representations may be made by the holder of the licence to the Commissioners with respect thereto, and shall consider all such representations duly made to them within that time. A notice under this paragraph may be given by post.

(3) A revocation of a standard licence under paragraph (1) above shall be regarded as a revocation under section 127(7) of the Act of 1960.

(4) In the event of the death, or physical or legal incapacity, of the holder of a standard licence (being an individual) or of the transport manager required for the licence, or in the event of the transport manager ceasing for some other reason to be employed by the holder of the licence, the Commissioners may suspend the revocation of the licence under paragraph (1) above for such period as seems to them to be reasonably required for enabling the road passenger transport undertaking of the licence holder to be transferred to another person, or for enabling a new transport manager (with appropriate qualifications) to be appointed, as the case may be, and may extend such period of suspension, but nothing in this paragraph shall affect the operation of Regulation 12 (death of holder of licence) of the 1952 Regulations in a case where that Regulation applies.

(5) For the purpose of paragraph (4) above "legal incapacity" means—

(*a*) in relation to the holder of a standard licence, that he is incapable by reason of mental disorder, within the meaning of the Mental Health Act 1959(**a**), of carrying on his road passenger transport undertaking, and

(*b*) in relation to a transport manager, that he is incapable by reason of mental disorder within the meaning of the said Act of performing the duties of a transport manager.

Exchange of Licences

8.—(1) The holder of a restricted licence relating to a passenger service vehicle may, on surrendering that licence to the Commissioners by whom it was granted, be granted by them a standard licence relating to that vehicle for a period corresponding to the unexpired period of the restricted licence and such standard licence may authorise the vehicle to which it relates to be used on both international and national transport operations or on national transport operations only.

(**a**) 1959 c. 72.

(2) The holder of a standard licence which authorises a vehicle to be used on national transport operations only may, on surrendering that licence to the Commissioners by whom it was granted, be granted by them a standard licence authorising the vehicle to be used on both international and national transport operations for a period corresponding to the unexpired period of the surrendered licence.

(3) The provisions of Regulations 4 to 7 relating to applications for, and to the grant or revocation of, standard licences shall apply to standard licences applied for and granted under this Regulation on the surrender of a licence in the same way as they apply to standard licences otherwise applied for or granted.

Permits—modifications of 1952 Regulations

9. In its application to a vehicle in relation to which a standard licence is in force Regulation 20 of the 1952 Regulations (hired vehicles) shall have effect subject to the following modifications: —

(*a*) where the vehicle is, or is to be, used by the person in possession of it, under a hiring or hire purchase agreement, for providing public passenger transport services—

(i) that person shall not, by virtue of the fact that he already holds a public service vehicle licence for another vehicle, be deemed by the said Regulation 20 to be the holder of the standard licence unless the public service vehicle licence for that other vehicle is itself a standard licence covering the types of transport operations for which the first mentioned vehicle is to be used,

(ii) that person shall not, by virtue of a permit, be deemed by the said Regulation 20 to be the holder of the standard licence unless the provisions of Regulation 4 have been complied with by that person in relation to that permit in the same way as if the permit were itself a standard licence covering the types of transport operations to which the actual standard licence relates;

(*b*) the joint operators of any public passenger transport service provided by the vehicle shall not by virtue of paragraph (3) of the said Regulation 20 be deemed to be the holders of the standard licence issued to any of them and relating to the vehicle unless the operator, or each of the operators, to whom the licence was not issued holds in respect of the vehicle a permit granted in the same manner and subject to the same provisions with respect to granting and revocation as a permit under paragraph (1) of the said Regulation 20, being a permit in relation to which the provisions of Regulation 4 have been complied with by him in the same way as if the permit were itself the standard licence.

(*c*) where, by virtue of paragraph (*a*)(ii) or (*b*) above, the provisions of Regulation 4 are required to be complied with in relation to a permit, Regulations 5 to 7 shall apply in relation to that permit as if it were a standard licence and for the purposes of such application the references in those Regulations to the applicant for, or the holder of, a standard licence shall be construed as references to the applicant for, or the holder of, the permit and the references to section 127(7) of the Act of 1960 shall be construed as references to the said Regulation 20;

(*d*) a permit shall, unless previously revoked by the Commissioners who granted it, continue in force for such period, not exceeding one year from the date on which it is expressed to take effect, as those Commissioners may determine.

Determination of reputation, financial standing and professional competence

10.—(1) This Regulation applies for the purposes of the operation of Regulations 4 to 9.

(2) For the purpose of determining whether or not a person is or is not of good repute regard shall be had in particular to the existence and number of any relevant convictions relating to him during the period of 5 years ending with the date on which the matter falls to be determined.

(3) A person shall be regarded as having appropriate financial standing if he has, or will have, available to him sufficient financial resources to ensure the proper administration of his road passenger transport undertaking (including, where a new undertaking is being launched, the launching of that undertaking).

(4) Only an individual can be professionally competent.

(5) The professional competence requirement, as respects a corporate body, can only be satisfied by the employment by that body of a transport manager who is of good repute and is professionally competent.

(6) Where a standard licence, or a permit relating to a vehicle for which a standard licence is in force, is applied for by, or granted to, two or more individuals who are trading in partnership, the applicant, or as the case may be, the licence or permit holder, shall be regarded as professionally competent if one or more of the partners is professionally competent and a partner who is professionally competent has effective responsibility for the management of the transport operations of the partnership.

(7) An individual shall be regarded as professionally competent—

(*a*) if he was engaged in road passenger transport operations before 1st January 1975 and has been so engaged after 31st December 1969;

(*b*) if he is the holder of a certificate issued by a body approved for the purposes of this Regulation by the Secretary of State, to the effect that he possesses skills in the subjects listed in Part A of the Annex to the Community instrument, and in a case where his qualification is relevant for the purpose of a standard licence or a permit which covers international transport operations, also to the effect that he possesses skills in the subjects listed in Part B of the Annex to that instrument (the subjects all being subjects recognised by that body as required by article 2(4) of that instrument); or

(*c*) if he is the holder of any other certificate of competence, diploma or other qualification recognised for the purpose of this paragraph by the Secretary of State.

(8) An individual whose engagement in road passenger transport operations began on or after 1st January 1975 but before 1st January 1978 shall, by virtue

of such engagement, be regarded as professionally competent until 1st January 1980, but shall then cease to be so regarded unless before that date he has—

(*a*) been engaged in such operations for a period of, or for periods amounting in the aggregate to, two years, or

(*b*) become the holder of any such certificate as is mentioned in paragraph (7)(*b*) or (*c*) above.

Consequential adaptation of enactments

11.—(1) The power of the Secretary of State to make regulations under section 158 of the Act of 1960 with respect to procedure in connection with public service vehicle licences, or under section 160 of that Act for the purposes of Part III thereof, may also be exercised with respect to such procedure as altered or supplemented by these Regulations, or for carrying into effect the said Part III as modified and supplemented by these Regulations.

(2) Section 128 of the Act of 1960 (certifying officers and public service vehicle examiners) shall apply for the purpose of securing that the provisions of Part III of that Act, as modified and supplemented by these Regulations, are observed.

(3) Section 161(1) of the Act of 1960 (restriction on institution of proceedings) shall apply in relation to offences under any provision of these Regulations as it applies in relation to proceedings for an offence under Part III of that Act.

(4) The references in section 233(1)(*a*) (forgery) and section 235(1) (false statements) of the Act of 1960 to a licence under any part of that Act shall include a reference to a public service vehicle licence under Part III of that Act, and to a permit under Regulation 20 of the 1952 Regulations, as modified and supplemented by these Regulations and shall also include references to a certificate, diploma or other qualification referred to in Regulation 10(7) of these Regulations.

(5) For the purposes of section 235(1) of the Act of 1960 a statement made by a transport manager to his employer, or to his prospective employer, with a view to the inclusion of the information contained in that statement in a declaration or further declaration to be made by that employer or prospective employer under Regulation 4, or in any further information to be furnished by him under Regulation 5, shall be regarded as a statment made by the transport manager for the purpose of obtaining the grant of a public service vehicle licence to that employer or prospective employer.

(6) Section 244 of the Act of 1960 (time for commencing summary proceedings for certain offences) shall apply in relation to an offence under Regulation 5 as it applies to an offence under section 235 of that Act.

Signed by authority of
the Secretary of State

26th August 1977.

John Horam,

Parliamentary Under Secretary of State,
Department of Transport.

EXPLANATORY NOTE

(This Note is not part of the Regulations.)

1. These Regulations implement, in relation to Great Britain, the obliga-tions of the United Kingdom under Council Directive 74/562/EEC of 12th November 1974 (O.J. No. L308/23) on admission to the occupation of road passenger transport operator in national and international transport operations.

2. For the purpose of this implementation public service vehicle licences under Part III of the Road Traffic Act 1960 (public service vehicles) are divided (see Regulation 3) into two classes as from 1st January 1978—

(*a*) standard licences—which are to be required for passenger service vehicles used for the provision of public passenger transport services, and

(*b*) restricted licences—which will apply to public service vehicles which are not passenger service vehicles and to passenger service vehicles not used for the provision of public passenger transport services.

Passenger service vehicles are defined in Regulation 2 as meaning motor vehicles which are constructed and equipped to carry more than 9 persons (including the driver) and are intended for that purpose, and public passenger transport services are defined as meaning passenger transport services pro-vided for the public, or for specified categories of users, in return for payment. Passenger transport services by means of vehicles constructed or adapted to carry not more than 17 persons (including the driver) are, however, excluded from the definition of public passenger transport services if they are provided otherwise than in the course of a business of carrying passengers or are pro-vided by a person whose main occupation is not the provision of road passenger transport services.

3. Standard licences may authorise the vehicles to which they relate to be used for providing public passenger transport services on both international and national transport operations or on national transport operations only (Regulation 3).

4. It is to be an offence punishable on summary conviction by a fine not exceeding £100 for a person to cause or permit a passenger service vehicle to be used on a road for the provision of public passenger transport services unless he is, or is deemed to be, the holder of a standard licence relating to that vehicle (Regulation 3(5)). It is also to be an offence, punishable on summary conviction by a fine not exceeding £50, for a person to cause or permit a passenger service vehicle to be used for providing public passenger transport services on international transport operations if the standard licence relating to that vehicle covers national transport operations only (Regulation 3(6)).

5. In general, the provisions of Part III of the Road Traffic Act 1960 continue to apply to restricted licences without any amendment, but in their application to standard licences those provisions have effect as modified and supplemented by these Regulations which lay down more stringent require-ments as respects repute and financial standing and impose new requirements as respects professional competence.

6. In Regulation 4 provision is made for requiring the applicant for the first standard licence he applies for to the Traffic Commissioners for a particular traffic area in any year after 1977 to submit to the Commissioners a declaration as to matters bearing on his fitness to hold the licence, his financial standing and his professional competence or the fitness and professional competence of his transport manager. On subsequent applications for standard licences in any year after 1977 the applicant must indicate any changes which have occurred in these matters since the first application was made, and Regulation 5 imposes a general obligation on applicants for, and holders of, standard licences to inform the Commissioners of changes in the particulars contained in the licence declaration when they occur. Failure, without reasonable excuse, to furnish this information is an offence, punishable on summary conviction by a fine not exceeding £100.

7. Where an applicant for a standard licence fails to satisfy the Traffic Commissioners as to his repute and financial standing and the professional competence of himself or his transport manager, the Traffic Commissioners are required by Regulation 6 to reject the application and if at any time during the currency of a standard licence it appears to the Traffic Commissioners that the holder of the licence and (where appropriate) his transport manager do not satisfy the relevant requirements on these matters, they must revoke the licence (Regulation 7). Refusal of an application and revocation of a licence are to be treated as taking place under section 127(7) of the Road Traffic Act 1960, thus giving rise to a right of appeal to the Secretary of State under section 143 of that Act.

8. Provision is made (Regulation 8) for enabling restricted licences to be exchanged for standard licences and for enabling standard licences which cover national transport operations only to be exchanged for standard licences which cover both international and national transport operations.

9. Regulation 9 modifies Regulation 20 of the Public Service Vehicles (Licences and Certificates) Regulations 1952 (S.I. No. 900) under which certain persons who are not holders of public service vehicle licences are deemed to be the holders of such licences. The changes made secure that a person cannot, by virtue of Regulation 20 of the 1952 Regulations, become, in effect, the holder of a standard licence unless the provisions of the present Regulations about applicants for, and holders of, standard licences have been complied with.

10. Regulation 10 contains provisions for explaining how the requirements as to fitness, financial standing and professional competence are to be met. Only individuals can be professionally competent. The professional competence requirement is met by a corporate body if that body has a professionally competent transport manager. Individuals who were engaged in the road passenger transport industry in a responsible position before 1st January 1975 and who have been so engaged after 31st December 1969 are to be regarded as professionally competent by virtue of their experience. Individuals whose engagement in the road passenger transport industry in responsible positions began after 31st December 1974 but before 1st January 1978 will cease to be treated as being professionally competent on 1st January 1980 if they have not before that date had at least 2 years' experience in such positions, or obtained from a body approved by the Secretary of State a certificate as to their skills in certain subjects specified in the Annex to the Council Directive, or obtained some other certificate of competence, diploma

or other qualification recognised by the Secretary of State. Individuals whose engagement in the industry in responsible positions begins on or after 1st January 1978 will be required in all cases to have such a certificate of competence, or such diploma or other qualification, if they are to meet the professional competence requirements prescribed for the holder of a standard licence or for his transport manager.

11. Consequential amendments to certain enactments are made by Regulation 11.

STATUTORY INSTRUMENTS

1977 No. 1462

ROAD TRAFFIC

The Goods Vehicle Operators (Qualifications) Regulations 1977

Made - - - -	*26th August* 1977
Laid before Parliament	*8th September* 1977
Coming into Operation	*29th September* 1977

The Secretary of State for Transport, being a Minister designated **(a)** for the purposes of section 2(2) of the European Communities Act 1972**(b)** in relation to the regulation and supervision of qualifications of persons engaged in road transport, in exercise of the powers conferred by that section, hereby makes the following Regulations:—

Citation and Commencement

1. These Regulations may be cited as the Goods Vehicle Operators (Qualifications) Regulations 1977, and shall come into operation on 29th September 1977.

Interpretation

2.—(1) In these Regulations, unless the context otherwise requires—

"the Act of 1968" means the Transport Act 1968**(c)**;

"the Community instrument" means Council Directive (EEC) 74/561 of 12 November 1974**(d)** on admission to the occupation of road haulage operator in national and international transport operations;

"company" and "holding company" have the same meaning as in section 154 of the Companies Act 1948**(e)**;

"international transport operations" means transport operations involving the use, for carrying goods for hire or reward, of goods vehicles on journeys which take place in part in the United Kingdom and in part elsewhere;

"national transport operations" means transport operations involving the use, for carrying goods for hire or reward, of goods vehicles on journeys in the United Kingdom only;

"relevant convictions", in relation to an applicant for, or the holder of, a standard operator's licence or to a transport manager, means any such convictions as are mentioned in section 69(4) of the Act of 1968 (taking the references in that subsection to the holder of the licence as including references to the applicant for the licence or the transport manager, as the case may require);

(**a**) S.I. 1975/1707 (1975 III, p. 5814).   (**b**) 1972 c. 68.   (**c**) 1968 c. 73.
(**d**) O.J. No. L308/18 of 12.11.74.   (**e**) 1948 c. 38.

"responsible road transport employment," in relation to an individual, means employment which is employment in the service of a person who carries on a road transport undertaking and is employment in a position where that individual has responsibility for the operation of goods vehicles used under an operator's licence;

"road transport undertaking" means an undertaking which involves the use of goods vehicles under an operator's licence;

"standard operator's licence" and "restricted operator's licence" have the meanings respectively given in Regulation 3;

"transport manager," in relation to an applicant for, or a holder of, a standard operator's licence, means a person who is, or is to be, employed in full time employment by the applicant, or, as the case may be, who is employed in full time employment by the holder, in a position where he is responsible for the operation of vehicles used under the licence, and references in relation to a transport manager to his employment or his being employed by the applicant for, or the holder of, a standard operator's licence are references to his full time employment in the service of the applicant or holder, as the case may be;

and any expression not defined above which is also used in Part V of the Act of 1968 has the same meaning as in that part of that Act.

(2) For the purposes of these Regulations a person who is an applicant for, or a holder of, a standard operator's licence, or who is a transport manager, shall be regarded as being engaged in road transport operations, if the person in question is—

(a) the holder or, if an individual, one of the joint holders, of an operator's licence, or

(b) the subsidiary of the holder of an operator's licence, being a subsidiary to which goods vehicles used under the licence belong or in whose possession they are, or

(c) if an individual, in responsible road transport employment.

(3) For the purposes of these Regulations, the driver of a vehicle, if it belongs to him or is in his possession under an agreement for hire, hire-purchase or loan, and in any other case the person whose servant or agent the driver is, shall be regarded as the person using the vehicle; and references to using the vehicles shall be construed accordingly.

(4) Any reference in these Regulations to the holder of an operator's licence is a reference to the person to whom the licence was granted.

(5) Any reference in these Regulations to any enactment or instrument is a reference to that enactment or instrument as amended or extended by or under any subsequent enactment or instrument (including these Regulations).

(6) Any reference in these Regulations to a numbered Regulation is a reference to the Regulation having that number in these Regulations.

(7) The Interpretation Act 1889(a) shall apply for the interpretation of these Regulations as it applies for the interpretation of an Act of Parliament.

(a) 1889 c. 63.

Classification of operators' licences

3.—(1) For the purpose of enabling the Community instrument to be implemented in Great Britain operators' licences granted under Part V of the Act of 1968 so as to take effect on or after 1 January 1978 shall be divided into two classes, namely—

(a) standard operators' licences—that is to say licences under which goods vehicles may be used on a road for the carriage of goods—

(i) for hire or reward, or

(ii) for or in connection with any trade or business carried on by the holder of the licence; and

(b) restricted operators' licences—that is to say licences under which goods vehicles may be used on a road for the carriage of goods for or in connection with any trade or business carried on by the holder of the licence, not being the trade or business of carrying goods for hire or reward.

(2) Where the holder of an operator's licence is a company, any trade or business carried on by—

(a) the holding company of that company, or

(b) a subsidiary of that company, or

(c) another company which is also a subsidiary of that company's holding company,

shall, for the purposes of paragraph (1) above, be regarded as a trade or business carried on by the holder of the licence.

(3) Standard operators' licences may authorise goods vehicles to be used for the carriage of goods for hire or reward—

(a) on both international and national transport operations, or

(b) on national transport operations only.

(4) A statement shall appear—

(a) on the face of each operator's licence, for indicating whether it is a standard operator's licence or a restricted operator's licence, and

(b) on the face of each standard operator's licence, for indicating whether it covers both international and national transport operations or national transport operations only.

(5) The Secretary of State may, by regulations under section 91 of the Act of 1968 (regulations and orders for the purposes of Part V of that Act), make provision—

(a) for requiring a person who applies for an operator's licence to state in his application whether he is applying for a standard operator's licence or a restricted operator's licence,

(b) for requiring a person who applies for a standard operator's licence to state in his application whether the licence is to cover both international and national transport operations or national transport operations only,

(c) with respect to the means by which goods vehicles may be identified—

    (i) as being vehicles used under a standard operator's licence or under a restricted operator's licence, and

    (ii) if used under a standard operator's licence, as being vehicles authorised to be used for both international and national transport operations or for national transport operations only, and

(d) with respect to the appropriate form of licence for reflecting the above distinctions.

(6) A person who uses a goods vehicle under a restricted operator's licence for carrying goods for hire or reward shall be guilty of an offence and shall be liable on summary conviction to a fine not exceeding £200.

(7) A person who uses a goods vehicle under a standard operator's licence which covers national transport operations only, for carrying goods for hire or reward on international transport operations shall be guilty of an offence and shall be liable on summary conviction to a fine not exceeding £100.

(8) In section 68(1) of the Act of 1968 (variation of operators' licences)—

(a) in sub paragraph (c), after the words "section 65 of this Act" there shall be added the words "or specified for the purposes of the Goods Vehicle Operators (Qualifications) Regulations 1977 in a standard operator's licence as defined in Regulation 3 of those Regulations", and

(b) after sub paragraph (d) there shall be added the following:— "or (e) that a restricted operator's licence as defined in Regulation 3 of the said Regulations of 1977 be converted into a standard operator's licence as defined in that Regulation, or vice versa.".

(9) Section 69 of the Act of 1968 (which relates to revocation of operators' licences) shall be amended as follows: —

(a) in subsection (1)(b)(i) for "paragraphs (a) to (f)" substitute "paragraphs (a) to (fff)";

(b) after subsection (3) insert new subsection as follows: —
"(3A) Where the ground mentioned in subsection (1) of this section consists of a conviction mentioned in paragraph (ff) of subsection (4) of this section and there has been, within the 5 years preceding that conviction, a previous conviction of the holder of the licence of the offence referred to in that paragraph, the licensing authority shall give a direction under this section to revoke the licence";

(c) in subsection (4), after paragraph (f), insert the following paragraphs: —

    "(ff) a conviction of the holder of a licence of an offence under Regulation 3(6) of the Goods Vehicle Operators (Qualifications) Regulations 1977;

    (fff) a conviction of the holder of the licence of an offence under Regulation 3(7) of the Goods Vehicle Operators (Qualifications) Regulations 1977:".

(10) In section 232(1)(*b*) of the Road Traffic Act 1960(**a**) (duty to give information as to identity of drivers) the reference to section 60 of the Act of 1968 shall include a reference to Regulation 3(6) and (7) of the Goods Vehicle Operators (Qualifications) Regulations 1977.

(11) Nothing in this Regulation shall apply to any operator's licence which takes effect before 1 January 1978.

(12) Except as provided in this Regulation and in Regulation 7, the provisions of these Regulations shall not affect the application of Part V of the Act of 1968, or of any regulations thereunder, to restricted operators' licences.

(13) Part V of the Act of 1968, and any regulations thereunder, shall have effect in relation to standard operators' licences subject to the provisions of these Regulations.

Applications for standard operators' licences

4.—(1) The provisions of this Regulation shall have effect for enabling the licensing authority to determine, in relation to an applicant for a standard operator's licence, whether, in the cases where these requirements apply, the applicant—

(a) is of good repute,

(b) has appropriate financial standing, and

(c) is professionally competent or will employ one or more transport managers who are of good repute and are professionally competent.

(2) Subject to paragraph (4) below, every applicant for a standard operator's licence shall—

(a) include in his application (without being specifically required by the licensing authority to do so) particulars of the matters specified in paragraphs (*d*), (*e*), (*f*) and (*g*) of section 62(4) of the Act of 1968 (information about activities, convictions, financial resources and other matters),

(b) in a case where the applicant relies on his own professional competence for satisfying the professional competence requirement, include in his application particulars of his professional competence qualifications, and

(c) in a case where the applicant does not so rely, include in his application—

(i) particulars of the name, address and place of work or intended place of work of his transport manager or, if the applicant has more than one operating centre and the licensing authority requires him to have more than one transport manager, particulars of the name, address and place of work or intended place of work of each transport manager so required, and

(**a**) 1960 c. 16.

    (ii) particulars, in relation to such, or each such, transport manager, of his professional competence qualifications and of any relevant convictions of his during the 5 years preceding the making of the application.

(3) Where particulars of a transport manager are, in accordance with paragraph (2)(c) above, included in an application, the applicant shall forthwith notify the licensing authority if there occurs, in the interval referred to in section 62(4A) of the Act of 1968 (convictions during interval between application and date on which it is disposed of), a relevant conviction of the transport manager; and subsection (4B) of the said section 62 (offence of failing to give information as to convictions) shall apply in relation to this paragraph as it does in relation to subsection (4A) of that section.

· (4) Paragraph (2)(a) above shall not apply in relation to an application for a standard operator's licence by a person, or by a partnership firm of which at least one of the partners is a person, who satisfies the licensing authority that he was engaged in road transport operations before 1 January 1978.

(5) Nothing in this Regulation shall prejudice the right of the licensing authority, in relation to an application for a standard operator's licence, to require the applicant under section 62(4) of the Act of 1968 to give particulars of the matters referred to in paragraphs (d), (e), (f) and (g) of that subsection in a case where the licensing authority would have done so if these Regulations had not been made.

Decisions on applications for standard operators' licences

5.—(1) The licensing authority shall refuse to grant to an applicant a standard operator's licence unless he is satisfied that—

    (a) the applicant is of good repute,

    (b) the applicant has appropriate financial standing, and

    (c) the applicant is himself professionally competent or will at all times during the currency of the licence have in his employment a transport manager who is of good repute and is professionally competent or, if the applicant has more than one operating centre and the licensing authority requires him to have more than one transport manager, such number of transport managers who are of good repute and are professionally competent as are so required.

(2) A refusal of a standard operator's licence under paragraph (1) above shall be regarded for the purposes of Part V of the Act of 1968 as a refusal under section 64(3) of that Act.

Conditions to be attached to standard operators' licences

6.—(1) Subject to paragraph (3) below, the licensing authority, when granting a standard operator's licence, shall attach to the licence conditions for requiring the holder of the licence to inform him of the happening of any such event as is referred to in paragraphs (a) to (c) of section 66(1) of the Act of 1968, which—

(a) occurs during the currency of the licence,

(b) affects the holder of the licence or a transport manager of his, and

(c) is relevant to the performance by the licensing authority of his duties under these Regulations in relation to the licence or the performance by some other licensing authority of that authority's duties under these Regulations in relation to another standard operator's licence granted to that holder.

(2) A condition attached by a licensing authority to a standard operator's licence under paragraph (1) above shall, for the purpose of Part V of the Act of 1968, be regarded as having been attached under section 66 of that Act.

(3) A condition attached by a licensing authority to a standard operator's licence under paragraph (1) above, in a case where the holder of the licence is a company, shall not require the holder to inform the licensing authority of any change in the persons holding shares in the company unless the change is such as to cause a change in the control of the company.

(4) For the purposes of paragraph (3) above a change in the control of a company occurs when the controlling interest (as defined in section 69(11) of the Act of 1968) passes from one person to another person or from one group of persons to a wholly or substantially different group of persons.

Variation of licences

7.—(1) The provisions of Regulations 4, 5, and 6 shall apply to an application to vary a restricted operator's licence by directing that it shall be converted into a standard operator's licence, to the making of the direction and to the imposition of conditions as those provisions respectively apply to an application for a standard operator's licence, the decision to grant such a licence and the imposition of conditions on the occasion of the grant of such a licence, and for the purposes of this application the references in those Regulations to the application or the applicant for, or the grant of, a standard operator's licence shall be construed respectively as references to the application or the applicant for such variation or to the making of such variation.

(2) If the holder of a standard operator's licence which covers national transport operations applies for the licence to be varied so that it shall also cover international transport operations—

(a) the applicant shall include in his application the particulars as to professional competence which would be required by Regulation 4(2)(b) or (c) if the application were an application for the grant of a standard operator's licence covering both types of operations, and

(b) the licensing authority shall refuse to direct the variation applied for unless the authority is satisfied with respect to the professional competence qualifications of the relevant person or persons (including, in particular, in a case where Regulation 9(7)(b) is relied on for a professional competence qualification, the holding of a certificate as to skills in the subjects listed in Part B of the Annex to the Community instrument).

Revocation of standard operators' licences

8.—(1) Subject to paragraphs (4) and (5) below, where, at any time during the currency of a standard operator's licence, it appears to the licensing authority by whom that licence was granted, whether from information given to him pursuant to section 62(4), 63 or 66(1) of the Act of 1968 or to these Regulations, or otherwise obtained by him, that—

(a) the licence holder is not of good repute, or

(b) the licence holder does not have appropriate financial standing, or

(c) the licence holder is not professionally competent and does not have such one or more transport managers who are of good repute and professionally competent as is or are required by the licence,

then the licensing authority shall, whether or not he has power to give a direction for the revocation of the licence under section 69(1) of the Act of 1968, direct that the licence shall be revoked.

(2) Before directing under paragraph (1) above that a standard operator's licence shall be revoked the licensing authority shall give notice in writing to the holder of the licence that he is considering its revocation, and shall state in the notice the grounds on which revocation is being considered and the time within which written representations may be made by the holder of the licence to the licensing authority with respect thereto, and shall consider all such representations duly made within that time.

(3) A direction to revoke given by a licensing authority under paragraph (1) above shall, for the purposes of Part V of the Act of 1968, be regarded as being given under section 69(1) of that Act, but subsection (3) of that section shall not apply in relation thereto.

(4) In the event of the death, or physical or legal incapacity, of the holder of a standard operator's licence (being an individual) or of a transport manager required by the licence, paragraph (1) above shall not require the licensing authority to revoke the licence during such period, not exceeding 6 months, from the occurrence of the event in question, as the licensing authority may determine, or during such further period, not exceeding 6 months from the end of the first mentioned period, as the licensing authority may determine.

(5) In a case where a transport manager required by a standard operator's licence ceases to be employed by the holder of that licence (otherwise than by reason of his death or physical or legal incapacity), or where there occurs a relevant conviction of such a transport manager, paragraph (1) above shall not require the licensing authority to revoke the licence during such period, not exceeding 6 months from the cessation of employment or the occurrence of the conviction, as the licensing authority may consider reasonable for enabling the holder of the licence to engage a new transport manager who is of good repute and is professionally competent or to make suitable alternative arrangements with respect to his transport manager or managers.

(6) For the purposes of paragraphs (4) and (5) above, "legal incapacity"—

(a) in relation to the holder of a standard operator's licence means that he is incapable by reason of mental disorder, within the meaning of the Mental Health Act 1959(a), of carrying on his road transport undertaking,

and

(b) in relation to a transport manager, means that he is incapable by reason of mental disorder within the meaning of the said Act of performing the duties of a transport manager.

(7) Nothing in this Regulation shall restrict the power of a licensing authority to direct the revocation of a standard operator's licence under section 69(1) of the Act of 1968 in a case where that authority would do so if these Regulations had not been made.

Determination of reputation, financial standing and professional competence

9.—(1) This Regulation applies for the purposes of the operation of Regulations 4 to 8.

(2) For the purpose of determining whether or not a person is or is not of good repute regard shall be had in particular to the existence and number of any relevant convictions relating to him during the period of 5 years ending with the date on which the matter falls to be determined.

(3) A person shall be regarded as having appropriate financial standing if he has available to him sufficient financial resources to ensure the proper administration of his road transport undertaking (including, where a new undertaking is being launched, the launching of that undertaking).

(4) Only an individual can be professionally competent.

(5) The professional competence requirement, as respects a company, can only be satisfied by the employment by that body of one or more transport managers who are of good repute and are professionally competent.

(6) Where a standard operator's licence is applied for by, or granted to, two or more individuals trading in partnership, the applicant, or as the case may be, the licence holder, shall be regarded as professionally competent if one or more of the partners are professionally competent, and a partner who is professionally competent is responsible for the operation of the vehicles used under the licence.

(7) Subject to paragraph (8) below, an individual shall be regarded as professionally competent—

(a) if he was engaged in road transport operations before 1st January 1975; or

(b) if he is the holder of a certificate issued by a body approved for the purposes of this Regulation by the Secretary of State, to the effect that he possesses skills in the subjects listed in Part A of the Annex to the Community instrument, and in a case where his qualification is relevant for the purpose of a standard operator's licence which covers

(a) 1959 c. 72.

international transport operations, also to the effect that he possesses skills in the subjects listed in Part B of the Annex to that instrument (the subjects all being subjects recognised by that body as required by article 3(4) of that instrument); or

(c) if he is the holder of any other certificate of competence, diploma or other qualification recognised for the purpose of this paragraph by the Secretary of State.

(8) An individual shall not be regarded as professionally competent by virtue of paragraph (7)(a) above after 31st December 1979 unless he is the holder of a certificate which has been issued by a licensing authority before that date and which states that the authority is satisfied that he was engaged in road transport operations as mentioned in the said paragraph (7)(a).

(9) An individual whose engagement in road transport operations began on or after 1st January 1975 but before 1st January 1978 shall, by virtue of such engagement, be regarded as professionally competent until 1st January 1980, but shall then cease to be so regarded unless before that date he has become the holder of any such certificate, diploma or other qualification as is mentioned in paragraph (7)(b) or (c) above.

Holding companies and subsidiaries

10. In a case where the applicant for, or the holder of, a standard operator's licence is a holding company and the goods vehicles to be used, or used, under the licence belong to, or are in the possession of, a subsidiary of that holding company, the provisions of these Regulations shall apply as if—

(a) the road transport undertaking and any operating centre of the subsidiary were the road transport undertaking and an operating centre of the holding company,

(b) for purposes of, or relating to, the reputation and financial standing of the holding company, the activities, relevant convictions and financial resources of the subsidiary were activities, convictions and resources of the holding company, and

(c) in relation to a transport manager, his employment by the subsidiary were employment by the holding company.

Consequential adaptation of enactments

11.—(1) In section 84 of the Act of 1968 (evidence by certificate) the reference to Part V of that Act shall include a reference to these Regulations, and references to that Part in sections 87 (inquiries), 88 (Transport Tribunal) 90 (appointment of officers), 91 (regulations and orders) and 92 (interpretation) shall be construed as references to it as modified or supplemented by the provisions of these Regulations.

(2) Without prejudice to Regulation 3(5) and paragraph (1) above, the power of the Secretary of State to make Regulations under section 91 of the Act of 1968 for the purposes of carrying Part V of that Act into effect may be exercised for the purposes of carrying into effect that Part as modified or supplemented by the provisions of these Regulations.

(3) In sections 233 (forgery) and 235(1) (false statements) of the Road Traffic Act 1960 the references to Part V of the Act of 1968 shall be construed as references to that Part as modified by these Regulations and the references to a licence under Part V of the Act of 1968 shall include references to a certificate, diploma or qualification referred to in Regulation 9(7) and to the certificate provided for in Regulation 9(8).

(4) In Section 56 of the Road Traffic Act 1972(a) (power to inspect goods vehicles for certain purposes) the reference to Part V of the Act of 1968 shall include a reference to these Regulations.

Signed by authority of
the Secretary of State
26th August 1977.

John Horam,
Parliamentary Under Secretary of State,
Department of Transport.

(a) 1972 c. 20.

EXPLANATORY NOTE

(This Note is not part of the Regulations.)

1. These Regulations implement, in relation to Great Britain, the obligations of the United Kingdom under Council Directive 74/561/EEC of 12th November 1974 (O.J. No. L308/18) on admission to the occupation of road haulage operator in national and international transport operations.

2. For the purpose of this implementation operators' licences under Part V of the Transport Act 1968 (regulation of carriage of goods by road) granted so as to take effect on or after 1st January 1978 are divided (see Regulation 3) into two classes—

(a) standard operators' licences—under which goods vehicles may be used either for hire or reward or for or in connection with a trade or business carried on by the holder of the licence, and

(b) restricted operators' licences—under which goods vehicles may only be used for or in connection with a trade or business carried on by the holder of the licence (not being the trade or business of carrying goods for hire or reward).

Standard operators' licences may cover the carriage of goods for hire or reward on both international and national transport operations or may cover such carriage on national transport operations only. It is to be an offence punishable on a summary conviction by a fine not exceeding £200 for the holder of a restricted operator's licence to use the vehicles to which the licence relates for carrying goods for hire or reward, and if the licence holder is convicted of this offence more than once in a period of 5 years the licensing authority must revoke his licence (Regulation 3(6) and (9)). It is to be an offence punishable on summary conviction by a fine not exceeding £100 for the holder of a standard operator's licence which covers national transport operations only to use the vehicles to which the licence relates for international transport operations, and if the licence holder is convicted of this offence the licensing authority will have power (but not a duty) to revoke his licence (Regulation 3(7) and (9)).

3. In general, the provisions of Part V of the Transport Act 1968 continue to apply to restricted operators' licences without any amendment, but in their application to standard operators' licences those provisions have effect as modified and supplemented by these Regulations which lay down more stringent requirements as respects repute and financial standing and impose new requirements as respects professional competence.

4. In Regulation 4 provision is made for requiring the applicant for a standard operator's licence to include in his application particulars of matters bearing on his fitness to hold the licence, his financial standing and his professional competence or the fitness and professional competence of the transport manager or managers in his full time employment, and Regulation 5 requires the licensing authority to refuse to grant a standard operator's licence to an applicant unless the licensing authority is satisfied on these matters. Regulation 6 requires the licensing authority to attach certain conditions to a standard operator's licence. Regulation 7 deals with the case where the holder of a restricted operator's licence applies to have it converted into a standard operator's licence and the case where the holder of a standard

operator's licence which covers national transport operations only applies to have it extended to cover international transport operations. Regulation 8 imposes an obligation on the licensing authority to revoke a standard operator's licence if it appears to that authority that the relevant requirements as to reputation, financial standing or professional competence of the holder of the licence or as to the fitness or professional competence of his transport manager or managers are not being met. A refusal by the licensing authority to grant a standard operator's licence, a decision by the licensing authority to attach conditions to such a licence and the revocation of such a licence by the licensing authority, under Regulations 5, 6 and 8 respectively, are to be treated as having taken place under the relevant provisions of Part V of the Transport Act 1968, thus giving rise to a right of appeal to the Transport Tribunal under section 70 of that Act.

5. Exemption from certain of the requirements of Regulation 4 is conferred on persons engaged in the road transport industry before 1st January 1978 (Regulation 4(4)) but the existing requirements in Part V of the 1968 Act remain applicable to such persons.

6. Regulation 9 contains provisions for explaining how the requirements as to fitness, financial standing and professional competence are to be met. Only individuals can be professionally competent. The professional competence requirement is met by a company if that company has one or more professionally competent transport managers in its full time employment. Individuals who held responsible positions in the road haulage industry before 1st January 1975 are to be regarded as professionally competent, but this qualification, based on experience, will, in general, avail after 31st December 1979 only if the individual concerned obtains from a licensing authority before that date a certificate confirming that that authority is satisfied that he was engaged in the industry, in an appropriate position, before 1st January 1975. Individuals whose engagement in the road transport industry in responsible positions begun after 31st December 1974 but before 1st January 1978 will cease to be treated as being professionally competent on 1st January 1980 if they have not before that date obtained from a body approved by the Secretary of State a certificate as to their skills in certain subjects specified in the Annex to the Council Directive, or obtained some other certificate of competence, diploma or other qualification required by the Secretary of State. Individuals whose engagement in this industry begins on or after 1st January 1978 will be required in all cases to have such a certificate of competence, or such diploma or other qualification, if they are to meet the professional competence requirement prescribed for the holder of a standard operator's licence or for his transport manager or managers.

7. Regulation 10 deals with cases where a standard operator's licence is applied for or held by a holding company but the goods vehicles used under it belong to, or are in the possession of, a subsidiary of that company.

8. Consequential amendments to certain enactments are made by Regulation 11.

APPENDIX
OF CERTAIN INSTRUMENTS
NOT REGISTERED AS S.I.

Orders in Council,
Letters Patent
and Royal Instructions

relating to the Constitutions etc. of
Overseas Territories or to appeals to the Judicial
Committee,

Royal Proclamations, etc.

THE TUVALU (AMENDMENT) ORDER 1977

At the Court at Buckingham Palace

THE 11th DAY OF MAY 1977

PRESENT,

THE QUEEN'S MOST EXCELLENT MAJESTY
IN COUNCIL

Her Majesty, by virtue and in exercise of the powers in Her Majesty vested, is pleased, by and with the advice of Her Privy Council, to order, and it is hereby ordered, as follows:

1.—(1) This Order may be cited as the Tuvalu (Amendment) Order 1977 and shall be construed as one with the Tuvalu Order 1975(**a**) including the Constitution set out in Schedule 2 thereto.

(2) This Order shall be published in Tuvalu by exhibition at the Public Office of the Commissioner and printed in the Gazette as soon as may be after the date of such publication and, subject to the provisions of this section, shall come into operation on such day (in this Order referred to as "the appointed day") as the Commissioner, acting in his discretion, by notice published and printed in like manner respectively, shall appoint.

(3) The provisions of section 3 of this Order shall come into operation on the dissolution of the House of Assembly next following the appointed day.

2. In this Order, "the Constitution" means the Constitution of Tuvalu set out in Schedule 2 to the Tuvalu Order 1975.

3. The Constitution is amended—

(a) in section 42(a), by substituting for the word "eight" the word "twelve";

(b) in section 61, by substituting for the word "six" wherever it appears the word "eight".

4. Notwithstanding that section 3 of this Order has not come into operation, provision may be made by or in pursuance of regulations made by the Commissioner, acting in his discretion, for giving effect or enabling effect to be given to the provisions of the Constitution relating to the election of the elected members of the House of Assembly as they will have effect when the said section 3 comes into operation.

N. E. Leigh,
Clerk of the Privy Council.

(**a**) 1975 III, p. 8537.

EXPLANATORY NOTE

(This Note is not part of the Order.)

This Order increases the number of elected members of the House of Assembly of Tuvalu from eight to twelve when the House is next reconstituted, and makes provision for the adaptation of the laws of the territory in anticipation of this change.

ANGUILLA.

THE ANGUILLA ROYAL INSTRUCTIONS 1977.

Dated: 10th June 1977.　　　　　*ELIZABETH R.*

INSTRUCTIONS To Our Commissioner in Anguilla or other Officer for the time being appointed by Us to act in the office of Commissioner.

We do hereby direct and enjoin and declare Our will and pleasure as follows:—

PART I

INTRODUCTORY

Citation, commencement and publication.

1.—(1) These Instructions may be cited as the Anguilla Royal Instructions 1977.

(2) These Instructions shall be published in the Official Gazette for Anguilla, and shall come into operation on 10th June 1977.

Interpretation.

2. The provisions of section 72 of the Constitution of Anguilla shall apply to the interpretation of these Instructions as they apply to the interpretation of that Constitution.

Instructions to be observed by deputy.

3.—(1) These Instructions, so far as they are applicable to any functions to be performed by a deputy to the Commissioner appointed under section 20 of the Constitution, shall be deemed to be addressed to and shall be observed by such deputy.

(2) Any such deputy may, if he thinks fit, apply to Us through a Secretary of State for instructions in any matter; but he shall forthwith transmit to the Commissioner a copy of every despatch or other communication by which he applies for any such instructions.

PART II

THE COMMISSIONER

Leave of absence for Commissioner.

4. Except when there is a subsisting appointment of a deputy under section 20 of the Constitution, the Commissioner shall not quit Anguilla without first having obtained Our permission through a Secretary of State.

Commissioner to correspond with Secretary of State.

5. The Commissioner shall correspond with a Secretary of State on all subjects connected with his office, shall transmit to a Secretary of State all reports and information touching his office, and shall apply to a Secretary of State for all such instructions as he may require for his guidance.

Part III

Legislation

6. In the making of laws the Commissioner and the Assembly shall observe, as far as practicable, the following rules:— Rules for the enactment of laws.

(*a*) All laws shall be styled "Ordinances" and the words of enactment shall be "Enacted by the Legislature of Anguilla".

(*b*) All Ordinances shall be distinguished by titles, and shall be divided into successive sections consecutively numbered, and to every section there shall be annexed in the margin a short indication of its contents.

(*c*) The Ordinances enacted in each year shall be distinguished by consecutive numbers, commencing in each year with the number one.

(*d*) Matters having no proper relation to each other shall not be provided for by the same Ordinance; no Ordinance shall contain anything foreign to what the title of the Ordinance imports; and no provision having indefinite duration shall be included in any Ordinance expressed to have limited duration.

(*e*) All Ordinances shall be published by Government Notice in the Official Gazette.

(*f*) Copies of all Ordinances shall be printed, and shall bear the following:—

    (i) particulars of the days on which each Ordinance was enacted and published by Government Notice; and

    (ii) particulars of the day on which each Ordinance came into operation or, if that day has not been determined, a reference to any provision in the Ordinance whereby it may be determined.

7.—(1) The Commissioner shall not, without having previously obtained Our Instructions through a Secretary of State, assent to any Bill within any of the following classes, unless the Bill contains a clause suspending its operation until the signification of Our pleasure thereon, that is to say:— Certain Bills not to be assented to without Instructions.

(*a*) any Bill for the divorce of married persons;

(*b*) any Bill whereby any grant of land or money or other donation may be made to himself;

(*c*) any Bill affecting the currency of Anguilla or relating to the issue of bank notes;

(*d*) any Bill establishing any banking association or altering the constitution, rights or duties of any banking association;

(*e*) any Bill imposing differential duties;

(*f*) any Bill the provisions of which shall appear to him to be inconsistent with obligations imposed upon Us by treaty;

(*g*) any Bill interfering with the discipline or control of Our forces by land, sea or air;

(*h*) any Bill whereby persons of any community or religion may either:—

    (i) be subjected or made liable to disabilities or restrictions to which persons of other communities or religions are not subjected or made liable; or

    (ii) be granted advantages which are not enjoyed by persons of other communities or religions;

(*i*) any Bill of an extraordinary nature and importance whereby Our prerogative, or the rights or property of Our subjects not residing in Anguilla, or the trade, transport or communications of any part of Our dominions or any territory in which We may for the time being have jurisdiction may be adversely affected;

(*j*) any Bill containing provisions to which Our assent has once been refused or which has been disallowed by Us:

Provided that, if the Commissioner is satisfied that urgent necessity requires that any Bill falling within any of the classes described in this clause (other than a Bill appearing to him to be inconsistent with obligations imposed upon Us by treaty) be brought into immediate operation, he may assent to the Bill without such Instructions as aforesaid and although the Bill contains no such clause as aforesaid, but he shall, at the earliest opportunity, transmit the Bill to Us together with his reasons for so assenting.

Private Bills.

8.—(1) Every Bill, not being a Government measure, intended to affect or favour a particular person, association or corporate body, shall contain a provision saving the rights of Us, Our Heirs and Successors, all bodies politic and corporate, and all others except such as are mentioned in the Bill and those claiming by, from or under them.

(2) (*a*) No such Bill shall be introduced into the Assembly until due notice has been given by not less than three successive publications of the Bill by Government Notice in the Official Gazette; and the Commissioner shall not assent to the Bill unless it has been so published.

(*b*) A certificate under the hand of the Commissioner signifying that such publication has been made shall be transmitted to Us when the Bill or Ordinance is forwarded in pursuance of these Instructions.

Ordinances and reserved Bills to be sent through Secretary of State.

9. When any Ordinance has been enacted or any Bill has been reserved, the Commissioner shall forthwith transmit to Us, through a Secretary of State, for the signification of Our pleasure, a transcript in duplicate of the Ordinance or of the Bill duly authenticated under the Public Seal and by his own signature, together with an explanation of the reasons and occasion for the enactment of the Ordinance or for the passing of the Bill.

Ordinances to be published.

10. As soon as practicable after the commencement of each year the Commissioner shall cause a complete collection of all Ordinances enacted in Anguilla during the preceding year to be published for general information.

PART IV

MISCELLANEOUS

Audit.

11. The Commissioner shall take all necessary steps to ensure that all public accounts maintained by the Commissioner or by officers under his control and the accounts of all courts in Anguilla shall be audited and reported upon at least once in every year by fit and proper persons.

12.—(1) Before disposing of any land or building belonging to Us in Anguilla the Commissioner shall cause it to be surveyed and such reservations to be made thereout as he may think necessary for any public purpose.

(2) The Commissioner shall not either directly or indirectly purchase for himself any land or building belonging to Us in Anguilla without Our special permission given through a Secretary of State.

13.—(1) Whenever any offender has been condemned by any civil court in Anguilla to suffer death, the Commissioner shall cause a written report of the case of that offender from the judge who tried the case, or if this is impossible, such other report as he sees fit, together with such other information derived from the record of the case or elsewhere as the Commissioner may require, to be taken into consideration at a meeting of the Executive Council.

(2) The Commissioner shall not pardon or reprieve the offender unless it appears to him expedient to do so, upon receiving the advice of the Executive Council thereon; but he is to decide either to extend or to withhold a pardon or reprieve according to his own deliberate judgment, whether the members of the Council concur therein or not; causing, nevertheless, to be entered in the minutes of the Council a statement of his reasons, in case he should decide any such question in opposition to the judgment of the majority of the members thereof.

14. The Commissioner may, whenever he thinks fit, require any person holding public office to make an oath or affirmation of allegiance in the form set out in the Schedule to the Constitution and shall either administer the oath or affirmation or cause it to be administered by some other person holding public office.

Given at Our Court at St. James's this tenth day of June 1977
in the twenty-sixth year of Our Reign.

THE GILBERT ISLANDS (AMENDMENT) ORDER 1977

At the Court at Buckingham Palace

THE 26th DAY OF JULY 1977

PRESENT,

THE QUEEN'S MOST EXCELLENT MAJESTY
IN COUNCIL

· Her Majesty, by virtue and in exercise of the powers in Her Majesty vested, is pleased, by and with the advice of Her Privy Council, to order, and it is hereby ordered, as follows:—

1.—(1) This Order may be cited as the Gilbert Islands (Amendment) Order 1977 and shall be construed as one with the Gilbert and Ellice Islands Order in Council 1915(**a**), the Gilbert Islands Order 1975(**b**), and the Gilbert Islands (Amendment) Order 1976(**c**).

(2) This Order shall be published in the Gilbert Islands by exhibition at the Public Office of the Governor and printed in the Gazette as soon as may be after the date of such publication and, subject to the provisions of this section, shall come into operation on such day (in this Order referred to as "the appointed day") as the Governor, acting in his discretion, by notice published and printed in like manner respectively, shall appoint.

(3) The provisions of section 3 of this Order shall come into operation on such day as may be prescribed by resolution of the House of Assembly, which day shall not be earlier than the dissolution of the House next following the appointed day.

(4) The provisions of section 4 of this Order shall come into operation on the dissolution of the House of Assembly next following the appointed day.

2. In this Order, "the Constitution" means the Constitution of the Gilbert Islands set out in Schedule 2 to the Gilbert Islands Order 1975 as amended by the Gilbert Islands (Amendment) Order 1976.

3.—(1) Section 31 of the Constitution is amended by substituting for paragraph (*a*) the following—

"(*a*) the Chief Minister, who shall be elected as such in accordance with regulations made by the Governor, acting in his discretion;".

(**a**) S.R. & O. Rev. 1948, IX p. 655.   (**b**) S.I. 1975 III, p. 8487.
(**c**) S.I. 1976 III, p. 6280.

(2) Section 33(2) of the Constitution is amended—

   (*a*) by substituting for paragraph (*a*) the following—

      "(*a*) at such time after a general election as may be prescribed by regulations made by the Governor, acting in his discretion;";

   (*b*) in paragraph (*f*), by substituting for the words "the provisions of Part 1 of Annex 1 to" the words "regulations made under section 31(*a*) of".

(3) Section 34(1) of the Constitution is amended by substituting for the words "the provisions of Part 2 of Annex 1 to" the words "regulations made under section 31(*a*) of".

(4) Annex 1 to the Constitution is revoked.

4.—(1) Section 44(*a*) of the Constitution is amended by substituting for the word "twenty-one" the word "thirty-six".

(2) Section 63 of the Constitution is amended by substituting for the word "twelve" wherever it appears the word "nineteen".

(3) Paragraphs 7 and 8 of Part 1 of Annex 1 to the Constitution are amended by substituting for the word "eleven" wherever it appears the word "nineteen".

5. Notwithstanding that section 4 of this Order has not come into operation, provision may be made by or in pursuance of any law made under section 52 of the Constitution for giving effect or enabling effect to be given to the provisions of the Constitution relating to the election of the elected members of the House of Assembly as they will have effect when the said section 4 comes into operation.

N. E. Leigh,
Clerk of the Privy Council.

EXPLANATORY NOTE

(This Note is not part of the Order.)

This Order amends the Constitution of the Gilbert Islands by increasing the number of elected members of the House of Assembly from 21 to 36 when the House is next reconstituted, and by enabling fresh provision to be made for the election of the Chief Minister.

BY THE QUEEN

A PROCLAMATION

APPOINTING MONDAY, 2ND JANUARY 1978 AND MONDAY, 1ST MAY 1978 AS BANK HOLIDAYS IN ENGLAND, WALES AND NORTHERN IRELAND AND TUESDAY, 27TH DECEMBER 1977 AND MONDAY, 29TH MAY 1978 AS BANK HOLIDAYS IN SCOTLAND.

ELIZABETH R.

Whereas We consider it desirable that Monday, the second day of January and Monday, the first day of May in the year 1978 should be bank holidays in England, Wales and Northern Ireland and that Tuesday, the twenty-seventh day of December in the year 1977 and Monday, the twenty-ninth day of May in the year 1978 should be bank holidays in Scotland.

We, therefore, in pursuance of section 1 (3) of the Banking and Financial Dealings Act 1971, do hereby appoint Monday, the second day of January and Monday, the first day of May in the year 1978 to be bank holidays in England, Wales and Northern Ireland and Tuesday, the twenty-seventh day of December in the year 1977 and Monday, the twenty-ninth day of May in the year 1978 to be bank holidays in Scotland.

Given at Our Court at Windsor Castle this twenty-ninth day of July in the year of our Lord One thousand nine hundred and seventy-seven and in the twenty-sixth year of Our Reign.

GOD SAVE THE QUEEN

HONG KONG

THE HONG KONG ADDITIONAL INSTRUCTIONS 1977

Dated, 17th August 1977.   *ELIZABETH R.*

ADDITIONAL INSTRUCTIONS to Our Governor and Commander-in-Chief in and over Our Colony of Hong Kong and its Dependencies or other Officer for the time being Administering the Government of Our said Colony and its Dependencies.

We do hereby direct and enjoin and declare Our will and pleasure as follows:—

1.—(1) These Instructions may be cited as the Hong Kong Additional Instructions 1977 and shall be construed as one with the Hong Kong Royal Instructions 1917 as amended (hereinafter called "the principal Instructions"). — Citation and construction.

(2) The Hong Kong Royal Instructions 1917 to 1976 and these Instructions may be cited together as the Hong Kong Royal Instructions 1917 to 1977.

2. Clause XIII of the principal Instructions is amended by substituting for the word "eighteen" the word "twenty", and for the word "twenty-three" the word "twenty-five" — Amendment of clause XIII of principal Instructions.

Given at Our Court at St. James's this seventeenth day of August in the Twenty-sixth year of Our Reign.

Modifications to Legislation

Year and Number (or date)	Act or instrument	How affected
1838	Judgement Act (c. 110)	s. 17 **am.**, 1977/141
1845	Companies Clauses Consolidation Act (c. 16)	s. 146 **am.** (N.I.), 1977/426 (N.I. 4)
	Railways Clauses Consolidation Act (c. 20)	ss. 95, 144 **am.** (N.I.), 1977/426 (N.I. 4)
1846	Fatal Accidents Act (c. 93)	**r.** (N.I.), 1977/1251 (N.I. 18)
1847	Gasworks Clauses Act (c. 15)	**r.** (N.I.), 1977/596 (N.I. 7)
	Cemeteries Clauses Act (c. 65) ...	s. 58 **r.** (N.I.), 1977/426 (N.I. 4)
	Town Police Clauses Act (c. 89) ...	s. 67 **r.** (N.I.), 1977/426 (N.I. 4)
1851	Summary Jurisdiction (I.) Act (c. 92)	s. 9 para. 7 **am.** (N.I.), 1977/426 (N.I. 4)
1854	Boundary Survey (I.) Act (c. 17) ...	s. 7 **am.** (N.I.), 1977/426 (N.I. 4)
1859	Sale of Gas Act (c. 66)	**r.** (N.I.), 1977/596 (N.I. 7)
1860	Sale of Gas Act (c. 146)	**r.** (N.I.), 1977/596 (N.I. 7)
1861	Malicious Damage Act (c. 97) ...	**r.** (N.I.), (exc. ss. 35, 36, 47, 48, 58, 72), 1977/426 (N.I. 4)
	Offences Against the Persons Act (c. 100)	ss. 4 **am.**, 16 **replaced**, 1977/1249
1864	Fatal Accidents Act (c. 95)	**r.** (N.I.), 1977/1251 (N.I. 18)
1868	Regulation of Railways Act (c. 19)	ss. 11, 12 **r.**, 22 **am.**, 23, 26, 34, 39 **r.** (N.I.), 1977/599 (N.I. 10)
1871	Gasworks Clauses Act (c. 41)	**r.** (N.I.), 1977/596 (N.I. 7)
1875	Explosives Act (c. 17)	s. 82 **am.** (N.I.), 1977/426 (N.I. 4)
		s. 21 **am.** (E. and W.) (S.), 1977/918
1878	Weights and Measures Act (c. 49) ...	ss. 37, 41, 66 **r.** (N.I.), 1977/596 (N.I. 7)
	Public Health (I.) Act (c. 52)	s. 273 **r.** (N.I.), 1977/426 (N.I. 4)
1883	Explosive Substances Act (c. 3) ...	s. 3(1) **am.**, 1977/1249
1886	Guardianship of Infants Act (c. 27)	s. 5A **inserted**, 1977/1250 (N.I. 17)
1889	Weights and Measures Act (c. 21) ...	**r.** (N.I.), 1977/596 (N.I. 7)
	Regulation of Railways Act (c. 57)	s. 5(1)(3) **am.** (N.I.), 1977/599 (N.I. 10)

Year and Number (or date)	Act or instrument	How affected
1898	Merchant Shipping (Mercantile Marine Fund) Act (c. 44)	sch. 2 scale of payments **replaced,** rule (1), **replaced,** (7) **am.,** 1977/430
1909	Weeds (I.) Act (c. 31)	**r.** (N.I.), 1977/52 (N.I. 1)
1911	Railway Companies (Accounts and Returns) Act (c. 34)	**r.** (N.I.), 1977/599 (N.I. 10)
1912 1750	Rules of the Scottish Land Ct. (Rev. XII, p. 235)	**am.,** 1977/657
1915 769	Naval Medical Compassionate Fund, standing orders and regs.—O. in C. (Rev. XVI, p. 857)	**am.,** 1977/819
1917 1018	New Hebrides Maritime O. in C. (Rev. XIV, p. 36)	**am.,** 1977/424
14 Feb.	Hong Kong R. Instructions	**am.,** Addnl. Instructions 1977 (II, p. 4365)
1920	Gas Regulation Act (c. 28)	**r.** (N.I.), 1977/596 (N.I. 7)
1250	Writs of Fieri, Facias, sherrifs' or sherrifs' officers' fees—O. (Rev. XX, p. 734)	**am.,** 1977/416
1921 827	Sherrifs' and sherrifs' officers' fees—O. (Rev. XX, p. 736)	**am.,** 1977/416
1923	Industrial Assurance Act (c. 8) ...	s. 23(1)(a) **am.,** 1977/1144
1925	Settled Land Act (c. 18)	s. 113(3) **am.,** 1977/600
	Administration of Estates Act (c. 23)	s. 46(1) **am.,** 1977/415
1927 289	Transit of Animals O. (Rev. II, p. 259)	**am.,** 1977/944
1928 133	Foot-and-Mouth Disease O. (Rev. II, p. 499)	**am.,** 1977/944
205	Pleuro-Pneumonia O. (Rev. II, p. 567)	**am.,** 1977/944
206	Cattle Plague O. (Rev. II, p. 472) ...	**am.,** 1977/944
681	Quarantine Stations (Regulation) O. (No. 2) (Rev. II, p. 443)	**r.,** 1977/944
1929 186	Quarantine Stations (Regulation) O. (Rev. II, p. 445)	**r.,** 1977/944
246	Quarantine Stations (Regulation) O. (No. 2) (Rev. II, p. 447)	**r.,** 1977/944
1930 922	Animals (Importation) O. (Rev. II, p. 331)	**r.,** 1977/944

Year and Number (or date)	Act or instrument	How affected
1930		
923	Animals (Sea Transport) O. (Rev. II, p. 284)	**am.,** 1977/944
1931		
294	Animals (Importation) (Amdt.) O. (Rev. II, p. 354)	**r.,** 1977/944
1932		
505	Hops Marketing Scheme (Rev. I, p. 203)	**am.,** 1977/1280
1933		
19	Animals (Importation) (Amdt.) O. (Rev. II, p. 331)	**r.,** 1977/944
48	Sherrifs' ordinary and small debt cts., forms of procedure—A.S. (Rev. XX, p. 829)	**am.,** 1977/402
789	Milk Marketing Scheme (Rev. I, p. 224)	**am.,** 1977/900
1934		
567	Local Govt. (Alteration of Areas) (Notices) Regs. (Rev. XII, p. 453)	**r.,** 1977/293
1935		
488	Sherrif Ct., solicitors', etc. fees—A.S. (Rev. XX, p. 880)	**am.,** 1977/969
1936	Old Age Pensions Act (c. 31)	**r.** (N.I.), 1977/610 (N.I. 11)
626	County Ct. Rules (1936 I, p. 282) ...	**am.,** 1977/604, 615, 1206
1937	Local Govt. Superannuation Act (c. 68)	**r.** (exc. ss. 28, 29, 30(3), 35, 36(6), 38, 40(1), 42, sch. 2. Pt. V and certain ·provns.), 1977/1341 s. 40(1) **am.,** 1977/1341
820	Importation of animals, Iceland— Amdg. O. (Rev. II, p. 331)	**r.,** 1977/944
1152	Animals (Importation) Order of 1930—Amdg. O. (Rev. II, p. 331)	**r.,** 1977/944
1938		
196	Sheep Scab O. (Rev. II, p. 602) ...	**r.,** 1977/1173
229	Sheep Pox O. (Rev. II, p. 588) ...	**am.,** 1977/944
488	Local Authies. (Transfer of Enforcement) O. (Rev. VII, p. 115)	**r.,** 1977/746
558	Land Drainage (Election of Drainage Bds.) Regs. (Rev. XI, p. 857)	**am.,** 1977/366
1434	Foot-and-Mouth Disease (Infected Areas Restrictions) O. (Rev. II, p. 528)	**am.,** 1977/944
1435	Foot-and-Mouth Disease (Controlled Areas Restrictions) General O. (Rev. II, p. 520)	**am.,** 1977/944
1939	Local Govt. Staffs (War Services) Act (c. 94)	ss. 3, 9 **r.** (E. and W.), 1977/1341

Year and Number (or date)	Act or instrument	How affected
1939		
56	Local Govt. Superannuation (Mental Hospital, etc., Employment) Regs. (Rev. XVII, p. 824)	**r.** (certain provns.), *see* 1977/1341
57	Local Govt. Superannuation (Service of Registration Officers) Regs. (Rev. XVII, p. 834)	**r.,** 1977/1341
1940		
1251	Brucellosis Melitensis O. (Rev. II, p. 468)	**am.,** 1977/945
1944	Education Act (c. 31)	ss. 114(1), 118 **am.,** 1977/293
119	Prevention of Fraud (Investments) Act Licensing Regs. (Rev. XVIII, p. 461)	**am.,** 1977/1067
1945	Water Act (c. 42)	sch. 3 s. 19(1)(b) **replaced** (exc. W.), 1977/293
666	Regulations for Scholarships and Other Benefits (Rev. VI, p. 378)	**r.,** 1977/1443
1946		
36	Bretton Woods Agreements O. in C. (Rev. III, p. 165)	**am.,** 1977/825
2157	Private Legislation Procedure (S.) General O. (Rev. XVIII, p. 719)	**am.,** 1977/132
1947		
1354	New Towns (Particulars and Forms of Orders and Notices) Regs. (Rev. XXII, p. 847)	**r.,** 1977/549
1948	National Assistance Act (c. 29) ...	s. 57 **r.** (N.I.), 1977/610 (N.I. 11)
	Superannuation (Misc. Provns.) Act (c. 33)	ss. 6, 7 **r.** (E. and W.), 17(1) **am.,** 1977/1341
	Companies Act (c. 38)	sch. 6 Pt. II form **replaced,** 1977/1368
	Representation of the People Act (c. 65)	s. 72 **r.** (E. and W.), 1977/1341
1	Statutory Instruments Regs. (Rev. XXI, p. 498)	**am.,** 1977/641
83	Sheep Scab O. (Rev. II, p. 638) ...	**r.,** 1977/1173
688	Scholarships and Other Benefits Amdg. Regulations No. 1 (1948 I, p. 754)	**r.,** 1977/1443
898	Electricity (Consultative Council) (Areas) Regs. (Rev. VI, p. 837)	**am.,** 1977/710
2223	Scholarships and Other Benefits Amdg. Regulations No. 2 (1948 I, p. 755)	**r.,** 1977/1443
2573	Falkland Is. (Legislative Council) O. in C. (Rev. VII, p. 591) ...	**am.,** 1977/423
2768	Residential Special Schools and Orphanages (S.) Grant Regs. (Rev. VI, p. 719)	**am.,** 1977/953

Year and Number (or date)	Act or instrument	How affected
1948		
2770	Industrial Assurance (Premium Receipt Books) Regs. (Rev. VIII, p. 915)	**am.**, 1977/1353
3 Dec.	Falkland Is. R. Instructions	**am.**, Addnl. Instructions 31.3.1977
1949	Representation of the People Act (c. 68)	s. 23(7) **am.**, 1977/293
330	Companies (Winding-up) Rules (1949 I, p. 789)	**am.**, 1977/365, 1395
382	Companies (Forms) O. (1949 I, p. 714)	**am.**, 1977/530, 1369
628	Local Govt. Superannuation (Break of Service) Regs. (1949 I, p. 3054)	**r.**, 1977/1341
1897	A.S. (Sheriff Ct. Jury Trials) (1949 I, p. 3966)	**r.**, 1977/402
2441	Business Names Rules (1949 I, p. 531)	**am.**, 1977/537
4 Feb	A.S. (Register of Sasines Procedure)	**am.**, 1977/70
1950		
376	Coal Industry Nationalisation (Superannuation) Regs. (1950 I, p. 356)	**am.**, 1977/1452
842	Local Authies. (Transfer of Enforcement) (Amdt.) O. (1950 I, p. 656)	**r.**, 1977/746
1952	Customs and Excise Act (c. 44) ...	s. 28(2)(cc) **inserted,** 1977/1091
	Visiting Forces Act (c. 67)	sch. para. 3(h) **inserted,** 1977/426(N.I.4)
900	Public Service Vehicles (Licenses and Certificates) Regs. (1952 III, p. 2907)	**am.**, 1977/1461
2113	Bankruptcy Rules (1952 I, p. 213) ...	**am.**, 1977/364, 1394
1953	Local Govt. Superannuation Act (c. 25)	**r.** (E. and W.) (exc. ss. 1(1)(3)(c)(d)(4)(c)(5), 18, 21, 27, 29, sch. 4), 1977/1341 s. 1(6), 18(5) **am.,** 1977/1341
	Post Office Act (c. 36)	s. 57 **am.** (N.I.), 1977/426 (N.I. 4)
1954	Protection of Birds Act (c. 30) ...	sch. 1 Pts. I, II **am.,** 1977/496 2 **am.**, 1977/403
1048	Local Govt. Superannuation (Benefits) Regs. (1954 II, p. 1595)	**r.** (certain provns.), 1977/1341
1192	Local Govt. Superannuation (Administration) Regs. (1954 II, p. 1570)	**r.**, 1977/1341
1211	Local Govt. Superannuation (Reckoning of Service on Transfer) Regs. (1954 II, p. 1676)	**r.**, 1977/1341
1212	Local Govt. Superannuation (Transfer Value) Regs. (1954 II, p. 1723)	**r.** (certain provns.), *see* 1977/1341

Year and Number (or date)	Act or instrument	How affected
1954		
1227	Local Govt. Superannuation (Mental Hospital, etc., Employment) (Amdt.) Regs. (1954 II, p. 1674)	**r.** (certain provns.), *see* 1977/1341
1237	Local Govt. Superannuation (Limitation of Service) Regs. (1954 II, p. 1672)	**r.,** 1977/1341
1955	Air Force Act (c. 19)	ss. 97(4) **inserted,** 99A **mod.,** 108, 111 **am.,** 132(3) **mod.,** 1977/88 s. 17(2), 20(1)(5) **am.,** 1977/1097
1041	Local Govt. Superannuation (Benefits) (Amdt.) Regs. (1955 II, p. 1825)	**r.** (certain provns.), 1977/1341
1310	Animals (Landing from Channel Is., Is. of Man, N.I., and Republic of Ireland) O. (1955 I, p. 190) ...	**r.,** 1977/944
1956	Agriculture (Safety, Health and Welfare Provns.) Act (c. 49)	ss. 3(1)(5)(7)(a), 5 **am.,** 11 **r.,** 24(1) **am.,** (3) **r.,** 25(3) **am.,** (8)(9) **r.,** (10) **am.,** 1977/746
	Medical Act (c. 76)	s. 7(1)(2) **replaced,** 7A, 7B **inserted,** 8(2)(3) **replaced by new** 8(2), sch. 3 **renumbered** sch. 3 Pt. I, Pt. II **inserted,** 1977/827
1750	Swine Fever (Infected Areas Restrictions) O. (1956 I, p. 180)	**am.,** 1977/944
1766	Coal and Other Mines (Electricity) Regs. (1956 I, p. 1314)	**am.,** 1977/1205
1914	Imprisonment and Detention (Army) Rules (1956 I, p. 310)	**am.,** 1977/90, 91
1981	Imprisonment and Detention (Air Force) Rules (1956 II, p. 2118)	**am.,** 1977/93
1957		
948	Artificial Insemination of Cattle (E. and W.) Regs. (1957 I, p. 165)	**r.,** 1977/1260
1954	Artificial Insemination of Cattle (S.) Regs. (1957 I, p. 168)	**r.,** 1977/1230
1958	Import Duties Act (c. 6)	s. 7 **r.** (*saving*), 10(1) **am.,** 1977/910
	Agricultural Marketing Act (c. 47) ...	s. 34(2)(3) **am.,** 1977/899
1975	Import Duty Reliefs (No. 3) O. (1958 I, p. 795)	**am.,** 1977/971

Year and Number (or date)	Act or instrument	How affected
1959	County Cts. Act (c. 22)	ss. 39–41, 44, 45, 47(1)(a)(b)(1A) (a)(b), 52, 68, 80 **am.,** 1977/600 87(1) **am.,** 1977/344 102(3)(c), 146 **am.,** 1977/600 148(1) **am.,** 1977/601 sch. 1 **am.,** 1977/600
277	Milk and Dairies (General) Regs. (1959 I, p. 1351)	**am.,** 1977/171
365	Handicapped Pupils and Special Schools Regs. (1959 I, p. 1024)	**am.,** 1977/278
366	Special Schools and Establishments (Grant) Regs. (1959 I, p. 1051)	**am.,** 1977/278
763	A.S. (Adoption of Children) (1959 I, p. 649)	**am.,** 1977/977
1063	Town Development (Exchequer Contributions) (S.) Regs. (1959 I, p. 1616)	**am.,** 1977/273
1098	Condensed Milk Regs. (1959 I, p. 1305)	**am.,** 1977/928
1115	Condensed Milk (S.) Regs. (1959 I, p. 1311)	**am.,** 1977/1027
1960	Films Act (c. 57)	s. 4(3) **am.,** 1977/1306
105	Movement of Animals (Records) O. (1960 I, p. 302)	**am.,** 1977/944
250	Cycle Racing on Highways Regs. (1960 III, p. 3047)	**am.,** 1977/270
974	Weights and Measures (Cran Measures: Verification and Marking Fees) O. (1960 III, p. 3952)	**r.,** 1977/55
2147	Beet Eelworm O. (1960 II, p. 2687)	**r.,** 1977/988
1961	Diplomatic Immunities (Conferences with Commonwealth Countries and Republic of Ireland) Act (c. 11)	s. 1 **am.,** 1977/821
	Carriage by Air Act (c. 27)	s. 3 **am.** (N.I.), 1977/1251 (N.I. 18)
	Factories Act (c. 34)	ss. 8 **r.,** 153, 181 **am.,** sch. 5 **am.,** 1977/746
	Army and Air Force Act (c. 52) ...	ss. 13(1)–(3) **am.,** sch. 2 **am.,** 1977/1097
	Trustee Investments Act (c. 62) ...	sch. 1 Pt. II **am.,** 1977/831
	Clergy Pensions Measure (No. 3) ...	s. 1(6) **r.,** 4(3), 10(1)(7) **am.,** 15, 41(1) **r.,** 42(1), 46(1) **am.,** sch. 1 Pt. I **am.,** 1977/1146
1931	Lead in Food Regs.	**am.** (17.11.78), 1977/927
1942	Lead in Food (S.) Regs.	**am.** (17.11.78), 1977/1026
2402	Independent Schools Tribunal (S.) Rules	**r.,** 1977/1261

Year and Number (or date)	Act or instrument	How affected
1962	Health Visiting and Social Work (Training) Act (c. 33)	sch. 1 para. 1 **am.,** 4 **replaced,** 7–9 **r.,** 10 **am.,** 11 **replaced,** 21 **inserted,** 1977/1240
757	Animals (Landing from Channel Is., Is. of Man, N.I., and Republic of Ireland) (Amdt.) O.	**r.,** 1977/944
884	Oil Heaters Regs.	**r.,** 1977/167
2044	Building Societies (Authorised Investments) O.	**r.,** 1977/851
2497	Beet Eelworm (Amdt.) O.	**r.,** 1977/988
2556	Drainage Rates (Forms) Regs. ...	**r.,** 1977/357
1963	Weights and Measures Act (c. 31) ...	s. 22(2) **mod.,** sch. 4 Pts. VIII, XI **mod.,** 1977/558 sch. 4 Pt. III **r.** (1.3.78), XI para. 3(2A) **inserted,** 1977/1335
	Offices, Shops and Railway Premises Act (c. 41)	ss. 52(1)–(4)(6)(7), 89 **r.,** 90 **am.,** 1977/746
133	A.S. (Alteration of Sheriff Ct. Fees) ...	**r.,** 1977/402
736	Animals (Landing from Channel Is., Is. of Man, N.I., and Republic of Ireland) (Amdt.) O.	**r.,** 1977/944
792	Location of Offices Bureau O.	**am.,** 1977/1296
1142	Town and Country Planning (New Towns Special Development) O.	**r.,** 1977/665
1571	Milk (Special Designation) Regs. ...	**r.,** 1977/1033
1964	Plant Varieties and Seeds Act (c. 14) ...	s. 16(3)(f) **am.,** 1977/1112
	Police Act (c. 48)	sch. 4 paras. 5(1)–(3)(6)(7) **r.** (exc. certain provns.), sch. 11 para. 3 **r.** (exc. certain provns.), 1977/1341
	Public Libraries and Museums Act (c. 75)	sch. 1 paras. 1(1)–(3), 3 **r.** (exc. certain provns.), 5 **am.,** 1977/1341
671	Building Societies (Authorised Investments) (Amdt.) O.	**r.,** 1977/851
760	Soft Drinks Regs.	**am.** (17.11.78), 1977/927
767	Soft Drinks (S.) Regs.	**am.** (17.11.78), 1977/1026
1033	Legal Officers Fees O.	**am.,** 1977/1149
1109	Tuberculosis (S.) O.	**am.,** 1977/957
1150	Tuberculosis (Compensation) O. ...	**am.,** 1977/947
1151	Tuberculosis O.	**am.,** 1977/948
1152	Tuberculosis (Compensation) (S.) O. ...	**am.,** 1977/990
1294	Scholarships and Other Benefits Amdg. Regs.	**r.,** 1977/1443

Year and Number (or date)	Act or instrument	How affected
1964		
1892	Land Drainage (Compensation) Regs.	**r.**, 1977/339
19 Sept.	Disablement and Death Pensions, etc. (Military) 1914 World War Service, and Service subsequent to 2 Sept. 1939, R. Warrant (1964 III, p. 5257)	**am.**, R. Warrant 11.3.1977
24 Sept.	Disablement and Death Pensions, etc. (Air Forces), 1914 World War Service, and Service subsequent to 2 Sept. 1939, O. (1964 III, p. 5361)	**am.**, O. 15.3.1977
25 Sept.	Disablement and Death Pensions, etc. (Naval Forces), 1914 World War Service, and Service subsequent to 2 Sept. 1939, O. in C. (1964 III, p. 5466)	**am.**, O. in C. 9.3.1977
1965	Cereals Marketing Act (c. 14)	s. 24 **am.**, 1977/181
	Museum of London Act (c. 17) ...	s. 10 **r.**, 1977/1341
	Compulsory Purchase Act (c. 56) ...	s. 27(4) **am.**, 1977/293
	Redundancy Payments Act (c. 62) ...	sch. 5 paras. 2, 3, 9, 12 **am.**, 1977/1321
321	A.S. (Rules of Ct., consolidation and amdt.)	**am.**, 1977/71, 472, 978
363	Dried Milk Regs.	**am.**, 1977/928
444	Land Drainage (Election of Drainage Bds.) Amdt. Regs.	**r.**, 1977/366
543	Police (Discipline) Regs.	**r.** (*saving*), 1977/580
544	Police (Discipline) (Deputy Chief Constables, Assistant Chief Constables and Chief Constables) Regs.	**r.** (*saving*), 1977/581
618	Police (Appeals) Rules	**r.** (*saving*), 1977/759
621	London Authies. (Superannuation) O.	**r.** (certain provns.), 1977/1341
1007	Dried Milk (S.) Regs.	**am.** (1.7.78), 1977/1027
1046	Merchant Shipping (Pilot Ladders) Rules	**am.**, 1977/252
1103	Merchant Shipping (Passengers Ship Construction) Rules	**am.**, 1977/252
1105	Merchant Shipping (Life-saving Appliances) Rules	**am.**, 1977/229, 252
1106	Merchant Shipping (Fire Appliances) Rules	**am.**, 1977/252
1283	Police (Appeals) (Amdt.) Rules ...	**r.** (*saving*), 1977/759
1307	Shipowners' Liability (New Hebrides) O.	**am.**, 1977/50
1525	Collision Regulations (Ships and Seaplanes on the Water) and Signals of Distress (Ships) O.	**r.**, 1977/982, 1257
1550	Merchant Shipping (Signals of Distress) Rules	**r.**, 1977/1010
1555	Milk (Special Designation) (Amdt.) Regs.	**r.**, 1977/1033

Year and Number (or date)	Act or instrument	How affected
1659	Town and Country Planning (New Towns Special Development) (Amdt.) O.	r., 1977/665
1776	Rules of the Supreme Ct. (Revision) ...	am., 1977/344, 532, 960
1929	Public Record Office (Fees) Regs. ...	r., 1977/288
1966	Finance Act (c. 18)	s. 1 r. (*saving*), 1977/910
164	Pneumoconiosis, Byssinosis and Misc. Diseases Benefit Scheme	am., 1977/380, 992, 1063, 1104
165	Workmen's Compensation (Supplementation) Scheme	am., 1977/991, 1063
588	Oil Heaters Regs.	r., 1977/167
1032	Development Areas O.	am., 1977/683
1065	Supplementary Benefit (General) Regs.	r., 1977/1141
1067	Supplementary Benefit (Claims and Payments) Regs.	r., 1977/1142
1338	Building Societies (Authorised Investments) (Amdt.) O.	r., 1977/851
1967	General Rate Act (c. 9)	sch. 5 para. 1 am., 1977/585
	Parliamentary Commr. Act (c. 13) ...	sch. 2 am., 1977/816
	Antarctic Treaty Act (c. 65)	sch. 2 annx. B am., 1977/1235
	Road Traffic Regulation Act (c. 76) ...	ss. 22, 23, 55, 61, 80 **mod.**, 1977/548
	Criminal Justice Act (c. 80)	ss. 9(2)(8), 11(10) **am.**, 1977/86 9(2)(c)(d) **am.**, (5)(8) **replaced**, 10(5) **mod.**, 11(1) **am.**, (3) **replaced**, (6)(8) **am.**, 1977/88
	Clergy Pensions (Amdt.) Measure (No. 1)	s. 2 r., 1977/1146
29	Teachers (Colleges of Education) (S.) Regs.	am., 1977/634
171	Animals (Land from Channel Is., Is. of Man, N.I., and Republic of Ireland) (Amdt.) O.	r., 1977/944
185	Police (Discipline) (Amdt.) Regs. ...	r. (*saving*), 1977/580
186	Police (Discipline) (Deputy Chief Constables, Assistant Chief Constables and Chief Constables) (Amdt.) Regs.	r. (*saving*), 1977/581
422	Supplementary Benefit (Claims and Payments) Amdt. Regs.	r., 1977/1142
434	Local Authies. (Sinking Funds) Regs.	r., 1977/293
1018	Army Terms of Service Regs.	am., 1977/701
1045	Supplementary Benefit (General) Amdt. Regs.	r., 1977/1141

Year and Number (or date)	Act or instrument	How affected
1967		
1330	London Authies. (Superannuation) (Amdt.) O.	**r.** (certain provns.), 1977/1341
1658	Legal Officers Fees O.	**am.**, 1977/1149
1905	Fugitive Offenders (Bermuda) O. ...	**am.**, 1977/47
1906	Fugitive Offenders (British Honduras) O.	**am.**, 1977/47
1907	Fugitive Offenders (British Solomon Is. Territory) O.	**am.**, 1977/47
1909	Fugitive Offenders (Gibraltar) O. ...	**am.**, 1977/47
1911	Fugitive Offenders (Hong Kong) O. ...	**am.**, 1977/47
1913	Fugitive Offenders (Montserrat) O. ...	**am.**, 1977/47
1915	Fugitive Offenders (Virgin Is.) O. ...	**am.**, 1977/47
1916	Fugitive Offenders (Sovereign Base Areas of Akrotiri and Dhekelia) O.	**am.**, 1977/47
1968	Administration of Justice Act (c. 5) ...	s. 1(1)(c) **am.**, 1977/602
	Trade Descriptions Act (c. 29) ...	**mod.**, 1977/1140
	Overseas Aid Act (c. 57)	s. 3(2) **am.**, 1977/485
	Gaming Act (c. 65)	s. 48 **am.** (E. and W.), 1977/570 (3)(4) **am.** (S.), 1977/633
	Medicines Act (c. 67)	s. 7(5) **am.**, (7) **inserted**, 8(3) **replaced by** 8(3)(4), 18(3) **inserted**, 20(1)(b) **am.**, 24(1A) **inserted**, (2) **am.**, 28(3)(j) **inserted**, 1977/1050
25	Police Cadets Regs.	**am.**, 1977/1005
43	Removal and Disposal of Vehicles Regs.	**am.**, 1977/354
69	Oversea Companies (Accounts) (Exceptions) O.	**r.**, 1977/1370
112	Fugitive Offenders (Cayman Is.) O. ...	**am.**, 1977/47
113	Fugitive Offenders (Falkland Is. and Dependencies) O.	**am.**, 1977/47
183	Fugitive Offenders (British Indian Ocean Territory) O.	**am.**, 1977/47
184	Fugitive Offenders (St. Helena) O. ...	**am.**, 1977/47
185	Fugitive Offenders (Turks and Caicos Is.) O.	**am.**, 1977/47
208	Police Cadets (S.) Regs.	**am.**, 1977/1131
577	Double Taxation Relief (Taxes on Income) (Netherlands) O.	**am.**, 1977/1300
657	Building Societies (Authorised Investments) (Amdt.) O.	**r.**, 1977/851
884	Fugitive Offenders (Pitcain) O. ...	**am.**, 1977/47
887	Antarctic Treaty (Contracting Parties)	**r.**, 1977/1234
888	Antarctic Treaty (Specially Protected Areas) O.	**am.**, 1977/1235

Year and Number (or date)	Act or instrument	How affected
1968		
1077	Cinematograph Films (Collection of Levy) Regs.	**am.,** 1977/1330
1091	Fugitive Offenders (New Hebrides) O.	**am.,** 1977/47
1163	Pensions Commutation Regs.	**am.,** 1977/108
1230	Legal Aid in Criminal Proceedings (Fees and Expenses) Regs.	**am.,** 1977/875
1919	Magistrates' Cts. (Forms) Rules ...	**am.,** 1977/1175
1920	Magistrates' Cts. Rules...	**am.,** 1977/1174
1969	Finance Act (c. 32)	sch. 18 Pt. I **am.,** 1977/347, 919
	Children and Young Persons Act (c. 54)	s. 23(2)(3) **mod.,** 1977/420
18	Conveyance in Harbours of Military Explosives Regs.	**r.,** 1977/890
19	Conveyance by Rail of Military Explosives Regs.	**r.,** 1977/889
20	Conveyance by Road of Military Explosives Regs.	**r.,** 1977/888
47	General Medical Council (Registration Regulations) O. of C.	**am.,** 1977/1266
77	Teachers Superannuation (S.) Regs. ...	**r.,** 1977/1360
85	Motor Cars (Driving Instructions) Regs.	**r.,** 1977/1043
293	Supplementary Benefit (Claims and Payments) Amdt. Regs.	**r.,** 1977/1142
294	Supplementary Benefit (General) Amdt. Regs.	**r.,** 1977/1141
310	Electrical Appliances (Colour Code) Regs.	**am.,** 1977/931
413	London Authies. (Superannuation) (Amdt.) O.	**r.,** 1977/1341
483	Prov. of Milk and Meals Regs.	**am.,** 1977/385, 1193
659	Teachers Superannuation (S.) (Amdt.) Regs.	**r.,** 1977/1360
713	Motor Cars (Driving Instruction) (Amdt.) Regs.	**r.,** 1977/1043
785	Teachers Superannuation Account (Rates of Interest) (S.) Regs.	**r.,** 1977/1360
793	National Insurance (Mod. of Local Govt. Superannuation Schemes) Regs.	**r.,** 1977/1341
841	Education Authy. Bursaries (S.) Regs.	**am.,** 1977/1150
854	Antarctic Treaty (Special Protected Area) O.	**r.,** 1977/1235
888	"Pelican" Pedestrian Crossings Regulations and General Directions	**mod.,** 1977/548
905	Representation of the People (N.I.) Regs.	**am.,** 1977/96
1021	Plant Breeders' Rights Regs.	**am.,** 1977/146

Year and Number (or date)	Act or instrument	How affected
1969		
1169	Supplementary Benefit (Claims and Payments) Amdt. (No. 2) Regs.	r., 1977/1142
1339	Import Duty Reliefs O.	r., 1977/971
1342	Savings Contracts Regs.	am., 1977/1456
1487	Traffic Signs (Speed Limits) Regulations and General Directions	am., 1977/952
1626	Assistance for House Purchase and Improvement (Increase of Subsidy) O.	am., 1977/1336
1787	Police Federation Regs.	am., 1977/583
1970	Income and Corporation Taxes Act (c. 10)	s. 65(1) **am.**, 1977/662
16	County Ct. Districts O.	am., 1977/149, 348, 1189
73	Rate Product (Passenger Transport Authies.) Rules	r., 1977/454
294	Merchant Shipping (Certificates of Competency as A.B.) Regs.	am., 1977/627
301	Vehicle and Driving Licences (Compensation to Officers) Regs.	r., 1977/1316
400	Labelling of Food Regs.	am., 1977/928
548	Wireless Telegraphy (Broadcast Licence Charges & Exemption) Regs.	am., 1977/1286
789	Exchange Control (Purchase of Foreign Currency) O.	am., 1977/920
887	Act of Adj. (Fees in the High Ct. of Justiciary)	am., 1977/72
966	Motor Cars (Driving Instruction) (Amdt.) Regs.	r., 1977/1043
1127	Preservatives in Food (S.) Regs. ...	am., 1977/1026, 1027
1288	Export of Goods (Control) O.	am., 1977/104, 1190
1312	Exchange Control (Purchase of Foreign Currency) (Amdt.) O.	r., 1977/920
1784	Supplementary Benefit (Decimalisation of the Currency) Regs.	r., 1977/1141
1839	Public Record Office (Fees) (Amdt.) Regs.	r., 1977/288
1971	Misuse of Drugs Act (c. 38)	sch. 2 Pt. I para. 1 **am.**, (b)(c) **inserted,** 1977/1243
	Mineral Workings (Offshore Installations) Act (c. 61)	s. 11(2) **am.** (N.I.), 1977/1251 (N.I. 18)
	Town and Country Planning Act (c. 78)	s. 290(1) **am.**, 1977/293 schs. 5 Pt. I **mod.**, 6 **mod.**, 1977/469, 1364
62	Legal Aid (General) Regs.	am., 1977/1293
133	Police (Discipline) (Amdt.) Regs. ...	r. (*saving*), 1977/580
134	Police (Discipline) Deputy Chief Constables, Assistant Chief Constables and Chief Constables) (Amdt.) Regs.	r. (*saving*), 1977/581
156	Police Regs.	am., 1977/582, 1006

Year and Number (or date)	Act or instrument	How affected
1971		
218	Land Tribunal for Scotland Rules ...	am., 1977/432
220	Jurors' Allowance (S.) Regs.	r., 1977/445
226	Family Income Supplements (General) Regs.	am., 1977/324
249	Residential Establishments (Payments by Local Authies.) (S.) O.	am., 1977/656
340	National Health Service (Charges) Regs.	am., 1977/279, 434
351	Motor Cars (Driving Instruction) (Amdt.) Regs.	r., 1977/1043
392	District Registries O.	am., 1977/152, 351, 1216
415	Agricultural and Horticultural Co-operation Scheme	am., 1977/846
450	Road Vehicles (Registration and Licensing) Regs.	am., 1977/230
491	Judgement Debts (Rate of Interest) O.	superseded, 1977/141
510	Royal Air Force Terms of Service Regs.	r., 1977/1097
656	County Cts. (Bankruptcy and Companies Winding-up Jurisdiction) O.	am., 1977/151, 350
792	Motor Vehicles (International Motor Insurance Card) Regs.	am., 1977/895
972	Medicines (Standard Provns. for Licences and Certificates) Regs.	am., 1977/675, 1039, 1053
973	Medicines (Applications for Products Licences and Clinical Trial and Animal Test Certificates) Regs.	am., 1977/1051
974	Medicines (Applications for Manufacturer's and Wholesale Dealer's Licences) Regs.	am., 1977/1052
987	Matrimonial Causes (Costs) Rules ...	r., 1977/345
1037	Milk (N.I.) O.	am., 1977/858
1038	Milk (G.B.) O.	am., 1977/1441
1152	County Cts. (Admiralty Jurisdiction) O.	am., 1977/150, 349
1303	Land Drainage (Compensation) (Amdt.) Regs.	r., 1977/339
1326	Medicines (Importation of Medicinal Products for Re-exportation) O.	am., 1977/640
1331	Supplementary Benefit (Claims and Payments) Amdt. Regs.	r., 1977/1142
1524	"Zebra" Pedestrian Crossing Regs. ...	am., 1977/548
1537	Milk and Meals (Education) (S.) Regs.	am., 1977/362, 1203
1549	Supplementary Benefit (General) Amdt. Regs.	r., 1977/1141
1717	Brucellosis (Area Eradication) (E. and W.) O.	r., 1977/1284
1752	Brucellosis (Area Eradication) (S.) O. ...	am., 1977/958
1775	Teachers Superannuation (Family Benefits) (S.) Regs.	r., 1977/1360
1954	Divorce County Cts. O.	am., 1977/939

Year and Number (or date)	Act or instrument	How affected
1971		
1995	Teachers Superannuation (S.) Amdt. Regs.	r., 1977/1360
2085	Industrial Relations (Nominations) Regs.	r., 1977/789
2102	Extradition (Hijacking) O.	am., 1977/1237
2103	Extradition (Tokyo Convention) O. ...	am., 1977/1239
2118	Tokyo Convention (Certification of Countries) O.	r., 1977/1258
1972	Superannuation Act (c. 11)	sch. 6 paras. 49, 50 r., 1977/1341
	Road Traffic Act (c. 20)...	ss. 168, 181 mod., 1977/548 128(1) paras. (b)(c), 129(1) para. (c), 131(1) para. (c) am., 1977/1043
	Road Traffic (Foreign Vehicles) Act (c. 27)	sch. 2 am., 1977/777
	Carriage by Railway Act (c. 33) ...	s. 3(4) am. (N.I.), 1977/1251 (N.I. 18)
	Trade Descriptions Act (c. 34)	mod., 1977/1140
	Legal Advice and Assistance Act (c. 50)	s. 1 am., 1977/507 sch. 1 am., 1977/213
	Town and Country Planning (S.) Act (c. 52)	schs. 3, 4 r. (prosp.), 1977/794
	European Communities Act (c. 68) ...	s. 6(5) am., 1977/910
	Local Govt. Act (c. 70)	s. 154(1)(b) **replaced**, 1977/1341
	Clergy Pensions (Amdt.) Measure (No. 5)	s. 1 r., 1977/1146
137	Exchange Control (Purchase of Foreign Currency) (Amdt.) O.	r., 1977/920
196	Registration of Restrictive Trading Agreements (Fees) Regs.	r., 1977/612
210	Ironstone Restoration Fund (Rates of Contribution) O.	r., 1977/134
316	Rules of Procedure (Army)	am., 1977/92
330	Supplementary Benefit (General) Amdt. Regs.	r., 1977/1141
355	Royal Air Force Terms of Service (Amdt.) Regs.	r., 1977/1097
419	Rules of Procedure (Air Force) ...	am., 1977/94
421	Intermediate Areas and Derelict Land Clearance Areas O.	am., 1977/683
442	Teachers Superannuation (Family Benefits) (S.) Amdt. Regs.	r., 1977/1360
550	Overseas Service (Pensions Supplement) Regs.	r., 1977/320
551	Teachers Superannuation (Financial Provns.) (S.) Regs.	r., 1977/1360

Year and Number (or date)	Act or instrument	How affected
1972		
595	New Street Byelaws (Ext. of Operation) O.	**expired** [31.4.77]
641	Savings Certificates Regs.	**am.,** 1977/545, 1448
673	Copyright (International Conventions) O.	**am.,** 1977/56, 830, 1256
765	Premium Savings Bonds Regs.	**am.,** 1977/1447
809	Collision Regulations (Traffic Separation Schemes) O.	**r.,** 1977/982, 1257
877	Pensions Increase (Federated Superannuation System for Universities) Regs.	**am.,** 1977/286, 863
904	Town and Country Planning (Industrial Development Certificates) Regs.	**am.,** 1977/682, 705
916	Family Provns. (Intestate Succession) O.	**superseded,** 1977/415
918	Merchant Shipping (Crew Agreements, Lists of Crew and Discharge of Seamen) Regs.	**am.,** 1977/45
919	Merchant Shipping (Crew Agreements, Lists of Crew and Discharge of Seamen) (Fishing Vessels) Regs.	**am.,** 1977/45
960	Extradition (Tokyo Convention) (Amdt.) O.	**r.,** 1977/1239
969	Aircraft (Exemption from Seizure on Patent Claims) O.	**r.,** 1977/829
971	Hovercraft (Application of Enactments) O.	**am.,** 1977/1257
1102	Extradition (Hijacking) (Amdt.) O. ...	**r.,** 1977/1237
1103	County Cts. (Administration Order Jurisdiction) O.	**superseded,** 1977/601
1117	Milk (Special Designation) (Amdt.) Regs.	**r.,** 1977/1033
1169	Value Added Tax (Self-Supply) (No. 2) O.	**am.,** 1977/1259
1173	Brucellosis (Area Eradication) (E. and W.) (Amdt.) O.	**r.,** 1977/1284
1174	Brucellosis (Area Eradication) (E. and W.) (Extension) O.	**r.,** 1977/1284
1239	Teachers Superannuation (Financial Provns. and Family Benefits) (S.) Regs.	**r.,** 1977/1360
1295	Merchant Shipping (Seamen's Documents) Regs.	**am.,** 1977/1181
1344	Value Added Tax Tribunals Rules ...	**am.,** 1977/1017
1362	Town and Country Planning (Listed Buildings and Buildings in Conservation Areas) Regs.	**r.** (*saving*), 1977/228
1371	Anti-Dumping Duty (No. 2) O. ...	**r.,** 1977/1072
1413	Diseases of Animals (Approved Disinfectants) O.	**am.,** 1977/36, 1139

Year and Number (or date)	Act or instrument	How affected
1972		
1493	Supplementary Benefit (General) Amdt. (No. 2) Regs.	**r.,** 1977/1141
1500	Brucellosis (E. and W.) Compensation O.	**am.,** 1977/946
1502	Conveyance in Harbours of Military Explosives (Amdt.) Regs.	**r.,** 1977/890
1503	Conveyance by Rail of Military Explosives (Amdt.) Regs.	**r.,** 1977/889
1504	Conveyance by Road of Military Explosives (Amdt.) Regs.	**r.,** 1977/888
1521	Brucellosis (E. and W.) O.	**r.,** 1977/1284
1538	Brucellosis Compensation (S.) O. ...	**am.,** 1977/989
1577	Building Societies (Designation for Trustee Investment) Regs.	**am.,** 1977/1207
1613	Immigration (Exemption from Control) O.	**am.,** 1977/693
1652	Town and Country Planning (Determination of appeals by appointed persons) (Prescribed Classes) Regs.	**am.,** 1977/477
1675	Overseas Service (Pensions Supplement) (Amdt.) Regs.	**r.,** 1977/320
1873	Merchant Shipping (Official Log Books) (Fishing Vessels) Regs.	**am.,** 1977/628
1922	Royal Air Force Terms of Service (Second Amdt.) Regs.	**r.,** 1977/1097
1980	Swine Vesicular Disease O.	**am.,** 1977/944
2012	Jurors' Allowances (S.) Amdt. Regs. ...	**spent**
1973	Counter-Inflation Act (c. 9)	sch. 3 paras. 2(1)(2) **am.,** (3) **inserted,** 3(1)(2), 5(1)–(3), 7 **am.,** 4 paras. 1(5) **inserted,** 2(1) **am.,** 3(6) **inserted,** 5(1) **am.,** 1977/1220
	Social Security Act (c. 38)	sch. 27 para. 111 **r.** (N.I.), 1977/1251 (N.I. 18)
	N.I. (Emergency Provns.) Act (c. 53) ...	sch. 4 Pt. I paras. 3, 5(a)–(n)(p) **r.,** 13B **inserted,** note 1A **r.,** 5 **inserted,** 1977/426 (N.I. 4) para. 6(aaa), 13C **inserted,** note 2, 5 **am.,** Pt. II para. 13(d) **inserted,** 1977/1265
24	Motor Vehicles (Construction and Use) Regs.	**am.,** 1977/154, 790, 791, 792, 809, 1401
31	Town and Country Planning General Development O.	**r.,** 1977/289

Year and Number (or date)	Act or instrument	How affected
1973		
180	Motor Cycles (Wearing of Helmets) Regs.	**am.,** 1977/129
237	Sea Fish (Conservation) (Is. of Man) O.	**am.,** 1977/1244
273	Town and Country Planning General Development (Amdt.) O.	**r.,** 1977/289
334	Income Tax (Employments) Regs. ...	**am.,** 1977/700
349	Legal Advice and Assistance Regs. ...	**am.,** 1977/182
350	Matrimonial Causes (Costs) (Amdt.) Rules	**r.,** 1977/345
424	Common Agricultural Policy (Protection of Community Arrangements) Regs.	**am.,** 1977/1287
547	Superannuation (Teachers and Teachers' Families) (S.) Regs.	**r.,** 1977/1360
621	Counter-Inflation (Notices and Orders) Regs.	**r.,** 1977/1222
660	Counter-Inflation (Validity of Transactions) O.	**r.,** 1977/1225
762	Extradition (Tokyo Convention) (Amdt.) O.	**r.,** 1977/1239
796	Misuse of Drugs (Designation) O. ...	**r.,** 1977/1379
797	Misuse of Drugs Regs.	**am.,** 1977/1380
944	Forest Reproductive Material Regs.	**r.,** 1977/891
988	Brucellosis (Eradication Area) (W.) O.	**r.,** 1977/1284
1065	Counter-Inflation (Designated Officers) (No. 2) O.	**r.,** 1977/1223
1108	Forest Reproductive Material (Amdt.) Regs.	**r.,** 1977/891
1199	Motor Vehicles (Type Approval) Regs.	**am.,** 1977/1402
1268	Redundant Mineworkers and Concessionary Coal (Payments Schemes) O.	**am.,** 1977/524
1286	National Health Service (Regional and Area Health Authies.: Membership and Procedure) Regs.	**am.,** 1977/1103
1345	Welsh National Water Development Authy. (Establishment and Constitution) O.	**am.,** 1977/724
1401	Public Record Office (Fees) (Amdt.) Regs.	**r.,** 1977/288
1414	Matrimonial Causes (Costs) (Amdt. No. 2) Rules	**r.,** 1977/345
1450	Registration and Enrolment Rules ...	**r.,** 1977/176
1469	Occupational Pension Schemes (Preservation of Benefit) Regs.	**am.,** 1977/1187
1521	Fertilisers and Feeding Stuffs Regs. ...	**am.,** 1977/115
1678	Civil Aviation (Route Charges for Navigation Services) Regs.	**am.,** 1977/287
1686	Jurors' Allowances (S.) Amdt. (No. 2) Regs.	**spent**

Year and Number (or date)	Act or instrument	How affected
1973		
1756	Extradition (Protection of Aircraft) O.	**am.**, 1977/1238
1758	New Hebrides O.	**am.**, 1977/49
1793	Overseas Service (Pensions Supplement) (Amdt.) Regs.	**r.**, 1977/320
1822	Medicines (Pharmacies) (Applications for Registration and Fees) Regs.	**am.**, 1977/511
1887	Sea Fish (Conservation) (Is. of Man) (No. 2) O.	**r.**, 1977/1244
1997	Exchange Control (Purchase of Foreign Currency) (Amdt.) O.	**r.**, 1977/920
2013	Motor Cars (Driving Instruction) (Amdt.) O.	**r.**, 1977/1043
2016	Matrimonial Causes Rules	**r.** (*saving*), 1977/344
2037	Anti-Dumping and Countervailing Duties O.	**am.**, 1977/1072, 1073
2069	Commonwealth Preference (Standstill Area) Regs.	**am.**, 1977/1081
2071	Origin of Goods (Petroleum Products) Regs.	**r.**, 1977/972
2078	Teachers Superannuation (Family Benefits) (S.) Amdt. Regs.	**r.**, 1977/1360
2106	Heating Appliances (Fireguards) Regs.	**am.**, 1977/167
2130	Control of Hiring O.	**r.**, 1977/770
2215	General Optical Council (Registration and Enrolment Rules) (Amdt.) O. of C.	**spent**
1974	Legal Aid Act (c. 4)	s. 1(1)(a) **am.**, 1977/446 4(3) **am.**, 1977/183
	Prices Act (c. 24)	sch. paras. 5(2)(3) **am.**, 15 **inserted**, 1977/1224
	Consumer Credit Act (c. 39)	s. 139(5) **am.**, 1977/600 sch. 3 **gen. am.**, paras. 5, 7, 44, 45 **am.**, 1977/325
	Housing Act (c. 44)	s. 64(3) **am.**, 1977/1211 sch. 6 Pt. **I replaced,** 1977/1212
	Solicitors Act (c. 47)	s. 69(3) **am.**, 1977/600
	Road Traffic Act (c. 50)...	ss. 1, 3–5 **mod.**, 1977/548
	Trade Union and Labour Relations Act (c. 52)	sch. 1 para. 16 **mod.**, 1977/500
	Petroleum and Submarine Pipe-Lines Act (c. 74)	s. 30(1) **am.** (N.I.), 1977/1251 (N.I. 18)
2	Importation of Wood (Prohibition) (G.B.) O.	**r.**, 1977/901
9	Prescription Pricing Authy. (Establishment and Constitution) O.	**am.**, 1977/1102
28	Export of Goods (Control) (Amdt.) O.	**r.**, 1977/104
62	Milk (Special Designation) (Amdt.) Regs.	**r.**, 1977/1033

Year and Number (or date)	Act or instrument	How affected
1974		
82	Scottish Local Elections Rules ...	**am.**, 1977/120
364	Rate Product Rules	**am.**, 1977/454
376	Teachers Superannuation (Misc. Amdts.) (S.) Regs.	**r.**, 1977/1360
418	Town and Country Planning General Development (Amdt.) O.	**r.**, 1977/289
447	Local Govt. (Allowances) Regs. ...	**am.**, 1977/107
479	Conveyance in Harbours of Military Explosives (Amdt.) Regs.	**r.**, 1977/890
492	Social Security (Contributions) Regs.	**am.**, 1977/544
520	Local Govt. Superannuation Regs.	**am.**, 1977/1121, 1341
522	National Health Service (Charges) (S.) Regs.	**am.**, 1977/471
628	Local Authies., Cemeteries O. ...	**r.**, 1977/204
645	New Street Byelaws (Ext. of Operation) O.	**expired** [31.4.77]
648	Representation of the People Regs. ...	**am.**, 1977/105
797	Crown Roads (Royal Parks) (Application of Road Traffic Enactments) O.	**r.**, 1977/548
818	Royal Air Force Terms of Service (Amdt.) Regs.	**r.**, 1977/1097
830	Dutch Elm Disease (Local Authies.) O.	**r.**, 1977/1074
832	Medicines (Renewal Applications for Licences and Certificates) Regs.	**am.**, 1977/180
877	Forest Reproductive Material (Amdt.) Regs.	**r.**, 1977/891
942	Misuse of Drugs (Licence Fees) Regs. ...	**am.**, 1977/587
1019	Commonwealth Preference (Standstill Area) (Amdt.) Regs.	**r.**, 1977/1081
1107	Extradition (Hijacking) (Amdt.) O. ...	**r.**, 1977/1237
1108	Extradition (Protection of Aircraft) (Amdt.) O.	**r.**, 1977/1238
1135	Teachers Superannuation (Added Years and Interchange) (S.) Regs.	**r.**, 1977/1360
1166	Weights and Measures Act 1963 (Sugar) O.	**am.**, 1977/1333
1202	Crown Roads (Royal Parks) (Application of Road Traffic Enactments) (Amdt.) O.	**r.**, 1977/548
1262	British Solomon Is. O.	**am.**, 1977/590
1265	Central Council for Education and Training in Social Work O.	**r.**, 1977/1240
1336	Town and Country Planning (Listed Buildings and Buildings in Conservation Areas) (Amdt.) Regs.	**r.** (*saving*), 1977/228
1377	National Health Service (Remission of Charges) Regs.	**am.**, 1977/434
1386	Industrial Tribunals (Labour Relations) Regs.	**am.**, 1977/911

Year and Number (or date)	Act or instrument	How affected
1974		
1387	Industrial Tribunals (Labour Relations) (S.) Regs.	**am.,** 1977/912
1416	Supplementary Benefit (General) Amdt. Regs.	**r.,** 1977/1141
1418	Town and Country Planning (Industrial Development Certificates) Regs.	**r.,** 1977/682
1440	National Health Service (Remission of Charges) (S.) Regs.	**am.,** 1977/471
1461	Jurors' Allowances Regs.	**r.,** 1977/4
1475	Fixed Penalty (Procedure) (No. 2) Regs.	**am.,** 1977/311, 548
1484	Jurors' Allowances (S.) Amdt. (No. 2) Regs.	**spent**
1816	Dutch Elm Disease (Local Authies.) (Amdt.) O.	**r.,** 1977/1074
1837	Legal Officers Fees O.	**am.,** 1977/1149
1867	Overseas Service (Pensions Supplement) (Amdt.) Regs.	**r.,** 1977/320
1890	Collision Regulations (Traffic Separation Schemes) (Amdt.) O.	**r.,** 1977/982, 1257
1974	Police (Discipline) (Amdt.) Regs. ...	**r.** (*saving*), 1977/580
1993	Teachers Superannuation (Misc. Amdts.) (S.) (No. 2) Regs.	**r.,** 1977/1360
1994	Teachers Superannuation (Contributions) (S.) (No. 2) Regs.	**r.,** 1977/1360
2000	Motor Cycles (Protective Helmets) Regs.	**am.,** 1977/128
2003	Savings Banks (Registrar's Fees) Warrant	**am.,** 1977/482
2004	Improvement Grant (Eligible Expense Limits) O.	**r.,** 1977/1211
2059	Social Security (Widow's Benefit and Retirement Pensions) Regs.	**am.,** 1977/342, 343
2079	Social Security (General Benefit) Regs.	**am.,** 1977/342, 343, 956
2100	Supplementary Benefit (Claims and Payments) Amdt. Regs.	**r.,** 1977/1142
2168	Matrimonial Causes (Amdt.) Rules ...	**r.** (*saving*), 1977/344
2211	Rabies (Importation of Dogs. Cats and Other Mammals) O.	**am.,** 1977/361
1975	Finance Act (c. 7)	s. 55(1) **am.,** 1977/753
	Social Security Act (c. 14)	ss. 4(1), 7(1)(5), 8(1), 9(2), 10(1) **am.,** 1977/113
		s. 37A (5) **am.,** 1977/1229
		ss. 30(1). 45(3), 66(4) **am.,** sch. 4 Pts I, III, IV, V **replaced,** 1977/1325

Year and Number (or date)	Act or instrument	How affected
1975	Social Security (N.I.) Act (c. 15) ...	**mod.** (Austria), 1977/54 ss. 1(5), 18(2)(b), 24(2), 25(3), 26(3) **am.,** 29(10A) **inserted,** 30(2), 31, 36(2)(b), 37(3)(b), 43(2)(b), 45(4), 65(2)(b), 66(5), 71(3)(b), 72(4)(a), 73(3), 80 **am.,** 93(1)(e) **inserted,** 120 **am.,** 124(3) **r.,** 127(5), 156(3)(a) **am.,** sch. 1 paras. 4(a), 17 **am.,** 1977/610 (N.I. 11)
	Industrial Injuries and Diseases (Old Cases) Act (c. 16)	ss. 2(6)(c), 7(2)(b) **am.,** 1977/1325
	Social Security (Consequential Provns.) Act (c. 18)	sch. 2 para. 99 **am.,** (N.I.), 101(a) **r.** (N.I.), 1977/610 (N.I. 11)
	H. of C. Disqualification Act (c. 24) ...	sch. 1 Pt. II **am.,** 1977/53
	N.I. Assembly Disqualification Act (c. 25)	sch. 1 Pt. II **am.,** 1977/53
	Ministerial and other Salaries Act (c. 27)	s. 1(2) **am.,** schs. 1 Pts. I–IV **am.,** 2 Pt. I **am.,** 1977/1295
	Remuneration, Charges and Grants Act (c. 57)	s. 1(1) **am.,** *see* 1977/1294
	Social Security Pensions Act (c. 60)	s. 44(6) **mod.,** 1977/1188 6(1)(a) **am.,** 1977/1325
	Child Benefit Act (c. 61)	Pt. I **mod.** (N.I.), 1977/7 **mod.,** 1977/592, 593
	N.I. (Emergency Provns.) (Amdt.) Act (c. 62)	sch. 2 paras. 3, 9 **r.,** 1977/426 (N.I. 4)
	Sex Discrimination Act (c. 65)	s. 43(3)(4) **replaced** by new s. (3), 1977/528
	Employment Protection Act (c. 71) ...	ss. 42(1), 44(1) **am.,** 1977/622
51	General Optical Council (Registration and Enrolment Rules) (Amdt.) O. of C.	**spent**
55	Dutch Elm Disease (Local Authies.) (Amdt.) O.	**r.,** 1977/1074
73	A.S. (Fees of Sheriff Officers)	**r.,** 1977/568
74	A.S. (Fees of Messengers-at-Arms) ...	**r.,** 1977/567
98	Teachers Superannuation (Family Benefits) (S.) Amdt. Regs.	**r.,** 1977/1360
136	Clergy Pensions (Amdt.) Regs. ...	**am.,** 1977/1146
203	Movement and Sale of Pigs O.	**am.,** 1977/944

Year and Number (or date)	Act or instrument	How affected
1975		
212	Wireless Telegraphy (Broadcast Licence Charges & Exemption) (Amdt.) Regs.	r., 1977/1286
224	Royal Air Force Terms of Service (Amdt.) Regs.	r., 1977/1097
287	Public Trustee (Fees) O.	r., 1977/508
308	Public Health (Infectious Diseases) (S.) Regs.	am., 1977/206
313	Exchange Control (Purchase of Foreign Currency) (Amdt.) O.	r., 1977/920
330	Fishing Vessels (Safety Provns.) Rules	am., 1977/252, 313, 498
368	Anti-Dumping Duty O.	am., 1977/1073
430	Carriage by Air (Parties to Convention) O.	superseded, 1977/240
458	Social Security (Misc. and Consequential Provns.) Regs.	am., 1977/343
485	Foreign Passenger and Goods Vehicles (Recording Equipment) Regs.	r., 1977/777
492	Social Security (Contributions) regs. ...	am., 1977/114, 638
497	Social Security (Child's Special Allowance) Regs.	am., 1977/342
498	Misuse of Drugs (Designation) (Amdt.) O.	r., 1977/1379
499	Misuse of Drugs (Amdt.) Regs.	am., 1977/1380
515	Social Security (Guardian's Allowances) Regs.	am., 1977/342
528	Social Security (Categorisation of Earners) Regs.	am., 1977/1015
546	Housing (Limits of Rateable Value for Improvement Grants) (S.) O.	r., 1977/523
553	Social Security (Maternity Benefit) Regs.	am., 1977/343
554	Social Security (Overlapping Benefits) Regs.	am., 1977/342
555	Social Security (Hospital In-Patients) Regs.	am., 1977/342, 956
556	Social Security (Credits) Regs.	am., 1977/788
559	Social Security (Industrial Injuries) (Benefit) Regs.	am., 1977/341, 342, 343
560	Social Security (Claims and Payments) Regs.	am., 1977/342, 1288, 1361, 1444
563	Social Security Benefit (Persons Abroad) Regs.	am., 1977/342
564	Social Security (Unemployment, Sickness and Invalidity Benefit) Regs.	am., 1977/342, 343, 1362
565	Social Security (Death Grant) Regs.	am., 1977/342
570	Jurors' Allowances (Amdt.) Regs. ...	r., 1977/4
571	Exchange Control (Authorised Dealers and Depositaries) O.	r., 1977/501
598	Social Security (Attendance Allowance) (No. 2) Regs.	am., 1977/342, 1361

Year and Number (or date)	Act or instrument	How affected
1975		
637	Sheriff Ct. Districts Reorganisation O.	am., 1977/672
659	Local Authies. (Property etc.) (S.) O.	am., 1977/277
674	Justices Allowances (S.) Regs. ...	am., 1977/40
686	Local Authies. (Allowances) (S.) Regs.	am., 1977/119
712	Control of Hiring (Amdt.) O.	r., 1977/770
739	Heavy Goods Vehicles (Drivers' Licences) Regs.	r., 1977/1309
747	Jurors' Allowances (S.) Amdt. Regs.	spent
803	Extradition (Hijacking) (Amdt.) O. ...	r., 1977/1237
804	Extradition (Protection of Aircraft) (Amdt.) O.	r., 1977/1238
850	Representation of the People (S.) Regs.	am., 1977/111
869	Oil Pollution (Compulsory Insurance) Regs.	r., 1977/85
872	Teachers Superannuation (War Service) (S.) Regs.	r., 1977/1360
879	Family Income Supplements (Computation) Regs.	r., 1977/586
931	Teachers Superannuation (Family Benefits) (S.) Regs.	r., 1977/1360
1026	Costs in Criminal Cases (Allowances) Regs.	am., 1977/407
1036	Merchant Shipping (Oil Pollution) (Parties to Convention) O.	am., 1977/826
1054	Further Education Regs.	am., 1977/887
1058	Social Security (Non-Contributory Invalidity Pension) Regs.	am., 1977/342, 343, 1312, 1362
1087	Legal Officers Fees O.	am., 1977/1149
1090	Coroners (Fees and Allowances) Rules	am., 1977/406
1091	Jurors' (Coroners' Cts.) Allowances Regs.	am., 1977/408
1101	National Health Service (Health Authies.: Membership) Regs.	r., 1977/1103
1163	Dutch Elm Disease (Local Authies.) (Amdt.) (No. 2) O.	r., 1977/1074
1173	Measuring Instruments (E.E.C. Requirements) Regs.	am., 1977/27
1184	Civil Aviation (Navigation Service Charges) Regs.	r., 1977/1437
1196	Civil Aviation (Air Travel Organisers Licensing) (Reserve Fund) Regs.	am., 1977/1331
1198	Direct Grant Grammer Schools (Cessation of Grant) Regs.	am., 1977/1443
1207	Local Education Authies. Awards Regs.	r., 1977/1307
1225	Students' Dependants' Allowances Regs.	r., 1977/1308
1234	Oil Pollution (Compulsory Insurance) (Amdt.) Regs.	r., 1977/85
1260	Overseas Service (Pensions Supplement) (Amdt.) Regs.	r., 1977/320

Year and Number (or date)	Act or instrument	How affected
1975		
1322	Rent Rebate and Rent Allowance Schemes (Students) (S.) Regs.	am., 1977/1310
1328	County Ct. Fees O.	am., 1977/1451
1329	Elections (Welsh Forms) Regs. ...	am., 1977/106
1335	Supplementary Benefit (General) Amdt. Regs.	r., 1977/1141
1346	Matrimonial Causes Fees O.	am., 1977/346
1352	Teachers Superannuation (Service Credit) (S.) Regs.	r., 1977/1360
1359	Matrimonial Causes (Amdt.) Rules ...	r. (*saving*), 1977/344
1434	Jurors' Allowances (S.) Amdt. (No. 2) Regs.	spent
1487	Preservatives in Food Regs.	am., 1977/645, 927
1495	Exchange Control (Authorised Dealers and Depositaries) (Amdt.) O.	r., 1977/501
1508	Fugitive Offenders (Tuvalu) O. ...	am., 1977/47
1512	Fugitive Offenders (Gilbert Is.) O. ...	am., 1977/47
1537	Social Security (Industrial Injuries) (Prescribed Diseases) Regs.	am., 1977/250, 342
1558	Remuneration of Teachers (Primary and Secondary Schools) (No. 2) O.	r., 1977/915
1573	Mobility Allowance Regs.	am., 1977/342, 1229
1582	Export of Goods (Control) (Amdt. No. 2) O.	r., 1977/1190
1598	Preservatives in Food (S.) Regs. ...	am., 1977/860, 1026
1631	Civil Aviation (Navigation Service Charges) (Amdt.) Regs.	r., 1977/1437
1646	Herring (Celtic Sea) Licensing O. ...	r., 1977/290
1686	Welfare Food O.	r., 1977/25
1697	Local Education Authies. Awards (Amdt.) Regs.	r., 1977/1307
1731	Heavy Goods Vehicles (Drivers' Licences) (Amdt.) Regs.	r., 1977/1309
1744	Import Duties (General) (No. 5) O.	am., 1977/184, 280, 555, 569, 616, 666, 713, 716, 861, 921, 983, 1077
1759	Oil Pollution (Compulsory Insurance) (Amdt. No. 2) Regs.	r., 1977/85
1791	Import Duty Reliefs O.	r., 1977/971
1848	Act of Adj. (Fees in the High Ct. of Justiciary) (Amdt.)	r., 1977/72
1849	A.S. (Fees in Ct. of Teinds)	r., 1977/73
1850	A.S. (Rules of Ct. Amdt. No. 4) ...	r., 1977/71
1855	Social Security (Contributions) Consequential (Amdt.) Regs.	am., 1977/543
1900	Royal Air Force Terms of Service (Second Amdt.) Regs.	r., 1977/1097
1904	Dutch Elm Disease (Restriction on Movement of Elms) O.	r., 1977/1075

Year and Number (or date)	Act or instrument	How affected
1975		
1905	Dutch Elm Disease (Local Authies.) (Amdt.) (No. 3) O.	**r.,** 1977/1074
1936	Jurors' Allowances (S.) Amdt. (No. 3) Regs.	**spent**
1940	Justices Allowances (S.) Amdt. Regs.	**superseded,** 1977/40
1968	Civil Aviation (Navigation Services Charges) (Second Amdt.) Regs.	**r.,** 1977/1437
1984	Local Govt. (Allowances) (Amdt.) Regs.	**r.,** 1977/107
1993	Sex Discrimination (Formal Investigations) Regs.	**am.,** 1977/843
1995	Building Societies (Authorised Investments) (Amdt.) O.	**r.,** 1977/851
2002	Oil Pollution (Compulsory Insurance) (Amdt. No. 3) Regs.	**r.,** 1977/85
2016	Jurors' Allowances (Amdt. No. 2) Regs.	**r.,** 1977/4
2048	Sex Discrimination (Questions and Replies) O.	**am.,** 1977/844
2056	Import Duties (Turkey) (Reductions and Exemptions) O.	**am.,** 1977/616, 1046
2057	Import Duties (Greece) (Reductions) O.	**am.,** 1977/838
2069	Town and Country Planning (Listed Buildings and Buildings in Conservation Areas) (S.) Regs.	**am.,** 1977/255
2074	Import Duties (Faroe Is.) (Reductions and Exemptions) O.	**am.,** 1977/616
2077	Import Duties (Egypt) (Reductions) O.	**r.,** 1977/1093
2080	Export of Goods (Control) (Amdt. No. 3) O.	**r.,** 1977/104
2094	Import Duties (Development Countries) (No. 4) O.	**am.,** 1977/616, 713
2098	Industrial Tribunals (Non-Discrimination Notices Appeals) Regs.	**r.** (*saving*), 1977/1094
2099	Industrial Tribunals (Non-Discrimination Notices and Appeals) (S.) Regs.	**r.** (*saving*), 1977/1095
2100	Origin of Goods (Certain Mediterranean Countries) Regs.	**r.,** 1977/1081
2101	Occupational Pension Schemes (Contracting-out) Regs.	**am.,** 1977/1188
2123	Consumer Credit Act 1974 (Commencement No. 1) O.	**am.,** 1977/325
2126	Social Security (Relaxation of Earnings Rules) Regs.	**am.,** 1977/343
2140	Control of Hiring (Amdt. No. 2) O. ...	**r.,** 1977/770
2159	Army, Air Force and Naval Discipline Act (Continuation) O.	**spent**
2181	Merchant Shipping Act 1974 (Jersey) O.	**am.,** 1977/1242

Year and Number (or date)	Act or instrument	How affected
1975		
2182	Merchant Shipping Act 1974 (Guernsey) O.	**am.**, 1977/1241
2194	Merchant Shipping (Light Dues) (No. 2) O.	**r.**, 1977/430
2204	Value Added Tax (General) Regs. ...	**am.**, 1977/205
2226	Community Drivers' Hours Rules (Deferment of Operation) Regs.	**superseded**, 1976/998
17 Sept.	Gilbert Is. O.	**am.**, 0. 1977 (II p. 4362)
1976	National Coal Bd. (Finance) Act (c. 1)	s. 2(3)(b) **replaced**, 1977/542
	Lotteries and Amusements Act (c. 32)	sch. 3 para. 18 **am.** (E. and W.), 1977/1176 (S.), 1977/1179
	Agriculture (Misc. Provns.) Act (c. 55)	**mod.**, 1977/1215 Pt. II s. 18(1A) **inserted**, (4)(e) **am.**, 19A **inserted**, 22 **mod.**, 23(1) **am.**, (2) **replaced** by (2A), (3) **am.**, (9) **inserted**, 24 **am.**, 1977/1215
	Supplementary Benefits Act (c. 71) ...	sch. 1 Pt. II paras. 7, 8 **replaced**, 10(1)(a)(b), 11(1)(b) **am.**, 1977/1326
	Endangered Species (Import and Export) Act (c. 72)	schs. 1 Pts. I, II **am.**, 2 **am.**, 3 paras. 9 **am.**, 18A **inserted**, 1977/153
14	A.S. (Sessions of Ct.)	**spent**
16	Exchange Control (Authorised Dealers and Depositaries) (Amdt.) O.	**r.**, 1977/501
19	Community Land (Outstanding Material Interests) O.	**am.**, 1977/148
56	Carriage by Air (Parties to Convention) (Supplementary) O.	**superseded**, 1977/240
106	Ironstone Restoration Fund (Standard Rate) O.	**r.**, 1977/133
107	Ironstone Restoration Fund (Rates of Contribution) (Amdt.) Regs.	**r.**, 1977/134
123	Plant Breeders' Rights (Fees) Regs. ...	**r.**, 1977/359
124	Seeds (National Lists of Varieties) (Fees) Regs.	**r.**, 1977/358
143	Contracted-out Employment (Notifications, Premium Payment and Misc. Provns.) Regs.	**am.**, 1977/118
154	Oil Pollution (Compulsory Insurance) (Amdt.) Regs.	**r.**, 1977/85

Year and Number (or date)	Act or instrument	How affected
1976		
157	General Optical Council (Registration and Enrolment Rules) (Amdt.) O. of C.	**spent**
212	Exchange Control (Purchase of Foreign Currency) (Amdt.) O.	**r.,** 1977/920
215	Consular Fees O.	**r.,** 1977/46
220	Foreign Compensation (Financial Provns.) O.	**spent**
244	Brucellosis (Area Eradication) (E. and W.) (Amdt.) O.	**r.,** 1977/1284
301	Town and Country Planning General Development (Amdt.) O.	**r.,** 1977/289
324	Sugar Beet (Research and Education) O.	**superseded,** 1977/338
331	Community Land (Excepted Development) Regs.	**am.,** 1977/743
347	Medicines (Fees) Regs.	**am.,** 1977/1056, 1374
350	Housing (Limits of Rateable Value for Improvement Grants) (Variation) (S.) O.	**r.,** 1977/523
369	Civil Aviation (Navigation Service Charges) (Third Amdt.) Regs.	**r.,** 1977/1437
375	A.S. (Amdt. of Fees in the Scottish Record Office)	**r.,** 1977/976
409	Social Security (Invalid Care Allowance) Regs.	**am.,** 1977/342, 343
419	Local Loans (Increase of Limit) O. ...	**superseded,** 1977/753
421	Air Navigation (Overseas Territories) O.	**r.** (*saving*), 1977/422
432	Fishing Vessels (Safety Provns.) Amdt. Rules	**am.,** 1977/313
465	Prevention of Terrorism (Supplemental Temp. Provns.) O.	**am.,** 1977/271
466	Prevention of Terrorism (Supplemental Temp. Provns.) (N.I.) O.	**am.,** 1977/455
473	Heavy Goods Vehicles (Drivers') ...	**r.,** 1977/1309
474	Approved Schools (Contributions by Local Authies.) Regs.	**r.,** 1977/473
517	Welfare Food (Amdt.) O.	**r.,** 1977/25
526	Improvement Grant (Rateable Value Limits) O.	**r.,** 1977/1213
530	Employment Protection Act 1975 (Commencement No. 4) O.	**am.,** 1977/82
545	Control of Hiring (Amdt.) O.	**r.,** 1977/770
585	Personal Injuries (Civilians) Scheme ...	**am.,** 1977/404
592	Gaming Act (Variation of Fees) O. ...	**r.,** 1977/570
597	Animals (Importation from Canada) O.	**r.,** 1977/944
606	Matrimonial Causes (Costs) (Amdt.) Rules	**r.,** 1977/345
607	Matrimonial Causes (Amdt.) Rules ...	**r.** (*saving*), 1977/344

Year and Number (or date)	Act or instrument	How affected
1976		
623	Gaming Act (Variation of Fees) (S.) O.	r., 1977/633
652	Control of Office Development (Exemption Limit) O.	r., 1977/848
656	Remuneration of Teachers (Primary and Secondary Schools) (Amdt.) O.	r., 1977/915
667	Medicines (Pharmacies) (Applications and Fees) Amdt. Regs.	am., 1977/511
695	Sheep Scab (Amdt.) O.	r., 1977/1173
732	Control of Pollution (Licensing of Waste Disposal) Regs.	am., 1977/1185
734	Dutch Elm Disease (Restriction on Movement of Elms) (Amdt.) O.	r., 1977/1075
766	Employment Protection (Offshore Employment) O.	am., 1977/588
769	Extradition (Hijacking) (Amdt.) O. ...	r., 1977/1237
770	Extradition (Protection of Aircraft) (Amdt.) O.	r., 1977/1238
776	Animals (Landing from Channel Is., Is. of Man, N.I., and Republic of Ireland) (Amdt.) O.	r., 1977/944 r., 1977/944
801	Family Income Supplements (Computation) Regs.	r., 1977/586
838	Import Duties (Outward Processing Relief) Regs.	am., 1977/910
857	Oil Pollution (Compulsory Insurance) (Amdt. No. 2) Regs.	r., 1977/85
873	Butter Prices O.	r., 1977/786
910	Teachers Superannuation (Misc. Provns.) (S.) Regs.	r., 1977/1360
937	Motor Vehicles (Type Approval) (G.B.) Regs.	am., 1977/1438
939	Pool Competitions Act 1971 (Continuance) O.	superseded, 1977/997
962	Child Benefit (Determination of Claims and Questions) Regs.	am., 1977/1048
965	Child Benefit (General) Regs.	am., 1977/534
975	Dutch Elm Disease (Local Authies.) (Amdt.) O.	r., 1977/1074
976	Import Duties (Certain Mediterranean Countries) O.	am., 1977/1093
988	Diseases of Animals (Misc. Fees) O. ...	am., 1977/377, 962
995	Origin of Goods (Certain Mediterranean Countries) (Amdt.) Regs.	r., 1977/1081
998	Community Drivers' Hours Rules (Deferment of Operation) Regs.	superseded, 1977/312
1029	Social Security Benefits Up-rating O. ...	r., 1977/1325
1032	Carriage by Air (Sterling Equivalents) O.	superseded, 1977/1

Year and Number (or date)	Act or instrument	How affected
1976		
1039	Merchant Shipping (Oil Pollution) (Parties to Conventions) (Amdt.) O.	r., 1977/48
1069	Social Security Benefits Up-rating Regs.	r., 1977/1362
1073	Police (S.) Regs....	am., 1977/1016
1075	Heavy Goods Vehicles (Drivers' Licences) (Amdt.) (No. 2) Regs.	r., 1977/1309
1076	Motor Vehicles (Driving Licences) Regs.	am., 1977/871
1077	Motor Cars (Driving Instruction) (Amdt.) Regs.	r., 1977/1043
1087	Local Education Authies. Awards (Amdt.) Regs.	r., 1977/1307, 1308
1089	N.I. Act 1974 (Interim Period Extension) O.	expired [12.7.77]
1098	Merchant Shipping (Fees) (No. 2) Regs.	am., 1977/627
1100	Anti-Dumping Duty (No. 2) O.	r., 1977/695
1135	Hire-Purchase and Credit Sale Agreements (Control) O.	am., 1977/771
1151	Consular Fees (Amdt.) O.	r., 1977/46
1159	Carriage by Air (Parties to Convention) (Supplementary) (No. 2) O.	superseded, 1977/240
1170	Counter-Inflation (Price Code) O.	r., 1977/1272
1171	Counter-Inflation (Notification of Increases in Prices and Charges) O.	r., 1977/1281
1172	Counter-Inflation (Prices and Charges) (Information) O.	r., 1977/1281
1177	Oil Pollution (Compulsory Insurance) (Amdt. No. 3) Regs.	r., 1977/85
1179	Countervailing Duty O.	am., 1977/1073
1192	Remuneration of Teachers (Primary and Secondary Schools) (Amdt. No. 2) O.	r., 1977/915
1202	Trustee Savings Banks (Interest-bearing Receipts) O.	r., 1977/216
1204	Paraffin (Maximum Retail Prices) O.	am., 1977/2
1215	Junior Ministers' and other Salaries O.	r., 1977/1295
1218	Compulsory Acquisition by Public Authies. (Compensation) O.	am., 1977/741
1219	Acquisition from the Crown (Grants) O.	am., 1977/742
1242	Rent Rebates and Rent Allowances (Students) (E. and W.) Regs.	am., 1977/1290
1245	Social Security Benefits Up-rating (No. 2) Regs.	r., 1977/1362
1267	Child Benefit and Social Security (Fixing and Adjustment of Rates) Regs.	am., 1977/1327, 1328
1268	Household Flour Prices O.	am., 1977/192, 935
1269	Tea Prices O.	r., 1977/934

Year and Number (or date)	Act or instrument	How affected
1976		
1275	Exchange Control (Authorised Dealers and Depositaries) (Amdt.) (No. 2) O.	r., 1977/501
1288	Rent Rebate and Rent Allowance Schemes (Students) (S.) Amdt. Regs.	r., 1977/1310
1322	Herring (North Irish Sea) Licensing O.	r., 1977/1388
1323	Herring (Is. of Man) Licensing O. ...	r., 1977/1389
1324	Fishing Nets (North-East Atlantic) O.	r., 1977/440
1377	Counter-Inflation (Prices and Charges) (Information) Order 1976 (Amdt.) O.	r., 1977/1281
1378	Counter-Inflation (Notification of Increases in Prices and Charges) Order 1976 (Amdt.) O.	r., 1977/1281
1396	Civil Aviation Authy. (Charges) Regs.	am., 1977/647
1440	Oil Pollution (Compulsory Insurance) (Amdt. No. 4) Regs.	r., 1977/85
1465	Motor Vehicles (Type Approval and Approval Marks) (Fees) Regs.	am., 1977/1440
1466	Motor Vehicles (Type Approval) (G.B.) (Fees) Regs.	am., 1977/1439
1519	Overseas Service (Pensions Supplement) (Amdt.) Regs.	r., 1977/320
1564	Exchange Control (Purchase of Foreign Currency) (Amdt.) (No. 2) O.	r., 1977/920
1659	National Assistance (Charges for Accommodation) Regs.	r., 1977/1069
1670	National Assistance (Charges for Accommodation) (S.) Regs.	r., 1977/1359
1682	Welfare Food (Amdt. No. 2) O. ...	r., 1977/25
1712	Anti-Dumping (Prov. Charge to Duty) (No. 3) O.	superseded, 1977/60
1726	Medicines (Labelling) Regs.	am., 1977/996
1736	Social Security (Misc. Amdt.) Regs. ...	am., 1977/343
1776	Air Navigation (Overseas Territories) (Amdt.) O.	r., 1977/422
1782	Registration of Title O.	r. (1.2.78), 1977/828
1783	Air Navigation O.	am., 1977/1255
1798	Acquisition of Land (Rate of Interest after Entry) (No. 4) Regs.	r., 1977/300
1799	Opencast Coal (Rate of Interest on Compensation) (No. 4) O.	r., 1977/302
1800	Acquisition of Land (Rate of Interest after Entry) (S.) (No. 4) Regs.	r., 1977/301
1830	Overseas Service (Pensions Supplement) (Amdt.) (No. 2) Regs.	r., 1977/320
1831	Seeds (Fees) (No. 2) Regs.	r., 1977/1049
1840	Paraffin (Maximum Retail Prices) (Amdt.) O.	superseded, 1977/2
1856	Welfare Food (Amdt. No. 3) O. ...	r., 1977/25
1871	Community Land (Register of Land Holdings) (W.) Regs.	am., 1977/450

Year and Number (or date)	Act or instrument	How affected
1976		
1906	Anti-Dumping Duty (No. 3) O. ...	am., 1977/1073
1929	Cheese Prices O.	am., 1977/193
1937	Butter Prices Order 1976 (Amdt.) O. ...	r., 1977/786
1938	Household Flour Prices (Amdt.) (No. 2) O.	r., 1977/192
1939	Rate Support Grants (Adjustment of Needs Element) Regs.	am., 1977/1342
1961	Medicines (Pharmacies) (Applications for Registration and Fees) Amdt. (No. 2) Regs.	am., 1977/511
1970	Medicines (Certificates of Analysis) Regs.	r., 1977/1399
2013	Overseas Service (Pensions Supplement) (Amdt.) (No. 3) Regs.	r., 1977/320
2026	Value Added Tax (Machine Tools) O. ...	am., 1977/818
2059	Milk (G.B.) (Amdt.) (No. 3) O. ...	r., 1977/859
2060	Milk (N.I.) (Amdt.) (No. 2) O. ...	r., 1977/858
2077	Import Duties (General) (No. 10) O. ...	am., 1977/435, 616, 713, 1087
2079	Import Duties (Egypt) (Reductions) (Amdt.) O.	spent
2084	Civil Aviation (Navigation Services Charges) (Fourth Amdt.) Regs.	r., 1977/1437
2096	Import Duties (Temp. Reductions and Exemptions) (No. 26) O.	am., 1977/155, 274, 653
2113	Import Duties (Temp. Reductions and Exemptions) (No. 27) O.	am., 1977/274
2128	Bread Prices (No. 2) O.	am., 1977/1166
2166	Matrimonial Causes (Amdt. No. 2) Rules	r. (*saving*), 1977/344
2167	Matrimonial Causes (Costs) (Amdt. No. 2) O.	r., 1977/345
2177	Anti-Dumping (Prov. Charge to Duty) (No. 7) O.	r., 1977/954
2204	Overseas Service (Pensions Supplement) (Amdt.) (No. 4) Regs.	r., 1977/320
2207	Counter-Inflation (Price Code) Order 1976 (Amdt.) O.	r., 1977/1272
2208	Exchange Control (Authorised Dealers and Depositaries) (Amdt.) (No. 3) O.	r., 1977/501
2226	Motor Vehicles (Designation of Approval Marks) Regs.	am., 1977/1400
2228	Remuneration of Teachers (Primary and Secondary Schools) (Amdt. No. 3) O.	r., 1977/915
2238	N.I. (Various Emergency Provns.) (Continuance) (No. 2) O.	expired [24.7.77]
2242	Motor Cycles (Wearing of Helmets) (Amdt.) O.	r., 1977/129

Year and Number (or date)	Act or instrument	How affected
1977	Social Security (Misc. Provns.) Act (c. 5)	s. 21 (1) **mod.**, 1977/1188 sch. 1 paras. 7, 8 **am.**, 1977/991,992
24	Endangered Species (Import and Export) Act 1976 (Commencement) O.	spent
39	Agriculture (Misc. Provns.) Act 1976 (Commencement No. 1) O.	spent
48	Merchant Shipping (Oil Pollution) (Parties to Conventions) (Amdt.) O.	r., 1977/826
68	Local Govt. (Misc. Provns.) Act 1976 (Commencement) O.	spent
85	Oil Pollution (Compulsory Insurance) Regs.	am., 1977/497
116	Development of Rural Wales Act 1976 (Commencement No. 2) O.	spent
165	Companies Act 1976 (Commencement No. 2) O.	spent
172	Medicines (Bal Jivan Chamcho Prohibition) O.	superseded, 1977/670
184	Anti-Dumping (Provisional Charge to Duty) (No. 2) O.	am., 1977/793
190	Fatal Accidents and Sudden Deaths Inquiry (S.) Act 1976 Commencement O.	spent
192	Household Flour Prices (Amdt.) O. ...	r., 1977/535
200	Norway Pout (Prohibition of Fishing) O.	r., 1977/1291
212	Licensing (S.) Act 1976 (Commencement No. 2) O.	spent
248	Costs in Criminal Cases (Central Funds) (Appeals) Regs.	am., 1977/709
252	Merchant Shipping (Smooth and Partially Smooth Waters) Rules	am., 1977/632
290	Herring (Celtic Sea) (Prohibition of Fishing) O.	r., 1977/1377
294	Health and Safety at Works etc. Act 1974 (Commencement No. 4) O.	spent
300	Acquisition of Land (Rate of Interest After Entry) Regs.	r., 1977/720
301	Acquisition of Land (Rate of Interest After Entry) (S.) Regs.	r., 1977/721
302	Opencast Coal (Rate of Interest on Compensation) O.	r., 1977/722
322	Maternity Pay (Rebate) Regs.	am., 1977/668
336	Control of Pollution Act 1974 (Commencement No. 8) O.	spent
340	Civil Aviation (Navigation Services Charges) (Fifth Amdt.) Regs.	r., 1977/1437

Year and Number (or date)	Act or instrument	How affected
1977		
341	Social Security (Industrial Injuries) (Benefit) (Amdt.) Regs.	**r.**, 1977/343
342	Social Security (Child Benefit Consequential) Regs.	**am.**, 1977/343, 417
343	Social Security Benefit (Dependency) Regs.	**am.**, 1977/620
360	Bread Prices (No. 2) Order 1976 (Amdt.) O.	**r.**, 1977/769
363	Insolvency Act 1976 (Commencement No. 2) O.	**spent**
401	National Health Service (Charges) (S.) Amdt. Regs.	**r.**, 1977/471
409	Lotteries Act 1975 (Commencement No. 2) O.	**spent**
422	Air Navigation (Overseas Territories) O.	**am.**, 1977/820
433	Employment Protection Act 1975 (Commencement No. 7) O.	**spent**
470	Town and Country Planning Act 1971 (Commencement No. 36) (South Hampshire) O.	**spent**
476	Control of Pollution Act 1974 (Commencement No. 9) O.	**spent**
506	Anti-Dumping (Prov. Charge to Duty) (Extension) (No. 2) O.	**spent**
509	Litigants in Person (Costs and Expenses) Act 1975 (Commencement) (N.I.) O.	**spent**
529	Companies Act 1976 (Commencement No. 3) O.	**spent**
535	Household Flour Prices (Amdt.) (No. 2) O.	**r.**, 1977/935
586	Family Income Supplements (Computation) Regs.	**r.**, 1977/1324
617	Social Security (Misc. Provns.) Act 1977 (Commencement No. 1) O.	**spent**
618	Social Security (Misc. Provns.) Act 1977 (Commencement No. 2) O.	**spent**
621	Supplementary Benefit (General) Amdt. Regs.	**r.**, 1977/1141
623	Fishing Boats (Specified Countries) Designation O.	**expired** [31.5.77]
624	Sea Fishing (Specified Foreign Boats) Licensing (No. 2) O.	**expired** [31.5.77]
652	Energy Act 1976 (Commencement No. 3) O.	**spent**
680	Race Relation Act 1976 (Commencement No. 1) O.	**spent**
683	Assisted Areas O.	**am.**, 1977/706

Year and Number (or date)	Act or instrument	How affected
1977		
713	Import Duties (General) (No. 3) O. ...	**am.,** 1977/1087
720	Acquisition of Land (Rate of Interest after (Entry) (No. 2) Regs.	**r.,** 1977/876
721	Acquisition of Land (Rate of Interest after (Entry) (S.) (No. 2) Regs.	**r.,** 1977/877
722	Opencast Coal (Rate of Interest on Compensation) (No. 2) O.	**r.,** 1977/878
769	Bread Prices (No. 2) Order 1976 (Amdt.) (No. 2) O.	**r.,** 1977/1166
774	Companies Act 1976 (Commencement No. 4) O.	**spent**
778	Social Security Pensions Act 1975 (Commencement No. 8) O.	**spent**
802	Consumer Credit Act 1974 (Commencement No. 3) O.	**spent**
840	Race Relations Act 1976 (Commencement No. 2) O.	**spent**
859	Milk (G.B.) (Amdt.) O....	**r.,** 1977/1441
891	Forest Reproductive Material Regs. ...	**am.,** 1977/1264
897	Armed Forces Act 1976 (Commencement) O.	**spent**
910	Inward Processing Relief Regs. ...	**am.,** 1977/1404
921	Customs Duties and Drawbacks (Tobacco) O.	**am.,** 1977/1058, 1315
936	Employment Protection Act 1975 (Commencement No. 8) O.	**spent**
941	Fishing Boats (Specified Countries) Designation (No. 2) O.	**expired** [30.6.77]
942	Sea Fishing (Specified Foreign Boats) Licensing (No. 3) O.	**am.,** 1977/1083
943	Local Govt. Act 1974 (Commencement No. 2) O.	**spent**
949	Brucellosis (Area Eradication) (E. and W.) (Amdt.) O.	**r.,** 1977/1284
982	Collision Regulations and Distress Signals O.	**am.,** 1977/1301
984	Local Land Charges Act 1975 (Commencement) O.	**spent**
1036	Children Act 1975 (Commencement No. 2) O.	**spent**
1068	Medicines Act 1968 (Commencement No. 6) O.	**spent**
1084	Fishing Boats (Specified Countries) Designation (No. 3) O.	**am.,** 1977/1292
1092	Customs Duties (E.C.S.C.) O. ...	**am.,** 1977/1117
1122	Dock Work Regulation Act 1976 (Commencement No. 1) O.	**spent**
1124	Diseases of Animals Act 1975 (Commencement No. 4) O.	**spent**

Year and Number (or date)	Act or instrument	How affected
1977		
1141	Supplementary Benefits (General) Regs.	**am.,** 1977/1226
1150	Education Authy. Bursaries (S.) Amdt. Regs.	**am.,** 1977/1356
1162	Returning Officers (S.) Act 1977 (Commencement) O.	**spent**
1268	Rent (Agriculture) Act 1976 (Commencement No. 2) O.	**spent**
1307	Local Education Authy. Awards Regs.	**am.,** 1977/1409
1311	Social Security Act 1975 (Commencement No. 3) O.	**spent**
1348	Companies Act 1976 (Commencement No. 5) O.	**spent**
1363	Town and Country Planning Act 1971 (Commencement No. 37) (Gwynedd) O.	**spent**
1365	Criminal Law Act 1977 (Commencement No. 1) O.	**spent**
1375	Insolvency Act 1976 (Commencement No. 3) O.	**spent**
1403	Social Security Pensions Act 1975 (Commencement No. 9) O.	**spent**
1405	Administration of Justice Act 1977 (Commencement No. 1) O.	**spent**
1426	Criminal Law Act 1977 (Commencement No. 2) O.	**spent**

Index to Parts I and II

Volume
Reference

Printed by Her Majesty's Stationery Office

at Reprographic Centre, Basildon

41094 K6 11/77

HORACE BARKS
REFERENCE LIBRARY

STOKE-ON-TRENT

S.O.
HMSO
£36.75
for 2 vols.